MARRIAGE AND
THE FAMILY

A Comprehensive Reader

MARRIAGE
AND THE
FAMILY

Edited by

Jeffrey K. Hadden
TULANE UNIVERSITY

Marie L. Borgatta
UNIVERSITY OF WISCONSIN

F. E. PEACOCK PUBLISHERS, INC. • ITASCA • ILLINOIS

Preface

No SINGLE BOOK can do all things, but that does not keep authors and editors from trying. This volume attempts to give a comprehensive base for a course in marriage and the family. Materials are presented that emphasize the theory and research in this field of study, but materials have also been selected to convey in a descriptive way the complexity of social forms. The balance of materials presented may leave some areas only lightly covered and some omitted entirely, and no apology can be made for this. Within the limitations of space, some things had to be omitted. We are impressed that some topics have had vogue and are now of lesser prominence, such as research on the "rating and dating" complex, early marriages, and marriage prediction scales.

The volume may be used to augment texts, and we have given some attention to provide materials in such a way as to cover the basic outlines of the more popular texts and to provide some depth in a number of topics. At the same time, the volume has been composed with the idea that some instructors may want to use their own lecture notes (with no assigned text). It was this last objective that made decisions to provide balance so much more difficult than merely trying to provide a set of interesting readings.

We are indebted to Edgar F. Borgatta, who in the long run was probably more a help than hindrance to this project. We are grateful to Susan Beggs for her help in preparing the manuscript. We are especially indebted to scholars who responded to calls for assistance and advice, and who volunteered help in many cases. Michael J. Armer, Paul C. Glick, Elizabeth Herzog, Mary Keyserling, Clyde V. Kiser, Ida C. Merriam,

Wyatt C. Jones, Martin Loeb, Ivan Nye, and many others should be mentioned for their generosity. Finally, we are most grateful to the authors and publishers who have made this book possible. The *Journal of Marriage and the Family*, Marvin B. Sussman, Editor, and the National Council on Family Relations especially deserve our gratitude for letting us draw so heavily from their materials.

Contents

THE CONTEMPORARY FAMILY AND THE FAMILY CYCLE

VII. FAMILY INTERACTION 265

VIII. FERTILITY: TRENDS AND CONTROL 317

IX. FAMILIES WITH CHILDREN AND CHILD DEVELOPMENT 357

X. FAMILY EXTENSION 409

SELECTED FACTORS

Introduction

T HE OBJECTIVES OF STUDYING the family may be characterized by two emphases: Those that are relevant primarily to sociology as a science and those that are of social or practical importance. What is sociologically relevant may also have a direct bearing on what is considered to be important by the society or vice versa, but the distinction focuses on the abstract character of the science as compared to the problem orientation of society.

The scientific study of the family involves the examination of regularities in the forms and structures of the group. The family represents a broad class of groupings, and at one level sociology is concerned with those properties of behavior that are associated commonly to all types of groups. For example, the behavior that is possible in any group is to some extent determined by the number of members. Hence, studying the factor of group size and how it affects the behavior of group members is something that would have meaning in families, but also in committees, cliques, work groups, or casually formal groups. Admittedly, however, the family ordinarily has rather well-defined sets of expectations. For example, once formed, the family is not a voluntary association but one to which by definition the members have a commitment to permanence, although, of course, there may be formalized procedures for breaking the family ties. But in spite of its unique features, there are many ways in which the family may be viewed as simply another type of small group; it is as such we study its processes and patterns.

Research interest in the family contributes to general knowledge about the behavior of people in groups. In a similar way research on the family may also center on gaining more knowledge about individuals; it may very well be that different types of families produce different types of individuals. For example, differences in personality may be due to the number of siblings that a person has in his family as he grows up. A first-born may differ systematically from a third-born. Such influences might be expected to be relatively stable irrespective of the culture in which they are observed. There are other important issues that may be studied directly through the family, however, such as the distinction between a theory of personality that emphasizes the importance of "role models" for the growing child as contrasted, say, to the importance of interaction with given types of individuals. Findings of this sort would have generality beyond the study of the family.

Viewed from the other side one may ask: "What can be learned from the comparative study of families, both within a culture and across cultures?" The answer has to involve what we already know about cultures and variations even within a culture. The anthropologist's exploration of the far corners of the world have taught us to expect grossly different behavior patterns between cultures. But there is also an important matter of discovering regularities and patterns that persist across many or all cultures, and it is such regularities that form the nucleus of a scientific theory of human society. There is only limited value in establishing that family types in one culture are different from family types in another. But, when this is put on a general comparative basis, and many cultures are observed, the culture becomes the unit of sampling. If there is sufficient variation of cultures and if there are a sufficient number of cultures, presumably something may be said about the concomitants of particular family forms with regard to the other social phenomena in the culture, and also with regard to processes within the culture. The comparative study of cultures, thus, provides the opportunity of charting the concomitants of family types.

It needs to be emphasized that concomitants do not necessarily mean causal relationships. If it is found that there is more hostility in a society in which there are less intimate social relationships between husband and wife pairs, this does not mean that the lack of closeness *causes* (through some mediating process) greater hostility in the society. The concomitants may arise from a common process and may have no direct causal relationship in the ordinary sense. It would be a far-fetched generalization to suggest from such a study that increasing the closeness in family relations between husband and wife pairs would reduce the amount of hostility in the society.

This is not to negate the possibility that causal relationships of this type can occur. Quite to the contrary, the explicit interest in finding concomitants is the expectation that among these will be found causal relationships that will permit the prediction and control of behavior under given circumstances.

Let us return to the question of studying the family from a problem orientation, the second emphasis mentioned above. Practical concern with families may occur at several levels. The simplest and most direct is that any society attempts to control the deviant behavior within it, or to maintain behavior within certain bounds. Whenever deviance occurs beyond a certain limit, mechanisms to handle it arise, or the society changes. There are general social values to which the individual members of the society are expected to conform; the degree of homogeneity in the society determines whether well-defined values can be easily identified. In some "primitive" cultures that have had very little contact with the outside world, the patterns of behavior and expectations are so consistent from generation to generation that little deviation from a family type is found. There is, however, much variation in family types among cultures, which range from the monogamous to the polygamous, and from the conjugal to the extended. And, within some nations variation is great—for example, in modern-day Israel the family types range from the modern conjugal family type to the Moslem polygyny which permits four wives.

A major interest of a society with regard to families within it centers on how to handle deviant families that are considered a "problem" by the society. Within any community there is usually some degree of consensus as to what constitutes a problem or significant deviation from established family patterns. But some communities are less willing than others to define and sanction deviance. Moreover, there may be reluctance to impose sanctions for deviance on certain members of the community, either because they are viewed as too powerful or because they are so marginal and isolated from the community that they do not pose a threat to the established patterns of behavior. The study of community variations in defining deviance as well as the differential application of sanctions immediately takes us beyond interest in the family as a social problem. Yet, understanding this process is of considerable importance to both the theorist and the person who is concerned about the practical problems of families.

It may be worthwhile to look at some ideals in American society as a point of departure for examining social concern with the study of the family. To begin with, obviously the American family has been shifting in character, constantly and rapidly, since colonial times. This has not been a matter simply of the American scene but a concomitant of the general industrialization and rapid advance of technology during the past two centuries. Among general values, however, there has been a rather strong insistence on the permanence of the marital unit and the importance of "blood" ties.

During this extensive period there have been great shifts in terms of preparation for and the means of gaining livelihood. The large extended family that could manage a farm and other interests in the community has virtually disappeared during this period. From a primarily rural state, for example, New York has changed so markedly that in 1960 only four percent of families were formally listed as farm families. The values that made children important on a farm are largely not present in urban areas. Thus, there may be conflicting values present that say children are good because they are useful and others that say children are hindrances because they constitute a significant economic burden. Children on farms may not wish to remain there and may develop values in school (especially with modern consolidated schools) that are more properly associated with urban areas. This may be the source of some conflict in families in rural areas. Within the urban areas the general assessment of children as desirable may be economically an impractical burden for many, conflicting with other values within the urban community.

There are other socially important problems that foster research on the family. Irrespective of the question of whether rural or urban values are involved, the permanence of the marriage relationship is a value that is common to most religions and to most philosophies of life. Yet, in the more modern scene of America there has been a considerable amount of family disruption. As education progresses, presumably the age of emancipation occurs later; yet on the average, marriages occur earlier today than they did, say, at the turn of the twentieth century. It should be noted that, paradoxically, biological maturation, at least for females, is occurring 3 to 4 years earlier than in colonial times. In colonial times the education of females was at least in part a luxury, and education for careers was a masculine orientation. Today there is relatively little discrimination in the education of males and females, except at the professional level. This has some bearing on the expectations of husbands and wives in their relationships, and more generally in the ordering of the dominance relationships in the family. Should husbands and wives complement each other, or are they intrinsically in a competitive situation? Should a hierarchy develop and should it be in the tradition of the male-centered family? Or have we become irreversibly child-centered?

All these are self-conscious questions that occur in American society. Today, there is less tolerance for allowing family forms to develop haphazardly or to proceed largely as a consequence of a general development of the society; rather, there is emphasis on implementing values in a positive way. This orientation places a heavy stress on a need for additional study of family life.

It remains to be said that there is also an immediate practical value in studying marriage and the family for any individual in a society. This, of course, underlies much of the motivation in offering "family courses" at both the high school and college levels. Basically, information about what behavior is considered proper and what actually happens can be valuable in itself. With the high value placed on individual choice rather than on censorship and ignorance, the obvious contribution of such study is in providing the individual with the tools for making his own decisions on the basis of knowledge rather than on the basis of ignorance. In this sense, the general study of family forms, both cross-culturally and within a culture, is important to all persons.

An Example of Sociological Interest

While the social sciences may be viewed as relatively recent in development, they have already begun to accumulate a considerable knowledge and experience. Knowledge about social phenomena becomes woven into sociological theory, which is both speculative and also cognizant of the current status of empirical validation. While well-established theory such as is found in the physical sciences does not yet occur among the social sciences, there are instances where a high degree of specialized attention has led to reasonably clear delineation of empirical generalizations.

One aspect of social science that has received considerable attention in more recent decades is identified with the "formalistic" interest in sociology. We may illustrate this interest by pointing to the variable of group size. If we examine the differences in behavioral organization that are *possible* in groups of sizes from two to five, for example, we notice that they are striking. In groups of size two there are only two ways in which the members may orient themselves about a decision—either they can agree or they disagree. If they agree, then the two persons may be seen as forming a unitary (unanimous) group. In a group of size two, obviously, if one person totally withdraws, implicitly the group no longer exists. Therefore, there are particular bounds that occur for the behavior of individuals to keep from disrupting the group. If this is a casual group, the group may come apart and together relatively easily on the basis of agreement or disagreement, except that experience tends to reinforce itself and therefore two persons who have parted in their ways may reinforce this separation rather than attempt to meet again; for once the channels of communication are broken, how can they be re-established without the person making the overtures placing himself in a position where he can be rejected?

On the other hand, the situation with an American married couple begins with the supposition that the group cannot be torn asunder because there is a legal bond maintaining it. Under these conditions there presumably is greater tolerance for hostility, antagonism, and emotional involvement within the pair, since these in themselves do not break the bond. Phrased differently, if a person throws a tantrum, a casual acquaintance might walk away thinking that person is out of his head and not the kind with whom he wants to associate. In the case of the married couple, the person throwing the tantrum may threaten the relationship, but if the second person walks away, the legal relationship is not broken, and the legal relationship and what it implies give continuity to the marriage, the tantrum being merely one episode.

Moving to the three person group, there are three ways in which the group may be ordered. It is possible for the three individuals to hold three separate positions with regard to some issue. It is more likely, however, that most issues are polar, and this predisposes for certain types of arrangement. For example, there may be two persons on different sides of the issue with a third person "in between," taking the position of a mediator. It may be that the organization of the group will be of two persons forming a coalition (or a unitary pair) in opposition to the third. It is also possible that the three persons may be in total agreement on the issue. If one person leaves the triad, the group does not lose its identity entirely. The two persons still constitute a group and, in one sense at least, continuity is maintained. In studying the family, the relevance of generalizations in the abstract as above can be explored in the more specific positions of the family. The husband and wife pair generally represent a coalition, however benevolent, with regard to the child. But alignments of coalitions may shift, and, as one example, the mother-child pair may become a dominant coalition in the unit. The unit of husband-wife pair and wife's mother may be analyzed in similar terms, and need not be just a matter of mother-in-law jokes.

In an abstract sense, the groupings within the four person group may take on several forms. The group may be divided equally into two halves; thus, a situation arises in which two coalitions may meet with balanced opposition, members presumably having equal relevance in the group. This may form a deadlock, or it may create a situation within the group in which two hostile camps operate independently. By analogy to a familial group this could be the association of one parent with one child and the other parent with a second child, each pair in this case concerned primarily with its own point of view. The husband-wife pair versus two children, obviously, is not a balanced opposition. There is always the possibility that there are four positions that are held independently by the members but this postulates a rather chaotic type of organization and, again, issues are rarely drawn in this fashion. If one person is in isolation and in opposition to three others, the opposition he meets is more formidable than when there are only two others. Numbers may make the opposition overwhelming but adding even more numbers to the opposition will have a decreasingly important impact; a law of diminishing returns may come into effect. The possibility of a unanimity always exists with the four person group but obviously, the larger the number of individuals involved in a group, the more difficult it will be to have unanimity on any issue on which individuals may differ.

The striking feature of the four person group is the possibility for the two opposing coalitions. How important is this structure of opposing coalitions? In terms of our empirical research experience, the answer is ambiguous, but it is likely that such structures cannot be permanent in a group of four persons without actually splitting it. Many issues occur that must be handled by the group and the coalitions are probably transitory rather than permanent, with many realignments, even when one set of coalitions is more likely than another. If the group is not to be torn asunder it will organize around maintaining an unbalanced and dominating opposition. The net consequence may be of de-emphasizing the importance of any individual in the group and emphasizing the structure.

In contrast to the four person group, the five person group presents the unique circumstance where two coalitions may occur with either of two mediating circumstances present. The two coalitions may be of two persons each, with the fifth person standing as a mediator between them. Or, the coalition may be of two persons against three persons, but this is no longer the antagonistic situation of the four person group because the majority is indicated. A majority situation in the five person group may not be as drastic in its consequences as in the three person group, since the minority may still consist of a coalition that is to some extent self-supporting and provides its own security. The five person group, thus, has some unique characteristics that might make it particularly advantageous for purposes of joint decisions or cooperative work.

It needs to be remarked further that there are certain characteristics that are associated with group size, *per se*. For example, in a large group a person may "stand out" as a leader by contrast because he happens to be delegated to that position. The delegation, implicit or explicit, may be for efficiency, since joint action becomes less feasible as the group gets larger. Delegation of responsibility or differentiation of roles thus becomes associated with largeness of the group. But largeness of the group provides for other things as well. For example, one cannot be anonymous in a two person group, and one can hardly be anonymous in a three person group, but in a five person group one may already begin to have an opportunity to retire and become inconspicuous without threatening the operation of the group. The group depends less heavily on the participation of any single member for its smooth operation.

These suggested generalizations appear to have a logical basis, but in fact most have some verification in empirical laboratory observation. Moreover it may be demonstrated that some of this theory and research carries over to the study of the family. The carry-over, however, is not direct or complete because the family situation is one that is circumscribed by statuses and roles that are ordinarily well-defined and dictate the overall patterns of interaction. The status of father in American society has particular expectations associated with it, and likewise the status of mother, daughter, and son. The expectations are found in the general culture, and depending upon the variability of the culture the specificity of the expectations will be either high or low. The coalition of father and mother as dominating the family during those periods when the children are in the formative stage is ordinarily prescribed in American society. Variation from this would constitute a pattern of behavior that would be defined as deviant. The researcher who finds that in certain middle class families there is child domination may further find that this fact has as much popular and practical interest as it does scientific interest.

The fact is, however, that groups in society are organized in many different ways, and not only in families. For example, the work group may be organized in terms of the boss, foreman, and the workers, and so forth, and there may be a great variety of work groups and organizations. Moreover, individuals in society belong to more than one group, and the goals and expectations of the various groups to which a person belongs may be in conflict. Assume, for example, that a husband and wife have experienced a period of considerable strain in their marital relationship. They have been looking forward to a week vacation during which time they hope to relax, get away from some of the sources of strain, and generally rediscover the basis of love and affection between them. On the day before the scheduled departure, the husband's boss calls and says that the company has a very good chance of acquiring a new client and that his services are needed to develop a proposal for the prospective client. What does our role-torn husband do? If he postpones the vacation he is almost certain to exacerbate the strain in his relationship with his wife—especially if too many hours at the office is one of the major sources of conflict. On the other hand, if he refuses to work on the proposal he may seriously jeopardize his job and relationship with his boss.

There can be literally hundreds of role conflicts in the course of a few months of a person's life. Many of these conflicts, obviously, will not be serious. But there are times when the conflicting expectations of groups to which an individual belongs can spell disaster or near disaster for an individual's relationship to one of these groups. Because marriage is a binding legal contract, there is probably a tendency on the part of most people to resolve conflicting intergroup expectations at the expense of the family. Repeated resolutions of this type may in time result in conflict within the family that reaches a point of no return and dissolution of the marriage. What is proposed here is simply a hypothesis. So far as we know, there is no study which empirically validates the tendency for conflicting intergroup expectations to be resolved at the expense of the family. But in any event, the question that is raised has theoretical implications that move us beyond the limited study of families.

Social science tends to be abstract and deals with groups in general, but it should be applicable to the study of the family. Conversely, the study of the family should contribute to the general status of knowledge in sociology.

Family Study and Change

The history of almost any science can be described as one moving from intuitive notions to more rigorous and accurate means of describing phenomena. At the level of intuition, there is dependence on belief in personal observation, and this is colored by the common beliefs in the culture. If one believes what everyone else believes, it is very difficult to move outside of this encompassing web. The progress of science seems to hinge on asking whether a belief corresponds to a given situation, or by trying to put beliefs into effect and finding that they do not work. This caricature fits the physical and biological sciences as well as the social sciences. The physical sciences did not begin with an abstract and sytematic representation of the phenomena as they are now understood.

The scientists of another generation concerned themselves with drugs to kill and to cure, with attempts to make gold out of base metals, with the refinement of implements to make life more comfortable for some. Their objectives were not necessarily lofty nor pure and it is of some interest that periods of material progress are very often identified (*post hoc*) with warfare and strife. What this raises as an issue is whether a science progresses because someone is interested in studying the abstract characteristics of trajectory, or because people want a catapult that will throw a massive stone over the defenders' wall.

While it is of dubious value to labor the question of causes, at least it can be said that a characteristic condition associated with the study of any phenomenon is the fact that some problems exist that call it to attention. From this point of view, interest in the study of the family is certainly as old as any other. The fact is, however, that the corresponding science, which we may call sociology, has not developed to a point where it is either as abstract or systematic as are the major physical sciences. There are many good reasons for this; the great variety, the apparent plasticity of families, and the ability of the community to operate under apparently radically different circumstances of family organization require attention only to the extent of maintaining a sufficient level of operation rather than an optimum level. This may be seen both from the point of view of the community and also from the point of view of the individual. Within any community the existing normative patterns indicate the bounds of what the family is. These normative patterns are rarely so rigorously defined that a considerable degree of variation is not found. Within the community the patterns tend to persist for any number of reasons but the most obvious is that this is the way things are done; besides, the patterns previously have worked so why should they not continue working? From the point of view of the individual, since the rules work for most, why shouldn't they work for a particular family? This is a view that says: As other families operate, so shall we, for we are of the same social fabric.

Of course, there is the proviso that if this is not possible, then something can be done, and most societies have means for the dissolution or revision of the family. Even within the most homogeneous community there will be individuals or situations that will deviate from the modal pattern or the ideal expectations of the community. The community defines what constitutes a problem for attention. On the one hand, the community may describe such a problem in relatively abstract terms, as, for example, in Aristotle's time, where the question of the proper form of government, the organization of the political state, was a focus of attention. Or the community may focus on a given type of deviance and judge this as a problem as, for example, in deviation from narrowly defined family values as prescribed by the Puritans. The existence of a problem by itself, however, does not lead to the development of science. While Aristotle may have concerned himself with questions of politics, the organization of the state and forms of constitutions, others participated in what today is commonly called social action and attempted to alter the problem situation into a form more acceptable to them. Similarly, the existence of deviation from the ideal family type among the Puritans need not lead to asking questions of why deviance might occur, but might lead directly to repressive measures to stamp out the evil in the aberration, possibly by eliminating the deviants; the cause of the deviation could be assumed as known (the devil), and inquiry into other possible causes might not occur as a serious possibility.

What is suggested here is that all human communities have a wisdom built into them that permits their effective change or the development of means for handling deviation in the family types. For these reasons it may be understood why the systematic study of the family, and for that matter, other social phenomena, need not have occurred systematically. On the other hand, the importance of deviation counter to expectations has certainly not been ignored. In fact, this is the common topic of moralistic history and the relationships of father and son and daughter, and of husband and wife, as prime examples, receive much emphasis in the Old Testament and other early recorded writings. But this is the recording of unique history and experience, rather than the abstraction of principles of organization. Much of this can provide information for the surface description of ideal and real patterns of behavior, but this does not provide the systematic information that is expected to lie at the base of social science. At best, the regularities that are recorded historically and that are sometimes intuitively well analyzed will be *understood* through a more exact social science.

Where Does the Study of the Family Begin?

What constitutes the family unit is defined by the culture, and not by the observer. From the point of view of the observer, the term refers to the identification of a complex that recurs with sufficient regularity through cultures to warrant inclusion under one concept, but not without a caution.

In every culture some unit of organization centers on the procreation and raising of children, and commensurate with the relatively long period of dependency, the unit tends to be enduring. This unit is the one that is commonly called the family, and the variety of forms it can take is staggering. A common (or core) feature of the unit is the existence of a mixed-sex responsible adult unit that actually begets the children; the variation on this score includes the well-defined husband-wife pair, the *polyandrous* group (one wife, more than one husband), the *polygynous* group (one husband, more than one wife), but also variations in which there is no formal status definition corresponding to husband. In the last case, while there may be no enduring mating unit established that is given formal recognition in the culture, the rules for mating may be explicit and well-defined with regard to *endogamy* and *exogamy*. The common pattern through cultures is that the procreation group also takes some responsibility for the procreated, and this is the core unit in defining the family.

The broad variety of forms of families, even in a relatively homogeneous culture, however, requires further caution and definition; for example, does a family exist if there are no children? In American culture, the husband-wife pairs are usually considered families, but in a culture where the core familial unit is the woman, her children, and a maternal uncle of the children, is there a family when there are no children? This becomes a sticky definitional question, since families have extensions in kinship and affinity, and the core units are embedded in larger complexes of the social fabric. In some cultures, the concept of family becomes less useful and intelligible than a concept like *household* in describing or understanding the operation of the social structure; but this implies only that a number of concepts may be useful or required in studying the area provisionally or intuitively identified by *family*.

The two features that we have thus far identified as commonly associated with the family are the mating unit and the parent-child unit. It needs to be stressed that in any culture these units do not occur in a vacuum. Among the folkways and mores that constitute the culture there are ways and means of identifying the persons within it, the system of identifying familial units or units of kinship and descent. Similarly, the notion that a familial unit exists at all implies that there are institutionalized patterns of belief and behavior with regard to the unit.

What Is a Society?

One of the ways to narrow down the definition of the family is to examine a larger unit within which it resides. What is meant by a society? What occurs within a society? First, in any society there is implicit existence over time. This implies a continuing supply of members of this society, and within the society there is ordinarily reproduction of the members, and social organization to maintain this. Similarly in the society there is continuity in the beliefs and behavior of the members, and hence the members must be socialized or indoctrinated into these beliefs and behavior patterns. In order for continuity to exist, obviously, there must also be persons, and a concomitant of survival is a provision of the basic biological requirements in the way of food, clothing, and shelter. If the society is of any size, ordinarily there will be some division of labor and specialization in production and distribution of goods and services. Similarly, implied in all this is that there is order and patterning to the behavior, or there is no society at all. Finally, either the society is in isolation or it must also be ordered with regard to other societies and therefore must provide means for regulation and communication in this direction.

In the statement that a society exists and has continuity there is no necessary implication that it has an underlying purpose in being, but commonly societies have expressions of such value orientations. Possibly, it is better said (tautologically) that a society's existence may be viewed from the point of view of the society as its main reason for existing.

In brief, the definition of a society might be outlined as follows:

  I. An aggregate of people

  II. Commonly identified with some territorial bounds (location)

  III. Existing through time with continuity
      Thus: A. Providing for the regulation of the relationships of
              the members (folkways, mores, and laws)

1. Providing for the physical needs of the members (food, clothing, shelter)
2. Providing for the means of continuing the numbers (reproduction and adoption)
3. Providing for socializing the members

B. Acting as a unit with regard to any externally defined force or threat

What society is excluded by this definition? Could a family also be a society? Yes, but this would be the limiting case. To some extent what is identified as the family does something in regard to each of the above.

From the point of view of the social scientist, within any society there are complexes of values and patterns of belief and behavior that are called institutional. The common ones are identified as the family, the economic, the political and the religious institutions, and these obviously correspond to some of the defining characteristics of a society. In addition, there are other kinds of institutions or institutional areas that are recognized in societies—for example, in American society we speak of institutional educational objectives. Peripherally, the family is the unit that concerns itself in some part with all of these societal defining aspects. Centrally, however, it is oriented toward the procreation and socialization.

The Context of Family Study

If one compares the interests likely to be expressed by students of the family during the present era with those of, say, 30 years ago, some evident changes are immediately apparent.

The college student of the thirties and forties was exposed to a standard fare, most likely, of a brief exposure to other forms of marriage—the more exotic the better with the new arrival, for all practical purposes, of an anthropological emphasis on the academic scene. He would probably be presented with various lists of what were considered "by Americans and for Americans" to be desirable "traits" among marriage partners, both individually and in combination with each other. John Dewey's philosophy influenced this field also in an oblique way, so that changes in child rearing and education were affecting the notion of the American marriage as a whole. If the student received a broad exposure, he would be lucky to be introduced to some of the legalistic concepts involved in marriage and the dissolution of marriage.

Control of fertility on the whole was pretty much restricted to the summary that Catholics were "against it." Sterilization as a means of preventing the "unfit" from propagating was considered an enlightened though restricted approach, not without its staunch supporters and vocal critics. The diaphragm as a contraceptive technique was the latest thing, but was rarely discussed publicly in a classroom situation. The "way out" subjects for discussion were usually considered to be trial marriages and the concepts of romantic love and its application to marriage.

As the world has expanded in communication and shrunk in size, a whole array of items relevant to the study of marriage and family institutions can be drawn from the same concerns that interest citizens as a whole. Poverty, for example, that common human misery, is seen as intimately related to any study of the family in general. Poverty as it affects size of family, utilization of resources in relation to the market place and consumer position, lending and borrowing procedures affecting place and character of homes and communities; poverty as it affects schooling, care of children, transmission of appropriate cultural values, racial attitudes, all these obviously first experienced and then developed within the family as well as affecting developments outside of it.

The point is that the family castle, once conceived of as the place into which one might escape the world is now generally viewed as totally related to the world at large. Family planning in Taiwan is related to family planning in the Smith household. The increased prevalence and kinds of contraceptive techniques have introduced the possibilities of whole new moralities which cannot be separated from the study of the family institution, its structure and functions in personal and societal ways.

PART 1
Some Bases of Family Study

CHAPTER I

The Origin of the Family

THE FIRST SECTION in this chapter, "Origins of the Family: Some Early Works," brings together materials that give the flavor of writings on family forms up to the beginning of this century. While some of the ideas are antiquated, these selections provide a broader perspective and a careful reading should yield an appreciation of the quality of early scholarship. As the student becomes more familiar with contemporary theories he will profit by going back and rereading these selections and asking where early theorists seem to have been right and where they seem to be wide of the mark. It is also interesting to observe the intellectual development of thought about the family. For example, Morgan's theories were incorporated into the work of Engel, and these were the bases of Freud's presentation on the origins of the incest taboo. Freud's speculations and instinct theories are not so uncritically accepted today as they were a decade or two ago, but the recency with which such theories have been taken literally seriously suggests their relevance for explanation of social forms.

The excerpt presented from Leslie A. White's "The Definition and Prohibition of Incest" basically reflects the anthropological view in the modern era, emphasizing the social bases of behavior. Anthropologists have subsequently considered questions of the situational factors that may lead to prohibitions on incest and other rules controlling mating. Review of such a topic in the anthropological journals during the last two decades makes an interesting intellectual exercise and demonstrates that interest in the study of incest is still very keen. It also provides insight as to how social scientists may examine predispositions for the social order built into the nature of man and his environment.

In the article by Gardner Lindzey titled "Some Remarks Concerning Incest and the Incest Taboo," the type of ingenious analysis reflected in the work of anthropologists is set to examining the biological consequences of inbreeding and the relationship of these to the incest taboo. After a number of decades of emphasis on the social, the importance of the biological factors is again being brought persuasively to the fore.

The final article in this chapter is Ira L. Reiss's "The Universality of the Family: A Conceptual Analysis." Consideration of the incest taboo and its origins and universality is highly related to the question of the universality of the family. Indeed, the question of universals *per se* is an old and recurring interest in the social sciences. In modern dress the question is frequently raised in terms of the functional prerequisites for human society, and the notion is that any universals which exist in human society must correspond to the functional prerequisites. Reiss questions the universality of the nuclear family as such. He argues that while nurturant-socialization is a functional prerequisite (and thus a universal), this process need not occur only through the nuclear family.

1.

ORIGINS OF THE FAMILY: SOME EARLY WORKS

One way of looking at the world is to see all within it as natural. Love, beauty, hate, and honor are all natural. This makes possible the statement that the cliff dwelling of modern super-apartments is as "natural" as living in a primeval forest. At the same time such a statement overshadows a question of concern to sociologists in earlier generations, and, in fact, of interest to sociologists today when phrased in a more sophisticated manner. The early formulation of the questions about the "natural" forms of the family, for example, included: What was the original form of family association? To some extent, these questions were well woven into others that referred more directly to the origins of human social behavior and the study of the evolution of societies, an important topic in early anthropology and sociology.

At this point it is easy to say glibly that concern with origins is futile, but this may be the naive rather than the sophisticated comment. The scholars of the time were brilliant, and we cannot blame them if they had intellectual diseases for which today we presumably have common cures. The academic climate fostered development of theories, concern with origins and evolution, and even involvement with one's own personal theory, which may have caused statements to become absolute that were intended in the formulation to be tentative hypotheses. Attention to the early writers in this field can be a fascinating and exciting study of watching an intellectual development.

The questions to which these writers (roughly including the period between 1860 and 1900) devoted themselves were not easy. What is the sequence of development of cultures? Certainly, as they so well pointed out, in terms of ma-

terial things a sequence must exist. The bow cannot be invented until there is string, or cord, or an equivalent artifact. And if material progress is orderly within certain bounds, should not the concomitant organization of people also be orderly? This, of course, is the rationale explicitly stated in Lewis Henry Morgan's An-cient Society (1878), and the stages of organization he provides center on material progress. But this only permitted the raising of hypotheses about stages, and hypotheses are not answers. What was the original form in the hypothetical state of nature? Here is where much of the early debate occurred.

The Darwinian proposal was of a group with a dominant male and his band. But this was disputed quickly and early. A notion that was more popular was of group living, with group marriage, as it were, and promiscuous relations among the adults. The rationale for this notion arose in several ways. In part, evidence for this was asserted through the interpretations of the Australian aborigines, who were judged among the most primitive and who were said to have a form of group marriage. But "evidence" was adduced from other sources as well. For example, an interpretation of the biblical story of origins required that there be no ban on brother-sister marriage, and this supported the notion of promiscuous relations in a primitive horde. Others, like Bachofen, proposed the notion of the importance of the unit of mother and child, and that this natural unit should be the pristine basis of organization.

What is often ignored by students of marriage and the family today is that much of concern of the early scholars centered implicitly on the questions of the limits of human behavior and organization, and these are not trivial questions. There necessarily also arose a considerable attention to the comparative study of forms of organization, and the variations on behavior that are imposed by different forms. In this light, considerable profit, aside from historical interest, is available in the writings of

Portions of this selection are reprinted from: Andrew Lang, *Social Origins;* and J. J. Atkinson, *Primal Law,* London: Longman's, Green, and Co., 1903 [Lang: excerpted and edited, pp. 21-33; Atkinson: excerpted and edited, pp. 219-38]; and Lewis H. Morgan, *Ancient Society,* New York: Henry Holt and Company, 1878 [excerpted and edited, pp. 498-509].

early writers like Darwin, Morgan, McLennan, Maine, Spencer, Tyler, Bachofen, Westermarck, Crawley, and others.

The question of origins could almost be looked at as if it were a game. If man was in his "natural" state, he had no social rules. Then how did he exist? Assuming there could be agreement on this, then, with regard to organization beyond this, what was the first rule that would need to occur? Inevitably, certain pressures must arise to cause change. The adults get older; the children become adults; the size of the unit changes; and so forth. These become the variables to consider in the game, or as it were, in the exchange between the early scholars, with the focus on the development of rules of family formation, of exogamy in particular.

Here we present a rather late suggestion in this arena of origins by J. J. Atkinson. This has been excerpted and the full argument is not presented. What is presented, however, well indicates how these questions of origin were conceived. Atkinson's materials are introduced posthumously in a book titled Social Origins *by Andrew Lang (1903), and the title of Atkinson's work was* Primal Law. *The primal law is the law of exogamy that prohibits marriage between brother and sister, and here we present the essence of the argument made by Atkinson.*

It should be noted in passing that Lang's review and introduction, which actually constitutes most of the published book, are critical and rather remarkable in pursuing logical analyses. Lang places some of the other writers on the topic in context, not always gently, and two examples of his comments follow before the main presentation of Primal Law.

THEORIES OF EXOGAMY

DR. WESTERMARCK'S THEORY

As to exogamy, Dr. Westermarck explains it by 'an instinct' against marriage of near kin. Our ancestors who married near kin would die out, he thinks, and they who avoided such unions would survive, 'and thus an instinct would be developed,' by 'Natural Selection.' But why did any of our ancestors avoid such marriages at all? From 'an aversion to those with whom they lived.' And why had they this aversion? Because they had an instinct against such unions. Then why had they an instinct? We are engaged in a vicious circle.

If the attention given to Westermarck by Lang is a little terse, that given to McLennan is precise but more extended. Here we indicate a section where Lang devotes his analysis specifically to McLennan's work.

MR. McLENNAN'S THEORY

Mr. McLennan's hypothetical first groups, like Mr. Atkinson's, were very low indeed. They developed exogamy, not (as in Mr. Atkinson's theory) through sexual jealousy on the part of the sires, but, first, through regular female infanticide. . . . Girl babies being mostly killed out, women became scarce. Neighboring groups being hostile, brides could only be procured by hostile capture. Each group thus stole all its brides and became exogamous, and marriage inside the group became a sin, by dint of 'a prejudice strong as a principle of religion.'

This theory of Mr. McLennan's is, I think, quite untenable. The prevalence of female infanticide, at the supposed very early stage of society, is not demonstrated, and did not seem probable to Mr. Darwin. Even if it existed, it could not create a prejudice against marrying the few women left within the group. Mr. McLennan, unhappily, was prevented by bad health, and death, from working out his hypothesis completely. His most recent statement involves the theory that the method of the Nairs of Malabar, living in polyandrous households (many men to each woman) was the earliest form of 'marriage.' But people who, like the Nairs, dwell in large households, are far indeed from being 'primitive.' 'A want of balance between the sexes' led, Mr. McLennan held, to a 'practice of capturing women for wives,' and was followed by 'the rise of the law of exogamy.' The first prohibition would be against capturing women of the kindred (marked by the totem), for such capture, if resisted, might involve the shedding of kindred blood. Women being scarce, through female infanticide, kindred groups would not give up or sell their women to each other (though to the males of the groups, such women could not be wives), nor could women be raided from kindred groups, as we saw. So they would be stolen from alien groups, 'and so marriages with kindred women would tend to go into desuetude.' The introduction of captured alien wives would change the nature of matrimonial relations. Under the Nair system 'a woman would live in the house of her mother, and under the special guardianship and protection of her brothers and her mother's brothers. She would be in a position of almost absolute independence of her husbands. . . .'

But really pristine man and woman can have had no houses, no matriarchal rule of women. The Nairs, not being primitive, have houses, and their women have authority: pristine man was not in their condition. However, captured alien wives would, Mr. McLennan argues, be property, be slaves; and men would find this arrangement (now obsolete) so charming that polyandry and the reign of woman would go out. The only real legal marriage would be wedlock with an alien, a captive, a slave woman. Marriage with a woman of the same stock would be a crime and a sin. It would be incest. Really it would be, at worst, concubinage.

This theory seems untenable at every point, community of wives, female infanticide, household life, supremacy of women in the household, living with a non-captive wife reckoning as incest, and, in short, all along the line. Even if the prejudice against marrying native women did exist, it could not be developed into the idea of sin—granting that the idea of sin already existed. To be sinful, endogamy within the group must have offended some superstitious belief, perhaps the belief in the totem, with its tabu.

While there is no question of the critical acumen of Andrew Lang in his review of the then current status of theories of origins, particularly with reference to exogamy, his volume and the work of Atkinson are not so well known as some of their contemporaries. Lang was not uncritical in his introduction of the work of Atkinson, probably because its rather well-formed lines of development were simple and could stand

the test. Here we reproduce, with minimal editing, the main argument of Atkinson (pp. 219–38).

PRIMAL LAW

Another difficulty in connection with the evolution of the so-called Primal Law of Avoidance between brother and sister from that early idea which we will presently disclose, seems to lie in the fact that if, as we uphold, such law was the first factor in the ascent of man, it must have taken its rise whilst he was still some ape-like creature. It remains, however, to be shown from its peculiar form that in its primitive application, the law would not have required for its intelligence greater mental power than is possessed by actual anthropoids. The law may indeed be said to be practically an inchoate fact, an actual if partial usage, for the regulation of the intersexual relations among most of the higher mammals. It could, at any rate, have come into full intelligent application as a well-defined social institution, in the actual sense of the term, whilst the anthropomorphic progenitor of man was still so little removed from the ape that

> His speech was yet as halting as his gait,
> Only less brutish than his moral state.

Briefly, the law of Avoidance concerns (more particularly) the relation 'inter se,' from a sexual point of view, of the male and female offspring of any given parents. In other words it determines the mutual attitude to the female within a (single) family group dominated by a male head.

Before entering into the argument in this connection, it will be desirable to make a paraphrase on Mr. Darwin's dictum as to the social condition of man in the animal stage in general, and more particularly in regard to his intermarital relations, and to compare this with that of actual mammals. It is to be noted that he does not pronounce definitely as to whether, in the era of pure animalism, the original type of man's ancestor was social or non-social in habit. But we may judge from the *Descent of Man* that Darwin evidently inclines to the opinion that, even primitively, he was a social animal, as seemingly more in accord with the present eminently social conditions.

The very significant counter-fact, however, remains, that none of the actual anthropoids, as far as regards the adult males, are in any way social or even gregarious; the conclusion thus seems evident that, like these his nearest compeers of today, man was on the contrary a non-social animal, and that, as with the gorilla, only one grown male would have been seen in a band. We must then imagine our more or less human ancestor, roaming the forest in search of daily food, as a solitary polygamous male, with wife or wives and female children; the unsocial head of a *solitary* isolated group.

With equal strength and probably already greater than any *actual* animal of to-day, he had perhaps acquired dominance over most of the other beasts of the field. The patriarch had only one enemy whom he should dread, an enemy with each coming year more and more to be feared—deadly rivals of his very own flesh and blood, and the fruit of his loins—namely, that neighbouring group of young males exiled by sexual jealousy from his own and similar family groups—a youthful band of brothers living together in forced celibacy, or at most in polyandrous relation with some single female captive. A horde as yet weak in their impubescence, they are, but they would, when strength was gained with time, inevitably wrench by combined attacks, renewed again and again, both wife and life from the paternal tyrant. But they themselves, after brief communistic enjoyment, would be segregated anew by the fierce fire of sexual jealousy, each survivor of the slaughter relapsing into lonely sovereignty, the head of the typical group with its characteristic feature of a single adult male member in antagonism with every other adult male. Now it can be shown that this vicious circle of the stream of social life is common to most mammals. The facts of the circumstance can be most easily observed amidst the half-wild, half-domesticated animals met with in colonial farming experience, in New Caledonia, for instance, where European horses and cattle have been allowed to return almost to a state of nature.

In this respect the economy of life in a herd of even such gregarious creatures as the bovine race, is a very curious and instructive study. There is no fact more striking than the subordination in which the younger bulls are kept; as long as they are at all tolerated in the herd by its patriarch, their intercourse with the females is most limited, and only takes place by stealth and at the risk of life and limb.

Nothing, as breeders are aware, is so fatal to the well-being of a herd, or leads so quickly to degeneration, as the perpetuation of the race by immature males. That procreation should be the act of the robust adult alone, is evidently an axiom with nature herself in successful production; it is doubtless of the highest importance to keep up the normal standard of strength and size. As a fact, the presence of the immature male among a herd of cattle is only permitted whilst he is still quite impubescent. Then banishment by the master of the herd is inevitable at a later stage. These exiles, although thus apart from the main herd, remain in touch with it, so to speak, and we find in consequence, in continual proximity of the troop of the patriarch and his females, a small band of males, which, as is evident from their colour and general physical resemblance, are its direct product. The relations between this mob and the old male are always strained, the latter has constantly to be on the watch to *shield his marital rights*.

For long the mere menace of his presence suffices for such protection, but with age—the young bulls becoming more bold—struggles take place which sooner or later, from mere force of numbers, end in the rout or death of the parent.

.   .   .

One important fact must here, however, be noted; that before such death or exile takes place, and the sons reach an age which enables them successfully to dispute the supremacy of the father, the daughters have reached puberty and borne produce to the sire—this matter, as will be seen later, has an important bearing on our general argument—on our theory of Primal Law. Amongst horses, again, which have become wild, exactly the same facts are to be observed. Each herd has one head, and this, as natural selection would imply, is the most powerful stallion; he is the master and owner of the females, and this mastery he retains until overpowered by other males, which, as before, are almost invariably his own progeny. In fact, any strange male would probably have first to run the gauntlet of this outlying herd of exiled sons before he could reach the father. It is, however, again to be noted that he is rarely thus overpowered by even the combined efforts of his sons, before his daughters have reached such an age as to have produced offspring to their father.

This system of sequence of generations in breeding is, indeed, so universal in a state of nature amongst all animals, as to seem to point to the fact that in-breeding between father and daughter cannot be so prejudicial as some believe. Its efficacy in type-fixing is at least very great, if, as experiments of my own in **pig**-breeding on these lines would lead me to think, the question of prepotency is merely a matter of such close in-breeding repeated for generations. We may note here that if, as is probable, the produce, on the contrary, of a full brother and sister are degenerate, nature seems to attempt to prevent its occurrence. On the succession of the sons to the father's rights, speedy conflicts from sexual jealousy arise amidst the former and lead to a rapid segregation of the herd, in which the chances of own brother and sister continuing to mate are slight. Until this segregation, however, does take place, nothing is more curious to watch than the attitude and relations of these young males among themselves, the oldest and strongest claiming prior marital rights, but no more.

The same phenomena in social economy may be observed with even greater intensity in lower ranks of life than the quadrupeds. For instance, in a large flock of game fowl which I had an opportunity to observe closely for several years, during which they had nearly relapsed into a state of nature, there was an exact reproduction of all these details. There existed the same division into small family groups, each headed by an adult male, the same subordination imposed on the junior males of their banishment at puberty, as also their inevitable combined attack, when sufficiently powerful, on their pa-. ternal enemy. His death resulted in the same communistic assumption of his rights, with a subsequent disruption, from jealousy, into the typical smaller and separate groups.

We thus find an identical condition of the sexual relations between the females of a group and its older and younger male members to be common in the animal world—the domination, in fact, of an idea that might, in the person of the senior male, confers marital rights over the female members of the family, and an inchoate rule of action resulting therefrom; which bars from the enjoyment of such right each junior male. To hold that man, whilst in the animal stage, should form an exception to the general rule seems unreasonable. If, as we are inclined to believe, he was originally a quite non-social animal, the fact becomes more possible still that, as with modern types of anthropoid apes, each adult as head of a group was at feud with every other. As regards the social evolution, it would indeed seem most natural that, as Mr. Darwin conceived, the first step in progress should have been taken by animals already united gregariously, and thus already imbued with some social feelings. Strange to say, the path in advance which the ancestor of man, in the light of our hypothesis, was destined to follow, disclosed itself as an indirect consequence of the very intensity of his non-social characteristic. . . .

Having ventured to differ from the great naturalist on this point, I would with deference take exception to his further statement—'That the younger males, being thus expelled and wandering about, would, when at last successful in finding a partner, prevent too close inter-breeding within the limits of the same family.' This, if I understand it rightly, would convey the idea that this youthful band quitted the scene of their birth, and deserted entirely their original habitat in the forest. I cannot help considering it an error to imagine that such wanderings could thus be without bounds. Nothing seems to me more remarkable and irrevocable in savage Nature than the rigid localisation of all living things in her realm. No fish in the sea, no bird in the air, but has its local habitation, which only becomes free to the stranger on the death of the occupant. No corner on earth but seems to hold its lawful tenant, and the bounds thereof are defined within rigid limits. Within, there is safety, with a sense of ownership; without, is the great unknown, possessed by others, fiercely ready to defend their rights, and threaten every danger and death to the stranger intruder—unless quite otherwise formidable than adolescent youth.

It is thus probable, in fact, that in common with the lower animals, the band of exiled young males of our anthropoid ancestor haunted the neighbourhood of the parent herd, remaining thus on familiar ground, and in hearing of friendly voices. For we must remember that their feud was only with the paternal parent. In the magic alembic of time the constantly increasing shadow of their presence would take sudden dreadful form, but in parricidal crime alone. The *sequel in disastrous incest, which Mr. Darwin would here conjecture at, Nature alone has ever been impotent to deal with.* The problem of an effectual bar to undesirable union between brother and sister was solved by man alone, and in the Primal Law. An effort of his embryonic intellect, thus early defiant of Nature, the law placed ethically, for once and for ever, a distinction between him and every other creature.

. . .

MAN VARYING FROM ANIMALS

In common, then, with their nearest congeners of to-day, we have found each male head of a group of our anthropoid ancestors in direct antagonism with every other male, and a consequent disruption of the family at each encounter with a superior force. This disruption, in its effects on a species of non-gregarious habits, would result not only in the dispersal of its members, but in the destruction of what material progress in the accumulation of property might have accrued. As this would have included all germs of mechanical discovery, again doubtless due solely to the superior constructive faculties of the male, it is evident that advance in a race thus socially constituted was quite impossible.

Now this antagonism of male with male, with all of its retrograde consequences, a struggle fierce enough in all animals, had a more

intense effect on nascent man than on any other creature that had ever existed. An added force was caused by the disappearance in the nascent human species of that season of physical and mental repose, granted by Nature to the rest of creation, when not actually in the moment or season of rut. This ever-recurring but limited period, ordinarily appearing for a certain fixed epoch in each year, by the exigencies of supply and demand in the necessarily abundant food required for nursing mothers, had lost its date-fixing power with this new creation—Man. With the very first steps in progress would come his adaptation to a more or less omnivorous and consequently more regular diet. The consequent modification would be profound in the matter of sexual habit and appetite. Man needed no longer to put limits to the season of love and desire. This was a crime against Nature, new in the history of the world, a crime which Nature would probably have avenged by race-deterioration or extermination, if the germs of mental power had not been already strong enough to lift him, Man, to be, of all creatures, almost completely beyond the influence of environment, thence of Nature herself.

The intensity of the evil led to its cure. In a state of society where literally every male creature's hand was against the other, and life one continual uproar from their contending strife; where not only was there no instant's truce in the warfare, but each blow dealt was emphasised (fatally) by the intellectual finesse which now directed it, it became a question of forced advance in progress or straight retreat in annihilation as a species. However difficult it may be to imagine by what path such a creature was ever to emerge from the materialistic labyrinth in which we thus find him involved, it is sure that he neither could nor did remain there. A forward step was somehow taken, some road out of the maze was somehow found.

It remains for us to trace, by what dim light of custom and tradition we may, the faint trail of those momentous footprints, which, however lame and halting, took the strait and difficult way to a higher life. We may expect to find, as is but natural, that the path was one before untrodden. As man followed it, at first unconsciously, from the shoulders of this new pilgrim, predestined to worthier burdens, would fall some of the heavy load of the mere animal nature.

There was now, in fact, to be a break in the economy of animal nature, as regards that vicious circle, where we found an ever-recurring violent succession to the solitary paternal tyrant, by sons whose parricidal hands were so soon again clenched in fratricidal strife. In the dawn of peace between this father and son we shall find the signpost to the new highway.

Before going further, we may here state our assumption that, when our ancestor had arrived at this crisis in his life, a crisis involving the vast psychological step in advance implied in the development of society, and the intelligence necessary for the evolution of the law in its regulation, he was already somewhat more than ape. The animal stage as forming part of the ladder of ascent from brute to man would be marked by degrees of progression, each a step further removed from the original type. These very earliest steps we indeed propose to examine later in detail, for the present we will suppose they have been taken, and that the influence of environment, under certain hypothetic conditions, to be also detailed hereafter, has fostered physical modifications toward the human type such as we found in the matter of rut. But in nature the relation is very close between the physical and the mental qualities. The advance in one would possibly lead to a corresponding development of the other. Each is the necessary complement of each. For instance, as Mr. Darwin has pointed out, while the lower extremities become more and more used for progression alone, so the upper, thus left free, would be specialised as prehensile organs, so becoming both valet and tutor to the nascent brain. To push our metaphor to an extreme, we may say that when Homo Alalus trod the new path, it was already as a biped in an upright attitude, thus leaving at least his hand free to point it out to others, for as yet his tongue, at least by the hypothesis, was inarticulate.

Our line of research as regards the new departure was at once narrowed when we indicated that it ended in the peaceful conjunction of father and son. Our path will lie in the examination of the question as to what possible series of natural circumstances, in the domestic life of the race, could lead to such conjunction, and what law in such an age could suffice for regulation of such association if formed. We shall have to examine more closely (as far as our imagination will aid us) the exact conditions of the family life of the semi-human group which we have supposed typical in that era, i.e., the small isolated band of anthropoids, composed of a single polygamous adult male with dependent wives and offspring. His possible relations with these, especially his attitude towards his male children, will interest us. Therein should certainly be found the desired series of circumstances entailing a critical situation, whose happy resolution shall furnish the clue to the problem of that possible aggregation on which all future progress depends. However strange it may appear, it will be found that the abnormal conditions imposed by the unnatural modifications of the sexual functions have served as a means to the end of advance in progress. And as, by their action in the past, anthropoid man had become the most sexually jealous and intractable of all creatures, so it may be expected that the series of causes which shall have for effect the restraint of such excess of passion, will possess further vast potentiality of action. Such latency in potentiality is evidently indispensable when we consider that there is here concerned the evolution of law in opposition to nature, and its triumph for all time over the mere brute.

But first as regards the fact of the association of adult males on friendly terms within the group, which fact has seemed to us to constitute the whole problem of progress, it would on a hasty view appear as if it had been already found in the band of exiled sons which we have seen haunting the parent horde. Here we meet with that aggregation of individuals whose combination in peaceful union should apparently be the result of some law in regulation. This idea would even seem to gain support from the fact that all the members being brothers, and living most probably in a state of polyandry, we here appear to find fulfilled exactly those genetic conditions of primitive marriage imperative according to Mr. McLennan's theory of the origin of society. It will not, however, be difficult to prove that, at least at this stage in evolution, such a group would lack the most essential elements of stability. Their unity, in fact, as has been already pointed out, could only endure as long as the youthfulness of the members necessitated union for protection, and their immaturity prevented the full play of the sexual passion. The horde would inevitably dissolve under the influence of jealousy at the adult stage, especially if, as is probable, the number of their female captives had increased with the gain in years and power. The necessary Primal Law which alone could determine peace within a family circle by recognising a *distinction between female and female* (the indispensable antecedent to a definition of marital rights) could never have arisen in such a body. It follows that if such law was ever evoked, it must have been from within the only other assembly in existence, viz. that headed by the solitary polygamous patriarch, 'the Cyclopean family.'

We have said that this family would be composed of the male head and his wives, the latter consisting of captured females, and further, let us note, of his own adult female offspring, accompanied by a troop of infants of both sexes. The absence of male offspring beyond those of tender years would be another most notable phenomenon. These sons would, as we have seen, have been banished at puberty from the herd, in common with the habit of most animals.

Now we have surmised that at this stage our subject has been modified, both physically and mentally, to a certain extent in approach to the human type, and there is precisely one special modification which would have been of paramount importance in view of the problem of advance in progress. For if we may thus infer a certain increase in the longevity of the nascent race at even so early a stage in evolution, then that evidently entails *a more prolonged infancy*. It follows that, however precocious, the young males before exile must have passed at least nine to ten helpless years under their mother's care. But, again, the rise of superior intellectual faculties in general presupposes a decided increase in the powers of

memory, and this agent, in connection with that of the longer companionship, would here set in movement, sooner or later, a psychological factor of strangely magnified force as compared with what it is in the mere brute—namely, human maternal love.

Separation, however caused, between this mother and her child would be far more severely felt than by any other animal. At the renewed banishment of each of her male progeny by the jealous patriarch, the mother's feelings and instinct would be increasingly lacerated and outraged. Her agonised efforts to retain at least her last and youngest would be even stronger than with her first-born. It is exceedingly important to observe that her chances of success in this case would be much greater. When this last and dearest son approached adolescence, it is not difficult to perceive that the patriarch must have reached an age when the fire of desire may have become somewhat dull; whilst, again, his harem, from the presence of numerous adult daughters, would be increased to an extent that might have overtaxed his once more active powers. Given some such rather exceptional situation, where a happy opportunity in superlative mother love wrestled with a for once satiated paternal appetite in desire, we may here discern a possible key of the sociological problem which occupies us, and which consisted in a conjunction within one group of two adult males.

We must conceive that, in the march of the centuries, on some fateful day, the bloody tragedy in the last act of the familiar drama was avoided, and the edict of exile or death left unpronounced. Pure maternal love triumphed over the demons of lust and jealousy. A mother succeeded in keeping by her side a male child, and thus, by a strange coincidence, that father and son, who, amongst all mammals, had been the most deadly of enemies, were now the first to join hands. So portentous an alliance might well bring the world to their feet. The family group would now present, for the first time, the till then unknown spectacle of the inclusion within a domestic circle, and amidst its component females, of an adolescent male youth. It must, however, be admitted that such an event, at such an epoch, demanded imperatively very exceptional qualities, both physiological and psychological, in the primitive agents. The new happy ending to that old-world drama which had run for so long through blood and tears, was an innovation requiring very unusually gifted actors. How many failures had doubtless taken place in its rehearsal during the centuries, with less able or happy interpreters! It is probable that, in the new experiment, success was rendered possible by the rise of new powers in nascent man. Some feeble germ of altruism may already have arisen to make its force felt as an important factor.

. . .

The love and care of a parent for his offspring is, after all, ethically speaking, the normal condition. Habitual desertion at too early an age would be fatal. Their dissociation, the abnormal and only one, took place under the influence of the strongest passion in nature, again largely exaggerated in primitive man. But in such an era purely physical characteristics would undoubtedly have also a vast influence in the development of the incident we have tried to depict. The fiercely solitary patriarch who first consented to the intrusive presence within his family circle of another adult male was, as I think we can prove, a being of abnormal physical power as compared with his fellows. For we have assumed satiety in desire to have been a powerful factor in the *innovatory* struggle we have witnessed. But such satiety implies extensive polygamy, and yet again a large harem composed exclusively of unwilling outside captives is incredible, escape for them in the primeval forest being too facile. Thus the harem would certainly be formed of the female offspring of the tyrant himself. These alone would need no watch or guard, for them the unknown outside world was hostile ground. But again very many adult daughters imply a father stricken in years. That one of such advanced age, in an epoch when force was all in all, could, defiant of rivals, still retain possession of his female kind, presupposes vast enduring physical power, or at least the protective tradition of past exceptional strength, still enduring in terror. If, again, at so early a date in the history of man we may be permitted to surmise

any development of the faculty of psychogenesis, then we may again perceive how extreme physical qualities might have facilitated the solution of the problem of the admission of the intrusive male. For it is credible that long undisputed supremacy of power as the result of personal vigour might, in its incredulous contempt of a possible rivalry, show a tolerance of a situation utterly impossible to a weaker nature.

. . .

EARLIEST EVOLUTION OF LAW

In what, then, we are willing to concede, must have been exceptional circumstances, may thus have been taken that first step in progress which was to lead to such vast advance. In a development of the *social* qualities depended the whole future of mankind, and here we seem to see their germ and birth.

When, however, we affirm that the triumph of maternal love in the continued companionship of a male child, constituted the solution of the social problem before us, we do not intend to convey the idea that it lay solely in the fact of a simple inclusion of male offspring within a group. Such a condition, however significant in the actual case, has nothing in itself but what is common to the family economy of many animals. It is the normal one, for instance, among many pithecoids, as baboons, etc., where we find the younger males still form an integral part of the horde, although denied marital rights. But, however inexorable among such species the temporary separation from the females during the actual season of rut, there is at other times a propinquity in amity as members of the same herd, which lessened doubtless the fierceness of the strife during the periodic play of passion, a truce in fact admitting of peace and alliance in offence and defence during most of the year.

With our ancestors there could be no such healing pause; the unnatural sexual modification of the race had rendered it impossible. The non-periodicity of the sexual function in rut would have made the whole year, with two adult males in presence, an interval of trial insupportable to the mere brute. With this race the banishment of the youth would be for all time, and the loss would be not only that of an ally, each exile would become an active enemy. Now we have hinted that the importance, in a potential sense, of a movement towards union, in such creatures, arose precisely from the fact that, on account of the intensity of the relations between male and male, and especially between father and son, their amicable conjunction was only possible under such exceptional conditions as would probably conduce to its stability whenever it did take place.

Indeed such inchoate rule or habit, a corollary of the early idea, as reigns in regulation of marital rights among lower creatures, would not be fully adequate for this higher creation. With lower creatures, might alone confers rights, which feebler force ever seeks each chance to invade, all stratagems being legitimate as a means to that end. With inchoate man such imperfect rule of action had become utterly impossible. The greater endowment in memory and reason entailed a too fatally added hate on non-compliance. For inchoate men the requisite law required such further exactness in definition as should leave no doubt of a meaning, not only to be understood, but to be accepted and obeyed unconditionally.

For between this father and son there was yet no real peace, only a truce, and that enduring but so long as the latter respected those marital rights of the former which we found extending over all that was feminine in the horde. The intelligent acceptance by the intruding junior of the sole right of the senior to union with the females of a group, was its *sine qua non*, which the dawn of intellectuality in the race as inevitably imposed as it happily permitted. Such a step in advance as a possible obedience, *ex animo*, to such a law would be immense. Therefrom would issue the vital point of a conception of moral reserves in marital rights as regards the other sex; the germ of a profound and fundamental difference between brute and man. For the first time in the history of the world we encounter the factor which is to be the leading power in future social metamorphosis, i.e., *an explicit distinction between female and female, as such*. The superlative fact, indeed, in relation to our general argument, appears—namely, that certain females are now to become sacred to certain males, and that

both (*nota bene*) are members of the same family circle.

But what shall be, in such an age, the notes of a law conveying this noble sentiment of sanctity, which, disarming jealousy, could permit peace where before strife reigned? How give the outer expression of the inner feeling, now aroused, of a change in the past intersexual attitude of certain group members? Whence borrow the eloquence which shall ordain rules in restriction of intercourse whilst yet, for Homo Alalus, they must needs be mute in expression. In the primal law alone, as I hope in its portrayal to show, can each condition be comprised and found as such. It will be marked and recognised by a physical trait whose presence is as significant and imperative as it is characteristic of the epoch. For a sentiment of restraint in feeling, whilst articulate speech was yet lacking, could only be expressed by restrictive checks in act and deed, requiring mere visual perception for interpretation—acts we may here note, which, as insulating the individual, would also inevitably tend to consecration.

Now we mentioned previously that, in connection with the primal law, certain cases of so-called avoidance, and especially that between near relatives, would have interest for us and probably afford aid in proof. We drew attention to the strange features marking these customs, which had rendered their origin a source of wondering conjecture to all inquirers. It may be that precisely the actual anomalism of these characteristics may render them eloquent in our case. In view of our past argument, in very deed, nothing now becomes insignificant in these quaint rules of non-propinquity between certain near relations; nothing inexpressive in the ordinance of non-recognition between individuals well known to each other; nothing not suggestive in the dread of mere contact between those whom nature would place closest together, no lack of import in the strange taciturnity so incongruous with our garrulous later days of unloosed tongues. There is a possible vestige of a past era of dumb show in their eloquent muteness; of connection in their actual utter unreason with a long dead past of all unfamiliar habits and manners. Further, is verily aught lacking, in these latter-day customs of avoidance, of the necessarily archaic features of a possible primeval law? If these in truth were still existent, would they not, with such traits in common, be simply classed with those? Undoubtedly so, as it seems to me.

Now in the course of our argument it has appeared that the inclusion of the son as the second adult male in a group would evolve, as the most primitive rule of action, restriction of intercourse between its component females and the intruder. But in such a group, the former would necessarily be to the latter in the relation of mother and sisters. Such restriction, again, taking the only possible form, would be avoidance of these relations, and thus there is a concurrence in resemblance with that particular habit of avoidance on which we enlarged in our first pages, viz. that between brother and sister (and now less strictly), between mother and son. Do we not thus seem to lay a finger on an actual law, still an everyday working factor in savage life, which is not only identical with, but is in very deed the primal law itself, in form at least? The acceptation of such intolerably irksome restraints as avoidance, in the daily economy of savage life, has seemed forcibly to imply a fundamental cause of profound depth. This cause now seems laid open to us. The unaccountable and seemingly unreasonable restrictions on intercourse which mark it thus betray their appropriate origin in a time of comparative unreason.

This then, the primal law—avoidance between a brother and sister—with appalling conservatism has descended through the ages (in conservance of form, if not of ultimate purpose). It ordained in the dawn of time a barrier between mother and son, and brother and sister, and that ordinance is still binding on all mankind [but in Egypt and Peru, for example, the opposite of this rule, for special reasons, has prevailed]. Between these forever, a bit was placed in the mouth of desire, and chains on the feet of lust. Their mutual relationship is one that has been held sacred from a sexual point of view, in most later ages. It only remains for us to repeat that it follows that this law, as applied in the group composed of a single family, is, as we pointed out, the parent of exogamy; continuance within the group neces-

sarily and logically entailed marriage without; but, again as we said, it was itself the offspring of the early idea. For this idea, in its assumption that sovereignty in marital right was compatible with solitude alone, was shaken to its depths when a second presence threatened rivalry, and demanded remedy in the action of law, which it has seemed to us could only take the form we have tried to portray in the primal law.

Atkinson's concern, it is seen, centers on the first step in the development of the human family as social. It queries analytically the logical possibility. This is quite different from tracing history, in the broad reaches of time particularly, as did some of his contemporaries and his precursors. As an example of the broader historical approach, here we reproduce a section from Lewis Henry Morgan's Ancient Society *(1878). Morgan was strongly influenced by Darwin, was well aware of the work of Maine, and in some ways represents a founding father of anthropology. Morgan's work, it should be noted, was the basis of Engel's famous treatise on the origins of the family, property, and the state, and as we noted earlier, the Freudian conception of the origins of the incest taboo essentially does not go beyond these sources. Additionally, Morgan is well known because other of his work centered on the American Indians and virtually opened this field of study.*

ANCIENT SOCIETY

SEQUENCE OF INSTITUTIONS CONNECTED WITH THE FAMILY

It remains to place in their relations the customs and institutions which have contributed to the growth of the family through successive forms. Their articulation in a sequence is in part hypothetical; but there is an intimate and undoubted connection between them.

This sequence embodies the principal social and domestic institutions which have influenced the growth of the family from the consanguine to the monogamian. They are to be understood as originating in the several branches of the human family substantially in the order named, and as existing generally in these branches while in the corresponding status.

First Stage of Sequence.

 I. Promiscuous Intercourse.

 II. Intermarriage of Brothers and Sisters, own and collateral, in a Group: Giving,—

 III. The Consanguine Family (First Stage of the Family): Giving,—

 IV. The Malayan System of Consanguinity and Affinity.

Second Stage of Sequence.

 V. The Organization upon the basis of Sex, and the Punaluan Custom, tending to check the intermarriage of brothers and sisters: Giving,—

 VI. The Punaluan Family. (Second Stage of the Family): Giving,—

 VII. The Organization into Gentes, which excluded brothers and sisters from the marriage relation: Giving,—

 VIII. The Turanian and Ganowánian System of Consanguinity and Affinity.

Third Stage of Sequence.

 IX. Increasing Influence of Gentile Organization and improvement in the arts of life, advancing a portion of mankind into the Lower Status of barbarism: Giving,—

 X. Marriage between Single Pairs, but without an exclusive cohabitation: Giving,—

 XI. The Syndyasmian Family. (Third Stage of the Family.)

Fourth Stage of Sequence.

 XII. Pastoral life on the plains in limited areas: Giving,—

 XIII. The Patriarchal Family. (Fourth, but exceptional Stage of the Family.)

Fifth Stage of Sequence.

 XIV. Rise of Property, and settlement of lineal succussion to estates: Giving,—

 XV. The Monogamian Family. (Fifth Stage of the Family): Giving,—

 XVI. The Aryan, Semitic and Uralian system of Consanguinity and Affinity; and causing the overthrow of the Turanian.

 A few observations upon the foregoing sequence of customs and institutions, for the purpose of tracing their connection and relations, will close this discussion of the growth of the family.

 Like the successive geological formations, the tribes of mankind may be arranged, according to their relative conditions, into successive strata. When thus arranged, they reveal with some degree of certainty the entire range of human progress from savagery to civilization.

A thorough study of each successive stratum will develop whatever is special in its culture and characteristics, and yield a definite conception of the whole, in their differences and in their relations. When this has been accomplished, the successive stages of human progress will be definitely understood. Time has been an important factor in the formation of these strata; and it must be measured out to each ethnical period in no stinted measure. Each period anterior to civilization necessarily represents many thousands of years.

 I. *Promiscuous intercourse.* This expresses the lowest conceivable stage of savagery—it represents the bottom of the scale. Man in this condition could scarcely be distinguished from the mute animals by whom he was surrounded. Ignorant of marriage, and living probably in a horde, he was not only a savage, but possessed a feeble intellect and a feebler moral sense. His hope of elevation rested in the vigor of his passions, for he seems always to have been courageous; in the possession of hands physically liberated, and in the improvable character of his nascent mental and moral powers. In corroboration of this view, the lessening volume of the skull and its increasing animal characteristics, as we recede from civilized to savage man, deliver some testimony concerning the necessary inferiority of primitive man. Were it possible to reach this earliest representative of the species, we must descend very far below the lowest savage now living upon the earth. The ruder flint implements found over parts of the earth's surface, and not used by existing savages, attest the extreme rudeness of his condition after he had emerged from his primitive habitat, and commenced, as a fisherman, his spread over continental areas. It is with respect to this primitive savage, and with respect to him alone, that promiscuity may be inferred.

 It will be asked whether any evidence exists of this antecedent condition. As an answer, it may be remarked that the consanguine family and the Malayan system of consanguinity presuppose antecedent promiscuity. It was limited, not unlikely, to the period when mankind were frugivorous and within their primitive habitat, since its continuance would have been improbable after they became fisherman and commenced their spread over the earth in dependence upon food artificially acquired. Consanguine groups would then form, with intermarriage in the group as a necessity, resulting in the formation of consanguine families. At all events, the oldest form of society which meets us in the past through deduction from systems of consanguinity is this family. It would be in the nature of a compact on the part of several males for the joint subsistence of the group, and for the defense of their common wives against the violence of society. In the second place, the consanguine family is stamped with the marks of this supposed antecedent state. It recognized promiscuity within defined limits, and those not the narrowest, and it points through its organism to a worse condition against which it interposed a shield. Between the consanguine family and the horde living in promiscuity, the step, though a long one, does not require an intermediate condition. If such existed, no known trace of it remains. The solution of this question, however, is not material. It is sufficient, for the present at least, to have gained the definite starting-point far down in savagery marked out by the consanguine family, which carries back our knowledge of the early condition of mankind well toward the primitive period.

There were tribes of savages and even of barbarians known to the Greeks and Romans who are represented as living in promiscuity. Among them were the Auseans of North Africa, mentioned by Herodotus, the Garamantes of Aethiopia, mentioned by Pliny, and the Celts of Ireland, mentioned by Strabo. The latter repeats a similar statement concerning the Arabs. It is not probable that any people within the time of recorded human observation have lived in a state of promiscuous intercourse like the gregarious animals. The perpetuation of such a people from the infancy of mankind would evidently have been impossible. The cases cited, and many others that might be added, are better explained as arising under the punaluan family, which, to the foreign observer, with limited means of observation, would afford the external indications named by these authors. Promiscuity may be deduced theoretically as a necessary condition antecedent to the consan-

guine family; but it lies concealed in the misty antiquity of mankind beyond the reach of positive knowledge.

II. *Intermarriage of brothers and sisters, own and collateral, in a group.* In this form of marriage the family had its birth. It is the root of the institution. The Malayan system of consanguinity affords conclusive evidence of its ancient prevalence. With the ancient existence of the consanguine family established, the remaining forms can be expalined as successive derivations from each other. This form of marriage gives (III.) the consanguine family and (IV.) the Malayan system of consanguinity, which disposes of the third and fourth members of the sequence. This family belongs to the Lower Status of savagery.

V. *The punaluan custom.* In the Australian male and female classes united in marriage, punaluan groups are found. Among the Hawaiians, the same group is also found, with the marriage custom it expresses. It has prevailed among the remote ancestors of all the tribes of mankind who now possess or have possessed the Turanian system of consanguinity, because they must have derived it from punaluan ancestors. There is seemingly no other explanation of the origin of this system. Attention has been called to the fact that the punaluan family included the same persons found in the previous consanguine, with the exception of own brothers and sisters, who were theoretically if not in every case excluded. It is a fair inference that the punaluan custom worked its way into general adoption through a discovery of its beneficial influence. Out of punaluan marriage came (VI.) the punaluan family, which disposes of the sixth member of the sequence. This family originated, probably, in the Middle Status of savagery.

VII. *The organization into gentes.* The position of this institution in the sequence is the only question here to be considered. Among the Australian classes, the punaluan group is found on a broad and systematic scale. The people are also organized in gentes. Here the punaluan family is older than the gens, because it rested upon the classes which preceded the gentes. The Australians also have the Turanian system of consanguinity, for which the classes laid the foundation by excluding own brothers and sisters from the punaluan group united in marriage. They were born members of classes who could not intermarry. Among the Hawaiians, the punaluan family was unable to create the Turanian system of consanguinity. Own brothers and sisters were frequently involved in the punaluan group, which the custom did not prevent, although it tended to do so. This system requires both the punaluan family and the gentile organization to bring it into existence. It follows that the latter came in after and upon the former. In its relative order it belongs to the Middle Status of savagery.

VIII. and IX. [Not considered here.]

X. and XI. *Marriage between single pairs, and the syndyasmian family.* After mankind had advanced out of savagery and entered the Lower Status of barbarism, their condition was immensely improved. More than half the battle for civilization was won. A tendency to reduce the groups of married persons to smaller proportions must have begun to manifest itself before the close of savagery, because the syndyasmian family became a constant phenomenon in the Lower Status of barbarism. The custom which led the more advanced savage to recognize one among a number of wives as his principal wife, ripened in time into the practice of pairing, and in making this wife a companion and associate in the maintenance of a family. With the growth of the propensity to pair came an increased certainty of the paternity of children. But the husband could put away his wife, and the wife could leave her husband, and each seek a new mate at pleasure. Moreover, the man did not recognize, on his part, the obligations of the marriage tie, and therefore had no right to expect its recognition by his wife. The old conjugal system, now reduced to narrower limits by the gradual disappearance of the punaluan groups, still environed the advancing family, which it was to follow to the verge of civilization. Its reduction to zero was a condition precedent to the introduction of monogamy. It finally disappeared in the new form of hetaerism, which still follows mankind in civilization as a dark shadow upon the family. The contrast between the punaluan and syndyasmian families was greater than between the latter and the monogamian. It was subsequent in time to the gens, which was largely instrumental in its production. That it was a transitional stage of the family between the two is made evident by its inability to change materially the Turanian system of consanguinity, which monogamy alone was able to overthrow. From the Columbia River to the Paraguay, the Indian family was syndyasmian in general, punaluan in exceptional areas, and monagamian perhaps in none.

XII. and XIII. *Pastoral life and the patriarchal family.* It has been remarked elsewhere that polygamy was not the essential feature of this family, which represented a movement of society to assert the individuality of persons. Among the Semitic tribes, it was an organization of servants and slaves under a patriarch for the care of flocks and herds, for the cultivation of lands, and for mutual protection and subsistence. Polygamy was incidental. With a single male head and an exclusive cohabitation, this family was an advance upon the syndyasmian, and therefore not a retrograde movement. Its influence upon the human race was limited; but it carries with it a confession of a state of society in the previous period against which it was designed to form a barrier.

XIV. *Rise of property and the establishment of lineal succession to estates.* Independently of the movement which culminated in the patriarchal family of the Hebrew and Latin types, property, as it increased in variety and amount, exercised a steady and constantly augmenting influence in the direction of monogamy. It is impossible to overestimate the influence of property in the civilization of mankind. It was the power that brought the Aryan and Semitic nations out of barbarism into civilization. The growth of the idea of property in the human mind commenced in feebleness and ended in becoming its master passion. Governments and laws are instituted with primary reference to its creation, protection and enjoyment. It introduced human slavery as an instrument in its production; and, after the experience of several thousand years, it caused the abolition of slavery upon the discovery that a freeman was a better property-making machine. The cruelty inherent in the heart of man, which civilization and Christianity have softened without eradicating, still betrays the savage origin of mankind, and in no way more pointedly than in the practice of human slavery, through all the centuries of recorded history. With the establishment of the inheritance of property in the children of its owner, came the first possibility of a strict monogamian family. Gradually, though slowly, this form of marriage, with an exclusive cohabitation, became the rule rather than the exception; but it was not until civilization had commenced that it became permanently established.

XV. *The monogamian family.* As finally constituted, this family assured the paternity of children, substituted the individual ownership of real as well as personal property for joint ownership, and an exclusive inheritance by children in the place of agnatic inheritance. Modern society reposes upon the monogamian family. The whole previous experience and progress of mankind culminated and crystallized in this pre-eminent institution. It was a slow growth, planting its roots far back in the period of savagery—a final result toward which the experience of the ages steadily tended. Although essentially modern, it was the product of a vast and varied experience.

XVI. *The Aryan, Semitic and Uralian systems of consanguinity.* They are essentially identical and were created by the monogamian family. Its relationships are those which actually existed under this form of marriage and of the family. A system of consanguinity is not an arbitrary enactment, but a natural growth. It expresses, and must of necessity express, the actual facts of consanguinity as they appeared to the common mind when the system was formed. As the Aryan system establishes the antecedent existence of a monogamian family, so the Turanian establishes the antecedent existence of a punaluan family, and the Malayan the antecedent existence of a consanguine family. The evidence they contain must be regarded as conclusive, because of its convincing character in each case. With the existence established of three kinds of marriage, of three forms of the family, and of three systems of consanguinity, nine of the sixteen members of the sequence are sustained. The existence and re-

lations of the remainder are warranted by sufficient proof.

The views herein presented contravene, as I am aware, an assumption which has for centuries been generally accepted. It is the hypothesis of human degradation to explain the existence of barbarians and of savages, who were found, physically and mentally, too far below the conceived standard of a supposed original man. It was never a scientific proposition supported by facts. It is refuted by the connected series of inventions and discoveries, by the progressive development of the social system, and by the successive forms of the family. The Aryan and Semitic peoples descended from barbarous ancestors. The question then meets us, how could these barbarians have attained to the Upper Status of barbarism, in which they first appear, without previously passing through the experience and acquiring the arts and development of the Middle Status; and, further than this, how could they have attained to the Middle Status without first passing through the experience of the Lower. Back of these is the further question, how a barbarian could exist without a previous savage. This hypothesis of degradation leads to another necessity, namely; that of regarding all the races of mankind without the Aryan and Semitic connections as abnormal races—races fallen away by degeneracy from their normal state. The Aryan and Semitic nations, it is true, represent the main streams of human progress, because they have carried it to the highest point yet attained; but there are good reasons for supposing that before they became differentiated into Aryan and Semitic tribes, they formed a part of the indistinguishable mass of barbarians. As these tribes themselves sprang remotely from barbarous, and still more remotely from savage ancestors, the distinction of *normal* and *abnormal* races falls to the ground.

This sequence, moreover, contravenes some of the conclusions of that body of eminent scholars who, in their speculations upon the origin of society, have adopted the patriarchal family of the Hebrew and Latin types as the oldest form of the family, and as producing the earliest organized society. The human race is thus invested from its infancy with a knowledge of the family under paternal power. Among the latest, and holding foremost rank among them, is Sir Henry Maine, whose brilliant researches in the sources of ancient law, and in the early history of institutions, have advanced so largely our knowledge of them. The patriarchal family, it is true, is the oldest made known to us by ascending along the lines of classical and Semitic authorities; but an investigation along these lines is unable to penetrate beyond the Upper Status of barbarism, leaving at least four entire ethnical periods untouched, and their connection unrecognized. It must be admitted, however, that the facts with respect to the early condition of mankind have been but recently produced, and that judicious investigators are justly careful about surrendering old doctrines for new.

Unfortunately for the hypothesis of degradation, inventions and discoveries would come one by one; the knowledge of a cord must precede the bow and arrow, as the knowledge of gunpowder preceded the musket, and that of the steam-engine preceded the railway and the steamship; so the arts of subsistence followed each other at long intervals of time, and human tools passed through forms of flint and stone before they were formed of iron. In like manner institutions of government are a growth from primitive germs of thought. Growth, development and transmission, must explain their existence among civilized nations. Not less clearly was the monogamian family derived, by experience, through the syndyasmian from the punaluan, and the still more ancient consan-

guine family. If, finally, we are obliged to surrender the antiquity of the monogamian family, we gain a knowledge of its derivation, which is of more importance, because it reveals the price at which it was obtained.

The antiquity of mankind upon the earth is now established by a body of evidence sufficient to convince unprejudiced minds. The existence of the race goes back definitely to the glacial period in Europe, and even back of it into the anterior period. We are now compelled to recognize the prolonged and unmeasured ages of man's existence. The human mind is naturally and justly curious to know something of the life of man during the last hundred thousand or more years, now that we are assured his days have been so long upon the earth. All this time could not have been spent in vain. His great and marvelous achievements prove the contrary, as well as imply the expenditure of long protracted ethnical periods. The fact that civilization was so recent suggests the difficulties in the way of human progress, and affords some intimation of the lowness of the level from which mankind started on their career.

The foregoing sequence may require modification, and perhaps essential change in some of its members; but it affords both a rational and a satisfactory explanation of the facts of human experience, so far as they are known, and of the course of human progress, in developing the ideas of the family and of government in the tribes of mankind.

2.

LESLIE A. WHITE

THE DEFINITION AND PROHIBITION OF INCEST

In the various interpretations, both sound and unsound, of the definition and prohibition of incest we have a neat example of a contrast between psychological explanations on the one hand and culturological explanations on the other. The problem simply does not yield to psychological solution. On the contrary, the evidence, both clinical and ethnographic, indicates that the desire to form sexual unions with an intimate associate is both powerful and widespread. Indeed, Freud opines that "the prohibition against incestuous object-choice [was] perhaps the most maiming wound ever inflicted . . . on the erotic life of man."[1] Psychology discloses an "incestuous wish" therefore, not a motive for its prevention. The problem yields very readily, however, to culturological interpretation. Man, as an animal species, lives in groups as well as individually. Relationships between individuals in the human species are determined by the *culture* of the group—that is, by the ideas, sentiments, tools, techniques, and behavior patterns, that are dependent upon the use of symbols[2] and which are handed down from one generation to another by means of this same faculty. These culture traits constitute a continuum, a stream of interacting elements. In this interacting process, new combinations and syntheses are formed, some traits become obsolete and drop out of the stream, some new ones enter it. The stream of culture thus flows, changes, grows and develops in accordance with laws of its own. Human behavior is but the reactions of the organism man to this stream of culture. Human behavior—in the mass, or of a typical member of a group—is therefore culturally determined. A people has an aversion to drinking cow's milk, avoids mothers-in-law, believes that exercise promotes health, practices divination or vaccination, eats roasted worms or grasshoppers, etc., because their culture contains trait-stimuli that evoke such responses. These traits cannot be accounted for psychologically.

And so it is with the definition and prohibition of incest. From psychology we learn that the human animal tends to unite sexually with someone close to him. The institution of exogamy is not only *not* explained by citing this tendency; it is contrary to it. But when we turn to the cultures that determine the relations between members of a group and regulate their social intercourse we readily find the reason for the definition of incest and the origin of exogamy. The struggle for existence is as vigorous in the human species as elsewhere. Life is made more secure, for group as well as individual, by cooperation. Articulate speech makes cooperation possible, extensive, and varied in human society. Incest was defined and exogamous rules were formulated in order to make cooperation compulsory and extensive, to the end that life be made more secure. These institutions were created by *social* systems, not by *neuro-sensory-muscular-glandular* systems. They were syntheses of culture elements formed within the interactive stream of culture traits. Variations of definition and prohibition of incest are due to the great variety of situations. In one situation, in one organization of culture traits—technological, social, philosophic, etc.—we will find one type of definition of incest and one set of rules of exogamy; in a different situation we find another definition and other rules. Incest and exogamy are thus defined in terms of the mode of life of a people—by the mode of sub-

This selection is reprinted from: Leslie A. White, "The Definition and Prohibition of Incest," *American Anthropologist*, 1948, 50, 416–435 [excerpt].

Reprinted with the permission of the author and publisher.

[1]S. Freud, 1930, *Civilization and its Discontents.* New York: p. 74.

[2]Cf. L. A. White, "The Symbol: The Origin and Basis of Human Behavior," *Philosophy of Science,* 1940, 7: 451–463.

sistence, the means and circumstances of offense and defense, the means of communication and transportation, customs of residence, knowl-edge, techniques of thought, etc. And the mode of life, in all its aspects, technological, sociologi-cal, and philosophical, is culturally determined.

3.

Gardner Lindzey

SOME REMARKS CONCERNING INCEST AND THE INCEST TABOO

This paper will be concerned with an examina-tion of the incest taboo with particular atten-tion being paid to theories of the origin of the taboo, the implications of the taboo for psycho-logical development, and the relation between these observations and the current status of psychoanalytic theory.

The existence of prohibitions against nuclear incest (and by this I mean sexual relations be-tween members of the nuclear family other than mother with father) long has been observed to be one of the few regularities in complex human behavior that transcends time and culture. The presence of such taboos appears to be almost exceptionless, and they are much more than ideal cultural patterns, inasmuch as the overt incidence of incest is believed generally to be very low. Given the extreme rarity of significant behavioral regularities that occur across all cul-tures, it is not surprising that anthropologists have shown intense interest in the study of this phenomenon. In contrast, one of the instiga-tions for the present talk is the relative sparse-ness of interest on the part of psychologists, other than psychoanalysts, in incest and its psy-chological significance.

Explanation of the incest taboo has attracted dozens of strongly partisan anthropological and sociological theorists who have attributed the phenomenon to a wide variety of simple and complex determinants. Moreover, this is an area of theorizing that has proven appealing to far more than its reasonable share of theorists who believe in what Gordon Allport has referred to as "simple and sovereign" formulations. It is a rare incest theorist who is willing to entertain seriously a multiplicity of instigating and sus-taining events, even though available facts point strongly in this direction. Examination of the merits and flaws of each of these theories would be time consuming, tedious, and an act of co-vert hostility toward any captive audience. In-stead, I propose to examine one particular set of determinants (the biological) which I believe by itself provides a *sufficient* explanation of the origin of the taboo. At the same time, I do not intend to imply that other mechanisms such as family cohesiveness, Malinowski (1927), de-velopmental immunization, Fox (1962), Wolf (1966), demographic-ecological factors, Slater (1959), enhancement of role learning, Parsons (1954), or the emergence of adaptive social structures, White (1948), may not have played some determining part. In my judgment, how-ever, most of these factors are likely to occupy a more significant role in explaining the *mainte-nance* of the taboo rather than its origin.

Very simply the formulation I am advancing

This selection is reprinted from: Gardner Lindzey, "Some Remarks Concerning Incest, the Incest Taboo, and Psychoanalytic Theory," *American Psychologist*, 1967, 22, 1051-1059 [a segment of the original article is omitted].

Reprinted with the permission of the author and publisher.

Address of the president to the Seventy-Fifth An-nual Convention of the American Psychological Association, Washington, D. C., September 2, 1967.

I am grateful for the valuable advice of Leslie Segner, H. D. Winston, Carol Ryan, Sheldon C. Reed, and Irving I. Gottesman. Preparation of the manuscript was facilitated by Grant MH 14076 from the National Institute of Mental Health. I appreciate the cooperation of the Institute for Sexual Research of Indiana University, in providing data reported in this paper.

argues that the biological consequence of inbreeding is a decrease in fitness. This decrement in fitness is present in all animals, but it is particularly pronounced in the case of man for a number of reasons including his slowness in reaching sexual maturity and his limited number of offspring. Given this lowered fitness a human group practicing incest operates at a selective disadvantage in competition with outbreeding human groups and ultimately would be unlikely to survive. Conversely, a group which prohibited inbreeding (presumably through some form of incest taboo) would be at an advantage in comparison to groups that permitted inbreeding. I assume that in the process of dealing with the problems posed by stable and intimate personal interactions, different human groups initially devised a variety of patterns of mating and family relations, with these variations determined by ecological factors, random factors, and other determinants that we can not hope to specify. Given this variation, however, one might expect over time that natural selection would lead to preservation of societies that practiced outbreeding (incest taboo) and elimination of those societies that favored, or were neutral to, the practice of incest. Consequently, what eventually remains is a substantial amount of variability in marriage rules and kinship structure across cultures, but with all varieties providing the basic minimum of outbreeding imposed by natural selection.

It should be understood that this formulation does not imply that early man necessarily understood the consequences of inbreeding when the incest taboo was established. Natural selection acting upon either morphological or behavioral characters is not mediated ordinarily by awareness on the part of the individual organism. Nonetheless, many of the deleterious consequences of human inbreeding are sufficiently rare, dramatic, and early in appearance (for example, albinism, some forms of mental deficiency, deaf-mutism, and major physical malformations such as dwarfism) so it is not altogether unlikely that in some cases the connection between incest and abnormality may have been noted by primitive man. Indeed an unpublished examination of incest myths in the Hu-

man Relations Area Files (Segner & Collins, 1967) revealed that in roughly one-third of the myths involving incest, deformed offspring or infertility were a consequence of the union. Such a substantial degree of association suggests that on occasion some degree of biological insight may well have accompanied the origin of the taboo.

Early scientific theories concerning the origins of the incest taboo emphasized biological or genetic explanations of the phenomenon, as illustrated by the formulations of Westermarck (1894) and the distinguished anthropologist, Lewis Morgan (1907). However, these positions were based upon pre-Mendelian conceptions of the process of inheritance, and inevitably they have been largely discredited by modern advances in the field of genetics. In spite of these early theories, and common belief among nonscientific observers, the negative effects of inbreeding are not widely accepted, or understood, by behavioral scientists today. Present day counterparts of the biological approach to understanding the incest taboo are few in number, and perhaps are best represented by the points of view of Aberle, Bronfenbrenner, Hess, Miller, Schneider, and Spuhler (1963) and Ember (1961) which are consistent in many important respects with the position advocated here.

Just what is the theory and evidence suggesting that inbreeding results in a reduction of fitness? The most relevant concepts here are *heterosis* or hybrid vigor—which refers to the relatively greater rate of growth, size, fertility, and comparable characters in hybrids when compared to their parents; and its mirror image—*inbreeding depression*, which designates the tendency of closely inbred animals to show a decline in such components of fitness as fertility and resistance to disease.

The most general theoretical observation that can be made in regard to the maladaptiveness of inbreeding concerns its effects upon genetic variability. Given nuclear incest (brother-sister or parent-child mating) it is commonly agreed (Falconer, 1960; Wright, 1933) that each successive generation of inbreeding leads to not less than a 19 percent reduction in degree of heterozygosis (number of chromosomal loci occupied by different alleles). With a few simplifying assumptions, this trend implies that approximately 20 generations of such inbreeding will produce individuals who are at the asymptote for homozygosity—that is to say, at each locus all alleles are identical. The fact that the paired chromosomes present identical alleles to be included in the genome of the individual offspring means that environmental forces have very limited opportunity to exercise selection in favor of particular genotypes. Consequently, changes in selection pressure, including cultural changes, would encounter a population or breeding group that was rigidly specified and relatively incapable of varied biological response to environmental demands. This is true in spite of a potentially greater variability in the individual organism's response to environmental variation (Lerner, 1954). As all of this suggests, genetic diversity is the raw material upon which changing environmental settings operate to select the biological variations that make the organism better adapted to its environment. Because inbreeding reduces this variability, it may be seen as interfering with the normal evolutionary process and to be powerfully maladaptive for the groups involved.

A further relevant formulation concerns the capacity in a heterozygotic condition for dominant genes to mask or suppress the action of deleterious or lethal recessive genes. It is generally accepted that since mutations, spontaneously occurring genetic changes, are continuously occurring, the genes resulting from mutations are ordinarily deleterious, because those mutations that lead to adaptive alleles already will have been retained through selection in the past (Dobzhansky, 1952). Moreover, those mutations leading to deleterious genes that are dominant would be phenotypically expressed and hence immediately subjected to negative selection, with the result that they would disappear. Deleterious genes that are recessive, however, would be maintained at some constant proportion because they would not be exposed to selection when paired with dominant genes. Thus, it is reasoned, and there is strong supporting empirical evidence (Lerner, 1958; Morton, 1961), that recessive genes are generally maladaptive in their effects. In addition, we know

that inbreeding will have the effect of increasing the likelihood that recessive alleles will be paired with other recessive alleles and thus their deleterious or lethal effects will be given expression. In brief, inbreeding eliminates or minimizes the masking of deleterious recessive genes by dominant genes, a process which occurs frequently in the normal, outbred state.

A final consideration is that groups of genes, commonly called polygenes, that have a combined effect upon the phenotype may have been jointly selected for over time because of their mutual (epistatic) and interacting positive effects. These balanced or coadapted systems, which represent a kind of genetic homeostasis (Lerner, 1954), are readily disrupted by inbreeding with a resultant loss in adaptiveness or fitness. It should be noted that some observers, especially Lerner (1954), have considered that even aside from the factors just discussed, homozygosity is intrinsically maladaptive. This view suggests that there is a level or balance of homozygosity below which the individual or group is severely penalized by a decreased likelihood of survival regardless of the nature of the specific recessive genes involved. As Gottesman (1965) has remarked, nature may not only abhor a vacuum but also a homozygote.

Thus, there are a variety of theoretical reasons for anticipating that inbreeding will have maladaptive effects. Let us turn now to the most pertinent empirical data suggesting the negative impact of inbreeding. Findings in regard to morphological and reproductive heterosis have been available for many years concerning a variety of characters and types of subjects (Dinsley, 1963; Falconer, 1960; Gowan, 1952; Lerner, 1954). For example, it has been shown for the mouse that hybrids generally have larger litters (Green, 1931); live longer (Gates, 1926); are larger (Law, 1938; Marshak, 1936); and are more resistant to disease. With chickens, hybrids have been shown to exceed the relatively inbred parental strains in egg size, hatchability of fertile eggs, number of eggs laid, and body size in adulthood. Comparable demonstrations have been made for many other species including rats, honey bees, silkworms, and drosophila.

It is only very recently, however, that we

have begun to obtain firm evidence concerning behavioral heterosis. During the past ten years a number of studies from our laboratory and elsewhere have produced results suggesting or demonstrating that relatively heterozygous animals are superior to their homozygous counterparts in terms of such behavioral characters as appetitive learning (Winston, 1964), aversive learning (Winston, 1964), exploratory behavior (Bruell, 1964b), and activity (Bruell, 1964a; Mordkkoff & Fuller, 1959). Although such findings are not observed for all behavioral attributes, they appear highly characteristic of those traits that are plausibly linked to natural selection and evolution. I believe that all of these results provide factual, although indirect, evidence for the folly of a social system that includes no proscription against incest.

Most interesting of the modern evidence are the findings that imply a strong buffering effect of heterosis upon the negative effects of noxious, early experience. The first of these studies was carried out in our laboratory by Winston (1963, 1964) using *Mus musculus,* or the common house mouse, as the target population. In this experiment the highly homozygous members of three inbred strains were subjected in infancy to an intense, high frequency, auditory stimulus. The maze learning of these groups in adulthood was found to be inferior to that of control animals not subjected to the intense, noxious stimulus. In contrast, when outbred and heterozygous F_1 animals, produced by crossing the three strains, were exposed to infantile trauma and compared with controls in their adult learning capacity, there were no observed differences. Thus, it appeared that the heterotic condition had the effect of introducing a damping or buffering effect that minimized the maladaptive consequences of noxious, early experience. This general finding has been replicated partially, under somewhat different conditions, in another laboratory, by Henderson (1966, 1967). He also found that for some treatment conditions infantile treatments that produced adult effects in inbred mice did not produce such effects in their hybrid offspring. If such findings could be generalized to human populations, they might imply that the relatively inbred and relatively homozygous creature

would operate at a markedly impaired level of functioning, because of the increased probability that negative early experiences would have a disabling or impairing effect upon adult adjustment. These findings are consistent with a large amount of evidence (Dinsley, 1963) indicating that homozygotes generally are more influenced by environmental variation than comparable heterozygotes.

Parenthetically it should be noted that there is considerably less than consensus in the animal literature as to whether the effects of noxious, infantile stimulation upon adult behavior are benign or malignant (Dennenberg, 1962; Hall & Whiteman, 1951; Levine, 1962; Lindzey, Lykken, & Winston, 1960; Lindzey, Winston, & Manosevitz, 1963). Undoubtedly one of the poorly controlled parameters that has contributed to these confusing, and variable, findings has been variation in the degree of heterozygosity of animals under study.

There is ample evidence from a wide variety of sources for the operation of inbreeding depression in lower animals (Dinsley, 1963; Falconer, 1960; Lerner, 1954, 1958). Characters such as rate of growth, resistance to disease, physical size, life span, and fertility are all negatively influenced by inbreeding. These findings are consistent across many different species including mice, swine, poultry, sheep, and cattle. Such effects are most marked in connection with fertility and viability of offspring, with the result that in many species inbreeding typically leads to failure to reproduce and loss of the strain in a relatively short number of generations.

Although controlled evidence for heterosis is very difficult to obtain for human subjects, there are considerable data bearing upon the effects of inbreeding (consanguinity) on fitness. These findings provide strong evidence of inbreeding depression. The data are most compelling in the case of disease entities such as phenylketonuria, amaurotic idiocy, and albinism where, under conditions of consanguineous marriages, the incidence of the disorders departs markedly from population figures. Among the many relevant studies in this area (cf. Morton, 1958, 1961; Morton, Crow, & Muller, 1956; Penrose, 1938; Schull, 1958; Stern, 1960; Sutter, 1958) perhaps the most impressive is the extensive investigation by Schull and Neel (1965). This study involved the comparison of offspring from more than 2300 consanguineous marriages with the offspring of over 2000 nonconsanguineous marriages. It was facilitated by the fact that in Japan approximately five percent of all marriages are between first cousins (Okazaki, 1941). The data were collected in Nagasaki and Hiroshima, and in selection of the samples and analysis of the data every effort was made to minimize the potential contribution of contaminating factors such as socioeconomic status. When the inbred sample was compared to an outbred group, there was clear, although not dramatic, evidence for inbreeding depression in incidence of loss of child during pregnancy, mortality in the first year of life, age at which child first walked and talked, visual and auditory acuity, physical stature, measures of neuromuscular and intellectual functioning (IQ), and incidence of major physical defects. It is worth emphasis that these effects were observed with a sample subjected to much less intense inbreeding than that involved in parent-child or brother-sister reproduction.

The findings most directly relevant to our present interest resulted from a very recent study by Adams and Neel (1967) in which they compared the children of 18 nuclear incest matings (12 brother-sister and six father-daughter) with 18 control matings, rather closely matched with the incest group for age, weight, stature, intelligence, and socioeconomic status. At the end of six months they found that of the 18 children of an incestuous union, five had died; two were severely mentally retarded, were subject to seizures, and had been institutionalized; one had a bilateral cleft palate; and three showed evidence of borderline intelligence (estimated IQ 70). Thus, only seven of the 18 children were considered free of pathology and ready for adoption. On the other hand, none of the 18 control children had died or were institutionalized, none was severely mentally retarded, only one had a major physical defect, and 15 were considered ready for adoption. Roughly comparable findings have been observed in an unpublished study by Sheldon C. Reed.

Perhaps it should be noted that the impressive and growing body of empirical findings (for example, Gottesman & Shields, 1966; Kringlin, 1966) concerning genetic variation and mental disorder has general implications for the maladaptiveness of incestuous matings. If any of the various genetic theories of schizophrenia, especially the autosomal recessive theory of Kallman (1953), should prove to be consistent with reality, it alone would provide powerful reasons for inhibiting or minimizing the incidence of inbreeding among humans.

A number of writers (for example, Aberle et al., 1963; Murdock, 1949) have implied that under some conditions, or with some species, inbreeding may produce a superior strain or race of animals. I know of no evidence to support this contention and there is much evidence to the contrary. Such animals may be superior in regard to one or a few characters, particularly if there has been controlled selection for these characters, but they regularly suffer the general loss of fitness that is a dependable consequence of lowered genetic variability.

Thus, there is compelling theoretical rationale, and a variety of empirical data at both human and lower-animal levels, to imply that the consequences of inbreeding are sufficiently strong and deleterious to make it unlikely that a human society would survive over long periods of time if it permitted, or encouraged, a high incidence of incest. In this sense, then, one may say that the incest taboo (whatever other purposes it may serve) is biologically guaranteed.

Given this biological mandate against inbreeding, one may ask whether the resultant prohibition is likely to be the basis for inducing serious conflict. Here the essential question is: Do we have evidence for the existence of strong and pervasive incestuous impulses that would be interfered with by such a taboo?

One may argue persuasively that the mere universal existence of the incest taboo, together with the powerful effects or emotions that are associated with its violation, constitute convincing evidence for the existence of a set of general tendencies that are being denied. It seems unlikely that there would have been universal selection in favor of such a taboo if there were not rather widespread impulses toward expression of the prohibited act. Cultures seldom focus upon the inhibition of behavior which few individuals feel compelled to display.

It should be mentioned, although not emphasized, that there is substantial clinical support in the raw material of therapeutic exchanges and case histories for the existence of incestuous impulses. Indeed, although I know of no controlled investigation, my impression from contact with clinicians and dream investigators is that overt incestuous dreams are by no means uncommon. To this infirm evidence can be appended the central and recurrent role that has been assigned to incestuous relations in the world of the theater and novel from the time of Sophocles until today. Even among nonliterate societies incest themes have occupied a prominent position because of their extremely high frequency in myths, as several studies (Kluckhohn, 1960; Moore, 1964) have shown.

More dramatic and undeniable evidence of the existence of incestuous impulses is presented by the occurrence of consummated incest. In spite of the strong and universal operation of the incest taboo, there is a detectable, although small, incidence of overt acts. The figure generally referred to in the literature is less than one case per million persons in modern western societies (Riemer, 1940; Weinberg, 1955). This index is obviously an extreme underestimation in view of the fact that it refers to reported or detected cases, and it seems evident that the majority of such cases go unreported and/or undetected by persons other than the participants.

Surprisingly enough the best available evidence has not been introduced in such discussions in the past. I am referring here to data collected by Kinsey, Gebhard, and their collaborators (Gebhard, Gagnon, Pomeroy, & Christenson, 1965; Kinsey, Pomeroy, & Martin, 1948; Kinsey, Pomeroy, Martin, & Gebhard, 1953). There are two relevant sets of data, one collected from a group of over 3500 subjects who were imprisoned for sexual offenses and the other a noncriminal sample of almost 12,000, comprising the large number of subgroups included in the main Kinsey study. For the criminals the incidence of incest was roughly 30 cases for each 1000 persons in the sample, while in the noncriminal group the incidence was approximately five cases for each 1000 persons. Even for these groups the available figures may be taken as substantial understatements (since forgetting and voluntary deception would be expected to play some significant role). Nevertheless, they vastly exceed the customarily cited index of "less than one case per million." More important, when this appreciable incidence is viewed against the background of powerful inhibiting forces, it provides strong support for the existence of frequent, if not invariable, incestuous impulses. It is worth further note that although the figures conventionally cited indicate that father-daughter incest is most common, the Kinsey-Gebhard data indicate that in the general population brother-sister incest is five times as common as the next most common variety (father-daughter relations).

Another relevant data domain is the substantial evidence indicating that personal attractiveness and interpersonal choice are mediated, or determined, by similarity in attitudes, values, needs, and background factors (Lindzey & Byrne, in press). To all of this can be added the relatively massive literature indicating that positive social choice is strongly facilitated by physical or geographc proximity (for example, Festinger, Schacter, & Back, 1950). These findings clearly support the contention that heterosexual choice within the family would be the easiest and most congruent alternative for most or many individuals. Likewise the evidence indicating homogeneity in mate selection (Tharp, 1963) far outweighs the occasional support advanced for a need-complementarity hypothesis (Winch, 1955). Again it seems that most of what we know about assortative mating in the human suggests that in the absence of the incest taboo, mate selection within the nuclear family would be a high frequency choice. The evidence in regard to association and mating preference at a lower animal level is somewhat more mixed (Beck & Lucas, 1963; Cairns, 1966; Mainardi, 1965; Mainardi, Marsan, & Pasquali, 1965; Warriner, Lemmon, & Ray, 1963), but again there is considerable hard data suggesting that like prefers and copulates with like.

I have suggested . . . that an examination of available data, leavened only modestly with speculation, implies that the evolutionary achievement of the incest taboo (a biological necessity) has resulted in the imposition of a developmental crisis upon the human organism. An immature individual, endowed with only limited capacity for diverse and integrated adaptive acts, is faced with the imperative that he must reorganize and channel in new directions his sexual impulses—one of the most powerful of human motives. The image that I am attempting to convey is one of an organism that is wired for sexual choice along dimensions of proximity and similarity, encountering a society or culture that is necessarily programmed for destructon or inhibtion of these natural tendencies. Moreover, the person first encounters this fundamental opposition at a time when he is poorly equipped to devise mediating and compromising patterns of response.

REFERENCES

ABERLE, D., BRONFENBRENNER, U., HESS, E., MILLER, D., SCHNEIDER, D., & SPUHLER, J. The incest taboo and the mating patterns of animals. *American Anthropologist*, 1963, 65, 253–265.

ADAMS, M. S., & NEEL, J. V. Children of incest. *Pediatrics*, 1967, 40, 55–62.

BECK, S. L., & LUCAS, J. J. Breeding characteristics of two strains of mice in a competitive situation. *Genetics*, 1963, 48, 833.

BRUELL, J. H. Heterotic inheritance of wheel running in mice. *Journal of Comparative and Physiological Psychology*, 1964, 58, 159–163. (a)

BRUELL, J. H. Inheritance of behavioral and physiological characters of mice and problems of heterosis. *American Zoologist*, 1964, 4, 125–138. (b)

CAIRNS, R. B. Attachment behavior of mammals. *Psychological Review*, 1966, 73, 409–426.

DENNENBERG, V. H. The effects of early experience. In E. S. E. Hafez (ed.), *The behaviour of domestic animals*. Baltimore: Williams & Wilkins, 1962, 109–138.

DINSLEY, M. Inbreeding and selection. In W. Lane-Petter (ed.), *Animals for research*. London: Academic Press, 1963, 235–259.

DOBZHANSKY, T. Nature and origin of heterosis. In J. W. Gowen (ed.), *Heterosis*. Ames: Iowa State College Press, 1952, 218–223.

EMBER, M. The incest taboo and the nuclear family. Paper presented at the meeting of the American Anthropological Association, Philadelphia, November, 1961.

FALCONER, D. S. *Introduction to quantitative genetics*. New York: Ronald Press, 1960.

FESTINGER, L., SCHACHTER, S., & BACK, K. *Social pressure in informal groups: A study of human factors in housing*. New York: Harper & Row, Publishers, 1950.

FOX, J. R. Sibling incest. *British Journal of Sociology*, 1962, 13, 128–150.

GATES, W. H. The Japanese waltzing mouse: Its origin, heredity and relation to the genetic characters of other varieties of mice. (No. 337) Washington, D. C.: Carnegie Institution, 1926, 83–138.

GEBHARD, P. H., GAGNON, J. H., POMEROY, W. B., & CHRISTENSON, C. V. *Sex offenders: An analysis of types*. New York: Harper & Row, Publishers, 1965.

GOTTESMAN, I. I. Personality and natural selection. In S. G. Vandenberg (ed.), *Methods and goals in human behavior genetics*. New York: Academic Press, 1965, 63–74.

GOTTESMAN, I. I., & SHIELDS, J. The twins of schizophrenics: 16 years of consecutive admissions to a psychiatric clinic. *Diseases of the nervous system* (Monogr. Suppl.), 1966, 27, 11–19.

GOWAN, J. W. (ed.) *Heterosis*. Ames: Iowa State College Press, 1952.

GREEN, C. V. Size inheritance and growth in a mouse species cross (*Mus musculus* × *Mus bactrianus*): I. Litter size. *Journal of Experimental Zoology*, 1931, 58, 237–246.

HALL, C. S., & WHITEMAN, P. H. The effects of infantile stimulation upon later emotional stability in the mouse. *Journal of Comparative and Physiological Psychology*, 1951, 44, 61–66.

HENDERSON, N. D. Inheritance of reactivity to experimental manipulation in mice. *Science*, 1966, 153, 651–652.

HENDERSON, N. D. Prior treatment effects on open field behaviour of mice: A genetic analysis. *Animal Behaviour*, 1967, 15, 364–376.

KALLMANN, F. J. *Heredity in health and mental disorder*. New York: Norton, 1953.

KINSEY, A. C., POMEROY, W. B., & MARTIN, C. E. *Sexual behavior in the human male*. Philadelphia: Saunders, 1948.

KINSEY, A. C., POMEROY, W. B., MARTIN, C. E., & GEBHARD, P. H. *Sexual behavior in the human female*. Philadelphia: Saunders, 1953.

KLUCKHOHN, C. Recurrent themes in myth and myth making. In H. A. Murray (ed.), *Myth and myth making*. New York: Braziller, 1960, 46–60.

KRINGLIN, E. Schizophrenia in twins. *Psychiatry*, 1966, 122, 809–818.

LAW, L. W. Studies on size inheritance in mice. *Genetics*, 1938, 23, 399–422.

LERNER, I. M. *Genetic homeostasis*. London: Oliver & Boyd, 1954.

LERNER, I. M. *The genetic basis of selection*. New York: John Wiley & Sons, Inc., 1958.

LEVINE, S. Psychophysiological effects of infantile stimulation, In E. L. Bliss (ed.), *Roots of behavior*. New York: Hoeber, 1962, 246–253.

LINDZEY, G., & BYRNE, D. Measurement of social choice and interpersonal attractiveness. In G. Lindzey & E. Aronson (eds.), *Handbook of social psychology.* Vol. 2 (rev. ed.). Reading, Mass.: Addison-Wesley, in press.

LINDZEY, G., LYKKEN, D. T. & WINSTON, H. D. Infantile trauma, genetic factors, and adult temperament. *Journal of Abnormal and Social Psychology,* 1960, *61,* 7–14.

LINDZEY, G., WINSTON, H., & MANOSEVITZ, M. Early experience, genotype, and temperament in *Mus musculus. Journal of Comparative and Physiological Psychology,* 1963, *56,* 622–629.

MAINARDI, D. Unesperimento nuovo sul determinismo delle preferenze sessuali nell femmina di topo (*Mus musculus* domesticus). *Bool Zool.,* 1965, *32.*

MAINARDI, D., MARSAN, M., & PASQUALI, A. Assenza di preferenze sessuali tra ceppi nel maschio di *Mus musculus* domesticus. *Instituto Lombardo,* (Rend, Sc.) 1965, *B99,* 26–34.

MALINOWSKI, B. *Sex and repression in savage society.* London: Routledge, Kegan Paul, 1927.

MARSHAK, A. Growth differences in reciprocal hybrids and cytoplasmic influence on growth in mice. *Journal of Experimental Zoology,* 1936, *72,* 497–510.

MOORE, S. F. Descent and symbolic filiation. *American Anthropologist,* 1964, *66,* 1308–1321.

MORDKOFF, A. M., & FULLER, J. L. Heritability in activity within inbred and cross-bred mice: A study in behavior genetics. *Journal of Heredity,* 1959, *50,* 6–8.

MORGAN, L. *Ancient society.* New York: Holt, Rinehart & Winston, Inc., 1907.

MORTON, N. E. Empirical risks in consanguineous marriages: Birth weight, gestation time, and measurements of infants. *American Journal of Human Genetics,* 1958, *10,* 344–349.

MORTON, N. E. Morbidity of children from consanguineous marriages. In A. G. Steinberg (ed.), *Progress in medical genetics.* New York: Grune & Stratton, 1961.

MORTON, N. E., CROW, J. F., & MULLER, H. J. An estimate of the mutational damage in man from data on consanguineous marriages. *Proceedings of the National Academy of Science,* 1956, *42,* 855–863.

MURDOCK, G. P. *Social structure.* New York: Crowell Collier and Macmillan, Inc., 1949.

OKAZAKI, A. *Kekkon to jinkō.* Tokyo: Chikura Shobō, 1941.

PARSONS, T. The incest taboo in relation to social structure and the socialization of the child. *British Journal of Sociology,* 1954, *5,* 101–117.

PENROSE, L. S. A clinical and genetical study of 1280 cases of mental defect. *Great Britain Medical Research Council, Special Report Series,* 1938, *229,* 1–159.

RIEMER, S. A research note on incest. *American Journal of Sociology,* 1940, *45,* 554–565.

SCHULL, W. J. Empirical risks in consanguineous marriages: Sex ratio, malformation, and viability. *American Journal of Human Genetics,* 1958, *10,* 294–343.

SCHULL, W. J., & NEEL, J. V. *The effects of inbreeding on Japanese children.* New York: Harper & Row, Publishers, 1965.

SEGNER, L., & COLLINS, A. Cross-cultural study of incest myths. Unpublished manuscript, University of Texas, 1967.

SLATER, M. Ecological factors in the origin of incest. *American Anthropologist,* 1959, *61,* 1042–1059.

STERN, C. *Principles of human genetics.* (2nd ed.) San Francisco: Freeman, 1960.

SUTTER, J. *Recherches sur les effects de la consanguinite chez l'homme.* Lons-le-Saunier: De-clume Press, 1958.

THARP, R. G. Psychological patterning in marriage. *Psychological Bulletin,* 1963, *60,* 97–117.

WARRINER, C. C., LEMMON, W. B., & RAY, T. S. Early experience as a variable in mate selection. *Animal Behaviour,* 1963, *11,* 121.

WEINBERG, S. K. *Incest behavior.* New York: Citadel, 1955.

WESTERMARCK, E. *The history of human marriage.* London: Macmillan, 1894.

WHITE, L. The definition and prohibition of incest. *American Anthropologist,* 1948, *50,* 416–435.

WINCH, R. F. The theory of complementary needs in mate selection: Final results on the test of general hypotheses. *American Sociological Review,* 1955, *20,* 552–555.

WINSTON, H. Influence of genotype and infantile trauma on adult learning in the mouse. *Journal of Comparative and Physiological Psychology,* 1963, *56,* 630–635.

WINSTON, H. Heterosis and learning in the mouse. *Journal of Comparative and Physiological Psychology,* 1964, *57,* 279–283.

WOLF, A. P. Childhood association, sexual attraction, and the incest taboo: A Chinese case. *American Anthropologist,* 1966, *68,* 883–898.

WRIGHT, S. Inbreeding and homozygosis. *Proceedings of the National Academy of Sciences,* 1933, *19,* 411–420.

4.

IRA L. REISS

THE UNIVERSALITY OF THE FAMILY:
A CONCEPTUAL ANALYSIS

During the last few decades, a revived interest in the question of the universality of the family has occurred. One key reason for this was the 1949 publication of George Peter Murdock's book *Social Structure*.[1] In that book, Murdock postulated that the nuclear family was universal and that it had four essential functions which it always and everywhere fulfilled. These four functions were: (1) socialization, (2) economic cooperation, (3) reproduction, and (4) sexual relations. Even in polygamous and extended family systems, the nuclear families within these larger family types were viewed as separate entities which each performed these four functions.

The simplicity and specificity of Murdock's position makes it an excellent starting point for an investigation of the universal functions of the human family. Since Murdock's position has gained support in many quarters, it should be examined carefully.[2] Brief comments on

Murdock's position appear in the literature, and some authors, such as Levy and Fallers, have elaborated their opposition.[3] The present paper attempts to go somewhat further, not only in testing Murdock's notion but in proposing and giving evidence for a substitute position. However, it should be clear that Murdock's position is being used merely as an illustration; our main concern is with delineating what, if anything, is universal about the human family.

The four functions of the nuclear family are "functional prerequisites" of human society, to use David Aberle's term from his classic article on the topic.[4] This means that these functions must somehow occur for human society to exist. If the nuclear family everywhere fulfills these functions, it follows that this family should be a "structural prerequisite" of human society, i.e., a universally necessary part of society.[5] The basic question being investigated is not whether these four functions are functional prerequisites of human society—almost all social scientists would accept this—but whether these four functions are necessarily carried out by the nuclear family. If these functions are not everywhere carried out by the nuclear family, then are there any functional prerequisites of society which the nuclear family or any family form does fulfill? Is the family a universal institution in the sense that it always fulfills some functional prerequisite of society? Also, what, if any, are the universal structural features of the family? These are the ultimate questions of

This selection is reprinted from: Ira L. Reiss, "The Universality of the Family: A Conceptual Analysis," *Journal of Marriage and the Family*, 1965, 27, 443-453.

Reprinted with the permission of the author and publisher.

[1]George P. Murdock, *Social Structure* (New York: Crowell Collier and Macmillan, Inc., 1949).

[2]Many of the textbooks in the family field fail to really cope with this issue and either ignore the question or accept a position arbitrarily. The census definition also ignores this issue: "A group of two persons or more related by blood, marriage, or adoption and residing together." The recently published *Dictionary of the Social Sciences*, ed. by Julius Gould and William Kolb (New York: The Free Press, 1964), defines the nuclear family as universal. See pp. 257-259. Parsons, Bales, Bell and Vogel are among those who also seem to accept Murdock's position. See: Talcott Parsons and Robert F. Bales, *Family, Socialization and Interaction Process* (New York: The Free Press, 1955); Talcott Parsons, "The Incest Taboo in Relation to Social Structure and the Socialization of the Child," *British Journal of Sociology*, January 1954, 5, 101-117; *A Modern*

Introduction to the Family, ed. by Norman Bell and Ezra Vogel (New York: The Free Press, 1960).

[3]Marion J. Levy, Jr. and L. A. Fallers, "The Family: Some Comparative Considerations, *American Anthropologist*, August, 1959, 61, 647-651.

[4]David F. Aberle *et al.*, "The Functional Prerequisites of a Society," *Ethics*, January, 1950, 60, 100-111.

[5]*Ibid.*

importance that this examination of Murdock's position is moving toward.

Murdock's contention that the nuclear family is a structural prerequisite of human society since it fulfills four functional prerequisites of human society is relatively easy to test. If a structure is essential, then finding one society where the structure does not exist or where one or more of the four functions are not fulfilled by this structure is sufficient to refute the theory. Thus, a crucial test could best be made by focusing on societies with rather atypical family systems to see whether the nuclear family was present and was fulfilling these four functions. The more typical family systems will also be discussed. A proper test can be made by using only groups which are societies. This limitation is necessary so as not to test Murdock unfairly with such subsocietal groups as celibate priests. For purposes of this paper, the author accepts the definition of society developed by Aberle and his associates:

> A society is a group of human beings sharing a self-sufficient system of action which is capable of existing longer than the life-span of an individual, the group being recruited at least in part by the sexual reproduction of the members.[6]

A TEST OF MURDOCK'S THESIS

One of the cultures chosen for the test of Murdock's thesis is from his own original sample of 250 cultures—the Nayar of the Malabar Coast of India. In his book, Murdock rejected Ralph Linton's view that the Nayar lacked the nuclear family.[7] Since that time, the work of Kathleen Gough has supported Linton's position, and Murdock has accordingly changed his own position.[8] In letters to the author dated April 3, 1963, and January 20, 1964, Murdock

took the position that the Nayar are merely the old warrior caste of the Kerala society and thus not a total society and are more comparable to a celibate group of priests. No such doubt about the societal status of the Nayar can be found in his book. Murdock rejects the Nayar only after he is forced to admit that they lack the nuclear family. In terms of the definition of society adopted above, the Nayar seem to be a society even if they, like many other societies, do have close connections with other groups.

The matrilineage is particularly strong among the Nayar, and a mother with the help of her matrilineage brings up her children. Her husband and "lovers" do not assist her in the raising of her children. Her brother typically assists her when male assistance is needed. Assistance from the linked lineages where most of her lovers come from also substitutes for the weak husband role. Since many Nayar women change lovers rather frequently, there may not even be any very stable male-female relation present. The male is frequently away fighting. The male makes it physiologically possible for the female to have offspring, but he is not an essential part of the family unit that will raise his biological children. In this sense, sex and reproduction are somewhat external to the family unit among the Nayar. Very little in the way of economic cooperation between husband and wife occurs. Thus, virtually all of Murdock's functions are outside of the nuclear family. However, it should be noted that the socialization of offspring function is present in the maternal extended family system. Here, then, is a society that seems to lack the nuclear family and, of necessity, therefore, the four functions of this unit. Even if we accept Gough's view that the "lovers" are husbands and that there really is a form of group marriage, it is still apparent that the separate husband-wife-child units formed by such a group marriage do not here comprise separately functioning nuclear families.

One does not have to rely on just the Nayar as a test of Murdock. Harold E. Driver, in his

---

[6]*Ibid.*, 101.

[7]Murdock, *op. cit.*, 3.

[8]For a brief account of the Nayer, see: E. Kathleen Gough, "Is the Family Universal: The Nayar Case," pp. 76–92 in *A Modern Introduction to the Family, op. cit.* It is interesting to note that Bell and Vogel, in their preface to Gough's article on the Nayar, contend that she supports Murdock's position on the universality of the nuclear family. In point of fact, Gough on page 84 rejects Murdock and actually deals primarily with the marital and not the family institution. See also: *Matrilineal Kinship*, ed. by David M. Schneider and Kathleen Gough (Berkeley: University of California Press, 1961), chaps. 6 and 7. A. R. Radcliffe-Brown was one of the first to note that the Nayar lacked the nuclear family. See his: *African Systems of Kinship and Marriage* (New York: Oxford University Press, Inc., 1959), 73.

study of North American Indians, concludes that in matrilocal extended family systems with matrilineal descent, the husband role and the nuclear family are often insignificant.[9] It therefore seems that the relative absence of the nuclear family in the Nayar is approached particularly in other similar matrilineal societies. Thus, the Nayar do not seem to be so unique. They apparently demonstrate a type of family system that is common in lesser degree.

A somewhat similar situation seems to occur in many parts of the Caribbean. Judith Blake described a matrifocal family structure in which the husband and father role are quite often absent or seriously modified.[10] Sexual relations are often performed with transitory males who have little relation to the raising of the resultant offspring. Thus, in Jamaica one can also question whether the nuclear family exists and performs the four functions Murdock ascribed to it. Socialization of offspring is often performed by the mother's family without any husband, common law or legal, being present. Naturally, if the husband is absent, the economic cooperation between husband and wife cannot occur. Also, if the male involved is not the husband but a short-term partner, sex and reproduction are also occurring outside the nuclear family.

The above societies are all "mother-centered" systems. A family system which is not mother-centered is the Israeli Kibbutz family system as described by Melford Spiro.[11] Here the husband and wife live together in a communal agricultural society. The children are raised communally and do not live with their parents. Although the Kibbutzim are only a small part of the total Israeli culture, they have a distinct culture and can be considered a separate society by the Aberle definition cited above. They have been in existence since 1909 and thus have

shown that they can survive for several generations and that they have a self-sufficient system of action. The function which is most clearly missing in the Kibbutz family is that of economic cooperation between husband and wife. In this communal society, almost all work is done for the total Kibbutz, and the rewards are relatively equally distributed regardless of whether one is married or not. There is practically no division of labor between husbands and wives as such. Meals are eaten communally, and residence is in one room which requires little in the way of housekeeping.

Here, too, Murdock denies that this is a real exception and, in the letters to the author referred to above, contends that the Kibbutzim could not be considered a society. Murdock's objection notwithstanding, a group which has existed for over half a century and has developed a self-sufficient system of action covering all major aspects of existence indeed seems to be a society by almost all definitions. There is nothing in the experience of the Kibbutzim that makes it difficult to conceive of such groups existing in many regions of the world or, for that matter, existing by themselves in a world devoid of other people. They are analogous to some of the Indian groups living in American society in the sense that they have a coherent way of life that differs considerably from the dominant culture. Thus, they are not the same as an average community which is merely a part of the dominant culture.

Melford Spiro concludes that Murdock's nuclear family is not present in the Kibbutz he and his wife studied. He suggests several alterations in Murdock's definition which would be required to make it better fit the Kibbutz. The alterations are rather drastic and would still not fit the Nayar and other cultures discussed above.[12]

[9]Harold H. Driver, *Indians of North America* (Chicago: University of Chicago Press, 1961), 291–292.

[10]Judith Blake, *Family Structure in Jamaica* (New York: The Free Press, 1961). Whether Jamaicans actually prefer to marry and have a more typical family system is a controversial point.

[11]Melford E. Spiro, *Kibbutz: Venture in Utopia* (Cambridge, Mass.: Harvard University Press, 1956); and Melford E. Spiro, *Children of the Kibbutz* (Cambridge, Mass.: Harvard University Press, 1958).

[12]Spiro suggests that "reference residence" be used in place of actual common residence. The kibbutz children do speak of their parents' room as "home." He suggests further that responsibility for education and economic cooperation be substituted for the actual doing of these functions by the parents. The parents could be viewed as responsible for the education of their children, but since nothing changes in economic terms when one marries, it is difficult to understand just what Spiro means by responsibility for economic cooperation being

There are other societies that are less extreme but which still create some difficulty with Murdock's definition of the nuclear family. Malinowski, in his study of the Trobriand Islanders, reports that except for perhaps nurturant socialization, the mother's brother rather than the father is the male who teaches the offspring much of the necessary way of life of the group.[13] Such a situation is certainly common in a matrilineal society, and it does place limits on the socialization function of the nuclear family *per se*. Further, one must at least qualify the economic function in the Trobriand case. The mother's brother here takes a large share of the economic burden and supplies his sister's family with half the food they require. The rigidity of Murdock's definition in light of such instances is apparent. These examples also make it reasonable that other societies may well exist which carry a little further such modifications of the nuclear family. For example, we find such more extreme societies when we look at the Nayar and the Kibbutz.

Some writers, like Nicholas Timasheff, have argued that the Russian experience with the family evidences the universality of the nuclear family.[14] While it is true that the Communists in Russia failed to abolish as much of the old family system as they wanted to, it does not follow that this demonstrates the impossibility of abolishing the family.[15] In point of fact, the family system of the Israeli Kibbutz is virtually identical with the system the Russian Communists desired, and thus we must admit that it is possible for at least some groups to achieve such a system. Also, the Communists did not want to do away with the family *in toto*. Rather, they wanted to do away with the patriarchal aspects of the family, to have marriage based on love, easy divorce, and communal upbringing of children. They ceased in much of this effort during the 1930's when a falling birth rate, rising delinquency and divorce rates, and the depression caused them to question the wisdom of their endeavors. However, it has never been demonstrated that these symptoms were consequences of the efforts to change the family. They may well have simply been results of a rapidly changing social order that would have occurred regardless of the family program. Therefore, the Russian experience is really not evidence pro or con Murdock's position.

The Chinese society deserves some brief mention here. Marion Levy contends that this is an exception to Murdock's thesis because in the extended Chinese family, the nuclear family was a rather unimportant unit, and it was the patrilineal extended family which performed the key functions of which Murdock speaks.[16] Regarding present day Communist China, it should be noted that the popular reports to the effect that the Chinese communes either aimed at or actually did do away with the nuclear family are not supported by evidence. The best information indicates that the Chinese Communists never intended to do away with the nuclear family as such; rather, what they wanted was the typical communist family system which the Israeli Kibbutzim possess.[17] The Communists in China did not intend to do away with the identification of a child with a

---

part of the family. Spiro also would alter Murdock's definition of marriage so as to make emotional intimacy the key element.

[13]Bronislaw Malinowski, *The Sexual Life of Savages in North-Western Melanesia* (New York: Harvest Books, 1929).

[14]Nicholas S. Timasheff, "The Attempt to Abolish the Family in Russia, pp. 55–63 in Bell and Vogel, *op. cit.*

[15]Timasheff refers to the family as "that pillar of society." But nothing in the way of convincing evidence is presented to support this view. The argument is largely that since disorganization followed the attempt to do away with the family, it was a result of that attempt. This may well be an example of a *post hoc ergo propter hoc* fallacy. Also, it should be noted that the love-based union of parents that the early communists wanted might well be called a family, and thus that the very title of Timasheff's article implies a rather narrow image of the family. For a recent account of the Soviet family see: David and Vera Mace, *The Soviet Family* (New York: Doubleday & Co., Inc., 1963); and Ray Bauer *et al.*, *How the Soviet System*

Works (Cambridge, Mass.: Harvard University Press, 1959).

[16]Levy and Fallers, *op. cit.*, 649–650.

[17]Felix Greene, *Awakened China* (New York: Doubleday & Co., Inc., 1961), esp. pp. 142–144. Philip Jones and Thomas Poleman, "Communes and the Agricultural Crisis in Communist China," *Food Research Institute Studies*, February, 1962, *3*, 1–22. Maurice Freedman, "The Family in China, Past and Present," *Pacific Affairs*, Winter, 1961–62, *34*, 323–336.

particular set of parents or vice-versa. If the Israeli Kibbutz is any indication, it would seem that a communal upbringing system goes quite well with a strong emphasis on affectionate ties between parent and child.[18] However, it is well to note that the type of communal family system toward which the Chinese are striving and have to some extent already achieved, clashes with Murdock's conception of the nuclear family and its functions in just the same way as the Kibbutz family does.

Over-all, it appears that a reasonable man looking at the evidence presented above would conclude that Murdock's position is seriously in doubt. As Levy and Fallers have said, Murdock's approach is too simplistic in viewing a particular structure such as the nuclear family as always, in all cultural contexts, having the same four functions.[19] Robert Merton has said that such a view of a very specific structure as indispensable involves the erroneous "postulate of indispensability."[20] Certainly it seems rather rash to say that one very specific social structure such as the nuclear family will always have the same consequences regardless of the context in which it is placed. Surely this is not true of specific structures in other institutions such as the political, religious, or economic. The consequences of a particular social structure vary with the socio-cultural context of that structure. Accordingly, a democratic bicameral legislative structure in a new African nation will function differently than in America; the Reform Jewish denomination has different consequences in Israel than in America; government control of the economy functions differently in England than in Russia.

The remarkable thing about the family institution is that in so many diverse contexts, one can find such similar structures and functions. To this extent, Murdock has made his point and has demonstrated that the nuclear family with these four functions is a surprisingly common social fact. But this is quite different from demonstrating that this is always the case or necessarily the case. It should be perfectly clear that

the author feels Murdock's work has contributed greatly to the advancement of our knowledge of the family. Murdock is used here because he is the best known proponent of the view being examined, not because he should be particularly criticized.

A safer approach to take toward the family is to look for functional prerequisites of society which the family fulfills and search for the full range of structures which may fulfill these functional prerequisites. At this stage of our knowledge, it seems more valuable to talk of the whole range of family structures and to seek for a common function that is performed and that may be essential to human society. What we need now is a broad, basic, parsimonious definition that would have utility in both single and cross-cultural comparisons.[21] We have a good deal of empirical data on family systems and a variety of definitions—it is time we strove for a universal definition that would clarify the essential features of this institution and help us locate the family in any cultural setting.

Looking over the four functions that Murdock associates with the nuclear family, one sees that three of them can be found to be absent in some cultures. The Nayar perhaps best illustrate the possibility of placing sex and reproduction outside the nuclear family. Also, it certainly seems within the realm of possibility that a "Brave New World" type of society could operate by scientifically mating sperm and egg and presenting married couples with state-produced offspring of certain types when they desired children.[22] Furthermore, the raising of children by other than their biological parents is widespread in many societies where adoption and rearing by friends and relatives is com-

---

[18]Spiro, *op. cit.*

[19]Levy and Fallers, *op. cit.*

[20]Robert K. Merton, *Social Theory and Social Structure* (New York: The Free Press, 1957), 32.

[21]Zelditch attempted to see if the husband-wife roles would be differentiated in the same way in all cultures, with males being instrumental and females expressive. He found general support, but some exceptions were noted, particularly in societies wherein the nuclear family was embedded in a larger kinship system. Morris Zelditch, Jr., "Role Differentiation in the Nuclear Family: A Comparative Study," in Parsons and Bales, *op. cit.* The kibbutz would represent another exception since both mother and father play expressive roles in relation to their offspring.

[22]Aldous Huxley, *Brave New World* (New York: Harper & Row, Publishers, 1950).

mon.[23] Thus, it seems that sex and reproduction may not be inexorably tied to the nuclear family.[24]

The third function of Murdock's which seems possible to take out of the nuclear family is that of economic cooperation. The Kibbutz is the prime example of this. Furthermore, it seems that many other communal-type societies approximate the situation in the Kibbutz.

The fourth function is that of socialization. Many aspects of this function have been taken away from the family in various societies. For example, the Kibbutz parents, according to Spiro, are not so heavily involved in the inculcation of values or the disciplinary and caretaking aspects of socialization. Nevertheless, the Kibbutz parents are heavily involved in nurturant socialization, i.e., the giving of positive emotional response to infants and young children. A recent book by Stephens also reports a seemingly universal presence of nurturance of infants.[25] It should be emphasized that this paper uses "nurturance" to mean not the physical, but the emotional care of the infant. Clearly, the two are not fully separable. This use of the term nurturant is similar to what is meant by "expressive" role.[26] Interestingly enough, in the Kibbutz both the mother and father are equally involved in giving their children nurturant socialization. All of the societies referred to above have a family institution with the function of nurturant socialization of children. This was true even for the extreme case of the Nayar.

The conception of the family institution being developed here has in common with some other family definitions an emphasis on socialization of offspring. The difference is that all other functions have been ruled out as unessential and that only the nurturant type of socialization is the universal function of the family institution. This paper presents empirical evidence to support its contention. It is important to be more specific than were Levy and Fallers regarding the type of socialization the family achieves since all societies have socialization occurring outside the family as well as within. It should be noted that this author, unlike Murdock, is talking of *any* form of family institution and not just the nuclear family.

As far as a universal structure of the family to fulfill the function of nurturant socialization is concerned, it seems possible to set only very broad limits, and even these involve some speculation. First, it may be said that the structure of the family will always be that of a primary group. Basically, this position rests on the assumption that nurturant socialization is a process which cannot be adequately carried out in an impersonal setting and which thus requires a primary type of relation.[27] The author would not specify the biological mother as the socializer or even a female, or even more than one person or the age of the person. If one is trying to state what the family must be like in a minimal sense in any society—what its universally required structure and function is—one cannot be too specific. However, we can go one step farther in specifying the structure of the family group we are defining. [The family is here viewed as an institution, as an integrated set of norms and relationships which are socially defined and internalized by the members of a society. In every society in the world, the institutional structure which contains the roles related to the nurturant function is a small kin-

[23]See: *Six Cultures: Studies in Child Rearing*, ed. by Beatrice B. Whiting (New York: John Wiley & Sons, Inc., 1963). Margaret Mead reports exchange of children in *Coming of Age in Samoa* (New York: Mentor Books, 1949). Similar customs in Puerto Rico are reported in David Landy, *Tropical Childhood* (Chapel Hill: University of North Carolina Press, 1959).

[24]Robert Winch, in his recent textbook, defines the family as a nuclear family with the basic function of "the replacement of dying members." In line with the present author's arguments, it seems that the actual biological production of infants can be removed from the family. In fact, Winch agrees that the Nayar lack the family as he defined it because they lack a permanent father role in the nuclear family. See: *The Modern Family* (New York: Holt, Rinehart & Winston, Inc., 1963), pp. 16, 31, and 750.

[25]William N. Stephens, *The Family in Cross Cultural Perspective* (New York: Holt, Rinehart & Winston, 1963), p. 357. Stephens discusses the universality of the family in this book but does not take a definite position on the issue. See Chapter 1.

[26]Zelditch, *op. cit.*, 307–353.

[27]The key importance of primary groups was long ago pointed out by Charles Horton Cooley, *Social Organization* (New York: Charles Scribner's Sons, 1929).

ship structured group.[28] Thus, we can say that the primary group which fulfills the nurturant function is a kinship structure. Kinship refers to descent—it involves rights of possession among those who are kin. It is a genealogical reckoning, and people with real or fictive biological connections are kin.[29]

This specification of structure helps to distinguish from the family institution those nonkin primary groups that may in a few instances perform nurturant functions. For example, a nurse-child relation or a governess-child relation could, if carried far enough, involve the bulk of nurturant socialization for that child. But such a relationship would be a quasi-family at best, for it clearly is not part of the kinship structure. There are no rights of "possession" given to the nurse or the child in such cases, and there is no socially accepted, institutionalized, system of child-rearing involving nurses and children. In addition, such supervisory help usually assumes more of a caretaking and disciplinary aspect, with the parents themselves still maintaining the nurturant relation.

Talcott Parsons has argued, in agreement with the author's position, that on a societal level, only kinship groups can perform the socialization function.[30] He believes that socialization in a kin group predisposes the child to assume marital and parental roles himself when he matures and affords a needed stable setting for socialization. Clearly other groups may at times perform part of the nurturant function. No institution in human society has an exclusive franchise on its characteristic function. However, no society exists in which any group other than a kinship group performs the dominant share of the nurturant function. Even in the Israeli Kibbutz with communal upbringing, it is the parents who dominate in this area.

Should a society develop wherein nonkin primary groups became the predominant means of raising children, the author would argue that these nonkin groups would tend to evolve in the direction of becoming kin groups. The primary quality of the adult-child relation would encourage the notion of descent and possession. Kin groups would evolve as roles and statuses in the nonkin system became defined in terms of accepted male-female and adult-child relationships and thereby became institutionalized. Once these nonkin groups had institutionalized their sex roles and adult-child (descent) roles, we would in effect have a kinship-type system, for kinship results from the recognition of a social relationship between "parents" and children. It seems that there would be much pressure toward institutionalization of roles in any primary group child-rearing system, if for no other reason than clarity and efficiency. The failure of any one generation to supply adequate role models and adequate nurturance means that the next generation will not know these skills, and persistence of such a society is questionable. The importance of this task makes institutionalization quite likely and kinship groups quite essential. To avoid kinship groups, it seems that children would have to be nurtured in a formal secondary group setting. The author will present evidence below for his belief that the raising of children in a secondary group setting is unworkable.

In summation then, following is the universal definition of the family institution: *The family institution is a small kinship structured group with the key function of nurturant socialization of the newborn.* How many years such nurturant socialization must last is hard to specify. There are numerous societies in which children six or seven years old are given a good deal of responsibility in terms of care of other children and other tasks. It seems that childhood in the West has been greatly extended to older ages in recent centuries.[31] The proposed definition focuses on what are assumed to be the structural and functional prerequisites of society which the family institution fulfills. The precise structure of the kinship group can vary quite radically among societies, and even within one society it may well be that more than one small kinship group will be involved in nurturant socialization. The definition seeks to avoid the

---

[28]The structural definition is similar to Levy and Fallers, *op. cit.*

[29]Radcliffe-Brown, *op. cit.*

[30]Parsons, *op. cit.*

[31]Phillippe Aries, *Centuries of Childhood* (New York: Alfred A. Knopf, 1962).

"error" of positing the indispensability of any *particular* family form by this approach. Rather, it says that any type of kinship group can achieve this function and that the limitation is merely that it be a kinship group. This degree of specification helps one delimit and identify the institution which one is describing. Some writers have spelled out more specifically the key structural forms in this area.[32] Adams has posited two key dyads: the maternal dyad and the conjugal dyad. When these two join, a nuclear family is formed, but these dyads are, Adams believes, more fundamental than the nuclear family.

There are always other functions besides nuturant socialization performed by the kinship group. Murdock's four functions are certainly quite frequently performed by some type of family group, although often not by the nuclear family. In addition, there are some linkages between the family kinship group and a larger kinship system. But this is not the place to pursue these interconnections. Instead, an examination follows of evidence relevant to this proposed universal definition of the family institution.

EVIDENCE ON REVISED CONCEPTION

The evidence to be examined here relates to the question of whether the definition proposed actually fits all human family institutions. Three types of evidence are relevant to test the universality of the proposed definition of the family. The first source of evidence comes from a cross-cultural examination such as that of this article. All of the cultures that were discussed were fulfilling the proposed functional prerequisite of nurturant socialization, and they all had some sort of small kinship group structure to accomplish nurturant socialization. The author also examined numerous reports on other cultures and found no exception to the proposed definition. Of course, other functions of

these family groups were present in all instances, but no other specific universally present functions appeared. However, the author hesitates to say that these data confirm his position because it is quite possible that such a cross-cultural examination will reveal some function or structure to be universally *present* but still not universally *required*. Rather, it could merely be universally present by chance or because it is difficult but not impossible to do away with. As an example of this, one may cite the incest taboo. The evidence recently presented by Russell Middleton on incest among commoners in Ptolemaic Egypt throws doubt on the thesis that incest taboos are functional prerequisites of human society.[33] We need some concept of functional "importance," for surely the incest taboo has great functional importance even if it is not a prerequisite of society. The same may be true of the functional importance of Murdock's view of the nuclear family.

If being universally present is but a necessary and not a sufficient condition for a functional prerequisite of society, then it is important to present other evidence. One source of such evidence lies in the studies of rhesus monkeys done by Harry Harlow.[34] Harlow separated monkeys from their natural mothers and raised them with surrogate "cloth" and "wire" mother dolls. In some trials, the wire mother surrogate was equipped with milk while the cloth mother was not. Even so, the monkeys preferred the cloth mother to the wire mother in several ways. The monkeys showed their preference by running more to the cloth mother when threatened and by exerting themselves more to press a lever to see her. Thus, it seemed that the monkeys "loved" the cloth mother more than the wire mother. This was supposedly due to the softer contact and comfort afforded by the cloth mother. One might speculatively argue that the

[32]Richard N. Adams, "An Inquiry into the Nature of the Family," pp. 30–49 in *Essays in the Science of Culture in Honor of Leslie A. White,* ed. by Gertrude E. Dole and Robert L. Carneiro (New York: Thomas Y. Crowell Company, 1960).

[33]Russell Middleton, "Brother-Sister and Father-Daughter Marriage in Ancient Egypt," *American Sociological Review,* October, 1962, 27, 603–611.

[34]See the following articles, all by Harry F. Harlow: "The Nature of Love," *American Psychologist,* December, 1958, 13, 673–685; "The Heterosexual Affection System in Monkeys," *American Psychologist,* January, 1962, 17, 1–9; (with Margaret K. Harlow), "Social Deprivation in Monkeys," *Scientific American,* November, 1962, 206, 1–10.

contact desire of the monkeys is indicative of at least a passive, rudimentary nurturance need. Yerkes has also reported similar "needs" in his study of chimpanzees.[35]

Further investigation of these monkeys revealed some important findings. The monkeys raised by the surrogate mothers became emotionally disturbed and were unable to relate to other monkeys or to have sexual relations. This result was produced irreversibly in about six months. One could interpret this to mean that the surrogate mothers, both cloth and wire, were inadequate in that they gave no emotional response to the infant monkeys. Although contact with the cloth mother seemed important, response seemingly was even more important. Those laboratory-raised females who did become pregnant became very ineffective mothers and were lacking in ability to give nurturance.

Harlow found that when monkeys were raised without mothers but with siblings present, the results were quite different. To date, these monkeys have shown emotional stability and sexual competence. In growing up, they clung to each other just as the other monkeys had clung to the cloth mother, but in addition they were able to obtain the type of emotional response or nurturance from each other which they needed.

Harlow's evidence on monkeys is surely not conclusive evidence for the thesis that nurturant socialization is a fundamental prerequisite of human society. There is need for much more precise testing and evidence on both human and nonhuman groups. Despite the fact that human beings and monkeys are both primates, there is quite a bit of difference in human and monkey infants. For one thing, the human infant is far more helpless and far less aware of its environment during the first few months of its life. Thus, it is doubtful if placing a group of helpless, relatively unaware human infants together would produce the same results as occurred when monkeys were raised with

siblings. The human infant requires someone older and more aware of the environment to be present. In a very real sense, it seems that the existence of human society is testimony to the concern of humans for each other. Unless older humans care for the newborn, the society will cease to exist. Every adult member of society is alive only because some other member of society took the time and effort to raise him. One may argue that this care need be only minimal and of a physical nature, e.g., food, clothing, and shelter. The author believes that such minimal care is insufficient for societal survival and will try to present additional evidence here to bear this out.

One type of evidence that is relevant concerns the effect of maternal separation or institutional upbringing on human infants. To afford a precise test, we should look for a situation in which nurturant socialization was quite low or absent. Although the Kibbutzim have institutional upbringing, the Kibbutz parents and children are very much emotionally attached to each other. In fact, both the mother and father have expressive roles in the Kibbutz family, and there is a strong emphasis on parent-child relations of a nurturant sort in the few hours a day the family is together.

A better place to look would be at studies of children who were raised in formal institutions or who were in other ways separated from their mothers. Leon J. Yarrow has recently published an excellent summary of over 100 such studies.[36] For over 50 years now, there have been reports supporting the view that maternal separation has deleterious effects on the child. The first such reports came from pediatricians pointing out physical and psychological deterioration in hospitalized infants. In 1951, Bowlby reviewed the literature in this area for the World Health Organization and arrived at similar conclusions.[37] More recent and careful studies have made us aware of the importance

---

[35]Robert M. Yerkes, *Chimpanzees* (New Haven: Yale University Press, 1943), esp. 43, 68, 257–258; and Robert M. Yerkes and Ada W. Yerkes, *The Great Apes* (New Haven: Yale University Press, 1929), passim.

[36]Leon J. Yarrow, "Separation from Parents During Early Childhood," pp. 89–136 in *Review of Child Development*, ed. by Martin L. Hoffman and Lois W. Hoffman (New York: Russell Sage Foundation, 1964), Vol. 1.

[37]John Bowlby, *Maternal Care and Mental Health* (Geneva: World Health Organization, 1951).

of distinguishing the effects of maternal separation from the effects of institutionalization. Certainly the type of institutional care afforded the child is quite important. Further, the previous relation of the child with the mother before institutionalization and the age of the child are important variables. In addition, one must look at the length of time separation endured and whether there were reunions with the mother at a later date. Yarrow's view is that while there is this tendency toward disturbance in mother separation, the occurrence can best be understood when we learn more about the precise conditions under which it occurs and cease to think of it as inevitable under any conditions. In this regard, recent evidence shows that children separated from mothers with whom they had poor relationships displayed less disturbance than other children. Further, infants who were provided with adequate mother-substitutes of a personal sort showed much less severe reactions. In line with the findings on the kibbutz, children who were in an all-day nursery gave no evidence of serious disturbance.

Many studies in the area of institutionalization show the importance of the structural characteristics of the institutional environment. When care is impersonal and inadequate, there is evidence of language retardation, impairment of motor functions, and limited emotional responses toward other people and objects.[38] Interestingly, the same types of characteristics are found among children living in deprived family environments.[39] One of the key factors in avoiding such negative results is the presence of a stable mother-figure in the institution for the child. Individualized care and attention seem to be capable of reversing or preventing the impairments mentioned. Without such care, there is evidence that ability to form close interpersonal relations later in life is greatly weakened.[40] As Yarrow concludes in his review of this area:

It is clear from the studies on institutionalization that permanent intellectual and personality damage may be avoided if following separation there is a substitute mother-figure who develops a personalized relationship with the child and who responds sensitively to his individualized needs.[41]

The evidence in this area indicates that some sort of emotionally nurturant relationship between the child in the first few years of life and some other individual is rather vital in the child's development. Disease and death rates have been reported to rise sharply in children deprived of nurturance. The author is not rash enough to take this evidence as conclusive support for his contention that nurturant socialization is a functional prerequisite of human society which the family performs. Nevertheless, he does believe that this evidence lends some support to this thesis and throws doubt on the survival of a society that rears its children without nurturance. In addition, it seems to support the position that some sort of kin-type group relationship is the structural prerequisite of the nurturant function. Indeed, it seemed that the closer the institution approximated a stable, personal kinship type of relationship of the child and a nurse, the more successful it was in achieving emotional nurturance and avoiding impairments of functions.

SUMMARY AND CONCLUSIONS

A check of several cultures revealed that the four nuclear family functions that Murdock states are universally present were often missing. The nuclear family itself seems either absent or unimportant in some cultures. An alternate definition of the family in terms of one functional prerequisite of human society and in terms of a broad structural prerequisite was put forth. The family was defined as a small kinship structured group with the key function of nuturant socialization of the newborn. The nurturant function directly supports the personality system and enables the individual to become a contributing member of society. Thus, by making adult role performance possible, nurturant socialization becomes a functional prerequisite of society.

[38]Yarrow, *op. cit.*, 100.
[39]*Ibid.*, 101–102.
[40]*Ibid.*, 106.
[41]*Ibid.*, 124–125.

Three sources of evidence were examined: (1) cross-cultural data, (2) studies of other primates, and (3) studies of effects on children of maternal separation. Although the evidence did tend to fit with and support the universality of the new definition, it must be noted that much more support is needed before any firm conclusion can be reached.

There is both a structural and a functional part to the definition. It is theoretically possible that a society could bring up its entire newborn population in a formal institutional setting and give them nurturance through mechanical devices that would reassure the child, afford contact, and perhaps even verbally respond to the child. In such a case, the family as defined here would cease to exist, and an alternate structure for fulfilling the functional requirement of nurturant socialization would be established. Although it is dubious whether humans could ever tolerate or achieve such a means of bringing up their children, this logical possibility must be recognized. In fact, since the evidence is not conclusive, one would also have to say that it is possible that a society could bring up its offspring without nurturance, and in such a case also, the family institution as defined here would cease to exist. The author has argued against this possibility by contending that nurturance of the newborn is a functional prerequisite of human society and therefore could never be done away with. However, despite a strong conviction to the contrary, he must also admit that this position may be in error and that it is possible that the family as defined here is not a universally required institution. There are those, like Barrington Moore, Jr., who feel that it is largely a middle-class sentimentality that makes social scientists believe that the family is universal.[42] It is certainly crucial to test further the universality of both the structural and functional parts of this definition and their interrelation.

The definition proposed seems to fit the existing data somewhat more closely than Murdock's definition. It also has the advantage of simplicity. It affords one a definition that can be used in comparative studies of human society. Further, it helps make one aware of the possibilities of change in a society or an institution if we know which functions and structures can or cannot be done away with. In this way, we come closer to the knowledge of what Goldenweiser called the "limited possibilities" of human society.[43] If nurturance in kin groups is a functional and structural prerequisite of society, we have deepened our knowledge of the nature of human society for we can see how, despite our constant warfare with each other, our conflicts and internal strife, each human society persists only so long as it meets the minimal nurturant requirements of its new members. This is not to deny the functions of social conflict that Coser and others have pointed out, but merely to assert the importance of nurturance.[44]

In terms of substantive theory, such a definition as the one proposed can be of considerable utility. If one views the marital institution, as Malinowski, Gough, Davis, Radcliffe-Brown, and others did, as having the key function of legitimization of offspring, then the tie between the marital and family institution becomes clear.[45] The marital institution affords a social definition of who is eligible to perform the nurturant function of the family institution. However, it is conceivable that a family system could exist without a marital system. This could

---

[42]Barrington Moore, Jr., *Political Power and Social Theory* (Cambridge, Mass.: Harvard University Press, 1958), chap. 5.

[43]Alexander A. Goldenweiser, *History, Psychology, and Culture* (New York: Alfred A. Knopf, 1933), esp. 45–49.

[44]Lewis Coser, *The Functions of Social Conflict* (New York: The Free Press, 1956).

[45]See Gough, *op. cit.*; Kingsley Davis, "Illegitimacy and the Social Structure," *American Journal of Sociology*, September, 1939, 45, 215–233; A. R. Radcliffe-Brown, *op. cit.*, p. 5. The structure of the marital institution is not specified in terms of number or sex, for there are cultures in which two women may marry and raise a family. See: B. E. Evans Pitchard, *Kinship and Marriage Among the Nuer* (London: Oxford University Press, 1951), 108–109. It is well to note here that Murdock stressed a somewhat different view of marriage. He focused on sexual and economic functions, and the woman-woman marriage found in the Nuer would not fit this definition. Morris Zelditch recently has used this legitimacy function as the key aspect of his definition of the family rather than marriage. Such a usage would, it seems, confuse the traditional distinction between these two institutions. See p. 682 in *Handbook of Modern Sociology*, ed. by Robert Faris (Chicago: Rand-McNally, 1964).

be done by the state scientifically producing and distributing infants or, as Blake believes occurs in Jamaica, by the absence of socially acceptable marriage for most people until childbirth is over.[46]

There may be other universally required functions of the family institution. Dorothy Blitsten suggests universal family contributions to the social order.[47] Kingsley Davis posits several universal functions, such as social placement, which are worth investigating further.[48]

One major value of the approach of this paper is that it has the potentiality of contributing to our ability to deal cross-culturally with the family. Surely it is useful to theory building to ascertain the essential or more essential features of an institution. Such work enables us to locate, identify, and compare this institution in various cultural settings and to discover its fundamental characteristics. In this respect, Murdock has contributed to the search for a cross-cultural view of the family by his work

in this area, even though the author has taken issue with some of his conclusions. It should be clear that this "universal, cross-cultural" approach is not at all presented as the only approach to an understanding of the family. Rather, it is viewed as but one essential approach. Research dealing with important but not universal functions is just as vital, as is empirical work within one culture.

Also of crucial importance is the relation of the family institution to the general kinship structure. It does seem that every society has other people linked by affinal or consanguineal ties to the nurturant person or persons. It remains for these aspects to be further tested. The family typologies now in existence are adequate to cover the proposed definition of the family, although a new typology built around the nurturant function and the type of kin who perform it could be quite useful.

The interrelations of the marital, family, and courtship institutions with such institutions as the political, economic, and religious in terms of both important and essential functions and structures is another vital avenue of exploration. One way that such exploration can be made is in terms of what, if any, are the functional and structural prerequisites of these institutions and how they interrelate. It is hoped that such comparative research and theory may be aided by a universal definition of the family such as that proposed in this paper.

---

[46]Blake, *op. cit.*

[47]Dorothy R. Blitsten, *The World of the Family* (New York: Random House, Inc., 1963), esp. chap. I.

[48]Kingsley Davis, *Human Society* (New York: Crowell Collier and Macmillan, Inc., 1950), 395. Davis lists reproduction, maintenance, placement, and socialization of the young as universal family functions. Social placement is the only function that differs from Murdock's list. One could conceive of this function as part of the marital rather than the family institution.

CHAPTER II

Examples of Family Systems

AN IMPORTANT APPROACH TO KNOWLEDGE about the principles that underlie social organization and behavior is to view societies and cultures comparatively. The systematic comparative analysis of social structure is ancient and is found at least as early as the work of Aristotle. The lessons learned from the method, however, are often lost in practical experience. So, for example, in contrast to a comparative approach, there are *ethnocentric* and *particularistic* approaches which disdain examining social behavior in perspective and often are replete with assertions of the "right" way of doing things from a single point of view. Ethnocentrism of this form contrasts with *cultural relativism,* which is often a consequence of a comparative approach to the study of social forms.

In this chapter examples of family systems in greatly diverse cultures are presented. However, it should be noted that the diversity demonstrated is of two types. First, materials are presented on the Hebrew family as described from Biblical sources. The Judeo-Christian tradition dominates the western world, but it is a tradition that in retrospect is often selected as encountered when moralists view current behavior. Modern concepts of marriage tend to ignore prior forms of permissive behavior, or even the fact that the Bible is itself a record of changes of custom. The laws and ceremonies of today are frequently viewed as though they always existed in exactly the form they are now encountered, in the same way that a particular view of morality is accepted by any age as though it were the natural and rational way of life. In the materials that are presented on the Hebrew family, the Biblical writings are analyzed as documents recording historical patterns of social behavior. It is illuminating to examine this historical basis of western civilization.

A second historical presentation is the description of the Roman family. Possibly the notions of the Roman family are more dominant in modern western society than other influences. But, before judging how directly the Romans provided this influence, it is well to examine in some detail the complexity of family structure in that ancient society. In most nations of western civilization, family ties are loosely marked and informal by comparison. In the presentation of the Roman family the reader will encounter several types of information that are important in the comparative study of families. First of all, there are relatively detailed presentations of the types of kinship ties. Second, a common method for schematizing family structures is illustrated. Third, the modification of language, such as *pater familias*, which has a relatively simple meaning today may be seen in the complexity of its implications in the period when the concept was a pivotal one in the definition of relationships in families and society.

The third presentation of family systems emphasizes cross-cultural rather than the historical variation. The article by Tara Patel and Vimal Shah summarizes a description of family types in present-day India. This presentation is important because it emphasizes the vast variety within India, noting the contrast between Hindu and Moslem cultures, which have existed side by side for generations. Special emphases are provided such as the historical note on the Nairs and on the joint family. The Moslem family tends in some way to be relatively homogeneous. Its most interesting characteristic to a student in American society is that in most Moslem structures, polygyny (plural wives) is accepted and often practiced by those who can afford it. Those who read the news from distant lands may occasionally find reference to plural marriages in the comments on the personal affairs of some national leaders.

The fourth presentation, on the Japanese family, includes two units. The Japanese family is of particular interest since it is one with many varieties and with great subtlety of definition within the society. As different religions existed in Japan, so do different kinship systems. And, concomitant with this highly complex structure of kinships rapid modernization has occurred, modifying but not completely rejecting earlier family traditions. Japan represents, especially in the urban areas, a system in which some predictable changes have necessarily occurred in the family. What is perhaps more interesting is how resistant Japanese culture has been to other types of change. By way of minor illustration, while there have been youth movements with more vocal statements, the intrinsic value on respect for the older generations seems not to have altered greatly among the Japanese. Still, rapid changes in Japan include some remarkable innovations. Theirs is a system where abortions are, within a definition of health standards, available to all women at their own discretion, and contraceptive information is widely available. An additional article giving perspective on family patterns in Japan will be found in Chapter 4.

Finally, we have included a presentation on African marriage. Many possible selections could be used to suggest the variety of tribal variations in marriage patterns. However, the intent of the volume is not to give an anthropological presentation of the variety of marriage and family forms so much as to illustrate that major population areas vary considerably in marriage forms. The selection on the African family suggests transitional problems that have occurred in some African areas as the black population has moved into urban settings. The presentation has a second value. Often anthropological descriptions are recorded not only by anthropologists, but by doctors, civil servants, and missionaries. This selection by a modern missionary contrasts native cultural and religious values with those of an external Christian mission.

The study of family forms requires the same objectivity that is necessary in any good sociological analysis. Marriage and the family in other cultures are to be studied, not judged in a moral sense. And, the object of comparative analysis is to examine what is "natural" and what is not. In essence, a comparative study will illustrate that many things that we, from a single culture and not necessarily familiar with the rest of the world, might judge as unnatural, immoral or otherwise strange is natural, moral, and in no way strange to other people within the context of their own society. Our own customs may be equally unnatural, strange, and immoral to members of other cultures. If there are moral lessons to be derived from such analyses, they are those of self-questioning. For example, how much of our behavior is habitual and learned in an unquestioning way? How sure should we be in our judgment of what is natural and what constitutes human nature? How can we be justified in judging what is "right" and "moral" if other civilized peoples think quite differently?

5.

Earle Bennett Cross

THE HEBREW FAMILY IN BIBLICAL TIMES

Since the Christian religion has established the type of relations between the sexes in the form of monogamy, it might be supposed that throughout the Bible which has been the basis of Christian thought, there would be a consistent adherence to monogamy. This is not the case. Nowhere in the Old Testament do we find monogamy exalted as the normal or ideal type of relation between men and women. The story of the creation of woman from the rib of man has often been cited to support the contention that the Old Testament teaches monogamy. Certainly, the narrative describes the creation of but one man and one woman; but this is hardly an argument for monogamy. . . . It is probable that for the great majority of Hebrews monogamy was the form of sexual union into which they entered, because of the limitations of their ability to support a larger number of wives. Toward the end of the period covered by the Old Testament, there appears to be a subcurrent of social feeling in favor of monogamy. Yet even in the Book of Proverbs, which seems to rest upon monogamist ideas, there is no clear statement exalting monogamy as the type. One looks in vain for some line in lawcode or in sermon, such as "Thou shalt take to thyself but one wife." Polygamy was practiced especially by the rulers and the affluent.

MARRIAGE BY PURCHASE

The prevailing manner of marriage was by the purchase of a wife on the part of the man. Patronymic ideas dominate the pages of the Old Testament, even as these ideas ruled the social order throughout the historic period of Hebrew life. The man was the important figure

This selection is reprinted from: Earle Bennett Cross, *The Hebrew Family: A Study in Historical Sociology*, Chicago: The University of Chicago Press, 1927 [excerpted and edited from pp. 114–170].

in the family. Woman was secondary always, and for a long period of time she was no more than the possession of her husband in sequence to her subordination to her father. The marriage ceremony was simplicity itself. Payment was made to the father of the bride, and the woman was taken to the domicile of the man, her husband. We have no trace of any religious ceremony, nor even of the simplest ritual of a wedding.

The term used for the payment made for a woman was *mohar*. . . . This word is wrongly rendered in our English versions of the Old Testament by the word "dowry." Properly speaking, a "dowry" is a gift to the bride made by her father, and is in the nature of a marriage portion. Such a gift, a dowry proper, is noted as occurring now and then among the Hebrews. One such instance is recorded of Caleb, who had given his daughter Achsah to Othniel. "And Caleb said unto her, 'What wouldest thou?' And she said, 'Give me a blessing; for that thou hast set me in the land of the South, give me also springs of water.' And he gave her the upper springs and the nether springs." (Joshua 15:18, 19.)

The dowry in this case consisted of springs of water, a very important item to nomadic folk. The word used by the bride in making request of her father for a gift is *berachah*, which our English version has rendered literally as "blessing." It might be translated as the margin of the Revised Version suggests by the word "gift." In this particular connection, the context indicates that a more adequate rendering would have been "dowry."

Frequently, the dowry was a maidservant, if we may judge from the story of Rachel. "And Laban gave to Rachel, his daughter, Bilhah to be her handmaid." (Genesis 29:29.) Leah also had received Zilpah as a dowry.

The *mohar* was variable. Othniel secured

Achsah, daughter of Caleb, to wife by capturing the town of Kiriath-sepher in the course of the conquest of Canaan by the Hebrew tribes. (Joshua 15:15-19.) Saul required of David a *mohar* of "an hundred foreskins of the Philistines" in payment for Michal. (I Samuel 18:25.) In both of these instances, the *mohar* required is a deed of valor. The payment made by the servant of Abraham to the relatives of Rebekah appears to have been similar to the gifts which were made to the bride, namely jewels of silver and gold and raiment. (Genesis 24:53.) Jacob rendered service for his wives. Seven years he labored for Laban in payment for each of the two wives, Leah and Rachel. (Genesis 29:20, 30.) The more usual form of payment would probably be cattle, sheep, or goats in the nomadic period, and grain, wine, oil, or the like after the agricultural life had begun. Money payments might have been made, if there had been such a thing. Certainly, jewels and gold and silver might have figured in the *mohar* at any period of Hebrew history.

Since the wife was the purchase of the husband, it was natural that the Hebrew word for husband should be "master," *ba'al*. Hosea in one of his sermons depicts the redeemed Israel as wedded to Yahweh, and in the delight of true love transforming the usual *bi'ali*, "my master," into the phrase *'ishi*, "my man." There is no reason for doubting the existence of sincere affection between a man and his purchased wife in those far off days; but the very form by which a wife came into the married relation with her man savored of slavery. In fact, the only difference between the wife and the female slave was one of degree of privilege. A female slave was subject to sexual relations with her master. In the "Book of the Covenant," there is explicit provision for the defence of the rights of a female slave, sold by her father. It appears to be expected that she will be subject to sexual relations with her master or with his son. (Exodus 21:7ff.) Even the maidservant who was given to a bride as dowry might come into sexual relations with her mistress' husband. Such relations are apparently subject to the approval of the mistress, however, as in the cases of Zilpah and Bilhah, handmaidens of Leah and Rachel respectively, who had children by Jacob

with the permission of their mistresses.

Marriage by purchase of the wife on the part of the groom prevailed throughout most of the historic period of Hebrew life. We have noted that the wealthy men of the community would probably have a considerable harem, because their economic status would permit them to support a number of wives. The conditions of life were hard for most of the people, however, and it is doubtful if polygamy was practised by very large numbers. The poorer element in the social order would be driven to form irregular unions, even as they do in modern society. Many of these unions were of a type which would not be recognized as legitimate in our day, but which were not beyond the pale of the social standards of their time.

"BEENA" MARRIAGE

Unions such as the metronymic type known as "beena" marriages would provide sexual satisfactions to those who could not afford to maintain an establishment even with a single purchased wife. There would be certain expenditures involved in such unions. Intercourse between husband and wife would occur only at intervals. The husband would be relieved of the support of the wife and also of the support of any children that might be born of the union. On the other hand, he would be deprived of the services of children when such had grown to maturity. The poor must needs be content with such immediate satisfactions as they can command; it is the well-to-do only who can plan for the distant future.

TEMPORARY MARRIAGE

Other unions of a patronnymic type, in which the wife is introduced into the house of the husband, but only for a limited period of time. would also serve the purpose of the impoverished. Such temporary unions would be in the nature of agreements, and the term of the union would be settled upon by the parties concerned. One might say that such marriages are hardly worthy of the name, since they are little removed from prostitution. To our modern sensibilities, they are primitive and intolerable. Yet to the people of that distant time, they were legitimate and obviously necessary for some in the exigencies of their economic situation. From the point of view of the times, they were marriages in legitimate type. They were of a higher grade of morality than modern prostitution at least in that they were sufficiently suited to the conditions of the social order to warrant the sanction of the group. Prostitution may be tolerated, but it is not sanctioned by society. . . .

The relations between Samson and the Philistine woman Delilah appear to be of a more permanent character than his affair with the woman of Gaza. The latter is called a harlot, *zonah*, which is word from a root denoting mere sensual relations. Samson's relations with this woman were but for a night. Such connections cannot be classed even with the comparatively transient relations which we are describing as temporary marriage. (Judges 16:1ff.) In the case of Delilah, however, Samson appears to have had relations with her for a considerable period. The narrators have not said of Delilah, as they did of the woman of Gaza, that she was a harlot. This may be merely a chance omission, but in such close proximity as the two stories stand, it is significant that Delilah is spared the title of shame. The implications of the context would lead the reader to think that Samson lived permanently with Delilah, and he certainly lived openly with her. The details of the story are lacking in those specific facts by which we could establish conclusively that this was a temporary marriage. The narrator is not concerned with this and, as is natural, gives but the details which make for the clarity and progress of his story. (Judges 16:4ff.)

An instance of temporary marriage in which the details are more clearly drawn is that case of the Levite whose wife was brutally and shamefully murdered by the roisterers of Gibeah. Throughout this story in the nineteenth and twentieth chapters of the Book of Judges, the woman is called the "concubine" of the Levite. The translators are doing the best they can with an Hebrew word of rather infrequent use and of uncertain origin. The word is *pi'leghesh*. Some have seen in the word a transliteration of the Greek word which passed into

the Latin in the form *pellex*, the meaning of which is "young girl." Greek influences are very dubious, however, in the Hebrew prior to the exile especially. The word *pi'leghesh* occurs in the late writings, in Chronicles, Esther, and the Song of Songs; but it also occurs in the earliest document of the Hexateuch, so that we shall have to call in question its Greek origin. Others have found its origin in the Hittite. Of this much we may be certain, that it is a thoroughly acclimatized word in the Hebrew. It is used of the members of the harems of the kings of Israel, who had not quite the full status of wives. The phrase in reference to the harem of Solomon will serve to give the typical form of expression. "And he (Solomon) had seven hundred wives, princesses, and three hundred concubines." (I Kings 11:3.) The *pi'legheshim* were evidently members of the harem who had not the status of princesses, but were none the less in the relation to Solomon of serving his sexual requirements. The word is also used of the lesser wives of the patriarchs. Thus "it came to pass, while Israel dwelt in that land, that Reuben went and lay with Bilhah, his father's *pi'leghesh*. And Israel heard of it." (Genesis 35:22.) As we have noted before, Bilhah was given to Jacob as a lesser wife by Rachel her mistress, and Jacob had children by her, namely, Dan and Naphtali. These facts lead readily to the conclusion that a *pi'leghesh* was in a somewhat abnormal sexual relationship, a wife of lesser status in the family group than the regularly purchased wife. . . .

CAPTIVE WOMEN

In primitive barbaric days when wars were commonplace in human existence, the women of captured people were appropriated ofttimes by their captors to be their wives. The most specific law concerning the taking of a captive woman to wife occurs in the code of Deuteronomy. The provisions of this law, as in the case of many others in this comparatively late code, undoubtedly were framed to mitigate the lot of such captives. "When thou goest forth to battle against thine enemies, and the Lord thy God delivereth them into thy hands, and thou carriest them away captive, and seest among the captives a beautiful woman, and thou hast a desire unto her, and wouldest take her to thee to wife; then thou shalt bring her home to thy house, and she shall shave her head and pare her nails, and she shall put the raiment of her captivity from off her, and shall remain in thy house, and bewail her father and her mother a full month. And after that thou shalt go in unto her, and be her husband and she shall be thy wife. And it shall be, if thou have no delight in her, then thou shalt let her go whither she will, but thou shalt not sell her at all for money. Thou shalt not deal with her as a slave, because thou hast humbled her." (Deuteronomy 21:10-14.) There is no doubt that women had suffered in all the wars of conquest in which Israel engaged. Sexual license and the violation of the women of the defeated enemy have throughout history attended the plunder of hamlets and the sack of cities. Not indignities only, but death, were too often the fate of women of a captured city or an invaded country. The ideal set up by the code of Deuteronomy seems almost ridiculously high for the semi-barbaric Hebrew soldier flushed with victory and lustful for all manner of spoils. It is to be feared that the law was idealistic. No earlier code touches on the subject. Yet there is every reason to suppose that whatever violence may have been wrought upon captive women, their captors may have in many instances taken them for slaves at least, and this implies sexual relationship. . . .

SUMMARY

In conclusion, be it said that the normal and usual form of marriage in Hebrew society was by purchase. The usual process was patronymic in that the wife was taken into the family group of the husband. Marriage of captive women taken in wars was probably not an uncommon event. When a man's economic condition did not warrant him in trying to maintain even one wife permanently, he might contract temporary marital relations with some woman, or he might enter into a metronymic type of union, by which also he would be relieved of the economic burden of supporting either wife or family. As to the rite or ceremony by which marriage was

contracted, we are quite without knowledge, and we may even doubt if there was among the Hebrews anything corresponding to the ceremonial of weddings in our modern times. The later Jews did have a wedding ceremonial, for use at which the Song of Songs is supposed to be a collection of poems. We have, however, no evidence on this point in connection with the ancient Hebrew life, unless it be the feasting which occurred at the home of the Levite's woman when he went to remarry her. (Judges 19.)

PROSCRIPTION OF MARRIAGE WITH NEAR KIN

Considerable variance appears in different periods of Hebrew history with regard to the degrees of kinship within which marriage was forbidden. Generally speaking, the lines were more strictly drawn as civilization developed. Particularly strict were the Jews of the exile and restoration.

In the earliest times . . . it was permissible for a man to marry his half-sister. Abraham and Sarah were reputed to stand in this degree of kinship with each other according to the E document of the Hexateuch. The J document which was put into written form slightly prior to the E document, however, is silent as to this relationship between the patriarch and his wife. In a genealogical table from the J document, Sarah's father is not named, although the genealogy of Milcah, Nahor's wife, is given. (Genesis 11:29.) This is a strange silence, since Milcah, whose father is named, was of less import to the Hebrews as the wife of Abraham's brother than Sarah, Abraham's wife. If the mention of the father of either was to be omitted, it would naturally be the less important name which would be ignored. We may infer that the name of Sarah's father was not given because she was a member of the group, as Terah's daughter, and half-sister of Abraham, so that her relationship would be well-known. Milcah, coming from without the group, needed specific mention of her descent. From the two narratives, the one in the J document and the other in the E, we gain the information with regard to this kinship of Abraham and Sarah. In the story of the J document, however, there is nothing to indicate that the representation that Sarah is his sister is anything more than a subterfuge on the part of Abraham, in the nature of a "white lie" to safeguard his own life from the attacks of such as might covet his fair wife. It is in the E document that the narrator specifically advises his readers of the fact by placing in Abraham's mouth the words, "And moreover she is indeed my sister, the daughter of my father, but not the daughter of my mother." (Genesis 20:12.) There is no reason to doubt this statement, and as the genealogy in the J document may possibly imply, the silence of that document is due to the fact that the kinship of the two was well-known.

. . . [We note] also the implication in the story of Amnon and Tamar, children of David by different mothers, that marriage between these two would have been possible. (II Samuel 13:13.) The fact would seem to be that such marriages persisted until a comparatively late date in Hebrew history. They are a relic of a metronymic system in which the two parties to the marriage would really not be close kin. With increasing stringency, the code of the Deuteronomic period and the later Holiness code forbade such marriages. The ascendency of the patronymic idea made them ever more inappropriate.

If we consider the story of Jacob as embodying the actual experiences of an individual as well as portraying tribal movements, we must see in his marriage with Leah and Rachel an instance of marriage between cousins, and the union between Isaac and Rebekah in the preceding generation was a marriage between second cousins, to employ modern terms in description of the relationship. Such marriages are nowhere forbidden even in the codes, where specific lines are drawn defining the forbidden degrees of consanguinity.

There are cases of marriage recorded, however, in the narrative portions of some of the documents, which were within the degrees of kinship proscribed by the laws of the same documents. The recorders seem to have faithfully set down the traditions which came to them, even when they involved unions on the part of the national progenitors which would

not have been permissible in the days when the documents were written. . . .

The seventh century code of Deuteronomy contains prohibition of marriage between a man and his father's wife. "A man shall not take his father's wife, and shall not uncover his father's skirt." (Deuteronomy 22:30.) This is further supplemented by a law against sexual intercourse with a father's wife. "Cursed be he that lieth with his father's wife, because he hath uncovered his father's skirt." (Deuteronomy 27:20.) Of course the reference is not to a man's own mother, but to the other wives of his father. The polygynous family made such unions a possibility without the feeling against incest rising in protest. Such marriages must have been entered into, otherwise the presence of the law forbidding them would be difficult to account for. In fact, we have the record that it was the usual practice for kings upon their accession to the throne to appropriate the harems of their fathers. Absalom by the counsel of Ahithophel proclaimed his usurpation of the throne of his father David by having intercourse with the women of David's harem. (II Samuel 16:20ff.) The family relationships of kings are anomalous, however, and we cannot argue from such acts of the royalty that marriage with the wife of a father was a general practice with the Hebrews. Even the laws which we have cited may have been directed against the procedure of royalty, which we have noted, and may not have had cause for enactment in the conduct of the ordinary citizen.

When we consider the laws of the P document, however, we find reiteration of the prohibition against marriage with the wife of one's father. (Leviticus 18:8.) Here is added also the specification against marriage with one's own mother. The P document is strictest of all and most detailed in its proscriptions. There may possibly have been need for enactment of laws even such as this prohibition against incest, for the times were raw and licentious out of which the P document came. One has but to read the vivid and plain-spoken sermons of Jeremiah or of Ezekiel to comprehend the slough of immorality into which the Hebrews had plunged at the period of the exile. We quote a few lines from Ezekiel. "Behold the princes of

Israel, every one according to his power, have been in thee to shed blood. In thee have they set light by father and mother. In the midst of thee have they dealt by oppression with the sojourner. In thee have they wronged the fatherless and the widow. Thou hast despised my holy things, and hast profaned my sabbaths. Slanderous men have been in thee to shed blood. And in thee they have eaten upon the mountains. In the midst of thee they have committed lewdness. In thee have they uncovered their father's nakedness. In thee have they humbled her that was unclean in her impurity. And one hath committed abomination with his neighbor's wife, and another hath lewdly defiled his daughter-in-law, and another in thee hath humbled his sister, his father's daughter." (Ezekiel 22:6-11.) These lines are definite charges against the social order of that day which gave evidence of the necessity for such laws even as those which proscribe incest. . . .

ENDOGAMY AND EXOGAMY

Marriages between members of different Hebrew tribes appear to have had the sanction of the social order at all periods. There is no evidence that there was any restriction on such unions. On the other hand, there is no reason for supposing that marriage between members of the same tribe was proscribed.

In the earlier stages of Hebrew history, there appears to have been freedom of marriage between Hebrews and other peoples of Palestine. The J document states that "the children of Israel dwelt among the Canaanites. . . . and they took their daughters to be their wives, and gave their own daughters to their sons, and served their gods." (Judges 3:6.) The last phrase of this passage contains a note which was of the utmost import in the development of a spirit of endogamy among the Hebrews. The religious element among the Hebrews feared for the purity of the national religion and with increasing severity frowned upon marriages with members of other races and peoples. We can trace the development of this antagonism to marriage abroad through the Deuteronomic into the P document. The latter

is particularly strenuous in its opposition to foreign marriages.

The records show that Moses contracted a marriage with a woman of the Midianites. (Exodus 2:21.) The J document which contains the information does not indicate any sentiment against such a union. The result of this marriage was the migration of at least one Midianite clan with the Hebrews into Canaan. "And Hobab the Kenite, Moses' brother-in-law, went up out of the city of palm trees with the children of Judah into the wilderness of Judah, which is in the south of Arad; and they went and dwelt with the people." (Judges 1:16.) We have made a correction of the text in quoting this verse, reading "Hobab" instead of "the children of"; but the sense is not materially altered by this modification.

We are somewhat perplexed to account for the narrative from the E document in the twelfth chapter of the Book of Numbers, in which it is stated that Moses had married a Cushite woman. In consequence, Miriam and Aaron called in question his leadership. The God Yahweh vindicated Moses by causing Miriam to be afflicted with leprosy. (Numbers 12:1-15.) We have no other record that Moses married a Cushite woman. A Cushite elsewhere in the Old Testament would mean an Ethiopian. It is very strange to have such a statement in the story. If it stated that Moses had married a Midianite woman, the fact would be consonant with the other incidental references to Moses' matrimonial venture. Some would regard the verse as a marginal gloss. It is hard to account for its appearance even in the margin. If it is not an original part of the narrative, then it has no bearing on the matter with which we are concerned. If it is an integral part of the story, then it testifies to the fact that Moses made not one only but two marriages with women who were not Hebrews.

As apostasy spread, and the worship of Yahweh appeared to be endangered by the intermarriage of Hebrews with the tribespeople who worshiped other deities, there arose an increasing opposition to marriages of that nature. The Deuteronomic code of the seventh century prohibits marriage between Hebrews and the other inhabitants of Palestine. One passage alone will suffice to give the tone of many others which might be cited. "When the Lord thy God shall bring thee into the land whither thou goest to possess it, and shall cast out many nations before thee, the Hittite, and the Girgashite, and the Amorite, and the Canaanite, and the Perizzite, and the Hivite, and the Jebusite, seven nations greater and mightier than thou . . . thou shalt make no covenant with them . . . neither shalt thou make marriages with them, thy daughter thou shalt not give unto his son, nor his daughter shalt thou take unto thy son." (Deuteronomy 7:1-3.) Even the kings were denounced for such foreign marriages. . . .

At the time of the restoration under Ezra and Nehemiah after the long exile in Babylonia, there came a most vigorous effort to root out the evil of foreign marriages, which seems to have become flagrant. The list of those who had contracted marriages with women other than Hebrews is found in the tenth chapter of the Book of Ezra. A decision was reached that all who had thus trespassed should put away their foreign wives and the children born of them. . . .

This effort to purge the restored Jewish nation of all admixture of foreign blood was not made without opposition. . . .

HEBREW HOUSEHOLD

The Hebrew household in nomadic days was a considerable establishment. It included two or three generations of the family proper together with the servants or slaves, and also the animals. With the development of settled life and the entry into city dwellings, there would come a tendency to break up the larger household into smaller units more after the fashion of our modern civilized life. The larger familiar household persisted, however, to a large extent. When we consider that the wives of the head of the household as well as those of his sons were bought, the position of slaves in the household appears in somewhat clearer light. The slave was also purchased, or born into the possession of the master. While the slave was at the disposal of the master, his lot would not be deplorable as a rule. Life for all the household is a struggle under primitive conditions.

In speaking of slaves, the Book of the Covenant, which is one of the earliest codes of law extant from Hebrew life, calls the slave his master's "money." The slave's life was in the master's hand. Probably, he could do what he would with him in the earliest times. This Book of the Covenant, however, provides several clauses in protection of slaves from violence at the hands of their masters. "And if a man smite his man-slave or his woman-slave with a rod, and he die under his hand, he shall surely be punished. Notwithstanding, if he continue a day or two, he shall not be punished, for he is his money." (Exodus 21:20, 21.) While this law is far from being humanitarian, if it be judged by the standards of our modern social order, yet it was no doubt a move toward the moderation of severities which might be shown to slaves by ill-tempered masters. The same code further extends defense to the slave. "And if a man smite the eye of his man-slave, or the eye of his woman-slave, and destroy it, he shall let him go free for his eye's sake. And if he smite out his man-slave's tooth, or his woman-slave's tooth, he shall let him go free for his tooth's sake." (Exodus 21:26, 27.) These clauses in the law may serve to indicate what slaves might suffer at the hands of their masters. Much would depend upon the nature of the master. Even children suffer somewhat at the hands of some parents. We are not attempting to justify the obnoxious custom of slavery, but we would indicate that the slave's position was not very different from that of the other members of the ancient Hebrew household.

Slaves were introduced into the household by capture in war, or by purchase from captors. In many cases, poverty-stricken parents would sell their children, or even themselves with their children in order to save themselves from starvation. The laws in the Book of the Covenant and also in the P document, which are purposed to mitigate the circumstances of such Hebrew slaves, reveal the fact that servitude of this kind must have been common. (Exodus 21:7; Leviticus 25:47-49.)

MALE SLAVES

We consider the case of the male slave first. By the terms of the Book of the Covenant which was composed in the ninth century, the Hebrew slave could be held for a term of six years only, after which in the seventh year he was to be freed. He was to "go out as he came in." That is to say, if he were unmarried when he was bought into slavery, he alone was to be set free. If he had married while he was a slave, his wife and children were to be left in the possession of the master. Under these circumstances, the only way for him to retain his wife and children would be for him to submit to life-long slavery with them, and to have his ear bored through with an awl in token of his permanent servitude. If, however, the wife had been bought with the slave, his wife should go out of slavery with him in the seventh year.

This code may be an idealization rather than a law which was enforced. If one may judge by the modifications which appear in the subsequent codes, the seventh year of release for slaves was not acceptable to slave-owners, who probably evaded it whenever they could. Yet the Deuteronomic code of the seventh century practically restates the law of the Book of the Covenant. Many pious incentives are added to the clause by the Deuteronomist, urging masters to observe the law, to send the slave away with a plentiful supply of food and the like. (Deuteronomy 15:12-18.) The code in the P document of the fifth century, following the exile, modifies the term of seven years. This suggests the inference that the term had proved to be too short in practice. This late code requires that the slave shall be released in the year of the jubilee, which came around every 50 years. He and his family together shall be liberated. If he has fallen into the hands of an owner who is not a Hebrew, his relatives are to buy him back at the year of jubilee. The foreign owner could hardly be expected to observe the Hebrew law, for we have now passed to the time when Hebrew national life had crashed into ruin, and the people have been exiles for a long time and returned to Palestine only to struggle for existence in the midst of foreign neighbors. (Leviticus 25:39-52.) If these laws were enforced at all, slaves might go free at length. Possibly with the new start in life, they might prove slavery to have been a blessing in relieving their extreme need. . . .

FEMALE SLAVE

The situation of the female slave was somewhat different from that of the male. She would undoubtedly be subject to sexual relations with the master. In view of the fact that the regular wives of the household were purchased, the female slaves of the master would stand only in a position subordinate to the other women. The position of a female slave in any social order is such as to make her subject to the will of her owner in any matter. That a poor Hebrew should sell his daughter to be a slave seems at first a heartless act. When it is viewed in the light of the common marriage customs of the time, it is not as distressing. Probably for a poor girl, such a transaction became a splendid settlement. The wealthy maiden also was purchased, but for a larger sum and with the understanding that her social position would be such as to surround her with luxuries consonant with the status of her husband.

The Book of the Covenant provides a ruling for the treatment of female slaves, which reads as if the woman would consider herself disgraced or treated "deceitfully," were she not taken into sexual relations with the master. After he had had sexual relations with her, if he no longer cared to continue them, he could let her be bought back by her family, but he had no right to sell her to any foreigner. He might give the woman to one of his sons, in which case he must treat her as he would one of his own daughters. If he took another woman, the master might not diminish in any way the rights of the first to food, raiment, or the privilege of sexual intercourse with him. Should he take another woman and fail to continue the dues of the first, the slave woman might go free without buying her freedom.

The later law codes of Deuteronomy and the P document do not make any provisions for female slaves as distinct from males. There is, however, a clause in the code in Leviticus which shows that female slaves were held in possession as slave-wives. The passage refers to the treatment of a slave-woman, who had been purchased by a man, who had not given her her freedom, nor allowed her to be redeemed. If she had sexual relations with another man, it was not regarded as adultery except in the second or third degree, so to speak. The usual penalty for adultery was death for both parties. In this case, however, inquisition was to be made. The implication is that the master of the woman might deal with her as he saw fit, since she was his property. The guilty man was to make ceremonial reparation for his guilt before the priest. The whole clause indicates the subordinate status of a slave-woman as compared with a purchased wife, and evidences the fact which we have been substantiating from the records, that slave-women were in relation to their masters as subordinate wives. (Leviticus 19:20-22.)

THE VIOLATION AND DISSOLUTION OF MARRIAGE

Marriage among the Hebrews at least before the exile was an affair of purchase. The wife, or wives, were therefore, the property of the purchaser, or husband. This economic phase of the marriage relation did not of necessity rob it of romance or of true love according as the parties to the transaction were capable of emotion or romance. The fact of material payment for the right of ownership of the woman does, however, give a thoroughly economic cast to the marriage relation. . . . The father of a girl would require satisfaction in material recompense for the loss of her chastity. In a sense, he would regard the violation of a daughter as an economic loss. This economic aspect of marriage among the Hebrews must have tinged the attitude of a husband with regard to the fidelity of his wife or wives. From the earliest times of which we have record, the penalty for adultery was most severe. When it was supposed that Tamar, daughter-in-law of Judah, had been faithless to her betrothal to Shelah, she was condemned to death by burning. This was not a case of adultery in the simplest definition of that term. Tamar had twice been widowed, and was living in her father's house as a widow, until such time as she should be given to Shelah, younger brother of her deceased husband, whose responsibility it was to fulfill the custom of the levirate and raise up some sons to carry on the name of his brother. In fact, Tamar was bound

to Shelah, and the penalty for her infidelity by having sexual intercourse with another was the same as that for adultery.

ADULTERY

The earliest legislation with regard to adultery is that of the decalogue attached to the Book of the Covenant in Exodus. "Thou shalt not commit adultery." (Exodus 20:14.) There is no penalty attached to the clause, even as there is none connected with the other items of the decalogue. If, however, the case just cited of Tamar be regarded as bearing on the crime of adultery, as we think it to be, the unwritten custom of the early days may be regarded as requiring the penalty of death for those who committed adultery.

In the seventh century code of Deuteronomy, the interdict against adultery appears again in the decalogue which is attached to the code, and also in the body of the law. "If a man be found lying with a woman married to a husband, then they shall both of them die, the man that lay with the woman and the woman. So shalt thou put away the evil from Israel." (Deuteronomy 22:22.) Nothing is said as to the manner of execution of the death penalty, which is set for both parties to the crime. Possibly, this decision was left for the elders, who would by normal process serve both as jury and judges on the crime. Stoning appears to have been the most common manner of executing a death penalty, although as we noted in the case of Tamar burning by fire was also practised.

In the P document from the fifth century, the crime of adultery is punishable by death. "And the man that committeth adultery with another man's wife, even he that committeth adultery with his neighbor's wife, the adulterer and the adulteress shall surely be put to death." (Leviticus 20:10.) Again the code is silent as to the method of the execution. A passage in the prophet Ezekiel's work, however, may throw light on the custom of that late time. In depicting the doom of Israel, whom he has been describing as the wife of God, the prophet concludes in a vigorous passage, which is doubtless imaginative, yet may be taken to be composed of elements from the life of the times. "And I will judge thee, as women that break wedlock and shed blood are judged; and I will bring upon thee the blood of wrath and jealousy. I will also give thee into their hand, and they shall throw down thy vaulted place, and break down thy lofty places, and they shall strip thee of thy clothes, and take thy fair jewels, and they shall leave thee naked and bare. They shall also bring up a company against thee, and they shall stone thee with stones, and thrust thee through with their swords." (Ezekiel 16:38-40.) This may be taken as a hint confirming the impression that death by stoning was commonly the penalty for adultery.

The man is never regarded as guilty except as he transgresses the rights of some other man to a woman. This is the usual patronymic attitude, in which everything is considered from the point of view of the master, man. If there rose suspicion in the mind of a husband that his wife had been unfaithful to him, he might proceed to discover whether she were guilty or not by a ceremonial prescribed in a section of the P document. This represents the late period of Jewish history, yet it may be that there is preserved in the enactment a process which had long prevailed among the people. The notable thing is that the woman alone is regarded as being under suspicion. Not a hint is given that the woman could ever charge her husband with the guilt of adultery. The double sexual standard prevailed. . . .

A woman charged with adultery by a suspicious husband was obliged to prove her innocence, even as a father was obliged to give evidence of the virginity of his daughter at the time of her marriage, if ever the husband raised a question in that regard. The trial for the woman suspected of adultery was by ordeal. She was obliged to drink a bitter mixture of water and dust from off the floor of the sanctuary. If she were guilty, her body was expected to swell and her thigh fall away. If she were innocent, the water would not harm her. The husband risked nothing in the accusation. In this, he is at an advantage over the husband who raised question as to the virginity of his wife at the time of her marriage. The latter had to settle with his father-in-law. The husband

who suspected his wife of adultery had but himself to reckon with, for the wife was wholly his property.

DIVORCE

Previous to the time of the Deuteronomic law, divorce appears to have consisted in the simple process of dismissal of the wife by the husband. We have few cases to cite by way of illustration. One outstanding instance of divorce concerns a subordinate wife, or slave-wife, and may not be typical of the procedure with regard to a wife in full status. We refer to the dismissal of Hagar by Abraham at the request of Sarah, the first wife. Abraham gave Hagar but a skin of water with some bread and sent her away in the wilderness, where she almost perished together with her boy, Ishmael. . . .

Remarriage of the divorced man and woman might occur, if circumstances brought them together again. At least in the case of Michal and David, remarriage recurred. This took place after the accession of David to the throne of Judah, however, and as a rule the affairs of kings are exceptional. This particular case was a remarriage after a divorce to which the husband did not agree, in which he was obliged by the exigencies of life or death to concur. Yet every divorce and remarriage is peculiar. Such disruptions of the normal processes of life can hardly be expected to follow a routine. David's actions in matters of sex relationship were not always commendable even to the people of his own time, rude as those people may seem to us moderns. Yet even as we recognize that the instance may be far from typical of ordinary cases, we recite it as one of the shreds of evidence which we have to throw light on the obscure procedures of divorce in the earlier period of Hebrew history. When David had gained the throne of Judah, Abner held the dominant hand in the territory of Israel to the north where had been the stronghold of Saul, now dead on the battlefield of Gilboa. Abner recognized the growing power of David and sent to make overtures of submission. David agreed to the reconciliation between north and south on the proviso that Michal, his former wife, should be restored to him by Abner. A pitiful tale it is. Almost by force, Abner took Michal from her husband, Paltiel ben Laish, to whom Saul had given her. "And her husband went with her, weeping as he went, and followed her to Bahurim. Then said Abner unto him, 'Go, return.' And he returned." (II Samuel 3:16.) As we read, we wonder whether romance bred in those ancient days as it has in the interval. Paltiel seems to have loved Michal, and David had not forgotten her. Had the story come to us from the hand of someone whose heart was quick to sense, and whose hand was inspired to tell of, earthly loves, there might have been spread upon the records here a romance to match the classics.

It is not surprising that divorce should have been a simple process and wholly at the will of the husband. The entire social fabric of the family in those days was built around the man as the centre and motivating agent of all the life and activity of the group. So much for the earliest period.

The code of Deuteronomy in the seventh century has a clause on divorce. This required that divorce be allowable only when a reason is given by the husband for the divorce. Furthermore, the husband is required to give to the divorced woman a document written in evidence of her marriage. "When a man taketh a wife and marrieth her, then it shall be if she find no favor in his eyes, because he hath found some unseemly thing in her, that he shall write her a bill of divorcement and give it in her hand and send her out of his house." (Deuteronomy 24:1.) This made divorce a legal affair. The very process of making out a formal document of divorce would give the husband time to "think twice." The law thus would protect the woman from caprice and temporary whim. The law goes on to specify that the woman might marry another man after her divorce. If, however, this second husband should divorce her, or should he die, the first husband is forbidden to remarry the woman. This enactment is reflected in the words of a contemporary prophet, Jeremiah. In charging the people with brazen, wanton apostasy from Yahweh, the prophet depicts their desperate straits in terms of the divorced woman who may not be remarried to her first husband. "If a man put away his wife, and she go from him, and become another man's, can there be a return to him?" (Following a revised text.) (Jeremiah 3:1.)

In a prophet of the days following the exile, there is the first note of disapproval of divorce. The statement in opposition to the divorce comes in connection with a recital of the reasons for the disaffection of Yahweh toward his people. One of the reasons was "because the Lord hath been witness between thee and the wife of thy youth, against whom thou hast dealt treacherously, though she is thy companion and the wife of thy covenant. . . . 'Therefore take heed to your spirit, and let none deal treacherously against the wife of his youth. For I hate putting away,' (divorce) saith the Lord, the God of Israel, 'and him that covereth his garment with violence,' saith the Lord of hosts. Therefore take heed to your spirit, that ye deal not treacherously." (Malachi 2:14-16.)

We are able, therefore, to trace a gradual effort to make the practice of divorce more difficult, and the growth of a sentiment against divorce especially in the minds of religious leaders.

WIDOWS

The woman whose marriage was dissolved by the death of her husband was in a difficult position. Many passages appeal to the Hebrew to be considerate of widows and orphans, and not to oppress them or do them injustice in any regard. (Exodus 22:21, 23; Deuteronomy 24:17; Isaiah 1:23; 10:2; Jeremiah 7:6; 22:3; Ezekiel 22:7; Malachi 3:5; Zechariah 7:10; Psalms 68:6; 146:9; Job 22:9; 24:3, 21.) In the earlier times, a second marriage followed frequently soon after the death of the first husband. Thus Abigail married David at once upon the death of her churlish husband Nabal. (I Samuel 25:39ff.) If the widow did not marry at once, she would return to her father's house. There she would remain probably until a second marriage was contracted. Thus Tamar returned to her girlhood home upon the death of Er and Onan, to wait till Shelah the third son of Judah was old enough to contract the responsibilities of the levirate and marry his brother's widow. (Genesis

38:11.) The same procedure is noted in the P document as being proper for the widowed daughter of a priest. (Leviticus 22:13.) From this, we infer that when it was possible, the widow went back to her family for protection and a home on the death of her husband.

THE LEVIRATE

The law of the levirate worked out for the protection and benefit of widows as well as to the advantage of the family in the perpetuation of the deceased's name through an heir by fiction. The material from which we can gather information concerning the practice of the levirate among the Hebrews is not very plentiful. Nevertheless, there is quite enough to substantiate the practice.

The earliest instance in the records is that of the sons of Judah. The eldest son, Er, married Tamar. Upon Er's death, it fell to Onan his next younger brother to take Tamar and beget a son who should bear the name and inherit the titles and privileges of Er. Onan evaded his duty and suffered the penalty of death at the hands of the deity. It thus developed upon Shelah, the third brother, to marry Tamar. The purpose of this custom as it is represented in this narrative was "to raise up seed" to the deceased. (Genesis 38:8.) Nothing is said about inheritance in this connection. The whole purpose seems to be the perpetuation of the name, or line, of the dead. This may be due to the fact that the background of life surrounding the family of Judah is pastoral and not agricultural. Until the agricultural stage had been reached, the matter of inheritance of land did not loom up as an element supplementing the purpose of the levirate to continue the name of the family. In the other instances of the custom, however, the matter of safeguarding the inheritance does not figure either. The natural conclusion is that inheritance of property did not figure in the custom among the Hebrews.

The most definite formulation of the custom appears in the code of Deuteronomy. There is no reason for supposing that this statement is not adequate for the custom as it was practised in all periods of Hebrew history. The clause deserves full quotation. "If brethren dwell together, and one of them die and have no son, the wife of the dead shall not be married without unto a stranger. Her husband's brother shall go in unto her, and take her to him to wife, and perform the duty of a husband's brother unto her. And it shall be that the first-born that she beareth shall succeed in the name of his brother that is dead, that his name be not blotted out of Israel. And if the man like not to take his brother's wife, then his brother's wife shall go up to the gate unto the elders and say, 'My husband's brother refused to raise up unto his brother a name in Israel. He will not perform the duty of a husband's brother unto me.' Then the elders of his city shall call him and speak unto him. And if he stand and say, 'I like not to take her,' then shall his brother's wife come unto him in the presence of the elders, and loose his shoe from off his foot, and spit in his face. And she shall answer and say, 'So shall it be done unto the man that doth not build up his brother's house.' And his name shall be called in Israel, 'The house of him that hath his shoe loosed.' " (Deuteronomy 25:5-10.) It appears, therefore, that the obligation to carry out the custom of the levirate might be evaded, but only at considerable cost in social obloquy. This was the formulation of the custom as it was in vogue just before the exile.

After the exile, there was an attempt to eliminate the custom of the levirate from Jewish life. The law defining the custom is conspicuous by its absence from the code of the P document, which was composed during the exile, and the years immediately subsequent. Furthermore, in the laws defining the proscribed degrees of kinship within which marriage might not take place, the law specifically states that a man may not marry his brother's wife. "And if a man shall take his brother's wife, it is impurity. He hath uncovered his brother's nakedness. They shall be childless." (Leviticus 20:21.) "Thou shalt not uncover the nakedness of thy brother's wife. It is thy brother's nakedness." (Leviticus 18:16.) Twice, the specific interdict of this kind of marriage appears, therefore, in the code of the later period of Jewish life. As we have noted perviously, the P document in its law codes sought to extend the forbidden degrees of consanguinity for persons intending marriage. The custom of the levirate ran counter to the ideal of the formulators of the new laws, and they stood against it.

There was opposition to this new law by many. Such opposition was natural, in view of the conservative tendencies of humanity. . . .

MUTUAL RELATIONS OF PARENTS AND CHILDREN

Frequent stress is laid in the Old Testament on the duty of children to honor their parents. The familiar clause in the decalogue will come to mind at once. "Honor thy father and thy mother, that thy days may be long in the land which the Lord thy God giveth thee." (Exodus 20:12; also Deuteronomy 5:16.) The ninth century Book of the Covenant laid the death penalty upon the person who smote either his father or his mother. (Exodus 21:15.) The same penalty was set also for the person who cursed his father or his mother. (Exodus 21:17.) How far we have traveled from such a primitive law! This is not the place to moralize upon the direction in which we have been moving. Certainly, the death penalty would not be reinvoked by moderns as a means of securing honor to parents.

The Deuteronomic code was as usual more specific in its statement of the law defining the attitude of children toward their parents. The death penalty was exacted also in this code for failure to show the proper respect for their wishes. Disobedience and failure to respond to the voice of parents made a man liable to trial before the elders in the gate. If the case was proven, the culprit was to be stoned to death. (Deuteronomy 21:18-21.) One of the clauses in the curses which were to be pronounced from Ebal upon the immigrant Hebrews, to offset the blessings from Gerizim, was the phrase, "Cursed be he that setteth light upon his father or his mother." (Deuteronomy 27:16.) This is no doubt a section introduced by writers of a much later date than the Deuteronomic period. The blessings which were composed to be pronounced upon Gerizim are of a much different tone and content from these curses. Even so,

the composition of editors in the period following the exile is illuminating as to the point of view of their time and mind on the relation of parents and children.

The P document also contains the law requiring honor of parents at the penalty of death. "Every one that curseth his father or his mother shall surely be put to death. He hath cursed his father or his mother. His blood shall be upon him." (Leviticus 20:9. Cf. 19:3.) And while the penalty of death is not mentioned in the Book of Proverbs, this one of the latest compositions to find a place in the canon of the Old Testament includes many an injunction upon children to have regard for parents. "Hearken unto thy father that begat thee, and despise not thy mother when she is old." (Proverbs 23:22.)

CARE FOR CHILDREN

Care and affectionate regard for children is taken for granted on the part of parents. From the fact that the social order was patronymic, it would be natural to suppose that boys would be of more value in the sight of parents than girls. Girls are rarely mentioned in genealogical lists. Girls would have a certain economic worth in the periods when marriage by purchase prevailed. The poor man, however, could not expect much return from the marriage of his daughters, unless they chanced to win the attention of some of the nobility or wealthy. In extreme poverty, it would be the girls who would be disposed of first as slaves to some more fortunate Hebrew family. In some instances, sale of children might be made to foreigners. We should not think of the parents who sold their children as heartless. Sometimes under well-tempered masters, the enslaved children would be in far better circumstances than they would have been in the pangs of starvation conditions at home. The maidens also as slave-wives of the right sort of masters would not be in the worst of circumstances. Nevertheless, the break of ties so close as those of parents and children could never be made without grief. A classic passage in illustration of the woe entailed by the custom is to be found in Nehemiah. "Then there arose a great cry of the people and of their wives against their brethren the Jews. For there were that said, 'We, our sons and our daughters are many. Let us get grain, that we may eat and live.' Some also there were that said, 'We are mortgaging our fields, and our vineyards and our houses. Let us get grain because of the dearth.' There were also that said, 'We have borrowed money for the king's tribute upon our fields and our vineyards. Yet now our flesh is as the flesh of our brethren, our children as their children. And lo, we bring into bondage our sons and our daughters to be servants, and some of our daughters are brought into bondage already. Neither is it in our power to help it, for other men have our fields and our vineyards.'" (Nehemiah 5:1-5.)

6.

HAROLD WHITSTONE JOHNSTON

THE ROMAN FAMILY

FAMILIA

THE HOUSEHOLD

If by our word family we usually understand a group of husband, wife, and children, we may acknowledge at once that it does not correspond exactly to any of the meanings of the Latin *familia*, varied as the dictionaries show these to be. Husband, wife, and children did not necessarily constitute an independent family among the Romans, and were not necessarily members even of the same family. Those persons made up the Roman *familia*, in the sense nearest to its English derivative, who were subject to the authority of the same head of the house (*pater familiās*). These persons might make a host in themselves: wife, unmarried daughters, sons real or adopted, married or unmarried, with their wives, sons, unmarried daughters, and even remoter descendants (always through males), yet they made but one *familia* in the eyes of the Romans. The head of such a family—"household" or "house" is the nearest English word—was always *suī iūris* ("independent," "one's own master"), while the others were *aliēnō iūrī subiectī* ("dependent").

This selection is reprinted from: Harold Whitstone Johnston, *The Private Life of the Romans*, Chicago: Scott, Foresman and Company, 1903 [excerpted and edited from pp. 21-34 and 49-55].

The authority of the *pater familiās* over his wife was called *manus*, over his descendants *patria potestās*, over his chattels *dominica potestās*. So long as he lived and retained his citizenship, these powers could be terminated only by his own deliberate act. He could dispose of his property by gift or sale as freely as we do now. He might "emancipate" his sons, a very formal proceeding (*ēmancipātiō*) by which they became each the head of a new family, though they were childless themselves or unmarried or even mere children. He might also emancipate an unmarried daughter, who thus in her own self became an independent family. Or he might give her in marriage to another Roman citizen, an act by which she passed by early usage into the family of which her husband was head, if he was *suī iūris*, or of which he was a member, if he was still *aliēnō iūrī subiectus*. It must be carefully noticed, on the other hand, that the marriage of a son did not make him a *pater familiās* or relieve him in any degree from the *patria potestās*: he and his wife and their children were subject to the same head of the house as he had been before his marriage. On the other hand, the head of the house could not number in his *familia* his daughter's children: legitimate children always followed their father, while an illegitimate child was from the moment of birth in himself or herself an independent family.

THE SPLITTING UP OF A HOUSE

Emancipation was not very common and it usually happened that the household was dissolved only by the death of the head. When this occurred, as many new households were formed as there were persons directly subject to his *potestās* at the moment of his death: wife, sons, unmarried daughters, widowed daughters-in-law, and children of a deceased son. The children of a surviving son, it must be noticed, merely passed from the *potestās* of their grandfather to that of their father. A son under age or an unmarried daughter was put under the care of a guardian (*tūtor*), selected from the same *gēns*, very often an older brother, if there was one. The following diagram will make this clearer:

OTHER MEANINGS OF FAMILIA

The word *familia* was also very commonly used in a slightly wider sense to include in addition to the persons named above all the slaves and clients and all the property real and personal belonging to the *pater familiās*, or acquired and used by the persons under his *potestās*. The word was also used of the slaves alone, and rarely of the property alone. In a still wider and more important sense the word was applied to a larger group of related persons, the *gēns*, consisting of all the "households" who derived their descent through males from a common ancestor. This remote ancestor, could his life have lasted through all the intervening centuries, would have been the *pater familiās* of all the persons included in the *gēns*, and all

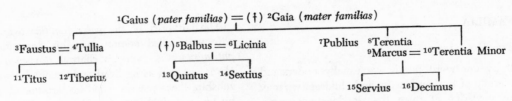

FIGURE 6-1.

It assumed that Gaius is a widower who has had five children, three sons and two daughters. Of the sons, Faustus and Balbus married and had each two children; Balbus then died. Of the daughters, Terentia Minor married Marcus and became the mother of two children. Publius and Terentia were unmarried at the death of Gaius, who had emancipated none of his children. It will be noticed:

1. The living descendants of Gaius were ten (3, 7, 8, 10, 11, 12, 13, 14, 15, 16), his son Balbus being dead.
2. Subject to his *potestas* were nine (3, 4, 6, 7, 8, 11, 12, 13, 14).
3. His daughter Terentia Minor (10) had passed out of his *potestas* by her marriage with Marcus (9), and her children (15, 16) alone out of all the descendants of Gaius had not been subject to him.
4. At his death are formed six independent families, one consisting of four persons (3, 4, 11, 12), the others of one person each (6, 7, 8, 13, 14).
5. Titus and Tiberius (11, 12) have merely passed out of the *potestas* of their grandfather Gaius to come under that of their father Faustus.

would have been subject to his *potestās*. Membership in the *gēns* was proved by the possession of the *nōmen,* the second of the three names that every citizen of the Republic regularly had.

Theoretically this *gēns* had been in prehistoric times one of the *familiae,* "households," whose union for political purposes had formed the state. Theoretically its *pater familiās* had been one of the heads of houses who in the days of the kings had formed the *patrēs,* or assembly of old men (*senātus*). The splitting up of this prehistoric household, a process repeated generation after generation, was believed to account for the numerous *familiae* who claimed connection with the great *gentēs* in later times. The *gēns* had an organization of which little is known. It passed resolutions binding upon its members; it furnished guardians for minor children, and curators for the insane and for spendthrifts. When a member died without leaving natural heirs, it succeeded to such property as he did not dispose of by will and administered it for the common good of all its members. These members were called *gentīlēs*, were bound to take part in the religious services of the *gēns* (*sacra gentīlicia*), had a claim to the common property, and might if they chose be laid to rest in the common burial ground.

Finally, the word *familia* was often applied to certain branches of a *gēns* whose members had the same *cognōmen*. For this use of *familia* a more accurate word is *stirps*.

Agnati. The children of a daughter could not be included in the *familia* of her father, and that membership in the larger organization called the *gēns* was limited to those who could trace their descent through males. All persons who could in this way trace their descent through males to a common ancestor, in whose *potestās* they would be were he alive, were called *agnātī*, and this *agnātiō* was the closest tie of relationship known to the Romans. In the list of *agnātī* were included two classes of persons who would seem by the definition to be excluded. These were the wife, who passed by *manus* into the family of her husband, becoming by law his agnate and the agnate of all his agnates, and the adopted son. On the other hand a son who had been emancipated was excluded from *agnātiō* with his father and his father's agnates, and could have no agnates of his own until he married or was adopted into another *familia*. The following diagram will make this clearer:

and Tiberius the sons of Faustus, Quintus and Sextius the sons of Balbus, and Servius and Decimus the sons of Terentia Minor). Gaius has emancipated two of his sons, Balbus and Publius, and has adopted his grandson Servius, who had previously been emancipated by his father Marcus. There are four sets of *agnātī*:

1. Gaius, his wife, and those whose *pater familias* he is, viz.: Faustus, Tullia the wife of Faustus, Terentia, Titus, Tiberius, and Servius, a son by adoption (1, 2, 3, 4, 8, 11, 12, 15).
2. Balbus, his wife, and their two sons (5, 6, 13, and 14).
3. Publius, who is himself a *pater familias*, but has no agnati at all.
4. Marcus, his wife Terentia Minor, and their child Decimus (9, 10, 16). Notice that the other child, Servius (15), having been emancipated by Marcus is no longer agnate to his father, mother, or brother.

Cognati. On the other hand, cognati were what we call blood relations, no matter whether they traced their relationship through males or females, and regardless of what *potestās* had been over them. The only barrier in the eyes of the law was loss of citizenship, and even this was not always regarded. Thus, in the table last given, Gaius, Faustus, Balbus, Publius, Terentia, Terentia Minor, Titus, Tiberius, Quintus, Sextius, Servius, and Decimus are all cognates with one another. So, too, is Gaia with all her descendants mentioned. So also are Tullia, Titus, and Tiberius; Licinia, Quintus, and Sextius; Marcus, Servius, and Decimus. But hus-

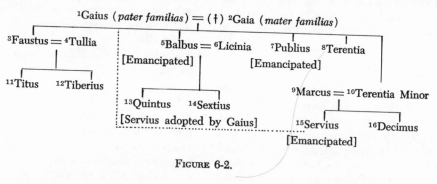

FIGURE 6-2.

It is supposed that Gaius and Gaia have five children (Faustus, Balbus, Publius, Terentia, and Terentia Minor), and six grandsons (Titus

band and wife (Gaius and Gaia, Faustus and Tullia, Balbus and Licinia, Marcus and Terentia Minor) were not cognates by virtue of their

marriage, though that made them agnates. . . .
It must be understood, however, that *cognātiō*
gave no legal rights or claims under the Republic.

Adfines. Persons connected by marriage only
were called *adfinēs,* as a wife with her husband's
cognates and he with hers. There were no formal degrees of *adfinitās,* as there were of *cognātiō.* Those *adfinēs* for whom distinctive names
were in common use were: *gener,* son-in-law;
nurus, daughter-in-law; *socer,* father-in-law;
socrus, mother-in-law; *prīvignus, prīvigna,* stepson, step-daughter; *vitricus,* step-father; *noverca,* step-mother. If we compare these names
with the awkward compounds that do duty for
them in English, we shall have additional proof
of the stress laid by the Romans on family ties:
two women who married brothers were called
iānitrīces, a relationship for which we do not
have even a compound. The names of blood
relations tell the same story: a glance at the
table of cognates will show how strong the
Latin is here, how weak the English. We have
"uncle," "aunt," and "cousin," but between
avunculus and *patruus, mātertera* and *amita,*
patruēlis and *cōnsōbrīnus,* we can distinguish
only by descriptive phrases. For *atavus* and
tritavus we have merely the indefinite "forefathers." In the same way the language testifies to the headship of the father. We speak of
the "mother country" and "mother tongue," but
to the Roman these were *patria* and *sermō*
patrius. As the *pater* stood to the *fīlius,* so stood
the *patrōnus* to the *cliēns,* the *patriciī* to the
plēbēiī, the *patrēs* (= senators) to the rest of
the citizens, and *Iūpiter* (Jove the Father) to
the other gods of Olympus.

THE FAMILY CULT

It has been said that *agnātiō* was the closest tie
know to the Romans. The importance they attached to the agnatic family is largely explained
by their ideas of the future life. They believed
that the souls of men had an existence apart
from the body, but not in a separate spirit-land.
They conceived of the soul as hovering around
the place of burial and requiring for its peace
and happiness that offerings of food and drink
should be made to it regularly. Should these
offerings be discontinued, the soul would cease
to be happy itself, and might become perhaps
a spirit of evil. The maintenance of these rites
and ceremonies devolved naturally upon the
descendants from generation to generation,
whom the spirits in turn would guide and
guard.

The Roman was bound, therefore, to perform these acts of affection and piety so long
as he lived himself, and bound no less to provide for their performance after his death by
perpetuating his race and the family cult. A
curse was believed to rest upon the childless
man. Marriage was, therefore, a solemn religious duty, entered into only with the approval of the gods ascertained by the auspices.
In taking a wife to himself the Roman made
her a partaker of his family mysteries, a service
that brooked no divided allegiance. He therefore separated her entirely from her father's
family, and was ready in turn to surrender his
daughter without reserve to the husband with
whom she was to minister at another altar. The
pater familiās was the priest of the household,
and those subject to his *potestās* assisted in the
prayers and offerings, the *sacra familiāria.*

But it might be that a marriage was fruitless, or that the head of the house saw his sons
die before him. In this case he had to face the
prospect of the extinction of his family, and his
own descent to the grave with no posterity to
make him blessed. One of two alternatives was
open to him to avert such a calamity. He might
give himself in adoption and pass into another
family in which the perpetuation of the family
cult seemed certain, or he might adopt a son
and thus perpetuate his own. He usually followed the latter course, because it secured
peace for the souls of his ancestors no less than
for his own.

ADOPTION

The person adopted might be either a *pater*
familiās himself or, more usually, a *fīlius*
familiās. In the case of the latter the process
was called *adoptiō* and was a somewhat complicated proceeding by which the natural parent
conveyed his son to the other, the effect being
to transfer the adopted person from one family to the other. The adoption of a *pater*
familiās was a much more serious matter, for

it involved the extinction of one family in order to prevent the extinction of another. It was called *adrogātiō* and was an affair of state. It had to be sanctioned by the *pontificēs,* the highest officers of religion, who had probably to make sure that the *adrogātus* had brothers enough to attend to the interests of the ancestors whose cult he was renouncing. If the *pontificēs* gave their consent, it had still to be sanctioned by the *comitia centuriāta,* as the adrogation might deprive the *gēns* of its succession to the property of the childless man. If the *comitia* gave consent, the *adrogātus* sank from the position of head of a house to that of a *fīlius familiās* in the household of his adoptive father. If he had wife and children, they passed with him into the new family, and so did all his property. Over him the adoptive father had *potestās* as over a son of his own, and looked upon him as flesh of his flesh and bone of his bone. We can have at best only a feeble and inadequate notion of what adoption meant to the Romans.

THE PATRIA POTESTAS *Power of one's native condr*

The authority of the *pater familiās* over his descendants was called usually the *patria potestās,* but also the *patria maiestās,* the *patrium iūs,* and the *imperium paternum.* It was carried to a greater length by the Romans than by any other people, a length that seems to us excessive and cruel. As they understood it, the *pater familiās* had absolute power over his children and other agnatic descendants. He decided whether or not the newborn child should be reared; he punished what he regarded as misconduct with penalties as severe as banishment, slavery, and death; he alone could own and exchange property—all that his descendants earned or acquired in any way was his: according to the letter of the law they were little better than his chattels. If his right to one of them was disputed, he vindicated it by the same form of action that he used to maintain his right to a house or a horse; if one was stolen, he proceeded against the abductor by the ordinary action for theft; if for any reason he wished to transfer one of them to a third person, it was done by the same form of conveyance that he employed to transfer inanimate

things. The jurists boasted that these powers were enjoyed by Roman citizens only.

Limitations. But however stern this authority was theoretically, it was greatly modified in practice, under the republic by custom, under the empire by law. King Romulus was said to have ordained that all sons should be reared and also all firstborn daughters; furthermore that no child should be put to death until its third year, unless it was greviously deformed. This at least secured life for the child, though the *pater familiās* still decided whether it should be admitted to his household, with the implied social and religious privileges, or be disowned and become an outcast. King Numa was said to have forbidden the sale into slavery of a son who had married with the consent of his father. But of much greater importance was the check put upon arbitrary and cruel punishments by custom. Custom, not law, obliged the *pater familiās* to call a council of relatives and friends (*iūdicium domesticum*) when he contemplated inflicting severe punishment upon his children, and public opinion obliged him to abide by their verdict. Even in the comparatively few cases where tradition tells us that the death penalty was actually inflicted, we usually find that the father acted in the capacity of a magistrate happening to be in office when the offense was committed, or that the penalties of the ordinary law were merely anticipated, perhaps to avoid the disgrace of a public trial and execution.

So, too, in regard to the ownership of property the conditions were not really so hard as the strict letter of the law makes them appear to us. It was customary for the head of the house to assign to his children property, *pecūlia* ("cattle of their own"), for them to manage for their own benefit. And more than this, although the *pater familiās* held legal title to all their acquisitions, yet practically all property was acquired for and belonged to the household as a whole, and he was in effect little more than a trustee to hold and administer it for the common benefit. This is shown by the fact that there was no graver offense against public morals, no fouler blot on private character, than to prove untrue to this trust, *patrimōnium prōfundere.* Besides this, the long continuance of the *potestās* is in itself a proof that its rigor was more apparent than real.

Extinction of the Potestās. The *patria potestās* was extinguished in various ways:

1. By the death of the *pater familias.*
2. By the emancipation of the son or daughter.
3. By the loss of citizenship by either father or son.
4. If the son became a *flamen dialis* or the daughter a *virgo vestalis.*
5. If either father or child was adopted by a third party.
6. If the daughter passed by formal marriage into the power (*in manum*) of a husband, though this did not essentially change her dependent condition.
7. If the son became a public magistrate. In this case the *potestas* was suspended during the period of office, but after it expired the father might hold the son accountable for his acts, public and private, while holding the magistracy.

MANUS

The subject of marriage will be considered later; at this point it is only necessary to define the power over the wife possessed by the husband in its most extreme form, called by the Romans *manus.* By the oldest and most solemn form of marriage the wife was separated entirely from her father's family and passed into her husband's power or "hand" (*conventiō in manum*). This assumes, of course, that he was *suī iūris;* if he was not, then though nominally in his "hand" she was really subject as he was to his *pater familiās.* Any property she had of her own, and to have had any she must have been independent before her marriage, passed to him as a matter of course. If she had none, her *pater familiās* furnished a dowry (*dōs*), which shared the same fate. Whatever she acquired by her industry or otherwise while the marriage lasted also became her husband's. So far, therefore, as property rights were concerned the *manus* differed in no respect from the *patria potestās:* the wife was in *locō fīliae,* and on the husband's death took a daughter's share in his estate.

In other respects *manus* conferred more limited powers. The husband was required by law, not merely obliged by custom, to refer alleged misconduct of his wife to the *iūdicium domesticum,* and this was composed in part of her cognates. He could put her away for certain grave offenses only; if he divorced her without good cause he was punished with the loss of all his property. He could not sell her at all. In short, public opinion and custom operated even more strongly for her protection than for that of her children. It must be noticed, therefore, that the chief distinction between *manus* and *patria potestās* lay in the fact that the former was a legal relationship based upon the consent of the weaker party, while the latter was a natural relationship antecedent to all law and choice.

DOMINICA POTESTAS

The right of ownership in his property (*dominica potestās*) was absolute in the case of a *pater familiās* and has been sufficiently explained in preceding paragraphs. This ownership included slaves as well as inanimate things, and slaves as well as inanimate things were mere chattels in the eyes of the law. The influence of custom and public opinion, so far as these tended to mitigating the horrors of their condition, will be discussed later. It will be sufficient to say here that there was nothing to which the slave could appeal from the judgment of his master. It was final and absolute.

MARRIAGE AND THE POSITION OF WOMEN

EARLY FORMS OF MARRIAGE

Polygamy was never practiced at Rome, and we are told that for five centuries after the founding of the city divorce was entirely unknown. Up to the time of the Servian constitution (date uncertain) the patricians were the only citizens and intermarried only with patricians and with members of surrounding communities having like social standing. The only form of marriage known to them was the stately religious ceremonial called, as will be explained hereafter, *cōnfarreātiō.* With the direct consent of the gods, with the *pontificēs* celebrating the solemn rites, in the presence of the accredited representatives of his *gēns,* the patrician took his wife from her father's family into his own, to be a *māter familiās,* to rear him children who should conserve the family mysteries, perpetuate his ancient race, and extend the power of Rome. By this, the one legal marriage of the time, the wife passed *in manum virī*, and the husband acquired over her practically the same rights as he had over his own children and other dependent members of his family. Such a marriage was said to be *cum conventiōne uxōris in manum virī*.

During this period, too, the free non-citizens, the plebeians, had been busy in marrying and giving in marriage. There is little doubt that their unions had been as sacred in their eyes, their family ties as strictly regarded and as pure, as those of the patricians, but these unions were unhallowed by the national gods and unrecognized by the civil law, simply because the plebeians were not yet citizens. Their form of marriage was called *ūsus*, and consisted essentially in the living together of the man and woman as husband and wife for a year, though there were, of course, conventional forms and observances, about which we know absolutely nothing. The plebeian husband might acquire the same rights over the person and property of his wife as the patrician, but the form of marriage did not in itself involve *manus*. The wife might remain a member of her father's family and retain such property as he allowed her by merely absenting herself from her husband for the space of a *trinoctium* each year. If she did this the marriage was *sine conventiōne in manum*, and the husband had no control over her property; if she did not, the marriage like that of the patricians was *cum conventiōne in manum*.

At least as far back as the time of Servius goes another Roman form of marriage, also plebeian, though not so ancient as *ūsus*. It was called *coēmptiō* and was a fictitious sale, by which the *pater familiās* of the woman, or her guardian (*tūtor*) if she was *suī iūris*, transferred her to the man *mātrimōniī causā*. This form must have been a survival of the old custom of purchase and sale of wives, but we do not know when it was introduced among the Romans. It carried *manus* with it as a matter of course and seems to have been regarded socially as better form than *ūsus*. The two existed for centuries side by side, but *coēmptiō* survived *ūsus* as a form of marriage *cum conventiōne in manum*.

Ius Conubii

While the Servian constitution made the plebeians citizens and thereby legalized their forms of marriage, it did not give them the right of intermarriage with the patricians. Many of the plebeian families were hardly less ancient than the patricians, many were rich and powerful, but it was not until 455 B.C. that marriages between the two orders were formally sanctioned by the civil law. The objection on the part of the patricians was largely a religious one: The gods of the state were patrician gods, the auspices could be taken by patricians only, the marriages of patricians only were sanctioned by heaven. Their orators protested that the unions of the plebeians were no better than promiscuous intercourse, they were not *iūstae nūptiae*; the plebeian wife was taken *in mātrimōnium*, she was at best an *uxor*, not a *māter familiās*; her offspring were "mother's children," not *patriciī*.

Much of this was class exaggeration, but it is true that at this early date the *gēns* was not so highly valued by the plebeians as by the patricians, and that the plebeians assigned to cognates certain duties and privileges that devolved upon the patrician *gentīlēs*. With the *iūs cōnūbiī* many of these points of difference disappeared. New conditions were fixed for *iūstae nūptiae*; *coēmptiō* by a sort of compromise became the usual form of marriage when one of the parties was a plebeian; and the stigma disappeared from the word *mātrimōnium*. On the other hand patrician women learned to understand the advantages of a marriage *sine conventiōne* and marriage with *manus* gradually became less frequent, the taking of the auspices before the ceremony came to be considered a mere form, and marriage began to lose its sacramental character, and with these changes came later the laxness in the marital relation and the freedom of divorce that seemed in the time of Augustus to threaten the very life of the commonwealth.

It is probable that by the time of Cicero marriage with *manus* was uncommon, and consequently that *cōnfarreātiō* and *coēmptiō* had gone out of general use. To a limited extent, however, the former was retained until Christian times, because certain priestly offices (*flāminēs maiōrēs* and *rēgēs sacrōrum*) could be filled only by persons whose parents had been married by the confarreate ceremony, the one sacramental form, and who had themselves been married by the same form. But so great became the reluctance of women to submit to *manus,* that in order to fill even these few priestly offices it was found necessary under Tiberius to eliminate *manus* from the confarreate ceremony.

Nuptiae Iustae

There were certain conditions that had to be satisfied before a legal marriage could be contracted even by citizens. It was required:

1. That the consent of both parties should be given, or of the *pater familias* if one or both were *in potestate.* Under Augustus it was provided that the *pater familias* should not withhold his consent unless he could show valid reasons for doing so.
2. That both parties should be *puberes;* there could be no marriage between children. Although no precise age was fixed by law, it is probable that fourteen and twelve were the lowest limit for the man and woman respectively.
3. That both man and woman should be unmarried. Polygamy was never practiced at Rome.
4. That the parties should not be nearly related. The restrictions in this direction were fixed rather by public opinion than by law and varied greatly at different times, becoming gradually less severe. In general it may be said that marriage was absolutely forbidden between ascendants and descendants, between other cognates within the fourth degree, and the nearer *adfines.* If the parties could satisfy these conditions they might be legally married, but distinctions were still made that affected the civil status of the children, although no doubt was cast upon their legitimacy or upon the moral character of their parents.

If the husband and wife were both Roman citizens, their marriage was called *iūstae nūptiae,* which we may translate "regular marriage," their children were *iūstī līberī* and were by birth *cīvēs optimō iūre,* "possessed of all civil rights."

If but one of the parties was a Roman citizen and the other a member of a community having the *iūs cōnūbiī* but not the full *cīvitās,* the marriage was still called *iūstae nūptiae,* but the children took the civil standing of the father. This means that if the father was a citizen and

the mother a foreigner, the children were citizens; but if the father was a foreigner and the mother a citizen, the children were foreigners (*peregrīnī*) with the father.

But if either of the parties was without the *iūs cōnūbiī,* the marriage, though still legal, was called *nūptiae iniūstae* or *mātrimōnium iniūstum,* "an irregular marriage," and the children, though legitimate, took the civil position of the parent of lower degree. We seem to have something analogous to this in the loss of social standing which usually follows the marriage of a person with one of distinctly inferior position.

Betrothals

Betrothal (*spōnsālia*) as a preliminary to marriage was considered good form but was not legally necessary and carried with it no obligations that could be enforced by law. In the *spōnsālia* the maiden was promised to the man as his bride with "words of style," that is, in solemn form. The promise was made, not by the maiden herself, but by her *pater familiās,* or by her *tūtor* if she was not *in potestāte.* In the same way, the promise was made to the man directly only in case he was *suī iūris,* otherwise to the head of his house, who had asked for him the maiden in marriage.

The word *spondeō* was technically used of the promise, and the maiden was henceforth *spōnsa.* The person who made the promise had always the right to cancel it. This was usually done through an intermediary (*nūntius*), and hence the formal expression for breaking an engagement was *repudium renūntiāre,* or simply *renūntiāre.* While the contract was entirely one-sided, it should be noticed that a man was liable to *īnfāmia* if he formed two engagements at the same time, and that he could not recover any presents made with a view to a future marriage if he himself broke the engagement. Such presents were almost always made, and while we find that articles for personal use, the toilet, etc., were common, a ring was usually given. The ring was worn on the third finger of the left hand, because it was believed that a nerve ran directly from this finger to the heart. It was also usual for the *spōnsa* to make a present to her betrothed.

THE DOWRY

It was a point of honor with the Romans, as it is now with some European nations, for the bride to bring to her husband a dowry (*dōs*). In the case of a girl *in potestāte* this would naturally be furnished by the head of her house; in the case of one *suī iūris* it was furnished from her own property, or if she had none was contributed by her relatives. It seems that if they were reluctant she might by process of law compel her ascendants at least to furnish it. In early times, when marriage *cum conventiōne* prevailed, all the property brought by the bride became the property of her husband, or of his *pater familiās*, but in later times, when *manus* was less common, and especially after divorce had become of frequent occurrence, a distinction was made. A part of the bride's possessions was reserved for her own exclusive use, and a part was made over to the groom under the technical name of *dōs*. The relative proportions varied, of course, with circumstances.

ESSENTIAL FORMS

There were really no legal forms necessary for the solemnization of a marriage; there was no license to be procured from the civil authorities, the ceremonies simple or elaborate did not have to be performed by persons authorized by the state. The one thing necessary was the consent of both parties, if they were *suī iūris*, or of their *patrēs familiās*, if they were *in potestāte*. It has been already remarked that the *pater familiās* could refuse his consent for valid reasons only; on the other hand, he could command the consent of persons subject to him. It is probable that parental and filial affection (*pietās*) made this hardship less rigorous than it now seems to us.

But while this consent was the only condition for a legal marriage, it had to be shown by some act of personal union between the parties; that is, the marriage could not be entered into by letter or by the intervention of a third party. Such an overt act was the joining of hands (*dextrārum iūnctiō*) in the presence of witnesses, or the escorting of the bride to her husband's house, never omitted when the parties had any social standing, or in later times the signing of the marriage contract. It was never necessary to a valid marriage that the parties should live together as man and wife, though this living together of itself constituted a legal marriage.

7.

TARA PATEL AND VIMAL SHAH

FAMILY IN INDIA

INTRODUCTION

The family as an association exists all over the world, but its forms and functions vary from one society to another as well as from one time to another in the same society. This is also true about the family patterns in India. India is a land of many castes, tribes, languages and regional subcultures and there is an enormous amount of variation in the customs and ceremonies practised. But, there is also an underlying uniformity in behavior patterns and organizational structures.

Marriage and family are so closely related that it is difficult to separate one from the other. Family as an organization is a consequence of marriage, and therefore, the patterns of marriage determine several organizational and functional characteristics of the family. Similarly, the pattern of marriage of an individual is determined, to a great extent, by the structural and functional characteristics of the family in which he is born. For example, among the Hindus, the emphasis placed upon procuring a male child suggests a somewhat subordinate status of women in a Hindu family. Similarly, the pattern of arranged marriages suggests the authority of the parents over their children, and the pattern of marriage at an early age requires that the children, even after their marriage, be supported in the parental family rather than through their own nuclear family. This, in turn, means that parents play an important role in mate selection, and the qualities desired in a mate include those which are most likely to facilitate living in a joint family. It should not be surprising from all this that the traditional family organization of the Hindus has always been of the joint and patrilineal type of family. In historical times, however, we also find joint or extended matrilineal types of family in some tribal groups.

We shall describe here, in general, the marriage and family patterns of the Hindus not only because the Hindus form the largest segment of the population but also because some of the major characteristics of the Hindu social organizations are shared by other groups. A brief account of the marriage and family patterns of the Muslims in India will be given at the end of this chapter.

THE HINDU IDEAL OF MARRIAGE

The Hindu scriptures describe four stages of life, namely *brahmacharyashrama* (period for celibacy and study), *gruhasthashrama* (period for householder's life), *vanaprasthashrama* (period for retirement from the worldly affairs and forest-dwelling), and *sanyasashrama* (period for renunciation). In the *Vedas* (the four ancient and sacred books of the Hindus) and other religious literature, *gruhasthashrama* is given considerable importance because the life of the people in the other three stages depends on the people in the householder's stage. Unlike Christianity, which permits marriage because of the fear of fornication (Stephens, 1963, 240), the *gruhasthashrama* is highly recommended and praised by the Hindu script-writers. Celibacy is ordained up to a certain age, and virginity is considered a virtue, but marriage is imperative for the Hindus, especially for women. It is only through marriage that a Hindu woman can become a partner in the daily religious rites and attain *moksha* (salvation), and it is through marriage that a Hindu man can fulfill all his duties and obligations to human beings and living creatures as well as to gods and ancestors.

Marriage is one of the sixteen *samskaras* (ceremonial purifications) that a Hindu performs during his life time. The aims of a Hindu marriage are *dharma* (duty), *praja* (progeny), and *kama* or *rati* (sensual pleasure). *Dharma* is the highest ideal of a Hindu marriage and marriage is recommended as a means for practising *dharma*. It is, therefore, a sacrament and not a contract; it is generally irrevocable. In brief, the Hindu scriptures recommend marriage as a social and moral duty towards the family, the community, and the society. Consequently, the interests of the individuals entering into a marriage are given secondary or little importance in the mate selection procedures.

Eight forms of marriage are mentioned in the religious books of the Hindus. They are labelled as Brahma, Daiva, Arsha, Prajapatya, Asura, Gandharva, Rakshasa, and Paishacha. Only the first four forms of marriage are called *dharmya* (according to religion), and hence they are recognized by all *Smritis* (also known as *Dharma-sastras;* Hindu religious treatises written during the period from 200 B.C. to 900 A.D.). In these forms of marriage, a girl is married to a suitable person by her parents. Except for a small exchange of gifts as a token of affection, no dowry is paid. The *Smritis* are divided in their opinion about the remaining forms of marriage. In the Asura form of marriage, the payment is given primary consideration. The Rakshasa and the Paishacha forms of marriage refer respectively to the abduction of a girl against her wish and to the seduction of a girl while she is drugged or unconscious. These three forms of marriage are, therefore, most criticized and considered undesirable. The Gandharva form of marriage is considered as the best marriage by Vatsyayana and some other religious authorities, but a majority of the Hindu law-givers (cf. Pandey, 1949, 280) discourages it on religious and moral grounds. Some script-writers object to the Gandharva form of marriage because no religious rites are performed in a Gandharva marriage.

Manu recommends that the first four forms of marriage should be practised by the people of all castes. In addition, the Kshatriyas may practise the Rakshasa form of marriage, and the Vaishyas and the Shudras may practise the Asura form of marriage. Manu does not approve the Gandharva form of marriage because it "springs from desire and has sexual intercourse for its purpose" (cf. Buhler, 1886, 81). Some script-writers suggest that the first four forms of marriage were prevalent among the Aryans while the latter were common among the non-Aryans (the original inhabitants of India). Only the Brahma and the Asura forms of marriage are in practice today. In addition, a marriage based on love and self-selection can be considered as a variant form of the traditional Gandharva form of marriage. Similarly, the practice of bride-price in some low castes and tribal groups suggests the traditional Asura form of marriage.

MONOGAMY, POLYGYNY, AND POLYANDRY

The Hindu ideal of marriage is monogamy. There are some references in the Vedic literature which suggest that polygyny (plural wives) was not unusual among the rich and royal families, but an explicit and categorical aversion to polygyny is found in the post-Vedic era. The Hindu script-writers allow a man to have a second wife only under certain circumstances. The emphasis placed on the presence of a male child for *pitrutarpana* (offerings to the ancestors) seems to be the major consideration for polygyny among the Hindus. Although polygyny was socially accepted, the idea of monogamy acted as a restraining factor on its prevalence, and the number of wives, even if a man was polygynous, was generally limited to two (Kapadia, 1966, 99). In the middle ages, however, the practice of polygynous marriages became a symbol of social prestige. Royal families, wealthy people, and big landlords generally practised polygynous marriages. Even some people from lower social strata practised polygynous marriages in order to obtain additional labor force which could be used in the house as well as in the field. Perhaps the most extreme pattern of polygynous marriages was found among the Kulin Brahmins of Bengal where the practice of hypergamy (marriage of a lower-status girl with a higher-status boy) led to a scandalous proportion of polygynous marriages. A succession of legal measures since the later half of the nineteenth century indicates the growing rejection of polygyny as an accepted marriage pattern. The Hindu Marriage Act of 1955 stipulates that neither party to the marriage may already have, at the time of marriage, a living spouse, and that any marriage which violates this condition is void. Moreover, bigamy is punishable under the Indian Penal Code. In brief, although some polygynous households may be found here and there in India, the polygynous marriages have been on a decline for a long time, and are now disappearing almost entirely.

Polyandry (plural husbands) is generally supposed to have been customary among the pre-Dravidian or the Dravidian people of the Indian subcontinent. Relying on the classical example of Draupadi (the heroine of the famous Hindu epic Mahabharata) having the five Pandava brothers as her husbands, polyandry is also suggested as a trait of the Brahmanic culture. Kapadia (1966, 52-57), however, very elaborately and convincingly suggests that Draupadi's case is not a clear evidence of polyandry. Some of the reports, inferences, and suppositions of old travellers and administrators regarding polyandrous groups are of questionable reliability. Sometimes, the reports of travellers, explorers, administrators, and clergymen often mentioned as "polyandrous" any system in which there was some tolerance of sexual access to a brother's wife. It seems that although polyandry was practised by some groups, especially the Nairs and the Irvas of Malbar, the Khasas of U.P., the Todas and Kotas of Nilgiri Hills, and the Coorgs, it was not an accepted practice of the Hindus. Polyandry among these different groups and tribes indicates different patterns and has different origins and developments.

In absence of reliable reports, it is difficult to generalize regarding the presence, type, and extent of polyandry in India. In 1901, polyandry was already falling into disrepute among the Nairs. At that time it was still found among the Todas, but since that period there has been a gradual shift to polygyny and monogamy, with some persistence of polyandry (Goode, 1963, 224). According to Kapadia (1966, 63), polyandry has almost died out among the Khasas except for a few small areas. The gradual disappearance of polyandry, in whatever form it existed in some communities in India, seems evident. The Hindu Marriage Act of 1955 makes polyandry as well as polygyny illegal, and in the opinion of many social scientists, this act merely sets the seal on a process which was well under way before the law was passed (Goode, 1963, 225).

EXOGAMY AND ENDOGAMY

The exogamous rules (rules prohibiting marriage within certain kinship and locally prescribed relationships) of the Hindus go beyond the incest taboos found in almost all societies. The Hindus are tabooed to marry in their own *gotra, pravara,* or *sapinda* relationships. *Gotra, pravara,* and *sapinda* relationships are variously defined as clan, sib, or lineage; however, they refer to a group of individuals descended from a paternal or maternal ancestor and carrying on a particular name.

Notwithstanding the exogamous rules which do not allow marriage of two persons related within certain generations on the father's or the mother's side, the practice of cross-cousin marriages has been prevalent and preferred in certain communities in India. Altekar, Kapadia and Karve have mentioned several castes and regions in which the practice of cross-cousin marriages was followed (Goode, 1963, 220). While sufficient quantative data are not available, it seems that matriline cross-cousin marriages have been fairly common and some other forms of cousin marriage are also to be found here and there in India (Goode, 1963, 221). Besides Kapadia (1966, 134) mentions that the kinship terminology of the Nagas of Assam suggests that at one stage they must have practised marriage with the sister's daughter. This form of marriage is also found among the Telugus, the Kannadigas and the Tamilians.

The Hindu Marriage Act of 1955 has removed the exogamous codes based on *gotra* and *pravara* from the requirements for a valid marriage, but it stipulates that the parties must not be *sapindas* of one another, unless the custom or usage governing each other permits of a sacramental marriage between the two. According to the Hindu Marriage Act of 1955, the marriage between two persons related within five generations on the father's side and three on the mother's is void unless permitted by local custom (Kapadia, 1966, 130).

Endogamy (practice of marrying within one's own caste or social group) is a very important characteristic of the Indian caste system. There are over three thousand castes, and each of these is endogamous. Until recently, breaches of caste endogamy were punished by excommunication from the caste. Since the caste exercised a tremendous influence over its members and since the excommunication and other types of punishment imposed by the caste for breaking the caste norms would virtually paralyse the life of an individual residing in a small orthodox community, intercaste marriages were practised only rarely. Current legislation has removed the legal barriers to recognizing marriage between Hindus on the basis of differences in religion, caste, subcaste, or sect. However, as Kapadia (1966, 119) observes, the moral force of caste is still so great, and Hindus are still so casteminded, that the legislation has only limited immediate effect, although the number of intercaste marriages is gradually increasing, especially among the educated people and in the urban areas. Quantitative data on the proportion of intercaste marriages in India are not available. There is apparent at least a gradual increase in the number of people who are willing to accept or tolerate the intercaste marriages of their friends or family-members under certain circumstances.

HYPERGAMY AND HYPOGAMY

The endogamous rules of marriage among the Hindus were based on the *varna* system (fourfold classification of the Hindus into Brahmins, Kshatriyas, Vaishyas, and Shudras) in the early Indian society. With the emergence of the caste system, more rigid rules came into force, and the field of marriage became restricted to small local subcastes composed of only a few hundred families. Although the norm for endogamous marriages prevailed, the early Hindu scriptwriters institutionalised inter-*varna* marriages in two ways. They allowed the *anuloma* and the *pratiloma* marriages under certain circumstances. The marriage of a woman from a lower *varna* with a man from a higher *varna* is known as the *anuloma* (hypergamous) marriage, and the marriage of a woman from a higher *varna* with a man of a lower *varna* is known as the *pratiloma* (hypogamous) marriage. However, the wife from a lower *varna* was considered no better than a mistress, and the marriage of a Brahmin woman and a low caste man was considered the basest of all types of marriage.

The hypergamous marriages took altogether a different turn in the caste society. With the growth of the endogamous character of sub-caste and prestige determined by social hierarchy, the hypergamous marriages were increasingly desired. It is a general tendency among the people all over the world to marry their daughters into families with higher social class origins. But, in India, where the marriages have been generally arranged by the parents, the practice of hypergamy led to several undesirable social evils, especially among the Kulin Brahmins of Bengal, the Khedaval and Audichya Brahmins, Rajputs, and the Anavils and Leva Patidars of Gujarat. The practice of dowry or groom-price became prevalent. Young men with low economic or low caste backgrounds were unable to find mates, and young women with low economic or social backgrounds remained unmarried or sometimes even committed suicide because their parents could not afford to pay a large dowry and adult unmarried girls were severely stigmatized. On the other hand, surveys and comments in the early part of the nineteenth century assert that some Kulin Brahmin men married fifteen or twenty wives, and occasionally cases were found of those who married as many as eighty. In these cases, the husband did not ordinarily live with all these women, but only visited them at their parents' home, where he was received at each visit with a gift, expressing the caste deference embodied in the marriage itself.

MATE SELECTION

From ancient times, the responsibility of finding a suitable mate has always been placed on parents or older relatives. Except for a few

incidents of the Gandharva type of marriage and some scattered illustrations of love before marriage, the pattern of mate selection in India has always been that of arranged marriage. Young and unmarried youths did not have opportunities to come in close contact with members of the other sex, since the western practice of dating has been nonexistent in India.

In any society, when marriages are arranged by the parents, it is natural that the criteria for mate selection conform to its traditional and ideal-type norms. There are several descriptions in the Hindu religious literature suggesting the age at marriage, the desired qualities of mates, how marriages should be arranged, and so on. Caste, religion, region, family, its economic status, and the appearance of the prospective mates were generally mentioned and practised as major considerations in arranged marriages.

Although no uniform view is found in the Hindu scriptures regarding the proper age at marriage, it seems that early marriages were preferred and generally practised. Kapadia (1966, 142) suggests that early marriages were not prevalent in early centuries of the Christian era, but later on when the religious and social sanctions were accorded to pre-puberty marriages, child-marriages spread faster and took deeper roots among the higher castes. Once it became a pattern with the Brahmins, it soon tended to become the norm for the Hindu community as a whole. During the medieval period, the age at marriage of the girls became lower and lower, and examples were found when the infants, or even children in their mother's womb, were betrothed. Towards the end of the nineteenth century the age at marriage began to increase. The Child Marriage Restraint Act of 1929 prohibited the marriage of a male under eighteen years and a girl under fourteen years. The Hindu Marriage Act of 1955 accepts fifteen as the minimum age at marriage for a girl and eighteen for that of a boy, but several studies indicate that there has been a distinct change in the outlook of the people and there has been a gradual rise in the age at marriage. It seems that legislation is lagging behind popular opinion with respect to the prescribed minimum age at marriage.

With the gradual increase in the age at marriage and the spread of high school and college education, youths in India now participate more in the selection of their mate. A trend for arranged marriages with the consent of the parties concerned seems to be developing. Also, marriages based on self-choice with the consent of the parents are increasing, especially among the urban and educated people.

DOWRY, GROOM-PRICE AND BRIDE-PRICE

Generally, the practice of giving dresses, ornaments, and other gifts to the bride at the time of her marriage is known as dowry. Sometimes, a dowry is also given to the groom in the form of cash, ornaments, and other precious articles by the bride's family. Dowry and groom-price have gradually become synonymous to the extent that the bride's parents are forced to give certain articles or a large sum of money to the bride, groom, or both. The custom of dowry was nonexistent in the Aryan society, and it was also not widely practised until medieval times. In the pre-British periods, the dowry system was almost absent among the peasants, artisans, and other lower and middle class people. However, the dowry system was prevalent generally among the royal and rich families, especially the Kshatriyas, in order to maintain or increase their social prestige. In the late nineteenth and the early twentieth centuries the dowry system spread among other castes and generated many social evils. In certain castes the dowry reached fantastic amounts. At times, the dowry system was accompanied by female infanticide and incredible negligence toward baby girls. The dowry system sometimes involves inappropriate marriage-matches, spinsterhood for some for lack of a dowry, and quarrels arising out of promised dowries. The enmity between two families increases in the latter disputes and the bride may be harassed and mistreated by her in-laws.

In 1961, an official attempt was made to abolish the dowry system by an act which actually provides punishment in fines or imprisonment for giving, taking, demanding, or abetting in the giving or taking of a dowry, but so far this act does not seem to have had much effect. The dowry system is currently found among many high-caste Hindus who follow hypergamy. Generally, the price is determined on the basis of the groom's academic qualifications, appearance, and age, as well as on the wealth and prestige of his family. Public opinion is developing against the dowry system, and some educated men are refusing to accept a dowry. Still, sometimes the increasing level of education, instead of mitigating the evil, has worsened it to a scandalous proportion (Kapadia, 1966, 137).

The practice of bride-price was prevalent in many early civilizations. A reason commonly given for the bride-price is that the bride's parents should receive some compensation for losing the services of their daughter. This practice existed among some untouchables and low castes and tribes for whom the bride usually became an additional worker in the family. Generally, a customary, nominal, and fixed price is given to the bride's family. However, among some higher castes, a high price for the bride is paid when an older man marries a relatively young girl. Some writers are of the opinion that polyandry in India is a consequence of the practice of high bride-price. Many non-polyandrous groups, however, follow the practice of bride-price. In certain groups, the bride-price reimburses the wife's family for the loss of her services, and it also gives a financial help to the family in arranging their son's marriage. In such cases, although a direct exchange of brides (or bride-prices) is not involved, the practice of bride-price seems to achieve that purpose.

Another custom known as *pallu, stridhan,* or trousseau refers to the payment given to the bride by the bride's or the groom's family, or both. In many castes, the *stridhan* consists of equal amounts contributed by both the bride's and the groom's family. Only the bride has the sole rights over her *stridhan*. The custom of *stridhan* or *pallu* seems to serve, to a certain extent, the purpose of social security in the event that the bride is divorced, widowed, or is in other adverse circumstances.

MARRIAGE AS A SACRAMENT

In matters of divorce, widowhood, and remarriage, we find quite different norms and practices among the high-caste and low-caste Hindus. Further, there were unequal or double standards for men and women, especially among the high-caste Hindus. Thus, while the low-caste Hindus customarily allowed divorce and practised remarriage, the high-caste Hindus proscribed divorce and remarriage for widows.

A Hindu marriage is considered sacred, and it is generally irrevocable. Although some scriptwriters suggested that a marriage could be dissolved under certain exceptional circumstances, this was never an accepted practice among the high-caste Hindus. Of course, a man could replace his wife or have nothing to do with her, but he still allowed her to continue living in the same household. Similar privileges were not granted to a Hindu wife. For her, marriage was binding not only during the lifetime of her husband, but also after his death. The ideal of *pativrata* (being devoted to the husband alone) suggested that a wife has no individuality of her own; as a river merges in the sea, a woman's individuality merges with that of her husband. Besides, an ideal of Sati (immolation on her husband's pyre) was placed before a Hindu wife. The practice of Sati gradually became so deep-rooted that it was not only customarily practised but something to which a Hindu wife aspired; it insured social prestige not only to herself but to the families on both sides. However, Altekar suggests that this "willingness" may have been due to many formal and informal sanctions visited against any woman who refused to die with her husband.

Since the Prevention of Sati Act of 1829, the practice of Sati has gradually died out. The Hindu Marriage Act of 1955 provides uniform codes for divorce and thus extends the customary practices of the low-caste Hindus to the high-caste Hindus. However, the conditions for obtaining divorce are strict, and divorce and remarriage are still looked upon as scandalous among high-caste Hindus. New legislation has actually created barriers to obtaining divorce for low-caste Hindus who customarily accepted divorce and remarriage.

THE NAIRS

Any discussion about marriage and family patterns in India would be incomplete without some consideration of the matrilineal and polyandrous systems prevalent among the Nairs of the Malabar Coast or Kerala in India. McLennan believed that polyandry among the Nairs was universal and of a nonfraternal type. Kapadia (1966, 76-78), however, argues that although the conjugal rights of a large number of persons over a woman were recognized in earlier times and that semiconjugal rights or functions in respect of these persons persisted down to recent times, polyandry did not necessarily exist as an institution among the Nairs. Without entering into any controversial discussion in this connection, we shall briefly refer to the marriage and family patterns of the Nairs, mostly as described by Goode (1963, 254-256) and Kapadia (1966, 76-85).

Among the Nairs, two distinct marriage ceremonies were performed. One ceremony known as *tali-kettu-kalyanam* was performed before a girl attained puberty. This was a kind of ritual marriage in which a man from one of the lineages linked to the girl's own lineage tied a gold ornament (*tali*) around her neck. After the ceremony the bride and the groom were secluded for three days, although sexual relations did not always take place. On the fourth day, the girl and the *tali*-tier would meet again before the members of their lineage, and the dress of the bridegroom would be torn, signifying thereby that the union between the two had come to an end. From that time, the girl was socially mature, had to avoid the men of her own lineage, and could begin to receive visiting husbands from her own caste or from a higher caste. On the death of the *tali*-tier the girl observed a pollution for fifteen days. The children born of this girl generally called the *tali*-tier 'little father.' As for the girl, virginity ceased with the performance of this ceremony. She was initiated into womanhood; she was called 'little Amma.'

The relation with visiting husbands was known as *sambandham,* the other type of marriage among the Nairs. A Nair girl could have *sambandham* not only with a Nair man of her caste or of a caste above her, but with a Brahmin and Kshatriya as well. *Sambandham,* though recognized as legal, was in theory dissoluble at will, and often it happened that due to misunderstanding or quarrels either of the partners would break off relations. Then the aggrieved party could, without further formality, marry somebody else. The *sambandham* implied no legal obligation of maintenance to the divorced wife. In the *sambandham* union, the husband did not live with the Nair girl nor did he support her or her children. He slept with her at night and left in the morning. If she became pregnant, one of the visiting husbands had to acknowledge paternity or she would become an outcaste or be killed. The Nairs being matrilineal and matrilocal, children born of *sambandham* belonged to their mother's *tarvad* (family of the Nairs) and inherited from the mother. The husband was simply a visitor to his wife's place, and children had no tie with him.

The Nair *tarvads* were each made up of four to eight property groups, headed by a male. The property was passed through the females, but the heads of the *tarvads* and property groups were the brothers of the women. The Nambudiri Brahmins were patrilineal. Only the eldest Nambudiri son married within his own caste, keeping the property intact within his patrilineal group. The others entered nonexclusive unions with Nair women and could not obtain control over the property. Thus, the *sambandham* practice of the Nair women and the custom of the younger Nambudiri Brahmins to marry outside their caste were complementary.

By the end of the nineteenth century, the sex life of the Nair women had become more restricted, and a series of laws were passed both to recognize the peculiarities of the system and to introduce gradual changes toward the usual Hindu system. The polyandrous marital patterns of the Nair women have now disappeared. The mother's brother has lost his power and authority as the property group has dissolved. The father commonly has more authority over his children and his emotional tie with them is closer than that in the past.

THE HINDU JOINT FAMILY

A comprehensive operational definition of the traditional Hindu joint family suggests the following characteristics (Shah, 1965, 73):

1. It consists of a group of individuals constituting more than one nuclear family unit, who generally (a) live under one roof, (b) eat food cooked at one hearth, (c) hold and manage their property in common, (d) belong to a common family worship, or *gotra*, and (e) are related to one another as kin by birth, marriage, or adoption.

2. The final authority in decision-making regarding family matters (for example, management of finances, or arrangement of marriages of the sons and the daughters in the family) is vested in the older members of he family.

3. The role of men is to earn and provide for the economic needs of the family, and the role of women is to look after household work.

4. There is a relationship of dominance-subordination among the members of the family on the basis of age, sex, and ties of relationship, irrespective of the individual qualities of the members.

5. Life is personalized through ties to relatives, and their claims often take precedence over individual interests and stability as well as over the impersonal and abstract demands of work and career.

While the above definition is comprehensive in suggesting the structural as well as functional and relational characteristics of the traditional Hindu family, the fact that this is an ideal-type definition should not be overlooked.

The traditional Hindu joint family was not merely a set of nuclear families linked by kinship, possibly headed by an elder male, but structurally it was a group of adult co-parceners (joint heirs). Family property was inherited through sons. The income of all members in the family was pooled and used according to the needs of the family as a whole. The history of the Hindu law of property shows the gradual development of individual property and women's rights to property. The Gains of Learning Act of 1930 permitted an individual to keep for his own the acquisitions that he made, even though the joint family had paid for his education or the support of his family. The Hindu Woman's Right To Property Act of 1937 entitled a widow to share the property of the joint family on an equal basis with that of her husband, and the Hindu Succession Act of 1956 also granted joint inheritance rights to daughters. These legal changes represent major alterations in the traditional joint family.

In theory, not only the living members of a Hindu joint family but the ancestors and the children to be born are also considered to be the members of the joint family. The living members are expected to fulfill their obligations towards the ancestors by performing the *shrad-*

dha (oblations) ceremonies, and the children to be born are also entitled to a share in the ancestral joint property. The birth of a child, especially that of a son, is a major occasion for delight in the family. Generally, the children are treated with kindness and affection. However, a male child is considered to be an asset, while a female child is considered to be a liability. Not only is a son expected to take care of his parents during their old age, but only a son can perform the religious rites after their death. Therefore, it is not unusual to find differences in the upbringing of and the treatment given to sons and daughters in a Hindu joint family. The attitudes of the children towards their parents and other elders are generally indicative of reverence and obedience. The father is a symbol of authority, but relationships of close intimate attachments are found between the child and mother.

Ideally, the joint family is based on the authority and sharing of relations among adult males rather than on the conjugal bonds between a married couple (Goode, 1963, 240-241). Love and affection between spouses does not play a major role, since marriages are arranged. The husband and wife are not supposed to show affection toward one another in public and have only limited opportunities to be alone. The relation of respect between elder and younger generations makes it improper, if not uncommon, to have an extremely emotional relationship between them. The sexes are segregated even in the areas of daily work. This segregation is also a means of teaching children the importance of restraint and chastity. In traditional households, men eat first separately from women.

The status of women in a Hindu family is generally subordinate to that of men. A daughter has a status inferior to her brother's. A wife has a status inferior to her husband's, and she is supposed to be submissive to her husband. A good wife is not supposed to argue with her husband, and a revolt is unimaginable. In the classical Hindu literature, a mother is much praised and considered to be even above heaven. But in actual practice, it is always the father, the husband, the elder son, or other male member who is head of the family, and the role of the wife or the mother is at the most restricted to that of a consultant and a counselor whose advice and suggestions may or may not be carried out.

The major advantages of such a family system are that it ensures some kind of social, economic, and psychological security for its members. Each member is expected to contribute to the family pool according to his own ability, and each member is expected to receive from the family pool according to his needs. The joint family unit can absorb the young girl-wife who is not yet equipped to handle the full-time job of homemaker and mother and to care for the newly married young man who cannot yet support himself. However, the joint family has many problems. It cannot escape responsibility for the incompetent, the helpless, and the parasite. In spite of the great solidarity among brothers and between sons and parents, quarrels among the wives of the brothers or between mother and daughters-in-law create tensions and ill-feelings. Individually, the wives who come from different families and who are expected to live together sometimes feel that their own husbands contribute more than they receive and that their own children do not receive a fair share. Such quarrels along with the increasing geographical mobility provide both excuses and opportunities to establish separate hearths, especially after the father's death.

The joint family system was prevalent among the Hindus, especially the high-caste and landed Hindus. And, even among the low-caste Hindus, where separate hearths were not infrequent, the sentiments and solidarity of the traditional joint family generally maintained the reciprocal relationships among the members of the joint family. In other words, many families, which were not structurally joint, were functionally joint.

Gradual changes are taking place in the structure and functions of the Indian family in modern times. There is increasing demand for individuality and personal freedom on the part of the younger generation. The status of women is changing fast, especially in the cities and among the educated people. However, a majority of the Indian population living in the rural areas still follow the conventional patterns of family living. While Goode (1963, 268) believes that there is a steady progress in the direction of some form of the conjugal system, the ideological sentiments in favor of the joint family system are deep-rooted among the Indian people and it seems unlikely that a majority of the Indian people will follow the western style of conjugal family in the near future.

MARRIAGE AND FAMILY AMONG THE MUSLIMS IN INDIA

The Muslims constitute the largest minority group in India. According to the Indian census reports, the Muslims numbered 35.4 million or about 10 percent of the total population in 1951, and 46.9 million or about 11 percent of the total population in 1961. Certain distinct influences of the Hindu social institutions on the customs and practices of the Muslims are found in India. For example, Islam stresses equality, devotion, and fraternity; it repudiates birth-conferred privileges, and considers the worth of a man on his piety as reflected in his conduct. But in actual practice, certain elements of the caste system are found among the Muslims in India (Misra, 1963, 129-149). In U.P. and Bengal, the untouchable communities which embraced Islam did not significantly improve their position or come to be regarded as clean castes and such groups were hardly integrated within the Muslim system. Although the institutionalization of the Muslim hierarchy has been haphazard and partial, the hierarchy has been accepted with all its concomitants, such as endogamy and status ascription to higher group.

In pre-Islamic days, women were treated as chattel, were not given any right of inheritance, and were absolutely dependent. Their guardians could contract their marriage with whomsoever they liked, and their consent was not asked. Only marriages with very close consanguine relations were prohibited. However, in the *muta* type of marriage, a woman was free to choose her husband, and the marriage was contracted through the mutual consent of the parties, for a specific period. Polygyny was prevalent, and there was no restriction as to the number of wives one could have. Women captured in warfare were either married or kept as mistresses. Marriage could also be contracted by paying *mahr* (bride-price) to the father or kin of a woman. In both methods, the prominent idea was of the husband's right to the woman captured or purchased. The privileges of the husband over his wife relate to the sharing of his conjugal rights with others, inheritance of his widow by his heir, and his absolute discretion to divorce his wife at pleasure (Kapadia, 1966, 200). The Prophet brought about a complete change in the position of women, by restricting polygyny to a maximum of four wives ["You may marry two, three, or four wives, but not more; but if you cannot deal equitably or justly with all you shall marry only one." (Saksena, 1954, 134)], by condemning female infanticide, by assigning a share of inheritance to women, by declaring *mahr* as a gift to the bride and by reorienting the Arab law of marriage and divorce in favor of woman.

Most of the customs, prevailing practices, and laws regarding the marriage and family patterns of the Muslims in India, like those of the Muslims elsewhere, are rooted in the Koranic injunction and the sayings of the Prophet. According to Islamic law, a marriage is a civil contract and not a sacrament as among the Hindus. Its spiritual value is, however, recognized. "It enjoins it as a religious duty incumbent on all who possess the ability" (Westermarck, 1926, 40). Thus, it is ordered in the Islamic law that a marriage is an act of worship and every capable individual should marry.

Abu Hanifa, the jurist whose legal system is the one accepted in India, emphasizes the doctrine of *kifa'a* (suitability) in which priority is given to the interests of the family in arranging a marriage. The suitability, especially of the husband, is based on six considerations, namely, Islam, free status, lineage, financial suitability, suitability in rectitude and piety, and occupation (Misra, 1963, 150).

The exogamous rules among the Muslim are based on consanguinity, affinity, and fosterage. When a child under the age of two years has been suckled by a woman other than its own mother, the woman becomes the foster-mother of the child. It is as much a prohibition to marriage as consanguinity, because the act of suckling is regarded as equal to the act of procreation. There are other temporary restrictions. For instance, it is not lawful for a man to marry a woman undergoing *iddat* (period during which a woman is prohibited from remarrying after the dissolution of her first marriage) of her previous marriage. Such a marriage would be invalid but not void. Also, a woman who has been divorced three times is prohibited to marry the same husband until she has been married to someone else, has lived with him, and has been divorced.

As a general rule, the Muslims have a close endogamous pattern of marriage. A Muslim woman cannot contract a valid marriage with a non-Muslim. However, a Muslim male can contract a valid marriage not only with a Muslim woman but also with a *kitabia* (a Jew or a Christian woman believing in Scriptures, the sacredness of which is acknowledged by the Muslims). The Special Marriage Act, which empowers a person belonging to one sect or religion to contract a valid marriage with a person belonging to a different sect or religion, does not apply to Muslims. In addition to the religious endogamy, various groups in the Muslim system of hierarchy (Syeds, Shaikhs, Pathans, Mughals, Rajputs, Bohras, Khojas, Memons, and many others) are generally endogamous on local and regional lines. The two broad sections, the Sunnis and the Shiahs, do not intermarry. Many of the lower castes, especially the occupational ones, are strictly endogamous and marriage outside the close groups entails excommunication. The practice of hypergamy is, however, prevalent among the Muslims. Misra (1963, 151) is of the opinion that it is becoming more common in the upper, more well-to-do groups to pay greater attention to the social, economic, and educational standards of a family than to its former affiliation with the community.

The practice of cross-cousin marriages has been preferred among the Muslims. It is most popular among the Pathans, Shaikhs, Mughals, and the Syeds, and least popular among the indigenous Muslim groups such as the Garasias and the Rajputs. Among cousin marriages, the commonest form is parallel cousin-marriage, to one's mother's sister's daughter. The next in order is the marriage to the mother's brother's daughter. The marriage with the father's sister's daughter and father's brother's daughter are less common but not rare. Such a system of marriage alliance is directly responsible in strengthening links within the family as also between different families, but it may also lead to serious rifts. It is customary among the Muslims to 'ask' for a girl from her parents and in case a claim which has been built up on the basis of cousin relationships is set aside without due cause, serious rifts may occur (Misra, 1963, 153).

A valid Muslim marriage is a contract made between two major persons in the presence of two sane Muslim adult male witnesses or one male and two female witnesses. No particular ceremonies are required for a marriage. The question of marriage is one of fact. Since marriage is a civil contract, it is possible for the parties to attach reasonable conditions to the matrimonial contract. On breach of any of such conditions, the court will have power to set aside the marriage. The conditions, whether they are ante-nuptial or post-nuptial, have the same effect in the eye of law. Marriages may also be contracted through agents or by proxies, and a person who is sane and has attained puberty can act as an agent or proxy. However, the agent cannot go beyond the power given or the directions or instructions laid down in the deed of power.

Matrimony under Muslim law, being a civil contract, may, like any other contract, be terminated by mutual consent. Each sex has certain rights regarding the other, but there are differences in the rights and obligations of a man and a woman during their married life and with respect to divorce. The man can, of his own accord, divorce the woman under certain formalities against her will; in such a case, the deferred dower becomes due and she has certain rights, such as of residence and maintenance and of inheritance for a stated period. In this type of divorce, a man can dissolve the marriage simply by speaking three times the word *'talaq'*. When the pronouncement is clear and the words are expressed, the divorce is valid, even if it is under compulsion or in a state of voluntary intoxication or fit of anger. The woman cannot, of her own accord, divorce her husband against his will, unless she has this power by an ante-nuptial or a post-nuptial contract with him. However, by means of *khula* (a divorce purchased by the wife from the husband for a price) she can induce her husband to grant her freedom, and she can for certain reasons obtain a judicial divorce or judicial separation without forfeiting her dower or, for a certain period, her rights to maintenance and inheritance.

A Muslim girl remains under the control and care of her parents, but on attainment of puberty she obtains all the rights and privileges which belong to her as an independent human being. She is entitled to a share of the inheritance of her parents along with her brothers, though in different proportions. On her marriage, her individuality is not lost and she remains a distinct member of the society; her existence or personality is not merged into that of her husband. Her property remains hers as an absolute individual right.

Muslim women are given equality in many respects, but their freedom in public movement and social intercourse is restricted by the custom of *purdah*. Muslim women are obliged by the rules of their religion to observe *purdah*, that is, veil themselves in the presence of all males except their closest relatives. Whenever they leave their house they wear a veil known as *burkha*, a garment which falls from the crown of the head to the ground.

In short, a Muslim woman occupies a superior legal position in comparison to a Hindu woman. But, in actual life, the conditions of a Muslim woman are not better than those of a Hindu woman. In India, most women, whether Hindu or Muslim, are still illiterate and ignorant of their rights and privileges; they are generally not in a position to exert their will, and only a few attempt to exercise their legal rights and privileges.

The joint family is not an institution of the Muslims, and a Muslim joint family is not taken as a legal entity (Saksena, 1954, 89). The entire conception of a joint Hindu family, its constitution, and the rights and obligations of its component parts are foreign to a Muslim joint family. A Muslim joint family simply implies that a group of individuals may have a common resi-dence, kitchen, business, and property. But, in a so-called Muslim joint family there may be some males and females who have no interest in the joint property, or there may be some other person who may have an interest in the joint property but who are not members of the family. For example, the married daughters of a deceased male co-owner would fall in the latter category. Notwithstanding this legal structure, it is not uncommon to find Muslims who live surrounded by Hindus and who have absorbed and adopted the Hindu way of living in a joint family. Misra (1963, 153-155) mentions that the family organization among the Muslim communities in Gujarat appears parallel to the Hindus' in the sense that the same type of patrilocal, patrilineal family system prevails in both. He found many large households which included several married and unmarried brothers and their other relatives living under the same roof and presided over by the father. It seems that although the legal structure of the Muslims provides for a distant family organization, the Muslim families in India manifest certain structural and functional characteristics which are similar to those of the Hindus.

REFERENCES

BUHLER, G. *The Laws of Manu*. Oxford: The Clarendon Press, 1886.

GOODE, WILLIAM J. *World Revolution and Family Patterns*. London: The Free Press of Glencoe, 1963.

KAPADIA, K. M. *Marriage and Family In India*. Bombay: Oxford University Press, Third ed., 1966.

MISRA, S. C. *Muslim Communities In Gujarat*. Bombay: Asia Publishing House, 1963.

PANDEY, RAJ BALI *Hindu Samskaras: A Socio-religious Study of the Hindu Sacraments*. Banaras: Vikrama Publications, 1949.

SAKSENA, KASHI PRASAD *Muslim Law As Administered In India and Pakistan*. Delhi: Eastern Book Company, Third ed., 1954.

SHAH, VIMAL P. "Attitudinal Change and Traditionalism In the Hindu Family," *Sociological Bulletin 14* (March), 77–89, 1965.

STEPHENS, WILLIAM N. *The Family In Cross-Cultural Perspective*. New York: Holt, Rinehart and Winston, Inc., 1963.

WESTERMARCK, E. A. *A Short History of Marriage*. London: MacMillan & Co. Limited, 1926.

8.

EDNA COOPER MASUOKA, JITSUICHI MASUOKA AND NOZOMU
KAWAMURA

ROLE CONFLICTS IN THE MODERN JAPANESE FAMILY

Japanese scholars are in agreement that: (1) the *ie* has influenced Japanese society for more than three and a half centuries, but the conscious elaboration of it into an ideology of *Kokka*—nation and *ie* as a single social organism—came only after the Meiji restoration (1868); and (2) with the development of modern capitalism in Japan in the 20's the change in the *ie* has been definitely in the direction of the nuclear family, and this transformation has become more pronounced since 1946. Along with this "great transformation" there has emerged in the society a mesh of new values and attitudes accompanied by role conflicts, revealing of the fact that cultural roles shaped in the *ie* and new attitudes and values which emerged in the postwar Japan stand in opposition in the arena of family life. In this paper we seek to point out some of the critical role determinants, and to indicate the areas of role conflicts. To do so it is necessary at the outset to make more explicit the concept of *ie*.

Clearly *ie* did not refer to a concrete physical structure, a house, nor to the togetherness of all blood- or pseudo blood-related members. *Ie* was a conception. It referred to a highly institutionalized set of statuses and roles, which defined for the constituent members their respective duties and responsibilities as well as specified for the individuals what norms were to be maintained and what values to be cherished. The *ie* continued through unbroken succession of lineage groups based on *kasan*

This selection is reprinted from: Edna Cooper Masuoka, Jitsuichi Masuoka, and Nozomu Kawamura, "Role Conflicts in the Modern Japanese Family," *Social Forces* 1962, *41*, 1–6.

Reprinted with the permission of the authors and publisher.

This is a revision of a paper read at the twenty-fourth annual meeting of the Southern Sociological Society, Miami Beach, Florida, April, 1961.

(family wealth), and the *raison d'etre* of its existence was the collective well-being. The guiding principle of relationship between individuals and between the collectivities (one household vis-à-vis another) was ascribed status. The institution of *ie* had status in the community, and was buttressed on all sides with religio-ethical values: its stability was, therefore, dependent chiefly upon the stability of culture and of the wider community.[1]

The *kacho* occupied the most important position in the *ie*, and the extent of his responsibilities (also obligations) and the degree of his authority (also power) varied directly with the importance of the *ie*-status or *iegara* in the community. He was responsible for continuing the family lineage, preserving *wa* (peace and harmony within his own household as well as between households bound by lineage ties), managing *kasan*, and maintaining *ie*-status in the community. In the name of *ie*, he demanded absolute obedience from all its members. Society recognized his rights to regulate marriage, divorce, adoption and disinheritance. As custodian of the *kasan*, he was not a free agent—even though in law he had the right to dispose of the family property. In exercising his rights, he was hemmed in on all sides by moral and institutional constraints. The

[1]The legal concept of the *ie* is different from the one given here. Until November 5, 1945, when the new constitution was promulgated, the *ie* was also a legal entity. From the legal point of view, the *ie* was a unit of living individuals whose names appeared on a single *koseki*, or family register, kept at a local government office. A common residence or domicile was not a prerequisite for membership in the *ie*. Definite legal rights and obligations were spelled out for the *kacho* and lesser attention was paid to subordinate members. According to the old civil codes, members entered the *ie* by birth, marriage, or adoption; they left the *ie* by marriage, adoption, expulsion, and death, as well as by establishment of a branch family.

bigger the *kasan*, or its equivalent the higher the *ie*-status, the greater were the constraints on him to maintain and preserve the *ie*. Such forces were strongest in rural society where hereditary land ownership was the basis of *ie*-status.

The *chonan*, or eldest son, occupied a position second only to the *kacho* since he was the heir presumptive. By others, the *chonan* was called *atotsugi* (a successor to the headship) and was given special treatment and respect due to his status. He was expected to conduct himself appropriately to his ascribed status. Vis-à-vis his younger brothers, he was constantly reminded that he should conduct himself as *nisan* (older brother)—"nisan rashiku" or "nisan rashiku-nai" was the expression frequently heard to indicate his conduct which was or was not in accordance with his ascribed status.[2]

In relation to the *chonan*, the *jinan* and *sannan* (the second and third sons respectively) occupied lower rank in the family, and the community at large regarded them lightly and referred to them as *hiyameshi kui* (cold rice eater) designating their lower ranks. As members of the main household, they were expected to contribute their share of labor—in return, they could expect help in establishing a *bunke*, or branch family. In some instances, they were adopted by other families, generally relatives.[3]

To be sure, the status of women was low in the *ie*, but the *shufu* (housewife) enjoyed a superior position vis-à-vis other female members. There were two distinct stages in her adjustment—the stage of the *yome* and that of *shuto*. It was in the first stage that she experienced the greatest strain in relationships, and the most critical one was with her *shuto* or mother-in-law. In addition to showing obe-

dience and respect to all family members, she was expected to labor hard and to give birth to an heir to insure *ie*-continuity. Her blind conformity to *kafu or ie*-ways and her attitude of dependency on the *shuto* were praised as the highest virtues. In her relations with her husband, the *yome* was expected to maintain a cool demeanor and show very little affection—this was necessary to avoid arousing the *shuto's* jealousy. The husband's expectations of his wife were: (1) competence in family management but of course not too much competence, and (2) skillfulness in maintaining harmony between herself and the *shuto*. The *yome's* expectation of her husband was that he play his *ie*-role well, thereby preserving family *wa*. When the *yome* satisfactorily fulfilled all these expectations, her position in the family became secure and her security was greatly enhanced when she herself became the *shuto*.[4]

Next to the *shuto*, but above the *yome*, was the position occupied by *shuto's* daughters. Their stay in the family was temporary as they eventually married into other *ie's*. There was, however, no evidence of rebellion on their part since their entire training at home, in the community, and in the school prepared them for their future role. Within the *ie* daughters were strictly trained by the *shuto* in order to prepare them to take their places successfully as *yome* in other *ie*. In brief, within the Japanese *ie*, role behavior of the individual fitted neatly into cultural roles.

The literature on the functional approach to the study of the modern Japanese family is extremely meager or rarely attempted. One is at a loss to find a systematic study showing the impact of technological changes on the family. One might hypothesize that in spite of urbanization and industrialization there has been no important loss in family functions. Therefore, we shall touch upon legal and educational reforms in postwar Japan, increased mobility incident to urbanization and indus-

---

[2]Should the eldest son prove to be incompetent to assume the role of househead, the civil codes of Japan laid down specific causes for disinheriting the heir presumptive. In such a case, a second or subsequent son might be selected as heir. In the absence of any other male heir one might be adopted.

[3]In addition to the *kacho* and his sons, other males might also be members. Their statuses and roles would be based upon their age and upon degree of relationship to the *kacho*. A retired father, or *inkyo*, might be present and in this case he was consulted by the *kacho* on important *ie* matters.

---

[4]If the *yome* proved unsatisfactory prior to the registration of the marriage in the *koseki*, she was sent home without the necessity for a divorce. Ordinarily some time elapsed before a socially approved marriage was registered; this was usually completed before or at the time of the birth of the first child.

trialization, and change in the status of women, as these have created conditions wherein role conflicts manifest themselves.⟩

LEGAL CHANGES

The new constitution and revised civil codes clearly show the *ie* is no longer recognized. The nuclear family receives legal recognition and the equality of sexes is also affirmed.[5]

Should the laws of inheritance be strictly observed, there is little need for distinguishing status-wise the heir from other children or to give him special training in affairs of the family. In fact a large majority of rural families (even a majority of urban families) show little change in regard to inheritance practices.[6] The practice of the *chonan* inheriting the largest share of the property is still adhered to and he is still trained in terms of former ascribed status. He is expected to furnish the sole support for his aged parents and to aid his younger siblings. As long as he fulfills his role well, rarely is an appeal made to the courts by others legally entitled to inheritance.[7] Where there is no substantial family property, as in many urban areas, there is no obstacle to equal division of property.[8] The *chonan* in such a situation is

not given rigorous preferential treatment or special training.

Under the new law the selection of marriage partners is a prerogative of the two persons involved and no parental consent is needed unless they are minors. Marriage selection offers a potential source of conflict in the family. In 1959 the Ministry of Labor made a study of the kinds of marriage and found that *miai* marriage (literally seeing each other—a necessary step in arranging marriage—but generally used to mean arranged marriage) constituted 73 percent of all marriages in the large cities, 86 percent in the farming district, and 84 percent in fishing districts. "Love marriages," on the other hand, constituted 25 percent in the large cities, 13 percent in farming districts and 12 percent in fishing districts. In 1956 the Prime Minister's Office inquired whether one's own choice of a spouse was preferable. Young urban males showed the highest proportion of preference for their own choice. Why then does *miai* marriage constitute so large a proportion of all marriages? While the persons involved might prefer to choose their own mates, there is as yet no satisfactory means open for them to meet potential mates; in the end they request employers, persons of importance, family or friends to find a suitable spouse.

Educational Reforms of 1947 recognizes coeducation as desirable.[9] Its immediate effects are that for the first time boys and girls are given the same education, and contact between adolescent boys and girls is feasible outside their family circles. This may result in the *miai* as "the bridge" to bring together a young man and woman becoming less important. This, however, in no way minimizes the importance of the *nakodo* (go-between).

[5] Relevant sections of the constitution state: *Article 13.* "All of the people shall be respected as individuals. Their right to life, liberty, and the pursuit of happiness shall, to the extent that it does not interfere with the public welfare, be the supreme consideration in legislation and in other governmental affairs." *Article 14.* "All of the people are equal under the law and there shall be no discrimination in political, economic or social relations because of race, creed, sex, social status or family origin." *Article 24.* "Marriage shall be based only on the mutual consent of both sexes and it shall be maintained through mutual cooperation with the equal rights of husband and wife as a basis." With regard to choice of spouse, property rights, inheritance, choice of domicile, divorce and other matters pertaining to marriage and the family, laws shall be enacted from the standpoint of individual dignity and the essential equality of the sexes.

[6] Takashi Koyama, "Changing Status of Japanese Women" (unpublished manuscript, 1960), pp. 54–56 and R. H. Beardsley, et al., *Village Japan* (Chicago: University of Chicago Press, 1959), 236–237, 471.

[7] Sometimes the potential heirs register with the Domestic Court resignations of their inheritances thereby clearing up any potential legal difficulties. General Secretariat, Supreme Court, *Annual Report of Judicial Statistics* (Tokyo, 1957).

[8] R. P. Dore found in his study of a Tokyo ward

that there was less differentiation of the roles of children—elder son from younger son and sons from daughters—than was common in the *ie*. See *City Life in Japan. A Study of a Tokyo Ward* (London: Routledge and Kegan Paul, 1958), chapter 9.

[9] *Article 3* of the Fundamental Law of Education stated: "All people shall be given equal opportunities of receiving education according to their ability, and they shall not be subject to educational discrimination on account of race, creed, sex, social status, economic position, or family origin." *Article 5* reads: "Men and women shall respect and cooperate with each other. Coeducation of both sexes shall be recognized."

Educational Reforms also abolished the morals course—the course which had indoctrinated children in the virtues of filial piety, loyalty to emperor, submission to elders, and proper conduct in the community—and replaced it with a social studies course. This marks a sharp break between the school and the family in the sense that the school now teaches individualism, freedom, and democracy. In this situation school teachers are the target of attack from conservative elements of the society as well as from family members.

MIGRATION, URBANIZATION, AND INDUSTRIALIZATION

A steady flow of people from country to city has been going on in Japan since the late nineteenth century. In 1888, there was 87.1 percent of the total population living in the country (areas under 10,000), three decades later the percentage decreased to 68.1 percent, and by 1950 it was 46 percent. This rural to urban migration was associated with an increase in the number of workers in industry, commerce, and other urban occupations. Despite this large population movement, the divorce rate (per 1000 total population) in Japan actually declined from 3.0 in 1887 to 0.8 in 1958.[10] However, the rate of individual demoralization is on the increase in the six large cities—Tokyo, Yokohama, Kyoto, Osaka, Nagoya, and Kobe.

Migration in Japan is still linked closely with the household and the village community. Since migration is regarded as a means to take the pressure off the limited land supply, migrants do not sever their family ties and those who migrate do so with their fathers' consent.[11] Often these young men and women live in the homes of distant kin and in many cases work for them in household industries. When the time comes for them to marry, their families in the country generally find for them suitable girls from the village.

In the late prewar and the postwar periods (roughly from 1935 to the present) the small factories were combined into giant industrial developments through the program of "rationalization of industry." With this the distance of migration has increased, involving more interprefectual migrants than formerly. Long distance migration terminating in large industrial cities provides a greater opportunity for migrants to come in contact with other workers as individuals. While marriages of such migrants are still arranged by the family, relatives or a go-between, there appears to be an increasing number of requests for one's superior in the place of employment to act as the *nakodo* or *baishaku-nin* and arrange a marriage. Such an intermediary is especially desired by an ambitious young man since having a person of higher status as *nakodo* accords him and his family greater prestige and also helps him in his career.

There is generally a high correlation between urbanization and the decline in family size. It is pointed out by many Japanese scholars that the modern urban Japanese family is smaller and less complex in size; this may be true in large metropolises like Tokyo. However, no statistical proof based on a nation-wide study now exists that would permit us to give a definitive answer.[12] If it is indeed true that the

---

[10]It is recognized that a divorce rate computed with number of marriages as the base would be preferable, but as yet there is no reliable way to secure such a base. Taeuber and others believe, however, that such a divorce rate would also show a decline. She suggests that the lowering of the divorce rate may be due in part to the later age at marriage and in part to the reluctance of families in a commercial economy to take back their daughters after dissolution of a marriage. See Irene Taeuber, *The Population of Japan* (Princeton: Princeton University Press, 1958) 229-230.

[11]A rural girl who went to work in a large textile factory when her labor was not needed in the household labor force did so after the *kacho* made the arrangements with the factory recruiters. Her wages were paid directly to the *kacho* who arranged her marriage when the time came. She lived under careful supervision in the factory dormitory with other girls like herself. No one expected her work to be permanent.

[12]No nationwide study has been made of family size and composition since Professor Toda's analysis of the 1920 census, *Kazoku kosei*, (Tokyo: Kobundo shobo, 1937). Census material is tabulated on the basis of households rather than families. Takashi Koyama's "Study of Modern Family in Japan" (Tokyo, 1960), involves very small numbers but show little variation from Toda's 1920 findings when nuclear families were already in the majority all over Japan but were much more common in the large cities than in rural areas. Professor Dore's study (*op. cit.*) of families in a Tokyo ward showed about the same family size as that found in 1920 for urban families.

present-day urban family is becoming less complex, one can expect readjustments of role definitions and the elimination of generation-conflicts growing out of the presence of three or more generations living together.

An obvious effect of urbanization and industrialization is the creation of what is called "rolelessness of the aged." The retirement age may come as early as 55, rarely later than 60 or 65, for urban workers who are not self-employed. At the same time life expectancy has been increasing.[13] In the traditional *ie*—especially those engaged in farming and small businesses—the aged were honored and appropriate lighter duties were assigned to them. In the city there is little that a retired man can do to contribute to the family's well-being. No suitable role definition has been evolved as yet for the aged.

WOMEN IN THE GAINFUL LABOR FORCE

Prior to World War II the employment of women was largely either in household enterprises or controlled by the *ie*. Daughters of the higher social classes did not engage in employment either before or after marriage. Since the last World War more and more women have been pressed into employment—in small business, factories, and in clerical and other white collar jobs. The necessities of the war and immediate postwar period opened up more occupational opportunities for women.

Social expectations are that women workers leave the labor force upon marriage. In spite of this, there is an increasing number of married women in gainful work. The proportion of married women workers increased from nine percent in 1948 to 17.4 percent in 1957. This appears to be not so much an attempt to exercise newly found legal equality on the part of women as an effort to insure the economic survival of the family. Of 1724 female clerks and laborers employed on a permanent basis in Tokyo firms, 16 percent of them reported

that they were responsible for the entire family's support, and another 38 percent gave as their reason for working "to supplement inadequate family income." Only small proportions gave such reasons as "to earn money for my personal use," "to have a knowledge of society," or "to render service to society through my work."[14] Although women have entered professional and technical work in increasing numbers, they are concentrated largely in the teaching profession at the lower levels and as technicians, largely midwives and nurses, in the medical field. This professional and technical category accounts for only 3.9 percent of the total female labor force. As a group, women are still concentrated in lower occupations requiring less skill—agriculture, retail trade, manufacturing, and domestic service.

In the eyes of the law women are equal now to men. An increasing number finish senior high school and attend college. They may run for and hold local, prefectual, or national political offices. All of these changes have made the better educated woman more conscious of her rights and probably more prone to experience internal conflicts. However drastic these changes, occupational opportunities are still not extensive enough on a permanent basis to encourage many women to seek life careers and forego marriage. By and large, the Japanese people (including women) still conceive of an adult woman's place as in the home and in a position subordinate to that of her husband.

CONCLUSIONS

Before concluding the paper, the paucity of literature on family role conflicts may be noted. A survey of the existing literature on the Japanese family in transition clearly reveals the absence of any systematic treatise on role conflicts in the family, though there has always been conflict between *kacho* and *chonan*, *shuto* and *yome*, husband and wife, brothers and sisters, or *honke* and *bunke*. These strifes and conflicts were attributed often to genic and psychogenic or temperamental factors and thus were not a worthy subject for scholars to probe into. These

[13]Life expectancy at birth has increased from 42.1 years for males and 43.2 years for females in 1920-25 to 62.8 years for males and 66.8 years for females in 1954-55. See Taeuber, *op. cit.*, 355.

[14]National Public Opinion Research Institute. *Women and Work* (Tokyo, 1948.)

problems were viewed as arising from faulty training and thus were treated as family comedy and tragedy for the artists to portray. On a somewhat different level, others viewed family conflicts and tensions as strains between customs and new economic forces. Here the problem was one of realignment of groups to resolve contradictions in folkways and mores.

In a society where the institution of the *ie* was all important and the *ie* and the *kuni* (state) were viewed as a single organism, the ever-present conflict between social institution and human nature was hardly given serious attention by students of social science. One may also note that psychoanalysis and psychiatry have not as yet gained the prominence given them in the western nations. In short, the concept of the family as "a unit of interacting personalities with history" has not received recognition. The neglected area of the study of the Japanese family is still the dynamic study of the institution, spelling out among other things role conflicts and their adjustments.

9.

Thomas O. Wilkinson

FAMILY STRUCTURE AND INDUSTRIALIZATION IN JAPAN

FAMILISM IN JAPANESE SOCIETY

Though signs of the dissolution of feudalism were visible earlier, historians usually mark the beginning of Japan's modern period from Commodore Perry's visit in 1853. In facing the difficulties of modernizing their nation, the Japanese leaders of the new era (the Meiji) recognized the effectiveness of the traditional family system. Their approach essentially was to alter the overt, material aspects of Japan through industrialization, while preserving significant elements from the covert, non-material system as mechanisms of social control. Individual life was to become subordinate to the familial unit (*ie*); the *ie* was to be the essential institution in a way of life that would maintain the social structure and values of an agrarian past in an industrializing present.[1]

Confucian familial philosophy formed the framework within which ancestor worship and classical martial ethics (*bushidō*) could serve to create and preserve the family line and cultural traditions. Parental control of marriage, primogeniture, and adoption were principal social techniques for maintaining this family ideal. The presence of family shrines in the home reinforced family cohesion through both Buddhist and Shinto emphases. In addition, more formal mechanisms were used. Family relationships and organization were formally defined and incorporated into the legal system. Nongovernmental social security was accomplished by making children legally responsible for the maintenance of aged parents. In like manner, police functions were served where the household head was accountable legally for the behavior of family members. The requirement that divorces be considered first in family councils revealed a judicial function assigned to the family. The family registration records (*koseki*)

This selection is reprinted from: Thomas O. Wilkinson, "Family Structure and Industrialization in Japan," *American Sociological Review*, 1962, 27, 678–682 [a segment of the original article is omitted], with the permission of the author and the American Psychological Association.

The census data cited in this paper are selected from materials processed with grants from the Population Council and the Research Council, University of Massachusetts.

[1]Irene B. Taeuber, *The Population of Japan* (Princeton: Princeton University Press, 1958), chapter VI.

were the focus about which members of the family found legal identity. The *koseki* were, as well, a source of official statistics on population changes and vital rates. In short, Meiji leaders recognized the value of traditional family organization and were loath to see it lose its force as an effective means of social control and stability in a time of rapid change in the economic and political spheres.

FAMILISM AND URBAN-INDUSTRIALIZATION

The relevance of these facets of Japanese family structure for the urban-industrialization of the nation lies in their creation of channels for the shift of individuals from agrarian to industrial pursuits. Given the family organizational traits cited above, this shift represented for the individual worker a change in means of earning a living which entailed a rather narrow range of reorientation in his mode of existence. Even after his migration to the city for new employment, all significant changes in his social status (e.g., marriages, births, divorces, and deaths) were referred to the family register in his place of origin. The urban-industrial labor force thus expanded, but it carried with it significant ties to traditional social groupings. The dislocations of World War II and the occupation-sponsored revisions of the civil code weakened traditional family attitudes. However, there remains sufficient evidence to continue terming Japan essentially familistic in outlook.[2]

The economic organization created to administer Japan's modern industrialization reflects clearly this basic familism. The emergence of an industrial élite was not so much the result of a rational, competitive sorting of individuals as it was the cooperation of strategically placed family units. The great commercial houses (*zaibatsu*) bear the family names of the kinship groups who own and administer them. The principal channels for participation at the upper

levels in these enterprises are birth and marriage into the controlling family units. These powerful kinship units are the descendants of the group of energetic former members of the warrior class (*samurai*) who were largely responsible for initiating the opening of Japan and administering the early steps toward modernization. Meiji policies of modernization were evolved largely through the cooperation of the government and these economically powerful familial groups.[3]

Abegglen's[4] post-World War II study traces recruitment policies for the executive levels of Japanese industry and shows that young candidates for employment at these levels are the products of particular schools and professors who have maintained placement relationships with specific companies for decades. Once the man is employed, his tie to the company is a permanent one both with respect to his loyalty to the employer and the employer's loyalty to him. Occupational advancement is conceived as possible exclusively within the channels of the particular company of one's original employment. The permanence of employment is recognized as a lasting commitment assumed by the employer for the laborer as well. In times of falling production, the employee is furloughed at a reduced wage, but with the understanding that he is to be recalled when labor force needs again rise. There are striking echoes of the relationships of the pre-Restoration feudal lord with his warrior staff and his agrarian workers in those of the modern Japanese employer and his employees.

THE JAPANESE FAMILY AS COMMERCIAL AND INDUSTRIAL UNIT

Even this brief summary of the interplay of Japanese family organization and industrial development supports the recognition of Japanese familism as a channel for the flow of feudal-

---

[2]Attitude surveys in contemporary Japan reveal a continuation of traditional outlooks especially in the area of family relationships; see, for example, Shio Sakanishi, "Women's Position and the Family System," *The Annals of the American Academy of Political and Social Science*, November, 1956, *308*, 130–140.

[3]Thomas C. Smith, *Political Change and Industrial Development in Japan: Government Enterprise, 1868-1880*, (Stanford: Stanford University Press, 1955), and William W. Lockwood, *The Economic Development of Japan*, (Princeton: Princeton University Press, 1954).

[4]James G. Abegglen, *The Japanese Factory: Aspects of Its Social Organization* (New York: The Free Press, 1958).

tinged outlooks and organizational techniques from the agrarian past into the industrial present. Our task now is to verify these traditional elements through the use of specific indices.

First, let it be noted that the tenacity of traditional familial elements was not fostered merely by a nostalgic attachment to the past; there were valid economic reasons for their retention. From the beginnings of Japan's modernization her most abundant resource has been manpower, and her most scarce resource has been investment capital. An economic organization which could substitute labor for capital was the one most likely to be successful. If traditional handicraft industry, with its emphasis upon hand labor, could be turned from subsistence to market production, the profits could be invested in new heavy industries which demand large capital outlay. At the risk of oversimplification, this is, in large measure, the policy followed in Japanese industrial development. The traditional handicraft production unit, which significantly was also a strong family unit, was made an integral part of Japan's industrial structure.

The industrial and commercial organization of modern Japan shows clearly the consequences of these policies: In 1954, 50 percent of Japanese industrial establishments, employing 12 percent of her industrial labor force, had less than five workers. In the same year, 87 percent of her trade establishments with 55 percent of the labor force in trade were of this size. The census of 1955 shows that a significant propor-

tion of these small economic units were family units. This census reports "unpaid family workers" as "persons who work without pay in the business, farm, trade or professional enterprise operated by a member of the household in which they live. Persons helping their relatives in their works without pay are included in this category, even if they do not belong to the proprietor's household." These, then, are persons doing not merely housework but engaging rather in a more genuine occupational activity. Approximately one-third (30.5 percent) of Japan's 1955 labor force were in this category. In contrast, the United States had 2.5 percent (1959) and Great Britain 0.2 percent (1950) in this category.

The figures for unpaid family workers refer to the total labor force, including those in agriculture where this type of employment is to be expected. Our primary concern, however, is with that segment of the employment structure specifically associated with urban industrialism. If we consider the two largest urban concentrations in Japan, Tokyo-*to* and Osaka-*fu*, we note that the proportion cited for the nation as a whole decreases, but also that the role of unpaid family workers is still a significant one, especially in the commercial area (Table 9-1).

The contribution of unpaid family employment to the economic structure of urban areas is shown in more detail in Table 9-2. Here, the proportion of unpaid family workers active in administratively defined cities is presented by

TABLE 9-1. PERCENTAGE DISTRIBUTION OF UNPAID FAMILY WORKERS BY INDUSTRY, TOKYO-TO & OSAKA-FU, 1955

Industrial Category	Percent of total employed in industry who are unpaid family workers		Percent distribution of total unpaid family workers in area	
	Tokyo	Osaka	Tokyo	Osaka
Extractive (Agriculture, For., Fish., Min.)	55.1	48.8	28.7	37.8
Mfg. (Incl. Const.)	3.9	4.4	20.5	18.5
Wholesale Trade (Incl. Fin., Ins. & R.E.)	3.8	5.6	3.9	4.8
Retail Trade	16.7	22.4	36.7	30.1
Transp. & Communication	0.2	0.6	0.3	0.5
Services	3.7	6.2	9.9	8.3
Total	7.3	10.2	100.0	100.0

Source: *1955 Population Census of Japan*, Prefectural Volumes V–13, V–27, Table 10.

TABLE 9-2. MEDIAN PERCENTAGE OF LABOR FORCE EMPLOYED AS UNPAID FAMILY WORKERS BY
SEX AND CITY SIZE, 1955

		Unpaid family workers			
		Males		Females	
City Size	No. of Cities	Median	Range	Median	Range
Under 50,000 253		17.6	2.1–30.5	67.9	11.5–80.2
50,000–74,999 103		12.2	2.1–27.7	49.8	11.2–76.5
75,000–99,999 37		17.3	2.1–20.8	46.2	12.0–69.7
100,000–249,999 73		8.4	2.3–21.1	38.2	17.5–62.4
250,000–499,999 18		5.6	2.6–12.4	25.7	15.7–41.4
500,000–749,999 1		5.0	....	21.4	....
750,000–999,999 1		3.9	....	20.3	....
1,000,000 & over 5		4.5	3.1–6.1	20.8	13.6–22.7

Source: *1955 Population Census of Japan,* Prefectural Volumes V–1 through V–46, Table 10.

size of city. There is a clear inverse relationship between city size and participation of unpaid family workers in the labor force. We conclude that an increasing intensity of urbanization, as measured by size, tends to weaken the force of familial production units in Japanese industrial organization. However, urban industrialization does not destroy these channels for agrarian traditions, for historical and present necessities keep them as basic to Japanese industrial structure. This does not mean that Japanese economic organization is therefore inefficient. A distinction between organizational efficiency and technological efficiency is useful here. Japanese indus-

try is certainly in some segments technologically inefficient—machine tools could vastly increase production of those goods and services now produced by hand and hand tools. The organizational efficiency of Japanese industry, however, is just as certainly of a high order. The utilization of hand labor absorbs much of the oversupply of laborers who otherwise would be unemployed. By integrating them into the economic system, modern Japanese industry quite efficiently substitutes labor for scarce capital. In the process, the social environment of Japan's urban centers evolves a unique blending of the present and the past.

10.

THOMAS PRICE

AFRICAN MARRIAGE

SAFEGUARDS OF THE MARRIED STATE

The sharp transition which the European wed-

This selection is reprinted from: Thomas Price, *African Marriage,* I. M. C. Research Pamphlets No. 1, London: SMC Press Ltd., 1954 [excerpted from pp. 14–39], with permission of SMC Press, Ltd., and the Friendship Press, New York.

ding day marks between maid and matron, independent bachelor and responsible man, the single and the married state, is not generally so marked in tribal custom. Elder kinsfolk of the pair who will set up household come to a formal agreement that the marriage will be desirable and proper. The pair are then regarded as betrothed, on a broader foundation than simple exchange of promise to marry between themselves. During this period they are under obligations to the families that will be united by their marriage, and are excluded from the full range of associations with others of their own age which are open to those not yet betrothed. Satisfactory behaviour through a betrothal period leads to permitted entry on cohabitation, which is frequently marked by a ceremony; but among the Gusii of Kenya, for example, a honeymoon period is followed by return of the bride to her parents for a period of about a month, during which either partner may withdraw from the marriage. The final ceremony which raises the wife to full secure matronly status may be deferred for years.

Such apparently insecure unions are guaranteed against breakdown, through emerging personal defects or the appearance of rival attractions, by the material bond of the bride-price, paid by the husband to the wife's kinsfolk. As he frequently has not yet acquired wealth himself, he received the means to pay the bride-price from his own kin, who accordingly have an immediate interest in seeing that he does not lightly forfeit the advantages and rights acquired through its payment. Since payment may not be completed at once, or even within a short period, the security of the union depends to a great extent on the mutual regard of the couple. If it breaks down, it can be dissolved by sending the wife, if she is blamed, back to her people, and claiming return of the bride-price; if the husband is at fault, the wife's kin may receive her back but until the bride-price is returned the husband is not free from his obligations.

The bride-price is not originally for the purchase of the wife's person. It has been rather recompense to her kin for the children she is expected to bear and who will reinforce the husband's group. The wife's people can and do employ the wealth so acquired to pay for a wife from another group for one of their young men, to restore the balance. At the same time, the fact that wealth came to them in virtue of the first marriage enlists their interest to maintain it in face of disturbance; and since claim for repayment is based on the wife's default, not simply on any kind of breakdown, their

interest is both in discouraging her from misbehaviour, and defending her against mere aspersions. The bride-price too is security for her well-being once she has left her family group.

Thus among the cattle-herding tribes the bride-price consists of a recognized number of cattle. All the husband's kinsmen who contribute to make up that number have claims on the bride, and so an interest in maintaining her position among them. If the husband behaved in such a way as to break up the union, and they were unable to restrain him, they had to permit her to return to her people without receiving back the bride-price; but she could not take her children. If the marriage were dissolved through the fault of the wife, her kinsfolk had to return the number of cattle they had received, but were allowed to retain a proportion if there were children left with the father. The numbers of beasts paid and deducted was regulated narrowly by local custom.

There is evidence, from the tribes of the Nyanza Province of Kenya for example, that the bride-price creates a special link between a woman and the brother whose wife was acquired with the wealth paid on her account. He has to discharge special responsibility as protector of her interests and guardian of her children. Against the social usefulness of such a definite allocation of responsibility we have to set the tendency for daughters to be pressed into early marriage so that the father may add to his herd, while sons are withheld from marriage as far as possible, to delay the paying out. Since youths are more in haste to attain full status of manhood as husbands than are girls to leave the security of their accustomed home, households tend to be racked with resentments as the children grow up—a parallel to the adolescent stresses of modern European life. Custom provides for the possibility, though it does not expect, that coerced girl brides may resort to suicide.

Among the cultivator tribes of the forested and tsetse-fly infested areas of Central and West Africa, who count descent and inheritance by the mother's line, the bride-price takes the form of a succession of gifts, and the devotion of the young husband's services to the interests of his wife's people. He goes to live at his wife's village, thus placing himself substantially at the mercy of her kinfolk. The gifts which have led up to his acceptance by them are traditionally such metal goods as copper bracelets and iron hoe blades, with contributions of food to provision the required formal assemblies of relatives. A ceremony of breaking bachelor associations and the exclusive ties with his own kin precedes his admission to the status of husband by his wife's people. Nevertheless men never accepted this position of dependence and service as final, but looked forward to establishing independent households as soon as they could contrive it.

In these societies the gifts were not of much intrinsic value, so that when foreign teaching and example showed that this was not the only system which was recognized in the world, it had little material hold on rebels. The advantage from the husband's labour was enjoyed only by the head of the household that the wife belonged to, and no others were much interested in enforcing the bond. But in small tribal communities the loss to the husband's kin of his services was so keenly felt that they required that a brother of the bride may marry a sister of the bridegroom, thus restoring the manpower of the group. This is the so-called sister-exchange marriage.

Where the bride joined her husband at his village, and the children belonged of right to his kindred, but the bride-price was paid in consumable goods and not in cattle, the final payment which marked the full recognition of the husband's rights took on much of the nature of a commercial transaction. But until the birth of a child gave conclusive evidence that the union was satisfactory, the marriage was still insecure.

These are the patterns which still lie at the back of African minds as standards of marital duty and propriety. Some of them depart from Anglo-Saxon customs and ideals, but they are nothing worse than open to abuse. They do not exclude anything that we reckon desirable, and in the circumstances in which they developed they foster the stability and discipline which we admire. But now in their own field they have been distorted in their application by the European introduction of cash and new markets for cattle and field produce, and by the assembly of immigrant individuals in new towns. Presents have no longer simply symbolic values, signifying submission or inflating the receiver's social repute. Bracelets and hoes, cattle and fowls, all have known cash values, and their cash equivalents can be offered or demanded. But once cash is handed over it is readily spent by the recipient, and no longer exists in a form that recalls its origin or the conditions implied in accepting it. The bride-price seldom survives in a form available to coerce the blameworthy or support the wronged when a marriage develops trouble.

The traditional receivers of bride-price try to push the cash equivalents to the highest possible figures. Young men find the demands far beyond their means, and their kinsfolk no longer willing to contribute their own spending money to a sum which will promptly be treated as spending money and placed beyond recall by those who get it. The wife-seeker is compelled to meet the demands of the bride's guardians by making his own money by his own exertions. Very often he has to enter employment far from home; and having earned enough to meet the demand by serving foreign and uninterested employers, he feels that he is discharging and not entering into an obligation in paying the bride-price. Each has bought a wife for himself, without more responsibility to her or her kin than in making any other purchase. The most that remains of the old idea is that the bride-price is still a child-price, empowering the husband to hold the children whatever the wife may do; but he now holds them for himself rather than as representative of an enduring kinship unit.

This development is inevitable if he stays in an industrial location where his neighbours are simply individuals of many tribes and countries, all without relations of longer duration than the period of their stay there. Households are set up by men and women who pair without the traditional observances, because the persons required for them are not available. These unions are under no social pressure to persist, and are exposed to extraordinary strains: the pair may belong to different tribes, and so offend each other while they try to observe their different ideals. Outside the household there is no comforting background of familiar routine and accustomed demands which when met guarantee security.

If the customary regulation of marriage is capable of developing to meet these circumstances it has not yet done so. African opinion recognizes this failure, and the more thoughtful of those involved in such situations are looking for some social development which may restrain the evils of promiscuous association and refusal to accept the responsibilities that marriage should impose. They may reasonably turn to the Christian churches. It is their agents that have preached a better way of life than the tribal one. It is members of Christian nations if not of the churches that have recruited the location-dwellers from their villages. The Africans may presume that people who claim to have made so much progress have the solution to the troubles of detribalized life.

The missionary activities of the churches have established within the pagan populations Christian communities, whose members in seeking baptism have undertaken to adopt new ways of life. Christian marriage is part of this new prescription of custom. As such, it has had attached to it some non-essential but highly valued accessories, which have taken African fancy in the course of observing weddings of Europeans. The wedding day assumes importance as the occasion for conspicuous consumption and even waste, such as marked the handing over of bride-price or the feasts at various stages of the tribal marriage transactions. But the tribal expenditure was that of perishable local produce or of objects of limited and mainly symbolic value which circulated within the sphere of marriage transactions. The expenditure at Christian weddings is not only of money, often acquired by refusing to purchase necessary goods of everyday life, or by borrowing; but it is further based on the example of European expatriates who have both more to spend and fewer occasions over which to spread their spending than they would have in their own country. As a result, expenditures on a Christian wedding may leave a sequel of debt or initial poverty which reacts on the success of the married life; or the requirements of expenditure may prevent those who are poor, and unable

or unwilling to borrow, from considering being married by Christian rites. Christianity, therefore, as it has developed in fact rather than in principle, does not provide a binding marriage rite which is accessible to all; nor is it desirable for all those who contrive to achieve it. The customary marriage procedure of Christians is not free from flaws by Christian standards.

The administrations in colonial territories accept the customs of the people as they are, so far as they promote peaceable relations and good order, and are not repugnant to undefined standards of, for example, 'natural justice, equity, and good conscience' (Sierra Leone), or to 'principles of public policy and natural justice' (South Africa). The tribal customs are accepted as establishing the marital state and rights where dispute arises between natives, but are not generally regarded as conferring married status on persons not born into the communities regulated by them. Legal proof of such marriages has to depend on the testimony of witnesses who know both the persons concerned and the tribal custom, for the marriages are not generally registered. Where members of different tribes marry, and in dispute can invoke different systems of customary law, the state takes the rites observed at the marriage as determining which tribal law is relevant to later developments.

But administrations also provide by statute for the performance of marriages by lay or ecclesiastical marriage officers. The couple undertake certain responsibilities, in particular to live from that time forward in monogamy, which are laid down by the state. These marriages, which may be civil when entered into before a lay officer, or may be celebrated by a clergyman under a marriage ordinance, are registered, and are sanctioned by the state, not by a local community or tribal court. The civil marriages, provided for those who do not desire to identify themselves too closely with the locally available churches, have not proved popular. Observers give various reasons. General dislike of anything novel and untried is thought to be greatly responsible. It is known that Africans find it troublesome and derogatory to have to procure an enabling certificate, as is generally required, from some prescribed native or European authority, vouching that the parties may properly contract such a marriage. Another factor is that the ceremony is brief and bare, devoid of any introduction or preparation. Only a very sophisticated pair are likely to have the confidence to risk such a sudden, crude entry into a new stage of their life. It is in fact adopted mainly by urban employees who require official proof of their married status in order to claim special allocations, such as married quarters.

The obvious bridge between acceptable but socially inadequate customary marriage and legally effective statutory marriage is to require all marriages to be registered; but it is apparent that it is often scarcely possible to determine at what point a marriage is firmly enough based to be regarded as registrable. Government would be compelled to concern itself with just rates of bride-price, for example, to prevent rupture of an early-registered marriage by no fault of the spouses; and it is held that this would be regarded as intrusion, exciting defiance and trying the native courts too high. Many missionary policies also oppose such registration of customary marriage as likely to establish patterns that ought to be left to die out with the rest of heathen barbarism.

The position is, then, that the various authorities who can sanction marriages have each effective influence over a more or less narrow range of the population in African territories. In every section of the population victims of changing circumstance are left without adequate support, and irresponsible individuals find it possible to escape control, entering on unions which can hardly be expected to develop into stable households and assured family life. The wiser observers, native and foreign, agree that something must be done; but it has still to be ascertained what would be both widely effective and generally acceptable.

HOW MANY WIVES?

African customary law recognizes that a man may legally have more wives than one, and prescribes no limit beyond which he must not go. On the other hand, no church which retains its connection with European missionary founders will celebrate marriage for anyone who is al-

ready married to another person than the one with whom he seeks the rite. To be, or to become, a polygamist bars a person from church membership. This is the most contentious field of conflict between Christian and customary conceptions of sin. Most other sins are agreed on both sides to be harmful, but here there is no general agreement. Insistence on a right to contract polygamous marriages is responsible for most disciplinary expulsions from the churches, and for the setting up of independent local sects. These claim, as a rule specifically in the titles they adopt, to be Christian bodies, but do not sway orthodox opinion. On the whole statutory marriage requirements follow European standards.[1]

Polygamy appears to express one aspect of the effort to build up, at a primitive level of social organization, the largest possible unit of production and defence. The mutual responsibilities between a man and his wife's kinsfolk extended the field in which he could move with assurance and security. The more wives he acquired, the wider that field. Moreover, each wife could be expected to bear a family of her own, and these together would make a large body of producers under a single direction and contributing to a single centre. These factors enhanced the prestige of the polygamist who could command them, and at the same time produced the wealth which enabled him to meet the demands that his prestige attracted. Thus it became the mark of a chief to have many wives, and a guarantee of social eminence in others.

The polygamous household need not be a single cluster of dwellings. Cattle-herding people in particular would set up each wife in a place of her own, at which she would be visited by her husband. In these circumstances the common and well-founded objection to polygamy, that it leads to jealous bickering between wives and their groups of children, loses some of its weight. Nor is a polygamous household always the result of wife-seeking or wife-buying by its head. It offers a solution to the problem of accommodating widows who have lost their

---

[1]Philips, Arthur (ed.), *Survey of African Marriage and Family Life* (London: Oxford University Press, 1953), 249 ff.

husbands and with them their guaranteed social place. The successor to the husband's place in the society, or some near kinsman of his, may be expected to accommodate the relicts in his household technically as his wives, in practice as dependents. The polygamist is not then of necessity either a very lustful or an excessively self-assertive and selfish person.

Nor is marriage by tribal custom invariably a proclamation of complete exclusion of the married pair from sexual relations outside their own union. (Equally little is it a mere form which scarcely bridles promiscuous intercourse.) Procreation in a specific line of descent, which is determined by the marriage, is more vital than denial of access to the wife by any other man than the husband. This view permits a proxy father to beget children in the name of an impotent husband, whose marriage is thus enabled to fulfill itself in the bringing up of another generation. On the wife's side, her sister may accompany her to live in her household, help to look after her children, and bear children to the husband if the original wife proves barren. In African eyes marriage is less a matter of the particular persons concerned than a social arrangement to ensure that a new generation appears to take over from the present one, and that its members are brought up to fill smoothly the various established places.

But for many Africans the conditions in which their polygamous system developed, and for which it provided, are passed away. Mechanical equipment even of simple hand-operated type has reduced the amount of crude manpower needed in food production. The growth of population has covered the free land, and to a great extent ended the scope for enlarging holdings on which large family groups could be employed. The European administrations have reduced the powers, the economic responsibilities, and the scope for competition between native magnates. The use of money has made individual enterprise and mental alertness more important than accumulations of perishable produce. The successful modern man travels light, and is ready and free to move where new opportunities offer. Thus both the enterprising and unenterprising find that the old ideal of the largest possible family establishment has lost its

practical justification, though it lingers as a basis for revolt against imposed foreign notions.

At the same time, the religious teaching of the Europeans has undermined concern about the ancestors as spirits still dependent on their living successors. The need to provide recognized lawful successors to take up in turn the necessary observances of invocation and offering has lost force. The way is open for more weight to be given to such considerations already existing as, for example, the value of the companionship provided by the marriage relation. This factor is specifically mentioned by observers of Northern Rhodesian tribes, whose informants would say, 'Your wife is the best friend you have.'[2]

Defenders of polygamy against Christian insistence that marriage makes the spouses one flesh in exclusive union, have argued that it solves problems of unwilling spinsterhood in communities with fewer men than women, and of male deprivation imposed by lactation taboos which forbid sexual intercourse with a nursing wife, and that it multiplies the bridges between social groups which otherwise tend to develop antagonisms. It is argued that it is preferable to prostitution, which becomes a serious social problem wherever European influence, including that of the Christian prohibitions, is introduced. But it is not the only answer to these problems, which are in fact matters of personal restraint and not of social pressure; and it has not proved a prophylactic against failures of restraint where it has survived into otherwise 'civilized' conditions.

A case perhaps not to be settled with so much assurance is that of the member of an already polygamous household who comes to seek admission to a Christian church. The missions of the older churches all require the candidate for baptism to renounce all connection with polygamy, and make church membership conditional on faithfulness to that standard. In human terms, it is a great deal to ask of a person who has entered on a polygamous union as a normal right procedure, and has shared the responsibilities and the mutual support of the members of the household. It is estimated to have prevented acceptance of full Christian

---

[2]Philips, *op. cit.,* 94.

status by many hearers of the first missionary generations. There have indeed been considerable divergences in the rigour with which individual missionaries and different missionary groups have applied this regulation. Different people have made different assessments of the balance between principle and the extent and intensity of the hurt that its application would cause. But it is to the interest of none that this inconsistency should persist, and those who have undertaken the Christian direction of Africans should reach some firm conclusions from a review of all the factors that have caused or may cause doubt and hesitation.

Meanwhile the African disregard of insistence on monogamy derives some reinforcement from the entry into their territories of Europeans who reject Christian observances and discipline. Those whose example shows little sense of marital responsibility and restraint are no doubt in a minority, but it is news in African gossip and overshadows the unobtrusive decency of the majority. The Christian churches are put in the position of imposing on Africans more than they have rendered acceptable to, or can impose on all their own people. If they protest that no community consists entirely of 'good' people amenable to the church's direction, they have abandoned evangelization for debate. In any case, such European examples undermine the claim that the church's teaching is a unity embodying a gospel. The danger that there may appear to be one standard for white men, and another stricter one for black ones, faces in particular the national churches which also provide European chaplaincies.

Statutory law does not at present provide any acceptable middle way between acceptance of customary and potentially polygamous marriage and a type of marriage derived from Christian spiritual conceptions. The former is stabilized by the provisions of custom which is steadily becoming obsolete and inapplicable to changing circumstances. The latter is registered by the state and sustained by the official magistrates' courts, but as a rule involves or implies acceptance of some code of Christian tenets and church discipline. Yet it is apparent that there is need for some method of getting married, appropriate to the new conditions of living on earned money and being free to move about as employment offers, yet not demanding a spiritual profession which the parties concerned may not be prepared seriously to make. Between custom and the new religion there has appeared a gap. Different temperaments have turned to different aspects of development away from tribalism, and the material appeal of economic individualism has perhaps made quicker converts than has the spiritual appeal of a universal faith and ethical system. Lay civilization has not provided for the social situation for which it is responsible, by making available devices to take the place of polygamous customs which are generally recognized to be inconsistent with accepted standards of personal being in modern life.

THE CONSEQUENCES OF MARRIAGE

Under whatever system a marriage is contracted it sets up a new unit in the society, with resources derived at first in great part from what earlier generations have handed on, which will in due course be replaced or augmented by the efforts of members of the new unit itself. Normally it grows by birth of children who bring into it new contributions and new claims. No society therefore can afford to let marriage be regarded as simply the satisfaction of the mutual desires of two individuals for as long as the desires may endure. Any marriage is a social investment, absorbing some resources, with prospect of replacing them at least. It imposes new responsibilities on the pair concerned and may require of each new individual qualities. It guarantees the common good against the breaches of trust and expectation that arise from capricious self-concern.

But tribal custom does not recognize the autonomy of the new unit as sharply as civilization does. It embodies the new association as part of the going concern of the family life of seniors, adding it to an existing household. The wane of the powers of the seniors as they grow aged allows the young household to grow into self-determination. Until that stage is reached the resources of the junior family are subject to claim by the kinsmen to whom it is attached, and these claims may extend to disposal of the wife's reproductive powers, and of other magical qualities inherent in her as woman. Looking at them from that point of view, it is possible to be more patient with such practices, repugnant to Europeans, as levirate marriages regardless of the inclinations of the individuals concerned, and including among wifely duties that of initiating the husband's brother into sexual practices.

Matrilineal inheritance and residence at the wife's original home do not confer prestige and authority on the wife over the husband, or on women generally over men. They simply make the husband more accessible to pressure by the men of his wife's kin. He is still in a position to require that his wife be faithful to him as husband, in accordance with the local rules of fidelity; and he is empowered to restrain and discipline his wife if she demonstrably inclines to misbehave.

On the other hand, in tribal conditions, wives are seldom wholly dependent on their husbands for maintenance. Among the cattle-keeping tribes, the garden crops are the special concern of the wives; and among the peasant cultivators, they often have rights to special plots under their own control. They may grow for sale at a market, or keep in their own stores provisions which they can withhold from household use if they think fit. Where the rule of inheritance in the mother's line holds, the wife's brother has a close interest in the children, which may amount to guardianship. Where marriage by sister-exchange links families of the same generation, or cross-cousin marriage brings it about that a man's maternal uncle is also his father-in-law, the parent-child relationship is not so distinct from that of junior to senior in general as it is with Europeans. All these factors contribute to a general African picture of relationships not very strictly delimited, and of widely spread family responsibility.

So far as there has been a degree of female dependence due to male control of the bride-price, that also is breaking down as women come to be trained for suitable remunerative employment as nurses, teachers, and domestics, away from the sphere of marriage. During the war married women receiving allowances from

husbands on service were able to redeem the bride-prices paid on their behalf, or to reimburse marriage payments made to their kinsfolk by their husbands' people. The suppression of internal wars and tribal aggression has permitted them to trade in markets and earn a cash income of their own while still holding their positions as wives and mothers. This new situation calls for the exercise of male tact which is not always offered by men looking back to the good old days. It has also produced some female irresponsibility.

Children also can now become wage- or tip-earners at an early age, particularly in townships and locations. In these places not only are they able to contribute to straitened family resources, but there is little other commendable occupation for them. The village employments of herding and hunting are impossible, schools are inadequately provided to take in and give occupation to all who could profit by them, and neither parent can as a rule spare time from wage-earning to attend to the children who are grown up enough to go about by themselves.

In such modern circumstances as these the whole tribal scheme of subordination and responsibility has broken down. Each person's life can be what he or she makes it; and many, who would prefer not to have the obligation laid on them, have to shoulder it without much confidence, because there is no authority left that can give them direction. All are in a situation of experiment, and any good outcome depends on personal integrity. Such integrity provides the stability in detribalized family relations.

In tribal areas where a large proportion of men leave home as migrant labourers, work and responsibility similarly fall on women and children. The work is necessarily performed on a low standard, for lack of sheer physical strength; and families grow up with inadequate domestic discipline, since one male generation is not effectively at hand. Such help as the absentees afford comes in the form of cash remittances. These are readily turned to the immediate personal account of whoever happens to cash them, and once so spent have passed out of more general control. Custom has no relevance to the new opportunities and temptations. Community is breaking down in a scramble for personal gratifications and evasions. Marriage in such a village no longer opens a period of settling down and rearing a family, but may easily become little more than a passing incident.

Colonial administrations have been acutely aware of the need to support the validity of marriage as it is constituted by the various tribal customs. They are careful to avoid the possibility that enactments of theirs should break down the respect for any recognized mode of contracting marriage. But customary law is personal to those born into and recognizing each set of customs, and can be invoked only in cases concerning such persons.

Further, certain persons entitled to have recourse to a tribal law may choose to submit their case to decision by the administration's law. Nor is customary law fixed and limited by traditional judgments. It is expressed by the findings of chiefs and elders looking at each case in the light of the interests and decencies of the community that they represent. So far as custom is law, it is fluid and develops to meet cases as they arise; but it has not been able to keep up with events.

Polygamy, which is an offence in European law, is not included under the repugnancy clauses as a condition to be abolished. As a rule, however, only one wife is recognized for purposes of concessions and allowances made by European agencies to married men. A few direct attempts to forbid polygamous marriage have been made by European civil authorities and by Christian chiefs, but to little effect. While there have been such moves toward discouraging the practice, rights and obligations due under customary law in respect of wives and children of polygamous households are enforceable. The conflict of ideals is not allowed to work to the advantage of the selfish and irresponsible.

The interest of the state is to ensure that dissensions can be settled on a commonly admitted basis. In matrimonial causes the essential step is to establish beyond dispute that a legal union has existed. This is most readily done where the marriage has been registered. Various administrations have given attention to

the business of having customary marriages registered, and have found some opposition and a great deal of simple disregard of the requirement; but the idea makes its way in time. Marriages performed by appointed marriage officers are necessarily registered. In British dependencies Christian clergymen are officially recognized as marriage officers, and Christian marriages are registered. This last type of marriage does not remove the married pair completely from the field in which customary law holds good, however.

The specific legal consequences of statutory marriage are the obligation of monogamy, and the removal of dissolution of the marriage from the jurisdiction of tribal authorities. Customary law would however be invoked in disputes over place of residence, the enforcement of domestic discipline or, on the other hand, assurance of reasonable freedom. Consequences of the marriage affecting third parties, such as rights of succession, and the devolution of property, are treated differently in different territories; but on the whole customary law determines all that is not covered by special additional arrangements such as ante-nuptial contract or a will disposing of recognized personal property.[3]

One test of the effectiveness of statutory marriage is how far it makes possible the founding of a family on the civilized pattern of western Christendom. It formally relieves the African woman of impositions and disabilities not recognized in civilization, such as compulsion to enter levirate marriage, or to pass as part of an inheritance to be wife to a kinsman of her husband on his decease. In Kenya and Rhodesia this release from subjection has been reinforced by direction to the husband's family to make provision for her to live as widow. This, however, does not give her a right to her husband's property. Customary law is usually left to deal with the concerns of any children who may be left fatherless; but where doubt or dispute arises, a magistrate's court will prescribe in the interests of their moral and material welfare, whatever native custom may run to the contrary.

From the Christian point of view marriage

---

[3]Philips, *op. cit.*, 281–286.

offers a fresh beginning for the lives of the marrying pair. It withdraws them from inherited bonds and involuntary associations, and sets them in a union of common intention and adult liberty to deal with a fresh situation. It offers opportunity to construct a new pattern of life on the foundation of custom which has been broken up where its effect was undesirable; and the good intention of the married couple has been mystically reinforced by a sacramental celebration. The churches may advance the claim that at least the recognition which is given to the customary marriages of the tribes should be given by the state to the marriage form which holds within the community of Christians; and that it should support enforcement of the consequences understood and accepted by the spouses. They deny that in pressing the state to legislate for Christian marriage they are seeking the state's backing to impose on Africans by force what they have failed to get generally accepted by persuasion. They hold rather that they are requiring due recognition of the proper aspirations of enlightened Africans, and reasonable support for them against the pressure of the more backward among their people, and of selfish interests in maintaining corrupted old ways.

Critics suggest that the churches are unduly hasty in calling in the power of the state, since it appears that insufficient positive instruction is given on the requirements, values and consequences of entry into Christian marriage, as part of the preparation for it. It may be thought that these are adequately covered by general ethical teaching, so that it is sufficient with reference to marriage to state the sinfulness of polygamy and rightness of monogamy. This general statement does not deny that there have been individual and local exertions to give more extended direct preparation for Christian marriage. It points to the absence of a common policy and method. The expected influence of the good example of immigrant European households with a tradition of Christian marriage is to a great extent nullified by the social segregation of European from African, and by the isolation of the European households from their own kindred. The relations within the household are to some extent

observable; the discharge of members' responsibilities to the families from which they derive, and the interplay of consideration and restraint are generally a matter of long-distance correspondence not open to observation.

There is a case for increasing efforts to ensure that Christian marriage is entered upon with real seriousness. At present it is the resort of some who want principally to escape from tribal restrictions, who carry into it an attitude of truculence to all authority. When it is apparent that a sufficient proportion of those entering a Christian marriage do so in a proper spirit and with adequate resolution, the state will be able to legislate to reflect an existing social attitude, rather than to impose adherence to engagements which were not fully realized or accepted. As things are, the particular consequences of Christian marriage as distinguished from other unions are: a demand for more rigorous personal self-restraint, an engagement to give the first place to Christian instruction and discipline, and to literate education, in bringing up the family. Of these only the last is matter for legislation, and even there the value of legislation to the Christian interests depends on what agents are found to undertake the instruction. There is no escaping the conclusion that Christian marriage, like every other facet of the Christian life, must derive its vigour and purity from the common life of the Christian churches. The most that legislation can do is to remove notorious stumbling blocks as experience reveals them to be generally noxious. It is valuable assistance, but it is of necessity negative.

DISTURBANCE AND DISSOLUTION OF MARRIAGE

The conflict of Christian requirements with tribal custom or the law of the state appears most acutely in respect to the procedure adopted when relations between the married couple become strained; and particularly when one or other partner wishes to end the marriage. So long as the life of the pair and their offspring goes on smoothly, all outside interests are substantially satisfied, and it is not necessary to analyse the nature of the union. As in the physical world, it is disease of the organism that provokes attention to its constitution.

It is apparent on such analysis that there is almost inevitable clash between the conceptions of two persons separating themselves from their youthful ties in order to 'cleave . . . and be no more twain,' and the inescapable demands of a scheme of life built round the maintenance of the kinship group into which each person is born. Old ties have still the force of duty, old associations are more than matter of sentiment. Under customary law marriage is dissolved by separation which is upheld and enforced by the kinsfolk of the aggrieved spouse. They may be challenged before the native court, but such cases are usually concerned with economic adjustments to the new situation, in respect of bride-price paid over and recoverable. Attempts to prevent the breakdown have preceded the recourse to the court and have obviously been ineffective. Or it may be that disgruntled kinsfolk, feeling that the spouse received among them is not meeting obligations to them, magnify ordinary difficulties of making personal adjustment to a new way of life, until the incomer is turned out of their community or withdraws from an unbearable situation.

Recognized grounds for divorce in customary law were, on the husband's side, laziness on the part of the wife which threw an undue share of the burdens of the household on the husband or his people; and suspicion that the wife was practising witchcraft. Childlessness could be but was not necessarily a ground for divorce, since the physical factors responsible could be circumvented by the husband taking a supplementary wife or wives; or by permitting or enjoining extramarital intercourse of certain other men with the wife of an impotent man. Distinction was kept between such permitted access to the wife, and her own deliberate lapse into promiscuity or intercourse with a paramour, which gave grounds for the husband to end the marriage. Divorce was never a concern only of the married pair, but involved to a considerable extent their kinsfolk who had shared in making the marriage to forward interests of their own. When a customary marriage has broken down, restoration of the

household involves more than just personal reconciliation of the spouses. The original offence would affect more than the other partner, and by the time separation had taken place a number of other people would see it as advisable or necessary in their own interests.

On the wife's side, harshness or niggardliness on the part of the husband can hardly be dealt with effectively in any other way than by getting away from the situation that he controls. This power of the husband is particularly hard to challenge in societies where the wife leaves her kin to go to the husband's place, as under patrilocal marriage and in township locations. On the other hand, meanness and brutality have a narrow range of effect. If the man can be induced to amend, or the wife to recognize that she had been asking too much indulgence, nobody else is deeply concerned. In these circumstances personal reconciliation may be effective. But if the husband's character has become notorious, and he has clung to his ways in defiance of the pressure of public opinion in his own society, reconciliation will call for a good deal of faith and spiritual courage on the part of the wife—a factor connected with sincere religious profession.

Modern conditions have introduced a new pattern of broken but not dissolved marriage. A husband who leaves home to seek employment in some of the areas of European settlement may be lost to communication for a long period, particularly if he cannot write. Since customary law is essentially local law, he may act as though uncommitted by his position at home, and within the sphere of customary laws there is no means of reaching agreement on the reasonable outcome of such a situation. Even where husband and wife emigrate together to a centre of employment, the lack of sufficient housing for family groups may compel them to separate and find different places of accommodation. This breaks the day-to-day function of the wife as cook to the household and deprives each party of the feeling of association. Numerous divorces follow such enforced separations, as simply making formal a division which is in being and has no prospect of being ended.

In the locations round industrial centres

there is no traditional community which would maintain accustomed decencies and restraints. There is no indication that their present condition is temporary and that there will soon be scope for ordinary family life and a secure future for which to train children. The material as well as the moral background of life in such places is makeshift and hand-to-mouth. It is estimated that divorces in some African urban communities amount to about 70 to 80 percent of the marriages. Many of the informal unions which are not marriages are nevertheless something more enduring than mere liaisons; but even so, few of the women who enter them are in their first association with a man.

There is a general impression that divorce is now more common than it was in pre-European African society. This is not improbable, since the teaching of the European preceptors has encouraged individuals to take freedom to act as they think fit and has attacked automatic submission to social regulations; there is, however, field evidence that in most tribes divorce was never very difficult, but was dealt with quietly within the groups of kinsmen concerned on both sides. More separations are being brought to public notice as the result of the transfer of social responsibilities by administrations to native authority courts, which are higher centres with a wider territorial range of authority than the kin groups had. As people become accustomed to the courts and see the effect of their powers, they resort to them in increasing numbers. Legislators have to deal today more with an old social attitude finding new expression than with a decline from antique virtue.

Appeal lies from the decisions of native courts, where the law is personal and customary, to courts under European magistrates. They also have regard to custom, but to custom more or less formalized by having been written out in standard form. Grounds for divorce in customary marriages are laid down in few territories, at present; but the observations and records on which that will no doubt be done are being accumulated and studied. Adultery has not the same prominence as a ground for divorce that it has in European law—it has been rather an occasion to take proceedings against a wife's paramour for compensation. It is now, however, developing more importance as justifying divorce. Where Africans have entered into statutory marriage, it is a general principle that power to dissolve or annul such marriage should not lie with native authority courts, but with the magistrates' courts. As the standards of efficiency and impartiality of native authority courts rise, it is possible that their powers may be extended in future.

The colonial law of divorce is normally closely parallel to that of the metropolitan country, and Africans who contract a statutory marriage are precluded from resorting to native law to have it dissolved. It does not follow that opportunity to contract legal monogamous marriage, civil or religious, ought to be linked to all the fluctuations of legal opinion as time brings varying viewpoints. The narrow prescriptions of British colonial legislation tend to impose the changing views at the metropolis on peoples who are much more in need of broad consistency. South Africa meets this dificulty by providing special native divorce courts, where persons sufficiently versed in both native and non-native law can adjudicate on matters involving both.

A clergyman, solemnizes marriage not only in the hope, but in the expectation, that it will endure. The terms in which he calls on the parties to face their responsibilities before they bind themselves exclude most of the common grounds of separation. In the eyes of Roman Catholics they exclude them all absolutely for the duration of bodily existence. The churches naturally try to bring other agencies up to this high level of expectation, and to eliminate as far as possible temptations offered to wavering individuals. Among these are legal provisions for giving permission to depart from the solemn engagements of the marriage vows.

In Africa particularly, where statutory provisions have prestige rivalling that of the ordinances of the churches, they may have unintended influence on behaviour. A high rate of marriage breakdown is one index of inadequate spiritual conviction; but all churches recognize that a measure of external discipline may properly reinforce good intention. They therefore are in the main prepared to bless such forms of customary marriage as do not depart from standards acceptable to Christians; and they sometimes seek official recognition of the special quality of such specially recognized customary marriages. With more confidence they seek civil recognition of Christian marriages, celebrated between professing Christians with the rites of their particular church; but they are not unanimous about what is meant by a 'Christian': some restrict it to the baptized; some extend it to catechumens. The state may properly require more agreement on the basic concepts among the Christian bodies before it admits criticisms of its lack of sympathy and failure to co-operate with them.

Meanwhile the churches are faced with the difficult practical situation that there are several coexisting standards of marital responsibility. It is a fact that a type of marriage for which their ethical training prepares their adherents, which they regard as a sacrament or divinely sanctioned engagement to live in unity, and which has attained much popular appeal and prestige as a socially important occasion, can be dissolved by a different and morally less exigent authority. The result of such dissolution is that such

concerns as the material security of the wife and the custody and upbringing of the children, which are directly considered in constituting the marriage, are left to the direction of authorities who need not be in sympathy with the church's aims and point of view. It is impossible to discern at the time of marriage those who genuinely accept its conditions and those who do not look beyond the immediate matter of entering into permitted association with a partner attractive for the time being. The only indication of intention is that the persons concerned ask for Christian marriage and accept such conditions and formulae as are then presented to them. The problem of divorce cannot be met by being wise before the event and excluding from the Christian rite those who will not live up to its responsibilities.

It is apparent that the question of divorce cannot be solved in isolation by the churches. It must be included in the whole complex of precept and example by which the rounded Christian life commends itself. Such example opens channels for the grace of God, than which in the last resort there is no other effective power over men's lives.

CHAPTER III

Approaches to
Family Research

To THE EXTENT THAT SOCIOLOGY ASPIRES to be a science, theory must be based on empirical facts. These facts derive from many different sources, including the wisdom of all types of observers and chroniclers, past and present. So, much insight into family operations and problems may come from novels, from commentaries of essayists, and from other literary sources. These are insights that may be helpful to persons who are building a science, but they are not a substitute for the science itself. Indeed, one of the problems in using literary sources for knowledge is the fact that, to be attractive to an audience, they very often emphasize situations or characteristics of people to *make* them notable; at the level where journalism is literary production, what constitutes news is the unusual rather than the commonplace. The serious study of marriage and the family requires an appreciation of scientific methodology and research. The same rules of evidence that are used for science in the physical and biological sciences must apply in social science, although the variables and circumstances may be quite different.

This book cannot devote space to instructing the reader in statistics and methodology; it must be assumed that the reader has some sophistication in these areas. At the same time, selections that will be encountered in subsequent chapters occasionally involve presentations that help to convey the flavor of science in the study of marriage and the family. The reader should be warned, however, that drawing causal inferences in social behavior is a most hazardous enterprise. Social events are generally viewed as multiply-determined, and themselves are seen as having multiple effects on subsequent events. Theories of social behavior are inevitably complex, and it would be presumptuous to suggest that in the field of marriage and the family there are well-developed theories. Science is at an early stage in the study of marriage and the family, so it is still important to be concerned with theory construction to guide research and to systematize knowledge. In this context, the article by Reuben Hill titled "Contemporary Developments in Family Theory" is appropriate to indicate both the types of theories that must be considered and also the types of theories that exist.

The article by Ivan Nye and William Rushing titled "Toward Family Measurement Research" emphasizes the problem of conceptualization in theory and research. The essence of theory construction for a science is that concepts correspond to measures. The emphasis of the presentation is on assessing the current status of measurement, with attention given to concepts of validity, reliability, and applicability.

Implicitly, other issues in research and theory construction will be encountered in subsequent chapters. It is appropriate, however, to recognize that problems in measurement must be deliberately and systematically explored; the methodological bases for acquiring knowledge are also the bases for evaluating the current status of the discipline.

11.

Reuben Hill

CONTEMPORARY DEVELOPMENTS IN FAMILY THEORY

WHAT IS MEANT BY FAMILY THEORY?

This presentation uses the term "theory" broadly and generically rather than narrowly and precisely. Here theory encompasses not just the body of laws which have been formulated from experimental science (so far as the author knows, there are none of this type about the family), but also generalizations of lesser explanatory power, including the information-packed descriptions in which our family literature is quite rich. Modifiers can be used to designate the kinds of theory under discussion. *Descriptive theory* maps and charts the phenomenon in which we are interested, and *explanatory theory* tells why the phenomenon occurs. One is as much theory as the other, although our aim is to increase the proportion of explanatory theory. Within explanatory theory, we can further differentiate *partial theory* from *grand theory*. The former offers limited explanations of specific aspects of the family phenomenon, most of which have grown out of empirical studies searching for orderly relationships in selected corners of the family arena. The latter —grand theory—has sought for universal and total explanations.

What is excluded by this use of the word "theory"? It excludes theory as social thought—the anthologies of sociological classics, as Zetterberg has termed them. It excludes theory as social commentary and criticism, the counterpart of literary criticism. It excludes at least one of the dictionary definitions, *ex cathedra* assertions based on speculation and conjecture, as in the distinction between factual and "that's just theory."

What about the "family" part of family theory? This refers to the family phenomenon in all of its manifestations in behavior, overt or covert, associational or institutional, interactional or ideological. The scope ranges widely from macroscopic issues of institutional changes in structure and function to microscopic propositions about coalition formation in family groups of varied sizes and sex composition. In this overview, however, interest remains more frequently with the family phenomenon as consequent, rather than as determinant. The theory discussed is more concerned about family behavior as a dependent variable to be explained, rather than as a determinant of personality development, social change, or community disorganization, important though these latter issues may be to other social scientists.

"Family theory" as used here ranges from small, modest generalizations about selected aspects of the family phenomenon, both descriptive and explanational, to more involved propositions approximating partial theories, to grand theories about the origins and evolutionary development of family forms. The components of family theory will be identified as concepts; conceptual frameworks, which are the classification and interdefinition of concepts; and propositions, which are statements about the interrelationships of the concepts within the framework.

WHAT ISSUES ARE WE CURRENTLY CONFRONTING?

Issues encountered in the family theory field today include the following:

1. The identification of extant conceptual frameworks appropriate for family study, including their properties, underlying assumptions, uses, and limitations.

This selection is reprinted from: Reuben Hill, "Contemporary Developments in Family Theory," *Journal of Marriage and the Family*, 1966, 28, 10-26 [a segment of the original article is omitted].

Reprinted with the permission of the author and publisher.

This paper is a revised version of the Ernest W. Burgess Award Lecture at the National Council on Family Relations annual meeting, Toronto, October, 1965.

2. The improvement of these frameworks as taxonomic cross-classifications of conceptual dimensions, by formulating new concepts to fill out empty cells in the taxonomic array of concepts.

3. The formulation of needed bridging concepts to link the configuration of family terms with concepts about personality and with concepts dealing with other collateral systems in the society.

4. The reduction of redundancy in the frameworks by interdefining concepts as a necessary step toward developing conceptual models.

5. The development of partial theories from discrete propositions about the interrelations of concepts within the current taxonomic frameworks.

6. The creation of theoretic paradigms or models from the interrelation of selected parts of the taxonomic frameworks as a more systematic test of partial theories.

Discussion of each of these issues follows in some detail to illustrate the problems we are encountering in improving the quality and explanatory power of family theory.

BUILDING BETTER CONCEPTUAL FRAMEWORKS FOR FAMILY STUDY

The first four of the issues identified fall under the general rubric of building better conceptual frames of reference appropriate for family study: the identifying of viable frameworks, the tidying up of these frameworks by discovering and/or coining new concepts, the building of bridging concepts to permit linking of the family and other systems, and the interdefining of concepts to reduce redundancy and to move toward better conceptual integration.

Conceptual frameworks are the intellectual lenses which we use to render some aspects of the family phenomenon clear and focused, other aspects less clear, and still others almost unseeable, as if in using such a frame we had put on blinders. The psychologist, utilizing any one of the frames of reference available to his discipline, finds himself focusing almost exclusively on the developing and responding child. His framework rarely permits him to include in his vision the many other positions, and the family as a group to be studied in its own right is absent from all of the psychological frames of reference we have analyzed to date. With this illustration as background, a definition of a conceptual framework as utilized by most family theorists might be: a cluster of interrelated, but not as

yet interdefined, concepts for viewing the phenomenon of marriage and family behavior and for describing and classifying its parts.

The frameworks used in family study have been inferred from the content analysis of several hundred American publications going back in time to 1920. Substantial progress has occurred in the identifying of current conceptual frameworks. The initial work of Hill, Katz, and Simpson in naming seven frameworks and their users in 1957[1] was followed in 1962 by a much more detailed specification by Hill and Hansen,[2] in which the chief conceptional properties and basic underlying assumptions of five frameworks were provided in taxonomic tables. Three categories of concepts were specified in these tables: type of behavior treated, social space in which it occurs, and the dimension of social time. The frameworks delineated were: the institutional, the structure function, the symbolic interactional, the situational, and the family developmental.

In making the requirement that, to be included, a framework must possess concepts for the description of the family, either as group or as institution, Hill and Hansen added no new frameworks to the Hill-Katz-Simpson list, and dropped two (learning theory and consumption economics). This initial work has stimulated dozens of articles in Asia and Europe as well as in America and has since been followed by the production of four chapters in Christensen's already classic *Handbook of Marriage and the Family*[3] which provide the intellectual history of each of these five frameworks, the chief researches utilizing the approach, and the generalizations which have flowed from these researches.

The most recent effort at extending the identification and specification of conceptual frameworks for family study is the work of Ivan Nye

---

[1] Reuben Hill, Alvin M. Katz, and Richard L. Simpson, "An Inventory of Research in Marriage and Family Behavior: A Statement of Objectives and Progress," *Marriage and Family Living*, February, 1957, *19*, 89–92.

[2] Reuben Hill and Donald A. Hansen, "The Identification of Conceptual Frameworks Utilized in Family Study," *Marriage and Family Living*, November, 1962, 24:4, 299–311.

[3] *Handbook of Marriage and the Family*, ed. by Harold T. Christensen (Chicago: Rand McNally, 1964), chaps. 2–5, 33–215.

and associates . . .[4] Nye's group built on the work of Hill-Hansen to specify further the underlying assumptions, the value positions of those using the frameworks, and the contributions and limitations of the framework for research, theory, and practice. Nye and his associates have also added, to the basic five noted by Hill and Hansen, six frameworks which cope with aspects of the family, even though these frameworks would not all qualify as possessing the concepts necessary for the study of the family as a group or institutional phenomenon. These are the anthropological, the psychoanalytic, the social psychological, the economic, the legal, and the Western Christian. Of these additions, the writer is particularly challenged by the anthropological, the psychoanalytic, and the economic, which Hill and Hansen also considered and rejected but which may well warrant further attention.

Having identified these frameworks and classified the concepts which make up their content, what deficits do we discover? We find, on the one hand, empty cells in the taxonomy of concepts, semantic lacks; and, on the other hand, we find redundancy, multiple concepts for the same cells with slightly different shades of meaning.

SEMANTIC DEFICITS

A first example of a serious semantic deficit is the limited vocabulary available for describing the behavioral properties of the family as a small group. For lack of adequate terms, we personalize families, ascribing to them concepts appropriate only for individuals. The sports writers have done better in developing a terminology which differentiates between the performance of the athletic team and the achievements of individual players than social scientists have done in developing a terminology appropriate for the study of whole families. Handel has turned to this problem in a recent provocative article addressed to psychologists, "The Psychological Study of Whole Families."[5]

Years ago a talented journalist writing up a story for *McCall's* about the author's research on war-separated families suggested, from a reading of the cases, that the families which adjusted best were more "intelligent" and less likely to get "rattled" in the face of emergencies. For purposes of communication to a mass audience, this personalizing of family behavior may have been justified. Do we have, however, family group equivalents to intelligent, easily rattled, masochistic, happy? What is the family equivalent for motivation, appetite, drive? Families may develop a style of living, may build a reputation, but do families develop identities? These are examples, at the most prosaic level of our need for a terminology which is distinctively at the group level to deal with whole family behavior.

If we turn to the issue of diagnostic terms, the confusion is even more apparent. Is it appropriate to speak of a family as having a personality of its own, as in terms like "the neurotic family," or "the schizophrenic family"?

Families may be diagnosed on the basis of types of interaction which are neurosis-producing, such as "scapegoating" or "isolating" members, but it is hardly appropriate to describe such families as "neurotic." Families may be characterized as having prestige structures, types of communication channels, and systems of role allocation which produce withdrawal patterns in some members, but should such families be then tagged as schizophrenic? We require diagnostic terms for those families which, because of their peculiarly maladaptive interactional patterns and alignments, produce schizophrenia, acting-out reactions, or suicide in members.

The problem of our impoverished vocabulary may be illustrated further by trying to take into account that the family is a special kind of group possessing both a history and a future. Are the same terms appropriate for the childless companionate before children (the incipient family), the family in the childbearing and child-rearing stages, and the postparental companionate? What of married couples who never have children—are they also a family? Should they be called an arrested family? How are the wife's parental family, the husband's parental family, the couple's immediate family, and the families of their married children to be distinguished

---

[4]*Conceptual Frameworks for the Study of the Family,* ed. by Ivan Nye and Felix Berardo (New York: Crowell Collier and Macmillan, 1966).
[5]Gerald Handel, *Psychological Bulletin,* January, 1965, *63*:1, 19–41.

from one another in discussing families of the same line over three generations?

We also lack group terms for family transactions with external agencies, where the internal system of the family is left residual and one concentrates on the network of relationships external to the family. What vocabulary of terms can characterize these exchanges, reciprocities, and interdependencies? None of the conceptual frameworks identified to date provides such a vocabulary for whole families.

Of quite a different order of deficits is the paucity of bridging concepts as links between family and personality and family and society. The concepts of role, norm, and value are good examples of bridges which join family and personality reasonably well, since each concept is anchored in both family and personality. Roles, for example, are defined, clarified, ascribed, and sanctioned by *the family* as a group, but are perceived, learned, taken, and enacted by individuals as family members. Values are similarly defined and integrated as part of the family's private culture and are often shared, but they are perceived, held, and expressed by persons. Bell and Vogel have demonstrated that the concept of function also performs such a bridging service between the family system and society since it is anchored in both the family and several other social systems.[6]

In their research on whole families, Hess and Handel[7] have found it necessary to develop a number of concepts which simultaneously refer to the personalities of the individual family members and to the characteristics of the family as a group. To quote from Handel's more recent appraisal of their work:

. . . *separateness and connectedness* are the underlying conditions of a family's life. . . . a basic family process is the effort to achieve a satisfactory pattern of separateness and connectedness. . . . in the course of establishing [such] patterns each member develops an image of each other member. . . . A second process is that behavior in a family may be viewed

as the family's effort to attain a satisfactory congruence of images through the exchange of suitable testimony. This family interaction comes to be centered around a particular theme in each family. Themes found in the families reported include: flight from insecurity, equanimity and its vicissitudes, dynamics of disconnectedness, demonstration of constructive independence, and the comforts and crises of companionship.[8]

From this brief excerpt, a number of relevant bridging concepts developed by Hess and Handel can be identified: pattern of separateness and connectedness, congruence of images, testimony exchanges, and family themes. Additional bridges rendered salient by these students include the concepts of boundary setting and maintenance, seen in the boundaries set for members in limiting the family's world of experience and, internally, the concept of "centering and dispersing of interactions," seen in the *patterns of alignment* and *coalition* of members.

As a way of summarizing this discussion of conceptual deficits, Chart 11-1 shows the basic dimensions with which a fully developed conceptual framework for studying the family as a social group should cope. It has been a helpful guide for remedying framework deficits. Of the conceptual frameworks we have analyzed to date, none provide us with concepts adequate for dealing with Section 4a, Structural Changes in the Family Over the Life Span, especially hierarchical changes, constellation changes, and changes in interdependencies.

REDUNDANCY OF CONCEPTS

The issue of semantic deficits may be turned completely around now to deal with the issue of semantic duplication and overlapping, or redundancy. In our conceptual frameworks, we have terms which are not quite synonymous which crowd into the same cells of our taxonomies. An excellent example is the cluster of concepts denoting location in the family structure: status, position, rank, station, and role. Each of these terms has been used by family theorists in describing the hierarchical and horizontal placement of family members with respect to one another. What if in geography there were five terms for locating the latitude

---

[6] *A Modern Introduction to the Family*, ed. by Norman W. Bell and Ezra F. Vogel (New York: The Free Press, 1960). See especially their discussion of interchanges between the nuclear family and several collateral systems, 8–19.

[7] R. D. Hess and G. Handel, *Family Worlds: A Psychological Approach to Family Life* (Chicago: University of Chicago Press, 1959).

[8] Handel, *op. cit.*, 27–28.

CHART 11-1. OUTLINE OF DIMENSIONS FOR AN ADEQUATE
TAXONOMIC CONCEPTUAL FRAMEWORK

Social Space Type Concepts

1. Boundaries, Spatial Limits of the System Treated
   a. What is included?
   b. What is residual?
2. Structure
   a. Number of units
   b. Location of units
   c. Hierarchy of units (power, resources)
   d. Configuration of units (closeness, sociometric)
   e. Interdependence of units (interrelatedness by function, service)
   f. Normative demands on units and the system

Systemic Behavior Type Concepts

3. Behavior Patterns
   a. Of total system with other systems, transactional behavior
   b. Of units within the system, interactional behavior
   c. Of a single unit, actional behavior

Social Time Type Concepts

4. Orderly Growth and Development Over Life Span of Group
   a. Structural changes in group
      i. Size
      ii. Age composition and locational structure
      iii. Hierarchical changes
      iv. Constellation changes
      v. Normative changes, role shifts
      vi. Changes in interdependencies
   b. Changes in unit members
      i. Expectations, age graded (cultural)
      ii. Maturation, age graded (biological)
   c. Behavioral changes over the life span
      i. Group in transaction with community, by stages
      ii. Interaction of members, by stages
      iii. Individual achievements, by stages

Bridging Type Concepts

5. Bridges Between Systems
   a. Between group and larger systems (community)
   b. Between group and collateral systems (school, etc.)
   c. Between group and smaller units (personality, members)
6. Bridges Between Observed and Inferred
   a. From action and interaction
      i. Concrete observable segments of behavior
      ii. Patterns of behavior
      iii. Behavior themes
   b. From expectations and norms
      i. Stated wishes, desires, objectives
      ii. Shared values and norms
      iii. Role structure
   c. Between behavior patterns and normative structure
      i. Role performance
      ii. Discrepancy between achievement and expectation
7. Bridges from Overt Objective Level of Interaction to Feeling Subjective Level of Definition and Perception
   a. Groups definitions of situations and imperatives
      i. As applied to group performance
      ii. As applied to age-graded positions
   b. Individual perceptions of
      i. Norms and expectations, of family and members
      ii. Behavior of others, distortions of performance

or longitude of a city? Another such confusing cluster involves the phenomenon of tightness or looseness of the ties binding family members: family cohesion, integration, solidarity, unity, adjustment, agreement, consensus, concordance, and concurrence. These are but a few of the terms used, each with its special shade of meaning.

The method which appears most promising to reduce the redundancy of concepts in a framework is the technique of interdefining basic concepts. In his classic work *The Human Group*,[9] Homans has done this for an important trio of concepts: activity, interaction, and sentiment. Frederick Bates[10] has performed such a service for the quartet of concepts: group structure, position, role, and norm.

Some progress has occurred in interdefining basic concepts for family theory, but only one of the five frameworks identified by Hill and Hansen has been subjected to this process as yet. Ann Blalock[11] some years ago utilized the

principle of parsimony to eliminate redundancy among concepts, ending up with three classes of concepts: 1) those referring to individuals and to the family group, 2) those referring to behavior and to structure, and 3) those which can be observed and those which need to be inferred. Chart 11-2 names and locates Blalock's basic concepts: action and interaction, expectations and norms, and position and structure. She was able to interdefine these six concepts, each in terms of the others, and thereby adduce propositions for family theory about their interrelations as Homans had earlier done with the concepts of activity, interaction, and sentiment.

Hill and Rodgers[12] have described some of the later attempts at interdefinitions within the family development framework. What was sought was the interdefinition of concepts coping with the orderly sequences of development. Beginning with Bates's interdefined concepts of family structure, position, role, and norm, the family development theorists have utilized Irwin Deutscher's interdefined concepts of role cluster, role complex, and role sequence to build toward Farber's intriguing view of the family

[9]George C. Homans, *The Human Group* (New York: Harcourt, Brace & World, Inc., 1950).
[10]Frederick Bates, "Position, Role and Status: A Reformulation of Concepts," *Social Forces,* 1956, 34, 313–321.
[11]Ann Blalock, "A Conceptual Scheme for Analyzing Families as Small Groups," unpublished M.A. thesis, University of North Carolina, 1954.

[12]Reuben Hill and R. H. Rodgers, "The Developmental Approach," in *Handbook of Marriage and the Family, op. cit.,* 178–185.

CHART 11-2. CLASSIFICATION SCHEMA FOR INTERDEFINITION OF CONCEPTS (BLALOCK)*

	Individual as Unit		Group as Unit	
	Observational Concepts	*Inferred Concepts*	*Observational Concepts*	*Inferred Concepts*
Behavioral Concepts	ACTION	EXPECTATIONS	INTERACTIONS	NORMS
Structural Concepts	......	POSITION	......	STRUCTURE

Note: It should be pointed out that *expectations* and *norms* have been selected from among other classes of covert behavior—the choice is not meant to imply that these two concepts are the most important or that no others exist. They seemed to be the most useful in the study of families from a sociological point of view. "Emotions," "beliefs," "goals," "values," and so on, are other important classes of covert behavior but will not be included in the scheme.

Also, it is not implied that individual concepts are to individuals as group concepts are to groups. It is important to avoid the assumption that individuals and groups are analogous. The idea of a group having "behavioral characteristics" (*interaction*) may be misleading unless it is made clear that no implication is made that "groups act." Perhaps it will help to say that using the individual as a unit for study means merely that the *focus* is on a *single individual;* when the group is taken as the unit, the *focus* is on a *plurality of individuals.*

The *plurality* does not behave as if it were a single individual. The concept *interaction* cannot be applied to the individual, and yet is an important concept in sociology; also, it refers to the behavior of individuals with respect to one another, and consequently fits the "behavioral concept" category better than the "structural."

*From Ann Blalock, "A Conceptual Scheme for Analyzing Families as Small Groups," M.A. thesis, U. of North Carolina, 1954, p. 12.

as a set of mutually contingent careers. A needed bridging concept, positional career, was coined as the intercontingency of role sequences within a position. Since the stages of family development had already been defined as changes in the family's position-role complex, the concept of family career became the intercontingency of the positional careers of family members.

One consequence of interdefining concepts will be to greatly reduce the sheer number of concepts of slightly different meanings within a framework, and to open the way for their utilization in the development of explanational theory urged by Zetterberg.[13]

THE UTILIZATION OF TAXONOMIC FRAMEWORKS FOR THEORETIC PURPOSES

We are being encouraged from within and outside the family fold to move beyond the identifying and creating of conceptual schemes. Conceptual frameworks enable us primarily to name and classify family phenomena, to map and specify the range and distribution of those family behaviors which our conceptual lenses open up for observation. If we are to go beyond journalistic-type descriptive writing, we must move to the level of explanation and verification; that is, to the formulation of propositions about the phenomena we are observing.

No one has expressed this theme better than Hans Zetterberg,[14] who sees most sociological theorizing stalled on the plateau of taxonomic description, and who has brilliantly delineated the steps required to move off this plateau and begin constructing what he terms theoretical sociology. Some work by students of family theory is already underway at this higher level of theory construction, but it has rarely been systematically and self-consciously undertaken.

In a recent article which he has appropriately entitled, "Toward a Theory of Family Development," Rodgers[15] has assessed the progress in theory building within family development against Zetterberg's criteria. Rodgers describes

the phases of transformation from what he terms the Family Development *Approach,* to the Family Development *Framework,* and on to the beginnings of Family Development *Theory.*

The transformation of a conceptual scheme or framework into a theoretical scheme occurs piecemeal as the descriptive statements, which follow from the naming and classifying of behaviors, give way to explanatory propositions which array these behaviors in co-variant or antecedent-consequent rhetoric. These three types of statements may be illustrated from the author's work on family crises:

1. A *descriptive statement:* The course of family adjustment to crisis follows a roller-coaster type pattern beginning with a downward skidding of disorganization, followed by trial-and-error recovery attempts, and ending with an equilibrium level of readjustment. *NB.*

2. A *statement of co-variance:* Crisis-proneness increases as a family's integration decreases.

3. An *antecedent-consequent statement:* If the breadwinner of a middle class family becomes unemployed, *then* his authority in the family declines.

It is apparent from these illustrations that the descriptive statement describes the variation of only one concept (which we call a variable), using time as the means to divide the family behavior observed into phases. The co-variance statement places in juxtaposition *two* concepts which have been operationalized into variables and specifies the way they co-vary. Such a statement does not specify which variable is determined but suggests interdependence. The antecedent-consequent statement is also two-variate, and introduces the notion of sequence into the proposition. Since the determinant variable and the resultant are identified, the resulting hypothesis is thus prepared for later experimental verification.

Zetterberg[16] has classified theoretical propositions into five types:

1. Univariate vs. multivariate
2. Reversible vs. irreversible
3. Stochastic vs. deterministic
4. Sequential vs. co-extensive
5. Interdependent, of two subtypes:
     Contingent vs. sufficient
     Substitutable vs. necessary

All of these five types of propositions can be

[13]Hans L. Zetterberg, *On Theory and Verification in Sociology* (Totowa, N. J.: Bedminster Press, 1963), 1–5.
[14]*Ibid.,* 10–84.
[15]R. H. Rodgers, "Toward a Theory of Family Development," *Journal of Marriage and the Family,* August, 1964, 26:3, 202–270.
[16]Zetterberg, *op. cit.,* 11–25.

illustrated from the hypotheses that are currently being tested in family research. This should indicate that family theory in 1965 is not limited to sheer naming and classifying of family behaviors. We are indeed developing more and more encompassing propositions, which, when linked together, permit the deduction of higher-order partial theories.

The basic materials for the construction of explanatory family theory are now abundantly available. Indeed, the volume of research findings in propositional form produced annually in the United States alone is sufficient to baffle the research librarian. Many of these propositions, upon examination, may prove to be invalid, unreliable, or nongeneralizable because of faulty sampling and data collection methodology; or, equally disheartening, to be theoretically uninteresting. They are often marginal to any of the extant conceptual frameworks within which accretive theory is likely to be built.

Need for Codification

What is required to deal with this mass of uneven findings is a program of inventorying, which would analyze the content of the several studies which have been published, specifying the research procedures employed, the conceptual frameworks used, and the substantive findings. Where possible, these research findings would be organized into higher-order theoretical propositions which, together with other related propositions, might be shown to support a partial theory. This task of inventorying and codification has been the chief mission of the Inventory of Research on Marriage and Family Behavior now located at the University of Minnesota, and a number of publications have demonstrated the feasibility of its procedures. William J. Goode and his associates at Columbia University have also been engaged in a program of codification of research propositions. His publications to date illustrate the higher-order theory made possible by mining the cross-cultural propositions about romantic love and social structure,[17] illegitimacy and social structure,[18] and

social mobility and personality structure.[19]

Hill and associates, in their Inventory, have developed procedures for annotating and arraying research propositions in the chronology of their development, to demonstrate how progressively more encompassing propositions evolve as a consequence of researchers building cumulatively on their predecessors' work. Katz and Hill have made the most explicit attempt to illustrate and test these procedures.[20] The authors examined over 20 pieces of research on residential propinquity and mate selection published over a 30-year period, and chose 14 of these to illustrate the evolution of an improved methodology for measuring the phenomena and the increasing sophistication of explanatory theory. The codifiers began with the original and most primitive statement of the theory by James Bossard, based on findings in Philadelphia, that the more propinquitous the residences, the more likely people would be to marry. Each of the studies cited made some refinement in methodology and/or in the phrasing of explanatory theory. Norm-segregation theory was a first major advance in that it gave a more satisfactory sociological explanation and encompassed some of the deviant findings not covered by residential propinquity theory. Norm-segregation theory in turn was modified by the theory of intervening opportunities, borrowed from Stouffer's job-migration theory. Finally, the authors developed a chain of propositions termed "norm-interaction theory" which appeared to encompass more of the variance in marital selection than either residential propinquity, norm-segregation, or intervening opportunities theory did separately.

The Minnesota Inventory has not been working on this task of assessment alone. The past decade has seen the production of a number of excellent codification papers which have both summarized research findings and pointed to the emergence of higher-order theories. A number of these papers may be found in the bibliography at the end of this article.

[17]William J. Goode, "The Theoretical Importance of Love," *American Sociological Review*, 1959, 24, 38–47.

[18]William J. Goode, "Illegitimacy in the Caribbean Social Structure," *American Sociological Review*, February, 1960, 25, 21–30.

[19]William J. Goode, *Family and Mobility* (New York: Institute of Life Insurance, 1963). See also his "Achievement Aspiration and Family Structure," *Research Forum*, February, 1964.

[20]Alvin Katz and Reuben Hill, "Residential Propinquity and Marital Selection: A Review of Theory, Method and Fact," *Marriage and Family Living*, February, 1958, 20, 27–35.

The highest quality reviewing of research propositions and constructing of theory in the family field has been done on mate selection, with a book-length publication by Winch[21] and a psychological assessment by Tharp[22] setting a high standard for subsequent writers. The treatment by Jacobsohn and Matheny[23] is the best codification the author has seen to date. These men have reviewed over 250 publications and have identified ten firm propositions about mate selection in closed marriage systems. These propositions form a chain whose links cumulatively relate socialization to role acquisition, role performance to family structure, familial relationships to kinship patterns, and kinship patterns to the social system as a whole. With equal care, the authors have also reviewed and provided the links for mate selection theory in open marriage systems, looking successively at the *referents* of mate selection, the *functions* of mate selection, and the *determinants* of mate selection. These latter are multifactional, including demographic, statutory, socio-economic, referent networks, and personal attribute-type factors. These codifiers conclude that, despite a wealth of information concerning the determinants of mate selection, the findings are, with some notable exceptions, not cumulative, nor do they coalesce into a unitary theoretical framework. Three major conceptual foci encompass these determinants: 1) Simple Convergence, within which propinquity and homogamy theories fall; 2) Perception and Affect, within which the phenomenological theory of the congruity of self and other perceptions, empathy theory, and Newcomb's Theory of Interpersonal Attraction are found; and 3) Interaction Process. Bolton's[24] recent conceptualization of interaction process, developed explicitly for the study of mate selection, covers better than any other framework to date the chief miniature theories.

For example, it encompasses Waller's *summatory* process, Cavan's *winnowing* process, Kerckhoff's *filtering* factors, Heider's *balance* theory, and Newcomb's *principle of interpersonal attraction*. Mate selection is thus seen by Bolton as a "problematic process"; that is, as an end product of a sequence of interactions characterized by advances and retreats along the paths of available alternatives. Interaction process analysis, because it emphasizes a relationship rather than the behavior of two individuals, can encompass numerous variables which hitherto have had to be studied in isolation. In Bolton's hands, it has yielded three modes of interaction which, in combination, determine the sequence and course of a relationship: episodes of interaction, forms of interaction, and turning points. This procedure has also produced five distinct types of developmental interaction processes, suggesting the likelihood of multiple explanations for mate selection.

Selected high-quality reviews ending with higher-order theoretical constructions may also be found with respect to age at marriage,[25] unmarried parenthood,[26] family planning,[27] and family authority patterns.[28] Theoretical propositions of some sophistication about family transactions with kindred,[29] neighbors, and collateral systems, stressing open and closed networks, will also qualify shortly as incipient middle-range theories.[30] Each of the scholars working in these areas has brought his own style of

[21]Robert F. Winch, *Mate Selection* (New York: Harper & Row, Publishers, 1958).

[22]Roland G. Tharp, "Psychological Patterning in Marriage," *Psychological Bulletin*, March, 1963, 60:2, 97–117.

[23]Peter Jacobsohn and Adam R. Matheny, "Mate Selection in Open Marriage Systems," *International Journal of Comparative Sociology*, III:1, 98–124.

[24]Charles D. Bolton, *The Developmental Process in Love Relationship*, Ph.D. dissertation, University of Chicago, 1959.

[25]J. Joel Moss, "Cross-National Trends and Sociological Factors in the Decision of When To Marry," *Journal of Marriage and the Family*, May, 1965, 27:2, 230–243.

[26]Clark E. Vincent, *Unmarried Mothers* (New York: The Free Press, 1961).

[27]Ronald Freedman, *The Sociology of Human Fertility: A Trend Report and Bibliography*, in *Current Sociology*, 1961-62, 10-11:2.

[28]James M. Rollins, "Two Empirical Tests of a Parsonian Theory of Family Authority Patterns," *Family Life Coordinator*, January-April, 1963, 12:1-2, 5–79. See also the excellent review of types of nuclear family role structure by Morris Zelditch in *Handbook of Modern Sociology*, ed. by Robert E. L. Faris (Chicago: Rand McNally, 1964), 699–715.

[29]Marvin B. Sussman and Lee Burchinal, "Kin Family Networks: Unheralded Structures in Current Conceptualizations of Family Functioning," *Marriage and Family Living*, August, 1962, 320–332.

[30]Robert W. Habenstein and Allan D. Coult, *The Function of Kinship in Urban Society* (Kansas City: Community Studies, Inc., 1965).

deriving propositions and arraying them developmentally. Some have been more interested than others in moving to construct chain propositions and partial theories, but all have left their readers with a better grasp of the present state of theory in their area of endeavor.

THE CREATION OF THEORETIC PARADIGMS OR MODELS

The preceding discussion has briefly delineated the way family scholars are coping today with five issues in theory construction, ending with an overview of the attempts to derive middle-range theories by interrelating research propositions. A case has been made for the utility of tidying up current conceptual frameworks, and for interdefining the interrelated concepts in these frameworks, both to reduce redundancy and to permit their use for developing theoretic models.

Whereas the entire range of concepts in a conceptual framework may be put to use in the descriptive photographing of family behaviors, particularly in case history writing, the theoretician constructing theoretical propositions or developing partial theories will usually utilize a limited sector of the taxonomic table of concepts. Similarly, although a researcher who is challenged by a research idea will want to consider which of several frameworks will be most likely to welcome his idea as theoretically relevant and illuminate best its possible contributions, he will not draw from the entire framework in designing his research problem. In the fortunate case where the concepts of the framework have been interdefined, the researcher will be able to select and arrange concepts from the framework relative to his problem to formulate with dispatch what Merton has termed "a theoretic paradigm." The process is often more complicated than appears here, because concepts and categories of the frameworks are not like fruit on a tree waiting to be picked and arranged in a bowl; they are at various levels of abstraction and visibility. The delineation, moreover, of concepts into those which are linked unidirectionally, those which are interdependent, and those which are independent, presumes specification about the interrelations of concepts

to a degree not yet attained for any framework. The paradigm produced is often at best a tentative statement of the interrelation and interdependence of its parts. The paradigm, furthermore, should not be mistaken for the conceptual framework from which it has been drawn, since usually only a selected few of the total range of concepts have been utilized, and these have been realigned entirely to conform to the demands of a specified and limited theoretical problem.

Merton provides a description of the functions and advantages of the paradigm. It should be noted, however, that his thoughts antedate the current work in identifying conceptual frameworks for family study. His paradigm therefore partakes somewhat of the properties of a conceptual framework and does not anticipate the possibilities we have today of utilizing a delineated framework as an aid in the development of an analytic paradigm:

First, paradigms have a notational function. They provide a compact parsimonious arrangement of the central concepts and their interrelations as these are utilized for description and analysis. Having one's concepts set out in sufficiently brief compass to permit their *simultaneous* inspection is an important aid to self-correction of one's successive interpretations, a result difficult to achieve when one's concepts are scattered and hidden in page after page of discursive exposition. . . .

Second, the explicit statement of analytic paradigms lessens the likelihood of inadvertently importing hidden assumptions and concepts, since each new assumption and each new concept must be either logically *derivable* from the previous terms of the paradigm or explictly *incorporated* in it. The paradigm thus supplies a pragmatic and logical guide for the avoidance of *ad hoc* (i.e., logically irresponsible) hypotheses.

Third, paradigms advance the *cumulation* of theoretical interpretation. . . .

Fourth, paradigms, by their very arrangement, suggest the systematic cross-tabulation of presumably significant concepts and may thus sensitize the analyst to types of empirical and theoretic problems which might otherwise be overlooked. They promote *analysis* rather than concrete description. They direct our attention, for example, to the components of social behavior, to possible strains and tensions among these components, and thereby to sources of departure from the behavior which is socially expectable.

Fifth, and in this accounting, finally, paradigms

make for the codificaton of methods of *qualitative* analysis in a manner approximating the logical, if not the empirical, rigor of *quantitative* analysis.[31]

⌊This type of paradigm is a device for raising the conceptual framework to the level of explanatory theory by arranging the selected relevant concepts into their determinant-consequent relationships and by specifying linkages and directions among concepts.⌉This was done by Stycos[32] in designing a paradigm for rendering explicit the antecedents of high fertility in the exploratory phase of research in Puerto Rico. Chart 11-3 illustrates the possibilities of this device. The format enables the reader to see at a glance the major categories of influences being brought to bear, as well as their hypothesized directions. This paradigm served both as a guide to the research undertaken in Puerto Rico and as a way of designating the direction of the empirical outcomes.

More frequently used for such a schema today is the term "model," which Jackson recommends should be changed from "conceptual model" to "measurement model" after the concepts within the schema have been operationalized for measurement.[33] The conceptual model usually is expressed graphically, with arrows to designate direction and other graphic devices to portray process and movement. These directional features are not, of course, found in the taxonomic cross-classification format of the conceptual framework from which the concepts have been drawn.

To date, few rules or procedures have been developed to aid the student in the creation of such theoretical schemas before he undertakes his research. My colleagues and I have developed three principles for arraying concepts in the conceptual model. We first cluster the concepts into categories, keeping those referring to value orientations and attitudes in one row, and those referring to behavior patterns in another, and array these in blocks along a continuum of specificity-generality and of degrees of conceptual distance from the dependent variable to be explained. These principles are illustrated by the format found in Chart 11-4. It is the conceptual model developed for the second phase of the study of the family factors in effectiveness of family planning in Puerto Rico.[34] The conceptual framework from which these concepts were drawn was the interactional framework because of the great emphasis in this study on the interactional components of effective family decision-making. It has been termed an "accounting model" (from its objective to account for as much variance as possible in the dependent variable). This format portrays graphically the interplay of concepts by placing the determinant or independent variables on the left of the chart and the dependent variables on the extreme right. In between are the variables which the theory suggests mediate and explain the impact of the independent variables.

The accounting model depicted in Chart 11-4 is a highly visual format for arranging concepts which, when operationalized, can be easily adapted for a factor analytic and partial- and multiple-correlation series of analyses. This fulfills the "accounting" purpose of the model to ascertain how much of the variance in the dependent variables is accounted for by each block of antecedent variables singly, and what the combined influence is of all blocks.

The "accounting model" used in the Puerto Rican study incorporates some of the advantages of the "causal-sequence model" developed by University of Michigan social scientists, which is well illustrated by James Morgan's schema for portraying the chain of sequences of influences preceding a consumer decision.[35] The causal-sequence model seeks to specify the extent of the causal jump between allegedly determinant variables and the dependent variable.

[31]Robert K. Merton, *Social Theory and Social Structure* (New York: The Free Press, 1957), 14–15.

[32]J. M. Stycos, *Family and Fertility in Puerto Rico* (New York: Columbia University Press, 1955), 249.

[33]Jay Jackson, *A Conceptual and Measurement Model for Norms and Roles* (Lawrence: University of Kansas, 1963).

[34]Reuben Hill, J. M. Stycos, and K. W. Back, *The Family and Population Control* (Chapel Hill: University of North Carolina Press, 1959), 220.

[35]See especially Charts II.3 and II.4 in James N. Morgan, "Household Decision-Making," in *Models of Household Decision-Making*, ed. by Nelson N. Foote (New York: New York University Press, 1961), 88, 92.

CHART 11-3. A PARADIGM OF THE ANTECEDENTS AND CONSEQUENCES OF HIGH FERTILITY

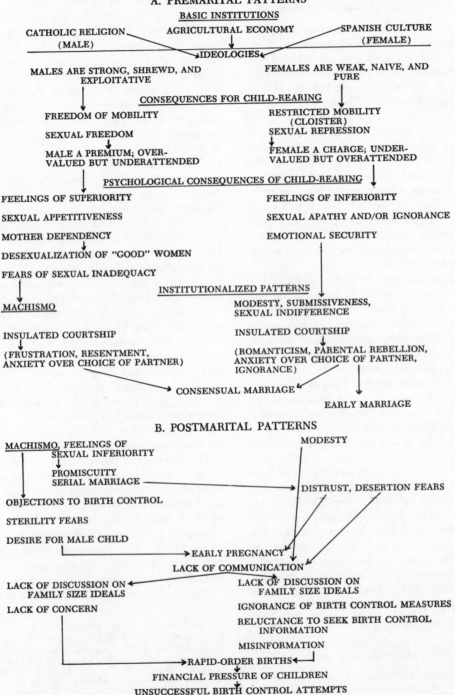

A. PREMARITAL PATTERNS

BASIC INSTITUTIONS

CATHOLIC RELIGION   AGRICULTURAL ECONOMY   SPANISH CULTURE
(MALE)   (FEMALE)

IDEOLOGIES

MALES ARE STRONG, SHREWD, AND   FEMALES ARE WEAK, NAIVE, AND
EXPLOITATIVE   PURE

CONSEQUENCES FOR CHILD-REARING

FREEDOM OF MOBILITY   RESTRICTED MOBILITY
                                       (CLOISTER)
SEXUAL FREEDOM   SEXUAL REPRESSION

MALE A PREMIUM; OVER-   FEMALE A CHARGE; UNDER-
VALUED BUT UNDERATTENDED   VALUED BUT OVERATTENDED

PSYCHOLOGICAL CONSEQUENCES OF CHILD-REARING

FEELINGS OF SUPERIORITY   FEELINGS OF INFERIORITY

SEXUAL APPETITIVENESS   SEXUAL APATHY AND/OR IGNORANCE

MOTHER DEPENDENCY   EMOTIONAL SECURITY

DESEXUALIZATION OF "GOOD" WOMEN

FEARS OF SEXUAL INADEQUACY

INSTITUTIONALIZED PATTERNS

MACHISMO   MODESTY, SUBMISSIVENESS,
                                       SEXUAL INDIFFERENCE

INSULATED COURTSHIP   INSULATED COURTSHIP

(FRUSTRATION, RESENTMENT,   (ROMANTICISM, PARENTAL REBELLION,
ANXIETY OVER CHOICE OF PARTNER)   ANXIETY OVER CHOICE OF PARTNER,
                                       IGNORANCE)

CONSENSUAL MARRIAGE

EARLY MARRIAGE

B. POSTMARITAL PATTERNS

MACHISMO, FEELINGS OF   MODESTY
SEXUAL INFERIORITY

PROMISCUITY
SERIAL MARRIAGE   DISTRUST, DESERTION FEARS

OBJECTIONS TO BIRTH CONTROL

STERILITY FEARS

DESIRE FOR MALE CHILD

EARLY PREGNANCY

LACK OF COMMUNICATION

LACK OF DISCUSSION ON   LACK OF DISCUSSION ON
FAMILY SIZE IDEALS   FAMILY SIZE IDEALS

LACK OF CONCERN   IGNORANCE OF BIRTH CONTROL MEASURES

                                       RELUCTANCE TO SEEK BIRTH CONTROL
                                       INFORMATION

                                       MISINFORMATION

RAPID-ORDER BIRTHS

FINANCIAL PRESSURE OF CHILDREN

UNSUCCESSFUL BIRTH CONTROL ATTEMPTS

DESERTION, EXTRAMARITAL RELATIONS,
STERILIZATION, CHILD DISPERSAL

CHART 11-4. SCHEMA SPECIFYING THE HYPOTHETICAL INTERRELATIONSHIPS OF SELECTED ANTECEDENT, INTERVENING, AND CONSEQUENT VARIABLES IN FERTILITY PLANNING.

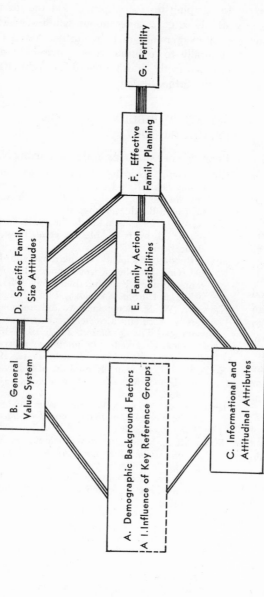

A. DEMOGRAPHIC BACKGROUND FACTORS
Residence
Occupation
Education
Religion
Economic status (rental value)
Type of marital union
Age at marriage

A1. INFLUENCE OF KEY REFERENCE GROUPS
Resident referents
Occupation colleagues
Classmates
Fellow parishioners, etc.
Extent of social participation
Patrons of birth control clinics

B. GENERAL VALUE SYSTEM
Fatalism-striving
Traditionalism-modernism
Aspirations for self and children
Tendencies toward general planning

C. INFORMATIONAL AND ATTITUDINAL ATTRIBUTES
Information on methods
Attitudes toward birth control
Extent of agreement on birth control

D. SPECIFIC FAMILY SIZE ATTITUDES
Attitudes toward importance of children
Ideal family size (present and past)
Summary index of family size preferences
Sense of pressure of fertility on family resources
Interest in spacing children

E. FAMILY ACTION POSSIBILITIES
Marital happiness
Agreement on general issues
Sexual satisfaction
Communication on general issues
Communication on family size ideals and birth control
Modesty handicaps
Familistic organization types:
  Degree of wife autonomy
  Degree of male dominance
Extent of prohibitions exercised by husband
Family readiness for action on birth control

F. EFFECTIVE FAMILY PLANNING
Proportion using birth control methods
Length and regularity of use
Success rate

G. FERTILITY
Different measures

This schema is fully discussed by Hoffman and Lippitt, who ascribe many of the conflicting research findings about the interrelations between family and child behavior variables in the family literature to the breadth of the causal jump between these variables. In their words: "Perhaps one of the most frequent problems with existing research is the size of the 'causal jump' in the sequential framework. Too broad a jump, without operationalizing the intervening steps, makes it difficult to infer whether any particular finding may be regarded as evidence for one or another linking process."[36]

There are probably as many other ways to depict models as there are useful analogies to draw from. Farber[37] has organized his book around a conceptual model of conflict between demands of a *closed system of orderly replacement*, maximizing intergenerational continuity, and an *open system of permanent sexual availability* of all adults, maximizing personal choice. The stimulation to theory construction of such a novel conceptual model has made for a challenging treatise. Mary Brodbeck[38] has discussed the many confusing uses to which the term "model" has been put and would be distressed to hear the uses to which it has been put here. She would restrict the use of "model" to isomorphic theories where two theories whose laws have the same form are isomorphic or structurally similar to each other. If the laws of one theory have the same form as the laws of another theory, then one may be said to be a *model* for the other. Family theory probably has no profitable uses for the term "model" within this restricted meaning. What phenomenon is sufficiently similar in its form to family behavior that we might better study it in order to better understand the laws which govern familial actions?

The loose use of the term "model" is really analogous to the "working model" which is put together and tested before being standardized for large-scale application. The model is ideal for shaping up for empirical test one or more middle-range theories about families which, if confirmed, might then be further tested cross-culturally to ascertain their universality or be returned to the drafting board for slight changes before further testing.

SELECTED BIBLIOGRAPHY ON FAMILY THEORY

RECENT APPRAISALS OF FAMILY THEORY

CHRISTENSEN, HAROLD T. Development of the family field of study. In *Handbook of marriage and the family*, ed. by Harold T. Christensen. Chicago: Rand McNally, 1964.

GOODE, W. J. Horizons in family theory. In *Sociology today*, ed. by R. K. Merton *et al.* New York: Basic Books, 1959.

HILL, REUBEN. Sociology of marriage and family behavior, 1945-56: a trend report and bibliography. Oxford, England: Blackwell, 1958, published as *Current Sociology*, 1958, 7, 1, iv-98.

KEPHART, W. M. Some knowns and unknowns in family research: a sociological critique. *Marriage and Family Living*, 1957, 19, 7-15.

KIRKPATRICK, CLIFFORD. *The family: as process and institution.* New York: Ronald Press, 1963.

KOLB, W. L. Sociologically established family norms and democratic values. *Social Forces*, 1948, 26, 451-456.

KOMAROVSKY, MIRRA & WALLER, WILLARD. Studies of the family. *American Journal of Sociology*, 1945, 50, 443-451.

KONIG, RENE. Materialien zur soziologie der familie. *Schriftenreibe bettrage zur soziologie und sozialphilosophie.* I, Bem, Francke, 1946.

MOGEY, JOHN. Introduction: changes in the family. *International Social Science Journal*, 1962, 14, 411-424.

MOWRER, E. R. & MOWRER, HARRIET. The social psychology of marriage. *American Sociological Review*, 1951, 16, 27-36.

PARSONS, TALCOTT & BALES, ROBERT F. *Family, socialization and interaction process,* New York: The Free Press, 1955.

SCHELSKY, HELMUT. Die gegenwartige problemlage der familiensoziologie. In *Soziologische forschung in unserer zeit*, ed. by K. G. Specht. Köln, Westdeutscher Verlag, 1951, 282-296.

WINCH, R. F. Marriage and the family. In *Review of sociology*, ed. by J. B. Gittler. New York: John Wiley, 1957, 346-390.

ZELDITCH, MORRIS, JR. Family, marriage and kinship. In *Handbook of modern sociology*, ed.

---

[36]Lois W. Hoffman and Ronald Lippitt, "The Measurement of Family Life Variables," in *Handbook of Research Methods in Child Development*, ed. by Paul Mussen (New York: John Wiley & Sons, Inc., 1960) 947.

[37]Bernard Farber, *The Family: Organization and Interaction* (San Francisco: Chandler, 1964). See especially his discussion, Chap. 4, "A Conceptual Model of the Contemporary Family," 103-133.

[38]Mary Brodbeck, "Models, Meaning and Theories," in *Symposium on Sociological Theory,* ed. by L. Gross (New York: Harper and Row, Publishers, 1959), 373-403.

by R. E. L. Faris. Chicago: Rand McNally, 1964, 680–733.

CONCEPTUAL FRAMEWORKS FOR FAMILY STUDY

1. General Discussion

HILL, REUBEN & HANSEN, DONALD A. The identification of conceptual frameworks utilized in family study. *Marriage and Family Living*, 1960, 22, 299–311.

NYE, IVAN. Introduction. In *Conceptual frameworks for the study of the family*, ed. by Nye and Berardo. New York: Crowell Collier and Macmillan, Inc., 1966.

2. The Institutional Framework

KOENIG, DANIEL J. & BAYER, ALAN E. The institutional frame of reference in family study. *Ibid.*

SIRJAMAKI, JOHN. The institutional approach. In *Handbook of marriage and the family, op cit.,* 33–50.

3. The Structural Functional Framework

BELL, NORMAN F. & VOGEL, E. F. Toward a framework for functional analysis of family behavior. In *A modern introduction to the family*, ed. by Bell and Vogel. New York: The Free Press, 1960, 1–33.

McINTYRE, JENNIE. The structural functional approach to family study. In *Conceptual frameworks for the study of the family, op. cit.*

PITTS, JESSE R. The structural functional approach. In *Handbook of marriage and the family, op. cit.,* 51–124.

4. The Interactional and Situational Frameworks

BOSSARD, JAMES H. S. & BOLL, ELEANOR S. *Family situations.* Philadelphia: University of Pennsylvania Press, 1943.

BURGESS, E. W. The family as a unity of interacting personalities. *Family*, 1926, 7, 3–9.

RALLINGS, E. M. The situational approach. In *Conceptual frameworks for the study of the family, op. cit.*

SCHWENEVELDT, JAY. The interactional framework to the family. *Ibid.*

STRYKER, SHELDON. Symbolic interaction as an approach to family research. *Marriage and Family Living*, 1959, 21, 111–119.

STRYKER, SHELDON. The interactional and situational approaches. In *Handbook of marriage and the family, op. cit.,* 125–170.

WALLER, WILLARD & HILL, REUBEN. *The family: a dynamic interpretation.* New York: Holt, Rinehart & Winston, Inc., 1951.

5. The Developmental Approach

DUVALL, EVELYN M. *Family development.* Philadelphia: J. B. Lippincott Co., 1962.

HILL, REUBEN. Methodological problems with the developmental approach to family study. *Family Process*, March, 1964, 3, 1, 186–206.

HILL, REUBEN & RODGERS, R. H. The development approach. In *Handbook of marriage and the family, op. cit.,* 171–211.

RODGERS, R. H. Toward a theory of family development. *Journal of marriage and the family*, August, 1964, 26, 3, 262–270.

ROWE, GEORGE P. The development conceptual framework. In *Conceptual frameworks for the study of the family, op. cit.*

6. The Anthropological Approach

BERARDO, FELIX. The anthropological approach to the family. *Ibid.*

LEWIS, OSCAR. An anthropological approach to family studies. *American Journal of Sociology*, March, 1950, 468–475.

7. The Psychoanalytic Approach

ACKERMAN, NATHAN. *The psychodynamics of family life.* New York: Basic Books, 1958.

BAYER, ALAN E. The psychoanalytic frame of reference in family study. In *Conceptual frameworks for the study of the family, op. cit.*

SPIEGEL, J. P. & KLUCKHOHN, F. R. *Integration and conflict in family behavior.* Report No. 27, Topeka, Kansas: Group for the Advancement of Psychiatry, 1954.

8. Miscellaneous Approaches

BROWN, WILLIAM D. A social psychological conceptual framework for the study of the family. In *Conceptual frameworks for the study of the family, op. cit.*

DEAN, K. I. & KARGMAN, M. W. Is there a legal conceptual framework for the study of the American family? *Ibid.*

RICE, ANN SMITH. An economic framework for viewing the family. *Ibid.*

RIBER, S. R. Western Christian framework for viewing the family. *Ibid.*

ASSESSMENTS OF THEORETICAL DEVELOPMENTS IN SUBSTANTIVE AREAS

1. Mate Selection and Premarital Sex Behavior

BURCHINAL, LEE G. The premarital dyad and love involvement. In *Handbook of marriage and the family, op. cit.,* 623–675.

EHRMAN, WINSTON. Marital and nonmarital sexual behavior. *Ibid.,* 585–623.

GIRARD, ALAIN. *Le choix du conjoint.* Paris: Presses Universitaires de France, 1964.

JACOBSOHN, PETER & MATHENY, ADAM R. Mate selection in open marriage systems. *International Journal of Comparative Sociology*, September, 1962, 3, 1, 98–124.

KATZ, ALVIN & HILL, REUBEN. Residential propinquity and marital selection: a review of theory, method and fact. *Marriage and Family Living*, February, 1958, 20-1, 27–35.

THARP, ROLAND G. Psychological patterning in marriage. *Psychological Bulletin*, March, 1963, *60*:2, 97–117.

VINCENT, CLARK E. *Unmarried Mothers*. New York: The Free Press, 1961.

WINCH, ROBERT F. *Mate Selection*. New York: Harper & Row, Publishers, 1958.

2. *Marriage and Marriage Adjustment*

BERNARD, JESSIE. The adjustment of married mates. In *Handbook of marriage and the family, op. cit.*, 675–740.

BOWERMAN, CHARLES E. Prediction studies. *Ibid.*, 215–247.

LEVINGER, GEORGE. Marital cohesiveness and dissolution: an integrative review. *Journal of Marriage and the Family*, February, 1965, *27*, 1, 19–28.

MOSS, J. JOEL. Teen-age marriage: cross-national trends and sociological factors in the decision of when to marry. *Journal of Marriage and the Family*, May, 1965, *27*, 2, 230–243.

3. *The Family as Social Group*

FREEDMAN, RONALD. The sociology of human fertility: a trend report and bibliography. Oxford, England: Blackwell, 1962, issued as *Current Sociology*, 1961-62, *10-11*, 2.

HANSEN, DONALD A. & HILL, REUBEN. Families under stress. In *Handbook of marriage and the family, op. cit.*, 782–823.

KONIG, RENE. Family and authority: the German father in 1955. *British Sociological Review*, 1957, 5.

MORIOKA, KIYOMI. A critical review of studies in the family life cycle. ICU *Social Science Journal*, 1964, No. 5. Translated from Japanese by Y. H. Kim.

ROLLINS, JAMES M. Two empirical tests of a parsonian theory of family authority patterns. *Family Life Coordinator*, January-April, 1963, *12*, 1-2, 5–79.

TASCH, RUTH J. The role of the father in the family. *Journal of Experimental Education*, June, 1952, *20*, 319–362.

4. *The Family in Transaction With Collateral Systems*

BOTT, ELIZABETH. *Family and social network: roles, norms and external relationships in ordinary urban families*. London: Tavistock Publications, 1957.

MOGEY, JOHN. The family and community in urban-industrial societies. In *Handbook of marriage and the family, op. cit.*, 501–535.

SUSSMAN, MARVIN & BURCHINAL, LEE. Kin family networks: unheralded structures in current conceptualizations of family functioning. *Marriage and Family Living*, August, 1962, *24*, 3, 320–332.

5. *The Family and Personality*

BRIM, ORVILLE, G., JR. *Education for child rearing*. New York: Russell Sage Foundation, 1959.

BRONFENBRENNER, URIE. Socialization and social class through time and space. In *Readings in social psychology*, ed. by Eleanor Maccoby *et al.* New York: Holt, Rinehart & Winston, Inc., 1958, 400–425.

CLAUSEN, JOHN A. & WILLIAMS, JUDITH R. Sociological correlates of child behavior: family structure and socialization processes. *Sixty-second yearbook of the National Society for the Study of Education, Part 1, Child Psychology, 1963*. Chicago: University of Chicago Press, 1963, 62–107.

DAGER, EDWARD Z. Socialization and personality development in the child. In *Handbook of marriage and the family, op. cit.*, 740–782.

LENNARD, HENRY I., BEAULIEU, MAURICE R., & EMBREY, NOLEN G. Interaction in families with a schizophrenic child. *Archives of General Psychiatry*, February, 1965, *12*, 166–183.

SPIEGEL, JOHN P. & BELL, NORMAN W. The family of the psychiatric patient. In *The American handbook of psychiatry*, ed. by Sylvano Arieti. New York: Norton, 1959, *1*, 114–149.

6. *The Family and Social Structure*

BARDIS, PANOS D. Family forms and variations historically considered. In *Handbook of marriage and the family, op. cit.*, 403–462.

CAVAN, RUTH SHONLE. Subcultural variations and mobility. *Ibid.*, 535–585.

GOODE, W. J. The theoretical importance of love. *American Sociological Review*, 1959, *24*, 38–47.

GOODE, W. J. Illegitimacy in the Caribbean social structure. *American Sociological Review*, February, 1960, *25*, 21–30.

MICHEL, ANDREE. Famille et urbanisation: inventaire des recherches recentes. *Current Sociology*, 1963–64, *12*, 1, 107–121.

ZELDITCH, MORRIS, JR. Family, marriage, kinship. In *Handbook of modern sociology*, ed. by Robert E. L. Faris. Chicago: Rand McNally, 1964, 699–715.

12.

IVAN NYE AND WILLIAM RUSHING

TOWARD FAMILY MEASUREMENT RESEARCH

PRESENT STATUS

In titling this discussion "Toward Family Measurement Research," we are not suggesting that no research on family measurement has been done. On the contrary, researchers on family behavior and attitudes have been very active for many years in research strongly empirical in orientation. The result is that many measures have been developed. Straus has recently collected and briefly described over 200 of them. (1)

Even so, we feel justified in looking forward to projects specifically on family measurement because the voluminous research to date has, with only a very few exceptions, been directed toward describing family behavior or toward the exploration of relationships between family variables. The instruments that have been developed were developed as means to other ends. As a consequence, family measures have often been developed hurriedly, with inadequate pretesting and validation. Time devoted to their original construction has varied from a few days to a few weeks. The weaknesses in these instruments are, in our opinion, as much a consequence of inadequate time and concern as of inherent difficulties in the measurement of family properties. There are a few exceptions to the generalization that instruments have been only means to ends. It appears that the Hunt-Kogan (2) and the Geismar-Ayres (3) instru-

ments in social work and possibly two or three others in the field of sociology are exceptions, but whether there are two or three or five or six exceptions, the number is tiny, either with respect to the total number of instruments or the need for measurement of family properties.

The contrast with individual measurement is startling—in that field scores of instruments have been developed as central concerns of research and have been the focus of extensive validation research, critical reviews, and use in a variety of substantive research projects. This is not to say that we should be content with the level of methodological research in individual measurement. Since individual measurement developed first, family measurement is in a strategic position to avoid errors and to move beyond many of the limitations of instruments measuring the properties of individuals.

PROBLEMS AND OPPORTUNITIES IN CONCEPT CLARIFICATION

One of the problems in family measurement is the frequent lack of a clear and adequate statement of *what* is being measured. Recently we had an opportunity to see a particularly extreme example of this in the form of a sexual attitude "scale." It contained items related to premarital, extra-marital, and homosexual behavior, plus questions concerning the double standard and differences in male and female enjoyment of the sexual act. What did a total score represent (if anything)?

Although a majority of researchers have a clearer idea of what they are measuring, we feel that there is much room for improvement. This might be illustrated by one of the senior author's instruments that was constructed about seven years ago in studying the effects of maternal employment on family life. An objective was to determine how such employment affected

This selection is reprinted from: Ivan Nye, and William Rushing, "Toward Family Measurement Research," in Catherine S. Chilman (ed.), *Approaches to the Measurement of Family Change* (Welfare Research Report #4), Washington, D.C.: GPO, U.S. Department of Health, Education, and Welfare, 1966 [pp. 20–32. A segment from the original is omitted].

Scientific Paper 2566, Washington Agricultural Experiment Stations, Washington State University. Work on the paper was conducted under Project 1792 supported in part by a grant from the Welfare Administration of the Department of Health, Education, and Welfare.

the husband-wife relationship. The Burgess-Wallin multiple criteria scales were too long, so it was decided initially to employ single items to measure happiness, satisfaction, stability, and conflict. Since single item measures are not very reliable, these several items were scaled to see whether they, in fact, measured a single dimension. (4) They do, but what is it? Probably it is best termed marital adjustment but this is not a very specific concept. If the research were to be planned now, more attention would be devoted to concept clarification before beginning instrument construction.

To develop more clearly the issues and alternatives in concept clarification and specification, let us look at the concept of family integration. We select it as an example of a concept with some potential value to family research and action programs and one of sufficient breadth and complexity to illustrate the problems and opportunities for the researcher. In employing it as an example, we are not taking a position that it should necessarily have a high priority in instrument development.

CONCEPT IMAGERY

Lazarsfeld has stated that there are four steps in defining and measuring concepts in social research: 1) concept imagery; 2) concept specification; 3) selection of indicators (i.e., instruments to measure the concept); and 4) the construction of an index from the indicators. (5) Social research begins with imagery. The researcher begins by conjuring up certain images about that which he wants to investigate. What images does the concept, family integration, conjure up? What does it mean in an empirical sense? How does it differ from family cohesion or family solidarity? Since the family is a group, it will be well first to look at some of the ways in which the general concept of group integration has been used. At the outset, we will make no distinction between the terms group integration, group cohesion, and group solidarity. All have been used in the literature, but there appears to be significant difference in their uses.

One does not have to look hard to find a variety of definitions of group integration. Some

define it in terms of the field of "forces which are acting on members to stay in a group," (6) others prefer the notion of "sticking-togetherness" and use as an alternative definition the "resistance of a group to disruptive forces," (7) while still others define it as "the degree to which units of a social system are oriented toward optimizing rewards for other units of the system." (8) Certainly, group integration has no universal meaning. It has meant different things to different writers.

The same is true for the concept of family integration. In one study it is described in terms of "the degree to which the family functions as a unit in attaining common goals with the interest of the individual members being considered," (9) in another it is defined in terms of "the extent of shared activities," (10) and in a recent study it is defined "as the degree to which a family member is oriented toward optimizing rewards and satisfactions for other family members." (11) Clearly, more precision and agreement in defining and measuring this concept are indicated.

Nevertheless, these definitions, vague and general as they sometimes are, do conjure up certain images concerning the empirical referents of groups and family integration. All appear to be consistent with the view that integration refers to the linkages between individual family members and the linkage of the individual member of the family as a whole. Final conceptualization of group integration, as well as its operational definition, must be framed in terms of this imagery.

CONCEPT SPECIFICATION

The next step in the research process is to analyze the original imagery, to break it down into components or dimensions. This means that since integration refers to linkages among individuals and of individuals to the group, analysis of the concept of family integration must involve splitting family linkages and relationships into their various components, properties, or dimensions.

Specific dimensions of a general concept may be arrived at in several ways. They may be derived from the overall concept; one dimension may be derived from another; dimensions may be derived from reviewing the literature to see the various ways the overall concept has been defined; or they may be selected because empirically observed correlations between them have been reported in previous research. Regardless of the procedure employed, however, it is important that the overall concept be specified in some detail. This is especially true for a concept like family integration, because of its multi-dimensional character.

In writing about social integration in general, Landecker has said: "We do not know enough about social integration to postulate any one set of data as the index of integration as such." (12) That is, group integration is multi-dimensional —it consists of a complex combination of phenomena, rather than a simple and directly observable property of group life. Our search of the literature indicates that at least six distinct dimensions of group or family integration have been studied. (13)

1. Associational integration: The range of interaction in common activities. Associational integration refers simply to the frequency with which group members are in contact and interact.
2. Affectual integration: The degree of positive affect individuals express for each other. Concern here is with those sentiments which have significance for each group member's self—expressions of love, respect, appreciation, and recognition for each other.
3. Consensual integration: The degree of consensus among group members on beliefs and values. This has sometimes been called communicative integration.
4. Functional integration: The degree to which group members exchange services. That is, the degree of interdependence among group members. The opposite of functional integration is the self-sufficiency and autonomy of a group.
5. Normative integration: This dimension concerns the group's control over individual members. In general, it usually refers to the degree to which members conform to group norms.
6. Goal integration: The extent to which individual members subordinate their interests and goals to those of the group as a whole. In family research, this concept is often referred to as familism.

To our knowledge, only some of these have been used in research on family integration. Certainly all have not been employed in a single study. Too often in family research, as in social research generally, the multidimensional character of a concept is not recognized. (14)

Researchers purport to measure what is actually only one dimension of family integration but do not restrict their generalizations to this one dimension.

In the formulation of these dimensions of integration we have followed two guidelines. (1) The dimension must be conceptually consistent with the original imagery that family integration refers to the linkages and relationships among family members and of the individual member to the family as a whole. It seems to us that each dimension refers to separate ways in which family members may be linked together. (2) The dimension must have common usage in sociology and social psychology, or in studies conducted in the family research field. Since all six dimensions are taken largely from literature in these fields, they fulfill this requirement. Nevertheless, some persons may question the inclusion of one or more of these components as a form of family integration. Others may choose to modify these dimensions or add other dimensions. But all will probably agree that this specification of the concept of family integration results in more precise statements than do the more general and all-encompassing definitions.

The importance of concept specification should be clearly recognized, for the way the concept is specified will determine what the research discovers, since operational definitions will be based upon it. Concept specification accordingly has important implications for the problem of internal validity.

INTERNAL VALIDITY

The requirements of internal validity add up to the question: Does the operational definition lead to measurement of that which the study purports to measure? Specifically, is the instrument logically derived from the definition given to the concept? Is the selection of indicators rigidly controlled by the definition of the concept?

Much research in family integration cannot answer these questions in the affirmative. In one study, for example, family integration is defined in terms of family members optimizing the rewards and satisfaction of others, but included among items in the instruments are joint attendance at community events, joint attendance outside the community, and joint formal participation. Although joint activities may represent a form of integration, there are so many questions one may raise as to whether they represent members' efforts to optimize the satisfactions of each other that the intrinsic relationship between the conceptualization and the items in the instrument is tenuous, indeed. In other studies, we wonder if the instrument has anything at all to do with integration; in one study, integration is defined as "the mutual coordination of domestic roles" but is operationalized with responses to personality items.

Poor internal validity often results from one of two factors, or both. First, research procedure may go in a reverse direction; the researcher begins by collecting his data and then tries to formulate a concept to fit the items included in the instrument. This was obviously the case in a recent study of family integration. Sometimes this procedure may succeed, in that a form of logical consistency is achieved between conceptual and operational definitions. But often it does not; since the construction of the intsrument was not controlled by explicit conceptualization, the nature of the data may be at variance with the conceptual definition. Because data are already collected, the instrument cannot be modified.

Poor internal validity may also result from failure to specify the original overall concept. This may result in the operationalization of one dimension of integration, when in fact the researcher intended to measure another dimension. (This seems to be clearly the case in one of the examples mentioned above. Data were collected on joint participation in common activities, but the stated objective was to measure the degree to which family members optimized each others' rewards and satisfaction.)

Before outlining some guidelines which will help assure the internal validity of research on family integration, it is necessary to ask: What is the conceptual status of family integration, aside from the fact that it is a multidimensional concept? Zetterberg distinguishes between *basic* and *derived* concepts. (15) Basic concepts refer to relatively simple and uncomplicated phenom-

ena; the concepts of activity, attitudes, and sentiments are examples of basic concepts. These concepts as introduced are undefined; their meanings are conveyed by descriptions and examples from the empirical world. They represent nothing more than an assumption of an agreement that we may use certain words in certain ways. Basic concepts are the beginning points in terms of basic concepts. They refer to more complex phenomena; to phenomena that are combinations of the more elementary and uncomplicated phenomena. Since the concept of group integration consists of several components of group life, it is certainly a derived concept. (16)

We may illustrate how certain dimensions of group integration may be defined in terms of basic concepts. We can take the following as basic properties of all group life:

Members
Activities
Interaction
Sentiments (which group members have toward each other)
Values

As derived concepts we could have:

Associational integration, defined as the degree to which group members interact in common activities;

Affectual integration, defined in terms of mutual positive sentiment among group members;

Consensual integration, defined as the degree to which group members agree in their values.

Our present purpose is not to argue that family integration must be defined in terms of these precise concepts. Rather, it is to illustrate that family integration is a complex phenomenon composed of several basic family properties. Its definition must therefore be based on concepts which have reference to these basic properties.

It is, of course, possible to define concepts without making explicit distinctions between basic and derived concepts. Probably in more cases than not in social research, derived concepts are only implicitly defined in terms of basic concepts. We think it is essential that the process be made explicit. Otherwise, misunderstandings concerning the meaning of the derived concept are likely, since the derived concept is defined, explicitly or implicitly, in terms of basic concepts. Agreement on the meaning of the derived concept is more likely, once agreement on the meanings of the basic concepts is reached. In the above example, for instance, we are more likely to reach agreement on the meanings of associational, affectual, and consensual integration, once we have agreed on what we mean by members, activities, interaction, sentiments, and values.

To assure an affirmative reply to the question underlying the demands of internal validity—is the selection of indicators rigidly controlled by the definition of the concept?—the construction of an instrument to measure family integration must be carefully guided by the following considerations:

1. The concept must be specified in detail. This we have begun by formulating six dimensions of family integration. But each dimension in turn is defined in terms of more basic concepts. Therefore, items entering the instrument to measure family integration must be designed to measure these basic concepts—activities, interaction, values, and sentiments. Consequently, questions about what should or should not enter the instrument should be answered by referring back to these basic concepts, rather than by referring immediately to the concept of family integration.

2. Each of the basic concepts must be further broken down and defined within the context of the family. For example, there are many forms of association: eating together, going to church together, visiting relatives together, going to movies together, watching TV together, *ad infinitum*. The same can be said of the other basic concepts. It is imperative, therefore, that all items entering the instrument be rigidly controlled by a listing of family-relevant content for each basic concept. Furthermore, items entering the instrument must collect information that is of some significance for the family. For example, agreement or disagreement on the belief that movies are not as good as they used to be is probably of less significance than agreement or disagreement concerning the proper way to rear children.

3. Since the concept of family integration is concerned with relationships and interaction among family members, a logically valid instrument must obtain information from more than one member of the family. *Direct* measures of consensus or mutual affect, for example, can be obtained only when two or more members are included in the analysis. *Indirect* measures can be obtained through the study of only one member of the family, but these measures are of perceived consensus and perceived attitudes of others; they may or may not be accurate reflections of the group condition and others' attitudes.

While these three principles are, of course, not the only ones that must be heeded in constructing a valid research instrument, they must certainly be included.

This discussion of problems of clarifying and specifying the concept of family integration, as well as the problems of internal validity, does not exhaust the range of difficulties involved in developing clear conceptualizations and precise measurement in social research. It only illustrates some of the important problems that must be solved before these goals can be achieved.

OPERATIONALIZATION OF CONCEPTS

Obviously, there is not enough space nor the need to discuss all the problems in operationalization. We shall focus primarily on structured instruments, although some of the issues relate to observational and other techniques also. That items be selected on the basis of the dimension of the concept, that questions be clear and response categories adequate, that separate ideas requiring separate answers not be included in one question, and that the instrument be no longer than necessary are percepts widely understood but often inadequately executed. The net effect of inadequate measurement is that many research projects have concluded with findings of "no significant differences," obscuring the fact that the relationships that really exist were not disclosed by the instruments employed.

Less generally understood (or at least acknowledged) by sociologists in family research are systematic response distortion (sometimes termed response set) and halo effect. Possibly the greatest response distortion is caused by defensiveness. Most husband-wife and parent-child behavior is characterized by behavior and attitude patterns which are highly valued. For some it is difficult to admit hostile attitudes or conflict within one's family or within oneself. This reluctance may be at the conscious or unconscious level. Further complicating the picture is the occasional individual who is overly critical of himself and of his social relationships —a behavior pattern sometimes referred to as "plus-getting." The effect of such distortion is to produce a spurious correlation between a subjective measure and another measure, either subjective or objective, provided both possess a social desirability component. The same result is produced by "halo effect" when the same rater scores two measures on the same individual. Many "significant differences" reflect nothing more than response distortion or halo effect.

Obviously it is easier to recognize these problems than to cope with them. Possible remedies include lie scales, social desirability measures, indirect or disguised objective tests, possibly projective techniques, and other devices. We feel that these are serious problems which have been too often ignored and that in a program of methodological research they should receive major attention.

INTERNAL ANALYSIS: RELIABILITY AND INTERNAL CONSISTENCY

By employing either a split-half test or a test-retest procedure, sociologists generally have given attention to the problem of random error in testing instruments of family measurement. One or the other of these procedures is an adequate test of the reliability of an instrument in a given research operation. However, sociologists have done little in the way of having the instrument administered to different populations. All of these procedures deserve attention in a research project centered on the development of versatile instruments that can be used independently of the particular skills and knowledge of the person who developed them.

If a measure involves variation along a dimension, we are disposed to place considerable emphasis on rigorous tests of unidimensionality. We have recently seen a book dealing with harshness and leniency in discipline. There is a clear assumption of unidimensionality, but the only "test" of it is the opinion of a number of professional and nonprofessional people. With the availability of the Guttman scaling technique, such assumptions can be tested, and, if the scale does not measure up, it can be revised and improved. We must be especially

critical of item analysis in which the researcher feels that he has established internal consistency by finding statistically significant relationship between individual items and the scale score. Actually, there is enough response distortion in many family instruments to provide a statistically significant relationship, even if no relationship exists between the property measured by the item and that measured by the several other items in the "scale." Of course, not all measures assume a single dimension; and, for those that do not, there is no need for scale analysis.

EXTERNAL VALIDATION

Validation through association with established measures of family properties or groups known to be different has been rather rare. In some areas, such as marital relationships, perhaps the logic of the relationship has been sufficiently compelling so that it was usually felt to be unnecessary. Some exceptions do come to mind, for example, Locke's use of a sample of divorced couples and a sample of couples judged to be happily married to validate his measure of marital success. (17) Also, Burgess and Cottrell validated self-ratings of marital happiness by the judgments of another couple, (18) and Geismar and Ayres employed criterion groups.

We are disposed to take the position, at least initially, that in a family measurement project any measure developed should be subjected to external validation. It may be, of course, that there are useful family properties which are impossible to validate against external criteria, but we would be inclined to accept that conclusion only after exploring all alternatives. The external validation of family measures is one aspect of family measurement that has made little, if any, progress since the early work of Burgess, Cottrell, and Locke. Careful attention to this aspect of measurement is indicated.

APPLICABILITY: POPULATIONS, FUNCTIONS, AND ADMINISTRATIONS

In this area, family measurement (as well as other sociological measurement) has a distinctly provincial look. Sociological researchers have gathered the necessary data under specific research conditions for a specific purpose, often under conditions of anonymity. They have sometimes given serious attention to the validity and reliability of the instruments employed, insofar as their own project was concerned, but they have given little consideration to whether the instrument could be employed with other types of populations, by other persons, or for other than basic research purposes. In a broad sense, these are all problems of reliability, since they pose the question of whether the instrument measures without distortion under different conditions of measurement. If family research instrumentation is to progress, it is necessary to develop instruments that are versatile in that they are reliable under a wide set of conditions: anonymous or identified; applicable to the various social classes and ethnic groups, to a range of age categories, and to both sexes; *and* virtually self-administering. We see a special problem in adapting measures of private family attitudes and behavior, developed under conditions of anonymity, to client evaluation where the client (and perhaps the administrator of the instrument) has a stake in the outcome. There is no simple way of doing this, but a way must be found through experimentation with wording of measures and widespread and careful testing of instruments on different populations and under a wide variety of conditions.

One improvement can easily be made in the area of applicability by spelling out in detail the circumstances present when the instrument was administered: by whom, the special or oral instructions given, and the scoring system employed. Also, it should be specified whether special permission of school boards or other governing units was obtained, whether special sponsorship from local organizations was available, and whether problems were encountered in establishing rapport with organizations or in public relations. However, such details would meet only a very small part of the general problem of developing versatile instruments, reliable under a wide variety of conditions. To produce instruments of such versatility, however, will require a long period of sustained research, including a great deal of testing, revision, and more testing.

NORMS

Norms, in the sense of reference points such as those established by standardized measures of the individual achievement and behavior, are almost if not entirely absent for family research instruments developed by sociologists. This can be explained by the fact that development of instruments for use by others has not been a primary objective. Instruments have been developed for a particular project, and the researcher neither designed them for wide and varied use nor took the time to develop the potential that may have been latent in them. Quite possibly the question whether norms should be developed should be considered selectively, instrument by instrument, or perhaps a general affirmative answer can be given when the problems earlier considered are solved. This may be looking a considerable distance ahead in the development of family measurement.

REFERENCES

1. STRAUS, MURRAY A. *Family measurement instruments.* Minneapolis, Minn.: University of Minnesota Family Study Center, vol. I, 1961 (dittoed), vol. II, 1964 (dittoed).
2. HUNT, J. McV. Measuring movement in social casework. *Journal of Social Casework,* 1948, *XXIX,* 343–351.
3. GEISMAR, L. L. and LaSORTE, MICHAEL. *Understanding the multi-problem family.* New York: The Association Press, 1964, chap. 3.
4. NYE, IVAN and MacDOUGAL, EVELYN. The dependent variable in marital research. *Pacific Sociological Review,* 1959, *II,* 67–70.
5. LAZARSFELD, PAUL F. Evidence and inference in social research. *Daedalus,* 1958, *LXXXVII,* 99–130.
6. BACK, KURT W. Influence through social communication. *The Journal of Abnormal and Social Psychology,* 1951, *XLVI,* 9.
7. GROSS, NEAL and MARTIN, WALTER E. On group cohesiveness. *American Journal of Sociology,* 1952, *LVII,* 546–564.
8. HAMBLIN, ROBERT L. Group integration during a crisis. *Human Relations,* 1958, *XI,* 67–76.
9. WILKENING, EUGENE A. Change in farm technology as related to families. *American Sociological Review,* 1954, *XIX,* 30.
10. CLELAND, COURTNEY B. Familism in rural Saskatchewan. *Rural Sociology,* 1955, *XX,* 252.
11. ROGERS, EVERETT M. and SEBALD, HANS. Familism, family integration, and kinship orientation. *Marriage and Family Living,* 1962, *XXIV,* 27.

12. LANDECKER, WERNER S. Types of integration and their measurement. *American Journal of Sociology*, 1951, *LVI*, 332.

13. Some of these are identical to or parallel the types in Landecker's formulation. See *ibid.*

14. For an exception, see Wilkening, *op. cit.* Also, Bernard Farber included two dimensions in his study, "An Index of Marital Integration," *Sociometry*, 1957, *XX*, 117–134.

15. There have been a number of discussions of validity in the literature. In one well-known discussion, four types of validity are identified—construct, content, concurrent and predictive. See, *Technical Recommendations for Psychological Tests and Diagnostic Techniques*. Washington, D.C.: American Psychological Association, 1954. There have been several criticisms and attempts to amplify this scheme. See in particular, Bechtoldt, H. P., "Construct Validity: A Critique," *American Psychologist*, 1959, *XXIV*, 619–629. See also, Campbell, Donald T., "Recommendations for NAPA Test Standards Regarding Construct, Trait, or Discriminate Validity," *American Psychologist*, 1960, *XV*, 546–554. In our analysis of validity we follow Louis Guttman's distinction between internal validity and external validity, "The Problem of Attitude and Opinion Measurement," in Stouffer, Samuel, *et al., Measurement and Prediction*. Princeton: Princeton University Press, 1963, 57–59. See also, Zetterberg, Hans L., *On Theory and Verification in Sociology*, rev. ed. Totowa, N.J.: The Bedminster Press, 1963, 44–50. The essential difference between the two is that the former refers to a logical relationship between the concept or theoretical definition and the operational definition, while the other refers to an empirical relationship between the operational definition and some "criterion" that is presumably correlated with the phenomenon being measured. For this reason, some authors distinguish between logical and empirical validity. See, for example, Jahoda, Marie, Deutsch, Morton, and Cook, Stuart W., *Research Methods in Social Relations*. New York: Holt, Rinehart & Winston, Inc., 1951, 108–114.

16. ZETTERBERG, HANS L. *On theory and verification in sociology*. New York: Tressler Press, 1954, 18.

17. LOCKE, HARVEY J. *Predicting adjustment in marriage: a comparison of a divorced and a happily married group*. New York: Holt, Rinehart & Winston, Inc., 1951.

18. BURGESS, ERNEST W. and COTTRELL, LEONARD S. *Predicting success or failure in marriage*. New York: Prentice-Hall, Inc., 1939.

PART 2

The Contemporary Family and the Family Circle

CHAPTER IV

Life Cycle and
Characteristics of Families

SOME APPROACHES TO THE STUDY of social phenomena appear "natural." The *life cycle*, or life history, since it represents a unity for any individual, is such a concept for the study of the family. From the point of view of the life cycle, specific points of change or important events that are "typical" or tend to reoccur with great regularity may be described coherently. For example, one way of describing the life cycle is to emphasize the *changes* in roles individuals occupy. Thus, a sequence might be, beginning at birth: infant, creeper, toddler, small child, child, early adolescent, adolescent, young adult, mature adult, middle-aged, elderly, aged. Sometimes emphasis is placed on the *crises* in the role changes, such as the transition from child to adolescent, from adolescent to adult, etc. Emphasis may also be placed on characteristics of the *forms of interactions* involved. This approach might focus on changes of status that are associated with family forms. In the latter case, the stages frequently described start with the single person and continue to married couple, conjugal unit with one child, conjugal unit with several children, family with children growing up, family (moving to empty nest) with children leaving the home, the middle-aged couple becoming grandparents, the elderly couple, and frequently, the surviving widow or widower.

The article by Paul C. Glick and Robert Parke, Jr., titled "New Approaches in Studying the Life Cycle of the Family," emphasizes aspects of data collection and interpretation on aspects of the family cycle *per se*.

Some historical data are presented which show the difference in typical life cycles in recent years and before the turn of the century. The major differences, as is noted in their Figure 13-1, occur in the death of a spouse at a later age, something that is easily understood in the light of the increased life expectancy generally experienced in the United States. Another item of information of interest is the lower average age at first marriage for women. Such relatively simple information is only a part of the study of life cycles, however, especially when the cohort approach is involved. The authors provide an excellent introduction through their footnotes to literature in this area.

Life cycles that are typical for one culture may not be typical for another, as the previous discussion of cross-cultural approaches has noted. In the article titled "Life Cycle Patterns in Japan, China, and the United States," Kiyomi Morioka suggests that the idea of life cycle which is associated with the study of the conjugal family may not be directly applicable to the *stem* type of family in Japan. From the analysis, a different set of cycle stages from those ordinarily encountered in the description of conjugal families is developed. The article adds to the materials on the Japanese family presented in Chapter 2, and additionally a brief description is presented of the Chinese family before the Communist regime. The description is historically interesting and may serve as a beginning point for students who may wish to examine the sparse literature on Communist China to find changes that have occurred in family types in that culture as the result of political changes.

The final section of this chapter draws descriptive information directly from a U.S. government report. In some areas of social science the state and federal agencies have enormous investments in data collection and reporting. This is particularly true in those areas where the government is concerned with regulation and standards. These reports range from information on numbers of individuals for purposes of establishing voting districts to the recording of health and other statistics in the maintenance and development of public health policies. The sources from the government publications are primary and may have failings, but those familiar with the data collection processes are quick to point out that the resources involved frequently lead to degrees of accuracy in data collection in social matters that are higher than most other research organizations can afford to provide. Particularly in matters of registration and enumeration, these sources of information are invaluable. The section reprinted from the *Vital and Health Statistics Reports on Marriage Statistics Analysis,* United States, 1962, is representative of the professional work from such sources. Additional materials from government publications will be encountered in the body of this volume.

There are many aspects of descriptive statistics in the study of marriage and the family that cannot be presented in a volume with limited space. Some of these will be encountered in incidental ways in subsequent articles, but other items of information will only come to the attention of the student as he broadens his horizon and pursues readings beyond the limited information that can be presented directly here. There are many interesting aspects of change that tend to be defined as historical or episodic which could be used in exploring comparatively the consequences of certain types of changes in family form. There is a question about whether there is any historical period that can be taken as typical, but wars, depressions, inflations, and those occasional lulls in between, lead to the question of: What is typical? To take one illustration, during the period of the Great Depression, one of the consequences of the economic deprivation felt was "doubling up" of families, sometimes with unrelated families living together, although more often with related families living together, and even more often married couples living with one of the parental families. As the Depression passed, the tendency to double up decreased, but during World War II and immediately after, when there was a great increase in marriages with the return of veterans and a concomitant housing shortage, doubling up reached a high of seven percent of married couples living with relatives. In 1967, the latest year for which data are available at this writing, only 1.6 percent of married couples lived with relatives. Clearly, the life cycle for those who live with relatives and those who do not is different. These variations and the analysis of consequences on subsequent stability of family, behavioral characteristics and development of the children, and so forth, are aspects of research appropriate for study.

13.

PAUL C. GLICK AND ROBERT PARKE, JR.

NEW APPROACHES IN STUDYING THE LIFE CYCLE OF THE FAMILY

The life cycle of the family has been widely accepted as a framework for the study of the conjugal family.[1] This orientation provides a means for analyzing the changes which take place in the composition and economic characteristics of families from marriage through child-rearing, children leaving home, the "empty nest" period, and the final dissolution of the family. Over the decades for which data are available, marked changes have been observed in the age at marriage, in the size of completed family, and in life expectancy, and these changes have modified the characteristic ages at which husbands and wives reach the several stages of the family life cycle.

This selection is reprinted from: Paul C. Glick and Robert Parke, Jr., "New Approaches in Studying the Life Cycle of the Family," Demography, 1965, 2, 187–202.
Reprinted with the permission of the authors and publishers.
[1] Among the pioneers in using the concept of the life cycle of the family were the rural sociologists. See especially Charles P. Loomis and C. Horace Hamilton, "Family in Life Cycle Analysis," Social Forces, December, 1936, XV, 225–31. Earlier writings by Paul C. Glick on this subject include "The Family Cycle," American Sociological Review, XII, April, 1947, 2, 164–74; "The Life Cycle of the Family," Marriage and Family Living, XVIII, February, 1955, 1, 3–9; and American Families (New York: John Wiley & Sons, Inc., 1957), chaps. iii–v.
See also Paul C. Glick, David M. Heer, and John C. Beresford, "Family Formation and Family Composition: Trends and Prospects," in Marvin B. Sussman (ed.), Sourcebook in Marriage and the Family (Boston: Houghton Mifflin Company, 1963), 37–40. A comprehensive treatment of the subject is found in Evelyn M. Duvall, Family Development (2d ed.; Phila.: J. B. Lippincott Co., 1962). See also Roy H. Rodgers and Reuben Hill, "The Developmental Approach," in Handbook of Marriage and the Family, ed. Harold Christensen (Chicago: Rand McNally & Co., 1964), chap. v; Lowry Nelson, Rural Sociology (2d ed.; New York: American Book Co., 1955), 307–12; and Andrew Collver, "The Family Cycle in India and the United States," American Sociological Review, February, 1963, XXVIII, 86–96.

This paper features revised and updated estimates of the trends in the family life cycle stages during the twentieth century, based on the latest available survey data and on revised techniques for estimating the intervals between the stages. It also presents new data, based on the 1960 census, on the typical patterns of change in family composition and economic characteristics from the beginning to the end of the cycle and examines alternative methods of describing progression through the cycle.[2]

STAGES OF THE FAMILY LIFE CYCLE

The estimates of typical ages for family life cycle stages given here differ from earlier estimates published by the senior author in the following respects:

1. Estimates of age at first marriage, ages at birth of first child, and completion of childbearing are based on a recent survey of marriage and childbearing, whereas earlier estimates were based perforce on indirect methods of estimation.

2. The estimates are for birth cohorts of women rather than for a given point in time (e.g., 1890 or 1940).

3. Estimates of joint survival of husband and wife are calculated from approximations to cohort survival rates for men and for women, from one age to the next, rather than from figures on expectation of life at marriage.

[2] The chief sources of data used in this paper are as follows: U.S. Bureau of the Census, U.S. Census of Population; 1960; Detailed Characteristics, United States Summary, Final Report PC(1)-1D, Tables 177–82 and 224; Families, Final Report PC(1)-4B, Tables 4, 5, 10, 12, and 24; and Sources (2)-4A, Tables 4–6, 9, 13, 15, 46, and 58; Persons by Family Characteristics, Final Report PC(1)-4B, Tables 4, 5, 10, 12, and 24; and Sources and Structure of Family Income, Final Report PC(2)-4C, Table 1; also U.S. Bureau of the Census, "Marriage, Fertility, and Childspacing: August, 1959," Current Population Reports, Series P-20, No. 108, Tables 5–8, 13, 16, 17, and 23.

4. Explicit recognition is given to different reference points for the estimation of family life cycle stages and to the effect of the selection of reference points on the calculated age at occurrence of the next stage in the family life cycle.

MARRIAGE AND CHILDBEARING

Survey data on marriage and childbearing histories obtained in the Census Bureau's *Current Population Survey* in 1959 provide the best recently available basis known to the authors for calculating median ages of women at first marriage, birth of the first child, and birth of the last child for women who have passed, or nearly passed, through the childbearing ages. These data, together with other family life cycle measures, are shown in Figure 13-1 and Table 13-1. For young women who will not complete their childbearing until some time in the future, the data include projected medians (dotted lines) prepared from partial marriage and childbearing histories and assumptions about proportions ultimately marrying and final completed family size. Estimates based on the survey data differ little from those published earlier, on the basis of indirect estimates, for age at first marriage. For age at completion of childbearing, however, the differences are substantial.

The estimates of typical ages for the family life cycle stages are presented here for birth cohorts of women (women born in a given period), whereas earlier estimates were prepared for a given calendar year. The availability of data on age at marriage and age at birth of first and last child for birth cohorts of women made it natural to seek ways to cast figures on the later stages of the family life cycle in the same terms. In addition, the use of birth cohorts was chosen because it eliminated certain conceptual problems in the preparation of measures for a calendar year. The calendar year approach probably is satisfactory where patterns of marriage, childbearing, and survivorship are stable. Where, as in recent

TABLE 13-1. MEDIAN AGE OF WOMEN AT SELECTED STAGES OF THE FAMILY LIFE CYCLE, FOR WOMEN BORN FROM 1880 TO 1939, BY YEAR OF BIRTH

Subject	Year of birth (birth cohort) of women					
	1880 to 1889	1890 to 1899	1900 to 1909	1910 to 1919	1920 to 1929	1930 to 1939
First marriage	21.6	21.4	21.1	21.7	20.8[a]	19.9[a]
Birth of first child	22.9	22.9	22.6	23.7	23.0[b]	21.5[b]
Birth of last child	32.9	31.1	30.4	31.5	30.0–31.0[c]	(NA)
First marriage of last child[d]	56.2	53.5	51.9	53.0	51.5–52.0	(NA)
Death of one spouse:						
For all couples[e]	57.0	59.4	62.3	63.7	64.4	64.4
For couples surviving to first marriage of last child[f]	69.2	68.1	67.8	68.2	67.2–68.2	(NA)

[a]Projected from partial experience on assumption that 96 percent of the cohort will ultimately marry.

[b]Projected from partial experience on assumption that 90 percent of all women in the cohort (including single) will ultimately become mothers.

[c]Projected as follows: Assuming that 48 percent of all women in this cohort (including single) will ultimately have a third child, partial experience to date indicates an ultimate median age of women at birth of the third child of 28.1 years. The median age of mothers in the cohort of 1900–09 and 1910–19 at birth of their last child of any order exceeded the median age at birth of their third child by an average of 2.4 years. This figure added to 28.1 gives 30.5 years, the center of the projection range shown.

[d]Assumes woman has last child at median age for cohort and last child marries at estimated median age at first marriage for children (see text).

[e]Assumes wife first married at median age for cohort to husband 3 years older.

[f]Measure applies to couples surviving jointly to median age of women at marriage of last child.

American history, these patterns have altered substantially, the meaning of intervals calculated from available calendar year data is open to question.

For example, the women who married in the 1940's did so at a median age about one year older than the women who married in the 1950's. This difference is reflected in ages at completion of childbearing. A majority of the women who married in the 1940's completed childbearing in the 1950's, and this fact is reflected in the data presented here. A presentation organized in terms of calendar years, as in the earlier studies, would relate age at marriage in the 1950's to age at completion of childbearing in the 1950's, a period with a quite different pattern of age at marriage than the 1940's.

The trend in the median age of women at first marriage shown in Table 13-1 was downward from 21.6 years for women born from 1880 to 1889 to 21.1 years for women born from 1900 to 1909, after which it rose to 21.7 years for women born from 1910 to 1919, most of whom were first married in the depression of the 1930's. Thereafter it declined, and projections based on the partial experience of the women born from 1930 to 1939 indicate an ultimate median age at first marriage of 19.9 years for this cohort.

Figures for men are not available on a basis comparable with those for women in Table 13-1, but estimates based on census figures indicate that the long-term decline in age at first marriage has been greater for men than for women. For males, the median age at first marriage was 26.1 years in 1890 but dropped 3.3 years to a median of 22.8 by 1960. For females the 1890 figure was 22.0 years, as compared with a 1960 figure of 20.3 years, a drop of only 1.7 years.[3]

The trend in median age at birth of first child is shown by the line in Figure 13-1 immediately above that for median age at first marriage. The differences between these two lines provide an indirect measure of interval from first marriage to birth of the first child.

[3]U.S. Bureau of the Census, "Marital Status and Family Status: March 1962," *Current Population Reports,* Series P-20, No. 122, Table C.

Direct measures of this interval for birth cohorts of women are not available. For marriage cohorts, however, medians based on distributions of interval from first marriage to birth of first child are available from the 1959 survey

Year of First Marriage	Median Years Marriage to Birth of First Child
1900–09	1.5
1910–19	1.4
1920–29	1.5
1930–39	1.7
1940–49	1.6
1950–59	1.3

(see accompanying tabulation). These figures indicate stability in the median spacing of the first child at about 1.5 years after marriage for women who married during the first three decades of the current century, a high of 1.7 years for women who first married in the 1930's, and a subsequent decline to a low of 1.3 years for women who first married in the 1950's. The figure for marriages in the 1950's is projected from incomplete experience.

The figures on median age of mother at birth of last child, shown in Figure 13-1 and Table 13-1, show a major decline in age at completion of childbearing, followed by a partial reversal. For the oldest cohort shown, the median age of mother at completion of childbearing was 32.9 years.[4] The figure declines to 30.4

[4]Lower estimates of age at completion of childbearing published in previous articles by the senior author were based on calculations, from vital statistics, of the median age of mother at the birth of the nth child, where n represented the mean size of completed family. For instance, if women completed childbearing with an average of 2.5 children per mother, an interpolated figure based on the median ages of mothers at birth of the second and third child was taken as the estimate of the median age at completion of childbearing.

Information (from the 1959 study) which was not available when the earlier articles were written shows that this method of estimation results in substantial understatement when compared with the median age at completion of childbearing based on childbearing histories. The reason for this is a very large difference between the age of mother when the nth child is her *last* and her age if she goes on to have more children. For instance, the 1959 survey data show that, among white women born from 1900 to 1909, those with four or more children had their third child at a median age of only 25.8 years, whereas those for whom the third child

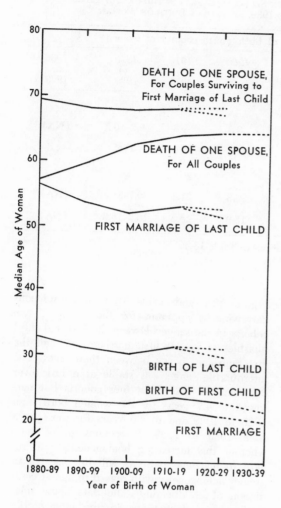

FIGURE 13-1. Stages of the family life cycle, for women born from 1880 to 1939. Source: Table 13-1.

years for mothers born from 1900 to 1909 and subsequently rose to 31.5 years for mothers born from 1910 to 1919, paralleling the increase in median ages at marriage and birth of first child for this cohort. This increase appears to have been a temporary phenomenon, attributable to the particular experience of this cohort, most of whose marriages occurred in the depression years of the 1930's.

The median age at completion of childbearing for younger cohorts is necessarily unknown. However, the projected figure (based on partial childbearing histories) for the women born from 1920 to 1929 indicate that, on the average, these women will have their last child at some time during the twelve-month period when the woman is thirty years old. If this projection proves to be fairly accurate, this group of women will complete childbearing at a younger median age than did the women born in the preceding decade.

The difference between the figures for median age at completion of childbearing and median age at first marriage provides a good index, if not an exact measure, of the median number of years from first marriage to completion of childbearing (Table 13.2).[5] This series follows a pattern of decline and partial recovery that is roughly parallel to the trend in completed family size. The 1959 survey, together with a projection for the youngest cohort shown, yields the figures shown in the accompanying tabulation for average number of children per woman ever married by the end of the childbearing period.

The relatively sharp increase in the fertility

was the last had their third child at a median age of 30.9 years. Differences of similar magnitude are found in other cohorts of women and for other birth orders. This pattern appears to result from the long average child-spacing intervals associated with small family size and, in particular, from the relatively long average spacing of the last child.

The foregoing observations account in large part for the fact that estimated median ages at completion of childbearing in the present paper are several years higher than those previously published in articles on the life cycle of the family; nonetheless, the patterns of change over time in median ages at completion of childbearing are quite similar in this and the earlier articles.

[5]Figures based on a differencing of median ages at first marriage and completion of childbearing compare favorably with median intervals from first marriage to completion of childbearing from the 1959 survey for marriage cohorts of women that correspond in an approximate fashion to the birth cohorts of 1880–89 to 1910–19:

Marriage Cohort	Median Interval (Year)
1900–09	11.6
1910–19	9.1
1920–29	8.1
1930–39	9.1

The movement of both series is similar, but the range of variation between the highest and lowest level is greater when marriage cohorts are used.

TABLE 13-2. MEDIAN NUMBER OF YEARS BETWEEN SELECTED EVENTS IN THE FAMILY LIFE CYCLE, FOR WOMEN BORN FROM 1880 TO 1939, BY YEAR OF BIRTH OF WOMAN

	Year of birth (birth cohort) of women					
Subject	1880 to 1889	1890 to 1899	1900 to 1909	1910 to 1919	1920 to 1929	1930 to 1939
For all couples:						
First marriage to birth of last child	11.3	9.7	9.3	9.8	9.2–10.2	(NA)
First marriage to death of one spouse	35.4	38.0	41.2	42.0	43.6	44.5
For couples surviving to marriage of last child:						
First marriage of couple to marriage of last child	43.6	32.1	30.8	31.3	30.7–31.7	(NA)
First marriage of last child to death of one spouse	13.0	14.6	15.9	15.2	15.2–16.2	(NA)

Source: Same calculations as Table 13–1.
(NA) Not available.

of the youngest cohort is not accompanied by any correspondingly sharp increase in the average interval from marriage to completion of childbearing projected for this cohort. This

Year of Birth of Woman	Completed Fertility
1880–89............	3.4
1890–99............	2.8
1900–09............	2.5
1910–19............	2.5
1920–29............	3.1

pattern may reflect, in part, a reduction in the average spacing interval per child, as compared with the cohort ten years older. It remains to be seen how figures on family size projected for even younger cohorts will affect the interval to completion of childbearing. Even assuming some shortening of the average spacing interval per child, it seems unlikely that the family size of 3.4 to 3.7 children per woman ever married projected for the women born in the 1940's can be achieved without lengthening the average period of childbearing and (barring unforeseen declines in marriage age) increasing the average age at completion of childbearing.

Although the presentation thus far has concentrated on median ages at first marriage and at childbearing, both marriage and childbearing are subject to ranges of variation as shown in

Figure 13-2 and Table 13-3. A conspicuous narrowing is apparent for the youngest two cohorts in the range between the first and third quartiles of age at first marriage; one-half the first marriages occur between these ages. The interquartile range was stable at a little over 6.0 years for the oldest four cohorts but narrowed to 4.7 years for the women born from 1920 to 1929 and to 4.0 years for those born from 1930 to 1939. It remains to be seen whether this increasing homogeneity with regard to marriage patterns will be reflected in greater homogeneity with regard to age at completion of childbearing. The data show relatively minor fluctuations in the interquartile range for age at birth of last child, but these data do not include the young cohorts who have not yet completed childbearing, among whom the greatest change may be expected in the future.

Some women, of course, bear no children. The general trend in childlessness for the cohorts shown in this paper has been downward. About 23 percent of all women (including single) in the cohort of 1880–89 bore no children. The figure rose slightly to 26 percent for the women born from 1900 to 1909 and has been consistently downward since then. Projections for the women now in the middle of their childbearing indicate that they may com-

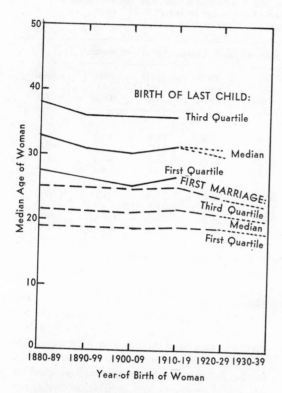

FIGURE 13-2. Quartiles of age at first marriage and age at birth of last child, for women born from 1880 to 1939. Source: Table 13-3.

plete childbearing with as few as 10 percent childless.

CHILDREN LEAVING HOME

The marriage of the last child in the family typically brings the number of members back down to the original couple, on the likely assumption that both the husband and wife have survived and are living together. Because of the variations in ages at marriage, size of family, spacing of children, and the spacing of the children's marriages, there can, of course, be a rather broad range of the ages of parents when their last child leaves home. Consequently, the data in Figure 13-1 and Table 13-1 for age of the mother when her last child marries and the associated number of years from the mother's marriage to that of her last child (Table 13-2) are more of an abstraction than the

values given for marriage and childbearing. The values for ages when the last child leaves home are actually illustrative figures that apply to mothers who had their last child at the median age for the cohort and whose last child first married at the estimated median age for children.[6]

Women born from 1920 to 1929 may be about 52 years old, on the average, when their last child marries. The corresponding age was about 56 years for the oldest cohort shown. The currently younger age of the parents when their children leave home reflects the combined effect of several factors. The effect of the declining age at first marriage is the most obvious. There is also some evidence that the women who were in the midst of childbearing at the time of this writing were spacing their children more closely than their predecessors. In addition, the trend in average family size, which has been downward for most of the cohorts shown, has tended to reduce the age of mothers when the last child leaves home. However, anticipated future increases in family size may very well result in some increase in this age.

DISSOLUTION OF THE FAMILY

Improving survivorship has resulted in revolutionary changes in the average duration of married life, and this factor, together with changes in patterns of marriage and childbearing, has resulted in some lengthening of married life after the last child leaves home.

Two measures of survivorship are shown in

---

[6]The median age of the last child at first marriage was assumed to be the median age at first marriage of women born 30 years after the cohort in question, plus an allowance for the difference between the median age at first marriage for females and that for all children. The following example of the calculation of median age of mother at marriage of the last child relates to the women born from 1890 to 1899:

Median age of mother at birth of last child,
cohort of 1890–99 .... 31.1
Median age at first marriage, cohort of
1920–29 .... 20.8
Allowance for difference between median age
at first marriage for females and that for all
children 1.6
Median age at marriage of last child 53.5

The median age at first marriage for the cohort of 1930–39 was used in estimating the median for children of the cohorts of 1900–1909 to 1920–29.

TABLE 13-3. QUARTILES OF AGE OF WOMEN AT FIRST MARRIAGE AND AGE OF MOTHERS AT BIRTH OF LAST CHILD, FOR WOMEN BORN FROM 1880 TO 1939, BY YEAR OF BIRTH OF WOMAN

Subject	Year of birth (birth cohort) of women					
	1880 to 1889	1890 to 1899	1900 to 1909	1910 to 1919	1920 to 1929	1930 to 1939
Age at first marriage*						
First quartile	18.9	18.9	18.5	18.8	18.7	18.1
Second quartile (median)	21.6	21.4	21.1	21.7	20.8	19.9
Third quartile	25.2	25.1	24.8	25.2	23.4	22.1
Interquartile range, year	6.3	6.2	6.3	6.4	4.7	4.0
Age at birth of last child						
First quartile	27.4	26.4	25.2	26.6	(NA)	(NA)
Second quartile (median)	32.9	31.1	30.4	31.5	30.0–31.0	(NA)
Third quartile	38.2	36.1	36.1	36.0	(NA)	(NA)
Interquartile range, year	10.8	9.7	10.9	9.4	(NA)	(NA)

Source: Derived from U.S. Bureau of the Census, Current Population Reports, Series P-20, No. 108.
(NA) Not available.
*Data for cohorts of 1920–1929 and 1930–1939 projected from partial experience on assumption that 96 percent of women will ultimately marry.

Figure 13-1 and Table 13-1. Both measures describe the age of the wife at the death of one spouse; that is, at her death or that of her husband, whichever comes first. (These measures assume that the marriage is not previously broken by divorce or annulment.) Median age of wife at the death of one spouse *for all couples* is an illustrative figure that applies to married couples in which the wife was first married at the median age for the cohort, shown in Table 13-1. The measure reflects mortality rates for all ages following first marriage. Median age of wife at the death of one spouse *for couples surviving to first marriage of last child* is an illustrative figure that applies to couples surviving jointly to the estimated median age of women at the marriage of the last child. This measure reflects mortality rates only for the ages of the couple after the last child marries.

Following the very useful comments of Robert J. Myers,[7] the figures on survivorship shown in the present paper were prepared from joint survival rates for husband and wife developed from life tables for men and women. In order to stay within the cohort framework adopted for the initial stages of the family life cycle, approximations were prepared of survival rates that would be yielded by cohort life tables. These approximations consisted of five-year survival rates calculated from United States life tables for successive years.[8] The products of the survival rates for husbands and wives yielded joint survival rates for successive five-year periods. These, in turn, were used to generate a

[7] Robert J. Myers, "Statistical Measures in the Marital Life Cycles of Men and Women," *International Population Conference: 1959* (Vienna: Christopher Reisser's Sons), 229–33.

[8] For instance, the women born from 1890 to 1899 who ultimately married, and who were enumerated in the 1959 survey, married for the first time at a median age of 21.4 years, and most of them married in the decade 1920–29. Survival rates from age 21.4 to age 26.4 and from age 26.4 to 31.4 were calculated from l_x values in life tables for 1919–21. Survival rates from age 31.4 to age 36.4 and from age 36.4 to 41.4 were calculated from life tables for 1929–31, and so forth. Survival rates for husbands were calculated in a similar fashion, on the assumption that the median age of the husbands was three years older than that of the wives.

Because the life tables used were for all persons regardless of marital status, the estimates of survivorship presented here assume no differential mortality by marital status. The estimates also assume independence of death probabilities for husband and wife.

distribution of couples surviving to the end of each five-year period since marriage. The figures on joint survival for all couples shown in Figure 13-1 and Table 13-1 represent the median of this distribution, expressed in terms of the age of the wife.

For some of the cohorts of women shown, most of the remaining lifetime lies in the future. Survival rates for future years were calculated from 1960 life tables. The figures for couples surviving to the marriage of the last child were also based on approximations of cohort survival rates, except that the starting points were the estimated median ages of the woman and her husband at the marriage of their last child rather than their first marriage.

In this century there has been an increase of nine years in the average number of years that husband and wife live together, according to the figures on median years between marriage and the death of one spouse for all couples shown in Table 13-2. In the oldest group of women, the median of 35.4 years of married life for all couples was only slightly greater than the median interval of 34.6 years for surviving couples between their marriage and the marriage of their last child. In the oldest group, in other words, only about one-half of all couples survived to the median age at which the surviving couples saw their last child married. The effect of the increase in survivorship has been to increase greatly the proportion of couples enjoying many years of married life after the last child leaves home.

Despite this fact, the average number of child-free years during middle age has increased only moderately for couples who survive jointly to the time when their last child marries. Under current conditions, a couple has perhaps sixteen more years together after the last child marries, as compared with thirteen years for the oldest cohort shown. The corresponding age of wife at dissolution of the couple through death has not shown a comparable rise—in fact, it is level or declining slightly, as shown by the top line of Figure 13-1 and by Table 13-1. This interesting result is a consequence of the decline in the median age of the mother when her last child marries.

The approach employed here is not amenable

to calculation of median ages at widowhood and still less to calculation of median duration of widowhood before death. The work of Myers, cited above, includes figures on these topics, although not for cohorts. Myers performed his calculations using survival rates for single years of age and expressed his results as means. A computation of his, using life tables for 1949–51, shows that 65.3 percent of brides eventually become widows at an average age of 61.2 years and that these widows have an average (mean) period of widowhood before death of 18.7 years. The corresponding figure for the period of widowerhood, in the event that the husband survives, was 14.2 years.

SUMMARY OF FINDINGS ON LIFE CYCLE STAGES

Changes during the twentieth century in age at marriage, size of completed family, spacing of children, and life expectancy have had substantial effects on the life cycle of the average family. The youngest women for whom data are available compare as follows, on the average, with women who are 40 to 60 years older: The youngest women marry one to two years younger and complete their childbearing two to three years younger; their age at the marriage of their last child is four to five years younger, and their length of married life is about nine years longer. As a consequence of the generally upward trend in fertility during the last two decades, present indications point to a return by women now in the midst of childbearing to an average family size not far from that of two generations ago but with the children spaced somewhat closer together.

CHANGES IN SOCIAL AND ECONOMIC CHARACTERISTICS DURING THE FAMILY LIFE CYCLE

As the family moves through its life cycle, marked changes generally occur in the family's place of residence, its composition, and its economic well-being. These changes tend to take place in a systematic pattern which is essentially the same when portrayed by various methods. In the modern day, the wife may work for a while after marriage, the couple establishes a separate home, children enter and eventually leave the family, and in the meantime the level of family income usually rises with the increasing skill and experience of the family's breadwinner(s) but eventually falls as gainful employment of the earner(s) becomes intermittent or discontinues.

Not all families display identical life cycle patterns, of course, because some families are larger than others, some have higher levels of income, and so on. A few of the differences will be illustrated, but an exhaustive treatment of the variations could not be presented within the scope of this paper.[9]

LABOR FORCE PARTICIPATION OF WIFE

Many of the family life cycle patterns, especially well exemplified by the labor force participation of the wife, occur in the form of a modified bell-shaped curve. The changing proportion of wives who are the labor force, shown in Figure 13-3,[10] deviates from the bell shape in the early years of marriage, when a larger proportion of wives is employed than a few years later when more of them are preoccupied with the rearing of children.

The basic similarity of the pattern when measured by two different methods is also illustrated by the labor force participation data in Figure 13-3.[11] Thus, regardless of whether the cycle is based on age of the husband or on number of years since the first marriage of the husband, essentially the same conclusion would be drawn about the characteristic rhythm of the labor force participation of wives outside the home. Yet there are some minor differences between the two curves, particularly for the younger families, which can be readily explained as an indication that labor force participation of young wives is somewhat more closely related to duration of marriage than to age of the husband.[12]

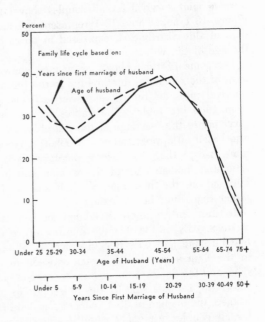

FIGURE 13-3. Percent of husband-wife families with wife in labor force (United States, 1960).

ESTABLISHING A HOME

The index chosen for demonstrating the gradual process of establishing a more or less permanent home is the proportion of husband-wife families which were living in the same house in both 1955 and 1960 (Figure 13-4).[13] As the age of the husband increased, the proportion of families in the same house rose continuously, with no decline at the upper ages. Specifically, only

---

[9]In this section the data presented were obtained directly or were derived from reports cited in n. 2. Specific sources of the following charts are given in footnotes below.

[10]Based on U.S. Bureau of the Census, *Families*, Tables 11 and 46.

[11]A third method of describing the family life cycle is used in Fig. 13-7.

[12]In plotting the two curves in Fig. 13-3, where the units of measurement of the independent variables are not the same, the distances on the horizon-

tal axis were determined by the percent of all husband-wife families which were in the specified age group or marriage-duration group. Thus, the points were plotted at the midpoints of the cumulative percentages of cases in the specified groups. The same procedure was followed in all subsequent groups for uniformity of presentation. John B. Lansing and Leslie Kish use this procedure in comparing different measures of the life cycles of the family in their article, "Family Life Cycle as an Independent Variable," *American Sociological Review* (1957), *XXII*, 512–19.

[13]Based on U.S. Bureau of the Census, *Families*, Table 58.

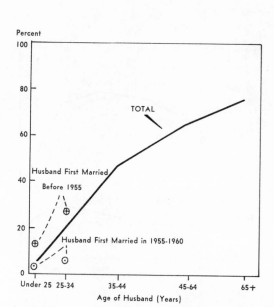

FIGURE 13-4. Percent of husband-wife families with husband in same house in 1955 and 1960 (United States, 1960).

and nearly three out of every four married 20 years or more. All but 13 percent of the married couples in 1960 who had been married less than a year had established a separate home (that is, a home which was not maintained by relatives or nonrelatives). Corresponding proportions for those married one, two, three or four, five to nine, and ten years or more were nine, six, four, two, and one percent, respectively.[14]

REARING CHILDREN

During the first 25 years of married life, more than one-half of the husband-wife families have young children in the home (Figure 13-5).[15] Of those married less than five years in 1960, two-thirds had one or more children. The peak of childrearing is between five and 20 years after marriage, when about 85 percent of the husband-wife families in 1960 had some sons

about 21 percent of the husbands 25-34 years old in 1960 were still living in the same home as five years earlier, whereas about 76 percent of those 65 and over remained in the same home. These figures provide a measure of the greater need and willingness of young than older families to resettle. The circled values shown in the graph demonstrate that extremely small proportions of young husbands who had been married during the five years before the 1960 census were still in the same house in which they had lived five years earlier—regardless of their ages in 1960.

Curves of increase in home ownership with advancing age of husband and with higher durations of marriage, not shown here, closely resemble the curve of residence in same house shown in Figure 13-4. In 1960, about one in every five of the couples married less than two years who had established a home also owned their home. This proportion rose to two in every five couples married two to four years, nearly three in every five married five to nine years,

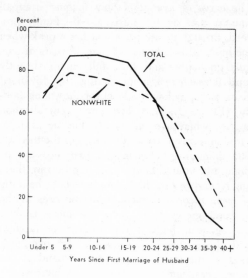

FIGURE 13-5. Percent of husband-wife families with own children under 18 years old (United States, 1960).

[14]See U.S. Bureau of the Census, *Families*, Tables 5 and 15, and *Persons by Family Characteristics*, Table 24.
[15]Based on U.S. Bureau of the Census, *Families*, Table 9.

or daughters under 18 at home. Thereafter the proportion with children still in the parental home drops off sharply.

Nonwhite families differ considerably from white families in the proportion with young children at home during the middle and late phases of the family life cycle. At the peak of the childbearing period, about ten percent fewer of the nonwhite than of the white husband-wife families in 1960 had any sons or daughters under 18 living with them. This fact is a reflection in part of the higher proportion of childlessness among nonwhite families. However, about twice as large a proportion of nonwhite than white husband-wife families with the husband married 30 to 40 years still had some of their young children at home. This, in turn, reflects the fact that a higher proportion of nonwhite mothers continue to bear children into the upper portion of the reproductive period and to have larger families.

Earning a Living

The curve of average family income from all sources rises as the husband-wife family proceeds through its life cycle, reaches a peak when the husband is between 45 and 55 years of age, falls gradually, and then falls more abruptly until it reaches a point during the advanced years that is below the level for the young family (Figure 13-6).[16] The same generalization applies when average family income is measured in terms of either the mean or the median. The difference between the two measures is slight for young families—among whom there are relatively few high incomes—but the ratio of mean income to median income rises as the husband grows older until the mean is over half again as high as the median for families with the husband 75 years old and over. For most of the families with the husband at the upper ages, family income consists increasingly of money obtained from sources other than employment.

Income per family member is, in some re-

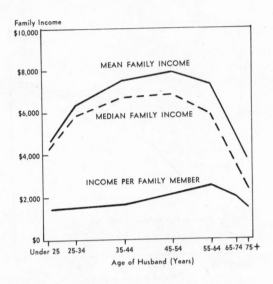

FIGURE 13-6. Mean and median family income and income per family member, for husband-wife families (United States, 1960).

spects, a better indicator of the changing economic well-being of the family at successive stages of the family life cycle than is income per family. As shown in Figure 13-6, income per family member rises very little during the period when the family is expanding in size, though income per family tends to rise more than one-half during the same period. Then, as family size contracts while family income remains at or near its peak, income per family member rises until it reaches its peak when the husband is 55-64 years old.[17]

The wide range in economic well-being of families in the upper as compared with the lower income strata during successive family

---

[16]Based on U.S. Bureau of the Census, *Detailed Characteristics, United States Summary*, Table 224; *Families*, Tables 4 and 13; *Persons by Family Characteristics*, Tables 5 and 12; *and Sources and Structures of Family Income*, Table 1.

---

[17]As indicated above, income per family reaches its peak when the husband is 45–54, on the average. Thereafter it declines as the husband grows older. Mean income per family member of the oldest age group of husbands is virtually the same as that for the youngest. If income per family member were computed from the median rather than the mean, it would be only about two-thirds as large for the oldest as the youngest husbands.

life cycle stages and the differences in age of husband at the time of peak family income are portrayed vividly in Figure 13-7.[18] Median

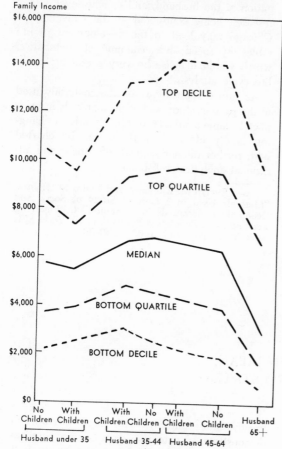

FIGURE 13-7. Dispersion of family income, for husband-wife families (United States, 1960).

family income for husband-wife families according to the 1960 census was just under $6000, whereas the lowest tenth of families had less than $2000 income and the top tenth had more than $12,000. Where the husband was under 35, upper income families tended to fare better economically if there were no children in the home, perhaps as a consequence in part at least of the greater freedom of childless wives than

<hr>

[18]Based on same sources as Fig. 13–6. Lansing and Kish, *op. cit.*, used a method similar to that shown here as their preferred method of describing the stages of the life cycle of the family.

mothers to work outside the home; yet young lower income families did not show a similar pattern, perhaps in part because childless wives in impoverished homes may have great difficulty finding employment. As may have been expected, the period of peak family income occurred later in the family life cycle for upper strata than for the lower. This fact evidently reflects the tendency for the incomes of white-collar workers to decline little, if any, before retirement and for that of manual workers to reach a peak around age 40 and then to decline. It may also reflect differences in the employability and earnings of the wives in the upper and lower strata of the population.

SUMMARY OF FINDINGS ON SOCIAL AND ECONOMIC CHARACTERISTICS

During recent years the proportion of wives in the labor force declines from about one-third for those in the first five years of marriage to one-fourth for those married five to nine years, then rises to about two-fifths for those married about 25 years (about the time their children are leaving home). Seven out of eight couples who are in their first year of marriage have set up homes apart from relatives; after ten years all but one percent have separate homes. A plateau of childrearing occurs between five and 20 years after marriage, when about 85 percent of the couples have some of their children in their home. Peak family income is found on the average among families with the husband 45–54 years old. Families in the lower economic strata are more likely to reach a peak of family income when the husband is around 40, but the corresponding age of husband for the upper strata tends to come much later. Because size of family usually declines at a faster rate than family income during the later stages of the family life cycle, the high point in income per family member is reached when the husband is 55–64 years old, on the average—about ten years after the peak in income per family.

DISCUSSION

The use of a cohort approach in developing direct measures of family life cycle stages for the present study has served as a check on the indirect measures used in earlier studies and has revealed that the last child in the family tends to be spaced considerably later after marriage than was shown by the earlier studies. Likewise, having data available for the first time on social and economic characteristics at successive phases of the family life cycle, which expressed the cycle in terms of interval since first marriage, permitted comparisons with data of the type shown in earlier studies, which expressed the cycle in terms of age of the husband. Showing ranges as well as averages of ages at reaching family life cycle stages and showing the range as well as the median family income at successive stages of the cycle have added perspective to the present analysis.

At the time of this writing, the Bureau of the Census is in the process of making tabulations of data on age at first marriage and child spacing, which would permit research into differential life cycle patterns of white and non-white couples by education of the wife, occupation of the husband, and income level. Other research being conducted at the University of Chicago may lead to the development of life tables by social and economic characteristics, which would likewise be very useful in family life cycle analysis.[19]

As future replications of the materials used in the present study and other materials in prospect become available, historic trends in changing family life cycle patterns can be charted with further methodological refinement and additional analytical substance.

[19]See Evelyn M. Kitagawa and Philip M. Hauser, "Methods Used in a Current Study of Social and Economic Differentials in Mortality," in *Emerging Techniques in Population Research* (New York: Milbank Memorial Fund, 1963), 250–66.

14.

KIYOMI MORIOKA

LIFE CYCLE PATTERNS IN JAPAN, CHINA, AND THE UNITED STATES

The present paper aims at clarifying characteristics of the life cycle pattern of the Japanese stem family in comparison with that of the Chinese joint family and of the American conjugal family and, by doing so, at widening the scope of the study of family development which has almost totally been confined to the conjugal family so far.[1] The developmental framework should not remain provincial, but be applicable to any family patterns. This paper attempts to demonstrate an extensive cross-cultural applicability of the emerging conceptual framework of family development.

From among a little more than a dozen existing life cycle studies of the Japanese family, three distinctive approaches to the subject can be identified. The three approaches are:

This selection is reprinted from: Kiyomi Morioka, "Life Cycle Patterns in Japan, China, and the United States," *Journal of Marriage and the Family,* 1967, 29, 595–606 [the conclusion section from the original article is omitted].
Reprinted with the permission of the author and publisher.
This is a revised version of a paper originally presented at the Sixth World Congress of Sociology, Evian, France, September, 1966.
[1]Among the few life cycle studies which treat a non-conjugal family system are: Horace Miner, St. Denis, *A French Canadian Parish* (Chicago: University of Chicago Press, 1939), 63–85, and Andrew Collver, "The Family Cycle in India and the United States," *American Sociological Review*, February, 1963, 28:1, 86–96. However, as George P. Rowe stated in his recent appraisal of the developmental framework, "To date no cross-cultural verification study has been attempted to test the universal applicability of this framework." See George P. Rowe, "The Developmental Conceptual Framework to the Study of the Family," in *Emerging Conceptual Framework in Family Analysis*, ed. by F. Ivan Nye and Felix M. Berardo (New York: Crowell Collier and MacMillan, Inc., 1966), 213.

1. The family composition approach, which emphasizes the changes in household composition and focuses on establishing a series of stages with the aid of a predetermined household typology, as best represented by Takashi Koyama's work.[2]

2. The approach whereby the life cycle is regarded as a demographic, independent variable. This approach, which is best exemplified by Eitaro Suzuki's pioneer study,[3] accentuates fluctuation in economic activities over a period of several decades in the family life history and elucidates the fact that the Japanese stem family undergoes a definite

cycle of prosperity and decline caused by regular changes in the household composition, even though economic conditions outside the family remain the same.

3. The approach which regards the life cycle as process, focusing attention on the role complex characteristic of each stage and tracing changes in it from the early stage to the later one mainly through a comparison of synchronic cross-sectional data on families in different stages.

The present writer has employed the third approach, for he finds it inadequate either to put emphasis on discovering a successive order of stages on the basis of a certain household typology or to try to find the existence of a cyclic regularity in family development without identifying stages; he regards it more important to clarify characteristics of the role complex associated with each stage of the cycle.[4]

---

[2]Takashi Koyama, "Cyclical Changes of the Family Composition," in *Ie: Its Structural Analyses*, ed. by Y. Okada and S. Kitano (Tokyo: Sobunsha, 1959), 67–83. This is the first longitudinal study ever attempted by a Japanese sociologist, making use of official documents of an agricultural neighborhood from 1802 to 1861 under the Tokugawa Shogunate which registered people by household for the purpose of religious inspection. Koyama classified a total of 1556 households appearing in the 60 books (one for each year) into seven types of households, and in each instance he carefully traced the transition of household types from one to another. Moreover, he delineated the main course of the transitions by highlighting the directions of change which occurred most often. The four stages thus made discernible are as follows:

1. The household with collateral relatives. This is a stage in which two couples in the family line cohabitate, the parents being retired and family headship lying with the younger generation. The unmarried sons and daughters are supported by their eldest brother, the family head, and leave the natal home as they marry or establish new branch families under his aid and protection. This stage lasts for 3.4 years on the average.

2. The household with lineal ascendants and descendants. This is also a stage of cohabitation of two couples with the headship in the hands of the younger generation. However, all siblings of the family head have now left home, and only lineal relatives remain. This lasts for 8.5 years.

3. The household with unmarried children. This is the stage in which the parents are dead and the family head and his wife live alone with their unmarried children. The family takes the form of a nuclear family household. This lasts for 8.7 years.

4. The household with married children. This is the stage in which two lineal couples live together, and the family headship is kept by the father rather than by his married heir. When the heir takes over headship, the household shifts back to the first stage and a new cycle starts. This lasts for 2.7 years.

[3]Eitaro Suzuki, *Principles of Japanese Rural Sociology* (Tokyo: Nippon-Hyoron-sha, 1940), 258–262. Also, Suzuki, "On Cyclical Regularity in Generational Development of the Japanese Family," in *Family and Rural Village*, vol. 2, ed. by T. Toda and E. Suzuki (Tokyo: Nikko-shoin, 1942), 1–50. Suzuki's inspiration came from Russian and American contributions to the subject, in particular from writings by P. A. Sorokin and C. E. Lively. He held that one would be able to identify a recurring cycle

in the course of changes in the composition of the stem family if basic demographic information were available. He further maintained that it would be possible to calculate a coefficient of consumption and productivity for each year of family development which would indicate the family's level of living and its changes. His ideas were embodied in a "scheme of cyclical development of the stem family" based on national averages of life expectancy, ages at the first marriage, the number of children, and infant mortality. Regularities he found through this procedure are as follows:

1. The length of each cycle is 59 years, including two family heads in successive generations.

2. The family when largest is made up of seven members, and when smallest is only three. The average family size during the whole cycle is 4.712 persons, which is close to the 1920 national average.

3. The family is made up of two generations of parents and children during a period of 40 years (68 percent of one cycle) and of three generations of grandparents, parents, and children for 19 years (32 percent of the cycle). Contrary to popular belief, the Japanese family exists in the form of a two-generation household for a longer period of time than it does in the form of a three-generation household.

4. The Japanese proverbs which read that "the family reaches its greatest poverty when the eldest son is 15" and "the family passes its height of prosperity when the youngest son is 15" are confirmed by the findings regarding the fluctuation of the coefficient of consumption and productivity during a cycle.

5. From the pattern of family development, three types of the Japanese family, namely, joint, stem, and conjugal, are identifiable.

[4]A fuller discussion of the three approaches is presented in Kiyomi Morioka, "A Critical Review of Studies in the Family Life Cycle" (2), *International Christian University Journal of Social Sciences*, September, 1964, 5, 1–26.

A life cycle study of the Japanese family ought to include demarcation of cycle stages as tools for further investigation. In this regard, there arises the problem of how to establish a set of stages which does not merely reflect transformations of a household, but represents major changes in a role complex. Dependence on a ready-made household typology as seen in Koyama's case does not offer a fully satisfactory delineation. One should remember that household typology and stages of a life cycle are of different nature, although they have some important elements in common and hence are interchangeable to a certain extent.

For the task of delineating cycle stages of the Japanese stem family, which is a supragenerational entity, it is necessary, first of all, to set aside the traditional notion of an endless continuation of the family line from generation to generation and instead to direct attention to its discontinuing aspect which has often been hidden from institution-oriented students; such a supragenerational continuance is possible only because couples from two or three generations live together under the same roof with the same family name. Here, with the aid of G. P. Murdock's useful concept of a composite form of the family,[5] the Japanese stem family is viewed as a vertically composite form of nuclear families, one from each generation. This position enables us to apply theories of the life cycle developed in the United States to the study

of the life cycle of the stem family in Japan and to solve the problem of stage delineation as well.

This idea was substantiated in the writer's first article treating the family life cycle,[6] with numerical data of 1950, according to which the average age at the first marriage was 25.9 for a man and 23.0 for a woman and the average life expectancy of a man was 67.2 and of a woman, 69.8. On the assumption that the first child or the second is an heir, one gets Figure 14-1. Since time is read from the left of the figure to the right, a horizontal line represents the duration of marriage, and generations come down from the top to the bottom.

In Figure 14-1, one can identify with little trouble the following two stages which appear alternately:

1. The period of two nuclear families of parents and the heir.
2. The period of a single nuclear family when parents are dead and the heir in the next generation remains unmarried.

This finding is consonant with Suzuki's view which referred to a cyclical regularity in the recurrence of the two stages.[7] But this preliminary demarcation of stages is inadequate, for the Japanese family is not a mere federation of nuclear families of different generations, but a single social entity that exists for generations.

[5]George Peter Murdock, *Social Structure* (New York: Crowell, Collier and MacMillan, Inc., 1949), 2.

[6]Kiyomi Morioka, "A New Approach to the Family Study: Theory and Method of Family Life Cycle," *Monthly Bulletin of Family Courts*, February, 1953, 5:2, 66–73.

[7]See (3) in footnote 3.

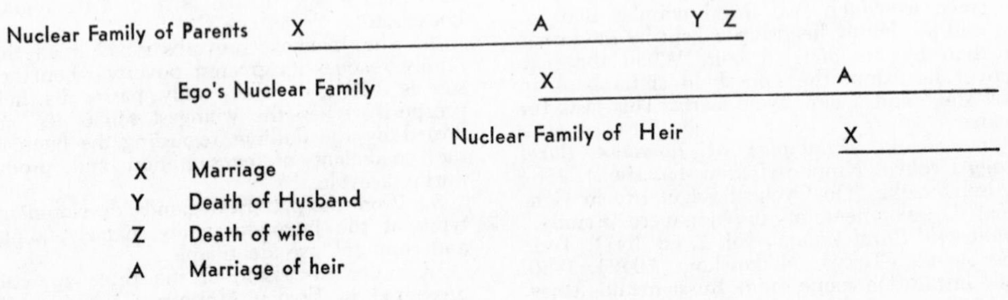

Nuclear Family of Parents   X _____ A   Y Z

       Ego's Nuclear Family   X _____ A

               Nuclear Family of Heir   X _____

      X   Marriage
      Y   Death of Husband
      Z   Death of wife
      A   Marriage of heir

FIGURE 14-1.

One should proceed further to take into consideration the succession of family headship which symbolizes the lineal continuity of the stem family. With the locus of the family headship as a criterion, life stages can be delineated as follows:

Stage I:
Two couples of successive generations cohabitate, but headship lies with the father (from A to Y in Figure 14-1).

Stage II:
The father has either retired or died, and the headship has been transferred to the son (from Y to Z).

Stage III:
The mother is dead also, and the nuclear family of the younger generation is left alone. Upon marriage of the heir, the stage is shifted to Stage I (from Z to A).

In this scheme, the period when two nuclear families of the parents and the heir overlap is divided into two stages and, thus, the period of a complete stem family household is separated largely from that of an incomplete stem family household. The above three stages can be said to reoccur in the life cycle of the stem family in Japan. Table 14-1 shows the length of each stage

TABLE 14-1. LENGTH OF STAGES IN
1930, 1950, AND 1960

Stage	1930 (in years)	1950 (in years)	1960 (in years)
I	5.5	14.4	15.7
II	4.0	5.5	6.5
III	20.0	7.0	6.8
Total	29.5	26.9	29.0

based on Suzuki's data for 1930[8] and census data for 1950 and 1960. It is due at least partly to prolonged life expectancy that Stage I has become longer, occupying a little more than half a cycle in 1960, and that Stage III has become correspondingly shorter.

The level of living of the family, as well as the household composition, changes with an advancement in the stages, but more important are the differences in the human relationships char-

acteristic of each stage. In Stage III, human relationships resemble those of the conjugal family, although special treatment toward and expectations of the heir can be fully explained in the context of the stem family. On the other hand, Stages I and II typically manifest the nature of the stem family. Characteristics of human relationships in these stages are focused upon in-law relations.

Stage I is an especially difficult period for a daughter-in-law and also an uncomfortable one for her husband and parents-in-law. Figure 14-2

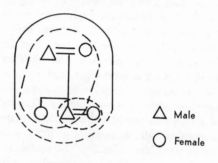

△ Male

○ Female

FIGURE 14-2.

illustrates the family composition at the time of receipt of a daughter-in-law. If adjustment between her and other members of her new family is not made, the dotted circle around the nuclear family of the parents-in-law or that of hers tends to become a solid circle. If the adjustment is made, the solid circle around the two nuclear families is completed at the bottom. Adjustment is mainly required of the daughter-in-law, because it is she who is to be adapted to the existing life patterns of the husband's family. But, since others are also required to readjust somewhat, there exists a special source of tension in the family at this stage. Moreover, this is also the stage in which daughters are to be married and sons to be matched and made independent of their parental family. This dual task may be expressed, as Figure 14-2 shows, in the task of linking generational discontinuity of component nuclear families to lineal continuity of the stem family. It is not an exaggeration to say that the

[8]The relative lengths of the stages are debatable, because the time of the heir's birth seems to have been much earlier in actuality than Suzuki had supposed in his calculation of lengths of the periods.

key to understanding the essence of the Japanese stem family (*ie*) lies here.

Next, Stage II is the one in which the young take up leadership and support their aging parents. The position of the young wife is already firmly established, and she assumes the responsibility of taking care of the consumption aspect of the household's life after the retirement of her mother-in-law. Naturally the relationship between mother-in-law and daughter-in-law also changes, and the mother-in-law, especially after the death of her husband, is placed in a weaker position.[9]

In Stage I and the early part of Stage II, the family tends to become prosperous enonomically and influential politically through the cooperation of father and son. On the other hand, in-law tensions often develop, sometimes leading to family discord or even separation or divorce, and thus economic deterioration ensues. Here the question arises as to why such a composite form of family can persist without disintegrating into component nuclear families in the regular fashion of the Chinese family. The reason is the institutional and ethical requirements placed on the traditional Japanese family, namely, the succession of the family line and the support of aged parents.

Family life cycle studies in the United States elucidate the following circumstance in answer to the present question. American farm families in the latter period of the second stage, in the early period of the third stage, and in the fourth stage—based on the classic four-stage theory—are especially vulnerable to economic stresses.[10] This would be true with Japanese farm families, too, if they retained the form of a nuclear family household without becoming a stem family household. In fact, economic stress would be felt much more strongly in general by Japanese farm families than by their American counterparts. (This is understandable, if one remembers that

the ratio per capita in production of calories between Japanese and American farmers was 100 to 1,060 for the period of 1926-1940.) In those days when the oldest child is about 15 years of age, a family is confronted with the heavy economic burden of bringing up children (the first period of financial pinch), and after the children have become married, the aged parents are not strong enough physically or financially to support themselves (the second period of pinch). In order to surmount these two financial squeezes, a family often needs social relief, but in Japan the popular way of living during these periods is to have the two nuclear families of parents and the heir cohabitate, sharing a single livelihood. The family overcomes these economic crises effectively, because the parents in the second pinch help their son in the first pinch by taking care of the grandchildren or providing extra hands for chores and family enterprises, while the son helps the aged parents by supporting them. In other words, the stem family performs the function of *concomitant mutual insurance,* in addition to that of mutual insurance between the parents and the son with an interval of about 30 years. This interpretation is applicable not only to farmers but perhaps to those engaging in other industries of low productivity, and provides a partial answer to why the stem family system continues.

THE LIFE CYCLE PATTERN OF THE CONJUGAL FAMILY AND OF THE JOINT FAMILY

A considerable number of life cycle studies of the conjugal family have been made in the United States since the early 1930's. In this section, the present writer will begin by summarizing American achievements insofar as they are relevant to his comparative review and then proceed to a discussion of life cycle patterns of the joint family as exemplified by the traditional Chinese family, making use of reports of first-hand studies conducted by Japanese scholars during the military invasion of the mainland of China.

THE AMERICAN FAMILY

When the conjugal family does not take any

---

[9]Paragraphs describing in-law relations overrepresent the prewar situation where a young wife was subjugated to her mother-in-law, accordingly more or less distorting the postwar picture. Nowadays the lengthened period of Stage I is balanced with the lessened control of a housewife over her daughter-in-law.

[10]G. W. Blackwell, "Correlates of Stages of Family Development among Farm Families on Relief," *Rural Sociology,* June, 1942, 7:2, 161–174.

composite form during its life span, it has a predictable natural history—from its formation at marriage, through the usual process of expansion and contraction in the number of positions and interpersonal relations, to total disappearance at the death of the original couple. One reason that scholars began life cycle studies of the conjugal family fairly early is the predictability of the history of this type of family which recurs with each newly married couple. On the other hand, life cycle studies in Japan developed later because of the difficulty of defining the life cycle of the stem family, which appears to have no predictable course of development and finality other than constant loss and addition of members.

Although there were some American scholars who observed variables in terms of the duration of marriage,[11] many divided the family cycle into stages of growth and development. The number of stages and criteria by which they delineated stages varied according to the various intentions of research. But generally speaking, studies in the 1930's and 1940's undertaken mostly by rural sociologists divided the cycle into four stages: the prechild family, the growing family, the contracting family, and the aging family. An appellation of stages was not, however, always the same.[12] Since about 1950, scholars have tended to identify six or more stages, probably in reflection of a shift of interest from household composition and the accompanying level of prosperity to more microscopic aspects of family life such as buying patterns, saving patterns, mobility patterns, role complex, and social participation including contact with relatives.[13]

This shift was concomitant with the spread of the use of this approach from rural sociology, where it had developed originally, to the study of urban families also.

The essential features of existing studies in this field are well-known to us elsewhere.[14] It would be enough, therefore, to pay passing attention to one of the latest investigations, that of Reuben Hill, which deserves special note. He developed an elaborate set of nine stages of the life cycle employing three criteria: numbers of positions in the family, the age composition as represented by the developmental stages of the oldest child, and the retirement of the husband-father from active employment. The stages thus differentiated are:

I. Establishment (newly married, childless); II. New Parents (infant to three years); III. Preschool Family (child three to six years and possibly younger siblings); IV. School-Age Family (oldest child six to 12 years, possibly younger siblings); V. Family with Adolescent (oldest 13-19, possibly younger siblings); VI. Family with Young Adult (oldest 20, until first child leaves home); VII. Family as Launching Center (from departure of first to last child); VIII. Postparental Family, The Middle Years (after the children have left home until father retires); IX. Aging Family (after retirement of father).

Hill views these stages of the family life cycle as distinctive in role complexes, anticipating peculiar types of family interaction for each of them.[15] What he has found from a comparative study of three generations of the same family lines would be changes in the decision-making pattern among the three groups—grandparents, parents, and married children—rather than over the life cycle. Nevertheless, the framework of the family cycle opens up the way for insights into

[11]C. E. Lively, *The Growth Cycle of the Farm Family*, Mimeographed Bulletin No. 51 (Wooster: Ohio Agricultural Experiment Station, 1932), 1–22. Allen Beegle and Charles P. Loomis, "Life Cycles of Farm, Rural-Nonfarm, and Urban Families in the United States as Derived from Census Materials," *Rural Sociology*, March, 1948, 13:1, 70–74.

[12]Pitirim A. Sorokin, Carle C. Zimmerman, and C. J. Galpin, *A Systematic Source Book in Rural Sociology*, vol. 2 (Minneapolis: University of Minnesota Press, 1931), 30–32. Lively, *op. cit.*; C. P. Loomis, "The Study of the Life Cycle of Families," *Rural Sociology*, June, 1936, 1:2, 180-199; and Blackwell, *op. cit.*

[13]James H. S. Bossard and Eleanor S. Boll, *Ritual in Family Living: A Contemporary Study* (Philadelphia: University of Pennsylvania Press, 1950), chapter 7. W. A. Anderson, *Rural Social Participation and the Family Life Cycle*, Part I: Formal

Participation (Memoir 314) and Part II: Informal Participation (Memoir 318) (Ithaca: Cornell University Agricultural Experiment Station, 1953). Robert O. Blood, Jr. and Donald M. Wolfe, *Husbands and Wives: The Dynamics of Married Living* (New York: The Free Press, a division of the Macmillan Co., 1960), 41–44. Reuben Hill, "Decision Making and the Family Life Cycle," in *Social Structure and the Family: Generational Relations*, ed. by Ethel Shanas and Gordon F. Streib (Englewood Cliffs: Prentice-Hall, Inc., 1965), 113–139.

[14]Reuben Hill and Roy H. Rodgers, "The Developmental Approach," in *Handbook of Marriage and the Family*, ed. by Harold T. Christensen (Chicago: Rand McNally, 1964), 171–211.

[15]Hill, *op. cit.*, 116–117.

changes taking place over the life span of the family.

Of the three sets of data as criteria, the first serves mainly to delineate the first and last stages in which the couple studied is childless, the second to demarcate the middle stages, and the third to divide the last stage into two parts, before and after retirement. While the third criterion represents a new approach to the study of the expanding postparental stage, the first two criteria have been applied before. The first, the most basic criterion, is quite simple to apply; but the second one, the age composition of the family, includes judgments as to which series of developmental stages of which child are best applied. The variety of stage delineations stems mainly from differences in these judgments.[16] Many, including Hill, used the oldest child; but some used all children,[17] and still others, the youngest child as the key child.[18]

In the demarcation of stages of the Japanese family, the first criterion has been employed in combination with the third, the retirement of the father from the position of family head, which is closely linked to his giving up active participation in the family enterprise. However, the content of the first criterion is not the same in Japanese and American families. In American conjugal families, expansion and contraction in the number of positions occur exclusively in the younger generation and not in the parents, because broken families are eliminated from the study of the life cycle.[19] On the contrary, changes in the number of positions take place in every generation in the Japanese family, and the changes in the number of positions which are relevant to stage delineation are confined to those in the family line—to the marriage of the heir and the addition of his wife to an existing household, to the death of the father, and later to that of the mother. The minor importance of noting changes in the number of the younger family members reduces the importance of the second criterion. This is not because the second criterion is regarded as unessential, but simply because its application would make the resultant set of stages too complicated. A similar consideration has prevented us from including changes in the number of the younger family members in the first criterion. The recent and rapid changes in the Japanese family, however, demand a reformulation of the stages by an application of the second criterion. This will be discussed later in more detail.

THE TRADITIONAL CHINESE FAMILY

The Chinese family to be discussed here is not the present-day family under the Communist regime, but the past one under Japanese military occupation. Thus, what is meant by the word "traditional" differs from the meaning intended by an American authority on the Chinese family.[20]

The Chinese family is a patrilineal, patrilocal family which can include all male descendants from common ancestors and their wives and children. However, this kind of very large household cannot endure for a long period of time, and family dissolution is inevitable. Since the Chinese family underwent steady growth as well as disintegration in almost every generation, it is obvious that the period from one disintegration to the next can be designated as the life span of a cycle. One cycle beginning with a nuclear family household may be divided into the following four stages:

I. The stage of a nuclear family household from the time it is formed to the marriage of its oldest son.

II. The stage of a stem family household from the time of the marriage of the oldest son to that of the second.

III. The stage of a joint family household from the time of the marriage of the second son to the death of his parents.

IV. The stage of a joint family household without common ancestors who are still alive.

[16]E. L. Kirkpatrick, R. Tough, and M. L. Cowles, *The Life Cycle of the Farm Family in Relation to its Standards of Living and Ability to Provide*, Research Bulletin 121, (Madison: University of Wisconsin Agricultural Experiment Station, 1934), 1–38. Blood and Wolfe, *op. cit.*

[17]Anderson, *op. cit.*, part I, 7–8.

[18]John B. Lansing and Leslie Kish, "Family Life Cycle as an Independent Variable," *American Sociological Review*, October, 1957, 22:5, 512–519.

[19]An exception is the conceptualization by R. H. Rodgers in his paper, *Improvement in the Construction and Analysis of Family Life Cycle Categories* (Kalamazoo: Western Michigan University, 1962).

[20]Marion J. Levy, Jr., *The Family Revolution in Modern China* (Cambridge: Harvard University Press, 1949), 41–42.

In Stage I there is no in-law relation living in the family. This comes into being in Stage II and becomes more and more complicated in Stage III with the addition of the son's wife who comes from a different clan, usually from a remote place. In spite of the existence of possibilities for internal discord, a family in Stage III is relatively stable because of the effective control exercised by the family head, the father. Stage IV, on the other hand, reveals a marked decline in the power of the family head over his younger brothers and sisters-in-law, and consequently, various forms of inner tension are manifested which finally lead to the splitting-up. The fact that most constituent family units have passed the first period of financial squeeze during this period and now are not so vulnerable may facilitate dissolution. It has been reported, however, that some families break down in Stage III before the death of the parents, and that many disintegrate in the latter part of the same stage, namely, after the death of the father while the mother is still alive. It is not a fixed rule, therefore, that an expanded family reaches its eventual dissolution in Stage IV. But, in view of the institutional requirement not to divide family property before the death of the parents, it is reasonable to set up the fourth stage. After this last stage, some constituent families begin a new cycle with Stage I and others with Stages II or III, depending on the degree of maturity of each family unit at that time.

Since averages of the age at the first marriage, of the number of sons born to a wife, and of life expectancy are not available for Chinese, the average length of each stage cannot be calculated. Instead, the writer presents one example of family development, which appears in the reports prepared by Megumi Hayashi[21] and which is the only relevant example the present writer has ever seen. It is the life history of the Wongs, a wealthy peasant family in an agricultural village in central China. In 1915 when the Wongs broke up into component family units, the whole family was in Stage IV, and the four independent families produced upon dissolution were all in Stage I, only one being childless. Hayashi traced the development of the family of the oldest brother, who had been the head of the family before it broke up, from 1915. In 1930, i.e., 15 years after the dissolution, his family was in Stage III and consisted of four nuclear families, one of his own and the others of his three sons. In the ten years following, he and his wife died and three independent nuclear households, those of his sons, appeared. Although the reports do not tell us whether the family disintegration occurred after the death of the parents or before, one can identify the stages of development through which the Wongs passed during the period of a quarter of a century. Those are Stages IV, I, II, III, IV, and I or IV, I, II, III, and I.

Why do all married sons of the Chinese family remain in the parental household with their wives and children? Answers to this question can be readily found in the Chinese custom of emphasizing dutiful service to one's parents and faithful performance of ancestor worship. But these ethical or religious motivations have economic and political foundations. The joint family household is preferred, because it can maintain the wealth of a family and its social status, which is dependent on the size of the family fortune, by preventing the partition of family property among the male descendants. It is also preferred for the accumulation of property which is facilitated by its efficient system of division of labor in production and by its economization of living expenses. It can furnish help with relative ease for the aged, the ill, the crippled, and the infirm. Further, in the days when political and military unrest prevailed, a large family far excelled a small family with only a single male adult in performing the role of protection and defense. These economic and political benefits in combination with the institutional requirements seem to have fostered the joint family system of China.

We have another question: Why does the Chinese family usually fail to maintain a joint

[21]Megumi Hayashi, "A Study of the Equal Division Inheritance in Chinese Peasant Families," in *Main Issues of Contemporary Sociology*, ed. by M. Hayashi *et al.* (Tokyo: Kobundo, 1949), 65–119. Also, Hayashi, "A Study of Large and Small Families Viewed from Population Census of Chinese Peasants," in *Main Issues of Sociology*, ed. by K. Komatsu *et al.* (Tokyo: Yuhikaku, 1954), 37–73.

family household over the generations, in spite of the negative sanction given to dissolution and the actual benefits derived from living together? The answers are both social-psychological and legal. Firstly, the failure is due partly to the tendency on the part of each component family unit to cohere within itself. (Naturally, there are institutional safeguards to defend the joint family against this tendency and to discourage cohesion of component units.) Secondly, the failure is due also to the legal right of male offspring to inherit an equally divided portion of family fortune. The fortune of a joint family is the accrued property, part of which each son assumes he will obtain sooner or later. The institution of equal division coupled with the coherence of constituent family units forms the basic impetus for family dissolution.

An explanation of cyclical dissolution of the Chinese family cannot be complete without a mention of the conditions that promote the aforesaid impetus. Those come from various types of internal discord. Japanese scholars in field interviews with Chinese peasants obtained the following as the conditions that led to dissolution.[22] Obviously, the first listed is the most important.

1. Quarrels among sisters-in-law, often over children or the unequal contributions of their husbands to the household.
2. Discord between mother-in-law and daughter-in-law.
3. Disharmony among brothers because of discrepancies in a variety of areas such as the degree of financial success, idleness versus diligence, frugality versus extravagance, and personal opinions. Sometimes, brothers' quarrels reflected those existing between their wives.
4. Tension between father and son, often closely linked to discord between mother-in-law and daughter-in-law.
5. Poverty. In cases where it was difficult to make a living, frustration on the part of sons or brothers tended to become so intense that the family was ready to find an outlet in quarrels.
6. Numerous family members, especially brothers. The existence of many brothers resulted in the inclusion of many sisters-in-law and complicated in-law relationships in the household. This was fertile soil for all manner of domestic discord.

Well-to-do families preferred to maintain themselves over generations without dissolution for reasons given in a foregoing paragraph. However, the larger the family size became and the more complicated the household composition, the greater the possibility for disharmony to occur and to lead to eventual disintegration. It was just for the purpose of avoiding such tensions that wealthy families had rules of avoidance or reserve and applied them as rigidly as possible.

The developmental cycle of the Chinese family suggests that the Japanese family would often fail to endure beyond a generation if all sons with their wives and children stayed in the natal household. A married son other than the heir may remain in the parental home, but only until the establishment of a new branch family.[23] It is the son's destiny to leave home before, at, or shortly after marriage and to find his own fortune, usually with financial aid from parents or the eldest brother, who lives with the parents and inherits almost all the property left by the former head. The institution to discourage all married sons except the heir from staying in the parental home for a long period of time minimizes possible in-law conflicts which are harmful for the continuation of the *ie,* the supragenerational entity. In this sense, the institution of primogeniture is a functional part of the stem family of Japan; and, similarly, that of equal division of property among coparceners is functionally linked to the cyclical growth and dissolution of the joint family of China.

COMPARATIVE REMARKS

Some comparative remarks have been made in the previous section. Here, the life cycle pattern of each of the major family types will be reviewed in terms of household types, and then the changes in the life cycle pattern of the contemporary Japanese families will be discussed from the cross-cultural standpoint.

---

[22]Noboru Niida, *Chinese Peasant Families* (Tokyo: University of Tokyo Press, 1952). Tomoo Uchida, *Family Dissolution in Rural China* (Tokyo: Iwanami-shoten, 1956).

[23]It is reported that joint family households existed very often in Japan's remote underdeveloped districts in the early part of the Edo period (1603-1867). They were, however, not joint-family-oriented but represented a variety of the stem family with a prolonged stay of married cadets in their parental households.

FAMILY TYPES, HOUSEHOLD TYPES, AND LIFE CYCLE PATTERNS

Employing composition as the criterion, the present writer classifies households into three types: the nuclear family household with no married offspring, the stem family household with a single married son or daughter, and the joint family household with two or more married offspring in one generation. Household is an actual manifestation, regulated by conditions of time and place, of the family as an institution. Household and family are not identical, but separate and yet interrelated orders. For example, the emergence of more nuclear family households does not necessarily indicate expanding support for the value of the conjugal family system.

With institutional orientation concerning household composition as the criterion, one can set up three family types, i.e., the conjugal family, the stem family, and the joint family, which have been employed in the present paper from the outset. As already suggested, a particular family type does not always take the form of a particular, seemingly corresponding household type. But, there is an undeniable link, of course, making exact correspondence likely. This correspondence can be explained by reference to the stages of the life cycle.

1. The conjugal family manifests itself mainly in the nuclear family household, seldom in the stem family household except in its incomplete form, and virtually never in the joint family household. The forms which a family takes over its life span are within the range of the nuclear family household.

2. The stem family demonstrates itself best in the stem family household, but often takes the form of a nuclear family household during its life cycle. It also occasionally appears as a joint family household but only when the married second or third son stays home temporarily. In Japan the intervention of a joint family household in a stem family household stage was more common formerly than today when the custom of married cadets remaining in the home has come to extinction.

3. The joint family demonstrates itself typically in the joint family household, but also takes the form of a stem family household when the family has only one married son. It also appears as a nuclear family household for some years immediately following the dissolution of the joint family household.[24]

Figure 14-3 summarizes the foregoing discus-

[24]Kiyomi Morioka, "Structure and Functioning of the Family," in *Family, Rural Village and City*, ed. by T. Fukutake *et al.* (Tokyo: University of Tokyo Press, 1957), 27.

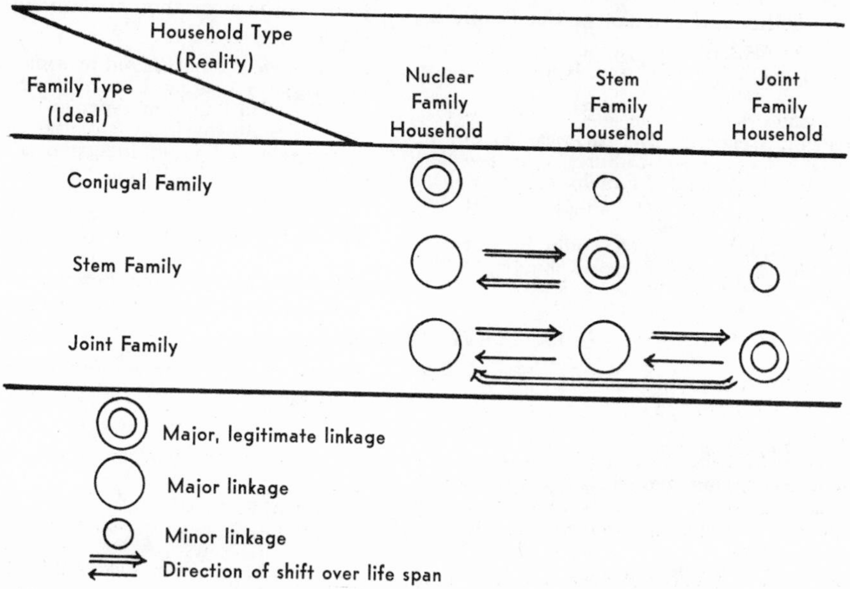

FIGURE 14-3.

sion. Since this figure is a device to describe the transformation of the stem family, it does not fit the conjugal family or the joint family as satisfactorily. However, it is useful in showing the relationship of family types, household types, and life cycle patterns.

THE CHANGING JAPANESE FAMILY AND ITS LIFE CYCLE PATTERN

In the previous subsection the present writer discussed tendencies of shifts in household types during the life span of a family, keeping the family type as a constant. With respect to changes in the family type, Conrad M. Arenberg has pointed out the irreversible trend of a shift from joint families to stem families and again from stem families to small (conjugal) families.[25] We can add the Japanese family to the list of examples in which a shift from the stem to the conjugal family has occurred or is occurring.

The conjugal family made inroads into Japan with official support in the wake of the last world war and has received widespread support. But it is hazardous to conclude that the traditional concept of the stem family has been displaced by this new pattern. There are rural-urban and generational variations in the attitudes toward this new concept of the family as illustrated in Takashi Koyama's comparative study of three districts in Tokyo.[26] The conjugal

family is popular in cities, and the younger generation is particularly enthusiastic about it. On the other hand, farmers and others with family enterprises handed down from forebears tend to adhere to the stem family. Naturally, the aged are suspicious of or even hostile toward this new invader. Even middle-aged urban white-collar workers who are converts to the new doctrine still retain some of the behavior patterns characteristic of the stem family. On the whole, we may say that the Japanese family is in a period of transition from the stem to the conjugal family.[27]

The changing status of the Japanese family permits us to compare it and the American family with regard to ages of wives at important events in the family's life. Table 14-2 is compiled from a combination of the numerical data prepared by Paul C. Glick on the American family[28] and my own materials on the Japanese family.

Although this table does not provide us with information which is completely comparable, nobody will miss some parallel trends in both countries. One is the decrease in the length of childbearing period, which is astonishing if the 1890 data for the U.S.A. are presented for comparison and which is undeniable with regard to Japan also, even though data for 1950 on this

---

[25]Conrad M. Arenberg, "The American Family in the Perspective of Other Cultures," in *Selected Studies in Marriage and the Family*, ed. by Robert F. Winch *et al.* (New York: Holt, Rinehart and Winston, Inc., 1962), 40–49.

[26]Takashi Koyama, (ed.), *A Study of Contemporary Families in Japan*, (Tokyo: Kobundo, 1960), 67–72.

[27]This view is not shared by some Japanese family sociologists including Kizaemon Ariga, who claims that the stem family of Japan is substantially maintained despite the impacts of the reformed postwar Civil Code and rapid industrialization since 1950. See K. Ariga, *The Japanese Family*, (Tokyo: Shibundo, 1965), 1–57.

[28]Paul C. Glick, "The Family Cycle," *American Sociological Review*, (April, 1947), 12:2, 164–174. Also, Glick, "The Life Cycle of the Family," *Marriage and Family Living*, February, 1955, 17:1, 3–9.

TABLE 14-2. AGES OF WIVES AT IMPORTANT EVENTS

Important Events	United States		Japan	
	1940	*1950*	*1950*	*1960*
First marriage (husband)	21.6 (24.3)	20.1 (22.8)	23.0 (25.9)	24.4 (27.2)
Birth of first child	22.6	. . .	. . .	26.3 28.7
Birth of last child	27.2	26.1	. . .	52.1
Marriage of first child	45.6	. . .	. . .	54.5
Marriage of last child	50.1	47.6	. . .	69.1
Death of husband	60.9	61.4	64.3	75.6
Death of wife	73.5	77.2	69.8	

point are lacking. Another is the remarkable expansion of the postparental period resulting from lengthened life expectancy and the shortened period of time for having children. In the United States the age at the time of marriage is another contributing factor to this trend, while in Japan it is a negative factor. Except for age at marriage, the American and the Japanese family reveal a similar trend so far as numerical data in Table 14-2 are concerned.

Another study which the present state of the Japanese family urges us to attempt is a reformulation of the set of life cycle stages. The one the present writer developed more than a dozen years ago is apt for the stem family, but not useful for the conjugal family. A new set should be applicable to both types; otherwise it cannot be useful for a study of the contemporary Japanese family which is changing from the stem to the conjugal family.

The procedure followed in the setting up of a new set of stages was, first of all, to divide a concrete family into component nuclear units and to record the number of units on the family line with the Roman numerals I, II, and III. ("I" means that the family is a nuclear family household, for example.) Then, eight stages of development were distinguished for each component nuclear unit and represented with the letters O, A, B, C, D, E, F, and G as follows:

Stage O (a newly married couple, prechild period); Stage A (the oldest child being an infant to six years old, preschool period); Stage B (the oldest child being seven to 12 years old, grade-school period); Stage C (the oldest child being 13 to 18 years old, middle-school period); Stage D (the oldest child being 19 years old or over until the last child leaves home, launching period); Stage E (after the last child has left home and until the father retires, post-parental period); Stage F (after the father has retired and until his death, aging period); Stage G (after the father has died and until the mother's death). This new set of cycle stages is obtained on the basis of Reuben Hill's three criteria and, therefore, it is, in substance, a Japanese translation of his nine stages.[29]

Then Roman numerals and letters were combined to designate household composition and stages of development of each component nuclear unit, as exemplified in the following lines:

IB:
A nuclear family household in the grade-school period.
IIF-C:
A stem family household with parents in the aging period and the son's nuclear unit in the middle-school period.
IIG-D-A:
A stem family household with a widowed grandmother, parents in the launching period, and the son's nuclear unit in the preschool period.

This new categorization is useful in describing the developmental status of particular families and in tracing in what generational combination of stages the shift from the stem to the conjugal family tends to occur. In a longitudinal panel study of about 50 stem family households in an agricultural neighborhood, in which this set of stages was applied, the present writer found that the departure of married heirs from parental households, which undermines the stem family, took place fairly often, however, only in the earlier stages of development, in O, A, or at latest B, and when the parents were in D, E, or F. In other words, pressures that bind a married heir to the natal household weaken during the period when his oldest child is about ten years old or under and his parents are still active enough to live without their son's help.[30] If the heir has taken advantage of this period and left for a job in a large urban center, which pays far more than farming, nobody can exactly predict, under present conditions of Japanese industrial growth and ideological climate, whether he will eventually return to his old home. He may come home to take care of his aged parents on the farm, or he may stay in town and have his parents join him if he is successful in business. When a farm family is uprooted, the concept of the stem family will gradually decline and fade away. This is because the primary props of the stem family of Japan are assumed to be family property and/or family enterprise handed down from the forefathers and the mutual aid network of the neighborhood in which families are interlocked by an endless number of payments and repayments over the generations.

[29]Hill, *op. cit.*

[30]Kiyomi Morioka, "Family Change and Reformulation of Cycle Stages," *International Christian University Journal of Social Sciences*, October, 1965, 6, 317–349.

15.

Carl E. Ortmeyer and Elizabeth F. Whiteman

MARRIAGE STATISTICS ANALYSIS, UNITED STATES

TRENDS IN MARRIAGES, MARRIAGE RATES, AND POPULATION, 1940–62

The years 1958-62 represent a "sea-level" shelf in the long-term trend in marriage totals and rates following a period of relatively marked ascents and declines. The marriage rate per 1000 resident population for the United States reached a peak (12.0) after World War I in 1920. It dropped to 10.3 in two years and except for two annual rates remained between 10.0 and 10.4 until 1929. During the first years of the economic depression of the early 1930's the rate dropped sharply to a low of 7.9 in 1932. There was an even sharper recovery by 1934 to a rate of 10.3 followed by a rise to 11.3 for 1937, a dip in 1938, and a moderate increase in 1939.

In 1940, the first year of the detailed analysis of trends in this report, the rate per 1000 resident population rose to 12.1, slightly above its peak after World War I of 12.0. By 1942 it reached 13.2 but then dropped to 10.9 by 1944 as young men moved from this country to the theaters of operations in World War II. The rate surged upward to a peak of 16.4 in 1946 during the demobilization of the Armed Forces after World War II. This rate was almost 25 percent higher than the peak in 1942 and 37 percent above the 12.0 peak after World War I. During the next three years the rate dropped successively by 15, 11, and 15 percent, continued to decline irregularly to 8.4 in 1958, and remained at 8.5 from 1959 to 1962.

The following analysis describes in somewhat more detail the interrelationships among trends in number of marriages and rates and their re-lationships to population growth and to changes in the age and sex composition of the population.

There are some limitations on the trend data used in the analysis. Distributions of brides and grooms by age are lacking except for one year, 1960. Were they available, both age-specific and age-adjusted rates could be computed. Estimates of the resident unmarried population, including Armed Forces living in barracks but not with their families, are not currently available for intercensal years (years other than those ending in 0). Age-specific marriage rates in 1960 for males and females by marital status prior to marriage could be estimated for the United States. The number of marriages expected on the basis of these 1960 rates could also be computed for each year since 1940, provided of course that the resident population by age, sex, and marital status could be estimated. Such annual expected totals would depict a trend based entirely on changes in the age, sex, and marital status composition of population. The difference between the trend in these expected totals and the trend in observed totals could then be definitely attributed to increases or decreases in specific rates of marriage. However, it would not be possible to estimate the degrees of change in any specified age, sex, or marital status groups.

· · ·

Although the marriage total was 51 percent larger in the peak year 1946 than the 1959-61 average, the rate per 1000 total population was 94 percent larger than its corresponding average. Thus overall population growth since about 1946 has exceeded the increase in number of marriages.

However, this growth in population has not been evenly distributed by sex and age. As shown in Figure 15-1, growth rates were greatest in the youngest age groups for both sexes

This selection is reprinted from: Carl E. Ortmeyer and Elizabeth F. Whiteman *Marriage Statistics Analysis, United States, 1962*, (Vital and Health Statistics, Series 21, No. 10), Washington, D.C., GPO: U.S. Department of Health, Education, and Welfare, 1967 [excerpted from the original report].

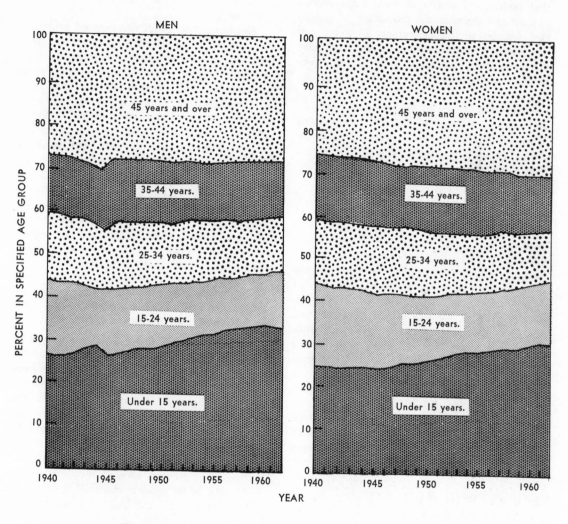

FIGURE 15-1. TRENDS IN PERCENTS OF RESIDENT MEN AND WOMEN
IN SPECIFIED AGE INTERVALS.

and in the oldest age group for women. Proportions of the population in the age groups
where most marriages occur declined. Only a
scattering of brides and grooms were under 15
years of age and 95 percent of all grooms and
97 percent of all brides in 1962 were less than
55 years of age. In 1940 the age group from
15 to 54 years included 60 percent of all males
and the same percent of females. By 1962 this
group included only 51 percent in each case.

During the years immediately following
World War II, 1946 to 1949, the rate per 1000
unmarried women 25 years of age and older
declined more sharply than did the rate per
1000 total women aged 15 years and over.
The former rate dropped from 79 percent to
19 percent above its 1959-61 level, while the
latter declined from 61 percent to 18 percent
above its 1959-61 level. This change in relationship between the trends in these two rates

during this four-year period reflects the fact that numbers of marriages were large enough to markedly decrease the proportion of unmarried females in the age group 15 years and over. Since 1949 the numbers of marriages have not been great enough to decrease this proportion appreciably or small enough to increase it.

Differences in trends in the rates for men and women 15 years of age and older during World War II show that many women waited until after the War to marry—the rate for women having declined more than that for men in 1943 and 1944.

A temporary imbalance in the sex ratio at peak marriage ages is occurring in the period of about 1960-68 since the large cohorts born around World War II are reaching the peak ages for first marriage (18 for women but 21 for men). There were marked increases in birth rates at the beginning of World War II and again in 1946 and 1947 after World War II. Women born in 1940 and 1941, and reaching age 18 in 1958 and 1959, were more numerous than men born in 1937 and 1938, who reached age 21 in 1958 and 1959. Similarly, women born in 1946 and 1947, and reaching age 18 in 1964 and 1965, were more numerous than men born in 1943 and 1944, who reached age 21 in 1964 and 1965. It may be that some women who would ordinarily marry at age 18 are delaying marriage until older ages. (Women who marry while in their twenties are more likely to marry men of the same age than are women who marry at ages under 20.)

. . .

AGE AT MARRIAGE

TRENDS, 1953-62

The predominant trend in age at marriage from 1953 to 1961 was a continuous increase in the percentage of brides and grooms who married when under 20. Between 1961 and 1962, however, this figure decreased from 41.7 to 39.7 percent. The 1962 figure is the same as that for 1958. In contrast, the percent of all brides in the age group 20-24 years increased from 31.8 in 1961 to 33.2 in 1962. The percent of brides marrying in this age group had changed little from 1959 to 1961. The percent of grooms

who were under 20 years of age at marriage remained at about the same level in both 1961 and 1962.

The proportion of all first-married brides under age 20 at marriage also decreased (from 52.2 percent in 1961 to 50.8 percent in 1962); the offsetting increase occurred chiefly in the group aged 20-24 years. The median age at first marriage of brides increased from 19.8 years in 1961 to 19.9 years in 1962 (Figure 15-2). Although the 1962 increase in median age was slight, it was the only increase in the ten-year period. The proportion of first-married grooms under age 20 was 18.3 percent, the same as in 1961. The percent of grooms aged 20-24 years also remained approximately the same in 1962, but the percent aged 25-29 years increased slightly. The median age at marriage of first-married grooms also increased slightly from 22.8 in 1961 to 22.9 in 1962.

. . .

MARRIAGES BY TYPE OF CEREMONY BY AGE OF BRIDE AND OF GROOM

The distribution of first marriages by type of ceremony performed shows that brides in the age groups 35-44, 45-54, and 55-64 years have the highest percentages of civil ceremonies. Brides in these age categories have almost twice as many civil ceremonies as brides married under 20 years of age (about 30 percent and 17 percent, respectively). For grooms, the age group 65 years and over has the highest proportion of civil ceremonies, followed by 45-54, 35-44, and 55-64 years in descending order.

The percentage distribution of remarriages by type of ceremony performed shows that grooms under 20 years of age have a high percentage (61.9) of civil ceremonies. This percentage declines as age increases, reaching 25.0 for ceremonies of grooms aged 65 and older. Between 38 and 40 percent of brides remarrying at all age levels under 45 years have civil ceremonies; this percentage declines to 18.7 for ceremonies of brides aged 65 and older.

For first marriages, brides and grooms in a peak marriage age group, 20-24 years, have the greatest proportion of religious ceremonies. In contrast, remarrying brides and grooms in the age category 65 years and over have the greatest proportion of religious ceremonies.

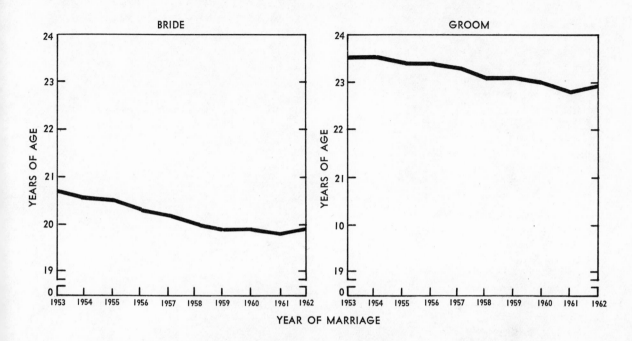

FIGURE 15-2. MEDIAN AGE AT FIRST MARRIAGE OF BRIDE AND OF GROOM:
TOTAL OF 19 SELECTED STATES.

CHAPTER V

The Woman in
Family and Society

IT IS MOST DIFFICULT to study the contemporary family and the family cycle without acknowledging that in the allocation of responsibilities, the role of women in society and in the family has changed markedly in the last century. This is not to say that the role of the husband has not also changed, for in some aspects the changes of male participation in the family have been relatively dramatic. It is probably impossible to have a change in the woman's role in the family without some sort of parallel or compensatory shift in the man's role.

As has often been pointed out, the traditional view of family life has kept the woman in the household. Most of the satisfactions available to her in the past were through her family. This was not the case for men, and thus the very nature of the participation in the family appears to have *altered* for women while it may have merely *shifted* for men.

In what sometimes is described as the movement from a father-dominated family to a democratically-oriented family, the role of the male has been considerably modified. He is still expected to be the primary breadwinner, but he no longer has the prerogative of autocratic rule with the expectation that wife and children will adhere to his demands. In the early industrial period the husband might not have been home very much because of the long hours and a six or seven day work week. But, when at home he was *the* authority. In modern suburban life, with the commuting distances and transportation problems that exist, the suburban father may not be at home much of the time. When he is home, the impact of his opinions may be relatively slight in comparison to those who are there more of the time.

For women, however, the changes are of a different order. The materials presented in this chapter are designed to emphasize some aspects of the new freedoms and also the new responsibilities assumed by women in the modern era. The ability to move out of the household is not an unmixed blessing, since conflicts arise for women. There is always a question of whether a woman should pursue a career if it means that the career competes directly with her ability to be a woman in the way society defines the role.

At best, the current era may be viewed as one of transition. In this chapter we explore some of the directions in which change is moving for women. In the article titled "The Status of Women in Modern Patterns of Culture," Jessie Bernard discusses the issues and problems associated over the globe with the defining of women's statuses in society. Questions of quality are prominent in these considerations, and the stage is set for examining in more detail some special aspects of women's place in the home and society.

One way of viewing the changes in women's roles is to examine the emergence of more similar behavior by both men and women. Charles Winick examines this type of orientation in his article titled "The Beige Epoch: Depolarization of Sex Roles in America" and notes that in play, boys and girls appear to be more similar than they have been in previous historical periods. Girls seem to demonstrate more sexual precocity and aggressiveness in aspects of behavior, and clothing appears to be moving in the direction of being more interchangeable with that of boys. Boys and girls are in some aspects of development exposed more uniformly to the same stimuli than in previous generations, and this may have consequences in many areas. The implications of such depolarization of sex roles for the future are explored in the article.

The article by Helena Znaniecki Lopata titled "The Life Cycle of the Social Role of Housewife," based on 1,000 depth interviews with urban housewives, examines three sets of life cycles. Emphasis is placed on concepts such as becoming a housewife, the expanding family circle, the peak stage where small children are present, the full house plateau, the shrinking family circle, and the miminal plateau or the final stage.

Some brief selections are presented from the *Report of the President's Commission on the Status of Women*, published in 1963. The first major summary report was titled *American Women* and heralded a new era of interest in examining the status of women as a minority group. It is of interest that in extending rights to minorities, the inclusion of rights for women has often been almost an afterthought. Even with the first report, changes in employment opportunities for women were noted; subsequent reports have been more specialized and less descriptive of the status of women, focusing particularly on areas in which advances of opportunities have occurred for women. These reports point out the double standard that exists in American society not only in sexual matters but in other important areas as well. The importance of women's economic independence has been emphasized by various branches of the government, especially by the *Women's Bureau,* but the existence of the President's Commission gave impetus to many government agencies to become concerned with the problem of women defined as a minority group.

One of the specialized reports from the President's Commission on the Status of Women was on *Civil and Political Rights.* The excerpt presented indicates some personal and property rights of married women. Some persons may be surprised to find that women and men are not equal under the law with regard to property rights, and that while the situation is one of inequity now, in prior times women's rights were even fewer and more tenuous.

Additional materials on women's status in the family and society will be found in other chapters. The chapter that follows on *Courtship and Mate Selection* obviously emphasizes the role of women, as courtship and related patterns have changed considerably even in the last few decades.

16.

JESSIE BERNARD

THE STATUS OF WOMEN IN MODERN PATTERNS OF CULTURE

I just happened to be in Kabul at the time when women began to appear in public with uncovered faces. The first ones were the airline stewardesses. They had been to Tashkent and New Delhi and seemed to feel no embarrassment, self-consciousness, or malaise in the exercise of their new freedom.

I was in Papeete a few years after its harbor was opened to tourist ships and the first air strips laid down. Already the young women performing in native dress for the tourists had begun to see themselves self-consciously, through tourist eyes, and knew how they looked to those people from beyond the seas. And the proud young women in Western dress bicycling to their jobs in shop and office had already acquired the tense expression resulting from schedules to keep and time to account for.

I was the recipient of the confidences of a wealthy young Arab flying back from the Middle East to school on the West Coast, anxious to see the American girl he hoped to marry. Yes, he would expect her to accept many of his ways; yes, he would expect to permit her many of her ways. No, he would not let her have a job for pay, certainly not one that involved contact with men. But what would he expect a university-trained girl to do all day? She could do volunteer work in a hospital. But he had said that she was interested in anthropology. Could she not, perhaps, do research? Work in a museum? Not if it meant dealing with men.

Last year's Christmas greetings from an old friend visiting in India included the announcement that his daughter, married to a Hindu, was getting a divorce and would return with her children to the United States; no ill will

on anyone's part. It had just not worked out.

I listened last year to a debate between two teams of African women at Howard University on the topic: "Resolved that polygyny should be officially sanctioned in Africa." The male judges, admitting that they had started with a prejudice on the positive side, awarded victory to the negative side.

I was the chairman of the doctoral committee of a young Pakistani who, like most graduate students, skated constantly at the brink of insolvency. Still, when his widowed mother wrote from Pakistan that he must go to Beirut and find a husband for his sister who was studying at a university there, he did—protesting, resentful, hostile, vowing that his was the last generation that would bow to the past, but obedient.

I have, puzzled, watched the ongoing efforts of sociologists and anthropologists to understand the relations between the sexes among the Caribbean peoples: are they to be interpreted in class or in cultural terms? It makes a difference if one is interested in change.

Revolution has become commonplace, daily fare, almost—incongruously—part of the status quo everywhere.

THE "STATUS OF WOMEN": A CHANGING MEDLEY

The term "status of women" refuses to sit still for its portrait; it is one of those evocative expressions which have no precise referent but which nearly everyone understands. It can refer to almost anything having to do with women. On December 14, 1961, President Kennedy charged that "we have by no means done enough to . . . encourage women to make their full contribution as citizens." He thought it appropriate, therefore, for us "to set forth before the world the story of women's progress

This selection is reprinted from: Jessie Bernard, "The Status of Women in Modern Patterns of of Culture," *The Annals,* 1968, 375, 3-14.

Reprinted with the permission of the author and publisher.

in a free, democratic society, to review recent accomplishments," but at the same time "to acknowledge frankly the further steps that must be taken." And this he rightly considered "a task for the entire nation." Accordingly, the President's Commission on the Status of Women was established by Executive Order 10980. Its reports covered the status water front, from restrictions on jury service to the degrading image of women projected by the mass media, from property rights to paid maternal leave.

Like the story of all reform movements, that of "women's rights" has had to do with both enacted rules (legislation and administrative rulings) and so-called crescive rules (mores, custom, tradition, and convention). Until well into the twentieth century, the first predominated. The term "status of women" referred primarily to the political and legal rights of women, that is, to the kinds of rights that legislators or administrators could do something about. Most of those rights have now been achieved, including, in the 1964 Civil Rights Act, the right to equal opportunity in employment. That battle is now a clean-up operation, bringing backward areas into the main stream. The term now has to do with such rights as the right to privacy and to contraception. The frontier battles have shifted from rights denied by enacted norms to rights denied by crescive norms.

Along with the movement for legal and political rights, there had been, even in the nineteenth century, a movement for "sexual emancipation." Sober demands by the more conservative leaders for the suffrage and for legal protection of women had been paralleled by demands of some, of the more radical, for "free love." Some Marxists—but not Karl Marx himself—had promised women this boon under socialism;[1] once women had achieved economic independence, they could also achieve sexual independence.

The two kinds of reform—political and sexual—were related, but by no means in a simple one-way manner. When lower-class women were

at the mercy of exploitative men of all classes, the sexual revolution needed to protect them was one which gave them, as well as upper-class women, the prerogative of "respectability." Steven Marcus has shown how Victorian puritanism had an elevating effect on the status of women.

Among the urban lower classes until well into the nineteenth century . . . life was degraded and often bestial; drink, violence, early and promiscuous sexuality, and disease were the counterparts of poverty, endless labor, and a life whose vision of futurity was at best cheerless. In such a context, the typical Victorian values, and indeed Victorianism itself, take on new meaning. It is not usual nowadays to regard such values as chastity, propriety, modesty, even rigid prudery, as positive moral values, but it is difficult to doubt that in the situation of the urban lower social classes they operated with positive force. The discipline and self-restraint which the exercise of such virtues required could not but be a giant step toward the humanization of a class of persons who had been traditionally regarded as almost of another species. Indeed, the whole question of "respectability" stands revealed in a new light when we consider it from this point of view. One of the chief components of respectability is self-respect, and when we see this young girl [in *My Secret Life*] resisting all that money, class, privilege, and power, we understand how vital an importance the moral idea of respectability could have for persons in her circumstances.[2]

But the wall of mores which protected some women was seen by others as a wall which cut them off from male prerogatives. They aimed their attack on the subtler rights denied them not by law or administrative rules, but by mores, custom, tradition, and convention. Why should men have more freedom than women? Why should women have to use the family entrance? Why could they not smoke and drink as men did? Why one standard of behavior for men and another for women? Why should women not be permitted as much sexual satisfaction as men? This relative emphasis on rights in the area of crescive norms, especially the mores, as compared with enacted norms, characterizes the status issues at the present time.

In discussing changes over time, it is important to remind ourselves of the enormous stability of social forms. The modal or typical

---

[1] For example, August Bebel, *Die Frau und der sozialismus* (Zurich, 1883). Translated by M. L. Stern in 1910 as *The Soul of Woman under Socialism*.

[2] Steven Marcus, *The Other Victorians* (New York: Basic Books, 1966), 146.

segments of a population show great inertia; they change slowly. The modal or typical college girl today is not astonishingly different from her counterpart of the 1940's—or even the 1930's or 1920's. What does change, and rapidly, is the form which the nontypical takes. It is the nontypical which *characterizes* a given time: that is, the *typical*, which tends to be stable, has to be distinguished from the *characteristic* or characterizing, which tends to be fluctuating. When we speak of "the silent generation" or "the beat generation" or the "anti-establishment generation" we are not referring to the typical member of any generation but to those who are not typical. To say, therefore, that the characteristic issues for young women of the 1960's are rights to privacy, to contraception, or to greater sexual freedom is not the same as saying that the typical young woman actively espouses these issues.

TECHNOLOGICAL CULTURE AND THE STATUS OF WOMEN

The term "culture" as popularly used has, like "status of women," only an imprecise referent which most people feel they understand until they try to define it. Actually, the norms which define the status of women constitute a considerable segment of any culture. They *are* major components of the culture—nonmaterial aspects, to be sure, but no less real for that. They act upon the material, especially the technological, aspects, as well as being themselves acted upon by them. If the mores had forbidden women to follow their work into the mills and factories, the technologies which depended on their work would have been retarded. But if the technology had not created the wage-paying jobs for them, the status of women would have continued to be one of universal dependence. It is a nice theoretical point to determine, in any one case, which way the influence operates. The emphasis for the most part has tended to be on the effect of material culture on the status of women rather than the other way round. And the effect, it has been found, has been great.

A generation ago, a team of cultural anthropologists surveyed the literature on the ma-

terial culture of "the simpler peoples" to see how it related to their institutions. So far as the position of women was concerned, they concluded that it was "not favorable as judged by modern standards."[3] It was a little worse among pastoral peoples than among hunting or agricultural peoples and worse in some areas of the world than in others, but "the preponderance of the negative type holds throughout."[4]

Not so among industrialized cultures. Among them, the status of women goes up along with that of the other formerly disadvantaged. With industrialization and urbanization, families everywhere tend to converge on the so-called conjugal system, a system which favors women:

Everywhere the ideology of the conjugal family is spreading, even though a majority does not accept it. It appeals to the disadvantaged, to the young, to women, and to the educated. It promises freedom and new alternatives as against the rigidities and controls of traditional systems. It is as effective as the appeal of freedom or land redistribution or an attack on the existing stratification system. It is radical, and is arousing support [even] in many areas where the rate of industrialization is very slight.[5]

The "material culture" which we call industrialism is the first, Goode reminds us, which permits women to hold independent jobs, to control the money they earn—a fact which greatly improves their bargaining position within the family—and to assert their rights and wishes within that group. In addition, the new system gives women allies in the outside world, third-party support for their demands within as well as outside the family.

Although there is nothing in the material culture of industrialized societies which precludes full equality for women, the actual prospects for full equality are not bright:

. . . we do not believe that any . . . system now in operation, or likely to emerge in the next generation, will grant full equality to women, although throughout the world the general position of women will improve greatly. The revolutionary philosophies

[3]L. T. Hobhouse, G. C. Wheeler, and M. Ginsberg, *The Material Culture and Social Institutions of the Simpler Peoples* (London: Chapman and Hall, 1915), 173.

[4]*Ibid.*, 174.

[5]W. J. Goode, *World Revolution and Family Patterns* (New York: Free Press, 1963), 369.

which have accompanied the shifts in power in Communist countries or in the Israel *kibbutzim* have asserted equality, and a significant stream of philosophic thought in the West has asserted the right to equality, but no society has yet granted it. Nor does the movement in Western countries, including the Communist countries, suggest that the future will be greatly different. We believe that it is possible to develop a society in which this would happen, but not without a radical reorganization of the social structure.[6]

TWO ROADBLOCKS TO EQUALITY

Two roadblocks, Goode finds, stand in the way of this radical reorganization of the social structure, essential for full equality:

1) The family base upon which all societies rest at present requires that much of the daily work of the house and children be handed over to women. Doubtless, men can do this nearly as well, but they have shown no eagerness to assume these tasks, and (2) families continue to rear their daughters to take only a modest degree of interest in full–time careers in which they would have equal responsibilities with men.[7]

With respect to the care of the home, modern technology has reduced the time and effort required to a very moderate level.[8] And whether or not men show any eagerness to assume household tasks, they do show at least willingness to assume them, as studies of the marriages of working women show.[9] In any event, no radical reorganization of the social structure would be called for if care of the house were the only roadblock in the path of equality.

The care of children is a more difficult one to deal with. The President's Commission on the Status of Women recognized the need for services to help mothers carry their responsibilities. They recommended a wide array of such services, including child-care services, health services, and services related to the home, as well as services related to employment.[10] And they placed the responsibility for providing these services on the local community, on voluntary organizations, on professional associations, and on federal and state governments.[11] These are among the new rights women ask for in the drive for equality.

Even without them, the care of children, though difficult, is manageable when we are dealing with, let us say, two children, whose intensive care takes only about ten years of a woman's life. But it becomes formidable when we are dealing with four, five, or six children, whose care covers a span long enough to preclude other life options.

MOTHERHOOD AND THE STATUS OF WOMEN

Although the existence of abortion and infanticide in many past societies shows that motherhood *per se* is no guarantee of high status for women, still in many societies, both Oriental and Western, there has been a strong tendency to honor and encourage motherhood. "Facts about the desirability of offspring should [therefore] always be noted in a study of the status of mother and wife."[12] Actually, there has always been a reverse relationship between the birth rate and status as measured by such

[6]*Ibid.*, 373.

[7]*Ibid.*, 373.

[8]Robert W. Smuts, *Women and Work in America* (New York: Columbia University Press, 1959), 26; W. F. Ogburn and M. F. Nimkoff, *Technology and the Changing Family* (New York: Houghton Mifflin Company, 1955), *passim*.

[9]The research literature is summarized in F. Ivan Nye and Lois W. Hoffman (eds.), *The Employed Mother in America* (Chicago: Rand McNally, 1963), chap. xv.

[10]U.S., President (Kennedy), Commission on the Status of Women, *Report of the Committee on Home and Community*, October, 1963, *passim*.

[11]No mention was made by the Commission of the responsibility of employers to supply help except in respect to paid maternity leave. For a discussion of employers' attitudes, see Nye and Hoffman (eds.), *loc. cit.*, chap. xxvi. Yet the question may well be raised with respect to motherhood: why should women have to pay the entire cost? When mechanization and automation began to deprive workers of their jobs, the same question was raised: why should one set of workers have to pay, with their unemployment, the entire cost of technological progress? Severance pay, retraining, and other devices were introduced to spread the costs. Perhaps the "right" of women to part-time jobs and to other concessions by industry to their peculiar career needs may be just around the corner. They may, in fact, constitute the radical reorganization of the social structure to which Goode referred.

[12]Elsie Clews Parsons, *The Family* (New York: G. P. Putnam's Sons, 1906), 229. Mary Wollstonecraft argued for the emancipation of women on the grounds of impaired maternity.

indexes as income, education, and occupation. This inverse relationship was, in fact, often invoked in the nineteenth century as an argument against the emancipation of women. Legal independence would create instability in marriage; economic independence would detract from motherhood or, worse still, lead to "race-suicide."[13] Such logic underlies the *Kirche, Küche, und Kinder* policy with respect to the status of women. Still, despite the jeremiads, the birth rate did go down and the status of women as measured in terms of political, legal, and economic rights did go up until well into the twentieth century.

STRANGE INTERLUDE: THE MOTHERHOOD MANIA, 1946–1957

In addition to the expectable trend fluctuations, there occurred at mid-century—between 1940 and 1957—an enormous upsurge in the fertility rate in the United States. The first phase can be fairly well "explained" in terms of expectable postdepression and postwar babies. But, on the basis of past experience, the trend should thereafter have resumed the long-time downward slope characteristic of the twentieth century or at least should have leveled off. But it did not. When, instead, it continued to increase at an almost unprecedented rate into the 1950's, demographers ran out of precedents for explaining it. For the first time since records had been kept, there was actually an upward secular trend (as contrasted with fluctuations with the business cycle and with war) in the birth rate.

One explanation offered for this strange interlude is the capture of the minds of women by the so-called feminine mystique, a psycho-analytically-spawned doctrine that one could be a woman only by having children, that women who sought self-fulfillment outside of the home were a lost sex.[14] A whole generation of women returned to weaving, baking, and food-preservation—along with extravagant motherhood—to validate their femininity. Another explanation was that the retreat into ma-

ternity was a revulsion against the anomie and impersonality of modern life. Prosperity was another stand-by explanation.

The sheer satisfaction of parenthood, a kind of "child-hunger," has recently also been invoked. Judith Blake, on the basis of world-wide demographic data, concludes that having children is more satisfying to many people as a way of life than are the alternatives; they are therefore willing to make economic sacrifices to achieve it.[15]

And women in the United States were willing to sacrifice more—education and careers and status-equality—for that way of life. For, whatever the causes of the mania for maternity may have been, the concomitants and consequences were adverse for the status of women. It was accompanied by a decline in graduate study[16] (see Figure 16-1), in career aspirations,[17] and, in general, in participation in the world.[18]

During the great baby boom, women expected to be envied by women and approved of by men when they had a fourth, fifth, or even sixth child. At the very least, they could expect to be excused from other responsibilities. The ability to afford many babies was, in effect, a "status symbol." But mounting costs for schools, health facilities, and other community provisions for the onrushing generation began gradually to puncture the euphoric mood —as did, also, the frightening threat of uncontrolled population growth.

We have now come full circle. Judith Blake tells us that we are going to have to find acceptable nonfamilial substitute roles for women, to supply the satisfactions that they find in motherhood. In a world that, faced with a population crisis, cannot permit women to indulge their "child-hunger," jobs are needed that can supply companionship, recreation, and creative activity as alternatives to motherhood. Partici-

---

[13]*Ibid.*, 357.

[14]Betty Friedan, in *The Feminine Mystique* (New York: W. W. Norton, 1963), summarized the literature on this curious phenomenon.

[15]Judith Blake, *Demographic Science and the Redirection of Population Policy* (Berkeley and Los Angeles: University of California Press, 1966).

[16]U.S., Department of Labor, Women's Bureau, *Trends in Educational Attainment of Women*, June, 1966.

[17]Ethel J. Alpenfels, "Women in the Professional World," in Beverly Benner Cassara (ed.), *American Women: The Changing Image* (Boston: Beacon Press, 1962), 73–89.

[18]*Ibid., passim.*

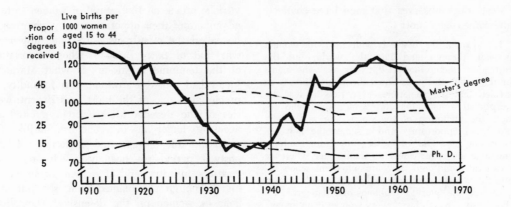

FIGURE 16-1. INVERSE RELATIONSHIP BETWEEN FERTILITY RATE AND PROPORTION OF ALL
ADVANCED DEGREES EARNED BY WOMEN*

*Sources: Fertility data: Population Reference Bureau, *Population Profile,* March,
1967; degree data: U.S. Department of Labor, Women's Bureau, *Trends in Educational Attainment of Women,* June, 1966, Chart C.

pation in the labor force, she notes, is the most relevant variable associated with family size in the Western world. If women can be deflected from familial roles, they may be satisfied with smaller families. "Until nonfamilial roles begin to offer significant competition to familial ones as avenues for adult satisfaction,"[19] we can expect Spencer's "genesis" to win over female "individuation."

ONLY A MODEST DEGREE OF INTEREST IN EQUAL RESPONSIBILITIES

Goode's second major roadblock to equality— lack of interest on the part of women in assuming equal responsibilities—can be documented by a respectable research literature[20] which suggests that most women would reject any radical reorganization of the social structure required for the achievement of full equality. Under the impact of the pressures of sympathetic men and activist women, much-publicized campaigns are inaugurated to find women for top positions in the federal government;

administrators are hounded by the White House to upgrade women staff members; honors are bestowed on top-level women; a President's Commission is appointed and labors long and industriously to improve the status of women— all with less than spectacular success.

Thoughtful leaders look with a jaundiced eye on the refusal or unwillingness of women to take full advantage of their opportunities.[21] They have little patience with the regression of women into maternity. Hear Margaret Mead:

We may well ask, in these days of great freedom, when education is as open to women as men, when the great professions of medicine and law, teaching and scientific research are open to women, how do we stand?

The answer is very simple; we stand very badly indeed. . . . And we may well ask why. Why have we returned, for all our great advances in technology, to the Stone Age arrangement in which women's main ambition is to acquire and hold a mate, to produce or adopt children who are to be the exclusive delight and concern of a single married pair, and in which work outside the home . . . holds no attraction in itself, unless it is subservient to the demands of an individual household. . . . Woman has returned, each to her separate cave . . . almost totally unaware of any life outside her door.[22]

[19]Judith Blake, quoted in *The Public Interest* (Spring, 1966), 128.

[20]Dael Wolfle, *America's Resources of Specialized Talent* (New York: Harper, 1954), 234–236; Jessie Bernard, *Academic Women* (University Park: Pennsylvania State University Press, 1964), chap. xii.

[21]Margaret Mead, "Introduction" to Cassara (ed.), *loc. cit.,* xi–xii.

[22]*Ibid.*

Pearl Buck observes that men have changed but women have not:

> The door of the house is wide open for women to walk through and into the world, but the stupendous scene beyond terrifies her. She slams the door shut and pulls down the shades. She is so terrified that she sometimes even rails against the exceptional woman, the daring individual who accepts the invitation of the open door and enters into wider opportunity and assumes the new responsibility. . . . Old prejudices are fading, intelligent men are eagerly seeking intelligence wherever it can be found and they are impatient when intelligent women continue to live in narrow ways, apart from the world's problems and dangers. . . . The question which faces every woman is no longer, "Do I want to?" or "How can I?" The answer is simple. "You must!"[23]

And Agnes E. Meyer says sternly: "I feel very strongly that the educated women of America are not taking their responsibility to the nation's strength and welfare seriously enough."[24] Ethel J. Alpenfels documents the recession of women from the professional world, noting the decline of women in the professions from one half in 1930 to about one third in the 1960's.[25] "The status of women deteriorates," she notes, "even while the administrative heads of their universities and colleges ponder the ways and means of salvaging lost talent."[26]

Even when women are themselves held responsible for their inferior status, men are often blamed for making women what they are. Thus, Marya Mannes: "Women are not by nature denied the ability to think creatively and abstractly. It is rather that this ability is unpopular with women because it is unpopular with men."[27] Or culture in the form of a "climate of opinion" is blamed. "It is not the individual young girl, or young wife or older woman who is to blame; it is the climate of opinion that has developed in this country."[28] The most

vitriolic attack on the refusal of women to take advantage of their opportunities, by what might be called the men-by-way-of-women approach, was that of Betty Friedan, whose excoriation of the feminine mystique, or what Margaret Mead had called a "retreat into fecundity,"[29] precipitated one of the most heated controversies of the decade. Miss Friedan pointed an accusing finger at everyone responsible for glorifying the exaggerated maternity of the postwar period—psychoanalysts, educators, advertisers, industry—and at women for succumbing.[30] Though she blamed men, she put millions of women on the defensive. Their lives *did* begin to look trivial under her unsympathetic eye; they *were* able-bodied; they *did* have little to do around the house; the children *did* resent too much meddling in their lives.

As frequently happens, the trends here attacked had already begun to moderate by the time they had been widely recognized and bemoaned. Five years before Betty Friedan's book appeared, women were already beginning to delay marriage,[31] return to college,[32] go on for graduate study,[33] as well as reduce the number of babies they bore.[34] Whether they would also now be willing to undertake full-time careers and assume equal responsibilities with men was still a question. It is too early as yet to discern trends. But the indications are that neither a full-time career nor unbridled motherhood will be the characteristic option. For even during the period that was dominated by the feminine mystique, there was almost a stampede of mothers back into the labor force; the

[23]Pearl Buck, "Changing Relationships between Men and Women," Cassara (ed.), *loc. cit.*, 8–9.

[24]Agnes E. Meyer, "Leadership Responsibilities of American Women," Cassara (ed.), *loc cit.*, 11.

[25]Ethel J. Alphenfels, "Women in the Professional World," Cassara (ed.), *loc. cit.*, 78–79.

[26]*Ibid.*, 79.

[27]Marya Mannes, "Female Intelligence—Who Wants It?," *New York Times Magazine,* January 3, 1960 (Cassara [ed.], *loc cit.*, 78–79).

[28]Mead "Introduction," Cassara (ed.), *loc cit.*, xiii.

[29]*Ibid.*, xii.

[30]Friedan, *op. cit., passim.*

[31]The age at first marriage: 1940 (21.5); 1947 (20.5); 1955 (20.2); 1960 (20.3); 1963 (20.5); 1965 (20.6); 1966 (20.5).

[32]Percentage of high school graduates who were first-time college enrollees: 1950 (31.3); 1954 (36.9); 1958 (40.0); 1962 (44.4); 1964 (45.0).

[33]Proportion of all master's and other second-level degrees granted to women: 1940 (38.2); 1950 (29.2); 1960 (31.6); 1964 (31.8). Proportion of doctorate and equivalent degrees granted to women: 1940 (13.0); 1950 (9.6); 1960 (10.5); 1964 (10.6).

[34]The rate of third births declined from 33 per 1000 in 1957 to 24.4 per 1000 in 1965; of fourth births, from 21 per 1000 in 1961 to 15.7 in 1965; of fifth babies, from 12 per 1000 in 1959–1962 to 9.3 in 1965. See "Baby Boom Ends," *Statistical Bulletin* of the Metropolitan Life Insurance Company, 47 (October 1966), 1.

feminine mystique did not keep millions of mothers from wanting jobs[35]—not, however, at the higher, more responsible levels. A job, not a career, was the trade-off in their dilemma. And even this compromise was far from achieving universal acceptance. Despite the urgent efforts of educators, counselors, and leaders, girls—and boys—are still unaware of the pattern of women's lives in this day and age. They "hold traditional attitudes about the place of women in modern society," and, as a result, "most of the girls will finish their education either unprepared or poorly prepared to take a place in society in which they will feel satisfied and fulfilled."[36] Goode's second roadblock stands firm.

SEXUALITY AND THE STATUS OF WOMEN

It was a standard argument against woman's rights in the nineteenth century that suffrage and political activity would "unsex" women. The converse was not usually articulated, namely, that emphasizing female sexuality would detract from serious participation in the outside world. But Agnes Meyer was making precisely this charge in the 1960's:

> It seems tragic that just when the challenge to women and their opportunities for service are greatest, the younger ones are so profoundly influenced by the overemphasis on sex now so prevalent in our whole culture that they are reverting to female rather than to womanly ideals.[37]

And Marya Mannes and Margaret Culkin Banning concurred. Miss Mannes noted that it was the *Playboy* Bunny and the whole *Playboy* psychology that degraded women;[38] and Mrs. Banning, that the emphasis on glamour tended to demote women.[39]

The men did not agree. They defended the idea of "an impossibly attractive, charming

. . . woman" as an ideal.[40] And even from the Soviet Union came word that feminine beauty was a worthy goal.

Soviet women were advised to pay more attention to their looks and charm. Men were told to look upon them as something more than a comrade worker. "We need an art which educates young boys to admire the miracle of beauty in women and young girls to aspire to imitate the examples of such beauty," said *Literaturnaya Gazeta* (Literary Gazette).

"Along with the full equality of women we need a cult of women's charm." The publication complained that Soviet women often are negligent about their appearance. There has been a tendency under communism to regard attention to clothes, cosmetics, and hairdo as a waste of time. But "the esthetics of woman's beauty is needed by the whole population, both men and women," the article contended. It was written by 68-year-old Ilya Selvinsky, a poet. A common theme, repeated by Selvinsky, is that legal equality does not mean that the sexes should behave and be treated exactly alike. The article urged not only that women become more feminine, but that they be idealized. "For a barbarian a woman is simply a person of the opposite sex," Selvinsky said. "But art teaches men to idealize women. This distinguishes civilized people from primitive ones."[41]

To be sure, Agnes Meyer, Marya Mannes, and Mrs. Banning are not talking to the same issue as is the Soviet poet, Selvinsky. But in his plea for feminine glamour there are reverberations of the nineteenth-century lady-on-a-pedestal, adored at a distance, and not permitted to demean herself by entrance into the male world. And, as the women sense, "to be looked up to" is not a substitute for equality.

CHANGING ISSUES

The issues that engage young women today have little to do with the traditional rights-for-women issues of the past. It is revealing of the changes in issues to note that on the same day (March 31, 1967), the press reported that, al-

---

[35]Nye and Hoffman (eds.), *loc. cit.*
[36]Kenneth K. Kern, "High School Freshmen and Seniors View the Role of Women in Modern Society," *The Bulletin on Family Development* (Family Study Center, University of Missouri, Kansas City, Mo.), 5 (Winter 1965), 11, 12.
[37]Agnes Meyer, in Cassara (ed.), *loc. cit.*, 11.
[38]"Portrayal of Women by the Mass Media," *Report of the President's Commission on the Status of Women*, 22.
[39]*Ibid.*

[40]*Ibid.*
[41]"Charm Comes to Comrade Olga: Will She Ogle Back?," *Washington Post*, April 13, 1967.

though only "a little over four years ago, Afghan women rarely set foot inside a mosque because, as many men said, 'their presence would interfere with sober prayer,' . . . today . . . that is all changed";[42] that in Korea today "instead of offering their daughters dowries and inheritances in cash and goods, farmers sell their land in order to send their daughters to college";[43] and that in the United States it was the right to the contraceptive pill that was being debated: "Any woman student over the age of 21 should be able to obtain contraceptive devices or prescriptions through the health service physician just as she could from the private physician."[44]

American women had never had to contend with religious exclusion; they have long since enjoyed the right to a college education; they are now asking for the right to get contraceptive help outside of marriage. There is little talk nowadays, as there was in the past, about "free love" but a considerable amount of discussion on the right to privacy, which may take the form of freedom from conventional controls. College students, for example, when interviewed about their position on the matter are often quoted as saying: "I don't care to indulge myself but I don't object if others do. They have a right to do it if they want to." The rights which the current generation of women seek are personal, private, and often sexual. And the confronting parties on these issues are not women versus men but one generation versus another. Young people of both sexes affirm their right to privacy, which amounts in many cases to a right to unregulated—though not promiscuous—sexual relations.

EQUALITY AND DIFFERENCES

How to equate differences in any area is a perennial and all-pervasive problem. As very young children, we are taught that we cannot

add apples and puppies and get fruits. A great deal of thought goes into ways to reduce different kinds of things to common units in order to deal with them logically, if not mathematically. In the area of sex differences, for example, we automatically adjust intelligence quotient (IQ) tests so that the average IQ of both sexes comes out 100.

Interesting in this connection is the trend among some young people in the mid-1960's toward a monosex or unisex, toward a convergence in dress and coiffure, toward a minimization of the usual, conventional sex distinctions. They emphasize their common status as human beings rather than their different statuses as males and females. Their stand could be interpreted as another aspect of the effort to remove all norms which make a distinction between the sexes in privileges, prerogatives, or responsibilities. But it seems to have little if any affinity with the traditional "woman's rights" movement which had the same goal. It is, however, as logical an outcome as the Equal Employment Opportunity Act of 1964.

A ZERO-SUM GAME?

There are even profounder aspects to the relationship between sexuality and the status of women. For women, the relevant problems have to do with the implications of sexuality for equality; for men, with the implications of equality for sexuality.

Some of the rights which women demanded in their movement for emancipation did not have the effect of seriously depriving men of their rights. Giving women the vote did not deprive men of theirs.[45] But granting other rights to women did deprive men. In such cases, it was a zero-sum situation. Laws, for example, which gave property rights took rights away from men. And laws which forbade discrimination in employment deprived men of an advantage in certain kinds of jobs. In a sense, any attempt to equalize unequal statuses can raise one only by lowering the other. In this sense, sexual equality is paid for by men.

---

[42]*Washington Post*, March 31, 1967.

[43]*Ibid.*

[44]*Ibid.* In the off-campus world, the issue of rights with respect to contraception took the form of the rights of relief recipients to such services. By the mid-1960's, this issue seemed to be settled; every woman had such a right, even young, unmarried women.

[45]Alan P. Grimes, *The Puritan Ethic and Woman Suffrage* (New York: Oxford University Press, 1967).

In the past, when the drive toward equality of the sexes dealt with a single standard, it was the feminine standard that was sought; in recent years, the male standard. A cultural pattern inherited from Victorian times prescribing a passive, recipient, nondemanding role for women in the sexual encounter was transmuted into one which, at least in some circles, called for active, even aggressive, sexual behavior on their part. There was to be no double standard so far as sexual satisfaction was concerned. Orgasm became almost a civil right. Women had sexual rights as well as men (whether they wanted them or not).

We have been so amazed at these phenomena, so concentrated on the changes in female sexuality, that until now we have not noticed the effect they were having on men. Recently, however, the psychological costs to men have received attention. It now appears that granting women the privilege of sexual initiative, not to mention aggressiveness, can have a sexually depressing effect on men. A growing literature alerts us to the "masculinity crisis" of modern men.[46] It raises the question: How much equality can the sexes stand? Women who prize male sexuality may be willing to pay a price to protect it; they will guard Goode's second roadblock; they will settle for less than complete equality. But others will want to know: Why should we?

There are certainly no easy answers.

[46]See, for example, Myron Brenton, *The American Male: A Penetrating Look at the Masculinity Crisis* (New York: Coward-McCann, 1966); Hendrik M. Ruitenbeek, *The Male Myth* (New York: Dell Publishing Co., Inc., 1967).

17.

HELENA ZNANIECKI LOPATA

THE LIFE CYCLE OF THE SOCIAL ROLE OF HOUSEWIFE

This article[1] is devoted to the analysis of the life cycle of the social role of housewife, and of its placement in the role cluster of performers at different stages in their life cycles.[2] It thus combines the concepts of social role and role cluster with three sets of life cycles: that of the role, that of the social person bearing the title of the role, and that of the participants in the social circle. The analysis is based upon the Znaniecki definition of social role as a set of patterned relations between a social person and participants of the social circle, involving sets of duties which are the functions of the role, and the sets of rights which enable their performance.[3] In all but new roles, a social role

definition

This selection is reprinted from: Helena Znaniecki Lopata, "The Life Cycle of the Social Role of Housewife," *Sociology and Social Research*, 1966, *51*, 5–22.

Reprinted with the permission of the author and publisher.

[1]Revised version of paper read in the Sociology of Aging session of the Midwest Sociological Society meetings in April, 1965, in Minneapolis, Minnesota.

[2]The major contributor to the concept of life cycle of the family is Paul Glick, both in his *American Families* (New York: John Wiley & Sons, Inc., 1957) and in articles, including: "The Family," *American Sociological Review*, April, 1947, *XII*, 164–174, and "The Life Cycle of the Family," *Marriage and Family Living*, February, 1955, *XVII*, 3–9. Most of the textbooks on the family rely on this concept.

This is a major focus of Evelyn Duvall's *Family Development* (Phila.: J. B. Lippincott Co., 2nd edition 1962) and Robert Winch uses it throughout his *The Modern Family* (New York: Holt, Rinehart and Winston, Inc., 1963). See also J. S. Slotkin's "Life Course in Middle Age," *Social Forces*, December, 1954, *33*, 171–76, for reference to the concept of "life course" developed in Germany by Charlotte Bühler.

[3]The definition and theoretical framework for the concept of social role are contained in the work of Florian Znaniecki. They first appeared in English in

(*Footnote continued on next page*)

is entered into when more than one "other" (or Parson's "alter") accepts a person into culturally defined relations after tests have indicated that he is fit to carry out the duties and to receive the rights. The title of the role is assigned to this person who is the center of the relations, toward whom rights are directed and from whom duties are expected. The role is based upon cultural expectations, but it is the actual set of relations. Members of the society and sociologists select only certain generalized and patterned actions in describing a role and in indicating it by the use of the title.

Although the title of a social role is assigned to the one person who is the center of the relations, the role does not exist if only that person carries out a system of actions.[4] It requires at least two more persons who interact within him because of the role. Thus roles require relational duties and, usually, task duties, but never the latter alone. The rights include the permission to carry out the duties, certain actions by circle members, and the facilities they provide in order to enable the functioning of the role.

Social roles can be located in a variety of systems. They are always assigned positions in status or prestige systems and, in the case of associational groups, in organizational charts.[5] They can also be seen as having location in clusters of all the social roles carried out by their participants. Each human being performs, usually, if not always, several social roles at any stage of his life, each role within a different social circle, but often among the same aggregates of human beings. The role clusters tend to be focused by the individual around a central role, with relative degrees of importance assigned by him to other roles which are placed in different locations from this center. Each role, of course, can take the center stage briefly every time attention is focused on it. However, it is the thesis of this paper that the individual tends to focus on one or at the most two, roles in any cluster he maintains. The life cycle of a human being can be seen as involving shifts in the components of his role cluster when new roles are added and old ones dropped, and shifts in the location of each role in the cluster. Modifications in the characteristics of each role occur as the individual enters different stages of its life cycle or changes his definition of the role, or as a consequence of shifts in the cluster. Changes in the role definition can, of course, be brought about by events external to the person, such as modifications in the components or characteristics of the social circle or in their definitions of the role or of their part in it.

The title "housewife" is assigned, in Western European and American societies, to women who are, or have been, married and who "run" their own households, clearly differentiating between them and daughters who care for the homes of their fathers, "housemothers" in sororities, or "housekeepers" running the households of their employers.[6] The matter of proprietal rights over the household is an issue in our society, as evidenced by the aged mother who feels that she has lost some vital rights as a housewife when she moves into the household of her daughter. A person may be designated as a housewife even when she no longer performs the role of wife, although it is assumed that only women who have been married are rightful holders of the title.

The social role of housewife is an indeterminate one, to use Mack's classification of occu-

---

The Method of Sociology (New York: Farrar & Rinehart, 1934) and were developed fully in his posthumous *Social Relations and Social Roles: An Unfinished Systematic Sociology.* (San Francisco: The Chandler Publishing Company, 1965). The last prior published reference to it is contained in "Basic Problems of Contemporary Sociology," *American Sociological Review,* October, 1954, *19,* 5, 519-42.

[4]The assumptions that a role can be limited to expectations of actions, or to the behavior of one person, or to the consequences of status placement is an important factor in the inability of sociologists to utilize it meaningfully in their analyses of social interaction. This deficiency results in an uneven and restricted use of a concept which could be vital to the field and renders comparisons of roles impossible or at best limited.

[5]See Helena Znaniecki Lopata, "A Restatement of the Relation Between Role and Status," *Sociology and Social Research,* October, 1964, *49,* for the theoretical foundation and definition of *status role.*

[6]American women often react negatively to the term "housewife." Women's magazines have used the word "homemaker" to accentuate creativity and action, but pilot interviews indicated that the women themselves find the term artificial and seldom use it to define their role. The objection to the term "housewife" is not due to the presence of a more satisfactory title, one suspects, but to the low level of prestige assigned to the role.

pations, binding together a variety of "others" through diversified sets of relations.[7] The role cannot be performed by a woman herself, although she may carry out many of the actions through which the maintenance of the home is accomplished without the immediate presence of others. It requires that several persons relate to the title holder through the duties and the rights. The housewife in modern American society maintains her home for and/or with the cooperation of: members of her family of procreation and other residents; guests, such as kin, neighbors, friends, husband's work associates, persons involved in the lives of offspring, members of voluntary associations, etc.; persons or groups who enter the home to provide services, such as servants, repair experts, or delivery men; and persons or groups whose services or goods she seeks outside of the home in order to maintain it.

The social role of housewife has an interesting cycle compared to other roles, involving relatively little anticipatory socialization, very brief time devoted to the "becoming" stage and a rather compressed and early peak. It can be performed during the major part of the life cycle of a women, yet its entrance, modifications, and cessation are usually not a consequence of its own characteristics or rhythm but of those of other roles.

BECOMING A HOUSEWIFE[8]

The first stage of any role which is to become important for the person is really composed of two phases, frequently lumped together under the term "novice." It involves not only the process of learning to perform the duties and to receive the rights in a satisfactory and unselfconscious or sophisticated manner, but also the process of gradual placement of the self within the role. The latter phase requires the ability to see the self as a "natural" center of a role

circle and the role as a part of one's own role cluster.

The dual aspect of the first stage are in great evidence in the social role of the housewife. In modern American society a young woman typically enters the role upon marriage, due to the neo-local residence of each family of procreation. The housewife is not "adequately" trained for the role according to Chicago urban and suburban women whose depth interviews collected over the past few years form the base of this paper,[9] and to numerous other commentators.[10] Although each young girl usually lives in a home run by her mother up till the time of marriage, the American system of education and occupation removes her from its walls for most of her conscious hours starting at the age of five, and even impinges upon her time within it. Training in "home economics" and the voluntary learning of homemaking skills are not highly evaluated by the society and especially by teenaged school-work-boy-leisure oriented girls. Attention tends to be directed "outside" of the home, and the focal point of interest in the role cluster of each teen-ager tends to be not a role, but the individual.

The process of becoming a housewife includes the phase of the learning the various skills used in maintaining the home and relating to those who are involved in its maintenance. The process of shifting identifications and space placements

---

[7]Raymond W. Mack, "Occupational Determinateness: A Problem and Hypotheses in Role Theory," *Social Forces*, October, 1956, 35, 20–24.

[8]The term "becoming" is not meant to indicate a teleological reaching for completed bloom of being, the closed frame of existentialistic writers. Howard Becker's "Becoming a Marihuana User," *American Journal of Sociology*, November, 1953, 59, 235–42, expresses more of the intended stress upon a process involving self-indication and placement.

[9]The study involves 1000 interviews with Chicago area housewives. The first 3000 were obtained with the help of funds from the *Chicago Tribune* and formed an area probability sample drawn from newly developed sections of 12 socioeconomically divergent suburbs. It included only full time housewives who owned their homes and had pre-high-school children. The additional 700 interviews came from as broad a range of racial, ethnic, socioeconomic, residential and role focusing women as available in the Chicago area and to Roosevelt University students.

[10]The most famous proponent of "home economics" training for women was Lynn White, Jr. His *Educating Our Daughters* (New York: Harper & Row Publishers, 1950) created a storm of controversy over the relative value of different systems of education for future homemakers. Practically every study of role expectations and preparation on the part of American girls concludes that training in housekeeping knowledge and skills is not a present focus of choice or even interest, although the popularity of "adult education" courses in related fields indicates increasing interest in later years.

is also important to the young woman. The stress upon the location of the self "inside" the home as opposed to "outside" life roles, or persons, so important to housewives in the next stage of the cycle, begins with a gradual shift of the image of the self from a rather functionally diffused "outside" existence to a role-focused and geographically placed identity within a home.

The newly married bride, still engaged in occupational or school roles typical of the American pattern, sees herself as located outside of the home. Living in her own place is important, but it is seen mostly as part of being a wife, and then in terms of primary relations with the husband, rather than as a potential center of multiple relations. She talks of her life in terms of personality changes and feelings to a degree not used again till very old age.

The role of housewife begins to enter her life pattern with a growing awareness of the complexity of duties involved in the role of wife, duties beyond those of primary attitudes, and, with shifting significance, the role of customer. The meaning of money does change, reflecting and perhaps even leading the changes in the role cluster. The role of worker becomes used more instrumentally than before, as a source of obtaining means for housekeeping activities. The role of consumer begins to involve purchasing for a unit, budgeting, and accounting to the self for expenditures. The role of customer no longer serves only the ends of personal pleasure and adornment. Although "fixing up the apartment" is accomplished with external eyes, the process of bringing the self and purchases "inside" the house begins to acquire a symbolic tone.

The shifting of roles into new clusters often results in the placement of the role of wife in the center, and in the pushing of the roles of daughter, worker, and colleague into the background. The role of housewife or "homemaker" and of consumer are gradually pulled into the foreground.

THE EXPANDING CIRCLE

The increase of importance assigned to the role of housewife in the role cluster comes with pregnancy. Outside employment "fades out" as an important role for most women, and the role of mother antecedes actual birth. The length of time involved in pregnancy performs the important function of "anticipatory socialization."

As LeMasters points out, and interviewees emphatically echo, the birth of the first child is a dramatic event, changing the whole life pattern of the woman.[11] One of the consequences is the shift of focus in the cluster of roles as new ones are added and old ones are dropped. Because of the utter dependence of newborn infants upon practically 24 hour care by an adult, the number of activities such care necessitates, and the society's preference for its being undertaken by the biological mother, the young housewife suddenly finds herself confined to her house, carrying on a variety of housekeeping tasks, often inexpertly and alone.

Not only does the infant require many housewifely actions, and its birth expand the social circle to include new people, but new sets of duties arise in new role relations with people already present in other circles. The husband now becomes also the father of the child and must relate to the mother on that level. The shift of attention often pushes the role of wife to the background, temporarily if not permanently.[12] One of the characteristics of the role of housewife is the fact that competence acquired· in the previous stage of the role may not actually help the new mother. A housekeeping schedule, for example, may be dysfunctional to, or made ineffective by, the demands of a newborn baby in a society which stresses its needs above those of adults.

THE PEAK STAGE

The stage of the role of housewife in which the woman has several small children, that is, the peak stage, varies considerably in actual

[11]E. E. LeMasters, "Parenthood as Crisis," *Marriage and Family Living*, November, 1957, *19*, 352–55.

[12]Two-thirds of the Chicago area women interviewed in this study, as reported in Helena Znaniecki Lopata, "Secondary Features of a Primary Relation," *Human Organization*, (Summer, 1965), 116–123, did not assign the role of wife first place when asked to list the roles of women in order of importance.

practice, depending on a combination of the following factors:

1. The number and ages of the children.
2. Their special needs.
3. The kinds of duties undertaken by the housewife in relation to these children, because of societal, circle, or self-imposed demands.
4. The kinds of duties undertaken by the housewife in relation to other members of the household.
5. The size of the home which must be maintained.
6. The number of items which must be maintained and the activities required to keep them in a desired condition.
7. The number of persons helping in the performance of the duties and the type of assistance each provides. Such assisting circle segments may include employees, relatives, friends and neighbors, and members of the household involved in a regular or emergency division of labor.
8. The number and variety of "labor-saving" devices or "conveniences" designed to decrease the effort or the time required to perform any of the tasks.
9. The location of the household and of each task in relation to the assisting segment of the circle and to the useful objects, plus the versatility of these services as a source of shifting duties and activities.

The role of housewife, being an indeterminate one, can be performed in a variety of styles, with great complexity or with simplified standards of care of the house and persons within it.

THE "FULL HOUSE" PLATEAU

The next major stage in the role of housewife starts, according to interviewers, when the youngest child enters school and ends when the children start leaving home to live somewhere else. The women with small, pre-school children had anticipated this stage with hopes for "relaxation" and "time for myself." Their statements reflected their reaction to the stage in which they were engaged, one of shift from "outside" to "inside," accompanied by the addition of new roles and hectic hours.

The stage when there are no babies in the home is not reached for most women as soon as the Glick tables of average life cycles led us to expect.[13] At least, the range of time between the birth of the first child and the year when

the youngest child starts school, for the 1000 Chicago interviewees, indicates wide variations in the ages of women when this stage occurs.

Furthermore the "full house" stage does not turn out to be as restful as the mothers of pre-schoolers had anticipated. It seems to be true that, as children grow older, the housewife tends to be relieved of certain household activities. A child's gradual increase in self-control, and in the ability to care for himself and his belongings, plus the decrease in the amount of time he actually spends in the home, may decrease the number or complexity of actions performed by the adult in the house. However, the presence of school-aged children often results in the expansion of the housewife's circle with additions of duties toward each member. Playmates, teachers, tutors, or organization leaders may ask for special attention or impose special demands upon the child, requiring more work of its mother. Other roles may impinge on the time she has to devote to housekeeping tasks. For example, many of the interviewed mothers stated that the supervision of their teen-aged daughters, who are entering a new stage of life, took more time than the supervision of small children. Allowing for the warping of memory and for the probability that these women are not really talking of the amount of time involved in direct supervision but of the amount of worry and conflict, we still must caution ourselves from accepting an oversimplified image of the "full-house" stage of the role of housewife—one of decreased activity and increased leisure.

The housewife's activities in this stage, when new members are not likely to be added to the household through birth, and when residing members are all still there and functioning in a relatively self-sufficient manner, are highly dependent on the size of the social circle, the cultural and personal demands as to what she must do for each person, the kind and amount of assistance provided her, and the time other roles leave her for this function.

For example, the career cycle of the husband is likely to have resulted in a consistent improvement of the family's economic position, due to increased expertness in occupational role performance or upward mobility in role sequences. Such affluence was frequently mentioned by

---

[13]Paul Glick, "The Life Cycle of the American Family," *op. cit.*, 4.

interviewees, but its consequences upon the role of housewife varied; it became a source of more work, if more objects were added for the sake of beauty, comfort or class status; or a source of less work if the money was converted into services or work simplifying objects.

Standard variations in the role of housewife in the "full-house" stage depend also on solutions to a "inside-outside" continuum of role clusters. The fact that the husband and the children are now all "outside" of the home a great deal of time, and have many outside identifications and orientations may leave the housewife as the only person with a basically "inside" location. She can continue focusing on any of the three roles of wife, mother, or housewife. An interesting focus is developed by women who generalize their relations with the husband and with each child into "family" relations, involving mostly the performance of duties for it. Such women tend to separate themselves, as performers of certain home maintaining actions, from those who are the recipients, defining all as "the family" and seldom during the interview, if ever, isolating individual relations. Such women speak of "cooking for the family," "sewing for the family," or "waiting for the family to come home."

Other women with growing children place themselves on the "outside" of the home for the majority of the day, taking full-time employment or devoting themselves with complete dedication to volunteer work. As a number of sociologists have pointed out, especially in the analysis of the working mother,[14] the kinds of outside roles undertaken, and the ways in which these are clustered depend on several factors. We can analyze the influence of these by seeing how they contribute to the balance between the pull of the activities and gains from each direction. Some women never become "inside-located," so

that the return to work or other community life after the birth of children is rapid and complete. Women who have placed themselves in the home and for whom the housewife role became important may be attracted to the outside or forced out of the inside by a feeling of obligation to help in the financial support of the family, or through crises such as widowhood. This study of housewives suggests that the factor of personal influence is very important in furnishing a bridge and an impetus for the breaking down of psychological barriers between the home and the rest of the world. The example and urging of friends and relatives who return to work help offset inertia of a woman who fears that she could no longer function in the occupational world. As in other instances of personal influence, decisions to undertake new roles requiring new skills and behavioral traits tend to take the form of fashion.[15]

Those who do not go out completely, but do so part-time, include women who have never cut off ties with the outside, or who develop new lines of connection. They most frequently combine both orientations through the addition of some outside roles, such as that of PTA member, or part-time worker, without letting such identifications grow into total commitments. They continue their focality of a home based role, such as a wife, mother, housewife or "carer" of the family. The women utilizing the last two categories of role foci tend, however, to least often combine inside with outside orientations, and they continue being home oriented.

One of the factors which must be considered

---

[14]The lack of importance given to their occupational roles, and especially to the task components of such roles, on the part of American women is a conclusion researched by many sociologists, as reported in F. Ivan Nye and Lois W. Hoffman, editors, *The Employed Mother in America* (Chicago: Rand McNally and Company, 1963). The same point is made by Cumming and Henry, especially in their chapter on "Retirement and Widowhood." Elaine Cumming and William E. Henry, *Growing Old* (New York: Basic Books, Inc., 1961).

[15]The Elihu Katz and Paul E. Lazarsfeld statement of the significance of informal communication appeared in *Personal Influence* (New York: The Free Press, 1955) and it has been the foundation of a great deal of research, especially in consumer behavior. I had the pleasure of participating in a search for an effective technique for getting to the content of "the recommendation process" through interviews, under the direction of Nelson Foote of General Electric in the summer of 1955. This experience, combined with the study of Polish-American associations, "The Function of Voluntary Associations in an Ethnic Community: Polonia" in Ernest Burgess and Donald Bogue, *Contributions to Urban Sociology* (Chicago: University of Chicago Press, 1964) and the study of housewives have convinced me of the importance of friends and other personal links between the woman and any form of "outside" activity.

in the analysis of role clustering on the part of women who no longer have small, dependent children and who have a choice in activities they may undertake is the low, if not negative, evaluation of the role of housewife in American society. Such an evaluation has been built up into whole systems of ideology by such writers as Betty Friedan.[16] The role tends to be seen as an instrumental, or servile one, whose function is to help other people perform more vital and interesting roles—away from the home.

Some prestige can come to a housewife if she runs the home of persons judged important by the society. The increase in the number of persons benefiting from the activities of a housewife is also a source of prestige, as it is assumed to increase the significance of what she does. So are, to some extent, the degree of dependency of these people, and the excellence of performance of the role.

All of these bases for prestige in the role of housewife make difficult the next stage for women who have invested their lives in that role, as many have, and who do not have alternative sources for the focusing of identity. The number of alternatives, however, decreases with increased separation from the "outside." The role of mother cannot become a satisfactory focus at this stage of the child's life, because, in American society especially, one of its basic functions is to decrease its own importance.

THE SHRINKING CIRCLE

The next stage in the social role of housewife starts when the first child is married or when he has left home. The previous years actually prepared the way for this stage, since modern American children tend to spend less and less time in the home as they progress through their teens. This stage can last for many years; and it often contains a pause after the last child has left and before the death of the husband.

The shrinking of the circle seriously affects the role. It removes many of the sources of prestige without any choice or control on the part of the woman whose identity is bound with it. No matter how well she performs it, how many and how important are the persons for whom it is performed, or how significant is the role in the lives of recipients, modern society automatically decreases the ability of the role of housewife to serve as a center of relations. The housewife ceases to perform the role at a peak, and even at a high plateau level, long before capacity to carry out its duties decreases, providing a reason or excuse for its cessation. Changes in the role come basically and primarily from changes in characteristics of the circle prior to any changes in her which could provide justification for decreasing functionality.[17]

The shrinking of the role importance of housewife and mother cannot always lead to a shift of self and of role-focus to a concentration on the role of wife, if such an emphasis was absent, since the husband tends still to be highly involved in his role of worker. Thus a gap develops between importance assigned to the husband's functions and those of his wife. She now has the time she desired before, but not necessarily the means of converting it into meaningful roles. An increase in self-directed or in house-directed activities is not a source of roles unless it is accomplished by entrance into new circles. In the case in which the woman does not have satisfactory role substitutions, or in which she does not have an acceptable reason for not being the center of several circles, the life cycle of the role and of the person are not synchronized. This withering of roles and circles leaves her feeling useless and functionless. It is within this stage of the role's cycle that a sharp difference in expressed life satisfactions occurs among different women because of availability of alternative activities and of expectations. Barring ill health, the women who can be located in the higher socioeconomic strata express greater enjoyment of their lives than their less well-positioned counterparts. They make frequent references to the tasks of entertaining and visiting, and to community activities. They look forward

---

[16]Betty Friedan, *The Feminine Mystique* (New York: W. W. Norton and Company, Inc., 1963). See also Simone de Beauvoir, *The Second Sex* (New York: Alfred Knopf, 1953).

[17]One must bear in mind that the fact the circle shrinks through a decrease in the number of persons within it may not automatically decrease the significance of the role to the person, even when the society evaluates roles by using the numbers game.

to their husband's vacations and future retirement. As one interviewee explained: "I have the ability, both physical and financial, to do and go pretty much as I please." On the other hand, women of the lower socioeconomic strata tend to list more dissatisfaction with life, and to either see the future in negative hues, or to refuse to predict changes in it.[18]

A source of satisfaction for some women whose circles inside the home had shrunk was that of grandmother. The interview did not specifically refer to this role, so we cannot know why so few women who had children 25 years of age or over, and who can be presumed to be grandmothers, actually spoke of the role. Older women tended to make more references to it, regardless of the age or number of children. Future studies will attempt to learn more of the significance of this role. An interesting hypothesis is that younger women do not identify with the role of grandmother, either because of its aging stereotype, or because they are so busy with other roles as not to assign much significance to it. The distance between the family units is, of course, one factor. It is possible that the present trends in marriage and childbearing are producing grandmothers who are too young to take up the role voluntarily until the grandchildren are too old to need them.

The role of worker does not draw positive comments from women in this stage of life, except on the part of the few who identify with their occupation, all of whom are in professional roles. Most women see their jobs as a source of money and personal contact, but, as they get older, they refer to the role more frequently as something they can leave, or from which they may retire. The comments bear some analysis, since they are very different from the desires of younger women with small children who see happiness in future roles away from home, and since they indicate a probable source of difference in attitudes of men and women facing retirement.

Women with shrinking housewife roles who are working outside the home frequently explain that they want to "return home" where they "belong," and where they "always wanted to be." They feel that they have been deprived of a certain set of rights because they "had to go to work." Previous complaints about home restrictions (if actually made by the same woman) are forgotten, and working away from home is seen as an imposition, not a choice. It is quite possible that the man, lacking this feeling of rightfully belonging in the home, has a much more difficult time adjusting to the substitution of this location of the "self" for one in the "world of work." Retirement automatically tends to place the focus of life inside the home. The woman who has always had the role of housewife, with its location "inside," as one of the roles in her cluster and sometimes as the focal role, finds herself inside the home more comfortably than the man for whom this focus is foreign.

The first phase of the "shrinking circle" stage in the social role of housewife ends with her adjustment to the absence of the last child to leave home. During the pause preceding the next stage when she is left alone in the home, before aging becomes a real problem, and if she is not bothered by special difficulties like ill health, the housewife tends to experience gradual changes due to the process of growing older. The factors bringing about these changes and the manner in which aging is evaluated by those who experience it, is of particular interest to modern society because of the increasing percentages of populations who do, or will, face the variety of problems connected with it. Sociological literature dealing with the process is recent, but expanding.[19] This study of the life

---

[18]The importance of a feeling of competence in life satisfaction has been of interest to several University of Chicago social scientists, including Nelson Foote, Robert Havighurst and Bernice Neugarten. Lee Rainwater, Richard Coleman and Gerald Handel contrast *The Workingman's Wife* (New York: Oceana Publications, 1959) whom they find filled with feelings of inadequacy, powerlessness, and incompetence with middle-class woman who expects to be able to deal with the world and to solve problems.

[19]The aging literature which is most pertinent to this study includes: James Birren, ed. *Handbook of Aging and the Individual* (Chicago: University of Chicago Press, 1959); Clark Tibbits, ed., *Handbook of Social Gerontology* (Chicago: University of Chicago Press, 1960, especially ch. 9 by Richard Williams; Clark Tibbits, Wilma Donahue, eds., *Process of Aging*, vol. I (New York: Atherton Press, 1963); E. W. Burgess, ed., *Aging in Western Society* (Chicago: University of Chicago Press,

Symptoms

cycle of the role of housewife indicates that there are several phenomena connected with not only the process but also with the societal and self definitions of its characteristics, stages, and consequences. Such definitions influence social roles in several different ways.

The roles a person performs are affected, of course, by physiological processes experienced in aging, since certain duties are no longer possible or have become modified. The interviewees who were in their latter 60's for example, frequently commented on the fact that they were getting "slower" or that it was taking them longer to do the things they had to do, although the evaluation of this fact ranged from negative, through neutral to even positive.

The societal definition of "symptoms" of aging and classification of a person who has reached a certain chronological age as "old" may have any of the additional consequences upon social roles:

consequences of aging

One, it may result in modifications in permitted duties or in rights offered within roles which the person is already performing. Fewer demands for help or for entertaining may be made on the part of offspring of a housewife. She may even be forbidden to perform certain actions. Women mentioned that they now were "eating out" a lot, or that husbands wouldn't let them shop alone.

Two, the person may be removed from certain social roles because of the assumption on the part of others, or of the self, that qualifications necessary for satisfactory behavior in those roles are lost. The interviewees frequently referred to retirement, or withdrawal, from active participation in voluntary associations and "community life," due to aging.

Three, the person may be assigned special social roles due to the societal assumption that the process of aging automatically develops qualities judged necessary for the roles. As many observers have pointed out, the American society has no social role for the aged person, not even a *status role*.[20] It does not have a function to be performed by an aged person. It does not even have a noun which could be the title of such a role, toward which preparatory stages would train the candidate.

Finally, it may make necessary a shift in the concentrations or clusters of social roles, with or without serious modifications of their components.

The aging housewife experiences all forms of changes but the process is gradual and the phenomena connected with it so complex that, until the final stages, its relation to the life cycle is not automatic and the manner in which it affects a particular woman depends upon many factors. A surprising finding was the level of satisfaction expressed by many women in their 50's and 60's who have remained healthy, have husbands still living and no serious problems. Aging frequently provides a rational and virtuous excuse for not expanding roles. Statements by women in this phase of the stage often lack the implication of emptiness and on nonfunctionality of statements made by women in the early phase of circle decrease. Fewer decision-making problems, a lack of pressure from demanding and often conflicting roles, satisfaction with past performance of the role of housewife and with the products of the role of mother, and prior adjustment to the lack of centrality in the lives of children, have all contributed to a relatively high degree of satisfaction contained in the interviews with women in this segment of the cycle. For those who are not widows, the focality of the role of wife is increased with the retirement, or "fade-out" from occupational roles on the part of the spouse. The roles of grandmother and of association member continue to provide sources of satisfaction but demand decreasing contribution. Actions are slowed down gradually so that regular self and house maintenance activities take more time and attention, and are less frequently seen as things which must be finished in order to clear the ground for something "important."

Widowhood causes a major transformation in the social role of housewife, especially if it occurs after everyone else but the couple have left the household. Being a widow with small children is very different from becoming one in later life, when the removal of the role of wife is likely to be permanent and when it adds to the effects of the prior withering of the social circle of housewife.

THE MINIMAL PLATEAU

The final stage in the role of housewife can be delineated as one in which she is the only person

---

1962); Peter Townsend, *The Family Life of Old People* (London: Routledge and Kegan Paul, 1957); Elaine Cumming and William E. Henry, *op. cit.* and Arnold Rose in Arnold and Warren Peterson, *Old People and their Social World* (Philadelphia: F. A. Davis Co., 1965).

[20]Helena Znaniecki Lopata, "A Restatement of the Relation between Role and Status," *op. cit.*

for whom the house is regularly maintained, though others still contribute to the performance of the role and enter it as guests or in order to provide services. It lasts until the death of the housewife, or until the time she breaks up *her* household and moves into a residence being "run" by someone else, be it an offspring or a paid administrator. For its duration the woman tends to devote decreasing energies to external affairs and she tends to see and relate to a decreasing number of persons, depending upon size and closeness (both social and geographic) of kin and friends.[21] The society expects of her lessening contributions while it increases her rights. No one seriously expects the "old widow" or "old woman" to be giving a role outside of her home the focal place in her cluster. The process involves some "disengagement" from organized "outside activities" but it basically changes role clusters.[22] The society, and, reflectively, she herself, justifies her existence in terms of itself, and her functionality in terms of self maintenance. The older she gets, the more pride she can gain from such tasks, and from continued contacts with others. Strain occurs if her expectation of what roles she should perform or what level of performance can be expected of her, does not match that of her social circle which either "restricts" her, or does not grant her "sufficient consideration" rights. The society has not, as the students of aging have pointed out, developed a satisfactory set of sub-roles or standardized variations of regular roles for its older persons. The lack of *status roles* or of other functional assignments for the aging may thus be only part of the problem facing the society and the person. It is possible that more attention ought to be paid by problem solvers to the development of, and training into, satisfactory modifications of on-going in addition to the creation of new roles for our aged population.

One of the basic problems leading to difficulties in role assignment or modifications is the fact that this stage of life is surrounded, as Goffman has pointed out, by "stigma" of such proportions that younger circle members are often incapable of understanding the needs of a mother, hostess, customer, etc., who obviously looks old.[23] The emphasis upon idiosyncratic characteristics of appearance and the suspicion of oncoming senility interfere with role relations.

The end result of this process of adjustment of performance is that no social role is expected to form the focus of the role cluster of the very aged. The person is considered as not "having to" or not "needing to" be vitally concerned with any role. The role of wife and mother have already been left behind entirely or significantly. The role of worker and association member are no longer a source of action or identity. The role of daughter as well as many others are impossible to maintain. Because of concerns with the self, because of the slowness with which tasks are performed, and because of the relative isolation of an old woman from the flow of active adult life, she is often described in terms quite similar to those assigned to teenage girls.[24]

---

[21]The importance of kin for the older person is indicated in the national and cross-cultural research of Ethel Shanas, in the Cumming and Henry and in the Townsend studies. Marvin Sussman and Eugene Litwak have also contributed to our understanding of the interaction with, and assistance dependencies of, members of a kin.

[22]The theory of disengagement, as developed by the several authors of *Growing Old*, suffers from a confused use of the concept of social role. Based on the ideal-typical Parsonian separation of roles on the basis of a single dimension, for example, "instrumental-emotional"—a separation that speaks only of the manner of behavior or attitude forming part of the duties or means—they neglect to distinguish between several forms of role-related phenomena. They thus speak of disengagement as involving the following processes as if they were all the same: a decrease in the number of duties which are performed, a change in the manner in which all duties are performed, a change in the manner in which rights are granted and received, shifts in the relation between one role and another performed simultaneously or in sequence by one person, the shifting focus of life from one role to another, the dropping of roles entirely, and the removal of persons with whom the individual is involved in a multiplicity of roles as if his absence eliminated only one role.

[23]Erving Goffman, *Stigma* (Englewood Cliffs, New Jersey: Prentice-Hall, Inc., 1963).

[24]Although Cumming and Henry draw a comparison between the old person and the child, my interviewees lead me to the comparison of the old woman to the teen-age girl because my population contained only housewives. Those women who were judged able to perform this role, to run a home, at least in a minimally effective manner, by those who would have had the right to remove them from the role, or to encourage or permit them to remove themselves had not disintegrated in their abilities sufficiently to warrant analogies of child-like behavior or attitudes.

The content and the location of the roles each undertakes in her cluster are almost exclusively different. Both women, however, are expected to be concerned mostly with themselves and society assigns neither a focal role nor a focal place in its scheme. The society excuses each if she neglects some aspect of a role and even expects negligence—if such behavior provides the active, often harried adult with a motivation to "keep his shoulder to the wheel." Role-oriented, wheel pushing activity belongs to those who prove virtue by non-negligence and who judge themselves as well as being judged by others on the basis of their performance within specific social roles, of the unique roles they select, or of the unique clusters they make of them.

A right which is often taken away from the aging housewife is that of running her own home or of deciding the duties she should undertake to run it. When this happens she loses one of the important rights by which housewives contrast this role to that of working outside, the right to "be my own boss," to "plan my own work."

SUMMARY

The social role of housewife is, in summary, peaked early in the life cycle of a woman, preceding sufficient anticipatory socialization, training, and identification. She must "be" a housewife before she has shifted her role clusters and herself inside the home through a process of "becoming." Placement of the self in the home as the center of its relations, because of house maintenance functions, is frequently a slow and painful process for the young American woman. Her successful adjustment to such placement may not, however, draw societal approval after the period of time judged normal, especially if it involves additions of "extra children." Some women never move inside. They do not build role clusters around the role of housewife or even assign it an important location. A number of women combine "inside" and "outside," especially after the peak stage, due usually to the influence of friends, neighbors or relatives, and to the outside location of husband and children. Most of the Chicago interviewees, even those who had full-time employment outside of the home, expressed an "inside" identity. Such a placement did not necessarily solve all strains as it involves several roles and is often combined with some external activities. Thus, in all but the last two stages the housewives felt rushed and busy, expecting the next stage to give them "time for themselves." Many expressed the desire to "go out," especially during the peak period, but not in terms of a complete shift in the role cluster.

18.

THE STATUS OF WOMEN

EDUCATION FOR THE MATURE WOMAN

Men and women are equally in need of continuing education, but at present women's opportunities are more limited than men's. In part, this is because neither the substantial arrangements for advanced training provided by businesses for their executives nor the educational

and training programs of the armed services are open to many women. In part, it is because counseling and training are of particular importance at times when new choices are likely to be made, and women's lives are less likely than man's to follow continuous patterns.

The woman who marries and is raising a family has urgent educational needs that have so far been badly neglected. During her intensive homemaking years, she should be encouraged to prepare for at least three decades of life after 40 when she will be relatively free to use her

This selection is reprinted from: *American Women*, Report of the President's Commission on the Status of Women, Washington, D.C., GPO: 1963 [excerpted from pp. 10–13, 27–30].

abilities and will wish to use them as constructively and as interestingly as possible. She also needs to continue her education in one form or another in order to provide the assistance, companionship, and stimulation needed by her husband and by her children as they develop.

The education required by mature women is at all levels. While illiteracy and near-illiteracy grow less year by year, almost four million adult women, alive in 1960, had had less than five years of schooling. In a society in which literacy is essential, they cannot follow a simple written instruction or fill out a simple form. In a time when automation is displacing workers far more qualified than they, their chances in the job market are slim indeed. Those with young children cannot help prepare them adequately for entry into today's world.

Similarly, over 11½ million adult women have started but failed to finish high school; less than half of all women 25 and over are high school graduates. Completion of high school would lift many out of the congested competition for declining jobs in unskilled employment.

Most single women work for a large part of their lives. Many young widows and married women from low-income families work outside the home even when they have young children. In 1963, more than half of all women in the 45- to 54-year age bracket were in paid employment. In the schools and out of the schools, a realistic, many-sided vocational program can reduce the tendency for women returning to the labor market, or entering it for the first time, to take the first job that comes along and remain in it. Their capabilities may be well above the level of competence which this job requires. Technical training for clerical, manual, and other skills is especially important to women of minority groups. During their school years they were not trained for fields that are now being opened to them.

Until recently, up to the college level, more young women than young men have stayed in school: in 1962, the median number of years of school completed was 12 for women as against 11.6 for men. Even in 1962, 872,000 in the nation's high school graduating classes were boys as against 966,000 girls.

But once the college level is reached, the girls begin to fall behind. The 437,000 women who enrolled in college in 1962 constituted only about 42 percent of the entering class. Women are earning only one in three of the B.A.'s and M.A.'s awarded by American institutions of higher learning, and only one in ten of the Ph.D.'s. Today's ratios, moreover, represent a loss of ground as compared with the 1930's, when two out of five B.A.'s and M.A.'s and one out of seven Ph.D.'s were earned by women.

Presentation of higher education in the form in which women with family responsibilities can take advantage of it quite clearly requires new adaptations.

To be usable by the large numbers of young women who marry in their late teens and early twenties, and by the mature woman in general, continuing education must be geographically available where the woman is. If she breaks away from school or college to marry, she is less likely to return after a gap than if practicable means of continued study are immediately at hand. . . .

The importance of vocational training to parallel academic courses is attested by the fact that increasing numbers of women are going to college and that almost 70 percent of women college graduates work for part of the second half of their adult lives. Many high schools offer vocational courses suitable for use by their graduates. Four-fifths of the larger junior and community colleges provide technical training under the National Defense Education Act. The opportunity to attain advanced skills to match national scarcities is clear from the very names of the courses: electronics, plastics, nucleonics.

For mature women using educational facilities at any level, part-time study is a likely pattern. Its legitimacy must be recognized both by institutions of higher education in accepting plans of study projected on this basis and by academic and other bodies determining eligibility for fellowships, scholarships, and loans.

Many current rigidities in regard to admission, academic prerequisites, residence, and the like, as well as scheduling, will have to yield to greater flexibility. For instance, proficiency testing should be widely available as a means of obtaining credit for knowledge acquired outside regular academic courses.

WOMEN IN EMPLOYMENT

American women work both in their homes, unpaid, and outside their homes, on a wage or salary basis. Among the great majority of women, as among the great majority of men, the motive for paid employment is to earn money. For some, work has additional—or even primary—value as self-fulfillment.

When America was an agricultural country, most of both man's and woman's work was an unpaid contribution to family subsistence. As production developed in factory and city centers, many women began to do outside, for pay, what they had formerly done, unpaid, in their homes—making textiles or garments, processing food, nursing the sick, teaching children. Women's participation in paid employment importantly increases the nation's labor force: one worker in three is a woman.

In any average month in 1962, there were some 23 million women at work; the forecast is for 30 million in 1970. Approximately three out of five women workers are married. Among married women, one in three is working; among nonwhites, almost one in two. Many of these women, nearly a third, work part-time; three-fifths of all part-time work is done by married women. Some 17 million women, in an average month, are full-time workers.

Their occupations range widely: the 1960 census recorded 431 geologists and geophysicists and 18,632 bus drivers. The largest concentration—seven million—is in the clerical field. Three other main groupings—service workers (waitresses, beauticians, hospital attendants), factory operatives, and professional and technical employees (teachers, nurses, accountants, librarians)—number between 3 and and 3¾ million each.

Though women are represented in the highly paid professions, in industry, in business, and in government, most jobs that women hold are in low-paid categories. Some occupations—nursing and household work, for instance—are almost entirely staffed by women. The difference in occupational distribution of men and women is largely responsible for the fact that in 1961, the earnings of women working full-time averaged only about 60 percent of those of men working full-time. But in various occupations where both sexes were employed, the levels of women's earnings were likewise demonstrably lower than those of men.

The existence of differentials in pay between men and women for the same kind of work has been substantiated by studies from numerous sources: an analysis of 1900 companies, for example, showed that one out of three had dual pay scales in effect for similar office jobs. . . .

The reasons given by employers for differential treatment cover a considerable range. Frequently, they say they prefer male employees because the nonwage costs of employing women are higher. They say that the employment pattern of younger women is in and out of the labor force, working for a time before marriage and thereafter putting family obligations first until their children are grown. They say that women's rates of sickness, absenteeism, and turnover are higher than men's; that the hiring of married women introduces one more element into the turnover rate because the residence of a married couple is normally determined by the occupation of the man. They say that though attendance rates of older women are often better than those of men, insurance and pensions for older workers are expensive, and that compliance with protective labor legislation applying to women is sometimes disruptive of schedules. They say that men object to working under women supervisors.

Because many personnel officers believe that women are less likely than men to want to make a career in industry, equally well-prepared young women are passed over in favor of men for posts that lead into management training programs and subsequent exercise of major executive responsibility.

Actually, situations vary far too much to make generalizations applicable, and more information is needed on rates of quits, layoffs, absenteeism, and illness among women workers and on the qualifications of women for responsible supervisory or executive positions. However, already available statistics on absenteeism and turnover indicate that the level of skill of the job, the worker's age, length of service with the employer, and record of job stability all are much more relevant than the fact that the worker is a man or a woman.

19.

CHARLES WINICK

THE BEIGE EPOCH: DEPOLARIZATION
OF SEX ROLES IN AMERICA

Perhaps the most significant and visible aspect of the contemporary American sexual scene is the tremendous decline, since World War II, in sexual dimorphism. Sex roles have become substantially neutered and environmental differences increasingly blurred.

Our Age of the Neuter begins to leave its mark on young people in their very tender years. Gender-linked colors like pink and blue for children's clothing are yielding to green, yellow, and other colors which can be used for either Dick or Jane. Such names, however, are less likely nowadays. A study of a large sample of given names reported in birth announcements in the *New York Times* from 1948 to 1963 concluded that almost one-fifth of them were not gender-specific, for example, Leslie, Robin, Tracy, Dana, Lynn, although the 1923-1938 period had few such names.[1] Since the name helps to position a person in his culture, many young people are starting out with an ambisexual given name.

The hair of little girls is shorter and that of little boys is longer, and such blurring is given fashionable designations, that is, the Oliver or Beatle haircut. Other kinds of his-hers appearances are chic for young people. Boys and girls may have similar toys, and the last few years have witnessed the popularity of dolls for boys (G.I. Joe and his many imitators).

Reading habits of young people are less related to gender than they were a generation ago. Both sexes are likely to enjoy the same books, for example, *The Moon Spinners* and *Island of the Blue Dolphins,* and there is less interest in books which are clearly sex-linked, like the *Nancy Drew* series for girls or the *Hardy Boys* for boys. School curricula are offering fewer subjects which are unique to each sex, and both sexes learn some subjects, for example, typing.

THE TEEN-AGER

Dating behavior of teen-agers reflects the crossing over of sex roles which pervades so much of the preadolescent years. The teen-age girl increasingly is looking for her own satisfaction and may want to be even more equal than her date. Such tendencies have become more important since the 1950's, which experienced the first movie about a sexually aggressive teen-ager (*Susan Slept Here,* 1954), an extraordinarily successful novel about a sexually sophisticated girl (*Lolita,* 1958), and, perhaps most important, a series of very popular mannequin dolls, beginning with Betsy McCall in 1954 and culminating in Barbie in 1959. Barbie is a sexy teen-ager, and playing with her involves changing costumes and thereby preparing for dates. During the last decade, an average of more than 6,000,000 mannequin dolls was sold each year.

The rehearsal for dating provided by Barbie and her imitators may even further accelerate the social development of their owners. By the time an owner is ready to engage in actual dating, she could be much more forward than her male companion. Studies of teen dating suggest that, not too long ago, the aggressiveness displayed by many contemporary teen-age girls was once found primarily in young men.[2]

So much time separated the nine-year-old

This selection is reprinted from: Charles Winick, "The Beige Epoch: Deplorization of Sex Roles in America," *The Annals,* 1968, 376, 18–24.
Reprinted with the permission of the author and publisher.

[1] Charles Winick, *The New People: Desexualization in American Life* (New York: Pegasus, 1968), chap. vi.

[2] Ira L. Reiss, "Sexual Codes in Teen-Age Culture," THE ANNALS, *American Academy of Political and Social Science,* November, 1961, 338, 53–62.

with an old-fashioned baby doll from her role as mother that she could enjoy fantasies about motherhood and not be concerned about doing something about them. But the distance in years that separates a Barbie fan from a socially active ten- or eleven-year-old girl is slight, and she can easily translate doll-play fantasies into real social life. Barbie owners may be more ready than any previous generation to take the traditional male role in teen-age courtship behavior.

CLOTHING AND APPEARANCE

The most conspicuous example of sexual criss-crossing is provided by clothing and appearance, which are important because the costume we wear reflects the customs by which we live. When World War II provided an urgent occasion for a re-evaluation of social roles, Rosie the Riveter, in slacks, became a national heroine. At the same time, many of the 14,000,000 men in uniform, who had a limited number of outlets for their money, began to buy fragrance-containing colognes, hair preparations, and after-shave lotion. Wearing the uniform probably helped to allay any fears that the products' users might be unmanly or were indulging themselves.

The most recent postwar impetus for men's fragrance products was the great success of Canoe in 1959. College men traveling abroad began to bring back the sweet and citrus-scented French cologne, used it for themselves—and gave it to their girl friends. The appetite of college students and teen-agers for strongly scented products in turn influenced their fathers, uncles, and older brothers.

Scent is a method of adornment by which a man of any age can unbutton his emotional self and attract attention, in frank recognition of women's growing freedom to pick and choose.[3] Very strong fragrances may have special appeal to men who are suffering from feelings of depersonalization. Just as anointing and incense helped to extend the body's boundaries and reach toward God, a man using a strong fragrance transcends his body's boundaries and

creates a unified atmosphere that projects him toward people. Other men who are confused about their body-image may use zesty essences as one way of reassuring themselves, in our deodorized age, that their body is recognizable and has exudations. For these and other reasons, men in the Scented Sixties spend three times as much money on fragrance-containing preparations as women do.

With men smelling so sweet, it is small wonder that the constitutionality of the New York state statute prohibiting a man from wearing a woman's clothes was challenged in 1964 for the first time. Apparel may oft proclaim the man, but many bells are jangling out of tune in the current proclamation. Men are wearing colorful and rakishly epauleted sports jackets, iridescent fabrics, dickies, and bibbed and pleated shirts of fabrics like batiste and voile.

Men's trousers are slimmer and in many instances are worn over girdles of rubber and nylon. Ties are slender and often feminine. The old reliable gray fedora has given way to softer shapes and shades, sometimes topped by gay feathers. Sweaters are less likely to have the traditional V-neck than a boat neck adopted from women's fashions. Padded shoulders on a suit are as out of date as wide lapels and a tucked-in waist. The new look is the soft, slender, straight-line silhouette that also characterizes the shift, which has been the major woman's dress style of the 1960's. Men accessorize their clothes with cuff links, tie bars and tacks, bracelets, rings, and watch bands.

Loss of gender is especially conspicuous in shoes, with women wearing boots or low-heeled, squat, square-toed, and heavy shoes at the same time that men's footwear has become more pointed, slender, colorful, and high-heeled. Men have adopted low-cut and laceless models from women's styles.

A modishly dressed couple might be walking along with the woman in hip-length boots, "basic black" leather coat, a helmet, and a pants suit or straight-line dress of heavy fabric. Her male companion might be wearing a soft pastel sack suit, mauve hat, and a frilled and cuff-linked pink shirt. He could sport a delicate tie and jewelry, exude fragrance, and wear tapered shoes with stacked heels. Both could have shoul-

[3]Charles Winick, "Dear Sir or Madam, As the Case May Be," *Antioch Review*, Spring, 1963, 23, 35–49.

der-length hair, and their silhouettes would be quite indistinguishable.

RECREATION AND LEISURE

The couple might be on the way to visit a family billiard center or bowling alley, now that both recreations have become somewhat feminized and have abandoned their connotations of the spittoon. Women are participating in many other previously male recreational activities, especially outdoor sports and competitive athletics. They accounted for 30 percent of our tennis players in 1946 but today represent 45 percent. The proportion of women golfers has risen from one-tenth to more than one-third in the same period. The pre-World War II golf club, which did not permit women, has become the family-centered country club. Men's city clubs have also substantially abandoned their formerly exclusionist attitudes toward women.

Social dancing has become almost a misnomer for the self-centered, nonrelational dances which have succeeded the twist since 1961 and have largely replaced traditional steps like the waltz and fox trot, in which the man led and the woman followed. In the frug and boogaloo and other current favorites, there is no leading or following. The man and woman do not even have to look at each other or start or finish together.

WORK AND THE HOME

We are so familiar with decreased resistance to the employment of women and their continually improving preparation for work that we may sometimes forget some implications of the trend. Well over one-third of our workers are women, and, every year, proportionately more married women enter the labor market. Over 2,300,000 women earn more than their husbands. Now that the United States is the first country in which the majority of jobs are in service industries, it has also become the first country where men may soon be competing for what were previously women's jobs.

Men are less and less likely to require physical strength on the job. They are also hardly likely to assume a traditional male role in the home. The husband must often take over house-

hold tasks that were once assigned to the wife. Over three-fifths assist in cooking. In many ways, the husband has become a part-time wife. As one result of this trend, initiative and aggressiveness may become less common in boys, who may have less opportunity to see their fathers functioning in either a traditional or masterful manner.

FOOD AND DRINK

As Talcott Parsons has so eloquently reminded us, the social structure constitutes a subtly interrelated and almost homeostatic series of interrelationships. At a time when the most basic difference in a society—between men and women—is dwindling, we might expect to find other differences becoming less significant. Extremes of taste sensation in food and drink have diminished as part of our culture's larger homogenization.

Blended whiskey's comparative lack of bouquet and flavor is probably the chief reason for its now accounting for over two-thirds of all domestic whiskey production. The most successful Scotches of the last 15 years have been brands which are light amber in color and possess a minimum of maltiness, smokiness, and body.

The dilution of distinguishing characteristics that is represented by "soft" whiskey and Scotch can be seen most dramatically in vodka, which jumped from one per cent of the 1952 domestic liquor market to ten percent in 1967. United States government regulations specify that it must be "without distinctive character, aroma or taste," so that its major appeal is a lack of the very qualities that traditionally make liquor attractive. Beer is also becoming "lighter" every year.

It would be logical to expect our great technological proficiency to have produced foods with an enormous range of taste, texture, and aroma. Yet our marriage of technology and convenience has led to wide acceptance of many foods with a blander and less explicit taste than in previous generations. Although access to more than 7,000 quick-preparation convenience items has exposed Americans to many new foods, the taste, aroma, and texture of such products tend to be more homogenized and less sharp than the fresh foods of earlier decades, as nonchemically treated fruits, home- or bakery-made bread, ethnic cooking, and many other contributors to strong taste experiences become less common.

INNER AND OUTER SPACE

In the Beige Epoch, color extremes are less welcome than they used to be. Even cosmetics stress paleness. The muted appearance of no-color color makes an ideal of "the suddenly, startlingly candid new beauties" whose makeup "turns on the immensely touching *au courant* look of the untouched, nude complexion."[4]

Beige has become the single most popular color for home interiors, carpeting, telephones, draperies. At the same time, interiors are less likely to have the heavy furniture, dark colors, and coarsely grained dark woods generally linked with men or the delicate furniture, light colors, and finely grained light woods that are associated with women.

Rooms with gender may soon be subjects for archaeologists, as a result of the continuing displacement of rooms by areas that merge into one another. And with the near-disappearance of masculine (for example, the leather club model) or feminine (for example, the chaise longue) chairs, foam rubber has become the Space Age's upholstering of choice. It is neutral and has no "give," in contrast to traditional upholstering's indentations after someone has been sitting on it.

Our manipulation of outer space, via architecture, reflects the blurring of gender which also characterizes how we use furniture in the organization of inner space. Few clearly feminine (for example, the Taj Mahal) or masculine (for example, the Empire State Building) structures have been built during the last generation. When men and women wear the same straight-line silhouette and are surrounded by furniture which avoids protuberances or padding, it is hardly surprising that their buildings so literally resemble "filing cases for people," although Frank Lloyd Wright intended his famous description to be only a metaphor.

[4]*Harper's Bazaar*, April, 1965, No. 3041, 214.

Function is almost as difficult to identify as gender in many new buildings. Hotel, bank, air terminal, lobby, store, office, and restaurant may look alike and play the same monotonous canned music, which provides a seamless wallpaper of sound.

THE PERFORMING ARTS

Men began to lose their dominant chairs at the head of the formerly rectangular dinner table at just about the time that they were yielding the center spotlight in each of the major performing arts to women. Caruso was the dominant figure of the Golden Age of Opera, but Birgit Nilsson, Joan Sutherland, Renata Tebaldi, Leontyne Price, and Maria Callas are typical of the divas who completely overshadow the male singers opposite whom they appear.

When Actors Equity celebrated its fiftieth birthday in 1963 by enacting some representative episodes from the recent past, not one actor did a major scene.[5] Lillian Gish, Helen Hayes, and Beatrice Lillie were the stars of the evening, performing excerpts from *Our Town, Victoria Regina,* and *Charlot's Review,* respectively. The male matinee idol (E. H. Sothern, John Barrymore, Richard Mansfield, John Drew, Joseph Schildkraut) took his final bow some decades ago. It would be nearly impossible to make up a list of "first men" of the contemporary theatre, but women have dominated our stage for about 40 years. Anne Bancroft, Geraldine Page, Kim Stanley, and Julie Harris are only a few younger current Broadway actresses who project characters with valid juices. Aggressive performers like Ethel Merman, Mary Martin, Barbra Streisand, Carol Channing, and Julie Andrews star in musicals which feature male leads who are either innocuous or nonsingers and are puny successors to the male singers, dancers, and comedians who made the American musical our happiest export.

The interrelationships and mutual reinforcement among the mass media are so pronounced that we might expect women to have assumed much greater importance in movie roles since

[5]Paul Gardner, "3 of Stage's First Ladies Salute Actors Equity on 50th Birthday," *New York Times*, May 6, 1963.

World War II. Death or retirement claimed Humphrey Bogart, Clark Gable, Spencer Tracy, William Powell, and other actors who shouldered through the "movie movies" of the 1930's. Actresses are now more important than ever before, and Doris Day has played more consecutive starring roles than any performer since talkies began 40 years ago. Marilyn Monroe became the unforgettable symbol of the child-woman, and Elizabeth Taylor is not only the highest paid performer in history ($2 million plus for *Cleopatra*) but also the prototype of the devouring Medusa in her private life. As in the earlier case of Ingrid Bergman, Miss Taylor made the key decision to leave one man for another, and both men acquiesced.

One of the most significant changes in the post-World War II performing arts was the emergence in the 1950's of the pianist Liberace as television's first and only superstar who had the qualities of a matinee idol. Liberace was not a particularly distinguished pianist, and much of his appeal seems to lie in his ability to communicate many characteristics of a five- or six-year-old child, of either gender.[6] His extraordinary rise to fame as America's biggest single concert attraction, barely 30 years after the disappearance of the virile stage idol in form-fitting doublet and dashing skin-tight breeches, is a striking commentary on changes in American fantasy needs.

WHY DEPOLARIZATION?

It would be possible to identify many other areas in which our society is manifesting a depolarization and bleaching of differences. Such neutering and role-blurring represent only one dimension in the dynamics of social change. It is possible that these trends necessarily develop in any society which becomes as highly industrialized as ours. There is reason to suspect that our acceptance of androgyny is, to some extent, one outcome of World War II. Studies of children from homes in which the father was absent during the war have suggested that many such children later exhibited considerable sex-role confusion.[7] Large numbers of such children could have been so affected by their fathers' absence and might be significantly represented in the ranks of today's young adults.

A fuller consideration of the conditions and factors producing neutering would include political, economic, technological, cultural, and demographic dimensions as well as rates of invention, acculturation, cultural diffusion, and resistance to change. Our no-war, no-peace situation, along with the blurring of categories in other fields, contributes to this condition.

The unique capacities of each sex are especially significant these days, when at least some quantitative aspects of a Great Society seem within reach. The emancipation of women and their greater equality and participation in the affairs of society were long overdue. But equality does not mean equivalence, and a difference is not a deficiency.

Multivalent, amorphous, and depolarized roles might theoretically lead to increased flexibility and options in behavior, but in actuality may tend to invoke uncertainty. Some tolerance of ambiguity is desirable for a healthy personality, but today's environment and culture are ambiguous enough to tax the adaptability of even the healthiest personalities.[8] The other extreme is represented by the completely polarized sex roles that we associate with the reactionary ideology of totalitarianism.

There is no evidence that any one kind of family structure is inherently healthier than any other, and history seems to suggest that almost any male-female role structure is viable, so long as there is clear division of labor and responsibilities. An equally important lesson of the past is that overly explicit roles can be pathogenic, because they do not permit the expression of individual differences or of a personal style. It is most disquieting to contemplate the possibility that the ambiguity of sex roles in our open society might ultimately prove to be almost as hazardous as the rigidities of authoritarianism.

[6]Charles Winick, "Fan Mail to Liberace," *Journal of Broadcasting*, Spring, 1962, 6, 129–142.

[7]Lois M. Stolz, *Father Relations of Warborn Children* (Palo Alto: Stanford University Press, 1951).
[8]T. W. Adorno, E. Frenkel-Brunswik, D. J. Levinson, and R. Nevitt Sanford, *The Authoritarian Personality* (New York: Harper & Row, Publishers, 1950), 480–481.

20.

PERSONAL AND PROPERTY RIGHTS OF MARRIED WOMEN

REGULATION OF OWNERSHIP AND CONTROL OF PROPERTY AS BETWEEN HUSBAND AND WIFE

There are basically two types of matrimonial property systems in the United States: in 42 states and the District of Columbia, earnings and property acquired during marriage are owned separately by the spouses; in eight states, all in the West or Southwest, earnings and most property acquired by either spouse during marriage are owned in common.

The systems of the separate property states derive from the English common law. The common law concepts of matrimonial property evolved from the needs of an agricultural, feudal society in which the husband was regarded as the head of the family and the guardian of his wife. A woman was considered as having lost her personal entity upon marriage, a fiction which furnished the basis for close to total legal disability of the married woman.

Under the common law, the husband had an "estate by marital right" in his wife's property during their joint lives. The husband could thus dispose of his wife's land without her consent and enjoy full possession and control of her rents and profits. In addition, he became the absolute owner of his wife's personal property. These common law rules have been modified by statute in most states, so that, today, the wife generally has full capacity to own and control her separate property. However, five states (Alabama, Florida, Indiana, North Carolina and Texas) still require the joinder of the husband in the conveyance of the wife's real property.

The eight community property states—Arizona, California, Idaho, Louisiana, New Mexico, Nevada, Texas, and Washington—adopted the French or Spanish civil law concept of community property. In general, under this system, whatever is acquired by the efforts of the husband or the wife during marriage constitutes part of a common fund. Management and control, however, generally vests in the husband. Either the husband or wife, or both, might also have "separate property," such as that belonging to either at the time of marriage or that acquired through gift, inheritance, or in exchange for other separate property. In these states, where the statute fails to cover a particular situation, common law rules prevail.

In most states, a wife is able to control her separate personal property independently of her husband. One exception is a Texas law requiring the husband to join in the transfer of his wife's stocks and bonds. In order to manage her estate independently of her husband, a Texas wife must file with the county clerk a statement that she elects to have the sole management, control, and disposition of her separate property.

All of the states, in varying degrees, have modified by statute some of the outmoded disabilities of married women. However, even the present state matrimonial property systems, as regulated by existing state law, may operate as an inequitable disadvantage to women. For example, in the separate property states, a wife has no legal rights to any part of her husband's earnings or property during the existence of the marriage, aside from a right to be properly supported. Hence, if she does not have earnings or property of her own, she is completely dependent upon the husband's largesse for anything above and beyond her support needs. On the other hand, under community property systems, while the wife has an interest in the commonly owned property, the husband generally has exclusive authority to manage and control the community property.

. . .

This selection is reprinted from: *Civil and Political Rights,* Report of the President's Commission on the Status of Women, GPO, 1963 [excerpted from pp. 15–20].

DOMICILE

A person's domicile or legal residence is important because it determines many personal rights and obligations. For example, the place of domicile determines in which state the right to vote may be exercised, where an individual may run for public office, where one may be called for jury service, where a divorce may be filed, where personal property and income taxes may be levied, where the assets of a decedent will be administered, where one might receive welfare benefits, and where one may be eligible for admission to state hospitals and other state institutions.

A person's domicile generally is the place which he intends to be his permanent home. However, this rule does not normally apply to married women; the common law rule with respect to the domicile of a married woman is that her domicile, by automatic operation of law, is the place of her husband's domicile, without regard to her intent or actual residence. This rule, if not modified, could operate to restrict basic rights of a married woman, particularly if for some reason she is not living in the same state as her husband. Thus, married women living apart from their husbands may be restricted in the exercise of their rights and obligations of citizenship—e.g., voting, running for public office, and jury service—because they lack the required domicile. Further, because state tax laws vary, a wife's personal property located with her in one jurisdiction may be taxed by a state with a higher rate if such happens to be the husband's domicile.

Today, there are apparently only four states (Arkansas, Delaware, Hawaii, and New Hampshire) which recognize a married woman's right to acquire her own domicile, independently of her husband, for all purposes, without limitation. Forty-two states and the District of Columbia permit a married woman to acquire an independent domicile for all purposes if she is living apart from her husband for cause; of these, only 18 permit a married woman to acquire an independent domicile if she is separated from her husband by mutual agreement or if her husband acquiesces to the separation. All states permit a married woman to establish a separate domicile for purposes of instituting divorce proceedings. However, in addition to Arkansas, Delaware, Hawaii, and New Hampshire, only 15 states permit, without limitation, a married woman to acquire her own domicile for the purpose of voting: six for the purpose of election to public office, five for the purpose of jury service, seven for the purpose of taxation, and five for the purpose of probate.

CHAPTER VI

Courtship and Mate Selection

THIS VOLUME has not been designed especially for a "functional" course in marriage and the family, that is, the course that tries to convey to students information that will be primarily useful to them in their own private lives. The objective of this volume as noted in the Introduction is to expose the student to the systematic study of the family. Still, it is difficult to present materials in the area of courtship and mate selection without mixing both functional and sociological aspects. It is hoped that some of the remarks and materials presented in this chapter will have practical value.

There are many cliches about what enters into the choice of a spouse. The extremes range from "opposites attract" to "birds of a feather flock together." While empirical research is far from clarifying which if either of these cliches may represent a more viable theory of mate selection, certain regularities in marriage selection patterns can be outlined briefly.

One overriding fact underlies marriage selection: some social contact must exist between two persons before they can marry. While this may appear self-evident, studies in residential propinquity as a factor in assortative mating have at times been reported almost as discoveries. Contact, however, must not be treated as an all or none proposition, and the amount of contact must be considered as a relative factor in mate selection. For example, the most casual contacts that an individual has with others in a crowd, in a train, or in other detached circumstances, have a very low probability (likelihood) of developing into more intimate social relations. How an individual's social networks develop is a complex

matter. In general, however, it seems more likely that intimate relationships will be developed through an existing network of social contact
and through situations in which persistent contact arises rather than
through haphazard or chance contact. Communities are not composed of
randomly distributed families with regard to the usual social classifications. Communities are defined by economic qualifications, by circumstances associated with their growth, including immigration and development of industries, and also by more subtle factors such as the designation
of one particular area as having an ethnic association, another being
close to a church, and so forth. There is a considerable likelihood that
an individual will be raised in the community that has many of his own
kind. Beyond this, being brought up in a community provides a type of
identification common for those in the community, even if they are different in some things. Residential propinquity in marriage thus is a
reflection of (a) the selective factors that occur in a community in accord
with degrees of homogeneity on important social characteristics, and
(b) the amount of contact that occurs between the members of the community. As children grow in the community, they become familiar with
the more general mores and expectations within it, but they also have
the opportunity to meet and see each other under a variety of circumstances not the least of which is school. Within the scope of the contacts
that are made during this period there is some likelihood that an individual's eventual marriage partner may be found.

A notion of propinquity as a factor need not be restricted to residence
only. A person may create the opportunities for finding marriage partners
in the selection of social circumstances. In joining the church in a community, the bachelor provides an opportunity for meeting members of a
community under socially approved conditions. This is an elective activity
on the part of the individual, and may be done purposively. Choice of a
job or an occupation may operate in a similar way for a young lady who
is looking for a husband, and money, prestige, and working conditions
are not the only factors that she might consider in taking a job; the opportunity of meeting eligible bachelors *might* have some relevance. Whether
it is done deliberately or not, however, the place of work is probably
an important place where individuals meet and may develop their contacts. Again, propinquity is not a simple factor in occupation either, and
some background factors also appear to be related to the selection of
occupations.

It needs to be emphasized, however, that the variable involved here
is the intensity or extensiveness of contact that is either developed in the
situation or required by it. Basically if a young man and a young woman
share an office all day long the important factor is not that they are together, but that they are alone. While two persons who are deeply in

love may be out of this world in a figurative sense, two persons who are isolated are so in a social sense, and this provides the opportunity for a development of more intimate contacts.

In the matter of mate selection, valued qualities of the individual often are important determinants of who will marry. This may be viewed almost in direct analogy to the operations of the economic marketplace. If a young man is handsome, tall, athletic, intelligent, well-educated, rich, and has all the desirable properties, he will be defined in our society as a "marriage catch." Since he is a desirable matrimonial prospect, it is likely that there will be some competition among women for his attentions. Inevitably, it is an unequal race. The women who have the most to offer become the most eligible marriage partners. The same, of course, is true for any woman who is pretty, intelligent, talented, feminine, and otherwise favorably viewed in society. In other words, there are self-selective processes that occur in a competitive field. Under such circumstances it would likely be found that the positively valued qualities in the society tend to be ordered in marriage selection. Since there are many valued properties in a society, and they are not equally valued at all points in time, and since there are other factors that operate, the correlation for husbands and wives on any of these factors cannot be expected to be large, but it should not be surprising that such correlations exist. These tendencies to similarity form the basis for theories of homogamy.

Some Restrictions on Marital Selection

There are many restrictions that occur in society on who a person's marriage partner may be. On one level there are the familial restrictions that prohibit marriage within certain degrees of kinship. Beyond this, however, there are other types of restrictions that appear to be important and pervasive definers of marriage lines. In American society, for example, there have been strong negative values among whites concerning intermarriage where a Negro and a white are involved. In fact, such prohibitions have been incorporated into the law in many states. Restrictions against marriage between races were one common concomitant of segregation laws. But of course the attitudinal climate in the society both makes these laws possible, and also governs the behavior of individuals generally in all the states. For example, in New York, probably the most cosmopolitan center in American society, residential segregation is an undeniable fact. Negroes tend to be restricted to or to restrict themselves to certain residential areas; but similar patterns occur for Puerto Ricans; there is a Chinatown, a "Little Italy," a "Polish Alley," and so forth. Segregation is not carried out merely by the attitudinal climate as reflected in the dominant culture (presumably the WASP's). To some extent segregation occurs on the basis of like selecting like, familiarity and similarity of background being important factors; lower socio-economic class is itself a factor involved in segregation, as people in some classes cannot afford a choice of where they live.

While there is intermarriage between members of different racial groups, the extent of it at this point of American society is very small. This is understandable on several grounds. To some extent, if there is a feeling of homogeneity for a given race, someone who married outside of it may be viewed as denying his kind. Both parties of a mixed marriage, thus, may find themselves rejected by the majority of their own race. Even in the case where two racial groups are ordered in society on the basis of dominance, the person who comes from the higher valued group may still be rejected by the lower valued race. For example, the white person in a mixed racial marriage may be viewed with suspicion and even hostility by family and friends of the spouse. With the rise of "Black Power" and group identity, the white person may be excluded from the spouse's social world.

There are other consequences which are equally important with regard to the mixed marriages. What is the place of children in such marriages? In American society the common practice identifies the children of marriages between a Negro and a white as Negro, between oriental and a white as oriental. From the point of view of the child, however, there may be some difficulty in being accepted in either of the two racial groups. In the case of the oriental, for example, cultural patterns that may be tightly knit with regard to the the specific oriental group may be lost to the child of the mixed marriage. Similarly, the physical difference in appearance for that child may make it difficult for him to experience fully the general white social culture.

Under these circumstances, it may reasonably be asked, "What factors make for such racial intermarriage?" In addition to the same factors that apply to any marriage, it may be that such a marriage in itself is a reflection of rebellion. Such marriages may involve a rejection of some common mores of society that arbitrarily place restrictions on humanity. Since the U.S. Supreme Court decisions on desegregation, the American scene on this matter has changed and is continuing to change. Where educational and residential segregation is reduced, social interaction between different peoples will increase, and patterns of marriage selection are also likely to change. Analysis of these trends and changes represents a potentially large area of research, especially in the urban scene. Speculation about this must be tempered by facts, however. While various devices have led to some desegregation of schools, for example, evidence is lacking that residential desegregation has occurred in any substantial way.

It is possible to summarize much of what has already been said by suggesting that wherever two definable groups exist, if at least one of them exerts pressure toward endogamy, this may be viewed as a barrier to intermarriage. This will be true for racial groups that may be identifiable on the basis of visible characteristics, but it will be true on other bases also. Ethnic groups may consider it inappropriate for children of their members to become interested in those from other ethnic groups. And, of course, the case of religious endogamy is fairly obvious in American society. With increased interaction among groups, where the interaction has social connotations and there is a denial of a rational basis for segregation, it is to be expected that eventually larger proportions of intermarriages will occur. This appears likely merely because the increased interaction diffuses the basis for the racial, ethnic, religious, or other identification, and thus more persons in each of the groups will have a lower identification with it. We may take as an example of this type of process a recently reported study. (Jerold S. Heiss, "Premarital Characteristics of the Religiously Intermarried in an Urban Area," *American Sociological Review*, 1960, 25, 47–55.) In his study Heiss found that the intermarried, when compared to a group of intramarried, reported less strong ties to religion in earlier ages, less satisfaction with early relationships with their parents, other characteristics associated with lower family integration, and greater emancipation from the parents at the age of marriage. In other words, those who are less a part of the homogeneous culture are less bound to be contained by it in their choice of marriage partners.

Many factors are involved in restricting the sphere of choices for marriage partners. In the above discussion we have emphasized *ascribed* characteristics. While there are differences in how the various characteristics operate, it should not be assumed that the ascribed characteristics are the only ones that operate to restrict marriage choices. Certainly there are aspects where ascribed and *achieved* characteristics are closely related, and achieved characteristics may indeed become more important in marriage selection than the ascribed characteristcs. An area of particular interest is associated with socioeconomic class and is a common concomitant of class. In particular, the impact of education on selective processes is enormous. The impact cannot be viewed as a simple one since socioeconomic class characteristics are strongly related to education. Phrased most simply, those with high income can afford to buy educations for their children, and thus in this sense there is a restrictive positive correlation. Similarly, the poor who must divert their energies into other channels may not have the money or time to acquire an education. Let us examine education as a pivotal characteristic and see how it operates in some aspects of marriage selection.

Educational Factors in Marriage Selection

While there is no question that a high value on education is an important American ideal, merely having more education does not necessarily make one a more desirable marriage partner. The amount of education that a person has is not the sole determinant of whom he or she will marry, but it may very well be part of a larger complex that does place serious implicit restrictions on marriage selection. For example, if a person is a member of some ethnic minority, and he leaves home to become educated, after a period of years of only limited contact with his home his values may alter significantly. In particular, if he has been accepted into the higher education groups, he may emulate both consciously and unconsciously the values of those who more commonly receive advanced education. Of course, this is an oversimplification; where he goes for his education, his prior relationships with the family, and many other factors are important in determining how he responds to this educational milieu. Nevertheless, it must be remarked that any person who becomes educated outside of the immediate scope of his background becomes marginal to it, and presumably this both increases a tolerance for persons who are different and also encourages a tendency to become more like them. This is one of the notions of the "melting pot" which has been so crucial to the development of an American culture.

Education tends to modify opportunities for marriage in other ways as well. A very important value in this regard is one that is romantically based and possibly is best identified as the Cinderella story. Women may have wonderful qualities that make them desirable to better men, and a good man may recognize a pearl who is beneath him in birth, status, and education. Rarely is there a corresponding legend of a man who has great latent qualities and is recognized—the man is really a prince and either by curse or volition temporarily exists as something else. The Horatio Alger story, to avoid confusion at this early point, requires that the man prove himself before he could win the beautiful damsel; that is, he must change his status to a higher level first. Phrased a little differently, we might examine two hypothetical plots for a novel and see which is the more reasonable. In one we have a college professor who visits a coal mining town and falls in love with the miner's daughter, and they marry and live happily ever after. In the second, we have a college professor (female) who visits a mining town and falls in love with a miner's son, and they marry and live happily ever after. The latter is conceivable only *if* one embroils the plot so that the female professor is interested in earthy things, or the miner's son is really an intellectual.

American values can accept the appropriateness for an American male to marry a female of his own education or a lower one, but tend to reject the notion of marriage of a male to a woman with higher education than his own. It is unlikely that a male American college graduate who is undistinguished in other ways will select a marriage partner from the professional ranks of females, such as doctors, lawyers, dentists, college professors, engineers, and architects. Women who have had this much education are more likely to marry other professional persons, and there are many things in the American scene that militate for this. The first and most obvious is that to become a professional person, one must spend time pursuing education. For women in American society, marriage may often interrupt the educational career. If a woman marries and is going to a professional school, it generally requires postponement of children as a practical matter; or the demands of the profession may require postponement of marriage altogether. If marriage occurs, it is likely to be in the context of the educational setting. The woman will want to marry someone who will understand what is involved in the advanced educational procedures and the most likely person in this case would be another professional person. In one minor sense, the relative numerical dominance of men in the professions provides a broader base to find husbands for the women who go on to become professionally trained. In fact, however, the marriage partner availability for the woman as she proceeds in her education is progressively restricted.

A common time for marriage is at the end of college or shortly after. The woman who is career-oriented tends not to marry at the end of college. The woman who marries at the end of college has a good likelihood of interrupting or stopping her education at that point since her husband may be taking a job or moving, and the wife ordinarily goes with the husband.

The educational values, and concomitants of these, operate in other ways as well. For example, in dating on campus, it is common to date someone who is in one's own class. A question may be raised when a senior male dates a freshman female, and there might even be some kidding about "robbing the cradle." This is a permissible pattern and not too infrequent, although the differences in education may militate against it; the interests of the seniors are likely to be different from those of freshmen. The reversed situation, however, is most unlikely. Senior females would be looked upon with a good deal of suspicion if they were to date freshman males. In effect, this system places the female at a disadvantage. A male may select his dates from his own class, from classes below him, and progressively may continue this process as he goes on in the educational sequence; and even after he leaves the institution he may continue selecting from a large crop of available females. The female, on the other hand, has a ceiling placed on her by common expectation. While she is available to be asked for dates by her elders, progressively as she moves up the educational sequence the number of those who are available to seek her out becomes more limited. Thus, in her senior year she commonly only has those yet unattached males in her class as potential marriage partners, while her male counterpart has all of the unattached females in the college as potential marriage partners.

There are points, thus, at which the educational discrepancy of males and females has important consequences for the selective processes in marriage. Not all the values that have been suggested here operate in a visible and direct way in American society; they may be subtle consequences of more complex and general situations.

There are other comments that need to be made. In the tradition of Western culture and American society, for example, a double standard of sexual conduct has been prevalent. At the level of education, this may mean surveillance of daughters by their parents, and often there is a notion of keeping a girl "good" and "pure" through extending and intensifying the educational process, especially if sexual segregation is involved. For sons in the society, on the other hand, manliness is a virtue and attempts may be made to manifest it in many ways, including rebellion of various sorts and autonomy in choosing or at least exploring educational and occupational opportunities. In a sense the values in society make it possible for the son to extend his educational and occupational preparations without necessarily limiting his breadth and scope of experience. Sheltering the son through education is probably less likely to occur in American society than thus sheltering the daughter. However, in times of an unpopular war, when deferments are given for education, one can speculate additionally on what the responses are.

It must be remarked that one of the major shifts that appears to be accompanying the increase in education for both sexes in American society is a breaking down of the values described above. This has already been noted in the previous chapter. Training beyond college tends to become professional, and as tolerance increases for women in professional work, administrative positions, and other white-collar locations previously reserved for males, men may feel *less* challenged or threatened by women with higher education. In fact, occupational selective procedures predispose for men making their marks in other ways than through educational achievement. Business acumen and success are highly valued as well as education, and the successful businessman may not be inhibited in selecting a professional wife. At one level, at least, recognition of education has become less threatening and has been integrated into American values. The school teacher, which is a position ordinarily occupied by women in American society, is not categorically excluded from the marriage market. But interestingly her education has increased progressively during the years, and at this point many educational systems require a master's or at least one year of post-graduate work for the school teacher. Such training is not considered to be debilitating in terms of potential marriageability. For women who are married and are already teaching, further training is not expected to have a deleterious effect on their marriages.

To return to our central assertion about American values, while education is considered to be good in itself, it should be recognized that it has not been considered equally good for all persons. The long time tradition has not been for education of the female at the higher levels, and certainly not at the professional levels. For women, thus, access to higher education has been uphill. The relative absence of higher education for females makes for a condition that tends to perpetuate itself. Persons who are highly trained and who are in the positions to train other highly trained persons tend to be men, and the institutions are run by them, and, in general, for their most frequent customers, other men. While there are special schools for women, the tradition of higher education has tended to make these "finishing schools" places for a woman to get an education rather than a place to train for professional life. This, of course, has changed in more recent years, but there is some difference of connotation when one says that someone has gotten a degree from Radcliffe and someone else has gotten a degree from Harvard. The former is a woman's degree in fact and also in connotation.

There are important questions, thus, that refer to the training circumstances available for women in American society. Who trains at the higher level has something to do with what the training is. Being a wife and a mother also becomes a *de facto* limitation on what education may be for a particular woman, and there are many other cultural concomitants that also operate and reaffirm the differences that exist in the educational outlook for women. Women are not only expected to specialize in particular areas, but they are also expected to behave differently from men in regard to education and the educational policies. As a final example, consider that there are but few campuses, and these are largely those of the urban areas, where young women are treated as equal to men, even on such obvious criteria as housing and dormitory restrictions.

❃   ❃   ❃

It is possible to examine the question of what the ideal characteristics of a marriage are for any culture. When the description is carried out, it may turn into something that is, to use non-technical jargon, "corny." The first article in this chapter is designed to give a very brief description of what appear to be "The American Ideals of Marriage." In reading this piece it should be noted that it does not represent what the editors think should be, but rather their perceptions of what American society appears to take as ideal. The reader may possibly have a number of further thoughts. The first is that there are obvious large variations possible on the pattern. Indeed, on contemplation the reader may even have the feeling that there are more exceptions than cases that correspond to the description. The description is, however, presented as a basis for discussion, and should be approached with the following question: If this is not the description of the American ideal of marriage, what does the ideal include?

Factors related to mate selection have already been discussed. The consequences of selection have been only casually considered, and more attention was given in passing to the factors involved in the selection itself. The article by Bruce K. Eckland titled "Theories of Mate Selection" reviews questions of selection in the light of both social and biological factors. Individualistic theories are described, particularly with reference to personality characteristics. The social cultural theories which have been discussed to some extent in these introductory notes are outlined more systematically. With regard to factors related to assortative marriage, students are advised to keep these theories in mind especially in subsequent examination of the factors associated with the dissolution of marriages.

Observers have noted that the selection procedures for marriage are varied, and may not have a great deal to do with "rational" selection. One aspect of these procedures has been associated with "dating," and it was noted early in the research literature that factors that are rated as important for dating desirability might have little to do with those related to selecting a spouse. The early literature in this area is reviewed briefly by Ira L. Reiss in his article titled "Social Class and Campus Dating," which examines the basic notion that dating actually tends to follow class lines and is related to class characterstics as defined by campus stratification and parental class identification. A broader perspective of the actual processes involved in the dating procedures on the campus results from this analysis.

The place of love in marriage is a matter of speculation, but it is also a matter for direct study. For example, a decade ago William J. Goode wrote an important paper indicating how love may be analyzed as an element of social action in the context of the social structure. He defined love as ". . . a strong emotional attachment, a cathexis, between adolescents or adults of opposite sexes, with at least the components of sex desire and tenderness." He noted that strong love attachments often are precursors to marriage, and thus are seen as requiring control or channeling. If love were not controlled, it could be disruptive of the stratification and lineage patterns, and thus while some variation is tolerated, the systems are oriented to control. Five types of control were enumerated by Goode: (1) Child marriage is restrictive of the interaction of the parties involved when they are unable effectively to oppose authority. (2) Kinship rules may exist to define the class of eligible marriage partners, and choice can occur only within very restricted definitions. (3) Younger people can be isolated, that is, a social segregation of sexes may be enforced. (4) Individuals may be closely watched and guarded, as through a chaperonage system. (5) Choice may be formally free and love relationships an expected element in mate selection. In this system, noted to be particularly associated with the existence of adolescent peer group cultures, informal and more diffuse processes of selection are involved. (Goode, William J., "The Theoretical Importance of Love," *American Sociological Review*, 1959, 24, 38–47.)

In his article titled "Love and Marriage in Modern America: A Functional Analysis," Sidney M. Greenfield gives consideration to the place of love in American society. In another form, this expands the description of the ideal values, but it is more directly coupled to the limiting factors in the social situation. Romantic love is seen as motivating individuals into marriage and toward formation of families, a process essential to the persistence of the society. The analysis is directed to show how the system tends to perpetuate itself to maintain its continuity as a system.

With regard to the topic of mate selection, emphasis should be placed on the fact that it is an intriguing area of research and analysis, and since patterns of courtship and other relevant behavior appear to change historically, the topic is likely to be lively. One recent paper established a framework for analysis of dating based on the delineation of four types and noted how a knowledge of motivation in dating could be related to factors of degree of emotional involvement and instrumental orientation. Motivations for dating included: recreation, socialization (develop appropriate techniques of interaction), status grading or status achievement, and courtship. Then, a typology of motivations for couples may be described, and this may facilitate the analysis of particular social situations. In the particular report presented, the illustration used was an ecological restriction that brought nurses with courtship motivation into contact with college students and medical men having a primary motivation of recreation. (Skipper, James K., Jr., and Nass, Gilbert, "Dating Behavior: A Framework for Analysis and an Illustration," *Journal of Marriage and the Family*, 1966, 28, 412–420.)

Another recent research (Kephart, William M., "Some Correlates of Romantic Love," *Journal of Marriage and the Family*, 1967, 29, 470–474) illustrates another form of analysis where the romantic orientations of males and females are compared, and females are found to be more often involved in romantic experiences, even when age is taken into account. However, the difference is reduced as males approach the age (or fact) of marriage.

The final topic for consideration in this chapter deals with the double standard of sexual behavior and its apparent change in this century. In their article titled "The Decline and Fall of the Double Standard," Erwin O. Smigel and Rita Seiden note that while the double standard is declining, it has not yet disappeared. New studies currently in process confirm this differential, but it may be that in the next decade the double standard will decline at a somewhat accelerated rate. It has been noted that verbal acceptance of the decline may have to be strongly established in the mores before behavior will follow, since the practical fact of the matter is that social sanctions will continue to apply, formally and informally, so long as the double standard persists at an attitudinal level.

Consideration of the double standard involves many factors, and the shifting values in American society may be seen as part of a complex rather than a simple matter. For example, a proposed hypothesis would be that changing the age expectations of dating would have consequences on factors that follow dating. Thus, for example, studies reported in the literature indicate that early marriage is associated with early dating, early going steady, going steady more often, being in love a greater number of times, beginning more serious dating earlier and being involved more often, and so forth. (See, for example, Burchinal, Lee G., Does Early Dating Lead to School-Age Marriage?" *Iowa Farm Science*, 1959, *13*, 11–12.) Stated somewhat more simply, the hypothesis is that when an event is seen as a terminal point of a sequence (marriage follows courtship), then affecting the antecedents may have consequences for the event.

Involvement in sexual matters does not enter only at the time of courtship, nor only with the beginning of dating. Values governing sexual behavior in a culture are carried through the family, through the major institutions, and more abstractly through the value system of the society as a whole. The suggestion that premarital sexual intercourse is to be avoided is based largely on the belief that conventional people do conventional things, but it ignores changing conventions and behavior and the broad differences in values that may occur in different families. For example, if one family is deeply embedded in a religion that postulates that the legitimate purpose of sexual intercourse is to have children and that pleasure at best can only be incidental to this, it may be expected that these values will be carried by the children, particularly if the family exists in a neighborhood in which many like families exist. Another family may emphasize humanistic values, and premarital sexual intercourse might be defined in a radically different way. The position taken in the latter case may involve a belief that two mature adult persons should enter into relationships according to their own needs and expectations. This is in sharp contrast to a view that it is a *sin* to be involved in premarital intercourse.

The issue of "maturity" is a difficult one to handle in modern society. It supposes competence in regard to self and in regard to others. It is not a positively defined quality but something that is judged after the fact, after behavior and its consequences are observed. In modern American society, even in the most liberal circles, there are still difficulties associated with the handling of sexual matters even at the most rational level. Part of the problem is that values are applied inconsistently. For example, in a college newspaper an editorial may assert that sex on the campus is so commonplace as to be a part of the mores. This kind of statement does not take into account the distinction between permissive patterns and normative patterns at another level. Persons are not prepared to ask the corollary question: Is it immoral not to be involved in premarital sexual affairs? In many ways, the expression of values in the area of sex has to be phrased very carefully. This is particularly the case when discussing the double standard. One may almost border on the facetious to say that there is a "double" double standard that is applied at times by the dominant group, the males. Males may make the aggressive assertion that girls who do not feel liberated in sexual matters are maintaining the double standard. There would be little difficulty in maintaining this position if one could be sure that the males who make this assertion do not believe in the double standards themselves, something not altogether evident.

With societal values as they currently stand, there are still real problems associated with premarital sexual experience. One aspect of this has already been mentioned above, and this is that differentially motivated persons involved in a relationship may differentially gain or lose. This would be the case if the motive of the male is recreation and that of the female is courtship, a not uncommon occurrence. Another problem that arises is that emphasis on sensual and sexual matters is not necessarily a good basis for mate selection, although it certainly is a relevant one. Society being what it is, another common consequence is that sexual involvement may create other problems, both practical and psychological. Possibly the actual existence of a double standard may become more noticeable in the ages following the periods when most experimentation is likely to occur, in which case females may remain with feelings of having lost, been exploited, or been cheapened by previous experiences. Finally, premarital sexual involvement does not always occur under the best circumstances, and it may lead to certain attitudes toward sex itself that are not conducive to a good sexual adjustment subsequently. There are indeed many factors that must be considered, and maturity includes being aware of what the factors are. The real difficulty is that one may *think* one is aware of all the factors involved, but how can one be sure?

21.

JEFFREY K. HADDEN AND MARIE L. BORGATTA

THE AMERICAN IDEAL OF MARRIAGE

The United States has drawn its population from many nations and a rich range of cultural traditions. For this reason, it is not easy to delineate a composite set of values that describe an "ideal" marriage and family. The task of defining an ideal family is further complicated by the fact that our own values about marriage and the family have been changing rather dramatically during the past century. What might have represented an ideal set of values that described the American family at the turn of the century would hardly be adequate to describe the contemporary ideal family. Yet, given these rather serious limitations, a great deal of energy has been devoted to describing the dominant ideals of the American family. Many of the characteristics of the ideal family sound like platitudes. In fact, they are. Other characteristics call forth a nostalgia to reassert an ideal family of yesteryear which in reality may no more describe our ancestor's families than our own. Yet they represent an integral part of the imagery we carry around in our heads about the family and which we continue to transmit to new generations. Some of these ideal values appear to be outmoded and thus bear little relationship to the families we all know through personal experience. Other values appear to retain a dominant place in our culture and do seem to describe ideal features of the family. The purpose of this article is to outline a description of the "ideal" family. We leave to the reader the task of sifting nostalgia and myth from reality. We also pose a serious question for the reader: what are the consequences and implications of living with a set of ideal images about the family that do not correspond to reality?

Ideally, marriage in American society involves a male who is somewhat older than the female. When marrying it is assumed that the adults involved, though young, still have achieved some degree of maturity. They have finished their schooling, or he has a responsible job, has learned a good trade, or has demonstrated competence as an adult. The popular view is that if a person does not marry young, he still should marry sometime, for marriage is "a good thing." On the other hand, marriage should not take place between persons who are too young, for they are not yet worldly-wise and do not know what the challenge of tomorrow is. The very young, the adolescent, are not expected to understand love in terms of responsibilities and mutual satisfactions, and thus their affective ties are often called by names like "puppy love."

Persons who marry in American society should do so through their own choice, and the major value that is involved is mutual affection. Each person is expected to understand both self-needs and those of the other. In a way every marriage is personalized, and every marriage is unique. The persons in love and about to be married are expected to feel as though this were a new experience, and no one has ever felt it before. The persons in the couple were made for each other, and indeed this can be seen by the fact that they were even neighbors, went to school together, or met under casual circumstances and "found" each other. Sometimes they do not realize that they should be married until after a long acquaintance. Still it is assumed marriage is for two persons who are made for each other, and often this realization may come after a short period. It is not good to marry, however, after too short an acquaintance, because the persons may not have had an opportunity to really become acquainted and know each other. But on the other hand, marriages that are born in such an aura of romance must be destined to be successful.

While opposite personalities may find each other stimulating and attractive, it is more likely that persons who can understand each other and have similar backgrounds are likely to have happy marriages. On basic factors, including race, ethnic background, religion, and education, the couples should have some meeting ground and, if they don't, at least they must provide for handling their problems in these areas. Whether or not the persons in the couple are similar or different is really not important, if they are the "ideal" persons for the marriage. Each is expected to be mature and have the ability to adapt and transcend any particular situation. Each will be responsible and aware of his own motives and the needs of the other. Each will be rational and sensible, and, if not rational, will have those intuitions that make for the right decision. Each will have respect for the other and thus will not force values on the other, nor require the other to give up individuality. As the society requires the man nominally to be the head of the household, this is the primary ordering. But within this, the personalities and relationships are compatible and complementary, and decisions and participation are joint ones.

In this marriage situation each person will benefit in many ways. Each will have the companionship of the person with whom he is intimate. In this companionship there is no need for defensiveness, and communication can be open and unguarded. Each has, in a word, security in the other and the interpersonal support from the other that earmarks a good partnership. The two are together to share a life, to give to each other rather than to take from each other. And yet in this situation where each extends himself to the other there is the opportunity for personal development and all persons get better through marriage. In being able to extend oneself to the other, in reaching out, in just this way, there is growth for the person in the marriage. Maturity continues to develop. In the marriage there are many pleasures. Companionship is important, but in addition it is in the marriage that the sexual drives are gratified in a situation of kindness and understanding and freedom from guilt which can lead to ecstatic physical pleasure. Sexual gratification consists of physical pleasure, relief, serenity and closeness. Sex has a purpose

within the marriage, and it is not surrounded by taboos or negative sanctions. Each person should be relatively inexperienced in sex, and it is particularly expected that the female will be a virgin. In this world of turbulence and change, many are not, but the prior experiences were of exploration, of chance, of accident, or of error, and in effect this is the first true sexual involvement.

Having children is something that is normally expected in the marriage, and two or three are good numbers. The partners in the marriage shall decide how many children they shall have, and also when. It is good to have children early, but a couple should also be given an opportunity to enjoy themselves first so that children may be delayed somewhat. There may be some reasons why a couple will not have children, but in general having children is a way of fulfillment to a richer life, and each couple should contribute to the new generation.

As the couple proceeds through life they will achieve more responsibilities in their jobs and in other social contacts. They will have friends, and they will have friendly relationships with their parents. They will be dependent upon each other, however, for their primary gratifications. Their aspirations will grow in a realistic way and every couple is expected to be upwardly mobile in socio-economic status. While they started their life together in a tastefully decorated apartment with all the modern conveniences, they look forward to and provide themselves with more adequate and extensive housing in a stable suburban community as the family grows. Not only does the family improve its position in the community, but it accumulates less visible forms of security, such as savings and insurance.

As the children grow in the family the participation in the community becomes broader. Not only are there memberships through clubs, religious organizations, and community organizations, but the children have contact through the school and through clubs of their own that broaden the base in the community. The children are pleasant and well behaved, and while they may make mistakes, they are never delinquent. Each child does well in school and each child is popular in his own way among his peers. And each child has the opportunity and expectations of going through college. As the children grow older, they develop interests of their own. They may earn money for themselves, but not because they need it. They can stay dependent upon their parents for as long as they require, provided that they are improving themselves. In fact, the parents are always glad to help in whatever way they can to give their children a good opportunity for a better life.

The external view of the family by the community requires that they be successful. Bad examples and poor marriages embarrass the community, and license on the part of particular individuals may threaten the solidarity of each person's marriage. Lack of success along financial lines may cause burdens to the community, also. A family that has no children may be viewed as less than complete. And children should be well raised because even though poor starts may end well, good starts may end better, and what the community needs is more good citizens.

There may be many exceptions to these values, and mistakes may happen in marriages and in this case they should be terminated in understanding of the mistake. Women, and in some cases the couple, may not wish to have children, and if this is devoted to a good purpose or a career, this is permissible. Tolerance for deviation is considerable, but only when the deviation is not frequent and leads to other success which is also considered important.

The description could be continued, but the violinist is tiring in his rendition of "Hearts and Flowers."

22.

Bruce K. Eckland

THEORIES OF MATE SELECTION

This paper is devoted to a review and clarification of questions which both social and biological scientists might regard as crucial to an understanding of nonrandom mate selection. Owing to the numerous facets of the topic, the diverse nature of the criteria by which selection occurs, and the sharp differences in the scientific orientations of students who have directed their attention to the problem, it does not seem possible at this time to shape the apparent chaos into perfect, or even near-perfect, order and, out of this, develop a generalized theory of mate selection. Nevertheless, it is one of our objectives to systematize some of our thinking on the topic and consider certain gaps and weaknesses in our present theories and research.

Before embarking on this task, it would be proper to ask why the problem is worth investigating, a question which other speakers no doubt also will raise during the course of this conference. If the social and biological scientists had a better understanding of mate selection, what would happen to other parts of our knowledge or practice as a result? Despite the fact that our questions arise from quite different perspectives, there is at least one obvious point at which they cut across the various fields. This point is our common interest in the evolution of human societies, and assortative mating in this context is one of the important links between the physical and cultural components of man's evolution.

Looking first from the geneticists' side, at the core of the problem lies the whole issue of

This selection is reprinted from: Bruce K. Eckland, "Theories of Mate Selection," *Eugenics Quarterly*, 1968, *15*, 71–84.

Reprinted with the permission of the author and publisher.

natural selection. Any divergence from perfect panmixia, i.e., random mating, splits the genetic composition of the human population into complex systems of subordinate populations. These may range from geographically isolated "races" to socially isolated caste, ethnic, or economic groups. Regardless of the nature of the boundaries, each group is viewed as a biological entity, differing statistically from other groups with respect to certain genes. To the extent that different mating groups produce more or fewer children, "natural" selection takes place.

In the absence of differential fertility, assortative mating alone does not alter the gene frequencies of the total population. Nevertheless, it *does* change the distribution and population variance of genes (Stern, 1960) and this, itself, is of considerable importance. Hirsch (1967), for example, has stated:

As the social, ethnic, and economic barriers to education are removed throughout the world, and as the quality of education approaches a more uniformly high level of effectiveness, heredity may be expected to make an ever larger contribution to individual differences in intellectual functioning and consequently to success in our increasingly complex civilization. Universally compulsory education, improved methods of ability assessment and career counseling, and prolongation of the years of schooling further into the reproductive period of life can only increase the degree of positive assortative mating in our population. From a geneticist's point of view our attempt to create the great society might prove to be the greatest selective breeding experiment ever undertaken. (p. 128)

Long-term mate selection for educability or intelligence increases the proportion of relevant homozygous genotypes which over successive generations *tends* to produce a biotic model of class structure in which a child's educability and, therefore, future social status are genetically determined. Since these propositions hold whether or not everyone has the same number of children with exact replacement, assortative mating would seem to have consequences just as relevant as any other mechanisms involving the genetic character of human societies.[1]

Also from the biological point of view, it is probable that assortative mating is becoming an increasingly important factor relative to others affecting the character of the gene pool. Infant mortality, for instance, does not appear to exert the same kind of a selection pressure on the populations of Western societies today as did a hundred, or even fifty, years ago. Likewise, accompanying the rise of mass education and spread of birth control information, fertility differentials appear to have narrowed markedly, especially in this country (Kirk, 1966). For example, the spread is not nearly as great as it once was between the number of children in lower and upper socio-economic families. It is not altogether clear, of course, just how the relaxation of selection pressures of this kind would, in the long run, affect future generations. Yet, assuming, as some have suggested, that these trends will continue, then a broader understanding of the nature and causes of mate selection may eventually become one of the outstanding objectives of population geneticists. One reason is that the more the assortative mating, the greater the rate of genetic selection. If nearly all members of a society reproduce and most reproduce about the same number of children, and these in turn live to reproduce, it might then be just as important to know who mates with whom as to know who reproduces and how much.

The interest of social scientists in mate selection has been more uneven and much more diffuse. Some anthropologists undoubtedly come closest to sharing the evolutionary perspective of geneticists, as indicated by their work in a variety of overlapping areas which deal in one way or another with mating, e.g., genetic drift, hybridization, and kinship systems. In contrast, sociologists have been less sensitive to genetic theories. We share with others an evolutionary approach, but one that rests almost wholly on social and cultural rather than physical processes. Nonetheless, mate selection lies at the core of a number of sociological prob-

---

[1] I have attempted in the early part of this paper to place mate selection in an evolutionary perspective. The discussion later will focus on explanatory theories, treating assortative mating as the dependent variable. In another paper, I shall discuss in much greater depth than outlined here the social-

evolutionary consequences of mate selection. See Bruce K. Eckland, "Evolutionary Consequences of Assortative Mating and Differential Fertility in Man," in Theodosius Dobzhansky (ed.), *Evolutionary Biology*, vol. IV (New York: Appleton-Century, in press).

lems. These range, for example, from studies of the manner in which class endogamy is perpetuated from one generation to the next to studies in which endogamy is conceived as a function of marital stability. While sociologists have helped to ascertain many facts as well as having developed a few quasi-theories about assortative mating, it is rather difficult when reviewing our literature on the subject to distinguish between that which is scientifically consequential and that which is scientifically trivial. The general orientation of social scientists, in any case, is far from trivial and can be used instructively in the region of mate selection and in ways heretofore neglected by population geneticists. Some of their "theories" will be reviewed later in this paper.

EVOLUTION IN PARALLEL AND INTERACTION

Differences in the basic theoretical orientations of the social and biological sciences with respect to human evolution and assortative mating perhaps can best be understood in terms of the set of diagrams that follow. Figure 22-1 illustrates the usual manner in which investigators in either field approach their subject matter.

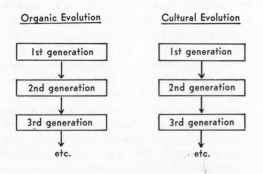

FIGURE 22-1. Evolution in parallel

The course of human development is traced on separate but parallel tracks. Some textbooks and elementary courses in sociology begin with a brief treatment of genetics, but it is soon forgotten. In a like manner, students in a course in genetics are told that the expression of the genetic character of an individual depends largely on environmental influences, after which no further reference to environment seems to be necessary (Caspari, 1967).

Evolution viewed in parallel has allowed each field to articulate its own theories and perspectives. Mate selection is only one case in point, but a good one. The anthropologist or sociologist typically begins with some universal statement to the effect that in no society is mate selection unregulated and then he may proceed to analyze the cultural controls that regulate the selection process. As he has defined his problem, there perhaps has been no need to consider physiological processes. The geneticist, on the other hand, typically introduces the topic with some statement about how mate selection alters the proportion of heterozygotes in the population (as we have done) and then proceeds to a discussion of allele frequencies or consanguinity. Because he is concerned almost exclusively with the nature of the genetic material, he does not care, for example, why tall people seem to prefer to marry tall people. I doubt that sociologists especially care either. There are, however, traits far more relevant than these, like education, which serve as a basis of assortative mating and to which sociologists have given considerable attention and the geneticists relatively little.

The gap about which I am speaking also can be illustrated by the manner in which some geneticists define assortative mating. To repeat a definition which appeared recently in the *Eugenics Quarterly*, assortative mating is "the tendency of marriage partners to resemble one another as a result of preference or choice" (Post, 1965). The reference to individual "preference or choice" illustrates one of the major weaknesses in the geneticist's understanding of the nature of culture and society. (It is not just this particular statement that is troublesome, but many others like it throughout the literature.)

Mate selection is *not* simply a matter of preference or choice. Despite the increased freedom and opportunities that young people have to select what they believe is the "ideal" mate, there are a host of factors, many *well* beyond the control of the individual, which severely limit the number of eligible persons from which to choose. As unpalatable as this proposition may be, it rests on a rather large volume of data which suggests that the regulatory system of society enforces in predictable ways a variety of norms and sometimes specific rules about who may marry whom. Perhaps the most important point I will have to make in this paper is that geneticists must begin to recast their assumptions about the nature of culture and society, just as sociologists must recast their thinking about genetics (Eckland, 1967).

Assuming that both geneticists and sociologists do reconsider their positions and assuming, too, that each discipline has a hold of some part of the truth, there still remains the unfilled gap in the kinds of knowledge needed to develop a set of interlocking theories between the social and biological sciences with regard to mate selection. I do not question that organic and cultural evolution can and, in many ways, must be studied as separate phenomena. The point is, however, that they do interact and this, too, should be studied; and to do so will require a much broader historical perspective than most geneticists and social scientists have exhibited up to now.

An interaction model of organic and cultural evolution must specify the precise nature of the relationships between the hereditary factors and environmental influences. Although certainly a very old idea, the notion of *interaction* has lain relatively dormant until recent years, probably largely due to the nature-nurture controversy and the racist arguments that covered most of the first half of the twentieth century. The expanded model in Figure 22-2 suggests a more elaborate system of causal paths along which there is continuous feedback between the genetic and cultural tracks from one generation to the next. As before, we are dealing with the processes by which generational replacement and change occur. However, in addition to the duplication of most genes and most cultural traits in each succeeding generation, new patterns invariably emerge through the interaction of heredity and environment. Briefly, and with no intent on my part to intimate either purpose or consciousness, (a) genes restrict the possible

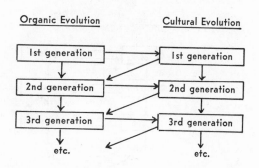

FIGURE 22-2. Evolution in interaction

range of man's development and (b) within these limits he alters his environment or cultural arrangements in such ways as to change the frequencies or distribution of genes in the next generation which (c) enables him to carry out further changes.

It is important to note here that the interaction of heredity and environment does not occur within the duration of a single generation, a point that social scientists, in particular, need to recognize. Holding for inspection a very short segment of the life span of a single cohort, as so often we do, it is not possible to observe, even to logically think about, heredity and environment in interaction. Within the span of one generation, the relationship appears only as a one-way process, with the genetic makeup of individuals determining the norms of reaction to the environment. The path from environment *back* to genetics which actually allows us to speak in terms of *interaction* appears only *between* generations, as in the above model. In other words, models of the sort abbreviated in Figure 22-3 do not fit reality. The cultural environment, of course, may have an immediate and direct effect upon an individual's endocrine system, as well as other physiological and morphological structures, but it cannot, as far as we know, alter his genes. Environment can only alter their phenotypic expression and, owing to selective mating, the genes of one's progeny in the next generation.

We have now moved into a position whereby we might raise two rather crucial questions re-

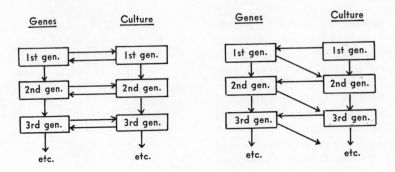

FIGURE 22-3. False models

garding the search for significant variables in mate selection, that is, significant in the context of an interaction model. The first is: What genotypes have social definitions attached to their behavioral manifestations or, conversely, what physical, personality, and social traits depend on our genes? The answer requires determining how much, if any, of the variance of a particular trait is due to heredity (and how much to environment). For example, taking the operational definition of intelligence we now employ, if none of the variance can be attributed to genetic sources, then no matter how intense assortative mating is for intelligence, we most certainly would exclude it from any further consideration in our model. Objections sometimes have been raised against partitioning the variance on the grounds that there is a strong interaction component in the development of most traits. It will be recalled, however, that our general model permits no interaction of this form between heredity and environment in the development of the intelligence or any other phenotype of an *individual*. Every character is determined during the lifetime of that individual, with genotypes determining part of the course of development and not the other way around. There are other problems to be encountered in any analysis of variance which attempts to sort out the hereditary component, but this is not one of them.

The second question is: What criteria for mate selection are *functionally* relevant within a particular population at a particular time?

This question, of course, raises some long-standing issues in genetics regarding the "adaptive" quality of characteristics which are genetically variable. It appears, for example, that some traits like the O, A, B, and AB blood types for the most part are adaptively neutral or, at least, it is not known how they affect the biological or social fitness of their possessors in any significant way. Likewise, there are traits like eye color which apparently have no clear functional value and yet seem to be involved in the sorting which unites one mate with another. By this, I do not mean that the search for socially relevant traits in mate selection should be directed toward putting the science of genetics to the service of human welfare. Rather, it is my belief that the discovery of socially relevant biological dimensions of human variation is likely to be of the sort, such as intelligence, which may be treated simultaneously as Mendelian mechanisms in the reproductive process and as sorting and selecting mechanisms in the allocation of social status and in the maintenance of boundaries between social groups, the discovery of which may serve to further our general understanding of human evolution. Any delimiting, therefore, of the class of mate selection variables we eventually must take into account should deal, on the one hand, with traits which are understood in terms of genetic processes and partly in terms of social and other environmental processes and, on the other hand, with traits whose survival or social value is at least partly understood.

NOTES ON TERMINOLOGY

Two basic forms of nonrandom mate selection are *assortative* mating and *inbreeding*. Assortative mating usually encompasses all character-specific mate selection which would not be expected to occur by chance. Inbreeding, on the other hand, encompasses all mating where departures from perfect panmixia involve the relatedness or ancestry of individuals. While some authors have used the terms in essentially this manner (e.g., Spuhler, 1962; Post, 1965), others have not (e.g., Allen, 1965; Warren, 1966). The latter have not restricted assortative mating to refer only to character-specific situations but have included inbreeding as one of its forms. Another variation is that some authors have used the labels *genotypic* assortative mating to refer to inbreeding and *phenotypic* assortative mating to refer to the nonrandom, character-specific form (e.g., Fuller and Thompson, 1960). Also, the terms *consanguine* and *conjugal* sometimes are used to make the same distinction.

Attention to the rules governing the selection of a spouse has led to another set of terms: the first, representing conformity to the norms, called *agathogamy;* the second, involving prohibited deviations from the norms, called *cacogamy* (Merton, 1964). *Incest,* a special case of inbreeding, involves prohibited deviations from the rules controlling matings between closely related persons and is also a special case of cacogamy since the latter includes other forms of socially disapproved matings as well, such as *mesalliance,* a marriage with one of an inferior position. Special cases of mesalliance are *hypergamy* to denote the pattern wherein the female marries upward into a higher social stratum (the male marries the one in the inferior position) and *hypogamy* wherein the female marries downward into a lower social stratum.

In common use are the more general terms *endogamy* and *exogamy* which refer to in-group marriages of almost any kind. Inbreeding is a special case of endogamy; *hybridization* and *admixture* are special cases of exogamy in which "racial" features are the implied criteria. *Interbreeding* and *intermarriage* also have about the same meaning as above, except the latter term is more frequently used in reference to traits dealing with categories other than race, such as *interfaith* marriages. Miscegenation, another form of exogamy, is the term usually applied to interbreeding between white and Negro or other intergroup matings (legitimate and illegitimate) wherein the contractants have violated cultural proscriptions; and, in this respect, miscegenation is also a form of cacogamy, as well as a form of mesalliance.

Still another term commonly employed to describe assortative mating is *homogamy* which denotes something about the likeness or similarity of the married couples, with or without specific reference to any particular set of characteristics. Thus, one may speak in terms of racial homogamy or social homogamy or, simply, homogamous marriages. The antonym, *heterogamy,* is not widely used but could logically refer to mixed matings, the tendency toward random mating, or selection for "dissimilar" traits. The latter, however, is more often called *negative* assortative mating; all other forms are called *positive* assortative mating.

The above discussion probably comes close to exhausting the arsenal of terms we employ. However, with few exceptions, the concepts which arise from their meaning do not appear to be especially useful for classifying mating patterns in such a manner as to provide a sound basis for bridging the gap between the organic and social models presented earlier. It is quite probable that not only do we need more knowledge of assortative mating upon which to base more generalized theories, but we very well might find it necessary either to develop a new set of concepts (and terms) or to undertake a major revision of those now used. At present, they are confusing and often redundant, many do not appear particularly relevant to our problem, and few perhaps mean the same thing to both the geneticist and social scientist.

In the remainder of this paper, I shall review briefly some of the current theories of mate selection. By no means a complete review, I have neglected, for example, the very large body of work of anthropologists and population geneticists dealing with inbreeding. Studies of consanguineous marriages provide important information about genetic processes, such as the mutation load which is especially sensitive to inbreeding. Also reported in this literature, but not here, are a number of theories that attempt to explain the cultural development of kinship systems in which inbreeding is permitted or prescribed. However, most, although not all, of this work tends to deal with small populations which have been isolated for many generations. It is not convenient for explaining assortative mating in large, relatively open, and highly mobile cultures. The following discussion, therefore, involves a search for those psychological and structural features which best show how assortative mating operates in contemporary societies.

INDIVIDUALISTIC THEORIES

The disappearance of unilineal kinship systems in Western societies has led to a decline of kinship control over mate selection. The resulting freedom which young people now enjoy has brought about an enormously complex system. No doubt, the selection process actually begins long before the adolescent's first "date." Moreover, under conditions of serial monogamy where it is possible to have many wives but only one at a time, the process for some probably never ends. Determining the "choice" are a myriad of emotional experiences and it is these experiences, along with a variety of subconscious drives and needs, upon which most psychological and other "individualistic" theories are based.

THE UNCONSCIOUS ARCHETYPE

Some of the earliest and perhaps most radical theories of mate selection suggested that what guides a man to choose a woman (it was seldom thought to be the other way around) is instinct. Scholars believed that there must be for each particular man a particular woman who, for reasons involving the survival of the species, corresponded most perfectly with him. A modern rendition of the same idea is Carl Jung's belief that falling in love is being caught by one's "anima." That is, every man inherits an anima which is an "archetypal form" ex-

pressing a particular female image he carries within his genes. When the right woman comes along, the one who corresponds to the archetype, he instantly is "seized" (Evans, 1964). However, no one, as far as we know, has actually discovered any pure biologically determined tendencies to assortative mating.

THE PARENT IMAGE

A psychoanalytic view, based on the Oedipus configuration, has been that in terms of temperament and physical appearance one's ideal mate is a parent substitute. The boy, thus, seeks someone like his mother and the girl seeks someone like her father. While it admittedly would seem reasonable to expect parent images to either encourage or discourage a person marrying someone like his parent, no clear evidence has been produced to support the hypothesis. Sometimes striking resemblances between a man's wife and his mother, or a woman's husband and her father, have been noted. Apparently, however, these are only "accidents," occurring hardly more frequently than expected by chance.

LIKE ATTRACTS LIKE

Another generally unproven assumption, at least with respect to any well-known personality traits, involves the notion that "likes attract." Cattell and Nesselroade (1967) recently found significant correlations between husband and wife on a number of personality traits among both stably and unstably married couples. The correlations, moreover, were substantially higher (and more often in the predicted direction) among the "normal" than among the unstably married couples. As the authors admit, however, it was not possible to determine whether the tendency of these couples to resemble each other was the basis for their initial attraction ("birds of a feather flock together") or whether the correlations were simply an outgrowth of the marital experience. Although the ordering of the variables is not clear, the evidence does tend to suggest that the stability of marriage and, thus the number of progeny of any particular set of parents, may depend to some extent on degrees of likeness.

THE PRINCIPLE OF COMPLEMENTARY NEEDS

Probably as old as any other is the notion that "opposites attract"; for example, little men love big women, or a masochistic male desiring punishment seeks out a sadistic female who hungers to give it. Only in the past 20 years has a definitive theory along these lines been formulated and put to empirical test. This is Winch's theory of complementary needs which hypothesizes that each individual seeks that person who will provide him with maximum need gratification. The specific need pattern and personality of each partner will be "complementary" (Winch, 1958). Accordingly, dominant women, for example, would tend to choose submissive men as mates rather than similarly dominant or aggressive ones. The results of a dozen or so investigations, however, are inconclusive, at best. More often than not, researchers have been unable to find a pattern of complementary differences. No less significant than other difficulties inherent in the problem is the discouraging fact that the correlation between what an individual thinks is the personality of his mate and the actual personality of his mate is quite small (Udry, 1966). Nevertheless, the theory that either mate selection or marital stability involves an exchange of interdependent behaviors resulting from complementary rather than similar needs and personalities is a compelling idea and perhaps deserves more attention.

No firm conclusions can yet be reached about the reasons for similarity (or complementariness) or personality and physical traits in assortative mating. (Even the degree of association or disassociation on most personality characteristics is largely unknown.) To state that "like attracts like" or "opposites attract," we know are oversimplifications. Moreover, few attempts to provide the kinds of explanations we seek have thus far stood up to empirical tests.

SOCIOLOGICAL THEORIES

In a very general way, social homogamy is a critical point in the integration or continuity of the family and other social institutions. It is a mechanism which serves to maintain the status quo and conserve traditional values and beliefs. And, because marriage itself is such a vital institution, it is not too difficult to understand why so many of the social characteristics which are important variables generally in society, such as race, religion, or class, are also the important variables in mate selection. Thus, most studies in the United States report a very high rate, over 99 percent, for racial endogamy, an overall rate perhaps as high as 90 percent for religious homogamy, and moderately high rates, 50 percent to 80 percent for class homogamy, the exact figures depending on the nature of the index used and the methods employed to calculate the rate.

One possible way of illustrating the conserving or maintenance function of social homogamy in mate selection is to try to visualize momentarily how a contemporary society would operate under conditions of *random* mating. Considering their proportions in the population, Negroes actually would be more likely to marry whites than other Negroes, Catholics more often than not would marry Protestants, and a college graduate would be more apt to marry a high school dropout than to marry another college graduate. In a like manner, about as often as not, dull would marry bright, old would marry young, Democrats would marry Republicans, and teetotalers would marry drinkers. What would be the end result of this kind of social heterogamy? A new melting pot, or chaos?

It seems that, in the absence of "arranged marriages," a variety of controls governs mate selection and, in the process, substantially reduces the availability of certain individuals as potential mates. Many structures in society undoubtedly carry out these functions, sometimes in quite indirect ways, such as, the subtle manner in which the promotion of an "organization man" may be based, in part, on how well his mate's characteristics meet the qualifications of a "company wife." Thus, despite the "liberation" of mate selection and the romantic ideals of lovers who are convinced that social differences must not be allowed to stand in their way, probably one of the most important functions of both the elaborate "rating and dating" complex and the ceremonial "engagement" is to allow a society to make apparent who may "marry upward" and under what conditions exogamy is permitted. We are referring here, then, not merely to a society's control over the orderly replacement of personnel, but to its integration and the transmission of culture as well.

Rather than reviewing any very well-formulated theories (since there may be none) in the remaining discussion, I have attempted to touch upon a fairly broad range of conditions under which homogamy, as a social fact, relates to other aspects of contemporary societies.

PROPINQUITY AND INTERACTION

Whether we are speaking about place of residence, school, work, or such abstruse features of human ecology as the bus or streetcar routes along which people travel, propinquity obviously plays a major part in mate selection since, in nearly all cases, it is a precondition for engaging in interaction. (The mail-order bride, for instance, is one of several exceptions.) A person usually "selects" a mate from the group of people he knows. Findings which illustrate the function of distance have been duplicated in dozens of studies. In Columbus, Ohio, it was once found that more than half of the adults who had been married in that city had actually lived within 16 blocks of one another at the time of their first date (Clarke, 1952). Cherished notions about romantic love notwithstanding, the chances are about 50-50 that the "one and only" lives within walking distance (Kephart, 1961).

As many authors have pointed out, people are not distributed through space in a random fashion. In fact, where people live, or work and play, corresponds so closely with one's social class (and race) that it is not quite clear whether propinquity, as a factor in mate selection, is simply a function of class endogamy or, the other way around, class endogamy is a function of propinquity. Ramsøy's (1966) recent attempt to resolve this issue, I want to note, misses the mark almost completely. Investigating over 5000 couples living in Oslo, Norway, she concludes that propinquity and social homogamy are "totally independent of one another" and, therefore, rejects the long-standing argument that "residential segregation of socioeconomic and cultural groups in cities represents a kind of structural underpinning both to propinquity in mate selection and to homogamy." More specifically, the author shows that "couples who lived very near one another before marriage were no more likely to be of the same occupational status than couples who lived at opposite sides of the city." This is astonishing, but misleading. The author equated the social status of the bride and, implicitly, her social class origin with *her* occupation at the time of marriage. No socioeconomic index other than the bride's occupation unfortunately was known to the investigator and, thus, it was a convenient although poorly considered jump to make. To most sociologists, it should be a great surprise to find in any Western society, including Norway, that the occupations young women hold before marriage give a very clear indication of their social status, relative either to the occupational status of men they marry or to their own places of residence.

EXCHANGE THEORY

An explanation often cited in the literature on mate selection, as well as in that on the more general topic of interpersonal attraction, deals in one form or another with the principle of exchange. A Marxian view, marriage is an exchange involving both the assets and liabilities which each partner brings to the relationship. Thus, a college-educated woman seldom brings any special earning power to the marriage, but rather she typically enters into contract with a male college graduate for whom her diploma is a social asset which may benefit his own career and possibly those of his children. In exchange, he offers her, with a fair degree of confidence, middle-class respectability. Norms of reciprocity might also help to explain the finding that most borderline mentally retarded women successfully marry and even, in some cases, marry upward, if they are physically attractive. This particular theory, however, has not been well-developed in regard to mate selection, despite its repeated usage. Also, it may be a more appropriate explanation of deviations from assortative mating or instances of negative mate selection than of positive selection.

VALUES AND BELIEF PATTERNS

In contrast to the inconclusive evidence regarding assortative mating in terms of personality characteristics, numerous studies do indicate that married couples (and engaged couples) show far more consensus on various matters than do randomly matched couples. Even on some rather generalized values, as in the area of aesthetics or economics, social homogamy occurs. Apparently, our perception that other persons share with us the same or similar value orientations and beliefs facilitates considerably our attraction to them (Burgess and Wallin, 1943).

The importance of norms and values in mate selection, part of the social fabric of every society, also can be illustrated in a more direct way by looking at some of the specific sanctions that we pass along from generation to generation. Without really asking why, children quite routinely are brought up to believe that gentlemen prefer blondes (which may be only a myth perpetuated by the cosmetic industry), that girls should marry someone older rather than younger than themselves (which leaves most of them widows later on), and that a man should be at least a little taller than the woman whom he marries (which places the conspicuously tall girl at an enormous disadvantage). Simple folkways as such beliefs presently are, they nevertheless influence in predictable ways the "choice" of many individuals.

SOCIAL STRATIFICATION AND CLASS ENDOGAMY

We have already noted that the field of eligible mates is largely confined to the same social stratum to which an individual's family of orientation belongs. Social-class endogamy not only plays a significant part in the process of mate selection, it may also help to explain other forms of assortative mating. For example, part of the reason why marriage partners or engaged couples share many of the same values

and beliefs no doubt is because they come from the same social backgrounds.

There are at least five explanations which can be offered for the persistence of class endogamy, each of which sounds reasonable enough and probably has a hold on some part of the truth.

First, simply to turn the next to last statement around, persons from the same class tend to marry *because* they share the same values (which reflect class differences) and not because they are otherwise aware or especially concerned about each other's background.

Second, during the period of dating and courtship most young people reside at the home of their parents. (Excluded here, of course, are the large minority in residential colleges and those who have left both school and home to take an apartment near their place of work.) The location of parental homes reflects the socioeconomic status of the family and is the general basis for residential segregation. With respect to both within and between communities, the pattern of segregation places potential mates with different backgrounds at greater distances than those with similar backgrounds. Thus, to the extent that the function of distance (or propinquity) limits the field of eligibles, it also encourages class endogamy by restricting class exogamy.

Third, class endogamy in some cases is simply a function of the interlocking nature of class and ethnicity. A middle-class Negro, for example, probably is prevented from an exogamous marriage with a member of the upper-class not so much because class barriers block it but because he (or she) is Negro. The majority of the eligible mates in the class above are whites and, in this instance, what appears to be class endogamy is really racial endogamy.

Fourth, ascriptive norms of the family exert a great deal of pressure on persons, especially in the higher strata, to marry someone of their "own kind," meaning the same social level. The pressures that parents exert in this regard sometimes are thought to have more than anything else to do with the process and certainly are visible at nearly every point at which young people come into meaningful contact with one another. Norms of kinship regarding the future status of a child may be involved, for example, in the parent's move to the right community, sending a child to a prep school, or seeing that he gets into the proper college.

Fifth, and an increasingly convincing argument, even as the structure of opportunities for social mobility open through direct competition within the educational system, class endogamy persists owing to the educational advantages (or disadvantages) accrued from one's family of orientation. Most colleges, whether commuter or residential, are matrimonial agencies. As suggested earlier, despite whatever else a woman may gain from her (or, more often, her parents') investment in higher education, the most important thing she can get out of college is the proper husband or at least the credentials that would increase her bargaining power in an exchange later on. Given the fact that men generally confer their status (whether achieved or ascribed) upon women and not the other way around (female proclamations to the contrary notwithstanding), marriage as a product of higher education has far more functional value for women than vocational or other more intrinsic rewards.

To carry this argument a bit further, access to college depends in large measure on the academic aptitude (or intelligence) of the applicants. Moreover, the hierarchical ordering of colleges which is based on this selectivity has led to a system of higher education which, in many ways, replicates the essential elements of the class structure. Differentiating those who go to college from those who do not, as well as where one goes to college, are *both* aptitude and social class. These two variables correspond so closely that despite the most stringent policies at some universities where academic aptitude and performance are the central criteria for admissions and where economic aid is no longer a major factor, students still come predominately from the higher socioeconomic classes. For whatever the reason, genetic and environmental, this correspondence facilitates the intermarriage of individuals with similar social backgrounds, especially on American campuses where the sex ratio has been declining. It is interesting to note in this context that Warren's recent study of a representative sample of adults showed that roughly half of the similarity in class backgrounds of mates was due to assortative mating by education (Warren, 1966).

ETHNIC SOLIDARITIES

While intermarriage is both a cause and consequence in the assimilation of the descendants of different ethnic origin, various writers claim that the American "melting pot" has failed to materialize. Religious and racial lines in particular, are far from being obliterated. In fact, the very low frequency of exogamous marriages across these lines itself underscores the strength

of the cleavages. Most authors also agree that nationality is not as binding as either race or religion as a factor in mate selection. Nation-type solidarities are still found among some urban groups (Italians and Poles) and rural groups (Swedes and Finns), but our public school system and open class structure have softened considerably what were once rather rigid boundaries. There is some evidence, too, that religious cleavages have been softening somewhat, and perhaps are continuing to soften as the functions of this institution become increasingly secular and social-problem oriented. On the other hand, racial boundaries, from the view of mate selection, appear to be as binding today as at any previous point in history; at least I have found no evidence to the contrary. The gains that Negroes have made in the schools and at the polls during the past ten years apparently have not softened the color line with respect to intermarriage.

Explanations of racial endogamy in America, some of which would take us back several centuries in time, are too varied to discuss here. It might be well to point out, however, that cultural and even legal prohibitions probably have relatively little to do with the present low rate of interracial marriage. As one author has stated, "the whole structure of social relationships between whites and Negroes in the United States has been organized in such a way as to prevent whites and Negroes from meeting, especially under circumstances which would lead to identifying each other as eligible partners. . . . Under these circumstances, the few interracial marriages which do occur are the ones which need explaining" (Udry, 1966).

For the population geneticist, too, it would seem that the deviant cases are the ones which require attention. Elsewhere I have suggested, for example, that genes associated with intelligence may simply drift across the white and Negro populations since it appears that only certain morphological features, like skin color, actually operate to maintain the color line (Eckland, 1967). In other words, if the skin of an individual with Negro ancestry is sufficiently light, he may "pass" (with no strings attached) into the white population. Even just a lighter-than-average complexion "for a Negro" probably enhances his chances of consummating what we socially define as an "interracial" marriage. In neither the first or second case, however, is intelligence necessarily involved.

If intelligence *were* associated in any predictable way with racial exogamy, the drift would not be random and we would then have a number of interesting questions to raise. For instance, do only the lighter *and* brighter pass, and, if so, what effect, if any, would this be likely to have on the character of the Negro gene pool? What, too, is the character of the inflow of genes from the white population? We do know that the great majority of legally consummated interracial marriages involve Negro men and white women. Does this information provide any clues? And, what about the illegitimate progeny of white males and Negro prostitutes? How often are they placed for adoption in white households and with what consequences? Before taking any of these questions too seriously, we would want to have many more facts. For obvious reasons, our knowledge is extremely meager.

PRECAUTIONARY NOTES

In conclusion, five brief comments may be made upon the present state of research and theories of mate selection as revealed in the foregoing discussion.

First, there is a great deal of evidence of homogamous or assortative mating but relatively few theories to explain it and no satisfactory way of classifying its many forms.

Second, nearly all facts and theories regarding mate selection deal with engaged or married couples and hardly any attention has been given to illegitimacy (including adultery) and its relationship to assortative mating. It may be, such as in the case of miscegenation, that some of the most important aspects of mate selection occur outside the bonds of matrimony.

Third, our heavy emphasis upon courtship and marriage has obscured the fact that people often separate, divorce, and remarry. Mate selection may be a more or less continuous process for some individuals, affecting the character of the progeny of each new set of partners.

Fourth, the relationships between fertility and assortative mating still must be specified. Are there, for example, any patterns of assortative mating on certain traits, like education, which affect the number of children a couple will have?

Fifth, most of the factors in mate selection appear to covary. We discussed some of the more obvious problems in this regard, such as the relationship between residential segregation (propinquity) and class endogamy. It would appear that much more work of this sort will need to be done.

In regard to the last point, it would also appear that it is precisely here that social scientists, and sociologists in particular, may best serve the needs of population geneticists. Through the application of causal (chain) models and multivariate techniques, it may eventually be possible to sort out the relevant from the irrelevant and to specify in fairly precise terms not only the distribution of assortative mating in the social structure with regard to any particular trait, but also the ordering of variables and processes which restrict the field of eligibles.

REFERENCES

ALLEN, GORDON. Random and nonrandom inbreeding. *Eugenics Quarterly*, 1965, *12*:181-198.

BURGESS, ERNEST W., and PAUL WALLIN. Homogamy in social characteristics. *American Journal of Sociology*, 1943, *49*:109-124.

CASPARI, ERNST. Genetic endowment and environment in the determination of human behavior: Biological viewpoint. Paper read at the annual meeting of the American Educational Research Association, February 17, 1967.

CATTELL, RAYMOND B., and JOHN R. NESSELROADE. "Likeness" and "completeness" theories examined by 16 personality factor measures on stably and unstably married couples. (Advanced Publication No. 7.) 1967, The Laboratory of Personality and Group Analysis, University of Illinois.

CLARKE, ALFRED C. An examination of the operation of residential propinquity as a factor in mate selection. *American Sociological Review*, 1952, *17*:17-22.

ECKLAND, BRUCE K. Genetics and sociology: A reconsideration. *American Sociological Review*, 1967, *32*:173-194.

EVANS, RICHARD I. *Conversations with Carl Jung.* Princeton: Van Nostrand, 1964.

FULLER, J., and W. THOMPSON. *Behavior genetics.* New York: John Wiley & Sons, Inc., 1960.

HIRSCH, JERRY. Behavior-genetic, or "experimental," analysis: The challenge of science versus the lure of technology. *American Psychology*, 1967, *22*:118-130.

KEPHART, WILLIAM M. *The family, society and the individual.* Boston: Houghton Mifflin Company, 1961.

KIRK, DUDLEY. Demographic factors affecting the opportunity for natural selection in the United States. *Eugenics Quarterly*, 1966, *13*:270–273.

MERTON, ROBERT. Intermarriage and the social structure: Fact and theory. In Rose L. Coser (ed.), *The family: Its structure and functions*. New York: St. Martin's, 1964, 128–152.

POST, R. H. (ed.). Genetics and demography. *Eugenics Quarterly*, 1965, *12*:41–71.

RAMSØY, NATALIE ROGOFF. Assortative mating and the structure of cities. *American Sociological Review*, 1966, *51*:773–786.

SPUHLER, J. N. Empirical studies on quantitative

human genetics. In The use of vital and health statistics for genetics and radiation studies. United Nations and World Health Organization, 1962, New York. 241–252.

STERN, CURT. *Principles of human genetics*. San Francisco: W. H. Freeman, 1960.

UDRY, J. RICHARD. *The social context of marriage*. Philadelphia: J. P. Lippincott, 1966.

WARREN, BRUCE L. A multiple variable approach to the assortative mating phenomenon. *Eugenics Quarterly*, 1966, *13*:285–290.

WINCH, ROBERT. *Mate selection*. New York: Harper and Row, Publishers, 1958.

23.

IRA L. REISS

SOCIAL CLASS AND CAMPUS DATING

GENERAL BACKGROUND OF THE RESEARCH AREA

About 30 years ago, there began to appear in the sociological literature accounts of dating practices on college campuses. Although earlier writers had mentioned the same phenomenon, it was a 1937 journal article by Willard Waller that has come to epitomize this early literature on campus dating customs.[1] Waller reported that the older accepted code of a courtship system that led to formal engagement and marriage in a predictable fashion had decayed and was being replaced by a thrill seeking and exploitive type of relationship which was not integrated with marriage. This new type of relationship was a dalliance relationship, needed to fill in the time it took to get a college education and establish oneself financially. Connected with this type of dating was the "rating-dating

complex" which was a set of customs that established one's prestige on campus and which in turn determined one's dating desirability. The key prestige variables were things like popularity, access to cars and money, and belonging to the best Greek organizations. Serious, marriage-oriented dating did not involve these prestige ratings. Thus, such prestige rating-and-dating was not viewed as "true" courtship. This campus dating system was discerned by Waller at the Pennsylvania State University in the early 1930's and was documented by discussion and interviews with students.

In order to clarify the place of my research, it may be well to recount very briefly a few of the relevant studies that followed the Waller article. In the 1940's Hollingshead brought forth considerable evidence indicating the social behavior of adolescents was functionally related to the social class of their parents.[2] Particularly relevant here was Hollingshead's finding that dating among high school students was heavily controlled by social class background. Then shortly after the war Harold Christensen, Robert Blood, and William Smith, in separate research

This selection is reprinted from: Ira L. Reiss, "Social Class and Campus Dating," *Social Problems*, 1965, *13*, 193–205.

Reprinted with the permission of the author and The Society for the Study of Social Problems.

[1]Willard Waller, "The Rating and Dating Complex," *American Sociological Review*, October, 1937, *2*, 727–734. Joseph K. Folsom was one of the sociologists who presented similar ideas before Waller's article.

[2]August B. Hollingshead, *Elmtown's Youth* (New York: John Wiley and Sons, Inc., 1949).

work, tested college students to see if the sort of rating factors (cars, money, dancing ability, etc.) which Waller found to hold at Penn State would also hold true in their samples.[3] They each found that the students in their sample largely rejected the "competitive-materialistic" items that Waller reported and instead favored "personality" factors such as "sense of humor, cheerful, good sport, natural and considerate."[4] Blood found that the type of value system Waller was speaking of was most likely to be found among the Greeks on campus but that even there it was not supported unanimously by any means. These findings brought into question Waller's own views.[5] Nevertheless, it must be borne in mind that Waller's observations may have been correct for the time and place they were made.

In 1960 Everett Rogers and Eugene Havens published a study done on Iowa State College students.[6] They had 11 judges rank the Greek organizations and the major residence on campus and then, by interviews with a random sample of 725 students and by checking the student newspapers, they gathered evidence regarding the relation of prestige to dating of various types. They found a high probability for people to date those who are ranked similar to them-selves. They concluded from this:

Therefore, Waller's hypothesis that prestige ranking governs casual campus dating but not more serious mate selection is not substantiated to any great degree by present findings. Instead, these findings indicate that students follow prestige lines at all stages of the mate selection process.[7]

A study of fraternity pledging at an Eastern college by Gene Levine and Leila Sussmann lent support to the Rogers and Havens findings on prestige factors in dating.[8] Levine and Sussmann found that it was the wealthier students who more often pledged and who more often were accepted into fraternities and who in addition had the "proper" attitudes toward fraternities. Thus, there seemed to be a class factor not only in campus ratings but in parental background that distinguished the Greek and non-Greek student.

In effect, these findings on campus dating radically revamped much of Waller's position. The "competitive-materialistic" system of values that Waller described seems to be present on college campuses today mainly as a sub-cultural element, most likely to be found among the Greek organizations. But the more recent findings on class prestige factors in dating are even more important theoretically. Waller's view of the prestige system at Penn State was not a view of people of different parental social classes dating along those class lines. Rather, Waller explicitly stated that he did not believe there were any basic social class background differences among the students.

The students of this college are predominantly taken from the lower half of the middle classes, and constitute a remarkably homogeneous group. Numerous censuses of the occupation of fathers and of living expenses seem to establish this fact definitely.[9]

The prestige that Waller spoke of was obtained by success in dating the highest ranked girls and boys. The rating-dating system was a popularity system in which having a good line, knowing how to dance, dressing nicely, all had a part.

[3]Harold T. Christensen, *Marriage Analysis* (New York: Ronald Press, 1958), 2nd edition, esp. 235–243, 261–264; Robert O. Blood, Jr., "A Retest of Waller's Rating Complex," *Marriage and Family Living*, February, 1955, *17*, 41–47; William M. Smith, Jr., "Rating and Dating: A Restudy," *Marriage and Family Living*, November, 1952, *14*, 312–317.

[4]See in particular Robert O. Blood, Jr., "Uniformities and Diversities in Campus Dating Preferences," *Marriage and Family Living*, February, 1956, *18*, 37–45. An interesting report of a similar research project on a Negro campus can be found in Charles S. Anderson and Joseph S. Himes, "Dating Values and Norms on a Negro College Campus," *Marriage and Family Living*, August, 1959, *21*, 227–229.

[5]At about this same time an article by Samuel H. Lowrie had questioned Waller's characterization of campus dating. See "Dating Theories and Student Responses," *American Sociological Review*, June, 1951, *16*, 334–340. A more recent discussion of this point can be found in Jack Delora, "Social Systems of Dating on a College Campus," *Marriage and Family Living*, February, 1963, *25*, 81–84.

[6]Everett M. Rogers and A. Eugene Havens, "Prestige Rating and Mate Selection on a College Campus," *Marriage and Family Living*, February, 1960, *22*, 55–59.

[7]Rogers and Havens, *ibid.*, 59.

[8]Gene N. Levine and Leila A. Sussmann, "Social Change and Sociability in Fraternity Pledging," *The American Journal of Sociology*, January, 1960, *65*, 391–399.

[9]Waller, *op. cit.*, 729.

It was, to Waller, based predominantly on dating desirability, and social class in any fundamental sense was not the basis of it. The system produced a sort of superficial rating-dating class of its own rather than depending on any more basic class system. Thus, one important question now is, is there a more fundamental class system both on and off campus with which the campus dating system is integrated and which Waller has overlooked? The Levine and Sussmann study of fraternities lends support to a positive answer to this question as does the Rogers and Havens study. Research on social class homogamy in marriage and engagement also strongly supports the view of the importance of social class in mating.[10] Careful research of this sort has not often been done on the college campus. In fact, some writers stress the democratization effects of college life and the homogeneity of social class on campuses.[11] Nevertheless, I am suggesting

that the social classes on campus are not simple "popularity" classes but that they are stable class structures based on many campus values and that they reflect parental social class and affect serious as well as casual dating.

THEORY AND HYPOTHESES

In its broadest sense the orientation of my research embodies the well-tested theory that *the dating patterns of a group will follow the social class lines of that group and thereby encourage class endogamous dating and mating.*[12] The implications of this theory have only rarely been tested on college campuses although it is often spoken about.[13] It follows from this theory that one should expect to find a stratified dating system on any campus, except those campuses where, due to extremely small size and homogeneity, there is no class distinction among the students. It also follows from our knowledge that student behavior reflects parental class, that the social class differences among students should reflect class differences among the parental adult population.[14] It is of theoretical value to know not only whether or not the

---

[10]The classic study establishing homogamy in mating is Ernest W. Burgess and Paul Wallin, *Engagement and Marriage*, (New York: Lippincott, 1953). There is an excellent account of the relation of parental class and student dating in Winston W. Ehrmann, *Premarital Dating Behavior* (New York: Holt, Rinehart & Winston, Inc., 1959), 144–169. For interesting evidence that sorority and fraternity people marry each other, see A. Philip Sundal and Thomas C. McCormic, "Age at Marriage and Mate Selection: Madison, Wisconsin, 1937-1943," *American Sociological Review*, February, 1951, *16*, 37–48, esp. p. 47. Sixty-one percent of the sorority girls married fraternity boys. A recent study reporting class homogamy in campus marriages and showing parental influence is Robert H. Coombs, "Reinforcement of Values in the Parental Home as a Factor in Mate Selection," *Marriage and Family Living*, May, 1962, *24*, 155–157. For a much older statement along these lines see Alan Bates, "Parental Roles in Courtship," *Social Forces*, May, 1942, *20*, 483–486. For evidence on the continued importance of social class in mate selection in general, see Simon Dinitz, Franklin Banks, and Benjamin Pasamanick, "Mate Selection and Social Class: Changes During the Past Quarter Century," *Marriage and Family Living*, November, 1960, *22*, 348–351; J. Daniel Ray, "Dating Behavior as Related to Organizational Prestige," (M.A. Thesis), Indiana University, 1942; Ernest A. Smith, "Dating and Courtship at Pioneer College," *Sociology and Social Research*, 1955, *40*, 92–98. Marvin Sussman has shown the ways parents control marriage in a New Haven study: Parental Participation in Mate Selection and Its Effect Upon Family Continuity," *Social Forces*, October, 1953, *32*, 76–81.

[11]Listed below is one such study that tested for class homogamy in campus marriages and found

little evidence of it. These authors believe that the campus is a democratizing influence which *reduces* class endogamy. Clark R. Leslie and Arthur H. Richardson, "Family Versus Campus Influences in Relation to Mate Selection," *Social Problems*, October, 1956, *4*, 117–121. The literature on intermarriage also mentions that the campus breaks through traditional barriers. See Albert I. Gordon, *Intermarriage* (Boston, Beacon Press, 1964). However, there could be a democratization concerning interfaith marriage, without affecting class endogamy.

[12]The references in footnote 10 are relevant here. Also, the role of stratification in love relations has been dealt with in William J. Goode, "The Theoretical Importance of Love," *American Sociological Review*, February, 1959, *24*, 38–47.

[13]For a relatively early statement in this area and an interesting test of courtship among college men see Robert F. Winch, "Interrelations Between Certain Social Backgrounds and Parent-Son Factors in A Study of Courtship Among College Men," *American Sociological Review*, June, 1946, *11*, 333–341, esp. p. 338. For a study showing similarities and changes in basic values see Robert McGinnis, "Campus Views in Mate Selection: A Repeat Study," *Social Forces*, May, 1958, *36*, 368–373.

[14]Hollingshead had found considerable evidence that the social class of one's parent was a good predictor of adolescent behavior. Hollingshead, *op. cit.*

campus is stratified but to know whether the class system tends to reflect in some ways the parental class lines. If it does, then one latent consequence of such a system may be to maintain some remnant of adult control over mating via the promotion of class endogamous marriages which parents generally seem to favor.

The Waller approach to campus dating focused on specific date-rating factors and took them to be the essence of the dating system. It is my contention that the rating factors are merely symptoms of basic campus and parental class distinctions and that the entire system can best be understood from this social class perspective. The rating-dating system of any sort, competitive or personality based, is believed to be a direct reflection of the campus and parental class system and a way of clarifying and identifying class differences. Such clarification is viewed as part of a serious mate-selection system. Thus, Waller's view that rating-dating is a dalliance system and not integrated with serious dating or mating is questioned.

In summary, I am proposing to test two hypotheses related to the basic "class-dating" theory: (1) serious dating on campus will be in line with an existing campus stratification system, and (2) campus dating will reflect the parental class system.

METHODOLOGY

The data on campus dating were gathered at a coeducational liberal arts college in Virginia. The 19 Greek organizations (ten fraternities and nine sororities) had 840 members and 151 pledges out of a total student body of 1800 single students. There were 809 single independent students. There was a relatively even sex ratio in both Greek and independent groupings. It was decided that full information on Greek serious dating practices would be obtained as one test of the stratification-dating theory. If in 19 highly organized fraternities and sororities there was no indication of the relation of social class and serious dating, then the theory and its derivative hypotheses would be brought into question. In addition to the sample of all seriously dating Greeks, I drew a random sample which I could use to rank all campus groups, to obtain information on parental social class, and to further test on a representative sample the relation of campus class to dating patterns in both independent and Greek student groups. The random sample was an important group since it represented the entire campus. The all Greek sample was used to give a fuller and more detailed picture of the serious dating patterns of the Greeks.

The Greek organizations all met on Monday nights and usually had over 90 percent attendance at meetings. I sent one student assistant to each Greek organization to obtain information regarding all "serious" dating relationships.[15] A serious dating relation was defined as a relatively exclusive dating relation such as going steady, being pinned or engaged. All such relations were reported to my informants together with information on the Greek, independent, or off-campus status of the dating partner. If class-dating were found in these serious relations it would be evidenced that serious dating relationships were not *just* based on "personality factors" but that these very personality factors could possibly be viewed as influenced by stratification factors.[16] Finally, if one wanted to check on the relation of mating to stratification then serious dating and not just casual dating must be checked.

The check of all 19 Greek organizations yielded 133 serious dating relations for sorority girls and 112 such relations for fraternity boys. About 30 percent of the Greek members were involved in serious relations. Sixty-two of these relations were between a sorority girl and a fraternity boy. (These figures are for members only, not pledges. Pledges were also investigated and they will be reported on later.) The 62 couples consisting entirely of Greeks on campus afforded a check on the reliability of our information. If our data were accurate the sororities and fraternities should each report 62 matched serious relations. This was the case.[17]

---

[15] The student assistants went back two more times to verify and check all information they had received the first time.

[16] Blood, *op. cit.*, Smith, *op. cit.;* both stress personality factors as crucial in dating.

[17] One additional couple broke up due to differences in the definition of their relationship that came to the foreground during the research.

In addition to this all-Greek sample, a random sample of all single students on the campus was drawn and given a questionnaire. One hundred forty-four questionnaires were obtained.[18] There were 25 non-responses who were mostly students who were not located by my research assistants. Questionnaires were given out and picked up within a few hours by my 19 assistants. The questionnaire asked the respondent to rank each of the ten fraternities as high, medium, or low, and to do the same for the nine sororities, and to give reasons for the rankings assigned. In addition, questions were asked concerning the students' background including income and occupation of father, their own dating behavior, and the relative rank they would give to male and female independents and Greeks.

The all-Greek sample containing all 245 seriously dating Greeks was used as one test of Hypothesis One concerning the congruence of the dating system with the campus class system. The random sample of the campus was used to further check this hypothesis for both Greeks and independents, to rank all campus groups, and also to check the second hypothesis con-

---

[18]There were 16 pledges and 5 No Answers on organizational membership which were not included in the general analysis of Greeks and independents in this paper. This left 123 respondents to be used in the general analysis. The pledges were analyzed separately.

cerning the relation of campus class to parental social class.

THE CAMPUS STRATIFICATION SYSTEM

If the first hypothesis is correct there should be a significant association between the rank of the various campus segments and the serious dating patterns of these groups. Table 23-1 presents information on all the Greek students who were involved in serious dating. The fraternities and sororities were listed according to the ranking assigned by the random sample of campus students. The majority of students agreed on all rankings, although the rankings on sororities were more unanimous than the rankings on fraternities. The fraternities were divided into five high and five low ranked groups and the sororities into five high and four low ranked groups. It should be noted that many other cuts were tried on these data and the results were the same, i.e., there is a significant and strong relation between one's organizational rank and that of one's serious date. This is particularly true for the high ranked Greeks.

Table 23-1 also shows that although all Greek organizations have roughly the same percent involved in serious dating, the high ranked Greek organizations (particularly the fraternities) have a significantly higher percent involved in serious dating with members of Greek or-

TABLE 23-1. PERCENTAGE DISTRIBUTION OF TYPES OF SERIOUS DATING PARTNERS AMONG GREEKS IN THE ALL GREEK SAMPLE*

	Percentage of Each Type of Partner				Number of Serious Dating Relations†
	High Ranked Greeks	Low Ranked Greeks	Off-Campus	Inde-pendent	
High ranked fraternities	63	12	17	8	(60)
Low ranked fraternities	14	19	23	44	(52)
High ranked sororities	44	8	48	0	(86)
Low ranked sororities	15	21	45	19	(47)

*Significant differences exist between high and low ranked Greeks in their choice of a Greek dating partner and in the percent dating Greeks and in the percent dating independents. Also, a significant difference exists between fraternities and sororities in percent dating off-campus.

†The percent of total members involved in serious relations is not significantly different for these four groups. Going from top to bottom of the table the percent is: 31, 27, 32, 25.

ganizations rather than with off-campus or independents. Serious dating within the Greek system is dominated by the high ranked organizations. The low ranked Greeks, for the most part, obtain their serious dates outside the Greek system. It should be noted here that the Greek dating reported by our random sample was very similar and this is evidence of the representativeness of our random sample.

When we look in Table 23-1 at the relation of sorority ranking to the choice of dating an off-campus or an independent male, the results are rather striking. Of the high ranked sorority girls who are not dating within the Greek system, all of them are dating off-campus and not one is seriously dating an independent male on campus. Whereas, of the low ranked sorority girls, 19 percent seriously date independent males. Since there are an equal supply of Greeks and independents on campus and an equal sex ratio, this pattern seems to imply an avoidance of independents, perhaps due to a low ranking on campus. This avoidance is particularly pronounced for the high ranked sororities.

If we look at fraternity members in Table 23-1 to see their choice of off-campus or independent dates, we find a pattern somewhat similar to that of the sororities. Table 23-1 shows that the high ranked fraternity men prefer off-campus dates significantly more than the low ranked fraternity men. In fact, the low ranked fraternity men date independent females more than they date off-campus girls. Here too, then, is evidence that the independents are ranked low particularly by high ranked Greeks, but it would seem that the independent females are not avoided to the extent that the independent males are. Our double standard culture dictates that in a dating relation, if one person is to be higher in status than the other, it should be the male; and perhaps this is why independent females are not avoided as much as independent males.[19]

There is direct evidence of the relative ranking of campus groups from our random sample which can be compared with the above evidence

from the Greek sample. We asked the random sample respondents to state their relative ranking of independent males and fraternity males and of independent females and sorority girls. Rankings were asked for in terms of one's personal views and not in terms of what one thought others would generally say. The results indicated that most individuals, except independent males, feel that independent males rank below fraternity males. The independent females were evenly divided regarding their own superiority, and the independent males closely agreed with them. However, most all the Greeks were convinced that sorority girls outranked the independent girls.[20]

It should be noted that this view of the independents is generally shared by both high and low ranked Greeks.[21] Thus, it would seem that when low ranked Greeks date independents, they believe they are dating "down" but are willing to do so for other compensatory reasons or, in the case of males, simply because they don't feel the distance is so great and that it is accepted for males to date down. Perhaps some of the low ranked fraternity males date independent females with sexual goals uppermost in mind. However, in serious dating relationships this is less likely to happen.[22]

Additional evidence on this relative campus ranking comes from a further look at serious dating patterns of the independents in our random sample.[23] If independent males are ranked lower than the independent females, then it follows that the independent females in our random sample should report more serious rela-

[19]For evidence and elaboration on the double standard see Ira L. Reiss, *Premarital Sexual Standards in America* (New York: The Free Press, 1960), esp. ch. 4.

[20]Eighty percent of the independent males thought they ranked higher than fraternity men but all other groups had over 80 percent who said the opposite. Fifty percent of the independent females felt they ranked higher than sorority girls. Although the independent males agreed, over 80 percent of the Greeks disagreed.
[21]Low fraternity as compared to high fraternity men are somewhat kinder in their ratings of independents whereas low sorority girls are almost unanimous in giving low rank to independents. These differences were not quite significant.
[22]For data on this see Winston W. Ehrmann, *op. cit.*, chs. 4 and 5.
[23]The independent females reported the largest group of friends from the other three campus groups, thereby further showing their pivotal positions and their tendencies to date both independent and Greek boys.

tions with the upper classes, namely, the Greeks. This was the case—of 19 independent females with serious dates, seven were with fraternity men. It should be noted that five of the seven fraternity men dating independent females were from low ranking fraternities. This, too, would be expected. There were 11 independent males with serious dates, and only one was with a sorority girl and this was with a girl from the lowest ranking sorority on campus. Further, the independent females are more likely to have their serious dates on campus than are the independent males. Only one-third of the serious dates were off campus for independent females, whereas two-thirds of the serious dates of independent males were off campus. Finally, the independent females are involved with fraternity men about as much as the low ranked sorority girls, while the independent males are involved with sorority girls much less than low ranked fraternity males. The evidence on independents here is based on a small number of cases. However, since the results are consistent with several other checks, the confidence in the findings is increased.

In sum then, the stratification system which emerges at this point is one in which the Greeks are clearly at the top, but the low ranked Greeks are more likely to date seriously outside the Greek part of the system. In addition, the independents seem stratified by sex, with females ranked higher than males; and here too it is noted that the females have their serious dates more within the total campus system and the independent males have their serious dates predominantly outside the entire campus system.

Casual dating was also checked in the random sample and proved to follow stratification lines quite similar to serious dating. Many independents, especially males, do not date at all in Greek organizations. Table 23-2 shows the distribution of those students who do date Greeks. The same relations among high and low Greeks and male and female independents prevail in casual dating as prevailed in serious dating.[24]

[24]Table 23-2 is composed of answers from those who do date in Greek organizations to the question, "In which Greek organizations have you dated the most?" Some respondents will include serious dating as well as casual. However, the bulk of the dating reported is casual. Further, when known serious

TABLE 23-2.
PERCENTAGE OF THOSE WHO DATE GREEKS, WHO ARE DATING IN HIGH RANKED GREEK ORGANIZATIONS, IN THE RANDOM SAMPLE

Group	Percent Dating High Ranked Greeks
High ranked Greeks	78 (41) *
Low ranked Greeks	54 (24)
Independent females	50 (20)
Independent males	20 (10)

$$X^2 = 8.95$$
$$P < .05$$
$$G = .53†$$

*The number to the right and below the percentage is the base for the percentage.
†G = Gamma or Index of Order Association devised by Goodman and Kruskal.

It may be argued that if casual dating and serious dating both show a similar relation to the campus rating system, then the rating system is integrated with serious dating and mating and is "true" courtship and not just a dalliance system as Waller contended.

An additional search was made via the questionnaire and campus records to see whether the above noted differences in campus prestige are related to differences in some key characteristics of the students in the four major campus groups. A comparison of age at which dating began among sorority and independent females revealed no significant differences. However, the same comparison of independent males and fraternity males revealed a moderately strong and almost significant difference.[25]

A stronger and a significant difference appeared between the fraternity and independent males when compared on whether they had been in love before. There was no significant differ-

dating is eliminated, the relationship still holds up the same as reported although a little weaker. Actually, the relation is understated since about 35 percent of the independent females and almost 60 percent of the independent males do not date Greeks at all. This fact supports the relation of social class and dating but is not presented in the table.

[25]Sorority girls had 74 percent who started dating by age 16 to the independent girls 66 percent. The percentages for fraternity and independent males were 65 and 41 respectively.

ence among females.[26] Thus, it seems the fraternity males started dating earlier and had more love experiences. This "sociability" factor is one that was found to characterize fraternity men in the Levine and Sussmann study referred to above.[27] Such "sociability" background may well represent a social class difference in this sample as it did in the Levine and Sussmann sample.

A check of attitudes toward pre-marital intercourse was also undertaken. The independent males were the most conservative male group. This somewhat fits with their lack of dating and love experience. The low fraternity males were the most liberal group with high fraternity males falling in the middle. All females were about equally conservative.

The reasons for the relative ranking of the fraternities and sororities given by the total random sample were also examined to see if independents and Greeks differed here. All groups agreed that high ranking was given to a Greek organization for things such as sociability, intelligence and maturity, and campus activities. These were the most frequently mentioned ranking factors. There is evidence that these reasons are accurate perceptions of differences among the Greek organizations. A search of school records revealed that the high ranked Greeks control the student assembly and its officers. All but seven of the 125 student assembly members during a three-year period preceding the study were Greeks, and of the 118 Greeks, 87 were from high ranked Greek organizations. Of 63 Greek class officers, 53 were high ranked Greeks. This relation held up for sororities as well as fraternities.

Good looks and good grades were evaluated differently by Greek and independent males. The Greeks stressed good looks and the independents stressed good grades. Available evidence generally fits these rankings. In the three years preceding this study, 30 beauty queens were chosen. Five of them were low ranked Greeks; 25 were high ranked Greeks; none of the beauty queens were independents. In terms

of academic grades, the high ranked sororities outdo the low ranked sororities. However, among males the situation is different and the high ranked fraternities do not outdo the low ranked fraternities in grades. The independent males are better than the fraternity males in grades; but the independent females are poorer than the sorority females. The academic grade records for a ten-year period were checked and verified that this was a stable patterning of grades.

Finally, independent males valued dancing, sports, and parties less than fraternity males. The differences among sorority and independent females in rankings were fewer than those between fraternity and independent males. The sorority females gave more importance to such items as good manners, dress, and dancing ability, but otherwise there was general agreement. So here, too, the independent females are closer to the Greek females than the independent males are to Greek males.

Some of the reasons for ranking Greek organizations are similar to the sort of factors about which Willard Waller wrote. In particular, this is true of such factors as "good dancer," "good dresser," "good looking." These factors were not the most frequently mentioned; nevertheless, here is evidence of the sort of rating-dating that Waller had in mind. However, and this is my major point here, to focus on these factors as the heart of the dating system and to conclude that the system is superficial and unintegrated with marriage is to miss the crux of the matter. I am suggesting that these factors are merely part of the complex of factors which defines what sort of organization the high ranked students on campus achieve. These prestige factors are some of the variables that go with belonging to a certain campus social class and serve to identify that class. They are merely symbols of campus class status, and it is that class status that is crucial, not the symbols.[28]

I should add here that an examination of the dating behavior of the 151 pledges in the Greek organizations revealed a very similar pattern to

---

[26]Sorority girls had 84 percent who had been in love to the independent girls 94 percent. The percentages for fraternity and independent males were 96 and 60 respectively.

[27]Levine and Sussman, *op. cit.*

[28]For a discussion of how fashion in dress symbolizes status see Bernard Barber and Lyle S. Lobel, "Fashion in Women's Clothes and the American Social System," *Social Forces*, December, 1952, **31**, 124–131.

that of Greek members. This examination involved all pledges from all Greek organizations. Also, a study checking Greek rating and dating was done on this same campus in 1954 with quite similar results.[29] Thus, the stratification we are describing has roots in the past and our examination of pledges indicates that it is being extended into the future.

CAMPUS SOCIAL CLASS AND PARENTAL SOCIAL CLASS

Although other studies have shown that parental social class affects dating and mating, there is very little data on the relation of campus social class to parental social class. Evidence from our own sample is relevant here, although our testing of this hypothesis is nowhere near as thorough as was our testing of Hypothesis One. We have shown above that the fraternity men are more socialized in terms of dating and love experience. There is also evidence showing that Greeks value elements such as dress, parties, dancing, sports, and drinking activities more than independents. Such values are again part of a "socialized" image of man which the Greeks promote and which Levine and Sussmann have identified as part of the middle classes.[30]

In the random sample, I also have information on fathers' income and occupation. Here too some differences appear among the campus strata. As can be seen in Table 23-3 the overall occupations of Greeks are significantly higher than those of the independents. High status occupation here is defined as executive or professional. There is also a difference in occupation of father between high and low fraternities and high and low sororities. However, these differences are not quite significant. The differences in Table 23-3 reflect the general rank of each campus group as discussed in this paper.[31]

TABLE 23-3.

PERCENTAGE OF FATHERS WITH HIGH STATUS OCCUPATIONS FOR VARIOUS CAMPUS GROUPS IN THE RANDOM SAMPLE[*]

Groups	Percent of Fathers in High Status Occupations
High fraternity	69 (13) [†]
Low fraternity	54 (13)
High sorority	80 (25)
Low sorority	60 (10)
Independent female	42 (31)
Independent male	41 (22)

[*]Differences within the three pairs in this table are not significant but the difference between all Greeks and all independents is significant.

[†]The number to the right and below the percentage is the base for the percentage.

The females in sororities are somewhat higher in class background than the independent females and are also somewhat above the fraternity men. Females in college often come from higher class backgrounds than males. Possibly this is due to females' college attendance being considered of secondary importance to males' college attendance and so those females that do go to college come from wealthier homes.[32] This higher background may further explain the reluctance of sorority girls (particularly high ranked ones) to date independent males.

A check on income revealed one interesting relationship. Although the differences between high and low ranked Greeks and male and female independents were present, the difference between all independents and all Greeks disappeared.[33] Independent females in particular came out quite high on income. One might interpret these occupational and income results as indicating that although Greeks come from higher social classes as indicated by occupation,

---

[29]This unpublished study was done by two students: Withers Davis and Penny Hutchinson.

[30]Levine and Sussman, *op. cit.* Religious differences were also checked and the only religious difference discovered was that low fraternity men were highest on Catholic and Baptist members.

[31]An unpublished study by two of my students (Rusty Dietrich and Barbara Clarke) at this same college did show that, among freshmen, independent females as compared to sorority girls had lower income, less church attendance, and fewer parents who had been in sororities. No test of males was done in this study.

[32]Recent evidence of females' higher status on other specific campuses can be found in Leslie Richardson, *op. cit.*, p. 120, and Robert P. Bell and Leonard Blumberg, "Courtship Intimacy and Religious Background," *Marriage and Family Living*, November, 1959, *21*, 356–360, esp. p. 357.

[33]The mean income based on questionnaire response of the random sample is estimated to be: High fraternity, $12,400; Low fraternity, $9,400; High sorority, $12,600; Low sorority, $11,100; Independent females, $13,000; and Independent males, $12,400.

they do not come from wealthier homes. Thus, the overall campus class differences between Greeks and independents reflect the style of life of each group as related to occupational background more than income background. It may be argued that the occupation of a father affects male values more than female values. Thus, despite their wealth the independents, particularly the males, lack the values that go with the high occupational groupings and thus are ranked lower on campus. Although this *post factum* explanation does make sense of these findings, it must, of course, be tested in new research.

The question raised in Hypothesis Two asks how parental social class affects the relationship, found in Hypothesis One, between one's own campus rating and the campus class rating of one's date. Unfortunately, the more crucial tests of Hypothesis Two cannot be made with the existing data I have available. Such tests would involve checking the various possible relations between parental social class and campus social class dating more directly. For example it is possible that, even though high campus class individuals are more likely to come from high parental classes (see Table 23-3), parental social class does not affect the campus class dating system. For example, even though the higher parental class boys join the higher ranking fraternities, the reasons why these boys most often date equally high campus ranked girls may well be fully independent of their parental social class. This possibility does *not* fit with Hypothesis Two. On the other hand, it is possible that parental class would fully explain the tendency of high campus ranked boys to date high campus ranked girls. If so, when one held parental social class constant and looked at only one parental social class at a time, the relation showing high campus ranked boys dating high campus ranked girls would disappear. If this happened, then one could conclude that parental class fully explained why boys and girls dated as they did within the campus class system. This would fit with Hypothesis Two.

Finally, there is another possible way that the parental social class system could influence the campus class dating system. It could be that one's campus social class acts as an intervening variable between one's parental social class and one's choice of a dating partner. Possibly it is because one has high parental social class that one gets involved in high campus class groups and these high campus class groups might develop a style of life which in turn would make one more likely to date others from similar high campus groups. This eventuality would also fit with Hypothesis Two for it would show the influence of parental class on the campus social class dating system. It is hoped that future research will test these several possibilities and thereby afford us a more precise test of Hypothesis Two.[34]

In sum then, this check of Hypothesis Two shows that there is some evidence to support the hypothesis that the stratification system on the college campus reflects the stratification system of the students' parents. However, the evidence is surely more suggestive than conclusive and is not nearly as complete as that supporting Hypothesis One.

CONCLUSIONS

The importance of this theoretical approach is its relevance for much of the past work on campus dating. In part, it tests ideas often verbalized but seldom tested, and tries to organize the many *ad hoc* findings in this area into one theory. The theory bears on Waller's position in that it defines his "materialistic-competitive" system as but one set of rating factors that can be used to symbolize the class differences among students. The rating-dating system (whether "competitive" or "personality" based) doesn't block mating; it is more an indication of the presence of an underlying campus stratification system than it is an indication of a thrill centered, exploitative dating system unintegrated with marriage or social class. As a matter of fact, the rating system operates not

---

[34] I did ask each person in the random student sample to give me information on his or her parental social class, However, in order to make the checks suggested it would be necessary to have parental social class information on *both* the boy and the girl involved in a dating relationship. My random sample consisted mostly of students who were seriously dating someone else *not* included in the sample and this left us with a lack of knowledge about the parental class of their dates. Because of this we could only perform the partial testing of Hypothesis Two which appears in the text and in Table 23-3.

only on casual dating but in serious dating also and therefore seems well integrated with marriage. The manifest consequences of this dating system may well be involved with the establishment of one's rating, as Waller suggested, but the latent consequences are the support of campus and parental class endogamy. It may further be hypothesized that since parents usually favor matings within the same social class, then another latent consequence is to aid in achieving such parental goals. Awareness of such latent consequences is crucial to the understanding of the campus dating system. Without this awareness the system may appear to be merely an "irrational" system of dalliance.

There is need for several types of additional research. First it would be important to examine a more representative sample of American college students to see how this theory and its derivative hypotheses fare on different types of campuses. Stratification on campuses without Greek organizations needs investigation. My data indicate that independents do indeed have hierarchical divisions just as Greeks do, but more investigation is needed. Testing this theory on various size campuses with differing

proportions of Greeks would also be valuable. In addition, how individual choice operates within the limits of a stratification system should be conceptualized more clearly. There is the important problem of how such factors as propinquity, ideal mate image, parental images, basic values, and other variables operate in relation to social class and in relation to mate selection in general. Finally, the relation of other institutions such as the political, economic, and religious to campus dating and campus class should be explored.

It is particularly important in the analysis of a "free dating system," such as we possess, to keep in mind the ways in which the system is structured and the controls of a socio-cultural nature that are operative. It is all too easy to believe the cultural ideology that we have a "free" system. The theory put forth in this paper keeps the socio-cultural limitations of our dating system in the foreground. It is by focusing on such socio-cultural factors that we may obtain insight into the functional relations of mate-selection to the overall institutional structure of our society.

24.

SIDNEY M. GREENFIELD

LOVE AND MARRIAGE IN MODERN AMERICA: A FUNCTIONAL ANALYSIS

'*Voi, che cose e amor?*' asked Cherubino in Mozart's *Marriage of Figaro*. "Tell me, you know, what is this thing, love?" Cherubino was still a beardless adolescent and did not know the answer,

This selection is reprinted from: Sidney M. Greenfield, "Love and Marriage in Modern America: A Functional Analysis," *The Sociological Quarterly*, 1965, *6*, 361–377.

Reprinted with the permission of the author and publisher.

This article is a revised version of a paper presented at the annual meetings of the Central States Anthropological Society, Detroit, Michigan, May, 1963.

but he took it for granted that there was one. So have most other people, and many of them have tried to give it, but the most noteworthy feature about all their answers is how thoroughly they disagree. Sometimes, it seems, they cannot be referring to the same phenomenon, or even to related ones. After a while one wonders whether there is something wrong with the question itself, or whether perhaps it employs a word of no fixed meaning and can have no answer.[1]

[1]Morton M. Hunt, *The Natural History of Love* (New York: Alfred A. Knopf, 1959), 3.

Love, wrote Theodor Reik, "is one of the most overworked words in our vocabulary. There is hardly a field of human activity in which the word is not worked to death."[2] The literature on the subject, to say the least, is voluminous. However, "if it is true that science is the topography of ignorance," as Oliver Wendell Holmes once said, "then the region of love is a vast white spot."[3]

Most of what we know of love comes from the pens of poets, dramatists, novelists, and philosophers. What they have to say, however, is so variable, idiosyncratic, and full of contradictions that, in sum, it adds relatively little to our understanding of the subject.

Psychologists also have written about love. Most of what they have to say, however, is an elaboration upon, or modification of, Freud's notion that love is "aim inhibited sex."[4] Furthermore, most of their attention has been focused on therapy and counseling, and here they tend to be at one with the numerous sociologists and marriage counselors who have done work on the subject. The vast majority of these students and therapists, as Goode has recently stated, have "commented on the importance of romantic love in America and its lesser importance in other societies, and have disparaged it as a poor basis for marriage, or as immaturity."[5] Although they have helped us to specify and describe what love in the United States is—in the ethnographic sense—they have done very little in the way of analyzing their observations and contributing to our understanding of love. Instead, they have devoted their efforts to exposing the evils of romantic love and preaching against its practice.

The present paper is an attempt to apply modern sociological thinking to the analysis of the descriptive materials that have been accumulated on the subject of romantic love. In this sense then it is offered as a partial contribution to the understanding of the general phenomenon of love. More specifically, however, it is offered as an analysis of the place of love in modern American society. Following the lead of the family sociologists and marriage counselors, love will be treated not in the philosopher's or poet's sense of a "sweeping experience," not in the psychologist's sense of a universal physical power, and not in the sociologist's sense of a universal attribute of man. Instead, love shall be looked upon as a part of society, as a distinctive pattern of social behavior—as a specific culture trait. Thus we shall take the word to mean a given behavioral complex that exists in a specifiable social context. In this sense, our approach is ethnographic and synchronic. In this paper, therefore, the term love will be used to refer to a specifc culture trait that has been described in modern American society. Whether or not it exists in other societies—or in all human societies—in the same or a modified form is a matter to be demonstrated ethnographically and not assumed *a priori*.

The most abundant descriptive material available on the behavioral pattern called love comes from observations made in the contemporary United States—but restricted primarily to members of the middle class. Thus we shall limit our analysis to this segment of our own society and leave comparisons for another time.

Love, or romantic love, as it is called in the literature, is a behavioral complex composed of a series of specific features or elements. In the first place, it is a pattern that characterizes the behavior of adolescent and adult members of the middle class engaged in the quest of a mate.[6] Such individuals generally act in a distinctive way—distinctive with respect to the way in which individuals not in quest of a mate behave in the same society. In general, middle-class Americans are extremely sober and rational. These same people, however, when they are "in love" tend to be anything but.

Emotion, as opposed to reason, may be taken as characteristic of the thoughts and acts of a person in love; reason is believed to dominate at all other times. The quality of the emotions may be characterized best by a word such as

[2]Theodor Reik, *A Psychologist Looks at Love* (New York: Holt, Reinhart, and Winston, 1944), 3.
[3]*Ibid.*, 4.
[4]Sigmund Freud, *Group Psychology and the Analysis of the Ego* (London: Hogarth, 1922), 72.
[5]William J. Goode, "The Theoretical Importance of Love," *American Sociological Review*, 1959, 24:38.

[6]This is to differentiate from other behavioral complexes to which the same word is applied: love of art, money, God, and so forth.

"flighty." Phrases such as "walking on air, floating on cloud nine," and so forth, are used to describe both the feelings and the behavior of someone in love. The theatrical extreme, for example, has been stated by the heroine of a once popular musical comedy when she sang: "I'm as corny as Kansas in August, as high as a kite on the fourth of July. If you'll excuse an expression I use, I'm in love . . . ."

The song writer obviously overstated the case as dramatists often do to emphasize what is commonplace to their audience. Most Americans do not go around singing of their love as one might imagine after watching their movies and theater. However, they do tend to behave in a manner that by their normal standards may be considered flighty and irrational.

In the more exceptional cases, ungovernable impulses are overtly indulged. At times, the person in love can scarcely think of anything but his beloved. A great tenderness is experienced by the lover along with extreme delusions as to the nature of the loved person. On rare occasions all else but love seems to cease to matter to the lover; the emotion of the experience is all-consuming. As a French author once put it, one ceases to live when the loved person is absent, and begins again only when he or she is present once more.

Another aspect of the pattern is that one falls in love not by design and conscious choice, but according to some accident of fate over which the victim has no control. Of course it is a well known fact that individuals are taught to fall in love. Whether or not the pattern is learned, however, the significant factor is that individuals come to believe that love can and does strike at almost any time and in any place, and that when it does, the parties involved are helpless victims: they lose control, so to speak, over themselves, their actions and their reason, and they tend to behave emotionally and irrationally.

Directly related to this is the idea that there is one person, or lover for each man and woman in the society. Thus, if and when the paths of these two "right for each other" parties cross, they are helpless and must succumb to the "forces of the Universe."

The recent increase in the incidence of divorce has in no way challenged this belief. At most the pattern has been altered slightly so that there is now one "right one" at a time.

That the entire syndrome is atypical for the society may be seen in the inability of the individual to help falling in love. The general American belief is that man is able to master and control his environment. But in the realm of love, he is the victim of forces even stronger than himself.

Along with the idea of a "right one," goes the over idealization of the loved one. Once he or she is found, and the lovers succumb to their destiny, the real features of the loved one's character become lost in the emotional irrationality that dominates behavior. Love is said to be blind and the lovers are blinded to the faults of their new found mates.

Overriding everything is the belief that love is a panacea. Love is believed to "conquer all" and once it is experienced everything is expected to be better than it was before. One consequence of this is that it is both good and desirable to fall in love.

For middle-class Americans the expected climax of a love affair is marriage. "The sentiment of love," write Waller and Hill, "is the heart of . . . the family. In our culture, people customarily get married because they are in love; indeed it seems preposterous to us that anyone should marry for any other reason."[7]

The syndrome of features that constitutes the pattern, or culture trait, that has come to be called romantic love in American society then may be summarized as follows:

1. Two diligent, hard working, rational adolescents or adults of the opposite sex meet, most probably by accident, and find each other to be personally and physically attractive.
2. They soon come to realize that they are "right for each other."
3. They then fall victims to forces beyond their control, and fall in love.
4. They then begin—at least for a short time— to behave in a flighty, irrational manner that is at variance with the way in which they formerly conducted themselves.
5. Finally, believing that love is a panacea and that the future holds only goodness for them, they marry and form a new nuclear family.

---

[7]Willard Waller and Reuben Hill, *The Family* (New York: The Dryden Press, 1951), 101.

At this point we may note that sexual behavior in middle-class America, in general, is directly related to the romantic love complex. Sex, in the ideal, is restricted to people who are in love and then its practice is generally postponed until after marriage. Thus sexual gratification is linked to and becomes the culmination of the syndrome just described. In terms of ideal patterns we may state that sexual activity is to be engaged in only by people who are married to each other. We know, however, that the incidence of premarital and extramarital sexual behavior is relatively high, and is on the increase. It appears that in spite of this sex is still linked to the romantic love complex in that, by and large, middle-class couples who engage in premarital or extramarital sexual activity invariably believe—at the time—and behave as if they are in love with their illicit partners. Thus it appears that the tie between sex and love is strong though the restriction of sex to marriage is weakening.

Though the pattern is quite clear, most middle-class Americans, as Hunt reminds us, "are firmly of two minds about it all—simultaneously hardheaded and idealistic, uncouth and tender, libidinous and puritanical; they believe implicitly in every tenet of romantic love, and yet know perfectly well that things don't really work out that way."[8] As with other culture traits, however, individuals, to a greater or lesser degree, do tend to approximate the ideal presented above.

The behavior and sentiments associated with romantic love appear to be at odds with what may be taken to be the general characteristics of American society. People in love are flighty and irrational in contrast with the sober rationality that generally prevails.

Students of non-Western societies tend to agree that the pattern just described for the United States is non-existent, or at best very rare in the non-Western world.[9] The most quoted statement, probably because it is extreme, was made by Linton:

All societies recognize that there are occasional violent emotional attachments between persons of opposite sex, but our present American culture is practically the only one which has attempted to capitalize these and make them the basis for marriage. Most groups regard them as unfortunate and point out the victims of such attachments as horrible examples. Their rarity in most societies suggests that they are psychological abnormalities to which our own culture has attached an extraordinary value just as other cultures have attached extreme values to other abnormalities. The hero of the modern American movie is always a romantic lover just as the hero of the old Arab epic is always an epileptic. A cynic might suspect that in any ordinary population the percentage of individuals with a capacity for romantic love of the Hollywood type was about as large as that of persons able to throw genuine epileptic fits. However, given a little social encouragement, either one can be adequately imitated without the performer admitting even to himself that the performance is not genuine.[10]

In addition to being both cross-culturally infrequent and atypical in comparison with the general range of behavior in American society —and possibly abnormal—the trait also has been considered pathological. As Truxal and Merrill put it: "The state of being romantically in love exhibits many characteristics of certain pathological conditions known as trance or dissociation phenomena."[11]

But to middle-class Americans, falling in love is not only the right thing to do, it is a panacea, and right and good for its own sake. As Hunt indicates: "At no time in history has so large a proportion of humanity rated love so highly, thought about it so much, or displayed such an insatiable appetite for word about it."[12] As a sympathetic observer (De Sales) once remarked, this "appears to be the only country in the world where love is a national problem."[13] In no other country do people devote so much of their time and energy to a conscious attempt to experience love—atypical, abnormal, and pathological though it may be.

It is at this point that sociologists and marriage counselors generally begin to point out that this is not a good way to begin a relationship as important as marriage. They warn that

---

[8]Hunt, *op. cit.*, 363.

[9]For an opposing position, see Goode, *op. cit.*

[10]Ralph Linton, *The Study of Man* (New York: Appleton-Century, 1936), 175.

[11]Andrew Truxal and Frances Merrill, *The Family in American Culture* (New York: Prentice-Hall, Inc., 1947), 139.

[12]Hunt, *op. cit.*, 341.

[13]Raoul De Sales, "Love in America," *The Atlantic Monthly*, 1938, *161*:645-51.

the euphoria of love generally begins to wane after the first few months. Then the parties gradually return to their more normal way of thinking, feeling, and behaving. With the return of their more rational and sober perspective, however, the promised best of all worlds often begins to crumble as the actual characteristics of the chosen mate are noticed for the first time. Then, in an increasing number of cases, the newly formed family moves along the road of strife, conflict, and eventual separation and divorce.

True as this may be, romantic love has persisted in American society and, as we have already indicated, is as strong, or stronger today than it ever has been. Why this is so is the problem to which the remainder of this paper is devoted. In brief, our task is to account for, or to explain both the existence and strength of the romantic love complex in contemporary American society.

The type of explanation to be employed will be the one most used in modern sociological analysis. Functionalism, according to Kingsley Davis—who sees it as synonymous with sociological analysis—"is commonly said to *do* two things; to relate the parts of society to the whole, and to relate one part to another."[14] Four decades ago Radcliffe-Brown elaborated upon this as follows:

It is a mistake to suppose that we can understand the institutions of society by studying them in isolation without regard to other institutions with which they co-exist and with which they may be correlated, . . . no explanation of one part of the system is satisfactory unless it fits in with an analysis of the system as a whole.[15]

To employ functional analysis as an explanatory mechanism, however, requires the addi-

tion of something more. Carl Hempel provides this for us with the logical rigor of the philosopher of science:

The kind of phenomenon that a functional analysis is invoked to explain is typically some recurrent activity or some behavior pattern in an individual or a group; it may be a physiological mechanism, a neurotic trait, a culture pattern, or a social institution, for example. And the principal objective of the analysis is to exhibit the contribution which the behavioral pattern makes to the preservation or the development of the individual or the group in which it occurs. Thus, functional analysis seeks to understand a behavior pattern or a socio-cultural institution in terms of the role it plays in keeping the given system in proper working order and thus maintaining it as a going concern.[16]

To provide a functional explanation of romantic love then, we must examine next the relationships that exist between this trait, or complex of institutionalized behavior, and the other social patterns with which it coexists, and then demonstrate the contributions that it makes towards "keeping the system in proper working order and thus maintaining it as a going concern."

AMERICAN SOCIETY AS THE SOCIAL CONTEXT OF ROMANTIC LOVE

We may begin this brief examination of the institutions with which romantic love is functionally interrelated in American culture by noting, as most of the numerous observers of our society already have done, that materialism ranks high in our value system. The ever increasing accumulation of material goods and services—the economists commodities—may be taken as one of the primary goals towards which socialized adult members of the system consciously strive. Consequently, the production, distribution, and consumption of material goods and services—loosely called economic behavior—tends to take precedence over almost all other activities engaged in by the members of the society.

Correlated with, or perhaps underlying, this desire for goods and services is the existence of

[14]Kingsley Davis, "The Myth of Functional Analysis," *American Sociological Review*, 1959, 24:758. Though this form of analysis and the kind of explanation it results in restricts our understanding to a delimited period of time, it does add insights that cannot be gained, at least in the present stage of development of anthropology, by historical and evolutionary orientations. Thus we are not attempting to provide all the answers. However, within the range of its limitations, functional analysis has added and still can add to and enrich our comprehension of human behavior.

[15]A. R. Radcliffe-Brown, *Structure and Function in Primitive Society* (New York: The Free Press, 1952), 17.

[16]Carl Hempel, "The Logic of Functional Analysis," in *Symposium on Sociological Theory*, ed. by L. Gross (Evanston, Ill.: Row, Peterson, 1959), 278.

a highly complex industrial technology that helps to make available the valued commodities. Large and efficient factories rationally mass produce goods and are constantly being improved by the incorporation of new technological innovations. The result is that the United States has been able to produce more goods and services, cumulatively and per capita, than any other society in human history.

The complex and elaborate machines that are the core of the rationally organized technology require highly specialized and intensive human skills. The social system that has emerged to implement the technology has been successful in training and utilizing the members of the society in such a way that their material aspirations are met—though, almost by definition, they can never be satisfied.

The social groups that produce and distribute the valued commodities are voluntary associations, or organizations—universalistic instrumental achievement structures, in Parsons' terms.[17] The use of the association, or organization as the means of ordering human social relations leads to certain distinctive problems, however. All social organizations, for purposes of analysis, may be viewed as a series of social positions that have associated with them complexes or normative behavior—roles—that are performed by individuals when they occupy any specific one of the positions. For social systems to work—i.e., things to get done—the positions must be filled by persons able to perform the expected roles. The analytic problem then is: How are the positions filled?

In most of the societies reported on in the ethnographic record, individuals are assigned to specific social positions by means of kinship, age, sex, and so forth. The term "ascription" is conventionally used to refer to these ethnographically more prevalent cases in which individuals are placed in positions without reference to either specific talents, or their wishes. In contrast with this, the term "achievement" is used to refer to the instances in which persons come to hold positions as the result of desire and successful competition based upon their possessing special talents, skills, or abilities.

The voluntary association is a form of social organization that uses the achievement mechanism to fill its ranks. Associations are created to accomplish specific objectives. To obtain their goals a series of positions with specific roles are established. When persons able to perform the roles are recruited to fill the positions, the desired result, or goal, of the organization is achieved. The question remains: How are the positions within the association filled after they are created? That is, how are the proper individuals, those with the necessary talents and abilities, induced to fill the positions and to perform the designated tasks, or roles? In achievement-oriented societies there is a need for some mechanism or force sufficient to motivate individuals to want to fill the positions and perform the expected roles. Rewards are needed that will successfully motivate enough individuals with the right combination of skills to "get the job done." In the contemporary United States, money in the form of wages or income is the primary inducement offered to fill most social positions. Within this market-oriented society, money functions as a medium of exchange. That is, it stands for the valued commodities in that it can be exchanged in the market for goods and services. In a sense, however, it has come to be valued in its own right as the symbol of goods and services. "It is the universal agency for satisfying any desires that can be met by purchasable goods."[18] But there is more than this to the social function of money in American society. "It is the symbol and measure," as Santayana has pointed out, the American "has at hand for success, intelligence, and power. . . ."[19]

Robin Williams has elaborated upon the implications of this insight as follows:

In a society of relatively high social mobility, in which position in the scale of social stratification basically depends upon occupational achievement, wealth is one of the few obvious signs of one's place in the hierarchy. Achievement is difficult to index, in a highly complex society of diverse occupations, because of the great differences in abilities and effort

[17]Talcott Parsons, *The Social System* (New York: The Free Press, 1951), 182–91.

[18]Cooley, quoted in Robin M. Williams, Jr., *American Society* (New York: Alfred A. Knopf, 1960), 420.

[19]George Santayana, *Character and Opinion in the United States* (New York: 1920), 185.

required for success in various fields. At the same time, the central type of achievement is in business, manufacturing, commerce, finance; and since traditionalized social hierarchies, fixed estates, and established symbols of hereditary rank have had only a rudimentary development, there is a strong tendency to use money as a symbol of success. Money comes to be valued not only for itself and for the goods it will buy, but as symbolic evidence of success and, thereby, of personal worth.[20]

Money, then, along with the material goods and services that it can purchase, is itself an important value in the society.

The valued commodities then are produced in the United States by special purpose organizations. The positions in each organization are filled by offering rewards—generally income, or wages—sufficient to induce individuals to join the organization and to perform the tasks that have been laid out by the rational planners of industry. Membership in the organizations, as we have noted, is voluntary. One consequence of this is that there tends to be a competition both by persons for positions and by organizations for individuals with specific recognized skills.

Since all positions are not equal in importance, however, nor equally demanding, the income offered is not the same for all jobs. Those positions considered to be most important by the members of the society generally pay the highest incomes. For the multitude of other jobs there is a gradual decrease in rewards offered, with the least income going to those positions taken to be least important.[21]

In theory, anyone with the appropriate skills can achieve any position in the system—i.e., it is open. Since the primary reward, money, both stands for success and is convertible directly into the valued goods and services, the achieving of positions that offer more and more rewards is also desirable. Mobility thus is another dominant theme in the culture, as is an aggressive competition for positions that offer high salaries and other rewards.

Filling social positions by means of achieve-

ment, however, appears to be working so well in what is generally referred to as the industrial sector that it has been carried over as the dominant means of filling positions in other parts of the social system. Also, the organization, or voluntary association, tends to be the form taken by the vast majority of American social groups.

The material goods and services, so highly valued by the members of the society, can be obtained only in the market where these commodities are bought and sold for money. Money, however, can be obtained, in theory—and in most cases in fact—only as the result of achieving a position in an organization that produces goods and service, and performing, or executing its prescribed role.

The positions in the industrial sector, however, are restricted generally to the adult male members of the society—and, in an increasing but still small number of cases, to adult females.[22] All other persons—the majority of women and all children—do not have access to the income needed to obtain both subsistence and prestige goods and services.

For the system to work, then, there must be a means by which women and children are provided with the necessary and highly valued goods and services—both in terms of absolute survival requirements and culturally defined prestige wants. Another way of phrasing this

---

[22]Though many women are now in the labor force, and the percentage of females to males is increasing, it is still true that, for the population as a whole, the adult male (husband-father) is still the primary source of support. By and large, the contribution of women to the household income is in the form of extras, or prestige items that would not otherwise be available.

The crucial aspect of the adult male role as provider, however, is to be found by turning to the stratification system. Nuclear families are the units. They are distributed into a series of social classes. The primary determinant of any given family's place in the system is based upon the occupational achievement of its adult male. The rewards earned at a job, therefore, in addition to providing the group's material necessities, also determine its place in the prestige system. Though women may add to the material and social-psychological well being of the family, the task of placing it in the stratification system—determining its prestige—accrues to the occupant of the position husband-father; and this is based primarily upon his achieved position in the industrial sector.

---

[20]Williams, *op. cit.*, 420–21.

[21]Kingsley Davis and Wilbert E. Moore, "Some Principles of Stratification," *American Sociological Review*, 1945, 10:242–49.

is to ask: How are women and children articulated with the industrial sector that produces and distributes the material items in the culture? In the United States, the family, in addition to its other activities, serves as the needed link.

The American family is a small, nuclear kinship unit composed of parents and children. Each group ideally occupies its own dwelling unit, and in general, is structurally and functionally isolated from other kinship units in that contacts with related kin groups are generally kept to a minimum.

Within the family—which is the society's unit of consumption for economic goods—the position husband-father calls for its occupant to provide support for the entire group in the form of money with which to purchase goods and services. The money, as we have seen, is obtained by the occupant of the position husband-father holding a job in the industrial sector. Adult males, therefore, are expected to occupy a position in an industrial or occupational organization and a position in a family simultaneously. The role wife-mother, meanwhile, calls for its occupant to take the money earned by its specific male counterpart into the market to purchase the goods and services needed by the entire family.

Individuals are articulated with the culturally dominant economic system, and the highly valued goods and services are distributed to, and consumed by, all members of the society as long as all adult males hold both a position in an occupational group and the position husband-father in a nuclear family and adult females occupy the position wife-mother *vis à vis* a gainfully employed male.

The associations, or organizations in the industrial sector can and do produce and distribute the highly valued goods and services. Without the family, however, organized as it is, the socially desired commodities cannot be distributed to all of the members of the society without drastically modifying the total sociocultural system. Also, they would not be consumed were it not for the family.

A general requirement for the continued operation of the American system of producing, distributing, and consuming the valued goods

and services then, is that nuclear families be formed and that the role expectations of the positions husband-father and wife-mother be discharged. This activity or function of the family is in addition to its contribution in the area of reproduction and socialization. Our intent here is not to slight the importance of these contributions but rather to point up the role of the family in maintaining our distinctive economic arrangements. In this respect we may say that the reproductive and socialization activities of the American family are self-evident. It is commonly argued, however, that the modern family no longer performs economic functions. To us this appears to be a restricted view. The reason may be that the economic and, for that matter, stratification functions of the family are not very evident and in this era of sociological specialization they tend to be neglected. Furthermore, by emphasizing the economic tasks performed by the family the contribution of romantic love to maintaining the larger social system is made more apparent.

With respect to the distribution and consumption of goods and services then, once families are formed—the positions husband-father and wife-mother are filled—there are numerous legal and social mechanisms that can be employed to insure role performance in the event that the socialization process does not train people adequately. Before these sanctions can be involved, however, individuals in this achievement-oriented society must be induced to fill the aforementioned positions. In the United States the positions husband-father and wife-mother are filled—nuclear families are formed—by the marriage of two adolescents or adults of the opposite sex. Our next problem, therefore, is to inquire as to why and how people get married.

We have already seen that achievement is the general mechanism used to fill social positions. Individuals learn to compete with each other for the rewards—generally money—that are associated with most positions. What rewards, we may ask, are offered to induce people to marry? Negatively we may note that the rewards used to fill the broad range of social statuses are not offered as inducements to fill the positions husband-father and wife-mother. In fact, it is generally considered improper to offer money, or other material items as inducements for marriage; most Americans would be shocked at the idea and such behavior probably would be regarded as indecent.

In the United States, however, there are no prescribed marriage patterns. Cousin marriage, the sororate, the levirate, etc., are not practiced. There are no extended kinship groups to pressure individuals into getting married.[23] Also, there are no institutionalized matchmakers. Moreover, in this affluent, market-oriented society all basic needs can be satisfied in the market. That is, there is no fundamental sexual division of labor that leads men and women to marry because they cannot survive without the services of a mate. Everything from food and clothing to sexual gratification can be purchased in the market.

One consequence of the combination of the materialistic values—specifically the desire of individuals, when presented with choices, to select the alternatives that maximize their material rewards—and the requirements of the husband-father and wife-mother roles within the family, which actually deprive the individuals of goods and services that they otherwise might have been able to obtain, is that, other things being equal, individuals would be negatively motivated toward marriage. In fact, in terms of the logic or rationale of the culture of the contemporary United States, in many instances getting married might well be considered an irrational choice of action.

If individuals do not marry, however, nuclear families would not be formed; and without them the mechanism for distributing and consuming the valued goods and services, reproducing and socializing the population, and maintaining the stratification system, among other things, would cease to operate. In brief, the social system, as it is presently constituted, would cease to operate.

What appears to be necessary for the maintenance of American culture in its present form then, is a special mechanism that would induce these generally rational, ambitious, and calculating individuals—in the sense of striving to max-

imize their personal achievement—to do what in the logic of their culture is not in their own personal interest. Somehow they must be induced—we might almost say in spite of themselves—to behave emotionally and irrationally and to desire and to occupy the positions husband-father and wife-mother. In conformity with the emphasis on achievement, it appears that something valued, to serve as a reward, is needed to motivate otherwise reluctant individuals to want to compete and to achieve these particular positions.

The negative aspects of the roles often require their occupants to dissipate rather than accumulate commodities, and to do so in a manner that does not bring prestige to the consumer (such as paying doctor and hospital bills for the birth of a child, or purchasing the host of specialized artifacts that we have come to believe are needed for adequate care and rearing of children), indicates, however, that it is necessary to establish a special reward in that individuals are being motivated to perform what in other circumstances would be considered irrational acts. Only by the institutionalization of a separate pattern of both rewards and behaviors, appropriate only in this special setting it appears, can the positions be filled. But, we may ask, how can an entire population, at a specific point in the life cycle of the individual —i.e., when searching for a mate—be induced to behave in a manner that can be considered abnormal and irrational within the context of their culture, and like it?

What we are suggesting is that the romantic love complex in middle-class America serves as the reward-motive that induces individuals to occupy the structurally essential positions of husband-father and wife-mother. As the pattern was described above, it provides what may be considered institutionalized irrationality that can be compartmentalized and separated conceptually and behaviorally so that it is not dysfunctional with respect to the operation of the rest of the culture. Individuals may behave strangely and not in accord with their own material interests, but they do so for only a short time. Soon they recover and get back to work. But while in this separable realm of cultural reality they respond to rewards, both real and symbolic, that

---

[23]An exception, however, may be found in the behavior of women toward their mature, unmarried daughters.

motivate them to do what must be done, and thus the incidence of marriage is at an all time high.⌡

The careful control of sex noted earlier, so that sexual gratification, ideally at least, is restricted to people in love and generally postponed until after marriage, serves to make sexual gratification a very real reward for those who marry.[24]⌈In addition, marriage, as the culmination of the love affair, offers affection, companionship, emotional security, and general happiness to those who enter into matrimony. As a reward to be achieved, this is significant in terms of what may be considered a counter trend in the value system.⌡ It is generally held that there should be something more to life than the accumulation of material goods. The content of this "more than" category, however, invariably is left unspecified. The romantic love complex subsumes many of the possibilities. Though at times it may imply an actual negation of material values, it is often interpreted as providing the unspecified other values. Culminating the love affair with marriage thus promises the values (or rewards) of affection, companionship, care, emotional security—in a society in which most activities are highly anxiety-provoking—and general happiness. This appears to be more than enough to motivate the members of the society. And though, as we have noted earlier, middle-class Americans are realistic enough to know that life does not always work out this way, they do give it a try hoping for the best. Thus romantic love may be considered as an almost separate realm of reality in which modern Americans are permitted (or permit themselves) to behave in response to a higher set of values than the material ones that motivate them in the ordinary work-a-day world.

With respect to the individual, love has thus come to be a thing that is a value in itself—its own reward. And it serves to motivate individuals to do what must be done so that the total social system can maintain itself as a going concern.⌈In short, romantic love induces Americans

to fill positions—in conformity with the general achievement orientations—that, though they are essential to the operation of society, they would not otherwise be motivated to fill. Furthermore, the very atypical, abnormal irrationality of romantic love is the very thing that enables it to work.

With respect to the individual, a person who falls in love and marries comes to believe that he or she is "doing the right thing" and takes understandable pride in doing so. If one is in love in contemporary middle-class America and then gets married it is considered good and proper. The individuals involved may come to have a feeling of satisfaction that goes with doing the right thing. This feeling is then given group support and validation by friends and relatives. The sentiments involved thus may be compared with those of the person in a kin oriented society who has made a "proper marriage"—a person, for example, who marries a cross-cousin in a society with a pattern of prescriptive cross-cousin marriage. This is the right thing and both the involved parties and those around them know it and rejoice in the feeling that goes with doing what is right.[25]

To conclude, then, the function of romantic love in American society appears to be to motivate individuals—where there is no other means of motivating them—to occupy the positions husband-father and wife-mother and form nuclear families that are essential not only for reproduction and socialization but also to maintain the existing arrangements for distributing and consuming goods and services and, in general, to keep the social system in proper working order and thus maintaining it as a going concern.

---

[24]Sexual gratification may be available in the market place, but if, as is the belief amongst middle-class Americans, love must accompany it to make it truly enjoyable, prostitution ceases to be a fully satisfying outlet. That is, it can never provide complete satisfaction.

[25]Before concluding we may note that in American society there are actual restrictions in the general pattern of romantic love. In theory, anyone is permitted to fall in love with anyone else. In fact, however, as Goode (*op. cit.*) has pointed out, falling in love has been structured so that lovers actually select each other not at random but from within specific cultural categories that have been defined as structural isolates. That is, not only is it right to fall in love, but it is "more right" to fall in love with and to marry someone who is a member of the same ethnic, racial, religious, educational, age, socioeconomic, etc. category as you are. This structuring of love not only gets people to marry and to occupy the positions husband-father and wife-mother, but also helps to maintain the structure of the society in accord with the categories.

25.

ERWIN O. SMIGEL AND RITA SEIDEN

THE DECLINE AND FALL OF THE DOUBLE STANDARD

To find meaningful correlations,[1] especially in a pluralistic society, between the multitude of social forces and sexual behavior is difficult; to determine these correlations accurately, when appropriate data on sexual behavior are not available, is impossible. Nonetheless, it is our assignment to examine these social forces in order to see what effect they have had on sexual behavior and attitudes—specifically on sexual behavior and attitudes of unmarried heterosexuals of college age and younger in the United States.

Most recent examinations of sexual behavior still cite Kinsey's data[2] (1938–1949) and/or Terman's[3] (1934–1935). No one has published a Kinsey-type study for the United States in the 1960's. However, a few limited studies[4] on premarital sexual behavior have been completed since Kinsey published *The Human Male* in 1948. The various studies of college students show percentages of premarital coitus for males and females which range from 54:35 in 1929;[5] 51:25 in 1938;[6] to 56:25 in 1951;[7] and, in 1953, 68:47, 41:9, or 63:14, depending on whose figures are accepted.[8] The most recent examination of sexual behavior puts the rate of college female premarital experience at 22 percent.[9] This is consistent with Kinsey's findings that 20 percent of all college women had had premarital intercourse.[10]

Most of the studies of sex completed after Kinsey's main works appeared have been limited to collecting statistics on attitudes. The most extensive of these studies, for which data was collected through 1963, was conducted by Ira Reiss, on sexual permissiveness.[11] Reiss's findings point to a coming together of sexual practices, and, for the young at least, of attitudes about sex. He found definite movement

This selection is reprinted from: Erwin O. Smigel, and Rita Seiden, "The Decline and Fall of the Double Standard," *The Annals*, 1968, 376, 6–17.
Reprinted with the permission of the authors and publisher.

[1] It is understood that even if it were possible to determine these correlations accurately, we would not have an explanation of causation.

[2] Alfred C. Kinsey, Wardell B. Pomeroy, Clyde E. Martin, Paul Gebhard *et al.*, *Sexual Behavior in the Human Female* (Philadelphia: W. B. Saunders, 1953). The data on the female subjects were collected from 1938 through 1949. Alfred C. Kinsey, Wardell B. Pomeroy, and Clyde E. Martin, *Sexual Behavior in the Human Male* (Philadelphia: W. B. Saunders, 1948). Data on the male subjects were collected from 1938 to 1947.

[3] Lewis M. Terman *et al.*, *Psychological Factors in Marital Happiness* (New York: McGraw-Hill Book Company, 1938).

[4] Gilbert Youth Research, "How Wild Are College Students?" *Pageant*, 1951, 7, 10–21; Ernest W. Burgess and Paul Wallin, *Engagement and Marriage* (Phila.: J. B. Lippincott, 1953); Judson T. Landis and Mary Landis, *Building a Successful Marriage* (3rd ed. rev.) (Englewood Cliffs, N.J.: Prentice-Hall, Inc., 1957); Winston Ehrmann, *Premarital Dating Behavior* (New York: Holt, Rinehart & Winston, Inc., 1959); Mervin B. Freedman, "The Sexual Behavior of American College Women: An Empirical Study and an Historical Study," *Merrill-Palmer Quarterly*, 1965, 2, 33–48; Ira L. Reiss, *The Social Context of Premarital Sexual Permis-*

siveness (New York: Holt, Rinehart & Winston, Inc., 1967), chap. vii. Reiss's primary purpose was not to examine behavior (at least not in this latest presentation); he was interested in attitudes. He asked 268 students (42 of them males) in an Iowa college about their behavior. What he did was to correlate expressed feelings of guilt with behavior, and found relationships with age and behavior and relationships between expressed standards and behavior. The Institute for Sex Research at Indiana University conducted a 1967 study of sex behavior among college students, but the final results have not as yet been published.

[5] Gilbert V. Hamilton, *A Research in Marriage* (1st ed., New York: Albert and Charles Boni, 1929; 2nd ed., New York: Lear, 1948), 348.

[6] D. D. Bromley and F. H. Britten, *Youth and Sex* (New York: Harper & Row, Publishers, 1938), 36.

[7] Gilbert Youth Research, *op. cit.*, 15.

[8] Burgess and Wallin, *op. cit.*, 330; Landis and Landis, *op. cit.*, 216 and 212; Ehrmann, *op. cit.*, 33–34 and 46.

[9] Freedman, *op. cit.*, 47.

[10] Kinsey, *The Human Female*, 288.

[11] Reiss, *op. cit.*

away from the orthodox double standard toward a standard of permissiveness with affection (shorthand for "premarital sex is acceptable when there is mutual affection between the partners").

The earlier statistics of Kinsey and Terman point up important differences in sexual behavior between the generation of women born before 1900 and the generation born in the following decade. Kinsey found that 73.4 percent of women born before 1900 had had no premarital intercourse, but among those born between 1900 and 1909, only 48.7 percent had been virgins at marriage. The figures for those born in the 1920–1929 generation are the same —48.8 percent.[12] Terman's findings are essentially in agreement. The statistics for both the Kinsey and Terman studies referred to here are for women of all ages, and not just for college women.[13] Terman found that 74 percent of the females born between 1890 and 1899 had had no premarital intercourse, whereas among those born between 1900 and 1909, the percentage of virgin brides had dropped to 51.2. His figures reveal that this trend also held for men: of those interviewees born between 1890 and 1899, 41.9 percent had had no premarital coitus, whereas of the interviewees born in the next generation, 32.6 percent had had no such premarital experience.[14] Clearly, the major

change in sex practices occurred in the generation born in the decade 1900–1909, which came to sexual age during or immediately after World War I, a period characterized by marked social change and innovation.

It may well be true that changes in sexual behavior and attitudes are related to the social changes which began in the late nineteenth century and accelerated rapidly over the past 67 years. It is not as clear, except perhaps for the post-World War I years, exactly what the effects of these social changes have been on sexual behavior. Reiss argues that, despite popular belief to the contrary, "the sexual revolution [is] a myth and the only basic change [is] a trend toward more equality between the sexes. . . . There has been less change than [is] popularly believed between modern American males and their Victorian grandfathers."[15]

It is generally thought, however, that the late-nineteenth-century break with Victorian morality was a tangential result of the Industrial Revolution, urban migration, war, the feminist movement, and the scientific study of once-taboo topics. Wilbert Moore, a leading authority on social change, credited industrialization with certain effects on the social structure;[16] and it is our opinion that industrialization affected sex attitudes and behavior as well. He specified increased social and geographic mobility; growth of industrial centers with concomitant concentration of population in urban areas; emphasis on rationality as a necessary part of an industrialized society (for example, a lessening of the influence of religion); transi-

---

[12]Ira L. Reiss, "Standards of Sexual Behavior," in Albert Ellis and Albert Abarbanel (eds.), *Encyclopedia of Sex* (New York: Hawthorne Books, 1961), 999. "These data were based on Kinsey (1953), but were especially prepared for [Reiss's] paper . . . [by] Drs. Gebhard and Martin of the Institute of Sex Research. These were based on 2479 women who either were or had been married by the time of the interview."

[13]Confirming this change are data reported by K. B. Davis, *Factors in the Sex Life of Twenty-two Hundred Women* (New York: Harper & Row, Publishers, 1929), 232. Of those women who attended college in the early 1900's (that is, were born before 1900), only seven percent had premarital intercourse. According to Bromley and Britten, *loc. cit.*, 25 percent of the college women of the 1930's had premarital intercourse. And according to Freedman, *op cit.*, p. 45: "The rate of premarital nonvirginity tripled from 1900 to 1930."

[14]Terman, *op. cit.*, 321; Kinsey, *The Human Male*, 395. Kinsey noted generational differences within his male sample; but the "generations" were formed by dividing his subjects into "younger" (under 33 years of age at the time of the interview) and "older" (over 33 years of age at the time inter-

viewed) groups. He did not compare them by decade of birth as he did the women. The median age of the younger group was 21.2 years, that is, born approximately between 1917 and 1926. The median age of the older group was 43.1 years, that is, born approximately between 1895 and 1904 (Kinsey, *The Human Female*, chap. vii). Information is provided here that premarital petting had increased with each generation since 1920 even though incidence of premarital coitus had not. One of the possible explanations for the continued relatively high number of virgins is that heavy petting is now very common, so that there are a large number of "technical" virgins who engage in almost everything except coitus.

[15]"Iowa Sociologist Calls Sex Revolution A Myth," *New York Times*, October 22, 1967, section I, p. 80.

[16]Wilbert E. Moore, *Social Change* (Englewood Cliffs, N.J.: Prentice-Hall, Inc., 1963), 100–103.

tion from extended (rurally located) families to nuclear (urban) families; emphasis on individualism resulting from the breakdown[17] of the extended kinship system; decreased family size accompanied by a decline in the economic significance of the family unit as the unit of survival; and, finally, increased education.

Each of these general effects of social change can be shown, at least theoretically, to have potential impact on sexual behavior and attitudes. As the population moves from small towns and intimate personal relationships to urban centers, old forms of social control break down. This disintegration and the accompanying anonymity is speeded by new and faster forms of transportation which further increase the possibilities of anonymity and independence. A rational society affects the individual's world view, and he tends to see his own life in terms of more rational standards. As the extended kinship system dissolves or loses its importance, mate-selection processes become a more personal responsibility, and increase the importance of peer group norms, which take precedence over family norms. In the evolving industrial society, women take a new and larger part in the working world, thereby securing greater independence for themselves and increased equality in male-female relationships. The general increase in education has made possible widespread dissemination of sex information to the public.

In sum, the family has declined in importance as the unit upon which or around which society is organized, and individualism, in relationship to the family, is in the ascendency. As individualism has grown, sexual behavior has become more a personal matter and is less exclusively influenced by family and procreational considerations.

The complex social changes discussed have been gradual, but the impact of war can be immediate and abrupt. This is clearly indicated in the data on sexual behavior during and immediately after World War I. In any war, the mores governing family life tend to decay. Removed from some of the responsibilities, restrictions, and supports of the family, removed from the all-seeing eye of the small town or the neighborhood, soldiers are suddenly subject only to the mostly approving observations of their fellow soldiers. In the face of death or the possibility of being severely wounded, hedonism becomes the prevailing attitude. This attitude appears to be contagious and spreads to the civilian population. In World War I, it particularly affected the young women who were working in factories, taking on roles and responsibilities that had once belonged exclusively to men, often for the first time alone in relative anonymity, and in many instances emotionally involved with men who were scheduled to be sent overseas. (This same hedonistic philosophy may be held by contemporary young people who are faced with the dangers of limited wars and the always present possibility of extinction by nuclear explosion.)

Many soldiers had contact with prostitutes and contracted venereal diseases. The United States Interdepartmental Social Hygiene Board reports: "Between September, 1917, and February 14, 1919, there were over 222,000 cases of venereal disease in the army and there were over 60,000 in the navy."[18] Venereal disease and the prostitute taught the soldier more about sex in his relatively short career in the armed services than he might normally have learned. The incidence of venereal disease was so high that it became a matter of both private and official army talk. The consequence was that most soldiers left the service knowing not only the protective effects but also the birth control uses of prophylactic sheaths. This kind of sex education became a standard part of the army curriculum.

The soldier who went abroad had new sexual experiences and came in contact with women whose behavior derived from different and

---

[17]In a recent article, Thomas K. Burch casts doubt on whether there has indeed been a breakdown of the extended family or a decline in the size of the family because of urbanization. See Thomas K. Burch, "The Size and Structure of Families: A Comparative Analysis of Census Data," *American Sociological Review*, 1967, 32, 347–363. We feel, however, that there can be little doubt about the relation between urbanization and changes in function and meaning of the family.

---

[18]T. A. Storey, "The Work of the United States Interdepartmental Social Hygiene Board" (New York: United States Interdepartmental Social Hygiene Board, 1920), 6.

more permissive sex norms; the returned veteran brought back with him sexual attitudes shaped by these new norms. Although they were not consciously intended for his mother, sister, wife, or wife-to-be, they tended to affect them as well.

War also tends to spread industrialization and to extend the need for women in industry, and, in turn, to increase their economic independence. The war and wartime experiences intensified the gradual way in which industrialization was changing the social structure.

War, industrialization, and an increase in political democracy seem to have led to the struggle for equal rights for women. The nineteenth-century feminists, who fought for financial and social rights and by 1920 had been enfranchised, were now also demanding more sexual freedom. Margaret Sanger, an American housewife, was a leader in this war. She waged a courageous battle for the control of pregnancy, and she was brought to trial for making birth control information available to interested persons. It was the trial, the wide publicity she received, and her persistence which helped to acquaint the public with the possibilities of birth control. She and other fighters for female sexual freedom were supported by a backdrop of the new norms of the returning soldiers, the effects of economic gains for women, and an increase in the scientific study of sex.

Although Krafft-Ebing,[19] Havelock Ellis,[20] and others were writing about sex pathology and sexuality, Freud's writings about the unconscious and the effect of sex on personality had the most influence upon American behavior and attitudes. Although *Studies in Hysteria,* written by Freud and Breuer, which made these ideas available to the public, was published in 1895, "it was not until after the war that the Freudian gospel began to circulate to a marked extent among the American reading public."[21] No one can estimate what popularization of psychoanalytic theory has done to free individuals—particularly women—from the puritan anxieties about sex. The fact of its influence, however, cannot be doubted. These studies by the sexologists and those by the sociologists, anthropologists, and psychologists studying and writing in the late 1920's and early 1930's provided the setting for the public acceptance of Kinsey's impressive work—which may in turn have had great influence on a society already impatient with Victorian sex mores. In any event, studies of sex were being undertaken, and they provided information about taboo topics which helped to free the average individual from the restraint against serious discussion of sexual behavior. Each generation of sex researchers has extended the study and broadened the understanding of sex, from Kinsey's counting of sexual outlets in the 1940's to Masters and Johnson's detailed study of human sexual response[22] in the early 1960's.

In addition to those factors already described, which have affected so many aspects of the social structure, other elements, although less powerful forces for general change, have also contributed to the alteration of sexual mores in a more immediate sense. Cultural interchange resulting from wartime contact since World War I and from the great increase in travel has led to a broadened participation with other societies. Furthermore, the disappearance of the chaperon undoubtedly created opportunities for sexual freedom which are not subject to the social sanctions of one's own society. The availability of the automobile, the affluent society which permits young people to live apart from their parents, and the growth of community size made privacy much more accessible. There has been a virtual removal of "fear-evoking" deterrents with the development of effective contraceptive devices.

All of these factors seem to be related to the change in sexual practices and to the apparent liberalization of sexual standards reflected in

---

[19]*Psychopathia Sexualis,* the best known work of Krafft-Ebing, was originally published in German in 1886. The first English translation was published shortly thereafter.

[20]*The Psychology of Sex,* which represents Ellis' main body of work, was published in English in six separate volumes from 1900 to 1910 by F. A. Davis, Philadelphia. Volumes I and II had appeared in French (1897) before they appeared in English.

[21]Frederick Lewis Allen, *Only Yesterday: An Informal History of the Nineteen-Twenties* (New York: Blue Ribbon Books, 1932), 98.

[22]William H. Masters and Virginia E. Johnson, *Human Sexual Response* (Boston: Little, Brown and Company, 1966).

TABLE 25–1. ATTITUDES TOWARD PREMARITAL INTERCOURSE (IN PERCENTAGES)

Approve of	1940 Cornell[*]			1947 Michigan State University[†]			1952–55 11 Colleges[†]			1958 University of Florida[‡]		
	M	F	Total	M	F	Total	M	F	Total	M	F	Total
1. Sex relations for both.........	15	6	9	16	2		20	5		42	7	25
2. Abstinence	49	76	65	59	76		52	65		20	86	52
3. Sex relations for men only......	23	11	16	10	15		12	23		33	0	17
4. Sex relations for engaged/in love	11	6	8	15	7		16	7		5	7	6
(N)	(73)	(100)	(173)			(2000)			(3000)	(45)	(42)	(87)

[*]Percentages are based on N of 173, but three percent (one percent male, two percent female) did not answer the question. The total percent appearing in Reiss is 101; therefore, ours totals 98.
[†]Separate N's for the male and female samples were not given; therefore, it was not possible to compute total percentage advocating each standard.
[‡]Total percentages were not shown by Reiss and were computed by the authors of this article.

Reiss's data.[23] Since these social forces are still operating in the same direction, we should also expect to see changes in the direction of permissive sexual attitudes and behavior to continue.

The data we have on sexual behavior are limited; but more data are available on attitudes.

The research statistics are analyzed in Tables 25-1, 25-2, 25-3, and 25-4.[24]

Reiss's later data, collected in 1959 and 1963,[25] confirm the trends evidenced in the findings of the earlier studies (see Table 25-2).

We can probably safely conclude from these data:

1. Abstinence and permissiveness with affection are the favored standards for both males and females.

2. There has been a rise in female approval of permissiveness with affection and a decline in approval of the abstinence standard.

3. Permisssiveness without affection, if we consider it comparable to a blanket endorsement of casual sex relations for both, is apparently on the decline—even more sharply for men than for women.

4. The orthodox double standard is also on the decline if we compare the Table 25-1 data (sex relations for men only) with the Table 25-2 data (orthodox double standard).

5. The percentage of men who favor permissiveness with affection has increased markedly while the female endorsement remains about the same. The redistribution of women's attitudes seems to be away from abstinence and the orthodox double standard toward greater endorsement of the transitional double standard—coitus is all right for men under any condition, but is acceptable for women only if they are in love. Therefore, while women still endorse abstinence more highly than other standards, they are coming to favor sexual relations in the context of affection. Reiss's 1963 data support the 1959 evidence which indicates an increasingly favorable

[23]Ira L. Reiss, *Premarital Sexual Standards in America* (New York: The Free Press, 1960), 219–221.

[24]These tables are rearranged in chronological order and condensed for our purposes from the ones appearing in Reiss, *The Social Context of Premarital Sexual Permissiveness*, 16–18. The categories used by L. Rockwood and M. Ford in their (1940) study of Cornell students, *Youth, Marriage, and Parenthood* (New York: John Wiley & Sons, Inc., 1945), 40, were used for classifying the data of the other studies. The 1947 and 1952-1955 studies were made by J. T. Landis and M. Landis and reported in *Building a Successful Marriage*, 215. Their categories were: "Sexual Relations: For both, none for either, for men only, between engaged only." The 1958 study by Ehrmann, *op. cit.*, 189, used the standards: "Double (comparable to sex relations for men only), conservative single (abstinence), general liberal single (sex relations for both), and lover liberal single (sex relations for those engaged or in love)" as categories.

[25]Reiss, *The Social Context of Premarital Sexual Permissiveness*, 25–27, tables 2.5, 2.6, and 2.7. The reverse double standard category has been omitted, for Reiss says that this "response is almost

certainly an error." For his discussion of this point, see *ibid.*, 24. Reverse double standard adherents are understood to believe that women should have greater sexual freedom than men. Percentage accepting this standard were: 1959—nine percent male, six percent female, seven percent total; 1963—zero percent male, five percent female, four percent total.

attitude on the part of females[26] toward sex with affection. Eighteen percent favor permissiveness with affection; one percent endorse permissiveness without affection; 56 percent support abstinence. The percentage endorsing the transitional double standard was not given.[27]

6. Succinctly: The percentage of both men and women who accept increased permissiveness with affection as their standard has increased (see Table 25-3).

TABLE 25-2. Percentage* Accepting Each Standard

Standard	1959‡		
	Male	Female	Total
Permissiveness with affection	24	15	19
Permissiveness without affection	13	2	7
Abstinence	28	55	42
Orthodox double standard	9	13	11
Transitional double standard†	18	10	14
N =	(386)	(435)	(821)

*Percentages of adherents to the reversed double standard have been omitted. Therefore, totals do not equal 100 percent.

†Transitional double standard means that sex relations are considered all right for men under any condition, but are acceptable for women only if they are in love.

‡The 1959 sample was drawn from the student populations of five schools: two Virginia colleges (one Negro, one white); two Virginia high schools (one Negro, one white); and one New York college.

Since the 1947, 1952-1955, and 1959 studies used the largest number of subjects and employed somewhat more rigorous sampling techniques, they are probably more reliable indicators of the trend in these attitudes. They strongly support the assumption that there has been an important change in attitudes toward sex in the direction of permissiveness.

In explaining the differences between statistics on sexual behavior and statistics on attitudes (namely, that behavior seems to have changed little since the 1920's, but attitudes have become more liberal), Reiss suggests that we are seeing a "consolidation process" taking place, that is, "a change in attitudes to match the change in behavior" is occurring.[28] Nelson Foote cites a variety of evidence which he claims indicates the decline of the double standard: decline in prostitution, increasingly equal sexual opportunities and experiences for women, increase in orgasm in marital sex relations, "the steady approach to equivalence of male and female premarital petting and marital sex play techniques," the increase of extramarital coitus, decreasing insistence on virginity in females at marriage, and "some decline in frequency of marital coitus implying more mutual consent and less unilateral demand."[29]

Finally, in line with both Reiss's and Foote's arguments that there is a trend toward a new

TABLE 25-3. Percentage Accepting the Standard

	1940		1947		1952–1955		1958		1959*		1963*	
Sex relations for Engaged/in love	M	F	M	F	M	F	M	F	M	F	M	F
	11	6	15	7	16	7	5	7	24	15	†	18

*We are considering Reiss's "permissiveness with affection" as equivalent to "sex relations for engaged/in love."

†Figure for men has been omitted as total number of male interviews is a small proportion of the total sample.

single standard of permissiveness with affection, Robert Bell suggests that for young adults, sex becomes acceptable today when the couple feels they are in love. Peer group members ac-

---

[26]*Ibid.*, 128. The data for males have not been utilized because the men represent only a small percentage of the total number of cases in the sample.

[27]Reiss reported 20 percent of the females endorsing the double standard, but did not break down the figure to show the percentage accepting the orthodox standard nor the percentage accepting the traditional standard.

---

[28]Reiss, *Premarital Sexual Permissiveness in America*, 233.

[29]Nelson N. Foote, "Sex As Play," *Social Problems*, 1964, *1*, 161.

TABLE 25-4. "MARITAL AND FAMILY STATUS AND PERMISSIVENESS IN THE ADULT SAMPLE°

Marital and Family Status	Percent Permissive	N
Single	44	(108)
Married		
No Children	23	(124)
All Preteen	22	(384)
Preteen and Older	17	(218)
All Teen and Older	13	(376)

°Reiss, *The Social Context of Premarital Sexual Permissiveness*, p. 142, Table 9.2 (some data omitted).

cept and approve of sex without marriage, but not of sex without love.[30]

For the unmarried, there is an increasing tendency to reject marriage as the arbitrary dividing line between "socially approved and socially disapproved sexual intimacy."[31] And in the same way that male and female roles have become more equal in other areas of life, greater equality has come to the area of sexual relations: "Fair play has been replacing chastity as the badge of honor in the interpersonal relations of the sexes."[32]

The results of the various studies of attitudes show two particularly interesting and possibly related findings:

First, there has been an increase in permissive attitudes toward sex since the 1940's. This may be due to the accumulating reforming influence of those social factors which was operating in the twentieth century. Certainly, the changed attitude shows itself sharply in the increase in sexual content of movies, the candid use of sexual lures in advertising, an increasing social sanctioning (if not precisely approval) of sexual material in popular literature, and a generally freer atmosphere which permits open talk about sex. But the new standard for coital involvement insists on permissiveness with affection.

Second, the parent generation (sampled in 1963 by Reiss) is far more conservative than the younger generation—and is apparently more conservative than it was when it was the younger generation. In Reiss's 1963 adult sample, only 17 percent endorsed permissiveness with affection for males and only five percent endorsed this standard for females.[33]

Apparently, the conservative parent generation refuse to endorse for their children standards of behavior in which members of their generation, and perhaps they themselves, engaged. What appears to be a "generation gap," however, is probably a manifestation of a change in role.[34] Reiss's data on his adult sample give a concise picture of the relationship between role position and attitudes.

Permissiveness evidently reaches its highest point on one curve (for the college student) while it reaches its lowest point on another curve (for the parents of the college student). What the data describe, then, are changes which occur as individuals come to occupy parental role positions, and they are not descriptive of differences between individuals of the post-World War II generation and their parents' generation.

In part, this information suggests that parents try to modify behavior in their children in which they themselves participated as young adults. This reaction may portend how the current young adult generation will feel when they are parents themselves. However, the qualification to be noted here is that the generation which came to maturity in the 1920's broke with previous generations in terms of behavior. The following generations continued in the same kind of practices but gradually came to express more liberal attitudes. The new liberalism of the younger generation may very well contribute to a shift in expressed adult values for the parent generations of the late 1960's and 1970's.

We know that sexual attitudes have changed and that sexual standards appear to be in a period of transition. "What was done by a female in 1925 acting as a rebel and a deviant can be done by a female in 1965 as a conformist."[35]

Data based on a large sample are available on sex behavior up to 1949 and on attitudes up to 1963. We do not know what has happened during the last five years or what is happening now. The general public impression

[30]Robert Bell, "Parent-Child Conflict in Sexual Values," *Journal of Social Issues*, 1966, 22, 38–39.
[31]*Ibid.*, 43.
[32]Foote, *op. cit.*, 161.
[33]Reiss, *The Social Context of Premarital Sexual Permissiveness*, 142. From Table 2.7.

[34]*Ibid.*, 140–143, and Bell, *op. cit.*, 38–39.
[35]Reiss, "The Sexual Renaissance: A Summary and Analysis," *Journal of Social Issues*, 1966, 22, 126.

is that there has been a very recent sexual revolution and that it is still going on. Most researchers do not believe that this is the case. The authors of this article, as social observers and recent reviewers of the literature on sexual behavior and attitudes toward sex, will attempt to "crystal ball" what has occurred during the last five years and what is occurring now. What follows, then, is not fact, but guess.

Past trends in social change, in behavior, and in attitudes toward sex are continuing. What seems to be taking place (except for pockets of our society) is a growing tendency toward more sexual permissiveness among the young unmarried. Sex with affection appears to be increasingly accepted. More and more this norm is based on personal choice, and it manifests itself for middle-class college youth in the form of trial marriage, for the girl, and for the boy at least as a stable, monogamous relationship, to the point of setting up housekeeping. Increasingly, this happens with parental knowledge though not necessarily with parental approval. If Kinsey repeated his study today, he would probably find premarital virginity slightly lower and figures for those who have had premarital intercourse only with their spouse, a circumstance which was already on the increase in 1947 (born before 1900, 10.4 percent; born 1920-1929, 27.3 percent),[36] somewhat higher.

Promiscuity, a word objected to by many young people, probably has lessened. Certainly the use of prostitutes has diminished. If we are correct in believing that more young people are living monogamously together, and if marriage for both men and women (the figures are: median age of first marriages in 1890 for brides was 22.0 and for grooms was 26.1;[37] for 1966, the median age for brides was 20.5 and for grooms 22.8[38]) is occurring at earlier ages, then the statistical probabilities of premarital promiscuity have lessened, except when it is a reflection of mental illness. Today, except for the "hippies," who, according to the press, indulge in group sex, promiscuity as a form of rebellion is significantly on the decline.

We are living in a much more permissive society, and we are much more vocal about sex. As Walter Lippmann put it, even as early as 1929: "It was impossible to know whether increased openness about sex reflected more promiscuity or less hypocrisy."[39] While we do not have much new evidence concerning sexual behavior, we do have nonsystematic overt indications about attitudes. It is seen in advertisements which are much more suggestive than they used to be. At one time, an advertiser would indicate to a male reader that, if he used a certain product, a pretty girl would kiss him. Now the ads suggest that she will have intercourse with him: "When an Avis girl winks at you she means business," and as Chateau Martin asks, leering only slightly, "Had any lately?" Movies have become less suggestive and more obvious; nudity as well as intercourse have become not uncommon sights. The Scandinavian picture, *I, A Woman*, for example, consists of a number of seductions with a number of different men. Perhaps what is more significant is that censorship boards, the courts, and power groups in this country have sharply amended their definitions of obscenity. The theater has, for some time, been more open about sex and its various ramifications, and four-letter words are becoming a theatrical cliché.

Another indicator of this generation's expressed attitudes toward sex are the omnipresent buttons, which express not only political, but also sexual opinions. The buttons are designed for fun and shock, and for public declaration for sexual freedom. Sold in large cities all over this country, they range from simple position-statements such as "Make Love Not War,"

[36]Reiss, "Standards of Sexual Behavior," *loc. cit.*
[37]U.S., Department of Health, Education, and Welfare, *Vital Statistics: National Summaries*, November, 1959, *50*, 28. Source: U.S., Department of Commerce, Bureau of the Census, "Population Characteristics," *Current Population Reports*, Series P-20, 105-3.
[38]U.S., Bureau of the Census, *Statistical Abstracts of the United States, 1967* (88th ed.; Washington, D.C.: U. S. Government Printing Office, 1967), Table 75: "Median Age at First Marriage, by Sex:

1920-1966." Source: U. S., Department of Commerce, Bureau of the Census, *Current Population Reports*, Series P-20, No. 159.
[39]Walter Lippmann, *A Preface to Morals* (New York: Crowell Collier and Macmillan, Inc., 1939; originally published in 1929; Beacon Press edition, 1960), p. 228.

repercussions.

"I'm for Sexual Freedom," or "Equality for Homosexuals," to invitations which read "Roommate Wanted," "Join the Sexual Revolution—Come Home With Me Tonight," to such shock jokes as "Phallic Symbols Arise," "Stand Up For S-X," and "Come Together."

More sophisticated young people feel that the dirty-word movements or the shock words no longer have any impact. In the October 26, 1967, *Washington Square Journal,* a New York University publication, the student reviewer of an off-Broadway production, *The Beard,* which freely uses four-letter words and ends with an act of cunnilingus on stage, says: "Unfortunately the force of the play rests on the anticipated violation of social taboo, and violating social taboos just isn't what it used to be."

Except for the rediscovered poor, the United States is a society of unprecedented abundance. Upper- and middle-class white Americans pamper their children, give them cars and money, send them to college and abroad, and set them up in their own apartments while they are going to school. These young people have leisure and the wherewithal to use it in amusing themselves—only the war is real, which gives a special significance to college as a way of avoiding the war. This abundance means that college-age men and women can travel together, live together, and have a sex life encouraged by their peers, whose opinions they have now come to value more than those of their elders.

Abundance for the young unmarrieds in the city has made it possible to meet other young unmarrieds in new ways. Apartment houses are being built for them; clubs are formed for them, but perhaps the most significant of all the developments is the use of bars, now often called pubs, which serve as meeting places where singles can meet without prejudice. A girl who visits the pub is under no obligation to "go to bed" with the man whom she meets and with whom she may leave. These pubs (and they begin to specialize in different kinds of singles), in a sense, institutionalize a system of bringing together like-minded people; they speed the dating and the trial-and-error process, for they offer this particular group of affluent young people a wide variety of partners to choose from, and they can choose quickly, independently, and frequently.[40]

Many observers of the current scene consider the "pill" the most significant single force for increased sexual freedom. A count of the articles listed in the *Reader's Guide to Periodical Literature* reveals that more articles were published about birth control in the period March 1965 to February 1966 than were listed in a ten-year sampling starting with 1925 and ending with 1957. The sampling yielded 89 titles. But we doubt that the pill has added materially to the increase in the numbers of young adults or adolescents who have had premarital sex. Effective techniques of birth control existed, and were used, before the pill. True, the pill makes birth control easier to manage (except for the memory requirement), but romantic love is still important; it makes taking the pill, when no definite partner is available, undesirable. What the pill does is to give sexual freedom to those who are having steady sexual relationships, for then the use of the pill adds to romantic love by making elaborate preparations unnecessary.

According to our crystal ball, which of course, may be clouded, we have not had a recent or current sexual revolution in terms of behavior. However, there probably has been some increase in the proportion of women who have had premarital intercourse. It is our guess that the increase has occurred largely among women who have had premarital sex only with their spouses-to-be. If there has been a sexual revolution (similar to the 1920's but ideologically different[41]), it is in terms of frankness about sex and the freedom to discuss it. Women have demanded and have achieved more education, more independence, and more social rights; one of these is the right to choose a partner for sex. Men are accepting many of these changes in the status of women and are tempering their insistence on what have generally been considered male prerogatives, for

---

[40]For an interesting comment on this phenomenon see "The Pleasures and Pain of the Single Life," *Time,* September 15, 1967, 26–27.

[41]See Bennett M. Berger, "The New Morality," Unpublished paper, read at the Plenary Session of the Society for the Study of Social Problems, August 27, 1967.

example, the right to demand that a bride be a virgin. Young men today are probably less promiscuous and more monogamous, and their relationships tend to be more stable. Both sexes are approaching a single standard based on sex with affection. We are still in a stage of transition. Despite the title of this article, the only indisputable conclusion which we can draw from the current scene is that we are witnessing the decline, but not yet the fall, of the double standard.

CHAPTER VII

Family Interaction

T HE STUDY OF PATTERNS of social interaction is sometimes taken as the core of sociology. There are regularities in how persons interact, and these regularities are organized according to aspects of the social structure in which the individuals participate. The differences between one structure and another may be illustrated with an example. Suppose one examines the interaction of couples, a male and a female, brought together on arbitrary bases to carry out an experiment. The experiment is a problem solving session, and the interaction is scored by one method. A certain amount of antagonism and hostility may be expressed during the session. A question that might be researched is: Do such unrelated couples express more or less antagonism than married couples? Many theoretical issues are raised by such a question. For example, the members of the unrelated couple have very little knowledge of each other, and thus cannot predict each other's reactions. Under these circumstances, they might tend to be cautious, defensive, and polite. By contrast, in the married couple communication might be less cautious, and less polite. Additionally, the married couple is tied by a legal bond, and aside from the greater knowledge of the other, interaction between the husband and wife may be less restricted merely on the basis that continuation of the relationship is a well-defined expectation. Additionally, in intimate relationships there is often a development of stylized responses, of joking relationships, and indeed sometimes hostile language (and its tolerance) is taken as an indication of intimacy. So, interaction in the two situations suggested, the unrelated couple as compared to the married couple, might have quite different characteristics.

There are many aspects of social interaction worthy of study in the area of marriage and the family. The materials presented in this chapter tend to be descriptive, emphasizing a variety of situations. In our example above, we illustrated a contrast in formal aspects of interaction. Before proceeding to the articles reprinted here, it is of value to examine how situations restrict and determine patterns of interaction. Consider the suburban family and some of the limitations it places on the nature of interaction within the family. The problem of time is often neglected in the description of family interaction, and in the example that follows we have attempted to indicate in the capsuled description how time is related to the nature of the interaction within the family.

The Suburban Family

Let us first look at the time schedule for the husband in the suburban family. If the door to door time of travel is an hour and a half each way, and the office hours are from 9:00 to 5:30, the husband must be absent from the house from 7:30 in the morning to 7:00 at night. He is up too early to have breakfast with his family, and he may come home too late to have dinner with them. He is the breadwinner but he may not be the dominant member of the family. Dominance of family, it should be remarked, does not depend entirely on how much time a member is at home. For example, when factory workers put in 12 hours a day, were the mothers of the household dominant in the family?

In the suburban community, the wife is viewed as the homemaker rather than the housewife, and for all practical purposes she sets the standards for the family. The husband is home on the weekend, but he is expected to devote some time to masculine tasks necessary to keep the house operative, to help with outdoor work, and to participate in the local social life. In addition, the husband is expected to demonstrate certain values in the community, some of these associated with male society. Possibly he bowls one night each week. He may like to play golf, fish, or boat, or to participate in some similar activity; if he does, he may be gone one or two afternoons of the weekend. The couple may go out occasionally, and if they do, they probably "make an evening of it." Thus, the next morning they may be tired. In fact, being a little tired may be chronic. Most evenings may be directed to relaxation that doesn't take too much effort, and the common retreat may be television. This is passive participation, and does not ordinarily involve interaction. In fact, spectator sports may invade the weekend to the point that when the husband is home, good weather notwithstanding, he may still spend his time indoors watching a ballgame. He not only may want to, but in a way he may need to do this, because what else do men talk about when they are together on a casual basis? Not keeping up with these activities means not knowing what has gone on that is relevant to ordinary male society.

How much time does the suburban husband spend with his family? How necessary is he for the family's development? How much does the family contribute to his personal development? This segmented picture of the husband is not sufficient to make the problems of suburbanism really graphic. The restrictions of time and activities are suggestive. Rather than to draw the rest of the description of the family, what we want to do here is to examine the dilemma situation for a wife who wants a career very badly, or thinks she wants it, but who also wants to be a wife and mother.

Suppose that the wife also works in the city, and thus is gone just as much as her husband. Her career is likely to be defined as a lesser one, but is equally important to her own sense of personal development. If she wants children, she may be able to arrange to take a short maternity leave and then return to work, having made appropriate arrangements for the care of the child. We oversimplify the situation with one child, for this is not the case where a society has implicit disapproval of raising "only children." Gone from the house as much as she is, she must make provision for care of the child or for full-time help of some sort. Sometimes this can involve a relative, but this type of arrangement is becoming less frequent in modern society, and so child care is likely to be provided by a practical nurse or just any available woman. Since the hours are long, it is likely the help will need to "live in." If a second child arrives, the situation becomes emphasized. It is probable that the wife is also expected to participate in the community, and possibly the husband and wife must work together in some community functions. Thus they will be out of the house evenings on occasion, and sometimes on weekends. Naturally, they must entertain as well and this too will occupy time. And, as the husband had some individual activities noted above, the wife will probably have some of her own.

Characteristic questions that may arise from the preceding description are: What is the family here? How much and what kinds of interaction occur between husband and wife and between parents and children? What is the role of persons who are raising the children with regard to the family? The answers are not given here, but clearly the situation is one in which time enters as an undeniable restrictive factor. Is there sufficient time for the development of intimate and relaxed relatonships between husband and wife in such circumstances? Is there sufficient time and contact with children necessary to build the kinds of relationships that are described as ideal?

*   *   *

The nature of the relationship in marriage, from the point of view of interaction, is established in part before marriage. As has been noted in earlier parts of this volume, the amount of knowledge that each gets about the other in courtship varies considerably from culture to culture. There may be virtually no contact between the married couple, or there may even be trial marriage. The honeymoon, or the period immediately following the marriage, has different significance also in different societies. In their article "New Light on the Honeymoon," Rhona and Robert N. Rapoport analyze the transitional period in the formation of the family. What does each of the pair have to learn in the early stage of marriage? What jointly must occur for the marriage relationship, seen within the value system of the society, to be fulfilled?

The article titled "Initial Adjustment Processes in Young Married Couples," by Beverly R. Cutler and William G. Dyer, examines what happens when the expectations of a young husband or wife are not fulfilled. They find that the predominant way of handling the situation is essentially to do nothing, hoping that an adjustment will occur with time. This "wait and see" strategy was found most prevalent for husbands when their expectations about the frequency of sexual intimacy were not fulfilled. Wives, by contrast, appeared to approach the situation more openly, attempting to effect adjustment by talking about the situation. Orientations of husbands and wives appeared to be adjustive, but husbands seemed more willing to respond in this way than wives.

The first two articles in this chapter emphasize the early adjustive processes in marriage. The process of adjustment—and this is the way that marriage may be viewed—is extended over the duration of marriage and involves aspects that may be associated with the life cycle. For example, one study found that in marriages described in favorable terms there appeared to be an increase in the sexual responsiveness of wives during the first five years of marriage. By contrast, in marriages characterized in negative terms, the sexual responsiveness of wives decreased in the later years. The nature of social interaction, the adjustive processes, and aspects of gratification obviously are tied together. (See: Clark, Alexander L., and Wallen, Paul, "Women's Sexual Responsiveness and the Duration and Quality of Their Marriages," *American Journal of Sociology*, 1965, 71, 187–196.) Another study indicates that a process of gradual reduction of marital satisfaction typically was found in the marriages studied. However, the reduction in marital adjustment was not accompanied by an apparent equal reduction of personal adjustment, and in this sense a concept of marriage as a "disenchantment" process is suggested. (See: Pineo, Peter C., "Disenchantment in the Later Years of Marriage," *Marriage and Family Living*, 1961, 23, 3–12.) Thus, the marriage process as viewed in the honeymoon may be seen as it extends into the more mature periods of family life.

In the excerpt titled "The Disclosure of Marital Problems," John Mayer makes a crucial interpretation: The intimate interactions of a nuclear family are largely unobservable to those on the "outside." Not only does this commentary point to the large gap in knowledge about actual family interaction, but it brings into focus the realization that the family is a relatively isolated unit. Since most of us have only a vague notion about what really goes on in this dyadic relationship (outside our own personal experience), it raises the question of how persons learn to be members of a husband-wife relationship. Without intimate knowledge of other families, how does an individual know what constitutes a "good" marriage? How does an individual know how other family units resolve conflict? How are family roles learned when people have such a limited exposure to role models? Three important sources occur for knowledge of the inner workings of other families: recollection of our parents; intimate conversations with others; and exposure to families through media and literature. Yet each of these sources provides only limited knowledge and perspective, for each of the exposures is selective. Parents are only partially accessible to children, others only reveal what they wish to reveal to their friends, and fictitious couples are whatever their authors choose to make them. In addition to the source reference for this article, students may wish to refer to a somewhat more general presentation of the topic in another article by the same author: Mayer, John E., "People's Imagery of Other Families," *Family Process*, 1967, *6*, 27–36.

If the period following marriage is described as one of adjustment, it is proper to ask the question, "Adjustment of what to what?" Obviously, differences must exist if an adjustment is required. Thus, one way of examining process in interaction is to focus on conflicts and how they are resolved. Robert O. Blood, Jr., examines some of the inherent characteristics involved in marital adjustment in his article titled "Resolving Family Conflicts." He examines sources of conflict, normative ways of preventing conflict, and the mechanism for resolving family conflicts.

In his article titled "Occupation and Family Differentiation," John Scanzoni presents a conceptual framework for types of conjugal families. The variables required for the framework are outlined, and they are then used to show differences between types of conjugal families. Classification of families by occupational and other characteristics is an important aspect of family study with reference both to processes of family formation and family development. Studies based on classifications of this sort may take many forms, and there have been studies that have described many aspects of families based on such categories. One study concludes that in a community professional and managerial couples appear characterized by "togetherness." By contrast, working class couples more often are involved in visiting relatives. (Adams, Bert N., and Butler, James E.,

Occupational Status and Husband-Wife Social Participation," *Social Forces*, 1967, 45, 501–507.)

The final article in this chapter is titled "Alienation and Family Crisis," authored by Florence Rosenstock and Bernard Kutner. The concept of alienation is examined, focusing on family response to crisis. What is the relationship of family stability to alienation? What are the responses to family crisis?

26.

RHONA RAPOPORT AND ROBERT N. RAPOPORT

NEW LIGHT ON THE HONEYMOON

The honeymoon is a custom in Western civilization that seems functionally equivalent to many of the practices thought of as *rites de passage* in the simpler, traditional societies of the world (Van Gennep, 1909). Though it is not in itself a ritual, in the sense of being rooted in the cultural logics and practices relating to the supernatural (Gluckman, 1963), it is a custom that is closely linked to marriage ritual and is an important segment of the cluster of customary practices associated with traversing the role transition of getting married.

Despite the widespread distribution of this custom, its association with the richly documented marriage and family field, and the intrinsic interest in it engendered by the idealization of romantic love in Western society, there is a relative dearth of writings on the honeymoon. In the social science and psychiatric literature serious treatment of the honeymoon is almost entirely lacking.[1] Even in fictional writing there are few works that exploit the potentialities of this human situation.[2]

For the social scientist the reticence may be connected in part with doubts about the ethical aspects of intrusion into this *sanctum sanctorum* of private human experiences. In part it may have had to do with the difficulties in gathering data on the topic. Again, neglect of the subject may reflect a culturally induced blind spot in the social scientist, as in other members of Western culture. The honeymoon has, in characteristic idealized fashion, tended to be seen as a tranquil, trouble-free episode from which one averts one's attention almost as a matter of instinctive human decency.

The viewpoint taken in this paper is that the honeymoon is a potentially fruitful area of scientific investigation. Marriage has long been recognized as a major life-cycle transition point, and the rituals associated with it have long been comprehended as helping individuals and society to sever old relationships and make new ones. It is also increasingly apparent that there is a range of variation (sometimes formally,[3] sometimes informally[4] recognized) within any given society as to adherence to any particular cultural pattern, and variants are frequent. Less well understood is the significance of different patterns of meeting such a critical role transition for the subsequent functioning of the individuals and social systems concerned. It is to throw

This selection is reprinted from: Rhona Rapoport, and Robert N. Rapoport, "New Light on the Honeymoon," *Human Relations,* 1964, *17,* 33–56 [a segment of the original article that includes a case study and a general discussion is omitted].

Reprinted with the permission of the authors and publisher.

This paper is based in part on a research program on family development in the Community Mental Health Program of the Harvard School of Public Health. The research is supported by a development grant from the United States Public Health Service, NIMH grant #MH-03442.

[1] Exceptions are Brav's 'Note on Honeymoons' (1947), some of the clinical observations of Freud (1953) and Marie Bonaparte (1953), and some of the social-psychological observations of Slater (1963) and Simpson (1960).

[2] Some examples are Alberto Moravia's 'Bitter Honeymoon' and Thomas MacIntyre's 'Wedding Hymn,' both short stories; Tennessee Williams' play *Period of Adjustment;* and Jules Romain's novel *The Body's Rapture.*

[3] For example, among the Hindus the most valued type of marriage is the *Brahma* marriage, arranged on the basis of social considerations by the parents. However, marriage by mutual choice (*Gandharva*), marriage by conquest (*Rakshasa*), by purchase (*Asur*), or by taking advantage of helplessness (*Paishacha*) are all explicitly recognized in Manu, though censured as not reflecting the social will (Tagore, 1927).

[4] For example, Spiro (1958) and Talmon (1963) note the informal development of an exogamous marriage pattern in Israeli kibbutzim, which functions, in part, in response to the quasi-sibling quality of relationship among kibbutz mates; Howitt (1903) reports the informal development of an elopement pattern among the Kurnai, which seems to have arisen in the face of excessive formal marriage interdictions within the group of potential sexual partners.

light on this problem that we examine the practice of the honeymoon.

CULTURAL PERSPECTIVES ON THE HONEYMOON

The literature associated with getting married, everywhere distinguished from mere mating, is voluminous. Accounts of the event bring out the richness of ceremonial symbolism associated with marriage and reflect its essential character as a critical role transition point which proliferates rituals of passage in the classical sense.

From the earliest days of exposure to exotic cultures, anthropolgists and others have been impressed with the profusion of symbolic practices immediately following marriage. Reports were plentiful on the widespread distribution of such practices as display of hymeneal blood, ordeals for the bride and groom, ritual defloration, ritual delay of intercourse, seclusion of one or both partners, and so on. (Crawley, 1902; Westermarck, 1891; Spencer & Gillen, 1904; Roscoe, 1911; and others).

The common themes that run through the complexes of practices associated with marriage reflect, on the one hand, the fundamental task of *separation* (i.e. in some degree loosening the ties binding the individual to premarital social groups), and, on the other, that of *joining* (i.e. intensifying the ties binding the individuals together in the new social grouping being formed through marriage) (Van Gennep, 1909; Rh. Rapoport, 1962). Many rituals emphasized the fact that marriage is not only an affair between individuals but, and this has been pre-eminently true in the smaller, more folk-like societies, an affair of the larger corporate groups to which they belong.

The separation dynamics were symbolically expressed, for example, by the various forms of mock-struggle between the bridegroom and the family of the bride, from which he took her. In the struggle the bride's family expressed their ambivalence about letting her go, and at the same time (in many cases) subjected the bridegroom to a symbolic test of strength and commitment. The payment of bridewealth ('progeny price,' 'suitor service,' etc.) seemed to deal with the economic loss that the bride's

family felt they were sustaining. It both compensated to some degree for this loss and provided an element of *joining* pressure in situations where the return of the bride entailed the return of the bridewealth by her family. More directly expressive of the joining dynamics were such rituals as the giving or exchanging of rings, the locking of hands or fingers, the tying together of clothing, and the sharing of food and drink from the same bowl, goblet, leaf, or melon. These smaller ritualized elements were often conducted in the framework of a large public feast in which social participation in and recognition of the changes that were occurring were ensured.

The set of practices with which we are focally concerned here are those involving the newly married persons immediately following the actual wedding ceremony. In general there was a great variety of practices, ranging from a relative absence of ritualized events (including practices associated with a period of withdrawal between the wedding and the establishment of the new family unit) to a relatively great elaboration of rituals following marriage.

Though it is beyond the scope of the present paper to analyse systematically the factors associated with the presence or absence of such rituals, we record some impressions of relevant variables.

First, cultures varied in the *degree to which the pair were physically segregated from their usual social environment* immediately following marriage. This seemed to relate to the degree of discontinuity the individuals experienced in leaving their unmarried roles and entering their married roles. In groups where considerable premarital sexual experimentation was allowed and the couple were publicly known to be intimately involved with one another, the actual marriage tended to be marked with little fanfare and little need for removal of the couple from their usual round of activities. The Eskimo and the Nuer are examples, at different levels of complexity of social structure, of cultures in which there was comparatively little emphasis on a segregated interlude for the newlyweds. Each of these groups allowed relatively free sexual experimentation (within the bounds of incest, adultery, and good form) prior to marriage, and each eased the transition into married life, though in different ways.[5]

Significant role discontinuities seemed to have been associated not only with the presence of a segregated interlude following marriage but with *ritual elaboration*. For example, the Bagan and the Nootka are typical of fairly elaborate postmarital ritualization.[6]

Another variable of interest in understanding the pattern taken by rituals in this period is the *degree to which they emphasize the unity of the couple as an autonomous unit* as against emphasizing their social imbeddedness in other structural units. It should be noted that

rituals of various kinds were to be found, expressing different aspects of the feelings of individuals concerned in this complex transition. Thus, even in the American case—which is probably one of the most extreme in its emphasis on the separateness and unity of the couple[7]—practices emphasizing group imbeddedness are found.[8] Perhaps intermediate and most common were such cases as the Nuer and the Baganda, in which expressions of imbeddedness were important, though secondary, accompaniments to the practices emphasizing separation.[9] In extreme cases, like the Nayar (Gough, 1961) and the Menangkabau (Loeb, 1935), the emphasis on imbeddedness was maintained as fundamental, even in the face of the formation of the new marital relationship.[10]

The sheer *length of seclusion of the pair* is another variable worth considering. It seems to be partly a function of economic wealth) In

---

[5]Among the Eskimos, the newly married couple simply set up a new nuclear household, but shared in the communal resources and enterprises in much the same way as prior to marriage. Among the Nuer, the transition into full married life was accomplished by a series of events, with sexual relations often having been established prior to the actual wedding and regular cohabitation of the couple commencing only after the birth of the first child (Evans-Pritchard, 1951).

[6]Among the Baganda the bride, after having been delivered to the compound of the groom by her relatives, remained in seclusion for several days following the marriage with the groom. During this period there were a number of ritualized elements of behavior, including some days' abstention from intercourse, following which the bridegroom sent a blood-stained bark-cloth to her relatives and later the bride performed ritualized demonstrations of tasks associated with her new role in the vicinity of her mother-in-law's house; subsequently she was either invited in or had grounds for dissolving the marriage (Roscoe, 1911). Among the Nootka there was also great ceremonial elaboration during and after the marriage. The Nootka marriage entailed the presentation, as dowry, of some of the bride's father's privileged names, special dances, potlatch seats, territorial rights, and other role elements marking the transition status. In the Baganda case, emphasis on propagation of lineage seemed to underlie the rituals, whereas among the Nootka it was their preoccupation with status and its symbols. Delay of consummation of the marriage is very widespread, giving ritualized recognition to the emotionally charged significance of the event of defloration. Among the Usambara, the bride and groom slept in a friend's house in two beds separated by a fire, and fasted for several days after the marriage. This custom was also found even in Europe, where it was referred to as 'Tobias nights' after the legendary piety of Tobias and Sarah. The 'holy state of matrimony' conception in current Western culture parallels the widespread recognition of the charged significance of this event—usually associated with premarital taboos on intercourse, supernatural sanctions against intercourse, and, often, ritualized methods of terminating the state of virginity.

[7]Philip Wylie (1952), deploring what he views as the malfunctional character of the American honeymoon with reference to the development of a love relationship, also notes the emphasis on couple autonomy. He caricatures this as follows: 'One would indeed presume . . . that the American honeymoon was the modern equivalent of some savage ordeal or tribal initiation ceremony. The newly-wed pair is first put under intense financial strain; it is then exhausted physically; it may also be submitted to a trial by alcohol. The pair is exposed to the frustrations of travel by public conveyance; it is thereafter exiled among strangers . . .'

[8]Slater (1963) notes that some of the stylized pranks played on honeymooners seem to contravene the explicit emphasis on separation of the couple—e.g. intrusion into their supposedly secret honeymoon retreat.

[9]For example, among the Baganda the bride is accompanied by a sister or close friend even after she is actually delivered to the groom's compound for the wedding. This companion stays with her through the rituals of joining and the ordeals of performance in her new role.

[10]Among the Nayar the bride's residence, activity patterns, and allegiances remained bound in with her matrilineal kin group's. Among the Menangkabau the bridegroom spent some nights with his wife, but remained closely tied to his own mother's house. After the actual marriage, this latter tie was expressed ritually in the return of the bridegroom to his mother's home, followed by his being ritually fetched back by a deputation of young men representing the bride. Clearly these rituals of imbeddedness related to the strength of corporate groupings within the society. Simpson (1960) notes the custom of the communal Amish, among whom the newly-weds spent the first several weeks visiting those who were guests at their wedding.

groups close to the bare subsistence level, e.g., certain Australian aboriginal groups, even where there was a segregated interlude the seclusion period tended to be confined to the time required for transporting the wife to her new home. In groups with greater surplus, the couple were often supported by relatives for a period of time, undergoing rituals to ensure fertility, to pay ritual respects to family gods, and so on. It is only among societies of relatively great affluence, as in post-industrial European and American society, that the prolonged withdrawal of the marital pair from their usual social obligations has developed.

THE AMERICAN HONEYMOON

In the context of the range of post-wedding practices known in human cultures, how can we understand the nature and functions of the honeymoon in Western, particularly American, culture?

The honeymoon, as we know it in Western society, is a phase of partial physical and social withdrawal of the newly married couple from the rest of the world, particularly the world of their prior social relationships. Traditionally, too, it reflects the expectation of a major discontinuity in sexual behavior, and it is overtly the occasion for the inauguration of sexual relations, ideally on the wedding night itself. It is relatively long, emphasizes the couple's autonomy to an extreme degree, and has a number of customary practices that are of interest in the context of our present discussion. As the etymology of the term suggests, the period is idealized as one of unparalleled bliss. The molten beauty of the full, 'honey' moon is used, according to this derivation, to characterize the psychological state of the newly wed couple. This psychological state, like the moon, has been characterized as inevitably beginning to wane no sooner than it is full.[11]

[11]Another derivation (see *Oxford Dictionary*) places the emphasis on the period of time, the term being a corruption of 'honeymonth,' referring to the fixed length of time traditionally set aside for newly-weds to go into retirement: e.g. Johnson. 'The first month after marriage when there is nothing but tenderness and pleasure.' This usage does not preclude the other derivation of the term, mentioned in the text here, but is rather a matter of emphasis.

Usually in Western civilization the honeymoon involves a trip away from parental families and others one knows well. In the theoretical speculations of early 'evolutionists' it was sometimes seen as a vestigial survival of the practice of marriage by capture, corresponding to the period during which the husband kept his wife in retirement to prevent her from appealing to her relatives for release (Avebury, 1870). Whatever the merits of this dubious theory, it is clear that the honeymoon in contemporary Western society serves none of the functions of the elopement as found still, for example, among some of the Australian aboriginal groups.[12]

Far from struggling against the bride's participation (except where the marriage is considered unsuitable) Western parents are expected to 'give the bride away' happily, and a very frequent form of parental wedding gift is the economic support of the honeymoon itself. The tears that parents are allowed to shed on this occasion are defined as mainly tears of happiness, and the true significance of the separation in a society practising neo-local residence is blurred by the cliché, 'I do not feel that I am losing a daughter (son) but gaining a son (daughter).' In the period of immediate post-marital seclusion that the honeymoon represents, there is anything but an interdiction of sexuality. Consummation is expected to occur on the first night if possible, and honeymooners are assisted in creating what are considered the ideal conditions for bringing this about.[13]

[12]The classical case of marriage by capture, Crawley (1902) was careful to maintain, is one in which there is no proper marriage at all, but rather the taking of a mate from a hostile tribe. This practice has been discussed in various anthropological contexts but it is clearly different from the situation in which there is a ritual tussle expressing the feelings of the bride's relatives at giving up their female group-member to a male from another group (cf. Firth, 1936). The Kurnai practice of elopement, which has been mentioned above, is still another kind of instance in which there is a situation of such in-breeding that no eligible marriage partners exist. In such a situation the killing of totems followed by a free fight and a reshuffling of social alignments makes new marriages possible, with elopment serving to remove the couples for a time from social sanctions pending their reabsorption on a new basis (Howitt, 1903).

[13]On the other hand, Slater (1963), viewing the honeymoon as a form of 'dyadic withdrawal', notes that the pranks often played on departing honey-

In the United States several elements seem to contribute to the elaboration of the honeymoon as a social institution. First of all there is the middle-class family life pattern, which is intensely nuclear in residence; this pattern both stimulates the child sexually (by proximity and intensity of living conditions and by the equalitarian, child-centered atmosphere) and simultaneously frustrates it by imposing a strict injunction against premarital sexuality, especially for the girl. It therefore makes functional sense to remove the newlywed couple from the intensive supervision of parental figures who have also been prohibited sexual objects. The familiar setting would seem, in this context, to be problematic for developing a good sexual basis for the marriage. Furthermore, the larger cultural setting is one of romantic idealization and commercial exploitation of love as manifested in so many Hollywood films. The honeymoon is both the apical expression of the romantic love complex and a ripe market for commericial promotion in an affluent society.

In the United States the honeymoon takes a variety of forms. There is the *lovers' nest* conception, as exemplified in the convergence of honeymooners in places such as Bermuda, Niagara Falls, and honeymoon camps in the Poconos and Florida. This seems to be a peculiarly North American custom, perhaps reflecting the general culture trait of 'other-directedness,' groupiness,' and the fear of intimacy noted by many observers of the American scene. Europeans tend to be astonished by this custom, noting that they would wish to get away from other people at such a time, certainly from others in the same situation.[14]

Another prominent type of honeymoon in the United States, superficially like that of the European but at a deeper level reflecting some of the same uniquely American traits mentioned above, is the *perpetuum mobile* honeymoon. Here a couple get into the omnipresent automobile and travel, often without predetermined plans, reservations, schedule, or itinerary, but with a budget and a date for return.[15]

The *vacation* type of honeymoon is also characteristic of American life, and here one finds as many sub-types of honeymoon within the category as there are conceptions of what constitutes an enjoyable vacation. Essentially, the honeymoon is defined as a kind of vacation and the criteria for having a good honeymoon get assimilated with those of having a good vacation. Those who like night-life and excitement seek a situation that will provide these diversions for their honeymoon; those who like camping and hiking seek that sort of a setting, and so on.

Within American culture, however, there is the idea that the honeymoon may be a hazard to physical health. It involves an expenditure of sexual energy, presumably under stressful conditions, involving proof of potency, overcoming intimacy fears, and surmounting any guilt that may surround sexuality, especially with a virginal female. It is expected to leave its mark, especially on the male. There is a good deal of teasing about how exhausted the male looks following the honeymoon, and the acquisition of a good tan on the honeymoon is sometimes jokingly remarked on as a way of covering up this condition.

On the other hand, it is also assumed that the period just prior to the wedding is one of great strain and that the honeymoon is necessary for recuperation, preparatory to facing the stresses of life as a married couple. From this point of view the couple are expected to extract from it as much relaxed enjoyment as possible. The general idea prevails that the honeymoon couple should be exempted from the pressures of life. It is considered bad form to ask where a honeymoon couple are going, and the assumption is made for a normal honeymoon that it will be taken by the couple alone, unaccompanied by friends or relatives, in a place segre-

mooners—e.g. tampering with their automobile—express the other side of the ambivalence felt at the event. The short story by MacIntyre (1903) brings out some of the problems associated with the expectation of sexual intercourse on the first night, and also some of the impingements on true privacy that commercialization of the honeymoon has made.

[14]However, in keeping with the general diffusion of many aspects of American culture, Britain now seems to have developed some honeymoon camps, e.g., in the Channel Islands and in some of the Butlin camps, that resemble the American phenomenon.

[15]Or, as in the case of Tennessee Williams's example of this in *Period of Adjustment,* a tentative date of arrival.

gated from their usual surroundings. It is a period of moratorium on usual stresses and strains, and seems to be characterized by two dominant themes: the first relates to the idyllic quality of the experience and the second surrounds the achievement of intimacy, especially sexual.[16]

Paradoxically, there is a strain entailed in the very pressures toward achieving the idyllic state—the 'honeyed' condition in the lovers' relationship. In American life there is a conspicuous tendency to deny the existence of difficulties in the way of achieving intimacy; and there is little overt recognition that marriage is based on many motives[17] and has many problems associated with it, and that the honeymoon could also be a period in which problems that have to be worked at in order to be solved could be confronted.

Another paradoxical source of strain is to be found in the sheer length of time allowed for the honeymoon by the affluence of our society. In many of the couples in our exploratory study,[18] an eagerness to get back home by the end of the honeymoon was observed. In some cases this was so great that the couple returned earlier than scheduled. This anxiety could be looked at in a number of different ways. To some extent it seems akin to the phenomenon often seen in people at the end of a vacation, of an eagerness to get back to normal routine,

the tasks of which may have been piling up. To the extent that the vacation is away from anyone one knows, there may be some anxiety about one's sense of belonging to a particular social group. To the extent that there may be guilt at experiencing pleasure and the absence of hard work, the anxieties may stem from this puritanical source. Personality differences among individuals affect the degree to which these phenomena are manifested (Tomkins, 1962). The majority of the honeymoon couples that we studied were young students just graduating from college; in most cases the individuals were without much prior sexual experience, and we were impressed with the extent to which the desire to return early seemed related to anxiety about the intimacy situation. If there is a lot of anxiety about being involved in an intimate two-person situation, one may expect a corresponding sense of relief or even eagerness at the prospect of returning to a more diffuse pattern of relationships. Getting back to the ordinary context provides, for such people, ways of handling their problems about intense intimacy. On honeymoons, the strain toward getting back to the regular social context is perhaps even more important than on ordinary vacations, because there is the anxiety about getting back to show oneself to one's social group and to test out the new basis for one's relationship with them. In addition to any personal threats that the honeymoon situation itself may hold for the individual, there is a pressure to get back to situations in which other bases for security and identity may simultaneously be felt to be in jeopardy. The extent to which there are career crises occurring in the occupational sphere of the male and/or female may also engender anxieties that aggravate the eagerness to return.

The culturally supported tendency, however, is to play these complexities down, emphasizing that marriage is a matter of free choice based on love between compatible individuals. The cultural tendency towards denying the strains inherent in making the initial adjustments may serve to delay the couple's facing them and dealing with them. Thus, the expression 'the honeymoon is over' may refer not only to the resumption of normal life situations, but also to facing the intimacies of sustained married life

---

[16]For Slater's observations, see footnoes 8 and 13 above.

[17]A cynical appreciation of the complexity of motives underlying the decision to marry is expressed by Wasserman in his novel *Laudin und die Seinen*. He states that the barrister Laudin could have written a treatise on how many marriages were based on 'frivolity and indiscretion, on hasty passion and blind sensuality . . . (on) ambition, vanity, financial gain, good natured weakness or mutual and temporary infatuation, . . . (on) complete indifference or disconsolate resignation. Some obtained their wives by craft (to pay their mistresses with their wives' money) . . ., and so on. This vividly communicates the kind of complexity that is involved in modern mate-selection which many of the more prosaic social science analyses of marital adjustment seek to deal with.

[18]The project to which we refer is the one mentioned in the first footnote. Of the dozen couples studied intensively during their engagement and after their marriage, about half were interviewed in detail about their honeymoon experience. [Footnote edited]

without the devices of vacation enjoyment and diversion that may help to avoid them.

THE HONEYMOON AS A PHASE IN THE CRITICAL TRANSITION OF GETTING MARRIED

Our point of departure is to view the honeymoon as a vital sub-phase of the *critical role transition* of 'getting married.' The honeymoon as a transitional event between the single state and the assumption of new familial responsibilities is an interlude of varying duration. It epitomizes the joining of the couple as a distinct new social unit in the world. In a way, the honeymoon is a moratorium on regular social participation with the expectation that the couple will use this time partly to prepare themselves for later entering and participating in society in their new social roles. The honeymoon also has a function for society, in that it gives others in the couple's social network time to prepare for the new relationship. Its transitional nature is thus fairly clear. Why do we call it critical?

The concept of *critical role transition* stems from work in social science and psychiatry which is loosely related in a body of writings referred to as 'crisis theory.' Studies stemming from the clinical tradition utilizing aspects of crisis theory have focused on traumatic crises of sudden onset (as with Lindemann's study [1944] of the effects of sudden bereavement), and on crises of an inherently disturbing nature which are negatively valued in our society (as with Janis [1958] or reactions to surgery, Kaplan & Mason [1960] and Caplan [1962] on responses of mothers to the birth of premature babies, Tyhurst [1951] on disaster, Fried [in press] on forced relocation, etc.). An attempt is now being made to apply aspects of crisis theory to normal but significant transitions from one social role to another in the life cycle of the individual in his family and work contexts (Rapoport, 1962).

In the context of the family developmental cycle, the major role transitions include the role changes involved in getting married, having a child, children leaving home, and one's spouse dying. In the more traditional societies these transition points tend to be marked by ceremonial elaboration of ritual activity. These rituals seem to function to ease the transition for all concerned by dealing with the psychic and social implications of the changes entailed (Van Gennep, 1909; Gluckman, 1963). Given the relative diversity of cultural norms, and the secularization of, and the rapidity of social changes in, modern urban life, each of these significant role transitions, however prosaic, involves some degree of uncertainty and tends to be unsupported by traditionally prescribed resolutions. Major transitions are seen as inherently disrupting events, providing for individuals new social environmental contexts within which they relate to one another. As an individual's social role changes, his image of himself is affected, the ways in which he is expected by others to behave are affected, and his legitimate expectations with regard to the behavior of others change. The norms, standards, and groups to which the individual refers his own behavior change as his roles change, and he may grow and develop under the impact of these new stimuli, or he may find them burdensome and distressing.

In short, our framework is one that places a focus on the points at which the evolution of personality systems is linked to social processes, in this case the process of development of the family of procreation. Unlike adolescence, which involves role changes as a consequence of biological growth processes (Blos, 1962; Erikson, 1959), getting married involves changes by virtue of a decision on the part of the individuals to take a step that is marked by an explicit legal transition point. In the case of adolescence, sociocultural transformations are drawn along in the wake of the psychobiological changes; in the case of getting married, the sociocultural change is independent and primary, having a complex relationship to psychobiological changes consequent to it. The two kinds of transition may have in common that the forces set in motion by them lead to deep and enduring consequences, positive or negative. What is certain is the urgency to change. Blos summarizes this viewpoint as present among some psycho-analytic theorists with reference to the topic of adolescence as follows:

The regressive processes of adolescence permit the remodeling of defective or incomplete earlier developments; new identifications and counter iden-tifications play an important part in this. The profound upheaval associated with the emotional reorganization of adolescence thus harbors a beneficial potential . . . Fenichel hinted at a similar concept: "Experiences in puberty may solve conflicts or shift conflicts into a final direction; more-over, they may give older and oscillating constella-tions a final and definitive form." Erikson . . . has suggested that we look at adolescence not as an affliction, but as a "normative crisis, i.e. a normal phase of increased conflict characterized by a seeming fluctuation in ego strength, and yet also by a high growth potential" . . . One might add that the definitive settling of conflicts at the end of adolescence means either that they lose their dis-turbing quality because they have been charac-terologically stabilized, or they solidify into per-manently debilitating symptoms or character disorder (Blos, 1962, p. 11).

Where adolescence has tended to be viewed by society as entailing more 'illness' and dis-turbance than appropriate (given this view of the period as one of transitional turbulence with many intrinsically positive potentials), the hon-eymoon has tended to be viewed by society as entailing more joy and harmony than seem appropriate. This may express a feeling of relief at the termination of a difficult period, or at least at the shifting of responsibilities from par-ents to spouse.

During the honeymoon, choices are being made as to how to structure the relationship. In modern urban cultures the wide range of latitude allowed may be stressful as well as helpful. Resolutions are made in response to various needs and pressures, often in an atmo-sphere of uncertainty. What people do at these times is seen as affecting their later behavior in future stages of the life cycle.

In general, we see the critical *role* transition as characterized by a change in the state of both the personal and the relevant social sys-tems of the individuals concerned. Before the new steady state is achieved, role-relational pat-terns are to some extent fluid and there may be more or less of a sense of personal disorganiza-tion. Undergoing a critical role transition carries connotations of significant change. It contrasts with living according to established routines. Once having been traversed, the critical role transition is a point of no return. The previous steady state can never again be attained in exactly the same way. The point in the life cycle once having been crossed, it can never be recrossed. In getting married, for instance, the individuals concerned undergo a change of role relationships from those that held for them as single, never-married individuals (perhaps liv-ing in their families of orientation) to those of becoming married individuals, constituting a new family of procreation. In our society this usually entails new living arrangements on a neo-local basis. Despite divorce, remarriage, and so on, the individual can never again be a single person who has never been married. If the girl forever loses her culturally defined status of virginal purity, the boy forever loses his status of a never-married bachelor, though he may once again become 'eligible' if he is divorced. Society redefines individuals who have been through this point, and though they may go through it again there is a sense in which the first transition is unique. The notion of critical role transition does not imply that the individ-uals concerned cannot accomplish many aspects of the role transition at other points in the life cycle. It does, however, imply that the tran-sition *must* be at this point and that the subse-quent state can be favorable or unfavorable, depending on how the work of making the tran-sition has been dealt with. Thus the critical role transition may or may not entail acute emo-tional disturbance, but it must entail disequilib-rium, followed by a restoration of a new steady state. We conceptualize the work of restoring the new steady state as a series of tasks, specific to each of the many critical role transitions that punctuate the flow of life. The fact that an individual performs the tasks of one role tran-sition satisfactorily does not necessarily imply that he can accomplish *all* role-transitional tasks with comparable ease or effectiveness. Each transition has tasks specific to it. The accom-plishment of these tasks affects outcome for the particular role transition. The outcome may be better than the previous state of equilibrium in some ways, it may leave things relatively un-changed, or it may be worse. In general, one would expect that favorable outcomes to life-cycle crises increase the chances for favorable outcomes to later crises in the life cycle, but this is not documented empirically and many anomalies are known to exist.

The honeymoon, then, is a culturally patterned event associated with a critical transition point. The transition point, getting married, is inherently disruptive of the steady states that had been established in the lives of the individuals concerned and in the social systems in which they are involved. While marriage differs for different couples according to their premarital relationships and the sort of early marriage they envisage, it is a transition point that must be reckoned with.[19] It is an event that has associated with it specific tasks defined partly by their culture, partly by themselves. The ways in which couples work through and accomplish these tasks hypothetically affect the subsequent stable state of affairs in the social systems of the family and in the personalities of the interacting individuals.

THE PHASE–SPECIFIC TASKS OF THE HONEYMOON

It is essential to our approach to delineate tasks that are *phase-specific*. Though much of the work—behavioral and intrapsychic—may have been done before the phase in which it becomes crucial to have accomplished the tasks, we postulate that failure to come to grips with them in the period for which they are specific will lead to deleterious consequences for the individuals and/or social systems concerned. For example, many individuals engage in sexual relationships before they marry, and many couples have sexual relations together before their

honeymoon. Though a certain amount of work toward task accomplishment may have been entailed for specific persons in this experience, in the context of our culture this is usually not defined as a role rehearsal, but as experimentation with individually meaningful behavior or the seeking of individually gratifying experience. In social psychological terms, the 'temporal gestalts' of individuals having premarital sexual relations differ from those of individuals engaging in similar behavior on their honeymoon in that the former have primarily individual life-cycle referents, perhaps being more backward-facing and parental-family oriented, whereas the latter are primarily forward-facing and oriented to the new social unit into which the individual is bound, his family of procreation.[20]

Four tasks are postulated as specific to the honeymoon. Two of these can be described as essentially intrapsychic or personal in nature, while the other two are interpersonal and focus on the interaction between the marital pair. They all relate directly to what is required for establishing a basis on which the ensuing husband-wife relationship will develop.[21]

---

[19]While couples who have had premarital sexual relations or have cohabited on a trial marriage basis or even more extended arrangement would seem to face a less challenging discontinuity at the point of their honeymoon than those who have never had any sort of sexual relations, it must not be taken as an absolute rule. Harmony between the couple may have depended on their not being married, the actual legal tie being felt as a constriction. (The relationship between Sartre and de Beauvoir is one of the more publicly known instances.) However, research is certainly needed on the question of factors that affect the actual pattern of honeymoon chosen, and the patterns of experience to be found on the honeymoon.

[20]Cf. Chein's classic paper on the genetic factor in a historical psychology for a discussion of the distinction between actual events in a person's life and how such events function in his awareness of his past (and future) at any given time. The task of the genetic psychologist (to which we would add 'and social scientist') is, Chein argues, 'the definition of crucial development periods within which, as a framework, the dynamic changes may be comprehended' (Chein, 1947).

[21]In our own, or any other, culture, the actual level of accomplishment of the tasks by the end of the honeymoon period, and the particular patterns of accomplishment that correlate with the various patterns of outcome, are as yet unknown. The empirical research from which data described in this paper are taken aims at discovering these correlations in the sample we use. Once these are known, it should be possible to predict mental health outcomes from a knowledge of task accomplishment in samples from similar subcultural backgrounds. These tasks are postulated as inherent in this stage of the marital transition. In cultures where the honeymoon does not exist, we would expect its *functions* to be met in other phases of the transitional process, either before or after the actual wedding. From what has been indicated above in the section on cultural perspectives, it would seem that some reformulation would be required to state the tasks in

(Footnote continued on next page)

Underlying the accomplishment patterns for these tasks are the deeper psychodynamic processes affecting the adjustment of two individuals to intimate living together. Prominent among these are the issues of dependence, interdependence, and independence in relation to one another. What happens in this period of adjustment will affect the course of whatever psychic processes are at work in the individuals at the time, e.g. their dealing with their identity problems. In Western society, much 'in the marriage relationship itself is wrought of the play of these opposite impulses—the regressive search for a "self-less" primary intimacy, and the drive towards individuation and responsible adulthood' (Pincus, 1960, p. 212). During the honeymoon, the individual may be faced for the first time with the conflicts contained in his intrapsychic needs and between his and his partner's needs on these dimensions.

Intrapersonal Task I: Developing a Competence to Participate in an Appropriate[22] Sexual Relationship with One's Marital Partner

For persons in our society this task appears to involve a review, conscious or unconscious, of one's feelings about intimate sexual relations in a familial setting and of one's attitudes to various sexual activities; it will involve coping with fears in this area and attempting to resolve them. Our exploratory work shows that young couples are often concerned about their sexual abilities. Women may be afraid of the pain of intercourse, of whether they will get past the initial period, whether they will be able to satisfy their husbands, whether their husbands will

be patient and gentle with them, and so on. The men's fears are expressed in terms of their ability or inability to be potent with their wives. For both husband and wife intrapsychic feelings of security are involved, feelings about whether their identity or autonomy will be threatened or enhanced by an intimate sexual relationship with another person in the context of marriage and its overtones of earlier childhood relationships.

During the honeymoon period individuals will be faced with the need to clarify some of their ideas about the place of sex in marriage: their preferences in relation to the character of the sex act; their recognition of the intensity or otherwise of their own sexual feelings, particularly towards their marital partner. For some individuals this task will also involve an initial review of themselves not only as a wife/husband but also as a potential father/mother. For some Catholic couples, for example, this is particularly important, since many begin their sexual life in the honeymoon without attempting to avert or delay conception of offspring. Here intrapsychic feelings associated with dependency, nurturance, and self-esteem are involved. Under this rubric we are concerned with individuals' attitudes and feelings about family planning, spacing of children, use of contraceptives, and so on.

It is felt that this task may also involve an initial clarification, explicit or implicit, of personal goals, values, and desires about a sexual life within marriage and outside it. Each person needs to understand his own ideas and feelings concerning the sexual aspects of marriage: such as the parts to be played by the male and female in the sex act with regard to position, frequency, initiation, and response; and expectations about the desirability for orgasm, its character, and its necessity or otherwise, for a satisfactory sexual life. Within our own culture there is a wide range of individual orientations to sexuality, from the view, on the one hand, that it is an unpleasant obligation, to the view that it is life's most treasured experience. In general, it would seem important for each person to begin to understand what he expects of the total sexual experience and to work out its place in relation

a universally applicable form. Thus, Intrapersonal Task II, 'Developing competence to live in close association with the marital partner,' might be rephrased to indicate that the degree of 'closeness' would be set by cultural prescriptions, with certain matrilineal groups, for example, requiring minimal alteration in this direction.

[22]The tasks are stated here in a form geared to conditions of Western society. However, our intention is to aim at isolating tasks that are universally relevant. There is a sense in which the tasks may be universally relevant, though the *behaviour* that will accomplish them will vary in different cultures. In this context, the qualification 'as appropriate in the particular subculture' is implicit in the statement of each task.

to procreation. This latter involves a consideration of family planning goals—or the lack of them—and some review of techniques for controlling conception and of attitudes and feelings towards such techniques.

INTRAPERSONAL TASK II: DEVELOPING COMPETENCE TO LIVE IN CLOSE ASSSOCIATION WITH THE MARITAL PARTNER

For most persons the honeymoon is the first time of living very closely with a person of the other sex. Even the experience of living in the single household with one's family of orientation is not directly transferable. Each person is likely to find that he has some feelings about this new situation, and sometimes these feelings are very strong. Once again a person's needs for autonomy, dependence, unity, and separation will be indicated in his capacity to live closely with another person. If he has a strong need to retain a separate identity he may have great difficulty in developing an ability to live closely with his partner. A person's feelings in this area are likely to show in his preference for a particular kind of honeymoon: where he wants to go, whether he wants to be alone with his spouse a great deal, whether he wants to be on the go much of the time, whether he wants to participate in a honeymooners' camp, and so on. On the actual honeymoon, feelings about sharing the same bed with the spouse, the mode of bathroom usage, feelings about undressing in front of the other person, will all provide clues to this area. The task, in general, involves the development of an understanding of one's own and the spouse's needs with respect to the elements of close day-to-day living; and of an ability to give up some of one's autonomy in favor of an adaptation to living with the spouse, i.e., working to adapt or 'harmonize' one's needs, values, and behavior to those of the spouse. During the honeymoon the range of areas where this is relevant is restricted since the couple are not involved in their usual pattern of activities. However, the honeymoon provides an opportunity for establishing the basis on which the later patterns can be developed. An essential aspect of this personal task is the development of a flexibility to act adaptively to the other person's needs.

INTERPERSONAL TASK I: DEVELOPING THE BASIS FOR A MUTUALLY SATISFACTORY SEXUAL RELATIONSHIP

It is postulated that some basic sexual relationship must be attained by the end of the honeymoon period, though couples will vary on the degree of intimacy[23] attained in the relationship and on other specific ways of relating to it. From one point of view, the honeymoon can be seen as the time *par excellence* for the couple to get to know each other in a sexual sense; they have the time and the license to indulge in lovemaking. It is during this period that it may be possible to lay the *basis* for their future sexual relationship. This does not mean that all problems will be ironed out or even that the level of intimacy achieved during this phase will not alter later—there is likely to be further development (or regression) in many couples. It is rather that during this time the couple have unprecedented opportunities for attending to the sexual relationship without other responsibilities of everyday life impinging on them.

In assessing accomplishment on this task we seek data on how each person feels about the sexual situation, on his anxieties and defenses, and on the way the partners relate to each other. Where there is a discrepancy in needs, we inquire into how discrepancies are dealt with and what feelings of satisfaction or otherwise the couple are left with. From this we rate couples on five aspects of their sexual relationship: the degree of mutuality in ideas about satisfaction expected from sexual roles; the degree of understanding of one another's sexual needs; their ability to cope with them; the degree of mutual arousal in sexual relations; and the degree of mutual satisfaction experienced.

[23]We are not at the point where we can postulate whether or not there is an actual degree of intimacy that goes with a good/poor outcome. The critical point is that whatever degree of intimacy is attained in the sexual relations, it must be mutually satisfactory. It seems clear that this issue is one basic to the honeymoon period and that what happens afterward in the marriage will probably be considerably affected by how it has been dealt with during the honeymoon.

INTERPERSONAL TASK II: HAVING A MUTUALLY
SATISFACTORY SHARED EXPERIENCE AS A BASIS
FOR DEVELOPING THE LATER HUSBAND–WIFE
ROLE RELATIONSHIP

From our case material and from the material in popular journals on the subject, it becomes apparent that a 'successful' honeymoon has great symbolic value. It would seem important that the couple have an experience which they both feel has been satisfactory and which provides them with a good start to their married life.

The task of having a 'good' honeymoon can be specified somewhat more dynamically than is implied in visualizing it as a period in which a happy time is cultivated to serve as a shared basis for future life together. The honeymoon couple are, after all, a kind of small group, subject to dynamic processes similar to all two-person groups. The new couple, detached from their former surroundings, with all the connotations of parental authority these contained, seem to have much in common with the kind of groups described by Bion (1961). Emotional drives of obscure origin seem to intrude themselves into the situation, affecting the capacity of individual couples to accomplish the tasks of the honeymoon. The honeymoon period is one in which these forces are rather actively at work, and the structure of the relationship that emerges can be seen partly as a defense against primitive anxieties stimulated in the new situation of intimacy.[24] The form taken by these

newly emergent interpersonal structures is not directly predictable from the personalities of the individual members.[25] As Asch (1952) points out, any sort of social interaction, if it is to develop into a relationship, is built on a sense of cooperation. And it is on this basis that family structure develops. In the honeymoon the elements of family structure described by Parsons & Bales (1956) can be seen to develop—with honeymoon couples tentatively establishing the bases for what later becomes their authority structure and their division of labor on the 'instrumental-expressive' axis of family life.

According to our postulate, then, the honeymoon should provide the couple not only with a shared experience of cooperation, but with the sense of an ability to cooperate. The beginning of the new cooperation, arising out of the living together as a marital pair for the first time, should provide the sense of it being possible to work out a structure for meeting subsequent tasks.

Obviously, the specifics of the experience will vary from couple to couple; our postulate is that those who have an experience which they feel was unsatisfactory become part of a population which is at greater risk for poor outcome.[26] The actual assessment of the degree of accomplishment of this task is based on data collected on several aspects of the task, including the managing of the various honeymoon arrangements, the feeling of 'harmony' the couple experience in their activities during the honeymoon, and the degree to which they see the experience as 'idyllic.' What appears to be

---

[24]The involvement of deep levels of personal dynamics in the forging of the honeymoon situation, especially among urban couples, is fostered not only because of the intimacy of the interaction but because of the increasing tendency for the major function of the family prior to the birth of children to be the 'stabilization of the adult personality' (Parsons & Bales, 1956, p. 16). An example of this kind of dynamic process at work in another context is seen in the work of Isabel Menzies (1960) on the socialization of young girls to the nursing role, where an unusually great degree of 'primitive' anxiety is aroused by the nature of the situation confronting the young girls, and the social structure provided by conventional nursing roles tends to be supported more because of its effectiveness in coping with these anxieties than because of its rationality in terms of modern medical care conceptions. The idealization of the honeymoon, and the relative inattention it receives as a topic for systematic concern, may be another form of defense in our culture.

[25]Emery, in reviewing the literature on what he terms ABX systems (i.e., two-person relationships, developed in reference to a particular external situation), concludes that in shared psychological fields one can thus detect the emergence of certain system characteristics—'of new possibilities for behaving, believing, and feeling and of determinants that cannot be traced back to the individual actor in isolation but must be referred to the ABX system *per se*' (Emery, 1962, p. 31).

[26]It should be remembered that here, as elsewhere in the paper, when we talk of risks for poor outcomes we are referring to statistical chances for populations in the public health sense, not to cases in the clinical sense. Thus, many couples who have an unsatisfactory honeymoon experience may have very good outcomes to their marriage without altering the overall pattern indicating that the chances of poorer outcomes increase when the experience is unsatisfactory.

focal here is the crystallization of some kind of positive emotional toning in relation to whatever pattern the relationship has taken by the end of the honeymoon. This emotional tone (e.g. of interpersonal trust, relaxation, security, admiration, or more negative counterparts) may form the basis for a set of stereotypes developing within the interpersonal relationship. The way one perceives one's spouse on one's honeymoon and the concomitant set of experiences seem to set up images and expectations between the couple that are later difficult to alter.[27]

COPING WITH THE TASKS OF THE HONEYMOON

Different conceptions of the honeymoon exist even within a culture and different couples approach the honeymoon experience with various expectations. What literature there is on the honeymoon tends to emphasize the uniformities of response within given sociocultural settings. In this section we attempt to indicate some of the processes that occur when individuals actualize their sociocultural and personal inclinations together in the new situation of the honeymoon. These coping processes give rise to a new set of factors which, we maintain, intervene significantly between the original inclinations of the individuals concerned and the eventual outcome when the honeymoon is over and the newlywed couple takes up its position as a new family.

Underlying our argument is that what happens on honeymoons tends to have important effects on the development of subsequent marital relationships. This seems particularly to hold for the bride; in our small research series there

was a definite tendency for couples to see the honeymoon as something the groom arranges for the bride, whereas the bride and her family were seen as the principal sponsors of the wedding ceremony.

'Coping' and 'task accomplishment' are differentiated concepts in the conceptual scheme we have been using. The former relates to the ways used in confronting and mastering the postulated tasks, whereas the latter relates to the degree to which the task is accomplished. Task accomplishment is regarded as the intervening set of variables between the individual and the collective resources of the couple, and their subsequent structuring of the marital relationship. This concept draws, on the one hand, from the developmental psychology of childhood and, on the other, from the 'crisis theory' of preventive intervention in the community mental health field; it is here extended to social process more generally.

Coping patterns are seen as ways of dealing with the flow of life circumstances. These patterns involve mechanisms of defense (in the psychoanalytic sense) and, more generally, patterns of cognition, motivation, and perception which individuals, in their sociocultural backgrounds, bring to bear on the situation. Coping patterns may thus be described as having contents, styles, approaches, and so on (Murphy, 1962). We are here concerned with coping patterns as *ways* of mastering the tasks specifically confronting the newlywed couple on the honeymoon, rather than with the degree of task accomplishment itself. It is likely that some coping patterns will be more closely associated with degrees of task accomplishment than others, but our interest in coping patterns is to understand *how* individuals and couples accomplish the specific tasks in hand as well as *how well* they accomplish them (White, 1959; Foote & Cottrell, 1955).

[27]A satirical husband-centered commentary on this aspect is provided in Froy's chapter on the honeymoon (1962). Froy cautions the male to be aware of the fact that the patterns initiated in the honeymoon constitute the 'thin edge of the wedge' by which life-long patterns are established. He cautions: 'All this sightseeing, lolling in gondolas, musing in museums, or cavorting in caves and other aberrations of nature is calculated only to take your mind off the serious campaign ahead. By squandering the little advantage of that well-known first careful rapture, you will make things far too easy for the missus. What, you may wonder, am I suggesting she is up to? . . . *she is laying the foundations of your future enslavement,* that's what the little dear is doing, and on your honeymoon too.'

REFERENCES

Asch, Solomon. *Social psychology.* New York: Prentice Hall, Inc., 1952.

Avebury, John L. *The origin of civilization and the primitive condition of man.* London: Longmans, Green, 1870.

Bertalanffy, Ludwig von. General system theory. *General systems,* vol. I. 1952.

BION, W. R. *Experiences in groups.* London: Tavistock Publications; New York: Basic Books, 1961.

BLOS, PETER. *On adolescence.* New York: The Free Press, 1962.

BONAPARTE, MARIE. *Female sexuality.* New York: International University Press, 1953.

BRAV, STANLEY, R. Note on honeymoons. *Marriage and Family Living,* 1947, *9,* 60.

CAPLAN, GERALD. Patterns of parental response to the crisis of premature birth. *Psychiatry,* 1962, *5,* 3–15.

CHEIN, ISIDOR. The genetic factors in a historical psychology. *J. Gen. Psychol.,* 1947, *36,* 151–72.

CRAWLEY, ERNEST. *The mystic rose: a study of primitive marriage.* London: Macmillan, 1902.

EMERY, FRED. In search of some principles of persuasion. London: Tavistock Institute Document No. T.10, 1962.

ERIKSON, ERIK. Identity and the life cycle, *Psychological Issues,* 1959, *1,* 1–171.

EVANS-PRITCHARD, E. E. *Kinship and marriage among the Nuer.* Oxford: Clarendon Press, 1951.

FIRTH, RAYMOND. *We the Tikopia.* London: Allen & Unwin, 1936.

FOOTE, NELSON & COTTRELL, LEONARD. *Identity and interpersonal competence.* Chicago: University of Chicago Press, 1955.

FREUD, SIGMUND. Contributions to psychology of love; the taboo of virginity. In E. Jones (ed.), *Collected papers.* London: Hogarth Press, 1953, vol. 4, 234.

FRIED, MARC. Transitional functions of working-class communities: implications for forced relocation. In M. Kantor (ed.), *Mobility and mental health.* (In press.)

FROY, H. *How to survive matrimony.* (Second edition.) London: Pan Books, 1962.

GENNEP, ARNOLD VAN. *Les rites de passage.* Paris: Emile Nourry, 1909.

GLUCKMAN, MAX (ed.). *Essays on the ritual of social relations.* Manchester: Manchester University Press, 1963.

GOUGH, K. Nayar: Central Kerala. In D. M. Schneider and K. Gough (eds.), *Matrilineal kinship.* Berkeley and Los Angeles: University of California Press, 1961, 298–384.

HOWITT, A. W. Native tribes of Southeast Australia. *American Antiquarian and Oriental,* 1903, *30,* 81–95.

JANIS, IRVING. *Psychological stress.* New York: John Wiley & Sons, Inc., 1958.

KAPLAN, D. & MASON, E. Maternal reactions to premature birth viewed as an acute emotional disorder. *American Journal Orthopsychiatry.* 30, 539–52.

LINDEMANN, ERIC. Symptomatology and management of acute grief. *Amer. J. Psychiat.,* 1944, *101,* 141–8.

LOEB, E. M. *Sumatra: its history and people.* Wien, 1935.

MACINTYRE, THOMAS. Wedding hymn. In *Short story international,* November, 1963, 19–30.

MENZIES, ISABEL. A case study in the functioning of social systems as a defence against anxiety. *Human Relations,* 1960, *13,* 95–122, Reprinted as Tavistock Pamphlet No. 3, 1961.

MORAVIA, ALBERTO. *Bitter honeymoon.* Harmondsworth: Penguin Books, 1961.

MURPHY, LOIS B. *The widening world of childhood: paths towards mastery.* New York: Basic Books, 1962.

PARSONS, TALCOTT & BALES, R. F. *Family, socialization and interaction process.* London: Routledge & Kegan Paul, 1956.

PINCUS, LILY (ed.) *Marriage: studies in emotional conflict and growth.* London: Methuen, 1960.

RAPOPORT, RHONA. Normal crises, family structure and mental health. *Family Process,* 1962, *2,* 68–80.

ROMAINS, JULES. *The body's rapture.* London: The Bodley Head, 1939.

ROSCOE, JOHN. *The Baganda.* London: Macmillan, 1911.

SIMPSON, GEORGE. *People in families.* New York: Thomas Y. Crowell Company, 1960.

SLATER, PHILLIP. On social regression. *American Journal Sociology,* 1963, *28,* 339–63.

SPENCER, WALTER B. & GILLEN, FRANCIS J. *The northern tribes of Central Australia.* New York & London: Macmillan, 1904.

SPIRO, MELFORD E. With the assistance of Audrey G. Spiro. *Children of the Kibbutz.* Cambridge, Mass.: Harvard University Press, 1958.

TAGORE, RABINDRANATH. The Indian ideal of marriage. In H. Keyserling (ed.), *The book of marriage.* London: Jonathan Cape, 1927, 98–122.

TALMON, YONINA. Exogamy in collective settlements. Paper read at 8th International Seminar on Family Research, Oslo, August 18–24, 1963.

TOMKINS, SILVAN. *Affect—imagery—consciousness,* vol. I. New York: Springer, 1962, London: Tavistock Publications, 1964.

TYHURST, JAMES. Individual reactions to community disaster. *American Journal Psychiatry,* 1951, *107,* 764–9.

WASSERMAN, JACOB. Bourgeois marriage. In H. Keyserling (ed.), *The book of marriage.* London: Jonathan Cape, 1927.

WESTERMARCK, EDWARD. *The history of human marriage.* New York & London: Macmillan, 1891.

WHITE, ROBERT W. Motivation reconsidered: the concept of competence. *Psychol. Rev.,* 1959, *66,* 297–333.

WILLIAMS, TENNESSEE. *Period of adjustment.* New York: New Directions, 1960.

WYLIE, PHILIP. Honeymoons are hell. *Redbook Magazine,* October, 1952.

27.

Beverly R. Cutler and William G. Dyer

INITIAL ADJUSTMENT PROCESSES IN YOUNG MARRIED COUPLES

The matter of "adjustment" in marriage is an area of discussion in almost every marriage textbook and class. A number of years ago, Kirkpatrick stated, "The investigation of marital adjustment is still almost a virgin field for sociological research. There is need for checking of previous research, for contributing additional fragments of evidence, and for a piecing together of the results of isolated studies into a meaningful whole."[1] This condition still appears to exist.

ADJUSTMENT AS PROCESS OR GOAL

In the literature on marital adjustment, two different approaches are often taken and sometimes intermingled indiscriminately. Some writers refer to adjustment as a state of marriage to be achieved,[2] while other writers refer to adjustment primarily as a process of interaction.[3]

Bowerman feels that both conditions are important. He says:

In addition to measures of overall evaluation of the marriage, there would seem to be considerable use, in both research and counseling, for measures of the *degree of adjustment* in the various aspects of the relationship, such as adjustment about financial matters, recreation, homemaking duties, etc. In studying the *processes of adjustment* in marriage,

it is necessary to take into account the relationship between different kinds of adjustment which must be made, how these types of adjustment are differentially affected by the various forces affecting the marriage, and how each contributes to the evaluation of the marriage as a whole.[4]

When seen as a goal, marital adjustment is commonly equated with such conditions as marital success, marital satisfaction, and marital happiness. It would seem that these terms are all referring to the same end condition which is arrived at through some interactive process. Research-wise it is much easier to develop a measure of marital adjustment or success and then relate a series of independent variables to this dependent condition and discover which variables are most highly related to the condition of adjustment, than it is to investigate the processes couples go through to arrive at the end condition. This paper is an attempt to add "an additional fragment of evidence" to the matter of adjustment as a process. Very little research actually shows the process married couples go through to achieve adjustment.

The focus of this research report is centered on the question, "When a young married person finds that his spouse engages in behavior that violates his expectations, what kinds of actions does he engage in to deal with this disturbance in the relationship?" Adjustment, generally speaking, is the process used in successfully reducing disturbance in a relationship.

ADJUSTMENT POSSIBILITIES USING ROLE THEORY

In a previous paper, a theoretical analysis of marital adjustment using role theory was pre-

This selection is reprinted from: Beverly R. Cutler and William G. Dyer, "Initial Adjustment Processes in Young Married Couples," *Social Forces,* 1965, *44,* 195–201.

Reprinted with the permission of the authors and publisher.

[1]Clifford Kirkpatrick, "Factors in Marital Adjustment," *American Journal of Sociology,* November 1957, *43,* 270.

[2]Judson T. Landis, "Length of Time Required to Achieve Adjustment in Marriage," *American Sociological Review,* December 1946, *11,* 666–677.

[3]Clifford Kirkpatrick, "Marriage as a Process," *The Family* (New York: Ronald Press, 1955), 443–448.

[4]Clark Bowerman, "Adjustment in Marriage, Overall and in Specific Areas," *Sociology and Social Research,* March-April 1957, *41,* 257–263.

sented.[5] This formulation is the basis for the following analysis.

Adjustment is defined as the bringing into agreement the behavior of one person with the expectation of another accompanied by a feeling of acceptance of the modified behavior by the one making the adjustment.

From the point of view of role behavior, when conflict in marriage occurs because one person has violated the expectations of his spouse the possible adjustments are:

1. The husband (or wife) can change his role performance completely to meet the role expectations of his partner.
2. The husband (or wife) can change his role expectations, completely, to coincide with the role performance of the partner.
3. There can be a mutual adjustment, each partner altering some. The husband (or wife) can alter his role to a degree and the partner alters his role expectations to a similar degree so that role performance and role expectations are compatible. In each of the above cases the end result is an agreement between role performance and role expectations.
4. There is also another type of adjustment possible. In some cases the couple might recognize a disparity between role performance and role expectations or between norms and also acknowledge that change is difficult or impossible and could "agree to disagree." In such cases the one partner recognizes and respects the position of the other without accepting or adjusting to it. This pattern of "agreeing to disagree" is not adjustment in the same sense as the others listed above. The "adjustment" comes from both partners agreeing that a certain area is "out of bounds" as far as the application of sanctions are concerned. There is no change in behavior but some change in expectations in that each now expects certain areas not to be raised as issues and that no sanctions will be applied over these "out of bound" issues.[6]

This study focuses on the following problems:

1. Are the initial reactions of young married partners to violations of role expectations (in the sense described above) adjustive or non-adjustive?
2. Do husbands and wives differ in their adjustment processes?
3. Do couples use different adjustments in different areas of marriage?

---

[5]William G. Dyer, "Analyzing Marital Adjustment Using Role Theory," *Marriage and Family Living*, November 1962, *24*.
[6]*Ibid.*, 374.

METHODOLOGY

Following an initial pilot study of depth interviews with ten couples, an extensive questionnaire on marital adjustment was administered to a random sample of young married couples at Brigham Young University during the fall and winter of the 1962-63 school year. Couples were selected on the basis of the husband's enrollment in the university. Since the study was aimed at the adjustment in young married couples, only those couples were selected where the husband was under 23 years of age. There were 75 couples in the sample. Fifteen couples were eliminated for various reasons leaving 60 couples in the study. Participants were asked to fill out the questionnaire separately and privately and not consult the marital partner.

DESCRIPTION OF THE SAMPLE

Eighty-five percent of the couples had been married less than three years. Fifty-five percent had no children while 35 percent had one child. All of the couples were members of the L.D.S. (Mormon) church. Seventy-four percent of the couples had known each other for more than one year prior to marriage. Only 13 percent of the husbands and 18 percent of the wives were reared in communities over 100,000. While all of the husbands were in college, 30 percent of the wives had not attended college.

The following areas of marriage were examined in the questionnaire:

1. Verbal expressions of affection.
2. Frequency of sexual intimacy.
3. Spending time at home.
4. Sharing ideas.
5. Care of the home.
6. Personal neatness and appearance.
7. Spending family income.

From the pilot study, it was indicated that the above represented the primary areas within which couples were making adjustments to each other. The questionnaire was constructed to determine the following:

1. The expectations of husbands and wives towards each other in the areas listed above.
2. The ways these expectations are violated by husbands and wives.

3. The responses by the marriage partner when the spouse has violated one's expectations.

4. The reaction of the spouse to the initial responses of the marriage partner.

5. The current feelings of the couple about the area of marriage following the initial adjustment responses and reactions.

For each of the seven areas of marriage examined in the study, the following questions were asked concerning responses to the violation of expectations:

(1) In what ways has your spouse failed to live up to your expectations? What has he (she) done to violate your expectations you held for him (her) concerning this aspect of your marriage relationship? (2) If your spouse did not meet your expectations, what did you do? (3) When you responded as indicated in the previous question, what did your spouse do in return?

Initial responses and subsequent reactions were judged either adjustive, non-adjustive, or non-action. An adjustive response is one that brings behavior and expectations closer together and reduces the degree of negative sanction. A non-adjustive response is one that either does not reduce the disparity or sanction or may actually intensify the difference. A third type of response was noted in the pilot study, namely non-action. The problem is recognized but no action is taken in hopes that the problem will resolve itself through the passing of time. One might conclude that non-action is a non-adjustive response, but the non-adjustive response actually represents a behavioral strategy that was being attempted in some type of behavior. There was no behavior strategy being attempted in non-action, only the hopes were that it would be adjustive in the long run, hence, the decision to make this a special category.

In addition to being adjustive or non-adjustive, responses and reactions to responses were categorized in terms of two dimensions: sharing and valence. This gave the following possible responses in the coding guide:

1. *Adjustive Response*

A. shared positive response—This is a response that is shared with the marriage partner and positive in the sense that it appears to be directed toward achieving adjustment.

B. non-shared positive—This is a non-shared response but also adjustively centered.

2. *Non-Adjustive Response*

A. shared negative—This is a shared response but apparently not given with the idea of facilitating adjustment, hence, a negative valence.

B. non-shared negative—A non-shared response not geared toward facilitating adjustment.

3. *Non-Action*—A non-shared response with suspended valence.

Following are examples of the various possible responses: Respondents would check these categories in response to the question "If your spouse did not meet your expectations, what did you do?"

A. Shared positive response: "Talked it over rather openly and calmly."

B. Non-shared positive: "Didn't say anything at all; just accepted the situation as it was—didn't let it bother me."

C. Shared negative: "Got upset and argued, quarreled, pouted or sulked with spouse."

D. Non-shared negative: "Got upset, worried about it, cried, or felt sorry for myself; but didn't say anything to my spouse."

E. Non-action: "Didn't say anything at first; just waited to see if things would work out."

DISCUSSION OF FINDINGS

A. INITIAL REACTIONS TO EXPECTATION VIOLATIONS

Husbands. From Table 27-1, the totals indicate that the generally most prevalent strategy adopted by husbands when they felt their wives had violated their expectations was a non-action response. The husbands indicated they initially took a "wait and see" stance but these data do not tell us how the wives perceived these same responses.

The next most prevalent response of the husbands, as perceived by themselves, was an open talking about the problem in a calm manner. These shared, adjustive type responses were followed numerically by non-shared adjustive responses. These two adjustive type responses account for 51 percent of all responses made by husbands. Husbands felt that only five percent of their initial responses were of a non-adjustive type.

For each of the areas taken separately, some differences appear. The non-action strategy is most apparent in Area 2 which is frequency

TABLE 27-1. INITIAL RESPONSES OF HUSBANDS AND
WIVES TO VIOLATIONS OF EXPECTATIONS

Type of Response	Verbal Expression of Affection	Frequency of Sexual Intimacy	Spending time at home	Sharing ideas	Care of home	Personal neatness, appearance	Spending family income	Total
Husband	I	II	III	IV	V	VI	VII	
S+	3	5	2	6	6	4	7	33
NS+	8	0	1	3	1	1	1	15
Non-Action	8	14	0	5	9	3	2	41
S−	0	1	0	1	0	0	1	3
NS−	0	2	0	0	0	0	0	2
Total	19	22	3	15	16	8	11	94
Wife	I	II	III	IV	V	VI	VII	
S+	8	12	6	6	10	9	6	57
NS+	5	0	2	2	4	0	1	14
Non-Action	9	6	6	8	5	2	5	41
S−	1	0	4	2	5	0	2	14
NS−	2	2	1	1	1	0	1	8
Total	25	20	19	19	25	11	15	134

of sexual intimacy. There were more violations of expectations in this area than any of the others, yet this is the one area where no husband checked a non-shared adjustive response—that is, "didn't say anything at all; just accepted the situation as it was—didn't let it bother me." While non-adjustive responses were rarely indicated at all, this area, more than any other, was one where some husbands admitted making some non-adjustive responses.

Area 1—(Verbal Expressions of Affection) appears to be the area most easily accepted by the husband without talking it over with his wife. Eight out of 19 husbands with non-met expectations in this area indicated that they accepted this situation as it was—didn't let it bother them.

Area 7—(Spending Family Income) appears to be the area most easily talked about openly and calmly. Seven of 11 violations were met in this manner. Area 3—(Spending Time at Home) was the area of least violations. Apparently most of these new husbands were satisfied with the amount of time the wife was spending in the home. Such is not the case, however, with the wives.

Wives. While 44 percent of the husbands' initial reactions were of the non-action variety, only 31 percent of the responses of the wives were in this category. Wives indicated they responded initially with more shared, adjustive type responses than their husbands and also with more non-adjustive type responses than were admitted by their spouses. Again it should be remembered, this is how the wives perceived their initial responses—not how the spouse experienced it.

Rather consistently, the pattern for the wives in most areas was one of more open sharing in contrast to the non-action strategy which characterized many areas for the husbands. This is especially true in the area of frequency of sexual intimacy. Husbands indicated they generally took a "wait and see" approach, while the wives initial response was to talk about the problem. Interestingly enough this sensitive area resulted in only two admitted non-adjustive type initial responses. Like the husbands, this was one area where no wife adopted a non-shared adjustive response.

As with the husbands, Area 1—(Verbal Expressions of Affection) was the area where more wives adjusted internally without talking about this with their spouses.

Areas 1 and 5 had the highest number of violations marked. These are Verbal Expressions of Affection and Care of the Home, respectively. Area 5 is also the area with more non-adjustive reactions than any other. It should be remembered that this does not indicate which of the areas was the most important to the couple, only which areas showed the most number of violations of expectations. Care of the Home had the most non-adjustive type reactions on the part of the wife. This may indicate not that she felt strongest about this, but that she felt freer to express her negative feelings about this than any other area.

The area with the fewest expressed violations of expectations was number Area 6—(Personal Neatness and Appearance). This was followed by Area 7—(Spending the Family Income).

As indicated above, the biggest area of disparity in terms of numbers of violations in the areas was in Area 3—(Spending Time at Home). Wives checked violations in this area six times as often as did the husbands. The other areas were relatively similar with some noticeable difference occurring in Area 5—(Care of the Home), where the wives had more non-met expectations than did the husbands at a ratio of 25 to 16.

B. SUBSEQUENT REACTIONS TO INITIAL RESPONSES

Table 27-2 shows the subsequent reactions to the initial responses as perceived by the spouse

TABLE 27-2. SUBSEQUENT REACTION TO INITIAL RESPONSES

	Verbal Expressions of Affection	Frequency of Sexual Intimacy	Spending time at home	Sharing ideas	Care of home	Personal neatness and appearance	Spending income of family	Total
Wife's Reaction to Husband (as perceived by husband)								
	I	II	III°	IV	V	VI°	VII	
Adj.	14	10		6	9		5	44
No Action	2	5		2	1		2	12
Non Adj.	5	7		7	6		3	28
Total	21	22		15	16		10	84
Husband's Reaction to Wife (as perceived by wife)								
	I	II	III	IV	V	VI	VII	
Adj.	14	13	10	12	19	6	7	81
No Action	2	2	4	0	0	0	0	12
Non Adj.	5	5	4	2	5	5	6	32
Total	21	20	18	18	24	11	13	125

°too few responses to be tabulated.

making the initial response. Both husbands and wives felt that the majority of their spouse's reactions to them were of an adjustive nature. In the questionnaire subjects were asked, "When you responded as indicated in the previous question, what did your spouse do in return?" Adjustive responses were the following:

1. "Made a real attempt to change and meet my expectations."

2. "We agreed that we differed, but we have tried to accept this difference."
3. "Said he (she) was sorry and would try to do better, but didn't really change."

This last response was considered to be an adjustive type response even though the spouse with the non-met expectations felt the other had not "really changed." The initial part of of adjustment had begun—the spouse knew of the violation, had expressed regret for this and indicated a willingness to "do better." Final adjustment does not come until expectation and behavior are in agreement, but this response indicates that perhaps adjustment has started.

Subjects were also asked to list other responses. Considered as adjustive were such responses as: "He is patient with me and tries to be understanding." "Made a genuine effort to change every now and then." "Got professional doctor's help and counseling."

It is interesting to note that while 44 percent of the husbands' responses and 31 percent of the wives' initial responses were of the non-action type, there were very few subsequent non-action responses. One would normally think that a non-action response would be followed by non-action. This may indicate that when one's expectations are violated, one really does give off certain cues about his feelings to which the spouse subsequently responds. A non-action response to the initial reaction was: "(Spouse did) Nothing, since he (she) didn't know how I felt."

Thirty-three percent of the wives' subsequent reactions were felt by the husbands to be non-adjustive, while 26 percent of the husband's reactions to the wife were seen by the wife as non-adjustive. Non-adjustive responses were as follows:

1. "Got upset and argued, complained, or grumbled back."
2. "Suggested that I accept him (her) as he (she) was."
3. "I told him (her) but nothing happened—we just dropped it."

Considered as non-adjustive were written in comments such as: "We quarrel occasionally about it." "He thought it was funny and persisted more strongly."

Some interesting patterns are indicated when

we examine the non-adjustive responses and the behavior that elicits a non-adjustive pattern. Nearly half of the non-adjustive responses for both husbands and wives came as a result of an initial shared adjustive reaction. This immediately raises the question—why should a shared adjustive initial reaction result in non-adjustive responses? There are at least these possibilities:

1. While the one reacting initially thinks he is reacting in an open, adjustive way, the marriage partner may not experience this in the way the first intended. The partner may see the initial reaction as critical and punitive while the reacting party thinks he is just talking it over "openly and calmly."

2. The initial reaction may be an open, calm sharing of one's feelings about a problem situation but an adjustive response from the mate presumes such conditions as an adequate level of maturity of the mate, proper timing and suitable circumstances for sharing sensitive information, and a non-threatening method of presenting the information.

3. The shared information may be presented calmly and openly but the information may be a hard blow to the self-image of the partner and the response may be immediately defensive and not adjustive.

4. Sharing sensitive information may be a violation of the expectations of the other partner. He or she may not expect such things to be talked about and when this is done, non-adjustive type responses result.

Seven non-adjustive responses for both husbands and wives came as a result of initial "non-action." This is another apparent contradiction. How can a non-response result in any type of reaction? The problem here may be in the weakness of the questionnaire in carefully sorting out the sequence of reactions. (Or it may be, as indicated above, that cues as to how the person feels are given off even though he feels there was no response made). There are indications in examining the data that a person filling out the questionnaire coming to the question, "What was your initial response?" marked a non-action category. The next question asked, "What did your spouse do in return?" It appears that a number of subjects jumped the time sequence and checked what may have been a response later in time. Thus, it appears that a non-adjustive reaction followed a non-action response. This same condition may account for

non-shared reactions eliciting non-adjustive responses.

Percentage-wise, the biggest number of non-adjustive responses came as a result of initial negative type reactions for both husbands and wives. There were five negative reactions listed by husbands and these resulted in three non-adjustive reactions. In fact, all three shared negative initial reactions resulted in non-adjustive responses.

Wives indicated 22 negative type reactions initially and these resulted in 11 non-adjustive type subsequent responses from the spouse.

One would tend to predict that a negative reaction would result in further negative type reactions. The data from the husbands in this study are too limited in this area to allow for any support of this generalization. For the wives, it shows from a limited number of responses, that about 50 percent of the time negative responses on their part resulted in non-adjustment on the part of the other. The data here do not tell us how the other partner feels about making an adjustment to a negative reaction by his spouse. It would seem that adjustments that came from shared positive type responses would be made out of a more positive feeling than adjustments that resulted from negative reactions.

SUMMARY

This study was designed to investigate the initial adjustment processes in young, married couples attending college. Adjustment was conceptualized in terms of role expectations, response to expectation violations and the subsequent reaction to the initial response. The data indicate the following trends in these couples:

1. Husbands, more than wives, appear to adopt a "wait and see" strategy when their wives violate their expectations, according to their self-perceptions. Wives say they more often meet a violation of expectation with an open sharing or talking about the situation or reacting negatively.

2. When difficulties occur, the several areas of marriage appear to be handled differently by married couples. Husbands say they talk openly about violations of expectations in the area of finance but not in the area of frequency of sexual intimacy.

3. Wives and husbands differ in the number of

expectation violations in certain areas of marriage. In the area of spending time at home, wives checked a violation of expectations in this area six times more frequently than did husbands. Wives also had more non-met expectations in the area of care of the home.

4. While a considerable number of both husbands and wives reacted to an initial violation of expectations with a non-action response—a "wait and see" strategy—subsequent reactions to the spouse's initial response were very infrequently found in this category. Husbands more than wives felt their spouses' reaction to them were non-adjustive in nature.

5. The data of this study indicate that nearly half of the non-adjustive responses for both husbands and wives came as a result of an open sharing of the feelings about the violation of expectations. Contrary to what might be expected, an open talking about the violation of expectations does not always lead to an adjustment.

6. The data, especially for wives, also show that in a large percentage of times, a negative reaction on the part of one partner does result in an adjustive response by the other. Negative reactions are apparently not always followed by reciprocal negative reactions.

28.

JOHN E. MAYER

NON-OBSERVABILITY OF FAMILY LIFE

Early in our efforts to delineate a promising area of research, we were struck by the "fact" that individuals in our society seem to know a great deal about their particular families, but very little about the inner workings of other people's families. How do husbands and wives in other families get along, how do they feel about each other, how do they treat their children? Topics such as these are not apt to be matters of common knowledge. The point is well illustrated by the remarks of a wife interviewed in another study:[1]

I do at times wonder . . . what *does* go on in other people's lives? We all respect each other's privacy to the point where we're really ignorant. It's not that I want to pry into my friends' and relatives' and neighbors' lives—but it's that when I remain ignorant, I have no way of knowing what really is . . .

We have been unable to locate any systematic data bearing on the discernibility of family life. However, certain characteristics of life in this country strongly suggest that a state of pluralistic ignorance exists.[2] Judging from the vast amount of time that individuals spend gossiping and conjecturing about the family life of those around them and the number of TV serials and magazine articles devoted to family life, one must conclude that Americans are vitally interested in what occurs within other people's families. Informal discussions typically abound with such exchanges as: "Why does she put up with him?" "Why don't they make their children behave better?" And so forth. The fact that so much conversation is devoted to family life and so much attention paid to the topic in the mass media is presumably a by-product of the fact that the family life of those around us is not overly exposed to view. Our curiosity about other people's family life seems to be an outgrowth of the fact that we know so little about it.

The countless courses on marriage and parent-

This selection is reprinted from: John E. Mayer, *The Disclosure of Marital Problems*, Institute of Welfare Research, New York: Community Service Society of New York, 1966 [excerpted from pp. 4–8]. Reprinted with the permission of the author and publisher.

[1]John F. Cuber and Peggy B. Harroff, *The Significant Americans* (New York: Appleton-Century, 1965), p. 36.

[2]The notion of "pluralistic ignorance," originally introduced by Floyd Allport, refers here to instances in which individuals have vague, rather than erroneous, conceptions of each other's family life.

hood which are given on college campuses and current efforts to extend the range of "family life education" are also symptomatic of the non-observability of family life. No doubt, if those who are expecting to marry or raise a family in the near future felt more knowledgeable about these topics, there would be less need for discussion and instruction. Interestingly enough, however, there has been a growing demand for marriage and family life courses in recent years.[3]

Our interest in the non-observability of family life, or what we took to be its non-observability, inevitably led us to wonder about its consequences. If members of a given family do not know how other husbands, wives, and children interact, how will this lack of knowledge affect their own interaction? What bearing, if any, will it have on the way in which they perform their roles within their own family? In general, we know that individuals are affected by the manner in which those in similar positions perform their roles; for example, doctors, lawyers, and teachers are affected by the behavior of their colleagues, just as adolescent are affected by their peers. But in the situation at hand, the apparent non-discernibility of family life prevents family members from observing, and thus reacting to, the behavior of their counterparts.

By way of illustration, let us consider one type of effect that might flow from conditions such as those described. For example, assuming that married couples know very little about the marital interaction of their contemporaries, whom will the couples utilize as a point of reference for their own behavior? To whom will they compare themselves? Whom, if anyone, will they utilize as models?

Perhaps they will become more independent upon the image of family life that is projected by the mass media. Maybe they will compare themselves, though not necessarily in a self-conscious manner, to the fictitious couples who appear in popular magazines and in the many TV depictions of family life. Some years ago, incidentally, a survey of why people listen to radio soap operas revealed that many in the audience hoped to obtain advice which would help them to solve their own problems.[4]

Another possibility, and a very likely one, is that each member of the couple will utilize his parents' marriage—or rather his recollections of it when he was growing up—as a point of reference for his own behavior. Husbands and wives may have firm impressions of how their parents interacted: how they treated each other, how they reached decisions, what they expected of each other. The very fact that they have a clear picture of marital life in this instance, coupled with their unawareness of what is happening within the homes of their contemporaries, may lead them to fall back upon their parents' marriage as a point of reference for their own behavior. While they may not be fully aware of it, they may nonetheless utilize their parents' marriage as a yardstick against which to judge their own behavior or as a model which should either be followed or rejected.

As a general proposition, we would anticipate that the less individuals know about the family life of their contemporaries, the more dependent, in a cognitive sense, they will be on their parents' marriage. In this connection, a process which seems to take place when disturbed couples receive group therapy is worth noting. It is possible that, as the couples get to know a lot about each other's marriages as a result of being in the same group, they become less dependent on their image of their parents' marriages as a point of reference for their own behavior. We would speculate further that this shift in reference group comprises one of the reasons why group therapy is often successful.

The essential point we are making here is that the particular reference group which a married person selects will have bearing on his marital interaction. Consider a husband who is reflecting about the amount of time he devotes to his children. If he compares himself to his father, he may be of the opinion that he is doing more than enough; as a result, he may very likely resent any attempts on the part of his wife to get him to do more. On the other

[3] Nelson N. Foote and Leonard S. Cottrell, Jr., *Identity and Interpersonal Competence* (Chicago: University of Chicago Press, 1955), p. 10.

[4] Herta Herzog, "Psychological Gratifications in Daytime Radio Listening," in Newcomb and Hartley (eds.), *Readings in Social Psychology* (New York: Henry Holt, 1947), pp. 561–66.

hand, if he compares himself to other husbands in his milieu—who happen to be very active fathers—he may conclude that he should do more; as a result, he may comply more readily with his wife's requests. The differences in reaction are a function, as least in part, of the particular reference group he has utilized.

The non-observability of family life would not only affect an individual's selection of reference group but would have other direct and indirect effects on his familial interaction. For example, if an individual's familial interaction is not subject to outside surveillance, what leads him to fulfill his role prescriptions? If other people, for instance, do not know how a husband treats his wife and children, what, aside from conscience and emotional ties, prevents him from doing pretty much as he pleases? In other situations, the anticipated disapproval

of others is an important mechanism of control, one that plays a vital role in curbing deviant tendencies. Yet, in the situation at hand, this mechanism is largely inoperative. As a result, possibly more deviation in marriage and family life takes place than is generally realized. On the other hand, perhaps there are special mechanisms which, while they may not be recognized as such, nonetheless serve to keep family members "in line."[5]

[5]It is possible that gossip operates as a mechanism of control. For example, it is a cliche that wives spend a lot of time discussing the marital foibles, shortcomings, and transgressions of other wives. One of the possible latent functions of such activity is that it curbs the gossipers from behaving like the transgressors. Because the absent party and her behavior are discussed in such a haughty or derisive or pious manner, the gossipers reinforce each other's views that such behavior is "wrong" and thus reduce the likelihood that the same offense will be committed by them.

29.

ROBERT O. BLOOD, JR.

RESOLVING FAMILY CONFLICTS

INTRODUCTION

Aside from the inner conflicts of the individual person, the family is the smallest arena within which conflict occurs. Since the scale of conflict is so much smaller than occurs between the great powers of the world, can the ways in which families resolve their conflicts ever apply to international conflict?

The present article deals primarily with the inherent characteristics of family conflict, some of them diametrically opposite to international conflict. Nevertheless, the study of small-scale conflict seems most likely to yield new hypothe-

ses relevant to large-scale conflict if the family is studied on its own terms. Were we to limit ourselves to facets of obvious relevance, new ways of looking at international conflict might be missed. In any case, a general theory of conflict must eventually embrace all ranges of social systems, from the largest to the smallest. Hence family conflict has potential interest for its similarities with, and its differences from, large-scale conflict.

Conflict is a widespread and serious problem in the contemporary American family. Roughly, one marriage in every four ends in divorce, which is usually preceded, and often caused, by the failure of family members to avoid or solve their conflicts. Many additional families survive their periods of stress only at great cost to their physical and mental health. Many a husband's ulcers, a wife's headaches, and a child's nervous

This selection is reprinted from: Robert O. Blood, Jr., "Resolving Family Conflicts," *Journal of Conflict Resolution*, 1960, *4*, 209–219.

Reprinted with the permission of the author and publisher.

tics are traceable to domestic tension and warfare.

How does it happen that conflict afflicts so many families?

SOURCES OF FAMILY CONFLICT

Families everywhere tend to have certain characteristics which lay them open to potential conflict.

COMPULSION

For one thing, a family is not a voluntary organization (except for the husband and wife). Children do not choose their parents. When the going gets tough, they cannot resign their membership. Even the parents are under heavy pressure to stick with the group no matter what.

Such involuntary participation tends to intensify conflict, once it originates. Because they have to continue living in the same house year in and year out, family members can develop deep antipathies for one another. What began as a mere conflict of interest easily turns into emotional hatred through the accumulation of grievances between two family members. Once such hostility has arisen, conflict often becomes self-perpetuating.

INTIMACY

The conflict potentialities inherent in the involuntary membership of the family are accentuated by the intimacy of contact within the family. In school or church or business physical distance and social formality are maintained at some minimum level. Moreover, contact is restricted to a limited range of relationships, such as teacher-pupil, priest-parishioner, or boss-secretary.[1]

By contrast, relationships within the family are functionally diffuse. Family members lay all sorts of claims on one another for economic maintenance, recreational companionship, sexual responsiveness, sympathetic understanding, love and affection, etc. The comprehensiveness of these claims points to additional potential sources of conflict.

[1] This is what Talcott Parsons calls "functionally specific relationships" (8).

When conflict does occur within the family, it lacks the restraint imposed by concern for public opinion. If a man's home is his castle, it is also the place where his dungeons of despair are. A man who would never strike a woman in public finds his fury uncontrollable when goaded by a nagging wife behind closed doors. A child who would be patiently admonished in a public park needs a pillow in his pants for the same behavior at home. The very privacy which makes possible the most uninhibited embrace within the bedroom permits an equally uninhibited tongue-lashing. Intimacy of contact, therefore, contributes to both the extensity and the intensity of conflict within the family.

SMALLNESS

While families everywhere are characterized by compulsory membership and intimate contact, the American family's small number of children further magnifies the problem of conflict, especially between siblings. In a large family, one child's share of his mother's attention and affection is so limited that it matters little whether he has it or not. In a two-child family, however, one child can monopolize the parent simply by vanquishing his sole sibling. Under these circumstances sibling rivalry becomes acute.

Similarly, among three siblings, the inherent instability of the triad typically leads the two older children to battle for the pawn. Again limited size dictates who the potential enemy shall be, makes him highly visible in the small group, and leads to the development of long-term feuds.

CHANGE

The above family features would not be so bad were it not for the rapidity with which the family situation changes. Given fixed ingredients, a stable equilibrium might be sought. But families change so fast that a moving equilibrium is the best than can be hoped for.

Families change rapidly in size. Census figures show that newlyweds typically have hardly more than a year in which to work out their marital relationship before it is altered by the nausea of pregnancy. Then the children come every two years—bing, bing, bing. A decade and a half later they leave for college or its working-class equivalents with similar rapidity (5).

Meanwhile the family may have maintained the same size, but the needs of its members were rapidly changing. Every time a new child starts to crawl, to climb, to wander across the street, to go to school, to experience puberty, or to drive a car, the pattern of family living must be readjusted. The changing "developmental tasks" of growing individuals create corresponding "family developmental tasks." Even parents' needs change as, for example, when the mother loses her figure or the father fails to get the raise he expected. Since the American family specializes in personality development and personal need fulfillment, such individual changes tend to disrupt the family equilibrium.

Given so many potentialities for conflict, what mechanisms exist for preventing the total disruption of what is so often called the "basic unit" in society?

NORMATIVE MECHANISMS FOR PREVENTING FAMILY CONFLICT

No society can afford to turn its back on family conflict. The family is too indispensable a unit of social structure and too necessary a means for the transmission of culture to the oncoming generation to be allowed to fall apart.

Consequently, every society tends to develop patterned ways of inhibiting the emergence of conflict. With the passage of time, these mechanisms tend to acquire the force of norms. That is, social pressures are mobilized to increase the likelihood that these mechanisms will be utilized, and social sanctions are imposed on those who violate them.

Different preventive mechanisms are found in various societies, depending partly on the points at which their family system is especially vulnerable to conflict. The following analysis classifies particular taboos and requirements in broad categories of general interest.

(1) *Avoidance of probable sources of conflict.* Many societies have devices for keeping apart potential or actual family members who otherwise would be likely to come into conflict with each other. By "potential family members" are meant couples who are not yet married. Societies have many ways of screening out those most

predisposed to conflict. The traditional "publishing of the banns" allowed triple opportunities for objections to be raised to an inappropriate partnership. The formal engagement notifies parents and friends of the couple's intentions, providing a last opportunity for pressures to be brought to bear in disapproved cases. Studies of broken engagements show that such pressures often successfully prevent what would presumably be conflict-laden marriages (4, pp. 275–76).

Studies of "mixed marriages" of many sorts show a greater incidence of conflict due to the contrasting cultural values, expectations, and behavior patterns of the partners (6). Church organizations mobilize their resources to discourage interfaith marriages, and informal social pressure tends to prevent heterogamous marriages across racial, national, or class boundaries. Although a majority of all mixed marriages succeeds, such social pressures presumably break up in advance those mixed marriages which would be least likely to succeed.

New preventive mechanisms in our society are marriage education and premarital counseling. An estimated ten percent of American college students now take a course in preparation for marriage, one of whose main purposes is to rationalize the process of mate selection through emphasizing numerous ways of testing compatibility (3). Most such courses operate on the premise that young people are liable to contract incompatible marriages if they are not careful. Hence the chief value of compatibility testing is to detect which relationships are incompatible.

One of the main functions of premarital counseling, similarly, is to provide couples in doubt with an opportunity to look objectively at the conflicts already apparent in their relationships and to provide them with emotional support as they go through the process of deciding to avoid each other in the future.

Two legal moves designed to avoid domestic difficulties are almost universal among the 50 states. One of these is the five-day waiting period between the time of applying for a marriage license and the date of the wedding. This provides an opportunity for those intoxicated with wine or perfume to sober up and reconsider. Similarly, the age at which couples can marry without the blessing of their parents has been increased to 18 for the bride and 21 for the groom. Since teen-age marriages have a conspicuously higher divorce rate, raising the minimum age probably reduces the number of marriages which get off to a bad start.

Once the marriage has been contracted, one of the widespread sources of difficulty is the in-law relationship. Since marriage involves a drastic shift in allegiance from parents to spouse, newlyweds often have ambivalent feelings which are reflected in interspousal jealousy and conflict. This marital tension makes its correspondingly difficult for couples to get along with their parents-in-law.

Our society reduces friction in this area by warning couples not to move in with their in-laws if they can possibly avoid doing so. Some societies prescribe even stricter avoidance by restricting or prohibiting social intercourse with the mother-in-law. Especially taboo is the familiarity of joking with the mother-in-law. Reserve and formality are frequently required. Sometimes complete avoidance is the rule—one must neither talk with nor even look at the mother-in-law.[2] Although there may be social losses, such mechanisms of avoidance effectively rule out the possibility of conflict between potentially hostile individuals.

Allocation of rights and duties to particular roles. A second way in which societies prevent conflict is by distributing the authority, privileges, and responsibilities of family members according to a fixed pattern. In so doing, these societies predetermine the outcome. In fact, they short-circuit the conflict process completely because they take the issue out of the area of legitimate controversy. Henceforth only in socially deviant families does conflict ever occur over the allocated matters. For example, the incest taboo allocates sexual privileges exclusively to the husband and wife. Murdock and other anthropologists believe that the reason why this allocation pattern is found universally is because it is essential to family harmony (7, pp. 295–96). It functions to prevent sexual jealousy and rivalry within the family which

would exist if more than one member of the family were allowed access to the same sexual partner.

Similarly, authority in the family is seldom distributed evenly among family members or (vaguer yet) left to each new member to decide for itself. Almost every society centralizes legitimate power in one role, usually that of the father. This is not to say that the wife and children are necessarily excluded from consultation in the decision-making process. Indeed, consideration for the wishes of the members of his family may be enjoined on the patriarch. However, a patriarchal family system specifies that in a showdown—when husband and wife cannot agree on mutually exclusive alternatives —the husband's wishes should prevail. The beauty of this system lies not in male superiority but in the fact that a ready out is available from any deadlock which may arise. It could as easily be the wife (and is in a few societies). It is handy, however, to have a way of avoiding prolonged crises within the family.

Authority need not be allocated entirely to one role. Each partner may have certain areas of family living in which he has autonomous jurisdiction. For example, most Detroit husbands make the final decision about what car to buy, while the typical wife decides how much money to spend on food for the family.[3] Whenever people grow up expecting the husband or the wife to make decisions on their own in the "proper" areas, those areas are effectively removed from the domain of conflict.

Herein lies the problem of the democratic family. Whenever two or more family members believe they ought to share in making a certain decision, they have added another potential conflict to their portfolio. The American family has been drifting in the direction of a "companionship" ideology, which specifies that an increasing number of decisions should be made jointly. A good example is the family vacation, which 66 percent of all Detroit housewives report is planned 50-50. In the long run, mutual planning is likely to produce results which at least partly

---

[2]Most of the cross-cultural examples in this paper are drawn from George P. Murdock (7).

[3]All references to Detroit families are drawn from the writer's 1955 interview study of 731 housewives (a representative sample of the Detroit Metropolitan Area) (2).

please both partners. And, according to our democratic philosophy, this is an improvement over the old system of fully pleasing one partner at the expense of the other.

But the process may be painful. The trend "from institution to companionship" has opened a whole Pandora's box of potential new conflicts. These do not necessarily materialize; under the classical patriarchate, they could not.

The blurring lines in the division of labor similarly open the way to more conflict. In a time when women did the dishes without question, dishwashing was not a topic for cartoons (symptoms of sore spots in any society). But, as men and women alike begin to wonder whether and how much men should help out in the kitchen, a new area of controversy is added to the list. Thus a clearly defined division of labor, like a clear-cut allocation of authority, may be a social device for preventing conflict.

Equality of treatment within the family. The allocation of authority to particular members of the family does not mean the right to wield it arbitrarily. Despotic power creates unrest within the body domestic just as much as in the body politic. To prevent such unrest, the centralization of authority must be coupled with a bill of rights for the weaker family members to protect them from discriminatory treatment.

The exercise of power within the family takes two forms:

(1) influencing or forcing the individual to alter his behavior (either by doing something he does not want to do or by stopping what he would like to do) and (2) granting or withholding favors. Even though the ability to exercise both types of power may be vested primarily (or ultimately) in the father, it is well to remember that the mother is a powerful figure for her children, especially when they are small. Indeed, every member of the family has the power to grant or withhold his attention, love, and respect regardless of how weak he may be in other respects. Therefore, when we speak of the necessity of equal treatment, we are not referring to the father alone.

How does equal treatment manifest itself in the family? The illustrations are endless. If Johnnie gets a story before he goes to bed, so must Jane. If he has to pick up the living-room floor, she has to be forced to do her share. If Tom gets to use the family car on Friday, then Dick has a right to it on Saturday. Children

and parents alike recognize the justice of such claims and can appeal to the moral value of fair play to secure equality. Insofar as equality is achieved, conflict tends to be avoided.

The administrative problem is complicated, however, by the fact that siblings are rarely of the same age. As a result, the principle of equality cannot always mean uniformity of treatment at any particular time. If John stays up until 9:00 P.M., that does not mean Jane can—being two years younger, she must have extra sleep. Accepting such seeming discrepancies is not easy for younger children. However, parental emphasis on the idea that, "when you are ten years old, you will be able to stay up until 9:00 P.M., too" is often effective.

Age-graded equality is likely to prevent conflict especially well when the system for moving from one notch to the next is clearly understood by all concerned. For instance, if every child's allowance automatically increases a nickel on his birthday, the younger siblings can feel confident that they will receive their "just deserts" when the proper time comes.

In the light of what was said earlier about the conflict-preventing function of the incest taboo, it is apparent that the custom of polygyny presents very serious problems. Whenever there are several wives but only one husband, the danger of jealousy and conflict among the wives is very acute. It is not surprising therefore, that polygynous societies have devised all three types of measures for preventing the outbreak of such conflict.

(1) Avoidance is achieved by placing each wife and her children in a separate hut. (2) Authority over subsequent wives is usually allocated to the first wife—her position is thereby less threatened, and the loss of exclusive wifehood is offset by the addition of maid service. (3) More important for our present purposes is the common requirement that the man treat his wives equally, that he not play favorites among them. This often takes the form of requiring the husband to follow a strict schedule of rotation among his wives, spending an equal number of nights with each in turn. No society can effectively control the warmth or coolness with which he treats an unpopular wife; however, this merry-go-round rule at least spares her the humiliation of public knowledge of her husband's disfavor.

Equality of treatment is not an easy achievement, especially where intangibles like affection and attention are involved. Only the childless couple can completely avoid conflict from this source. As soon as the first child arrives, competition for the time and interest of the mother is created. Since she does not have enough time to go around, she must be prepared to say to her son, "I played with you last night, so tonight you should not object to my going out with your father." Even the child whose oedipal wishes have not been effectively resolved may accept such a statement if the norm of family equality has been adequately learned.

Avoidance, allocation, and equality—not separately but in combination—are the inventions which cross-cultural research shows to have been practical ways by which societies have prevented family conflict.

INSTRUMENTAL MECHANISMS FOR RESOLVING FAMILY CONFLICTS

Despite the existence of preventive mechanisms, and wherever those mechanisms do not exist, conflict occurs. The means of ending those conflicts seem far less often culturally prescribed. Rather there seem to be a number of optional procedures, in the United States at least, which are available to families as ways out of their dilemmas. These mechanisms are instrumental in the sense that they can be employed as means to achieve certain ends, if the family so desires.

Increased facilities for family living. When conflict results from scarce facilities, it is sometimes possible to satisfy both the conflicting parties by increasing the resources at the family's disposal. For example, sibling jealousy often originates from the mother's preoccupation with the new baby on her return from the hospital. An extra "mother" in the form of grandmother or nurse relieves the real mother of part of her work load so that she can give more attention to her displaced child.

Those societies with an extended family system have built-in grandmothers, aunts, and cousins who flexibly replace the mother when her attention is unavailable. Ethnographers report a general lack of sibling rivalry under this multiple mothering.

Conflict in the American home often centers around the use of scarce physical facilities. The current trends to a second car, a second television set, and a second telephone result not only in increased profits for the corresponding manufacturers but in decreased tension for family personnel who can now use parallel facilities simultaneously instead of having to compete for control of single channels. Similarly, the new-fangled recreation room provides the rest of the family with a retreat when daughter decides to throw a party in the living room, taking the tension off competition for "the only room in the house where I can entertain my friends."

Priority systems for the use of limited facilities. When enlargement of facilities is impossible, family conflict often becomes chronic—there is perpetual tension between family members, perennial jockeying for position, and fear that the competitor is getting ahead or taking advantage. Such feuding can often be seen among young children and is difficult to end by rational means. With older family members, war weariness may eventuate in a desire for peace at any price. Conflict may then be ended by facing the issues and arriving at decisions in some fashion or other.

The product of such decision-making is often a priority system governing the use of the scarce facility. If the bone of contention is the television set, a schedule for the whole week, born of a major showdown, may take the place of petty conflict "every hour on the hour." If the scarcity has been financial, the record of decisions takes the form of a budget. Here the mutual recriminations sparked by overdrawn bank accounts can be obviated by advance planning about where the money is to be spent.

The beauty of a budget, as of any other system, is that personal control ("I say you must") is replaced by impersonal control ("The budget says you must"). The process of agreeing on a budget is still liable to plenty of conflict, but, once formulated, a budget tends to divert attention from the hostile antagonist to the operational code.

Enlargement of areas of autonomy. Analogous in many ways to the method of effecting an absolute increase in the facilities available to family members is the chopping-up of existing facilities into smaller units which can then be made available exclusively to different members of the family. This results in a relative increase in the facilities at the disposal of the individual without the necessity of securing the consent of other family members. Hence potential conflict is avoided. For example, some couples plague themselves with difficulty by trying to arrive at joint decisions about the disposition of the scarce commodity of money. Worse yet, each partner may endlessly reproach the other for the petty expenditures he has already made. Such bickering can be ended by granting each partner an allowance to be spent as he sees fit without the necessity of accounting to the other for his whims and fancies. This innovation correspondingly restricts the area in which decision-making (and potential conflict) must occur to more critical areas of financial management.

The method of granting autonomy is not limited, however, to the use of scarce facilities. The problem of adolescent-parent conflict may be resolved by judicious increases in the amount of autonomy granted the teen-ager. Some parents clash head-on with their high-school sons and daughters in attempting to curb their adoption of the latest fads in dress and speech. Certainly, the easiest way out of this dilemma is to recognize that teen-agers are old enough to decide for themselves what to wear and how to talk.

Similarly, conflict may result from undue stress on total-family activities. The mother who worries about finding recreation which both her four-year-old and her 14-year-old will enjoy may be troubling herself unduly, since almost anything she chooses evokes dissent from one child or the other. Autonomy under such circumstances need not mean a complete atomization of the family but simply a willingness of a subgroup within the family to enjoy singing nursery rhymes without feeling the necessity of compelling disinterested members to join.

Safety valves for reducing tension between family members. Insofar as conflict within the family is precipitated or accentuated by accumulated interpersonal resentment, various means are available for reducing the level of this tension. Vacations are one such resource. Of course, a family may find plenty of things to quarrel about on a vacation, but at least they are new issues. As far as the old problems are concerned, a change of scenery makes it possible to forget about them for a while, and on return they may even have lost their power to provoke antagonism.

A change in personnel may be just as effective. Adding a pal or two for the morning play period may so restructure relationships within the sibling group that the old feuds are disrupted at least for the time being.

For some purposes, however, it is most effective to get away from the family group completely. One reason we speak of harried housewives but not of harried husbands is that wives (and especially mothers) are so often tied down to the four walls and the four faces of the home. The piling-up of petty irritations into peaks of tension results in perennial irritability and conflict-proneness. Then little issues provoke major crises because of the loading of accumulated tension.

Under these circumstances escape mechanisms are not childish but sensible. Getting out of the house produces a sense of relief. A television farce or romance produces the right kind of distraction. Even "going home to mama" may be useful provided mama does not take daughter's troubles too seriously.

There may be corresponding value in masculine and children's expeditions. The husband's "night out with the boys" may be resented by his wife but is likely to result in a new look in marital relations. And the children need not always be on the receiving end for personnel changes but may find welcome escape from the network of conflict by visiting their friends in return.

There is also what the psychologists call "catharsis"—the reduction of tension through telling one's troubles to someone else. There is little doubt that "unloading" one's difficulties on someone else genuinely lightens the burden of conflict for most people. In so doing, it reduces the necessity for purposeless vindictiveness which prolongs the conflict. In effect, catharsis (like the other safety valves) helps to break the vicious circle of attack and retaliation which so often characterizes families with a long history of conflict.

The only problem involved in the use of catharsis is the selection of the target. Among the shoulders which might conveniently be cried on are those of the husband (provided he is not the antagonist in the conflict), the mother, and the neighbor. Providing a sympathetic ear for the spouse is one of the major steps in accomplishing what I like to call the "mental hygiene function" of marriage. Mothers and neighbors can usually be counted on to be sympathetic—but sometimes too much so, tending to jump into the conflict, too, starting a mobilization race on both sides.

Because of these dangers in lay friendships, couples in serious conflict sometimes find it useful to turn to a professional third party, for instance, a clergyman, doctor, or family counselor. These functionaries are accustomed to providing people with discreet opportunities for catharsis.

Whatever the specific safety valve opened, the reduction of the head of steam facilitates the tolerance of frustration and a patient approach to finding satisfactory solutions to the basic sources of conflict.

PROCESSES OF RESOLVING FAMILY CONFLICT

So far we have been ducking the main issue of what happens when two parties to a family conflict collide head-on. To treat this problem, it is necessary to assume that the two partners (for it is most often the husband and wife who find themselves in this position) think of each other as equals. Hence the problem cannot be solved by appeal to differential authority.

One obstacle to resolving family conflict is that it is often dyadic in nature. Hence voting is impossible. Or at least there is no way to break the inevitable tie. Some families have found that conflicts of limited importance can be settled by ordinary voting procedures—especially if there is an odd number of children in the family. But this easy way out is available at best during a small fraction of the total family life-cycle.

What, then, to do in case of a deadlock?

DISCUSSION

The natural first step is to talk things over, to outline the various possible solutions, to weigh the pros and cons in an attempt to arrive at some sort of solution. This process of decision-making has been studied and analyzed too well elsewhere to need detailed treatment here (1, pp. 225–51). Suffice it to say that there are three major types of solutions which can be reached:

(1) *consensus*—that is, mutual agreement by both partners that a vacation at the lake would be best for both of them; (2) *compromise*—one week at the lake and one week in the mountains so that both partners gain part and lose part of their objectives; (3) *concession*—two weeks in the mountains, not because the wife is convinced that that would be most enjoyable, but because she decides to end the conflict by dropping her own demands.

Most families solve most of their problems by such processes of communication followed by decision-making.

MEDIATION

Occasionally, couples need outside help in arriving at a decision. Here relatives and friends can seldom qualify because they are usually more closely aligned with one partner than the other. Hence professional personnel are almost the only resort.

The function of the third party in this case is seldom to take over the decision-making process. Rather he acts as a catalytic agent, enabling the couple to become more objective and more rational by his very presence. If conflict is serious and hostile feelings have accumulated, he may work with each partner separately for a long time. Only after self-insight and mutual empathy have been achieved might it be productive for the couple to be seen jointly. Meanwhile the couple may discover on their own that they have already acquired the ability to settle their conflict, aided by the new skills and understandings gained in counseling. Even when only one partner turns to a third party, the beneficial repercussions of the counselor's collaboration may be felt throughout the family.

ACCOMMODATION

In one sense, accommodation might be listed as a type of decision. More accurately, however, it represents the recognition of a failure to agree. In the classic phrase, we "agree to disagree" or to "live and let live." In the specific case of the summer vacation, this could mean separate vacations for husband and wife (though so much autonomy runs heavily counter to American mores).

It is not always possible for the parties to a family conflict to go their separate ways. If the issue at hand is the need for a new car, one either gets one or one does not. But if John likes to play tennis while Mary likes to go to concerts, Mary could accommodate herself to going it alone while John finds a different partner.

Essentially, accommodation involves adopting a philosophical attitude of resignation—coming to the conclusion that further attempts to influence the partner are just not worth the conflict they provoke. Hence expectations of mutuality are abandoned in favor of accepting the partner as he is.

SEPARATION

If neither discussion, mediation, nor accommodation succeeds in settling family conflict, the last resort is separation. In a sense, separation does not really settle conflict at all, but it usually does end it. If the antagonists are no longer within shooting distance of each other, their attention is soon likely to be diverted from the point at issue.

The term "separation" is usually applied to husband and wife. If they cannot live together in peace, few there are who would force them to go on living in conflict. Even those groups who are most opposed to divorce and remarriage recognize that separating the marriage partners is sometimes preferable to prolonging the agony.

Separation can also occur between parents and children. The military academies of this country are populated by boys whose parents were unable to arrive at peace treaties with them. And the older adolescent who leaves home for college, job, or marriage sometimes only thus terminates his or her revolutionary war.

Separation is the most drastic way out of family conflict, yet those who have tried it often say that peaceful loneliness is an improvement over perpetual conflict.

CONCLUSION

Returning now to the question of the similarities and differences between family conflict and con-

flict in other settings, it is apparent that the sources of family conflict are largely distinctive. Families are uniquely small and intimate. The structure and developmental tasks of the family are transformed with unusual speed. Only in the involuntary nature of world society is there a close analogy.

Much as the sources of conflict may differ between the family and the world community, the mechanisms for preventing and resolving conflict have more in common. International "mechanisms of avoidance" include the United Nations Emergency Force sealing the border between Israel and Egypt and the proposals for disengagement in Central Europe. The "allocation of authority" to a world court and a world government would alter the naked struggle of sovereign nations among themselves. "Equality of treatment" is just as difficult a problem among nations differing in size, wealth, and maturity as among children differing in age. However, the admission of all nations to membership in the United Nations might achieve minimal equality and bring excluded nations within the sphere of authority of the international organization. Rotation systems in key international offices tend to reduce international jealousy.

"Increased facilities" for international living are provided through economic development, reducing the envy of the "have" nations by the "have-nots." "Priority systems" for the use of limited facilities apply to such international waterways as rivers and harbors on which multiple countries depend. "Enlargement of areas of autonomy" reduces international conflict as colonial powers become independent. International "safety valves" include the opportunities for catharsis provided by the open forum of the General Assembly and by smaller-scale talks at or below the summit.

Big-power rivalry between East and West is closely analogous to the conflict between husband and wife. Voting has little value when the conflicting parties perennially deadlock or veto each other. The focus under such circumstances must be on the same processes that enable families to resolve their deadlocks. Discussion through negotiation and diplomatic talks may lead to consensus, compromise, or concession internationally as well as familially. The General Secretary of the United Nations has increasingly become an international mediator, as have many of the smaller powers. Accommodation to the status quo has been the outcome of many an international crisis that for a time threatened to disturb the peace. But separation, in a shrinking world, is one process not open to national societies, for much as they may dislike each other, they must go on forever living in the same international "house."

REFERENCES

1. BLOOD, ROBERT O., JR. *Anticipating your marriage.* New York: The Free Press, 1955.

2. BLOOD, ROBERT O., JR., & WOLFE, DONALD M. *Husbands and wives: the dynamics of married living.* New York: The Free Press, 1960.

3. BOWMAN, HENRY A. *Marriage education in the colleges.* New York: American Social Hygiene Association, 1949.

4. BURGESS, ERNEST W., & WALLIN, PAUL. *Engagement and marriage.* Philadelphia: J. B. Lippincott Co., 1953.

5. GLICK, PAUL. "The life cycle of the family," *Marriage and Family Living,* 1955. *XVII,* 3–9.

6. LANDIS, JUDSON T. "Marriages of mixed and nonmixed religious faith," *American Sociological Review,* 1949, *XIV,* 401-7.

7. MURDOCK, GEORGE P. *Social structure.* New York: Crowell Collier and Macmillan, Inc., 1949.

8. PARSONS, TALCOTT. "The social structure of the family." In RUTH NANDA ANSHEN (ed.), *The family: its function and destiny.* New York: Harper & Row, Publishers, 1949.

30.

JOHN SCANZONI

OCCUPATION AND FAMILY DIFFERENTIATION

Beginning with Ogburn, the place of economic factors within the modern conjugal unit has been minimized.[1] It has been argued that the major dimension of the current nuclear unit is the affective, the emotional, the expressive. The very term "marital adjustment" connotes that external constraints are less vital than the "ability" of the couple to "work out" interpersonal problems. The observers leaped from the data—the decrease of joint economic participation between husbands and wives—to the inference that modern marriage coheres or collapses almost solely on the basis of affective elements. Parsons has recently restated and expanded this position by asserting that "it is of course a commonplace that the [my italics] American family is predominantly . . . an urban middle-class family . . . there has emerged a remarkably uniform, basic type of family."[2] For Parsons, this "uniform family" rests chiefly on personality variables which he analyzes in a psychoanalytic context.

It may be that except at the most general structural level, Parsons' "uniform family" may be as unfortunate a term as was his "isolated family" of a decade ago. For it is also possible to leap from the data to the alternative hypothesis that economic factors still play a vital role within the conjugal family albeit in a differentiated form. Is it not strange to realize that an inherent feature of modern society is complexity, specialization, and differentiation, and that this can be seen in every part of society—every part, that is, except the conjugal family system? Here we are told that there is "remarkable" homogeneity based on the "indispensable function" of expressive gratifications.

This selection is reprinted from: John Scanzoni, "Occupational and Family Differentiation," *The Sociological Quarterly,* 1967, *8,* 187–198. Reprinted with the permission of the author and publisher.

[1] See Robert F. Winch, *The Modern Family* (New York: Holt, Rinehart & Winston, Inc., 1963), chap. 1.

[2] Talcott Parsons, "The Normal American Family," in Seymour M. Farber, Piero Mustacchi, Roger H. L. Wilson, *The Family's Search for Survival* (New York: McGraw-Hill, 1965), 31–50.

It seems just as simple and perhaps more logical to assume the opposite, viz., that increasing societal complexity should be related to a more complex family system. In any event, given the ever-increasing complexity of our society, the burden of proof is on those who argue that the conjugal family is going the other way. From common-sense observation, we know that the almost infinite variety of occupations today is a far cry from the few types of agricultural and related supporting occupations of the last century. Yet while agricultural occupations were supposedly inextricable from the family, the impact of modern occupations is largely ignored and thus unexplored.

Therefore, the purpose of this paper is to set forth a conceptual schema which indicates that there is significant differentiation among types of conjugal families, and that this differentiation is based on differing relationships to the occupational structure. First, we will outline the five sets of variables within our schema; second, we will attempt to present a rationale for these particular kinds of variables; and finally, we will try to link them in ways that meaningfully demonstrate differentiation between conjugal families.

CONCEPTUAL FRAMEWORK

1. Economic Ideas and Behavior
   a) Success and economic aspirations
   b) Levels of achievement values, norms, behaviors (degree of commitment to norms and behavior usually associated with achievement)
   c) Perceived alienation (degree to which one perceives he is or is not part of the "opportunity structure")
   d) Level of life-style (long or short range consumption patterns, tangible vs. intangible symbols, kinds of tangible symbols)
   e) Meaning of work (duty or moral obligation, means to "success" or to "get ahead," means of survival, necessary evil, means to satisfaction, or service, or money, etc.)
   f) Gap (anomie) if any, between success goals and actual position
   g) Evaluation and reaction to this gap (disappointment, frustration, acceptance, indifference)
2. Social Status (homogamy, hypogamy, hypergamy of pair)
   a) Background (education, occupation, income of each parent of both partners)

b) Current (education, occupation, income of each partner)
3. Self-Esteem (of husband and of wife)
4. Nonwork Ideas and Behavior
   a) Expressive Conjunctiveness or Disjunctiveness of husband and wife (degree of joint leisure activities or companionship; degree of joint interests)
   b) Leisure-significant-others (mutually shared friends vs. individually-held friends)
   c) Objective of leisure (to what extent is it "alter-directed," i.e., toward other family members vs. "ego-directed," i.e., toward reinforcement of male self-esteem not reinforced through occupational achievement?)
   d) Meaning of leisure (traditional ascetic Protestant attitudes of suspicion; indifference; restorative; Grecian idea of intrinsic worth; escape from work; center of existence, etc.)
5. Perceived Situational Satisfaction (global evaluation of husband and of wife)

In graphic form, the model is as shown in Figure 30-1. Self-esteem is the intervening vari-

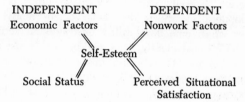

FIGURE 30-1.

able which links the structural and cultural variables to interpersonal and individual variables.

RATIONALE FOR THE FRAMEWORK

The basis for the kinds of economic variables selected stems from our earlier work.[3] A sample of "disorganized" marriages (those which had been dissolved by divorce, or separation plus a current suit) was compared with a sample of "organized" marriages (the absence of legal dissolution or threats thereto). Among organized marriages we found strong evidence of consensus between husbands and wives over achievement levels, success goals, and life-style. Among disorganized marriages there was inten-

---

[3]In press.

sive conflict between spouses over these same kinds of orientations. Wives from these marriages whose husbands held manual occupations were consistent in their dissatisfaction with what they defined as underachievement, i.e., wives possessed higher levels of achievement and life-style than their husbands. (Most of these wives had married hypogamously.) Wives from nonmanual disorganized marriages defined their husbands' occupational behavior as overachievement, i.e., in an attempt to obtain success goals, he performs his occupational behaviors to the almost total exclusion of conjugal roles.

This and later work with adolescents (discussed below under "homogamy and stability") leads us to suggest that the issue of family organization-disorganization-differentiation may be linked to that growing body of theory and research dealing with sources and consequences of achievement, success, anomie, alienation, etc.[4] Certainly part of the major ethos of a modern society is the "achievement motive," or what some have called "instrumental activism." Consequently, it would be highly useful to be able to subsume this substantive area under a theoretical rubric which seems to hold some promise of explanatory power in other substantive areas. It is generally agreed that in a pre-modern society, joint economic participation by husbands and wives is a major determinant of nuclear unit organization. Furthermore, Murdock argues that marriage does not exist apart from two essential bases: the economic *and* the expressive.[5] In a modern, achievement-oriented society, it may be that husband-wife congruence or conflict over achievement values and life-style serves as a kind of "functional equivalent" of joint economic participation. Essentially, therefore, the different patterns of familial organization discussed below are derived from manipulation of these kinds of economic variables in combination with the remaining four sets of variables.

The correlation between homogamy and "marital stability" is well known, but its theoretical explanation is lacking. Concomitantly, Goode, Roth and Peck, among others, have shown that hypogamy (wife marries downward) is highly related to dissolution and to "poor adjustment."[6] Hypergamy (wife marries upward) has been shown to be more related to "stability" than hypogamy, but not as strongly as homogamy. Among our earlier studies was one concerning adolescents which suggests that the explanation for these associations may lie in certain kinds of socialization experiences that have a relation to the development of achievement levels, which, in turn, are brought by both partners into the marriage.

For example, we found that the middle-class girl (this included daughters of upper-manual foremen and skilled workers) is socialized in ways similar to those of middle-class boys, thus resulting in value consensus over achievement levels when these people marry homogamously. When the girl marries a lower-class boy, there is a clash over achievement values because (as a vast literature indicates) he has been socialized in ways that hinder achievement.[7] Likewise, there is some evidence which suggests that the socialization of lower-class girls is more like that of middle-class youth, and thus these girls sometimes develop higher achievement levels than lower-class boys. Therefore, there may sometimes exist a kind of "subjective hypogamy" in which the lower-class girl who marries a lower-class boy actually marries "downward" in terms of achievement levels and life-style. On the other hand, due to her essentially middle-class achievement values, the probability of disorganization is less when she marries upward than when she marries downward.[8]

It has been argued that male self-esteem is

[4]For a thorough summary, see Ephraim Mizruchi, *Success and Opportunity* (New York: The Free Press, 1964).

[5]George P. Murdock, *Social Structure* (New York: Crowell Collier and Macmillan, Inc., 1949), 8–9.

[6]William J. Goode, *After Divorce* (New York: The Free Press, 1956), 97 ff. Julius Roth and Robert F. Peck, "Social Class and Social Mobility Factors Related to Marital Adjustment," *American Sociological Review*, August, 1961, *16*, 478–82. Jessie Bernard, *Marriage and Family Among Negroes* (Englewood Cliffs, N.J.: Prentice-Hall, Inc., 1966), 90 ff.

[7]David C. McClelland, *The Achieving Society* (Princeton, N. J.: D. Van Nostrand & Co., Inc., 1961).

[8]Goode, *After Divorce.*

largely a function of occupational achievement, thus the import of its inclusion here.[9] What the equivalent is for the female in our society is uncertain, but perhaps it can be traced to a number of factors for different categories of women. In some cases it may be the life-style or expressive satisfactions provided by the husband, or her own attainments in job, religious, or community activities, or perhaps even something else. As we shall note below, the impact on family organization and differentiation, wife self-esteem, as well as that of the husband, cannot be overlooked.

Though in the past much attention has been given to husband-wife companionship, expressive conjunctiveness, etc., less attention has been paid to the theoretical notion that these specific behaviors fall under the heading of nonwork interaction in general. As such, they should be analyzed in connection with other forms of nonwork behaviors (i.e., leisure in general), and with work behaviors as well. For example, Goode suggests that "economic strain" may be transferred negatively on to expressive relations between spouses, and we also found this to be true from our earlier studies.[10] A concomitant factor is that of leisure-significant others, i.e., to what extent do husbands and wives share the same friends, or else have individual friends? Further, to what extent does the husband look on leisure as a means to bolster a self-esteem unsupported by the occupational realm vis-à-vis leisure as a means to support and bolster other family members? Finally, Berger has suggested that we should define leisure activities in terms of the constraint and importance they hold for the individual—a view which he asserts was the Grecian concept of leisure.[11] This he contrasts with the Puritan view that only work activities are worthy to be a constraint to the individual. What might be the import of these contrasting views and their intermediate stages on expressive interaction between husbands and wives?

At first one might question the concept of

"perceived situational satisfaction" on the grounds that it partakes of the older "adjustment" and "marital success" nations, but this is not the case. Actor's perceived satisfaction with *any* type of situation is a statement of what "is," and as legitimate scientific data it is in no way related to any value-judgments an onlooker might have. Its meaning is interpreted in the light of Farber's argument that our society currently defines marriage as a situation in which "personal welfare" and individual interests and needs are supposed to be met.[12] Thus, satisfaction with the *global* marital situation reflects the degree to which one perceives that his welfare, interests, and needs are actually being met.

FAMILY DIFFERENTIATION

By manipulating these variables, it is possible to derive at least five different categories or patterns of organized marriages. Other patterns are certainly possible, but space limits us to a discussion only of the following.

1. The husband has a nonmanual or upper-manual occupation. The husband and wife are fairly homogamous in terms of background and current social status, especially education. They share similar orientations with regard to success goals, levels of achievement, life-style, meaning of work, and degree of alienation-integration into the opportunity structure. These orientations are essentially the dominant middle-class ethos of an achievement-oriented society which stresses and rewards individualism and "instrumental activism." Neither spouse perceives a gap between relative success goals and present position, hence there is not likely to be disappointment or frustration over such a gap. Since, in our society, male self-esteem is generally dependent on occupational achievement, his is probably high, and not likely to be threatened by conflict with his wife because of what she might consider as underachievement. As a function of homogamy, the level of wife self-esteem is probably comparable to that of the

[9]Mizruchi, *op. cit.*
[10]Goode, *After Divorce.*
[11]Bennett M. Berger, "The Sociology of Leisure: Some Suggestions," *Industrial Relations,* February, 1962). *1,* 31–45.

[12]Bernard Farber, *Family: Organization and Interaction* (San Francisco: Chandler Press, 1964), chap. 4.

husband, and neither does it seem to be in danger of threat due to structural sources such as inadequate life-style.

Consensus with regard to achievement and life-style probably results in expressive conjunctiveness, as well as in a large number of mutually-held significant others. Nonwork activities tend to be alter-directed (toward wife and children) rather than an attempt to bolster a self-esteem unreinforced by occupational achievement. Leisure is defined as a "restorative" in terms of more efficient work, but certain leisure activities also take on a sense of constraint, worth, and inherent importance. Thus, there is a "constraint" to interact in certain expressive ways with wife and children. It is considered obligatory to allow occupational roles to go unfulfilled at certain times in order to fulfill conjugal roles.[13] Satisfaction of both partners with the global marital situation is probably quite high due to congruence over the bases of marriage, viz., the economic and the expressive, and the absence of any threat to the self-esteem of either partner.

2. Husband has a nonmanual occupation, the union is hypergamous (wife upward) but the possibility of homogamy of background or current status is allowed. The husband holds norms different from the wife regarding achievement behaviors and different values regarding success goals and the meaning of work. To him, work is a kind of moral obligation, duty, or compulsion (e.g., Whyte's *Organization Man* executives, or certain sect clergy)[14] rather than merely the road to success. He perceives a continual gap between success goals and present occupational position—his duty is never ending. He feels he must be striving continually. The wife, while she highly values success goals, de-

---

[13]See A. Paul Hare, *Handbook of Small Group Research* (New York: The Free Press, 1962, 119–21), for a discussion on resolution of conflict between occupational and conjugal roles.

[14]From William H. Whyte, Jr., *The Organization Man,* quoted in Jackson Toby, *Contemporary Society* (New York: John Wiley & Sons, Inc., 1964), 119–21; Whyte, (*ibid.,* 119), refers to a union executive who works 70 to 80 hours a week and who says "I feel I'm part of a crusade, making the world a better place in which to live. . . . The incentive isn't monetary gain."

fines work as a means to obtain success and not as an end in itself nor as a "duty." She perceives no continual gap between success goals and present position, and defines his current work behavior as "overplayed."

It is possible that the husband "overachieves" vis-à-vis wife expectations because of his low self-esteem that no amount of objective "success" can raise, or because of ascetic Protestant values (whether secularized or sacred). In any event, the husband tends to give low priority to nonwork expressive behaviors with wife and children, and to fulfill these kinds of behavior only minimally.

If the wife does not actively conflict with her husband over his economic and expressive behaviors, this removes one possibility of a threat to the "overachiever" with low self-esteem, as well as to the "duty-bound" worker. She may define the rewards inherent in the situation as sufficient compensation for deprivations she encounters, e.g., affluence (the executive), "honor" (political or military occupational roles), "spiritual-moral-ethical," etc. (religious or humanitarian occupational roles). It is quite possible that this type of reaction may vary with high self-esteem on the part of the wife. She does not define the situation as a threat either to herself or to her interests. Consequently, she is less likely to conflict with her husband over his behavior.

If she defines the compensations as insufficient or unsuitable (this definition may vary with the wife's low self-esteem), she may choose to enter into conflict with her husband. This would pose a further threat to male self-esteem in those cases where it is already low, but not necessarily if it is high and work is a duty. Threatened self-esteem might be displaced even further onto already tenuous expressive and interpersonal relations and deepen definitions of alter as an undesirable partner. In these cases, satisfaction with the marriage is likely to be low for both partners. Where husband's self-esteem is not threatened, negative definitions of alter's desirability are probably not deepened as much, though the economic conflict itself may result in further expressive strains. In any event, situational satisfaction of both partners is again likely to be low, though perhaps not as low as where husband self-esteem is seriously threatened.

3. Husband has either a manual or nonmanual occupation, and the union is likely to be either hypogamous or hypergamous, though homogamy cannot be ruled out. There is no basic cleavage between husbands and wives over economic factors. Nonetheless, the husband has low self-esteem (1) despite relative objective economic success (nonmanual), or (2) because of what he defines as the large gap between success and his actual position (manual), and because of frustration or disappointment over his gap. His wife perceives no such gap, hence experiences no frustration. In this situation, he tends to seek for sources that will bolster his self-esteem—sources which, analogous to the occupation, are external to the marriage.

Given the generalization that male self-esteem is so much a function of occupational achievement, the belief that one is not "achieving" or "succeeding" leads to the effort to "achieve" outside the ascriptive confines of the conjugal setting. (Connected with this is the possibility that for workers who experience this frustration either subjectively or objectively, leisure activities become a means of "escape," a means to "get away" from work disappointments. These kinds of activities tend to be "ego-directed," a means to bolster self-esteem not reinforced in the occupational sphere, rather than being alter-directed.) As a result, the husband may begin to define expressive conjugal interaction as less desirable and exciting, since these are the kinds of behaviors which flow from these ascriptive roles. Furthermore, he may assume that because *he* defines his occupational achievement as unsatisfactory, his wife does also, though in fact she may not. This contributes even more toward expressive strain and a definition of his wife as a less desirable expressive companion.

For the nonmanual worker, extrafamilial achievement may take the form of immersion in voluntary associations, and for the manual worker, large amounts of time and energy are invested with his "male buddies" in "masculine activities" such as hunting, car-racing, etc. Little time or energy is left for conjugal companionate behaviors. It may be that in this situation wives with low self-esteem are apt to conflict more often and more intensely with their husbands and to perceive low situational satisfaction. His satisfaction with the marriage is problematical since his major life interests lie outside it, but it would seem that as conflict with his wife over these issues increases, his satisfaction will decrease. On the other hand, if she does not conflict, this may be related to her high self-esteem as well as satisfaction with the situation regardless of her husband's evaluations.

A further complicating factor is the possible impact that the legitimacy of this type of behavior might have on wife self-esteem. It seems probable that the wife of the manual worker is less likely to consider the above type of behavior as a threat to her self-esteem, since extensive husband interaction with nonconjugal male significant others is part of lower-class life.[15] She is thus less likely to engage in frequent and intensive conflict. Since within nonmanual strata, extensive, noneconomic, extrafamilial behavior is less legitimate, its actual appearance may pose more of a threat to wife self-esteem, thus resulting in more frequent and intense conflict.

In those cases where either manual or nonmanual workers attempt to "achieve" in terms of the "other woman" (or women), the wife is quite likely to conflict and to define her situation as unsatisfactory. The resultant conflict will probably increase husband dissatisfaction as well.

4. Husband is a manual worker, the union is hypogamous, and there is basic economic cleavage between partners. The wife possesses higher levels of achievement norms and behaviors than her husband, and she defines work as a means to "get ahead" whereas he defines it chiefly in monetary terms, as a means to "economic survival." She tends to favor a life-style or consumption pattern that is long-range, middle-

---

[15]Mirra Komarovsky, *Blue-Collar Marriage* (New York: Random House, Inc., 1962), chap. 9.

class, characterized by deferred gratifications; whereas he favors short-range considerations and immediate gratifications. He feels alienated from the opportunity structure, she does not. He may or may not perceive a gap between success goals and his actual position, but his wife does so very keenly. His self-esteem is probably already low due to his position in the occupational structure, and if his wife chooses to conflict over what she defines as his "under-achievement," he probably feels even more threatened. The frequency and intensity of wife conflict are probably related to the extent of the perceived threat that her husband's occupational behavior and the kind of life-style he provides, pose to her self-esteem. A strongly threatened self-esteem may result in her employment in spite of her husband's objections, and if her role becomes defined as "breadwinner," these strains may be transferred strongly to expressive interaction, causing husband and wife to define each other as undesirable companions.

For as Goode suggests, while married women work in ever-increasing numbers, their role is not defined as "breadwinner," except in those situations where the wife defines her husband as "underplaying" his breadwinning role.[16] This kind of definition accompanied by the wife working in order to attain the life-style he cannot or will not provide, (especially at a higher status job than her husband's) is a very serious threat to male self-esteem. Given this complex situation, it is quite likely that both partners define it as unsatisfactory.

As has been shown empirically, the probability of disorganization becomes quite high at this point,[17] but some marriages may nevertheless remain "organized" due to variations in the intensity with which wives hold to certain achievement levels, or the extent to which they press the conflict due to the degree of threatened self-esteem. Thus, if she conflicts only minimally, does not work, or if she does, her role is not that of breadwinner, there are less serious threats to male self-esteem. Consequently, there is an absence of severe economic

strain, resultant expressive disjunctiveness, and situational dissatisfactions. Only the usual male and kin significant others pose any threat to expressive relations.

Some recent observers have noted the existence of this fourth pattern among many Negro families. Pettigrew and Bernard have commented on the relative integration of Negro females into the societal opportunity structure vis-à-vis Negro male alienation. The more achievement-oriented female, often able to hold a higher-status job than her husband's (if he holds any job at all) is quite likely to conflict with her husband because of his "underachievement." Pettigrew writes: "The Negro wife in this situation can easily become disgusted with her financially dependent husband, and her rejection of him further alienates the male from family life."[18] Theoretically, the same general notions hold for certain white marriages as well.

5. Finally, there is the lower-lower stratum. Of late, increasing attention has been given to that segment of the population where both males and females are effectively alienated from almost all aspects of the larger society. "Achievement," "success," are meaningless terms, and Schwartz has argued that even the notion of male self-concept as a function of occupation can be seriously questioned.[19] Whites as well as Negroes are to be found within this category. Work may be viewed negatively, as a threat, because in comparison to unemployment or relief checks, it is less rewarding and more uncertain.[20] Not only are stable economic patterns for the nuclear family missing, so are meaningful expressive patterns. Nonwork activities become the center of one's existence, the major sources of one's identification. Self-esteem, for the male in particular, comes almost totally from significant male others in the same situation. The source of female self-esteem is em-

---

[16]*Op. cit.*, 1956, 60–64.
[17]In press.

[18]George F. Pettigrew, *A Profile of the Negro American* (Princeton, N.J.: D. Van Nostrand, 1964), 16; Bernard, *op. cit.*
[19]Michael Schwartz, "The Northern United States Negro Matriarchy: Status vs. Authority," *Phylon*, 1965, *26*, No. 1, 18–24.
[20]Louis A. Ferman, "Sociological Perspectives in Unemployment Research," in Arthur B. Shostak and William B. Gomberg, *Blue-Collar World* (Englewood Cliffs, N.J.: Prentice Hall, Inc., 1964), 504–14.

pirically uncertain. With both bases for the maintenance of the nuclear family missing, marriage, in the larger societal sense, hardly exists.[21]

It is well known that marital patterns of this sort account for the highest rates of desertion, illegitimacy, and dependency. However, as Goode has shown, the United States, in comparison to many Latin American countries, has a far lower incidence of these types of phenomena.[22]

SUMMARY

In this paper an attempt has been made to show that the notion of a "uniform American family" based chiefly on expressive gratifications is theoretically sterile and misleading substantively. In view of the inherent tendency toward complexity and differentiation within a modern society, it seems logical to look for evidence of these same processes within the conjugal family. Uniformity of family structure and interaction is quite apparent in a pre-modern society due to the dominance of agriculture. The joint participation of husband and wife in agricultural behaviors obviously contributed to marital organization.

In a modern society the occupational structure is highly differentiated, and the congruence of husband-wife relationships toward that structure becomes problematic. The essence of these relationships changes from joint behavior *per se* to joint (or conflicting) ideas about occupational behavior of the husband and also

of the wife. These relationships are in large measure a consequence of the class backgrounds of the husband and wife. (In a modern society, mate-selection is less controlled, less systematic, and more random than in a pre-modern setting. The probability is less that partners will have a homogeneous background.) These occupational relationships have a strong interactional effect with the self-esteem of both husband and wife. In turn, these complex elements have varying degrees of negative or positive consequences on the affective, expressive, emotional, etc., dimensions of marriage, as well as on one's perceived satisfaction with the total situation. Note that this approach does not ignore the place of expressive dimensions. Instead, it seeks out the conditions under which they are weakened or strengthened. Another useful feature is that it combines several levels of analysis: structural-cultural, social psychological, interpersonal, and individual.

We suggest at least five different patterns or differentiated forms that the conjugal family can take in connection with different kinds of relationships to the occupational structure. (On the basis of census data, one could argue that these marriages within these patterns would have differing rates of disorganization. As we move from patterns one to five, we would expect the rates of disorganization to increase correspondingly.) There may be other major patterns, and there are undoubtedly several other variations within all these patterns. The actual usefulness of this framework can, of course, be determined only through empirical research. In any event, it is hoped that these few suggestions will stimulate systematic investigation into the relationships between occupation and conjugal family, to see what kinds of linkages do, in fact, exist.

---

[21]Murdock, *op. cit.*
[22]William J. Goode, "Illegitimacy, Anomie, and Cultural Penetration," *American Sociological Review*, December, 1961, *26*, 910–25.

31.

FLORENCE ROSENSTOCK AND BERNARD KUTNER

ALIENATION AND FAMILY CRISIS

References to alienation abound in both technical literature of the behavioral sciences and journalistic attempts at social diagnosis. Although the concept of alienation may, in fact, be applicable to a range of settings, widespread and impressionistic usage has tended to overemphasize the dramatic aspect of the term while obscuring its basic connotations. If alienation is actually to become a useful analytic tool, therefore, its definitions must be clarified and its theoretical relevance for different settings must be systematically explored. We begin this paper by pointing out the uniqueness of alienation as a psychosocial concept, and thus distinguishing it from alienation as used in a strictly clinical sense. Following this, we allude briefly to two of the major articles in the social sciences which have sought to define psychosocial alienation and to demonstrate its utility. Finally, we attempt to clarify the alienation concept further by setting it in the theoretical framework of an ongoing social system, namely, the nuclear family in the process of response to family crisis. In this context, alienation is designated as one possible mode of crisis response, and the implications of this pattern are discussed.

ALIENATION AS A PSYCHOSOCIAL CONCEPT

Certain basic assumptions differentiate the use of alienation as a psychosocial concept from its application as a clinical description. Within the clinical fields of psychiatry and psychoanalysis, alienation refers to a pervasive individual pathology—a state of defective personality functioning that is the outgrowth of a neurotic developmental process.[1] The origins and characteristics of this condition were discussed initially in the works of Karen Horney and have been further elucidated in more recent writings of other investigators.[2]

For the social scientist, in contrast, a diagnosis of alienation does not denote a pervasive personal state. Rather, it always implies reaction to a particular social system or context, and thus it is situation-relevant. One may point out here that to be alienated from a social context is different from being away from, apart from, or unaware of it. Such absence may in some circumstances constitute a response to alienation. The condition of alienation itself, however, is a negative form of involvement in a social system: an individual is present within, cognizant of, or somehow implicated by the system, although he perceives that it cannot fulfill his goals or provide the outcomes he values.

The other major distinction between the clinical and the psychosocial uses of the alienation notion is this: while alienation from any particular group or system is a subjective experience, it is not necessarily pathological, nor painful, nor need it render an individual dysfunctional. Rather, it may enhance the quality or meaning, or increase the salience, of his involvement in other systems. Moreover, it may incorporate a conscious and deliberate decision regarding the most likely sources of satisfaction for him.

This selection is reprinted from: Florence Rosenstock and Bernard Kutner, "Alienation and Family Crisis," *The Sociological Quarterly*, 1967, *8*, 397–405.

Reprinted with the permission of the authors and publishers.

The research on this paper was done at the Center for Social Research in Rehabilitation Medicine, a unit supported by Grant RD-1634-P, Vocational Rehabilitation Administration.

[1]Karen Horney, *Neurosis and Human Growth* (New York: W. W. Norton, 1950).

[2]*Ibid.*; Karen Horney, *Our Inner Conflicts* (New York: W. W. Norton, 1945); *American Journal of Psychoanalysis*, 1961, *21*.

OTHER APPROACHES TO THE CONCEPT OF PSYCHOSOCIAL ALIENATION

Psychosocial alienation has been systematically examined at two levels, best represented by the following questions:

1. What are the subjective components of an alienated individual's perceptions of a particular social system and his relationship to it?
2. What are the characteristics of or circumstances within a system that give rise to such perceptions?

In his comprehensive summary article, Melvin Seeman has identified five possible attitudinal components of alienation: powerlessness, normlessness, meaninglessness, social isolation, and self-estrangement.[3] The historical background of each dimension is reviewed in the article, and a set of social-psychological operational definitions is proposed.[4] These different aspects of alienation seem to relate to the individual's perceptions of his relationships to larger social systems—to society in general, to work, to the political arena. Seeman points out in addition, though, that "the five variants of alienation . . . can be applied to as broad or as narrow a range of social behavior as seems useful."[5] Presumably, then, one might also study alienation in the family, the club, or in other primary groups organized for different purposes.

The individual dimensions of alienation identified by Seeman have been incorporated in an interesting conceptual model proposed by F. B. Waisenen.[6] He points out that both the social system and the self systems of individual members are goal-oriented and are organized, on the basis of roles, to facilitate goal attainment.[7] If the goals of the two systems are in accord—that is, if individuals perceive that the goals toward which they are directed are goals that can be fulfilled by their participation as system members—then a condition of stability is pres-

ent.[8] If, however, a discrepancy occurs between the self-goals of members and the goals that they perceive as being satisfied by the system, the condition that obtains is alienation.[9] Waisenen indicates that alienation in these terms can also be viewed from the standpoint of dissonance theory.[10] He quotes Festinger's comment that cognitive dissonance refers to a situation in which "a person knows two things —for example, something about himself and something about the world in which he lives— which somehow do not fit together."[11]

Waisenen links his formulation with that of Seeman by noting that the subjective dimensions of powerlessness, normlessness, meaninglessness, estrangement, and isolation are, in fact, likely to be the feelings that reflect such a perception of discrepancy between self and social system.[12] The presence of these feelings for an individual, in turn, may provoke one or another attempt to reduce the alienative discrepancy and restore consonance or stability.[13] As possible modes of adaptation to alienation Waisenen lists those which Merton has proposed in his typology of responses to anomie— innovation, rebellion, retreatism, conformity, and ritualism—and adds also adjustment.[14]

ALIENATION IN THE FAMILY SYSTEM

Waisenen's approach integrates and unifies a number of previously developed theoretical points, and provides a lucid and interesting guide for understanding how feelings of alienation may accrue to participants in, presumably, any social system. As a framework for a more intensive examination of alienation in a particular system, we take as our point of departure the nuclear family, both because it has been relatively neglected in terms of systematic research on alienation and because it is a salient

[3]Melvin Seeman, "On the Meaning of Alienation," *American Sociological Review*, December, 1959, *24*, 783–91.

[4]*Ibid*, 784–91.

[5]*Ibid.*, 788.

[6]F. B. Waisenen, "Stability, Alienation, and Change," *Sociological Quarterly*, Winter, 1963, *4*, 18–31.

[7]*Ibid.*, 21.

[8]*Ibid.*

[9]*Ibid.*, 22.

[10]*Ibid.*, 26.

[11]Leon Festinger, *A Theory of Cognitive Dissonance* (New York: The Free Press, 1957), cited in Waisenen, *op. cit.*

[12]Waisenen, 23.

[13]*Ibid.*, 24.

[14]Robert K. Merton, *Social Theory and Social Structure* (New York: The Free Press, 1949), 23.

primary reference group for most individuals at a number of possible points during the life cycle. We have chosen the process of family response to crisis as the context within which to study the dynamics of alienation.

Two questions now emerge at this point of specific application. First, what are the factors or circumstances which provoke the movement of a family system away from a condition of stability? And secondly, once a change process has been initiated in a system, can there conceivably be outcomes or resolutions other than alienation? For example, can a family act to avert alienation before it fully materializes, or, on the other hand, can an alienative process proceed beyond the point where adaptation is possible and lead instead to family breakdown? The model to be presented in this paper proposes some possible answers to the questions of change stimuli and alternative resolutions.

The goals of a family derive from two sources. Some goals relate to the functions performed by the family for larger society: these may include socialization of children and preparation for adult role performance, the transmission of cultural patterns, and the fulfillment of various personal needs of individual members.[15] Other goals may be introduced by individuals into the family context or may develop as part of the family's shared experiences.[16]

The structural elements of the family system, as indeed with any social system—the roles, sanctions, norms, and facilities—constitute the inputs necessary for goal fulfillment.[17] Family structure tends to develop relative to a number of areas of family life and in accordance with goals. These areas may include the division of labor and performance of tasks, the distribution of authority and the means employed for decision-making, the contents and patterns of communication, the boundaries of the family world and experience, the "lifespace" and relationships to other social groups, the rituals engaged in by the family and the symbols adopted, the manner and range of provision of emotional support, and the perpetuation of personal, idiosyncratic roles within the family.[18]

Family stability rests upon the maintenance of role complementarity. Ackerman defines complementarity as consisting of "specific patterns of family role relations that provide satisfactions, avenues of solution of conflict, support for a needed self-image, and buttressing of crucial forms of defenses against anxiety."[19] It must, however, be pointed out that while it will be used in a generic sense here, the concept of complementarity incorporates a great deal of variation. Different families 'fit together' in different ways and the nature and level of 'relatedness' may vary both in its adequacy for goal fulfillment, and in the satisfactions which it affords.[20]

Certain processes of change are institutionalized within the family system in terms of its characteristic as a socializing agent. "As the child grows older and becomes more socialized, obviously his roles in the family change. . . . Further . . . if the child's role changes, that of the parents must also change in complementary fashion, if the family as a system is not to be disorganized."[21] Similarly, other changes in the roles or the capacities for role performance by individuals in different family circumstances must be complemented by changes in roles and expectations of other members. It is likely that a process of disruption and restoration of complementarity goes on continuously in most families, with varying degrees of success or ease depending upon the magnitude of each necessary change, the amount of forewarning, and the adaptability of individual family members.

Should a necessary adjustment in expectations fail to occur over any protracted length

[15]Scott Briar, "The Family as an Organization: An Approach to Family Diagnosis and Treatment," *Social Science Review*, September, 1964, *21*, 248–54.
[16]*Ibid.*, 249.
[17]Waisenen, 20.

[18]Briar, 252–54.
[19]Nathan Ackerman, *The Psychodynamics of Family Life: Diagnosis and Treatment of Family Relationships* (New York: Basic Books, Inc., 1958), 86.
[20]An interesting delineation of patterns of complementarity and their implications has been provided by Wynne, Rycoff, Day, and Hirsh in their article "Pseudomutuality in the Family Relations of Schizophrenics," *Psychiatry*, May, 1958, *21*, 205–20.
[21]Talcott Parsons, *The Social System* (New York: The Free Press, 1951), 195.

of time, however, the process of role change may lead to alienation of members from the family system. Parsons describes this situation: "Alienation of the actor from his collectivity will exist where the various categories of qualities . . . are differently assessed; that is, where the expectations of the actor concerning himself do not correspond to the expectations which others have formed concerning him."[22] In circumstances where such dissonance occurs, Parsons continues, the individual may experience internal conflict as well as disruption of his relationships with other system members.[23]

THE CRISIS EVENT

To the extent that it causes role change, any event constituting a crisis may threaten family stability and thus may represent a potential precipitant toward alienation among family members. Hill defines crisis as "an event that strains the resources which families possess, cannot be solved by the repertory of ready-made answers provided by the mores or built up out of the families' previous experience with trouble, and require the family to find new (and usually expedient) ways of carrying on family operations."[24] He points out that "one major effect of crisis is to cause changes in . . . role patterns. Expectations shift, and the family finds it necessary to work out different patterns. In the process, the family is slowed up in its affectional and emotion-satisfying performances until the new patterns are worked out and avenues of expressing affection are opened once more."[25] Here, then, is a situation in which there may occur a discrepancy between the goals of individuals and the goals that can be met by the family system. Hill has proposed a useful classification of crisis situations based on their implications for the family role configuration. He identifies crises of dismember-

ment, crises of accession, crises of demoralization, and crises of demoralization plus dismemberment or accession.[26]

PATTERNS OF RESPONSE TO FAMILY CRISIS

In Hill's view, the general process of crisis resolution may be thought of as having four steps: the crisis event, disorganization, recovery, and reorganization. These stages occur in what he terms a "roller coaster" profile.[27] Hill indicates, however, that the actual pattern of adjustment varies among families, and according to the particular crisis.[28]

By introducing a few additional concepts into Hill's schema, it becomes possible to chart some of the complexity and individual variation in crisis response. First, it is apparent that not every family that experiences a period of disorganization following crisis will recover from it. Thus, dissolution ought to be included as a possible outcome of the process of family crisis resolution. Secondly, and more significantly, since a crisis has been designated as a situation that causes role change and may alter the goal-fulfilling capacities of the family, it would appear that alienation may also represent a mode of crisis response. Figure 31-1 illustrates this proposed elaboration of the paths by which family crisis may be resolved.

Referring to Figure 31-1, one notes that the period of postcrisis disorganization may have different outcomes. The family unit may quickly and totally dissolve, thus resolving the crisis. Such dissolution would be characterized by relinquishing the family home and by permanently intended separation of family members. Or family disorganization may give rise directly to the condition of alienation, that is, to a discrepant relationship between members' goals and the goals that they perceive the family can satisfy at that point. As indicated before, such perception of discrepancy is likely to be manifested in some combination of the attitudes of

---

[22]Talcott Parsons (ed.), *Toward a General Theory of Action* (Cambridge, Mass.: Harvard Univ. Press, 1951), 151.
[23]*Ibid.*
[24]Willard Waller, *The Family: A Dynamic Interpretation*, rev. by Reuben Hill (New York: Holt, Rinehart & Winston, Inc., 1951), 465.
[25]*Ibid.*, 464.

[26]*Ibid.*, 458.
[27]*Ibid.*, 465.
[28]*Ibid.*, 464.

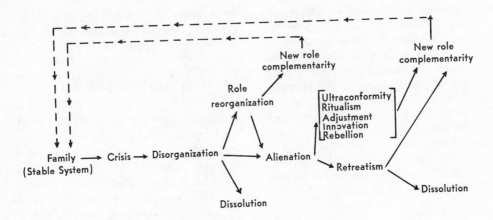

FIGURE 31-1. The role of alienation in the resolution of family crisis.

powerlessness, meaninglessness, normlessness, estrangement, and isolation.

Another alternatively attempted mode of crisis response emerging from a period of family disorganization may be role reorganization. The two general paths of response illustrated in Figure 31-1 may be construed as elaborations of Hill's concept of reorganization. Following one such path, a new complementarity of roles and role expectations may be developed collectively by family members, thus resolving the crisis and restoring the family to a stable functional level. Branching in the other direction, altered role expectations may develop in a conflicting or discrepant manner, initiating or perpetuating a process of alienation among family members.

The concept of alienation appears in Hill's discussion of divorce as a crisis. However, he uses the term largely in describing only the marital dyad, and identifies alienation not only in terms of response to crisis, but also as the precipitant of crisis and even as the crisis itself.[29] The present schema, somewhat differently, designates alienation specifically as a response to crisis and to the accompanying disorganization and role change. This model is proposed as a guide for empirical research and increased understanding, and is generally applicable, we believe, to all categories of crises—

those caused by external factors as well as those precipitated by interpersonal conflict.

The condition of alienation, whether it derives from a state of family disorganization or from an attempt at role reorganization, may give rise to the different responses described by Waisenen and shown in Figure 31-1. Retreatism, for example, as a mode of response to alienation following crisis, consists generally of the individual's abandonment of social system goals and commitment solely to the self system. This may involve the voluntary or involuntary separation of alienated members from one another or from the rest of the family, or the social and psychological withdrawal of such members even though they are physically present.[30] Either form of retreatism may, as indicated in Figure 31-1, then conceivably either lead to family dissolution or else permit the establishment of a new family role complementarity. Such complementarity may either exclude the alienated members or assign them passive roles.

Ultraconformity may be viewed as the opposite response: the individual attributes high salience to the goals of the social system, while disregarding self goals.[31] Here, alienated family members might assume martyr roles, presumably replacing the feelings of alienation

---

[29]Waller, rev. by Hill, chap. 23.

[30]Waisenen, 23.
[31]*Ibid.*, 27.

with attitudes of altruism and family commitment.[32]

The adaptive mode of ritualism represents "routinized behavior dissociated from both the goals of the self system and the goals of the social system. The individual 'goes through the motions.' "[33] In an adaptation of this type, active feelings of alienation may be replaced by more pervasive attitudes of detachment or passive resignation.

More positive responses to alienation would seem to be those in which deliberate alteration of either the self system or the social system occurs. Innovation and rebellion as adaptive modes would involve the introduction of changes in the goals or the norms of the social system.[34] For the family in which a crisis is experienced, these forms of adaptation imply change in the conduct of family life to coincide with needs and expectations of those individuals experiencing alienation. Adjustment as a pattern of adaptation to alienation implies change by the alienated members of their own goals and expectations, such that they are in accord with their own perceptions of goal ful-

filling properties of the family system.[35]

Any of the six adaptive modes described would, by reducing alienation, permit the reestablishment of some level of role complementarity and the return of the family system to a stable state.

In summary it must be noted that the concepts of complementarity, alienation, and stability, used here in a general, illustrative sense, are complex notions implying substantial variation. The nature of the complementarity achieved by a family following a crisis, and the level of stability thereby engendered, may or may not differ greatly from that which was characteristic beforehand. Similarly, the amount of subjective alienation that can be borne or managed by members in a family system without jeopardizing system functioning may vary from time to time, and from member to member.

We have attempted, in this paper, to work toward clarifying the meaning of alienation and demonstrating its utility as a conceptual tool. It is hoped that the model presented will stimulate the further theoretical speculation and the methodological refinements that are necessary before the dynamics of the alienation and crisis processes can more fully be understood.

---

[32] *Ibid.*
[33] *Ibid.*
[34] *Ibid.*, 26.

---

[35] *Ibid.*, 27.

CHAPTER VIII

Fertility:
Trends and Control

T HE STUDY OF FERTILITY has many facets, and a book on marriage and the family can only touch on some of the most pertinent ones. For example, the biological aspects of fertility are of interest, but except for casual reference they are beyond the scope of this volume. Our emphasis here will be on some of the many social and psychological factors that affect fertility.

With regard to social factors, the most basic variables associated with fertility performance are income and education. The socioeconomic variables, however, are complex. Attention has to be given to aspirations for social mobility, and indeed to actual changes in status with regard to the socioeconomic factors. Some variables, such as race and ethnic variables, are related to the socioeconomic factors, but since such differences often are of a cultural type, they also may have additional relationship to fertility performance. Regional differences, and differences between rural and urban areas, similarly may be associated with fertility performance. Religion also enters into the matrix of factors in a complex way, since some religions are specific in their concerns with the control of fertility. Other social factors may enter into the picture, such as age at marriage, size of the source family or family of orientation, the happiness of the family of orientation, and so forth.

Personal characteristics may also affect fertility performance. For example, the adjustment level of individuals may be involved in their orientations toward fertility. Attitudes toward sex and attitudes toward the sex roles, liking for children, health orientation, and personality characteristics and values may also be relevant to fertility performance. Once the marriage is contracted other factors may become involved, such as adjustment or happiness in the relationship, frequency and the nature of sexual intercourse, the amount of communication within the couple, knowledge of and availability of contraceptives, and so forth. The list is incomplete, but the presence of complexity should be reasonably demonstrated.

Questions about fertility control and family planning have come to the fore in the last decade. In the report of the President's Commission on the Status of Women in 1963, titled *American Women,* an unambiguous statement was made about the place of family planning in American life. In 1968, a five-year report titled *American Women, 1963–1968* was issued by the Interdepartmental Committee on the Status of Women. The report included the following on family planning:

"Women should have opportunity for education about sex and human reproduction in the context of education for family responsibility."--*American Women,* p. 17.

Popular attitudes and public policies on family planning have radically changed since this recommendation was published in *American Women* in 1963. During this period the Federal Government has encouraged and supported family planning programs in an effort to provide freedom of choice in this matter.

President Johnson was the first President to deal forthrightly with the question of family planning. He included it in his State of the Union Messages of 1965 and 1966, and on March 1, 1966, in a Message to Congress on Domestic Health and Education, he said: "We have a growing concern to foster the integrity of the family, and the opportunity for each child. It is essential that all families have access to information and services that will allow freedom to choose the number and spacing of their children within the dictates of individual conscience."

As Secretary of Labor Willard Wirtz put it in October of 1966, 'Discussion of the planning of the Family of Man (and Woman) has been raised almost suddenly from the level of a whisper to that of open decisions openly arrived at.'

Under the Social Security Amendments of 1967, States are obligated to offer family planning services to appropriate clients. Moreover, the amendments make it possible for all social workers in departments of welfare to discuss contraception with people who frequently have inadequate or grossly erroneous knowledge of both procreation and contraception.

In July 1967, the Manpower Administration of the Department of Labor in a memorandum to sponsors of training projects recommended that all enrollees be given information on personal hygiene, the reproductive process, and family planning, and that arrangements be made for agencies or medical authorities to provide specified enrollees with planning information, services, and supplies— including contraceptive devices and drugs.

In 1968, the Secretary of Health, Education, and Welfare established a priority program within his department and set up a new post to serve as the focal point for family planning policy and coordination. On July 16, 1968, President Johnson appointed a Committee on Population and Family Planning to review Federal policies and programs in relation to worldwide and domestic needs in the area of population and family planning.

The Supreme Court handed down a significant decision in 1965 which held that the Connecticut statute prohibiting the use of contraceptives, or the giving of medical advice or information to prevent conception, was unconstitutional because it invaded the right of marital privacy.

Factors associated with fertility control cannot be underestimated. Aside from motivational factors, if people do not have correct or usable information with regard to techniques, we cannot expect very effective fertility control or planning. In a recent study on a liberal university campus, for example, slightly less than a fifth of the underclass students were *uninformed* about contraceptive techniques entirely, and in the upper class group less than two-thirds of the girls understood such female-oriented techniques of fertility control as the rhythm method or the douche, and less than a fifth of them understood a method such as the use of a diaphragm. (Grinder, Robert E., and Schmitt, Sue S., "Coeds and Contraceptive Information," *Journal of Marriage and the Family,* 1966, 28, 471–479.) With the arrival of oral contraceptives on the scene, knowledge of techniques of control appears to be of a different order. Information about the existence of the "pill" is easily communicated, and, by contrast to techniques such as the use of a diaphragm, instruction on use does not involve detailed discussion. Studies of the dissemination of information and use of oral contraceptives are in process, and preliminary findings appear to be consistent with a report from the *National Fertility Study, 1965,* which surveyed aspects of reproductive behavior for a national sample of married women living with their husbands and less than 55 years of age. It was found that younger and more educated women were using the "pill" more often, and indeed a majority of the young women with college training had already used it. The authors projected an increased use and note the acceptance of this new technique for controlling fertility. It is interesting to speculate, however, as to the effect of knowledge about the pill. Will the near universality of knowledge about the pill lead to a general reduction in knowledge about other methods? If so, will this have any significant impact on unplanned fertility? (Ryder, Norman B., and Westhoff, Charles F., "Use of Oral Contraception in the United States, 1954," *Science,* 1966, *153,* 1199–1205.)

The reader should not get the impression that questions of fertility control revolve only around matters of knowledge and motivation. Questions about fertility control have been a matter for public discussion in recent decades, and in the 60's, particularly, because of the controversy within the Catholic Church on the matter of morality and official Church policy.

Probably the most prominent force resisting the dissemination of birth control information has been the Catholic Church. This in itself represented a more permissive attitude by the higher levels of the clergy than has been encountered any time previously in the United States. Implications of the Catholic concern carry over into the morality of communities, and pockets of vested interests have created resistance to liberalization of laws prohibiting the dissemination of contraceptive information.

It may be that the position of the Catholic Church is shifting on matters of birth control, but on other matters the position seems to be more fixed and less subject to change in the immediate future. For example, on the matter of liberalizing anti-abortion laws, the Church still takes a fairly conservative position, holding that this is contrary to "natural law," and that the rights of unborn infants must be protected. However, dissent even on this issue is beginning to emerge from within the Church. Public opinion on this matter is not as uniformly in favor of making abortions available without legal restrictions as is the case in the liberalization of laws prohibiting the dissemination of birth control information. Still, examining the historical period in the United States, laws prohibiting or severely restricting abortions in the United States are somewhat in the same position that the laws prohibiting the dissemination of contraceptive information were just a few years ago.

One may examine what some organizations state regarding the removal of anti-abortion laws.

An organization most concerned with the health of the nation, the American Public Health Association, passed a resolution in 1968 as follows: "The APHA urges that access to abortion be accepted as an important means of securing the right to spacing and choosing the number of children wanted . . ."

"To this end, restrictive laws should be repealed so that pregnant women may have abortions performed by qualified practitioners in medicine and osteopathy."

The point made was that all women should have a right to safe legal abortions without qualifications. The full text of the resolution was reported as follows:

It is generally accepted that individual women and couples should have the means to decide without compulsion the number and spacing of their children.

The personal right has been supported and enhanced through governmental action at all levels.

The APHA and many other groups have joined with public agencies to secure this right and to make widely available those services that will provide a range of choice of contraceptive methods consistent with personal beliefs and desires.

However, contraceptive methods vary among users in effectiveness and suitability. Pregnancies sometimes occur due to rape, incest and difficulties in obtaining contraceptives and sometimes because of contraceptive failures.

In order to assure the accepted right to determine freely the number and spacing of children, safe legal abortion should be available to all women.

Further, the provision of abortion within the usual channels of medical care will reduce the well-known adverse health effects of illegal abortion.

The APHA urges that access to abortion be accepted as an important means of securing the right to spacing and choosing the number of children wanted.

From a comparative point of view, it must be noted that the proposal of the APHA is neither new nor untried. Several nations do not legally restrict the availability of abortions, the most notable example being Japan. Experience in those nations where abortions are freely available as desired, indicates increases in the number of legal abortions carried out and also indicates other things as well. It has become quite clear that abortion is not the most desirable way of controlling pregnancies, and thus the dissemination of contraceptive information and use of contraceptives becomes more widespread. Many issues of moral ethics, and religious values are raised along with the question of abortion. At least one interesting perspective that must be raised in such considerations is how the morality of Japan, let us say, has been affected since it has accepted the notion of available legal abortions for all those who desire them. This will be left for the exploration of the readers, but one question may be raised rather directly: Has Japan become an immoral nation through its action? We rather think not.

While the APHS may be concerned with the medical factors associated with abortion and the rights of women particularly around such a concept, the American Civil Liberties Union traditionally has given attention to the constitutional rights of individuals. Its position on the matter of abortion is similar to that of the APHS. A segment of the policy statement from the ACLU follows:

The American Civil Liberties Union asserts that a woman has a right to have an abortion—that is, a termination of pregnancy prior to the viability of the fetus—and that a licensed physician has a right to perform an abortion, without the threat of criminal sanctions. In pursuit of this right the Union asks that state legislatures abolish all laws imposing criminal penalties for abortions performed, for whatever reason, by a licensed physician. The effect of this step would be that any woman could ask a doctor to terminate a pregnancy up to the time that the fetus becomes viable. (The exact moment at which this happens is not known, but the medical profession does agree that a fetus could not possibly live apart from the mother until sometime after the 20th week, and as a practical matter, even with the best medical care now available, not until several weeks later.) In this turn, a doctor could accede to the woman's request in accordance with his professional judgment without fear of criminal prosecution. Thus, the decision whether or not to continue a pregnancy would become one of the woman's personal discretion and the doctor's medical opinion. Both would be free to follow their private consciences in determining whether their religious or moral standards were being violated. No fear of criminal punishment would enter into the decision.

The ACLU holds that every woman, as a matter of her right to the enjoyment of life, liberty and privacy, should be free to determine whether and when to bear children. It is not a matter for the state to control. As long as criminal sanctions are attached to the performance of abortions, however, this freedom will not be realized. Even the recognition of special "hardship cases"—danger to the life and mental or physical health of the mother, probable fetal deformity, pregnancy resulting from rape or incest—fall short of satisfying the rights of life, liberty and privacy. Although it is true that a number of well-established religious and moral doctrines forbid abortion, we do not believe that the state has the power to force these particular religious and moral standards upon the entire community. The Union itself offers no comment on the wisdom or the moral implications of abortion, believing that such judgments belong solely in the province of individual conscience and religion. We maintain that the penal sanctions of the state have no proper application to such matters.

In this volume we present an article concerned with the problem more generally from a sociological point of view. Elmer H. Johnson examines the many-faceted problem in his article titled "Abortion: A Sociological Critique." The issues involved in public policy are not resolved, but the forces and factors involved in the formation of public policy are examined.

Topics related to religious issues in the control of fertility are many. A number of hypotheses have been phrased on what the expected Catholic fertility performance will be. A recent study sampled households in six metropolitan areas and provided information that appears consistent with a hypothesis that the Catholic population is likely to move in the directions of the larger and more secularized aspects of American society. While it was found that Catholics had larger families, shorter time intervals between children, and a longer period of involvement in actual fertility performance than Protestants, it was found that in the suburban areas where a maximum of urbanization is implicit, the Catholic-Protestant differences tend to be very small. (Zimmer, Basil G., and Goldscheider, Calvin, "A Further Look at Catholic Fertility," *Demography*, 1966, 3, 462–469.) The conclusion is part of a general assumption that greater communication and a broadening of the base of secular education moves groups toward convergence in their characteristics.

Similarly, a recent study indicated that while differences in fertility between rural and urban areas persist, the conclusion reached is as follows: "As the population continues to become more highly urbanized then as socioeconomic differences are further diminished, rural-urban differences in fertility will doubtless continue to narrow." (Beegle, J. Allen, "Social Structure and Changing Fertility of the Farm Population," *Rural Sociology*, 1966, *31*, 415–427.

Up to this point we have emphasized the factors involved in fertility. We have not actually indicated what the fertility changes have been. To illustrate these, we reproduce a figure that indicates the fertility rates for whites and non-whites for women in the childbearing years in the period from 1920 to the middle of the 1960's. Readers may wish to refer to the original source, a pamphlet titled *Natality Statistics Analysis, United States–1964,* published by the National Center for Health Statistics, U.S. Department of Health, Education & Welfare (Series 21, Number 11), 1967. The consequences of fertility may be viewed as the current status of population in the nation, and such information may be obtained from government publications like: *Population Estimates,* Bureau of the Census, U.S. Department of Commerce (Series P-25, Number 381), 1967. In the latter publication population projections and their relationship to fertility performance are provided, along with analyses of the composition of the population on the bases of age, sex, color, and other characteristics. Government sources in these matters are excellent, and provide detailed information in many aspects of fertility and population research even down to such matters as an analysis of multiple births. To wit:

The Hellin-Zeleny hypothesis for the frequency of multiple deliveries states that if twins occur once in N deliveries, then triplets will occur once in N^2 deliveries, and quadruplets once in N^3 deliveries.

The observed ratio of twin to total deliveries for all races in 1964 was 1/96. From this, the expected frequency of triplets is 1/9216. The actual frequency of 1/9977 was slightly lower (by about 8 percent) than the expected frequency. The actual frequency of quadruplets, 1/663,470, was 33 percent greater than the hypothesis 1/884,736. (*Multiple Births, United States–1964,* National Center for Health Statistics, U.S. Department of Health, Education & Welfare (Series 21, Number 14), 1967.)

✿   ✿   ✿

In the remaining two articles, emphasis is placed on the study of fertility in a broader context. The article by Norman D. Ryder titled "The Character of Modern Fertility," examines what has happened to fertility rates generally and how these are measured, the general modes for regulation of fertility, and future prospects. An indication is given in this article about the relationship of fertility performance to trends for nations. The area of demography to which this would refer is enormous, and a subject matter in its own right. Students who are interested in studying the "demographic transition" may find it useful to refer to literature in the field of demography. An example for a specific nation is: Freedman, Ronald, "The Transition from High to Low Fertility: Challenge to Demographers," *Population Index,* 1965, *31*, 417–430. Dealing with fertility at the level of nations, the question of how programs can be developed and managed is an important one. An article on this topic to which students may wish to refer suggests that such problems are entirely possible. It examines some problems involved in introducing programs, and includes the beliefs about popuation dynamics and lower class cultures. (Stycos, J. Mayone, "Obstacles to Programs of Population Control—Facts and Fancies," *Marriage and Family Living,* 1963, 25, 5–13.) The consequence of the "demographic transition" if fertility is not brought under control is the "population explosion." The question of whether or not the explosion will ever come under control is often debated in the literature. The consensus is alarmist, and most writers are concerned that fertility control cannot become effective in time to avoid massive problems in the entire world. At least one scholar takes exception to the majority view. He writes: "The trend of the nationwide movement toward fertility control has already reached a state where declines in death rates are being surpassed by declines in birth rates. Because progress in death control is slackening and progress in birth control is accelerating, the world has already entered a situation where the pace of population growth has begun to slacken. The exact time at which this 'switch-over' took place cannot be known exactly, but we estimate it to have occurred about 1965. From 1965 onward, therefore, the rate of world population growth may be expected to decline with each passing year. The rate of growth will slacken at such a pace that it will be zero or near zero at about the year 2000, so that population growth will not be regarded as a major social problem except in isolated and small 'retarded' areas." (Bogue, Donald J., "The End of the Population Explosion," *The Public Interest,* 1967, No. 7, 11–20.)

We have alluded to many aspects of fertility performance and its consequences on demographic characteristics of a nation. We have introduced a few sparse pieces of information on this topic here. Thus, it is appropriate that the last article in this chapter provide a more systematic review of the topic. The article is by David M. Heer and is titled "Economic Development and the Fertility Transition."

Additional materials on fertility control will be found in Chapter XI, which deals with economic factors in family life.

32.

LOIS WLADIS HOFFMAN AND FREDERICK WYATT

SOCIAL CHANGE AND MOTIVATIONS FOR HAVING LARGER FAMILIES: SOME THEORETICAL CONSIDERATIONS

In recent years there has been an increase in the size of the American family. This is especially marked in the middle class where more families have three or four children than formerly. Furthermore, it has been established that this increase is due not only to medical advances or to ineffective family planning; it is largely the result of choice. Freedman, Whelpton, and Campbell (8), interviewing a national sample of married women between 18 and 39, found that almost three-quarters of their sample *expected* to have families of two, three, or four children; a similar number felt that three or four children would be *ideal*. The authors also reported that the number of children considered ideal has increased even since 1941 when 27 percent considered four or more children ideal; in 1955, as many as 49 percent considered four or more ideal.

The increase in family size is usually assumed by writers on the subject to be the result of technological advances and economic prosperity which have removed some of the hardships of parenthood. This view assumes that there is a relatively unchanging desire for large families and that fertility rates are determined by whether the current social setting facilitates or impedes the expression of this desire. However, it is possible that the very *motives* for reproduction are not fixed but respond to social change, and that the current increase in family size is in part a reflection of increased motivations for larger families.

Studies of motivations for reproduction can be broadly classified as psychoanalytic and demo-

graphic. The psychoanalytic studies (1, 2, 3, 5) have been concerned with motivations for pregnancy *per se* rather than for having large families, and all of them have tended to view the motivation for reproduction as fixed—more or less unresponsive to the social milieu. The demographic studies dealing with psychological motivations (12, 14, 16, 17, 19, 20, 21, 22) have been interested in family size and in fertility *trends*, but they have not related the psychological motivations investigated to social change.

The approach presented in this paper deals specifically with motivations for having larger families and with the social changes that may underlie these motivations. (Thus, only those facets of the motive for reproduction which might be seen as responsive to recent social change and which seem most relevant to having three or more children will be taken up.[1]) We will consider three groups of social trends that may have influenced women's attitudes toward maternity: changes that have occurred in the woman's role; changes in the parent role and the concept of parenthood; and the loneliness and alienation that seem to characterize individuals in our society.

CHANGES IN THE WOMAN'S ROLE

Technological advances have brought about the following changes:

This selection is reprinted from: Lois Wladis Hoffman and Frederick Wyatt, "Social Change and Motivations for Having Larger Families: Some Theoretical Considerations," *Merrill-Palmer Quarterly*, 1961, 6, 235–244.

Reprinted with the permission of the authors and publisher.

[1]Mishler and Westoff (14) point out that decisions concerning the first and third births are especially significant for population trends. The decision regarding the first child is usually one of timing. This would probably affect eventual family size only in that it influences the age and circumstances of the couple when the decision for the third child is made. Thus, it seems more parsimonious in the present context to consider these factors as they influence the decision about a third child at the time the decision is made, rather than to study the original reasons for the timing of the first birth.

1. Housework has become less time-consuming.
2. The remaining household tasks are the dullest and most uncreative (e.g., dusting). Areas where formerly a woman could make a special contribution as homemaker have been lost through the greater availability of commercial products (e.g., package mixes) and through standardization of techniques (e.g., the modern cookbook).
3. There are more women employed outside the home and greater opportunities for women to find such employment.
4. A housewife's time has potential monetary value, and, because of mass production efficiencies, performance of tasks in the industrial setting is more efficient than their performance in the home. In most cases, it is more economical for the woman to work for wages and buy commercial products than to spend her time making the products at home for her own family.

These conditions mean that being a housewife without children or a mother whose children are all in school is not a full-time job, not a creative job, and not a functionally efficient job.[2] This was not the case 30 years ago, nor is it true today for the woman who has a preschool child.

At the same time a change has taken place in the notions of what a woman should expect from life. There seem to be more opportunities and desires for personal happiness and self-fulfillment. Perhaps "choice" and "freedom" are the key words. A woman's life has become much less circumscribed. There are more choice points in her life, more paths available, more opportunities for activity and impulse expression; and the possibility that she will make the accompanying decisions for herself is greater. These are not, however, unmixed blessings; presumably they can produce doubt and anxiety, as Fromm, among others, has suggested (9).

In addition, the Protestant ethic seems to be still very much alive in the United States.[3] In some ways it may be stronger than ever. The present-day "idle rich" are more likely to be involved in public works than in the pursuit of sheer pleasure. The conspicuous use of leisure seems to have become the creative or efficient use of leisure. The do-it-yourself projects are not just an answer to inflation but have become a sign of the productive use of leisure time and a great source of prestige and esteem. There seems to be an orientation toward a full and useful life which combines creativity and contribution.

To these we add another consideration: the woman of today who has borne two children is younger, more attractive, healthier, and more energetic than her mother or grandmother was after her second child, and she has a longer life ahead of her.

What can this young and vigorous woman look forward to when her second and last child enters school? If she does not choose employment, she can anticipate a life of housework which she very likely considers dull, or at least an insufficient contribution to her family or the world. For some women, particularly in the upper middle or upper class, unpaid work in voluntary organizations may fill out their lives. Many women, however, who do not choose employment, may feel they have chosen a path of "boon-doggling," and their neighbors will disapprovingly concur. Work is virtue. The mother of five children and the employed mother are both hard workers, but the mother of two school-age children who is not employed is a woman of leisure.

In contrast, having a child is highly creative —both in the physical sense of producing it and in the social sense of molding it. The decision to have another baby is a decision to break the established daily routines. With a new baby the woman introduces a major change in her life and in the lives of her family. Furthermore, the care of the infant provides an area where the woman is not replaceable. In America, few other persons would be entrusted with the total care of an infant. In addition, the care of a very young child is a full-time job, and while it often may not seem efficient, there are no acceptable alternatives.

Thus, the third (or later) child may be the expression of a need for creativity or for change. This child may be an escape from outside employment, boredom, unwelcome leisure, guilt about inactivity or non-contribution, and censure. It may also be an escape from independence, impulsivity, and, very much as Fromm discusses it, an "escape from freedom."

[2]These points are discussed in more detail by Cyrus (4), and data supporting them have been reported by Hoffman (11).

[3]Empirical evidence for this is presented by Morse and Weiss (15).

In addition there is today a considerable diffusion of sex roles and the definition of the woman's role is ambiguous. Bearing and mothering children are important as proofs of femininity. Not only is this the traditional feminine role, but it is now especially important because it enables the woman to avoid entering the occupational role. Employment may involve competition with one's husband and the woman may want to avoid this, not for fear of losing, but for fear of winning. The need to perceive the man as more competent is deeply rooted, and, if the woman's employment is a potential threat to this perception, it will be avoided in order to preserve the woman's sense of femininity, the man's masculinity, and the integrity of the marriage.[4] Thus, since employment is such a viable alternative, some women will be motivated to have a large family in order to avoid employment.

Mishler and Westoff (14) offer the hypothesis that excessive dependency needs are incompatible with the desire for pregnancy. The formulation presented here would lead to a different expectation. The third child can be seen as a prolongation of the period of the mother's dependency in relation to the husband. Not only is pregnancy itself an opportunity for the legitimate expression of dependency needs, but to the extent that remaining at home is a more dependent relationship to the husband than employment, prolonging this period prolongs dependency. This is assuming that we are not dealing with pathological dependency where legitimacy of roles is not a consideration. While extreme dependency needs might allow the woman to languish in the traditional role of full-time homemaker with no young children, occupation, or community activities, she must be prepared to defend this position to herself and her friends or acknowledge her self-indulgence. Furthermore, personality needs are usually not unidimensional, and seemingly opposite tendencies often coexist. Thus, for some women the dependency dimension is a salient one but it involves both needs for being dependent on others and having others dependent on oneself. For such women, the ideal situation might be

---

[4]This point is discussed in more detail by Hoffman (10, 11).

having an infant dependent on them while, at the same time, both the infant and the mother are dependent on the father.

CHANGES IN THE PARENT ROLE

In the past decade the United States has become increasingly a child-centered culture, and a closely related development is the popularization of psychology. The role of the parent in socializing the child has been emphasized in the popular culture to the point where theories about heredity are now rarely heard. The stress on child-rearing and the widespread conviction that a child is what his parents have made him have had two important effects on the parental role. First, they have added challenge and importance to the child-rearing function, making it a creative and ego-involving area, for mothers at least. Being a "good mother" no longer means simply keeping the children fed and clothed but implies that one is skilled in a mysterious and difficult art. The creative aspect of the mother role is particularly important when highlighted against the background of the increased standardization and mechanization of the housewife role and the increased desire for self-fulfillment, mentioned earlier. Thus some women will be motivated for motherhood because of the challenge it imposes, this challenge being all the greater in contrast to other aspects of the woman's role.

At the same time, and largely because the skills for being a good mother are not being communicated at the same rate as is the emphasis on being a good mother, the child-rearing function is fraught with anxiety. Paradoxically, this very anxiety may operate as a motivation for reproduction, particularly for later pregnancies. The rare mother who is satisfied with her performance in rearing the first and second child may either have more children because of the gratifications it offers, or cease to, in the knowledge that she has done well. Many mothers, however, will, consciously or unconsciously, be disappointed with their handiwork, guilty and anxious about their failures. People respond differently to anxiety, but the situation often limits the possibilities. For example, the mother cannot run away from the child who is

(margin annotation: challenge to motherhood)

the focal point of her anxiety. A more appropriate solution is either to try to do better with the next one or bury her anxiety in activity. Both of these are well served by having many children. With many children, she has less involvement in one, more chances to alleviate her own sense of responsibility through the individual variations offered by her products, and less time to experience anxiety. Furthermore, it is likely that her job performance does improve with practice and so this particular defense may be reinforced by reality. In addition, the attention of others, and perhaps even her own involvement, may become focused on the quantity rather than the quality.

A trend that is closely related to the emphasis on the parent's responsibility for the child's personality and to the filtering of psychology to the grass roots is an increased acknowledgment of hostile feelings toward one's own parents. Analytic writers have sometimes discussed the first pregnancy as a hostile wish to replace one's mother. There is a modern way that child bearing can express hostility toward the mother. Today's young woman who has more children than her own mother and who often does so with a show of greater ease (e.g., being physically active throughout her pregnancy) says in effect to her mother: "What was all the fuss about? I can do a better job, on a bigger scale, and with very little effort on my part." Thus, the larger family may be an expression of hostility toward the mother. Such inter-generational conflict may not be new except in form. It is possible that the generation which mothered two-child families had exactly the same motivation, but since their mothers had large families instead of small, the form of their protest was different. These women may have been saying in effect to their mothers: "I am intelligent enough, genteel enough, and sufficiently in control of my own life, that I can have only one or two children instead of seven."

There is one other way in which the particular emphasis on child rearing might operate as a stimulus to the motivation for larger families. The modern young mother is neither drudge nor disciplinarian but warm, active, and a companion to her children. This is a more attractive model for a woman and, hence, the mother role

is a becoming one. The slim, vigorous, well-groomed woman with four children has an advantage over another woman who is not a mother. This latter point may be true only because of the transitional nature of the present situation where the stereotype of the haggard mother still exists as a contrast. Attractiveness in a mother seems doubly attractive, and the more children, the greater the emphasis to her attractiveness.

THE LONELINESS AND ALIENATION THEME

Several contemporary writers have discussed a "loneliness" and "alienation" quality as characterizing modern life. Briefly, this is described as feeling insignificant, lost and alone. This is not a new trend on the social scene, nor is it new to social scientists. Durkheim discussed it over 50 years ago (7). Like Fromm after him (9) he attributed it, in part, to Protestantism and to the lack of group affiliation. More recently, Riesman has similarly discussed it in connection with the breakdown of moral traditionalism (18). The loneliness and alienation of modern man have also been attributed to changes in productive modes, the complexity of modern politics, urbanism, the loss of religious conviction, the absence of extended family ties, and increased geographical mobility. Thus, while it is not a new trend, it may be an evergrowing one, and we will consider it as a possible basis for fertility motives.

Pregnancy itself is in some ways the fulfilled fantasy of the lonely child. The pregnant woman has a secret companion who is hers alone. The companion is always with her and communicates only to her. Like the imaginary friend of the lonely child, it is a creature of her own making.

Even after the child is born, elements of this fantasy continue. The infant's total dependency on the mother may suggest almost a fusion of the mother with the child. This is related to our earlier suggestion: for some women, having a child totally dependent on them is highly gratifying; at the same time they find it gratifying to be dependent themselves. Both circumstances involve close relationships, the antithesis of loneliness. Although these motives may not be readily articulated, they may help to make pregnancy and mothering pleasurable experiences both in the past and in anticipation.

Furthermore, a child may represent a tie between the mother's life and "immortality." Modern man may feel himself to be insignificant—sometimes acutely and depressingly aware of the evanescent quality of life. The creation of a child may involve the feeling that something of the self will continue after death. This theme has been explicitly put forth in certain religions, and it may operate independently among many persons. This motivation for fertility is not a new one, but it may be one that has become increasingly important as the belief in the "hereafter" loses ground. Another motive for pregnancy may be the desire to recreate the self. The child represents to the mother herself as a child. This brings the mother still closer to "immortality" and at the same time involves a connection to the past: the child that the mother once was is re-created and will live on after she is dead.

Since the child develops out of the mother and is at first entirely a part of her, the mother is sometimes able to envisage herself in two roles at the same time. She can feel as *mother* with all attendant rewards of status and self-regard and she can feel as the *child*. She can in this way relive her own childhood and give herself as child all the love and affection which she wanted in her own life, but did not always receive. In short, by having a baby, a mother has an opportunity for remaking her own life in fantasy. She can treat her infant as she wanted her mother to treat her. Women also imagine sometimes that in the child they are reproducing the husband in order to be his mother. In all these instances women repeat characteristic fantasies of their own early girlhood.

There is one more motivation for children which seems to have significance for avoiding feelings of aloneness. Participation in a secret ritual and entering into a special status group have often been thought of as means by which aloneness is avoided through merging the self with the group. Both Durkheim (6) and Fromm (9) talk of this in explaining the existence of certain social institutions. Motherhood itself is

such a group; the ritual is the bearing of a child. Through childbirth and child rearing the woman joins a special society. The society has many members and with each of them she automatically has common bonds. Kluckhohn (13) has discussed the advantages a woman has in an unfamiliar culture in establishing rapport with other women. These advantages come from sharing a common status with similar role prescriptions. Thus, simply by becoming a mother, a woman becomes part of a group and has a bond with many other persons. Furthermore, with successive children one joins more exclusive groups with whom there are even closer bonds and one does not lose membership in the larger group. In fact, with each successive child one gains a certain amount of status as an expert ("Yes, it was that way with my first, but you'll find with the second . . .").

Most of the motivations that have been organized around the loneliness theme do not deal specifically with motivations for successive children. However, the gratification of these needs with the first birth may make pregnancy and mothering events of great pleasure. Thus the motivation for later pregnancies may be the recapturing of this gratifying experience.[5]

SUMMARY AND IMPLICATIONS

It is our view that the recent increase in family size in America may reflect in part a change in women's motivations for reproduction and that this change may be a response to certain social trends. The first group of trends we discussed dealt with some of the changes in the role of women which have resulted from technological developments. Thus, for many women the role of housewife has ceased to be a satisfying or even legitimate full-time pursuit. In addition, maternal employment has increased to the point where it is a conscious possibility to most women

---

[5]Also of relevance to the theme discussed in this section is a point made by Ronald Freedman that the family itself is important as a primary group anchor in avoiding loneliness and alienation. The family of procreation has become the only primary group with any permanence. Therefore, the desire for the larger family may be a response not only of women, for whom reproduction has a special significance, but also of men.

when their youngest child enters school. In combination, these trends mean that the woman may have to choose between the housewife role and the employment role. For those women who view both alternatives negatively, having another baby can postpone the choice. The new baby represents an opportunity for the woman to avoid employment and leisure, to have a socially acceptable role which is creative and demands her very special attention, and also enables her to remain dependent and to continue in a traditionally feminine and circumscribed pattern.

We have also taken the cultural emphasis on child-rearing and the prevalent belief in environmentalism and the importance of the mother's role as a social trend that may influence fertility rates. Thus creativity and significance have been added to the role of mother just at the time they are disappearing from the housewife role. Even the anxiety which many mothers feel as a result of this emphasis may provide a motivation for larger families through the desire to have a less intensive investment in one child and to bury the anxiety in activity. Furthermore, modern child-rearing notions with their greater emphasis on warmth and companionship have made the mother role a more becoming one. Thus, technological advances have removed much of the drudgery from both the mother role and the housewife role, but modern views of child rearing have added new meaning to the mother role while the housewife role has been left empty of potential gratifications.

Several social trends have been seen by social scientists as leading to feelings of loneliness and alienation. We have pointed out how pregnancy and motherhood might provide satisfactions for the needs induced by these feelings. Thus a new baby or a large family may mean to the mother companionship, a fusion of the self and the child, a tie with immortality, and a meaningful status in society.

We would not expect that these social factors will affect all women equally. First of all, fertility is not always a matter of free choice. Subfecundity, religious attitudes against birth control, and ignorance about contraceptive methods may all influence fertility rates. Secondly,

social trends may affect certain segments of society more than others. There may be some subgroup variations in the amount of time required by the housewife role and in its potential for creative satisfactions; for some groups the employment alternative will be more viable than for others; child-rearing beliefs are not uniform; and social conditions that lead to alienation vary. Thirdly, there are personality differences that are relatively independent of the social trends although they interact with them in determining the attitude of the mother toward having another child or toward planning a large family. Thus, for example, a need for dependency may provide a motive for pregnancy only because of the existence of pressure toward employment.

Because of these subgroup differences and individual personality differences, much of this theory could be tested within the current social setting. Specified groups could be compared as to attitudes toward pregnancy and toward having another child as well as to actual fertility rates. These groups would be defined in terms of their social situation (e.g., the child-rearing beliefs prevalent in the individual's social milieu, maternal employment rates, geographical mobility, ties to the extended family) and in terms of personality factors (e.g., the woman's feelings about leisure, impulsivity, femininity). We would expect these social and personality variables, which reflect and interact with the social trends, to influence the meaning of a new baby and a large family.

In addition, the theory presented here has certain implications for social prediction. It suggests that the recent increase in family size, particularly in the middle class, reflects not only economic affluence but also an increased desire for children. It is not merely that having children is less burdensome; they are actually wanted more. If this is so, it has considerable significance for predicting population shifts. For example, if certain social trends have brought about an increased desire for reproduction, an economic recession without a corresponding change in these trends might fail to bring about a decrease in family size. If the motivation for large families is strong enough, many other "luxuries" might be given up before giving up the "luxury" of a third or fourth child. On the other hand, if economic hardship succeeded in bringing about a decrease in family size, this response might prove costly in terms of mental health.

REFERENCES

1. BENEDEK, THERESE. *Psychosexual functions in women.* New York: Ronald Press, 1952.
2. BENEDEK, THERESE. Parenthood as a developmental phase. *Journal of American Psychoanalytic Association,* 1959, 7, 389–417.
3. BIBRING, GRETA. Some consideration of the psychological process in pregnancy. In, *The psychoanalytic study of the child.* Vol. 14. New York: International Universities Press, 1951. Pp. 113–121.
4. CYRUS, DELLA. Problems of the modern homemaker-mother. In J. T. Landis and M. C. Landis (Eds.), *Readings in marriage and the family.* New York: Prentice-Hall, Inc., 1952. Pp. 392–402.
5. DEUTSCH, HELENE. *The psychology of women.* 2 vols. New York: Grune and Stratton, 1944.
6. DURKHEIM, E. *The elementary forms of the religious life.* (Trans. J. W. Swain.) London: Allen and Unwin, 1915.
7. DURKHEIM, E. *Suicide.* (Trans. J. A. Spaulding and G. Simpson.) New York: The Free Press, 1951.
8. FREEDMAN, R., WHELPTON, P. K., and CAMPBELL, A. A. *Family planning, sterility, and population growth.* New York: McGraw-Hill Book Company, 1959.
9. FROMM, E. *Escape from freedom.* New York: Reinhart, 1941.
10. HOFFMAN, LOIS W. Effects of the employment of mothers on parental power relations and the division of household tasks. *Marriage and Family Living,* 1960, 22, 27–35.
11. HOFFMAN, LOIS W. The motivation of mothers for outside employment. In I. Nye and Lois W. Hoffman (Eds.), The working mother. In preparation.
12. KISER, C. V., MISHLER, E. G., WESTOFF, C. F., and POTTER, R. G., JR. Development of plans for a social psychological study of the future fertility of two-child families. *Population Studies,* 1956, 10, 43–52.
13. KLUCKHOHN, FLORENCE. The participant observer technique in small communities. *American Journal of Sociology,* 1940, 46, 331–343.
14. MISHLER, E. G., and WESTOFF, C. F. A proposal for research on social psychological factors affecting fertility: concepts and hypotheses. *Current Research in Human Fertility* (Proceedings of a Round Table at the 1954 Annual Conference). New York: Milbank Memorial Fund, 1955, 121–150.
15. MORSE, NANCY C., and WEISS, R. S. The function and meaning of work and the job. *American Sociological Review,* 1955, 20, 191–198.
16. NOTESTEIN, F. W., MISHLER, E. G., POTTER, R. G., JR., and WESTOFF, C. F. Pretest results of a new study of fertility in the United States. *ISI Bull.,* 1958, 36 (Pt. 2), 154–163.
17. PRATT, LOIS V. The relationship of non-familial activity of wives to some aspects of family life. Unpublished doctoral dissertation, University of Michigan, 1955.
18. RIESMAN, D., GLAZER, N., and DENNY, R. *The lonely crowd.* New York: Doubleday & Co., Inc., Books, 1953.
19. WESTOFF, C. F., MISHLER, E. G., and KELLY, E. L. Preferences in size of family and eventual fertility twenty years after. *American Journal of Sociology,* 1957, 62, 491–497.
20. WESTOFF, C. F. The social-psychological structure of fertility. *Proceedings of the International Population Conference, Vienna, 1959.* Pp. 355–366.
21. WHELPTON, P. K. and KISER, C. V. Social and psychological factors affecting fertility: VI. The planning of fertility. *Milbank Memorial Fund Quarterly,* 1947, 25, 63–111.
22. WHELPTON, P. K. and KISER, C. V. (Eds.). *Social and psychological factors affecting fertility. Vol. 4. Further reports on hypothesis and other data in the Indianapolis study.* New York: Milbank Memorial Fund, 1954, 801–1086.

33.

ELMER H. JOHNSON

ABORTION: A SOCIOLOGICAL CRITIQUE

Induced abortion usually is viewed as the sum total of individuals who resort to this means to rid themselves of an unwanted pregnancy because it is clearcut evidence of sexual transgressions. In this view, induced abortion is symptomatic either of the deviant's failure to maintain an inner purity or the failure of the socialization process to prepare the individual for social conformity. Under either assumption, the individual *per se* is the object of major attention in the search for causes of the misbehavior. This individualistic orientation affords the fundamental rationalization for resort to the criminal law to repress and control induced abortion as a deviant reaction to a personal problem.

A fundamental error of the individualistic orientation is failure to recognize that induced abortion is a social phenomenon. This paper will review the difficulties raised when the criminal law becomes the societal instrument for dealing with induced abortion as a social problem. In the course of the discussion, the paper will demonstrate that abortions are a product of social interactions within groups which influence the decision that the pregnancy is unwanted and the choice of induced abortion as the means of resolving the culturally-structured dilemma.

The nature of the sociocultural organization influences the choice of particular behaviors to be defined as criminal. The criminal law reflects the values and attitudes characteristic of the society. Certain behaviors are regarded as so harmful socially that they are penalized as crimes. The particular set of cultural values affords the setting within which the political evaluation is made that these particular acts threaten group survival. The concern over abortion stems from the intimate relationship of the problem with procreation of the next generation. Major moral and religious issues are raised because induced abortion strikes at fundamental values which counterindicate the taking of human life, sexual relations outside marriage, and undermining of the vital functions of the family in communal life. Demographic and political issues are raised because abortion is among the techniques for balancing economic resources and population size.

Seeing the criminal law as facing a crisis in values, Hermann Mannheim believes that it must change with the values upon which it rests. Otherwise, the law becomes a petrified body, maintained by tradition and habit and unable to cope with the endless problems created by a dynamic world. Crime is *anti-social* behavior, he asserts, and no form of human behavior which is not anti-social should ever be treated as a crime.[1] In the case of abortion, the problem is to narrow the criminal law to those facets which are anti-social.

There are signs of a growing dissatisfaction with the employment of the criminal law as the means of societal reaction to induced abortion. One such indication is the scheduling of today's program. Moral condemnation of abortion is so ingrained in our official ethic that public discussion itself is evidence of the degree of dissatisfaction. The word "abortion" itself has emotional impact creating doubts about its use in decent conversation. Disagreement over the current policies is a phase of the process of social change and the retooling of social institutions to keep pace with changing human needs. Through debate, even though rather heated, the facts of the problem are revealed and the relative merits of alternative solutions

This article is reprinted from: Elmer H. Johnson, "A Sociological Critique," *Criminologica*, 1967, *4*, 20–28.

Reprinted with the permission of the author and publisher.

[1]Hermann Mannheim, *Criminal Justice and Social Reconstruction* (New York: Oxford University Press, 1946), 2–5.

are weighed. Ultimately, some compromise solution will be reached and included within the normative structure of social institutions. The increased discussion of abortion as a social problem indicates that this process is under way.

Abortion is only one aspect of the broader question of the place and function of criminal law as a means of controlling sexual behavior. This use of the criminal law is a by-product of the moral condemnation by the community of abortion. This emphasis assumes a sharp demarcation between the law-violators and the law-conformists in behavior and motivation. The emphasis assumes a universal disapproval by a homogeneous community of the behavior penalized through criminal law.

A different orientation is expressed in the American Law Institute's Model Penal Code and England's Wolfenden Report which would punish only those acts that are socially dangerous, independent of their moral character. This orientation separates public and private morality and makes a distinction between illegality and immorality. The law would be limited to those activities which offend against public order and decency or expose the ordinary citizen to what is offensive or injurious. It is contended that law does not build character. Rather it sets limits on obligations, thereby stunting the sense of moral obligation. Coerced behavior is not the equivalent of righteous behavior. In fact, by dealing with immorality as such through criminal statutes, the state sharply limits the potential usefulness of psychological strategies in dealing with the particular evil. Critics contend that employment of the criminal law to regulate sin as such invades private morality which properly is the province of the church. The principle of privacy in our political traditions is indicated by the concern over wiretapping.[2] In a multi-values society, this principle is a vital safeguard against moral imperialism.

Major difficulties result when the criminal law becomes the means of expressing moral condemnation:

1. Even in primitive communities, the conception of a universal response to deviation

---

[2] Joseph Fletcher, "Sex Offenses: An Ethical View," *Law and Contemporary Problems*, Spring 1960, 25, 244–257.

was overdrawn. The diversity of moral sentiments in the modern community makes the conception even more unrealistic. The diversity may be explained in part by conflicting themes within American culture which stem from, on one hand, the ascetic ideals of the early church and, on the other hand, the romantic movement's conception of sex relations in terms of personal response rather than social obligation. The conflict has been aggravated by the effect of the Industrial Revolution on relationships between the sexes.

Resort to the myth of normative universality is largely stimulated by fear of the consequences following elimination of the discrepancies between individual behavior as a reality and verbalized support of the official morality. To challenge this myth openly, it is feared, would endanger community unity and to appear indifferent to morality. There is concern that any legal means of eliminating unwanted pregnancy will undermine the social values of premarital virginity and the restriction of parenthood to marriage. Other myths are brought to the support of normative universality in order to maintain public support of statutes proscribing abortion. The dangers and complexity of the medical techniques are exaggerated. The motives for abortion are defined indiscriminately as clearly and completely antisocial. Attention is directed to the act of abortion and away from the broad range of social circumstances which stimulate such acts. Reliance on such fallacious beliefs as the basis for policy complicates the task of determining accurately and reliably the fundamental facts of the problem.

2. In the absence of universal condemnation of abortion, the processes of adjudication result in great disparities in the application of criminal laws. Responses to abortion depend heavily on the social status of the offenders, the social psychology of the individuals making official decisions determining whether prosecution will be undertaken, and the degree of tolerance a given community applies to abortion at the given time. As in the case of capital punishment, a fundamental flaw in the operation of abortion laws is the gross inequities which result in administration when the laws are framed in a spirit heavily charged with emotions.

3. There is a remarkable lack of enforcement of abortion laws because of the inherent unenforceability of a statute that attempts to prohibit a private practice where all parties concerned desire to avoid its restrictions. Because most sexual activity is clandestine, it is not easily subjected to control by public policy. Although pregnancy is obvious evidence of sexual activity, criminal prosecution is handicapped because moral values must be translated into the precise rationale of legal evidence, especially when a broad discrepancy exists between moral precept and actual practice. After reviewing several American and English studies, Glanville Williams concludes that convictions for abortion are "certainly only a minute fraction of the number of offences."[3]

Edwin M. Schur includes induced abortion under his concept of "crime without victims" which he defines as the willing exchange, among adults, of strongly demanded but legally proscribed goods or services.[4] He emphasizes the exchange situation because the woman's seeking of a proscribed service blurs the identification of the offender and victim, respectively, as in robbery, rape, and murder. Because the woman as "victim" is reluctant to testify, the state has a difficult time in obtaining proper evidence. Her reluctance may be explained by her gratitude in being rid of an unwanted pregnancy. But, even if this were not true, she is unlikely to accept the social risk of presenting herself as a reluctant mother and, possibly, an immoral person. The conviction proceedings function as status-degradation ceremonies which define the woman and other participants in the abortion situation as criminals regardless of their own self-conceptions. Here is a fundamental danger in handling of abortions as a crime because the participants are exposed to the "criminalization of deviance." The official definition of the person as a criminal has psychological impact on the deviant to move his self-image nearer the sphere of genuine criminal.[5]

4. Definition of induced abortion as a crime tends to exaggerate the differences in behavior and motivations of those persons subject to legal penalties and those not subject. Sociologists regard criminals as "normal" in that their personalities were developed through the same processes by which noncriminal personalities were developed. Instead of regarding offenders generally as biologically and psychologically abnormal, criminality is expained as a product of learned behavior in the course of social interaction.

In the case of abortion, repressive legislation is based on the fallacious assumption that such behavior is exceptional and pathological. There is ample evidence that the assumption is erroneous. In his anthropological study, George Devereux concluded: "There is every indication that abortion is an absolutely universal phenomenon, and that it is impossible even to construct an imaginary social system in which no woman would ever feel at least impelled to abort."[6]

Although scientifically valid research is not available, the statistics committee of the Planned Parenthood Federation of America estimated in 1955 that there were between 200,000 and 1,200,000 induced abortions per year in the United States.[7] Even the smaller estimate refutes the belief that abortions are exceptional. Furthermore, the practice is not confined to illegitimate pregnancies, but is widespread among the married in all races, religions, and socioeconomic classes.[8]

The motives for abortion are of extreme variety, but all operate within a sociocultural environment. Economic motives may center around threats to social status when another child would impair the family standard of living or interfere with employment of the mother outside the home. One study found that illegal abortions among married women composed a consistently greater proportion of pregnancies as the ordinal number of pregnancies increased.[9]

---

[3]Glanville Williams, *The Sanctity of Life and the Criminal Law* (New York: Alfred A. Knopf, 1957), 206–212.

[4]Edwin M. Schur, *Crimes Without Victims* (Englewood Cliffs, N.J.: Prentice-Hall, Inc., 1965), 169.

[5]*Ibid.*, 5–7.

[6]George Devereux, *A Study of Abortion in Primitive Societies* (New York: Julian Press, 1954), 161.

[7]Mary S. Calderone (ed.), *Abortion in The United States* (New York: Hoeber-Harper, 1958), 180.

[8]Glanville Williams, *op. cit.*, 210; and Schur, *op. cit.*, 12.

[9]P. K. Whelpton and C. V. Kiser, "Social and Psychological Factors Affecting Fertility: The Comparative Influence on Fertility of Contraception and Impairments of Fertility," *Milbank Memorial Fund Quarterly*, 1948, 26, 182–236.

Similarly, psychological motives involve social correlates. When fear of the effect of motherhood on youthful beauty is the motive, female vanity, as a product of the cultural emphasis on youth, becomes the stimulus for abortion. Social motives are more direct in the case of fear of illicit births or the coming of the child so early in marriage that premarital sex relations are revealed. Children may come at the "wrong time" for the father's educational or other career plans. Having a child or additional children may place the couple at odds with what is "fashionable" in their social clique.

5. Legal prohibitions, in the face of a desperate demand for such services, has created circumstances favorable to the development of a complex illicit system for providing abortions. Negative sanctions divert abortion-seekers from legal channels and favor the development of criminal institutions. There are high costs for the clients and the community. The clients are forced to pay excessive fees, to risk social stigmatization as criminals, to undergo the psychological consequences of guilt feelings, and to risk inadequate medical care. Successful operation of a criminal system on a long-term basis depends ultimately upon referrals from legitimate medical practitioners and indifferent law enforcement. These requirements imply corruption of individuals occupying status positions within the community as a whole.

The possibilities of corruption are indicated by the degree of structuring found in the operation of abortion mills. Jerome E. Bates finds similarities in practices of abortion mills qualify them as deviant types of crescive institutions. When the operation is on a large scale, the mill is structured around a hierarchy of roles. The physician-abortionist requires a secretary who evaluates the client to set the fee at what the traffic will bear and to forestall intrusion by government investigators. The business agent handles the payment of bills, salaries, splitting of fees with persons who refer clients, and bribes of officials. The contact man serves as an intermediary with sources of referral who largely are local druggists and general practitioners. Continuous anxiety over police intervention patterns abortion mill practices. Commercial linen service is avoided for fear of supplying evidence. The abortionist operates behind a surgical mask without conversing with the patient. All negotiations and preparations are conducted by others.[10]

6. Women differ in the risk that they will experience an unwanted pregnancy. First, although it would be an oversimplification to claim that universal use of contraceptives would eliminate the abortion problem, access to knowledge, and opportunity to employ contraceptives affect the probability of pregnancy. Differential access to birth control techniques is related to government policies, public mores, religious belief, and economic means. Second, attitudes toward illegitimacy differ among cultures and subcultures. Where her reference group strongly censures illegitimacy, the potential unwed mother will have greater incentive to seek abortion. Third, the coming of an additional child is more likely to precipitate an economic crisis for families with a submarginal income and a high fertility tradition. Fourth, the pregnant divorcee or widow is in a particularly vulnerable position. Fifth, with economic factors ruled out, the married woman's definition of pregnancy as unwanted will depend upon the coincidence of her self-image and the role of mother. To an important degree, her self-image is a product of her personality conditioning in earlier years and the norms of her current reference group.

7. Since induced abortions are performed in spite of legal prohibitions, a situation is created whereby some categories of applicants have greater access to the service than other categories. There is a subterranean system whereby induced abortions can be obtained. However, because pregnant women differ in their relative opportunity to gain access to this system, a form of social discrimination is produced by the legal controls.

Because of attitudes toward illegitimacy, unwed women are less likely to obtain a therapeutic abortion than married women. However, even among married women, the major difference between being labeled as a criminal or a woman receiving medical services without stigma may be their relative access to a cooperative physician and to sufficient funds for the fee.[11] To obtain illicit services, the applicant must

[10] Jerome E. Bates, *Criminal Abortion* (Springfield, Illinois: Charles C. Thomas, 1964), chapter 5.
[11] Calderone, *op. cit.*, 133.

have means to gain referral to the abortionist. A further inequity is the range of skills found among abortionists. Bates lists five types of abortion practitioners: the physician-abortionist, the abortionist with some medical training, the unlicensed general practitioner of medicine with little or no formal medical training, the amateur drawn from a variety of occupations unrelated to medicine, and the self-abortionist.[12] As the pregnant woman moves down the list in quality of service she obtains, she increases her medical risk.

8. The social structure contributes to criminal abortions by creating pressures toward deviance by women occupying particular positions in the structure. This is the theme of Robert K. Merton's "means-ends" theory. He calls attention to the possibility that crime may result from a contradiction between ends in the form of cultural values and the means by which the social structure provides for achieving them.[13]

In support of this theory, we have noted that differences among women exist in risk of experiencing an unwanted pregnancy and in the means available to meet the personal problem without resort to criminal abortion. In other words, status position in the social structure influences the degree of pressure exerted on the woman to seek a criminal abortion. Nevertheless, the criminal law would deal with the social problem of abortion as though environmental pressure were a constant factor.

Urbanization has brought changes in values which contribute to the possibility of contradiction between culturally prescribed aspirations and socially structured avenues for realizing these aspirations. Urbanization has increased material values and hence has tended to downgrade parenthood as a supreme end in life. Although acquisition of goods is held up as a universal goal, a fundamental discrepancy is created because there is not an equivalent uniformity in degree of access to these goals. When the child conflicts with material goals, the motivation to avoid motherhood is greater. The impersonality of urban relationships has promoted individualism in pursuit of goals. Marriage is

sought for sake of ego gratification through romantic love rather than in terms of acceptance of social obligations. Greater emphasis is given on relationships between husband and wife without children in the early period of marriage and upon minimizing the size of family throughout marriage. The urban mores of the middle class have increased the price to be paid for illicit birth. Abortion laws have restricted the means of avoiding births in compliance with these urban values.

9. The reputable physician is subjected to serious medico-legal problems by definition of abortion as a crime. Although the laws vary among the states, legal abortions are limited to those necessary to preserve the life of the mother. As Schur points out,[14] medical advances have narrowed the magnitude of cases qualifying in a strictly medical sense in spite of an increase in psychiatrically indicated abortions. "Therapeutic abortion" usually refers to intentional termination of pregnancy for reasons of medical necessity. This term covers a broader range of cases than legal abortions. Consequently, there is a fringe area between the two terms which restricts the doctor's freedom. Fear of legal difficulties has made hospitals reluctant to grant abortions on humanitarian (such as forcible rape) or eugenic grounds.

Physicians disagree among themselves whether non-medical factors, such as the plight of the victim of rape or the family with too many children for their economic means, should be recognized in applications for abortion. But the fact remains that physicians are placed in the situation of ignoring the plight of their patient, performing an illegal abortion, or referring the patient to an abortionist. Furthermore, the illegality of abortion has implications concerning privileged communication when his patient confides that she has perpetrated a crime through previous abortions.

10. Abortion is but one phase of the American women's effort to control when they shall bear children. Legal prohibitions can have the effect of forcing women to bear unwanted children and, in this sense, be means to further

[12]Jerome E. Bates, op. cit., 35.
[13]Robert K. Merton, Social Theory and the Social Structure (New York: The Free Press, 1949), 125–146.

[14]Edwin M. Schur, "Abortion and the Social System," in Edwin M. Schur (ed.), The Family and the Sexual Revolution (Bloomington: Indiana University Press, 1964), 371–379.

women's subservient social status in an age when emancipation of women is a major cultural theme. Associated with this aspect of abortion are the implications on the personality development of the unwanted child and the closing of all escape from the status of the illegitimate mother without penalizing equally the illegitimate father.

11. If the issues raised by abortion are to be resolved effectively, policy-making must be based on reliable facts. But examination of the literature on the subject reveals an absence of valid and reliable information on even the most general dimensions of abortion as a social problem. We do not know precisely how many induced abortions are perpetrated each year, the characteristics of the women who are aborted, the circumstances of the situations which lead to the quest for abortions, and the relative importance of various kinds of consequences in terms of effects on individuals and the community as a whole. The literature offers speculations and fragmented studies based on data of doubtful sampling reliability. In short, careful study of the abortion problem involves the researcher in the same difficulties faced by scientific inquiry in any phase of criminology: a lack of a body of fundamental data for measurement of the extent of criminal behavior and for testing of hypotheses concerning the causes and treatment of that behavior.

The inadequacy of information stems largely from the definition of abortion as a crime and the spirit of moral condemnation applied indiscriminately to all individuals involved in such behavior. Criminalization of this form of deviance forces the behavior underground even when it is consistent with values generally regarded to be prosocial. Official reports on arrests and convictions are more a description of administrative actions than of the incidence of criminal abortions. Irregular and incomplete enforcement of statutes distorts the descriptions so that comparisons among jurisdictions have little meaning.

In conclusion, the employment of the criminal law to control induced abortion raises many unanticipated problems and does little, at best, to eliminate induced abortion. Criminologists are interested in this dilemma because it is but one example of extending criminal penalties for conduct in which the social threat is innocuous but the moral condemnation intense. Other examples include drug addiction, alcoholism, homosexuality, vagrancy, and wayward minors.

Paul W. Tappan has warned against indiscriminate extension of the criminal laws to control human behavior without recognition of the dual aspect of our system of justice: "on one hand, it avoids imputing an injurious stigma to individuals whose conduct is not distinctively offensive to the community, and on the other, the stigma of conviction facilitates effective control where the conduct is truly dangerous."[15] The application of criminal law raises difficulties because this dualism is not respected. The stigma of crime is applied to too broad a range of deviants. Reform involves statutory revision and legal recognition that most aspects of the abortion should be determined largely on medical grounds. However, before such specific reforms can be affected, the general attitudes toward abortion should be freed of the indiscriminate moral condemnation of abortion regardless of circumstances. It is toward this latter purpose this paper is directed.

---

[15]Paul W. Tappan, *Crime, Justice, and Correction* (New York: McGraw-Hill Book Company, 1960), 15.

34.

NORMAN B. RYDER

THE CHARACTER OF MODERN FERTILITY

In the past hundred and fifty years, all countries which are now urbanized and industrialized have experienced a transition from a relatively high to a relatively low fertility pattern. Differences in reproductivity within this set of nations through time have been a consequence primarily of the differing dates at which they embarked on the diminution of childbearing, and these in turn were largely reflections of the extent of modernization of the country. The general character of the socioeconomic development has prescribed a single low modern fertility level.

In this essay we describe the movements of the relevant demographic indices during this transition, outline the variant modes of fertility regulation responsible for these changes, develop an argument concerning the etiology of transition, and speculate on the future of modern fertility.[1]

THE BIRTH RATE

A crude birth rate of 30 per thousand per annum dichotomizes fertility levels conveniently between high and low.[2] The nations of the world today are sorted into two clusters with respect to their birth rates: the less developed nations with rates well above 30; the more developed nations with rates well below 30. The data employed in this paper concern 28 modern nations, selected on the criteria of low fertility, substantial population size, and good information covering a reasonable span of time.[3] These nations are listed in Table 34-1, showing the decade in which the birth rate of each passed permanently below the value of 30.

TABLE 34-1. DECADE OF TRANSITION TO LOW FERTILITY

1830's:	France
1840's:	Ireland
1880's:	Switzerland, Belgium
1890's:	Sweden, Denmark, England and Wales, Scotland, Australia, New Zealand
1900's:	Netherlands, Norway, Germany, United States
1910's:	Canada, Finland, Austria, Hungary, Czechoslovakia
1920's:	Italy, Spain, Portugal
1930's:	Poland, Bulgaria, Rumania
1940's:	Soviet Union
1950's:	Yugoslavia, Japan

Although these countries have all participated in the decline of the birth rate, their particular paths towards low fertility have differed in various ways. For example: They did not begin their decline from a common high level: birth rates were much higher in eastern

This selection is reprinted from: Norman B. Ryder, "The Character of Modern Fertility," *The Annals*, 1967, *369*, 26–36.

Reprinted with the permission of the author and publisher.

[1]The task has been simplified by contributions to the subject from many participants in the World Population Conference, Belgrade, 1965. In addition, the author is indebted to the writings of Ronald Freedman and Kingsley Davis. See, for example, Kingsley Davis, "The Theory of Change and Response in Modern Demographic History," *Population Index*, October, 1963, *29*, 4, 345–366; Ronald Freedman, "The Sociology of Human Fertility," *Current Sociology*, 1961–1962, *10/11* 2, 35–68; Ronald Freedman, "Norms for Family Size in Underdeveloped Areas," *Proceedings of the Royal Society*, B, 1963, *159*, 220–245.

[2]The crude birth rate for a population is the ratio of the number of live births occurring within a specified time period to the number of person-years of exposure of the total populaton, expressed conventionally on a per thousand basis. For interpreting various values of the crude birth rate in terms of the life cycle, it is approximately true that the average number of births per married couple is one-sixth of the birth rate.

[3]The notable omissions are Argentina, Greece, Israel, and Uruguay. Nothing said here would have to be changed appreciably by what is known of fertility movements in these four countries.

than in western Europe. Nor did they experience the same tempo of transition: the more recently the nation embarked on decline, the more rapidly the birth rate was to fall. Japan accomplished in a few years what it had taken England many decades to do.

The data are adequate to permit a detailed appraisal of movements since 1900. Table 34-2

TABLE 34-2. MEDIAN CRUDE BIRTH RATES AND INTERQUARTILE DEVIATIONS, 1900–1965

Period	Median	I.Q.D.
1900–04	31.7	6.7
1905–09	31.0	6.3
1910–14	28.9	8.4
1915–19	24.0	6.4
1920–24	26.0	9.1
1925–29	23.0	11.3
1930–34	19.7	10.9
1935–39	19.4	7.3
1940–44	20.4	4.2
1945–49	22.4	5.7
1950–54	21.6	6.4
1955–59	18.8	5.9
1960–64	18.4	4.6
1965	18.3	2.6

contains two convenient measures of these changes for the set of 28 nations: the median birth rate and its interquartile deviation.[4]

Two major changes are manifest in Table 34-2. First, the median has declined continuously (by more than 40 percent since 1900) except for the experience at the ends of the two world wars, and a trough coincident with the depression. Second, the dispersion among the countries rose to a peak in the middle of the era, and has since declined steadily, again except for the wartime periods. An examination of movements of the crude birth rate nation by nation provides one important footnote. It appears that almost every nation has experienced a small rise following its era of major decline, although the disturbing effects of the depression and the Second World War often obscure the slight revival.

[4]The median birth rate is that which divides the list of birth rates for the various countries in half, when ranked in order of size. The interquartile deviation is the range of values required to bracket the middle half of the same ordered list.

Thus, the observations support the basic thesis of decline accompanying modernization and spreading from nation to nation until all are lodged firmly within the low-fertility category. In 1965 no country in the group considered as "modern" had a birth rate as high as 23; in 1900 only France was (a little) below this figure. Certainly there is diversity in the paths followed by individual nations—no less could be expected of societies with widely variant traditions and with differential exposure to war, revolution, and migration. What is surprising is the extent of current equality. As for the concave shape of the time series for the interquartile deviation, this is what would be expected in a model in which nations are successively transferred from the higher to the lower fertility category.

REFINEMENTS OF THE BIRTH RATE

The crude birth rate may give a distorted view of fertility variations through time and space because its level depends on the numbers of women in each childbearing age relative to the total population. The index customarily used to obviate this impediment is the gross reproduction rate.[5] Table 34-3 presents the distribution of modern countries by gross reproduction rate as estimated for 1965. Thus, with two high

TABLE 34-3. ESTIMATED GROSS REPRODUCTION RATES, 1965

1.80–1.89: Ireland
1.70–1.79: New Zealand
1.60–1.69:
1.50–1.59: Canada
1.40–1.49: Netherlands, Australia, United States, Scotland, Norway, Portugal, France
1.30–1.39: England and Wales, Spain, Denmark, Austria
1.20–1.29: Belgium, Italy, Yugoslavia, Finland, Switzerland, Sweden
1.10–1.19: West Germany, Czechoslovakia, Poland, Soviet Union
1.00–1.09: Japan, Bulgaria
0.90–0.99:
0.80–0.89: Rumania, Hungary

[5]If birth rates are calculated separately for the subpopulations of women in each age, with the numerators restricted to female births, then the sum of these rates for all ages is the gross reproduction rate.

and two low exceptions, the gross reproduction rates are now concentrated within some 20 percent of the mean value of 1.30. The conclusion that their fertility is highly similar has not been modified by introducing a control for differences in age distributions.

The gross reproduction rate does provide an important corrective to some false impressions derived from birth rate variations. Between the late 1930's and the early 1960's for example, the United States birth rate rose 21 percent, but the gross reproduction rate rose 58 percent. Evolution of the age distribution is responsible for this difference. The point can be generalized as follows. The chief determinant of the age distribution with respect to the current birth rate is the direction of movement of the birth rate in the preceding several decades. Because fertility was low in most countries during the 1930's, their birth rates today are artificially depressed by age distributions which are temporarily unfavorable to childbearing. Those countries which did not achieve low fertility until after the war still have an age distribution favorable to childbearing. Thus Japan's birth rate is the same as that of England and Wales, yet Japan's gross reproduction rate is 30 percent lower. On the same grounds, comparisons of the birth rate will soon be unfavorable to Japan.

As well as the general pattern of association with the sequence of prior births, the age distribution can be misshaped, in ways which depress the birth rate, by war mortality (the Soviet Union is the outstanding contemporary case) and by emigration. Despite Ireland's high gross reproduction rate, its birth rate is moderate, in large part because more than half of each cohort of Irish babies leave their homeland before completing their reproductive lifespan. This is one effective if perverse way of restricting population growth.

Even as the birth rate is faulted by defects relative to the gross reproduction rate, so is the latter technically flawed. In particular, the reproduction rate will register more fertility from year to year than the participant couples experience during their lifetimes, whenever there is a trend toward earlier childbearing. Since just such a trend has characterized most mod-

ern nations recently, the fertility levels recorded in Table 34-3 tend to be spuriously high. This is not now the case for the United States. For 20 years American fertility was distorted upward by a trend toward earlier childbearing. Now that trend has ended, the spurious surplus has vanished, and the gross reproduction rate has consequently declined.[6] The general import of this example is that we must exercise due circumspection when tempted to infer from year-to-year movements of fertility the advent of new family values, new birth control techniques, or other changes.

MODES OF FERTILITY REGULATION

The *modus operandi* of fertility reduction must take one of three forms: reduction of the probability of intercourse; reduction of the probability of conception if intercourse occurs; reduction of the probability of birth if conception occurs.[7] The first of these is control through nuptiality (in the form of higher age at marriage or lower proportions ever-married); the latter two constitute control of marital fertility.

It is presumed, on admittedly sketchy evidence, that fertility throughout Europe was once as high as it is now in the still underdeveloped nations, because of early and nearly universal marriage, and high marital fertility. Then, some five hundred years ago, marriage patterns changed in western Europe, toward a new pattern of rather high age at marriage and low proportions eventually marrying.[8] The consequence for this region was a moderately high birth rate (about 35), the level at which west-

[6]Cf. Norman B. Ryder, "The Reproductive Renaissance North of the Rio Grande," *The Annals*, March 1958, *316*, 18–24.

[7]This is actually not a complete list. The birth rate can also be reduced by the emigration of young adults. Although only one country, Ireland, has practiced this mode of fertility regulation on a more than temporary basis, it has been the general rule for rural *vis-à-vis* urban areas within nations.

[8]Hajnal presents evidence that this change occurred between the fourteenth and the seventeenth centuries, to the west of a line running from Leningrad to Trieste. John Hajnal, "European Marriage Patterns in Perspective," in D. V. Glass and D. E. C. Eversley (eds.), *Population in History* (London: Edward Arnold, 1965), 101–143.

ern (but not eastern) European nations entered the modern demographic era. In the past 150 years, the predominant transformation has been a decline in marital fertility, beginning in France and a little later in the United States, and now pervasive in the modern world. Although the data do not permit confident assertion, the modern nations now appear to be embarked on yet a fourth phase of transition: to a combination of low marital fertility and high nuptiality, again beginning in France and a little later in the United States. This is part of the explanation for the recent small rise in fertility in most modern societies. For western Europe and its overseas heirs, the sequence, in summary, has been: high nuptiality and high marital fertility; low nuptiality and high marital fertility; low nuptiality and low marital fertility; and finally high nuptiality and low marital fertility. Apparently, the nations of eastern Europe (but not Japan and probably not the Soviet Union) have abbreviated the sequence by omitting the two intermediate stages.

Patterns of age at marriage relative to present fertility levels are most diverse at present, probably because the evolution is not everywhere complete and because there are differences in the choices societies have made in their drive toward lower fertility. Gross reproduction rates are relatively high in New Zealand (with high nuptiality) and in The Netherlands (with low nuptiality); gross reproduction rates are relatively low in Japan (with low nuptiality) and in Bulgaria (with high nuptiality). But the predominant tendency seems to be convergence toward the early marriage of nearly everybody, and the careful regulation of subsequent childbearing.[9]

It is well known that the predominant mode of fertility regulation is contraception, the reduction of the probability that intercourse will result in conception.[10] So well known is it indeed that demographers have until recently ignored the importance of the alternatives of nuptiality control and abortion. Until the last few decades, information about the means being employed to restrain marital fertility has been fragmentary and anecdotal. It is generally agreed, however, that efficacious procedures (like *coitus interruptus*) have long been known and used by most if not all populations. In explaining the historical decline in marital fertility, much less weight is given to technical improvement of means (such as condom and diaphragm) than to the increased employment of these and other means.[11]

As a supplement or alternative to contraception, abortion has probably been significant always and everywhere, despite its associated danger and moral opprobrium. Because it has been illegal, the magnitude of its influence on variations in fertility through time and space is unknown and likely to remain so. Nevertheless, the more we learn of the ineffectuality of most efforts at contraception, the more we are inclined to suspect a major covert role for abortion as a second line of defense against the unwanted birth.

In the past two decades, abortion has been legalized in a number of countries characterized by insufficient and inefficient contraception and by a lot of illegal abortion. First Japan, then the Soviet Union, and subsequently all countries of eastern Europe except East Germany (and Albania) permitted abortion on socioeconomic grounds. Legal abortions rose to a high level, and birth rates dropped rapidly; the lowest fertility in the world today is found among these countries. Controls associated with legalization have reduced the health risks appreciably. Nevertheless, and entirely apart from moral considerations, abortion is an expensive alternative to contraception. Consequently, we may expect a persistent effort to induce a shift from abortion to contraception.

Although different reproductive strategies were adopted by modernizing nations in their particular paths toward the common goal, it is unquestionable that the consequent decline in fertility has everywhere been intentional and

[9]The important exceptions are Ireland, Spain, and Portugal, where tardy economic development and influential Catholicism prevail.

[10]This result can also be achieved by sterilization, but the practice has nowhere yet become quantitatively important.

[11]There may be a different judgment of the impact of the modern contraceptives—the oral progestins and intra-uterine devices because of their extraordinarily high acceptability and efficacy.

not, for instance, the outcome of the working of mysterious biological forces. Equally clear is that, with the sole exception of recent provisions legalizing abortion—which have the force of facilitating individual intent—the reproductive decisions and actions have been taken by individual couples rather than by governments or religious bodies. Indeed, what has happened has happened despite the persistent efforts by such agencies to thwart the will of the populace.

The next question to be answered, then, is: Why did couples systematically reduce the numbers of babies they were bringing into the world, in every country experiencing modernization? Despite broad agreement among demographers on the general sociocultural dimensions involved, there persists a feeling of intellectual dissatisfaction that the complex of interdependent elements remains far too diffuse to permit confident specification of the necessary (let alone the sufficient) conditions for modern fertility regulation. The sketch which follows is a preliminary attempt to identify what seem to the writer to be the basic components of the explanation.

HIGH FERTILITY NORMS

No society can afford indifference to reproductive behavior. Every society maintains fertility norms: standardized solutions to the problems of sex and procreation. The society indoctrinates its members into conformity with these norms, by explicit and implicit rewards and punishments. The norms are necessary to direct the behavior of individuals into channels which are desirable from the standpoint of the sources of the norms, rather than leave it to take forms which, however appealing from the standpoint of the individuals concerned, might be prejudicial to group interests.

And yet to say that a society has high fertility because it has high fertility norms is to run the risk of lapsing into circularity. Nor is it satisfactory to say that fertility was once high because it was the tradition to have many babies, but now tradition has been replaced by rationality and the reasonable family size is small. It would be a crude misreading of social history to interpret the decline of fertility as

a straight-forward consequence of the growth of intelligence and understanding.[12]

The fact is that high fertility norms prevailed because they were rational: they were intelligible orientations of means toward ends, given particular conditions. These conditions were high mortality, and the family farm as the basis of productive organization. In such circumstances, high fertility was mandatory from the standpoint of societal survival and desirable from the standpoint of the leaders of the kinship group. In the practical affairs of life, where human labor was the principal source of energy, children were necessary as helpers in the fields, as defenders against attacking tribes, and as sources of security in their parents' later years. Children were raised frugally and put to work early. From the viewpoint of the family, they were essential productive assets.

In underdeveloped areas, couples have many births, not precisely because they want them, but because the groups to which they are responsible want them, and secure them through the enforcement of high fertility norms. The fundamental clue to the explanation of fertility decline is not the introduction of rationality, but change in the locus of the goals toward which rational acts are directed: the ends of the family have been replaced in the reproductive calculus by the ends of the individual.

In peasant societies, marriage is characteristically arranged at a very early age, and the young couple incorporated within the larger kinship economic unit. Since the economic context is one in which extra labor is an important asset, the couple are enjoined to produce children for the greater good of the group as a whole. But in the European family type which developed some 500 years ago, the independent nuclear family was the norm. The *quid pro quo* of autonomy was the responsibility of each couple for the support of its own children. Accordingly, marriage had to be delayed until these responsibilities could be met. Since the parents controlled access to the principal eco-

---

[12]A similar misrepresentation is to ascribe low fertility to the advent of materialism. No orientation could be more materialistic than that essential to a subsistence economy.

nomic opportunities (the land they held), the time of marriage rested in their hands. Thus, the system provided control over the relationship between population and resources. In addition, agriculture was typically labor-extensive: there was a lower demand at the margin for additional labor than in peasant societies.[13]

The western European system set the stage for modern fertility by counterpoising the interests of parents and children, and the interests of one sibling and another, at the time of movement from family of orientation to family of procreation.[14] The specific stimuli which brought pressure to bear on these points of structural strain were two: mortality decline and urban economic development.

Social arrangements had been adapted to high mortality. High levels of fertility were required to produce small families (in terms of the numbers surviving to adulthood) because spouses were likely to die prematurely, and infant and child mortality was commonplace. Mortality decline produced the large family for the first time. Its size grew both in numbers and in years; the labor force on the family farm was increased, often beyond the point of efficient utilization of the extra hands; the parents had more years to live, prolonging the time when the property passed to the children, and thus raising the age of marriage; and more siblings survived to adulthood, so that each had a smaller share of the patrimony.

At the same time as mortality decline was putting pressure on the relationships between parent and child and between sibling and sibling, there was economic development and a rise in income expectations. The growth of urban industry and the opening of the new world provided employment opportunities alternative to the long wait for part of the family farm. Migration to the cities of Europe and to the cities and farmlands of America mounted to major proportions. In consequence, the bearing and rearing of children became a much less

rewarding activity for the parents who stayed on the farm, spatial and social distance grew between family of orientation and family of procreation, and postponement of marriage became avoidable.[15]

Then the crucial normative transformation occurred. Society intervened to institutionalize the rights of the individual vis-à-vis the family and thus to provide the basis for building the kind of citizenry appropriate to a modern economy. Three developments were particularly pertinent to the creation of a low fertility climate: legislation prohibiting child labor, legislation prescribing education of children, and establishment of a higher status for women. Large families had been the outcome of a system of sharp inequality between the generations and between the sexes. Children were no longer mass-produced once they were withdrawn from the farm and the factory and put into school.

The transfer of the focus of work organization from the rural family to the urban society had many implications for reproduction. The cost of raising children is higher in cities than in rural areas because necessities cost more, the preparation of children for urban jobs is more expensive, and the income once he takes a job belongs to the child, and not his parents. Moreover, the woman in the urban society is provided the opportunity of seeking satisfactions elsewhere than in motherhood. Her weight in the reproductive decision increases; the relevance of this is that the burdens of bearing and rearing children have always fallen more directly and heavily on women than on men.

Thus, the locus of authority has moved away from the family in two directions: toward the individual and toward the formal organizations which characterize the modern state. The society has replaced the family as the instrument of education, the avenue of employment, and the source of social security for the individual. No longer are the worthwhile things of life, and the rights and responsibilities of power, the province of the parents; the new contract is directly between the individual and his society.

---

[13]Norman B. Ryder, "Fertility," in Philip M. Hauser and O. Dudley Duncan (eds.), *The Study of Population* (Chicago: University of Chicago Press, 1959), 400–436.

[14]A person's family of orientation is the one in which he is born; his family of procreation is the one in which he is a parent.

[15]Under these circumstances there may even have been some rise in fertility for the time being, at least in some parts of Europe.

These are not simply the manifestations of a higher morality; they are recognitions of the many ways in which the interests of the individual are co-ordinate with the interests of the modern economy. Strong family relationships, on the contrary, are incompatible with the rational allocation of human resources. Yet, the character of the society which replaces the family at the center of life is not irrelevant. Rulers of nations who are obsessed with the strength of the collectivity to the disregard of individual well-being have always been opposed to fertility regulation. The more scope a society provides for individual initiative and responsibility, the more likely is a low level of fertility.

A postscript is worthwhile on the roles played by formal public instruction. In an approximate way, the decline of illiteracy has everywhere accompanied the decline of fertility (although there seems to be no crucial proportion of literates which can be said to trigger that decline). The educational system represents a societal alternative to the family as a source of new normative orientations, and an enhancement of vision beyond the limited boundaries of the local community. Education equips children with the means for exploiting new economic opportunities, and in the process increases the expense to the parents. Education reinforces the prospects for continued mortality decline, and improves the access of individuals to the efficient modes of contraception with which to attain new reproductive goals. Children are separated from their parents for most of their preadult life, and girls and boys are treated with approximate equality. Education is the cutting edge of the modern world; the school is the arena within which the new alliance between individual and society is contracted.

THE BASIS FOR MODERN FERTILITY

Throughout the modern world there is now a remarkable demographic consensus. Marriage occurs at a rather early age, and the couple proceeds to have a small number of children at regulated intervals. Both celibacy and voluntary infertility are highly improbable, and, at the other extreme, the large family is an anachronism. The range of fertility differences among modern nations depends essentially on the question of whether the proportion of couples who have three children is greater or less than the proportion who have two children.

Given the cogency of the argument we have advanced concerning the decline of the family in relation to the interests of the individual and the society, an explanation is required for the continuation of adequate reproduction. As a general argument, although the functions performed by the family are much more narrowly circumscribed than they once were, its remaining contributions are not only valuable but essential. Even in the economic sphere, it may be true that the family is no longer an important production unit (although this is belied by the picture of the housewife with her array of capital equipment for the provision of services), but it continues to serve as a distribution center for the products of the economy.

More to the point, the family has become specialized as a producer of noneconomic goods. We have argued that the normative transformation underlying fertility decline took the form of termination of the individual's service to his family's interests; this says nothing about the extent to which the family can serve the individual's interests. There is no present substitute for the family as the instrument of child socialization. The family provides stable, diffuse, and unquestioning support for the personality of the individual on his return from participation in the competitive impersonal environment of modern occupational and educational life. The family is an oasis for the replenishment of the individual personality. One piece of evidence for this view is a further characteristic of modern family life—the prevalence of resort to divorce if the family is not providing the individual with what he or she expects and requires as a person. The demographic structure required to fulfill the task of maintaining the individual's emotional equilibrium is difficult to specify, but it would not seem to require more than a few children. Perhaps it is pertinent to the sociopsychological balance of the modern family that most parents desire one child of each sex.

Above and beyond the satisfactions the individual may find in the parental role, the society has a vital interest in the production of citizens. On the implicit level, positive sanctions encourage marriage and childbearing, and negative sanctions penalize the sterile and the celibate, as a reflection of deepseated norms undoubtedly associated with the requisite of societal survival. Explicitly, the society subsidizes the family. The bearing, rearing, and educating of children are too expensive for the individual couple. Society supports reproduction through family allowances, tax exemptions, and facilities for health and education; it assumes the responsibility for employment and relief when unemployed, for protection and defense, and for security throughout the low points of life. Without such intervention, children would be a luxury beyond the reach of most couples. The ability of society to influence the reproductivity of its citizens is essential to its future. The difference between two children and three may have small salience for the couple concerned, but the aggregate outcome has overwhelming import for social and economic progress.

The role played by religion in contemporary fertility is difficult to assess. Notwithstanding the cleavage in contraceptive doctrine, Catholic and non-Catholic populations differ little in their birth rates—although the former are more likely than the latter to employ nuptiality control in striving for the common objective of low fertility. In some nations, religious leaders have supported legislation which has probably slowed somewhat the dissemination of contraceptive knowledge and means. Yet perhaps the major effect religion has had on the pace of fertility decline has been indirect, through modification of the choice of reproductive strategies among the alternative modes of regulation, through support for the authority of the family with respect to the individual, and through the implicit effects on economic development of its support for the traditional virtues.

In a similar vein, it would seem that ideological orientation has played a distinctly sec-

ondary role in demographic developments. Modernizing stimuli have yielded the same demographic responses in socialistic as in capitalistic societies. The reproductive significance of the type of politico-economic structure must be sought in its implications for the pace of economic development, and for the scope offered the individual for the pursuit of personal well-being.

SPECULATIONS ON THE FUTURE

It appears unlikely, on the basis of current developments, that the average level of fertility in these 28 modern nations will change much. The trend toward similarity will probably continue: those countries with the lowest birth rates cannot be expected to tolerate the subjective and objective implications of reproduction at a subreplacement level—at least no country yet has—and those countries with birth rates which are high despite low per capita income (Spain, Portugal, and Ireland) should show further declines as economic development continues.

Relevant to the future of modern fertility is the availability of efficient contraception. Only in the 1960's has modern contraception become available. The intra-uterine contraceptive device and the oral contraceptive deserve to be called modern because they are the first procedures which separate the acts of contraception and sexual intercourse. Fertility decline has recently been observed in those countries, largely the English-speaking nations, where oral contraception is beginning to be employed extensively. Although the analysis required to substantiate the argument is incomplete, there is reason to believe that the principal impact of oral contraception has been to permit couples to delay the births of their children—a type of behavior which has the effect of reducing the birth rate in the absence of changes of completed family size. Knowledge about the practice of family planning is most comprehensive for the United States. Here, although most pregnancies are unplanned, they are typically failures of timing. Problems of excess fertility which could be solved by the modern contraceptives are small from the standpoint of the total population, although not for the most deprived levels within the society.

The most likely consequence of the adoption of contraceptive innovations is a transformation of the regulatory pattern away from abstinence (in the form of delayed marriage) and abortion. The advent of more efficient contraception will probably cause the most decline in nations where there is now the greatest discrepancy between the numbers of children intended and the numbers achieved, as a consequence of the ineffectiveness of the methods currently being used. The point is that the improvement of regulatory means is not necessarily associated with fertility decline, but rather with a reduction in the gap between reproductive intent and reproductive achievement. Unfortunately, we cannot tell whether current international differences in marital fertility represent differences in goals or differences in success in achieving goals.

It is well known that the richer nations of the world have much lower fertility than the poorer ones, and that rising per capita income as a consequence of economic development has been associated with fertility decline. But within the group of modern nations there is today no relationship between level of development and level of fertility. If, as seems probable, this is the outcome of effective means to somewhat higher reproductive goals in the more developed nations and ineffective means to somewhat lower reproductive goals in the less developed nations, we may expect a direct rela-tionship between fertility level and income level to become established as the gap between intentions and achievements is reduced by more effective fertility regulation.

It would seem to follow that a rise in per capita income through time would be associated with a rise in fertility. But rising fertility means an increased rate of population growth, with its attendant sacrifice of irreplaceable economic and noneconomic resources universally regarded as essentials of the good life. It is difficult to believe that a successful society would permit demographic despoliation to continue; it is equally difficult to contemplate the precise ways in which reproductive restraint could be achieved, given the disparity in perspective between the individuals who make reproductive decisions and the social aggregate which is exposed to the consequences. One point does seem clear: improved ability to determine fertility will lead to greater sensitivity of response to instability in the environment, and therefore to the risk of fertility fluctuations of even greater amplitude and more embarrassing consequences than we have seen in the recent past.

To conclude, it seems that the future fertility of modern nations will depend primarily on the relative success with which their respective governments can bring individual decisions about child-bearing into correspondence with the demographic requirements of the society. Strait is the gate and narrow is the way between too much and too little fertility. There may well be few that find it.

35.

David M. Heer

ECONOMIC DEVELOPMENT AND THE FERTILITY TRANSITION

1968.

Population theorists have developed contrasting views concerning the effect that economic development, or increase in per-capita income, has on fertility. One school contends that economic development inhibits fertility. This view, perhaps predominant in recent years, is expressed most succinctly in the theory of demographic transition set forth by Warren S. Thompson, C. P. Blacker, Kingsley Davis, Frank Notestein, and others.[1] According to this theory, a nation's demographic process depends on its stage of industrialization and, by implication, its level of economic development. Warren Thompson and Kingsley Davis, for example, divide the nations of the world into three classes. Class I nations are highly industrialized, have low fertility and mortality, and show little or no population growth; Class II nations are beginning the process of industrialization, have declining although still high fertility, rapidly declining mortality, but, in net balance, a high rate of population growth; Class III nations are not yet industrialized, have both high fertility and high mortality, and, at most, only moderate population growth. The theory of demographic transition, popularized around the time of World War II, is congruent with the generally inverse association between fertility level and degree of industrialization among nations today. Indeed,

fertility levels of industrialized nations are lower than they were before the nations became industrialized.

A second school of thought, however, argues that economic development promotes fertility. Perhaps the foremost representative of this viewpoint was the English economist, T. R. Malthus. He believed that an increase in the demand for labor increased the proportion of persons marrying and reduced the average age at marriage, and that this change in marriage pattern led in turn to an increase in fertility.[2] Because Malthus lived during the middle of the Industrial Revolution in England, his views were presumably colored by what he conceived to be recent trends in fertility in his own country. Later critics of Malthus, considering his views on the relation between fertility and economic development to be erroneous, generally attributed the large acceleration in population growth which accompanied the Industrial Revolution exclusively to lowered mortality. Several historical demographers have, however, recently produced evidence indicating that fertility may well have increased during England's period of industrial development in the early nineteenth century,[3] and that similar increases may have occurred in parts of the Netherlands.[4]

Support for the school of thought linking fertility increase to economic development has also been supplied by studies indicating a relationship between birth and marriage rates and

This selection is reprinted from: David M. Heer, "Economic Development and the Fertility Transition," *Daedalus*, 1968, 97, 447–462.

Reprinted with the permission of *Daedalus*, the Journal of the American Academy of Arts and Sciences, Boston, Mass., Spring 1968, "Historical Population Studies."

[1]See Warren S. Thompson, *Population and Peace in the Pacific* (Chicago: 1946), 22–35; C. P. Blacker, "Stages in Population Growth," *Eugenics Review,* October, 1947, 39, no. 3, 88–102; Kingsley Davis, *Human Society* (New York: 1949), 603–608; Frank W. Notestein, "The Economics of Population and Food Supplies," *Proceedings of the Eighth International Conference of Agricultural Economists* (London, 1953), 15–31.

[2]Thomas R. Malthus, *An Essay on Population* (New York: 1914), vol. 1, 167, 277–78; vol. 2, 27–28, 132, 140, 230–31.

[3]J. T. Krause, "Some Implications of Recent Work in Historical Demography," *Comparative Studies in Society and History,* January, 1954, *1,* no. 2, 164–88; H. J. Habakkuk, "English Population in the 18th Century," *Economic History Review,* December, 1953, *6,* no. 2, 117–33.

[4]William Petersen, "The Demographic Transition in the Netherlands," *American Sociological Review,* June, 1960, *25,* no. 3, 334–47.

business cycles.[5] Virginia Galbraith and Dorothy Thomas have demonstrated that business cycles in the United States between 1919 and 1937 affected both marriages and births. With an appropriate time lag, marriages and births of each parity increased when business conditions improved and declined when business fell off.[6] Dudley Kirk analyzed the situation in Germany during the 1920's and arrived at similar conclusions.[7] Researchers working with such data from other countries have in all cases shown a positive correlation between birth and marriage rates and the height of the business cycle.[8]

Evidence that economic development promotes fertility also comes from other types of studies. From his analysis of both the influence of general business conditions on fertility and the effects of the relative demand for labor on young persons of reproductive age, Richard Easterlin hypothesizes that the high wage and salary levels of persons 20 to 29 years old was one of the prime factors sustaining the American baby boom of the 1950's. The number of persons in this age group was exceptionally low because of the small number of babies born during the Depression. The supply of new entrants to the labor force was, therefore, abnormally reduced during the 1950's, a period when demand for labor was high. Moreover, the group entering the labor force in the 1950's was exceptionally well educated in comparison with older age groups and thus had a competitive advantage in employment during a period in which educational qualifications became increasingly important.[9]

A recent study by W. Stys further supports the conclusion that a high economic level increases fertility. Stys has shown that for Polish peasant women born during the latter half of the nineteenth century, average completed family size varied directly with size of farm. Among landless peasants, the average number of births per mother was 3.9; on farms of more than seven hectares, the average number was 9.1. The difference in fertility by size of farm results mostly from variations in the mother's age at marriage. There was, nevertheless, some tendency for births per year of marriage to be slightly higher among women living on the larger farms.[10]

The results of surveys conducted by Gordon De Jong imply that respondents of each social class would increase their fertility as their economic circumstances improved and would reduce it were their economic circumstances to decline. De Jong asked respondents in the Southern Appalachian region of the United States what they considered to be the ideal number of children for the average young couple today, for a "well-off" young couple, and for a "not well-off" couple. The respondents in the study believed that the ideal number of children for the "not well-off" couple would be 1.5; for the average couple, 2.79; and for the "well-off" couple, 4.2. Similar results were obtained separately for respondents of each social class.[11]

Deborah Freedman has been concerned with the extent to which the husband's "relative income" affects fertility of individual married couples in the United States.[12] (By "relative income" she means the degree to which the husband's actual income exceeded or was exceeded by that of men in his socio-economic reference group—that is, men of similar age, occupation, income, and region of residence.) Her analysis was made with data from a national probability

[5] In citing studies whose conclusions can be interpreted as lending support to the Malthusian theory of a direct relation between economic development and fertility, I do not wish to imply that the authors of the studies necessarily themselves subscribe in whole or in part to Malthus's views in this regard.

[6] Virginia Galbraith and Dorothy S. Thomas, "Birth Rates and the Interwar Business Cycles," *Journal of the American Statistical Association,* December, 1941, *36,* 465–76.

[7] Dudley Kirk, "The Relation of Employment Levels to Births in Germany," *Milbank Memorial Fund Quarterly,* April, 1942, *28,* 126–38.

[8] For further bibliography on this topic, see Ronald Freedman, "The Sociology of Human Fertility," *Current Sociology,* 1961–62, *10/11,* no. 2, 108.

[9] Richard Easterlin, *The American Baby Boom in Historical Perspective* (New York: 1962).

[10] W. Stys, "The Influence of Economic Conditions on the Fertility of Peasant Women," *Population Studies,* November, 1957, *11,* no. 2, 136–48.

[11] Gordon De Jong, "Religious Fundamentalism, Socio-economic Status, and Fertility Attitudes in the Southern Appalachians," *Demography,* 1965, *2,* 540–48.

[12] Deborah S. Freedman, "The Relation of Economic Status to Fertility," *American Economic Review,* June, 1963, *53,* no. 3, 414–26.

sample of fecund, white, nonfarm wives 18 to 39 years old married at least five years. After controls for 13 other relevant variables, she found that the number of children born to the wife was positively related to the magnitude of the husband's relative income. After ten years of marriage, wives whose husband's relative income was low had .42 less children than would have been expected on the basis of the other variables; conversely, wives whose husband's relative income was high had .21 more children than would have been expected.

The two contrasting views concerning the effect of economic development on fertility obviously demand reconciliation. I have elsewhere hypothesized that economic development directly increases fertility, although various other factors usually accompanying the process of economic development serve to reduce fertility.[13] The indirect effects of economic development tending to reduce fertility are often, albeit not invariably, stronger than the direct effect tending to raise it. Thus, economic development frequently results in fertility decline.[14] Making use of data for 41 nations during the 1950's, I found that

[13]See David M. Heer, "Economic Development and Fertility," *Demography*, 1966, 3, no. 2, 423–44, where I set forth a theory which attempts to harmonize these contrasting views and offer empirical evidence of a new theory's validity.

[14]Actually there are four possible versions of this hypothesis. In the first version, we refer to one national population over time and examine the effect of aggregate economic development and the aggregate factors accompanying it on aggregate trends in fertility. In the second, we look at the effect of the aggregate level of economic development and its accompanying factors on the aggregate level of fertility in a set of national populations at a particular time. In a third version, we look at the effect of economic development and its accompanying factors on an individual basis—individual change in income and style of life associated with that income—on individual fertility for a group of persons over time. In the fourth version, we examine the effect of the individual level of economic development and its accompanying factors on individual fertility for a group of persons at a given moment in time. Ansley Coale has correctly pointed out that a demonstration of the truth of one of these versions does not necessarily constitute proof of any other version. The results contained in my article "Economic Development and Fertility" are pertinent only to the second version, whereas my main interest in this paper is the first version of the hypothesis. Some of the other studies I have cited are pertinent to the third and fourth versions.

the average level of national fertility was inversely associated with per capita net national product when no other variables were held constant. The relation between the two variables was slightly positive, however, after instituting controls for other relevant variables— the level of infant mortality, per capita newspaper circulation, population density, and the recent percentage increase in per capita energy consumption. Controlling for these other variables, I found that per capita newspaper circulation and population density were inversely related to fertility, and that infant mortality and recent increase in per capita energy consumption were directly related. After control for other variables, infant mortality showed a stronger relation to fertility than any of the other four variables. Increase in educational attainment, for which per capita newspaper circulation is a good index, and decline in infant and early childhood mortality are, of course, two of the most pervasive phenomena accompanying economic development.

An understanding of the biological factors which constrain fertility is necessary to any analysis of fertility change. Nevertheless, fertility cannot be fully explained unless voluntary decisions concerning future children are also considered. Biological factors clearly place an upper bound on the fertility of each individual. Below the limit of biologically maximum fertility (probably around 12 births for the average woman[15]), each individual is more or less free to choose how many babies to have. Excess fertility can always be avoided even though the price for doing so may be great. To consider two extreme examples, couples can refrain from sexual intercourse to avoid further pregnancy, and the pregnant woman can decide to abort the fetus even at the risk of her own life.

Joseph Spengler has devised an excellent conceptual scheme for analyzing the factors affecting the decision to have children.[16] He considers the decision to have an additional child to be a function of three variables: the preference sys-

[15]See J. W. Eaton and A. J. Mayer, "The Social Biology of Very High Fertility Among the Hutterites," *Human Biology*, 1953, 25, 206–63.

[16]Joseph J. Spengler, "Values and Fertility Analysis," *Demography*, 1966, 3, no. 1, 109–30.

tem, the price system, and income. Provided these terms are given a broader definition than they usually receive in economic literature, the three concepts provide a complete classification of all factors that affect such a decision. The preference system simply describes the value a married couple places on an additional child relative to the value of goals they might otherwise achieve. The price system delineates the cost of an additional child relative to the cost of attaining other goals that might be achieved were the decision to have another child not made. Costs must be broadly defined to include not only monetary costs, but expenditures of time and effort. Income, too, must be broadly defined so that it encompasses monetary income as well as the total amount of time and energy available to a couple in their pursuit of possible goals. (Because the term *resources* fits the definition more closely than the term *income*, I shall henceforth refer to the former rather than the latter.) Given these definitions, the probability of deciding in favor of another child will vary directly with the relative value anticipated from that child, inversely with the predicted relative cost, and directly with the

amount of resources foreseen as available for all goals.[17]

Spengler's scheme should prove to be useful in analyzing the long-term changes in fertility in the now developed countries during the last century or so and in demonstrating further the thesis that economic development directly enhances fertility, but has indirect effects that lead to fertility decline. Any explanation of the variables accounting for the long-term fertility change in the developed nations should, however, be postponed until the magnitude of this change has been described. The accompanying graph shows, for example, the change in the total fertility rate for white women in the United States between 1800 and 1965. The total fertility rate for a given year is a summary measure of fertility, which can best be described as the total number of children a woman would have were she to live through the entire reproductive period and bear children at the average

[17] I shall ignore the possibility that children are an "inferior good" so that as income rises children are substituted for more desirable objects which give the same sort of satisfaction only in higher degree. I do not consider this to be a realistic assumption.

FIGURE 35-1. TOTAL FERTILITY RATE FOR THE WHITE POPULATION OF THE UNITED STATES 1800–1965

Sources: Ansley J. Coale and Melvin Zelnik, *New Estimates of Fertility and Population in the United States* (Princeton: 1963), p. 36; U. S. National Center for Health Statistics, *Monthly Vital Statistics Report*, February, 1967, *15*, no. 11, supplement.

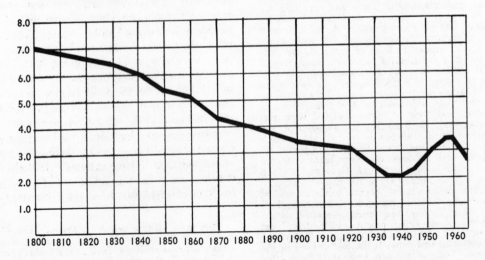

rate for that time. As one can see from this graph, the decline in the total fertility rate from 1800 to 1965 has been very pronounced. The regularity of the decline, however, is distinctly marred by the dramatic fertility rise during the 1940's and 1950's. Since 1957, the trend of fertility decline has been renewed, and from 1964 to 1965 the United States experienced the sharpest annual percentage fertility decline in its entire history (almost 8 percent).

It should not be supposed that the temporal pattern of fertility decline has been identical in all of the developed nations. The magnitude of the decline was greater in the United States than in Europe. Furthermore, fertility reduction began much earlier in France and the United States than in Great Britain, where decline dates only from 1876,[18] even though England industrialized much earlier. Moreover, the baby boom following World War II was much more pronounced in the United States than it was in Europe.

The developed nations have a long history of increasing per capita monetary income. According to Simon Kuznets, the average decennial rate of growth in per capita national product in the United States between 1839 and 1960-62 was more than 17 percent, a rate sufficient to increase per capita product 4.9 times per century.[19] The developed nations also have a long history of decreasing hours devoted to gainful employment and increasing amounts of leisure time. Had there been no change in either the price or preference system, one might have expected that the long-term trend in fertility would have been upward. Since fertility has tended over the long run to go down rather than up, changes in the preference and price system must have discouraged rather than encouraged fertility to an extent that they counterbalanced the elevating effects of increased money and leisure time.

On the other hand, the developed nations which did not suffer severely from World War II (United States, Canada, Australia, and New Zealand) underwent a substantial rise in fertility during the 1940's and 1950's. As I have noted earlier, Easterlin has provided extensive documentation that this period of rising fertility was also one of rapid rise in monetary income for young adults in the United States.[20] During the period of the baby boom in the United States, the amount of time, money, and effort available for child-rearing activities was markedly expanded by the increased willingness and ability of grandparents to help their married children in child-care responsibilities. The grandparents of the postwar baby crop had had relatively few children themselves and, therefore, probably welcomed the chance to share in the work of raising their grandchildren. Moreover, even though the number of children per parent was quite high during the 1950's, the number per grandparent was not large since the number in the parental generation was so small. Thus, grandparents could make a large contribution to the rearing of each grandchild in a way that will not, for example, be possible for the grandparents of the 1970's. We may therefore presume that during the period of the baby boom the elevating effects of rising resources more than counterbalanced any depressing effects of changes in the preference or price system.

In the last hundred years or so, several changes in the preference system of the developed nations have undoubtedly tended to reduce family size. One of the most important of these is the decline in mortality, which has of course been pronounced. In the United States for example, the mean expectation of life at birth increased from 47.3 years in 1900 to 70.2 years in 1964.[21] The secular (long-term) decline in mortality has had greater relative effect in infancy and childhood than adulthood. If fertility had not declined, the reduction in mortality would have tended to increase somewhat the number of living children per living parent. The United Nations estimates that for a population with high fertility (a gross reproduction rate of 2.5) and very high mortality (life expectation at birth of 20 years), the ratio of

---

[18]A. M. Carr-Saunders, *World Population: Past Growth and Present Trends* (London: 1964), 92.

[19]Simon Kuznets, *Postwar Economic Growth: Four Lectures* (Cambridge: 1964), 64.

[20]Easterlin, *The American Baby Boom in Historical Perspective.*

[21]U. S. Public Health Service, *Vital Statistics of the United States, 1964,* 2, section 5, Life Tables, p. 12.

population under 15 years to that aged 15 to 59 years is 0.56. When the expectation of life at birth is increased to 70 years with no change in fertility, the ratio is increased to 0.83.[22] Thus one would expect the value of an additional birth to wane as the level of mortality declines.

There is also a possible connection between the level of mortality and the amount of emotional energy that parents invest in each of their children. It may be supposed that the pain of bereavement at a child's death is directly proportional to the amount of emotional energy that the parents have invested in the child. Where mortality levels are high, one might expect parents, in the interest of self-protection, to develop relatively little emotional involvement in any one child. A reduction in mortality encourages parents to place more libido in the existing children and thus should reduce their desire to have an additional child, since they have limited amounts of emotional energy.[23]

Lowering the mortality level should also reduce the desire for additional children because parents can be more certain of having a specified minimum number of children survive to maturity. When mortality is high, one cannot be sure that any of one's existing children will survive to maturity. When mortality is as low as it is in the developed nations, parents can be highly certain that their child will survive from birth to maturity. Thus, a decline in mortality reduces the value of an additional child as insurance against the possibility that one or more of the existing children may die. The effect of mortality reduction in this respect can be quantitatively measured. If one assumes that each couple is capable of bearing 12 children, that a perfect means of birth control is available and utilized, and that all couples want to be 95 percent certain of having at least one son who will survive to the father's 65th birthday, the gross reproduction rate will fall from 5.2 when the expectation of life at birth is 20 years to

0.95 when the expectation of life rises to 74 years.[24]

A second long-term change in the preference system relates to the value which parents can derive from the productive labor of their children. In the agrarian society of the United States in the eighteenth century, when the supply of land was practically unlimited, children could be productive assets to their parents at a very early age. As the amount of land per capita declined, as it did in the United States during the nineteenth century, the value to the farmer of the labor of an additional child probably declined correspondingly. In all of the developed nations, industrialization substantially reduced the value of child labor. Although such labor was quite common in many of the early factories, the situation of the child in the factory was much less satisfactory than it was when he worked under the direction of his father on the family farm. As a result, strong moral sentiment developed against child labor, and legislation restricting it emerged in all of the developed nations. In each nation, the development of this legislation was very gradual, and the early regulations were much less restrictive than later laws. The first such legislation in England, passed in 1817, merely banned children under nine years of age from working in cotton mills. In the United States, the first mildly restrictive legislation appeared in a few northern states about the middle of the nineteenth century.[25] Only in 1938 did the United States federal government enact child-labor regulations; these prohibited the employment of children under 16 in manufacturing or mining and banned the employment of children under 14 from all industry, except agriculture, which engaged in interstate commerce.[26]

The utility of child labor was further reduced by compulsory education laws which, as they increased in severity, also lowered the productive value to the parents of an additional child.

[22]United Nations, Department of Economic and Social Affairs. *The Aging of Populations and Its Economic and Social Implications* (New York: 1956), 26–27.
[23]This idea was first advanced in an oral communication by Dr. Laila Sh. El Hamamsy, director of the Social Research Center, American University, Cairo, Egypt.
[24]David M. Heer and Dean O. Smith, "Mortality Level and Desired Family Size," *Indian Population Journal*, 1967, *1*, no. 1.
[25]United States Children's Bureau, *Child Labor: Facts and Figures*, Publication No. 197 (Washington, D. C., 1930), 2–5.
[26]Florence Taylor, *Child Labor Fact Books: 1900–1950* (New York: 1950).

Prussia, under the leadership of Frederick the Great, became in 1763 the first nation to legislate compulsory attendance at schools for all persons five to 14 years of age. The first law establishing compulsory school attendance in England was enacted in 1876. In the United States, Massachusetts became in 1852 the first state to demand school attendance; similar legislation did not become universal until 1918, when attendance was finally made compulsory in Mississippi.[27]

The development of formal institutions to support the elderly has also brought about substantial changes in the value of an additional child. In the pre-industrial period and in the early stages of the Industrial Revolution, the elderly could expect to receive financial support only from their own kin—mainly from their sons. Gradually business corporations and governments developed social-security schemes for the aged and for widows. In the United Kingdom, legislation establishing old-age pensions for needy persons was first enacted in 1908, and in 1925 a contributory system covering all workers was established. In the United States, the first federal legislation concerning old-age, survivors' or disability pensions dates from 1935, although many private corporations provided pensions and insurance systems much earlier.[28] With the full development of social security, it became unnecessary for parents to bear children in sufficient number to assure that one or more sons would support them in their old age. Thus, the value to parents of additional children has been further diminished.

The preference system has also been altered by the decline in social rewards for bearing a large number of children. When mortality was high, a high rate of fertility was a positive necessity if the population was not to decline. Governmental and religious authorities who did not wish to see the nation's population reduced encouraged a high level of fertility. As mortality declined, however, a high level of fertility was no longer necessary to maintain the existing population level. As a result, many governments and religious bodies have shifted from a position favoring large families to one of neutrality or even opposition. A historic landmark was reached when the Church of England admitted at its Lambeth Conference of 1930 that mechanical or chemical means of contraception were not necessarily immoral.[29] Since that time, the Protestant churches have, for the most part, ceased to extol the virtue of large families, and in the present decade the Roman Catholic Church has been faced with a great internal struggle, as yet unresolved, concerning this question. Although no European government has become alarmed about problems of excess fertility—all, in fact, encourage large families through their programs of family allowances— the United States has for the first time, under the Johnson administration, provided federal funds for the establishment of family-planning clinics, thus indicating that it no longer wishes to encourage large families, at least among the poor.

A fifth possible change in the preference system may be the result of a tendency for economic development to shift the criteria for social status from ascribed characteristics (such as birth into a particular family) to achievement. While status is ascribed at birth, one need spend little effort in advertising one's status to others; where status is achieved, its level tends to be transitory, and individuals may develop an intense need for conspicuous consumption to demonstrate their rank. If the preference for conspicuous consumption increases, the preference for children, who do little to publicize one's status, should decline. J. A. Banks has provided extensive documentation to show that during the latter years of the Victorian Era, the British middle class felt an increasing need to engage in conspicuous consumption, and that English fertility first began its decline during this period.

The tremendous development of new and improved methods of birth control over the last century has not only reduced the relative preference for children, but has also increased their price relative to that of other goals. When avail-

---

[27]H. G. Good, *A History of Western Education* (New York: 1960), 318, 356, 450; "Education in the United States," *Collier's Encyclopedia* (1959), vol. 7, 79–93.

[28]"Social Security," *Encyclopaedia Britannica* (Chicago, 1967), vol. 20, 762–69.

[29]Richard M. Fagley, *The Population Explosion and Christian Responsibility* (New York: 1960), 194–95.

able methods of birth control are crude and undeveloped, or knowledge of better methods is lacking, the decision not to have an additional child involves substantial inconvenience, interference with sexual pleasure, or even some hazard to health and life incurred by resort to a primitive means of abortion. Some of the major landmarks in the development of contraceptive technology during the last century were the manufacture of rubber condoms in the late-nineteenth century, the invention of a diaphragm by Mensinga in 1880, and in the 1930's the appearance of the latex condom, which was cheaper and better than its rubber predecessor.[30] Increasing use of the highly effective oral contraceptives in the United States and other nations during the 1960's reduced the penalties in deciding against another child and may have been one of the major reasons for sharp fertility decline. Although the "pill" was placed on the United States market only in 1960, by 1965 it was the most popular contraceptive, the method used most recently by 24 percent of white wives 18 to 39 years of age.[31] Abortion has also been one of the principal means of birth control, and improvements in its technology have probably affected the preference for children. Little has been written about this, however, and it is difficult to ascertain the history of abortion techniques in those nations where the purposeful disruption of pregnancy is for the most part illegal.

Economic development has produced other changes in the price system affecting desired family size. Urbanization has been one of the most important concomitants of economic development. In the United States, the proportion of the population classified as urban increased from five to 70 percent between 1790 and 1960.[32] In general, urbanization results in a rise

in the relative price of living space. Since rearing of children demands considerable living space, the relative cost of children no doubt rises with each increase in the relative price of living space. Although the relative cost of living space has in general been increasing over the last hundred years, the rise has, perhaps, not been invariant. One may speculate that the increasingly widespread use of the automobile in the United States during the 1940's and 1950's, together with governmental policies which subsidized home ownership, made possible the acquisition of suburban houses at a relative cost probably substantially lower than prevailed during previous decades. Part of the American baby boom of the 1940's and 1950's may be explained by this short-term change in the relative cost of living space.

The tendency for the labor cost of child care to rise relative to the labor cost of producing material goods no doubt is a factor affecting desired family size. While economic development makes possible a much larger production of factory goods per man-hour of labor, the number of man-hours necessary to supervise and socialize a child has certainly not declined and most probably has risen. When a married couple are deciding whether to have another child, they can assume that an additional child will burden the wife with the responsibilities of child care for about three years. Moreover, with another child to supervise, she will have to work harder during the period when the older children are still under her care. This increased effort must be set against the possible remuneration from a job. Since the amount of material goods which can be bought with each hour of labor outside the home has steadily increased with each advance in national economic level, there has been a substantial long-term increase in the price of child-care services relative to the price of material goods.

A final long-term change in the price system affecting the decision to have children concerns the quality of education which parents demand for their children and which is socially imposed. A society more and more oriented to a complex technology requires that children be given an increasingly lengthy education. Parents recognize that their own child will be at a substantial

---

[30]For extensive accounts of the history of contraception, see Norman E. Himes, *Medical History of Contraception* (New York: 1963), and Elizabeth Draper, *Birth Control in the Modern World* (London: 1965).

[31]Charles F. Westoff and Norman B. Ryder, "United States: Methods of Fertility Control, 1955, 1960, & 1965," *Studies in Family Planning*, February, 1967, no. 17.

[32]U. S. Bureau of the Census, *United States Census of Population, 1960* (Washington, D.C.), vol. 1, part 1, p. 4.

disadvantage unless his education meets society's new norm. Even where the direct cost of education is met by the state, longer education increases the cost to the parent in terms of more years of child dependency. Hence the secular rise in the standard of education has no doubt helped to depress family size.

The factors connected with industrial development which I have listed have, in my opinion, tended to depress fertility to such an extent that the actual trend has usually been downward despite the elevating effect increased revenues have had on fertility. It is not yet possible to evaluate the importance of the role each of these factors has played in the temporal changes in fertility in the developed nations during the past century or more. Although their relative importance may never be well established, further historical research may be of great value. I would recommend, in particular, detailed study correlating fertility change with such matters as the development of social-security systems, the decline in the prevalence of child labor, increases in the proportion of children attending school, changes in the relative cost of living space, and augmentation of the relative labor cost of child care.

Analysis of the past can be of some help in predicting the future course of fertility in both the more developed nations and in those currently less developed. For the economically advanced nations, certain of the factors which have operated in the past will in the future operate with much diminished force. It is, for example, impossible for infant and childhood mortality to drop much further. Again, provision for old-age security is now almost completely divorced from the extended kin-group, and little further shift from kin-group responsibility can be expected. Moreover, child labor has been practically eliminated, and additional change in this will be of no further importance to fertility. Thus, for the economically developed nations, at least three factors important in the past reduction of fertility will have little impact on the course of future fertility.

This might tempt one to predict that if per capita income continues to rise in these nations, fertility will also rise. We should, however, be able to count on the continuation of certain trends which in the past have been inimical to high fertility. Most of these trends affect the price system. Since the ideal means of birth control has not yet been invented, we can anticipate some decline in fertility with each successive step toward this ideal. We can also predict that the mother's opportunity cost for spending time in child-rearing activities will continue to climb since the price of material goods will most probably continue to fall relative to that of providing child-care services. The demand for a higher level of education will in all likelihood also continue. Unless the cost of such education is completely socialized, this demand should constitute additional pressure for fertility decline. Barring unforeseen developments in transportation technology, increasing population density should make inevitable a further increase in the relative cost of living space, an important component of the total cost of rearing children. Finally, we can, I think, be fairly confident that public opinion will take an increasingly negative stance toward large family size. A withdrawal of social rewards for a large number of children might have a substantial effect on fertility preference. I believe that the public will be more and more aware of the taxes necessary to support population growth, of the ways in which a larger population aggravates urban congestion and crowds detract from the enjoyment of places of prime interest and scenic interest. If, however, the level of international tension is exacerbated, a contrary pressure in favor of larger families might ensue since each nation might fear that its power relative to other nations would diminish were its relative population size to fall.

The long-run fertility trend in the now industrialized nations will, I think, not be upward. Nevertheless, it is certainly plausible to assume that fertility may rise in several of these nations for certain short-run periods. For the less developed nations, it seems very probable that further progress in economic level should bring substantial fertility decline. In these nations, economic development should have all of the indirect effects that it had previously in Europe and North America. In many of these nations, there will also be governmental programs encouraging small families. Furthermore, the technology of birth control is now more advanced than it was when fertility first began to decline in the West; thus, the mere introduction of the new birth-control methods may bring moderate fertility reduction into populations only weakly motivated to reduce family size. The real question for the less developed nations is whether they will be able to attain a further measure of economic development. It is, of course, not impossible that in at least some of these nations population growth will outstrip the increase in the means of subsistence. If lower living standards ensue, the level of mortality may be greatly affected. Given a rise in infant and childhood mortality, it may then be impossible to obtain fertility decline.

CHAPTER IX

Families with Children and Child Development

THIS CHAPTER centers on the family when children arrive. There are two foci, one on the dyadic group becoming a triadic group with a dependent infant, and the second on the infant and its development through childhood and participation in the society. The latter area receives specialized attention under fields such as child psychology, child development, socialization process, and education.

The first event, the transition to parenthood, receives surprisingly little attention in the field of marriage and the family. Indeed, it is almost as though it is assumed that all families "become whole" by an instant process, that the process is so easy or natural that research is not required to understand this phase of the life cycle or that it creates few if any problems for the family. There has been only a meager literature in the study of this transition. However, the research literature that does exist in this area indicates that parents do tend to see the transition from the marital dyad to the first child triad as a crisis (LeMasters, E. E., "Parenthood as Crisis," *Marriage and Family Living*, 1957, *19*, 352–355.) At least one study confirmed that of LeMasters, but more recently other studies indicate that early parenthood is not necessarily a stressful experience. (Hobbs, Daniel F., Jr., "Transition to Parenthood: A Replication and an Extension," *Journal of Marriage and the Family*, 1968, *30*, 413–417.) The findings, since they deal with different levels of response, are not unambiguous. It can at least be said that the arrival of the first child is associated with stress for the dyad; in the readjustment, there are additional costs both literally and in terms of the time and freedom of the marriage partners, and many subtle changes occur to redefine relationships between the partners.

In her article titled "Transition to Parenthood," Alice S. Rossi presents a structural analysis of the parental role cycle. She points out that the transition to parenthood may be more difficult than other types of adjustments at roughly the same period in life for the young adults, such as the marital adjustments themselves and occupational adjustments. There are constraints on the regulation of parenthood that the couple may feel. The adult woman's life is radically shifted by the pregnancy; childbirth itself is an abrupt transition in status, and in all these matters there are only few guidelines to becoming a successful parent. Whether either sex is adequately prepared for parenthood is called into question.

What is it that parents must adjust to with the arrival of a child? Certainly the social circumstances are changed, but what of the child itself? In his article titled "Social and Emotional Behavior of Infancy: Some Developmental Issues and Problems," Henry N. Ricciuti discusses some aspects of child development. What are the inherent characteristics of the child as an organism, and how does it develop in its social environment? These processes are stressed with regard to infancy. The generalized process of becoming a social person from the point of view of symbolic interactionism is described by Edgar F. Borgatta in a brief excerpt titled "The Socialization Process."

Many topics dealing with the problem of socialization are not presented here. There is, for example, enormous literature on the impact of birth order on the personality of the child. One is reminded of the fact that parents are least experienced in child rearing with their first-born, and one may encounter in the sardonic literature of cultures such expressions as: "First-born on whom parents practice should be thrown away." It is not surprising that differences should be found between first-born or only children and subsequent children. If such differences exist and are pronounced, this raises some interesting questions about the structural impact on personality and behavior for nations where family size ideals are for small one- and two-children families. By contrast, comments on large family size often indicate that the youngest are at least partially raised by the oldest children in a family. Thus, in traditions of large families and of extended families, the introduction to child-rearing practices and the management of children may be structurally more adequately built into the system. Another relevant area of research is the involvement of children in their own socialization. While peer cultures have frequently been studied, Donald P. Irish indicates in his article, "Sibling Interaction: A Neglected Aspect in Family Life Research," that the interaction among children within the family has yet to receive adequate attention.

The question of peer relationships and parental relationships may be approached in any number of ways. One way may be to examine the types of parental orientations toward children's behavior. In this area, for example, the Fels Parent Behavior Scales provided an analysis about three decades ago of how parents react toward the family, and particularly toward the child. (Champney, H., "The Variables of Parent Behavior," *Journal of Abnormal and Social Psychology*, 1941, 36, 529–542.) Subsequently, there have been technical factor analyses of these types of data, leading to various empirical typologies of the orientations of parents. A simple one dealing with the most global concepts involved three "second-order factors": the orientation toward fostering dependence on the part of the child; orientation toward democratic practices and values; and orientation toward maintaining strict orderliness in the home. Interest in the Fels instrument has persisted, and a considerable research literature has subsequently developed.

A good deal of analysis of family life involving parents and children is described either as conflict or struggle. Many factors are involved in the conceptualization of these relationships, including the homogeneity of the culture within the society, the homogeneity of expectations between youth culture and adult culture, and even values about the appropriateness of certain types of child-rearing practices. In the public mind, concepts of child rebellion and originality are sometimes only hazily distinguished, and confusion is often a major problem for inexperienced— as well as experienced—parents. Where the lines are drawn between parents and children on values, describing the situation as conflict or battle may indeed become appropriate. In discussing this problem, one author related it directly to the manner in which changes in western civilization have affected forms of authority. He noted that there are conflicting norms, competing authorities, little explicit institutionalization of aspects of parental authority and localization of authority within the small family rather than in a more extended system. Further, there may be conflict of values because of different aspirations, and struggle precipitated by changing values, such as in the area of sex where a generational lag occurs if the mores are becoming more liberal. (Davis, Kingsley, "The Sociology of Parent-Youth Conflict," *American Sociological Review*, 1940, 5, 523–535.) Some of these may be emphasized. For example, the different cultures in which parents and children live can be illustrated by the secularization and greater involvement of children in education outside the home. This may be phrased simply as saying that as children become involved in activities with their peers, they are increasingly responsive to peer values. If youngsters are not oriented toward their families and identify with the family norms and values in a strong way initially, they are likely to be more susceptible to persuasion away from the family values. (See, for example: Bowerman, Charles E., and Kinch, John W., "Changes in Family and Peer Orientation of Children between the Fourth and Tenth Grades," *Social Forces*, 1959, 37, 206–211.) Our readings include an article which suggests aspects of the parent-child conflict. It is by Robert R. Bell, titled "Parent-Child Conflict in Sexual Values," and reviews research and issues dealing with the problem. The relevance of this article to materials in Chapter VI, which deals with courtship and mate selection, will be evident.

The final paper in this chapter is somewhat different from other materials, and is designed to indicate the cross-cultural approach to child-rearing. We have already had considerable emphasis on the cross-cultural approach in the examination of materials in Chapters 1 and 2 with regard to differences in family systems. Here we present an article by Larry D. Barnett titled "The Kibbutz as a Child-Rearing System: A Review of the Literature." The kibbutz has certain unique features with regard to child-rearing, yet is part of a culture that may be viewed as having firm contacts with modern western civilization. Thus, findings about child-rearing in this quite different familial setting are of interest to persons concerned with hypotheses about parental influence on child personality characteristics.

36.

ALICE S. ROSSI

TRANSITION TO PARENTHOOD

THE PROBLEM

The central concern in this sociological analysis of parenthood will be with two closely related questions. (1) What is involved in the transition to parenthood: what must be learned and what readjustments of other role commitments must take place in order to move smoothly through the transition from a childless married state to parenthood? (2) What is the effect of parenthood on the adult: in what ways do parents, and in particular mothers, change as a result of their parental experiences?

To get a firmer conceptual handle on the problem, I shall first specify the stages in the development of the parental role and then explore several of the most salient features of the parental role by comparing it with the two other major adult social roles—the marital and work role. Throughout the discussion, special attention will be given to the social changes that have taken place during the past few decades which facilitate or complicate the transition to and the experience of parenthood among young American adults.

FROM CHILD TO PARENT: AN EXAMPLE

What is unique about this perspective on parenthood is the focus on the adult parent rather than the child. Until quite recent years, concern in the behavioral sciences with the parent-child relationship has been confined almost exclusively to the child. Whether a psychological study such as Ferreira's on the influence of the

pregnant woman's attitude to maternity upon postnatal behavior of the neonate,[1] Sears and Maccoby's survey of child-rearing practices,[2] or Brody's detailed observations of mothering,[3] the long tradition of studies of maternal deprivation[4] and more recently of maternal employment,[5] the child has been the center of attention. The design of such research has assumed that, if enough were known about what parents were like and what they in fact did in rearing their children, much of the variation among children could be accounted for.[6]

The very different order of questions which emerge when the parent replaces the child as

This selection is reprinted from: Alice S. Rossi, "Transition to Parenthood," *Journal of Marriage and the Family*, 1968, 30, 26–39.

Reprinted with the permission of the author and publisher.

This paper was presented to the American Orthopsychiatric Association, Washington, D.C., March 22, 1967.

[1]Antonio J. Ferreira, "The Pregnant Woman's Emotional Attitude and Its Reflection on the Newborn," *American Journal of Orthopsychiatry*, 1960, 30, 553–561.

[2]Robert Sears, E. Maccoby, and H. Levin, *Patterns of Child-Rearing* (Evanston, Illinois: Row, Peterson, 1957).

[3]Sylvia Brody, *Patterns of Mothering: Maternal Influences during Infancy* (New York: International Universities Press, 1956).

[4]Leon J. Yarrow, "Maternal Deprivation: Toward an Empirical and Conceptual Re-evaluation," *Psychological Bulletin*, 1961, 58:6, 459–490.

[5]F. Ivan Nye and L. W. Hoffman, *The Employed Mother in America* (Chicago: Rand McNally, 1963); Alice S. Rossi, "Equality Between the Sexes: An Immodest Proposal," *Daedalus*, 1964, 93:2, 607–652.

[6]The younger the child, the more was this the accepted view. It is only in recent years that research has paid any attention to the initiating role of the infant in the development of his attachment to maternal and other adult figures, as in Ainsworth's research which showed that infants become attached to the mother, not solely because she is instrumental in satisfying their primary visceral drives, but through a chain of behavioral interchange between the infant and the mother, thus supporting Bowlby's rejection of the secondary drive theory of the infant's ties to his mother. Mary D. Ainsworth, "Patterns of Attachment Behavior Shown by the Infant in Interaction with His Mother," *Merrill-Palmer Quarterly*, 1964, 10:1, 51–58; John Bowlby, "The Nature of the Child's Tie to His Mother," *International Journal of Psychoanalysis*, 1958, 39, 1–34.

the primary focus of analytic attention can best be shown with an illustration. Let us take, as our example, the point Benedek makes that the child's need for mothering is *absolute* while the need of an adult woman to mother is *relative*.[7] From a concern for the child, this discrepancy in need leads to an analysis of the impact on the child of separation from the mother or inadequacy of mothering. Family systems that provide numerous adults to care for the young child can make up for this discrepancy in need between mother and child, which may be why ethnographic accounts give little evidence of postpartum depression following childbirth in simpler societies. Yet our family system of isolated households, increasingly distant from kinswomen to assist in mothering, requires that new mothers shoulder total responsibility for the infant precisely for that stage of the child's life when his need for mothering is far in excess of the mother's need for the child.

From the perspective of the mother, the question has therefore become: what does maternity deprive her of? Are the intrinsic gratifications of maternity sufficient to compensate for shelving or reducing a woman's involvement in non-family interests and social roles? The literature on maternal deprivation cannot answer such questions, because the concept, even in the careful specification Yarrow has given it,[8] has never meant anything but the effect on the child of various kinds of insufficient mothering. Yet what has been seen as a failure or inadequacy of individual women may in fact be a failure of the society to provide institutionalized substitutes for the extended kin to assist in the care of infants and young children. It may be that the role requirements of maternity in the American family system extract too high a price of deprivation for young adult women reared with highly diversified interests and social expectations concerning adult life. Here, as at several points in the course of this paper, familiar problems take on a new and suggestive research dimension when the focus is on the parent rather than the child.

------

[7]Therese Benedek, "Parenthood as a Developmental Phase," *Journal of American Psychoanalytic Association*, 1959, 7:8, 389–417.

[8]Yarrow, *op. cit.*

BACKGROUND

Since it is a relatively recent development to focus on the parent side of the parent-child relationship, some preliminary attention to the emergence of this focus on parenthood is in order. Several developments in the behavioral sciences paved the way to this perspective. Of perhaps most importance have been the development of ego psychology and the problem of adaptation of Murray[9] and Hartmann,[10] the interpersonal focus of Sullivan's psychoanalytic theories,[11] and the life cycle approach to identity of Erikson.[12] These have been fundamental to the growth of the human development perspective: that personality is not a stable given but a constantly changing phenomenon, that the individual changes along the life line as he lives through critical life experiences. The transition to parenthood, or the impact of parenthood upon the adult, is part of the heightened contemporary interest in adult socialization.

A second and related development has been the growing concern of behavioral scientists with crossing levels of analysis to adequately comprehend social and individual phenomena and to build theories appropriate to a complex social system. In the past, social anthropologists focused as purely on the level of prescriptive normative variables as psychologists had concentrated on intrapsychic processes at the individual level or sociologists on social-structural and institutional variables. These are adequate, perhaps, when societies are in a stable state of equilibrium and the social sciences were at early stages of conceptual development, but they become inadequate when the societies we study are undergoing rapid social change and we have an increasing amount of individual and subgroup variance to account for.

Psychology and anthropology were the first to join theoretical forces in their concern for

------

[9]Henry A. Murray, *Explorations in Personality* (New York: Oxford University Press, 1938).

[10]Heinz Hartmann, *Ego Psychology and the Problem of Adaptation* (New York: International Universities Press, Inc., 1958).

[11]Patrick Mullahy (ed.), *The Contributions of Harry Stack Sullivan* (New York: Hermitage House, 1952).

[12]E. Erikson, "Identity and the Life Cycle: Selected Papers," *Psychological Issues*, 1959, *1*, 1–171.

the connections between culture and personality. The question of how culture is transmitted across the generations and finds its manifestations in the personality structure and social roles of the individual has brought renewed research attention to the primary institutions of the family and the schools, which provide the intermediary contexts through which culture is transmitted and built into personality structure.

It is no longer possible for a psychologist or a therapist to neglect the social environment of the individual subject or patient, nor is the "family" they are concerned with any longer confined to the family of origin, for current theory and therapy view the adult individual in the context of his current family of procreation. So too it is no longer possible for the sociologist to focus exclusively on the current family relationships of the individual. The incorporation of psychoanalytic theory into the informal, if not the formal, training of the sociologist has led to an increasing concern for the quality of relationships in the family of origin as determinants of the adult attitudes, values, and behavior which the sociologist studies.

Quite another tradition of research has led to the formulation of "normal crises of parenthood." "Crisis" research began with the studies of individuals undergoing traumatic experiences, such as that by Tyhurst on natural catastrophes,[13] Caplan on parental responses to premature births,[14] Lindemann on grief and bereavement,[15] and Janis on surgery.[16] In these studies attention was on differential response to stress—how and why individuals vary in the ease with which they coped with the stressful experience and achieved some reintegration. Sociological interest has been piqued as these studies were built upon by Rhona and Robert Rapoport's research on the honeymoon and the engagement as normal crises in the role transitions

to marriage and their theoretical attempt to build a conceptual bridge between family and occupational research from a "transition task" perspective.[17] LeMasters, Dyer, and Hobbs have each conducted studies of parenthood precisely as a crisis or disruptive event in family life.[18]

I think, however, that the time is now ripe to drop the concept of "normal crises" and to speak directly, instead, of the transition to and impact of parenthood. There is an uncomfortable incongruity in speaking of any crisis as normal. If the transition is achieved and if a successful reintegration of personality or social roles occurs, then crisis is a misnomer. To confine attention to "normal crises" suggests, even if it is not logically implied, successful outcome, thus excluding from our analysis the deviant instances in which failure occurs.

Sociologists have been just as prone as psychologists to dichotomize normality and pathology. We have had one set of theories to deal with deviance, social problems, and conflict and quite another set in theoretical analyses of a normal system—whether a family or a society. In the latter case our theories seldom include categories to cover deviance, strain, dysfunction, or failure. Thus, Parsons and Bales' systems find "task-leaders" oriented to problem solution, but not instrumental leaders attempting to undercut or destroy the goal of the group, and "sociometric stars" who play a posi-

[13] J. Tyhurst, "Individual Reactions to Community Disaster," *American Journal of Psychiatry*, 1951, *107*, 764–769.

[14] G. Caplan, "Patterns of Parental Response to the Crisis of Premature Birth: A Preliminary Approach to Modifying the Mental Health Outcome," *Psychiatry*, 1960, *23*, 365–374.

[15] E. Lindemann, "Symptomatology and Management of Acute Grief," *American Journal of Psychiatry*, 1944, *101*, 141–148.

[16] Irving Janis, *Psychological Stress* (New York: John Wiley & Sons, Inc., 1958).

[17] Rhona Rapoport, "Normal Crises, Family Structure and Mental Health," *Family Process*, 1963, *2*:1, 68–80; Rhona Rapoport and Robert Rapoport, "New Light on the Honeymoon," *Human Relations*, 1964, *17*:1, 33–56; Rhona Rapoport, "The Transition from Engagement to Marriage," *Acta Sociologica*, 1964, *8*, fasc, 1-2, 36–55; and Robert Rapoport and Rhona Rapoport, "Work and Family in Contemporary Society," *American Sociological Review*, 1965, *30*:3, 381–394.

[18] E. E. LeMasters, "Parenthood as Crisis," *Marriage and Family Living*, 1957, *19*, 352–355; Everett D. Dyer, "Parenthood as Crisis: A Re-Study," *Marriage and Family Living*, 1963, *25*, 196–201; and Daniel F. Hobbs, Jr., "Parenthood as Crisis: A Third Study," *Journal of Marriage and the Family*, 1963, *27*:3, 367–372. LeMasters and Dyer both report the first experience of parenthood involves extensive to severe crises in the lives of their young parent respondents. Hobbs's study does not show first parenthood to be a crisis experience, but this may be due to the fact that his couples have very young (seven-week-old) first babies and are therefore still experiencing the euphoric honeymoon stage of parenthood.

tive integrative function in cementing ties among group members, but not negatively expressive persons with hostile aims of reducing or destroying such intragroup ties.[19]

Parsons' analysis of the experience of parenthood as a step in maturation and personality growth does not allow for negative outcome. In this view either parents show little or no positive impact upon themselves of their parental role experiences, or they show a new level of maturity. Yet many women, whose interests and values made a congenial combination of wifehood and work role, may find that the addition of maternal responsibilities has the consequence of a fundamental and undesired change in both their relationships to their husbands and their involvements outside the family. Still other women, who might have kept a precarious hold on adequate functioning as adults had they *not* become parents, suffer severe retrogression with pregnancy and childbearing, because the reactivation of older unresolved conflicts with their own mothers is not favorably resolved but in fact leads to personality deterioration[20] and the

transmission of pathology to their children.[21]

Where cultural pressure is very great to assume a particular adult role, as it is for American women to bear and rear children, latent desire and psychological readiness for parenthood may often be at odds with manifest desire and actual ability to perform adequately as parents. Clinicians and therapists are aware, as perhaps many sociologists are not, that failure, hostility, and destructiveness are as much a part of the family system and the relationships among family members as success, love, and solidarity are.[22]

A conceptual system which can deal with both successful and unsuccessful role transitions, or positive and negative impact of parenthood upon adult men and women, is thus more powerful than one built to handle success but not failure or vice versa. For these reasons I have concluded that it is misleading and restrictive to perpetuate the use of the concept of "normal crisis." A more fruitful point of departure is to build upon the stage-task concepts of Erikson, viewing parenthood as a developmental stage, as Benedek[23] and Hill[24] have done, a perspective carried into the research of Rausch, Goodrich, and Campbell[25] and of Rhona and Robert Rapoport[26] on adaptation to the early years of marriage and that of Cohen, Fearing *et al.*[27] on the adjustments involved in pregnancy.

ROLE CYCLE STAGES

A discussion of the impact of parenthood upon the parent will be assisted by two analytic devices. One is to follow a comparative approach, by asking in what basic structural ways the

---

[19]Parson's theoretical analysis of the family system builds directly on Bales's research on small groups. The latter are typically comprised of volunteers willing to attempt the single task put to the group. This positive orientation is most apt to yield the empirical discovery of "sociometric stars" and "task leaders," least apt to sensitize the researcher or theorist to the effect of hostile non-acceptance of the group task. Talcott Parsons and R. F. Bales, *Family, Socialization and Interaction Process* (New York: The Free Press, a division of the Macmillan Co., 1955).

Yet the same limited definition of the key variables is found in the important attempts by Straus to develop the theory that every social system, as every personality, requires a circumplex model with two independent axes of authority and support. His discussion and examples indicate a variable definition with limited range: support is defined as High (+) or Low (−), but "low" covers both the absence of high support and the presence of negative support; there is love or neutrality in this system, but not hate. Applied to actual families, this groups destructive mothers with low-supportive mothers, much as the non-authoritarian pole on the Authoritarian Personality Scale includes both mere non-authoritarians and vigorously anti-authoritarian personalities. Murray A. Straus, "Power and Support Structure of the Family in Relation to Socialization," *Journal of Marriage and the Family*, 1964, 26:3, 318–326.

[20]Mabel Blake Cohen, "Personal Identity and Sexual Identity," *Psychiatry*, 1966, 29:1, 1–14; Joseph C. Rheingold, *The Fear of Being a Woman: A Theory of Maternal Destructiveness* (New York: Grune and Stratton, 1964).

[21]Theodore Lidz, S. Fleck, and A. Cornelison, *Schizophrenia and the Family* (New York: International Universities Press, Inc., 1965); Rheingold, *op. cit.*

[22]Cf. the long review of studies Rheingold covers in his book on maternal destructiveness, *op. cit.*

[23]Benedek, *op. cit.*

[24]Reuben Hill and D. A. Hansen, "The Identification of a Conceptual Framework Utilized in Family Study," *Marriage and Family Living*, 1960, 22, 299–311.

[25]Harold L. Raush, W. Goodrich, and J. D. Campbell, "Adaptation to the First Years of Marriage," *Psychiatry*, 1963, 26:4, 368–380.

[26]Rapoport, *op. cit.*

[27]Cohen, *op. cit.*

parental role differs from other primary adult roles. The marital and occupational roles will be used for this comparison. A second device is to specify the phases in the development of a social role. If the total life span may be said to have a cycle, each stage with its unique tasks, then by analogy a role may be said to have a cycle and each stage in that role cycle, to have its unique tasks and problems of adjustment. Four broad stages of a role cycle may be specified:

ANTICIPATORY STAGE

All major adult roles have a long history of anticipatory training for them, since parental and school socialization of children is dedicated precisely to this task of producing the kind of competent adult valued by the culture. For our present purposes, however, a narrower conception of the anticipatory stage is preferable: the engagement period in the case of the marital role, pregnancy in the case of the parental role, and the last stages of highly vocationally oriented schooling or on-the-job apprenticeship in the case of an occupational role.

HONEYMOON STAGE

This is the time period immediately following the full assumption of the adult role. The inception of this stage is more easily defined than its termination. In the case of the marital role, the honeymoon stage extends from the marriage ceremony itself through the literal honeymoon and on through an unspecified and individually varying period of time. Raush[28] has caught this stage of the marital role in his description of the "psychic honeymoon": that extended postmarital period when, through close intimacy and joint activity, the couple can explore each other's capacities and limitations. I shall arbitrarily consider the onset of pregnancy as marking the end of the honeymoon stage of the marital role. This stage of the parental role may involve an equivalent psychic honeymoon, that post-childbirth period during which, through intimacy and prolonged contact, an attachment between parent and child is laid down. There is a crucial difference, however, from the marital role in this stage. A woman

[28]Raush *et al., op. cit.*

knows her husband as a unique real person when she enters the honeymoon stage of marriage. A good deal of preparatory adjustment on a firm reality-base is possible during the engagement period which is not possible in the equivalent pregnancy period. Fantasy is not corrected by the reality of a specific individual child until the birth of the child. The "quickening" is psychologically of special significance to women precisely because it marks the first evidence of a real baby rather than a purely fantasized one. On this basis alone there is greater interpersonal adjustment and learning during the honeymoon stage of the parental role than of the marital role.

PLATEAU STAGE

This is the protracted middle period of a role cycle during which the role is fully exercised. Depending on the specific problem under analysis, one would obviously subdivide this large plateau stage further. For my present purposes it is not necessary to do so, since my focus is on the earlier anticipatory and honeymoon stages of the parental role and the overall impact of parenthood on adults.

DISENGAGEMENT-TERMINATION STAGE

This period immediately precedes and includes the actual termination of the role. Marriage ends with the death of the spouse or, just as definitively, with separation and divorce. A unique characteristic of parental role termination is the fact that it is not clearly marked by any specific act but is an attenuated process of termination with little cultural prescription about when the authority and obligations of a parent end. Many parents, however, experience the marriage of the child as a psychological termination of the active parental role.

UNIQUE FEATURES OF PARENTAL ROLE

With this role cycle suggestion as a broader framework, we can narrow our focus to what are the unique and most salient features of the parental role. In doing so, special attention will be given to two further questions: (1) the impact of social changes over the past few decades in facilitating or complicating the transition to and experience of parenthood and (2) the new interpretations or new research suggested by the focus on the parent rather than the child.

CULTURAL PRESSURE TO ASSUME THE ROLE

On the level of cultural values, men have no freedom of choice where work is concerned: they must work to secure their status as adult men. The equivalent for women has been maternity. There is considerable pressure upon the growing girl and young woman to consider maternity necessary for a woman's fulfillment as an individual and to secure her status as an adult.[29]

This is not to say there are no fluctuations over time in the intensity of the cultural pressure to parenthood. During the depression years of the 1930's, there was more widespread awareness of the economic hardships parenthood can entail, and many demographic experts believe there was a great increase in illegal abortions during those years. Bird has discussed the dread with which a suspected pregnancy was viewed by many American women in the 1930's.[30] Quite a different set of pressures were at work during the 1950's, when the general societal tendency was toward withdrawal from active engagement with the issues of the larger society and a turning in to the gratifications of the private sphere of home and family life. Important in the background were the general affluence of the period and the expanded room and ease of child rearing that go with suburban living. For the past five years, there has been a drop in the birth rate in general, fourth and higher-order births in particular. During this same period there has been increased concern and debate about women's participation in politics and work, with more

women now returning to work rather than conceiving the third or fourth child.[31]

INCEPTION OF THE PARENTAL ROLE

The decision to marry and the choice of a mate are voluntary acts of individuals in our family system. Engagements are therefore consciously considered, freely entered, and freely terminated if increased familiarity decreases, rather than increases, intimacy and commitment to the choice. The inception of a pregnancy, unlike the engagement, is not always a voluntary decision, for it may be the unintended consequence of a sexual act that was recreative in intent rather than procreative. Secondly, and again unlike the engagement, the termination of a pregnancy is not socially sanctioned, as shown by current resistance to abortion-law reform.

The implication of this difference is a much higher probability of unwanted pregnancies than of unwanted marriages in our family system. Coupled with the ample clinical evidence of parental rejection and sometimes cruelty to children, it is all the more surprising that there has not been more consistent research attention to the problem of *parental satisfaction*, as there has for long been on *marital satisfaction* or *work satisfaction*. Only the extreme iceberg tip of the parental satisfaction continuum is clearly demarcated and researched, as in the growing concern with "battered babies." Cultural and psychological resistance to the image of a nonnurturant woman may afflict social scientists as well as the American public.

The timing of a first pregnancy is critical to the manner in which parental responsibilities are joined to the marital relationship. The single most important change over the past few decades is extensive and efficient contraceptive usage, since this has meant for a growing proportion of new marriages, the possibility of and increasing preference for some postponement

---

[29]The greater the cultural pressure to assume a given adult social role, the greater will be the tendency for individual negative feelings toward that role to be expressed covertly. Men may complain about a given job but not about working *per se,* and hence their work dissatisfactions are often displaced to the non-work sphere, as psychosomatic complaints or irritation and dominance at home. An equivalent displacement for women of the ambivalence many may feel toward maternity is to dissatisfactions with the homemaker role.

[30]Caroline Bird, *The Invisible Scar* (New York: David McKay Co., Inc., 1966).

[31]When it is realized that a mean family size of 3.5 would double the population in 40 years, while a mean of 2.5 would yield a stable population in the same period, the social importance of withholding praise for procreative prowess is clear. At the same time, a drop in the birth rate may reduce the number of unwanted babies born, for such a drop would mean more efficient contraceptive usage and a closer correspondence between desired and attained family size.

of childbearing after marriage. When pregnancy was likely to follow shortly after marriage, the major transition point in a woman's life was marriage itself. *This transition point is increasingly the first pregnancy rather than marriage.* It is accepted and increasingly expected that women will work after marriage, while household furnishings are acquired and spouses complete their advanced training or gain a foothold in their work.[32] This provides an early marriage period in which the fact of a wife's employment presses for a greater egalitarian relationship between husband and wife in decision-making, commonality of experience, and sharing of household responsibilities.

The balance between individual autonomy and couple mutuality that develops during the honeymoon stage of such a marriage may be important in establishing a pattern that will later affect the quality of the parent-child relationship and the extent of sex-role segregation of duties between the parents. It is only in the context of a growing egalitarian base to the marital relationship that one could find, as Gavron has,[33] a tendency for parents to establish some barriers between themselves and their children, a marital defense against the institution of parenthood as she describes it. This may eventually replace the typical coalition in more traditional families of mother and children against husband-father. Parenthood will continue for some time to impose a degree of temporary segregation of primary responsibilities between husband and wife, but, when this takes place in the context of a previously established egalitarian relationship between the husband and wife, such role segregation may become blurred, with greater recognition of the wife's need for autonomy and the husband's role in the routines of home and child rearing.[34]

There is one further significant social change that has important implications for the changed relationship between husband and wife: the increasing departure from an old pattern of role-inception phasing in which the young person first completed his schooling, then established himself in the world of work, then married and began his family. Marriage and parenthood are increasingly taking place *before* the schooling of the husband, and often of the wife, has been completed.[35] An important reason for this trend lies in the fact that, during the same decades in which the average age of physical-sexual maturation has dropped, the average amount of education which young people obtain has been on the increase. Particularly for the college and graduate or professional school population, family roles are often assumed before the degrees needed to enter careers have been obtained.

Just how long it now takes young people to complete their higher education has been investigated only recently in several longitudinal

new households during the early months of marriage. Indeed, natural childbirth builds directly on this shifted base to the marital relationship. Goshen-Gottstein has found in an Israeli sample that women with a "traditional" orientation to marriage far exceed women with a "modern" orientation to marriage in menstrual difficulty, dislike of sexual intercourse, and pregnancy disorders and complaints such as vomiting. She argues that traditional women demand and expect little from their husbands and become demanding and narcissistic by means of their children, as shown in pregnancy by an over-exaggeration of symptoms and attention-seeking. Esther R. Goshen-Gottstein, *Marriage and First Pregnancy: Cultural Influences on Attitudes of Israeli Women* (London: Tavistock Publications, 1966). A prolonged psychic honeymoon uncomplicated by an early pregnancy, and with the new acceptance of married women's employment, may help to cement the egalitarian relationship in the marriage and reduce both the tendency to pregnancy difficulties and the need for a narcissistic focus on the children. Such a background is fruitful ground for sympathy toward and acceptance of the natural childbirth ideology.

[32] James A. Davis, *Stipends and Spouses: The Finances of American Arts and Sciences Graduate Students* (Chicago: University of Chicago Press, 1962).

[33] Hannah Gavron, *The Captive Wife* (London: Routledge & Kegan Paul, 1966).

[34] The recent increase in natural childbirth, prenatal courses for expectant fathers, and greater participation of men during childbirth and postnatal care of the infant may therefore be a *consequence* of greater sharing between husband and wife when both work and jointly maintain their

[35] James A. Davis, *Stipends and Spouses: The Finances of American Arts and Sciences Graduate Students, op. cit.;* James A. Davis, *Great Aspirations* (Chicago: Aldine Publishing Company, 1964); Eli Ginsberg, *Life Styles of Educated Women* (New York: Columbia University Press, 1966); Ginsberg, *Educated American Women: Self Portraits* (New York: Columbia University Press, 1967); National Science Foundation, *Two Years After the College Degree—Work and Further Study Patterns* (Washington, D.C.: Government Printing Office, NSF 63-26, 1963).

studies of college-graduate cohorts.[36] College is far less uniformly a four-year period than high school is. A full third of the college freshmen in one study had been out of high school a year or more before entering college.[37] In a large sample of college graduates in 1961, one in five were over 25 years of age at graduation.[38] Thus, financial difficulties, military service, change of career plans, and marriage itself all tend to create interruptions in the college attendance of a significant proportion of college graduates. At the graduate and professional school level, this is even more marked: the mean age of men receiving the doctorate, for example, is 32, and of women, 36.[39] It is the exception rather than the rule for men and women who seek graduate degrees to go directly from college to graduate school and remain there until they secure their degrees.[40]

The major implication of this change is that more men and women are achieving full adult status in family roles while they are still less than fully adult in status terms in the occupational system. Graduate students are, increasingly, men and women with full family responsibilities. Within the family many more husbands and fathers are still students, often quite dependent on the earnings of their wives to see them through their advanced training.[41] No matter what the couple's desires and preferences are, this fact alone presses for more egalitarian relations between husband and wife, just as the adult family status of graduate students presses for more egalitarian relations between students and faculty.

IRREVOCABILITY

If marriages do not work out, there is now widespread acceptance of divorce and remarriage as a solution. The same point applies to the work world: we are free to leave an unsatisfactory job and seek another. But once a pregnancy occurs, there is little possibility of undoing the commitment to parenthood implicit in conception except in the rare instance of placing children for adoption. We can have ex-spouses and ex-jobs but not ex-children. This being so, it is scarcely surprising to find marked differences between the relationship of a parent and one child and the relationship of the same parent with another child. If the culture does not permit pregnancy termination, the equivalent to giving up a child is psychological withdrawal on the part of the parent.

This taps an important area in which a focus on the parent rather than the child may contribute a new interpretive dimension to an old problem: the long history of interest, in the social sciences, in differences among children associated with their sex-birth-order position in their sibling set. Research has largely been based on data gathered about and/or from the children, and interpretations make inferences back to the "probable" quality of the child's relation to a parent and how a parent might differ in relating to a first-born compared to a last-born child. The relevant research, directed at the parents (mothers in particular), remains to be done, but at least a few examples can be suggested of the different order of interpretation that flows from a focus on the parent.

Some birth-order research stresses the influence of sibs upon other sibs, as in Koch's finding that second-born boys with an older sister are more feminine than second-born boys with an older brother.[42] A similar sib-influence interpretation is offered in the major common finding of birth-order correlates, that sociability is greater among last-borns[43] and achievement

[36]Davis, *Great Aspirations, op. cit.*; Laure Sharp, "Graduate Study and Its Relation to Careers: The Experience of a Recent Cohort of College Graduates," *Journal of Human Resources*, 1966, *1*:2, 41–58.

[37]James D. Cowhig and C. Nam, "Educational Status, College Plans and Occupational Status of Farm and Nonfarm Youths," U.S. Bureau of the Census Series ERS (P-27). No. 30, 1961.

[38]Davis, *Great Aspirations, op. cit.*

[39]Lindsey R. Harmon, *Profiles of Ph.D.'s in the Sciences: Summary Report on Follow-up of Doctorate Cohorts, 1935–1960,* (Washington, D.C.: National Research Council, Publication 1293, 1965).

[40]Sharp, *op. cit.*

[41]Davis, *Stipends and Spouses, The Finances of American Arts and Sciences Graduate Students, op. cit.*

[42]Orville G. Brim, "Family Structure and Sex-Role Learning by Children," *Sociometry*, 1958, *21*, 1–16; H. L. Koch, "Sissiness and Tomboyishness in Relation to Sibling Characteristics," *Journal of Genetic Psychology*, 1956, *88*, 231–244.

[43]Charles MacArthur, "Personalities of First and Second Children," *Psychiatry*, 1956, *19*, 47–54; S. Schachter, "Birth Order and Sociometric Choice,"

among first-borns.[44] It has been suggested that last-borns use social skills to increase acceptance by their older sibs or are more peer-oriented because they receive less adult stimulation from parents. The tendency of first-borns to greater achievement has been interpreted in a corollary way, as a reflection of early assumption of responsibility for younger sibs, greater adult stimulation during the time the oldest was the only child in the family,[45] and the greater significance of the first-born for the larger kinship network of the family.[46]

Sociologists have shown increasing interest in structural family variables in recent years, a primary variable being family size. From Bossard's descriptive work on the large family[47] to more methodologically sophisticated work such as that by Rosen,[48] Elder and Bowerman,[49] Boocock,[50] and Nisbet,[51] the question posed is: what is the effect of growing up in a small family, compared with a large family, that is attributable to this group-size variable? Unfortunately, the theoretical point of departure for sociologists' expectations of the effect of the family-size variables is the Durkheim-Simmel tradition of the differential effect of group size

---

Journal of Abnormal and Social Psychology, 1964, 68, 453–456.

[44]Irving Harris, *The Promised Seed* (New York: The Free Press, 1964); Bernard Rosen, "Family Structure and Achievement Motivation," *American Sociological Review*, 1961, 26, 574–585; Alice S. Rossi, "Naming Children in Middle-Class Families," *American Sociological Review*, 1965, 30:4, 499–513; Stanley Schachter, "Birth Order, Eminence and Higher Education," *American Sociological Review*, 1963, 28, 757–768.

[45]Harris, *op. cit.*

[46]Rossi, "Naming Children in Middle-Class Families," *op. cit.*

[47]James H. Bossard, *Parent and Child*, (Philadelphia; University of Pennsylvania Press, 1953); James H. Bossard and E. Boll, *The Large Family System* (Philadelphia: University of Pennsylvania Press, 1956).

[48]Rosen, *op. cit.*

[49]Glen H. J. Elder and C. Bowerman, "Family Structure and Child Rearing Patterns: The Effect of Family Size and Sex Composition on Child-Rearing Practices," *American Sociological Review*, 1963, 28, 891–905.

[50]Sarane S. Boocock, "Toward a Sociology of Learning: A Selective Review of Existing Research," *Sociology of Education*, 1966, 39:1, 1–45.

[51]John Nisbet, "Family Environment and Intelligence," in *Education, Economy and Society*, ed. by Halsey *et al.* (New York: The Free Press, a division of the Macmillan Company, 1961).

or population density upon members or inhabitants.[52] In the case of the family, however, this overlooks the very important fact that family size is determined by the key figures *within* the group, i.e., the parents. To find that children in small families differ from children in large families is not simply due to the impact of group size upon individual members but to the very different involvement of the parent with the children and to relations between the parents themselves in small versus large families.

An important clue to a new interpretation can be gained by examining family size from the perspective of parental motivation toward having children. A small family is small for one of two primary reasons: either the parents wanted a small family and achieved their desired size, or they wanted a large family but were not able to attain it. In either case, there is a low probability of unwanted children. Indeed, in the latter eventuality they may take particularly great interest in the children they do have. Small families are therefore most likely to contain parents with a strong and positive orientation to each of the children they have. A large family, by contrast, is large either because the parents achieved the size they desired or because they have more children than they in fact wanted. Large families therefore have a higher probability than small families of including unwanted and unloved children. Consistent with this are Nye's finding that adolescents in small families have better relations with their parents than those in large families[53] and Sears and Maccoby's finding that mothers of large families are more restrictive toward their children than mothers of small families.[54]

This also means that last-born children are more likely to be unwanted than first- or middle-born children, particularly in large fami-

---

[52]Thus Rosen writes: "Considering the sociologist's traditional and continuing concern with group size as an independent variable (from Simmel and Durkheim to the recent experimental studies of small groups), there have been surprisingly few studies of the influence of group size upon the nature of interaction in the family," *op. cit.*, p. 576.

[53]Ivan Nye, "Adolescent-Parent Adjustment: Age, Sex, Sibling, Number, Broken Homes, and Employed Mothers as Variables," *Marriage and Family Living*, 1952, 14, 327–332.

[54]Sears *et al.*, *op. cit.*

lies. This is consistent with what is known of abortion patterns among married women, who typically resort to abortion only when they have achieved the number of children they want or feel they can afford to have. Only a small proportion of women faced with such unwanted pregnancies actually resort to abortion. *This suggests the possibility that the last-born child's reliance on social skills may be his device for securing the attention and loving involvement of a parent less positively predisposed to him than to his older siblings.*

In developing this interpretation, rather extreme cases have been stressed. Closer to the normal range, of families in which even the last-born child was desired and planned for, there is still another element which may contribute to the greater sociability of the last-born child. Most parents are themselves aware of the greater ease with which they face the care of a third fragile newborn than the first; clearly, parental skills and confidence are greater with last-born children than with first-born children. But this does not mean that the attitude of the parent is more positive toward the care of the third child than the first. There is no necessary correlation between skills in an area and enjoyment of that area. Searls[55] found that older homemakers are *more* skillful in domestic tasks but experience *less* enjoyment of them than younger homemakers, pointing to a declining euphoria for a particular role with the passage of time. In the same way, older people rate their marriages as "very happy" less often than younger people do.[56] It is perhaps culturally and psychologically more difficult to face the possibility that women may find less enjoyment of the maternal role with the passage of time, though women themselves know the difference between the romantic expectation concerning child care and the incorporation of the first baby into the household and the more realistic expectation and sharper assessment of their own abilities to do an adequate job of mothering as they face a third confinement. Last-born chil-

dren may experience not only less verbal stimulation from their parents than first-born children but also less prompt and enthusiastic response to their demands—from feeding and diaper-change as infants to requests for stories read at three or a college education at eighteen —simply because the parents experience less intense gratification from the parent role with the third child than they did with the first. The child's response to this might well be to cultivate winning, pleasing manners in early childhood that blossom as charm and sociability in later life, showing both a greater need to be loved and greater pressure to seek approval.

One last point may be appropriately developed at this juncture. Mention was made earlier that for many women the personal outcome of experience in the parent role is not a higher level of maturation but the negative outcome of a depressed sense of self-worth, if not actual personality deterioration. There is considerable evidence that this is more prevalent than we recognize. On a qualitative level, a close reading of the portrait of the working-class wife in Rainwater,[57] Newsom,[58] Komarovsky,[59] Gavron,[60] or Zweig[61] gives little suggestion that maternity has provided these women with opportunities for personal growth and development. So too, Cohen[62] notes with some surprise that in her sample of middle-class educated couples, as in Pavenstadt's study of lower-income women in Boston, there were more emotional difficulty and lower levels of maturation among multiparous women than primiparous women. On a more extensive sample basis, in Gurin's survey of Americans viewing their mental health,[63] as in Bradburn's reports on happiness,[64] single men are

---

[55]Laura G. Searls, "Leisure Role Emphasis of College Graduate Homemakers," *Journal of Marriage and the Family*, 1966, 28:1, 77–82.

[56]Norman Bradburn and D. Caplovitz, *Reports on Happiness* (Chicago: Aldine Publishing Company, 1965).

[57]Lee Rainwater, R. Coleman, and G. Handel, *Workingman's Wife* (New York: Oceana Publications, 1959).

[58]John Newsom and E. Newsom, *Infant Care in an Urban Community* (New York: International Universities Press, 1963).

[59]Mirra Komarovsky, *Blue Collar Marriage* (New York: Random House, Inc., 1962).

[60]Gavron, *op. cit.*

[61]Ferdinand Zweig, *Woman's Life and Labor* (London: Camelot Press, 1952).

[62]Cohen, *op. cit.*

[63]Gerald Gurin, J. Veroff, and S. Feld, *Americans View Their Mental Health* (New York: Basic Books, Monograph Series No. 4, Joint Commission on Mental Illness and Health, 1960).

[64]Bradburn and Caplovitz, *op. cit.*

less happy and less active than single women, but among the married respondents the women are unhappier, have more problems, feel inadequate as parents, have a more negative and passive outlook on life, and show a more negative self-image. All of these characteristics increase with age among married women but show no relationship to age among men. While it may be true, as Gurin argues, that women are more introspective and hence more attuned to the psychological facets of experience than men are, this point does not account for the fact that the things which the women report are all on the negative side; few are on the positive side, indicative of euphoric sensitivity and pleasure. The possibility must be faced, and at some point researched, that women lose ground in personal development and self-esteem during the early and middle years of adulthood, whereas men gain ground in these respects during the same years. The retention of a high level of self-esteem may depend upon the adequacy of earlier preparation for major adult roles: men's training adequately prepares them for their primary adult roles in the occupational system, as it does for those women who opt to participate significantly in the work world. Training in the qualities and skills needed for family roles in contemporary society may be inadequate for both sexes, but the lowering of self-esteem occurs only among women because their primary adult roles are within the family system.

PREPARATION FOR PARENTHOOD

Four factors may be given special attention on the question of what preparation American couples bring to parenthood.

Paucity of preparation. Our educational system is dedicated to the cognitive development of the young, and our primary teaching approach is the pragmatic one of learning by doing. How much one knows and how well he can apply what he knows are the standards by which the child is judged in school, as the employee is judged at work. The child can learn by doing in such subjects as science, mathematics, art work, or shop, but not in the subjects most relevant to successful family life: sex, home maintenance, child care, interpersonal competence, and empathy. If the home is defi-

cient in training in these areas, the child is left with no preparation for a major segment of his adult life. A doctor facing his first patient in private practice has treated numerous patients under close supervision during his internship, but probably a majority of American mothers approach maternity with no previous child-care experience beyond sporadic baby-sitting, perhaps a course in child psychology, or occasional care of younger siblings.

Limited learning during pregnancy. A second important point makes adjustment to parenthood potentially more stressful than marital adjustment. This is the lack of any realistic training for parenthood during the anticipatory stage of pregnancy. By contrast, during the engagement period preceding marriage, an individual has opportunities to develop the skills and make the adjustments which ease the transition to marriage. Through discussions of values and life goals, through sexual experimentation, shared social experiences as an engaged couple with friends and relatives, and planning and furnishing an apartment, the engaged couple can make considerable progress in developing mutuality in advance of the marriage itself.[65] No such headstart is possible in the case of pregnancy. What preparation exists is confined to reading, consultation with friends and parents, discussions between husband and wife, and a minor nesting phase in which a place and the equipment for a baby are prepared in the household.[66]

Abruptness of transition. Thirdly, the birth of a child is not followed by any gradual taking on of responsibility, as in the case of a professional work role. It is as if the woman shifted from a graduate student to a full professor with little intervening apprenticeship experience of slowly increasing responsibility. The new mother starts out immediately on 24-hour duty,

[65]Rapoport, "The Transition from Engagement to Marriage," *op. cit.;* Raush *et al., op. cit.*

[66]During the period when marriage was the critical transition in the adult woman's life rather than pregnancy, a good deal of anticipatory "nesting" behavior took place from the time of conception. Now more women work through a considerable portion of the first pregnancy, and such nesting behavior as exists may be confined to a few shopping expeditions or baby showers, thus adding to the abruptness of the transition and the difficulty of adjustment following the birth of a first child.

with responsibility for a fragile and mysterious infant totally dependent on her care.

If marital adjustment is more difficult for very young brides than more mature ones,[67] adjustment to motherhood may be even more difficult. A woman can adapt a passive dependence on a husband and still have a successful marriage, but a young mother with strong dependency needs is in for difficulty in maternal adjustment, because the role precludes such dependency. This situation was well described in Cohen's study[68] in a case of a young wife with a background of co-ed popularity and a passive dependent relationship to her admired and admiring husband, who collapsed into restricted incapacity when faced with the responsibilities of maintaining a home and caring for a child.

Lack of guidelines to successful parenthood. If the central task of parenthood is the rearing of children to become the kind of competent adults valued by the society, then an important question facing any parent is what he or she specifically can do to create such a competent adult. This is where the parent is left with few or no guidelines from the expert. Parents can readily inform themselves concerning the young infant's nutritional, clothing, and medical needs and follow the general prescription that a child needs loving physical contact and emotional support. Such advice may be sufficient to produce a healthy, happy, and well-adjusted preschooler, but adult competency is quite another matter.

In fact, the adults who do "succeed" in American society show a complex of characteristics as children that current experts in child-care would evaluate as "poor" to "bad." Biographies of leading authors and artists, as well as the more rigorous research inquiries of creativity among architects[69] or scientists,[70] do not portray childhoods with characteristics currently endorsed by mental health and child-care authorities. Indeed, there is often a predominance of tension in childhood family relations and traumatic loss rather than loving parental support, intense channeling of energy in one area of interest rather than an all-round profile of diverse interests, and social withdrawal and preference for loner activities rather than gregarious sociability. Thus, the stress in current child-rearing advice on a high level of loving support but a low level of discipline or restriction on the behavior of the child—the "developmental" family type as Duvall calls it[71]—is a profile consistent with the focus on mental health, sociability, and adjustment. Yet the combination of both high support and high authority on the part of parents is most strongly related to the child's sense of responsibility, leadership quality, and achievement level, as found in Bronfenbrenner's studies[72] and that of Mussen and Distler.[73]

Brim points out[74] that we are a long way from being able to say just what parent role prescriptions have what effect on the adult characteristics of the child. We know even less about how such parental prescriptions should be changed to adapt to changed conceptions of competency in adulthood. In such an ambiguous context, the great interest parents take in school reports on their children or the pediatrician's assessment of the child's developmental progress should be seen as among the few indices

[67]Lee G. Burchinal, "Adolescent Role Deprivation and High School Marriage," *Marriage and Family Living,* 1959, *21,* 378-384; Floyd M. Martinson, "Ego Deficiency as a Factor in Marriage," *American Sociological Review,* 1955, *22,* 161–164; J. Joel Moss and Ruby Gingles, "The Relationship of Personality to the Incidence of Early Marriage," *Marriage and Family Living,* 1959, *21,* 373–377.

[68]Cohen, *op. cit.*

[69]Donald W. MacKinnon, "Creativity and Images of the Self," in *The Study of Lives,* ed. by Robert W. White (New York: Atherton Press, 1963).

[70]Anne Roe, *A Psychological Study of Eminent Biologists, Psychological Monographs,* 1951, 65:14, 68 pages; Anne Roe, "A Psychological Study of Physical Scientists," *Genetic Psychology Monographs,* 1951, *43,* 121–239; Anne Roe, "Crucial Life Experiences in the Development of Scientists," in *Talent and Education,* ed. by E. P. Torrance (Minneapolis: University of Minnesota Press, 1960).

[71]Evelyn M. Duvall, "Conceptions of Parenthood," *American Journal of Sociology,* 1946, *52,* 193-203.

[72]Urie Bronfenbrenner, "Some Familial Antecedents of Responsibility and Leadership in Adolescents," in *Studies in Leadership,* ed. by L. Petrullo and B. Bass (New York: Holt, Rinehart, & Winston, Inc., 1960).

[73]Paul Mussen and L. Distler, "Masculinity, Identification and Father-Son Relationships," *Journal of Abnormal and Social Psychology,* 1959, *59,* 350-356.

[74]Orville G. Brim, "The Parent-Child Relation as a Social System: I. Parent and Child Roles," *Child Development,* 1952, 28:3, 343-364.

parents have of how well *they* are doing as parents.

SYSTEM AND ROLE REQUIREMENTS: INSTRUMENTALITY AND INTEGRATION

Typological dichotomies and unidimensional scales have loomed large in the search by social scientists for the most economical and general principles to account for some significant portion of the complex behavior or social organization they study. Thus, for example, the European dichotomy of *Gemeinschaft* and *Gesellschaft* became the American sociological distinction between rural and urban sociology, subfields that have outlasted their conceptual utility now that the rural environment has become urbanized and the interstices between country and city are swelling with suburban developments.

In recent years a new dichotomy has gained more acceptance in sociological circles—the Parsonian distinction between *instrumental* and *expressive*, an interesting dichotomy that is unfortunately applied in an indiscriminate way to all manner of social phenomena including the analysis of teacher role conflict, occupational choice, the contrast between the family system and the occupational system, and the primary roles or personality tendencies of men compared to women.

On a system level, for example, the "instrumental" occupational system is characterized by rationality, efficiency, rejection of tradition, and depression of interpersonal loyalty, while the "expressive" family system is characterized by nurturance, integration, tension-management, ritual, and interpersonal solidarity. Applied to sex roles within the family, the husband-father emerges as the instrumental rational leader, a symbolic representative of the outside world, and the wife-mother emerges as the expressive, nurturant, affective center of the family. Such distinctions may be useful in the attempt to capture some general tendency of a system or a role, but they lead to more distortion than illumination when applied to the actual functioning of a specific system or social role or to the actual behavior of a given individual in a particular role.

Take, for example, the husband-father as the instrumental role within the family on the assumption that men are the major breadwinners and therefore carry the instrumentality associated with work into their roles within the family. To begin with, the family is not an experimental one-task small group but a complex, ongoing 24-hour entity with many tasks that must be performed. Secondly, we really know very little about how occupational roles affect the performance of family roles.[75] An aggressive courtroom lawyer or a shrewd business executive are not lawyers and businessmen at home but husbands and fathers. Unless shown to be in error, we should proceed on the assumption that behavior is role-specific. (Indeed, Brim[76] argues that even personality is role-specific.) A strict teacher may be an indulgent mother at home; a submissive wife may be a dominant mother; a dictatorial father may be an exploited and passive worker on the assembly line; or, as in some of Lidz's schizophrenic patients' families,[77] a passive dependent husband at home may be a successful dominant lawyer away from home.

There is, however, a more fundamental level to the criticism that the dichotomous usage of

---

[75] Miller and Swanson have suggested a connection between the trend toward bureaucratic structure in the occupational world and the shift in child-rearing practices toward permissiveness and a greater stress on personal adjustment of children. Their findings are suggestive rather than definitive, however, and no hard research has subjected this question to empirical inquiry. Daniel R. Miller and G. Swanson, *The Changing American Parent* (New York: John Wiley & Sons, Inc., 1958).

The same suggestive but nondefinitive clues are to be found in von Mering's study of the contrast between professional and nonprofessional women as mothers. She shows that the professionally active woman in her mother role tends toward a greater stress on discipline rather than indulgence and has a larger number of rules with fewer choices or suggestions to the child: the emphasis is in equipping the child to cope effectively with rules and techniques of his culture. The nonprofessional mother, by contrast, has a greater value stress on insuring the child's emotional security, tending to take the role of the clinician in an attempt to diagnose the child's problems and behavior, Faye H. von Mering, "Professional and Non-Professional Women as Mothers," *Journal of Social Psychology*, 1955, 42, 21–34.

[76] Orville G. Brim, "Personality Development as Role-Learning," in *Personality Development in Children*, ed. by Ira Iscoe and Harold Stevenson, (Austin, Texas: University of Texas Press, 1960).

[77] Lidz *et al.*, *op. cit.*

instrumentality and expressiveness, linked to sex and applied to intrafamily roles, leads to more distortion than illumination. The logic of my argument starts with the premise that every social system, group, or role has two primary, independent, structural axes. Whether these axes are called "authority and support," as in Straus's circumplex model,[78] or "instrumental and expressive" as by Parsons,[79] there are tasks to be performed and affective support to be given in all the cases cited. There must be discipline, rules, and division of labor in the nation-state as in the family or a business enterprise *and* there must be solidarity among the units comprising these same systems in order for the system to function adequately. *This means that the role of father, husband, wife, or mother each has these two independent dimensions of authority and support, instrumentality and expressiveness, work and love.* Little is gained by trying to stretch empirical results to fit the father role to the instrumental category, as Brim[80] has done, or the mother role to the expressive category, as Zelditch has done.[81]

In taking a next logical step from this premise, the critical issue, both theoretically and empirically, becomes gauging the *balance* between these two dimensions of the system or of the role. Roles or systems could be compared in terms of the average difference among them in the direction and extent of the discrepancy between authority and support; or individuals could be compared in terms of the variation among them in the discrepancy between the two dimensions in a given role.

An example may clarify these points. A teacher who is all loving, warm support to her students and plans many occasions to evoke integrative ties among them but who is incompetent in the exercise of authority or knowledge of the subjects she teaches would be judged by any school principal as an inadequate teacher. The same judgment of inadequacy would apply to a strict disciplinarian teacher, competent and informed about her subjects but totally lacking in any personal quality of warmth or ability to encourage integrative and cooperative responses among her students. Maximum adequacy of teacher performance requires a relatively high positive level on both of these two dimensions of the teacher role.

To claim that teachers have a basic conflict in approaching their role because they are required to be a "bisexual parent, permissive giver of love and harsh disciplinarian with a masculine intellectual grasp of the world," as Jackson and Moscovici[82] have argued, at least recognizes the two dimensions of the teacher role, though it shares the view of many sociologists that role *conflict* is inherent wherever these seeming polarities are required. Why conflict is predicted hinges on the assumed invariance of the linkage of the male to authority and the female to the expressive-integrative roles.

It is this latter assumed difference between the sexes that restricts theory-building in family sociology and produces so much puzzlement on the part of researchers into marriage and parenthood, sex-role socialization, or personality tendencies toward masculinity or femininity. Let me give one example of recent findings on this latter topic and then move on to apply the two-dimension concept to the parental role. Vincent[83] administered the Gough Femininity Scale along with several other scale batteries from the California Personality Inventory to several hundred college men and women. He found that women *low* on femininity were higher in the Class I scale which measures poise, ascendancy, and self-assurance, and men *high* in femininity were higher in dominance, capacity for status, and responsibility. Successful adult men in a technological society are rarely interested in racing cars, soldiering, or hunting; they are cautious, subtle, and psychologically attuned to others. So too, contemporary adult women who fear windstorms, the dark, strange places, automobile accidents, excitement, crowded par-

---

[78]Straus, *op. cit.*
[79]Parsons and Bales, *op. cit.*
[80]Brim, "The Parent-Child Relation as a Social System: I. Parent and Child Roles," *op. cit.*
[81]Parsons and Bales, *op. cit.*

[82]Philip Jackson and F. Moscovici, "The Teacher-to-be: A Study of Embryonic Indentification with a Professional Role," *School Review*, 1963, 71:1, 41–65.
[83]Clark E. Vincent, "Implications of Changes in Male-Female Role Expectations for Interpreting M-F Scores," *Journal of Marriage and the Family*, 1966, 28:2, 196–199.

ties, or practical jokes (and are therefore high on femininity in the Gough scale) will be inadequate for the task of managing an isolated household with neither men nor kinswomen close by to help them through daily crises, for the assumption of leadership roles in community organizations, or for holding down supplementary breadwinning or cakewinning jobs.

When Deutsch[84] and Escalona[85] point out that today's "neurotic" woman is not an assertive dominant person but a passive dependent one, the reason may be found in the social change in role expectations concerning competence among adult women, not that there has been a social change in the characteristics of neurotic women. In the past an assertive, dominant woman might have defined herself and been defined by her analyst as "neurotic" because she could not fill the expectations then held for adequacy among adult women. Today, it is the passive dependent woman who will be judged "neurotic" because she cannot fill adequately the expectations now set for and by her. What is really meant when we say that sex role definitions have become increasingly blurred is that men are now required to show more integrative skills than in the past, and women more instrumental skills. This incurs potential sex-role "confusion" only by the standards of the past, not by the standards of what is required for contemporary adult competence in family and work roles.

Once freed from the assumption of a single bipolar continuum of masculinity-femininity,[86]

authority-integration, or even independence-dependence,[87] one can observe increased instrumentality in a role with no implication of necessarily decreased integration, and vice versa. Thus, an increasing rationality in the care of children, the maintenance of a household, or meal planning for a family does not imply a decreasing level of integrative support associated with the wife-mother role. So, too, the increased involvement of a young father in playful encounters with his toddler carries no necessary implication of a change in the instrumental dimensions of his role.

The two-dimensional approach also frees our analyses of parenthood on two other important questions. Brim has reviewed much of the research on the parent-child relationship[88] and noted the necessity of specifying not only the sex of the parent but the sex of the child and whether a given parent-child dyad is a cross-sex or same-sex pair. It is clear from his review that fathers and mothers relate differently to their sons and daughters: fathers have been found to be stricter with their sons than with their daughters, and mothers stricter with their daughters than with their sons. Thus, a two-dimensional approach to the parent role is more appropriate to what is already empirically known about the parent-child relationship.

Secondly, only on a very general overview level does a parent maintain a particular level of support and of discipline toward a given child: situational variation is an important determinant of parental response to a child. A father with a general tendency toward relatively

---

[84]Helene Deutsch, *The Psychology of Women: A Psychoanalytic Interpretation*, vol. 1 (New York: Grune and Stratton, 1944).

[85]Sibylle Escalona, "The Psychological Situation of Mother and Child Upon Return from the Hospital," in *Problems of Infancy and Childhood: Transactions of the Third Conference*, ed. by Milton Senn, 1949.

[86]Several authors have recently pointed out the inadequacy of social science usage of the masculinity-femininity concept. Landreth, in a study of parent-role appropriateness in giving physical care and companionship to the child, found her four-year-old subjects, particularly in New Zealand, made no simple linkage of activity to mother as opposed to father. Catherine Landreth, "Four-Year-Olds' Notions about Sex Appropriateness of Parental Care and Companionship Activities," *Merrill-Palmer Quarterly*, 1963, 9:3, 175–182. She comments that in New Zealand "masculinity and femininity appear to be comfortably relegated to chromosome rather

than to contrived activity" (p. 176). Lansky, in a study of the effect of the sex of the children upon the parents' own sex-identification, calls for devising tests which look at masculinity and femininity as two dimensions rather than a single continuum. Leonard M. Lansky, "The Family Structure Also Affects the Model: Sex-Role Identification in Parents of Preschool Children," *Merrill-Palmer Quarterly*, 1964, *10*:1, 39–50.

[87]Beller has already shown the value of such an approach, in a study that defined independence and dependence as two separate dimensions rather than the extremes of a bipolar continuum. He found, as hypothesized, a very *low* negative correlation between the two measures. E. K. Beller, "Exploratory Studies of Dependency," trans., *N.Y. Academy of Science*, 1959, *21*, 414–426.

[88]Brim, "The Parent-Child Relation as a Social System: I Parent and Child Roles," *op. cit.*

little emotional support of his son may offer a good deal of comfort if the child is hurt. An indulgent and loving mother may show an extreme degree of discipline when the same child misbehaves. Landreth found that her four-year-olds gave more mother responses on a care item concerning food than on bath-time or bedtime care and suggests as Brim has,[89] that "any generalizations on parent roles should be made in terms of the role activities studied."[90]

Let me illustrate the utility of the two-dimensional concept by applying it to the parental role. Clearly there are a number of expressive requirements for adequate performance in this role: spontaneity and flexibility, the ability to be tender and loving and to respond to tenderness and love from a child, to take pleasure in tactile contact and in play, and to forget one's adultness and unselfconsciously respond to the sensitivities and fantasies of a child. Equally important are the instrumental requirements for adequate performance in the parental role: firmness and consistency; the ability to manage time and energy; to plan and organize activities involving the child; to teach and to train the child in body controls, motor and language skills, and knowledge of the natural and social world; and interpersonal and value discriminations.

Assuming we had empirical measures of these two dimensions of the parental role, one could then compare individual women both by their levels on each of these dimensions and by the extent to which the discrepancy in level on the two dimensions was tipped toward a high expressive or instrumental dimension. This makes no assumptions about what the balance "should" be; that remains an empirical question awaiting a test in the form of output variables—the characteristics of children we deem to be critical for their competence as adults. Indeed, I would

predict that an exhaustive count of the actual components of both the marital and parental roles would show a very high proportion of instrumental components in the parental role and a low proportion in the marital role and that this is an underlying reason why maternal role adjustment is more difficult for women than marital role adjustment. It also leaves as an open, empirical question what the variance is, among fathers, in the level of expressiveness and instrumentality in their paternal role performance and how the profile of fathers compares with that of mothers.

It would not surprise many of us, of course, if women scored higher than men on the expressive dimension and men scored higher on the instrumental dimension of the parental role. Yet quite the opposite might actually result. Men spend relatively little time with their children, and it is time of a particular kind: evenings, weekends, and vacations, when the activities and mood of the family are heavily on the expressive side. Women carry the major burden of the instrumental dimension of parenting. If, as Mable Cohen[91] suggests, the rearing of American boys is inadequate on the social and sexual dimension of development and the rearing of American girls is inadequate on the personal dimension of development, then from the perspective of adequate parenthood performance, we have indeed cause to reexamine the socialization of boys and girls in families and schools. Our current practices appear adequate as preparation for occupational life for men but not women, and inadequate as preparation for family life for both sexes.

However, this is to look too far ahead. At the present, this analysis of parenthood suggests we have much to rethink and much to research before we develop policy recommendations in this area.

---

[89]*Ibid.*
[90]Landreth, *op. cit.*, 181.

---

[91]Cohen, *op. cit.*

37.

HENRY N. RICCIUTI

SOCIAL AND EMOTIONAL BEHAVIOR IN INFANCY: SOME DEVELOPMENTAL ISSUES AND PROBLEMS

My major concern in the present discussion will not be to offer a broad summary of the principal literature dealing with social and emotional development in infancy. A number of excellent reviews and discussions of some of the most salient topics in this broad area have appeared within the past several years (e.g., Yarrow's review of the effects of maternal separation [1964], Bronfenbrenner's paper on early deprivation in mammals and man [1968], Rheingold's discussion of the development of social behavior in infancy [1966], etc.). Rather, my main purpose will be to point out and discuss what seem to me to be some important current research issues and areas of investigation which hold particular promise for advancing our understanding of the nature and development of social and emotional behavior in human infancy. At the same time, I would like to indicate both the historical contrast, as well as the continuity, between these contemporary research issues and those which represented some of the main concerns of earlier investigators in the field of child development. I shall therefore precede my discussion of current research emphases with a brief summary of the early descriptive studies of social and emotional behavior and development in infancy.

SOME DEFINITIONAL NOTES

Thus far I've used the terms "social" and "emo-

This selection is reprinted from: Henry N. Ricciuti, "Social and Emotional Behavior in Infancy: Some Developmental Issues and Problems," *Merrill-Palmer Quarterly*, 1968, *14*, 82–100.
Reprinted with the permission of the author and publisher.
This paper was presented at The Merrill-Palmer Institute Conference on Research and Teaching of Infant Development, February 9–11, 1967. The conference was financially supported in part by the National Institute of Child Health and Human Development.

tional" rather glibly, as though they were either closely related, or possibly even interchangeable. This usage of the two terms in close juxtaposition, which one finds quite commonly, reflects the fact that there is indeed a close relationship between social and emotional behavior. A great many significant social interactions in infancy involve important affective or emotional components; similarly, some of the most potent instigators of emotional responses are "social" stimuli, i.e., stimuli emitted by another person. On the other hand, if one regards social behavior, broadly considered, as any behavior that is evoked, maintained, and modified by the behavior of another person (Rheingold, 1966), obviously much social behavior is not associated with significant emotional responses; at the same time, important emotional responses are evoked by a wide range of non-social stimuli. In the present discussion, I shall be concerned with emotional behavior whether instigated by social or non-social stimuli; with respect to social behavior, however, my primary reference will be to social responses which typically have significant emotional or affective components associated with them.

The problem of defining the precise nature of what is meant by the "emotions" or "affects" has been a major concern of many philosophers, psychologists, and physiologists for a good many years. At this point in our discussion, it would be helpful to have at least a brief working definition of emotional behavior. I have found the following conceptualization, distilled from a variety of sources, to be particularly meaningful: we tend to regard a particular behavior as "emotional" when it represents an appreciable change from some typical "baseline," or characteristic level or mode of response, *and* where the behavioral change is accompanied by physiological or visceral changes and by a change in subjective or experiential state, generally along a pleasure-displeasure or hedonic continuum. Thus, we might say that an emotion typically has a behavioral or action component, a physiological or arousal component, and a subjective or hedonic component (Hamburg, 1963). This last component, that of subjective state or feeling, is obviously the most troublesome and controversial one conceptually, and as expected, it poses particular problems for us when we try to analyze the nature of emotions in infants. A final definitional note: while the terms "emotional" and "affective" are often used interchangeably, in common usage the latter usually implies some reference to the subjective component, whereas the former may not.

EARLY DESCRIPTIVE STUDIES OF SOCIAL AND EMOTIONAL BEHAVIOR IN INFANCY

Early studies of social and emotional behavior in infancy tended to be primarily descriptive in nature, and were addressed particularly to the question of what sorts of social and emotional responses were typically observable in children at successive age levels. The major historical change, as in many areas of study in child development, has been the transition from this descriptive focus to the contemporary emphasis on analytic studies, which are primarily concerned with understanding the nature of social and emotional behavior, and with the question of how particular patterns of developmental change come about. While it has become somewhat fashionable in recent years to speak rather disparagingly of studies which are primarily descriptive in nature, I would like to emphasize the very real importance of these early studies, which provided so many insightful observations and questions concerning social and emotional behavior, often foreshadowing a good deal of the content of contemporary research in the area.

Three major sources of data on social and emotional development are provided by these early studies in the field. First, there are the informal, but detailed qualitative observations and descriptions reported by such early investi-

gators as Charles Darwin, whose classic treatise on "The Expression of the Emotions in Man and Animals," written nearly a hundred years ago (1873) is still an essential reference in the field; James Sully, writing in England in 1895, and Stern in Germany about 30 years later (1924), describing and speculating about the nature of young children's fear of strange, novel, or unusual objects; James Baldwin in America (1895), describing what he called "organic bashfulness" in the latter part of the first year of life, when the infant turned away from the stranger and toward the mother; and finally Karl and Charlotte Buhler in Austria, in the late 1920's and early 1930's, describing the affective pleasure infants derive from simple motoric movements, and from mastery of simple motoric tasks (i.e., "function pleasure") (1930).

The second source of descriptive information on social and emotional behavior is provided by the systematic normative data collected in the development and standardization of the various infant tests, beginning with Buhler (1935) and Gesell (1928) in the 1920's. While social and emotional responses represented only a small part of the total pool of items included in most of the early baby tests, we still depend very much on such data for descriptive information regarding the age of appearance of particular behaviors such as smiling and cooing in response to the adult face, showing displeasure at the removal of a toy, engaging in playful social imitation, etc. (e.g., Gesell, 1940, Griffiths, 1954).

The third major source of data is found in the relatively large number of systematic descriptive or quasi-experimental studies which began to appear mainly in the early and middle 1930's. These investigations typically involved the collection of information concerning the age of appearance of a variety of specific emotional and social behaviors, based on observations or parental records and reports for fairly large samples of children. (For example, see Bridges, 1932; Blatz and Millichamp, 1935; Jersild and Holmes, 1935; Jones and Jones, 1928.)

Given this threefold body of literature, what is the general portrayal of the over-all course of social and emotional development in the first two years of life which emerges therefrom? First, with respect to the infant's changing social responsiveness, the general picture provided by these studies remains a fairly reliable one, although it is limited to rather gross developmental changes. Very briefly, clear-cut pleasureful social responses to other people do not appear until approximately the end of the second month, when any human face readily instigates smiling and other indications of positive affect. This indiscriminate positive social response to humans continues until approximately the fifth or sixth month, after which smiling at strangers seems to be considerably reduced. Moreover, toward the end of the first year there is a rather marked tendency for infants to respond to the approach of a stranger with considerable distress and anxiety. Simultaneously, affectional attachments to specific adults such as the parents become more marked and clearly delineated, and this trend continues into the second year, during the latter part of which one also sees increasing social and affectional interactions with other children. While the general pattern of development change just outlined seems reasonably well established, we sorely need more precise descriptions of these changes in social responsiveness and their variations, as well as systematic analyses of the various major influences which function as determinants of such changes. A concern with precisely these sorts of questions represents one of the major emphases of contemporary research in the field.

Turning next to a consideration of the somewhat more general problem of emotional behavior and development, it is probably fair to say that a good many of the specific issues and questions raised by early investigators in this field are still very much with us. Many of the early studies were concerned with such questions as what emotional responses, if any, are present in the neonate (Watson, 1917); at what points in subsequent development is it possible to identify specific emotions (or emotional behaviors, we would prefer to say nowadays); how are these expressed; what are the stimulus situations which evoke responses of a particular sort; etc.

Again there are a few broad, empirical generalizations emerging from these studies which most people would probably regard as reasonably acceptable today. In the neonate, one can only differentiate between states of quiescence and undifferentiated excitement (according to Bridges, 1932), or between quiescence and a primitive sort of "unpleasure" (Spitz, 1950). By the end of the first month one can more readily distinguish between quiescence and what Bridges calls "distress" reactions, but it is not until the end of the second or third month that clear "pleasurable" responses are seen, chiefly in the smiling, increased vocalizations, and bodily activity constituting the positive social response to people. From this point on, with increasing development, more highly differentiated forms of positive as well as negative emotional behaviors occur. Just how distinct these are, and how one can best conceptualize, observe, and measure them are thorny problems that are very much in the forefront of our current thinking and research today (e.g., Escalona, 1963; Spitz, 1963; Tomkins, 1962, 1963; Wolff, 1966).

SOME CONTEMPORARY RESEARCH EMPHASES AND SIGNIFICANT AREAS OF INVESTIGATION

Having reviewed very briefly the general nature and major outcomes of the primarily descriptive earlier studies of social and emotional development in infancy, let us consider next two rather broad areas of contemporary research activity which appear to me to involve particularly promising lines of empirical as well as theoretical investigation.

One of the major emphases characterizing a large body of current research is a concern with more detailed analyses of the role of stimulus and situational determinants of social and emotional responses. This emphasis is particularly well represented in recent research on the development of attachment behavior in infants, and in research concerned with specifying the role of various stimulus cues as elicitors, and sometimes as reinforcers, of responses involved in adult-infant interaction. In both instances, we find a great deal of significant research currently being undertaken not only with humans, but with various species of infra-human mammals and birds as well.

Much of the recent and contemporary work aimed at specifying the processes involved in the development of the infant's attachment to familiar adults has been greatly influenced, if not stimulated, by Bowlby's theoretical writings on the nature of the mother-infant tie (1958) and the related problem of separation anxiety (1960). Bowlby suggested that certain innate response systems in the infant's repertoire play an important role in establishing the initial "tie" with the mother, since these responses are readily elicitable by appropriate stimuli and help to ensure proximity to and caretaking by mother. Included among such response systems are sucking, clinging, and visual or locomotor following behavior, as well as smiling and crying, the last two serving as particularly effective stimuli for eliciting social or caretaking responses from mother. The infant's first manifestations of protest and distress reactions on separation from mother are regarded as a form of "primary anxiety," associated with the persistent activation of such response systems as crying, clinging, and following under circumstances (i.e., isolation from mother) which prevent their normal termination (i.e., proximity to mother). Bowlby goes on to point out the importance of the connection between these separation reactions and the infant's fear or fright responses to stimuli instigating escape or freezing, such as sudden noise, strangeness, etc. Observations of infants of many species indicate that relatively intense fear reactions are terminated not by mere flight alone but by escape to a particular "haven of safety" (e.g., a home nest, another animal, or the mother). Thus, after the infant has developed specific attachments to adults, being frightened and at the same time separated from mother poses for the infant a situation where the terminating or distress-reducing situation both for the escape behaviors instigated by the fright stimulus, and for the crying, clinging, and following responses instigated by separation is essentially the same, i.e., closeness to mother. Circumstances such as these place the infant in a situation of "double exposure" to distress reactions which specifically require mother for their alleviation.

Several recent studies provide good illustrations of contemporary investigations in which problems of the sort just indicated are being investigated empirically under circumstances that permit one to examine rather closely some of the relevant stimulus and situational determinants of the behavior under investigation. Morgan and Ricciuti (1968) examined changes in infants' affective responses to a stranger during the period from four to twelve months, employing a laboratory situation in which a male and female stranger systematically approached the infant, who was sometimes on mother's lap, sometimes four feet away from her. Generally speaking, the younger the infants, the more positive the responses to the stranger, and it was not until the 12-month level that one could characterize the reactions as generally more negative than positive. Prior to eight months of age, the infants were equally positive in their responses regardless of their proximity to mother. From that point on, however, closeness to mother began to play an increasingly important role, with the responses to the stranger being significantly less positive or more negative when the infant was separated from mother (as one would expect from Bowlby's theory). The younger infants responded more positively as the stranger initiated closer and more active social contact, whereas the opposite was true for the older infants. Finally, the female stranger elicited more positive and less negative reactions from the infants at all ages than the male stranger.

Another example of research concerned with specifying the role of particular situational variables may be found in an interesting series of experiments by Rheingold (1968) in which she examined the emotional and exploratory behavior of 9½-month-old infants in a strange laboratory room whose characteristics were systematically varied. Infants placed alone in the room when it was either empty, contained a few toys, or contained a strange young female about six feet away, showed a good deal of emotional distress and inhibited normal locomotor activity. In contrast to this group, babies who found their mothers present in the otherwise empty room produced non-distress vocalizations rather than crying, and explored the room freely. In short, Rheingold concludes, mother's presence seemed to neutralize the strangeness of the environment confronting the infant. There was some evidence, also, suggesting that the strange room was most distressing when it contained the unfamiliar person.

These findings, that proximity to mother attenuates the infants' negative responses to strange stimuli and supports positive emotional responses and exploratory behavior, are strikingly paralleled in recent animal studies, even when the "mother" happens to be a cloth-covered surrogate to which infant rhesus monkeys had become "attached" (Harlow, 1961), or a green styrofoam rectangle to which Peking ducklings had been imprinted (Stettner and Tilds, 1966). It seems quite clear that our understanding of the complex factors involved in the interplay between the infant's developing attachment to specific adults and the nature of his responses to separation and to fear-eliciting stimuli will be considerably facilitated as we continue to find ways of studying objectively the specific influence of various major determinants of the social and emotional behaviors involved.

Thus far we have been discussing recent analyses of stimulus and situational determinants of social and emotional responses at given points in development. There is obviously great need for a more complete understanding of how initial patterns of response are subsequently modified through experience and learning. This is particularly true in regard to the development of the complex, mutually adaptive response patterns involved in infant-adult attachment behavior. A number of investigators have been concerned with the role of specific stimuli as elicitors and reinforcers of some of the social and emotional responses involved in mother-infant interaction, within a learning framework. It has been shown, for example (Rheingold, Gewirtz, and Ross, 1959), that three-month-old infants made increasingly frequent vocalizations to an adult when such vocalizations were immediately followed by the adult smiling broad-

ly, making "tsk, tsk" sounds, and touching the infant lightly on the abdomen. When such "reinforcement" no longer followed the infants' vocalizations, their frequency decreased substantially.

The study just mentioned was concerned with the effects of adult reinforcement of infant vocalizations under controlled, experimental conditions. Can learning analyses of this sort by employed profitably in the study of naturally occurring infant-adult interaction? The recent work of Gewirtz and Gewirtz (1968) provides an excellent illustration of a research strategy aimed at facilitating learning analyses of infant-adult interaction occurring in "natural" settings. These investigators began by making detailed observational records of the sequential behaviors of infants and mothers (or other adult caretakers) in several different environments. Analysis of these records then permits them to define and compare the caretaking environments, in terms of the availability of specific stimuli of various sorts as potential elicitors and/or reinforcers of infant social responses (e.g., specific caretaking behaviors of adults, physical characteristics of the environment, etc.). Further analyses make it possible to determine the relative frequency of occurrence of various infant responses to particular adult behaviors, and vice versa. Some preliminary analyses indicate, for example, that the likelihood of an infant's vocalization being followed by an adult's smile varied from .21 to .42 for different adult-child pairs, whereas the likelihood that the infant's smile would elicit an adult smile was considerably greater, from .46 to .88. Further work, either under way or planned, is aimed at more refined evaluations of the degree to which various adult responses are made contingent upon particular infant behaviors, and at methods for handling longer sequential interaction "chains." Although complicated and time consuming, this approach holds great promise for both defining more precisely the salient features of the environment impinging on the infant, and for understanding how the infant and adults in his environment begin to modify one another's behavior.

The last problem just mentioned has been

under investigation in a somewhat different manner in the earliest weeks of life by Sander and Julia (1966). By employing procedures which permit continuous 24-hour monitoring of the infant's motility, crying, periods of sleep and wakefulness, as well as various interventions by the nurse-caretaker, these investigators are able to examine relationships between the infants' rhythm patterns and the caretaker's interventions as these become modified over a period of weeks, in the direction of increasing or decreasing regulation and adaptation in the adult-infant interaction.

Turning from our discussion of research focused mainly on infant-adult interaction, I want to make brief reference to the increasing attention being directed to the problem of identifying the particular stimulus elements or cues which account for the apparent effectiveness of certain relatively complex stimulus configurations as elicitors of early social and emotional responses in infants, often a presumably unlearned sort. (This line of approach has traditionally been employed to advantage by ethologists in their analysis of the stimulus determinants of behavior in various species of animals and birds—e.g., Hinde, 1966; Thorpe, 1963.) For example, it has long been known that one of the most potent elicitors of the smiling response in early infancy is the face of the human adult, particularly when it is animated by talking and smiling. In recent years, investigators have been trying to specify more precisely which particular cues in this stimulus configuration are primarily involved in instigating smiling behavior at various points in the infant's development, beginning with the first few weeks of life (Ahrens, 1954; Wolff, 1963, 1966).

Paralleling this line of inquiry is a concern with exploring the social or emotional response-eliciting characteristics of a rather broad range of stimuli in various modalities. Salzen (1963), for example, working with one infant, found that at eight weeks of age relatively simple, non-human visual stimuli elicited smiling responses (e.g., a black-and-white cardboard oval, particularly when rotated slowly). By the 12th week such simple stimuli failed to elicit smiling, but "novel" combinations of visual and auditory cues, such as a rattle or clock, would do so. Wolff (1963) was readily able to elicit smiling as well as positive vocalizations in four- to five-week-old infants by placing the infant's hands in his own, and bouncing his hands together three times in rapid succession (as though playing "pat-a-cake"), while keeping his face out of sight of the infant. A particularly interesting recent investigation by Kistiakovskaia (1965) was concerned with determining the stimulus conditions which elicit and help to establish the "positive emotional complex of responses" in infants during the first weeks and months of life. Her interpretation placed particular emphasis upon the role of rather prolonged visual fixation of immobile target objects, and of convergence and divergence responses to an object being moved toward and away from the infant, as basic instigators of the earliest positive emotional responses of smiling, vocalization, and animated movements.

While the last several studies mentioned were directly concerned with stimulus determinants involved in the elicitation of smiling and other positive emotional responses, they can actually be regarded as part of several broader lines of currently active research dealing with the general problem of characteristics of incoming stimulation as they affect a variety of behavioral responses. It is to these lines of investigation that I would now like to turn.

The second broad area of contemporary research which I regard as having particularly promising implications for our understanding of the nature and role of emotional behavior in infancy is represented by studies dealing with the following set of discrete but related topics: (a) approach-withdrawal processes; (b) exploratory behavior, curiosity, and intrinsic motivation; and (c) arousal or activation, orienting and alerting responses. By way of introductory comment, let me say that I believe that studies of these problems, which are very much under investigation currently with both humans and animals, are extremely relevant for the study of affect and emotional behavior, even though many of the investigations have not been directly concerned with affect or emotion as such to begin with. What these studies have in common, despite often diverse initial aims, is a concern with the behavioral orientation of the infant (or animal) toward particular types of external stimulation, as well as a concern with explaining such orientation in terms of the nature of the stimulus information impinging upon the subject, and the manner in which such information is "processed" as a function of the previous experience or current state of the infant. Since we regard emotions or affects as having a physiological arousal or activation component, and a behavioral or action component which often takes the form of a heightened orientation toward or away from the salient object, the relevance of studies of the problems just mentioned should be obvious. At the same time, it seems to me that research on these very problems would often be enhanced by more direct efforts to isolate and study the affective or pleasure-displeasure components involved in the behavior being investigated.

Let me give you a few examples of some relevant issues and problems being considered in the general areas of research I have just mentioned.

APPROACH AND WITHDRAWAL PROCESSES

While many of the previously discussed studies of infant-adult attachment dealt with approach and withdrawal responses of various types, I would like to speak here of research which reflects a more general concern with the nature of such processes. It is pretty generally agreed by many investigators that the response systems which mediate appropriate approach and withdrawal responses to stimuli of varying intensities (or qualities) are among the most fundamental, from the point of view of both phylogenetic and ontogenetic development. In attempting to integrate the results of many studies in this area into a broad theory of approach-withdrawal processes, Schneirla (1965) has argued that it is the intensity of stimulation which is crucial: a broad range of low stimulus intensities (or small changes in intensity) tends to instigate approach responses while a broad range of high stimulus intensities (or large intensity changes) produce withdrawal responses. Stimulus intensity is not definable entirely ob-

jectively, but it is rather a matter of "effective stimulus input," which is a function of such factors as the particular species involved, as well as age, previous experience, adaptation, etc. In the case of higher animals, intensity of stimulation is the crucial determinant early in life, while the qualitative features of different objects and stimuli become salient as a result of subsequent development and learning.

This point of view, of course, is directly opposed to the idea that animals (and human infants) are capable of manifesting approach or withdrawal responses to innately perceived qualitative features of stimuli (e.g., particular visual patterns or shapes). Schneirla has argued, for example, that the distress responses shown by ducklings to a moving hawk-shaped silhouette, and not to the same silhouette moving in the opposite direction (with the simulated appearance of a goose), can be explained in terms of differences in the magnitude of the changes in retinal stimulation produced, rather than by assuming an innate discrimination of the hawk from the goose configuration. A recent study (Green, Green, and Carr, 1966) provides some confirmatory evidence for ducklings responding selectively to the configurational properties of the hawk silhouette. Recent studies with human neonates, of course, also provide increasing evidence of preferential visual responses to shape and pattern (Fantz and Nevis, 1967).

There seems to be no doubt about the central importance of stimulus intensity and intensity change as one of the important determinants of approach and withdrawal responses (particularly the latter). At the same time, there is good evidence that qualitative or structural features of stimuli play a salient role even very early in development, both with humans and some lower species. One of the crucial problems which Schneirla was attempting to deal with and which most current investigators are still struggling with, is that of how best to conceptualize and define the relevant characteristics of "the stimulus," so that we can look for more meaningful relationships between the infant's approach and withdrawal behavior, or emotional responses, and the nature of the stimulation impinging upon him.

EXPLORATORY BEHAVIOR, CURIOSITY,
AND INTRINSIC MOTIVATION

One of the people who has been very much concerned with defining characteristics of stimulation which instigate approach behaviors such as exploration and curiosity is Berlyne (1960, 1966). In searching for a motivational explanation of such behavior in rats as well as in human infants, Berlyne proposed that there are certain "collative" properties of stimuli which induce curiosity and specific exploratory (or information seeking) activity. These properties include such characteristics as novelty, surprisingness, incongruity, and complexity. They are referred to as "collative" properties since they require that the animal collate or compare information from different stimulus elements which appear in some sense to be discrepant or incompatible, either with other elements in the same stimulus or with previously perceived stimuli. According to Berlyne, it is this uncertainty or incompleteness of information which generates the state of discomfort he regards as perceptual curiosity, and the function of specific exploratory behavior is to provide the additional information needed to reduce this discomfort. (Note the persistent influence of drive reduction theory here!)

Berlyne has gone considerably farther than Schneirla in attempting to specify a number of clearly important qualitative characteristics of stimuli which appear to elicit approach behavior, and in providing a hypothesized explanation of such behavior in terms of its information-seeking function. On the other hand, the collative properties of stimuli are still extremely difficult to define and measure objectively, in part because they depend to some extent on the subject's previous experience with the stimuli. Another perplexing problem, which has been with us for a long time, is that some novel, surprising, or incongruous stimuli produce conflicting approach and withdrawal reactions, or clear escape and fear responses. Some examples of this are the human infant's fear responses to strangers toward the end of the first year of life, and the chimpanzee's marked fear reactions to cadavers or skulls of chimpanzees (Hebb, 1946).

This problem has been dealt with by a number of people, including Hunt (1965) who considers the issue in considerable depth as part of his recent detailed discussion of the role of "intrinsic motivation" in psychological development (i.e., motivation not dependent on primary drive reduction, but intrinsic to such "spontaneous" activities as play, exploration, problem solving, etc.). Hunt includes the collative stimulus properties proposed by Berlyne under his generic concept of "incongruity," which is a central part of his theory of intrinsic motivation and early development. In this broader context, incongruity represents a discrepancy between stimulus information impinging on the infant at any given time and some relevant standard of comparison, which may be either "external" to the subject, in terms of ongoing or concurrent stimulation, or "internal" in the sense of its being based upon the stored information or "schemata" resulting from previous experience. (See also Hunt, 1961, pp. 267–269.)

Hunt proposes that the notion of an "optimal level of incongruity," which has been suggested in various forms by other theorists as well, may be the best way to account for the broad range of responses we find to various novel, surprising, or strange stimuli. According to this model, stimuli representing optimal levels of incongruity would be generally attractive for the infant, and might be regarded as generating an "optimal" level of arousal or physiological activation. Stimuli constituting extreme degrees of incongruity would instigate withdrawal or escape responses, while stimulus conditions representing levels well below the optimal (e.g., conditions of minimal or unchanging stimulation) would elicit attempts to seek interaction with the environment providing higher levels of incongruity. Presumably the affective state or hedonic tone associated with optimal incongruity levels would be generally positive, while that associated with either of the extreme levels would be generally negative.

This "optimal level" model we have been discussing has seemed to many of us to be a basically reasonable and heuristically valuable one. On the other hand, it is extremely difficult to define levels of incongruity objectively in our specific research endeavors, and one has to guard against the tendency to base one's stimulus definitions, even in part, upon the nature of the infant's or animal's responses. As Hunt himself puts it, the concept of incongruity is "operationally slippery" (1965, p. 213). For example, Morgan and I found (1968) that while our infants began to respond less positively or more negatively to the strange experimenter as we moved from the eight-month to the 12-month level, they appeared increasingly to enjoy both a realistic and a grossly distorted mask of the human face which we presented at the end of a rod. How do we determine objectively whether the strange examiners or the masks were the most incongruous stimuli, representing the greater discrepancy from the infant's "schemata" of familiar faces or persons? There is also the problem, of course, of determining what other motivational or experiential factors might have been operating, in addition to incongruity as such. As we begin to find better solutions to specific questions like these, we ought to be able to gain a better understanding of the determinants of the infant's behavior, and to confirm, or elaborate on, the optimal level of incongruity notion.

AROUSAL OR ACTIVATION; ORIENTING AND ALERTING RESPONSES

Generally speaking the concepts of arousal or activation refer to such characteristics as excitation, alertness, or responsivity, which are manifested in a complex of physiological changes (e.g., in heart rate, respiration, electrical activity of the brain, muscle action potentials, etc.), as well as in such behavioral properties as activity level, motility patterns, postural responses, attentiveness to stimuli, etc. The question of the levels and patterns of arousal associated with various forms of approach and withdrawal reactions, exploratory behavior, and other intrinsically motivated behaviors, is obviously a very important one.

An increasing amount of systematic research attention is being directed to the general problems of arousal and activation in infants as well as animals, both in the context of the kinds of problems we've been discussing, as well as in other contexts (e.g., Duffy, 1962; Lynn, 1966).

Much of the contemporary research in this area has been stimulated by the extensive Russian studies of the physiological and behavioral responses associated with the "orientation reaction" (when the animal responds to a stimulus with the mobilization of a complex of responses which appear to make him maximally alert to and prepared to deal with the stimulus. The differential response patterns associated with "defensive reactions," generated by too intense or too sudden stimuli, has also been under investigation. (See Lynn, 1966, for a summary of this Russian work.)

While there are many technical as well as conceptual problems involved in the securing and utilization of physiological measures as indices of arousal or activation, a good deal of hard and generally promising work is being done on the development and use of such measures, often in association with related behavioral indices. Changes in heart rate, respiration, or electrical skin potential, for example, are being employed as indices of degree of responsiveness or attention to both visual and auditory stimuli in neonates and in older infants (Brackbill, *et al.*, 1966; Graham and Clifton, 1966; Lewis, *et al.*, 1966; Stechler, Bradford and Levy, 1966; Steinschneider, Lipton, and Richmond, 1966).

There has also been a great deal of recent effort directed toward more precise assessment of the behaviorally observable arousal or activation characteristics of newborns and very young infants (sometimes referred to as the "state" variable), either as a relatively stable characteristic of the individual infant (Birns, 1965; Escalona, 1962), or as an important "baseline" condition which must be specified for any infant at the time when his responses to particular stimulation are being observed and evaluated (Escalona, 1965; Prechtl, 1965; Wolff, 1966).

In such studies of arousal in very young infants it seems pretty clear that we are often dealing with at least rudimentary precursors of emotional behavior. It is interesting to note, for example, that the highest level of behavioral arousal in these studies is usually judged by the presence of marked crying, agitation, and irritability, or what some of us might be quite willing to call a state of hedonically negative excitation. As a matter of fact, the general question of the aversiveness or attractiveness of different levels of arousal or activation is a very fundamental one which has concerned psychological theorists for a long time. Closely paralleling the notion of "optimal levels of incongruity," which we discussed earlier, is the point of view that much of the organism's behavior is directed toward obtaining or maintaining optimal levels of arousal or activation, since levels which are either too high or too low are aversive, and in some sense hedonically or affectively negative. (See Hunt, 1965, for a theoretical discussion of these issues.)

While the reduction of aversively high levels of arousal (or drive) has long been accepted as a prime motivational determinant of behavior, the notion that animals or humans will behave so as to increase their levels of arousal, incongruity, or stimulation, is a more recent arrival on the experimental scene. The precise circumstances under which such behavioral events will take place and why they take place, are questions that are far from being answered to everyone's satisfaction. For example, are some forms of exploratory behavior and simple problem solving activities engaged in by infants primarily because they are intrinsically pleasurable and perhaps generate an "optimal level of arousal" (as Buhler, 1930 or Hunt, 1965 might argue), or because they serve to reduce the discomfort of boredom drive or perceptual curiosity (as Berlyne might put the matter), or are both factors operative at different points in the ongoing behavior? Are some forms of perceptual or investigatory activity sustained because the organism is biologically and psychologically constructed to operate on incoming stimulus information until it is somehow meaningfully "processed" and assimilated with previously stored information (as Piaget, 1952 or Hunt, 1965 might put it), with the hedonic or affective state accompanying such activities often being essentially neither positive nor negative, though the infant may be operating at a relatively high level of arousal and alertness?

In the course of reviewing the impressive body of literature on approach and withdrawal processes, exploratory behavior, intrinsic motivation, and arousal or activation phenomena, it has seemed to me that some of the issues raised by research in these areas, including the specific questions I've just posed, might be approached more fruitfully if we attempted to specify more directly the hedonic, or pleasure-displeasure characteristics associated with the behaviors we are attempting to understand. Admittedly this is not always an easy task, particularly if we try to identify behavioral indicators of pleasure-displeasure (or affective tone) which are distinguishable from the responses we are utilizing as indicators of approach or withdrawal, and of arousal or activation, as I think needs to be done.

What are some of the alternatives to this approach? One alternative followed by some investigators, is to ignore the issue of hedonic qualities, on the grounds that these pleasure-displeasure components cannot be specified objectively anyway, although one might still be perfectly willing to employ expressive responses like the distress calls of pups or ducklings as objective indicators of avoidance reactions, and the smile of the infant as an indicator of approach behavior or attention. Other alternatives, shown in some of the theoretical discussions already cited, involve making a number of implicit assumptions about the qualities of aversiveness or attractiveness, pleasure or displeasure, which might be associated with various forms of approach and withdrawal behavior, and with various levels of arousal. Clearly, however, we'd be considerably better off if we had more direct measures of the pleasure-displeasure characteristics associated with these behaviors.

These are some of the reasons why, in our own current research[1] on emotional behavior in the first year of life, we are directing some of our major efforts to the problem of identifying, hopefully by independent criteria, appropriate behavioral indicators of the three essential characteristics of the infant's responses which we've been discussing, namely: (1) the approach-

[1]This research, now underway at Cornell University, is supported in part by the U.S. Office of Education as part of the National Laboratory in Early Childhood Education (Contract No. OEC-1-7-070083-2867).

withdrawal, or "directional" qualities of the behavior (distinguished as stimulus maintaining and enhancing, stimulus seeking, stimulus terminating and avoiding, much in the manner suggested by Schneirla, 1965 and Ambrose, 1963); (2) the arousal or activation characteristics (in terms of activity and motility increases or inhibition, intensity of responses, and eventually, selected physiological responses); and (3) the pleasure-displeasure, or hedonic qualities (as reflected in facial behavior, smiling, laughing, crying, other qualities of vocalizations and accompanying movements). Our hope is that if we can more adequately identify and assess these specific qualities of the infant's responses, we should be in a much better position to examine empirically the patterns of relationship among them, as components of what we regard as emotional behavior. At the same time, we ought to be able to arrive at more meaningful descriptions and analyses of the many ambiguous and conflictful or mixed reactions one observes so often in infants as they are confronted with such "incongruous" stimuli as unfamiliar or unexpected object movements or sounds, strange adults or strange environments, distortions of familiar stimuli, novel or "surprising" stimuli of various sorts, etc.

SUMMARY

In summary, my major purpose in this paper has been to point out and discuss some contemporary research issues and emphases which appear to me to be of particular significance in regard to the general problem of social and emotional behavior and development in infancy. I have tried to indicate very briefly the historical contrast, as well as the continuity, between these current research issues and some of the central concerns of early investigators in the field. One pervasive and important research emphasis has been a concern with more precise analyses of stimulus and situational determinants of social and emotional behavior, as shown in the many studies of infant attachment behavior in both humans and animals, and in analyses of the eliciting as well as the reinforcing effects of salient stimuli involved in infant-adult interaction.

Another set of very important issues is being investigated widely in connection with research on approach and withdrawal processes; exploratory behavior, curiosity and intrinsic motivation, and arousal or activation. These problem areas are particularly relevant to our concern with emotional behavior in infancy, since they deal essentially with the directional and the arousal characteristics of the infant's responses, both of which we regard as important components of emotional behavior. I have suggested that if we can combine our studies of these aspects of the infant's responses with better assessments of the pleasure-displeasure, or hedonic qualities involved in such behavior, our research efforts in this area should be considerably enhanced.

One of our main problems is still that of adequately conceptualizing the nature of emotional processes early in life, and the transformations undergone by these processes and their precursors during ontogenesis, beginning with birth. Some of the most perceptive discussions of these difficult issues may be found in the recent writing of Spitz (1963) and Wolff (1966, pp. 74–80). Concurrent with these conceptual problems are those we face in attempting to assess the most salient behavioral indicators of emotional responses in infants at different points in development. It seems to me that as we make further progress along these basic lines, investigations focussed on the influence of major "independent" variables on emotional and social development in infancy will be considerably more fruitful.

Finally, I think that it is probably obvious by now that we cannot adequately study social and emotional behavior in infancy independently of other basic psychological processes involved in the infant's behavior and development. Perceptual-cognitive and learning processes clearly play a major role in determining what social or emotional responses will be elicited by particular stimulus conditions, as well as how such responses will be expressed in behavior. Much of the contemporary research we've discussed has been very much concerned with just this sort of interaction. Conversely, social and emotional factors play a significant role in the development of perceptual-cognitive behavior and of various motivational systems. One of the significant features of the contemporary research scene is that many investigators are increasingly inclined to examine the role of the *various* psychological processes which may be involved in particular transactions of importance between the infant and his environment.

REFERENCES

AHRENS, R. Beitrag zur entwicklung der physiognomie und mimikerkennens. *Zeit. fur. exp. und ang. Psychol.*, 1954, 2, 414–454; 599–633.

AMBROSE, J. A. The age of onset of ambivalence in early infancy: indications from the study of laughing. *Journal Child Psychology & Psychiatry*, 1963, 4, 167–187.

BALDWIN, J. M. *Mental development in the child and in the race.* New York: Crowell Collier and Macmillan, Inc., 1895.

BERLYNE, D. *Conflict, arousal and curiosity.* New York: McGraw-Hill Book Company, 1960.

BERLYNE, D. Curiosity and exploration. *Science*, 1966, 153, 25–33.

BIRNS, BEVERLY. Individual differences in human neonates' responses to stimulation. *Child Development*, 1965, 36, 249–256.

BLATZ, W. E. & MILLICHAMP, D. A. The development of emotion in the infant. *University of Toronto Studies, Child Development Series*, 1935, 4.

BOWLBY, J. The nature of the child's tie to his mother. *International Journal Psychoanalysis*, 1958, 39, 350–373.

BOWLBY, J. Separation anxiety. *International Journal Psychoanalysis*, 1960, 41, 89–113.

BRACKBILL, YVONNE, ADAMS, GAIL, CROWELL, D. H., & GRAY, M. LIBBIE. Arousal level in neonates and preschool children under continuous auditory stimulation. *Journal of Experimental Child Psychology*, 1966, 4, 178–188.

BRIDGES, K. M. B. Emotional development in early infancy. *Child Development*, 1932, 3, 324–341.

BRONFENBRENNER, U. Early deprivation: a cross-species analysis. In Grant Newton (ed.), *Early experience and behavior.* Springfield, Ill: Charles C. Thomas, 1968.

BUHLER, CHARLOTTE. *The first year of life.* New York: John Day, 1930.

BUHLER, CHARLOTTE & HETZER, H. *Testing children's development from birth to school age.* New York: Farrar & Rinehart, 1935.

BUHLER, K. *The mental development of the child.* New York: Harcourt Brace & World, Inc., 1930.

CATTELL, PSYCHE. *The measurement of intelligence of infants and young children.* New York: Psychological Corporation, 1940.

DARWIN, C. (1873). *The expression of the emotions in man and animals.* New York: Philosophical Library, 1955.

DUFFY, ELIZABETH. *Activation and behavior.* New York: John Wiley & Sons, Inc., 1962.

ESCALONA, SIBYLLE K. The study of individual differences and the problem of state. *Journal of Child Psychiatry*, 1962, 1, 11–37.

ESCALONA, SIBYLLE K. Some determinants of individual differences. *Transactions New York Academy of Science*, 1965, 27, 802–816.

ESCALONA, SIBYLLE K. Emotional development in the first year of life. In Milton J. E. Senn (ed.), *Problems of infancy and childhood; transactions of the Sixth Conference, March 17 and 18, 1952.* New York: Josiah Macy, Jr. Foundation, 1953, 11–92.

FANTZ, R. L. & NEVIS, SONIA. Pattern preferences and perceptual-cognitive development in early infancy. *Merrill-Palmer Quarterly*, 1967, 13, 77–108.

GESELL, A. *Infancy and human growth.* New York: Crowell Collier and Macmillan, Inc., 1928.

GESELL, A. ET AL. *The first five years of life.* New York: Harper & Row, Publishers, 1940.

GEWIRTZ, HAVA B. & GEWIRTZ, J. L. Caretaking settings, background events, and behavior differences in four Israeli child-rearing environments: some preliminary trends. In B. M. Foss (ed.), *Determinants of infant behavior: IV.* London: Methuen; New York: John Wiley & Sons, Inc., 1968.

GRAHAM, FRANCES K. & CLIFTON, RACHEL K. Heart rate change as a component of the orienting response. *Psychological Bulletin*, 1966, 65, 305–320.

GREEN, MARSHA, GREEN, R., & CARR, W. J. The hawk-goose phenomenon: a replication and an extension. *Psychon. Sci.*, 1966, 4, 185–186.

GRIFFITHS, R. *The abilities of babies.* London: Univer. of London Press, 1954.

HAMBURG, D. A. Emotions in the perspective of human evolution. In P. H. Knapp (ed.), *Expression of the emotions in man.* New York: Internat. Univer. Press, 1963, 300–317.

HARLOW, H. F. The development of affectional patterns in infant monkeys. In B. M. Foss (ed.), *Determinants of infant behavior: I.* London: Methuen; New York: John Wiley & Sons, Inc., 1961, 75–97.

HEBB, D. O. On the nature of fear. *Psychology Review*, 1946, 53, 259–276.

HINDE, R. A. *Animal behavior.* New York: McGraw-Hill Book Company, 1966.

HUNT, J. McV. *Intelligence and experience.* New York: Ronald Press, 1961.

HUNT, J. McV. Intrinsic motivation and its role in psychological development. In David Levine (ed.), *Nebraska symposium on motivation, 1965.* Lincoln: Univer. Nebraska Press, 1965, 189–282.

JERSILD, A. T. & HOLMES, F. B. *Children's fears.* (Child development monograph No. 20.) New York: Teachers College Press, Columbia Univer., 1935.

JONES, H. E. & JONES, MARY C. A study of fear. *Childhood Education,* 1928, *5,* 136–143.

KISTIAKOVSKAIA, M. I. Stimuli evoking emotions in infants in the first months of life, *Sov. Psychol. Psychiat.,* 1965, *3,* 39–48.

LEWIS, M., KAGAN, J., CAMPBELL, HELEN, & KALAFAT, J. The cardiac response as a correlate of attention in infants. *Child Development,* 1966, *37,* 63–72.

LYNN, R. *Attention, arousal, and the orientation reaction.* London: Pergamon Press, 1966.

MORGAN, G. & RICCIUTI, H. N. Infants' responses to strangers during the first year. In B. M. Foss (ed.), *Determinants of infant behavior: IV.* London: Methuen; New York: John Wiley & Sons, Inc., 1968.

PIAGET, J. *The origins of intelligence in children.* New York: Internat. Univer. Press, 1952.

PRECHTL, H. F. R. Problems of behavioral studies in the newborn infant. In D. S. Lehrman, R. A. Hinde, & E. Shaw (eds.), *Advances in the study of behavior: I.* New York: and London: Academic Press, 1965, 75–98.

RHEINGOLD, HARRIET L. The development of social behavior in the human infant. In H. W. Stevenson (ed.), Concept of development: a report of a conference commemorating the fortieth anniversary of the Institute of Child Development, University of Minnesota. *Monogr. Soc. Res. Child Development,* 1966, *31,* No. 5 (Serial No. 107), 1–17.

RHEINGOLD, HARRIET L. The effect of a strange environment on the behavior of infants. In B. M. Foss (ed.), *Determinants of infant behavior: IV.* London: Methuen; New York: John Wiley & Sons, Inc., 1968.

RHEINGOLD, HARRIET, GEWIRTZ, J. L., & ROSS, HELEN W. Social conditioning of vocalizations. *Journal of Comparative Physiology & Psychology,* 1959, *52,* 68–73.

SALZEN, E. Visual stimuli eliciting the smiling response in the human infant. *Journal Genetic Psychology,* 1963, *102,* 51–54.

SANDER, L. W. & JULIA, H. Continuous interactional monitoring in the neonate. *Psychosom. Med.,* 1966, *28,* 822–835.

SCHNEIRLA, T. C. Aspects of stimulation and organization in approach/withdrawal processes underlying vertebrate behavioral development. In D. S. Lehrman, R. A. Hinde, & E. Shaw, (eds.), *Advances in the study of behavior: I.* New York and London: Academic Press, 1965, 1–74.

SPITZ, R. Anxiety in infancy. *International Journal of Psychoanalysis,* 1950, *31,* 138–143.

SPITZ, R. A. Ontogenesis: the proleptic function of emotion. In P. H. Knapp (ed.), *Expression of the emotions in man.* New York: Internat. Univer. Press, 1963, 36–64.

STECHLER, G., BRADFORD, SUSAN, & LEVY, H. Attention in the newborn: effect on motility and skin potential. *Science,* 1966, *151,* 1246–1248.

STEINSCHNEIDER, A., LIPTON, E. L., & RICHMOND, J. B. Auditory sensitivity in the infant: effect of intensity on cardiac and motor responsivity. *Child Development,* 1966, *37,* 233–252.

STERN, W. *Psychology of early childhood.* New York: Holt, 1924.

STETTNER, L. J. & TILDS, B. N. Effect of presence of an imprinted object on response of ducklings in an open field and when exposed to fear stimulus. *Psychon. Science,* 1966, *4,* 107–108.

SULLY, J. *Studies of childhood.* New York: D. Appleton, 1895.

THORPE, W. H. *Learning and instinct in animals.* London: Methuen, 1963.

TOMKINS, S. S. *Affect, imagery, consciousness.* Vol. I. The positive affects. Vol. II. The negative affects. New York: Springer, 1962, 1963.

WATSON, J. B. & MORGAN, J. J. B. Emotional reactions and psychological experimentation. *Americal Journal of Psychology,* 1917, *28,* 163–174.

WOLFF, P. H. The causes, controls, and organization of behavior in the neonate. *Psychological Issues,* 1966, *5,* No. 17.

WOLFF, P. H. Observations on the early development of smiling. In B. M. Foss (ed.), *Determinants of infant behavior: II.* London: Methuen; New York: John Wiley & Sons, Inc., 1963, 113–138.

YARROW, L. J. Separation from parents during early childhood. In M. L. Hoffman and Lois Hoffman (eds.), *Review of child development research: I.* New York: Russell Sage Found., 1964, 89–136.

38.

Edgar F. Borgatta

THE SOCIALIZATION PROCESS

In most general terms, the socialization process is characterized as follows: The infant is born a creature relatively undifferentiated in terms of the responses it can manifest, and relatively unable to differentiate among stimuli. For the infant, certain bodily states occur that tend to initiate activity (generalized stimuli) and these are commonly called drives. The generalized activity resulting from a drive such as hunger in the child must receive a response in the environment, for if the child is not fed it cannot survive. Thus, the mechanism for differentiation of response patterns in the organism is inherently stated in: (a) the existence of the various physically based drives that exist for the organism at issue and that are responded to differentially in the environment; and (b) the ability of the organism to respond differentially to certain kinds of stimuli that are externally defined. For example, the infant is able to respond with a sucking reflex on the basis of certain kinds of stimuli, and preferentially to some; similarly, food intake, liquid intake, etc., may be viewed to preferentially satisfy a hypothesized hunger drive; and, the organism can be put into a state of agitation (avoidance) by a wide variety of stimuli, such as loud sharp noise, bright flashes of light, burning, cutting, etc. A dialectic process, thus, of (a) test; (b) result; (c) result becomes part of experience for a new test, flows on the basis of drives primarily associated with the organism as a source and drives set into motion by external stimulation. (The sequence is obviously analogous to the conditioning sequence of modern S-R theory.) But the patterns of behavior the organism manifests to diminish

drives may themselves persist and become drives, thus multiplying the base on which the dialectic process occurs and, similarly, the range of stimuli it can differentiate increases.

The world into which the infant is born is already operative and, through a cumulative learning process such as the one alluded to above, the early infant develops forms defined as appropriate by the socially external world it meets. The external world serves as a limiting process, rewarding and punishing, recognizing or ignoring, but it also provides the circumstances of the cumulation and differentiation of response patterns.

The child's own view of himself and of the external process is not differentiated initially. At some point, however, the awareness of action occurs. Awareness, in terms of the behavior of the child, is constituted in its rudimentary sense when the child anticipates an entire cycle of the dialectic. For example, the child who is about to run into the wall stops short. In anticipation, the child presumably has gone through the procedure of bumping his head and the consequent pain. This awareness or generalization of learning involves the substitution of symbol for the stimulus, and such symbolization obviously need no longer involve the simple direct stimulus-receptor reactivity of the original dialectic. The visual stimulus may evoke the tactile and pain reactions of before, or at least some of the concomitants. But, if this is the case, awareness must also arise in less dramatic ways; the child sees himself move a finger or hears himself make a noise, and the child learns to duplicate his own behavior. On this basis of awareness, the parallelism of action associated with imitation may arise. If the child has learned to imitate himself, to the extent that the child sees behavior of others as the same (or in parallel) as his own, the child can imitate others.

It is in the very imitation that the development

This selection is reprinted from: Edgar F. Borgatta, "A Systematic Study of Interaction Scores, Peer and Self-Assessments, Personality and Other Variables," *Genetic Psychology Monographs*, 1962, *65*, 219–291 [excerpt].

Reprinted with the permission of the author and publisher.

of the "social" component occurs, for in b aving in parallel with an alter, the child may generalize the alter's experience as his own. In the parallelism, the child may feel hurt when it imitates another crying, for crying has been associated with certain bodily states for himself. In this sense, alter and self are inseparable, for one can only know another's experience through his own. "Conscience," as representative of the social, appears in the generalization that what one has done to me to make me feel in a given way must make another feel the same thing when I do it to him. This sort of generalization of self to other underlies the concepts of "taking the role of the other" and empathy, which are frequently taken as the base of the socialized self.

But, again, to return to the external limits on behavior development, a person can only have some notion of what he is by noticing how others respond to him. A person's identity is established for him in terms of others, and one crucial identification occurs in "testing" behavior used in parallel by others. Imitated behavior will work at one time and not another and, by learning when and where behavior that has this self-other reference point is used by himself and others, the child establishes an identity among selves.

39.

DONALD P. IRISH

SIBLING INTERACTION: A NEGLECTED ASPECT IN FAMILY LIFE RESEARCH

INATTENTION TO SIBLING INTERACTION

One of the earliest and most productive of the orientations still current in research is the theoretical approach in which the family is considered as a "unity of interacting personalities." Within that framework, there are several sets of structural relationships about which sociological research concerning life in the nuclear family can be organized: interactions between adult members, between parents and children, and among children.

The relationships laterally between husbands

This selection is reprinted from: Donald P. Irish, "Sibling Interaction: A Neglected Aspect in Family Life Research," *Social Forces*, 1964, *42*, 279–288 [a segment of the original article is omitted].

Reprinted with the permission of the author and publisher.

This exposition was prepared as a basis for analysis of data for a project supported by PHS research grant M-2045 from the National Institute of Mental Health, and was directed by Charles E. Bowerman.

and wives—the parent generation—have primarily occupied those family sociologists who for several decades have been most engrossed with the processes of mate-selection, marital adjustment and interaction, prediction studies of marital success, parenthood, and related matters.

Vertical connections between parents and children—intergenerational influences—have been investigated extensively by psychologists as well as sociologists. Among the concerns that have occupied numerous researchers interested in these vertical dimensions of family life have been the effects of differential child-training practices of parents on the development of designated personality traits in their children, parent-child interactions and adjustments, comparisons of the belief and behavior patterns of the elder and younger generations, the attainment of appropriate sex roles by the children with parents as models, and the achievement of various developmental tasks. These aspects are introduced with the advent of child-rearing.

The interactions between and among children in the home—the horizontal relationships within the younger generation itself—seem to have been given relatively little heed. An examination of the research literature for the decades since World War I provides very few examples of empirical studies focused primarily on sibling relations. The many investigations of ordinal position have usually examined the parent-child nexus—the variations in parental treatment of children because of their position in the birth order and the effects of such divergencies in child-rearing patterns and parental attitudes on the development of the children's personalities.[1] The multifarious discussions and studies of "sibling rivalry" likewise have tended to consider the relations of siblings to each other mainly in terms of the vertical dimension—the competition of children in the family for the love, attention, and favor of one or both parents.[2]

Among sociologists and social psychologists, Bossard and Boll contended that the security of children has been treated as if based almost exclusively on (1) the adequacy of parent-child (and often just mother-child) relationships and (2) the interactions with peers outside the home. They point out that

. . . the role of siblings has been considered chiefly in the light of "displacement" and "rivalry." It is rarely that one finds any but the negative aspects of sibling relationships, and warnings how to deal with them.[3]

Furthermore, they assert, while the contributions of peer groups to the socialization and psychic security of children have been recognized,

The differences in social situations obtaining as between a non-family and a family group have not been so appreciated . . . having come into prominence in an era of the small family system, the peer group has meant, exclusively, non-family peers.[4]

Some of the relationships existing among siblings in diverse cultures have been described by ethnologists interested in socialization and personality development, kinship patterns, family life as a cultural complex, and related aspects. As summarized by Murdock, in many societies:

Siblings are . . . bound to one another through the care and help given by an elder to a younger, through cooperation in childhood games which imitate the activities of adults, and through mutual economic assistance as they grow older. Thus, through reciprocal material services sons and daughters are bound to fathers and mothers and to one another. . . .[5]

For the most part, however, inquiry into the meaning siblings have for each other, and their interactions within the nuclear family, have not been the focus of attention in anthropological research.[6]

Numerous investigations of "individual psychology" have been conducted, using sibling position, number, and differentiation by sex as independent variables to examine the influence that particular sibship configurations may have

---

[1]Already, 30 years ago, Jones was able to list almost 100 research articles on order of birth and its relation to other traits in individuals. See H. E. Jones, "Order of Birth," in C. Murchison (ed.), *Handbook of Child Psychology* (Worcester, Mass.: Clark University Press, 1933). Also, Leonard Carmichael (ed.), *Manual of Child Psychology* (New York: John Wiley & Sons, Inc., 1954, second edition).

[2]For example, David M. Levy, "Hostility Patterns in Sibling Rivalry Experiments," *American Journal of Orthopsychiatry*, April, 1936, 6, 183–257; *Studies in Sibling Rivalry*, Monograph No. 2, published by American Orthopsychiatry Association, 1937; and his "Sibling Rivalry Studies in Children of Primitive Groups," *American Journal of Orthopsychiatry*, January, 1939, 9, 205–214.

[3]James H. S. Bossard and Eleanor Boll, "Security in the Large Family," *Mental Hygiene*, October, 1954, 38, 532.

[4]*Ibid.*, 553–534.

[5]George Peter Murdock, *Social Structure* (New York: Crowell Collier and Macmillan Inc., 1949), 9.

[6]The culture-personality specialists have examined extensively the consequences for basic personality structure of the child-rearing patterns prevalent in numerous societies, with some attention to birth order and sex roles. Anthropologists also have studied the socialization of children through age and sex-graded friendship and ritual groups. Some have explored the relationships between siblings in the small nuclear families of hunting bands in the simplest societies. Others have presented and explained the customary avoidance or preferential, joking or respect relationships among them. Many have reported about the custodial supervision of younger children by their older brothers and sisters.

It is recognized that, among many preliterate groups and some civilized societies, the frequency of polygamous marriage arrangements, often further complicated by the levirate or sororate, joint residence patterns, the commonality of adoption, and other influences, modify the intensity and extensity of sibling interactions and probably minimize their significance. It is perhaps in the simplest hunting and gathering cultures, most of all in those in which the nuclear family may be isolated to itself for a considerable portion of each year, that sibling relationships are of greatest importance, relatively.

upon the personality characteristics and competencies that persons manifest later during their life span. Krout long ago felt that "virtually every problem of socio-psychological importance has been studied" in terms of birth order.[7] Most of these inquiries, however, have focused merely on the relation of a structural sib-*position* to particular personality *traits*, as presumed end-products. Generally, they have failed to elucidate the intervening interactions among sibling roles.

Thus far, it would appear that very little empirical research has been conducted in any of these related fields regarding the interaction of siblings with each other either within the family setting during the years of childhood and youth when they reside together, or later among them when they have become adults.

THE SIGNIFICANCE ATTRIBUTED TO SIBLING RELATIONS

While the bonds between parent(s) and child(ren) are customarily strong within our nuclear family system, the ties between and among siblings will in most homes generally also be close, being second in strength only to the former. Pherson has suggested that "sibling solidarity" may be the "fundamental kinship bond" within bilateral systems, of which our own society is one illustration.[8] Cumming and Schneider found that some persons, particularly during certain phases of the life cycle, find sibling ties to be more meaningful than their spouse-bonds.[9] During childhood and adolescence the degree of affection between siblings, and sometimes toward cousins, may be second only to the mother-child ties.[10]

Within the immediate family, siblings constitute an important sub-"we-group" for research analysis. They comprise a significant portion of the family group structure distinct from other combinations that may be isolated for investigation. Three decades ago, Chapin recognized that both a manifest and latent structural pattern may be discerned in family interaction. The manifest factors—parent pattern, number of siblings, sex and age distribution of the children, and guests in the home, among others—have been given most attention. However, as Chapin pointed out:

> The latent structural pattern is of a subtler nature. It is revealed in the separate member roles and in the pattern of equilibrium of the whole family group. It has to be inferred from the common reciprocating attitudes of the individual members of the family group. . . . The manifest structure of the sibling group may determine the latent structure of the member role.[11]

Shortly thereafter, Sletto stated that differences in children's personality traits might be attributed to the divergent roles which they play in "intrasibship interaction," patterns associated with the sibling position of the children, as well as to the dissimilar treatments by the parents.[12] Siblings, Krout has pointed out, "create an ever-changing milieu in the family." A sibling "is not a silent witness of a drama in which the parent and another child participates."[13]

Toman likewise has recognized the influence of interactions among siblings as important supplements to the parent-child relationships. He has contended that a person can be characterized appropriately

> . . . in terms of the people who have been living with him the longest, most intimately, and most

[7]M. H. Krout, "Typical Behavior Patterns in Twenty-six Ordinal Positions," *Journal of Genetic Psychology*, 1939, 55, 5.

[8]R. Pherson, "Bilateral Kin Grouping as a Structural Type," University of Manila *Journal of East Asiatic Studies*, 1954, 3, 199-202; and also Helen Codere, "A Genealogical Study of Kinship in the United States," *Psychiatry*, February, 1955, 18, 65-79.

[9]Elaine Cumming and David M. Schneider, "Sibling Solidarity: A Property of American Kinship," *American Anthropologist*, June, 1961, 63, 498-507.

[10]P. Garigue, "French Canadian Kinship and Urban Life," *American Anthropologist*, 1956, 58, pp. 1090-1101. For a cogent, succinct delineation of American kinship structure, see Talcott Parsons, "The Kinship System in the Contemporary United States," *American Anthropologist*, January-March, 1943, 45, 22-28.

[11]F. Stuart Chapin, "The Experimental Approach: The Advantages of Experimental Sociology in the Study of Family Group Patterns," *Social Forces*, December, 1932, 11, 204. See Katherine Lumpkin, *Family Life: A Study in Member Roles* (manuscript, 1931) for one example of an analysis of member roles.

[12]Raymond F. Sletto, "Sibling Position and Juvenile Delinquency," *American Journal of Sociology*, March, 1934, 39, 657-669.

[13]Krout, *op. cit.*, 4.

regularly, and by incidental losses of such people—i.e., primarily his parents and siblings.[14]

This psychoanalyst recently set forth in exposition a schema for examining family constellations, using eight basic types of sibling positions in both the child and parent generations.[15]

Sibling relationships can perform a number of functions. Brothers and/or sisters spend many hours together and share a wide range of activities.[16] Such contacts within the nuclear family tend to be intimate and inclusive in character, and to constitute primary groups characterized by frankness, informality, cohesiveness, intensity, and extensity. Interaction with siblings functions as one avenue for the socialization of children. It helps bring them into social reality, gives them experience in resolving interpersonal conflicts, introduces them to the rights of others, and provides a "school of mirrors." On occasion, siblings may act as substitutes for parents. They may turn to each other when sufficient attention or understanding is not shown by an indifferent, harried, or uncomprehending parent. Sometimes siblings are more effective teachers than adults, particularly if youthful skills are involved. Siblings may often understand childhood problems and new situations better, in some ways, than do the parents they share. They are associates that can contribute importantly to emotional security; and, ordinarily, it is pleasant and helpful for children to have other children as companions. Siblings may serve as role models for one another; particularly may the younger observe the older siblings of the same sex. They can serve as challengers and stimulators. Finally, in the creation of a "sense of family," a psycho-

logical unity of members who perform the essential and peripheral tasks of habitation together, each person develops his niche in the total structure. The larger the family, the greater the number, variety, and degree of specializations that may develop in these roles.[17]

Of course, sibling associations can also be dysfunctional in their consequences. They may engender so much security and cohesiveness within the group that a member comes to feel insecure or "homesick" when away from it. Frequently, particularly in the larger families, the presence of many siblings may considerably increase the difficulty of the life struggle. Some siblings, we recognize, become bullies of the smaller and younger; while in other circumstances the latter may be coddled. The talents of some children in the family may be sacrificed to the needs or desires of others. Jealousy and rivalry may disrupt cordial relations and hinder the attainment of adequate personal and social adjustments both within and outside the family. Results such as these also require investigation in the study of the meaning of sibship.

RESEARCH STUDIES OF SIBLING INTERACTION

Sears has highlighted the two divergent but supplementary approaches to family study—the sociological and the psychological.[18] The former focuses on the family group, or portion of it, as a unit, recognizing that such entities have some properties that differentiate them from others—diverse structures of internal relationships, specified by roles, and contrasting status relations with others. The latter accepts the individual as focal and recognizes the family as a social structure in which the individual is enmeshed and with which he interacts. The family functions as an environment for life and learning. The contributions of several investi-

---

[14]Walter Toman, "Family Constellation as a Basic Personality Determinant," *Journal of Individual Psychology*, November, 1959, *15*, 199.

[15]Walter Toman, *Family Constellation* (New York: Springer Publishing Company, Inc., 1961). In addition, he developed some "formulas of family constellation," suggesting how certain sibling relationships might be algebraically represented and quantified.

[16]A number of publications have been prepared for parents, teachers, and children to guide them in sibling relationships. For example, Edith G. Neisser, *Brothers and Sisters* (New York: Harper and Row, Publishers, 1951); Frances Ullman, *Getting Along with Brothers and Sisters* (Chicago: Science Research Associates, 1950); and *Life with Brothers and Sisters* (Chicago: Science Research Associates, 1952).

[17]James H. S. Bossard and Eleanor S. Boll, *The Sociology of Child Development* (New York: Harper and Row, Publishers, 1960, third edition), Chapter 5: "Interaction between Siblings," 89–111; and in their "Security in the Large Family," *op. cit.*, 529–544.

[18]Robert R. Sears, "Ordinal Position in the Family as a Psychological Variable," *American Sociological Review*, June, 1950, *15*, 397–401.

gators who have focused most sharply on *sibling interaction* will be reviewed.

Krout began by accepting the proposition that "the attempt to explain behavior in terms of non-psychological factors such as birth order is thoroughly futile." He classified siblings by "ordinal *positions*" rather than by mere birth order, desiring thereby to "emphasize psychological position in the family, resulting from certain types of social constellations." Utilizing birth intervals, family size, sex of subject, and sex of sibling preceding and following, he delineated 26 such sibship positions, 13 for each sex. His 1093 subjects all lived with two parents in 432 family groups, and a college student was at least one subject in each home. The questionnaire used in the research secured a complete roster of family members and contained 24 statements concerning intra-family relations. From these data Krout derived a number of statistical relationships between personality traits and ordinal position.[19]

In a suggestive study, Paulette Cahn explored the use of a sociometric approach to sibling research. She found that preferences of siblings were most often directed to the youngest, except among children reared in institutions. Also, the strongest affective attitudes devloped between siblings of corresponding sex.[20]

Davis and Northway observed five pairs of siblings during a period of five years. They hypothesized that "each child uses his sibling as a means of his own self-definition." In observing their differences, siblings may strengthen their relationships while yet each one can enhance his own individuality. The researchers' data supported their contention, and they were able to interpret the everyday behavior of the siblings in terms of the hypothesis.[21]

The most frequent contributor to the sociopsychological literature of statistical research concerned with sibling relationships appears to be Helen Koch. Her major research interest in

this regard has been the effect on the personalities of children of various family constellation factors: sex of child, sex of sibling, ordinal position of child in sibship, and differences in age between subjects and their siblings. Her 498 subjects, half boys and half girls, averaged about six years in age, were enrolled in public and private Chicago schools, constituted the children in white two-child families, were free from any known mental or physical disabilities, and resided in every case with both natural parents, who were native born. She divided her group into three sib-spacing levels; and each level was, in turn, divided into eight possible sibling patternings. Fels Child Behavior Rating Scales, the California Behavior Inventory for Nursery School Children, Children's Apperception Test (CAT), teachers' ratings, and interviews provided the data for the total inquiry. Her extensive findings have been published in numerous separate articles[22] and have been even further analyzed by others.[23] The congruence of her findings in many regards led her to believe that the effects of sibling interactions were effectively

[19]M. H. Krout, *op. cit.*, 3–30.

[20]Paulette Cahn, "Experimentations Sociometriques Appliquees au Groupe Fraternal," (Sociometric Experiments on Groups of Siblings) *Cahiers International Sociologie*, 1952, *12*, 169–173; and in *Sociometry*, 1952, *15*, 306–310.

[21]Carroll Davis and Mary L. Northway, "Siblings —Rivalry or Relationship?" *Bulletin of the Institute for Child Study*, Toronto, 1957, *19*, 3, 10–13.

[22]Helen L. Koch, "The Relationship of 'Primary Mental Abilities' in Five and Six-Year Olds to Sex of Child and Characteristics of His Sibling," *Child Development*, 1954, *25*, 209–223; "The Relation of Certain Family Constellation Characteristics and the Attitudes of Children toward Adults," *Child Development*, 1955, *26*, 13–40; "Some Personality Correlates of Sex, Sibling Position, and Sex of Sibling among Five and Six-Year-Old Children," *Genetic Psychology Monographs*, 1955, *52*, 3–50; "Attitudes of Young Children Toward Their Peers as Related to Certain Characteristics of Their Siblings," *Psychological Monographs*, 1956, *70*, No. 426, 41 pages; "Sissiness and Tomboyishness in Relation to Sibling Characteristics," *Journal of Genetic Psychology*, 1956, *88*, 231–244; "Some Emotional Attitudes of the Young Child in Relation to Characteristics of His Sibling," *Child Development*, December, 1956, *27*, 393–426; Sibling Influence on Children's Speech," *Journal of Speech Disorders*, 1956, *21*, 322–328; "Children's Work Attitudes and Sibling Characteristics," *Child Development*, 1956, *27*, 289–310; "The Relation in Young Children between Characteristics of Their Playmates and Certain Attributes of Their Siblings," *Child Development*, 1957, *28*, 175–202; and "Der Einfluss der Geschwister auf die Persönlichkeitsentwicklung jungerer Knaben," (The Influence of Siblings on the Personality Development of Younger Boys), *Jb. Psychol. Psychother.*, 1958, *5*, 211–225.

[23]Orville G. Brim, Jr., "Family Structure and Sex Role Learning by Children: A Further Analysis of Helen Koch's Data," *Sociometry*, March, 1958, *21*, 1–16.

being probed. She, more than many others, has studied personality traits within the context of sibling relationships and roles.

Brim has suggested three propositions regarding the development of sex roles, which he based on Koch's evidence:

One would predict that cross-sex, as compared with same-sex, siblings would possess more traits appropriate to the cross-sex role.

. . . One would predict that this effect would be more noticeable for the younger, as compared with the older, sibling in that the latter is more powerful and is more able to differentiate his own from his sibling's role.

. . . on the assumption that siblings close in age interact more than those not close in age, one would predict that this effect would be more noticeable for the siblings who are closest together in age.[24]

He found that the data supported the first two hypotheses, but provided little evidence for the third. He suggested that more varied configurations would develop in families with more than two children. For example, in a four-child setting, with a three to one sex split, the parents might be relatively more influential in helping the one to find his role. In a two-by-two division, cross-sex interaction among siblings might be relatively minimized.

Several investigators have stimulated interest in sibling interactions through their concern for the "large family" as a social structure. Ellis and Beechley utilized data from 1000 child guidance case histories to study the characteristics of individuals from "large families" (seven or more children) compared with those from "medium" (two to six children) and "small," one-child families.[25] Their subjects, of course, were not a representative sample of all children in the area but included those involved in adoption procedures and those with behavior, emotional, or other problems. They did produce evidence that family size may be an important variable in mental hygiene.

Bossard and Boll have discussed the contrasts between large and small families most.[26] In a first report, based upon a study of 25 large families of diverse background and involving 222 children, Bossard and Sanger introduced the concept of the "interacting size of the family."[27] There, they contended that almost every facet of family life tends to be different in the large family and that a quite different type of personality is fostered. In such a family, the group rather than the individual tends to be stressed. The larger the family becomes, the more internal organization develops, and dominance of some one or two persons appears. The large family typically involves greater specialization and multiplicity of roles and functions—greater complexity. Children in a large family system discipline each other, adjustments being made relatively more often to intra-family peers.

The study was expanded to include 879 children living in 100 large families of diverse background and having six or more living children. The information was secured over a six-year period from persons within the families through the use of questionnaires, non-directive interviews, and written family-life documents. One of the queries reported in the 1955 publication concerned the specialization of sibling roles as seen by the other sibling respondents—descriptions of brothers and sisters as fully as possible as personality types. Distilled from these data were eight general, composite types of personality roles, not all of which would be found in each family. Bossard and Boll point out that there are only a limited number of role choices available to a sibling, even in a large family. They suggest that each child tends to develop his or her role on the basis of, and in relation to, the roles which have already been pre-empted by others in the family.

"Personality Types in the Large Family," *Child Development*, March, 1955, 26, 71–78; "Adjustment of Siblings in Large Families," *American Journal of Psychiatry*, 1956, 112, 889–892; and *The Large Family System* (Philadelphia: University of Pennsylvania Press, 1956).

[27]James H. S. Bossard and Winogene Sanger, "The Large Family System—A Research Report," *American Sociological Review*, February, 1952, 17, 3–9. Also Chapter 3: "Families by Size," pp. 47–67 in *The Sociology of Child Development, op. cit.*; and James H. S. Bossard, "Large and Small Families —A Study in Contrasts," *The Journal* of the American Society of Chartered Life Underwriters (Summer 1959), 221–241.

[24]*Ibid.*, 4–5.

[25]Albert Ellis and Robert M. Beechley, "A Comparison of Child Guidance Clinic Patients Coming from Large, Medium, and Small Families," *Journal of Genetic Psychology*, September, 1951, 79, 131–144.

[26]James H. S. Bossard and Eleanor S. Boll, "Security in the Large Family," *op. cit.*, 529–544;

An earlier study by Nye had indicated that adolescents from small families showed better relations with parents than did those from larger families.[28] Hawkes, Burchinal, and Gardner investigated the matter of adjustment further,[29] utilizing data from 256 fifth-grade children from rural areas and small towns in four Midwestern states, all of whom lived with both parents and had at least one sibling. These authors found, also, that children from the smaller families had more favorable relations to parents *and* to siblings than did those from larger families. Their data did not corroborate the notion that the larger family atmosphere is more favorable to personality adjustment. However, the small number of respondents precluded the application of controls for socio-economic class and other important variables.

Only recently have family sociologists begun to focus their research interests directly and with more emphasis upon sibling interaction. From an area sample of households in Cleveland, Sussman secured information concerning the interactions among the adult siblings and between parents and their mature children for the nuclear families selected. He examined the functions of ceremonial occasions, inter-family visitations, and help and services exchanged. That study is a precursor for a longitudinal study of urban family networks, "an investigation of the quantity and type of aid exchanged in connection with the movements of the immediate family through the life cycle."[30] Sussman believes that the notion of the atomized and isolated nuclear family is not being confirmed by empirical research findings.

In a somewhat similar study of randomly selected middle-class Boston families, Reiss also manifested interest in "the factors related to the frequency of interaction with extended kin and attitudes about the frequency of interaction."[31] He found that "females are in contact with relatives more than males, but males are in contact with in-laws more than are females." Further, he asserts:

As a consequence of this slight matrilineal tendency, interaction in those sibling relationships involving two sisters, or a brother and a sister, would be more frequent than that of two brothers. Paradoxically, ... the families of siblings with least contact with each other are those of two brothers, the only ones with the same last name—a residue of our now defunct patrilineal tradition.[32]

Farber has presented interesting insights into the meaning that normal and retarded siblings can have for one another. In a monograph, he reported that normal girls who interacted frequently with retarded siblings were more often rated by their mothers as possessing more neurotic or negative traits than did other girls who did not have as frequent contact with the retarded child.[33] In a second report, he examined the "life goals" of 83 boys and girls, aged 10-16, who lived with a retarded sibling.[34] He found that both boys and girls who interacted daily with such handicapped brothers and sisters showed less interest in goals related to success in personal relations.

Both boys and girls who had sustained interaction with their retarded siblings, ranked devotion to a worthwhile cause and making a contribution to mankind as high. Perhaps feeling that they are serving a welfare function in the family provides the frequent interactors with motivation to achieve in a welfare profession.[35]

His inquiry concluded with the suggestion that continual interaction with retarded siblings often may come to be considered as a duty by the normal children, and "in the performance of

[28]F. Ivan Nye, "Adolescent-Parent Adjustment: Age, Sex, Sibling Number, Broken Homes, and Employed Mother as Variables," *Marriage and Family Living*, November, 1952, 14, 328.

[29]Glenn R. Hawkes, Lee Burchinal, and Bruce Gardner, "Size of Family and Adjustments of Children," *Marriage and Family Living*, February, 1958, 20, 65–68.

[30]Marvin B. Sussman, "The Isolated Nuclear Family: Fact or Fiction," *Social Problems*, Spring, 1959, 6, 333–340.

[31]Paul J. Reiss, "The Extended Kinship System: Correlates of and Attitudes on Frequency of Interaction," *Marriage and Family Living*, November, 1962, 24, 333–339.

[32]*Ibid.*, 334.

[33]Bernard Farber, "Family Organization and Crisis: Maintenance of Integration in Families with a Severely Mentally Retarded Child," *Monographs of the Society for Research in Child Development*, 1960, 25, No. 1 (Serial No. 75).

[34]Bernard Farber and William C. Jenné, "Interaction with Retarded Siblings and Life Goals of Children," *Marriage and Family Living*, February, 1963, 25, 96–98.

[35]*Ibid.*, 97.

this duty, the normal sibling internalizes welfare norms and turns his life career toward the improvement of mankind or at least toward the achievement of goals which will require the most dedication and sacrifice."

A perusal of the literature has not revealed any empirical study of sibling relations among and between stepchildren and the other children of "reconstituted" families. In the studies reviewed, stepchildren and those with half-sibling relations have almost always been excluded.

40.

ROBERT R. BELL

PARENT-CHILD CONFLICT IN SEXUAL VALUES

The old cliché that as one grows older he becomes more conservative may be true, if premarital sexual values held by parents are compared with the values they held when they were younger. In this paper, the interest is in the nature of sex value conflict between parents and their unmarried late adolescent and young adult children. Our discussion will focus on values held by parents and by their unmarried children toward premarital sexual intimacy.

Conceptually, our approach focuses upon values related to a specific area of sexual behavior held by individuals from two very different role perspectives. The perspectives differ because parents and children are always at different stages in the life cycle, and while parents are highly significant in the socialization of their children, other social forces increasingly come to influence the child as he grows older. The various social values that influence the child's sexual behavior are often complementary, but they may also be contradictory. Furthermore, various types of influences on the acceptance of a given set of values may operate on the child only during a given age period. For example, the youngster at age 15 may be influenced by his age peers to a much greater extent than he will be at age 20.

Given their different stages in the life cycle, parents and children will almost always show differences in how they define appropriate behavior for a given role. Values as to "proper" premarital sexual role behavior from the perspective of the parents are greatly influenced by the strong emotional involvement of the parent with his child. Youth, on the other hand, are going through a life cycle stage in which the actual behavior occurs, and they must relate the parent values to what they are doing or may do. There is a significant difference between defining appropriate role conduct for others to follow and defining proper role conduct to be followed by oneself. Even more important for actual behavior, there is often more than one significant group of role definers to which the young person can turn to as guides for his sex role behavior. Therefore, our discussion will focus more specifically on parent values related to premarital sexual intimacy, the peer group values of youth, and how these two different age groups, as role definers, influence the sexual values and behavior of unmarried youth.

Limits of Discussion. For several reasons, our discussion will center primarily on the middle class. First, this class level has been highly significant in influencing changes in general sexual values and behavior. Second, and on a more pragmatic level, what little research has been done on parent-child conflict over sexual values

---

This selection is reprinted from: Robert R. Bell, "Parent-Child Conflict in Sexual Values," *Journal of Social Issues*, 1966, 22, 34–44.

Reprinted with the permission of the author and publisher.

has been done with middle-class groups. Third, the general values of the middle class are coming to include an increasing proportion of the American population. This also suggests that the values and behavior of college youth are of increasing importance as this group continues to expand in size and influence within the middle class.

A further limit is that our main focus is on the generational conflict between mother and daughter. The history of change in sexual values in the United States has been complexly interwoven with the attainment of greater sex equality and freedom by the female (2). Also, the relationship between the mother and daughter tends to be the closest of the possible parent-child relationships in the family socializing of the child to future adult sex roles. Furthermore, whatever the value system verbalized and/or applied by the girl, she often has more to gain or lose personally than the boy by whatever premarital sexual decisions she makes.

We also believe that any analysis of conflict over premarital sex between generations should center on *value* changes rather than *behavioral* changes. On the basis of available evidence, it appears that there have been no significant changes in the *frequency* of premarital sexual petting or coitus since the 1920's. Kinsey has pointed out that "there has been little recognition that the premarital petting and coital patterns which were established then (1920's) are still with us" (15, p. 300). Therefore, it is important to recognize that the parents and even some of the grandparents of today were the youth who introduced the new patterns of premarital sexual behavior about 40 years ago.

PARENT VALUES ABOUT PREMARITAL SEX

The transmission of sexual values by parents to their children is only a small part of all parent values passed on during the family socialization process. Most parents do a more deliberate and comprehensive job of transmitting values to their children in such areas as educational attainment, career choice, religious beliefs, and so forth than they do with reference to any aspect of sexual values. Often when parents do discuss sex with their children it may be from a "clinical, physiological" perspective with overtones of parental embarrassment and a desire to get a distasteful task over with.

But perhaps more important than the formal confrontation between the parent and child in sexual matters are the informal values transmitted by the parent. In the past girls were often taught that premarital sexual deviancy was dirty and shameful, and that nonconformity to premarital sexual chastity values would mean suffering great personal and social shame. This highly negative view of premarital sex is undoubtedly less common today, but the newer, more "positive" values may also have some negative consequences. Very often today the mother continues to place great value on the daughter's virginity, and stresses to the daughter the great virtues of maintaining her virginity until marriage. But the "romantic" view of the rewards for the girl who waits for coitus until after marriage are often highly unrealistic and may sometimes create problems by leading the girl to expectations that cannot be realistically met in marital sex. Morton Hunt writes with regard to this approach that "if the woman has been assured that she will, that she ought, and she *must* see colored lights, feel like a breaking wave, or helplessly utter inarticulate cries, she is apt to consider herself or her husband at fault when these promised wonders do not appear" (13, 114). Whether or not the "romantic" view of marital sex is presented by her mother the girl often encounters it in the "approved" reading list suggested by the adult world, which tells her about the positive delights of waiting for sex until after marriage. So, though premarital sexual control may be "positive" in that it is based on rewards for waiting, it can be negative if the rewards are unrealistic and unobtainable.

For many parents, a major problem as their child moves through adolescence and into early adult years centers around how much independence to allow the child. Because they often recall the child's younger dependency, it may be difficult to assess the independency of the same child who is now older. Also, over the years the growing child has increasingly become involved with reference groups outside—

and sometimes competing with—the family. In other words, the self-role definitions by the child and the parents' definitions of the child's role undergo constant change as the child grows older. For example, "The daughter in her younger years has her role as daughter defined to a great degree by her mother. But as she grows older she is influenced by other definitions which she internalizes and applies to herself in her movement toward self-determination. The mother frequently continues to visualize the daughter's role as it was defined in the past and also attaches the same importance to her function as mother in defining her daughter's role. But given the rapid social change associated with family roles the definer, as well as the definitions, may no longer be institutionally appropriate" (5, 388).

Parents may also be biased in their definitions of their child as less mature than they, the parents, were when they were the child's age. One can not recall experiences earlier in the life cycle free from influence by the events that have occurred since. This may result in many parents' thinking of their younger selves as being more mature than they actually were. At the same time the parents' view of their child's degree of maturity may be biased by their recall of him when he was younger and less mature. Thus, from the parents' perspective they may recall themselves as youngsters within the context of what has occurred since (more mature) and may see their offspring within the context of their earlier childhood (less mature).

There also may be some symbolic significance for parents who must define their children as having reached the age when something as "adult" as sexual behavior is of relevance. In part, viewing one's children as too young for sexual involvement may contribute to the parents' feeling young, while seeing their children as old enough to be involved in sexual activity may lead to some parents feeling forced to view themselves as aging. For example, the comment about a man seen out with a young woman that "she is young enough to be his daughter" may have implications for his self-role image if the young woman *is* his daughter. We have little research data on how the aging process of parents influences their defini-

tions of appropriate behavior for their young adult children.

In general, it is probable that most parents assume that their children, especially their daughters, accept the traditional restrictive values about premarital sexual behavior unless they are forced to do otherwise. Also, because of the great emotional involvement of parents with their own children, there is a common parental tendency to attribute sexual "immorality" to other youngsters. For many parents to face the possibility that their children do not conform to their values is to suggest some failure on the part of the parents. Often, rather than admit failure, the parents may define their children as having been forced to reject the parent values by other social influences or that their children have willfully let them down.

YOUTH VIEWS ABOUT PREMARITAL SEX

The importance of age peer group influence on the values and behavior of young people has been shown by a number of social scientists (see: 6, 9, 10, 11, 12, 14, 19, 20, 21, 22). Because youth subcultures are to some degree self-developing, they often have conflict points in relation to some dominant adult values. However, the inconsistency and lack of effective adult definitions for adolescent behavior have also contributed to the emergence of youth subcultural values. That adults often view the adolescent with indecision as to appropriate behavior means that sometimes given adolescent behavior is treated one way at one time and in a different way at another time. Since the young person desires some decisiveness and precision in his role definitions, he often develops his own role prescriptions. Often when he creates his own role expectations, he demands a high degree of conformity by other adolescents as "proof" of the rightness of his definitions. It is ironical that the adolescent often thinks of himself as a social deviant. What he fails to realize is that his adolescent group deviates from the adult world, but that the requirements for conformity within his youth subculture are very strong (1, 369–74).

Youth subcultures have developed great influence over many aspects of premarital male-female interaction. The patterns of dating and courtship, appropriate behavior, success and failure are for the most part patterns defined by the youth group and not by the adult world. Yet, heterosexual relationships of youth are often based on adult role patterns, and they are therefore an important part of the youth world because they are seen by the youth as symbolizing adult status. To many young people, who are no longer defined by the adult world as children, but are not yet given full status as adults, their involvement in what they see as adult roles is important to them in seeking for adult status and recognition.

A part of the American youth subculture has been the development of new values related to premarital sexual intimacy. Reiss suggests that, "It might well be that, since the 1920's, what has been occurring is a change in attitudes to match the change in behavior of that era" [premarital sexual behavior] (16, 233). The evidence suggests that for at least some college students new sex norms are emerging at the various stages of dating and courtship. One study found that "on the dating level necking is the norm for females and petting for males. During going steady and engagement, petting seems to be acceptable for both sexes. This would suggest that the young people both act and accept a higher level of intimacy than has generally been suggested by courtship norms." (3, 63).

In the past, emphasis was placed on the girl's virginity at the time of marriage; but today, many young people may only emphasize her being a virgin until she is in love, which may mean at the stage of going steady or engagement (8, Ch. 5 and 16, Ch. 6). If the girl is in love, some premarital sexual relations may be acceptable by peer group standards, although the dominant adult values—that love *and* marriage are basic prerequisites for coitus —continue. In the United States love as a prerequisite for sexual relations has long been a necessary condition for most middle-class females. The condition has not changed; rather, the point in the courtship-marriage process where it may be applied to sexual involvement has shifted. Hence, the major point of parent-child conflict over premarital sex centers around

the parent value that one should be in love *and* married before entering coitus and the modified value system of youth that an emotional and interpersonal commitment is important, but that this may occur before marriage.

There are two recent studies that provide some evidence on the nature of generational conflict; one study is of youth and adults in general and the other study is specifically concerned with mothers and their daughters. Reiss, in his extensive study of premarital sexual permissiveness, provides data on values held by adults as contrasted with values in a sample of high school and college students. The respondents were asked to express their beliefs about different combinations of intimacy and degree of interpersonal commitment for both unmarried males and females. Respondents were asked if they believed petting to be acceptable when the male or female is engaged. In the adult sample the belief that petting during engagement was acceptable for the engaged male was the response of 61 percent, and for the engaged female the response was 56 percent. Of the student responses 85 percent approved for the engaged male and 82 percent for the engaged female (17, 190-91); thus adult attitudes about petting during engagement were more conservative than those of the student population. It may also be noted that for both the adult and student groups there was a single standard—that is, the acceptance rates were essentially the same for both males and females.

Reiss also asked his respondents if they believed full sexual relations to be acceptable if the male or female were engaged. Approval was the response given by 20 percent of the adult group for males and 17 percent for females. In the student group acceptance was given by 52 percent for the male and 44 percent for the female (17, 190-91). Here, as with petting, there are significant differences between the adult and the student samples, and once again both respondent groups suggest a single standard of acceptance or rejection for both males and females.

A study by Bell and Buerkle compared the attitudes of 217 coeds with those of their mothers. Both mothers and daughters were asked to respond to the question, "How important do you think it is that a girl be a virgin when she marries?" Of the mothers, 88 percent answered "very important," 12 percent "generally important," and 0 percent "not important"; compared to 55 percent, 34 percent and 13 percent of the daughters (4, 391). Both the mothers and daughters were also asked: "Do you think sexual intercourse during engagement is: very wrong; generally wrong; right in many situations?" The percentages for each response category were 83 percent, 15 percent and 2 percent for the mothers; and 35 percent, 48 percent, and 17 percent for the daughters (4, 391).

Both of the above questions show sharp differences between the value responses of the mothers and daughters with reference to premarital chastity. Many mothers were undoubtedly influenced in their responses by having a daughter in the age setting where the questions had an immediate and highly emotional application. Nevertheless, the differences in mother and daughter responses indicate that the area of premarital sexual behavior is one of potentially great conflict. One means of minimizing conflict is for the daughter not to discuss her sexual values or behavior with her mother. In the Bell and Buerkle study it was found that only 37 percent of the daughters, in contrast with 83 percent of the mothers, felt daughters should freely answer questions from their mothers in regard to attitudes toward sexual intimacy (4, 392).

The area of sexual values appears to be highly influenced by emotion, especially for the mother with reference to her daughter. Generational conflict with regard to premarital sexual intimacy has a variety of implications. First, the conflict in values clearly suggests that the traditional morality is often not socially effective as a meaningful determinant of behavior. Social values have behavioral influence when they emerge as social norms with significant rewards and punishments. In the case of sexual norms, however, there are rarely clearly-articulated rewards, or positive consequences, for the conforming individual. In almost all situations the effectiveness of sexual norms is dependent upon their negative sanctions, or punishments.

For example, the traditional norm of female premarital chastity bases its behavioral influence on negative consequences for the girl who fails to conform. This negative means of control is most commonly found as a part of the adult value system. In effect, the major sanctions over premarital chastity are based upon punishments for the girl and for her family if she deviates. Yet, in most cases the girl who has premarital coitus is not discovered by her parents or by the community. The real danger for the girl often centers around premarital pregnancy, because if that occurs and becomes known there can be no denying premarital coitus. Vincent has suggested that an important part of the negative sanction toward premarital pregnancy is not the pregnancy itself, but rather that it symbolizes premarital coitus *and* getting caught (23, Ch. 1).

The available studies indicate that fear of pregnancy is not the major deterrent for most girls (7, 344 and 15, 315). The personal values of the girl appear far more important in restricting her from engaging in premarital coitus. Yet, within the privacy of the youth world, there may operate for some girls certain values positive toward premarital coitus. For example, there may be a strong emotional desire and commitment to the boy and a positive feeling by the girl of wanting to engage in greater sexual intimacy.

There is a tendency by parents, as well as many who give professional advice, to overlook the pleasurable aspects of sex at all ages, especially for the young who are experiencing sexual pleasure for the first time. Undoubtedly, many girls engage in premarital sexual intimacy to "compensate" for some need and many may suffer some negative consequences. But it is foolish to state categorically that the "artificial" setting of premarital sex always makes it negative and unpleasant for the girl. We would be much more honest if we recognized that for many girls premarital coitus is enjoyable and the participants suffer no negative consequences. This was illustrated in the Kinsey research; it was found that "69 percent of the still unmarried females in the sample who had had premarital coitus insisted they did not regret their experiences. Another 13 percent recorded some minor regrets" (15, 316). Kinsey also found that "77 percent of the married females, looking back from the vantage point of their more mature experience, saw no reason to regret their premarital coitus" (15, 316).

THE EXTENT OF GENERATIONAL CONFLICT

With the evidence suggesting strong conflict between generations with regard to premarital sexual values, our final consideration is: how permanent is this generational conflict? We can provide some evidence on this question by examining the values of college-educated females of different ages. This appears justified because higher-educated females are generally the most liberal in their views about sexual rights and expectations for women.

The evidence suggests that the premarital sexual liberalism of the college girl may be a temporary phenomenon. The coed's sexual liberalism must be seen as related to the interactional context of her being emotionally involved, and to a future commitment to an ongoing paired relationship. The Bell and Buerkle study (4) found that the values of daughters toward the importance of premarital virginity were very similar to those of their mothers, until they had spent some time in college. However, at "around age 20 there emerge sharp differences between mothers and daughters in regard to premarital sexual attitudes. Behavioral studies indicate that it is at this point that sexual activity is greatly intensified, perhaps because it is at this age that college girls are entering engagement. A suggested pattern is that the college girl of 20 or 21 years of age, in her junior or senior year and engaged, has a strong 'liberal' pattern toward premarital sexual behavior and attitudes" (4, 392 and 18, 696).

We can get some indication of the persistence of premarital sexual liberalism by comparing the values of mothers by education. In the mothers' views as to the importance of premarital virginity it was found that the college-educated mothers were actually as "conserva-

tive" as those mothers with lower levels of education (4, 392). It is quite possible that in the future the coeds will become as conservative as the college-educated mothers. This may occur when the coed's attitudinal rationales are not related to herself, but as a mother to her own daughter. It is therefore possible that the "sexual emancipation" of the college girl exists only for a short period of time, centering mainly around the engagement years.

Yet, even if the girl becomes more conservative as she grows older, and especially with reference to her own daughter, her temporary "liberalism" probably is contributing to some shift in adult values about premarital sexual intimacy. Certainly, today's parental generation accepts greater sexual intimacy as a part of the premarital heterosexual relationship. Probably most parents assume that their adolescent and young adult children are engaging in necking and even some petting. Most parents, as long as they don't actually see the sexual intimacy, don't concern themselves about it. However, to suggest that parents may be more liberal (or tolerant) of premarital sexual intimacy does not necessarily suggest that parents are liberal if the intimacy reaches coitus.

It also appears that there has been some reduction in the severity of negative sanctions by parents if the daughter deviates and is caught. Among middle-class parents today it may be less common to reject the unwed daughter if she becomes pregnant than in the past, and more common for the parents to help her. This is not to suggest that today's parents offer any positive sanctions for premarital pregnancy, but that they may be able to adapt (often painfully) to it, rather than respond with high rejection and anger.

If our suggestion is correct (that parents take a less totally negative view of "discovered" premarital coitus), then this further suggests that traditional sexual values are being altered, since, as we have suggested, in the past the values of premarital chastity were primarily based on the negative consequences for those who deviated and were caught. If these negative consequences have been reduced, then the social force of the traditional values has been reduced as a means utilized by parents to control premarital sexual deviancy.

CONCLUSIONS

Based on the available evidence, there are several general speculations that may be made about future generational conflict over premarital sex. In general we would suggest that conflict between parents and their adolescent-young adult children with regard to premarital sexual intimacy may decrease in the future, because of several trends.

1. The trend in the United States is toward a more liberal view of sexual behavior in general. This is reflected in the generally accepted professional opinion that the woman has a right to sexual satisfaction, and that sexual satisfaction is a desirable end in itself. The trend toward a belief in a single sexual standard for both men and women, even though within the setting of marriage, is bound to influence the beliefs and behavior of the unmarried. For the unmarried, there may be an increasing tendency to attach less importance to the marriage act as the arbitrary dividing line between socially approved and socially disapproved sexual intimacy.

2. Since the evidence suggests that over the past three or four generations the rates of female premarital coital experience have not changed, and since the younger generation has developed some value frameworks for its behavior, modification of traditional values and behavior may increasingly influence the values of parents to be more liberal. That is, it may become increasingly difficult for many parents to hold their children to a set of conservative values which they, the parents, did not hold to when they were younger.

3. Parents seem increasingly unwilling to strongly punish their daughters who sexually deviate and are caught. This parental reduction of punishment may be influenced by the increasing public attention directed at such social problems as illegal abortion. For example, many parents may be more willing to accept and help an unmarried pregnant daughter than take the risk of her seeking out an illegal abortion. The possible negative consequences of abortion may appear more undesirable than the premarital pregnancy.

4. Less generational conflict will occur if parents know less about the sexual activities of their children. A great part of the social activity of young people is carried out in the privacy of their age peer setting; what they do in the way of sexual intimacy is increasingly less apt to be noted by their parents. With the development and marketing of oral contraceptives, the risks of premarital pregnancy will be greatly reduced. In the future the rates of premarital coitus may remain the same, but with the chances of pregnancy reduced parents may be less aware of their children's premarital coitus.

Over time, then, the values of parents and the adult community in general may become more liberal and the conflict between generations reduced. (There seems little possibility that the opposite will occur; i.e., the younger generation's reducing the conflict by becoming more conservative.) But in the meantime, and certainly in the near future, it appears that parents and their children will continue to live with somewhat different value systems with regard to premarital sexual values. Parents will probably continue to hold to traditional values, and assume that *their* child is conforming to those values unless his actions force them to see otherwise. The youth generation will probably continue to develop their own modified value systems and keep those values to themselves, and implicitly allow their parents to believe they are behaving according to the traditional values of premarital sexual morality. For many parents and their children, the conflict about premarital sex will continue to be characterized by the parent's playing ostrich and burying his head in the sand, and the youth's efforts to keep the sand from blowing away.

REFERENCES

1. BELL, ROBERT R. *Marriage and family interaction.* Homewood, Ill.: The Dorsey Press, 1963.
2. BELL, ROBERT R. *Premarital sex in a changing society.* Englewood Cliffs, N.J.: Prentice-Hall, Inc., 1966.
3. BELL, ROBERT R. AND LEONARD BLUMBERG. Courtship stages and intimacy attitudes. *Family Life Coordinator,* 1960, 8, 60–63.
4. BELL, ROBERT R. AND JACK V. BUERKLE. Mother-daughter attitudes to premarital sexual behavior. *Marriage and Family Living,* 1961, 23, 390–92.
5. BELL, ROBERT R. AND JACK V. BUERKLE. Mother daughter conflict during the 'launching stage.' *Marriage and Family Living,* 1962, 24, 384–88.
6. BERNARD, JESSIE (editor). Teen-age culture. *Annals of the American Academy of Political and Social Science,* November, 1961, 338.
7. BURGESS, ERNEST AND PAUL WALLIN. *Engagement and marriage.* Phila.: J. B. Lippincott Co., 1953.

8. EHRMANN, WINSTON. *Premarital dating behavior.* New York: Holt, Rinehart & Winston, Inc., 1959.

9. GINSBURG, ELI. *Values and ideals of American youth.* New York: Columbia University Press, 1962.

10. GOTTLIEB, DAVID AND CHARLES RAMSEY. *The American adolescent.* Homewood, Ill.: The Dorsey Press, 1964.

11. GRINDER, ROBERT. *Studies in adolescence.* New York: Crowell, Collier and Macmillan, Inc., 1963.

12. HECHINGER, GRACE AND FRED. *Teen-age tyranny.* New York: Crest, 1962.

13. HUNT, NORTON M. *The natural history of love.* New York: Alfred A. Knopf, 1959.

14. KELLEY, EARL C. *In defense of youth.* Englewood Cliffs, N.J.: Prentice-Hall, Inc., 1962.

15. KINSEY, ALFRED C., WARDELL B. POMEROY, CLYDE E. MARTIN AND PAUL H. GEBHARD. *Sexual behavior in the human female.* Philadelphia: W. B. Saunders, 1953.

16. REISS, IRA L. *Premarital sexual standards in America.* New York: The Free Press, 1960.

17. REISS, IRA L. The scaling of premarital sexual permissiveness. *Journal of Marriage and the Family,* 1964, 26, 188–98.

18. REISS, IRA L. Premarital sexual permissiveness among Negroes and whites. *American Sociological Review,* 1964, 29, 688–98.

19. REMMERS, H. H. AND D. H. RADLER. *The American teenager.* New York: Charter, 1957.

20. SEIDMAN, JEROME. *The adolescent.* New York: Holt, Rinehart & Winston, Inc., 1960.

21. SMITH, ERNEST A. *American youth culture.* New York: The Free Press, 1963.

22. SYMONDS, P. M. *From adolescent to adult.* New York: Columbia University Press, 1961.

23. VINCENT, CLARK. *Unmarried mothers.* New York: The Free Press, 1961.

41.

LARRY D. BARNETT

THE KIBBUTZ AS A CHILD-REARING SYSTEM: A REVIEW OF THE LITERATURE

In recent years, several students of the family have advanced the question as to whether or not we should maintain a strictly conjugal family system of child-rearing. One such individual has suggested that a conjugal family is perhaps a different type of setting than a community and that therefore rearing children in the former creates behavior patterns dysfunctional for living in the latter. Consequently, he asks if we have placed "an impossible burden" upon families in requiring them to socialize youngsters for community life.[1] Certainly, recognizing that we are living in a generation in which techno-logical-economic and social-cultural conditions are very different from those of even 50 years ago, we should attempt to answer the question rationally in spite of the fact that it challenges some of our basic values.

A review of the literature on the Israeli kibbutz can possibly help to answer this question. In the kibbutzim, which are agricultural collective settlements, children live in their own quarters apart from their parents and are cared for and reared from birth by professionally trained nurses and teachers. These personnel assume all of the duties and responsibilities, including that of discipline, involved in caring for and training children. Parents and children are together about two hours a day, which time is generally devoted to play, and on holidays.[2] The value,

This selection is reprinted from: Larry D. Barnett, "The Kibbutz as a Child-Rearing System: A Review of the Literature," *Journal of Marriage and the Family,* 1965, 27, 348–349.

Reprinted with the permission of the author and publisher.

[1]David R. Mace, "Some Reflections on the American Family," *Marriage and Family Living,* May, 1962, 24, 109.

[2]With respect to the separation of children from their parents, the situation in the kibbutz does not

(Footnote continued on next page)

then, of studying the kibbutz as a child-rearing system is that it lies near the opposite end of the continuum from a conjugal family system such as exists in the United States at the present time.

A fundamental problem in evaluating the kibbutz is that of knowing precisely the rate of occurrence of a given form of behavior in *both* conjugal family and kibbutz systems. Some evidence suggesting that there may be differential rates of deviant behavior between persons reared in the two systems arises from the fact that kibbutz children and adolescents are typically not "emotionally disturbed"[3] and that characteristically, the relationship between parents and child (ren) in kibbutzim is "emotionally positive,"[4] but when neuroses develop among kibbutz children, the etiological factor in the majority of cases appears to be a disturbed parent-child relationship.[5] Although this would argue in favor of a form of child-rearing that does not depend upon the conjugal family, it

is indeed very weak evidence. Definitive evidence requires determining for both systems the rates of occurrence of behavior problems attributable to the method of upbringing.

Following is a brief look at research evidence allowing a comparison of the incidence of deviant behavior among children in conjugal family and kibbutz systems.

A study of some 400 kibbutz children ranging from seven through 12 years of age found that about six percent were "disturbed";[6] by way of comparison, 2.3 percent of elementary school students and 2.4 percent of junior high school students in California have been rated by their teachers as sufficiently "emotionally disturbed" to be in need of psychiatric assistance. In another survey, the teachers of 186 fourth-, fifth-, and sixth-grade classes (ages nine-12) estimated that "most of the time" 4.4 percent of their students were overly aggressive or defiant;[7] the study of kibbutz children found that aggression was a problem among two percent of the nine-11 year olds and six percent of the 11-12 year olds.[8]

Additional relevant evidence is available from studies comparing groups of kibbutz youth with groups of Israeli children of comparable age from conjugal families. The results of these studies indicate that there is no significant difference among adolescents in the two groups in self-concept and in concept of ideal self as measured by Q sorts and sentence-completion tests;[9] that there is no marked general difference among ten-year-old children in "personality" but that kibbutz children may have a superior perception of reality as measured by responses to Rorschachs;[10] that there are no profound

appear to be comparable to that in the traditional institution, such as an orphanage, where children often experience psycho-social deprivation. John Bowlby has written:
"Separation is a relative concept. As it appears in the kibbutz, it should not be thought of as identical with that of children brought up in foster homes or institutions away from their parents. . . . In the kibbutz there is a great deal of opportunity for close relationship between child and parents." John Bowlby, *Child Care and the Growth of Love* (London: Penguin Books, 1953), 45–46.

[3]G. Caplan, "Clinical Observations on the Emotional Life of Children in the Communal Settlements in Israel," in *Problems of Infancy and Childhood*, ed. by Milton S. Senn (New York: Josiah Macy, Jr., Foundation, 1954), 91–120; Elizabeth E. Irvine, "Observations on the Aims and Methods of Child-Rearing in Communal Settlements in Israel," *Human Relations*, August, 1952, 5, 273–274; Mordecai Kaffman, "Evaluation of Emotional Disturbance in 43 Israeli Kibbutz Children," *American Journal of Psychiatry*, Feburary, 1961, 117, 737; Melford E. Spiro, *Children of the Kibbutz* (Cambridge: Harvard University Press, 1958), 423; Marilyn Winograd, "Behavior Research in Collective Settlements in Israel: 3. The Development of the Young Child in a Collective Settlement," *American Journal of Orthopsychiatry*, July, 1958, 28, 557–562.

[4]Shmuel Golan, "Collective Education in the Kibbutz," *Psychiatry*, May, 1959, 22, 167–177; Yonina Talmon-Garber, "The Family in Israel," *Marriage and Family Living*, November, 1954, 16, 343–349.

[5]Shmuel Golan, "Behavior Research in Collective Settlement in Israel: 2. Collective Education in the Kibbutz," *American Journal of Orthopsychiatry*, July, 1958, 28, 549–556; Kaffman, *op. cit.*, 738.

[6]Kaffman data, published in Hebrew, cited by Shmuel Golan, "Collective Education in the Kibbutz," *Psychiatry*, May, 1959, 22, 174.

[7]Both surveys are reported in Eli M. Bower, *The Education of Emotionally Handicapped Children* (Sacramento: California State Department of Education, 1961), 3–4.

[8]Kaffman, *op. cit.*, 734.

[9]Amos Handel, "Self-Concept of the Kibbutz Adolescent," *Psychological Abstracts*, August, 1962, 36, 644.

[10]A. I. Rabin, "Personality Maturity of Kibbutz (Israeli Collective Settlement) and Non-Kibbutz Children as Reflected in Rorschach Findings," *Journal of Projective Techniques*, June, 1957, 21, 148–153.

differences among ten-year-old children in Oedipal intensity, positive identification, and sibling rivalry as measured by responses to the Blacky Test;[11] and that there is no significant difference among ten-year-old children in attitudes toward family, father, and mother as measured by the individual items on a sentence-completion test.[12] The latter study, however, obtained also a global evaluation of response to the sentence-completion test by having three judges read the sentence completions and make an over-all assessment. Evidence was found that kibbutz males (but not females) had significantly more positive attitudes toward the family and their mother than male children reared in the conjugal families, and that females (but not males) reared in conjugal families had more positive attitudes toward their fathers than did kibbutz females.[13] In addition, Rabin found that there was no significant difference between infants (with a mean age of 13 months) from kibbutzim and those from conjugal families on the Vineland Social Maturity Scale but that the kibbutz infants had a significantly lower mean score in the personal-social development area of the Griffiths Scales for Infants than did the infants from conjugal families. Finally, among ten-year-old Israeli children from kibbutzim and conjugal families, there was no significant difference between the groups on the Goodenough Draw-A-Man test.[14]

In summary, the weight of the evidence suggests that children reared in kibbutzim and children reared in conjugal families do not in general differ markedly in terms of rates of behavioral deviance. However, as Rabin advises:

The question of 'how good' is child rearing in the kibbutz cannot be answered categorically and out of the social context. The last 40 to 50 years have shown that kibbutzim have reared many young men and women for effective membership *in a kibbutz*. The effectiveness of this new generation is judged by kibbutz standards—by standards of the society which they perpetuate. How effective and how adequate a kibbutz-reared person may be in *another* social context is a question remaining for future investigation.[15]

By the same token, it remains to establish how well the kibbutz system of child-rearing would work in an urban, industrial setting. The kibbutz is an agricultural settlement, and no definitive evidence indicates that its method of child-rearing would function more effectively than the conjugal family in the urban, industrial environment.

[11]A. I. Rabin, "Some Psychosexual Differences Between Kibbutz and Non-Kibbutz Israeli Boys," *Journal of Projective Techniques,* September, 1958, 22, 328–332.
[12]A. I. Rabin, "Attitudes of Kibbutz Children to Family and Parents," *American Journal of Orthopsychiatry,* January, 1959, 29, 172–179.
[13]*Ibid.*

[14]A. I. Rabin, "Behavior Research in Collective Settlements in Israel: 6. Infants and Children Under Conditions of 'Intermittent' Mothering in the Kibbutz," *American Journal of Orthopsychiatry,* July, 1958, 577–586.
[15]Albert I. Rabin, "Kibbutz Children—Research Findings to Date," September, 1958, *Children, 5,* 184.

CHAPTER X

Family Extension

THIS CHAPTER focuses on family extension, the fact that the family ranges through many generations and extends laterally to involve many degrees of relationship. There has been a considerable amount of interest in the study of family extension in recent years. Part of this interest develops out of the idea that there has been a breakdown of extended family ties, and that kinship has become less important in the daily lives of individuals. The theoretical assumption maintains that in a complex urban society the ties that traditionally held kinship networks together are breaking down. Educational, social, and physical mobility tend to disperse kinship groups and interaction pivots more on interest and ideology than on physical proximity, kinship, and tradition. In short, all the pressures and structures of urban society work to reduce the importance of the extended family network.

However plausible this theory may appear, there is beginning to emerge a literature which challenges the assumption of the decline in the importance of the extended family. The literature is provocative enough to suggest that the extended family will not disappear as quickly as some sociologists and anthropologists thought.

In a study of urban middle-class families, one author found that older couples that had been married for longer periods of time had neither more nor less friends than those more recently married. And, frequent getting together with friends did not appear to have any relationship with how often relatives were seen; thus, an expected constraint was not found. (Babchuk, Nicholas, "Primary Friends and Kin: A Study of the Associations of Middle-Class Couples," *Social Forces,* 1965, *43,* 483–493.) A number of studies have questioned the notion that extended kinship systems have only a marginal existence in modern society, and many analyses studied the factors associated with kin interaction. (See, for example: Reiss, Paul J., "The Extended Kinship System: Correlates of and Attitudes on Frequency of Interaction," *Marriage and Family Living,* 1962, *24,* 333–339. And: Adams, Bert N., "Occupational Position, Mobility, and the Kin of Orientation," *American Sociological Review,* 1967, *32,* 364–377.)

Interest in the extended family has not merely centered on maintenance of contact with distant kins, but particular attention has also been given to the relatively new phenomenon of survival of the parents. In particular, it is not uncommon to encounter families in which there are four living generations, which prompts such levities as: "How can you go home to mother if your mother has gone home to her mother?" New situations to study are created by these developments. One of these is the phenomenon of the "empty nest." The article by Irwin Deutscher titled "Socialization for Postparental Life" deals specifically with the period of life in which parents become removed from their children. How do they adapt to this new status? What takes the place of the children? How are the parents viewed by their children?

What parents do after their children grow up and leave is only a part of the question of what happens as families grow older. Middle-aged couples eventually become elderly couples. In process there are many transitions and changes. Physical ability decreases and this has different consequences for different groups. For the poor it may mean a more precarious hold on an adequate standard of living. For the more well-to-do, it may mean a more relaxed life and other interests. Old age can run the gamut of everything from the most strained existence to the freest point in the couple's life. As social security and concepts of minimum standards of living develop, possibly the discrepancies will be diminished. In the present era, however, attention is generated by the problems of the aged, and this will probably increase in the next few decades. One way of conceptualizing some of the problems of the aged is to examine their access to privacy and individuality. This is a topic considered by John C. Beresford and Alice M. Rivlin in their article titled "Privacy, Poverty, and Old Age," which focuses on economic restrictions and old age.

In the article titled "Age Grouping and the Family Status of the Elderly," Mark Messer examines the last phase of the life cycle, that of the elderly. He analyzes some of the contemporary alternatives, including the development of age-concentrated living arrangements.

Age structures are still changing, and as persons live longer the problems of the aged will be more familiar and adaptations more regular. Some phenomena will be difficult to resolve simply. For example, if the differential death rates for males and females continue, the question of what aged widowed grandmothers and great-grandmothers should do will be constantly present. If people continue to grow older, but their health deteriorates and their physical abilities are not maintained, problems of what the elderly are to do in their infirm periods will become more prominent also. And, along with these, many other problems are implied. For example, for how long and to what extent should children be responsible for their parents? Indeed, who should be responsible for whom in a system when there are four generations of adults present? Since these aspects of society are continuing to change, they will provide intriguing topics for study.

42.

Irwin Deutscher

SOCIALIZATION FOR POSTPARENTAL LIFE

The notion of life careers—of a developmental process—as a perspective for viewing the etiology of individual or institutional behavior is not new (see 15). The word "career" itself carries the connotation of a progressively developing sequence of *work* experiences. It need not, however, be restricted to the experiences of individuals. The "natural history" approach to institutional development employs an identical perspective (14). In attempting to understand and describe the family career, or stages in the development of the American family, the concept of the "family cycle" has been frequently, although not intensively, employed (see 4, Chapter 2; 13; 22, Chapter 20). Perhaps more than any other analyst, Paul C. Glick has consistently exploited this concept in an effort to direct his analysis of demographic shifts in family structure (11, 12). In this paper some of the social-psychological problems of transition from one phase of the family cycle to another will be examined.[1]

THE POSTPARENTAL PHASE OF THE FAMILY CYCLE

The span of time from the beginning of a family with the marriage of a young couple, the bearing, rearing, and marrying of their children, through the time when they are again alone together, until the ultimate death of one or both of them, is referred to as the family cycle.

Cavan has described as thoroughly as anyone variations in family organization through the family cycle. She sees the cycle as "significant in that with each stage, changes occur in the family membership and consequently in family organization, roles, and interpersonal relationships." (3, pp. 262–263; 4, pp. 28–38) This paper focuses on the transition from the phase during which children are being launched into the adult world to the phase Cavan calls postparental: "The postparental couple are the husband and wife usually . . . in their forties and fifties. . . . The most obvious change is the withdrawal of adolescent and young children from the family, leaving husband and wife as the family unit." (3, p. 573)

In the family career pattern of a large segment of our adult urban population, this appears to be emerging as a new phase of the family cycle, largely as a result of two demographic shifts: the fact that these people can expect to live considerably longer than their parents or grandparents and the fact that they averaged fewer children over a shorter span of years than their parents or grandparents.[2] The typical couple of two generations ago had a life expectancy which enabled them to survive together for 31 years after marriage, two years short of the time when their *fifth* child was expected to marry. But, "the decline in size of family and the improved survival prospects of the popula-

This selection is reprinted from: Irwin Deutscher, "Socialization for Postparental Life," in Arnold Rose (ed.), *Human Behavior and Social Processes*, Boston: Houghton Mifflin Company, 1962, 506–525.
Copyright © 1962 by Houghton Mifflin Company. Reprinted by permission of the publisher.
[1]This paper is based on a part of the author's doctoral dissertation (6). The research was facilitated by a pre-doctoral research training fellowship from the Social Science Research Council and a grant from Community Studies, Inc., of Kansas City, Missouri.

[2]Although it may appear that, in terms of average number of children, the offspring of the current crop of postparental couples are reverting to the patterns of older generations, this reversion is more apparent than real: "The fact that the crude birth rate has been higher in the postwar period than in the 1930's is due primarily to the operation of two factors: a larger proportion of women have been marrying at younger ages, and more of those marrying have started their families relatively soon after marriage. These factors may have only a minor effect on the final average number of children that women will have borne by the end of the childbearing period . . ." (10, p. 215).

tion since 1890 not only have assured the average parents of our day that they will live to see their children married but also have made it probable that they will have one-fourth of their married life still to come when their last child leaves the parental home." (11)

THE PROBLEM OF TRANSITION

In her classic formulation of "Continuities and Discontinuities in Cultural Conditioning," Ruth Benedict highlighted the problem of socially structured impediments to continuous socialization through the life cycle. She begins with the observation that there are certain discontinuities in the life cycle which are facts of nature and inescapable; thus, "Every man who rounds out his human potentialities must have been a son first and a father later and the two roles are physiologically in great contrast." (1) The important point, however, is that there is a great deal of variability in the way in which the transition is effected in different societies. Moving from Benedict's focus on the transition between childhood and adulthood to a focus on the transition from the launching to the postparental stage of the family cycle, and shifting from the concepts of "culture" and "conditioning" to the concepts of "role" and "socialization," we have a perspective within which to view the problems of transition and the modes of adaptation to postparental life.

Theoretically, it might be expected that the transition to postparental life would be a difficult one for the middle-aged spouses to make. Since this is an emerging phase of the family cycle, few of those entering it can find role models; in most cases one of their own parents was dead before the last of their own siblings was launched. This lack of anticipatory socialization—the absence of an opportunity to take the role of a postparental spouse, to rehearse the part before having to play the role themselves —ought theoretically to make for an extremely difficult situation after the children leave home. Much of the descriptive literature indicates that this, indeed, is a dangerous time of life (2, p. 626; 5, p. 404; 9, p. 3; 16, pp. 353–354; 17; 18, p. 79; 21, p. 7; 22, p. 43). *Nevertheless, despite expectations based on both theory and clinical experience, when urban middle-class postparental couples describe their life, the hurdle does not appear to have been insurmountable and the adaptations are seldom pathological.*[3]

In discussing postparental life, middle-aged spouses clearly reveal that it is not sound to assume that anticipatory socialization is absent because this is a new stage of the family cycle —that is, because middle-aged couples of today have not had the experience of observing their parents make such a transition. In spite of the fact that the identical situation could not be observed and rehearsed—that there was no opportunity to learn to take the role of the other by observing others—*analogous* situations exist in one's own life. Sussman recognizes this when he suggests that "most parents are gradually prepared to some degree for the day when their children marry and leave home by their periodic absences away at school or elsewhere." (20)[4] Such periodic absences do not, however, represent the full extent to which such socialization by analogy can occur.

Situations such as these provide an opportunity for the parent to rehearse in his own mind what life will be like when his children are gone. Anomalously, he himself becomes the "other" whose role he has an opportunity to take. Even though these practice situations may not be considered as permanent, important, or serious (they are more nearly instances of "playing-at-roles" than "role-playing") it will be seen that they provide the continuity in role conditioning—the socializing opportunity—that is needed. The word "opportunity" is used advisedly. Individuals react to the socialization process in different ways; on some it "takes" and on others it doesn't. The simple fact that an individual is provided with a potentially socializing expe-

---

[3] Observations made and materials cited below are derived from intensive interviews with 49 urban middle-class postparental spouses. The investigator gathered sufficient data on family characteristics from approximately 540 middle-class households to determine whether or not they met his criteria of postparental. Those selected were between 40 and 65 years of age, had from one to four children all of whom had been launched, and both parents were alive and living together. Self-selection occurred in only two cases where the family refused to be interviewed.

[4] A similar perspective can be found in John Sirjamaki (19, p. 135).

rience does not necessarily result in his defining it as such or in his being socialized as a result of the experience. The remainder of this paper will be devoted to an examination of what these socializing opportunities are and the manner in which they appear to facilitate the transition to postparental life.

OPPORTUNITIES FOR ANTICIPATORY SOCIALIZATION

CHANGE AS A CULTURAL VALUE

One of the underlying cultural values of our contemporary society is the focus on change for its own sake. In a sense all Americans are socialized from early childhood to believe that change is both inevitable and good. The notion that things will not remain the same—politically, economically, or socially—is an integral part of our national ethos. Otherwise there could be no Horatio Alger myth. Otherwise the political slogan, "It's time for a change," could not have been so effective as it obviously was in 1952. Otherwise Southern segregationists would not concede that the best they can do is fight a *delaying* action against integration. Change apparently is accepted as something both natural and inevitable by the vast majority of the members of our society. Such a value provides a general conditioning for the acceptance of new and different situations regardless of their specific nature.

In our interviews, we find evidence that middle-class urban Americans have internalized this value and are able logically to relate it to the family cycle. One mother observes philosophically that "it seems like life spaces itself. You look forward to finishing up one space but then another space always pops up. When this is accomplished something else comes along." The clearest statements, however, come from two of the fathers. One of them, when asked how it felt to become a grandfather responded that "like most things in my life, it's just a matter of course. Things can be expected, like you expect changes in jobs and expect children to be married. Natural events come afterward and you take those things as a matter of course." This process, felt to be "natural" in

our society, is described in full detail by the other father:

Of course you hate to give up your daughter, but I think we all understand that is the way of life; you can't stand still; you can't be the same forever. Life moves on and that is the most natural thing. You see them grow. You see them graduate from high school. Then you see them graduate from college—you follow along. It is changing all the time. First it is childhood. You hold them on your lap then you go walking with them. Then you see them through high school. I was her chauffeur, all the time taking her to social functions. She went through music school, then she got a bachelor of arts, then we sent her for four years to Juilliard and she got her bachelor's and master's there. Then she comes out and teaches in college for one year and then she gets married and settles down.

It is clear that at least some people are aware of a life cycle and a family cycle and are resigned (if not committed) to a philosophy of change. Whether or not one is willing to accept the conditioning effect of a basic cultural emphasis on change *per se*, there remain several more specific types of experiences which provide parents with an opportunity for anticipatory socialization.

THE TEMPORARY DEPARTURE OF CHILDREN

Opportunities for middle-class parents at least to play at a postparental role frequently occur when the children leave home for college. However, such opportunities are exploited to varying degrees, or, to put it another way, the experience is defined differently by different couples. Some parents make no mention of the possibility of college as a socializing experience for themselves. Presumably many of these do not see that possibility. On the other hand, there are others who see clearly what is happening. A mother claims that, "The breaking point is when your children go away to college. After that you grow used to it. By the time they get married you're used to the idea of their being away and adjust to it."

The question, "Do you think your child was ready to marry when he did?" brought out the functionality of the college experience. One father responded, "Yes, I thought she was. She had already gone through college—those five years of college and two years working. She was ready to get married." More important is that the college experience meant that he was now ready for her to get married. This kind of projection—the notion that college is training for the child to get away rather than training for the parent to release him—is expressed most clearly by a mother:

It's only natural, when you have a family of three without any relatives near by, to notice a gap when she gets married. Of course, the first adjustment is when they go away to school; that's the first break. It's healthy for an only child to go far away to school. It makes them more self-sufficient. She had been in school away from home since she was 16 and I think she was very well adjusted. Being away like that she learned to be independent, and make her own decisions and take responsibilities on her own. It was a sort of training period which prepared her [*sic;* "us"?] for leaving us [*sic;* "her"?].

Another mother says of her recently married son, "We had gotten used to just being by ourselves while he was in the Navy and away at college." This brings us to another frequently occurring opportunity for parents to play at the postparental role: the departure of children for military service. Life experiences tend to be evaluated in comparison with other experiences. They are not just good or bad; they are better or worse. Apparently it is better to lose a child through marriage than through war: "My most unhappy time was around the war years when my boy was in service. I worried over him coming back; he was missing several times." This is the kind of socialization that gives a parent a sense of relief to have a child home and married. We learn from another mother that, "When he was sent overseas, I was so worried about him over there that it was a relief when he got married and settled down." The importance of this as a learning experience is illustrated by the mother whose three children are now married, but who says of the time when her son went into service and she still had two others at home, "I think that the lonesomest part of my life I ever had was when my son was in service. We missed our boy." Her husband, interestingly enough, explicitly states that the Army experience serves as preparation for marriage. When asked if he thought his children were mature enough to get married, he responded: "Well, I thought more so about the boy because he was in the Army, but

I did think that she (the daughter) should have waited."

Being in the armed forces serves both to wean the parents away from the children and the children away from the parents. Still another mother reports that:

After he came out of the service he had aged a lot. He used to confide in us about life and to tell us about everything that was happening in school. But after he went into service he changed. We always spent our afternoons together—both the children. We'd go out for drives or picnics or something like that. But after he came home from service he didn't do that anymore. He wasn't contented to be at home.

But then, after the anguish of wartime separation, another woman implies that it is good just to know that the child is safe and is in this country:

He was in the Second World War and he was overseas. And after having been so far away from home he feels like he's practically right here, because we can telephone and it's just 50 miles. After having been in Europe a couple of years, you know 50 miles away is "at home."

There are other experiences which, like college or service in the armed forces, give parents an opportunity to practice living without their children. Nearly a quarter of the families interviewed had parted with their children for extended periods of time while they were still in their teens. For example, there is the son who couldn't get along with his father: "My son used to say that as much as he would like to stay here, he couldn't take things off of his dad any longer. So I never insisted on him staying. He left a couple of times and would come back." Then there is the child with the wanderlust: "That boy wasn't interested in anything except to hitchhike—just to get as far as he could and to see what he could see. He was walking when he was eight months old and has been walking ever since." More common than either of these two experiences is the departure of children prior to marriage in search of work. Although this sometimes occurs with daughters, it is more frequently the sons who leave for this reason:

(Do you remember how you felt when you first found out he was going to get married?) Yes, he was the first one. Both of them are married now. It was all right. He was able to take care of himself.

He was away from home a lot. He and the oldest boy were up in Detroit on defense work. They have really been away from home a long time—ever since 1940.

(How did you find it when the children left? Did you have a lot of time on your hands?) Well, that came gradually. The war had something to do with that. They were both in the war before they got married and we were alone then. And the youngest one went to aviation school. He was just barely 18 when he got his first job in Texas. Then he went to Phoenix and then he came home and then he went into service. And the other boy was at home for awhile and then he had to go. So with their coming and going it kinda eased off gradually.

Finally, in connection with these temporary departures of children prior to marriage, a word should be said about the modern middle-class urban high school complex. In some cases it results in the home being little more than a place to sleep and certainly in infrequent contacts with the parents. This reaction was obtained only from fathers. Possibly mothers maintain closer contacts with their children—especially with daughters—during the high school years. Be this as it may, one father reports that:

There is a difference when they grow older—particularly when they went to high school. Naturally they got their own friends and you saw less of them than you did before. They'd come home from school late and then they'd have a game or maybe the girl would have a date and you might see them at dinner time, but you probably wouldn't see them until breakfast—or maybe after the game or date.

Another father stated that the "best years" were when his boys were around nine or ten: "(When they started to grow up did you feel that they were growing away from you?) No, but when they go to high school they have different ideas and interests than the people at home have." There is, however, another side to this coin. The proud father of a high school athlete was asked when was the happiest time of his life: "Oh—that kid of mine—the things he did when he was in high school. It was like living your life over again. I guess I really enjoyed that period."

On the basis of such observations, there is reason to believe that there are bridges—transitional learning experiences which aid parents in adapting themselves to postparental life. These appear to provide continuity in role conditioning. Such "rehearsals" are not as difficult as "opening night," the real and permanent departure of the children which will come later. They are defined as temporary and are broken by regular visits home or the expectation that the children will at some time again return to live at home. But the "temporary" can gradually shift into the permanent without any traumatic transition: "My daughter went to California, to Berkeley, to go to school. Then she decided to work there a while and then she got married out there and she has lived there ever since." The fact that these socializing experiences occur at a time when the parents are still extremely active with their own affairs should not be ignored. It is probably easier to prepare for and accept such a transition in early middle age than in later years when it will actually occur. When one mother was asked how she made out at home with the children all off to college, she shrugged off the question with, "Oh, I don't know. I was just too busy to be bothered about anything."

③ LIFE WITHOUT FATHER

If there are temporary departures of the children which provide parents with an opportunity to practice the postparental role, there is also a combination of recent historical events and cultural expectations which have provided middle-class fathers with an additional opportunity to practice this role. The historical events are the Great Depression and the Second World War; the cultural expectations are those related to the middle-class notion of "work." Unlike some of the temporary departures of children mentioned in the preceding section, a temporary shattering of the family constellation due to the exigencies of war, work, or economic depression can be rationalized as beyond the control of those involved—attributed to immitigable external forces. Such rationalization is not always possible when the family breakup results from a unilateral decision on the part of a child to leave home for reasons related to education or work. When opportunities to engage in these pursuits are locally available, the parents may view the child's decision as a rejection of themselves. Such a definition of the situation (whether accurate or inaccurate) is hardly conducive to promoting a smooth transition into postparental life.

Some fathers, owing to the press of circumstances, have lived for extended periods of time away from their wives and children.

I was having a rough time. I was six months or a year on WPA and when I got off that I couldn't find anything. But I had a brother in Portland, Oregon, so I went out there and it seems I was away from mother (wife) and the kids for close to a year and a half.

During the war my husband was on a swingshift and worked nights and then he was in the Hawaiian Islands for a year working for the Navy.

Let me tell you how it was. On a certain day I had $50,000 in the bank and a $25,000 home paid for and all the trimmings to go with it. Three months later I borrowed $25 to send my wife and children up to Kansas City (from Oklahoma). It was months before I got things straightened out enough to join them.

My huband was 38 and the company sent us to Ottawa (Kansas). The draft board there just had a high quota and they scraped the bottom of the barrel. That's how they got him.

Nearly one in every five of the families interviewed was broken for extended periods of time under circumstances similar to those described above. It is relevant that these experiences most often were narrated in response to questions about how close the father was to the children when they were growing up.

A somewhat more common experience (also usually discussed in relation to that same line of questioning) is the detachment of the father from his growing children and his lack of involvement in their activities as a result of his being "on the road." One third of these middle-class fathers found it necessary to travel regularly during some phase of their work career, and in all but one case this was defined as alienating the father from the children. When asked if she felt that she was closer to her children than her husband, one wife answered, "I think I was, definitely, because my husband is a traveling man. I really reared the children; most of the time he was only home Saturdays and Sundays." Other wives of traveling men tend to respond in like manner:

He travels from Monday to Thursday and he's

in Thursday evening until Monday morning. (Do you think this had anything to do with his relationship with the children when they were growing up?) Yes, quite a bit! They didn't have the companionship with their dad that I thought they should have had.

This is not a one-sided "mama's" point of view. As the following couplets excerpted from husband and wife interviews reveal, the husbands are in essential agreement on this matter:

(1) *Wife:* (Do you think your husband's occupation kept him away from the boys?) Very definitely! It was unfortunate too. He felt he was just not able to devote the time to them and it was not up to me to say what he should and should not do. (He was out of town a good part of the time?) Yes, when they were young he was gone a great deal. Then later on he had so much responsibility in the office. He was the kind that went early and stayed late. You see he had had considerable trouble when he was younger, seeing his mother working and slaving while his father was ill and he didn't want me to have to do the same thing. *That* result has been fine. But as for the boys, he never did have much time for them.

Husband: (Did you feel that your job kept you away from your children—that you didn't have enough time to spend with them?) I didn't have enough time to spend with them. When I was traveling I was away a great deal, and then when I went into the office my job there kept me on the job from early in the morning until dinner time and then I worked a good many nights at home. So I didn't have too much time with them.

* * *

(2) *Wife:* (Which one of you was closer to the children when they were younger?) I would say I was. For one thing, he was gone so much. He would only see them on weekends. So I would definitely say they were closer to me. They respect their father and think a lot of him, but they wouldn't bring their problems to him as much as they would to me.

Husband: (Tell me how your work affects your family life?) Well, like the average man gets up and goes to work every morning. *I* am out for a week! Now that we have better highways and faster cars you can make most all your territory in a week's time. I used to make a lot of two and three weeks' trips because we had slower cars and not very good highways and it took just that much longer.

Although improvements in transportation may have reduced the periods of absence, they still exist. However, simply because a man travels does not mean that he has become detached from his children and family. A railroader and his wife demonstrate how a family can be tightly knit because his absence for short periods results in his being home for five or six day "weekends." This traveling man had the opportunity to be closer to his family than most who do not travel:

(Do you think it took away from your family too much to be on the road?) Well, I was away from the family. Like a trip from here to Omaha and Colorado it was two nights and one day away and come in and sleep a day and then go right back out again when I had to make two round trips. So I was four nights off on the road, but then I'd come in and I'd have five days off one time and six the next.

And from his wife:

Yes, he was on the road a lot. He was on the Super Chief on the Santa Fe Main Line. He was on that train for 11 years. (Would you rather he worked at something that kept him home?) Oh my no! He liked his work. He was on the railroad for 44 years. (Do you think his being away from home affected his relationship with the children?) No, no; they were always regular companions—all of them. He knew the children as well as I did.

As has been indicated in some of the passages cited, even when father is at home, he may be so in body only, being engrossed in his work day and night whether on the road or in town. When this kind of commitment to work evolves, men whose work never takes them out of town may see less of their families than some who, like the railroader, travel a great deal. One mother generalizes: "I think most men are so occupied with their work that they sort of leave that (rearing of children) to the mother." A father whose work has never taken him out of town concurs: "I'm afraid I left most of bringing him up to his mother. Lots of times when he was growing up I had to work late. I wouldn't get home till 9:30 or 10:00 at night and I'd be out to the office at 5:00 in the morning."

It is important, however, that this parental detachment not be overemphasized. Not all middle-class fathers orient themselves to the work role so strongly. There are certainly some who leave their work at the office: "I have no night work. My work is at the office and when I leave the office I'm through until the next day, regardless of what I've got. I've never made a

practice of bringing work home." There are others who emphasize that, in spite of many temptations, they have steadfastly refused to take their work out of the office.

It would seem that there are a good many cases among urban middle-class families where life goes on without father during the years when the child is growing up. As dysfunctional as this may be to the family at that stage, it does provide the fathers with continuity in role conditioning which can stand them in good stead at the later postparental stage when the time comes for the children to depart permanently.

THE MOTHER-IN-LAW MYTH AS A CONDITIONING DEVICE

If the work role helps to condition fathers for the departure of their children, at least some mothers appear to be provided with a conditioning device which is the distinctive property of their sex. That device is the cultural myth of the mother-in-law: "As soon as my youngsters were born I made up my mind that I was not going to be a mother-in-law like you read about." Such a resolution, if intended seriously, could go far in preparing a mother to accept the departure of her children. In addition to the folklore on the mother-in-law, there is the reality of experience:

My son got married before he even finished his education. He was only 17 years old, but I did not say a word! I don't think it's good policy. That can be a very tender spot. I know because I went through it. I had a mother-in-law—well, she was just butting into everything all the time. I just resolved never to act like that myself. The Bible says something about to hold your peace. And that's not prose. That's just the way it should be. People when they get married should get away from relatives. Far enough away so that it takes three days for a postcard to get to them and three more for it to get back.

The following mother expresses the same opinion even more vehemently:

I'll go to the county home before I'll live with any of my children. I have very definite ideas on that. Because I had his mother with us every winter for 20 years whether I had room for her or not and it *doesn't* work and I very *definitely* will *not* do a thing like that! If I have to take a dose of strychnine first, I won't!

Humor is, of course, an effective form of social control—especially in an increasingly other-directed society. Mothers, like everyone else, are sensitive to the pleas of the mass media for conformity. They want to be "good" mothers-in-law and Evelyn Duvall's study indicates that they are—that the mother-in-law is not nearly the center of conflict in America that she is often thought to be (7). It is very possible that a more accurate statement would be that the mother-in-law is not nearly the center of conflict that she *used* to be. The pressures of experience and folklore as indicated in the passages cited above may have brought about a shift in the self-conception of mothers-in-law and in the role which they play. In any event, at least in some cases, these myths and experiences provide an opportunity for mothers to anticipate and prepare themselves for postparental life—a socializing opportunity.

⑤ SURVIVALS OF AN OLDER FAMILY PATTERN

The postparental phase of the family cycle was described earlier as a newly emerging phenomenon resulting from increasing longevity and decreasing fertility. No longer is it true, as it was at the turn of the century, that both parents will have died before the last of their children was launched. However, as with any emerging phenomenon, fragmentary survivals of the earlier pattern remain. In such cases, there is, in effect, no transition to make—these people have no postparental period. Take, for example, the couple with six children ranging in age from 31 to 44, with three of them married and residing in the metropolitan area and a fourth divorced and living at home. Their daily life remains essentially the same as it has always been, although the work is somewhat lighter and the economic situation somewhat more secure:

(Tell me just how you spend a typical day nowadays?) Well, I do my housework in the morning and then I get meals again, and the children will come in once in a while and sometimes I go down to one of my daughters'. That is all I do. I have a fine family. They are all good Christian children and I am just as proud of them as I can be.

Life has changed so little for this couple that they even argue about the same kinds of trivialities they did 30 years ago:

. . . take that rug there in the dining room. I didn't like the color but he bought it anyway because it was a good buy. It was a remnant. But it seemed to me that a rug is something that you have to live with for a long time and it ought to satisfy you. But he said that I had had my way with the wallpaper so he went ahead and bought it.

An extended family need not be one of procreation; even with few children, postparental couples may refer themselves to a large family of orientation. This older pattern manifests itself in the case of a couple one of whose two married children is now living in Minneapolis. In spite of this, there is a plethora of parental siblings, in-laws, nephews, nieces, and grandchildren—all part of a second- and third-generation Irish clan residing in the Kansas City area:

(Tell me what you do with your time these days?) Well, we are quite home people, that is, with the grandchildren, the daughter, and his (husband's) people. He has seven brothers and they are all living in Kansas City, and we are very close to one another—the husbands and wives. We have picnics, and we go from home to home for little parties and then I have my sisters too and they live here. You know, we just enjoy family. I have brothers and sisters and he has all brothers. So that gives me a lot of sister-in-laws too. So we are very family people—very home people.

This kind of extended family support appears to lessen the trauma of the disintegration of the family of procreation. Most families, however, find themselves far more isolated from "kinfolk" in the modern American city.

SUMMARY AND CONCLUSIONS

We have seen that several conditioning situations present themselves as potential aids in the socialization of parents for post-parental life. These situations provide an opportunity to anticipate postparental roles, not by taking the role of the other in the usual sense, but by experiencing analogous situations which are quasi-postparental and which enable the parents to play at anticipated roles. There is the underlying value in our society on change for its own sake—a value which can be applied to the particular case of change in the family structure; there are the temporary departures of children during the adolescent years for college, service in the armed forces, and a variety of other reasons; there is the modern complex of urban high school life, which can move the children into a world which is foreign to their parents; there are the exigencies of the work situation which often remove the middle-class father from the family during the years when the children are growing up; there is the myth and the reality of the mother-in-law which some mothers internalize as lessons for themselves. In addition, remnants of the older extended family pattern which tend to reduce the impact of the transition cannot be ignored.

It was stated earlier that *theoretically* this could be assumed to be a difficult transition to make, largely because of the absence of role models—the absence of socialization to play postparental roles. However, the middle-aged couples whose children have left home indicate that there are opportunities for them to learn these new roles before they are thrust upon them.

It was also stated earlier that much of the descriptive literature indicates that this is a difficult period of life. By and large such observations are based on clinical experiences with persons who have so much difficulty in making the transition that they must seek outside help. The small group of postparental spouses interviewed by the present writer represent a random sample of such people who discussed their lives in their own living room. Although definite conclusions cannot be drawn from the responses of this small fragment of the population, they have managed to provide us with some notion of the variety of alternative modes of anticipatory socialization available to their ilk. It would appear from their comments that it is reasonable to assume that people do have opportunities to prepare for postparental life and, in addition, that most of them take advantage of these opportunities.

This phase of the family cycle is seen by the majority of middle-aged spouses as a time of new freedoms: freedom from the economic responsibilities of children; freedom to be mobile (geographically); freedom from housework and other chores. And, finally, freedom to be one's self for the first time since the children came along. No longer do the parents need to live the self-consciously restricted existence of models

for their own children: "We just take life easy now that the children are grown. We even serve dinner right from the stove when we're alone. It's hotter that way, but you just couldn't let down like that when your children are still at home."

REFERENCES

1. BENEDICT, RUTH. Continuities and discontinuities in cultural conditioning. *Psychiatry*, 1938, *1*, 161–167.
2. BURGESS, ERNEST W., and LOCKE, HARVEY. *The family: from institution to companionship.* New York: American Book Co., 1945.
3. CAVAN, RUTH S. *The American family.* New York: Thomas Y. Crowell Company, 1953.
4. CAVAN, RUTH S. *Marriage and family in the modern world.* New York: Thomas Y. Crowell Company, 1960.
5. CHRISTENSEN, HAROLD. *Marriage analysis.* New York: The Ronald Press Company, 1950.
6. DEUTSCHER, IRWIN. Married life in the middle years: a study of the middle class urban postparental couple. Ph.D. dissertation, Department of Sociology, University of Missouri, 1958.
7. DUVALL, EVELYN M. *In-laws: pro and con.* New York: Association Press, 1954.
8. DUVALL, EVELYN M. Implications for education through the family life cycle. *Marriage and Family Living*, November, 1958, *20*, 334–342.
9. DUVALL, EVELYN M., and HILL, REUBEN. *The dynamics of family interaction.* National Conference on Family Life, Inc., 1948 (mimeographed).
10. FREEDMAN, RONALD, WHELPTON, PASCAL K., and CAMPBELL, ARTHUR A. *Family planning, sterility and population growth.* New York: McGraw-Hill Book Company, 1959.
11. GLICK, PAUL C. The family cycle. *American Sociological Review*, April, 1947, *12*, 164–169.
12. GLICK, PAUL C. The cycle of the family. *Marriage and Family Living*, February, 1955, *17*.
13. HILTNER, HELEN J. Changing family tasks of adults. *Marriage and Family Living*, May, 1953, *15*, 110–113.
14. HOUSE, FLOYD N. The natural history of institutions. In *The development of sociology.* New York: McGraw-Hill Book Company, 1936, 141–157.
15. HUGHES, EVERETT C. *Men and their work.* New York: The Free Press, 1959.
16. KINSEY, ALFRED, POMEROY, WARDELL B., MARTIN, CLYDE E., and GEBHARD, PAUL H. *Sexual behavior in the human female.* Philadelphia: W. B. Saunders Company, 1953.
17. LOWREY, LAWSON G. Adjustment over the life

span. In George Lawton (ed.), *New goals for old age.* New York: Columbia University Press, 1943, 8–9.

18. POLLAK, OTTO. *Social adjustment in old age.* New York: Social Science Research Council, Bulletin 59, 1948.

19. SIRJAMAKI, JOHN. *The American family in the twentieth century.* Cambridge, Mass.: Harvard University Press, 1953.

20. SUSSMAN, MARVIN B. Parental participation in mate selection and its effect upon family

continuity. *Social Forces,* October, 1953, *32,* 76–77.

21. TIBBITTS, CLARK. National aspects of an aging population. In CLARK TIBBITTS and WILMA DONAHUE (eds.), *Growing in the older years.* Ann Arbor, Mich.: The University of Michigan Press, 1951.

22. WALLER, WILLARD, and HILL, REUBEN. *The family: a dynamic interpretation.* New York: The Dryden Press. 1951.

43.

JOHN C. BERESFORD AND ALICE M. RIVLIN

PRIVACY, POVERTY, AND OLD AGE

Wants are relative. As people's incomes rise, they desire more and new kinds of goods and services. Rapidly rising incomes in the United States in the postwar period have brought new levels of demand for cars, toys, clothes, pleasure boats, entertainment, education, and hundreds of other goods and services. Almost overlooked in this plethora of consumer wants has been a major increase in Americans' demand for an item not ordinarily listed among goods and services, namely, privacy. By "privacy" we mean the occupancy by an individual or a nuclear family of a separate dwelling unit not shared with other relatives or nonrelatives.

The typical modern American apparently puts a high value on having a separate dwelling unit, into which he can retreat with his wife, if he has one, and his minor children but no one else, and close the door. He is reluctant to share a dwelling with relatives outside his nuclear family or to live as a roomer or boarder in the household of a nonrelative. Since World

War II, Americans have expressed these preferences by using part of their rising income to buy privacy. At all age levels, individuals and nuclear families have succeeded in obtaining not only more housing and better housing but housing separate from other people.

Privacy can be identified statistically as the proportion of households containing only one person or one nuclear family. Changes in the proportion of persons over 14 (or over 18) reported to the census as "head" or "wife of head" of the household also reflect changes in privacy.

Older persons and persons just beginning adult life are the individuals most likely to play a key role in determining the privacy standards achieved by families. The ability of young adults to set up their own households and of older persons to maintain their own households determines how much privacy all generations will experience. This discussion of privacy examines the living patterns of those age groups.

THE CHANGING HOUSEHOLD STATUS OF THE YOUNG

A marked increase in the proportion of young men who were heads of households occurred

This selection is reprinted from: John C. Beresford, and Alice M. Rivlin, "Privacy, Poverty, and Old Age," *Demography,* 1966, *3,* 247–258. Reprinted with the permission of the authors and publisher.

This is a revision of a paper presented at the meetings of the Population Association of America, April 23, 1965.

between 1940 and 1960.[1] In 1940, only one in five men aged 20–24 headed his own household; by 1960, two in five were household heads. In 1940, just over half the men aged 25–29 headed households; by 1960, the fraction had risen to three-quarters.

The proportionate increases in household heads were balanced by reductions in the proportion of young men living in the households of others. Men in their twenties were much less likely in 1960 than in 1940 to be living in their parents' household as "children of the head." They were also less likely to be grandchildren or other relatives of the head, although neither of these categories was large even in 1940. The proportion of men in their twenties living as nonrelatives of the head (lodgers or resident employees) also decreased between 1940 and 1960.

In the household population, the only category which showed an increase for young men was that of "head." Outside the household population, however, the "group quarters" population also showed a relative increase. For ages 15–24, the proportion of men in group quarters rose substantially, reflecting an increase in college enrollment and military service, as well as a shift in the method of enumerating college students. (In 1960, college students living in dormitories were enumerated at college. In 1940, an attempt was made to include them in their parental families.)

The household status of young women likewise altered radically over the two decades. Like men, women in their twenties were far less likely to be living as "children of the head" in 1960 than in 1940 and somewhat less likely to be other relatives, lodgers, or resident employees. But the major shift for women was not toward household headship. Although the proportion of young women who were household heads did rise, the position of household head was still rare for a young woman in 1960. The big increase between 1940 and 1960 was in the proportion of young women who were wives of heads. Some increase in the proportion of young women in group quarters also occurred at age 15–24.

[1] U.S. Bureau of the Census, U.S. *Census of Population,* PC(1)-1D, Table 183.

LIVING ARRANGEMENTS OF THE YOUNG IN 1885

Before examining in greater detail the shifts since 1940 in the living arrangements of the young, it would be useful to know whether the changes are recent or part of a long trend. Unfortunately, national data on household relationships are not available before 1940. For earlier years, it is necessary to turn to state censuses.

The Massachusetts census of 1885 is rich in detail on relationship to the head of the household, and from it information can be extracted and compared with 1940 and 1960 census data for Massachusetts. No inference should be drawn, of course, that the intervening years lay on a smooth trend line. There may have been ups and downs in the interim.

A dramatic change did occur between 1885 and 1960 in household relationships of young adults in Massachusetts, but most of the change seems to have taken place since 1940, as shown in Table 43–1. In 1960, over half the male population 20–29 had achieved the status of household head, compared with slightly more than one-quarter in that status in both 1885 and 1940. More than two-thirds of the women 20–29 were wives or household heads in 1960, and less than 40 percent were wives or household heads in 1885 or 1940.

As mentioned, college students living in dormitories in 1940 were enumerated at their parental homes. In 1885 and 1960, they were enumerated at college. This difference may explain, in part, a drop in the proportion of males 20–29 years old in group quarters which appears between 1885 and 1940 and a corresponding increase in the proportion of "children." "Children of the head" plus persons in group quarters constituted about 60 percent of the males in the age group in 1885 and 1940 and just over 40 percent in 1960.

In the case of young women 20–29 years old, a major shift did occur before 1940—the decline in the proportion of employees, which reflected the disappearance of live-in domestic help. Children and employees together accounted for just under half of the women in the age group in 1885 and 1940 but only a fifth in 1960.

TABLE 43–1. PERCENT OF PERSONS BY HOUSEHOLD STATUS IN THREE BROAD AGE
GROUPS BY SEX FOR MASSACHUSETTS, 1885, 1940, 1960

| Broad age group, sex and year | Total | Relationship to head for household members | | | | | | Persons in group quarters |
		Head	Wife	Child	Other relative	Lodger	Employee	
20 to 29								
Male								
1960	100.0	51.7	...	30.0	4.2	2.7	...	11.4
1940	100.0	27.0	...	56.9	7.4	4.4	0.2	4.1
1885	100.0	26.2	...	39.1	7.2	6.6	2.7	18.2
Female								
1960	100.0	4.9	63.0	21.4	3.2	2.1	0.3	5.1
1940	100.0	1.7	37.5	45.4	6.2	3.1	2.1	4.0
1885	100.0	1.1	34.0	34.2	7.0	3.5	14.3	5.9
30 to 60								
Male								
1960	100.0	87.3	...	5.2	3.3	1.2	*	3.0
1940	100.0	76.5	...	8.0	5.6	5.3	0.3	4.3
1885	100.0	77.6	...	6.8	3.7	3.4	1.0	7.5
Female								
1960	100.0	12.9	74.1	5.8	4.1	0.7	0.3	2.1
1940	100.0	11.7	65.0	9.1	6.1	2.8	1.9	3.5
1885	100.0	11.6	63.9	8.0	6.4	2.0	4.6	3.5
60 and over								
Male								
1960	100.0	82.6	...	0.2	9.5	2.4	0.1	5.2
1940	100.0	72.7	...	0.2	11.3	6.7	0.2	8.9
1885	100.0	81.9	...	0.3	10.3	1.2	0.5	5.8
Female								
1960	100.0	34.4	36.0	0.4	19.3	2.3	0.7	6.9
1940	100.0	30.2	32.7	0.2	22.1	5.9	1.7	7.2
1885	100.0	28.1	34.6	0.4	28.7	1.0	1.8	5.4

*Less than 0.05 per cent.
Sources: Census of Massachusetts: 1885, *Volume I, Population and Social Statistics*, Part I, Wright and Potter Printing Company, State Printers, p. 482; Sixteenth Census of the United States, 1940: *Volume IV. Characteristics by Age, Massachusetts*, Tables 13 and 14; U.S. Bureau of the Census, *U.S. Census of Population: 1960, Detailed Characteristics, Massachusetts*. Final Report PC(1)-23D, Tables 106, 107.

Unfortunately, the definition of "household" is not strictly comparable for 1885 and the other years being compared. The major effect of the difference is probably that many lodgers of 1885 would have been primary individuals in 1940 or 1960. However, even if all 1885 lodgers were converted to household heads, the conclusion that the increase in household formation occurred in recent years would not be altered.

There is no way to determine how closely family living arrangements in Massachusetts in 1885 correspond to those in the rest of the United States. It is known, however, that the changes found in Massachusetts between 1940 and 1960 mirror those in the country as a whole, and there is no obvious reason for thinking that Massachusetts was less typical of the whole country in 1885. Hence, it seems reasonable to conclude that the increase in privacy which occurred in the country as a whole after World War II was a new phenomenon, not a continuation of a long trend.

PRIVACY AND MARITAL STATUS
OF THE YOUNG

Much of what is called here the quest for privacy among the young was associated with earlier marriage. The median age at first marriage dropped sharply in the 1940's, and the proportion of young people who were married and living with their spouses rose accordingly. The proportion of men aged 20–24, for example, who were married and living with their spouses rose from 26 percent to 40 percent between 1940 and 1960.[2]

Since married men are far more likely to be household heads than unmarried men, an increase in marriage at early ages raises the proportion of young male household heads.

By no means all the increase in young households can be attributed to changes in marital status. There were 8.3 million households headed by persons 14–34 years old in 1940. Between 1940 and 1960, the population in this age group hardly increased at all. If the proportion of heads aged 14–34 in 1940 were applied to the 1960 population, about 8.7 million households would result. If marital status changes were taken into account and the 1940 proportion of heads age 14–34 by sex and marital status were applied to the 1960 population, about 10.4 million households would result. Actually there were 12.4 million household heads aged 14–34 in 1960, or 2 million more than can be explained by marital status changes alone.[3]

Most of the increase in separate living for married couples came after 1950, as shown in Table 43–2. During World War II, the proportion of young married women with their own household decreased.[4] By 1950 the proportion with households of their own had risen again

[2]Figures for the conterminous United States (*U.S. Census of Population, 1960,* PC(1)-1D, Tables 177 and 178).

[3]Household headship rates by marital status for ages 14–34 were as follows:

	1940	1960
	percent	percent
Males:		
Married, spouse present	86	96
Other	3	6
Females:		
Other (i.e., not married, spouse present)	5	10

Source: *U.S. Census of Population, 1960,* PC(1)-1D, Tables 178 and 183.

[4]Paul C. Glick, *American Families* (New York: John Wiley & Sons, Inc., 1957), 61.

TABLE 43–2. PERCENT OF MARRIED COUPLES WITH OWN HOUSEHOLD, BY AGE OF WIFE, CONTERMINOUS UNITED STATES, 1940, 1950, 1960

Age of wife	1940	1950	1960
All ages	93.2	93.6	97.9
Under 25	81.0	82.5	92.3
25 to 34	91.8	92.6	98.1
35 to 44	96.2	96.2	99.0
45 to 54	97.3	97.1	99.1
55 to 64	96.4	96.6	98.7
65 and over	93.0	93.4	97.2

Sources: 1940 and 1950 from Glick, *American Families,* 1960, p. 61, from PC(1)-1D, Tables 178, 182. Figures based on the decennial censuses do not correspond exactly to Current Population Sruvey data given in Current Population Report, P-20, No. 130.

to just above the prewar level. Then it rose sharply in the 1950's as housing became more available and incomes rose.

Among unmarried people the rising demand for privacy has been reflected in an increase in the proportion of primary individuals (persons maintaining their own households apart from relatives). Although primary individual status was not very usual for young people even in 1960, the number of young primary individuals increased considerably faster between 1950 and 1960 than the number of young people who were not in the "married spouse present" category. The largest relative increase was for young men 25–34 years old. Only about eight percent of the unmarried men in this age group were primary individuals in 1950, compared with 19 percent in 1960.[5]

In most age groups the increase in primary individuals was accompanied by a decline in secondary individuals. Among people 18–24 not living with their spouses, however, the likelihood of being a secondary individual actually increased between 1950 and 1960. Most of these young secondary individuals were probably college students and members of the armed forces.

Another manifestation of the demand for privacy among the young was the increase in families with young female heads. Families

[5]U.S. Bureau of the Census, *1950 Census of Population,* P-E No. 20, Table 1; *1960 Census of Population,* PC(2)-4B, Table 2.

headed by women under 35 increased much faster between 1950 and 1960 than did families with male heads in the same age group.[6] Since young women who head families are typically widowed, divorced, or separated, one is tempted to attribute the increase in female head families to increased marital disruption. The total number of young women with broken marriages, however, did not increase between 1950 and 1960. The total of widowed, divorced, and separated women aged 18–34 was actually slightly lower in 1960 than ten years earlier because a moderate increase in the number of divorcees was more than offset by a decline in the number of widows.[7] However, the living arrangements of young widowed, divorced, and separated women changed markedly. The proportion living separately (as primary individuals and heads of primary families) rose sharply, while the proportion living with others or in group quarters declined.

Although the number of widowed, divorced, and separated women in the younger age groups declined, the number married, with spouse absent for reasons other than marital discord, increased almost 60 percent—to over 500,000. Some of these women are wives of servicemen. Others are probably waiting to join their husbands in a new location. Others may be in transition to separation or divorce. These women were less likely to maintain their own households than widowed, divorced, or separated women of the same age, but they were more likely to live separately in 1960 than in 1950.

PRIVACY AND SCHOOL ENROLLMENT OF THE YOUNG

Perhaps the most surprising aspect of the increase in separate living among the young is that it has occurred simultaneously with a major increase in school enrollment. At a time when young people were staying in school longer and starting their working careers later, one might have expected a decrease in separate

living rather than the increase which has taken place.

The successive stages of independence for young people have been telescoped. "In the old days," a young man typically left school in his mid-teens and went to work. In general, he continued to live with his parents or with other relatives, but sometimes he lived as a lodger or an employee in the household of nonrelatives. Only after some years of work experience did he take a wife. The new people usually set up housekeeping by themselves, although they sometimes continued to live with relatives.

For women, the typical sequence involved an interval "at home" between school and marriage. Some women worked before marriage, but few worked after marriage. If the marriage was broken by death, divorce, or separation, the young woman went to live with her parents or with other relatives.

Since World War II, the typical sequences have been foreshortened and even mixed up. Both young men and young women stay in school longer, as shown in the first column of Table 43–3. But this does not mean that they stay out of the labor force. Labor force participation rates of young people failed to drop significantly for either sex between 1940 and 1960, despite the increase in school enrollment. In fact, labor force participation of the 16–19 age group increased appreciably for both sexes.

Although they stay in school longer, young people also marry sooner. The interval between school and marriage has been shortened for both sexes. Marrying before leaving school and returning to school after marriage are no longer uncommon.

The increase in marriage for women has not lowered their labor force participation. Women are more likely to work in the now-short interval between school and marriage and more likely to stay in the labor force after marriage than they were in 1940. Despite the increase in marriage and school enrollment, labor force participation rates of students and married women apparently combine to explain how young people have managed to marry and set up separate households at younger ages while at the same time staying longer in school.

The 1960 census statistics provide a close

---

[6]John C. Beresford and Alice M. Rivlin, "Characteristics of 'Other' Families," *Demography*, 1, No. 1.

[7]*Ibid.*

TABLE 43–3. SCHOOL ENROLLMENT, LABOR FORCE PARTICIPATION,
MARRIAGE, AND HOUSEHOLD STATUS OF YOUNG MEN
AND WOMEN, UNITED STATES, 1940 AND 1960

Sex, age, year	Percent enrolled in school or college	Percent in labor force	Percent married, spouse present*	Percent head or wife of head of household
Males				
16–19				
1940	49.4	41.4	1.6	1.2
1960	65.8	50.0	3.6	3.4
20–21				
1940	12.4	83.5	13.8	10.3
1960	25.8	81.4	26.1	25.9
20–24				
1940	5.3	91.1	33.6	28.5
1960	15.1	89.4	52.0	51.9
25–34				
1940	NA	95.2	66.5	62.1
1960	6.5	94.9	77.4	80.1
Females				
16–19				
1940	47.7	24.6	12.9	9.2
1960	60.8	32.6	16.3	14.8
20–21				
1940	8.7	47.4	38.0	30.0
1960	16.6	48.3	52.1	52.3
22–24				
1940	2.4	43.5	55.5	47.3
1960	5.3	42.6	71.5	73.9
25–34				
1940	NA	32.9	73.3	67.3
1960	2.7	35.3	82.5	87.9

*Ratio of spouse present to total married estimated from broader age-groups, 1940, for ages under 25.

Source: U.S. Bureau of the Census: *Sixteenth Census of the United States: 1940, Population,* Vol. IV, Part 1, Tables 9, 11, 14, 24; *Census of Population 1960,* PC(2)-5A, Table 8, 9.

look at the marital status, labor force participation, enrollment, and separate living for quite narrow age groups.[8] It is clear that enrollment was still a deterrent to marriage (or marriage to enrollment) even in 1960. Students were far less likely to be married than nonstudents, although the difference narrowed with increasing age. By age 22–24, over a third of male students were married and living with their spouses, compared with slightly over half the nonstudents of the same age.

Most married men headed their own households in 1960, even if they were students. Very young husbands (aged 16–19) were somewhat

more likely to be living with relatives if they were still in school, but this difference disappeared about the age of 20. At ages 20–24, nine out of ten married men headed households, whether they were students or not.

Most young married men were in the labor force, even if they were enrolled in school. Labor force participation rates of married nonstudents were almost 100 percent. Those of married students were lower but still surprisingly high. Over three-quarters of the student husbands were in the labor force. Moreover, the students' wives were far more likely to be labor force participants than were wives of nonstudents. Half the wives of students 22–24 were in the labor force, compared with about 30 percent of the wives of nonstudents in the

[8]U.S. Bureau of the Census, *1960 Census of Population,* PC(2)-5A, Tables 8 and 9.

same age group. If the student husband himself was not in the labor force, the chance that his wife was a participant rose to two out of three. In fact, only eight percent of the student couples in the 22–24 age group had neither member in the labor force, while 37 percent had both. It seems clear that the high labor force participation of married students and their wives had been an important factor in enabling couples to marry young and set up separate households even while the husband was still in school.

PRIVACY AT OLDER AGES

In the middle age groups (35–64), there was less room for a major shift in marital and household status than among the young. Even in 1940, the large majority of men and women in these age groups were married, and almost all married couples maintained their own households. Small increases in the proportions married and the tendency of married couples to maintain their own households did occur but did not produce large increases in the total number of households. The number of households headed by married men aged 35–64 living with their wives increased from 16.8 million in 1940 to 24.2 million in 1960.[9] Of the 7.4 million increase, 5.0 million would have resulted from the larger number of men in this age group, even if the proportion of men who were married and maintained their own households had remained constant. The additional 2.4 million were attributable to increases in the proportions married and living apart from relatives.

The proportion of unmarried people in the middle age groups declined between 1940 and 1960, but it was within this group that the most marked increases in privacy occurred. The proportion of household heads among unmarried men (i.e., men not in the category "married, spouse present") increased from 35 to 45 percent, and the corresponding percentage for women increased from 51 to 62 percent.

It should be remembered that the major impact of increased privacy for persons in the

middle age groups was not on their household status but on the composition of the households they headed. Because of the increased privacy of the young, households headed by persons 35–64 in 1960 were far less likely to contain grown children of the head than similar households in 1940. The tendency of elderly people (aged 65 and over) to maintain their own households also affected the middle generation.

The increasing tendency of older people to maintain separate households rather than to live with relatives or nonrelatives has been widely noted. In fact, this trend has been sometimes viewed with alarm. Contrasts can be drawn between the "old days" (say, 1940), when elderly people were somewhat more likely to be absorbed into larger family units as parents of a head, and the present, when they are supposedly thrust out to be heads on their own limited resources.

When viewed as part of the general increase in privacy, however, the tendency for older people to maintain separate households does not stand out as a phenomenon peculiar to that generation. The same changes found in other age groups—increases in proportions married and in the tendency of married and unmarried people to maintain their own households—also show up among the elderly.

In the elderly group, as in the middle age group, increases in the proportion married and living with spouse occurred between 1940 and 1960, although they were by no means as spectacular as the marital status changes of the young. The proportion of men aged 65 and over living with their spouses increased from 60 percent to 67 percent over the two decades, and the corresponding proportion for women, from 32 to 35 percent.[10] The proportion of elderly married couples maintaining their own households was already 94 percent in 1940. It increased to 98 percent in 1960. Older married couples without privacy were rare before World War II. They are even rarer now.

Among those not married spouse present, the proportion of household heads for men and women 65 and over has increased in the last two decades. Most of the increase in household

---

[9] U.S. *Census of Population, 1960,* PC(1)-1D, Tables 178 and 183.

[10] *Ibid.*

headship among unmarried older people was an increase in persons living as primary individuals. By no means all of these new primary individuals of 1960 were people who would have been living as relatives of the head under conditions prevalent in earlier years. Many would have been secondary individuals—resident employees and lodgers in households and group quarters.

The big increase in the number of older households in recent years was primarily a result of the increase in the proportion of older persons in the population, not of a radical shift in the living arrangements of older people. It should be noted that if elderly people had not increased the extent to which they maintained their own households, the privacy of the middle age groups would necessarily have been impaired. The older population increased faster than the middle age group (and will continue to do so for the next decade or so). Absorbing the increased number of older people into younger families over the last two decades would have meant a major increase in the frequency with which middle-aged families had older relatives living with them.

PRIVACY AND INCOME

The period of increasing privacy since World War II has also been a period of rising incomes. But this coincidence by itself does not establish any causal connection between rising income and an increased demand for privacy. After all, incomes rose substantially between 1885 and 1940, yet the Massachusetts census data do not indicate any significant shift toward separate household maintenance between these two dates. To assert that separate living has been associated with higher incomes since 1940, one must also assert that a basic shift in tastes occurred at about that time after which people tended to use their rising incomes to purchase additional privacy. (A "change in taste" is the economist's phrase for something he is unable to explain.)

A positive association between shortrun fluctuations in marriage rates and personal income (or employment) has often been demonstrat-

ed.[11] Here again, however, there is no convincing reason for attributing to rising income the major upward shift in proportions married at all ages which occurred after World War II. Incomes had been increasing for a long time without producing any noticeable change in marriage proportions.

Nevertheless, although the time series evidence is ambiguous, cross-sectional data for recent years suggest a strong connection between individual or family income and separate household maintenance. At a given age, a man is more likely to be married if his income is high than if it is low.[12] Presumably, men with higher incomes feel better able to afford the cost of marriage, but marriage itself undoubtedly provides an incentive to earn more income. Within the married group, moreover, the tendency to live separately rises with income, at least for the young. Couples in which the husband is under 25 are considerably more likely to maintain a separate household if their joint income is high than if it is low, but the effect dies out at older ages. A husband between 35 and 75 was almost always a household head in 1960, even if the couple had a low income.[13]

Young unmarried men were also more likely to maintain their own households in 1960 if their income was high than if it was low—a relationship which persisted at older ages. Comparable data are not available for unmarried women in 1960.

It would be helpful to have more than one cross-section to determine whether the relationship between living arrangements at various ages and income levels is changing over time. Steiner and Dorfman related the living arrangements of aged couples and unrelated individuals to their incomes in 1951.[14] They found aged couples and unrelated males somewhat more likely to be sharing a dwelling unit with

---

[11]For example, Orcutt *et al.*, *Microanalysis of Socioeconomic Systems* (Harpers, 1961), 84–85.

[12]See Glick, *op. cit.*, 156–58, for 1950 data. Comparable data for 1960 have not yet been published.

[13]U.S. Bureau of the Census, *Census of Population, 1960*, PC(2)-4B, Table 24.

[14]Peter O. Steiner and Robert Dorfman, *The Economic Status of the Aged* (Berkeley: University of California Press, 1957), Table 202, 244.

TABLE 43–4. LIVING ARRANGEMENTS OF WOMEN 65 AND OVER NOT LIVING
WITH A SPOUSE, UNITED STATES, 1952

Income in 1951	Percent living apart from relatives	Percent head of family	Percent parent or other relative of family head
Total	39.3	20.6	40.0
No income	21.6	20.0	58.5
$1–499	39.1	20.2	40.7
$500–999	55.3	19.9	24.8
$1000–1499*	64.4	25.4	10.2

*Higher income levels not shown because sample too small.
Source: Steiner and Dorfman, *op. cit.*, Table 202, p. 244.

TABLE 43–5. LIVING ARRANGEMENTS OF WOMEN 65 AND OVER NOT LIVING
WITH SPOUSE, UNITED STATES, 1960

Income in 1959	Percent living apart from relatives (primary and secondary individuals)	Percent head of family	Percent parent or other relative of family head
Total	46.6	17.6	36.1
No income	27.2	15.7	57.0
$1–999*	43.2	17.7	39.1
$1000–1499	59.9	16.7	23.4
$1500 and over	61.8	19.2	19.0

*Includes loss.
Source: *U.S. Census of Population, 1960*, PC(2)-8B, Table 1.

relatives (either as heads of families or as parents or other relatives of the family head) at very low levels of income and somewhat more likely to be living apart from relatives at higher income levels. The relationship was strongest, however, for unrelated females. Among women 65 and over who were not living with their spouses, Steiner and Dorfman found the relationship between income and living arrangements shown in Table 43–4.

Rough comparisons between 1960 census results and the Steiner-Dorfman data for unrelated females can be made if we subtract wives of family heads from all women over 65 and look at the living arrangements of the rest.[15] (Some women who are married and living with spouses who are not family heads are left in the "unmarried" group, but they are not numerous enough to affect the results appreciably.) Living arrangements by income level of

[15]U.S. Bureau of the Census, *Census of Population, 1960*, PC(2)-8B, Table 1.

women 65 and over who are not wives of family heads are shown in Table 43–5.

Table 43–5 is remarkably similar to the one prepared by Steiner and Dorfman eight years earlier. The similarity should not be taken too seriously, especially since no adjustment was made for price-level changes. Nevertheless, comparison does suggest that the probability of living as a parent or other relative of the family head at a given income level stayed pretty constant over this period for women 65 and over not living with their spouses. The probability of heading a family declined slightly and that of living apart from relatives increased at each income level, although the changes were not great. The results are at least not inconsistent with the hypothesis that rising incomes led to more separate living among the aged over the decade of the 1950's.

Comparisons of 1950 and 1960 census data on family status by income for men in all age groups are shown in Table 43–6. These lead to

TABLE 43–6. PERCENT OF MALES 14 YEARS OLD AND OVER BY
FAMILY STATUS, BY INCOME IN 1949 AND 1959, FOR
THE UNITED STATES: 1950 AND 1960
(Consumer Price Index Used To Convert
1949 Incomes to 1959 Prices)

Year and family status	Individual income (in 1959 prices)		
	Under $1500	$1500–2999	$3000
1959			
All males	100.00	100.0	100.0
Head of family	31.7	64.5	86.4
Relative of head	53.3	19.2	7.3
Unrelated individual	15.0	16.3	6.4
1949			
All males	100.0	100.0	100.0
Head of family	37.9	68.0	84.9
Relative of head	47.7	20.3	9.3
Unrelated individual	14.4	11.7	5.9

Source: *U.S. Census of Population: 1950,* Vol. II, Part 1, Ch. C., Table 140; *U.S Census of Population: 1960,* PC(1)-1D, Table 220.

similar tentative conclusions. The probability of being a family head for males rose with income in both years, while that of being a relative fell with income.

The probabilities for the two years are similar. The probability of being a head at very low income levels (under $1500) seems to have dropped for men over the decade, but this drop may be attributable to the changing age distribution of men in this low income group, who in 1959 were more likely to be teen-agers and less likely to be elderly than in 1949.

PRIVACY AND POVERTY

One interesting aspect of a changing level of privacy is its effect on measurable poverty. Poverty statistics generally refer to "families" and "unrelated individuals." Families are defined as groups of two or more related persons living under one roof. Unrelated individuals are persons living alone or with nonrelatives. Hence, the number of poor units (families and unrelated individuals) clearly depends on whether groups of relatives decide to live together or apart.

Consider a hypothetical family consisting of a couple with an income of $10,000, their son, who is a college student living at home and

has no income, and the wife's father, who lives with them and also has no income. This family of four is not "poor" by any usual definition. But suppose the son finds a part-time job which pays $1000 a year and decides to take a room by himself. The father gets a pension of $1000 a year and decides to stay on in his old house rather than come to live with his daughter. The total income of these four people is $2000 higher than that in the original example, but they no longer constitute a single unit. Now they are three units—one family and two unrelated individuals—and two of these units may be considered "poor."

If the old man and the student son are living alone on $1000 a year, their poverty is not fictitious. Both are poor in the sense that neither has sufficient resources to meet the minimum needs of an individual living alone. Various things might be done to alleviate their poverty, including having them move in with more affluent relatives; but, as long as the affluent relatives are not contributing to their support, their present poverty is real. If one is interested only in assessing the extent of present poverty, recent changes in the level of privacy may not be important.

If, on the other hand, the interest is in measuring changes over time, the prevalence of poverty, or in predicting the success of a program to eliminate it, one cannot ignore the impact of changes in privacy. Failure to consider the privacy phenomenon may lead to the conclusion that programs to increase the incomes of needy groups are unsuccessful because the number of poor units has not declined or has even increased.

To see how this might happen, consider the situation of 1000 elderly unmarried women with no income of their own. On the basis of the 1960 census data shown in Table 43–5, one would expect 272 of these women to be living apart from relatives, and this group can be clearly identified as poor. Another 157 would be found heading families. Some of these families have younger members who are earning enough income to keep the family as a whole above the poverty line. One can estimate from 1960 census data that about 78 of these women head poor families.[16] Another large group—about 570—would be living as parents or other relatives of the head. Some of them (about 131) live in poor families, but the rest do not. Altogether, out of the original 1000 elderly women with no income, about 481 could be classified either as poor or as members of poor families.

Now suppose that a new public program gives each of these women an income of $1200 a year. Suppose further that these women now behave like other women with incomes of $1200 a year. This supposition leads to the expectation that 599 of them will live apart from relatives (see Table 43–5). About 167 will be heads of families of which 90 will be poor families.

Another 234 will live as parents or other relatives—only 40 of them in poor families.[17] After spending $1.2 million to raise the income of these 1000 women, the number classified as poor or as members of poor families would increase from 481 to 729.

This hypothetical example should not be taken too seriously. The crucial assumption—that increasing the income of these women from zero to $1200 would lead them to make the same living arrangements as women who already have incomes of $1200—may well be false. Nevertheless, the example illustrates the real possibility that moderate increases in the incomes of the poor will enable them to live apart from relatives and hence will actually lead to increases in the number of people counted as poor. Their situation may be improving, in the sense that they have more income and are better able to afford the privacy and other commodities they desire, but the statistician engaged in counting poor households may not detect this improvement at all.

One implication of this analysis is that there are hidden, "second stage" costs for eliminating poverty. In this example, if a goal is set to raise the incomes of all families to $3000 and to raise the incomes of individuals living alone to $1500, then a realistic appraisal of the cost of achieving that goal must go beyond an estimate of the funds required to raise the incomes of existing units from their present levels to these targets. Among other things, an estimate must be made of the "second stage" costs of raising to target levels the incomes of additional units created as a result of the policy.

---

[16] 49.8 percent of female heads over 65 with no income headed families with less than $3000 in 1959 (*U.S. Census of Population, 1960*, PC[2]-8B, Table 2).

[17] *U.S. Census of Population, 1960*, PC(2)-8B, Table 2.

44.

Mark Messer

AGE GROUPING AND THE FAMILY STATUS OF THE ELDERLY

The conjugal or nuclear family structure which characterizes modern societies renders the family status of the elderly parent somewhat problematic. In terms of his relationship to those functions which define the family as a social institution, it appears that the parent whose children are themselves parents is in a position of having a family while not being in a family. His family of procreation (which clearly established his status as a parent) is now broken into as many nuclear units as the number of his children who are married. Having performed the core function of "replacing the population," his children are in a position to carry on this function themselves. He is now a grandparent—a kind of honorary parent—who, like an honorary president, is essentially functionless.

Beside the core function of procreation, however, the corollary functions of child socialization,[1] maintenance (instrumental functions), and nurturance or affection (consummatory functions) must also be considered in defining the family status of the elderly. Here again, an attrition in status seems to obtain.

With regard to the child socialization function, for instance, the fact that only a small minority of older people live in three generational households[2] reduces the possibility of sus-tained and significant grandchild socialization. Those studies which have investigated grandparents as socializers in modern American society have found more often than not that the consequences are dysfunctional for the child,[3] the conjugal family unit,[4] or the grandparents themselves.[5] It is likely, furthermore, that grandparent-grandchild interaction does not so much meet a socialization function[6] as it does a consummatory gratification function for both parties.[7]

Some recent cross-cultural research findings indicate that the vestiges of an extended kinship system are most evident in the maintenance function in the form of mutual help patterns between generations.[8] While substantial economic assistance from the older parents to the children is likely to produce more intergenera-

This selection is reprinted from: Mark Messer, "Age Grouping and the Family Status of the Elderly," *Sociology and Social Research*, 1968, 52, 271–279.

Reprinted with the permission of the author and publisher. This investigation was supported by funds from the Department of Housing and Urban Development and the Chicago Housing Authority.

[1]Ira L. Reiss, "The Universality of the Family," *Journal of Marriage and the Family*, November, 1965, 27, 443–53, argues that child socialization is the core function of the family. In this paper, however, we shall use the more conventional taxonomy presented by Robert F. Winch, *The Modern Family* (New York: Holt, Rinehart, and Winston, Inc., 1963).

[2]According to H. D. Sheldon, *The Older People of the United States* (New York: John Wiley & Sons, Inc., 1958), only 20 percent of people over 65 years of age in America actually live in the same household with relatives of any kind other than their spouses. For some persuasive historical data indicating that multi-generational households never have existed to any appreciable extent in America, see E. A. Friedmann, "The Impact of Aging on the Social Structure," in Clark Tibbetts (ed.), *Handbook of Social Gerontology*, (Chicago: University of Chicago Press, 1960), 130–33.

[3]See, for example, B. Borden, "The Role of Grandparents in Children's Behavioral Problems," *Smith College Studies in Social Work*, 1946, 17, 115–16.

[4]H. Vollmer, "The Grandparent: A Problem in Childbearing," *American Journal of Orthopsychiatry*, November, 1937, 7, 378–82.

[5]Bernard Kutner, *et al.*, *Five-Hundred Over Sixty* (New York: Russell Sage Foundation, 1956), 122.

[6]An important exception to this might be the American Negro family. See E. Franklin Frazier, *The Negro Family in the United States* (Chicago: University of Chicago Press, 1939); and "Ethnic Family Patterns," *American Journal of Sociology*, May, 1948, 53, 435–38.

[7]Dorrian Sweetser, "The Social Structure of Grandparenthood," *American Anthropologist*, August, 1956, 58, 656–63; and Vollmer, *op. cit.*

[8]Ethel Shanas, *et al.*, *Old People in Three Industrial Societies* (New York: Atherton Press, in press).

tional conflict than affection,[9] there is some evidence that this sort of interchange, as with the socialization of the grandchild, is motivated more by consummatory than maintenance needs.[10] Norms of filial responsibility (economic assistance from the married children to the elderly parents) seem to be increasingly consistent with conjugal family independence. In response to the question, "Who do you think should provide for the older person who has stopped working, if he needs help?" elderly subjects in the Cornell study of aging were more likely to choose the federal government, the state government, and the company for which they worked than the family.[11]

The corollary function of the family to provide affection and nurturance, then, seems most important in defining the family status of the elderly. The problem is whether or not a conjugal organization of the family can satisfactorily meet the consummatory needs of the elderly.

The possibility that shall be considered here is that extra-familial age grouping among the elderly is an appropriate arrangement for partially fulfilling this corollary function of the family.

AGE GROUPING: AN HYPOTHESIS

Some theorists have described the various phases of the life cycle in terms of appropriate patterns of role expectations and orientations.[12] These role patterns are characterized as predominantly "consummatory" for the child and old age phases, and predominantly "instrumental" for the productive middle years. Eisenstadt suggests that, in highly differentiated societies, the transition from the role patterns appropriate for the first stage of the life cycle

(consummatory roles met in the family context) to that set of instrumental role patterns appropriate for the productive years is met by adolescent age grouping.[13] These age-homogeneous structures (youth cultures) are said to be universal in advanced societies which serve the function of "phasing in" a generational cohort to that sector which characterizes such societies—productivity.

It seems that the "phasing out" mechanisms are not so well established.[14] There comes a time, nonetheless, when people disengage from the "productive" middle years of the life cycle. Such disengagement marks the return to consummatory role expectations and orientations.[15] The consummatory needs of the child may be thought of as "preengagement" needs and those of the elderly as "postengagement" needs. For the child, these needs can be met both by the family (of which he is still an integral part) and by his age peers. The extra-familial status of the older person, however, suggests the increased importance of age peers in meeting the appropriate expectations of disengagement. Accordingly, the following hypothesis is put forward: age grouping among the elderly might facilitate the transition from instrumental to consummatory role patterns and thereby serve as a functional alternative to the family in satisfying some of the consummatory needs.

METHOD OF DATA COLLECTION

Interview data from a larger study on the effects of age concentration in a sample of elderly residents of Chicago[16] were used for a preliminary test of this hypothesis. The major independent

[9]Mirra Komarovsky, "Functional Analysis of Sex Roles," *American Sociological Review,* August, 1950, *15,* 508–16; and Marvin Sussman, "The Help-Pattern in the Middle Class Family," *American Sociological Review,* February, 1953, *18,* 22–28.

[10]Sussman, *loc. cit.*

[11]Gordon F. Streib and Wayne E. Thompson, "The Older Person in a Family Context," in Tibbitts, *op. cit.,* 480.

[12]For a good review of this literature, see Leonard Caine, Jr., "Life Course and Social Structure," in Robert Faris (ed.), *Handbook of Modern Sociology* (Chicago: Rand McNally and Co., 1964), 279–309.

[13]S. N. Eisenstadt, *From Generation to Generation* (New York: The Free Press, 1956).

[14]Mark Messer, "The Third Generation: An Extension of Eisenstadt's Age-Homogeneity Hypothesis," paper at The Social Science Research Institute, University of Chicago, 1965.

[15]See Lois Dean and D. S. Newell, "The Evidence for Disengagement in Attitude and Orientation Changes," in Elaine Cumming and William Henry (eds.), *Growing Old,* (New York: Basic Books, Inc., 1961), 75–105; and Talcott Parsons, "Old Age as Consummatory Phase," *The Gerontologist,* March, 1963, *3,* 53–54.

[16]Mark Messer, "The Effects of Age-Concentration on Organizational and Normative Systems of the Elderly," unpublished Ph.D. thesis, Northwestern University, 1966.

TABLE 44–1. SAMPLE CHARACTERISTICS

	Age-Homogeneous Environment (N=51)	Age-Heterogeneous Environment (N=106)
		(Percentages)
Sex		
Male	35.3	29.2
Female	64.7	70.8
Age		
62-70	39.2	42.5
71-75	35.3	34.9
76-90	25.5	23.6
Race		
Negro	41.2	57.5
White	58.8	42.5
Education		
0-6th Grade	35.3	38.7
7th-8th Grade	39.2	39.6
9th Grade or more	25.5	21.7
Health		
"Good"	49.0	47.2
"Poor"	51.0	52.8

variable—relative age grouping—was operationalized by the nature of the sampling design. A probability sample of tenants of public housing projects occupied exclusively by people over 62 years of age was taken as the "age grouping" or age-homogeneous case. A sample of people who were themselves over 62 years old but who were living in public housing projects of mixed-age composition was used as a comparison group.

To control for differences in the feasibility of having intergenerational family contact, only those respondents who had children who were themselves parents and who lived within two hours' traveling distance of these children were included in the analysis. This left a sample of 157 (51 in an age-homogeneous environment and 106 in an age-heterogeneous setting). The sample characteristics of these two groups of respondents is reported in Table 44–1.

It should be noted that eligibility for public housing presupposes a relatively low income level (the mean annual income for the sample is $1298). The respondents are all retired (mostly from manual and factory-type jobs). For purposes of analyzing the data, this means that socioeconomic status is a controlled variable, but the limitations that this imposes on the generalizability of the findings must be considered.

Self-selection for one or the other housing situation is not a problem here, because the housing authority's policy is to locate applicants on the basis of their neighborhood and housing available at the time of application. Nevertheless, a measure of sampling equivalence was assured by premeasuring a subsample of people in each group before they moved into their respective housing modes. These data revealed no significant differences on the dependent variables of concern here.

The major dependent variable is the extent to which the consummatory needs of the elderly are being satisfied. No direct operational index to measure this rather ill-defined concept[17] was available, so the following indirect measures of "consummatory satisfaction" were used: morale, feelings of neglect from children, and social integration.

The conceptual hypothesis again is that age grouping will serve as a functional alternative to the family in satisfying the consummatory needs of the elderly. In operational terms, we

---

[17]Instrumental and consummatory role patterns are discussed extensively in the work of Talcott Parsons. Efforts to make these concepts usable in research, however, are few. One research attempt to empirically describe role orientations and expectations (but not the satisfaction of role needs) was carried out by Lois Dean, "The Pattern Variables: Some Empirical Operations," *American Sociological Review*, February, 1961, *26*, 80-90.

TABLE 44–2. MORALE BY AGE ENVIRONMENT AND FREQUENCY
OF INTERACTION WITH CHILDREN

| | Frequency of Interaction with Children | | | |
| | Once/wk or more Age environment | | Less than once/wk Age environment | |
Morale	All elderly	Mixed ages	All elderly	Mixed ages
	Percent	Percent	Percent	Percent
High	25.0	20.4	41.9	17.3
Medium*	55.0	55.6	45.2	51.9
Low	20.0	24.1	12.9	30.8
Total percent	100.0	100.1	100.0	100.0
No. of cases	20	54	31	52
	$X^2 = 0.22$, n.s.		$X^2 = 6.66, P < .01$	

*"medium" morale is left out of X^2 computations

are led to predict that those people living in an age-concentrated housing environment will show higher morale, will perceive less neglect from their adult children, and will be more integrated with the overall society than those living in mixed-age environments.

THE RESEARCH FINDINGS

Morale was measured by the life satisfaction scale used in the Elmira and Kips Bay studies of aging.[18] A score of 0-2 on the scale was rated as "low" morale, 3-5 as "medium," and 6-7 as "high" morale. As predicted, the age-homogeneous sample showed higher morale than the mixed-age sample. This tendency was maintained when race, age, sex, and health status were added to the analysis as control variables. The data presented in Table 44–2 support our hypothesis that age grouping serves as an effective functional alternative to the family in providing such consummatory satisfactions for the elderly as are reflected in having high morale. The extent of interaction with the subjects' children is introduced to present data directly comparing the importance of age environment and family involvement for morale in the elderly.

Among those who visit their children at least once a week, there is no statistically significant relationship between age environment and mo-

[18] A complete description of this scale is available in Kutner, *et al., op. cit.,* 48–54.

rale. More important for our purposes, however, among those who have less frequent familial interaction, morale goes down in the age-heterogeneous sample and up in the age-homogeneous sample. This relationship seems to suggest that the source of morale among the aged is moving away from intergenerational family interaction and toward the available age-peer group.

In response to the question, "Do you sometimes feel that your children neglect you?" those living in an age-heterogeneous setting, even though they had more frequent interaction with their children, were considerably more likely than the age-concentrated sample to answer in the affirmative (see Table 44–3).

The findings reported in Tables 44–2 and 44–3 taken together are interpreted to mean that older people living in a situation which lends itself to age-peer group formation rely less on the family for social support, but at the same time they do not feel more alienated from their families. Such a situation seems appropriate for the predominant system of conjugal family organization in complex societies.

The question arises, however, as to whether the kind of age-grading implied by separate living arrangements for the elderly might be divisive, creating feelings of detachment from the overall society. The family and other societal subsystems such as occupational groupings are said to mediate between the individual and the overall society thus creating societal inte-

TABLE 44–3. FEELINGS OF NEGLECT BY AGE ENVIRONMENT AND
FREQUENCY OF INTERACTION WITH CHILDREN

| | Frequency of Interaction with Children | | | |
| | Once/wk or more Age environment | | Less than once/wk Age environment | |
	All elderly	Mixed ages	All elderly	Mixed ages
	Percent	Percent	Percent	Percent
Feel that Children Neglect Them				
Yes	10.0	22.2	12.9	38.5
No	90.0	77.8	87.1	61.5
Total percent	100.0	100.0	100.0	100.0
No. of cases	20	54	31	52
	$X^2 = 1.44$, n.s.		$X^2 = 6.26$, P $<$ .02	

TABLE 44–4. SOCIAL INTEGRATION BY AGE ENVIRONMENT AND RACE

	Race			
	White		Negro	
	Age environment		Age environment	
	All elderly	Mixed ages	All elderly	Mixed ages
	Percent	Percent	Percent	Percent
Social Integration				
High	63.3	26.7	33.3	23.0
Low	36.7	73.3	66.7	77.0
Total percent	100.0	100.0	100.0	100.0
No. of cases	30	45	21	61
	$X^2 = 9.98$, P $<$ .01		$X^2 = 0.86$, n.s.	

gration, i.e., a kind of organic solidarity.[19] If, as is hypothesized here, age grouping is an effective functional alternative to the family for the aged, then it too should mediate between the older person and the larger society providing a sense of social integration rather than detachment.

To see if this was the case, we employed in our study Srole's scale of social integration.[20] This scale consists of five items which are said to measure the degree to which an individual feels alienated, powerless, or anomic vis-à-vis the general society. Analysis of the data indicated that age composition of the environment and race accounted for far more of the variation on social integration than any of the other variables on which we had data. Table 44–4 reports the findings from a simultaneous consideration of these variables.

Negroes were found to be considerably lower

[19]For theoretical discussion of the mediating function of societal subsystems, see Emile Durkheim, *Division of Labor* (New York: The Free Press, 1964), 1–31; Peter Blau, "Mediating Values in Complex Structures," *Exchange and Power in Social Life* (New York: John Wiley & Sons, Inc., 1964), ch. 10; and Robert Nisbet, *Community and Power* (New York: Oxford University Press, 1962).

[20]Leo Srole, "Social Integration and Certain Corollaries," *American Sociological Review*, December, 1956, *21*, 709.

than whites on social integration (though they were found to be higher on morale—a topic presently under investigation). More important here, however, is that age composition of the environment has a considerable effect on social integration and in the predicted direction (though this relationship reaches statistical significance only among the white respondents). Those living in an age-concentrated situation are found to sense less detachment from the larger society than those who, in effect, are living in closer proximity to a youth and middle-age biased societal structure. A grouping, then, seems to take on certain attributes of a genuine subculture. It mediates between the individual and the overall society and at the same time decreases rather than increases social distance.

SUMMARY

In this paper, it has been argued that, because of the dominant system of conjugal family organization in advanced societies, the elderly parent has, in many ways, an "extra-familial" status. In effect, he has a family but he is not in a family.

The last phase of the life cycle, however, is said to be characterized by consummatory needs, the satisfaction of which have traditionally been regarded as a corollary function of the family. It seems that nuclear family structure is not adequately suited for filling this function in the elderly.

Extending Eisenstadt's age-homogeneity hypothesis, we examined the possibility of age grouping among the elderly as a functional alternative to the family for consummatory gratification. Tentative findings (the severe limitation of the sample, for instance, must be borne in mind) suggest that (1) age grouping is associated with less dependence on the family as a source of morale, (2) this is not accompanied by feelings of familial neglect, and (3) age grouping serves as a mediator between the older individual and the overall society, providing a greater sense of social integration.

PART 3

Selected Factors

CHAPTER XI

Economic Factors in
Family Life

THE ECONOMICS OF EVERYDAY LIFE appear as a perennial problem of management for both the rich and the poor. It has been noted that even the well-to-do seem to think they need more money than they have to really live the way they need to, and similarly, most families, regardless of the amount of money they have, manage to share the experience of living up to their income and occasionally beyond it. There are realities both explicit and implicit to the management of family budgets.

The first section in this chapter focuses on "The Economics of Family Living," and illustrates how a young family might run into difficulties trying to live within its income. The income selected for the family may be a trifle low for the average urban family, but it should be noted that the selection is for the young family rather than for the mature family which may be at the peak of its earning capacity. Additionally, food costs have been underestimated because persons who have not experienced budgetary problems are often not aware of how much food actually costs in the maintenance of a family. Rent, on the other hand, is probably slightly overestimated for the budgetary situation, because of the likelihood that a young family will have recently moved into available housing, and recent construction of housing tends to cost more. In other words, bargains in housing are already likely to be occupied. Persons interested in what family budgets involve might find it useful to look at a recent article on the topic. (See, for example, Farnsworth, Gene E., and Lehman, John W., "A Moderate Family Living Standard—What It Is and What It Costs Today," *Business and Government Review*, 1968, 9, 5–12.)

The family cycle, which was discussed in Chapter 3, may be considered from the point of view of how family income develops through time. The issue of income development is particularly important if one wishes to consider how one might bolster incomes for the poor. The theoretical setting for this type of consideration is presented by Alvin L. Schorr in his article titled "The Family Cycle and Income Development."

A recent article which considers the special problems of budget for the retired couple and presents detailed information and analysis is: Orshansky, Mollie, "Living in Retirement: A Moderate Standard for an Elderly City Couple," *Social Security Bulletin,* 1968, *31,* No. 10, 3–17.

An additional economic consideration that is faced in all family study is whether there is a single income or whether there are multiple incomes. There has been a growing proportion of females in the United States labor force, and the increases have occurred for all statuses of women. From a societal point of view, however, one of the more interesting changes has been the increase in working mothers. The question of who the working mothers are is interesting because of the multiple pressures that exist for mothers to work. On the one hand, mothers may have to work as a matter of economic necessity; this could be true at the poverty line, or in circumstances where husbands are incapacitated, undependable, or periodically absent. On the other hand, mothers may also wish to work in order to maintain or develop aspects of their individuality. For example, mothers may feel they wish to continue career lines that they initiated. Mothers may also feel they wish to participate in the more general aspects of society, including earning a part of the income, on an equal setting with males. Here we provide an excerpt from a government publication indicating: "Who Are the Working Mothers?"

Concern with economic factors in family life centers on the ability of the family to control its own destiny. The latter frequently is defined in terms of the family's ability to plan its size, or to limit its size in order to maintain an adequate standard of living for the members. If limited resources have to be shared, the larger the number of participants the smaller the share. While there are benefits that may be derived in large families, it is often felt that the liabilities may be overriding. Especially in impoverished areas, uncontrolled fertility is viewed as self-defeating. In this chapter additional materials are presented on poverty that bear on family planning, and add to those already found in Chapter 8. Catherine S. Chilman, in the article titled "Poverty and Family Planning in the United States," provides a summary and overview of findings relating social and psychological factors to poverty and family planning. In an excerpt titled "Income and Reproductive Motivation," Judith Blake examines the question of the relationship of family-size preference and rising income.

Finally, an article is provided written by Elizabeth Herzog titled "About the Poor: Some Facts and Some Fictions," which examines some alternative questions about the poor. Is there a culture of poverty? Do the poor differ from the middle class on family values and sex patterns? Do Negroes differ from whites on family values and sex patterns? Some additional materials relevant to this last topic will be found in the next chapter on the Negro family.

45.

JEFFREY K. HADDEN AND MARIE L. BORGATTA

THE ECONOMICS OF FAMILY LIVING

One of the most difficult problems that a young married couple face is that of learning to live within their income. This is often a particularly acute problem for young college graduates. Most college students, whether married or single, have lived within a relatively frugal budget, at least in terms of cash flow. Only a few are aware of the many ways in which their style of living is being "subsidized" by the university in terms of such things as low cost housing and medical care or by parents who continue to buy a major proportion of their clothing or make available to them the old family car, etc.

Whether the starting salary on a first job is $7000 or even $10,000, balancing the budget after the first few months can be a rather shocking experience. What appeared to be a very comfortable income often turns out to be inadequate to meet the bills.

The purpose of this article is to provide an exercise in budget management. It represents a departure from the academic orientation of most of the volume. It is, nonetheless, serious in its intent and may be viewed as a "warning" to those who are tempted to rush into deficit spending to fulfill their desire to experience middle class affluency immediately upon college graduation. Too many marriages end up in frustration, unhappiness and even the divorce courts because of unrealistic expectations as to how far a starting salary will stretch.

There are a number of ways through which the income of families may be approached. Perhaps the most simple beginning is to look at the federal statistics on income of families. In a report from the Bureau of the Census (Series P-60, No. 53, December 28, 1967) it is indicated that for 1966, 68 percent of American families had total money incomes of $5000 or more. Twenty-five percent had incomes of $10,000 and over.

To some extent this under-represents the amount of actual income of families because the material income of farm families from their own products is not included as cash income, and farm families ordinarily tend to have lower reportable income. In addition, there is a lag between income and report, and the period involved is one in which incomes were rising about $500 per year on the average. Moreover, it may fail to represent the "typical" family because very young and older families often have much lower incomes.

We may examine the economics of family living by examining the expenditures of an "average" family based on an average budget for 1966. We will assume that the adults of the family are about twenty-five years of age and have two young children. They live in a metropolitan area; the husband is a white collar worker and his income is just about the national average—$7500 per year. For the sake of relevancy to the college student, we might further assume that the husband is a liberal arts college graduate. His starting salary upon graduation from college in 1963 was $5800, or somewhat above the average starting salary for liberal arts graduates in his class.

In our review of this family's budget, we shall work on the basis of a monthly salary, estimating costs for various budget items. In terms of the reader's own experience or particular location in this country, we may occasionally assign an excessive figure for a particular budget item. On the whole, however, our budget allocations are quite modest and for many families they will be inadequate.

To begin with, in this modern age federal taxes are ordinarily deducted at the source and so the earner is not likely to see a substantial portion of his income at all. If we assume that there is both a federal and a state income tax and that it is deducted from the salary, a reasonable estimate on the basis of current tax rates for the person with a $7500 income is approximately $1020 per year or $85 a month.

In addition to the taxes there will be an average monthly deduction of $24 as a contribution toward the federal social security plan (FICA). Another deduction that is very likely is a group health insurance plan, and this is likely to amount to an additional $15 per month if it is the common hospitalization and surgical plan.

Thus, before our family sees their $625 per month pay check, it is reduced to approximately $500, and this assumes there are no further deductions for group life insurance, United Fund giving, etc. But there are still plenty of fixed costs.

SUMMARY BUDGET

Taxes (Estimated Federal plus State)	$ 85.00
FICA	24.00
Health Insurance	15.00
Rent (Four rooms, marginal)	150.00
Utilities	15.00
Telephone	7.00
Medical bills, medicine, dental, optical, and other	15.00
Clothing	40.00
Cleaning	6.00
Food	150.00
Automobile	
Depreciation	40.00
Registration	2.00
Repairs, estimate	8.00
Insurance	12.00
Gas, oil, lubrication	10.00
Entertainment	
Going out and at home	13.00
Family outings	5.00
Vacation	15.00
Club, lodge, and other hobbies	3.00
Sub-total	615.00
Expendable home supplies, soaps, waxes, paper napkins, brushes, etc.	6.00
Tobacco	12.00
TOTAL	$633.00

Another fixed item that will immediately confront our family is paying the rent or mortgage payments on a home. Let us assume that the family has a four room apartment (only two bedrooms, which means the children are in the same room), and that they are willing to find an apartment that is marginal or close to marginal. In most metropolitan areas the prevailing rental rate for such an apartment is likely to be about $150. They might have conceivably gotten by for less, but in many cities they would have to be extremely lucky or look for a long time to find satisfactory accommodations for this figure. This figure is slightly lower than the old twenty five percent of income rule of thumb for housing.

At this rate, the rental will not include utilities, and thus another fixed cost will be for gas and electricity. With the assumption that the family has modern appliances the cost of these utilities will run a minimum of about $15. Regional differences in climate can affect costs, especially if heating costs are included. This would not usually be relevant in an apartment rental, but would be if a house rental or house ownership is involved.

Another common utility that almost every family has is a telephone. Assuming that our family makes only one relatively short long distance call per month, we can estimate that the charge for this utility will be about $7.

There will be many different types of requirements of a personal nature but those that are unavoidable or seem to occur consistently involve such things as medical bills (especially with two small children), and pharmaceutical supplies of various types. In addition to this there are recurring dental bills, plus additional bills for eye-glasses and the like. For all these suppose we again allot another $15 per month, which is a modest sum only possibly on the assumption of comprehensive health care plans or the fortune of good health.

Another major and persistent expenditure that our family must face is clothing. As a white collar person, it is essential that the head of the household be reasonably dressed, and ordinarily his family must also be dressed correspondingly. At the very least, the husband will require a new suit each year, a sport jacket every other year, and some other kind of light cover on the alternate year, probably one or two pairs of slacks each year, shirts, underwear, shoes, and probably a heavy outer garment every two, three, or four years.

A wife may be quite economical and make many of her own clothes, although this is not the typical pattern. In any event, she will have to have clothing and this involves suits, dresses, skirts, slacks, blouses, sweaters, undergarments, and hose. Women's styles tend to change quickly and hence the total expenditure for the wife's clothing may exceed that of the husband who must be presentable each day on the job. Growing children require relatively rapid replenishing of clothes. Hand-me-downs may help cut costs somewhat, but even so children tend to be hard on clothing and many articles of clothing are not fit to be handed down. Having children of the same sex is convenient, but not controllable.

It is highly unlikely that our family would require less than $500 per year for clothing, or approximately $40 per month. Today it is difficult to buy a suit of any quality for less than $75 and one can easily spend $125-$150. If one does not pay some attention to quality, the necessity to replace worn out articles will recur more frequently. Here too, differences in climate will affect expenditures.

In addition to this there are extensive cleaning bills that occur for most families. While most families do their laundry at home, the normal pattern is that shirts will be sent out. Suits, slacks, and much of the clothing of the family require dry cleaning periodically. An estimate of $6 per month for this is very modest.

We have as yet to mention that our family cannot do without food. It is difficult, of course, to give a fixed figure for food expenditures. However, with food costs rising virtually every month, it is difficult to imagine that a family of four could get by on less than $150 per month. This amounts to $5 per day for food for four persons. Even two quarts of milk per day amounts to one-tenth of this figure. Steak or a roast could easily exceed this daily budget allocation. Nor does the budget allow for occasional dining out. In any event, this is the figure we shall use here.

An additional large item that very few families do without is an automobile. If we assume that depreciation of an automobile is $500 per year (approximately 1/5 the cost of a moderately priced automobile) then we must allow approximately $40 per month for depreciation for the car, whether it is paid for with cash or bought on time payments. In the latter case, interest on the loan makes the actual cost substantially higher. A compact car could cut this

cost somewhat, but similarly many cars cost substantially more than $2500. Moreover, if our family feels that they must buy a new car every two, three, or four years, the cost of owning an automobile will go up accordingly, and this is hardly a trivial cost.

Most states place a charge on automobile registration that amounts to approximately $2 per month. A modest estimate for automobile repairs, even if traded in every other year, is probably $100 per year, or say $8 per month. Assuming the automobile is financed, there will be a requirement that insurance include the collision provision. Thus, the required insurance will be higher, but in any event, a family that cannot afford to be wrong may need to have collision insurance to protect themselves against total loss of their investment. Even utilizing a mutual or inexpensive insurance, a reasonable estimate for insurance would be $150 a year, but let us round it off to $12 per month. If one of the drivers is under 25 years of age or if the couple lives in a very large metropolitan area, insurance will run considerably higher. Assuming rather modest use of the car, gas, oil, and lubrication will probably cost about $10 per month.

Our family must do something by way of entertainment, aside from driving the family car, and we may assume that this can be categorized in three ways. First, the couple goes out on occasion, or they have company in. In either case, some expenses are involved. Going out to a movie, if they go to a neighbrhood theater, may cost only $3; if our couple has a beer and pizza afterwards, it is likely to cost another $3; and when they get home they will have to pay the baby sitter an additional $3. If company comes the hosts are likely to serve some delicacies and have drinks. (Going out to visit other persons is commonly reciprocated.) It is probably quite modest, thus to suggest allowing $13 per month for entertainment for this couple with a $7500 income. In addition, however, there are family outings, and the family goes to the beach or to an amusement park, to the zoo, or to some other place, and there are minor expenses involved with this. Let us suppose that for such outings we allot $5 per month. The third item is the vacation. Most families take vacations, and provision for vacations is made in most job situations. In the common occupations, vacations generally range from two weeks to one month, the latter becoming fairly prevalent for white collar persons. Let us say that it is likely that the family will take one week of the vacation going to some resort area, and let us suppose further that we allow $180 for the one week of splurge, or $15 per month pro-rated on a monthly salary basis. In addition, let us assume that the family, either through the husband, through the wife, or jointly, belongs to some community activity, like a club, lodge, or the like, and let us allow $3 for this other activity.

The sub-total of expenditures at this point is $615. This leaves $10 from the $625 available each month and we might indicate what an allocation for these $10 could be. For example, one item that has not yet been considered has been the constant expenditure that occurs with regard to expendable supplies in the home including such items as soaps, waxes, paper napkins, brushes, and so forth. For these let us allot $6 per month.

In addition, it must be recalled that smoking is a common habit, and we may thus allot $12, which constitutes a modest rather than an excessive amount of smoking on the part of the two adults in the family. These two items round out expenditures on the summary budget as indicated to $633, only $8 more per month than is earned.

It now remains to examine whether something has been omitted in this budget. Alas, it seems that there are a few things that are not as yet taken into account. For example, the husband must get haircuts and must have minor necessities including such things as razor blades. Similarly the wife must have certain personal items in regard to her toiletry, and there is a considerable encouragement in American society for visits to the beauty salon. For these purposes let us allot to each, in a democratic way, $3 per month.

The husband must go to work, and to do this he must either drive the automobile, in which case the mileage allowance provided in the estimate of the automobile is insufficient, or he must pay carfare. In an urban situation, let us assume that he is fortunate enough to have a single fare, and that the fare is reasonably small, say 15 cents each way; a total of 30 cents a day must be allotted for carfare. In addition, the husband must eat lunch at work, and while it is possible for him to bring a sandwich, in most white-collar situations it is more frequent that the husband will eat at a cafeteria or lunch counter, or in some other institutionalized place. Let us assume that he is extremely modest and always eats the "special," or eats very little and strategically, and let us allow him 65 cents per day for lunch. Carfare and lunch now total 95 cents per day, and to round this out let us allow him 5 cents each day to invest in frivolities like chewing-gum. In essence, thus, we are allocating $1 per day for the husband for pocket-money at work. This is a frugal sum, and must be estimated (excluding vacation time) at $20 per month.

Most families have relatives, and relatives have birthdays, anniversaries, and participate in such activities as holidays. There is an entire panel of expenditures of gifts for birthdays and other occasions within the family and at holidays, and exchange of gifts to persons outside the immediate conjugal family also. Assuming that this is done modestly and with extreme care in controlling expenditures, let us allocate $10 per month for this purpose, or $120 in all. This means, of course, that the purchase of a bicycle for one of the children places a crimp on all other purchases in the gift category. A gift for father or grandfather is not going to be a watch or anything of this sort, but is likely to be a tie or a pair of socks.

In any community, participation comes at a price, and this involves charity and other contributions. Assuming the family is churchgoing, for example, one might allot $1 for all four persons participating for each Sunday, or $4 per month, and say an additional dollar is allocated for all other contributions the family makes. This is a relatively small allowance in terms of the frequent image of American generosity, but our family is beginning to feel the pinch.

Insurance is something that is also commonplace in American society. In general there is a reasonable amount of investment that occurs for the protection of the family. Let us assume that the husband in this family has $10,000 insurance, representing somewhat less than twice his annual earnings, and that the type of insurance is a twenty year pay life policy. Let us assume the cost of this insurance is approximately $20 per month. Generally, less insurance is considered necessary for the wife; in this case let us allocate $10 per month for a policy one half the size of that of the husband. Insurance on the possessions of the family is also common, and in the case of this family would probably be minimal. Let us thus allow only one dollar per month for this purpose.

Next, let us have a category of odds and ends to include such things as newspapers, magazines, books, films, phonograph records, flowers, toys, pets, and other foolishness. For this let us allot approximately $2 per week, or $8 per month.

One last item must be added and this is the cost of depreciation or replacement of family possessions. These include the ordinary furnishings of the house—the furniture, rugs, soft goods including towels, linens, drapes, blankets and so forth, and the appliances including the more common ones that are owned by families such as the TV, refrigerator, washer, radios, phonograph, fans, clocks, toaster, mixer, and electric iron. For our family let us assume conservatively that the net worth of all these items at purchase price is $3000. Families are constantly adding new items and replacing other items, sometimes because things wear out and sometimes because they go out of style. Let us assume that there is a one hundred percent turn-over in family possessions in a period of ten years. This is not unlikely in a family where children are growing up and presumably where the parents are in the prime of their lives and are aspiring to be at least partially upwardly mobile in socio-economic status. Ten percent of three thousand dollars is three hundred dollars, or twenty-five dollars per month depreciation that should be allowed for this purpose.

A sub-total of these supplementary items comes to $105 per month. This is more per month than the family actually has to spend, however, and thus what is required for this family is a revision of the budget that reduces it by $105. Pardon the error—$113, we were

$8 over already. It should be recalled that in our procedure what we have done is to estimate modest to reasonable expenditures on the basis of expectations for a young white-collar family living in an urban environment. There have been no excesses introduced into this budget, and indeed the estimates have generally been modest or low. The budget has been designed in large part to anticipate the kinds of modest expectations that families have according to the general standards reflected in American values. Little things like allowances for the children and the like have not been included in a systematic way and yet they must come in some place. What then can be cut? The family can do without a vacation, and expenditures for entertainment can be curtailed. Possibly there is some scrimping and hesitancy in going to the doctor or the dentist. The clothing is made to last longer and corners are cut in other ways.

In this budget there is no room that has been provided for savings, and still we have excessive expenditures. Without savings this family is never going to get out of their apartment and into their own home. The situation is one in which following ordinary expectations concerning relatively minimal standards, a level of expenditures occurs that is above the earnings of the average family.

SUPPLEMENTARY BUDGET

Personal items for wife, toiletries, beauty treatments, etc. ....$	3.00
Husband's personal needs, haircuts, etc.	3.00
Lunch and other allowance for husband at work, pocket money	20.00
Gifts	10.00
Charity	5.00
Insurance on husband	20.00
Insurance on wife	10.00
Insurance on property	1.00
Odds and ends, newspapers, magazines, films, flowers, pets, and other foolishness..	8.00
Furniture, rugs, soft goods, TV, refrigerator, washer, and other appliances (depreciation)	25.00
Sub-total	105.00
Over expenditure on Summary Budget	8.00
GRAND TOTAL ($630.00 plus $113.00)..$743.00	

The crucial point that is illustrated here is that the average family must become involved in an intimate way in the planning of their expenditures, whether in a forward and controlled way or in a backward one of "making ends meet." Economic crises are difficult to avoid if planning is not forward and for control; but if attention is given to planning expenditures the families may feel constricted economically whether their income is the $7500 that is indicated, or considerably higher. In general, families tend to live up to their incomes, and often beyond them. Obviously, then, the economics of family living are an important aspect of study. The role of the day by day explicit and implicit budgeting of the expenditures of a family has been discussed in many places, and yet, there is relatively little that

is really known about the intimate part that such situational factors play in the development and maintenance of family relationships. The budget that has been presented here is not designed merely to serve as an indication of anticipated problems for the person who is to be married, or as a corrective for those who may not be aware of their expenditure problems in the family. It is designed as well to indicate the relationship of the economics of family living to expectations that are derived from the general values that occur in society with regard to what families should have and how families should live. Failure to handle this problem may spell disaster for young families.

46.

ALVIN L. SCHORR

THE FAMILY CYCLE AND INCOME DEVELOPMENT

It is, on the whole, a fact that most people who die poor were born poor. It is also a fact, though partial, that poor people show typical attitudes and behavior and transmit them to their children. Human manipulation has made from these observations a non-fact or artifact: The poor move about in a self-contained aura of attitudes that are more or less independent of their life experience; the attitudes themselves produce their poverty. It would be hard to imagine a more comfortable mystique for those who are not poor. It is less flattering and more taxing to the mind to grasp the play back-and-forth between facts of life and attitudes towards life, between what seems practical and what one aspires to. Yet this is the task facing those who want to understand at all how an income-maintenance program may influence its beneficiaries.

Some light might be shed on the mystique of the "culture of poverty" by a simple examina-

tion of the effect of poor food or poor housing on behavior. Ample evidence testifies to the capacity of such deficiencies to produce the type of attitudes associated with poor people.[1] However, it will serve the purpose better to take another approach, attempting to relate the stages through which a family passes over time to the development of family income. It is the progress of a child, over time, from poverty to adequacy that is sought. It is a family of some sort that will receive income from any program devised.

Available studies and statistics are poorly suited to outlining the family-income cycle. The problem may be simplified by talking only of poor families, but even so, no one knows whether there are one, two, or several typical modes of

---

[1] Alvin L. Schorr, *Slums and Social Insecurity*, Social Security Administration, Division of Research and Statistics (Research Report No. 1), 1963. Alvin L. Schorr, "The Non-culture of Poverty," *American Journal of Orthopsychiatry*, October, 1964, I. T. Stone, D. C. Leighton, A. H. Leighton, "Poverty and the Individual," paper presented at the University of West Virginia Conference on Poverty Amidst Affluence, May 3–7, 1965.

This selection is reprinted from: Alvin L. Schorr, "The Family Cycle and Income Development," *Social Security Bulletin*, February, 1966, 14–26.

TABLE 46–1. EDUCATION AND OCCUPATION OF HUSBAND BY AGE WHEN WIFE WAS
FIRST MARRIED, FOR FAMILIES IN WHICH THE WIFE WAS 35
YEARS OLD OR OVER IN 1960

Age of wife at first marriage	Percent of total number of families	Education of husband (percent)		Occupation of husband[*] (percent)	
		11 years of school or less	13 years of school or more	Operative, service worker, or laborer	Professional or technical worker, or manager, official, or proprietor
14–16	8	83	4	44	12
17 and 18	15	75	6	38	16
19 and 20	19	67	13	32	20
21 and 22	17	60	21	29	26

[*]For husbands with work experience since 1950.
Source: Derived from *U.S. Census of Population: 1960—Families*, Final Report, PC(2)4A, 1963, Tables 52 and 55.

development. It is clear only that not every family now poor necessarily started poor or will end poor. In order to attempt to discern a pattern, overlapping and partially sequential stages in family life will be identified. The stages are selected because they represent crises on two planes at once—family development and income development. If the wrong choice, in terms of future income, is made at the first stage, the right choice becomes progressively harder to make at each subsequent stage. The four stages are these: (1) timing and circumstances of first marriage or child-bearing; (2) timing and direction of occupational choice; (3) family cycle squeeze—the conflict of aspiration and need; and (4) family breakdown.

INITIAL MARRIAGE AND CHILD-BEARING

Women who married for the first time in 1960 were, on the average, about 20 years old. By 27 or 28, the median wife will have had her last child.[2] Within a general trend to young marriage and child-bearing, it appears that the very youngest will have lower incomes and less stable families. The evidence comes from studies that

are variously focused and of varying vintage. Arguing 40 years ago that society was moving towards a norm in which 18 would be the youngest age at which girls would marry, Mary Richmond and Fred Hall observed: "The daughter who in the Old Country would have been married at the first chance, must now, for a few years at least, delay marriage—often will wish to do so—in order to help in putting her own and her family's fortunes on a firmer foundation."[3] More recently: ". . . youthful marriages are less satisfactory to the participants and less stable than marriages contracted by persons who are out of their teens."[4] The incidence of poverty among families with heads 14 to 24 years old, already high by the end of World War II, had increased by 1960. "The honor of being called family head, bestowed too soon," observes Oscar Ornati, "brings with it a greater likelihood of poverty."[5] This observation shows only the relationship of early marriage to income shortly after marriage.

That the relationship of early marriage to low income persists over time can be seen in Table 46–1. Education and occupation are both significant indicators of income. The husbands

[2]Paul C. Glick, David M. Heer, and John C. Beresford, "Family Formation and Family Composition: Trends and Prospects," in *Sourcebook in Marriage and the Family*, ed., Marvin B. Sussman (Boston: Houghton Mifflin Company, 1963).

[3]Mary E. Richmond and Fred S. Hall, *Child Marriages* (Russell Sage Foundation, 1925).
[4]Lee G. Burchinal, "Research on Young Marriage· Implications for Family Life Education," in *Sourcebook in Marriage and the Family*, cited above.
[5]Oscar Ornati, "Poverty in America," National Policy Committee on Pockets of Poverty, Washington, D.C., 1964, 12.

of wives first married under the age of 17 are far more likely than other husbands, some 20 years or more later, to have the poorest education and work. Their chances of turning up with some college education or a professional or technical job are very small indeed. The age of women at marriage must be permitted to tell the story for their husbands, as the 1960 census distinguished between men who had married younger or older than 22, without distinguishing below that age. Even dealing with that comparatively advanced age, the data suggest the same conclusion. The men who married between 22 and 27 eventually held better jobs than those who married before 22.[6] It is not surprising to find, too, evidence suggesting that, ". . . early arrival of children is associated with less accumulation of capital by the family, even when adjustments are made for differences in age, education, inheritances, and unemployment experiences."[7] Putting together the two cross-sections, one shortly after marriage and the other a decade or two later, one may conclude that low income is likely to be a continuing experience for those who marry before 18.

The table understates the risk in young marriages. It deals with intact marriages and omits the women whose marriages did not last and who were not, in 1960, remarried. The omission is consequential, for the evidence is also clear that earlier marriages tend to be less stable. If they married before 17, for example, three out of ten women between 25 and 34 are remarried or their husbands are remarried. Only a fraction more than one out of ten who first married at 20 show the same result.[8] Paul Glick has observed that, after a lapse of 30 years, only half of the women married by 17 are still living with the first husband.[9]

These statistics are clear about the risks to income and stability in young marriages, but they do not begin to explain them. To understand the statistics, it is necessary to begin before the marriage takes place. It appears that a substantial number of children (perhaps 20 percent of all legitimate first children) are conceived before marriage.[10] Although the conclusion might once have been that one out of five marriages has been forced, it now appears that many young people who are planning to be married simply anticipate the ceremony. The situation is rather different among those who marry at 16 or 17. The girl and quite possibly the boy have not finished school. Even if they contemplated marriage, all sorts of practical difficulties would deter them. In fact, the percentage of premarital conceptions among youths is much higher than 20 percent. Studies in a variety of localities show premarital pregnancy rates that range upward from one-third of all school-age marriages to 87 percent where both parties were high school students.[11] The conclusion is that young marriages are, indeed, forced marriages.

Whether forced or not, young marriages face a number of practical problems. The table above shows that young marriage is associated with less education for the husband. In the climate of postwar attitudes, a young couple readily complete the husband's education while the wife works. If they are very young, however, and already have a baby, this is rather harder to bring off. Forty percent of girls dropping out of high school are willing to tell an interviewer that marriage or pregnancy is the reason.[12] Education and training are increasingly competitive requirements in a period when many youths are unemployed. At any given moment, one of five youths without a high school diploma is unemployed.[13] At least as many dropouts are probably not even seeking work.[14] Thus, the

---

[6]*U. S. Census of Population: 1960—Families,* Final Report, PC(2)4A, Table 48.

[7]James N. Morgan, *et al., Income and Welfare in the United States* (McGraw-Hill Book Company, 1962), 91.

[8]*U. S. Census of Population, op. cit.,* Table 51.

[9]Paul C. Glick, "Stability of Marriage in Relation to Age at Marriage," in Robert F. Winch, Robert McGinnis, and Herbert R. Barringer,, *Selected Studies in Marriage and the Family* (New York: Holt, Rinehart, and Winston, Inc., 1963).

[10]Harold T. Christensen and Hanna H. Meissner, "Premarital Pregnancy as a Factor in Divorce," in Robert F. Winch, Robert McGinnis, and Herbert R. Barringer, *op. cit.*

[11]Lee G. Burchinal, *op. cit.*

[12]Vera C. Perrella and Forrest A. Bogan, "Out-of-School Youth, February, 1963," Part I, *Monthly Labor Review,* November, 1964.

[13]Thomas E. Swanstrom, "Out-of-School Youth, February, 1963," Part II, *Monthly Labor Review,* December, 1964.

[14]Mollie Orshansky, "Who's Who Among the Poor: A Demographic View of Poverty," *Social Security Bulletin,* July, 1965.

young marriage is likely to start with unemployment compounded, when work turns up, by comparatively low wages.

The discussion has proceeded, thus far, as if all families begin with marriage and, of course, they do not. The prevalence of poverty among families headed by women is well documented; obviously, mothers who start out without a husband are no better off. Nor is it to be supposed that pregnancy before marriage or at a young age is the first cause and poverty follows from it, an automatic punishment for transgression. Sometimes, indeed, causality moves in this direction. For example, a pioneer study raised doubt about simple formulations of the relation between fertility and social class.[15] Yet it seemed clear that those couples whose incomes actually declined seemed to have been "selected for initial lack of fertility control."[16]

At the same time, it is known that those who are already uninterested in education may more usually engage in premarital relations or wish to get married at a young age. People's ambitions and efforts to achieve them flow together day by day. Whether lack of interest in school leads to marriage or vice versa must be knowledge to which only each youngster is privy, if indeed he knows himself.

When a couple start out together early, they are not only likely to have their first child earlier than usual; they are likely to have more children. White mothers who were married by the age of 18 have an average of 3.7 children by the time their families are completed, and Negro mothers 4.3 children.[17] By contrast, mothers married at 20 or 21 have 2.8 and 4.0 children, respectively. (The first pair of figures is

worth bearing in mind, for it will be suggested shortly that four children are qualitatively different than three.) The difference is not simply that the younger couples get a head start. Rather, those who marry young and are fated to be poor tend to have children early and late. The others concentrate their children in a few years and have fewer all told.[18]

Is it that poor people want to have more children? It seems not. All the evidence is that American families, whatever their income, want to have about the same number of children. Those who are poor do not manage to succeed in limiting the number.[19] A study of growth of American families puts the matter so:

Lower status couples don't have more children . . . simply because they want more. They have more children because some of them do not use contraception regularly and effectively. If the wife has a grade school education and if the husband has an income of less than $3000 a year, then 39 percent have excess fertility . . . The judgment that their fertility is too high is their own opinion.[20]

Describing the handicap to income that more children represent would take the discussion into another stage of the family-income cycle. For the moment, it is sufficient to observe that early marriage sets the stage for a large family. By the rigors of arithmetic alone, more income will be required to escape poverty.

Referring a quarter of a century ago to countless surveys already conducted, Richard and Kathleen Titmuss observed that "children . . . introduce insecurity into the home."[21] Young couples are likely to face the problem of providing for a child quite early. They are likely to face the problem of providing for more than the average number of children. They are likely to

---

[15]The theory of social capillarity, stated in 1890, appears regularly in other metamorphoses. Arsene Dumont's theory is stated as follows: "Just as a column of liquid has to be thin in order to rise under the force of capillarity, so a family must be small in order to rise in the social scale." *Dépopulation et Civilization*, Paris, 1890, quoted in Charles F. Westoff, "The Changing Focus of Differential Fertility Research: The Social Mobility Hypothesis," *The Milbank Memorial Fund Quarterly*, January, 1953, 30.

[16]Ruth Riemer and Clyde V. Kiser, "Social and Psychological Factors Affecting Fertility," *Milbank Memorial Fund Quarterly*, April, 1954.

[17]*U. S. Census of Population: 1960—Women by Number of Children Ever Born*, Final Report, PC(2)3A, 1964, Tables 18 and 19.

[18]*Ibid.*, Table 37.

[19]Ruth Riemer and Clyde V. Kiser, *op. cit.*, Ronald Freedman, Pascal K. Whelpton, and Arthur A. Campbell, *Family Planning, Sterility, and Population Growth* (New York: McGraw-Hill Book Company, 1959). Ronald Freedman and L. Coombs, "Working Paper on Family Income and Family Growth," Appendix B to Social Security Administration Grant Progress Report, June 1963, and "Working Paper on Changes in the Family Situation," Appendix C.

[20]Frederick S. Jaffe, "Family Planning and Poverty," *Journal of Marriage and the Family*, November, 1964.

[21]Richard and Kathleen Titmuss, *Parents Revolt* (London: Secker and Warburg, 1942).

face these problems with insufficient training and education. They are more than ordinarily likely to suffer separation or divorce. For a few families, fortunate in money or otherwise, these are no problems at all. The others are not barred, with early marriage, from developing decent income, but the rules of the game are changed for them.

OCCUPATIONAL CHOICE

By the time a wage earner reaches his mid-twenties, the limits of his lifetime income have in very large measure been established. He will have continued in school or not. The issue is not whether he drops out of school and returns, but whether he has left for several years and is unable to return. In the decade before retirement age a man who has completed college earns two-thirds more, on the average, than a man who has only completed high school and over twice as much as a man who has only completed grade school.[22] The diploma or degree (or qualities attached to getting it) counts for more than the prorated years of schooling it represents. The college graduate referred to earns over $10,000, but the man of the same age with one to three years of college earns $7000.

Quite apart from education, the young adult will have taken his first job and established a pattern of job movement. White-collar and professional workers (and readers) may be given to thinking of jobs in terms of choice. Studies of manual laborers, blue-collar workers, the lower class, or the working class, make it clear that their entry into the job market is compounded of accident and immediate necessity. A study of youths doing manual work in 1951 summarized their situation as follows:

Most youngsters (and their parents) approached the choice of a first job with no clear conception of where they were going; the great majority of first jobs were found in a very informal way, preponderantly through relatives and friends; the great majority of youngsters took the *first job* they found and did not make comparisons with any other job; their knowledge of the job before they took it was

in most cases extremely meager; and in most cases the job turned out to be a blind alley . . . ."[23] [Italics added.]

In 1964 other researchers were still trying to counter "the myth of occupational choice." S. M. Miller wrote that, on the contrary, working-class jobs are "a recurring and frequently unpredictable series of events in which 'choice' is frequently the obverse of necessity."[24] Despite its chance beginning, the first job is an excellent indication of what the last job will be. The first ten years of work—with exceptions, to be sure—foreshadow the rest.[25]

The choices that are made by people who are going to be poor may seem haphazard to the observer. The components of this approach to work have been well documented. However, their combined effect is as accidental as the path a trolley car takes. The youth enters upon work unready. He may have left school because he wanted to—whatever that says about his life situation. He may have left school because of sheer financial need. For example, a national study showed that withdrawing public assistance from families who needed it ended the schooling of some of the children.[26] The youth's bargaining power is not good and it is a doubtful favor to tell him otherwise. He knows astonishingly little about the consequences of his choice of job. In terms of immediate payoff, the difference between one job and another may not be great. Their long-range payoff is lost to him in scholarly studies and social administrators' offices. In one sense, help from parents is nonexistent and in another sense, all too available. Although parents tend to want much for their children, they know little about how to prepare for occupations other than their own. The links they can provide are to the work they have known. If one accepts the

[22]Bureau of the Census, *Current Population Reports;* "Consumer Income," Series P-20, No. 43, September 29, 1964, Table 22.

[23]Lloyd G. Reynolds, *Wages and Labor Mobility in Theory and Practice* (New York: Harper & Row, Publishers, 1951), 127–128.

[24]S. M. Miller, "The Outlook of Working-Class Youth,'" in Arthur B. Shostak and William Gomberg, *Blue-Collar World* (Englewood Cliffs, N.J.: Prentice-Hall, Inc., 1964).

[25]Seymour Martin Lipset and Reinhard Bendix, *Social Mobility in Industrial Society* (Berkeley: University of California Press, 1959). Lloyd G. Reynolds, *op. cit.*

[26]M. Elaine Burgess and Daniel O. Price, *An American Dependency Challenge* (Chicago: American Public Welfare Association, 1963).

interesting, though speculative, concept that careers develop according to a timetable that is learned from others, parents are also passing on not only advice and personal contacts that are limiting but a handicapping sense of the timetable that should normally be followed.[27]

Some youths stay in school only because of the high unemployment rate in their age group.[28] In the circumstances, those who are out of school believe they do well to seize the first job that is offered. Thinking of individuality and realistically, who is to gainsay this? Over a third of marriages involve boys who are 21 or under. Other boys have responsibilities to parents or brothers and sisters. They are not in a position to refuse even dead-end jobs. As for the rest, any beginning salary may look large compared with what they have had. One should not overlook that a youth may be immature. The penalties of the choice he is making may be hidden, but its benefits—cash in the pocket, independence, adult status—call to his deepest needs. Here is one of the homeliest advantages of higher education. Vocationally speaking, the late teens and early twenties tend to be a "floundering period."[29] The youngster without advanced education enters upon his career uncertain and immature. The youngster who has spent this period in college evaluates work from the vantage point of four more years.

By their middle twenties, youths have made other, interlocking decisions that bind them. Women have decided whether or not to work; in their schooling and in their first jobs they too have bounded the sort of work they may do later. Obviously, these decisions influence the family's income, but—equally significant in the long run—women who work will have fewer children.[30] Having a very small family is not typical of ambitious families starting out with

decent income. Having one child or none is typical, however, of families starting out with great disadvantage and determined to make their way at all costs.[31] For example, the higher their husband's income, the fewer white women reach menopause without having a child. But among nonwhite women, the largest percentage who are childless are in the $3000 to $7000 bracket.[32] Presumably, the struggle by nonwhites to attain a modest income is somehow connected with having no children at all. In nonwhite families with income above $7000, childlessness is not as common as in the moderate-income group; one senses that a balance point has been attained at which a child does not block the family's aspirations.

Young men, young women, and couples may also have faced a choice about moving where jobs are more readily available. Those who do move are less likely to be unemployed.[33] An English study observes that, in a depressed area, the ages from 20 to 30 are crucial for skilled workers. "Now is taken the vital decision to move or to stay." But for the unskilled, "before they are out of their teens some . . . are almost completely precluded from exercising any free choice in their careers."[34] The evidence in the United States is consistent with this. The highest mobility rate is in the years from 20 to 30; those who are better educated are more likely to have moved.[35] So, too, larger families are less likely to move.[36]

It was noted that young marriages run a high risk of dissolution. By the time the couples are in their mid-twenties, the determination of stability or separation is likely to have been made. Separation creates an obvious income problem for the mother and her children. The

---

[27]See Julius A. Roth, *Timetables* (Indianapolis: Ind.: The Bobbs-Merrill Co., Inc., 1963).

[28]W. G. Bowen and T. A. Finegan, "Labor Force Participation and Unemployment," Princeton Industrial Relations Section (undated).

[29]P. E. Davidson and H. D. Anderson, *Occupational Mobility in an American Community* (Stanford: Stanford University Press, 1937); Seymour Martin Lipset and Reinhard Bendix, *op. cit.*

[30]Ronald Freedman, "The Sociology of Human Fertility: A Trend Report and Bibliography," *Current Sociology*, 1961–62. V. X-XI, No. 2, Oxford, England.

[31]Ruth Riemer and Clyde V. Kiser, *op. cit.*

[32]*U. S. Census of Population: 1960—Women by Number of Children Ever Born*, Final Report, PC(2)3A, 1964, Table 37.

[33]Thomas E. Swanstrom, *op. cit.*

[34]Adrian Sinfield, "Unemployed in Tyneside," May, 1964 (mimeographed).

[35]John B. Lansing, Eva Mueller, William Ladd, Nancy Barth, *The Geographic Mobility of Labor: A First Report* (Ann Arbor, Mich.: Survey Research Center, April, 1963).

[36]Ronald Freedman and L. Coombs, "Working Paper on Changes in the Family Situation," Appendix C to Social Security Administration Grant Progress Report, June, 1963.

father has a problem too, unless he can escape it. He is probably liable for support payments which, if they look small to those who complain of growing irresponsibility, loom large to the father with limited income. Whatever the reason, the jobs of men who have been married only once show steady improvement in the first decade of marriage. In contrast, the status of men who remarry improves rather little.[37] Finally, not only is each job decision important; the sequence of jobs is also important. Harold Wilensky has carefully elaborated the consequences of an orderly work history in which "one job normally leads to another, related in function and higher in status."[38] The man with an orderly career shows strong attachment to his work and continues to make progress. The man who shifts about without apparent reason or benefit is likely to be dissatisfied and blocked.

The permutations of even key decisions are numerous, but perhaps several useful *and plausible* generalizations may be extracted from these disorderly patterns. First, occupational and family decisions may be subject matter for different professional disciplines but, as families live, they are a unity. The decision to marry and begin work, for example, is more likely to be one decision than two. Second, one can readily discern extreme family types, even at this early point. On one hand are the heroic families—overcoming their antecedents, husband and wife sticking together (with pleasure or without), studying and working and foregoing children. It is not to be assumed that all of these families achieve reasonable objectives, but obviously some do. Then there are the families defeated from the beginning—pregnant early, married early, dropped out of school, soon separated, and unlikely to have enough income at any time. In between are most poor families, undoubtedly encompassing two or three or several types. Third, the common problem that youths face about school, family, and work, lies in being forced to make decisions prematurely and unprepared. In the situation in which poor

youths find themselves, the alternative to one choice for which they are unprepared (completing school) is another choice for which they are also unprepared (early marriage or work). Perhaps what is required are devices to postpone the necessity for any of these choices at 17 or 18 or 20.

Although this conclusion is arrived at by a narrow consideration of occupational development, a parallel psychological argument may be made for providing a "psychological moratorium"—a period of delay in the assumption of adult commitment.[39] Because of change and shifting values, today especially youths require a period of relaxed expectation, of experimenting with various kinds of work, or even of introspection to locate their sense of adult identity.[40] The two lines of argument—occupational and psychological—link in the recognition that, in our society, the major source of social identity for men is work. Lee Rainwater has explored this point to argue that if a sense of identity is blocked by the route of work, it may be sought instead through expressive behavior—personal expression in speech, song, behavior, or idiosyncratic ideas. Rainwater observes that the expressive solution is only temporarily satisfying to low-income youths.[41] Given time and opportunity, they may shift to a sense of identity through work. By this line of argument too, one comes to the need for providing time before a youth is finally committed to the work he will do.

In any event, the stage 1 decision, if it begins a family, clearly governs stage 2 decisions: when to begin work and at what. Those who do not marry early retain more flexibility. At the close of stage 2 (say, between 25 and 30), those families who will be poor can be readily recognized. Early marriage and child-bearing, incomplete education, a poor first job, a chaotic work history—any two of these qualities mean a family

---

[37]Jessie Bernard, *Remarriage, A Study of Marriage* (The Dryden Press, 1956).

[38]Harold L. Wilensky, "Orderly Careers and Social Participation: The Impact of Work History on Social Integration in the Middle Mass," *American Sociological Review*, August, 1961, 522.

[39]Erik Erikson, "Youth and the Life Cycle," *Children*, March–April, 1960, 48.

[40]Erik Erikson, *Young Man Luther* (New York: Norton, 1958), and *Childhood and Society* (New York; Norton, 1950). David Riesman, "The Search for Challenge," *Kenyon Alumni Bulletin*, January-March, 1959.

[41]Lee Rainwater, "Work and Identity in the Lower Class," Washington University Conference on Planning for the Quality of Urban Life, November 25, 1964.

at high risk of being poor most of the time. Members of such a family are unlikely to change matters very much through their own efforts. A recent study in California, seeking to distinguish between people who receive public assistance and those who do not, confirms this conclusion:

The main factor involved in the unemployment, underemployment and dependency of the welfare group is not deviant attitude, or deviant personality, but the high-risk objective circumstances of being relatively under-skilled, under-educated, and over-sized. . . .

These high-risk circumstances are shared by a substantial segment of the population which is not currently on welfare . . . but is likely to be at any given time in the future.[42]

FAMILY-CYCLE SQUEEZE—THE CONFLICT OF ASPIRATION AND NEED

In a study of men who carry more than one job —moonlighters—Harold Wilensky found them to be not necessarily poor, or rich, or in between. Rather, the moonlighter was, typically, a man of any income, squeezed between not unreasonable ambitions and family needs he could never quite satisfy. The key, which Wilensky calls "life-cycle squeeze," is not the man's age but the stage of his family development and, especially, the number of his children.

The American man most likely to moonlight would be a young, educated Negro with many children, a job such as ward attendant, and a chaotic work history. His mother, a sales clerk whose husband deserted years ago, has fired him with old-fashioned ambition; his wife, a part-time cleaning woman, wants to escape from the ghetto. He is a clerk in his spare time.[43]

In the end, the moonlighter does not realize his ambitions. The needs of his family move more rapidly than he; he has neither surplus money nor energy. Typically, he is blocked and feels deprived.

For a special group, perhaps six percent of

workingmen, Wilensky has established a dynamic relationship between aspiration and need. (Because family structure determines the changing content of need, this relationship is here called family-cycle squeeze.) Almost all poor families must feel the squeeze and, obviously, most respond otherwise than by moonlighting. Some men, though they would take similar steps, work too many hours or too irregularly.[44] Some poor families send the mother to work, even when the children are relatively young. Some families take the opposite course; instead of expanding their income, they adjust need to their income. They may space their children so their needs can be absorbed. Those who are to be poor appear to have their second child three or four months closer to the birth of the first child than others do.[45] Families may restrict the number of their children, thus limiting need. That families take these steps has been demonstrated over and over again. Studies suggest that at least a number of these families manage to move up a step or two.[46] The variety of ways of meeting need illustrate what is, anyway, plausible. The more members in a family, the more income is needed. The necessity to devote all income and more to current needs is associated with inability to make progress.

Beyond this point, discussion frequently mires down in inability to demonstrate either, on one hand, that people have children for the same reasons that they are poor (a tendency to live

---

[42]Curtis C. Aller, "Toward the Prevention of Dependency: A Report on AFDC-U Recipients," preliminary report, pp. 16, 18. State of California, Department of Social Welfare, *First Annual Report*, January, 1965.

[43]Harold L. Wilensky, "The Moonlighter: A Product of Relative Deprivation," *Industrial Relations*, October, 1963, 119.

[44]*Ibid.*

[45]Lolagene C. Coombs, "Child Spacing and Family Economic Position," memorandum of May 31, 1965 (unpublished).

[46]Seymour Martin Lipset and Reinhard Bendix, *op. cit.* For other citations of studies relating status and fertility, see Ronald Freedman, "The Sociology of Human Fertility . . . ," cited above. Studies have produced inconclusive or negative results if their samples were small or special, if they did not discriminate between families that could afford children and families that could not, or if the hypothesis was formulated too grandly. For example, in the Indianapolis study the "economic tension" hypothesis was stated as follows: "The greater the difference between the actual level of living and the standard of living desired, the higher the proportion of couples practising contraception effectively and the smaller the planned families." (Ruth Riemer and Clyde V. Kiser, *op. cit.*) Large families, quite unrealistic about their aspirations, and small, quite realistic families would blur the findings when the hypothesis is so stated.

in the present, etc.) or, on the other hand, that the facts of poverty make it difficult to control the number of births. Poor people have not had the required attitudes, skills, or access to medical resources for effective birth control.[47] But these facts lend themselves to either interpretation. Indeed, the opposing interpretations are probably selective, somewhat biased summaries of the same facts. For, seen day by day, the family that cannot control its course does not seek to control its course, and the reverse is also true. The point here, however, is that the squeeze is felt every day. Whatever its origin, above some threshold the imbalance becomes a hindrance rather than a stimulus to self-improvement.

There is a sprinkling of evidence that the fourth or fifth child represents a point of no return for poor families. The California study cited above concluded that families with four or more children face a substantial risk of poverty.[48] A study of families during periods of unemployment concluded that families with four or more children "found it considerably more difficult to manage financially." The more drastic means of managing—"borrowing money, piling up bills, moving to cheaper quarters, and going on relief —all show sharp increases with size of family."[49] A third study notes that separations and desertions tend to occur at the time the wife is pregnant. "A major point of pressure for the low-income male," observes the authors, "appears to be an increase in family size with no comparable increase in family income or earning capacity."[50] If four- or five-children families face a special problem, one would expect the children to reflect it. About seven of every ten youths rejected for Selective Service come from families with four children or more.[51]

Table 46–2 sums up the risk of poverty in terms of family size. Adding a third or fourth child raises the incidence of poverty by six percentage points, but the next children raise the

TABLE 46–2. PERCENT OF FAMILIES WHO WERE POOR IN 1963, BY NUMBER OF CHILDREN

Number of related children under 18 years of age	Percent of families who were poor
None, 1 or 2	12
Three	17
Four	23
Five	36
Six or more	49

Source: Derived from Mollie Orshansky, "Counting the Poor: Another Look at the Poverty Profile," *Social Security Bulletin,* January 1965, table 8.

incidence by 13 percentage points. "For many families," writes the researcher who developed these figures, "a critical point in financial status may be the arrival of the fourth or fifth child."[52]

Although these figures make the point about risk, they are averages and inevitably crude. It is possible to get somewhat closer to various family types by examining the occupations of the men whose wives have had the most children. These figures (still averages, to be sure) hint at a more common-sense, though complex, relation of birth rate and income. The white men who have the most children work, in descending order, as farm laborers and foremen, miners, plasterers, carpenters, truck drivers, and physicians. These are the lowest- and highest-paid occupations listed by the census for which number of children can be determined. Their incomes fell, more or less, under $5000 or, for physicians, over $19,000. By contrast, families averaging about three children or fewer per mother are bunched in the occupational range between $4000 and $9,000, with a scattering up to $15,000.[53] (The pattern for Negro families does not show any high-fertility, high-income

[47]Lee Rainwater and Karol Kane Weinstein, *And the Poor Get Children* (Chicago: Quadrangle Books, 1960).

[48]State of California, *op. cit.,* Table 20.

[49]Wilbur J. Cohen, William Haber, and Eva Mueller, *The Impact of Unemployment in the 1958 Recession,* U. S. Senate, Special Committee on Unemployment Problems, June, 1960.

[50]Hylan Lewis and Camille Jeffers, "Poverty and the Behavior of Low-Income Families," paper presented to the American Orthopsychiatric Association, Chicago, May 19, 1964.

[51]The President's Task Force on Manpower Conservation, *One-Third of a Nation,* January 1, 1964.

[52]Mollie Orshansky, "Counting the Poor: Another Look at the Poverty Profile," *Social Security Bulletin,* January, 1965, 25.

[53]U. S. *Census of Population: 1960—Occupation by Earnings and Education,* Final Report, PC(2)7B, 1963, Table 1. U. S. *Census of Population: 1960— Women by Number of Children Ever Born,* Final Report, PC(2)3A, 1964, Table 33.

occupational groups. This is consistent with the observation made earlier that disadvantaged families moving up are more likely to restrict their family size severely.)

Obviously, several children are not necessarily a bar to decent income. Either income is high enough to support several children, however, or income is destined to be very low indeed. For families of four or five children or more, there is no in-between. Other evidence supports this point: the more children in a family under the Aid to Families with Dependent Children program, the more the mother owes.[54] In general, the more children in a poor family, the larger is the proportion of needed income that the family lacks.[55]

Children are the most significant element of the family-cycle squeeze, but they are not the only element. An explanation can be assembled for the special difficulty of large families. In finding housing, they experience great hardship; public housing, for example, is less likely to provide a resource. A mother with five children cannot as readily go to work as a mother with two. Yet the problem of a large family is only a midstream example of imbalance between need and resources. In the same sense, the 18-year-old couple with one child faces an imbalance. The problem of the mother without a husband may also be read as a type of family-cycle squeeze. She has very nearly the same need for income but much less in the way of resources than a mother with a husband. In the past decade the median income of such families has increased only about half as fast as that of all families.[56] Entirely apart from children, the relatives of those who are poor are also likely to be poor. As a mother or father approaches 40, *his* parents enter their sixties and may present serious need for financial or other kinds of care.[57] For example, study of families receiving public assistance shows that the majority of recipients

with relatives were giving rather than receiving help.[58]

For all these reasons, need may exceed resources by too wide a margin, forcing choices that are likely to defeat the family. The sorts of choices that are forced have already been named: limited education, limited mobility, dead-end jobs, and family breakdown. Moreover, the couple in their thirties have children growing into adolescence. The quality of their nurture, education, and family life has, no doubt, been affected right along. By adolescence, they begin to make the same categorical choices—more school or less, expect to begin a family early or not. The strains that are implicit in the life cycle of any family have been recognized for some time. But for poor families, whose need is likely continually to outpace resources, disadvantage goes around in a tight descending spiral. In the end, statistics reflect the spiral. The same people have many children, poor education, unemployment, broken families, and so forth. What else is new?

It may be useful at this point to illustrate the type of program question that can be raised on the basis of the family-income cycle. On the whole, public assistance tends to deal with families late in the game. Essentially the same families, with fewer children, are rejected for Aid to Families with Dependent Children (AFDC) who will be granted assistance later, when they have more children.[59] If accepted for assistance, smaller families receive it for a shorter period of time.[60] With stipulated exceptions in a number of states, a surplus of income over minimum requirements becomes the occasion for discontinuing assistance. Standards for minimum requirements are themselves low; in 1963 the standards were below the Social Security Administration definition of poverty in all but six states. In the majority of states, assistance will not be provided if a husband or other man is at home. In short, while the program

[54]Greenleigh Associates, *Facts, Fallacies, and Future* (New York: 1960).

[55]Mollie Orshansky, *op. cit.* (January, 1965).

[56]John Beresford and Alice Rivlin, "Characteristics of 'Other' Families," paper read at the Population Association of America, Philadelphia, April 19, 1963.

[57]Alvin L. Schorr, *Filial Responsibility in the Modern American Family*, Social Security Administration, 1961.

[58]Jane C. Kronick, "Attitudes Toward Dependency: A Study of 119 ADC Mothers," a report to the Social Security Administration, May 15, 1963 (unpublished).

[59]State Charities Aid Association, "Striving for Balance in Community Health and Welfare," Annual Report, New York, 1963.

[60]M. Elaine Burgess **and Daniel O. Price**, *op. cit.*

may relieve desperate need, it deliberately avoids any surplus that will provide room for maneuver. Thus, AFDC is a recognizable element of the poor family's world, relieving need but not providing the flexibility that will tend to alter the direction in which the family is moving. These policies reflect the necessity of distributing insufficient resources equitably, as well as the necessity of discouraging malingering. But from the point of view of objectives, such policies exhibit a curious ambivalence. In a wide variety of ways in the past few years, the program has been bent towards helping to prevent dependency. Yet, AFDC tends to operate too parsimoniously and too late to turn the tide of family-cycle squeeze.

FAMILY BREAKDOWN

With the material reviewed so far, it cannot come as news that many poor families in time become unable to maintain an intact family or a steady income. Some will have reached this stage by the age of 20, having already achieved two or three children and a chaotic family and work history. Others will have struggled doggedly, perhaps experiencing moments of hope, but yielding in the end. Some of the evidence of this outcome has already been seen; it requires now to be brought together.

It has been noted that early marriages tend to break up; only half the women married at 17 or earlier will still be living with the same husband 30 years later. It has also been noted that half of the women married at 17 will have (about) four children or more. Finally, large families create unbearable pressure for low-income men. These are not independent facts. Taken together, they suggest that mothers in broken families are likely to have more children than those in stable families. Although on the face of it, this may seem odd, it is indeed a fact. "Among those females who were mothers by 1960, wives had an average of 2.9 children ever born, and female heads [of families] had an average of 3.7 children ever born." (That the two groups were somewhat different in age and race accounted for only a third of the difference.)[61]

[61]John Beresford and Alice Rivlin, *op. cit.*

The pattern that these figures represent is not difficult to induce. The early, low-income marriage may begin poorly or it may begin well and earnestly. The problem is not necessarily in beginning but rather in providing the "means for the young adult to meet the demands of marriage and not become a marriage dropout."[62] However, with inadequate education and training, money becomes a grave problem. With a second or third child, the marriage may well show strain. When a middle-class marriage shows strain, the wife may settle for being supported comfortably, even if she is unhappy. The wife whose husband is poor does not have that particular alternative.[63] The situation would vary according to the actual economic position of the husband; it has been observed that even unmarried mothers will reject marriage if the man is viewed as an economic liability.[64] From the wife's point of view as well as from the husband's, strain may lead to separation or divorce.

Following separation, there may be reconciliation or the wife may make an arrangement with another man. Contrary to the general impression that only separation is more common among poor families, divorce is also more common.[65] In general, two-thirds of divorced women remarry,[66] and the younger the women are, the more likely they are to remarry. That is, whether a family is broken by separation or divorce, the chances are high that a new family will be formed. The pressures continue, however.

The likelihood that reasonable support will be forthcoming for children is very small and the parents are more heavily burdened than in

---

[62]Hylan Lewis and Camille Jeffers, *op. cit.*, 11.
[63]*Ibid.*
[64]Charles E. Bowerman, Donald P. Irish, and Hallowell Pope, *Unwed Motherhood: Personal and Social Consequences* (Chapel Hill, N.C.: University of North Carolina, 1963). Helen Icken Safa, "The Unwed Mother: A Case Study," in *Fatherless Families: Working Papers*, Youth Development Center (Syracuse, N.Y.: Syracuse University, 1965). G. B. Shaw, not quite the same sort of researcher, had his character say in *Housebreak House*: "If I can't have love, there's no reason why I should have poverty."
[65]Hugh Carter and Alexander Plateris, "Trends in Divorce and Family Disruption," *Health, Education, and Welfare Indicators*, September, 1963.
[66]Paul Glick, *American Families* (New York: John Wiley & Sons., Inc., 1957).

the initial marriage. Some of these second attempts work out, but more do not.[67] The path that opens before a family is a sequence of marriages or liaisons, with the notion of a stable, intact marriage, if it was present at the beginning, becoming fainter. One study of economically dependent families observes:

Many of the women who were currently divorced, separated or deserted had been in such situations previously and expected to have similar experiences in future . . . This repetition in behavior was hard for the women we interviewed to explain.[68]

How indeed, *explain* a response to circumstances that seems natural and even inevitable. The sound of this pattern is grim. The saving grace for the individuals involved may be that people who reflect such a pattern are sufficiently plentiful and walled off by neighborhood and communication patterns that many regard it as a common, fated way of life.[69]

Thus far, the pattern has been traced with families who were married young; although the overall chances are smaller, some who married later would follow the same course. It must be clear that progressive breakdown in family relations may be accompanied by breakdown in ability to secure a stable income. Without a husband, mothers are, of course, at a disadvantage. They may work, but their earnings are relatively low and they have special costs. If the man feels he must move, he may make a damaging job change. The process of divorce or separation itself involves costs (legal, dislocation) that are large to poor families. Confused legal relationships or casual work patterns may interfere with entitlement to survivors insurance, unemployment compensation, and so forth. Children may be pulled out of school, making for later difficulty. All these costs would be significant for any family; for poor families, they add to the squeeze that is already intolerable.

The discussion, in this stage as in others, has only hinted at extensive research into the feelings associated with deprivation.[70] Such material would reinforce the argument about the critical nature of each of the stages, but might tend to distract attention from the simple relationships of money and family development. As income is the point, this vital aspect has been foregone. Simply to bear in mind that feeling must accompany things and their absence, here is an excerpt from a researcher's interview with a woman who is supporting four children on $27.50 a week, in the stage described as family breakdown:

If a man has anything and offers to help you out, you don't say to him: "But you'll have to marry me first," she said. You take what he offers right off and offer what you have in return. Of course, you hope that some day he will want to make it legal. But beggars can't be choosers . . . I don't drink whisky but once in a while I'll get myself a half pint of gin . . . But that's about all I spend on myself. I ain't had a new dress for about three years . . . I don't go nowhere to need a new dress . . .

If there's one thing I want it's a back yard, fenced in, so my children don't have to play out in the street . . . I sure hope and pray that some day I can do better. But what can I do now?[71]

By definition, parents who reach their forties poor have not managed to achieve a decent income. A substantial percentage are no longer married and some of the rest have a troubled marriage. The two problems are interconnected. The income problem is a source of reinfection for each new marriage, and each marital failure is likely to add to the income problem.

STAGE FIVE

Only four stages of family-income development have been set forth here; stage five is actually stage one for the next generation. In each of the stages, children have been growing older.

---

[67]Jessie Bernard, *op. cit.*

[68]Paul R. Kimmel, Report on Welfare Administration Project No. 199, 1965 (unpublished).

[69]August B. Hollingshead and Frederick C. Relich, *Social Class and Mental Illness* (New York: John Wiley & Sons, Inc., 1958). Walter B. Miller, "Implications of Urban Lower-Class Culture for Social Work," *Social Service Review*, September, 1959.

[70]See John H. Rohrer, *et al., The Eighth Generation* (New York: Harper & Row, Publishers, 1960); Mirra Komarovsky and Jane H. Philips, *Blue Collar Marriage* (New York: Random House, Inc., 1964); Lee Rainwater and Karol Kane Weinstein, *op. cit.*; Frank Riessman, *The Culturally Deprived Child* (New York: Harper & Row, Publishers, 1962); Oscar Lewis, *The Children of Sanchez* (New York: Random House, Inc., 1961); Hylan Lewis and Camille Jeffers, *op. cit.*, and other articles by Hylan Lewis; Walter B. Miller, *op. cit.*, and other articles.

[71]Roscoe Lewis, unpublished report prepared for the Child-Rearing Study, Health and Welfare Council of the National Capitol Area, quoted in *The Washington Post*, January 12, 1964, p. E-5.

In the third and fourth stages for their parents, children are entering the first and second stages. Even if their parents have managed to avoid family breakdown and certainly if they have moved into stage four, the children would tend to begin families early and make a poor career choice. They would make the same mistakes as their parents for the same reasons: little help and example, not enough money to support longer-term alternatives, little hope of doing better, little practical access to ways of doing better. We spoke of the rules of the game changing at the end of stage one. For these children, growing through their parents' third and fourth stages, the rule reads: Go back to stage one and retrace the moves your parents made.

CONCLUSION

It is a platitude of occupational research that the father's occupation determines the son's. As one discerns the complex and powerful forces that shape choices related to income, one can make a more exact statement: The father's circumstances determine the son's and the circumstances that surround them both determine occupational choice.

This article has attempted to distinguish four critical stages in the family and income development of poor people. They may assist in visualizing the stream of life in poor families rather than seeing them always as fractions of a population or at a given point in time. The method of visualizing flow used here is easily as imperfect as an early kinescope. One projects a series of snatches of life and trusts the imagination to provide the intervals. Research that will provide a sharper, truer image is badly needed.

Apart from the detail that is offered here there are some general conclusions to be taken into consideration:

1. Money, as it is paid out, may be regarded as going to individuals. As money is received and spent in a poor family, however, every individual's income and arrangements affect pooled spending.

2. Minimum income for decent living may represent public policy that is responsible and even charitable. It does not necessarily represent a policy that is functional in terms of moving people out of poverty. For such a policy, there are times when surplus (money and time) is required; capital is required. The situation of families taking off from poverty is analogous to that of nations. Take-off awaits "the build-up *of social overhead capital*," together with the necessary skills and a drive for improvement.[72]

3. The stages of family-income development suggest that leverage may more readily be provided at some points than at others. As has been seen, each stage prejudices the next. Therefore, the two stages most open to influence from outside are, in rather different senses, the earliest. First is the period when the family sets out, when it may be induced to postpone childbirths and to make the wisest (and usually most expensive) choices about training and work. Second is the period after the family has 13- or 14-year-old children who may be led to postpone beginning a family of their own, at least until the girl is 18 or 19 and a boy somewhat older. These are not matters of regulating or simply advising against marriage but of making possible a total pattern in which early marriage and early and dead-end employment do not become attractive or necessary.

4. It is not simply availability of money at any given moment that influences the course poor families take, but their expectation that money will be available for certain purposes. Therefore, a *functional* program, in terms of setting them on a course out of poverty, will be predictable and, where necessary, continuous. Families will not only receive money but understand the comparatively simple conditions that determine whether they receive it. And income will not be subject to discontinuance because new policies are devised from year to year or the funds of a demonstration program run out.

5. The description of the family-income cycle may lead to increased understanding of poor people, but it is offered mainly for a narrower and more utilitarian purpose. It is intended to assist in judging the effectiveness and desirability of current and proposed income-maintenance programs. Management efficiency and cost may be appraised fairly readily. Methods are needed for appraising the effectiveness of programs in relation to the nation's qualitative objectives for the people who are served.

[72]W. W. Rostow, *The Stages of Economic Growth* (London: Cambridge University Press, 1960) [italics added].

47.

WORKING MOTHERS

The American woman, as part of the changing world about her, not only performs her basic role within the family unit but also assumes other obligations that are necessitated by the times in which she lives and by her sense of responsibility to the community as well as to her family. Today's woman is faced with new problems and new challenges. For many women, including those who have children, new life patterns include paid employment, although such work may be intermittent or on a part-time basis.

Among the 27.5 million women who were working or seeking work in March 1967 were 10.6 million mothers with children under 18 years of age. These mothers constituted 38 percent of the total number of women in the labor force and 38 percent of all mothers in the population.

Over the decades, social and economic forces have drawn more and more women into paid employment. Since the pre-World War II period, the trend has been accelerated; there is scarcely a workplace in the nation in which there are no women workers. The most striking rate of increase in employment has been among working mothers. Almost four out of ten mothers were in the labor force in March 1967 as compared with less than one out of ten in 1940.

The growing movement of women into paid employment, with its implications for family life and society, has focused a great deal of attention on the circumstances of women's working, particularly if there are young children in the family.

Why do mothers of young children work? For the great majority of working women with young children, economic need is the most compelling reason. This need, in large measure, is determined by the husband's earnings and the regularity of his employment. The higher his earnings, and the greater the security afforded by his job, the less likely the wife is to work. In fatherless homes and in homes where the husband is absent, the compulsion on a mother to seek work is obviously great. Her earnings are not supplementary; they are basic to the maintenance of her family. In this most affluent of nations, 37 percent of all families headed by a woman lived in poverty in 1966; many other such families lived in near poverty.

There are, of course, other factors that influence a mother's decision to seek work. These include the jobs in the community available to one with her education, training, or skills, and the hours that she is required to be on the job. Mothers with young children have a strong preference for part-time or part-year jobs.

In the final analysis, the decision whether to work outside the home rests with each mother. Usually, she bases her decision on the particular circumstances of her life. She may feel the choice is forced upon her, as in the case of critical financial necessity. But the choice is still her own in a society that puts great value on self-determination by the individual and on the individual's right to exercise free choice.

This selection is reprinted from: "Who Are The Working Mothers?" Leaflet No. 37, Washington, D.C., GPO: United States Department of Labor, Women's Bureau, 1968 [excerpt].

48.

Catherine S. Chilman

POVERTY AND FAMILY PLANNING IN THE UNITED STATES: SOME SOCIAL AND PSYCHOLOGICAL ASPECTS AND IMPLICATIONS FOR PROGRAMS AND POLICY

SUMMARY OF SELECTED SOCIAL AND PSYCHOLOGICAL RESEARCH

The chief sources of social and psychological research related to family planning and poverty in the continental United States derive, for the most part, from four major kinds of investigations: (a) studies of knowledge, attitudes and practices regarding family planning, (2, 8) (b) census data, (c) in-depth studies that might be considered anthropological in nature, (9) and (d) experimental action studies. (10, 11) While the focal point is the continental United States, other countries are also highlighted when evidence from research studies abroad yield important insights. (12, 13)

Some Limitations of Studies

All of these studies provide helpful information. The first group is the most extensive but presents certain limitations in terms of providing a national, current picture of family planning knowledge, attitudes and practices of all relevant segments of the population.

1. These studies are limited, for the most part, to married couples only.
2. Most of these investigations refer to a point in time which might now be called "antique"—i.e., before the simpler forms of contraceptives (the oral contraceptives and the intra-uterine device) were widely available and in general use.
3. Three studies refer to only one city (2, 3, 6, 7) and one study is almost 30 years old. (2)
4. One study focuses on formative families that are still small (two children). (4)
5. Most studies do not make fine enough distinctions between working class and very poor groups (unemployed or underemployed casual laborers).

This selection is reprinted from: Catherine S. Chilman, "Poverty and Family Planning in the United States," *Welfare in Review*, 1967, 5, No. 4, 3–15 [excerpted from pp. 3–8].

6. The nonwhite samples are either not included or are very small.
7. Women are the chief correspondents for the majority of these investigations.

Census data have been helpful in providing broad pictures of the relationship between family size and education, occupational level, income, marital status, and type of area (urban, rural, etc.). Of course, these data cannot provide in-depth information about such factors as attitudes, aspirations, contraceptive practices and the like.

In-depth studies. The in-depth studies related to the topic of family planning (9) provide insights and clues; they are limited, however, by lack of a national sample and by lack of scientifically rigorous research designs and statistical analysis of results.

Experimental action studies. Such studies that involve the use of newer forms of contraceptives, such as the "loop" or the "pill," are still in an early stage of development in terms of the numbers and kinds of experiments that have been carried out and completed to date. However, these studies offer considerable promise for the future, in providing guides to effective ways of setting up and operating family planning programs designed to reach those who have particularly lacked such services in the past, i.e., very poor families of rural residence or recent rural background. (5)

Psychological Studies. Only a few studies have attempted to get at such psychological factors as personality characteristics of persons who favor or disapprove of family planning or of persons who prefer large or small families. These investigations have failed to provide any clear-cut results. This failure may be associated with the lack of coherent theory on which some of the studies were built. (2) In one instance, problems may relate to the nature of the sample itself (couples still in the early process of family formation) and to the kinds of personality tests used. (4) In other earlier psychological studies, the methods of personality testing were still too rudimentary to yield satisfactory results. However, even today, reliable and valid methods of personality assessment for research purposes are still in their early and less-than-satisfactory stages of development.

A host of speculative theories have been advanced—mostly by behavioral theorists and clinicians—as to the psychological factors involved in the desire for no, a few, or many children. Hypotheses based on these theories have tended to cluster around such concepts as female anxiety over adequate sexuality, female resistance to woman's sex role, male concerns to prove virility, infantile impulsiveness and so on. There is, however, no research evidence to support these "hunches" and it is highly probable that psychological factors alone (2, 4) do not account for attitudes and behaviors in this matter. Family size preferences apparently are a complex matter involving interactions of psychological, physical, cultural, religious, economic and situational factors operating in the dynamic context of family life. In this context, the multiple characteristics of both husband and wife in their relationship with each other are among the salient factors that must be considered.

Studies of Life Styles of the Poor. Along with the social and psychological studies that have been specifically concerned with family planning, other important although somewhat indirect sources of evidence lie in investigations that have been concerned with: (a) the child-rearing and family life patterns of the very poor and (b) social and psychological factors associated with marital stability. (14)

Major Findings of Social Research Related to Family Planning

Despite the gaps and limitations in research-based knowledge, a good deal of information is available which should be useful to practitioners, administrators and researchers as they seek to develop effective family planning programs. Therefore, a summary of the major findings

from related social and psychological studies is presented below.

1. The great majority of people in the United States (about 90 percent) approve of the concept of family planning. (2-11)

2. At all socioeconomic levels in this country and in other countries studied—including some of the so-called disadvantaged nations—the average number of children desired is between two and four. (4-6, 12, 13)

3. The arrival of the fourth child seems to represent a critical point for a family. Even for those relatively few families which had previously expressed a desire for more than this number of children, this wish is apt to be revised after the arrival of the fourth child. (5, 6, 13)

4. Evidence is beginning to emerge that families with more than four children, even when controls are established for differences in socioeconomic level, are less likely to be viewed by the children as happy ones (15) and are less likely to produce self-reliant, outgoing youngsters who achieve well in school. (16) However, further studies are needed in this area, with careful consideration of possible associated variables, before one can be confident that family size plays such a crucial role.

5. The basic reason for limitation of family size given by couples in the United States and other countries is an economic one. (6, 9, 12) It is closely tied to a desire to provide a better quality of life for one's children. Considerations of maternal and child health are rarely given by respondents.

6. In this and other countries, desire for small families and for effective contraceptive practice is highly associated with: urbanization, education (in the United States, more than an eighth grade education) and high aspirations for one's children. In this country, however, urbanization has failed to have the sharp, distinctive impact on desire for small families and related contraceptive practice that was anticipated by urban sociologists. These anticipations were based on the experiences of Western European countries and Japan and on theories of urbanization. Urban and rural families in the United States are highly similar in generally

wanting between two and four children—and in having this number of children. The distinctively different group consists of those families living in the rural South and recent urban migrants from that region, especially nonwhite families. Although this group generally aspires to a small number of children, there are high rates of contraceptive failure.

Among the reasons for the general lack of differences in desired family size between most urban and rural people in this country may be: the high level of income available to most families; the growing urbanization of rural areas through improved transportation facilities, the availability of mass media and the mechanization of most farms; and the suburban and "exurban" living of numbers of our so-called urban families. It is well known that the suburban and exurban style of life is generally a family-centered one.

The relatively greater poverty, isolation and racial segregation of the rural South probably play a large part in the different family planning attitudes, information levels and practices found in this region. The severe problems of the urban in-migrants from the rural South and their isolation in the poverty "ghettos" of the city (particularly in the case of the non-whites) are directly related to their difficulties in family size limitation.

7. Poverty has a cluster of causes and effects that interact with, and exacerbate, each other. Cause and effect are so intertwined as to make it impossible to know which is which. The following are factors which are strongly associated with the poverty of families: low educational level of parents, lack of job skills, rural residence or rural origins, female-headed families, illegitimacy, minority group status, early marriage, children spaced closely together and large family size—especially families with five or more children.

8. Large families increase the problems of the very poor: a small income has to be divided into even more parts; harassed and inadequately prepared parents experience an added number of pressures; children suffer extra amounts of economic, physical, social and psychological deprivations; housing and homemaking problems are increased; the marriage is likely to be strained to the breaking point; and a new generation of children grow up with a tendency to be trapped in poverty and failure. (1)

9. Difficulties in effective family planning on the part of very poor people relate to the above and to the following factors: lack of money to pay for family planning services, isolation from such services, lack of relevant information, and their life-style (or subcultural) patterns. (14)

10. Contrary to much popular opinion, very poor people do not want large families; they simply have more difficulty in effective family planning. (3, 5, 9) Again, contrary to popular opinion, very poor families are not resigned to poverty for themselves and their children; particularly for their children they want the same things that other more fortunate parents want: a good education, good health, respectability, a secure and satisfying job, an attractive home and a happy marriage.

11. The life styles more typical (but *not* typical) of the very poor include elements that create a variety of problems for them and tend to stand in the way of their movement out of poverty. The conditions of poverty account, to a large extent, for these patterns, but these patterns tend to interact with adverse conditions to tighten the poverty trap. These life styles affect family planning attitudes and practices in a variety of ways. Attitudes of fatalism, magical thinking, personalism, apathy, lack of time orientation and hostile alienation from the more advantaged sector of society—especially its social institutions and authority figures—tend to stand in the way of active planning for marriage, child-spacing, family size and future goals for one's self and one's children. A lack of commitment to and faith in schools, clinics, social agencies, religious institutions and the advice and services emanating therefrom frequently prevents the use of such services. These attitudes also tend to undermine a belief in the efficacy of contraceptive methods. Such families which do use contraceptives tend not to start using them until they have had three or four children and then to use them sporadically. (5, 9)

Resistance to active participation in family

planning on the part of very poor families was much higher before the introduction of the simpler, less expensive contraceptive methods, such as "the pill" and "the loop." These methods, unlike earlier medically recommended ones such as the diaphragm, do not require specific preplanning regarding sex relations and direct communication and cooperation between marital partners. Moreover, these methods are easier and cheaper to use and are not so likely to require a knowledge and understanding of the physiology of human reproduction. Programs for low-income families which offer these newer methods are experiencing a far higher rate of sustained clinic attendance than was true in the past. Yet many people still are not reached, a number of patients drop out of the program and a number of unplanned births occur. Further efforts are required to help low-income groups achieve their goals of smaller families.

12. Other aspects of family life styles more prevalent among poverty groups are associated with their problems in family planning. A series of studies (9, 17-20) indicate that:

a. A larger proportion of working-class and middle-class families than very poor families report happy marriages and mutually satisfying sex relationships.

b. Low-income men and women tend to live in quite separate social and psychological worlds with very little communication between husband and wife, whereas communication and shared activities are clearly related to marital happiness, and sex satisfaction and communication and marital happiness are closely associated with effective family planning.

c. Hostile and mutually exploitative attitudes are likely to obtain between the sexes in low-income groups; the male tends to play an authoritarian role in the family; a larger number of marriages are broken by divorce, desertion and separation; very poor people have extremely limited knowledge about sex, reproduction and childbirth.

d. Sex relations—both in and out of marriage—are likely to be seen as proof of one's prowess as a man or women rather than as a part of an interpersonal relationship. Peer group pressures for premarital and extramarital sex experiences are strong.

e. Parents are apt to fear giving sex education to their children in the belief that this may lead to "trouble."

f. Illegitimacy is regarded as undesirable, and there is a marked preference for marriage if the opportunity for an economically secure and satisfying marriage presents itself. (22)

The very poor tend to adapt their values regarding sex to the conditions of poverty where jobs for men are scarce and wages are low, where public assistance policies in some states forbid aid to families in which an able-bodied man is present in the home, and where the struggle for existence often breeds an atmosphere of fear, violence and despair. The seeming impulsiveness of many of the very poor probably springs more from a depressed "can't care" attitude than an irresponsible "don't care" approach. Apparent sex freedom is more likely to be a symptom of underlying loneliness and hopelessness about one's self and others than a positive search for pleasure. The sex-related problems more characteristic of the very poor are apt to be a presenting symptom of the more basic cluster of problems that go with their disadvantaged life situation.

Life styles of the sort discussed above have been found to be associated with extreme poverty in such areas as Puerto Rico (21-24) and other Caribbean islands as well as in the continental United States. Although there are minor variations of these life styles from region to region, evidence is mounting that such patterns are strongly associated with poverty itself, wherever poverty exists.

13. The *conditions* of poverty are not the only factors creating the life styles frequently found among the very poor. The life styles of the more advantaged also play a part. Their attitudes toward the poor help to shape the attitudes of poverty groups towards themselves and the outer world. Fatalism and apathy *about* poor people, rejection of them as worthy human beings, separation and alienation *from* them, punitive attitudes toward their problems: middle-class life styles of this sort help to create the separate and troubled worlds of the very poor.

14. Nonwhites, compared to whites at the same poverty level, are more apt to suffer from the foregoing problems. Many explanations are advanced for this, including the fact that a larger segment of the nonwhite population is very poor and more nonwhites are recent new-

comers to cities. The effects of prejudice, discrimination and cumulative disadvantages over many generations on cultural patterns and personality formation (9, 25) are not given enough serious recognition by many writers who discuss the marital and family problems of non-whites. Although in some respects the situation of nonwhites has improved in recent years, the social-psychological effects of the past are not easily erased.

15. Women who are employed in the labor force, at all socioeconomic levels, are apt to have small, planned families. This is not chiefly associated with fertility problems but is more related to aspirations of the family for a higher standard of living. (6) It is also (probably) related to the fact that these women have found broader interests and a sense of personal significance through a range of experiences that go beyond having a large number of children.

16. Experimental programs designed to test the effectiveness of various methods of reaching very poor families with family planning services point to the conclusion that the person-to-person approach is the most effective, especially when the person has apparent competence in such professional fields as medicine or social work, and a warm, outgoing empathetic manner. Well-informed, enthusiastic members of the poverty group itself have also proved to be highly effective communicators concerning family planning. (10, 11) Communications via the mass media or special mailings in low-income neighborhoods tend to be helpful in shaping general community opinion and reinforcing the knowledge and convictions of persons already using family planning services. Such publicity efforts, however, apparently have little effect on those highly disadvantaged people who wish to plan their families but who are held back from initiating action through their lack of education, low reading ability, fear, distrust and sense of rejection by society.

REFERENCES

1. CHILMAN, CATHERINE S. Population dynamics and poverty in the United States: Implications for family planning programs. *Welfare in Review,* June-July, 1966. (Reprints available from Division of Research, Office of the Commissioner, Welfare Administration.)

2. KISER, CLYDE V. and WHELPTON, P. K. *Social and psychological factors affecting fertility.* Vol. V. New York: Milbank Memorial Fund, 1958.

3. BOGUE, DONALD. West side fertility report (mimeo). Community and Family Study Center, University of Chicago, 1965.

4. WESTOFF, CHARLES F. and others. *The third child.* Princeton, N.J.: Princeton University Press, 1964.

5. WHELPTON, PASCAL K., CAMPBELL, ARTHUR A. and PATTERSON, JOHN E., *Fertility and family planning in the United States.* Princeton, N.J.: Princeton University Press, 1966.

6. FREEDMAN, RONALD. Economic status, unemployment, and family growth (mimeo). Final report to Division of Research, Welfare Administration. Project 10703-043. This project, carried out by Dr. Freedman and associates at the University of Michigan, has been supported by research grants from the Welfare Administration and the Social Security Administration.

7. BEASLEY, JOHN D., M.D., HARTER, CARL L. and FISCHER, ANN. Attitudes and knowledge relevant to family planning among New Orleans Negro women. *American Journal of Public Health,* November, 1966, 56, No. 11, 1847-1857. This report is based on a larger research project supported by a grant from the Children's Bureau, Welfare Administration.

8. WESTOFF, CHARLES F., POTTER, ROBERT C., SAGE, PHILIP C., and MESHLER, ELIOT G. *Family growth in metropolitan America.* Princeton, N.J.: Princeton University Press, 1961.

9. RAINWATER, LEE. *Family design.* Chicago: Aldine Publishing Co., 1965.

10. BOGUE, DONALD. *Op. cit.;* and *The rural south: fertility experiments,* Report No. 1. Community and Family Study Center, University of Chicago, February, 1966.

11. POLGAR, STEPHEN. United States: the PPFA mobile service project in New York City. *Studies in family planning, No. 15.* New York: The Population Council. (Note: there is a vast literature of studies concerning family planning in other countries. A detailed summary is beyond the scope of this paper. Some of the major results are summarized in the volumes listed below.)

12. BERELSON, BERNARD and others. *Family planning and population problems.* Chicago: University of Chicago Press, 1966.

13. KISER, CLYDE V. *Research in family planning.* Princeton, N.J.: Princeton University Press, 1962.

14. CHILMAN, CATHERINE S. *Growing up poor.*

Welfare Administration, Department of Health, Education, and Welfare. Washington: U.S. Government Printing Office, 1966, 45 cents.

15. MOORE, BERENICE and HOLTZMAN, WAYNE. *Tomorrow's parents*. Austin, Texas: Hogg Foundation, University of Texas, 1965.

16. DOUVAN, ELIZABETH and ADELSON, JOSEPH. *The adolescent experience*. New York: John Wiley & Sons, Inc., 1966.

17. RAINWATER, LEE and WEINSTEIN, KAROL K. *And the poor get children*. Chicago: Quadrangle Books, 1960.

18. IRELAN, LOLA M., ed. *Low-income life styles*. Welfare Administration, Department of Health, Education, and Welfare. Washington: U.S. Government Printing Office, 1966, 35 cents.

19. KOMAROVSKY, MIRRA. *Blue collar marriage*. New York: Random House, Inc., 1964.

20. HERZOG, ELIZABETH. Some assumptions about the poor. *Social Science Review*. December, 1963, XXXVII.

21. HILL, REUBEN, STYCOS, J. MAYONE, and BACK, KURT W. *The family and population control*. Chapel Hill, N.C.: University of North Carolina Press, 1959.

22. RAINWATER, LEE. Some problems of lower class culture. Paper given at the University of Wisconsin, 1966.

23. LEWIS, OSCAR. *La vida*. New York: Random House, Inc., 1966. The research on which this book was based was supported in part by grants from the Welfare Administration and Social Security Administration.

24. RAINWATER, LEE. Marital sexuality in four cultures of poverty. *Journal of marriage and the family*, November, 1964, *26*, No. 4.

25. See, for example, *Mental health and segregation*, a series of papers, edited by Martin M. Grossack. New York: Springer Publishing Co., 1963.

49.

JUDITH BLAKE

INCOME AND REPRODUCTIVE MOTIVATION

Survey data on ideal family size for national samples of the white American population do not confirm the expectation of a rise in family-size preferences accompanying a rise in income. The theory of economic demand for consumer durables does not, therefore, appear to be a reasonable model for reproductive motivation. More credible is the expectation that family-size preferences are held in check despite added income because the direct and alternative costs of children are greater for the more prosperous. Examination of Catholic and non-Catholic fertility ideals reinforces our belief in the importance for reproductive motivation of rising child costs with rising income. Non-Catholics are either unresponsive in their ideals to increases in income, or they exhibit an inverse pattern of ideals in relation to income. Catholics, however, tend to prefer more children with more income, although even here the relationship is not usually linear. On the other hand, despite a highly ramified system of pro-natalist norms and enforcements, the Church's influence on the magnitude of family-size preferences among ordinary Catholics appears to be very limited. Only a minority of Catholics prefer families of a size that is beyond the normal non-Catholic range of preference—that is, more than four children.

Data for non-Catholics by white- and blue-collar occupational levels and income fit the hypothesis that the demands of an advancing style of life outweigh the potential 'consumption' of more children. White-collar workers generally prefer fewer children than do blue-collar workers even at similar income levels.

This selection is reprinted from: Judith Blake, "Income and Reproductive Motivation," *Population Studies*, 1967, *21*, 185–206 [excerpted from the original article].

Reprinted with the permission of the author and publisher.

Moreover, respondents at upper-income blue-collar levels have clearly smaller fertility ideals than do those among the blue-collar class having less income.

The data on ideal family size by religious affiliation and occupational status in relation to income thus bring us to an ironic conclusion concerning a strictly economic framework for modern fertility analysis. It appears that the relationship predicted by an *economic* interpretation of fertility—a rise in family-size preferences with rising income—is not likely to be found unless some powerful, pro-natalist *non-economic* influence is at work. Such a force is required to offset a class-oriented inflation of child costs with rising income—an inflation that

is itself basically non-economic since it is geared to the unlimited demands of a symbolic system of prestige and deference.

Finally, it is important to note that no major group in the population prefers really small families. Even the smallest ideals in this paper—those of upper-income white-collar non-Catholics—are approximately one-half a child ahead of the size family among married couples that would give us population stability (approximately 2 5 children). Findings such as these lead us to believe that effective population policy will have to concern itself not merely with birth-control instrumentalities but with reproductive motivation as well if our demographic expansion is to level off and stay that way.

50.

Elizabeth Herzog

SOME ASSUMPTIONS ABOUT THE POOR

The people discussed in this paper are commonly referred to by a number of names, preferably polysyllabic. They are called "the underprivileged," "the disadvantaged," "the culturally deprived," "the low SES group," "the low-income group," "the lower class," and so on. Recently, however, there has emerged a refreshing tendency to call them "the poor"—a usage that seems worth accepting, at least for present purposes.[1]

The main purpose of this discussion is not

to support or to attack, but rather merely to look at a few assumptions about the poor, to review some of the testimony for and against them, and to consider how it seems to stack up. The writer cannot claim to have reviewed all the evidence, but only to have pondered what has been reviewed. Moreover, others have had far more opportunity to check the written or spoken word against firsthand observation and contact.

Of course one problem is that, although certain kinds of experience must take precedence over hearsay, experience itself is not always reliable. This was demonstrated not long ago at a small, select conference of social scientists and physicians engaged in studies of child development. One of the physicians remarked, "Whenever you see Negroes you see happy people." When a fellow participant expressed surprise at so sweeping a generalization, a child psychologist chimed in: "That is absolutely true. I grew up in Africa, and I know." When asked whether they had read Richard Wright

---

This paper originally appeared in *The Social Service Review*, Dec. 1963, XXXVII, No. 4, 389–402; and was subsequently printed, in the slightly revised form in which it appears here, in Elizabeth Herzog, *About the Poor: Some Facts and Some Fictions* (Children's Bureau Publication No. 451), Washington, D.C.: GPO, U.S. Department of Health, Education, and Welfare, 1967, pp. 35–51.
[1]For ease of reference, those who are not poor will be called "the more prosperous," "the nonpoor," or "the middle class." For we know a good deal more about the middle class than about the upper class, and in some ways the middle class is the one that most embodies what is often called "the American way of life."

or James Baldwin or Claude Brown or Kenneth Clark they said they had. And one of them added: "Did you ever see them dance? Did you ever hear them sing? Anyone who dances like that and sings like that is happy." As far as they were concerned, their conclusion was based on evidence observed at first hand.

Most of us are familiar enough by now with problems of sampling and reliability and validity that there is no need to belabor the point that even firsthand observation needs to be systematically assembled and systematically checked. This is just one small example of the problems we confront when we try to assess evidence of any kind on any subject. In view of the fact that whatever we are studying is likely to change even while we study it—and sometimes even because we are studying it—there is some excuse for believing that truth is elusive and facts are slippery.

This, obviously, is no reason for giving up the chase. But any good hunter knows that understanding the nature and habits of his quarry is a necessary—though not a sufficient—prerequisite to tracking it down. The little example of the invariably happy Negro was startling because it happened in the sixties and involved social scientists committed to the rules of evidence. It is useful here merely as a reminder that it is respectable to distrust easy generalizations and to keep on looking for answers and continuing to test them even after they seem to be safe in the net.

We have heard a good deal recently about the culture of poverty and the ways in which those who have too little money are also cheated of some less tangible benefits. The recognition that poverty can be a disadvantage is not new. Even in biblical times it was not new, although the Bible took a somewhat more favorable view of poverty than do the commentators of the 1960's. Much later than the Bible, but a good deal earlier than the 1960's, Disraeli made a comment that might serve as a text today. A character in one of his novels declares that Queen Victoria reigns over not one nation, but two: ". . . two nations between whom there is no intercourse and no sympathy; who are as ignorant of each other's habits, thoughts, and feelings as if they were dwellers in different zones or inhabitants of different planets; who are formed by a different breeding, are fed by a different food, are ordered by different manners, and are not governed by the same law— The Rich and The Poor."[2] Michael Harrington was referring to that conversation when he titled his book *The Other America* and called the last chapter "The Two Nations."[3]

We have developed a number of assumptions about that other America. It will be possible to consider only three of them here and to give in each instance some basis for accepting the assumption and some basis for rejecting it or at least qualifying it. These are the three:

1. There is a culture of poverty.
2. The family and sex patterns of the poor differ from those of the middle class.
3. The family and sex patterns of poor Negroes differ from those of whites on the same socioeconomic level.

What is said here about these three statements will be confined to the United States and to the urban part of its population. Reference to the poor does not, of course, mean the lower layer of a three-way breakdown into upper, middle, and lower socioeconomic groups. We have had abundant evidence that this lower segment of the traditional three-way break is itself divided into a number of layers. We have evidence, too, that the life-ways of the very lowest layer differ from the others in this same band more than the so-called upper-lower differs from the lower-middle.

No effort will be made at this point to define precisely what is meant by "the poor," since this review draws on a wide range of studies, which themselves use a variety of indexes and cutting points. It should be said merely that those under discussion live at, or near, or considerably below what is commonly regarded as the subsistence level and that this group constitutes a much larger segment of the population than many had realized until recently. Estimates vary about the exact size of that segment. According to the poverty index of the Social Security Administration, 12 percent of the white families with children under 18, and 48 percent of the nonwhite families in 1964 could be cate-

[2]Disraeli, 1845.
[3]Harrington, 1962.

gorized as poor.[4] Among the poor, a much larger proportion of nonwhite than of white families and persons had annual incomes of less than $1500.[5] Money income is not the sole determinant of membership in this segment, but it is one of the easiest to define and establish and one of the few variables almost always used by investigators. Some others will be mentioned.

In general, the ill-defined group referred to as "the poor" does not include the stable, respectable working class. Nevertheless, some of the characteristics discussed below are derived from studies of the working class, since these particular characteristics have also been found in more marked degree among the poor. This blurring of class lines derives partly from life and partly from ignorance. It derives from life because, for all our insistence on differentiations, certain characteristics do seem to occur in inverse relation to income from top to bottom. It derives from ignorance because so much of our information comes from studies based on inadequate breakdowns, and we do not yet know enough to be as precise as we would like.

The term, "the culture of poverty," seems to have flared into prominence in the early sixties —at least in the field of welfare research. At the 1961 National Conference on Social Welfare, Oscar Lewis gave an excellent paper entitled "The Culture of Poverty."[6] At the same session another anthropologist, Thomas Gladwin, gave a paper on much the same subject; and an anthropologically inclined sociologist, Hylan Lewis, in addition to discussing Gladwin's paper, reported on his ongoing study of low-income families in Washington, D.C.[7] Anyone who listened to these three sessions probably came away with a fresher and deeper realization that in a number of respects the rules of life and the ways of living are different for the poor.

IS THERE A CULTURE OF POVERTY?

Oscar Lewis summarized succinctly his reasons for believing that there is a culture of poverty, when he said:

> In anthropological usage, the term culture implies, essentially, a design for living which is passed down from generation to generation. In applying this concept of culture to the understanding of poverty, I want to draw attention to the fact that poverty in modern nations is not only a state of economic deprivation, of disorganization, or of the absence of something. It is also something positive in the sense that it has a structure, a rationale, and defense mechanisms without which the poor could hardly carry on. In short, it is a way of life, remarkably stable and persistent, passed down from generation to generation along family lines. The culture of poverty has its own modalities and distinctive social and psychological consequences for its members.[8]

He was talking about a culture of poverty that cuts across national borders, including those of the United States, to which the present comments are confined. Our first question concerns his thesis: is there a culture of poverty?

One way to approach this question is to list a number of traits or characteristics attributed to the poor by different investigators and supported at least to some degree by evidence. The summary given below is by no means exhaustive. It does not include all the traits or characteristics attributed with supporting evidence. But none which is mentioned has been put forward without some supporting evidence, even though the quality and quantity of the evidence may have been far from conclusive.

The poor, by definition, are described as having little money, virtually no savings, no economic security. This means, among other things, buying often and in small amounts—and getting less for their money than do the rich. (One anthropologist threatened for years to write a treatise on "The High Cost of Poverty," an intention eventually carried out by a sociologist.[9])

Poverty involves underemployment and scattered, irregular, miscellaneous employment, often at undesirable occupations; it involves extensive borrowing through formal and informal sources, use of second-hand clothing and furniture, and overcrowded dwellings and lack of privacy. The poor have a higher death rate,

[4]Orshansky, 1966.
[5]U.S. Department of Commerce, 1967.
[6]Lewis, O., 1961.
[7]Gladwin, 1961; Lewis, H., 1961.

[8]Lewis, O., 1961.
[9]Caplovitz, 1963.

a lower life expectancy, lower levels of health—physical and mental—and of nutrition, than the prosperous; they depend more on home remedies and folk medicine, since medical care is expensive and frightening; they are relatively unlikely to be members of labor unions, political parties, and other organizations; they are more inclined to excessive drinking and to violence than the prosperous.[10]

These are familiar variables. Equally familiar is the inverse relation of education and income, the fact that education has been, at least until recently, the most useful single indicator of socioeconomic status. Sometimes it almost seems as if all the other differences flowed from that one, so overwhelming are its apparent results in the lives and thoughts and feelings of the poor. Associated with low education are low school achievement, inadequate verbal skills, lack of intellectual stimulation, lack of motivation to education—often coupled with unrealistic aspirations and unrealistic faith in education as an open sesame to getting on in the world.[11]

Because of the key importance of education, it seems appropriate to indulge in one quotation that suggests a good deal more than it says about this crucial variable. This is the comment of an unregretful school dropout, some years after he left school:

Well, I never wanted to do nothing but have my own business, and that's all I ever wanted; you know like a restaurant or something. I figured I just wanted a regular income of my own, you know, where I wouldn't have to get out and work for nobody else. . . . That's what I still want, so all I had in mind was any way that I could get a dollar. That was it. See, I couldn't see nothing in the book, because I used to tell the teacher, "Where am I gonna need no fractions?"—you know. If I have my own business, I don't need no fractions. All I need is whole penny—you know. And which right now is still the way I feel. I don't see why I need no fractions. If I got my own business I don't need that. You see at the time that's what I was thinking. If I got my own business, I don't need nothing else. Take French or something like that—

I said I don't need to learn no French. Cause all I ever wanted was a place of business to myself.[12]

Another set of variables having to do with family life, child rearing, and patterns of sex behavior will be discussed presently.[13] However, I know of no investigator who denies that there are characteristic and distinctive patterns of sex and family life among the poor.

PSYCHOLOGICAL CHARACTERISTICS ASSOCIATED WITH POVERTY

Less obvious but nevertheless supported by empirical evidence, are certain psychological characteristics attributed to the poor. A number of investigators have presented evidence to show that the poor tend on the whole to be more authoritarian than the prosperous; more given to intolerance and prejudice; more given to black-and-white thinking; more anti-intellectual; more prone to action and less to contemplation; more inclined to personal and concrete rather than impersonal and abstract thinking; more given to resignation and fatalism; more subject to anomie; more inclined to a concrete and magical emphasis in religion; more provincial and locally oriented in attitudes and opinions; more distrustful of governmental authority; more suspicious and hostile toward the police; less developed in imaginative and logical powers; more given to economic liberalism and more reactionary in noneconomic matters; less eager to preserve civil liberties, if they themselves are not members of a minority group.[14]

We are told, too, that among the poor we find more hostility, more tension, and more aggression than among those who live well above the subsistence level. One report comments that, in encouraging their children to fight back, these mothers show a realistic understanding of

---

[10]Axelrod, 1956; Brager, 1963; Conference, 1962; Harrington, 1962; Hollingshead, 1949; Hollingshead and Redlich, 1958; Lewis, O., 1961; Lipset, 1959; MacDonald, 1963; Malzberg, 1956; Miller and Riessman, 1961; Simmons, 1957; Stein and Cloward, 1958.

[11]Della-Dora, 1962; Masland *et al.* 1959; Reiss and Rhodes, 1958; Riessman, 1962; Toby, 1957.

[12]This and all the following comments by respondents are from field materials collected by the Child Rearing Study, directed by Hylan Lewis, sponsored by the Health and Welfare Council of the National Capital Area, and supported by Mental Health Projects Grants, 5-R11-MH278-4, from the National Institutes of Health, Public Health Service, U.S. Department of Health, Education, and Welfare.

[13]Bronfenbrenner, 1958; Chilman, 1966; Havighurst, 1961; Havighurst and Davis, 1955; Hollingshead, 1949; Kephart, 1955; Kohn, 1959.

[14]Lewis, O., 1961; Lipset, 1959; Miller and Riessman, 1961.

eg child rearing.

the social problems in their neighborhoods.[15] This view receives support from a low-income father who said of his son: "I . . . knock the hell out of him, 'cause he can't be no sissy and grow up in this here jungle."

Two other generalizations are often made and seldom challenged, though both of them have been challenged. One is that the poor have less belief in their control over their own destinies than the prosperous—less sense of autonomy. The other is that their time perspective is shorter, that they are present-oriented rather than future-oriented.[16]

This is an incomplete listing of various kinds of attributes that have been mentioned as differentiating the very poor from the more prosperous. They are listed here chiefly as background for considering the usefulness of that currently popular phrase, the culture of poverty.

All of the items on the list have a bearing on culture. No account of a culture could ignore these traits and those which cluster with them. If we accept—as this writer does—the relative accuracy of most of them in differentiating the prevailing patterns of the poor from the prevailing patterns of the prosperous, then it seems clear that cultural differences do exist—differences in family and sex patterns, in daily life, in model patterns of character, personality, and belief.

The question remains: Are there aspects of culture that are lacking from the picture known as the culture of poverty? The answer seems to be that a few minor ones and a major cluster are lacking. The classic account of a culture includes, for example, art and artifacts. A case could be made—though a rather flimsy one—for attributing some art forms to the poor. As for artifacts, the tools of living, the whole apparatus of the poor differs from that of the prosperous chiefly by default. Things are lacking or battered or old; but to the extent that they exist at all they differ from those of the prosperous only by being inferior, not by being different.

Lack of a distinctive technology and possibly of art forms constitutes a real but trivial defect in the concept of a culture of poverty. More

substantial is the lack of the basic core that gives to a culture its identity as a culture: the sense that its members have of belonging to a culture entity with its institutions, patterns, and shared beliefs; a sense of that entity as good— a sense of allegiance as well as of identity. There are cultures whose members want to break away, but if they do break away at least they have the feeling that they are separating themselves from an entity that exists and that claims them as members. Corollary to this is the sense of sharing and participating in the life of a broad group, of sharing in a system of beliefs and practices. This positive aspect of culture, the sense of belonging, with its corollary elements of sharing and of participating, seems to be absent from the so-called culture of poverty.

Some of the closest students of slum life emphasize the unincorporated quality of the individuals who make up the slums. There are gangs and cliques composed of some members; but the neighborhoods, they say, consist of people who happen to live near each other. The lack of worldly goods, according to these observers of large city slums, does not create a sense of community, of common institutions and customs, practices and beliefs.

The few people who challenge the idea of a culture of poverty assert that in great cities the poor live relatively isolated lives; that, as Disraeli said, "there is aggregation, but aggregation under circumstances which make it rather a dissociating than a uniting principle," and that the life-ways of the slum dwellers represent, not a system of culturally evolved patterns, but rather a series of disjointed pragmatic adjustments to exigencies perceived as unpredictable and uncontrollable.[17]

These represent the chief qualifications to the concept of culture applied to the poor. They do not destroy the usefulness of the concept, provided its limits are recognized. They do, however, reduce the usefulness if these limits are not recognized, for failure to recognize them invites a neostereotyping, which in turn invites distortion and misapprehension.

The culture-of-poverty concept is so helpful

---

[15] Wortis, 1963.

[16] For comment on time orientation, see *Problem Populations*, p. 1. [Herzog, 1968]

[17] Disraeli, 1845; Gladwin, 1961; Lewis, H., 1961.

that some of its sharpest critics would not block its acceptance even if they could. They would, however, urge that, in order to use it most constructively, one must remember that it represents an analogy or a simile rather than the thing itself. To the extent that the word "culture" is appropriate, the culture of poverty should be thought of as a subculture rather than as a culture in itself—a distinction made, in fact, by Oscar Lewis in the paper quoted above.

Whether we call it a culture or a subculture, it is always important to avoid the cookie-cutter view of culture, with regard to the individual and to the culture or subculture involved. With regard to the individual, the cookie-cutter view assumes that all individuals in a culture turn out exactly alike, as if they were so many cookies. It overlooks the fact that, at least in our urban society, every individual is a member of more than one subculture; and which subculture most strongly influences his response in a given situation depends on the interaction of a great many factors, including his individual makeup and history, the specifics of the various subcultures to which he belongs, and the specifics of the given situation. Thus, although we find prevailing regularities in what might be called culture-character and behavior, and although it is highly useful to recognize these irregularities, it is also useful to remember the vast range of individual differences that coexist with these prevailing patterns of thought, feeling, and behavior.

With regard to the culture as a whole, the cookie-cutter concept again assumes a spurious homogeneity. It forgets that within any one culture or subculture there are conflicts and contradictions and that at any given moment an individual may have to choose—consciously or unconsciously—between conflicting values or patterns. A familiar conflict in middle-class American culture, for example, is that between the value placed on family life and the value placed on success. Both are viewed as good, but at times an individual has to decide which should come first in a given situation.

The anti-cookie-cutters have to remember also that most individuals in varying degrees, have a dual set of values—those by which they live and those they cherish as best. We all have constant evidence of this duality in our own daily lives, although it is sometimes easier to observe in someone else. The classic example is the man who lectures his son about the evils of lying and then adroitly fixes up his own income tax. This point—duality of values—has been made and documented repeatedly about the culture of poverty. The poor, we are told, to a large extent accept and believe in the standards and values of the middle class, but many of the poor regard those standards as a luxury appropriate only to those who can afford it—like a yacht or a mink coat. And so it is possible, without too much discomfort, to behave as if these standards did not exist and at the same time to prefer those standards to one's behavior.[18]

Our tendency to look for statistically significant correlations and clutch them to us, like drowning men clasping a raft, sometimes leads us to forget that a small correlation, even if significant, reveals a large amount of variation and that even a strong correlation may coexist with a significant minority of deviant cases. The infinite variety of individual differences and of intracultural conflicts in values and behavior patterns tends to be forgotten in the cookie-cutter view of culture. Difficult as it is, somehow we have to be able to recognize and profit by the prevailing regularities to be found in any culture or subculture, and at the same time to remember the countermores, the value clashes, and the deviant cases.

With regard to our first statement, then, in the view of this writer the culture of poverty is a very useful concept, if and only if it is used with discrimination, with recognition that poverty is a subculture, and with avoidance of the cookie-cutter approach. It should be added that these provisos have been met by the investigators most responsible for giving it currency. They have been neglected chiefly by those who annex inspired phrases with less than the amount of blood, sweat, and tears required to make the most of inspiration.

[18]Goode, 1961; Powdermaker, 1939; Rodman, 1959.

FAMILY STRUCTURE AND SEX PATTERNS ASSOCIATED WITH POVERTY

Our second statement is that the family structure and sex patterns of the poor differ from those of the nonpoor. There is a good deal of empirical evidence for this statement. There is evidence that not only separation and desertion but also divorce vary in frequency in inverse proportion to income and that family size also varies inversely with income.[19] There is evidence, too, that families headed by women are far more frequent among the poor than among the prosperous and that births out of wedlock are also far more frequent among the poor. There is evidence that childrearing practices differ, with physical punishment and ridicule being more frequent as one descends the social-economic scale.[20] Few, if any, serious investigators would challenge these statements. Although a number could be added, these seem enough to justify accepting the second assumption—namely, that the family and sex patterns of the poor differ from those of the middle class.

This does not, of course, tell much about how they differ. When one gets into that question, one is bound to become involved in our third statement. Accordingly, it seems simpler to consider them together. The third is: The family and sex patterns of poor Negroes differ from those of whites on the same socioeconomic level.

One of the big obstacles to assessing that statement is the fact, mentioned before, that adequate controlling of socioeconomic factors is rarely found.[21] An example of inadequate control was found in a study of marriages among Negro and white working-class couples. All the subjects were of the group carefully classified as working class. Yet it was quite clear that most of the Negroes ranked below most of the whites in education and in occupational status. These differences were ignored in the analysis and the reader was presented with a contrast between two kinds of marriage, which were described as white and nonwhite; yet there was no adequate evidence that they did not in fact represent two somewhat different socioeconomic layers, even though both layers were in the segment marked "working class."

Another study compared the adjustment and achievement of Negro and white children of working-class parents. The investigator remarked that in education and in occupational status the Negroes were consistently at a disadvantage as compared with the whites; yet no account was taken of this in the analysis or conclusions and again the differences were presented as differences between white and nonwhite children. The same situation appeared in a large study of unmarried mothers in New York City. Differences were presented as differences between Negroes and whites, with no attempt to take socioeconomic discrepancies into account.

These are mentioned merely as a few examples of a practice that has been extremely widespread. They are mentioned, not by way of scolding about them, but as one explanation for saying we do not really know certain things that certain investigators thought they had demonstrated rather conclusively. It should be noticed that "thought" is in the past tense—because by now some of these very investigators may not be so sure, and some may even be trying to make more adequate comparisons.

We find, then, that some reports of differences in Negro and white family and sex patterns are based on inadequate matching. This does not mean that there are no differences, but merely that these particular studies have failed to document the existence and extent of differences. In each of these studies, it happened that the patterns usually ascribed to lower socioeconomic levels were stronger among the Negroes than among the whites.

A different kind of evidence comes from studies of available figures on marital stability and on fertility. Thomas Monahan, after careful analysis of statistics on divorce and on premarital pregnancy, came to the conclusion that there is higher incidence of divorce among Negroes than among whites, even when socioeconomic factors are controlled, but that the

[19]Epstein, 1961; Goode, 1965; Orshansky, 1966.
[20]Bronfenbrenner, 1958; Kohn, 1959.
[21]For one of the rare examples, see Gebhard *et al.* 1958.

slavery-legacy theory is probably not tenable.[22] Some others report that the differences seem wholly attributable to socioeconomic factors. Our National Vital Statistics Division reports fertility rates much higher among nonwhites than among whites—a finding generally accepted and often referred to.[23] On the other hand, a review of information on differential fertility, although it underwrites the familiar belief that fertility rates rise as one descends the socioeconomic scale, adds that when socioeconomic factors are controlled the alleged higher fertility rates among Negroes are revealed to relate to socioeconomic status rather than to race.[24] These are two very different kinds of variables, though they both relate to the color-versus-class question.

A few other researchers have tried to compare both by socioeconomic indexes and by color. Clark Vincent has attempted this in his studies of unmarried mothers, as have Jones, Meyer, Borgatta, and others.[25] The findings here showed that both color and socioeconomic status exerted an influence, but that the influence of socioeconomic status was considerably stronger. The studies are few enough and limited enough to cause one to want more evidence. Nevertheless they are encouraging steps in the direction of learning what we need to know.

A different group of studies is relevant here—namely, poverty studies that deal entirely or predominantly with white subjects. Again and again one reads descriptions of the lower class that sound exactly like patterns often ascribed to lower-lower class Negroes—and often (it might be inserted) ascribed to the heritage of slavery. *Plainville, U.S.A.* describes the group referred to by the citizenry as "people who live like animals.[26] No mention is made of color, but it is clear that those described are white. The same can be said of the lower-lower class described by Hollingshead, Warner, and others.[27]

Finally, there are some investigators who have studied both Negroes and whites and who

(so far) report no substantial differences in family and sex patterns at the same socioeconomic level. Walter Miller is one of these.[28] The published accounts of his Roxbury study reviewed so far do not make a point of differentiating between white and nonwhite; but in discussion he has been emphatic in the conviction that the patterns he describes are related to socioeconomic rather than to ethnic characteristics. Publications based on the study of low-income families in Washington, D.C., also favor the view that the family and sex patterns observed relate mainly to class rather than to color.[29]

Oscar Lewis, in describing what he means by the culture of poverty, lists some family characteristics that he ascribes to poverty in any urban Western society. He includes a trend toward mother-centered families, a relatively high incidence of the abandonment of mothers and children, a belief in male superiority with an accompanying cult of masculinity, frequent resort to violence in the settlement of quarrels, frequent use of physical punishment in the training of children, wife-beating, early initiation into sex, free unions, or consensual marriages. All of these characteristics are found in studies of our urban poor, whether white or Negro.

THREE "MARITAL AXIOMS"

The Washington study of low-income families directed by Hylan Lewis offers a feature seldom found among studies of the poor in this country—namely, repeated and extended interviews—sometimes as many as 20—with the same respondents with free use of tape-recording and with evidence of excellent rapport between interviewers and respondents. The respondents are predominantly Negro, but include some white families. Inevitably, in a study of this intensity, the number of respondents is small. In some respects the research method is closer to the classic anthropological than to the classic sociological approach.

From this and some other studies emerge three propositions about marriage that seem to

[22]Monahan, 1960.
[23]U.S. Department of Health, Education, and Welfare, 1966 (A).
[24]Dreger and Miller, 1960.
[25]Vincent, 1961; Jones *et al.* 1962.
[26]West, 1945.
[27]Hollingshead, 1949; Warner and Lunt, 1941.

[28]Miller, 1959.
[29]Lewis, H., 1967.

be regarded as axiomatic among the very poor. Available evidence suggests that the following three "marital axioms" represent points of convergence rather than differences between family and sex patterns among low-income whites and nonwhites.

The first is that a good marriage is far better than no marriage. The second is that a bad marriage is far worse than no marriage. The third is that for a girl to bear a child out of wedlock is unfortunate, but does not necessarily impair her chances for a good marriage.

The positive value put on a good marriage and the negative value put on illegitimacy have escaped a number of observers, because both differ from those found in the middle class. The social and psychological plus of a good marriage is extremely high. The negative value of birth out of wedlock, for mother and for child, although it exists, is not nearly so strong. (Sometimes we fail to recognize that a variable can be much stronger on the plus side than on the minus, or much stronger on the minus than on the plus.) Moreover, neither marriage nor birth out of wedlock stands as high on the value pyramid of the poor as do a number of other values. They are important, but not the most important.

All the mothers interviewed in the Washington study, white and nonwhite, were asked at some point how they would feel if a daughter of theirs became pregnant out of wedlock. The answer was unanimous: they would feel terrible. It would be pain and grief. "That's why I always prayed for boys," one mother said. But they were almost as unanimous in declaring that they would not urge the prospective parents to marry unless they really loved each other. "An unhappy marriage," they agree, "is worse than no marriage at all." But a good marriage is important.

The classic dream of marry-and-live-happily-ever-after is implicit in the remembered fantasy of an unmarried mother, who said:

Do you know something? It sounds so silly. But I played with dolls until I was thirteen. I always wanted to get married and have children—and sew for them. And my husband was going to have fine patches. That must have been from seeing my mother patching clothing. I, of course, was going to patch better. Needles were scarce. They'd hide the one or more we had away from me. Then I'd try to sew with a pin—and the head would tear holes in the cloth, and I'd cry. I could just see myself making little baby's clothes with real fine stitches.

Both the value put on a good marriage and the fact that out-of-wedlock pregnancy need not prevent a good marriage are evident in the following statements made by mothers about their daughters:

She's over 21, so if that's the way she wants it, that's the way she wants it! Sometimes I think she might have it in mind that, if he marries her now, it might look as if he had to. But if they just got married later, why then it would be what they wanted to do.

I had one child before I was married. I wouldn't marry his father. I told him I wouldn't have him. I didn't love him. I stayed with my mother.

Alice had three children without being married, before she straightened up. But she really did straighten up—I'll give her credit. And she's working hard, now, to help keep these straight. She tells them how being so fast and hardheaded had hurt her and everybody else.

Eloise was very lucky. Because she was in Buffalo, visiting, when she was pregnant with Alex, and she met her husband, Brown, there, and he fell for her. She told him all about it, and he waited until after Alex was born, and married her. Little Susie Jane is theirs. Brown's a wonderful man—steady and hardworking. And he's good to her and her children. All four of them go by the name of Brown.

Attitudes toward both marriage and illegitimacy are obviously interwoven with many other ingredients of that deceptively simple phrase, family and sex patterns. Two that must be mentioned are the war between the sexes and the cult of masculinity. They ought to be discussed at greater length, along with a number of others. But at least these two cannot be omitted.

There seems no doubt that the lower one goes on the social-economic ladder, the more overt and bitter becomes the war between the sexes. It seems clear also that this generalization cuts across the color line. The following observation was made about low-income whites:

For most of these women, men are seen as dominant and controlling. They are, like the rest of the external world, unpredictable, difficult to understand, and more powerful than the women.[30]

---

[30]Rainwater and Weinstein, 1960.

These observations were made about low-income Negroes:

> The middle-class emphasis on achievement and striving in relation to color is definitely replaced here by an axis of security and exploitation. These women do exploit men for security when they can, yet they see themselves rather as the victims of exploitation—an exploitation more sexual than racial or economic.

> While the matriarchy and the gang agree that sex is the most important of all social categories, it is clear that sex is seen in quite different terms by the two groups. What is for the women a matter of preserving family solidarity becomes for the man a question of individual assertive virility. . . . They (the women) see the difference between the sexes as the most basic of social categories, and they align themselves psychologically with their mothers in a solidary phalanx against men.[31]

These attitudes obviously affect attitudes toward marriage. One formerly married woman said:

> Men folks are rotten these days. You got to lick 'em to get along with them. You got to take so much off 'em. People down the line all say the same thing. (The interviewer asked if she was saying that she didn't want another husband.) She threw up her hands and said: "I don't *never* want another!"

If most men are beasts and most women are exploited by them, then a smart woman does not want marriage unless she can find that rare paragon, a really good husband. If she can find him, then she is successful. If she bears a child out of wedlock, that is a social misfortune. But illegitimate children do not necessarily preclude a good marriage, and lack of marriage does not necessarily preclude sex.

There may be differences in the degree and expression of the sex war and the cult of masculine superiority among Negroes and whites on the lowest socioeconomic level. Nevertheless, the similarities are striking.

With regard to the whole complex of family and sex patterns, one may say the same thing. Whether there are differences, and, if so, what they are, remains a question. On the basis of this somewhat telescoped discussion it seems reasonable to conclude two things: that the differences related to color, if they exist at all, are probably far slighter than has often been assumed; and that we do not yet have the kind of evidence that would give adequate

basis for a firm conclusion on the matter.

It may be added, as a speculation, that there probably are some differences related to ethnic background, but that probably they are dwarfed by the similarities related to socioeconomic status. One cluster of reasons for thinking that some differences exist has to do with the special status of Negro Americans today, including their history, their current situation, and the continuing struggle against discrimination being waged for them and by them. Another reason is based on the many discriminations that—to our shame and our regret—still exist. Analysis of Aid to Dependent Children caseloads in one state showed more abuse and neglect of children among white than among Negroes and "a higher proportion of white cases in which parents are deteriorated, with severe personality disturbances making it impossible for them to be adequate parents." Such a report suggests that the white people found on the lowest socioeconomic levels may be, on the average, less capable and more disturbed than the Negroes on this level. If so, it is probably because social and economic conditions make it easier for white people to rise from poverty, so that for them the screening process is more directly related to basic competence. In order to remain one of the poor, a Negro does not have to have something wrong with him. The speculation about prevailing likenesses and differences, however, remains speculative. It is offered in the hope that others will continue with studies that may help us all to inch toward conclusions without leaping to them.

At this point, I remember a certain man who, although friendly and tolerant in general, once exploded about an opinionated female relative: "No matter what she says, I always feel like disagreeing, because after she says it she always shuts her mouth like a trap." Perhaps the moral of our tale is that no matter what we say about the poor we are in no position to shut our mouths like a trap—or to shut our minds, either.

31Rohrer and Edmonson, 1960.

REFERENCES

Axelrod, Morris. Urban structure and social participation. *American Sociological Review*, February, 1956, *XXI*, 13–18.

BRAGER, GEORGE. Organizing the unaffiliated in a low-income area. *Social Work*, April, 1963, VIII, No. 2, 34–40.

BRONFENBRENNER, URIE, Socialization and social class through time and space. In MACCOBY, ELEANOR E., NEWCOMB, THEODORE M. and HARTLEY, EUGENE L., eds.: *Readings in social psychology*, third edition. New York; Holt, 1958.

CAPLOVITZ, DAVID. *The poor pay more: consumer practices of low-income families*. New York: The Free Press, 1963, 220 pp.

CHILMAN, CATHERINE S.: *Growing up poor*. U.S. Department of Health, Education, and Welfare, Welfare Administration, Washington, D.C. 20402: Government Printing Office, May, 1966, 117 pp.

Conference on Economic Progess. *Poverty and deprivation in the United States*. Washington, D.C.: The Conference, April, 1962.

DELLA-DORA, DELMO. The culturally disadvantaged: educational implications of certain social-cultural phenomena. *Exceptional Children*, May, 1962, XXVII, 467–472.

DISRAELI, BENJAMIN. *Sybil; or, the two nations*. London: H. Colburn, 1845.

DREGER, RALPH MASON and MILLER, KENT S. Comparative psychological studies of Negroes and whites in the United States. *Psychological Bulletin*, September, 1960, LVII, 361–402.

EPSTEIN, LENORE A. Some effects of low income on children and their families. *Social Security Bulletin*, February, 1961, 24, 12–17.

GEBHARD, PAUL H. et. al. *Pregnancy, birth, and abortion*. New York: Harper & Row, Publishers, 1958.

GLADWIN, THOMAS. The anthropologist's view of poverty. In *The social work forum*, 1961, 73–86.

GOODE, WILLIAM J. Economic factors and marital stability. *American Sociological Review*, December, 1951, XVI, 802–812.

GOODE, WILLIAM J. Illegitimacy, anomie, and cultural penetration. *American Sociological Review*, December, 1961, XXVI, 910–925.

HARRINGTON, MICHAEL. *The other America: poverty in the United States*. New York: MacMillan Co., 1962, 191 pp.

HAVIGHURST, ROBERT J. Conditions productive of superior children. *Teachers College Record*, April, 1961, XX, 524–531.

HAVIGHURST, ROBERT J. and DAVIS, ALLISON. A comparison of the Chicago and Harvard studies of social class differences in child rearing." *American Sociological Review*, August, 1955, XX, 438–442.

HERZOG, ELIZABETH: *About the poor: some facts and some fictions*. Department of Health, Education, and Welfare, Children's Bureau. Washington, D.C.: U.S. Government Printing Office, 1968, 85 pp.

HOLLINGSHEAD, AUGUST B. *Elmstown's youth—the impact of social classes on adolescents*. New York: John Wiley & Sons, 1949, 480 pp.

HOLLINGSHEAD, AUGUST B. and REDLICH, FREDERICK C. *Social class and mental illness: a community study*. New York: John Wiley & Sons, 1958, 442 pp.

JONES, WYATT C., MEYER, HENRY J. and BORGATTA, EDGAR F. Social and psychological factors in status decisions of unmarried mothers. *Journal of Marriage and Family Living*, August, 1962, XXIV, No. 3, 224–230.

KEPHART, WILLIAM M. Occupational level and marital disruption. *American Sociological Review*, August, 1955, XX, 456–465.

KOHN, MELVIN L. Social class and the exercise of parental authority. *American Sociological Review*, June, 1959, XXIV, 352–366.

LEWIS, HYLAN. Child-rearing practices among low-income families. *Casework Papers, 1961*. New York: Family Service Association of America, 1961.

LEWIS, HYLAN: Culture, class and family life among low-income urban Negroes. In Ross, ARTHUR, ed., *Employment, race and poverty*, New York: Harcourt, Brace & World, Inc., 1967 (A).

LEWIS, HYLAN. *Culture, class and poverty*. Washington, D.C.: Communicating Research on the Urban Poor (CROSS-TELL), Health and Welfare Council of the National Capital Area, February, 1967, 49 pp. (B).

LEWIS, OSCAR. *The children of Sanchez: autobiography of a Mexican family*. New York: Random House, 1961, 499 pp.

LIPSET, SEYMOUR MARTIN. Democracy and working-class authoritarianism. *American Sociological Review*, August, 1959, XXIV, 482–501.

MACDONALD, DWIGHT. Our invisible poor. *New Yorker*, January 19, 1963.

MALZBERG, BENJAMIN: Mental disease in relation to economic status. *Journal of Nervous and Mental Diseases*, March, 1956, CXXIII, 257–261.

MASLAND, RICHARD L. et al. *Mental subnormality: biological, psychological, and cultural factors*. New York: Basic Books, 1959, 442 pp.

MILLER, S. M. and RIESSMAN, FRANK. The working class subculture: a new view. *Social Problems*, Summer 1961, IX, 86–97.

MILLER, WALTER B. Implications of urban lower-class culture for social work. *Social Service Review*, September, 1959, XXXIII, No. 3, 219–236.

MONAHAN, THOMAS P.: "Premarital Pregnancy in the United States: A Critical Review and Some New Findings." *Eugenics Quarterly*, September 1960, pp. 133–147 (Vol. VII).

ORSHANSKY, MOLLIE. Recounting the poor—a five-year review. *Social Security Bulletin*, April, 1966, 29, No. 4, 20–37.

POWDERMAKER, HORTENSE. *After freedom: A cul-*

tural study in the deep South. New York: Viking Press, 1939, 408 pp.

RAINWATER, LEE and WEINSTEIN, KAROL KANE. *And the poor get children.* Chicago: Quadrangle Books, 1960, 202 pp.

REISS, ALBERT J., JR., and RHODES, ALBERT LEWIS. A socio-psychological study of conformity and deviant behavior among adolescents. Vanderbilt University Project 6399, Final Report, 1958. Mimeographed.

RIESSMAN, FRANK. *The culturally deprived child.* New York: Harper & Row, 1962, 140 pp.

RODMAN, HYMAN. On understanding lower-class behavior. *Social and Economic Studies,* December, 1959, *VIII,* 441–450.

ROHRER, JOHN H. and EDMONSON, MUNRO S. *The eighth generation: cultures and personalities of New Orleans Negroes.* New York: Harper & Row, 1960, 346 pp.

SIMMONS. OZZIE G. Implications of social class for public health. *Human Organization,* Fall, 1957, *XVI,* 7–10.

STEIN, HERMAN D. and CLOWARD, RICHARD A., eds. *Social perspectives on behavior,* esp. pp. 45–52. New York: Free Press, 1958, 666 pp.

TOBY, JACKSON. Orientation to education as a factor in the school maladjustment of lower-class children. *Social Forces,* March, 1957, *XXXV,* 259–266.

U.S. Department of Commerce, Bureau of the Census. *Current Population Reports,* Series P-60, No. 51, January 12, 1967, Washington, D.C.: Government Printing Office, 1967.

U.S. Department of Health, Education, and Welfare, Public Health Service, National Center for Health Statistics. *Vital Statistics of the United States, 1964—Volume I, Natality,* p. 1–4. Washington, D.C.: Government Printing Office, 1966 (A).

VINCENT, CLARK E. *Unmarried mothers.* New York: The Free Press, 1961, 308 pp.

WARNER, W. LLOYD and LUNT, PAUL S. *The social life of a modern community.* New Haven, Conn.: Yale University Press, 1941.

WEST, JAMES. *Plainville, U.S.A.* New York: Columbia University Press, 1945, 238 pp.

WORTIS, HELEN *et al.* Child-rearing practices in a low socio-economic group: the mothers of premature infants. *Pediatrics,* August, 1963, *XXXII,* 298–307.

CHAPTER **XII**

The Negro Family

Since the Negro family has frequently been described as culturally different from families in the mainstream of American life we have devoted a separate chapter to this topic. Because of highly visible cultural differences, it is not uncommon that we develop certain feelings or expectations about the family patterns of certain groups. A specific example may be a particular religious group because the teachings of their faith may have strong bearings on the relationships of husbands and wives, the married couple to their extended families, child-rearing practices, the control of fertility, and so forth. In the case of the American Negro, certain assumptions or stereotypes have arisen. For example, there are statements that the Negroes are more musical, more violent, childlike, unstable, sexually immoral or amoral, and so forth. In parallel, statements may be found that Jews are intellectual, clannish, scheming, and aggrandizing in the economic area. Italians may sometimes be described as hot blooded, romantic, and prone to become racketeers. While at various points in time and in certain locations there may be kernels of truth to such statements, in general they are statements of prejudice, often phrased in generalities because of lack of contact or knowledge of the groups. So, questions about the description of particular groups within American society have to be answered in a guarded way. For example, are there familial differences between different religious groups? The answer has to be that there must be some, at least in the way individuals orient themselves, otherwise when intermarriage occurs between religious groups we should not expect any greater difficulty in the maintenance of the marriage. If all that is involved is merely the set of beliefs relative to a religion and these do not affect major aspects of the family life, why should interfaith marriages have greater difficulty? Is it merely on the basis of the fact that children of the marriage are brought up in only one religion, or that there are differences among the parents on which religion this is to be? It seems unlikely that this is the only difference. The topic of intermarriage between religious groups received considerably more attention at an earlier point in time, but now seems to be a lesser topic for research, possibly because the notions of intermarriage have been disseminated into the population more generally as a set of permitted alternatives. Indeed, one might remark that in the last few decades a spirit of ecumenicism has been displayed. It is difficult to maintain an ecumenical point of view while insisting that persons of different religions should not mix and marry.

Aspects of factors involved in mate selection were noted earlier in Chapter 6, but the topic of intermarriage was not discussed formally. Recent literature seems to indicate no different or extraordinary processes involved in regard to Negro marriages, or to intermarriage between Negroes and Whites. For example, a recent study indicates that such an important variable as educational homogamy tends to exist among Whites, among Negroes, and among Negro-White intermarriages. (Bernard, Jessie, "Note on Educational Homogamy in Negro-White and White-Negro Marriages, 1960," *Journal of Marriage and the Family*, 1966, 28, 262–273.) The fact is that examination of what occurs in terms of *social processes* suggests that factors of propinquity, homogeneity of education, and other important variables appear to operate in similar ways in most groups and also when the groups interact.

Here materials are presented on the Negro family as such. Some pieces of information presented are objective, and reflective of general status differences rather than of cultural differences. For example, about three-fourths of all non-White families are headed by a man, as compared to nine-tenths of White families. But, the higher the income level, the closer the statistics are for Negroes and Whites. What are the concomitants to such facts? In an article titled "Is There a 'Breakdown' of the Negro Family?" Elizabeth Herzog examines some of the facts in the light of assumptions and raises questions that will require answering as time passes in order to ascertain whether or not there are really "group differences." In an article titled "The Negro Matriarchy," Mark Battle and Jeanne Barnett present an interpretation of current trends on the basis of matriarchally-centered family type. The final article in this chapter is by Ludwig L. Geismar and Ursula C. Gerhart titled "Social Class, Ethnicity, and Family Functioning: Exploring Some Issues Raised by the Moynihan Report." It illustrates how suppositions about group differences require direct empirical examination.

51.

ELIZABETH HERZOG

IS THERE A "BREAKDOWN" OF THE NEGRO FAMILY?

Much has been said of late—and often with great heat—about the Negro family. Despite prevailing consensus on a number of points, controversy has been generated with regard to other points because one man's fact is another man's fiction. Some points of consensus deserve mention before points of controversy. First, it is generally agreed that a harmonious two-parent home is better for children than a one-parent home—and better for parents, too, in this society. It is agreed also that fatherless homes are far more frequent among Negroes than among whites and that in both groups their frequency rises as income falls.

Another point of firm consensus is that strong action is needed to remedy adverse conditions that have existed far too long, especially for low-income Negroes; and that these conditions bear especially on the low-income Negro man, whose disadvantaged situation takes heavy toll of himself, his children, their mother, and the family unit as a whole. All these statements have long been accepted by serious students of Negro family life.[1]

NB The controversy centers mainly on the following points: (1) whether "the" Negro family is "crumbling" at a disastrous rate, (2) whether the amount of breakdown that exists is primarily due to poverty, or to cultural inheritance, or to a cycle of self-perpetuating pathology, (3) whether the remedy is to be sought primarily through improving the economic, social, and legal status of Negroes or primarily through conducting a remedial campaign aimed directly at the Negro family.

This selection first appeared in *Social Work*, Jan., 1966, XI, No. 1, pp. 3–10; and subsequently printed, in slightly revised form, in Elizabeth Herzog, *About the Poor: Some Facts and Fictions* (Children's Bureau Publication #451), Washington, D.C., GPO: U.S. Department of Health, Education, and Welfare, 1967, pp. 23–32.
[1] Drake and Cayton, 1945; Frazier, 1939; Lewis, H., 1960; Pettigrew, 1964.

THE MOYNIHAN REPORT

Impetus has been given to these and related questions by the much discussed "Moynihan report." Released to the general public in the late fall of 1965, this publication presents census figures and findings from some special studies to document the grim effects of poverty and discrimination and their impact on Negro families. It brings together all-too-familiar evidence that the frequency of broken marriage, female-headed families, births out of wedlock, and dependence on public assistance is much higher among Negroes than among whites. In doing so, it recognizes that these problems are most acute among the very poor and least acute at the middle- and upper-income levels. It points out also that they are more acute in cities than in rural areas and thus are intensified by continuing urbanization.

The report further documents the higher unemployment rates and lower wage rates among Negroes than among whites. It states, as others have done, the two-to-one Negro-white unemployment ratio that has persisted for years, the lower wages available to Negroes, and the fact that the median nonwhite family income is little more than half the median for white families. To this discrepancy is added the fact that the families of the poor tend to be larger than middle class families. "Families of six or more children have median incomes 24 percent below families with three.[2] Other sources tell how heavily this fertility differential bears on Negro families: in 1963, according to the Social Security Administration Index, 60 per cent of nonwhite children under 18 lived in poverty as compared with 16 percent of white children.[3]

The effect on marital and family stability of the man's economic instability is also discussed.

[2] U.S. Department of Labor, 1965.
[3] Orshansky, 1965(B).

483

The sad cycle has become familiar in the professional literature: the man who cannot command a stable job at adequate wages cannot be an adequate family provider; the man who cannot provide for his family is likely to lose status and respect in his own eyes and in the eyes of others—including his family. His inability to provide drains him of the will to struggle with continuing and insuperable family responsibilities. It is an incentive to desertion, especially if his family can receive public assistance only when he is gone.

A good deal of the Moynihan report is devoted to interpretation of the documented figures and, quite naturally, it is on the interpretation that opinions diverge.[4] It is not the purpose of this paper to summarize fully, to concur with, or to take issue with the report as such, but rather to consider some propositions that were in circulation before it was published and to which it has given increased currency. With regard to the report itself, its factual summary has shocked some Americans into new recognition of old and unpalatable facts about the toll exacted by poverty coupled with discrimination; and its interpretive sections have challenged us to an assessment of evidence—two substantial services. Some of the propositions attributed to it may be misinterpretations of the author's intended meaning. In any case, they have taken on a life of their own and are met frequently in other current writings. Accordingly, they will be considered here on their own merits, without reference to any particular document.

FATHERLESS FAMILIES

One recurrent proposition concerns the "rapid

[4]Midway between statistical report and interpretation is discussion of a "startling increase in welfare dependency," described as occurring at a time when employment was increasing. (U.S. Department of Labor, 1965, p. 12.) It would require extensive and sophisticated analysis to determine the extent to which this upswing in AFDC recipients related to changes in families, or to liberalization of AFDC policies following new legislation, or to changes in population distribution. Similarly, differentials in rates of juvenile delinquency would need to be controlled for income and analyzed in light of differential rates of apprehension and treatment of presumed offenders, white or nonwhite.

deterioration" of the Negro family, often referred to as "crumbling" and presumably near dissolution. The frequency of fatherless families is used as the primary index of family breakdown. Although questions can be—and have been—raised about this index, such questions do not dominate the mainstream of the argument and will be disregarded here. But if one accepts the proportion of fatherless homes as a primary index of family breakdown, does it then follow, on the basis of the evidence, that the Negro family is rapidly deteriorating?

It is important to differentiate between sudden acceleration of family crisis and relatively sudden perception of a long-chronic situation, since the diagnosis of a social condition influences the prescription for relieving it and the context in which the prescription is filled.

Actually, census figures do not justify an alarmist interpretation. It seems worth while to review these figures, not because there is no urgent need for remedial action—the need is urgent, especially in the area of jobs for low-income Negro men. Rather it is important to keep the problem in perspective and to avoid feeding prejudices that can all too readily seize upon statistical misconceptions as reason to delay rather than to speed such action.

As already noted, census figures do show much higher rates of fatherless families for Negroes than for whites. The 1965 figures show almost nine percent of white families headed by a woman as compared with 24 percent nonwhite families; a difference of this order has persisted for years.[5] The figures do not, however, document a rapid increase in those rates during recent years. On the contrary—and this is a point curiously slighted by commentators on both sides of the argument—they show a gradual increase from 1949 (19 percent) to 1959 (24 percent). Moreover, from 1959 to 1965 the proportion of female-headed families among Negroes showed virtually no net rise, standing at about 24 percent in 1965. The total rise from 1949 to 1965 was about five percentage points, that is, less than one-third of a percentage point

[5]These figures are available for white and nonwhite rather than for white and Negro families. However, most of the nonwhite (over 90 percent) are Negroes.

TABLE 51–1. FAMILIES HEADED BY A WOMAN AS PERCENT OF ALL FAMILIES BY COLOR
SELECTED PERIODS, 1949–65

Year	Families headed by a woman as percent of total		Year	Families headed by a woman as percent of total	
	White	Nonwhite		White	Nonwhite
1965	9.0	23.7	1957	8.9	21.9
1964	8.8	23.4	1956	8.8	20.5
1963	8.6	23.3	1955	9.0	20.7
1962	8.6	23.2	1954	8.3	19.2
1961	8.9	21.6	1953	8.4	18.1
1960	8.7	22.4	1952	9.2	17.9
1959	8.4	23.6	1950	8.4	19.1
1958	8.6	22.4	1949	8.8	18.8

Source: U.S. Department of Commerce, Bureau of the Census: Current Population Reports. P-20, No. 153, 125, 116, 106, 100, 88, 83, 75, 67, 53, 44, 33, and 26. Figures for 1963 and 1964 are drawn from U.S. Department of Labor, Bureau of Labor Statistics, Bulletin No. 1511, 1966.

a year. In 1940, the proportion was 18 percent.[6] Thus, an accurate description would be that during the past 25 years there has been a gradual, wavering rise, but not an acute increase in the overall proportion of broken homes among Negroes. (Table 51–1.)

ILLEGITIMACY

Another generalization also related to family breakdown is met so often that by now it threatens to attain the status of "fact," namely, that there has been an "alarming rise" in illegitimacy. It is true that the number of births out of wedlock has soared. In 1965 the number was 291,000 as compared with 176,600 in 1954.[7] This is a tremendous number, and the more distressing since there has been no services explosion to keep pace with the population explosion. However, in terms of people's behavior, the only relevant index of increase in illegitimacy is *rate*, that is, the number of births out of wedlock per 1000 unmarried women of childbearing age.

The rise in rate (as differentiated from numbers) was relatively steady over several decades. This rise represents a long-term trend and not a sudden upsurge. Moreover, in the last eight years reported (1958–1965) the rate has oscillated within about two points, at about the same level, rising or falling one point or less annually, but in effect representing an eight-year plateau. Since all national illegitimacy figures are based on estimates, with a number of states not reporting, very slight changes should not be regarded as significant. Thus, the current picture is a large rise in *numbers* and a leveling off in the *rate* of non-wedlock births.[8] (The ratio—the proportion of live births that are out of wedlock—has risen for both white and nonwhites. However, *ratio* is far less meaningful than *rate* as an index of change.)

The recent relative stability of rate does not diminish the problems caused by nonwedlock births but it should affect the conclusions drawn from the statistics, the measures taken to act on those conclusions, and the attitudes of those who ponder the meaning of the figures.

Over half the children born out of wedlock are non-white, although only 12 percent of the population are nonwhite. The reasons for this difference have been much discussed and need only be mentioned here. They include (1) less use of contraception, (2) less use of abortion, (3) differences in reporting, (4) reluctance to

[6]Percentages have been rounded. The exact rise was from 18.8 percent to 23.6 percent, or 4.4 percentage points. The 1940 figure was 17.8 percent, as recomputed according to the definition of "family" introduced in 1947. U.S. Department of Commerce, *Current Population Reports.* Series P-20 1949–1962); U.S. Department of Labor, 1966; U.S. Department of Commerce, 1943.

[7]U.S. Department of Health, Education, and Welfare, 1967(B); 1966(C).

[8]See Unmarried Mothers, p. 55. [Herzog, 1968].

lose a public assistance grant by admitting to a man in the house, (5) the expense of divorce and legal separation. It seems probable that, even if discount could be made for these and other factors, a difference would remain. It would be a much smaller difference, however, and conceivably could still relate more to income than to color.[9]

If further evidence were needed on this virtually unchallenged relation between income and illegitimacy rates, figures on rates in high- and low-income tracts should be sufficient. Pakter and associates, for example, found that the proportion of births out of wedlock in relation to total nonwhite births varied from a high of 38 percent in the Central Harlem district to a comparative low of nine percent in the Pelham Bay District.[10]

Attitudes toward illegitimacy and toward marriage are clearly linked with the economic position of the Negro male. A male head of house who is not a breadwinner and provider is a hazard to the happiness of the marriage, and his loss of economic status is so great a hazard to his intrafamily status that he may decamp, either to protect his own ego or to make his family eligible for support from AFDC. Some recent changes in the AFDC program are aimed against the latter reason for family desertion.

SLAVERY IS NOT THE EXPLANATION

Among the most frequent and most challenged generalizations relating to low-income Negro families is the assumption that their present characteristics are influenced more by the legacy of slavery than by postslavery discriminations and deprivations. One difficulty with this proposition is that slavery is a hundred years behind us—crowded years, during which many influences have affected the family life and sex patterns of us all. Another is that some characteristics lumped under the slavery-legacy label are characteristically found also among low-income whites.

This convergence is the less surprising when we consider that much of what is ascribed to the culture of slavery is inherent in what has come to be known as the culture of poverty. If Negroes had not been slaves in the plantation setting but had been in as depressed an economic situation as the majority of them have been during and since slavery, the behavior of the low-income segment would probably show some of the elements now ascribed to slavery.

Adequately controlled comparisons within different income levels show that the differences associated with income outweigh those associated with color. Family structure, for example, differs more between different income levels than between Negro and white families. The same is true of differences between Negro and white children in educational achievement, and —when income is controlled—the relative position of men with respect to women, economically and educationally, is the same for whites as for nonwhites.[11]

Descriptions of white families at the very low-income levels read very much like current descriptions of poor Negro families, with high incidence of broken homes, "mother dominance," births out of wedlock, educational deficit, crowded living, three-generation households, and failure to observe the norms of middle-class behavior.[12] Such families are described by Hollingshead and Redlich:

> Doctors, nurses, and public officials who know these families best estimate from one-fifth to one-fourth of all births are illegitimate.
>
> Death, desertion, separation, or divorce has broken more than half the families (56%). The burden of child care, as well as support, falls on the mother more often than on the father when the family is broken. The mother-child relation is the strongest and most enduring family tie.
>
> ❖ ❖ ❖ ❖ ❖
>
> Here we find a conglomerate of broken homes where two or three generations live together, where boarders and roomers, in-laws and common-law liaisons share living quarters. Laws may be broken and the moral standards of the higher classes flouted before the children's eyes day after day.[13]

These are descriptions of white families in

---

[9]Some of these elements are discussed in *Some Assumptions About the Poor*, p. 35. [Herzog, 1968].
[10]Pakter *et al.* 1961.

[11]Lefcowitz, 1965.
[12]Miller, 1959; Warner and Lunt, 1941; West, 1945.
[13]Hollingshead, 1949; Hollingshead and Redlich, 1958.

the North, with no heritage of slavery to explain their way of life. It seems unlikely that the slavery-specific thesis is needed to explain the occurrence among Negroes of patterns so similar to those produced in other groups merely by poverty, and so often described in other contexts as "the culture of poverty."[14]

It is difficult to be sure how much—if any—difference would remain in proportions of female-headed families if really sensitive comparisons were made between Negroes and whites on the same income level. Available income breakdowns employ rather broad groupings, and Negroes tend to be overrepresented at the lower layers of each grouping. It seems reasonable to assume that some differences between white and nonwhite would remain even with a more sensitive income classification. Yet it does not necessarily follow that they might be ascribed primarily to the legacy of slavery rather than to the hundred years since slavery. It seems more likely that differences between low-income white and Negro families, beyond that explained by income alone, may be attributed primarily to postslavery factors of deprivation and discrimination affecting every facet of life: occupation, education, income, housing, nutrition, health and mortality, social status, self-respect —the documented list is long and the documenting references myriad.[15]

The habit of analyzing data by color rather than by income level has helped to support the slavery-specific thesis. Since a much larger proportion of Negroes than of whites are on the lowest income levels, what look like statistically significant differences between Negroes and whites may also look like significant differences between different socioeconomic levels. But if the figures are presented only in one way, we don't find out about the other. Studies of prenatal care, for example, indicate that in effect one is comparing the prosperous with the poor in all three of the following comparisons: white mothers with nonwhite mothers; married mothers with unmarried mothers; all mothers who do, with all mothers who do not, obtain prenatal care.[16]

All the points mentioned here, and some not mentioned, are important. However, the emphasis on rapid deterioration is so central to current discussion of the low-income Negro family and to means proposed for alleviating its current problems that it deserves major emphasis— along with the slavery-specific thesis to which it is so often linked.

There has been little disposition to challenge the ample evidence that family structure and functioning in our society are strongly linked with social and economic status. The questions raised, as Robert Coles put it, have to do with which is the cart and which is the horse.[17] The alleged rapid acceleration of family breakdown has been cited as evidence that among low-income Negroes the family is the horse. Therefore it is important to recognize that, according to the chief index used by proponents of this view, no rapid acceleration of family breakdown is evident.

If there has been no substantial change in family structure during the past two decades, then there are no grounds for claiming that a new "tangle of pathology" has set up a degenerative process from within, over and above response to the long continued impact of social and economic forces from without; and that this process is specific to a Negro "culture" inherited from days of slavery.

TWO VIEWS—AND TWO REMEDIES

Both sides of the controversy agree that there is urgent need for strong action to increase the proportion of sound, harmonious two-parent homes among low-income Negroes. They disagree on whether that action should be focused primarily on intrafamily or extrafamily problems. The acute-crisis view suggests that primary attention be given to the family as such. The other view suggests that the best way to strengthen low-income families, as families, is to give primary attention to building up the economic and social status of Negro men.

According to this view, a number of noneconomic supports can and should be given to low-income Negro families, pending the time

---

[14]Lewis, O., 1961.
[15]U.S. Department of Labor, 1966; Schorr, 1963.
[16]Herzog and Bernstein, 1964.

[17]Coles, 1965.

when fewer of them are fatherless. Such helps should include, among other things, (1) aids for the overburdened mother in her multiple role as homemaker, child-rearer, and bread-winner; and (2) effective male models intro-duced into the lives of children—girls as well as boys. A number of new ways for providing both kinds of support have been proposed. In the long run, however, according to this view, what these families need most is jobs for Negro men—jobs with status, with stability, with fu-ture, and with fair wages. No one claims that this can be achieved easily, quickly, or cheaply; but many believe it can and must be done.

What is new for the white majority is not that it is suddenly faced with an explosive breakdown of "the" Negro family. What is new is the recognition of a long-standing situation, plus the determination to do something about it. If we are able to achieve that recognition and determination, however belatedly, then surely we must be able to act on this basis rather than to galvanize ourselves into action by believing that suddenly the Negro family is a bomb or a mine which will explode in our faces if it is not quickly defused. Surely we are able to act not because of panic but because action is long overdue, and inaction flies in the face of de-cency.

What is new for the Negro minority is not a sudden acceleration of family breakdown. What is new is an injection of hope that attacks apathy and fatalism and sparks insistence on full justice. It is not increased family breakdown that activates outbreaks like those in Harlem, Watts, and elsewhere. It is the recognition that the families of the "dark ghetto" no longer need to continue to accept the ghetto and what it does to them.

It must, of course, be recognized that "the" Negro family is itself a fiction. Different family forms prevail at different class and income levels throughout our society. In addition, at any given level a wide variety of families are found, each with its individual characteristics—some of which are not class linked. When the great diversity among low-income families is ignored, there is danger that the deplored characteristics of some will be imputed to all.[18] At the same time, most writers—including the present one—find it almost impossible to avoid falling into the oversimplified form of reference to "the" Negro family that constantly risks oversimplified thinking.

It is necessary also to caution one's self and others that, while problems must be discussed and attacked, strengths must not be forgotten. Problem-focused discussions, however necessary and constructive, also invite distortion. Not all fathers are absent fathers among the poor—in fact, about two-thirds of them are present among low-income Negro families. And, as Erik Erikson reminds us, there are impressive strengths in many Negro mothers.[19] Robert Coles, after living among low-income Negroes for months, wrote:

I was constantly surprised at the endurance shown by children we would all call poor or, in the current fashion, "culturally disadvantaged." . . . What enabled such children from such families to survive, emotionally and educationally, ordeals I feel sure many white middle-class boys and girls would find impossible? What has been the source of strength shown by the sit-in students, many of whom do not come from comfortable homes but, quite the contrary, from rural cabins or slum tene-ments?[20]

One may go on to speculate: What are the sources of strength and self-discipline that make possible a Montgomery bus boycott or a march on Washington, conducted without violence? We do well to ponder such questions, for we shall have to mobilize the strengths of families in poverty as well as the wisdom of accredited problem solvers, if we are at last "to fulfill these rights."

REFERENCES

COLES, ROBERT, There's sinew in the Negro family. Background paper for White House Confer-ence "To Fulfill These Rights." Washington, D.C., November, 1965. Reprinted from the *Washington Post*, October 10, 1965, p. E 1.

DRAKE, ST. CLAIR and CAYTON, HORACE R. *Black metropolis.* New York: Harcourt, Brace, and World, 1945, 809 pp.

ERICKSON, ERIK H. The concept of identity in race relations: notes and queries. *Daedalus*, Winter 1966, 145–171.

---

[18]Lewis, H., 1967 (B). See also *Some Assump-tions About the Poor*, p. 35. [Herzog, 1968].

[19]Erikson, 1966.
[20]Coles, 1965.

FRAZIER, E. FRANKLIN. *The Negro family in the United States.* Chicago: University of Chicago Press, 1939, 686 pp.

HERZOG, ELIZABETH. *About the poor: some facts and some fictions.* Department of Health, Education, and Welfare, Children's Bureau. Washington, D.C.: U.S. Government Printing Office, 1968, 85 pp.

HERZOG, ELIZABETH and BERNSTEIN, ROSE. *Health services for unmarried mothers.* Department of Health, Education, and Welfare, Welfare Administration, Children's Bureau. Washington, D.C.: U.S. Government Printing Office, 1964, 61 pp.

HOLLNGSHEAD, AUGUST B. *Elmstown's youth—the impact of social classes on adolescents.* New York: John Wiley & Sons, Inc., 1949, 480 pp.

HOLLINGSHEAD, AUGUST B. and REDLICH, FREDERICK C. *Social class and mental illness: A community study.* New York: John Wiley & Sons, Inc., 1958, 442 pp.

LEFCOWITZ, MYRON J. Poverty and Negro-white family structures. Background paper for White House Conference "To Fulfill These Rights," Washington, D.C., November, 1965.

LEWIS, HYLAN. The changing Negro family. In GINZBERG, ELI, ed. *The nation's children, vol. 1: the family and social change.* New York: Columbia University Press, 1960.

LEWIS, HYLAN *Culture, class and poverty.* Washington, D.C., Communicating Research on the Urban Poor (CROSS-TELL), Health and Welfare Council of the National Capital Area, February, 1967, 49 pp. (B).

LEWIS, OSCAR. *The children of Sanchez: autobiography of a Mexican family.* New York: Random House, 1961, 499 pp.

MILLER, WALTER B. Implications of urban lower-class culture for social work. *Social Service Review,* September, 1959, *XXXIII,* No. 3, 219–236.

ORSHANSKY, MOLLIE. Who's who among the poor: a demographic view of poverty. *Social Security Bulletin,* July, 1965, *28,* No. 7 (B), 3–32.

PAKTER, JEAN, ROSNER, HENRY J., JACOBZINER, HAROLD and GREENSTEIN, FRIEDA. Out-of-wedlock births in New York City: I—Sociological aspects. *American Journal of Public Health,* May, 1961, *51,* No. 5; II—Medical aspects. *American Journal of Public Health,* June, 1961, *51,* No. 6, 846–865.

PETTIGREW, THOMAS F. *A profile of the Negro American.* Princeton, N.J.: D. Van Nostrand Co., 1964, 250 pp.

SCHORR, ALVIN L. *Slums and social insecurity.* Social Security Administration, U.S. Department of Health, Education, and Welfare. Research Report No. 1. Washington, D.C.: Government Printing Office, 1963, 168 pp.

U.S. Department of Commerce, Bureau of the Census. *Current population reports,* Series P-20 (1949–1962). Washington, D. C.: Government Printing Office.

U.S. Department of Commerce, Bureau of the Census. *16th census of the U.S. 1940. Population—families—types of families,* 1943.

U.S. Department of Health, Education, and Welfare, Public Health Service, National Center for Health Statistics, Monthly Vital Statistics Report, Advance Report. *Final natality statistics, 1965,* 1967 (B).

U.S. Department of Health, Education, and Welfare, Public Health Service, National Center for Health Statistics. *Vital statistics of the United States, 1964—volume I, natality,* 4–8. Washington, D.C.: Government Printing Office, 1966 (C).

U.S. Department of Labor, Bureau of Labor Statistics. *The Negroes in the United States—their economic and social situation.* Bulletin No. 1511, June, 1966. Washington, D.C.: Government Printing Office, 1966, 241 pp.

U.S. Department of Labor, Office of Planning and Research: *The Negro family: The case for national action.* Washington, D.C. 20402: Government Printing Office, 1965, 78 pp.

WARNER, W. LOYD and LUNT, PAUL S. *The social life of a modern community.* New Haven, Conn.: Yale University Press, 1941.

WEST, JAMES. *Plainville, U.S.A.* New York: Columbia University Press, 1945, 238 pp.

52.

MARK BATTLE AND JEANNE BARNETT

THE NEGRO MATRIARCHY

A major by-product of the current drive to give Negroes first-class citizenship will be a change in the structure and functioning of the Negro subculture. Negroes, of course, welcome and demand the new opportunities for education and employment, but these very opportunities will topple the traditional and accepted patterns of behavior among Negro men and women in the lower-middle and lower-income classes.

For Negro men—if the new education and training programs work—the change will not be too difficult. For Negro women the hurdle may be greater.

Historically, the Negro subculture in the United States has been a matriarchal society. What little family life obtained during the years of slavery was the result of applied instinct by Negro women. Male slaves were separated from their families and sold without their wives and children. Owners were often kind enough to offer children for sale with their mothers.

Even after slavery was abolished, the matriarchal Negro society persisted. Women were the real family heads. It was easier for them to negotiate the system. It was easier for them to find jobs, if only as domestic servants. Women saw themselves as worthwhile persons. They brought into their marriages ideas gathered from their own childhood. They had seen their fathers without jobs or changing from one job to another. They had seen their mothers holding the family together.

These patterns and attitudes influenced the upbringing of their children. A Negro mother identified with her daughters and dreamed of better lives for them. She gave girls the better break, brought them up to hope for and aim toward the life of a "lady." She taught them how to fight for their rights. This attitude gave rise to an old saying among Negroes: "Only white men and Negro women are free."

A Negro mother encouraged her girls—rather then her boys—to achieve status. And, partly because Negro society as a whole could not hope for much wealth, status became associated with education. Traditionally, more girls than boys went to college. Even today, *two-thirds of all Negro college students are girls*. This process, repeating itself in generation after generation, established Negro women as the elite of their society.

Gunnar Myrdal has stated that Negroes have been permanent aliens in American society. We would go one step further: Negro men in the lower-middle and lower class have been aliens in Negro society as well.

The idea that Negro boys belonged at work —not in school—was reinforced by Negroes themselves. This happened partly because an educated Negro male did not have a great advantage over an uneducated Negro male in finding employment. It resulted also from the limited numbers of educated Negro men for boys to pattern their lives after. Boys rarely realized there was another way. In traditional Southern society the pretense that Negro men simply did not exist brought about the custom of referring to 80-year-old men as "boys." Negro fathers, if home, were usually dominated by their mothers or grandmothers; their education was meager; their jobs were transitory and unimportant. In short, their fathers were unimportant.

Negro men may not have liked the traditional role into which they were cast but until recently, there was little they could do to change it. They sought and gained power in their churches and fraternal organizations rather than in the world of work. They withdrew as workers, fathers and

This selection is reprinted from: Mark Battle, and Jeanne Barnett, "The Negro Matriarchy," *American Child*, 1965, *47*, No. 3, 8–10.
Reprinted with the permission of the publisher.

husbands. They withdrew because they could not find work. They withdrew to escape female domination. And sometimes they removed themselves physically from their family households when this desertion enabled their families to get essential economic help on relief rolls. While their withdrawal may appear to have been irresponsible, it should be understood that it frequently was the result of behavioral conditioning —nothing more was expected of them by their own families or by white society.

Of course, in reality, the resulting Negro society has never meshed. Girls trained to be teachers, social workers and nurses are not prepared to marry boys with little education who earn their living at menial work. Girls who are absorbing the value which American society places on white collar jobs are not ready to marry boys who come home dirty and work only seasonally. Girls, aware that their mothers look down on men, are sometimes reluctant to marry at all.

One unfortunate result of this situation is the disproportionately high rate of illegitimate births among lower-middle and lower-class Negroes. The solution increasingly offered is birth control, or, rather, birth control education. The assumption is that Negroes, with all their alleged sexual know-how, with all their much-attacked knowledge of drugs and narcotics, have somehow remained totally ignorant about methods of contraception. We suspect that this is usually not the case. Most Negro youngsters, like most whites, hear about contraceptives when they are still in elementary school. What is more likely is that the bearing and rearing of an illegitimate child has more positive meaning to a Negro girl than the public has suspected. For example, marriage may be the last thing desired by a girl trained to be distrustful and contemptuous of men. In contrast, becoming a mother may be her one way of proving herself a woman and of gaining a permanent tie to the future. These are only speculations, but what seems clear is that many other factors will have to be explored before we can assume we know how to decrease out-of-wedlock births.

Today Negro women who account for 40 percent of the total Negro labor force, also account for 61 percent of all Negroes in the professional world, 50 percent of Negro clerical workers, and 44 percent of Negro sales persons.

The average income of Negro men in the labor force is higher than that of women—primarily because the jobs they hold when they work pay higher wages. For example, of the Negroes working as domestics, 97 percent are women. But again status in the lower-middle and lower-class Negro culture is not based primarily on income.

As for Negro boys, despite generations of conditioning, they are now becoming increasingly aware, according to recent studies, that a job gives status. They yearn to be something in the professional world. The problem in the past has been that there were few opportunities for training, little reason to seek training, and no awareness of what training was needed. What we call lack of motivation may more realistically be termed lack of integrated preparation.

As patterns of education and expectations continue to change, Negro boys, brought up to think of themselves as working, responsible, law-abiding persons, will develop into working, responsible, law-abiding persons.

But what of the girls? What will happen? We suspect that part of the reason for the high unemployment among Negro teenage girls today —31 percent—results partly from the "ideal" still in the mind of the Negro girl. Many unskilled girls are unwilling to take just any job being offered—part of the myth that a Negro girl must always aim high. Many are unwilling to take available jobs as waitresses or domestics while unemployed boys, because of their outlook, will often grab any job—legal or illegal. When better jobs open up to all Negroes, will the girls jump in to compete with the boys?

Superimposed on the Negro subculture today is the conflict within the total American society on the role of women. Do we glorify homemakers? Do we glorify the career girl?

Will Negro girls and women, because of the traditions of their own society, have even greater conflicts within themselves than white women? In the Great Society in which Negro males hopefully at last will be first-class citizens, Negro males will be treated as men. Are Negro women ready for this?

53.

Ludwig L. Geismar and Ursula C. Gerhart

SOCIAL CLASS, ETHNICITY, AND FAMILY FUNCTIONING:
EXPLORING SOME ISSUES RAISED BY THE
MOYNIHAN REPORT

In March, 1965, the Office of Policy Planning
and Research of the United States Department
of Labor issued a 78-page document under the
title *The Negro Family—The Case for National
Action*.[1] This document is better known as the
Moynihan Report, after its chief author, Daniel

This selection is reprinted from: Ludwig L.
Geismar and Ursula C. Gerhart, "Social Class,
Ethnicity, and Family Functioning: Exploring Some
Issues Raised by the Moynihan Report," *Journal
of Marriage and the Family*, 1968, *30*, 480–487.
Reprinted with the permission of the authors and
publisher.
This is a revised version of a paper presented
at the National Conference of Social Welfare, May
22–26, 1967, in Dallas, Texas. The research for
this report was made possible by HEW Grant No.
190 from the U.S. Welfare Administration. Data
were collected from Fall, 1964 to December, 1965.
[1]Office of Planning and Research, *The Negro
Family—The Case for National Action*, Washington,
D.C.: U.S. Department of Labor, March, 1965.
Since its publication and review by the press, the
Moynihan Report has become one of the most
controversial government documents in recent years.
Although Chapter V of the report stating "The Case
for National Action" is nonspecific in its recommendation and its authors wish it understood that
"the object of this study has been to define a
problem rather than propose solutions to it," the
published study as a whole conveys a definitive point
of view on the role of the Negro family vis-à-vis
the problems of the Negroes. Moreover, the report
proposes, at least by implication, the action focus
which gives primary consideration to strengthening
the Negro family. Because both aspects of the report
touch some of the most sensitive issues of the problems besetting Negroes, the release of the study
predictably aroused a storm of controversy.
For a history of events surrounding the writing
and release of the report, see Lee Rainwater and
William L. Yancey, "Black Families and the White
House, the Political Implications of the Moynihan
Report Controversy," *Trans-action*, July/August,
1966, *3:5*, 6–11, and 48–53. For an answer to the
critics of the report, see Daniel P. Moynihan, "'The
President and the Negro: The Moment Lost," *Commentary*, February, 1967, *43:2*, 31–45.
See also Lee Rainwater and William L. Yancey,
*The Moynihan Report and the Politics of Con-
troversy*, Cambridge, Mass.: M.I.T. Press, 1967.

Patrick Moynihan, who was assistant secretary of
labor at the time of the writing.

The Moynihan Report places the broken and
unstable Negro family at the heart of the problem facing the Negro community, citing broken
families, illegitimacy, matriarchy, economic dependency, failure to pass armed forces entrance
tests, delinquency, and crime as evidence of the
Negro family's pathology.

The study's primary proof of the failure of
the Negro family resides in statistics on family
structure, economic dependency, deviant behavior, and educational attainment. In basing its argument on these data, the report makes the inference that basic structural and certain behavioral characteristics of the Negro family serve as
valid indicants of its functioning which is considered to be of a very problematic nature. That
condition, the report assumes, is a fundamental
source of weakness of the Negro community and
calls for action aimed at strengthening the
family.

The act of inferring functioning patterns from
some structural and official, recorded behavorial
characteristics is not as much the articulation
of a theoretical position as it is a form of research which grasps at available straws. Mean
Intelligence Quotients and school enrollment
rates, which favor children from homes with
both parents present, reveal little about the
quality of family life. The higher rate of economic dependency among Negro families is,
above all, testimony to their precarious economic position. Official statistics on crime and
juvenile delinquency have long been considered
a doubtful index of deviant behavior, and their
power as an indicant of the nature of the socialization process in the family is questionable.[2]

[2]John Kitsuse and A. L. Cicourel, "A Note on
the Use of Official Statistics," *Social Problems*,

The present paper examines the Moynihan findings by using data which appear to be more appropriate than the Moynihan statistics[3] for gaining an understanding of the nature of Negro family life relative to the family life of two other ethnic groups. The focus will be on the potential of the family environment for supplying a positive socializing experience for its children. It was E. Franklin Frazier, the noted Negro sociologist, repeatedly cited in the Moynihan Report, who held the Negro family to be deficient in that respect.[4]

SOURCE OF DATA

Data for this analysis are derived from the Rutgers Family Life Improvement Project, a research-action endeavor in which the social functioning of a random sample of some 500 young urban families, residents of an eastern seaboard city with a first child born in 1964 to a mother under age 30, is being studied longitudinally.[5] The study reported here relies on a subsample

of the aforementioned population, a stratified random sample of 133 cases, divided into 50 Negro, 50 white, and 33 Puerto Rican families. This method of sampling was designed to permit ethnic group comparisons on the relevant variables.

The primary source of the data was a two- to three-hour open-ended interview with the mother in the family's home. Data collected comprised family history, information on the parents' families of orientation, and an account of the family's social functioning. Some structured questionnaires on child-rearing attitudes and alienation from society were also administered.

Although the main emphasis of this report is on Negro-white differences, the inclusion of a sample of Puerto Rican families served two purposes: it provided much-needed information about one of our greatly neglected minorities and furnished comparative data on family structure and functioning for another low-income group with a high rate of migration and limited acculturation to urban life.

Before proceeding to a discussion of social characteristics of the three population samples, the reader should be reminded that we are dealing here with young families at the start of the family life cycle. Although this fact limits our ability to generalize about families in each ethnic group, the sample composition has the advantage of controlling the variable "stage of family development," thereby eliminating a confounding factor in the analysis.

A fair degree of sample representatives is claimed by virtue of the fact that names of respondents were drawn from the birth register of the city's vital statistics department. The interview rejection rate was low, 6.7 percent, but only 50 percent of the names drawn could be interviewed because of the high mobility rate of the young families. Preliminary findings from a comprehensive sample validation study now underway suggest, nonetheless, that cases interviewed were demographically similar to those which could not be located because the family had moved.[6]

Fall, 1963, 2:2, 131–139; James F. Short, Jr. and F. Ivan Nye, "Reported Behavior as a Criterion of Deviant Behavior," *Social Problems*, Winter, 1957–1958, 5:3, 207–213; James E. Price, "Testing the Accuracy of Crime Statistics," *Social Problems*, Fall, 1963, 14:2, 214–221; Sophia M. Robison, *Juvenile Delinquency, Its Nature and Control*, New York: Holt, Rinehart & Winston, Inc., 1960, 14–27; William M. Kephart, "The Negro Offender: An Urban Research Project," *American Journal of Sociology*, July 1954, 60:1, 46–50.

Elizabeth Herzog questions the validity of statistics on illegitimacy as an index of Negro family disorganization. See Elizabeth Herzog, "Is There a Breakdown in the Negro Family?" *Social Work*, January, 1966, 11:1, 3–10.

[3]The Moynihan Report and a more recent study by Jessie Bernard, using residential togetherness of marriage partners and frequency of husband's marriage as an index of family stability, serve as examples of the selection of readily available and representative statistics which are, nonetheless, an inadequate index of the chief research variable. Jessie Bernard, "Marital Stability and Patterns of Status Variables," *Journal of Marriage and the Family*, November, 1966, 28:4, 421–439.

[4]E. Franklin Frazier, "Problems and Needs of Negro Children and Youth Resulting from Family Disorganization," *Journal of Negro Education*, Summer, 1950, 276–277. A citation on the above subject from the foregoing article was given in *The Negro Family—The Case for National Action, op. cit.*, 48.

[5]For a more detailed account, see Ludwig L. Geismar and Jane Krisberg, "The Family Life Improvement Project: An Experiment in Preventive Intervention," *Social Casework*, November, 1966, Part I, 47:9, 563–570; December, 1966, Part II, 47:10, 663–667.

[6]Family Life Improvement Project, *Progress Report*, Graduate School of Social Work (New Brunswick, N.J.: Rutgers University, February, 1966), pp. 12–14, 15, 16 (mimeographed).

TABLE 53–1. RELATIONSHIP BETWEEN SOCIAL STATUS OF FAMILIES AND ETHNIC GROUP

Social Status	Whites		Negroes		Puerto Ricans		Total
	Percent	N	Percent	N	Percent	N	N
Class I to III	20.0	10	4.3	2	3.0	1	13
Class IV	20.0	10	10.6	5	18.2	6	21
Class V	54.0	27	48.9	23	33.3	11	61
Class VI	6.0	3	36.2	17	45.5	15	35
Total	100.0	50	100.0	47	100.0	33	130*

*Where total sample size is less than 133, data on the dependent variable were found missing from the number of cases constituting the difference between 133 and the total N shown in the table.

STRUCTURAL CHARACTERISTICS

At the time of the interview all families were residents of the city proper, for the research sample was drawn from a universe of city residents. The lower-class character of the community is reflected in the social-status distribution of the three ethnic groups (Table 53–1) which is based on a modified Hollingshead Two Factor Index of Social Position.[7] The ISP which differentiates among six instead of the usual five status groups shows the bulk of the young families concentrated in groups V and VI.

The striking difference in class position between the white families and the minority-group families[8] is in line with the differences in status distribution in the American urban community. For example, 40 percent of the whites, 15 percent of the Negroes, and 21 percent of the Puerto Ricans are found in classes I to IV;[9] by contrast six percent of the whites, 36 percent of the Negroes, and 46 percent of the Puerto Ricans are located in the bottom status group VI.

The three ethnic groups differ decidely in family composition. Two white families (four percent) as against four Puerto Rican families (12.1 percent) and 21 Negro families (42.0 percent) are headed by unmarried mothers. This distribution reflects in attenuated form the proportion of out-of-wedlock births to young

[7]The adaptation of the Index of Social Position was done by Professor William Wells of Rutgers University.

[8]The term "minority group" is actually a misnomer when applied to Negro representation within the community being studied, for between national censuses the Negro was becoming a majority group.

[9]Classes I to IV had to be combined for statistical analysis because of the small number of Negroes and Puerto Ricans in these status groups.

mothers in the community where the reasearch was done.[10] This study, recognizing the high incidence of one-parent families in the urban community, includes families headed by a woman as well as two-parent families.

The migration patterns of the three ethnic groups provide a telling picture of their differential mobility (Table 53–2). Over half the heads of Negro families had migrated from the South since 1955. Another 15 percent of the men and six percent of the women heading the families had migrated to the city from various sections of the United States other than the South. All the Puerto Rican male heads of families and 79 percent of the female heads had come from Puerto Rico, mostly since 1955. By contrast, 69 percent of the white fathers and 54 percent of the white mothers had always lived in the community. Only 14 percent of the former and 34 percent of the latter had migrated from another place in the American North. Of equal interest is the finding that between 41 percent and 93 percent of the minority-group parents as against seven percent of the white fathers and 27 per-

[10]In 1964, the year the sample was drawn, the percentage of out-of-wedlock births of the total number of first births to women under 30 was 77 percent for Negroes and 23 percent for whites. No data were available for Puerto Ricans. The above percentages for families headed by unmarried mothers reflect mainly differences in opportunities for placing children for adoption. The bulk of white mothers succeed in having their babies adopted; a few keep their babies either in a household headed by themselves or, following marriage, a two-parent household. For Negroes the opportunities for adoption are very limited. The smaller percentage of Negro homes headed by unmarried mothers as against the percentage of illegitimate births reflects both marriages of mothers and placements of children with relatives, usually without formal adoption.

TABLE 53–2. MIGRATION PATTERNS IN THREE ETHNIC GROUPS

Migration Pattern	Percent					
	White		Negro		Puerto Ricans	
	Fathers	Mothers	Fathers	Mothers	Fathers	Mothers
Geographic						
South to North	...	2.0	53.7	52.0	...	3.0
From Puerto Rico	...	...	...	...	100.0	78.9
From another country ...	16.3	10.0	...	...	...	3.0
Within North	14.3	34.0	14.6	6.0	...	3.0
Did not migrate	69.4	54.0	31.7	42.0	...	12.1
Total	100.0	100.0	100.0	100.0	100.0	100.0
	(N-49)	(N-50)	(N-41)	(N-50)	(N-33)	(N-33)
Type of Community						
Rural to city	...	2.0	13.8	9.3	44.8	28.1
Small town to city	6.5	24.5	27.6	32.6	48.3	43.8
City to city	19.6	18.4	13.8	9.3	6.9	15.6
Did not migrate*	73.9	55.1	44.8	48.8	...	12.5
Total	100.0	100.0	100.0	100.0	100.0	100.0
	(N-46)	(N-49)	(N-29)	(N-43)	(N-29)	(N-32)

*Percentages in this row differ slightly from those in the "did not migrate" category above because of variations in the N's on which information was available.

TABLE 53–3. SOCIAL-STATUS MOBILITY OF FAMILY OF PROCREATION VERSUS MATERNAL FAMILY OF ORIENTATION, IN THREE ETHNIC GROUPS

Social-Status Mobility of Family of Procreation	White		Negro		Puerto Rican		Total
	Percent	N	Percent	N	Percent	N	N
Lower than parents	28.1	9	16.7	5	20.0	6	20
Same as parents	34.4	11	33.3	10	36.7	11	32
Higher than parents	37.5	12	50.0	15	43.3	13	40
Total	100.0	32	100.0	30	100.0	30	92

cent of the white mothers had moved to the city from a rural area or a small town.

Social status mobility—as based on the modified Hollingshead ISP—from family of origin to family of procreation did not show the same striking contrast among ethnic groups. With data available on the maternal line[11] for nearly all Puerto Rican families but only on three-fifths of the Negroes and whites (see Table 53–3), the evidence points to a modal pattern of upward mobility in all groups and a somewhat larger percentage of downward mobility among the whites than among the Negroes and Puerto

Ricans.[12] One might speculate, since this research does not dispose over the demographic data required for testing the hypothesis, that the lesser upward mobility among white families indicates selective geographic (horizontal) mobility among the three ethnic groups. The upwardly mobile Negro or Puerto Rican is more likely to move to the city, whereas the upwardly mobile white may exchange the city for the suburbs, leaving the socially non-mobile or downwardly mobile more heavily represented among urban white families. The small differences in

[11]A similar distribution was shown for the parental line, but data on parental grandfathers were not sufficiently complete to justify reporting.

[12]Contrary to expectations, better jobs rather than more formal education for the young minority-group parents seems to be the explanation for their greater intergenerational status mobility.

TABLE 53–4. FAMILY FUNCTIONING IN THREE ETHNIC GROUPS

Family Functioning	White		Negro		Puerto Rican		Total
	Percent	N	Percent	N	Percent	N	N
Adequate	44.0	22	12.0	6	21.2	7	35
Near-adequate	40.0	20	22.0	11	33.3	11	42
Near-problematic	10.0	5	36.0	18	24.3	8	31
Problematic	6.0	3	30.0	15	21.2	7	25
Total	100.0	50	100.0	50	100.0	33	133

status mobility notwithstanding, the intergenerational movement between classes did little to minimize the status gap between white families on the one hand and Negro and Puerto Rican families on the other (Table 53–1).[13]

COMPARATIVE PATTERNS OF FAMILY FUNCTIONING

A better view of the family's ability to socialize its young, serve the welfare of its adult members, and carry out some society-serving tasks can be had by inquiring into its social functioning. The social functioning patterns of our research families were studied systematically with the aid of the St. Paul Scale of Family Functioning. Since space is limited and theory and technique of measurement are treated elsewhere,[14] let us for the sake of brevity state that the scale measures role performance in eight areas and 23 subareas along the dimensions of health-illness or pathology and conformity-deviance. In looking upon the family from a social functioning focus, we are asserting in effect that the family, like other social systems, has certain functional requirements which must be satisfied if it is to survive.[15]

[13]Status mobility, likewise, was not significantly related to the dependent variable of this study, family functioning. (This variable is discussed in the next section.)

[14]L. L. Geismar and Beverly Ayres, *Measuring Family Functioning, A Manual on a Method for Evaluating the Social Functioning of Disorganized Families*, St. Paul, Minnesota: Family Centered Project, 1960; L. L. Geismar, Michael A. LaSorte, and Beverly Ayres, "Measuring Family Disorganization," *Marriage and Family Living*, February, 1962, 24:1, 51–56; L. L. Geismar, "Family Functioning as an Index of Need for Welfare Services," *Family Process*, March, 1964, 3:1, 99–113.

[15]Norman W. Bell and Ezra F. Vogel, *A Modern Introduction to the Family*, New York: The Free Press, 1960, pp. 11 ff.

A rough comparison of the families' level of social functioning may be gleaned from Table 53–4. Levels 4 to 1 constitute four points on a continuum from Adequate Functioning, or behavior which meets physical, social, and emotional needs of family members and is more or less in line with community expectations, to Problematic Functioning, behavior which fails to meet many family needs and is contrary to community expectation.[16]

A sharp contrast in level of functioning among the three ethnic groups is clearly evident. Sixty-six percent of the Negroes, 46 percent of the Puerto Ricans, but only 16 percent of the whites reveal problematic or near-problematic family functioning. Adequate functioning on the other hand appears to be characteristic of 44 percent of the whites, 21 percent of the Puerto Ricans, and 12 percent of the Negro families. These differences are statistically very significant ($X^2 = 27.83$, 6 df, $p < .001$).

[16]For a fuller definition of the categories, see Ludwig L. Geismar and Jane Krisberg, "The Family Life Improvement Project, An Experiment in Preventive Intervention, Part I," *Social Casework*, November, 1966, 47:9, 563–570. As in other studies utilizing the St. Paul Scale, ratings on family functioning were carried out by three judges and subjected to reliability tests. In the present sample the reliability of rating categories and subcategories of social functioning with the aid of three independent judges is as follows:

	Main Categories		Subcategories	
	%	Number of Ratings	%	Number of Ratings
Three raters agreed on identical or adjacent scale positions.	93	996	92	2400
Three raters are more than one scale step apart.	7	73	8	198
	100	1069	100	2598

Because a host of studies done in recent years have shown such attributes as physical and emotional health, social adjustment, and psychosocial functioning to be class-related[17] and since our three study groups reveal sharply divergent status structures, we hold that the most meaningful way of comparing the family functioning of these ethnic groups is in terms of their social status level. In other words, their social functioning will be compared by holding class constant. The remainder of the paper is devoted to this comparison.

In an analysis with an N of 133 where the class variable is controlled, the unequal distribution of whites and nonwhites poses a problem of cell frequency attrition. To overcome this we replicated this particular cross-tabulation with comparable data available from a prior study of young metropolitan families done two years earlier. The N of this analysis is 206 composed of whites and Negroes.[18] Approximately one-third of this population were, at the time of the study, residents of the same city from which the aforementioned ethnic sample was drawn, while two-thirds lived in two nearby suburban communities with roughly 40,000 inhabitants. The earlier, like the later, sample (designated here as samples A and B) was drawn from the vital statistics registers of the communities by means of random selection. The techniques of rating family functioning and social class were identical. On other dimensions, however, the two studies did not run parallel, a fact which restricted the replication phase to an analysis of the relationship by class between ethnicity and family functioning.

Table 53–5 shows the degree of association between the aforementioned variables for status groups I to IV,[19] V, and VI. An inspection of percentage distributions shows a tendency for white families to function somewhat more adequately than the minority-group families. The trend is not completely consistent, for Negroes in the top status group (I-IV) of Sample B (N = 7) reveal somewhat greater adequacy than white families. Puerto Rican families, where included in the comparison, occupy an in-between position between whites and Negroes.

A further analysis of ethnic group differences on family functioning reveals that they are not statistically significant and probably due to chance, with one exception. Class V of Sample B, composed entirely of city families, shows differences in family functioning which are statistically significant beyond the five percent level.[20] Stated differently, we can make the following observations based on six cross-tabulations with data from two population samples: Negroes, Puerto Ricans, and whites differ slightly in the way they perform socially expected tasks, but when rated on the basis of social adequacy these differences do not permit us to conclude that ethnic group membership is a decisive factor. In the case of Class V families who reside in the city proper, a significant association between ethnicity and family functioning invites at least a tentative explanation of group differences.

An inspection of differences among the three ethnic groups in the components (categories and subcategories) of family functioning reveals[21] that Class V Negroes and Puerto Ricans in the city sample (B) evidenced more problematic behavior than whites in the family relationship area, in individual behavior and adjustment, and in source of income. No differences emerged in these areas or any others[22] for the higher status groups (I to IV) or Class VI at the bottom of the status hierarchy.

---

[17]The data of the present research sample show a correlation of (Gamma) + .65 ($X^2 = 44.05$, 6 df, p < .001) between social status and family functioning.

[18]The total number of Puerto Ricans in this earlier study was too small to justify their inclusion in the analysis.

[19]Because of the small number of Negroes and Puerto Ricans in the four top status groups, it was necessary for purposes of statistical analysis to combine the classes into one.

[20]$X^2 = 6.50$, 2 df, p < .05.

[21]Category and subcategory tables are not shown in this report but will be presented in a separate write-up.

[22]The one exception is in the area of health practices, where the top social-class whites revealed better functioning than the Negroes and Puerto Ricans. While the reason for this difference is not quite clear at this stage, a superficial perusal of interview data suggests that better preventive dental care on the part of the white families accounts for the higher ratings in health practices.

TABLE 53-5. RELATIONSHIP OF FAMILY FUNCTIONING TO ETHNICITY WITH SOCIAL CLASS HELD CONSTANT[a]

Family Functioning	White Social Class						Negro Social Class						Puerto Rican Social Class					
	I-V		V		VI		I-IV		V		VI		I-IV		V		VI	
	%	N	%	N	%	N	%	N	%	N	%	N	%	N	%	N	%	N
Sample A																		
Adequate	68.7	57	56.5	26	45.5	5	54.5	6	40.0	12	16.0	4						
Less than Adequate	31.3	26	43.5	20	54.5	6	45.5	5	60.0	18	84.0	21						
Total	100.0	83	100.0	46	100.0	11	100.0	11	100.0	30	100.0	25						
Sample B																		
Adequate	50.0	10	40.8	11	33.1	1	57.1	4	8.7	2	0	0	42.9	3	27.3	3	6.7	1
Less than Adequate	50.0	10	59.2	16	66.7	2	42.9	3	91.3	21	100.0	17	57.1	4	72.7	8	93.3	14
Total	100.0	20	100.0	27	100.0	3	100.0	7	100.0	23	100.0	17	100.0	7	100.0	11	100.0	15

[a]Chi-square values for ethnic differences do not reach the five percent level of significance except for Class V in sample B ($x^2 = 6.50$, 2 df, $p < .05$). Where the Chi-square tests on the original computer printout failed to meet all the requirements for the use of the test but the value was nonsignificant, the decision was made to accept the results of the test, since the more conservative Fisher Exact Test would not have altered the findings. See Hubert M. Blalock, Social Statistics, New York: McGraw-Hill Book Co., 1960, 224-225.

⸼ Class I-IV is constituted of middle-class families whose heads are fully employed in skilled blue-collar or white-collar occupations. These families share the American middle-class culture, which, judging by the lack of differences in social functioning, has a homogenizing effect. Class VI on the modified Hollingshead Scale is composed of families headed by unskilled laborers often with an unsteady employment record, the unemployed, and men and women receiving public assistance. Being part of the bottom-of-the-social-barrel group may likewise have the effect of imposing a class pattern of family behavior.

Class V by contrast is made up, to a large extent, of semiskilled workers with marginal incomes and non-tenure jobs. This is the group in which, because of discriminatory employment practices, whites have been enjoying an economic advantage over Negroes and Puerto Ricans. That advantage might be reflected in the differentials in overall social functioning. The absence of significant differences in social functioning among Class V families in Sample A (the mixed suburban and city sample), however, might be explained[23] as the result of a leveling effect of suburban living on the behavior of Class V families.

To argue, as we did earlier, that economic factors may account largely for differences in family functioning of Class V families in the city may at first glance seem farfetched in an analysis in which class was held constant. Vis-à-vis this argument it is worth recalling that Hollingshead's Index of Social Position constitutes only a broad categorization which combines educational and occupational factors. The respective status strata comprise a fair range of job opportunities and situations which might serve as partial determinants of various aspects of family behavior. In the economically marginal Class V, the consequences of occupational differences on family behavior may well be greater than in the higher- and lower-status groups.

Table 53–5 and findings from previous studies,[24] all of which showed a clear relationship between social status and family functioning, do suggest a nexus between economic situation and social functioning. Yet the lack of a consistent regression between status and social functioning and the relative adequacy in functioning of the economically disadvantaged Puerto Rican group suggest caution in interpreting the relationship between economic status and family functioning. Data on the occupational status of the three ethnic groups provide at least a clue about factors which may be intervening between economic situation and family functioning.[25]

The data analysis shows that 82 percent of the whites, 73 percent of the Puerto Ricans, but only 44 percent of the Negroes in the sample had a more or less steady source of income sufficient to their families' needs. This observation must be viewed against the fact that a status classification of jobs held by the heads of households in this study (using the Hollingshead occupational classification derived from his Two-Factor Index of Social Position) revealed that Negro and Puerto Rican wage earners held lower status jobs than whites (the mean indices were Negroes 3.62, Puerto Ricans 3.18, whites 2.26)[26] but that the occupational status difference between whites and Puerto Ricans was more than twice that between Puerto Ricans and Negroes.[27]

These figures suggest that, in spite of limited job opportunity and the necessity to accept low-status jobs, the Puerton Rican head of the family has less difficulty in holding a job than the Negro family head. As a possible explanation

---

[23]The small sample size precludes a separate analysis of city and suburban ethnic groups with class held constant. The fact that Negroes are greatly underrepresented in the higher- and whites are underrepresented in the lower-status groups constitutes the main barrier to such an analysis.

[24]Geismar and Krisberg, *op. cit.*, p. 568; Walda Ciafone, Florence Bernstein, *et al.*, *Relationship of Family Functioning to Anomie, Social Class and Other Related Factors,* unpublished M.S.W. thesis, Graduate School of Social Work, New Brunswick, N.J.: Rutgers University, June, 1963.

[25]The relatively small N's of the ethnic groups did not permit the specific cross-tabulations required for a thorough analysis of this issue.

[26]The higher the Index number, the lower the occupational status.

[27]A higher ratio of female heads of families among Negroes than among Puerto Ricans and whites accounts largely for the low occupational position of the Negroes. When we discount the occupational status of the mothers who are unskilled and do not work, Puerto Ricans and the Negroes occupy a similar position on the status scale.

we advance the argument that the former, a recent newcomer to the mainland United States, may have lower job expectations and perhaps lower expectations for standard of living in general than does the Negro head of the family, who has had a long exposure to the frustrating conditions which pervade his economic and social life in America.

INTERPRETATION

While ethnic samples ranging from 33 to 140 may not be impressive in size, their representativeness based on random selection lends strength to the findings. In generalizing on the basis of the foregoing data, it is well to remember that our universe of study is composed of young, urban families which, at the time of the interview, had only one dependent child.

Findings in this family study are at variance with some others which compared American whites and nonwhites (generally Negroes) on such variables as family structure and family stability.[28] Our own study, in contrast to those cited below, suggests that controlling for socioeconomic factors comes reasonably close to eliminating variances attributable to race. While we cannot dismiss the possibility that the limited representativeness of our study sample could account for the differences in findings, we tend to advance the more cogent argument that the crude structural census variables, which yield relatively little information on the families' ability to socialize the young, are more subject to variation from group to group than the variable "family functioning." Divorce and remarriage in particular are indices which are strongly affected by state laws, religion, ethnic traditions, and other factors. A significant conclusion to be drawn from the array of data assembled here is that social class is a more powerful influence than ethnicity in determining social functioning. The fact that family behavior of Negroes, Puerto Ricans, and whites in both the top and bottom strata of the status hierarchy shows a reasonably close resemblance within each group suggests

that social class acts as a great leveler. The leveling process is incomplete in Class V, although here differences among the ethnic groups are of a much lower magnitude than in a cross-tabulation of family functioning and ethnicity when class is not held constant. It seems safe to assume that differentials in economic opportunity among the ethnic groups studied may account at least in part for differences in their social functioning. The present analysis, nonetheless, points to factors other than economic opportunity as being related to differentials in family functioning.

The preceding analysis would suggest that it is the delicate interplay among social, economic, and psychological factors rather than the operation of any one of them which determines the social functioning of families in various ethnic groups. Within the context of our data, it is not economic opportunity alone but a group's response to such opportunity or lack of it, level of job expectation, etc. which affect families' ability to carry out their socially expected roles.

Any attempt to change social functioning patterns must address itself to the broad constellation of factors which serve to explain a given situation. It is improbable that major changes in any one of them can be effected without a simultaneous change in related factors.

The interconnectedness of the social status of the three ethnic groups and their families' functioning has become evident in this study. Migration patterns are likely to have a bearing on the families' ability to perform social roles. Certain social and psychological factors which appear to modify the relationship between social functioning and socioeconomic class can only be dealt with as change attempts are addressed to the existing class structure.

In returning to the issues raised by the Moynihan Report, we concede that this research did yield some direct evidence—by the study of families' social functioning—that the Negro family is handicapped in its ability to provide a home and socialize the young. However, that handicap is above all a function of socioeconomic position as evidenced by the fact that, in most strata of the social status hierarchy, Negroes are not functioning differently at a significant level from Puerto Ricans and whites. This means that the

[28]Bernard, *op. cit.*; J. Richard Udry, "Marital Instability by Race, Sex, Education and Occupation Using 1960 Census Data," *American Journal of Sociology*, September, 1966, 72:2, 203–209.

quality of family life, patterns of child socialization, economic functioning, personal and social deviancy, etc. were simply distributed among the ethnic groups in most class strata and differed radically only between class levels.

In the light of these observations, one may question whether strengthening the Negro family really gets at the heart of the problem of the Negro. To the contrary, our data suggest that the problems of the Negro family need to be viewed and treated within the context of the Negro's problematic position in society. Such an approach calls for massive action in the areas of jobs, education, housing, and civil rights. To the extent that characteristics of the Negro family may stand in the way of behavior changes to be affected by modifications in the social structure, these characteristics also need to become the focus of intervention.

To make the Negro family a special target of social action separate from a massive attack upon the socioeconomic structure of American society would be an exercise in futility similar to the war on poverty. Their common effect can only be to divert attention from the basic problems of the total American society and select a course designed to push palliatives rather than basic solutions. The unintended effect on the minorities—both the poor and the Negro— is their stigmatization, which can only serve to delay finding a solution to their problems and defer their integration into a larger society.

CHAPTER **XIII**

Stability of Marriage

I N CHAPTER VI, Courtship and Mate Selection, emphasis was given to who marries whom, and under what circumstances. This chapter deals with the factors which are associated with stability of marriage. Instability of marriage, or marriages that end in separation or divorce, are considered a social problem by the society. In American society we have come to accept the fact that a relatively large proportion of marriages will end in divorce and the stigma that was once associated with divorce has disappeared to a considerable extent. The large majority of Protestant clergy in America feel that divorce is preferable to unhappy marriages. The Catholic church still does not recognize divorce as a satisfactory means of resolving marital conflict, but even within Catholicism there is some evidence of pressures to change the official church position.

Even though divorce is more widely accepted today, the fact of the matter is that divorces involve serious problems of adjustment and dislocation in social relationships. As is well-known, it is relatively easy to get married in American society, but considerably more difficult to get divorced. While marriage is a relatively inexpensive proposition, divorce seldom is. Divorce involves many problems directly, such as the division of assets, decision on who will accept what kinds of responsibilities for the raising of children, provision for support of the children and the mother, alimony, reorientation, development of new social interests, and so forth. Even when divorce is a mutual decision, it almost never occurs without a great deal of frustration, alienation, bitterness and disruption of established behavioral patterns. For many people, divorce so basically disrupts their lives as to require months or even years before they are able to function as "normal" human beings.

Here we excerpt from a recent government publication prepared by Alexander A. Plateris titled "Divorce Statistics Analysis." This report presents an enormous amount of factual data on divorce. Study of these statistics may provide an indication of longer range trends. The statistics are sobering and implicitly, at least, raise many questions about courtship, mate selection and the process of establishing families in American society.

If one is asked what the most common reason is for divorce, the answer may come in legal terms like "mental cruelty." Such a concept communicates little of what the sources of discord were for the couples. In his article titled "Sources of Marital Dissatisfaction Among Applicants for Divorce," George Levinger compares marital complaints of husbands and wives for middle class and lower class marriages. Differences are found according to the social class, and as might be expected, husbands and wives do not have the same complaints.

In another article titled "Marital Cohesiveness and Dissolution: An Integrative Review," George Levinger presents a conceptual framework for analyzing marriage relationships. He suggests that the strength of the relationship for a married couple is related to social and psychological attraction and barrier forces inside the marriage, and inversely related to such influences when directed outside the married pair. Cohesiveness is a central concept in this analysis, which stresses "a group dynamics" orientation.

Many analyses that appear to be directed toward particular aspects of marriage are found to give simultaneous attention to divorce and instability of marriage. For example, a recent article on characteristics of young marriages notes in detail factors associated with "poor risk" for young marriages, including low socioeconomic status, limited education, meager economic basis, requirements for continued parental support, premarital pregnancy, and so forth. (Burchinal, Lee G., "Trends and Prospects for Young Marriages in the United States," *Journal of Marriage and the Family*, 1965, 27, 243–254.)

Another concern with stability of marriage is what happens after divorce. A recent article inventoried many of the concomitants, a few of which may be mentioned here. Of divorced women in early adulthood (say, under 30), almost all will remarry. About two-thirds of all women who get divorced and three-fourths of the men will eventually remarry. Rates of remarriage are higher among lower educated than among higher educated groups. Remarriage usually occurs within a short time after divorce, the median time lapse between divorce and remarriage being 2.7 years. Remarriages are more apt to end in divorce than first marriages.

While remarriage presents some problems for children, the balance of the evidence indicates that children in remarriages are not different from children in stable marriages. (Greater detail and references may be found in Schlesinger, Benjamin, "Remarriage—An Inventory of Findings," *The Family Coordinator,* 1968, 248–250.)

54.

ALEXANDER A. PLATERIS

THE STATISTICS OF DIVORCE

INTRODUCTION

FAMILY FORMATION AND DISSOLUTION

During the year 1963, 428,000 divorces and annulments were granted in the United States (2.3 per 1000 total population, or 9.6 per 1000 married women 15 years of age and over). Because some families were disrupted by the death of one spouse, these figures represent only a part of all family dissolutions that took place during the year. The total number of all family

judicial decree, and 19.7 percent to the death of the wife.

As shown in Figure 54–1, the total number of family dissolutions during 1963 (1,278,112) was smaller than that of new families established during the same period of time (1,654,000). This represents an increase of 375,888 in the total number of married couples. These figures are limited to family formation and dissolution that occurred within the United States and do not include couples that migrated to the United

TABLE 54–1. FAMILY FORMATION AND DISSOLUTION: UNITED STATES, 1940, 1949-51, and 1959-63.

		Family dissolution					
			Deaths of married persons			Divorces and annul- ments	Net increase in married couples
Year of occurrence	Marriages	Total	All deaths	Husbands	Wives		
1963	1,654,000	1,278,112	850,112	597,814	252,298	428,000	375,888
1962	1,577,000	1,235,099	822,099	576,277	245,822	413,000	341,901
1961	1,548,000	1,210,533	796,533	559,038	237,495	414,000	337,467
1960	1,523,000	1,190,769	797,769	558,801	238,968	393,000	332,231
1959	1,494,000	1,164,218	769,218	536,671	232,547	395,000	329,782
1951	1,594,694	1,066,800	685,800	464,105	221,695	381,000	527,894
1950	1,667,231	1,058,615	673,471	453,656	219,815	385,144	608,616
1949	1,579,798	1,059,987	662,987	443,573	219,414	397,000	519,811
1940	1,595,879	900,465	636,465	406,240	230,225	264,000	695,414

Data refer only to events occurring within the United States. Data on international migration are not included. Deaths of married persons include numbers published in sources listed in the appendix that have been adjusted by distributing proportionally the deaths of persons with marital status not stated.

dissolutions due to death was 850,112 in 1963 —597,814 by the death of the husband and 252-298 by the death of the wife (Table 54–1). Thus out of a total of 1,278,112 family dissolutions that occurred in 1963, 46.8 percent were due to the death of the husband, 33.5 percent to a

States; hence, the total increase in married couples was larger than 375,888. . . .

MEASURES OF FAMILY FORMATION AND DISSOLUTION

A set of comparable rates, all based on the same population and presenting a much clearer picture of the incidence of family formation and dissolution than rates computed using different populations, are shown in Table 54–2. Inasmuch as accurate data are not available for the population at risk—the population of all married

This selection is reprinted from: Alexander A. Plateris, *Divorce Statistics Analysis (United States— 1963)* (Vital and Health Statistics, Series 21, #13), Washington, D. C.; GPO: U. S. Department of Health, Education, and Welfare, October, 1967 [excerpted from pp. 1–40].

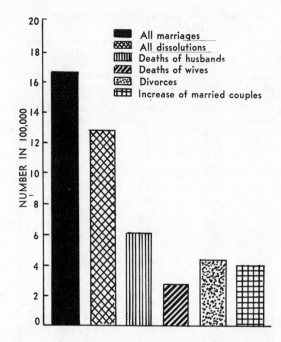

FIGURE 54-1. FAMILY FORMATION AND DISSOLUTION.

TABLE 54-2. RATES OF FAMILY FORMATION AND DISSOLUTION PER 1000 MARRIED MEN AND WOMEN: UNITED STATES, 1963.

Type of rate	Men	Women
	\textit{Rate per 1000 married persons}	
Marriage rate—rate of gross increase of married population	38.0	37.3
Total dissolution rate	29.2	28.6
Death rate of married population	19.4	19.0
Of husbands	13.6	13.3
Of wives	5.8	5.7
Divorce rate	9.8	9.6
Rate of growth of the married population	8.8	8.6

Data refer only to events occurring within the United States.

couples—the estimated numbers of married women were used as approximations.[1] (Na-

[1] Population bases given in Table 1 of U.S. Bureau of the Census. "Marital Status and Family Status, March 1964 and 1963," *Current Population Reports*, Series P-20, No. 135, Washington, D.C., April, 1965.

tional divorce rates per 1000 married women 15 years and over, which have been computed routinely, are shown in Table 54-3 for the years 1920 through 1963.)

TOTALS AND RATES

THE NATIONAL DIVORCE TREND

The national divorce total of 428,000 for 1963 was the highest annual number ever observed, except for the years 1945-47 when the post-World War II divorce peak occurred. The 1963 total represents an increase of 3.6 percent over the figure for 1962 and an increase of 8.9 percent over that for 1960. The 1963 divorce rate of 2.3 per 1000 population was much lower than that for the early postwar years, when the maximum rate of 4.3 was observed in 1946. The 1963 rate is close to the levels observed since 1955.

The trend of the divorce rate since 1867, the first year for which this rate was computed, showed a long-term increase that lasted 80 years, reaching a record peak in 1946. During this period, the rate increased from 0.3 to 4.3 per 1000 total population. The trend was accelerated by wars and reversed by economic depressions. During the 44 years shown in Table 54-3 and Figure 54-2, the rate first declined from the slight post-World War I peak, then resumed its upward trend (which was interrupted by the great depression), and almost doubled during the war and early postwar years—from 2.2 in 1941 to 4.3 in 1946. It declined rapidly afterwards, going back to 2.2 in 1957; since then it has remained approximately at the same level. At the present moment it is too early to say whether the slight increases of the rate found in 1961 and 1963 indicate the beginning of a new period of growth, but the provisional estimates of the national divorce totals for 1964 and 1965 (445,000 and 481,000, respectively, or 2.3 and 2.5 per 1000 population) suggest that the upward trend may have resumed.

The crude divorce rate, computed for the total population, depends in part on the proportion of married persons in the population, as married persons only are subject to the risk of divorce. Therefore the divorce rate per 1000 married women is a more refined measure of

TABLE 54–3. ESTIMATED NUMBER OF DIVORCES AND ANNULMENTS AND RATES, WITH PERCENT CHANGES FROM PRECEDING YEAR: UNITED STATES, 1920-63.

Year	Number	Percent change in number	Rate per 1000 total population*	Percent change in rate	Rate per 1000 married female population 15+ yrs.†	Percent change in rate
1963	428,000	+3.6	2.3	+4.5	9.6	+2.1
1962	413,000	-0.2	2.2	-4.3	9.4	-2.1
1961	414,000	+5.3	2.3	+4.5	9.6	+4.3
1960	393,000	-0.5	2.2	...	9.2	-1.1
1959	395,000	+7.3	2.2	+4.8	9.3	+4.5
1958	368,000	-3.4	2.1	-4.5	8.9	-3.3
1957	381,000	-0.3	2.2	-4.3	9.2	-2.1
1956	382,000	+1.3	2.3	...	9.4	+1.1
1955	377,000	-0.5	2.3	-4.2	9.3	-2.1
1954	379,000	-2.8	2.4	-4.0	9.5	-4.0
1953	390,000	-0.5	2.5	...	9.9	-2.0
1952	392,000	+2.9	2.5	...	10.1	+2.0
1951	381,000	-1.1	2.5	-3.8	9.9	-3.9
1950	385,144	-3.0	2.6	-3.7	10.3	-2.8
1949	397,000	-2.7	2.7	-3.6	10.6	-5.4
1948	408,000	-15.5	2.8	-17.6	11.2	-17.6
1947	483,000	-20.8	3.4	-20.9	13.6	-24.0
1946	610,000	+25.8	4.3	+22.9	17.9	+24.3
1945	485,000	+21.3	3.5	+20.7	14.4	+20.0
1944	400,000	+11.4	2.9	+11.5	12.0	+9.1
1943	359,000	+11.8	2.6	+8.3	11.0	+8.9
1942	321,000	+9.6	2.4	+9.1	10.1	+7.4
1941	293,000	+11.0	2.2	+10.0	9.4	+6.8
1940	264,000	+5.2	2.0	+5.3	8.8	+3.5
1939	251,000	+2.9	1.9	...	8.5	+1.2
1938	244,000	-2.0	1.9	...	8.4	-3.4
1937	249,000	+5.5	1.9	+5.6	8.7	+4.8
1936	236,000	+8.3	1.8	+5.9	8.3	+6.4
1935	218,000	+6.9	1.7	+6.3	7.8	+4.0
1934	204,000	+23.6	1.6	+23.1	7.5	+23.0
1933	165,000	+0.6	1.3		6.1	...
1932	164,241	-12.6	1.3	-13.3	6.1	-14.1
1931	188,003	-4.1	1.5	-6.2	7.1	-5.3
1930	195,961	-4.8	1.6	-5.9	7.5	-6.2
1929	205,876	+2.8	1.7	...	8.0	+2.6
1928	200,176	+2.0	1.7	+6.3	7.8	
1927	196,292	+6.3	1.6	...	7.8	+4.0
1926	184,678	+5.3	1.6	+6.7	7.5	+4.2
1925	175,449	+2.6	1.5	...	7.2	...
1924	170,952	+3.5	1.5	...	7.2	+1.4
1923	165,096	+10.9	1.5	+7.1	7.1	+7.6
1922	148,815	-6.7	1.4	-6.7	6.6	-8.3
1921	159,580	-6.4	1.5	-6.2	7.2	-10.0
1920	170,505	+20.5	1.6	+23.1	8.0	...

*Population enumerated as of April 1 for 1940, 1950, and 1960 and estimated as of July 1 for all other years; includes armed forces abroad for 1941-46.
†Population enumerated as of January 1 for 1920 and as of April 1 for 1930, 1940, 1950, and 1960 and estimated as of July 1 for all other years.
Data refer only to events occurring within the United States. Includes Alaska beginning 1959, and Hawaii, 1960.

the incidence of divorce. The divorce rate per 1000 married women was 9.6 in 1963—slightly higher than the 1962 rate of 9.4, equal to the 1961 rate, and higher than the rates for all years from 1954 to 1960. These differences indicate that the increase in the number of divorces was

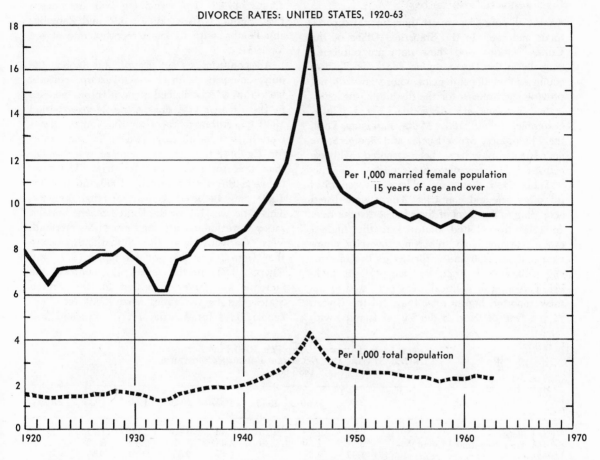

FIGURE 54–2. DIVORCE RATES: UNITED STATES, 1920-63.

partially due to reasons other than the growth of the married population. This statement can also be illustrated by ratios of the population to divorce: in 1963 a divorce was granted to one of every 104 married women, in 1962 to one of every 106, and in 1960 to one of every 109.

Inasmuch as the number of persons divorced is twice the number of divorces granted, 856,000 persons were divorced in 1963. In addition, 583,000 children of divorced couples were involved in divorce cases. This brings the total number of persons involved in divorce to 1,439,000. The involvement rate was 7.6 per 1000 population. Analogous figures for other years are shown in Table 54–4.

TABLE 54–4. NUMBER OF HUSBANDS, WIVES, AND CHILDREN INVOLVED IN DIVORCE AND RATES PER 1000 TOTAL POPULATION, WITH PERCENT CHANGE FROM PRECEDING YEAR: UNITED STATES, 1953-63.

Year	Total involved	Percent change	Rate
1963	1,439,000	+5.6	7.6
1962	1,363,000	+2.6	7.3
1961	1,329,000	+6.4	7.3
1960	1,249,000	−0.7	7.0
1959	1,258,000	+10.9	7.1
1958	1,134,000	−0.6	6.5
1957	1,141,000	+1.4	6.7
1956	1,125,000	+2.2	6.7
1955	1,101,000	+0.2	6.7
1954	1,099,000	−1.0	6.8
1953	1,110,000	...	7.0

INTERNATIONAL COMPARISONS

Almost all countries report their annual divorce totals and rates to the Statistical Office of the United Nations, and these data are published annually in the *Demographic Yearbook.* Twelve countries and dependencies whose laws do not provide legal means for the dissolution of legitimate marriages are Argentina, Brazil, Chile, Colombia, Ireland, Italy, Malta, Paraguay, Peru, the Philippines, Santa Lucia, and Spain. Some annulments may have been granted in these countries, but they were not reported.

Table 54-5 shows the official divorce rates for other selected countries. These were listed according to the level of their latest divorce rate. In 1963 the United States had the highest crude rate among the reporting sovereign countries, but in 1960 and earlier years the rate for the United Arab Republic (Egypt) was highest. Three minor political areas not listed in the table reported higher rates than did the United States. One of them is the Virgin Islands, with

a rate of 4.3. The remaining two areas were East Berlin, with a rate of 3.0, and Zanzibar and Pemba, with its latest reported rate of 4.4 for 1957.

All countries except Egypt and Japan, the only countries with a non-Western cultural background, experienced a considerable increase in the divorce rate during the 34-year period 1930-63. Although rates for the United States were highest for all years (except for some rates for Egypt), the relative increase was smaller than that for most other countries. The ratio between the divorce rate for 1963 and that for 1930 may be used to measure this increase. This ratio was 1.4 for the United States. Smaller ratios were found only for France, Switzerland, West Germany, and the Netherlands, where they were 1.3 or 1.4, and for Japan (0.9) and Egypt (0.8). In the remaining countries, the increase was larger than that for the United States—the largest ratios were 25.0 for Venezuela, 11.4 for Austria, 7.4 for England and

TABLE 54-5. DIVORCE RATES PER 1000 POPULATION:
UNITED STATES AND SELECTED FOREIGN COUNTRIES,
1930-63.

Country	1963	1960	1955	1950	1945	1940	1935	1930
United States	2.27	2.18	2.29	2.55	3.66	2.00	1.71	1.59
United Arab Republic (Egypt)[a]	[b]2.11	2.50	2.39	2.95	3.45	2.44	2.80	...
Romania	1.92	2.01	1.80	1.47	0.89	0.59	0.50	0.38
Hungary	1.82	1.66	1.63	1.21	0.22	0.50	0.63	0.64
Denmark	1.38	1.46	1.53	1.61	1.45	0.91	0.81	0.65
East Germany[c]	1.33	1.34	1.35	2.47	...	0.75	0.75	0.63
U.S.S.R.	1.3	1.3	...	...	...	...	...	...
Czechoslovakia	1.22	1.12	1.05	1.06	0.71	0.61	0.50	0.40
Austria	1.14	1.13	1.29	1.52	0.67	0.93	0.11	0.10
Sweden	1.12	1.20	1.21	1.14	0.97	0.55	0.44	0.36
West Germany[c]	0.84	0.83	0.85	1.57	...	0.75	0.75	0.63
Switzerland	0.82	0.87	0.89	0.90	0.84	0.73	0.73	0.67
Japan	0.73	0.74	0.85	1.01	...	0.67	0.70	0.79
Australia	0.68	0.65	0.73	0.90	0.97	0.46	0.36	0.28
England and Wales	0.67	0.51	0.59	0.69	0.36	0.18	0.10	0.09
France	0.63	0.66	0.67	0.85	0.62	0.28	0.51	0.49
Belgium	0.56	0.50	0.50	0.59	0.38	0.22	0.31	0.31
Mexico	0.50	0.43	0.41	0.31	0.43	0.22	0.24	0.10
Netherlands	0.49	0.49	0.51	0.64	0.50	0.33	0.35	0.36
Scotland	0.42	0.35	0.40	0.42	0.43	0.15	0.10	0.10
Canada[d]	0.41	0.39	0.38	0.39	0.42	0.21	0.13	0.08
Venezuela	0.25	0.25	0.18	0.14	0.15	0.09	0.04	0.01

[a]Beginning with 1955, data include revocable divorces among the Moslem population, which approximate legal separations.
[b]Provisional.
[c]Rates for 1930, 1935, and 1940 refer to Germany as a whole.
[d]Prior to 1950 excludes Newfoundland.
Based on the Demographic Yearbook of the United Nations, 1958, 1961, 1964, and 1965.

Wales, 5.1 in both Canada and Romania, and 5.0 for Mexico. From the available data, it is impossible to estimate how much of the change is due to a higher incidence of divorces and how much to improved registration practices in some of the reporting countries. Changes in crude rates may also reflect differences in age structure and marital status of the population.

Most of the reporting countries experienced a sharp increase of the divorce rate during or immediately after World War II. Afterwards, the rate declined in the United States and several other countries but continued to grow in others. This postwar growth was particularly pronounced in Hungary and Romania.

It is difficult to find an explanation for the differences in the divorce rates among various countries, except that most Communist countries have comparatively high rates. The usual explanations, such as differences in religion or in urbanization, do not seem to apply. It is particularly interesting to compare the United States and Canada, because Canada has always had one of the lowest rates listed in the *Demographic Yearbook* despite geographic proximity and cultural similarity. On the other hand, the Canadian rate grew much more rapidly than the American rate. In 1930 the ratio between the two rates was 19.9, but by 1963 it had declined to 5.5.

DIVORCES BY REGION, DIVISION, AND STATE

Variation in the incidence of divorce was more pronounced within the United States than among the other countries. In 1963 the rate for the United States (2.3 per 1000 population) was about nine times as high as the lowest rate (0.25 for Venezuela), but in the same year the rate for Nevada was 62 times as high as that for New York. The differences between the states were due in part to variations in the permissiveness of the divorce laws and to the concentration of migratory divorces (those granted to persons who came to the state solely for the purpose of obtaining a divorce decree rapidly). However, comparatively high divorce rates were also found in states where few if any migratory divorces occurred. It was observed before the beginning of this century that the divorce rate tended to increase from East to

West;[2] this generalization still holds. In 1963 the divorce rate was 0.9 for the Northeast, 2.2 for the North Central, 2.8 for the South, and 3.6 for the West. The rate for the West was approximately four times as high as that for the Northeast. . . .

MIGRATORY DIVORCES

Migratory divorces are divorce decrees obtained outside the usual state of residence of the parties in places where divorce laws are particularly permissive and/or judges interpret these laws to the advantage of the seekers of speedy divorce. Such places are often referred to as "divorce mills." Typically, the plaintiff moves to a divorce-mill state for the minimum period of time required to establish legal residence and to come under the jurisdiction of courts of that state, then leaves as soon as the decree is rendered, and, presumably, returns to his or her earlier state of residence.

Migratory divorces should be distinguished from divorces of migrants, i.e., divorces of people who migrate and obtain a decree in their new place of permanent residence. In the case of migratory divorce, the residence established in the divorce-mill state is a legal fiction necessary for taking advantage of the permissive divorce laws, while in the case of divorcing migrants, the plaintiffs honestly intend to live indefinitely in their new state of residence.

Migratory divorces should also be distinguished from those obtained outside the county of usual residence of the plaintiff but in his state of residence. Some persons may wish to be divorced where they are not known or may have other reasons for filing the divorce petition in another county. Such moves may result in the concentration of divorces in particular counties. These divorces are not considered migratory as long as the plaintiff does not cross a state line in order to obtain the decree.

The opinion is often expressed that low divorce rates in many Eastern states with strict divorce laws are due to large numbers of Easterners obtaining divorces in divorce mills and that variations among state rates would be much less pronounced if rates were computed by

[2]Wilcox, Walter F. *The Divorce Problem* (New York: Columbia University Press, 1897), 37-38, 42.

usual residence rather than by place of occurrence. In order to explore such possibilities, estimates of the numbers of migratory divorces have been prepared.

These estimates were based on variations among county divorce rates in states where the existence of divorce mills seemed likely. These states are characterized by permissive legal grounds for divorce, by short periods required to establish legal residence, and by the availability of various services useful to the divorce seekers. County rates were computed for states that possessed these characteristics, and one entire state and 26 counties in four other states were identified as probable divorce mills. Then divorces of the permanent residents of these areas were estimated and subtracted from the totals. . . . Because the method [of estimation] is based on divorce rates by counties, estimates were prepared only for 1960, a year for which county population figures were available from the census enumeration.

Altogether, 19,000 migratory divorces were estimated to have occurred in the United States in 1960. This is 4.8 percent of the national divorce total, or 0.1 per 1000 population (Table 54–6). Even if it were assumed that migratory divorces are underestimated by 100 percent, their number would be less than ten percent of the national total. However, there is no reason to believe that they have been substantially underestimated, particularly in view of the inclu-

sion of several marginal counties among the presumptive divorce mills. Some migratory divorces are granted to Americans in Mexico and in other foreign countries. These were not included in the estimate.

The comparative insignificance of the number of migratory divorces granted in the United States in 1960 can best be visualized when compared with divorces occurring in states from which, presumably, large numbers of divorce seekers come. If it is assumed that all migratory divorces that were granted in 1960 were exclusively to residents of New York, then the crude resident divorce rate for that state would have increased to 1.6 and still would have been considerably below the national rate of 2.2. Since many migratory divorces were granted to residents of states other than New York, the resident divorce rate for that state had to be much lower than 1.6. On the other hand, if it is assumed that all migratory divorces granted in Nevada were obtained exclusively by residents of California, then the resident rate for that state would have been 3.6 as compared with the observed rate of 3.1. Hence, the resident divorce rate for California, though above 3.1, was considerably below 3.6.

These figures indicate that the incidence of migratory divorce in 1960 was not as large as it is widely believed to be. Migratory divorces may have declined since 1960, as the state authorities and the Bar Association of Alabama

TABLE 54–6. TOTAL, RESIDENT, AND MIGRATORY DIVORCES AND RATES: UNITED STATES AND FIVE SELECTED STATES, 1960.

		All divorces		Estimated resident divorce		Estimated migratory divorce	
Area	Population	Number	Rate	Number	Rate*	Number	Rate
United States	179,323,175	393,000	2.2	374,000	2.1	19,000	0.1
Percentages	...	100.0	...	95.2	...	4.8	...
Total	1,338,740	23,307	17.4	4,082	3.0	19,225	14.4
Alabama, 8 counties	255,124	9,122	35.8	689	2.7	8,433	33.1
Arkansas, 8 counties	472,303	2,533	5.4	1,275	2.7	1,258	2.7
Florida, 7 counties	259,869	2,532	9.7	936	3.6	1,596	6.1
Idaho, 3 counties	66,166	665	10.1	212	3.2	453	6.9
Nevada, the state	285,278	8,455	29.6	970	3.4	7,485	26.2

*Estimated rates for resident divorces are rates for combined counties outside the divorce-mill areas for Alabama, Arkansas, Florida, and Idaho, and rate for the West region for Nevada.
Rates are per 1000 total population in area. For estimating methods, see appendix.

took action against unconstitutional granting of migratory divorce in that state. Following this action, the total number of divorces granted in Alabama declined from 17,320 in 1960 to 12,566 in 1963, a decline of 4,754 (or 27.4 percent), and the annual divorce rate declined from 5.3 to 3.7. However, it should be pointed out that the number of divorces in other states with divorce mills increased during the same period, but no information is available as to whether the increases were largely among migratory divorces.

ANNULMENTS

Divorce statistics shown in this report refer to absolute divorces and to annulments and exclude various limited matrimonial decrees such as divorces from bed and board, limited divorces, legal separations, decrees of separate maintenance, and others. The national total for 1963 included 12,701 reported annulments, which was 3.0 percent of the absolute divorces and annulments combined. These figures were incomplete because Idaho, Massachusetts, and Missouri failed to report divorces and annulments separately. The number of annulments granted in these three states is usually small; it was 229 in 1962 and 204 in 1961. In addition, for a small number of decrees reported by other states, it was not stated whether they were absolute divorces or whether they were annulments.

The number of annulments granted in most states was small—0 in Vermont, less than 100 in 31 states and the District of Columbia, and between 100 and 1000 in 13 states. California and New York were the only two states that reported more than 1000 annulments.

The 1963 annulment total for California was 6134 as compared with 5984 in 1962 and 5643 in 1961. The figure for 1963 represented 10.9 percent of all divorces and annulments granted in the state and almost one-half of all annulments reported in the United States. For New York 2284 annulments were estimated, 36.2 percent of the combined annual total of divorces and annulments for that state and 18.0 percent of the national annulment total. The annulment figures reported for past years from New York were 2331 in 1962 and 2310 in 1961. As in

prior years, about two-thirds of all annulments reported for 1963 were granted in California and New York.

DETAILED DIVORCE STATISTICS

Annual divorce and annulment totals were received from all states, even though some figures were incomplete or estimated, but detailed statistical information was limited to the 22 states included in the divorce-registration area (DRA). . . .

REPORTING OF AGE

Despite the importance of data on age, the reporting of this item was very incomplete. Information on age of the parties to divorce, their dates of birth, or both, is required from all registration states, but these items are often left blank on the certificates. For the entire DRA age was reported in 54 percent of cases, and only six states had a satisfactory level of completeness: Hawaii, Iowa, Missouri, Rhode Island, Tennessee, and Wisconsin. All of these states reported age on 93 percent or more of their divorce certificates. At the opposite extreme, four states reported age on less than ten percent of the certificates.

DISTRIBUTION OF AGE AT DECREE

The percent distribution of divorces and annulments by age of husband and of wife at time of decree was prepared only for the six states that reported this item with a high degree of completeness. The data indicate that at time of divorce the modal five-year age group was 25-29 years for husbands and 20-24 years for wives. These modal values held for all of these states except Hawaii, where the peak age group was 30-34 years for husbands. In general, approximately one-half of all divorces were granted to men and women between the ages of 20 and 35.

In the six states combined, teenagers represented 2.0 percent of the divorced husbands and 7.7 of the divorced wives; however, among the states the figures varied from 0.2 and 2.8 percent in Rhode Island to 2.5 and 9.2 percent in Missouri.

When the peak divorce age was passed, the

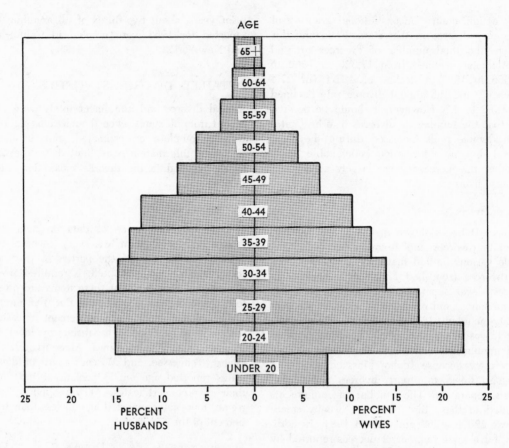

FIGURE 54–3. PERCENT OF DIVORCES AND ANNULMENTS, BY AGE OF HUSBAND AND OF WIFE AT TIME OF DECREE: TOTAL OF SIX SELECTED STATES, 1963.

percentages declined gradually and fairly consistently (Figure 54–3). The oldest age group (65 years and over) included 2.2 percent of husbands and 0.9 of wives in the six states.

The median age at decree in all registration states combined was 34.8 years for husbands and 31.3 years for wives as compared with 34.5 and 31.0 years, respectively, in 1962. For individual states the 1963 medians varied between a minimum of 31.5 and 26.4 years in Wyoming and a maximum of 37.0 and 33.5 years in Ohio. From 1962 to 1963 the median age of husbands increased in eight states and declined in 13; for wives it increased in ten states and declined in ten; and in one state the median did not change. . . .

DURATION OF MARRIAGE

REPORTING AND DEFINITION

The duration of marriage at time of decree was computed by subtracting month and year of marriage from month and year of divorce. When only the year of marriage was given on the divorce record it was assumed that the marriage occurred at the midpoint of the year. Information about the time of marriage is required in all registration states and is almost always reported. For the DRA information about duration of marriage was available for 97.1 percent of divorces granted in 1963, and this percentage was below 85 in two states only.

The time that elapses between marriage and

divorce comprises three distinct periods: (1) the period between marriage and final separation of the couple (there may have been earlier separations followed by reconciliations, but the important date is that when husband and wife ceased for the last time to live in the same household); (2) the time between separation and filing the petition for divorce, and (3) the time between filing the petition and the decree. The family functions as a social unit only during the first period, and, therefore, the date of the last separation is of great interest for the study of family disruption. . . .

The duration of the second period, that between the separation and the filing of the divorce petition, depends partly on the decision of the parties to start divorce proceedings and partly on laws that specify the time that must elapse in order for a certain legal ground for divorce to arise, e.g., desertion, voluntary separation, or insanity. The duration of the third period depends almost exclusively on laws. Thus it can be seen that the three periods into which the duration of marriage to decree is divided have different characteristics, and their length is caused by different factors. All of these factors affect the duration of marriage to decree.

DISTRIBUTION OF DIVORCES BY DURATION OF MARRIAGE

Data for the divorce-registration area indicated that the modal number of divorces occurred when the marriage had lasted more than one year but less than two years. Almost the same proportion of divorces took place when the marriage had lasted between one and three years, 8.6 and 8.4 percent, respectively. The number of divorces declined consistently with each additional year of duration (Figure 54–4); and when the marriage had lasted nine years (the last single year of duration for which data are available) the proportion had declined to 3.7 percent. . . .

The group of divorces that had a very short duration, less than one year, included 5.2 percent of all decrees granted in the DRA. As this duration included the time the case was pending in court, the divorced couples had an extremely short period of married life before

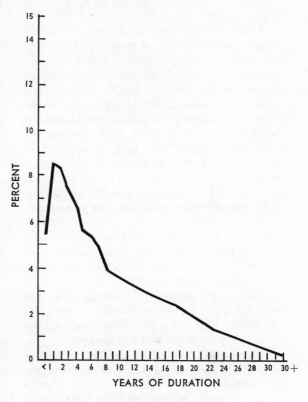

FIGURE 54–4. PERCENT OF DIVORCES AND ANNULMENTS, BY DURATION OF MARRIAGE TO TIME OF DECREE: DIVORCE-REGISTRATION AREA, 1963.

separation. The percentages of divorces after less than one year of married life showed very marked variation from state to state—from 0.4 percent in Virginia to 10.5 in Idaho. The regional factor is pronounced; all registration states in the Northeast region, in the northeastern part of the South region, and in the East North Central division of the North Central region had low proportions of divorces granted within less than one year—the highest percent being 4.3 in Ohio—while states in the remaining part of the country (including the West, the remainder of the North Central region, and the remainder of the South) had much higher percentages—the lowest being 6.0 percent in Hawaii. Thus all seven states in the first area had percentages lower than that for the DRA, and all states in the second area had higher percentages.

At the other extreme, 3.0 percent of divorced couples had a duration of marriage of 30 years or more, and this percentage ranged from 1.2 in Alaska to 4.9 in Alabama. Altogether 6.5 percent of the divorced couples had reached their silver wedding anniversary. Many of the states that had very low percentages of divorces after marriages with durations of less than one year had comparatively high percentages of those divorces after marriages with durations of 25 years or more and vice versa; the range was between 3.6 in Utah and 8.9 in Virginia. The regional distribution was also pronounced, with high percentages found in the Northeast and in the South between 6.3 and 8.9 percent), median percentages in the North Central (between 5.1 and 6.7), and low percentages in the West (between 3.8 and 5.2). . . .

The median duration of marriage at divorce was 7.5 years for the registration states combined; the figures for individual states ranged from 5.0 in Idaho to 10.3 in Maryland. . . .

The median duration of marriage at decree depends in part on the distribution of divorces by marriage order of husband and wife. Though data for 1963 are not available, information collected for earlier years indicates that the

duration is longer for first marriages than for remarriages for all age categories. . . .

CHILDREN INVOLVED IN DIVORCE CASES

NUMBER OF CHILDREN INVOLVED

It is estimated that the couples divorced in the United States during 1963 had a total of 583,000 children, or 1.36 children per divorce, and that 8.5 children were involved in divorce per 1000 children under 18 in the nation. Estimates of the number of children of divorced couples are available for 11 years, beginning with 1953. At that time, 330,000 children were involved in divorce cases, or 0.85 per divorce, and the involvement rate was 6.4 (Table 54–7).

Between 1953 and 1963, the number of divorce decrees granted annually increased by 9.7 percent, but the number of children involved increased by 76.7 percent; from 1962 to 1963 these increases were 3.6 and 8.6 percent, respectively. . . .

Some factors that contributed to the growth of the number of children involved in divorce cases are shown in Table 54–8. The proportion of divorces with children involved increased in the reporting states from 45.5 to 61.6 percent, while the number of children per divorce with

TABLE 54–7. ESTIMATED NUMBER OF CHILDREN INVOLVED IN DIVORCES AND ANNULMENTS: UNITED STATES, 1953-63.

Year	All divorces and annulments	Estimated number of children involved	Average number of children per decree	Rate per 1000 children under 18
1963	428,000	583,000	1.36	8.5
1962	413,000	537,000	1.30	8.0
1961	414,000	501,000	1.21	7.6
1960	393,000	463,000	1.18	7.2
1959	395,000	463,000	1.18	7.5
1958	368,000	398,000	1.08	6.5
1957	381,000	379,000	0.99	6.4
1956	382,000	361,000	0.95	6.3
1955	377,000	347,000	0.92	6.3
1954	379,000	341,000	0.90	6.4
1953	390,000	330,000	0.85	6.4

Refers only to events occurring within the United States. Figures for 1960-63 estimated from frequencies based on sample; those for other years estimating from total counts.

TABLE 54–8. PROPORTION OF DIVORCES AND
ANNULMENTS WITH CHILDREN INVOLVED: TOTAL
REPORTING STATES, 1953-63.

Year	Number of reporting states	Percent of decrees with children involved	Ratio of children per decree with children
1963	 22	61.6	2.16
1962	 21	60.2	2.14
1961	 20	60.3	2.06
1960	 50	56.7	2.08
1959	 16	59.1	2.00
1958	 12	55.1	1.96
1957	 23	50.9	1.95
1956	 22	48.9	1.93
1955	 22	48.1	1.92
1954	 22	47.8	1.88
1953	 22	45.5	1.86

Figures for 1960-63 based on sample data; those for
1953-59 based on total counts.

children involved increased from 1.86 to 2.16.
The increase in the proportion of divorced couples reporting children (or conversely, the decline in the proportion of childless couples in
divorce courts) was 35.4 percent, while the increase of the ratio of children per divorce with

children was 16.1 percent. This indicates that
the decline in the proportion of couples who
reported no children contributed most to the
increase in the number of children involved in
divorce.

. . . Almost two-thirds of all couples divorced
in 1963 reported children, and only 38.4 percent had no children under 18. The latter included couples that had no children because
they were only recently married, couples to
whom no children have been born irrespective
of the length of marriage, and couples that had
been married for many years and had grownup
children. Because of the composite character of
the childless group, there are many factors that
may have affected its decline during the last
decade. The proportion of couples reporting no
children varied considerably among the states,
from less than one-fourth (24.5 percent in Rhode
Island) to almost one-half (45.2 percent in Missouri). In no state did the divorces of childless
couples comprise more than one-half of all
divorces. In 1956 and earlier years, however,
in the reporting states combined this proportion
was more than 50 percent. This indicates a
rapid decline of the proportion of childless
divorced couples.

55.

GEORGE LEVINGER

SOURCES OF MARITAL DISSATISFACTION AMONG APPLICANTS FOR DIVORCE

To paraphrase Jean Jacques Rousseau, man's dissatisfaction results from an excess of his wants
over his abilities. This simple formula appears

both sensible and valid, but it covers a complex
topic. On the other hand, satisfaction and dissatisfaction are ever present qualifiers of human existence. On the other hand, they are

This selection is reprinted from: George Levinger,
"Sources of Marital Dissatisfaction Among Applicants for Divorce," *American Journal of Orthopsychiatry*, 1966, *36*, 803–807. Copyright, the American Orthopsychiatric Association, Inc. Reproduced
by permission.

This is a revision of a paper presented at the 1965
annual meeting of the American Orthopsychiatric
Association, New York. The work was supported in

part by grants from the Cleveland Foundation and
the National Institute of Mental Health (MH-
04653).

Appreciation is owed to officials of the Court of
Common Pleas, Cuyahoga County, Ohio; particularly to Dr. Mandel Rubin, director, and the other
staff of the Department of Marriage Conciliation.
Strict anonymity of applicants' names was ensured.

518 / *Stability of Marriage*

diffuse effects of a variety of often poorly understood determinants.

Marital satisfaction, too, is the composite of numerous factors, some permanent, others temporary. It not only depends on what one partner wants and can give, and the needs and capacities of the other spouse, but it also depends on the impact of the environment. Nevertheless, one may try to demarcate certain broad parameters, to outline some reasonably stable determinants or correlates of satisfaction.

In an earlier paper, based on a study of 60 urban middle-class couples, it was reported that husbands' and wives' marital goals and criteria for satisfaction were remarkably similar. (6) For example, both husbands and wives were equally prone to rank "companionship" and "affection" as the most important goals for a good marriage. And both spouses' actual happiness bore a far higher association with the fulfillment of social-emotional roles than that of success in work.

Nevertheless, evidence from a previous study by Farber (1) indicated that husbands and wives in a lower socioeconomic stratum tend to show some systematic dissimilarity in marital goals. Farber's husbands were significantly less concerned than their wives with the achievement of affection and companionship.

Further, dissatisfaction with marriage need not stem from the same determinants as does satisfaction. Both spouses may agree about the potential and actual rewards, but each may suffer from distinctively different problems when complaints do arise. The most extreme case of marital complaint occurs when partners are seeking dissolution—when a husband and wife are applying for divorce.

The present paper will deal with two general questions. First, to what extent do such husbands and wives differ in the bases of their marital dissatisfaction? Second, what differences can be noted across socioeconomic lines?

METHOD

The findings are based on a sample of 600 couples who were divorce applicants, representing marriages at the brink of dissolution. All these people were residents of Cuyahoga

County, Ohio (i.e., greater Cleveland). All had one or more children under 14 and had been seen jointly by an experienced marriage counselor at the Conciliation Department of the Domestic Relations Court of Cuyahoga County. The interviews were of a mandatory nature, required by rule of court for all divorce applicants with children under 14. The interview records of the marriage counselors were kept according to a standardized printed schedule.

The counselors' records were made available to us for analysis and a large number of characteristics were coded. Among the codable data, there was considerable information about each spouse's complaints about his partner.

Spouses' complaints were coded in one of the following 12 categories, with an intercoder reliability of 88 percent:

1. *Neglect of home or children:* frequent absence, irregular hours, emotional distance.
2. *Financial problems:* either inadequate support (by husband) or poor handling of family's money.
3. *Physical abuse:* committing overt physical hurt or injury to other partner.
4. *Verbal abuse:* profanity, namecalling, shouting.
5. *Infidelity:* attachment to an alternate partner, frequently sexual in nature, which excludes spouse; adultery.
6. *Sexual incompatibility:* reluctance or refusal of coitus, inconsiderateness and other sources of dissatisfaction.
7. *Drinking:* drunkenness or excessive drinking.
8. *In-law trouble:* Interference or pressure by in-laws, spouse's excessive loyalty to parental kin.
9. *Mental cruelty:* suspicion, jealousy, untruthfulness, and vague subjective complaints.
10. *Lack of love:* insufficient affection, communication, companionship.
11. *Excessive demands:* impatience, intolerance, strictness, possessiveness.
12. *Other:* miscellaneous category.

RESULTS

Let us examine the findings of the study. First, did husbands and wives differ in the number and the nature of their complaints?

Concerning the number of complaints, wives' reports exceeded husbands' by a ratio of almost 2:1. The 600 wives averaged 3.05 separate complaints; the husbands expressed a mean of 1.64 complaints.

As to the nature of complaints, Table 55–1 shows that wives complained 11 times more

TABLE 55–1. MARITAL COMPLAINTS AMONG 600 COUPLES APPLYING FOR DIVORCE, CLASSIFIED BY SEX AND BY SOCIAL POSITION OF RESPONDENTS

			Proportion of Complaints by Respondent Groups			
			Social Position of			
			Wives		Husbands	
Complaint	Wives Total[a]	Husbands Total[a]	Middle[b]	Lower[c]	Middle[b]	Lower[c]
Physical Abuse	.368***	.033	.228	.401**	.029	.035
Verbal Abuse	.238***	.075	.200	.245	.048	.082
Financial Problems	.368***	.087	.219	.402**	.124	.079
Drinking	.265***	.050	.143	.294**	.048	.051
Neglect of Home or Children	.390**	.262	.457	.374	.200	.276
Mental Cruelty	.403**	.297	.372	.408	.267	.306
In-Law Trouble	.067	.162**	.038	.074	.200	.153
Excessive Demands	.025	.040	.057*	.018	.057	.035
Infidelity	.240	.200	.324*	.223	.114	.198*
Sexual Incompatibility	.138	.200**	.124	.141	.267	.188
Lack of Love	.228**	.135	.324**	.206	.200*	.120

[a]N = 600; all husbands or wives.
[b]N = 105; "Middle" refers to Class I–III on Hollingshead's Index of Social Position. (4)
[c]N = 490; "Lower" refers to Class IV–V on the Hollingshead index. Note that 5 cases could not be categorized for social position, by dint of insufficient information.
***$p < .001$, indicating a significant difference in favor of the starred number in the pair, by t test (two-tailed).
**$p < .01$.
*$p < .05$.

frequently than husbands about physical abuse. That is, 36.8 percent of the wives and only 3.3 percent of the husbands said that their partner hurt them physically. Wives complained four times as often about financial problems and about drinking; three times as much about their spouse's verbal abuse. Wives' complaints significantly exceeded husbands' on three other categories, neglect of home and children, lack of love, and mental cruelty, but these ratios were less one-sided.

Husbands' complaints exceeded those of their mates on two counts. They were more apt to mention in-law trouble, by a ratio of 5 to 2; and they more often brought up sexual incompatibility, in a ratio of 3 to 2.

Let us now look at some social-class comparisons. Did complaint patterns differ across socioeconomic lines? The answer is a clear "yes."

To examine the matter, frequencies of complaints from 490 lower-class pairs—Class IV and V, according to Hollingshead's Two-Factor Index (4)—were compared with adjusted frequencies for 105 middle-class pairs (Class I-III).

In mean number of *total* expressed complaints, there was no difference between spouses from lower and those from middle socioeconomic position. However, Table 55–1 indicates that lower-status wives were considerably more likely than middle-status wives to complain about financial problems, physical abuse and drinking. Middle-class wives were significantly more prone to complain about lack of love, infidelity and excessive demands. Middle-class husbands paralleled the wives in their significantly greater concern with lack of love; on the other hand, they were significantly *less* likely than lower-class husbands to complain of the wife's infidelity.

Considering the sexual relationship, one may note that "sexual incompatibility" was a more frequently voiced complaint by middle-class than by lower-class husbands, while the reverse was true for wives. The opposite was found for "infidelity."

In general, the evidence indicates that spouses in the middle-class marriages were more concerned with psychological and emotional interaction, while the lower-class partners saw as most salient in their lives financial problems and the unsubtle physical actions of their partner.

DISCUSSION

The essence of the results suggests the following interpretation. When things are going well and the relationship is fruitful, husband and wife tend to obtain very similar satisfaction. After all, their marital satisfaction is derived from one another; it is a matter of mutuality and of reciprocation.

When matters are going badly, if positive mutuality breaks down, then husband and wife complaints may still be mainly directed toward their joint relationship, but the verbalized sources of friction are different for the partners. Wives complain about lack of love, neglect, physical or verbal abuse, or other matters included under the catch-all term of "mental cruelty." While husbands are also disturbed by neglect, lack of love, and emotional cruelty, they are more prone to express complaints about in-law interference or sexual mismatching.

These conclusions are similar to those in one major recent study of this general topic. From their 1958 national survey of mental health in America, Gurin, Veroff, and Feld (3) noted no dramatic differences among men and women in evaluating their marital adjustment. Married men and women were equally likely to mention some aspect of their interpersonal relationship, as opposed to their external environment. In that survey, women were also prone to acknowledge a somewhat higher proportion of marital problems, while men were more likely to deny the existence of such problems.

The survey findings have a second interesting implication for understanding our own results. In their random national sample the authors reported that the perceived source of marital problems was significantly connected with the educational level of the respondent. In other words, almost twice as many highly educated respondents as those with low education mentioned relationship-based problems or inadequacies in their marriage. This result accords with our own finding that occupational and educational status was linked to the nature of the spouses' goals, satisfactions and problem admission.

A study by Komarovsky, (5) published quite recently, underlines this issue in another way. Her research dealt intensively with 58 married couples, all with a "blue-collar" background. In her sample the high school educated spouses showed themselves to be more oriented toward marital communication and feeling disclosure than did the less educated persons. And the entire sample tended, on the average, to be less companionship-oriented than couples with white-collar socioeconomic status.

SOME INTERPRETATIONS

What integrating conceptions might help to deal with such facts? First, consider a quote from a recent paper by the economist Galbraith on "Economics and the Quality of Life"; and then let us turn to some notions about need hierarchies by the psychologist Maslow.

Galbraith (2) says:

> In the poor society, not only do economic considerations dominate social attitudes but they rigidly specify the problems that will be accorded priority (p. 117).

Maslow (7) has stated that each human being desires to fulfill a variety of needs, but he postulates the following categorical order in which they can be gratified. First and most basic are the subsistence needs of hunger, thirst and other physiological requirements. Second, there are the needs for safety and protection from external harm. Third, the individual wants love, belongingness and interpersonal warmth. Fourth are the needs for esteem and respect from other persons. Fifth, and only after the previous needs have been satisfied to a minimal extent, can the individual actively seek and achieve self-actualization.

Putting together the notions of Galbraith with those of Maslow, one may note that a large proportion of individuals, not only in the world at large, but also in the United States of America, are so heavily engaged with coping to satisfy needs at the first and second level (desire for subsistence and safety) that they are unable in their adulthood to worry about the achievement of mature love or interpersonal respect, not to speak of that rare quality of self-actualization.

The implications for preventive or curative treatment would be that our current verbal therapies, already known to be relatively unsuccessful with nonverbal people, may be not merely unsuccessful, but largely irrelevant to the needs of individuals striving at the basic levels. It may be important to consider the psychological hunger of a financially secure clientele and to learn to improve treatment practices. It is equally important to learn how other members of our population can be helped to satisfy their more basic needs, so that verbal therapy eventually might become relevant to them.

REFERENCES

1. FARBER, B. An index of marital integration. *Sociometry*, 1957, *20*(2), 117–134.
2. GALBRAITH, J. K. Economics and the quality of life. *Science*, 1964, *145*(2), 117–123.
3. GURIN, G., VEROFF, J. AND FELD, SHEILA. *Americans view their mental health.* New York: Basic Books, 1960.
4. HOLLINGSHEAD, A. B. *Two factor index of social position.* New Haven, Conn.: 1957, multilithed.
5. KOMAROVSKY, MIRRA. *Blue-collar marriage.* New York: Random House, 1964.
6. LEVINGER, G. Task and social behavior in marriage. *Sociometry*, 1964, *27*(4), 433–448.
7. MASLOW, A. H. *Motivation and personality.* New York: Harper & Row, Publishers, 1954.

56.

GEORGE LEVINGER

MARITAL COHESIVENESS AND DISSOLUTION: AN INTEGRATIVE REVIEW

What makes a marriage "stick"? And what breaks it apart? Such questions have answers, but the answers do not yet rest on an explicit theoretical base. There is an abundance of descriptive findings and of empirical generalizations, but as yet a scarcity of conceptual construction.[1]

Consider the following instance. In a review of "willed departures" in marriage, Goode[2] has summarized a number of variables related to divorce proneness "which seem to be based on good evidence": urban background, marriage at very young ages, short acquaintanceship before marriage, short or no engagement, marital unhappiness of parents, nonattendance at church, mixed religious faith, disapproval by kin and friends of the marriage, dissimilarity of background, and different definitions by spouses of their mutual roles. Goode also notes that husband's occupation and income are inversely related to divorce proneness.[3] Other writers have shown associations between di-

This selection is reprinted from: George Levinger, "Marital Cohesiveness and Dissolution: An Integrative Review," *Journal of Marriage and the Family,* 1965, *27*, 19–28.
Reprinted with the permission of the author and publisher.
This paper was written in connection with research on marital relationships, supported by a grant from the Cleveland Foundation and by Grant M-4653 from the National Institute of Mental Health.
[1]This state of affairs has not been uncommon in other areas of sociological investigation. See Hans L. Zetterberg, *On Theory and Verification in Sociology* (Totowa, N.J.: Bedminster, 1963).

[2]William J. Goode, "Family Disorganization," in *Contemporary Social Problems,* ed. by Robert K. Merton and Robert A. Nisbet (New York: Harcourt, Brace & World, Inc., 1961), 425.
[3]*Ibid.,* 417–418.

vorce proneness and childlessness,[4] low conventionality,[5] disjunctive affiliation networks,[6] and a series of other factors.[7]

It seems reasonable to seek a common conceptual base that will assist in explaining those findings. This paper presents such a conceptual frame, in which marriage is conceived as a special case of all two-person relationships. Marital cohesiveness becomes a special case of group cohesiveness in general. The findings from some major studies of divorce and of marital adjustment are interpreted according to this framework.

COHESIVENESS IN MARRIAGE

The marriage pair is a two-person group. It follows, then, that marital cohesiveness is analogous to group cohesiveness and can be defined accordingly. Group cohesiveness is "the total field of forces which act on members to remain in the group."[8] Inducements to remain in any group include the attractiveness of the group itself and the strength of the restraints against leaving it; inducements to leave a group include the attractiveness of alternative relationships and the restraints against breaking up such existing relationships. Thus the strength of the marital relationship would be a direct function of the attractions within and barriers around the marriage, and an inverse function of such attractions and barriers from other relationships.

In marriage, a spouse is attracted to his mate because of her intrinsic worth, her love, her charm, her ability to please his wants, or perhaps because she gains him external prestige or will further extrinsic goals. Barriers against a breakup emanate from other sources: the emotional, religious, and moral commitments that a partner feels toward his marriage or toward his children; the external pressures of kin and community, of the law, the church, and other associational memberships.

Thus marital strength is a function of bars as well as bonds. Yet the strength of barriers matters little if the partners' attraction is high enough. In many marriages, the barriers have trivial importance. The spouses' close attachment precludes that either one would seriously consider breaking the relationship.

In other marriages, though, barriers have crucial importance. In the absence of positive feelings, they maintain outward signs of marital togetherness. Goode has called the latter case an "empty shell" marriage:

. . . The atmosphere is without laughter or fun, and a sullen gloom pervades the household. Members do not discuss their problems or experiences with each other, and communication is kept to a minimum. . . . Their rationalization for avoiding a divorce is, on the part of one or both, "sacrifice for the children," "neighborhood respectability," and a religious conviction that divorce is morally wrong. . . . The hostility in such a home is great, but arguments focus on the small issues, not the large ones. Facing the latter would, of course, lead directly to separation or divorce, but the couple has decided that staying together overrides other values, including each other's happiness and the psychological health of their children.[9]

This illustration of an "empty shell" family evokes contrasting images of "full shell" and "no shell" families. To carry Goode's metaphor farther, a "full shell" marriage would be one in which not only the boundaries but also the attractions are strong for both partners; a marriage in which there is warm emotional interchange. In contrast, the "no shell" couple is in a state of dissolution; it consists of two disconnected individuals, living separate lives. In this latter instance, boundaries as well as attractions have been eroded by the events over time, until eventually alternatives to the marital state are

[4]Paul H. Jacobson, "Differentials in Divorce by Duration of Marriage and Size of Family," *American Sociological Review*, April, 1950, *15*, 235–244.

[5]Harvey J. Locke, *Predicting Adjustment in Marriage* (New York: Holt, Rinehart & Winston, Inc., 1951), 236–243.

[6]Charles Ackerman, "Affiliations: Structural Determinants of Differential Divorce Rates," *American Journal of Sociology*, July, 1963, *69*, 13–20.

[7]See also William J. Goode, *After Divorce* (New York: The Free Press, 1956); Paul C. Glick, *American Families* (New York: John Wiley & Sons, Inc., 1957); Hugh Carter and Alexander Plateris, "Trends in Divorce and Family Disruption," *HEW Indicators* September, 1963, v–xiv.

[8]Leon Festinger, Stanley Schachter, and Kurt Back, *Social Pressures in Informal Groups* (New York: Harper & Row, Publishers, 1950), 164.

[9]Goode, "Family Disorganization," *op. cit.*, 441–442.

preferred. Goode's metaphor is appropriate. It implicitly refers to two underlying continua: fullness-emptiness of attraction, and strength-weakness of boundaries.

Finally, consider the attractions and barriers outside the marriage. These are forces that pertain to relations with parents, children, lovers, friends, enemies, employers, employees, or any of a host of alternate persons. Husband or wife may be more or less attracted to any of these relationships, and he or she will have a varying sense of obligation to maintain them. Such alternate relationships can be fully compatible with the existence of a strong and stable marriage. The maintenance of relations with in-laws or employers, for example, does not necessarily conflict with the primary marital bond. However, an extreme commitment to such a relationship would interfere with the marriage; as would also, of course, a commitment to a third party that fully excludes the spouse.

COHESIVENESS AND DIVORCE

In studying marriage, high cohesiveness is far harder to detect than low cohesiveness. The privacy of the marital relationship prevents outsiders from judging how "truly happy" a particular union might be; even insiders, the spouses themselves, cannot be fully aware of all the attractions and restraints that they feel.

On the other hand, the extremes of low cohesiveness eventuate in the dissolution of the relationship. If divorce is the result, it is a public index that can be studied. For this reason, it is useful to give particular consideration to research on divorce to illustrate how the present framework can be applied.

Yet consideration of such research must note the distinction between (divorce) and (separation). In certain groups of our society, *de jure* separation (divorce) is a less likely occurrence than *de facto* residential separation. Undoubtedly, the less socially visible a couple is, the more likely it is to resort to informal procedures of separation. The less clear a family's ties to stable norms of kin and community, the less necessary it is to make a break formal. Thus desertion has been a far more common phenomenon in the

lowest socio-economic stratum than in the higher strata. This point must be remembered in interpreting findings on divorce rates.[10]

Possible differences in the forces affecting the two partners. The term *cohesiveness* is drawn from a physical analogy. The cohesiveness of a physical bond between two nuclei in a molecule may be indicated by the amount of energy required to break it. The physical model, though, assumes homogeneity in the forces among the nuclei. A social group model of bond strength cannot assume such homogeneity. Feelings of attraction and restraint can and do vary among the members of a group.

In marriage, too, the two partners' feelings are not identical. One spouse may consider separation, while the other remains fully bound to the relationship. Nevertheless, by definition, both partners must value another alternative over that of the present marriage before both will agree to a separation. Usually, the wife is plaintiff in divorce proceedings. Nationally, the figure is about 70 percent.[11] The preponderance of wife-initiated divorce suits results in part from cultural prescription, yet some of the author's unpublished evidence indicates that the balance of the wife's feelings is more important than the husband's as an indicator of divorce proneness.[12]

REVIEW OF FACTORS ASSOCIATED WITH DIVORCE

How do findings from actual studies illustrate the framework? Attractions that act to secure a marriage derive from love and money. The rewards that spouses receive are linked to their affection for each other, to their financial income and social position, and also to the degree that husband and wife share similar characteristics. Barriers against a breakup can be coordi-

---

[10]Glick, *op. cit.,* 156.

[11]Paul H. Jacobson, *American Marriage and Divorce* (New York: Holt, Rinehart & Winston, Inc., 1959), 119.

[12]Goode, *After Divorce, op cit.,* has pointed out that in many divorce cases, the husband has precipitated the break by providing reasons for the wife's complaint. Nevertheless, the wife's *tolerance* for the husband's normative deviation is a crucial determinant of the decision to seek a divorce.

TABLE 56–1. FACTORS FOUND TO DIFFERENTIATE BETWEEN HIGH AND
LOW COHESIVE MARRIAGES

Sources of Attraction	Sources of Barrier Strength	Sources of Alternate Attraction
Affectional rewards: esteem for spouse[11,14,17,24]• desire for companionship[4,20] sexual enjoyment[18,24,32] *Socio-economic rewards:* husband's income[(2),5,12,24,31,(32),34] home ownership[5,24,31] husband's education[10,28,35,36] husband's occupation[11,19,26,33,38] *Similarity in social status:* religion[4,6,8,21,29,30,38] education[4,13,20,39] age[4,5,24]	*Feelings of obligation:* to dependent children[11,15,27] to marital bond[25] *Moral proscriptions:* proscriptive religion[8,21,30] joint church attendance[9,11,24,31] *External pressures:* primary group affiliations[1] community stigma rural-urban[3,5,7,31,87] in legal and economic bars[16]	*Affectional rewards:* preferred alternate sex partner[11,14,18,24] disjunctive social relations[1,24] opposing religious affiliations[21] *Economic rewards:* wife's opportunity for independent income[12,16,23]

•Numerals pertain to positive findings in the corresponding references listed below. Numerals in parentheses indicate which studies reported an absence of a difference between High and Lcw cohesive couples.

[1]Charles Ackerman, "Affiliations: Structural Determinants of Differential Divorce Rates," *American Journal of Sociology*, July, 1963, *69*, 12–20.

[2]Jessie Bernard, "Factors in the Distribution of Success in Marriage," *American Journal of Sociology*, July, 1934, *40*, 49–60.

[3]Robert O. Blood, Jr. *Marriage* (New York: The Free Press, 1962).

[4]Robert O. Blood, Jr. & Donald M. Wolfe, *Husbands and Wives*, (New York: The Free Press, 1960).

[5]Ernest W. Burgess & Leonard S. Cottrell, Jr., *Predicting Success or Failure in Marriage* (Englewood Cliffs, N.J.; Prentice-Hall, Inc. 1939).

[6]Ernest W. Burgess & Paul Wallin, *Engagement and Marriage* (Philadelphia: J. B. Lippincott Co., 1953).

[7]Hugh Carter and Alexander Plateris, "Trends in Divorce and Family Disruption," *HEW Indicators*, September, 1963, v–xiv.

[8]Loren E. Chancellor and Thomas Monahan, "Religious Preference and Inter-religious Mixtures in Marriages and Divorces in Iowa," *American Journal of Sociology*, November, 1955, *61*, 233–239.

[9]Eustace Chesser, *The Sexual, Marital, and Family Relationships of the English Woman* (New York: Roy, 1957).

[10]Paul C. Glick, *American Families* (New York: John Wiley & Sons, Inc., 1957).

[11]William J. Goode, *After Divorce* (New York: The Free Press, 1956).

[12]William J. Goode, "Marital Satisfaction and Instability: A Cross-Cultural Analysis of Divorce Rates," *International Social Science Journal*, 1962, *14*,3, 507–526.

[13]Gilbert V. Hamilton, *A Research in Marriage* (New York: Boni, 1929).

[14]E. Lowell Kelly, "Marital Compatability as Related to Personality Traits of Husbands and Wives as Rated by Self and Spouse," *Journal of Social Psychology*, February, 1941, *13*, 193–198.

[15]Paul H. Jacobson, "Differentials in Divorce by Duration of Marriage and Size of Family," *American Sociological Review*, April, 1950, *15*, 235–244.

[16]Paul H. Jacobson, *American Marriage and Divorce* (New York: Holt, Rinehart & Winston, Inc., 1959).

[17]E. Lowell Kelly, "Marital Compatability as Related to Personality Traits of Husbands and Wives as Rated by Self and Spouse," *Journal of Social Psychology*, February, 1941, *13*, 193–198.

[18]William M. Kephart, "Some Variables in Cases of Reported Sexual Maladjustment," *Marriage and Family Living*, August, 1954, *16*, 241–243.

[19]William M. Kephart, "Occupational Level and Marital Disruption," *American Sociological Review*, August, 1955, *20*, 456–465.

[20]Clifford Kirkpatrick, "Community of Interest and the Measurement of Adjustment in Marriage," *The Family*, June, 1937, *18*, 133–137.

[21]Judson T. Landis, "Marriages of Mixed and Non-Mixed Religious Faith," *American Sociological Review*, June, 1949, *14*, 401–406.

[22]Richard O. Lang, *A Study of the Degree of Happiness or Unhappiness in Marriages as Rated by Acquaintances of the Married Couples*, M.A. thesis, University of Chicago, 1932 cited in Goode (11), 57.

[23]J. P. Lichtenberger, *Divorce* (New York: McGraw-Hill Book Company, 1931).

[24]Harvey J. Locke, *Predicting Adjustment in Marriage: A Comparison of a Divorced and a Happily Married Group* (New York: Holt, Rinehart & Winston, Inc., 1951).

[25]Thomas P. Monahan, "How Stable Are Remarriages?" *American Journal of Sociology*, November, 1952, *58*, 280–288.

[26]Thomas P. Monahan, "Divorce by Occupational Level," *Marriage and Family Living*, November, 1955, *17*, 322–324.

[27]Thomas P. Monahan, "Is Childlessness Related to Family Stability?" *American Sociological Review*, August, 1955, *20*, 446–456.

[28]Thomas P. Monahan, "Educational Achievement and Family Stability," *Journal of Social Psychology*, December, 1961, *55*, 253–263.

[29]Thomas P. Monahan & Loren E. Chancellor, "Statistical Aspects of Marriage and Divorce by Religious Denomination in Iowa," *Eugenics Quarterly*, September, 1955, *2*, 162–173.

[30]Thomas P. Monahan & William M. Kephart, "Divorce and Desertion by Religious and Mixed-Religious Groups," *American Journal of Sociology*, March, 1954, *59*, 454–465.

[31]Clarence W. Schroeder, *Divorce in a City of 100,000 Population* (Peoria, Ill.: Bradley Polytechnic Institute Library, 1939).

[32]Lewis M. Terman, *Psychological Factors in Marital Happiness* (New York: McGraw-Hill Book Company, 1938).

[33]U.S. Bureau of Census, *Marriage and Divorce: 1887–1906*, Bulletin 96, Washington, D.C.: Government Printing Office, 1908, 25–27.

[34]U.S. Bureau of Census, *U.S. Census of Population: 1950*, Vol. IV, *Special Reports*, Part 2, Chapter D, Marital Status. Washington, D.C.: Government Printing Office, 1953, Table 6, 47–48.

nated to the partners' feelings of obligation to their family, to their moral values, and to external pressures exerted on them from various sources—these are the sorts of pressures that serve to maintain the boundaries of their marriage. Finally, one can consider alternate sources of affectional and financial reward; these serve as a contrast to the internal attractions and have a potentially disruptive effect.

Table 56–1, together with its accompanying discussion, organizes published findings that pertain to marital cohesiveness under the three headings of attraction, barrier, and alternate attraction.

ATTRACTIONS IN MARRIAGE

Esteem for spouse. It appears obvious that marital cohesiveness is positively associated with the spouses' mutual esteem and affection. Yet in what areas is esteem most apparent, and in what forms is it present or absent? Locke (24)[13] has found that spouses in happy marriages described their partners' traits in a far more positive way than did divorced persons; the former were far more likely to report the mate's traits as superior or at least equal to their own. Kelly (17) also has reported that this tendency is positively related to marital happiness. Regarding negative esteem, Goode (11), Harmsworth and Minnis (14), and Locke (24) have reported a far higher incidence of complaints about the partner among divorcees or divorce applicants than among normally adjusted spouses.

Desire for companionship. In some cultures, such as the Japanese, marriage does not promote companionship with the spouse. However, two studies of American marriages by Blood and Wolfe (4) and Kirkpatrick (20) found that desire for companionship is strongly related to marital adjustment.

Sexual enjoyment. Locke (24) has reported

[13]Numerals in parentheses in this review section pertain to the references in the footnotes to Table 56–1.

that happy and divorced spouses differed significantly, both in their enjoyment of actual intercourse and in their desire for it. Terman (32) found that the most adjusted couples had the highest ratio of actual/preferred frequency of sexual relations. To qualify this finding, one should note Kephart's report (18) that concern with sexual incompatibility was found primarily among divorce applicants from the higher social strata. (The present author, in an unpublished study, has obtained a similar finding.) Sexual gratification is one vital source of marital attraction, but its lack apparently is less keenly felt among spouses who have not achieved a satisfactory material standard of living.

Husband's income. In Western nations, as Goode (12) has recently pointed out, divorce rates were greater for high-income than for low-income marriages until the advent of industrialization. However, since some unspecifiable transition point during the early part of this century, divorce rates have been negatively associated with husband's income (12). It would appear that the attractions within the marriage are lowest for the poor, and that attractions outside the marriage are relatively greater. With the reduction of legal obstacles and of economic costs of divorce, there has occurred a large increase in divorce among low-income couples.

These reasons, then, explain the inverse relation between income and divorce found in modern studies. One of the first studies to suggest this was Schroeder's (31) analysis of divorce rates in Peoria; by an ecological technique, he found a correlation of −.32 between divorce rates and average income in different districts of that city. Locke (24), in his comparison between happily married and divorced spouses, found that an income "adequate for the needs of the family" lessened the likelihood of divorce. Burgess and Cottrell (5) also found a moderate positive relationship. In contrast, neither Bernard (2) nor Terman (32) found such an association; however, their samples were probably too restricted in the range of

[35]U.S. Bureau of Census, *U.S. Census of Population; 1950*, Vol. IV, *Special Reports*, Part 5, Chapter B, Education, Washington, D.C.: Government Printing Office, 1953, Table 8, 63–64.

[36]U.S. Department of Health, Education and Welfare, *Vital Statistics—Special Reports*, September 9, 1957, 45:12, 301.

[37]U.S. Bureau of Census, *Current Population Reports*, Series 20, No. 87, November 14, 1958, 11–12.

[38]H. Ashley Weeks, "Differential Divorce Rates by Occupations," *Social Forces*, March, 1943, 21, 334–337.

[39]Edith W. Williams, "Factors Associated with Adjustment in Rural Marriage," Ph.D. Dissertation, Cornell University, 1938, 98, cited in Goode (11), 99.

financial income. When wide ranges of income and marital satisfaction are considered, as in studies of the entire U.S. population by the Census (34), there is a clear inverse correlation between income and divorced status, and even more between income and separated status.[14]

Home ownership. The proportion of couples who obtain a divorce is lower for owners than for nonowners of a home. This finding is reported by Schroeder (31), by Burgess and Cottrell (5), and by Locke (24). Much of the association may be a function of family income and of length of marriage. However, even if the influence of those two variables is controlled, home ownership itself probably contributes to the stability of family life.[15] It would seem that home ownership is not only a source of attraction, but also helps to stabilize the boundaries that hold the marriage together. All else being equal, the mere fact of owning a home probably increases a couple's reluctance to dissolve their relationship.

Husband's amount of education. The amount of the husband's education is higher for durable than for dissolved marriages. This is indicated by data reported by Glick (10), by Monahan (28), and by U.S. Census reports (35, 36). One would speculate, *ceteris paribus*, that a wife's attraction varies with her spouse's educational status. These findings, of course, are linked to variations in other variables, such as husband's income or prestige. His years of edu-

cation undoubtedly are correlated positively with prestige, with the husband's relative superiority over his wife, and with his ability to maintain a masculine role. If the husband's education is lower than his wife's, there is more likely to be a reversal in the male-female power balance with an ensuing loss of the husband's attractiveness as her marital partner.

Husband's occupation. Numerous studies have shown that divorce proneness is also inversely related to husband's occupational rank. Thus, Goode (11), Kephart (19), Monahan (26), and Weeks (38) have each shown that couples in which the husband's occupation ranks high have less divorce proneness than those where it ranks low. Part of this result may be attributed to the contribution of income, another part to the higher prestige of the professions and managerial occupations.

A third reason for the difference in divorce proneness among occupational groups relates to the stability of the husband's home life, as associated with his occupation. Thus Monahan (26) reported that physicians have a higher divorce rate than dentists, taxicab drivers a higher rate than truck drivers. One would hypothesize that the divorce rate of general practitioners or internists, whose home life is constantly disrupted, would be higher than that of doctors with regular working hours (e.g., pathologists, radiologists, or X-ray specialists); that it would be higher for long-haul truckers than for intra-city truck drivers. High degrees of instability would tend to reduce the attractiveness of the relationship and also to erode the boundaries that contain it.

Occupational differences may also be linked to differences in susceptibility to alternate attractions. Members of certain occupations (e.g., internists, taxicab drivers, or masseurs) have a greater than average probability for extended intimate contacts with members of the opposite sex. Thus they will have a greater opportunity to explore alternate attractions that would compete with their current marital relationship. In contrast, members of other occupations (e.g., clergymen or politicians) are particularly vulnerable to externally imposed norms about boundary maintenance, which would restrain

---

[14]A forthcoming paper by the author will report that income is also closely related to the outcome of *applications for divorce,* once such applications have actually been filed. This study avoids a criticism by Day, pertaining to some published studies of divorce. He points out that census enumerations of persons currently occupying the status "divorced" have sometimes been erroneously taken to represent the *rate* of divorce itself. He suggests that ". . . socioeconomic differences in rates of remarriage or in the interval between divorce and re-marriage could seriously affect the relative sizes of these ratios." See Lincoln H. Day, "Patterns of Divorce in Australia and the United States," *American Sociological Review,* August, 1964, 29, 509. Day's reminder, published after this paper was written, is well to bear in mind in assessing findings reviewed here.

[15]Unpublished data from the author's research indicate that homeowners are also more likely to dismiss an already filed divorce suit than are nonowners.

any proclivity toward divorce.[16]

Such additional considerations are important in weighing the impact of occupational factors in affecting marital stability. Future empirical studies may be able to distinguish among the separate influences of each of these components.

Similarity in social status. Many studies have linked marital adjustment to similarity of religious preference—particularly Chancellor and Monahan (8), Landis (21), Monahan and Chancellor (29), Monahan and Kephart (30), and Weeks (38). Burgess and Wallin (6) noted that frequency of broken engagements was lower for same-faith couples. Hamilton (13), Kirkpatrick (20), and Williams (39) have indicated that marital attraction is positively related to similarity in education. Burgess and Cottrell (5) and Locke (24) found that it is significantly associated with age similarity, particularly when the husband is older. Blood and Wolfe (4) have found that all three kinds of similarity relate positively to marital satisfaction. Undoubtedly, these are all different aspects of status similarity. Communication between the spouses would tend to be enhanced by relative likeness on these characteristics.

Sources of Barrier Strength

Sources of barrier forces exist both inside and outside the individual. The following examples of restraints against marital dissolution include some cases where the restraints are primarily internal, others where they are mainly external, and still others where their source is difficult to locate.

Obligation to dependent children. It is widely held that as long as there are no children involved, divorce is the couple's own affair. For that reason, one might expect that husbands and wives with children would feel a greater restraint than those without children—particularly minor children.

Early writings on divorce gave the impression that childless couples have indeed a vastly higher divorce rate,[17] but those studies neglected to adjust divorce rate by *duration* of marriage. More sophisticated analyses by Jacobson (15) and by Monahan (27) have shown that if length of marriage is controlled, the difference in separation rate between childless and child-rearing couples is much smaller, but still noticeable. According to Jacobson (15), between 1928 and 1948 this disparity decreased to a ratio of less than 2:1. Even the most skeptical analysis of this difference by Monahan (27) showed some excess of divorce frequency in the childless groups.

The real question is, perhaps, what obligations do the parents *feel* toward their children? To what extent do they feel that divorce of an unattractive marriage would either damage or promote their children's well-being? If parents believe the former, then the existence of children will create barrier forces; if they believe the latter, then they would be likely to be attracted to an alternative other than the present marriage. Goode (11), for example, has taken the position that, in an inevitably conflicted home, children may actually benefit from the divorce.

So far, there is no published evidence which differentiates between parents' feelings of obligation to children as *barriers* that prevent a breakup and such obligations as sources of *negative attraction* to the marriage. Until such evidence is obtained, the issue will remain unresolved.

---

[16]There are few good data to substantiate these predictions, because published divorce statistics do not generally reveal detailed occupational information. Possibly the best single source is a 1908 U.S. Census Bulletin (33), which relates occupation to divorce. Although its national returns were qualified as "incomplete and hardly acceptable," its New Jersey data for 1887–1906 covered 81.1 percent of all husbands divorced. New Jersey husbands occupied in agricultural, mechanical, and manufacturing pursuits showed lower than average divorce rates; those in professional or personal service or in trade and transportation had a higher rate. Particularly low were farmers, agricultural laborers, blacksmiths, carpenters, clergymen, engineers, and manufacturing officials. Clearly on the high side were actors, commercial travelers, musicians, bartenders, physicians and surgeons, sailors, and barbers and hairdressers, in that order. Husbands in the high-rate occupations seem to have been highly exposed to alternate attractions.

---

[17]E.g., Alfred Cohen, *Statistical Analysis of American Divorce* (New York: Columbia University Press, 1932); Walter F. Willcox, *Studies in American Demography* (Ithaca, N. Y.: Cornell University Press, 1940).

Obligations to the marital bond. In a large proportion of marriages, both partners are firmly committed to respect the marital contract, and divorce is not considered as a possibility. Each partner has certain qualms against even thinking of such a thing. On the other hand, if one or both have previously experienced a divorce proceeding, then either partner would be more likely to consider divorce. Thus, the barriers against the dissolution of the present marriage would be weaker. A study by Monahan (25) has indeed shown that first marriages are more resistant to dissolution than are second or later marriages. His data were confined to population statistics and did not pertain longitudinally to particular individuals. Nevertheless, it would be hypothesized that marriages of divorcees tend to have weaker boundaries than those of first-married spouses; further evidence is needed, however, to arrive at any sound generalization.

Proscriptive religion. It is popularly believed that Catholics are less likely to break their marriages than persons of other religious persuasions. This is only partly true. A more correct statement is that like-faith marriages in which both members are either Catholics, Jews, or reasonably strict Protestants have the lowest probability of divorce. This has been pointed out by studies of Chancellor and Monahan (8), Landis (21), and Monahan and Kephart (30). Such studies have also shown that persons of unconventional religious convictions are most prone to use divorce as a solution to their marital problems.

Joint church attendance. Various studies have shown that divorce proneness is inversely related to joint church attendance. Joint membership and regular attendance at church places a couple in a network of connected affiliations and exposes them to conventional values. One would assume that membership in such a net is a source of powerful external pressures. If necessary, such pressures would come into play to prevent the marriage from breaking up.

Reports by Chesser (9), Locke (24), and Schroeder (31) each indicate that, in their samples of couples, marital dissolution was less frequent among regular church attenders than among nonattenders. In his study of divorcees, Goode (11) found that (in his group of Cath-

olics) regularity of church attendance was positively associated with duration of marriage before separation.

Primary group affiliation. Affiliation with a church or with other sorts of organizations is one source of barrier forces; affiliation with kinfolk is another vital source. In a recent paper, Ackerman (1) has proposed that divorce rates vary across different cultures to the extent that the culture encourages "conjunctive" as opposed to "disjunctive" affiliations with kin. Ackerman defines the former case as one where husband and wife share a common network of kinfolk and friends; in the latter, their loyalties go in different directions. One would suppose that a conjunctive net of affiliations acts to restrain marital dissolution more than a disjunctive net. Ackerman's analysis of cross-cultural data shows empirical support for this supposition.

Community stigma. Another source of barriers against divorce is community disapproval. Such disapproval seems more characteristic of rural than of urban communities, which leads to the expectation that rural divorce rates are lower than urban ones. This expectation is borne out by 1955 census data (37) and by 1960 census data cited by Carter and Plateris (7). Also, studies by Schroeder (31) and by Burgess and Cottrell (5) have reported that divorced persons are less likely to be born and reared in a rural setting.[18]

Blood (3) has drawn attention to the importance of the visibility of the marriage relationship in the community where the couple lives. When both partners are known, when their behavior is observed, there are greater restraints against social transgressions such as extramarital affairs. Life in the country would seem more restrictive than that in the city; relations in the suburb more constraining than in the urban center.

In describing life in the modern suburb, Whyte has noted that it exerts a "beneficient effect on relations between husband and wife. The group is a foster family." Whyte quotes a

---

[18]William J. Goode (personal communication) has suggested that rural divorce rates in the United States may be low only for farmers, but higher for nonowners of farms.

minister as follows: "The kind of social situation you find here discourages divorce. Few people, as a rule, get divorces until they break with their groups. I think the fact that it is so hard to break with a group here has had a lot to do with keeping some marriages from going on the rocks."[19]

Legal and economic bars. It goes almost without saying that legal and financial considerations exert restraints against a breakup. The wide differences in divorce rates among different states can, in part, be accounted for by differences in divorce laws—as Jacobson (16) has pointed out. And, when considering differences between high- and low-income husbands, one notes that a high-income husband is likely to pay more, both absolutely and proportionately, to support his ex-wife after separation. Thus both legal and financial factors provide important restraints against going through with a divorce.

SOURCES OF ALTERNATE ATTRACTION

Popularly, it might seem that alternate attractions are the chief or the only reason for broken marriages. This impression is sustained by legal fiat, which emphasizes adultery as a reason for divorce. In one state, New York, adultery is the only legal grounds for dissolving a marriage contract.

It is logically necessary that the alternative environment be more attractive than the marital relationship, if the partners are to be willing to undergo the costs of divorce. However, it is not necessary that the attraction be "another woman" or "another man." The marital relationship itself may be so unattractive that any alternative condition—with or without another partner—is preferred.

Preferred other sex partner. Aside from reports on official complaints lodged with the court, which frequently are colored to sustain the legal fiction, relatively few studies contain data about spouses' alternate attractions outside the marriage. It is difficult to inquire about this without asking the parties to a divorce action to compromise their personal and legal position

vis-à-vis their spouse. Nevertheless, several published studies have reported that preference for an outside sexual partner does play a part in a significant proportion of divorce actions. The proportion may vary anywhere from 15 to 35 percent of all cases—e.g., Goode (11), Harmsworth and Minnis (14), Kephart (18), and Locke (24). Complaints about external sexual attachments are more frequently reported by wives; but when the husband reports them in a divorce suit, they may be even more serious.[20]

Disjunctive kin affiliations. Another source of outside attraction forces would be the loyalty toward one's kin or friends. If these ties conflict with those of the spouse, they will at the least lead to strain in the marriage. As mentioned earlier, Ackerman (1) has suggested that competing primary group affiliations are associated with divorce proneness. Locke (24) found that his "happy" couples frequently reported "a little" conflict with their own parents, i.e., (alternate) attractions to parents were at less than maximal strength. This source of marital disruption is worthy of fuller exploration in future studies of divorce.

In cases of disjunctive affiliation, one would hypothesize that the marital bond would be strengthened if the couple increases its physical and psychological distance from *both* sets of alternate affiliation groups, reducing thereby the disruptive forces. For example, partners in a heterogamous marriage that involves antogonistic in-laws would strengthen their relationship by moving away from the community where either set of parents resides. No systematic evidence to support this hypothesis can be cited, but it does coincide with informal observation.[21]

Opposing religious affiliations. What are the effects of obligations toward alternative com-

---

[19]William H. Whyte, Jr., *The Organization Man* (New York: Simon and Schuster, Inc., 1956), 392–393.

[20]In an unpublished study by the author, a comparison was made of two groups of divorce applicants, one set of whom later dismissed the action. It was found that husbands' complaints of "infidelity" were more frequent in the divorcing group, while wives' complaints of the husband's "infidelity" were more frequent in the group of couples who dismissed their action and rejoined their marriage.

[21]E. Lowell Kelly (personal communication) has reported anecdotal evidence from his own marriage research that substantiates this notion concerning mixed-religious marriages.

peting relationships? Little direct study of this question has been made. However, one bit of evidence indicates the direction in which the answer may lie.

Landis's (21) study of divorce rates in Catholic-Protestant marriages showed clearly that mixed-faith unions were less durable than same-faith marriages of Catholics or Protestants. However, Catholic-Protestant marriages were three times more likely to break up when the wife was Protestant than when the husband was Protestant.

This result is explainable by the framework as follows. Assume that both partners are attracted to their own religious group, but that the wife's feelings are stronger. Assume, also, that the children in each of these marriages are to be raised as Catholics, as is the usual agreement in Catholic-Protestant marriages. Finally, assume that the wife takes prime responsibility for child-rearing. It follows, then, that the Protestant mother is exposed to more conflict—negative attraction toward spouse's religion and disruptive pressure from own religion—than is the Protestant father. The strength of this conflict would depend on the strength of her religious identification—probably weakest in the lowest strata and strongest in the middle or higher strata. This line of reasoning has clear-cut empirical derivations and may well be testable in Landis's existing data. Additional studies of this question are desirable.

Wife's opportunity for independent income. One other important source of alternate attraction or repulsion lies in the possibility of the wife's separate financial maintenance. The more readily she can support herself outside the marital relationship or can be assured of such support from other means (including her ex-husband's), the more ready she would be to break the marriage.

In most cases where the husband's income is extremely low, and where the wife's earnings are a substantial proportion of family income, these conditions would seem to be met. In the upper economic strata, however, income differentials between wife and husband are large, and the wife has more reason to maintain the marriage (see Goode, 12, p. 516). In other words, wives in the lower strata appear to have less

to lose and more to gain from a divorce. Economic source of alternate attraction for the wife require further attention in research on divorce. Today, when certain forms of relief payment are contingent upon proof of the husband's nonsupport, it is particularly likely that economic factors exercise an influence on divorce proneness.[22]

Considering the wife's attraction to alternate relationships, one may also note interesting differences in divorce rates between the Eastern and Western states. Both Jacobson (16) and Lichtenberger (23) have reported that the Mountain, Southwestern, and Pacific states have had high rates, while the Middle Atlantic and New England states have had low rates. Traditionally, there has been a scarcity of women in the Western states, leading to greater opportunity for remarriage and also to greater female power.

CONCLUSION

This paper introduces an elementary framework for integrating the determinants of marital durability and divorce. The framework is based on merely two components—attractions toward or repulsions from a relationship, and barriers against its dissolution. The former correspond to Lewin's concept of "driving forces," which are said to drive a person either toward a positively valent object or away from a negatively valent one.[23] The latter correspond to Lewin's concept of "restraining forces," which act to restrain a person from leaving any particular relationship or situation.[24] These components

---

[22]In an article based on assumptions similar to Goode's and the present author's, Heer has recently dealt with propositions about the wife's relative power in marriage. David M. Heer, "The Measurement and Bases of Family Power: An Overview," *Marriage and Family Living*, May, 1963, 25, 133–139. Heer writes: ". . . the greater the difference between the value to the wife of the resources contributed by her husband and the value to the wife of the resources which she might earn outside the existing marriage, the greater the power of her husband, and vice-versa" (p. 138). We would propose that in cases of *low difference*, if the husband does not readily yield power within the marriage itself, the wife is inclined instead to dissolve the marriage.

[23]Kurt Lewin, *Field Theory in Social Science* (New York: Harper & Row, Publishers, 1951), 259.

[24]*Ibid.*, 259.

can be used to subsume a large diversity of published findings. For example, findings about the effects of both income differentials and kinship affiliation could logically be fitted within the same scheme. Marital cohesiveness was thus interpreted as a special case of group cohesiveness.

Both the limitations and the advantages of the present analysis should be noted.

Limitations. First, the scheme is based on a hypothetical conception of the attractions and barriers that affect the partners in a marriage. These influences can rarely be inferred directly from changes in overt indices. This is one reason why this paper has not attempted to examine the complex interaction effects between different sets of such influences.

Second, the concept of group cohesiveness, from which this scheme is drawn, is itself the subject of critique and reformulation.[25] Theoretically, it is difficult to define cohesiveness so that it describes under the same rubric the forces that act on both the group and the separate individuals who compose the groups.

Third, the present review of earlier studies has been illustrative rather than comprehensive. Some pertinent studies were omitted. The discussion was often limited to single findings of available studies that were occasionally taken out of their wider context.

Advantages. At this time, it is *not* intended to offer either a general theory or to present an entirely complete review. It *is* intended to understand existing studies at a more general level of abstraction. It is suggested that marriage research can fruitfully be linked to small group research, that simple general hypotheses can be derived in the beginning stages of such a linkage, and that existing evidence about marital dissolution is suitable for documenting such hypotheses.

The present approach draws on the insights of Goode and other writers on marriage and divorce. Yet it aims to go farther in several ways. First, it points to the development of a general framework, congruent with theories about all social groups. It avoids *ad hoc* theories about "marriage" or "family," but aims to integrate the subject with knowledge of social relationships in general.

Second, the scheme intends to deal not only with actuarial rates of divorce nor only with a particular cultural milieu. Its social-psychological concepts are, in principle, applicable to any given marriage in any society. Although marriages and societies differ in the constellation of forces that determine cohesiveness, it is assumed that these determinants ultimately will be measured and precisely described.

Third, and most important, the components of the present scheme are derived from one basic assumption about the existence of psychological and social forces. Such "forces" are hypothetical. They are not easily accessible to measurement. Yet the present statement aims to prepare for eventual measurement.

Previous attempts to explain divorce have sometimes precluded a clear operational assessment. For example, Goode recently accounted for differences in divorce rates in terms of *both* "social pressures from kinfolk and friends" and a culture-based "equalitarian ethos."[26] Yet his two concepts, kin pressures and cultural ethos, are on quite different levels of conceptualization; the former is vaguely contained in the latter. In contrast, the presently proposed framework offers an opportunity for describing the relations among such concepts. To obtain a precise estimate of the various factors which influence divorce, one would need eventually to establish some common measuring unit that would indicate the magnitude of each force.

The present interpretation does not aim at novelty, but it does attempt to prepare the ground for more advanced derivations. Consider one example of a derivation from the scheme. To increase the durability of a marriage, one can (1) increase its positive attractiveness, (2) decrease the attractiveness of

---

[25]For detailed discussions of conceptual and operational issues in research on group cohesiveness, see *Group Dynamics,* ed. by Dorwin Cartwright and Alvin Zander (Evanston, Ill.: Row Peterson, 1960), chapter 3; Annie Van Bergen and J. Koekebakker, "Group Cohesiveness in Laboratory Experiments," *Acta Psychologica,* 1959, *16,* 81–98; Neal Gross and William Martin, On Group Cohesiveness, *American Journal of Sociology,* May, 1952, *57,* 546–554.

[26]Goode, "Family Disorganization," *op. cit.,* 413–414.

alternate relationships, or (3) increase the strength of the barriers against a breakup. What would be the consequence of each of these?

Increase of marital attractions would renew the partners' interest in and affection for one another. It would further the spouses' turning toward each other for their gratification, and would promote the mutual consummation of the marital bond.

Decrease of external attractions would lessen the distractions of the outside environment; therefore, it would encourage the spouse to look toward his partner as an object of need gratification. Yet this is only an indirect way of enhancing marital satisfaction. It is neither a necessary nor a sufficient means for creating positive consequences for the relationship.

Increase of the barriers is the least likely means of making a lasting increase in marital cohesiveness. Without an increase of internal attraction, barrier maintenance does not heighten the satisfactions that partners gain from their marriage. In the absence of adequate marital satisfaction, high barriers are likely to lead to high interpersonal conflict and tension. In fact, the very severity often found in cases of marital conflict may derive from the high restraints society places against breaking up a marriage. Yet this method of keeping a marriage together is society's usual prescription for dealing with low marital cohesiveness.

If the above points are logically correct, then they should lead to empirical investigation of marriage relationships to verify them. For example, one might study marriages with equal degrees of marital satisfaction that differ in boundary strength; under conditions of low satisfaction, lower tension would be predicted in those relationships where the barriers are relatively low. Or is it possible to conceive longitudinal studies in which indices of attraction and barrier forces depict the course of the partner's relationships? Additional illustrations can be developed.

The generality of the present scheme makes it suitable also for analyzing friendship or quasi-marriage relationships. For example, relationships that emerge during courtship and engagement can be examined in these terms. What, for instance, are the determinants of broken engagements? How do broken engagements differ from broken marriages in the constellation of factors that influence the partners? These questions can be investigated by asking what the attractions and barriers are as seen by the partners, and by developing criteria to indicate the stability or persistence of such influences.

To summarize, a conceptual framework has been outlined for integrating research on marital cohesiveness and dissolution. The concepts are the same as those employed for understanding the cohesiveness of other social groups. The strength of the marital relationship is proposed to be a direct function of hypothetical attraction and barrier forces inside the marriage, and an inverse function of such influences from alternate relationships. The scheme was then applied to a review of some major findings about divorce, and its implications were discussed.

CHAPTER XIV

The Incomplete Family

I F A COMPLETE FAMILY is viewed as the nucleus of parents and children, there are a number of ways in which incomplete families can arise. The conjugal pair may be separated or divorced, or a parent may be lost through death. But, as deviations from the ideal, another way that an incomplete family may arise is if an unmarried woman has children. Additionally, never getting married, which is a relatively infrequent occurrence in American society, also creates an incomplete family. The spinster and the bachelor are viewed as anomalies, even if they apparently elect to remain unmarried after having tried the marriage state. Indeed, marriage is sometimes described as the conspiracy of all married persons against unmarried persons. Additionally, as we have noted earlier, the "empty nest" tends to leave a family with aspects of incompletion revealed; and of course, an acute aspect of incompletion arises when a person is left widowed and alone.

This chapter emphasizes the problems of incomplete families. The first article by Paul Glasser and Elizabeth Navarre titled "Structural Problems of the One-Parent Family," focuses on role definitions and constraints associated with particular structures. How do variations in the structure affect the socialization process? What is the relationship of poverty to the structure and how it operates? In what ways are opportunities restricted?

The second article in this chapter is drawn from another government publication authored by Alice J. Clague and Stephanie J. Ventura and is titled "Trends in Illegitimacy." In this publication emphasis is placed on the statistics of illegitimacy, and cross-national comparisons are indicated. The situation is noted of premarital pregnancies that end up as legitimate births because of marriage before parturition. Emphasis is placed on trends in the illegitimacy rates and the relationship of these to certain demographic factors, including the differentials in White and non-White rates. There are many topics that may be raised about the relationship of unmarried motherhood or illegitimate birth to family structure. For example, in a study of pre-pregnancy relationships for women who were not married when they had their first child, only a minority had a liaison unknown to and in isolation from social ties of the couple's family and friends. This study concluded that in general these relationships could not be characterized as deviant, exploitative, or isolated from normal social controls. (Pope, Hollowell, "Unwed Mothers and Their Sex Partners," *Journal of Marriage and the Family*, 1967, 29, 555–567.) Materials have also been published on other aspects, including the sex partners themselves. (See, for example, Vincent, Clark E., "Unmarried Fathers and the Mores," *American Sociological Review*, 1960, 25, 40–66.) Research has also focused on the social and psychological characteristics of unmarried mothers, and the factors involved in whether or not they keep their babies. (See for example, Jones, Wyatt C., Meyer, Henry J., and Borgatta, Edgar F., "Social and Psychological Factors in Status Decisions of Unmarried Mothers," *Marriage and Family Living*, 1962, 24, 224–230.) Finally, the other side of the coin, what happens when babies are adopted has been the subject of a considerable amount of research. (Fanshel, David, *Foster Parenthood: A Role Analysis*, Minneapolis: University of Minnesota Press, 1966.) Since unmarried mothers are viewed as a social problem of some importance in society, a vast literature exists of studies of the many aspects of the problem. The problem is accentuated in the study of the social welfare aspects since unmarried motherhood is frequently associated with indigency.

Another article in this chapter focuses on widowhood, a status that has become more problematic because of the greater average length of life for females. As we have noted in passing, the loss of a spouse in a stable family is disruptive in many ways, whether it is a widow or a widower that survives. When lives have been lived in a complementary dyadic situation, certainly the removal of one member from the pair leaves many gaps in the ordinary responses that satisfy one's daily needs for social interaction. Felix M. Berardo describes the problem for widows in his article titled "Widowhood Status in the United States: Perspective on a Neglected Aspect of the Family Life-Cycle." Problems of economic insecurity, the need for readjustment and possible employment, the management of children if they are present, and other problems are discussed.

The final selection in this chapter is titled "Bachelors and Spinsters," in which Paul C. Glick briefly outlines the statistics of bachelorhood. As noted above, only a very small percentage of the population never marries. It is of interest to note who the persons are who are delaying marriage and who remain unmarried.

57.

PAUL GLASSER AND ELIZABETH NAVARRE

STRUCTURAL PROBLEMS OF THE ONE-PARENT FAMILY

INTRODUCTION

Recent concern about the problems of people who are poor has led to renewed interest in the sources of such difficulties.* While these are manifold and complexly related to each other, emphasis has been placed upon the opportunity structure and the socialization process found among lower socioeconomic groups. Relatively little attention has been paid to family structure, which serves as an important intervening variable between these two considerations. This seems to be a significant omission in view of the major change in the structure of family life in the United States during this century, and the large number of one-parent families classified as poor. The consequences of the latter structural arrangements for family members, parents and children, and for society, is the focus of this paper.

One-parent families are far more apt to be poor than other families. This is true for one-fourth of those headed by a woman. Chilman and Sussman summarize that data in the following way:

About ten percent of the children in the United States are living with only one parent, usually the mother. Nonwhite children are much more likely to live in such circumstances, with one-third of them living in one-parent families. Two and a quarter million families in the United States today are composed of a mother and her children. They represent only one-twelfth of all families with children but make up more than a fourth of all that are classed as poor. . . .

*The conceptualization in this paper grew out of work on Project D-16, "Demonstration of Social Group Work With Parents," financed by a grant from the Children's Bureau, Welfare Administration, Department of Health, Education and Welfare.

This selection is reprinted from: Paul Glasser and Elizabeth Navarre, "Structural Problems of the One-Parent Family," *Journal of Social Issues*, 1965, 21, 1, 98–109.
Reprinted with the permission of the authors and publisher.

Despite the resulting economic disadvantages, among both white and nonwhite families there is a growing number headed only by a mother. By 1960 the total was 7½ percent of all families with own children rather than the six percent of ten years earlier. By March 1962 the mother-child families represented 8½ percent of all families with own children (4, p. 393).

When these demographic findings are seen in the context of the relative isolation of the nuclear family in the United States today, the structural consequences of the one-parent group takes on added meaning. It may be seen as the culmination of the contraction of the effective kin group.

This "isolation" is manifested in the fact that the members of the nuclear family, consisting of parents and their still dependent children, ordinarily occupy a separate dwelling not shared with members of the family of orientation. . . . It is, of course, not uncommon to find a (member of the family of orientation) residing with the family, but this is both statistically secondary, and it is clearly not felt to be the "normal arrangement" (9, p. 10).

While families maintain social contact with grown children and with siblings, lines of responsibility outside of the nuclear group are neither clear nor binding, and obligations among extended kin are often seen as limited and weak. Even when affectional ties among extended family members are strong, their spatial mobility in contemporary society isolates the nuclear group geographically, and increases the difficulty of giving aid in personal service among them (2, 6).

Associated with the weakening of the extended kinship structure has been the loss of some social functions of the family and the lessened import of others. Nonetheless, reproduction, physical maintenance, placement or status, and socialization are still considered significant social functions of the modern American family although they often have to be buttressed by other institutions in the community. At the same

536

time, however, the personal functions of the family, including affection, security, guidance and sexual gratification have been heightened and highlighted (3, 9). These functions are closely and complexly related to each other but can serve as foci for analysis of the consequences of family structure. In the one-parent family neither reproduction nor sexual gratification can be carried out within the confines of the nuclear group itself. But more importantly, the other personal and social functions are drastically affected also, and it is to these that this paper will give its attention. A few of the implications for social policy and practice will be mentioned at the end.

While it is recognized that all individuals have some contact with others outside the nuclear group, for purposes of analytic clarity this paper will confine itself to a discussion of the relationships among nuclear family members primarily. Two factors will be the foci of much of the content. The age difference between parent and children is central to the analysis. Although it is understood that children vary with age in the degree of independence from their parents, the nature of their dependence will be emphasized throughout. The sex of the parent and the sex of the children is the second variable. Cultural definitions of appropriate behavior for men and women and for girls and boys vary from place to place and are in the process of change, but nonetheless this factor cannot be ignored. Since the largest majority of one-parent families are headed by a woman, greater attention will be given to the mother-son and mother-daughter relationships in the absence of the father.

STRUCTURAL CHARACTERISTICS OF ONE-PARENT FAMILIES AND THEIR CONSEQUENCES

Task Structure

The large majority of tasks for which a family is responsible devolve upon the parents. Providing for the physical, emotional, and social needs of all the family members is a full-time job for two adults. If these tasks are to be performed by the nuclear group during the absence or incapacity of one of its adult members, the crucial factor is the availability of another member with sufficient maturity, competence, and time to perform them. The two-parent family has sufficient flexibility to adapt to such a crisis. Although there is considerable specialization in the traditional sex roles concerning these tasks, there is little evidence that such specialization is inherent in the sex roles. It is, in fact, expected that one parent will substitute if the other parent is incapacitated and, in our essentially servantless society, such acquired tasks are given full social approval. However, in the one-parent family such flexibility is much less possible, and the permanent loss of the remaining parent generally dissolves the nuclear group.

Even if the remaining parent is able to function adequately, it is unlikely that one person can take over all parental tasks on a long term basis. Financial support, child care, and household maintenance are concrete tasks involving temporal and spatial relationships, and in one form or another they account for a large proportion of the waking life of two adult family members. A permanent adjustment then must involve a reduction in the tasks performed and/or a reduction in the adequacy of performance, or external assistance.

In addition to limitations on the time and energy available to the solitary parent for the performance of tasks, there are social limitations on the extent to which both the male and the female tasks may be fulfilled by a member of one sex. If the remaining parent be male, it is possible for him to continue to perform his major role as breadwinner and to hire a woman to keep house and, at least, to care for the children's physical needs. If, however, the solitary parent be a female, as is the more usual case, the woman must take on the male role of breadwinner, unless society or the absent husband provides financial support in the form of insurance, pensions, welfare payments, etc. This is a major reversal in cultural roles and, in addition, usually consumes the mother's time and energy away from the home for many hours during the day. There is little time or energy left to perform the tasks normally performed by the female in the household and she, too, must hire a female substitute at considerable cost. The effect of this reversal of the sex role model in the socialization of children has been a matter of some concern, but the emphasis has been upon the male child who lacked a male role model rather than upon the effect of the reversal of the female role model for children of both sexes. In both cases, the probability seems great that some tasks will be neglected, particularly those of the traditionally female specialization.

The wish to accomplish concrete household tasks in the most efficient manner in terms of time and energy expenditure may lead to less involvement of children in these tasks and the concomitant loss of peripheral benefits that are extremely important to the socialization process and/or to family cohesion. Some tasks may be almost completely avoided, especially those which are not immediately obvious to the local community, such as the provision of emotional support and attention to children. A third possibility is to overload children, particularly adolescents, with such tasks. These may be greater than the child is ready to assume, or tasks inappropriate for the child of a particular sex to perform regularly.

Females are often lacking in skills and experience in the economic world, and frequently receive less pay and lower status jobs than men with similar skills. The probability of lower income and lower occupational status for the female-headed household is likely to lower the family's social position in a society which bases social status primarily upon these variables. If the family perceives a great enough distance between its former level and that achieved by the single parent, it is possible that the family as a whole may become more or less anomic, with serious consequences in the socialization process of the children and in the remaining parent's perception of personal adequacy.

COMMUNICATION STRUCTURE

Parents serve as the channels of communication with the adult world in two ways; first as transmitters of the cultural value system which has previously been internalized by the parents; and secondly, as the child's contact with and representative in the adult world. Except for very young children, the parents are not the sole means of communication, but for a large part of the socialization process, the child sees the adult world through the eyes and by the experience of his parents, and even his own experiences are limited to those which can be provided for him within whatever social opportunities that are open to his parents. More importantly, to the extent that the child's identity is integrated with that of the family, he is likely to see himself not only as his parents see him but also as the world sees his parents.

Since sex differences have been assumed in the ways men and women see the world and differences can be substantiated in the ways that the world sees men and women, the child can have a relatively undistorted channel of communication only if both parents are present. Therefore, whatever the interests, values, and opinions of the remaining parent, the loss of a parent of one sex produces a structural distortion in the communications between the child and the adult world and, since such communication is a factor in the development of the self-image, of social skills, and of an image of the total society, the totality of the child's possible development is also distorted.

The type and quality of experiences available even to adults tend to be regulated according to sex. In the two-parent family not only is the child provided with more varied experiences, but the parent of either sex has, through the spouse, some communication with the experiences typical of the opposite sex. Thus, the housewife is likely to have some idea of what is going on in the business or sports worlds even if she has no interest in them. The solitary parent is not likely to be apprised of such information and is handicapped to the extent that it may be necessary for decision making. The female who has taken on the breadwinner role may be cut off from the sources of information pertinent to the female role as she misses out on neighborhood gossip about the symptoms of the latest virus prevalent among the children, events being planned, the best places to shop, etc.

Finally, the solitary parent is likely to be limited in the social ties that are normal channels of communication. Most social occasions for adults tend to be planned for couples and the lone parent is often excluded or refuses because of the discomfort of being a fifth wheel. Her responsibilities to home and children tend to never be completed and provide additional reasons for refusing invitations. Lone women are particularly vulnerable to community sanctions and must be cautious in their social relationships lest their own standing and that of the family be lowered. Finally, the possible drop in social status previously discussed may isolate the family from its own peer group and place them among a group with which they can not or will not communicate freely.

POWER STRUCTURE

Bales and Borgatta (1) have pointed out that the diad has unique properties and certainly a uniquely simple power structure. In terms of authority from which the children are more or less excluded by age and social norms, the one-parent family establishes a diadic relationship, between the parent and each child. Society places full responsibility in the parental role, and, therefore, the parent becomes the only power figure in the one-parent family. Consequently, the adult in any given situation is either for or against the child. Some experience of playing one adult against the other, as long as it is not carried to extremes, is probably valuable in developing social skills and in developing a view of authority as tolerable and even manipulable within reason, rather than absolute and possibly tyrannical. In the one-parent family the child is more likely to see authority as personal rather than consensual, and this in itself removes some of the legitimation of the power of parents as the representatives of society.

Even if benevolent, the absolutism of the power figure in the one-parent family, where there can be no experience of democratic decision-making between equals in power, may increase the difficulty of the adolescent and the young adult in achieving independence from the family, and that of the parent in allowing and encouraging such development. Further, the adult, the power of authority figure, is always of one sex, whether that sex be the same sex as the child or the opposite. However, in con-

temporary society where decision making is the responsibility of both sexes, the child who has identified authority too closely with either sex may have a difficult adjustment. The situation also has consequences for the parent, for when the supportive reinforcement or the balancing mediation which comes with the sharing of authority for decision making is absent, there may be a greater tendency to frequent changes in the decisions made, inconsistency, or rigidity.

AFFECTIONAL STRUCTURE

The personal functions of the family in providing for the emotional needs of its members have been increasingly emphasized. There is ample evidence that children require love and security in order to develop in a healthy manner. Although there is nearly as much substantiation for the emotional needs of parents, these are less frequently emphasized. Adults must have love and security in order to maintain emotional stability under the stresses of life and in order to meet the emotional demands made upon them by their children. In addition to providing the positive emotional needs of its members, the family has the further function of providing a safe outlet for negative feelings as well. Buttressed by the underlying security of family affection, the dissatisfactions and frustrations of life may be expressed without the negative consequences attendant upon their expression in other contexts. Even within the family, however, the expressions of such basic emotions cannot go unchecked. The needs of one member or one sub-group may dominate to the point that the requirements of others are not fulfilled, or are not met in a manner acceptable to society. To some extent this danger exists in any group, but it is particularly strong in a group where emotional relationships are intensive. Traditionally, the danger is reduced by regulating the context, manner, and occasion of the expression of such needs.

Family structure is an important element both in the provision and the regulation of emotional needs. The increasing isolation of the nuclear family focuses these needs on the nuclear group by weakening ties with the larger kin group. Thus, both generations and both sexes are forced into a more intensive relationship; yet the marital relationship itself is increasingly unsupported by legal or social norms and is increasingly dependent upon affectional ties alone for its solidity. Such intense relationships are increased within the one-parent family, and possibly reach their culmination in the family consisting of one parent and one child.

In a two person group the loss of one person destroys the group. The structure, therefore, creates pressure for greater attention to group maintenance through the expression of affection and the denial of negative feelings, and in turn may restrict problem solving efforts. In a sense, the one-parent family is in this position even if there are several children because the loss of the remaining parent effectively breaks up the group. The children have neither the ability nor the social power to maintain the group's independence. Therefore, the one-parent family structure exerts at least some pressure in this direction.

However, where there is more than one child there is some mitigation of the pattern, though this in itself may have some disadvantages. In a group of three or more there are greater possibilities for emotional outlet for those not in an authority role. Unfortunately, there are also greater possibilities that one member may become the scapegoat as other members combine against him. In spite of the power relationships, it is even possible that the solitary parent will become the scapegoat if the children combine against her. This problem is greatest in the three person family as three of the five possible sub-groups reject one member (Figure 57–2). The problem is also present in the four person family, although the possible sub-groups in which the family combines against one member has dropped to four out of 12 (Figure 57–1). The relation of group structure to emotional constriction has been clearly expressed by Slater:

> The disadvantages of the smaller groups are not verbalized by members, but can only be inferred from their behavior. It appears that group members are too tense, passive, tactful, and constrained, to work together in a manner which is altogether satisfying to them. *Their fear of alienating one another seems to prevent them from expressing their ideas freely.* (Emphasis is ours.)

These findings suggest that maximal group satisfaction is achieved when the group is large enough so that the members feel able to express positive and negative feelings freely, and to make aggressive efforts toward problem solving even at the risk of antagonizing each other, yet small enough so that some regard will be shown for the feelings and needs of others; large enough so that the loss of a member could be tolerated, but small enough so that such a loss could not be altogether ignored (11, p. 138).

SUB-GROUP CHOICES AMONG GROUPS OF
VARYING SIZES*

1.	A,B,C,D	5.	B,C,D	9.	B,D
2.	A,B,C	6.	A,B	10.	A,D
3.	A,B,D	7.	C,D	11.	B,C
4.	A,C,D	8.	A,C	12.	All persons independent; no sub-group

Figure 57–1. The Four Person Group

1.	A,B,C	3.	A,B	5.	All persons independent; no sub-group
2.	B,C	4.	A,C		

Figure 57–2. The Three Person Group

*Persons designated by letter.

Interpersonal relationships between parents and children in the area of emotional needs are not entirely reciprocal because of age and power differences in the family. Parents provide children with love, emotional support, and an outlet for negative feelings. However, while the love of a child is gratifying to the adult in some ways, it cannot be considered as supporting; rather it is demanding in the responsibilities it places upon the loved one. Support may be received only from one who is seen as equal or greater in power and discrimination. Nor can the child serve as a socially acceptable outlet for negative emotions to the extent that another adult can, for the child's emotional and physical dependency upon the adult makes him more vulnerable to possible damage from this source. The solitary parent in the one-parent family is structurally deprived of a significant element in the meeting of his own emotional needs. To this must be added the psychological and physical frustrations of the loss of the means for sexual gratification. In some situations involving divorce or desertion, the damage to the self-image of the remaining parent may intensify the very needs for support and reassurance which can no longer be met within the family structure.

The regulation of emotional demands of family members is similar in many ways to the regulation of the behavior of family members discussed under power structure. As there was the possibility that authority might be too closely identified with only one sex in the one-parent family, there is the similar danger that the source of love and affection may be seen as absolute and/or as vested in only one sex. Having only one source of love and security, both physical and emotional, is more likely to produce greater anxiety about its loss in the child, and may make the child's necessary withdrawal from the family with growing maturity more difficult for both parent and child. Again, as in the power structure, the identification of the source of love with only one sex is likely to cause a difficult adjustment to adult life, particularly if the original source of love was of the same sex as the child, for our society's expectations are that the source of love for an adult must lie with the opposite sex.

One of the most important regulatory devices for the emotional needs of the group is the presence and influence of members who serve to deter or limit demands which would be harmful to group members or to group cohesion, and to prevent the intensification of the influence of any one individual by balancing it with the influence of others. Parental figures will tend to have greater influence in acting as a deterrent or balance to the needs and demands of other family members because of their greater power and maturity. The loss of one parent removes a large portion of the structural balance and intensifies the influence of the remaining parent upon the children, while possibly limiting the ability of this parent to withstand demands made upon her by the children. There is also a tendency for any family member to transfer to one or more of the remaining members the demands formerly filled by the absent person (8). There would seem to be a danger in the one-parent family that:

1. The demands of the sole parent for the fulfillment of individual and emotional needs normally met within the marital relationship may prove intolerable and damaging to the children, who are unable to give emotional support or to absorb negative feelings from this source, or

2. The combined needs of the children may be intolerable to the emotionally unsupported solitary parent. Since the emotional requirements of children are very likely to take the form of demands for physical attention or personal service, the remaining parent may be subject to physical as well as emotional exhaustion from the source.

When emotional needs are not met within the family, there may be important consequences for the socialization of the children and for the personal adjustment of all family members. Further, fulfillment of such needs may be sought in the larger community by illegitimate means. The children may exhibit emotional problems in school or in their relations with their play group. A parent may be unable to control her own emotions and anxieties sufficiently to function adequately in society. When there are no means for the satisfaction of these demands they may well prove destructive, not only to the family group and its individual members, but to society as well.

The consequences of the problems discussed above may be minimized or magnified by the personal resources or inadequacies of the family members, and particularly the solitary parent in this situation. But, the problems are structural elements of the situation, and must be faced on this level if they are to be solved.

IMPLICATIONS FOR SOCIAL POLICY AND PRACTICE

The introduction describes the growth of the number of one-parent families during the last generation. Chilman and Sussman go on to describe the financial plight of many of these families.

The public program of aid to families with dependent children (AFDC) that is most applicable to this group currently makes payments on behalf of children in nearly a million families. Three out of every four of these families have no father in the home. Less than half of the families that are estimated to be in need receive payments under the program and, ". . . with the low financial standards for aid to dependent children prevailing in many states, dependence on the program for support is in itself likely to put the family in low-income status. . . . The average monthly payment per family as reported in a study late in 1961 was only $112. . . .

"The overall poverty of the recipient families is suggested by the fact that, according to the standards set up in their own states, half of them are still in financial need even with their assistance payment" (4, p. 394; 10).

There is increasing evidence that both the one-parent family structure and poverty are being transmitted from one generation to the next.

"A recently released study of cases assisted by aid to families with dependent children shows that, for a nationwide sample of such families whose cases were closed early in 1961" more than 40 percent of the mothers and/or fathers were raised in the homes where some form of assistance had been received at some time. "Nearly half of these cases had received aid to families with dependent children. This estimated proportion that received some type of aid is more than four times the almost 10 percent estimated for the total United States population . . ." (4, p. 395; 10).

If poverty and one-parent family structure tend to go together, providing increases in financial assistance alone may not be sufficient to help parents and children in the present and future generation to become financially independent of welfare funds. Under the 1962 amendments to the Social Security Act states are now receiving additional funds to provide rehabilitation services to welfare families, and these programs have begun. Creative use of such funds to overcome some of the consequences of one-parent family structure is a possibility, but as yet the authors know of no services that have explicitly taken this direction.

A few suggestions may serve to illustrate how existing or new services might deal with the consequences of one-parent family structure:

1. Recognition of the need of the mother without a husband at home for emotional support and social outlets could lead to a variety of services. Recreation and problem-focused groups for women in this situation, which would provide some opportunities for socially sanctioned heterosexual relationships, might go a long way in helping these parents and their children.
2. Special efforts to provide male figures to which both girls and boys can relate may have utility. This can be done in day-care centers, settlement house agencies, schools, and through the inclusion of girls in programs like the Big Brothers. It would be particularly useful for children in one-parent families to see the ways in which adults of each sex

deal with each other in these situations, and at an early age.
3. Subsidization of child care and housekeeping services for parents with children too young or unsuitable for day-care services would provide greater freedom for solitary mothers to work outside the home. Training persons as homemakers and making them responsible to an agency or a professional organization would reduce the anxiety of the working parent, and provide greater insurance to both the parent and society that this important job would be done well.

More fundamental to the prevention of poverty and the problems of one-parent family status may be programs aimed at averting family dissolution through divorce, separation and desertion, particularly among lower socioeconomic groups. Few public programs have addressed themselves to this problem, and there is now a good deal of evidence that the private family agencies which provide counseling services have disenfranchised themselves from the poor (5). The need to involve other institutional components in the community, such as the educational, economic and political systems, is obvious but beyond the scope of discussion in this paper (7). Increasing the number of stable and enduring marriages in the community so as to prevent the consequences of one-parent family structure may be a first line of defense, and more closely related to treating the causes rather than the effects of poverty for a large number of people who are poor.

SUMMARY

One-parent families constitute more than a fourth of that group classified as poor, and are growing in number. Family structure is seen as a variable intervening between the opportunity system and the socialization process. The task, communication, power and affectional structure within the nuclear group are influenced by the absence of one parent, and the family's ability to fulfill its social and personal functions may be adversely affected. Some of the consequences of this deviant family structure seem related to both the evolvement of low socioeconomic status and its continuation from one generation to the next. Solutions must take account of this social situational problem.

REFERENCES

1. BALES, R. F. AND BORGATTA, E. F. Size of group as a factor in the interaction profile. In HARE, BORGATTA, and BALES, (eds.), *Small groups.* New York: Knopf, 1955.
2. BELL, W. AND BOAT, M. D. Urban neighborhoods and informal social relations. *American Journal of Sociology,* 1957, 43, 391–398.
3. BERNARD, J. *American family behavior.* New York: Harper & Row, Publishers, 1942.
4. CHILMAN, C. AND SUSSMAN, M. Poverty in the United States. *Journal Marriage and the Family,* 1964, 26, 391–395.
5. CLOWARD, R. A. AND EPSTEIN, I. Private social welfare's disengagement from the poor: the case of family adjustment agencies. Mimeographed, April, 1964.
6. LITWAK, E. Geographic mobility and extended family cohesion. *American Sociological Review,* 1960, 25, 385–394.
7. LUTZ, W. A. Marital incompatability. In COHEN, N. E. (ed.) *Social work and social problems.* New York: National Association of Social Workers, 1964.
8. MITTLEMAN, B. Analysis of reciprocal neurotic patterns in family relationships. In V. Eisenstein (ed.), *Neurotic interaction in marriage.* New York: Basic Books, 1956.
9. PARSONS, T. AND BALES, R. F. Family socialization and interaction processes. New York: The Free Press, 1954.
10. *Poverty in the United States.* Committee on Education and Labor, House of Representatives, 88th Congress, Second Session, April, 1964. U.S. Government Printing Office, Washington, D.C.
11. SLATER, P. E. Contrasting correlates of group size. *Sociometry,* 1958, 6, 129–139.

58.

ALICE J. CLAGUE AND STEPHANIE J. VENTURA

TRENDS IN ILLEGITIMACY

Over the years included in this study, the number of states asking for the legitimacy status of the child has declined. During the 1930's almost all states had the legitimacy item on their certificates. During the 1940's, however, a concern for the confidentiality of this item prompted a number of states to remove it. Today most state vital statistics offices take special care to insure the confidentiality of a child's legitimacy status.

The quality of illegitimacy statistics is affected by the completeness of birth registration as well as by the accuracy with which the legitimacy item is completed. Some of the recent increase in illegitimate births may be due to improvements in the registration of births. However, improved reporting could account for only a small part of the observed increase.

No attempt has been made to evaluate the accuracy with which the legitimacy question is completed. It is impossible to say whether the accuracy has varied over time, yet it is probable that variation in accuracy exists among different segments of the population.

It was noted above that only 34 states and the District of Columbia currently report illegitimacy. Among the nonreporting states are New York, California, and Massachusetts, together accounting for 21 percent of all births in 1964. In order to have national figures on illegitimacy, estimates are prepared for the number of illegitimate births occurring in these and other nonreporting states. To obtain national estimates, all states are grouped into nine geographic divisions. The combined ratio of illegitimate births per 1000 total live births for all reporting states in a single geographic division is then applied

This selection is reprinted from: Alice J. Clague, and Stephanie J. Ventura, *Trends in Illegitimacy; United States—1940-1965* (Vital and Health Statistics, Series 21, No. 15), Washington, D. C.: GPO, U. S. Department of Health, Education, and Welfare, 1968. [excerpted from pp. 1–17].

to all the live births occurring to residents of that division. This yields an estimate of illegitimate live births for the geographic division. This procedure is applied separately to white and nonwhite births. The sum of these estimates for the nine geographic divisions makes up the estimate for the United States.

This method assumes that the nonreporting states in a given geographic division have the same proportion of illegitimate births as the reporting states in that division. The reliability of the estimates is therefore influenced by the proportion of births to residents of the reporting states in each geographic division. In some divisions this proportion is small, particularly in the New England, Middle Atlantic, Mountain, and Pacific divisions. Therefore an independent estimate was made of the number of illegitimate births in the nonreporting states in 1964 in order to evaluate the usual estimation procedure. In general, the independent estimates of illegitimacy were remarkably consistent with the results obtained from the customary estimation procedure. . . .

The findings in this report are based largely on the illegitimacy rate, which is the number of illegitimate births per 1000 unmarried women aged 15-44 years. This rate is used to measure the likelihood that an unmarried woman will give birth.

INTRODUCTION

The steady increase in the annual number of illegitimate births since 1940 has led to widespread public concern for the causes and consequences of illegitimacy in the United States. The principal purpose of this report is to examine this trend and describe some of the factors associated with it.

The principal topics covered here are (1) trends and differentials in the incidence of illegitimacy, (2) factors accounting for these trends and differentials, and (3) differences in health between the legitimate and illegitimate newborn infants.

A number of special tabulations were prepared for 1964, the most recent year for which detailed data were available at the time this report was written.

The previous report on this subject was "Illegitimate Births: United States, 1938-1957." (1) In addition to the information in that publication, further detailed tables are shown in the annual report, *Vital Statistics of the United States*, Vol. 1.

SOURCE OF DATA AND METHODOLOGY

The source of data for this report is the certificate of live birth filed for each child born in the United States. The birth certificates of 34 states and the District of Columbia include an item asking for the legitimacy status of the child.

Other analytical measures that are sometimes used in describing patterns of illegitimacy will be discussed where appropriate. These include the illegitimacy ratio (the number of illegitimate births per 1000 total births) and the total illegitimacy rate (number of illegitimate births per 1000 total women aged 15-44 years).

THE ILLEGITIMACY RATE

COMPARISON OF THE UNITED STATES WITH ENGLAND AND WALES

Trends in the illegitimacy rate for the United States are available for a relatively short period of time, because all states were not included in the birth-registration area until 1933 and estimates for the states not reporting illegitimacy were not made until 1938. In England and Wales, where the registration system is older, comparable data are available since 1850. (2) The long historical trend shown in Figure 58–1 for this country gives some perspective to the picture presented by the United States for the shorter period. It suggests that illegitimacy may have been nearly as high in the past as it is now. In any case, we cannot assume that the currently high rates represent a phenomenon entirely without precedent in Western society.

In England and Wales, the illegitimacy rate declined fairly steadily from 18.3 during 1851-60 to a low of 5.5 illegitimate births per 1000 unmarried women in the early 1930's. There was relatively little change until the 1940's. Then the rate rose rapidly to 16.1 in 1945 and began

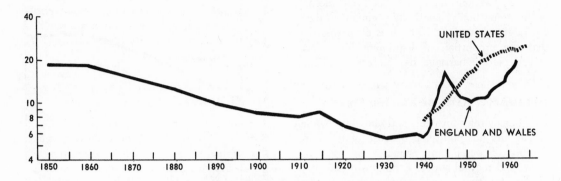

FIGURE 58–1. ILLEGITIMACY RATES: ENGLAND AND WALES, 1851–1962,[2] AND
UNITED STATES, 1940-65. (SEMILOGARITHMIC SCALE. RATES FOR THE UNITED STATES
ARE ESTIMATED.)

to decline immediately after the war to a level of about ten illegitimate births per 1000 unmarried women in 1950. After 1955, the rate began to increase rapidly and steadily, as it had during the early war years, until by 1962 it had reached a level of 18.9, almost the same as the rate observed during the 1850's.

The illegitimacy rate for the United States increased steadily from 1940 to 1957 (from 7.1 to 21.0) in contrast to the rise and fall in the illegitimacy rate experienced in England and Wales during the last two decades. There has been little change in rate during the period 1958-65: in some years the rate increased, while in others it declined slightly. In 1965 the rate was 23.5. Figure 58–1 indicates that during the 1950's the illegitimacy rates for both countries increased at about the same pace.

PREMARITAL CONCEPTIONS ENDING IN LEGITIMATE BIRTHS

Not all conceptions occurring before marriage result in illegitimate births. In many cases the couple marries before delivery and the child is registered as legitimate. Some inferential data on this pattern of behavior are presented in Table 58–1. These data are based on a survey of marriage, fertility, and childspacing conducted by the Bureau of the Census in 1959. (3) According to Table 58–1, the proportion premaritally pregnant has risen for white women mar-

TABLE 58–1. ESTIMATED PERCENT OF WOMEN
MARRIED IN SPECIFIED YEARS WHOSE FIRST CHILD
WAS BORN WITHIN EIGHT MONTHS OF MARRIAGE,
BY COLOR: UNITED STATES.

Marriage cohort and color	Percent
White women	
1955-59	16.0
1950-54	11.9
1945-49	10.3
1940-44	8.0
1935-39	8.6
1930-34	9.0
1925-29	8.1
1920-24	8.3
1910-19	8.9
1900-1909	7.4
Nonwhite women	
1950-59	41.3
1940-49	29.4
1930-39	25.5
1920-29	21.8
1910-19	20.7
1900-1909	11.8

NOTE: Figures based on data shown in tables 16 and 17 in U.S. Bureau of the Census, "Marriage, Fertility and Child-spacing, August 1959," by W. Grabill and R. Parke, Jr., *Current Population Reports*, Series P-20, No. 108, Washington, D.C., July, 1961.

ried since 1945. For example, among white women who first married during 1955-59, 16.0 percent had a first birth within eight months of marriage. This proportion is twice as great as the comparable proportion among white women who first married during 1940-44. For nonwhite women there has been an increase in the proportion premaritally pregnant in every marriage cohort since 1900. It is clear therefore that the proportion of legitimate births conceived before marriage has increased substantially.

ILLEGITIMACY RATES BY AGE AND COLOR

Illegitimacy rates for white and nonwhite women are usually not published because of the unreliability of population estimates by age, sex, color, and marital status. Estimates of the population by these demographic characteristics are available for the census years 1940 and 1950 and for each of the intercensal years since 1957. Since intercensal estimates of the numbers of unmarried women by age were obtained from a sample survey, they fluctuate widely from year to year. Therefore they were smoothed for the computation of illegitimacy rates.

There are large differences in the incidence of illegitimacy between white and nonwhite women as shown in Figure 58–2 and Table 58–2. In 1940 the illegitimacy rate for nonwhite women was 35.6, about ten times greater than the rate of 3.6 for white women. During the 1940's the rate rose more rapidly for nonwhite women than for white. By 1950 the rate for the former was 71.2, and that for the latter was 6.1. Since then the rise has been slightly more rapid for white women. Although the nonwhite rate for 1950 was about 12 times higher than the white rate, by 1965 this color differential (expressed as the ratio of the nonwhite to the white measure) had declined to slightly over eight times as high. In that year 9.8 percent of the unmarried nonwhite women and 1.2 percent of the unmarried white women had an illegitimate child. Actually, the illegitimacy rate for nonwhite women has shown a slight decline since 1960 (one percent during the period 1960-65) while the rate for white women has increased 26 percent. Trends in the illegitimacy rate for white and nonwhite, unmarried women are illustrated in Figure 58–2.

The illegitimacy rates for each age and color group indicate that the trend is generally the same for women of the same age within each

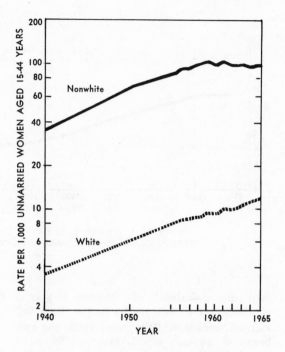

FIGURE 58–2. ESTIMATED ILLEGITIMACY RATES, BY COLOR: UNITED STATES, 1940, 1950, 1955-65. (SEMILOGARITHMIC SCALE)

color group except for the age groups 15-19 and 25-29 (Figure 58–3). Nonwhite teenagers have been the only group to show a sustained decline since 1957. Between 1957 and 1965, there was a net decline of 5.6 births per 1,000 in the illegitimacy rates for nonwhite women aged 15-19. In contrast rates for white teenagers showed an increase of 1.5 births per 1000.

Although it is commonly believed that teenagers have the greatest risk of bearing an illegitimate child (over 40 percent of the illegitimate children are born to mothers 15-19 years of age), these women actually have the lowest illegitimacy rates among women under 35 years of age (Table 58–2). In general the illegitimacy rates for women 25 years of age and over have increased more rapidly than those for younger

TABLE 58–2. ESTIMATED NUMBER OF ILLEGITIMATE BIRTHS PER 1000 UNMARRIED WOMEN 15-44, BY AGE AND COLOR OF MOTHER: UNITED STATES, 1940, 1950, 1960, 1964, AND 1965.

[Refers only to births occurring within the United States. Alaska and Hawaii included beginning 1960. Figures for age of mother not stated are distributed.]

Age and color	1965*	1964*	1960*	1950	1940
Total	Rate per 1000 unmarried women in specified group				
15-44 years†	23.5	23.0	21.6	14.1	7.1
15-19 years	16.7	15.8	15.3	12.6	7.4
20-24 years	39.9	39.9	39.7	21.3	9.5
25-29 years	49.3	50.2	45.1	19.9	7.2
30-34 years	37.5	37.2	27.8	13.3	5.1
35-39 years	17.4	16.3	14.1	7.2	3.4
40-44 years‡	4.5	4.4	3.6	2.0	1.2
White					
15-44 years†	11.6	11.0	9.2	6.1	3.6
15-19 years	7.9	7.3	6.6	5.1	3.3
20-24 years	22.1	21.2	18.2	10.0	5.7
25-29 years	24.3	24.1	18.2	8.7	4.0
30-34 years	16.6	15.9	10.8	5.9	2.5
35-39 years	...	...	...	3.2	1.7
40-44 years‡	4.9	4.8	3.9	0.9	0.7
Nonwhite					
15-44 years†	97.6	97.2	98.3	71.2	35.6
15-19 years	75.8	74.0	76.5	68.5	42.5
20-24 years	152.6	164.2	166.5	105.4	46.1
25-29 years	164.7	168.7	171.8	94.2	32.5
30-34 years	137.8	132.3	104.0	63.5	23.4
35-39 years	...	...	...	31.3	13.2
40-44 years‡	39.0	34.5	35.6	8.7	5.0

*Based on a 50 percent sample of births.
†Rates computed by relating total births, regardless of age of mother, to women 15-44.
‡Rates computed by relating births to mothers aged 40 and over to women aged 40-44.

women during the period 1940-65.

LIVE-BIRTH ORDER AND COLOR

By relating the number of first illegitimate births to the population of unmarried women, it is possible to determine the minimum number who became mothers of an illegitimate child for the first time in a given year. (Some additional women may have their first illegitimate birth sometime after the birth of one more legitimate children, but it is impossible to identify such women from information given on the birth certificate.) Table 58–3 shows that in 1964 1.2 percent of the unmarried women became mothers for the first time. The proportions were 4.3 percent for nonwhite women and 0.7 percent for white women.

It appears that the white-nonwhite differential has declined a little over the past ten years due to an increased tendency of white women to have illegitimate children of all orders. Figure 58–4 indicates that there has been little or no change in the rate of higher order illegitimacy among nonwhite women. In fact, most of the increase in illegitimacy rates since 1955 for both color groups can be attributed to an increase in first illegitimate births.

GEOGRAPHIC VARIATION

Each state has its own laws and regulations de-

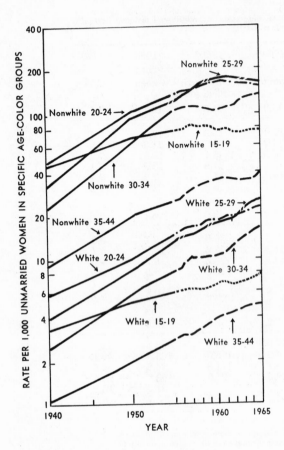

FIGURE 58–3. ESTIMATED ILLEGITIMACY RATES, BY AGE OF MOTHER AND COLOR: UNITED STATES, 1940, 1950, 1955-65.
(SEMILOGARITHMIC SCALE)

fining an illegitimate birth. In some states an illegitimate birth is a child whose mother reports that she is not currently married. The birth certificates in a few of these states ask only, "Is mother married?" The child is considered legitimate if she is married. In other states, a birth is classified as illegitimate if the child was conceived "out of wedlock" to an unmarried woman or to a married woman by a man who was not her husband. Every state assumes that a child born to a widowed or divorced woman is legiti-

mate if the mother and her husband were living together at the time of conception.

Since a high proportion of the illegitimate births are to women who have never been married, we can assume that any differences in the laws affect the legitimacy status of only a small proportion of all infants.

It is highly likely that the quality of reporting varies from state to state and from one locale to another within states. For example, it may be easier for a woman to hide the fact that she is not married if she lives in a large metropolitan area than if she lives in a small town. Therefore comparisons made between different geographic locations should be made with caution. Small differences may not mean a great deal.

Only in the census years is it possible to obtain estimates for each state of the number of unmarried women by age, estimates that are needed to compute illegitimacy rates. In 1960 there were 24 illegitimate births per 1000 unmarried women aged 15-44 years in the reporting states; in other words, 2.4 percent of the women "at risk" actually had an illegitimate child.

The highest illegitimacy rates were found primarily in the South Atlantic and in the East and West South Central divisions. Of the reporting states, Alaska was the only state outside these divisions with an illegitimacy rate above 25 per 1000. The highest reported rates of illegitimacy were for Mississippi (64.3) and the District of Columbia (60.0). South Carolina, Alabama, Florida, Alaska, Louisiana, and Delaware all had rates between 40.0 and 50.0. (See Figure 58–4 for greater detail.)

Most of the states with relatively low rates of illegitimacy were in the New England or Midwestern areas.

The rates for white women were highest in Hawaii (21.5), West Virginia (16.4), and Delaware (14.3) and lowest in Alabama (6.7), Mississippi (6.0), and New Jersey (5.3). There was relatively little correlation between rates for white and nonwhite women. Nonwhite women in Delaware (179.2), Florida (150.8), and Missouri (136.1) had the highest rates while those in Michigan (72.5), Washington (62.4), and Hawaii (22.6) had the lowest.

TABLE 58–3. ESTIMATED NUMBER OF ILLEGITIMATE BIRTHS AND ILLEGITIMACY RATES, BY LIVE-BIRTH ORDER AND COLOR: UNITED STATES, 1947, 1955, 1960, AND 1964.

[Refers only to births occurring within the United States. Live-birth order refers to number of children born to mother. Figures for live-birth order not stated are distributed. Due to rounding estimates to the nearest hundred, figures by color may not add to totals.]

		Live-birth order				
Year and color	Total	First	Second and higher	Total	First	Second and higher
Total		Number of illegitimate births			Illegitimacy rates	
1964*	275,700	147,500	128,000	23.0	12.3	10.8
1960*	224,300	110,300	114,000	21.6	10.6	11.0
1955	183,300	91,700	91,600	19.3	9.7	9.7
1947	131,900	81,800	50,100	12.1	7.5	4.6
White						
1964*	114,300	76,200	38,000	11.0	7.4	3.7
1960*	82,500	52,600	29,900	9.2	5.9	3.3
1955	64,200	42,100	22,100	7.9	5.2	2.7
1947†	60,500	44,600	15,900	...	...	...
Nonwhite						
1964*	161,300	71,200	90,000	97.2	42.9	54.2
1960*	141,800	57,700	84,100	98.3	40.0	58.3
1955	119,200	49,500	69,700	87.2	36.2	51.0
1947†	71,500	37,200	34,300	...	...	...

*Based on a 50 percent sample of births.
†Rates were not computed because no estimates of unmarried women by color are available for 1947.
NOTES: Figures for 1947 and 1955 based on data shown in Table H in National Office of Vital Statistics, "Illegitimate Births, United States, 1938-57," by J. Schachter and M. McCarthy, Vital Statistics—Special Reports, 47, No. 8, Public Health Service, Washington, D.C. September, 1960.
Figures by birth order for 1960 based on data from unpublished tabulations, Natality Statistics, National Center for Health Statistics.

TRENDS IN NUMBERS OF ILLEGITIMATE BIRTHS

The number of illegitimate births estimated for the entire United States has risen annually since 1940 with only one exception. During the 25-year period 1940-65, the estimated total more than tripled, from 89,500 in 1940 to 291,200 in 1965 (Table 58-4).

In analyzing trends in numbers of illegitimate births, it is necessary to consider not only changes in the "risk" that an unmarried woman will bear an illegitimate child (as measured by the illegitimacy rate) but also changes in the size of the population "at risk" (unmarried women of reproductive age). The years between 1940 and 1965 can be divided into two periods

with respect to trends in these components as follows:

Period	Trend in risk of illegitimacy	Trend in number of unmarried women 15-44 years of age
1940-57	Up	Down
1958-65	Stable	Up

The changes in the size of the unmarried female population can be explained as follows:

1. Although the total number of women increased during the 1940's and 1950's, an increasing proportion of women married in these years, causing the

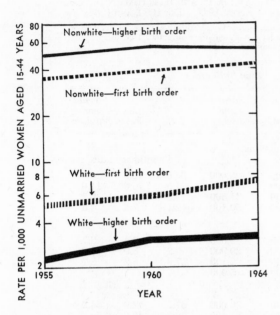

FIGURE 58–4. ESTIMATED ILLEGITIMACY RATES BY LIVEBIRTH ORDER AND COLOR: UNITED STATES, 1955, 1960, AND 1964.
(SEMILOGARITHMIC SCALE)

number of unmarried women to decline (see Table 58–5).

2. During the 1940's the annual number of births increased; by 1958 the girls born in those years began to reach age 15. In each year thereafter, there has been an increasing number of women reaching the younger ages of the reproductive period.

3. The declining age at marriage observed in the 1940's appears to have reversed in the late 1950's and the 1960's, thereby inflating the number of young women remaining unmarried.

It has already been shown that the "risk" of illegitimacy, as measured by the illegitimacy rate, has leveled off in the past seven years. If it is assumed that the age-specific illegitimacy rates continue at their 1965 levels and that the proportions of women unmarried by age for 1965 remain constant, then it is possible to project the number of illegitimate births that will occur in future years if only the *number* of unmarried women changes.

Figure 58–5 shows estimated numbers of unmarried women 15–44 years of age and of illegitimate births for 1940-65 and hypothetical

numbers of women and illegitimate births up to 1980. The projected figures, based on the assumptions stated above, indicate that the number of unmarried women of reproductive age will increase from an estimated 12,459,000 for 1965 to an estimated 16,173,000 for 1980. Even if the illegitimacy rates remain constant at their 1965 levels, the number of illegitimate births would increase from an estimated 291,200 in 1965 to 403,000 by 1980 (Figure 58–5).

ILLEGITIMATE BIRTHS AS A PROPORTION OF TOTAL BIRTHS

ANALYTICAL PROBLEMS ASSOCIATED WITH THE ILLEGITIMACY RATIO

The illegitimacy ratio (number of illegitimate births per 1000 total births) is the measure used when describing the proportion of all births classified as illegitimate. It is useful in judging the numerical impact of illegitimate babies on services provided for the newborn. This is an important function since the health of these infants is more precarious and their needs for social services greater.

However, the illegitimacy ratio has many shortcomings as an analytical tool. When using this measure, it is essential to remember that two independent factors affect the numerator and denominator. Illegitimate births (the numerator) are affected by the size of the unmarried female population and the rate of illegitimacy. The denominator (total number of live births) is primarily influenced by the factors that affect marital fertility, including changes in spacing and completed family size and the proportion of women who are married. If this changes, the ratio will change, even if the numerator remains the same.

For example, although the illegitimacy rate has remained fairly stable during the 1960's, the number of unmarried women has been increasing and more illegitimate children are being born. Simultaneously, there has been a general decline in marital fertility associated with the delay of births by married women. Therefore, there has been a substantial rise in the illegitimacy ratio. From 1959 to 1965, the illegitimacy ratio increased by 49 percent. The corresponding percentage increases among white and non-

TABLE 58–4. ESTIMATED NUMBER OF ILLEGITIMATE BIRTHS AND RATIO OF
ILLEGITIMATE BIRTHS TO TOTAL BIRTHS, BY COLOR: UNITED STATES, 1940–65.

[Refers only to births occurring within the United States. Alaska included beginning 1959, and Hawaii, 1960. Due to rounding estimates to the nearest hundred, figures by color may not add to totals.]

Year	Total	White	Non-white	Total	White	Non-white
	Number of illegitimate births			Illegitimacy ratios per 1000 live births		
1965°	291,200	123,700	167,500	77.4	39.6	263.2
1964°	275,700	114,300	161,300	68.5	33.9	245.0
1963°	259,400	104,600	154,900	63.3	30.4	235.5
1962°	245,100	94,700	150,400	58.8	27.0	227.8
1961°	240,200	91,100	149,100	56.3	25.3	223.4
1960°	224,300	82,500	141,800	52.7	22.9	215.8
1959°	220,600	79,600	141,100	52.0	22.1	218.0
1958°	208,700	74,600	134,100	49.6	20.9	212.3
1957°	201,700	70,800	130,900	47.4	19.6	206.7
1956°	193,500	67,500	126,000	46.5	19.0	204.0
1955	183,300	64,200	119,200	45.3	18.6	202.4
1954°	176,600	62,700	113,900	44.0	18.2	198.5
1953°	160,800	56,600	104,200	41.2	16.9	191.1
1952°	150,300	54,100	96,200	39.1	16.3	183.4
1951°	146,500	52,600	93,900	39.1	16.3	182.8
1950	141,600	53,500	88,100	39.8	17.5	179.6
1949	133,200	53,500	79,700	37.4	17.3	167.5
1948	129,700	54,800	74,900	36.7	17.8	164.7
1947	131,900	60,500	71,500	35.7	18.5	168.0
1946	125,200	61,400	63,800	38.1	21.1	170.1
1945	117,400	56,400	60,900	42.9	23.6	179.3
1944	105,200	49,600	55,600	37.6	20.2	163.4
1943	98,100	42,800	55,400	33.4	16.5	162.8
1942	96,500	42,000	54,500	34.3	16.9	169.2
1941	95,700	41,900	53,800	38.1	19.0	174.5
1940	89,500	40,300	49,200	37.9	19.5	168.3

°Based on a 50 percent sample of births.

white women were 79 and 21, respectively. Other measures of illegitimacy have changed as follows:

	Total	White	Non-white
	Percent change		
Number of illegitimate births	+32	+55	+19
Illegitimacy rate	+7	+26	−3

Similarly contrasting impressions of the incidence of illegitimacy can be shown with respect to age differentials. . . . The illegitimacy ratio has been highest at the youngest ages—for example, in 1965 the ratios per 1000 live births were 785.3 for women under 15 years of age, 208.3 for those 15-19, and considerably lower for all women over 20. As shown in Table 58–2, however, the illegitimacy rate has been higher at ages 20-24 and 25-29 than at ages 15-19.

Several factors contribute to the different pictures presented by the illegitimacy rate and ratio. Very few teenagers are married in comparison with older women. Therefore a smaller proportion of teenage girls are in a position to have a legitimate child. The result is that even though only a very small percent of the women aged 15-19 years have an illegitimate child (1.7

TABLE 58–5. NUMBER AND PERCENT OF UNMARRIED WOMEN 15-44, BY COLOR AND
AGE: UNITED STATES, 1940, 1950, AND 1960.

Color and age	1960	1950	1940	1960	1950	1940
	Number of unmarried women* in thousands			Percent of all women who are unmarried		
Total						
15-44 years	10,289	10,017	12,523	28.5	29.3	39.1
15-19 years	5,555	4,434	5,439	84.3	83.3	88.4
20-24 years	1,686	2,021	2,870	30.5	34.4	48.7
25-29 years	765	1,050	1,461	13.8	16.7	25.9
30-34 years	688	814	1,016	11.3	13.8	19.6
35-39 years	761	830	888	11.9	14.5	18.5
40-44 years	834	868	849	14.1	16.9	19.4
White						
15-44 years	8,802	8,779	11,142	27.7	28.9	39.1
15-19 years	4,868	3,907	4,863	84.3	83.9	89.3
20-24 years	1,422	1,781	2,599	29.5	34.4	49.7
25-29 years	618	911	1,298	12.8	16.3	25.9
30-34 years	599	711	892	10.4	13.5	19.3
35-39 years	631	715	759	11.1	14.1	17.8
40-44 years	704	753	730	13.3	16.3	18.5
Nonwhite						
15-44 years	1,486	1,238	1,381	34.8	32.4	39.3
15-19 years	687	527	576	84.2	79.4	81.7
20-24 years	264	240	271	37.8	34.3	40.4
25-29 years	147	138	163	21.1	19.8	25.7
30-34 years	129	104	124	17.6	16.9	23.0
35-39 years	130	115	129	18.3	18.3	24.0
40-44 years	130	115	119	21.0	22.1	27.9

*Population enumerated as of April 1 for each year.
NOTES: Figures for 1960 based on data shown in Table 176 in U.S. Bureau of the Census,
U.S. Census of Population, 1960, Detailed Characteristics, U.S. Summary, Final Report, PC(1)-1D,
Washington, U.S. Government Printing Office, 1963.
Figures for 1950 and 1940 based on data shown in Table 102 in U.S. Bureau of the Census,
U.S. Census of Population, 1950, Vol. II, Characteristics of Population, Pt. I, U.S. Summary, Ch. C.,
Washington, U.S. Government Printing Office, 1953.

percent in 1965), a much larger percent of all births to teenage mothers are classified as illegitimate. In contrast, a large proportion of women 20-24 years of age are married and having legitimate children. Therefore although the unmarried women of this age have a higher risk of bearing an illegitimate child than do those 15-19, they contribute only a small proportion of all births to mothers aged 20-24.

Although the illegitimacy ratio is helpful in indicating the proportion of infants requiring special services, its shortcomings impair its usefulness as an analytical measure.

TRENDS IN THE ILLEGITIMACY RATIO
BY COLOR

In 1940 the illegitimacy ratio was 37.9 per

1000 total live births; that is, almost four percent of the children born in that year were illegitimate. By 1965 the ratio had risen to 77.4.

The illegitimacy ratio for white infants has varied between 16 and 34 since 1940 (Figure 58-6). The ratio began to increase in 1953 and has risen quite rapidly through 1965.

For nonwhite infants the ratio has ranged between 163 and 263 per 1000; it has been rising steadily but slowly since 1948. In other words, the proportion of babies born each year that are illegitimate has been approximately six to ten times greater for the nonwhite than for the white population. Since the early 1950's, the color differential in the ratio has been diminishing, just as it has in the illegitimacy rate. In both cases, the declining differential is due to

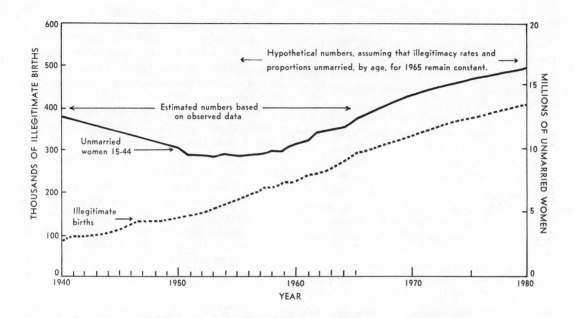

FIGURE 58–5. ESTIMATED NUMBERS OF UNMARRIED WOMEN 15-44 YEARS OF AGE
AND OF ILLEGITIMATE BIRTHS, 1940-65; AND HYPOTHETICAL NUMBERS OF UNMARRIED
WOMEN AND ILLEGITIMATE BIRTHS UP TO 1980: UNITED STATES.

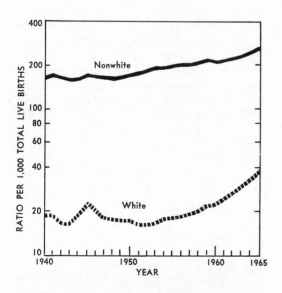

FIGURE 58–6. ESTIMATED ILLEGITIMACY RATIOS, BY
COLOR: UNITED STATES, 1940-65.
(SEMILOGARITHMIC SCALE)

a more rapid increase in the white than in the nonwhite measure.

Within the nonwhite population, the illegitimacy ratio for Negro births (270.9) was about 2½ times as great as that for the other nonwhite races (107.8). . . .

LIVE-BIRTH ORDER AND COLOR

The classification of illegitimate births by live-birth order indicates that the highest illegitimacy ratio in recent years has been for first births: 136 illegitimate births per 1000 in 1964, for example. In contrast, the illegitimacy ratios for all higher order births ranged from 40 to 58 per 1000.

For white births in 1964, the first birth illegitimacy ratio was 76 per 1000 while the ratio for all other birth orders was 20 or less. The comparable ratios for nonwhite births were 487 for first births and between 163 and 276 for second and higher births.

AGE OF MOTHER AND LIVE-BIRTH ORDER BY COLOR

For the younger mothers, those under 20 years, the highest illegitimacy ratios have been for first births, and the lowest for births of fifth or higher order. This has been true for both white and nonwhite births.

. . . The highest illegitimacy ratios for babies born to women over 20 have also been, with few exceptions, for first births. However, the lowest ratios for births to these women have been, in many cases, for third and fourth births. In some age groups, the ratio for fourth or fifth and higher order births has been nearly the same as that for first births. These relationships have been similar within each color group.

Between 1955 and 1964, the illegitimacy ratio increased most for first, second, and third births to women over 25. For white births the illegitimacy ratio rose most for births to older women, but for nonwhite births there were declines in the ratio for first births to mothers aged 30-40 and in the ratio for third and fourth births to mothers over 30.

VARIATION IN ILLEGITIMACY RATIOS BY PLACE OF RESIDENCE

If the level of illegitimacy as measured by the illegitimacy ratio is positively associated with the illegitimacy level indicated by the rate in a given state, we would expect the variation in illegitimacy ratios by place of residence to be similar to the variation in rates. Rank order correlation coefficients were computed for the relationship between the illegitimacy ratios and rates in 29 reporting states. There was a positive correlation of 0.95 between these measures of illegitimacy. For the white and nonwhite groups separately, the coefficients of correlation were +0.73 and +0.76, respectively. Only a few states showed marked differences in their rankings. . . .

Since the correlation between rates and ratios is so great, it is not necessary to restate the variations by age of mother and color.

METROPOLITAN AND NONMETROPOLITAN RESIDENCE

In order to compare the relative incidence of illegitimacy between metropolitan and nonmetropolitan areas, the illegitimacy rates for these two types of residence should be computed. Since the necessary population estimates for unmarried women have not been available, however, illegitimacy ratios have been used for the comparison.

In 1964 the illegitimacy ratio for women residing in metropolitan counties was 20 percent higher than that for women residents of nonmetropolitan counties—78.0 per 1000 total births compared with 65.0.

The difference by residence was 23 percent for white births, but for nonwhite births there was almost no difference (one percent). Among white births, those to mothers 15-19 years of age showed the greatest residential variation—119.7 for metropolitan births and 76.2 for nonmetropolitan births, a difference of 57 percent. . . .

Data classified by metropolitan and nonmetropolitan county of residence are available since 1962. From 1962 to 1964, the gap between metropolitan and nonmetropolitan counties widened slightly due to the more rapid rise of the illegitimacy ratios in metropolitan counties. Most of the 35 reporting areas followed the pattern of higher ratios in metropolitan counties. . . . However, there were a few states where the ratios were higher in nonmetropolitan counties.

The illegitimacy ratio is a very important indicator to a large city or metropolitan area health department of the amount of special services it will have to provide. . . . The proportion of births that were illegitimate in 150 standard metropolitan statistical areas in 1964 . . . varied from a high of 20 percent in Memphis, Tennessee, to a low of 1.3 percent in Provo-Orem, Utah. Among nonwhite births, generally those in need of the most services, the proportion of births classified as illegitimate was as high as 50 percent, as in York, Pennsylvania.

The trends in the illegitimacy ratio for specified urban places indicates that the ratio has been increasing in most places since 1955. . . .

For those people in the health professions who must provide immediate care to a mother and her child, there is little reassurance in knowing that the risk of having an illegitimate child has remained fairly constant in the past several years. Even if there is no increase in the illegitimacy rates, there will probably be larger and larger numbers of mothers and illegitimate children to care for in the years to come, simply because the number of young unmarried women is rising rapidly.

CHARACTERISTICS OF UNWED MOTHERS

According to data from the areas reporting legitimacy status (34 states and the District of Columbia), 44 percent of the unmarried mothers giving birth in 1964 were under 20 years of age (Table 58-6). A slightly larger proportion of the nonwhite unmarried mothers (45 percent) than of the white unmarried mothers (41 percent) were under 20. An additional 31 percent of all the unwed mothers in 1964 were 20-24 years of age. The proportion of unwed mothers in this age group was somewhat higher for white women (35 percent) than for nonwhite women (29 percent).

More than half (52 percent) of the unmarried mothers who had a child in 1964 reported that this was their first child; 17 percent, their second; and ten percent, their third (Table 58-7). The corresponding proportions differ substantially between the two color groups. For example, 66 percent of the white unwed mothers but only 44 percent of the nonwhite mothers reported that the baby was their first.

Between 1955 and 1964, these distributions have changed only slightly. The proportion of unwed mothers giving birth in 1964 who indicated that this was their first child increased by a small amount over the corresponding proportion in 1955. This was due primarily to an increase in the percentage of first births among nonwhite mothers.

As would be expected, the proportion of first births declined with each older age group of unmarried mothers. In 1964, 80 percent of the births among unwed mothers under 20 were first births. The corresponding proportion for mothers 20-24 was 45 percent. For the age group 25-29 years, the percentage declined to 16 percent.

Within each maternal age group, first illegiti-mate births accounted for a greater proportion of all illegitimate births for white than for nonwhite mothers. Among unwed mothers under 20 years of age, 92 percent of the births to white mothers and 73 percent of the births to nonwhite mothers were first born. The relative difference by color was greatest for unmarried mothers at ages 20-24; the percentages of first births were 64 and 31 for white and nonwhite, respectively.

FACTORS ACCOUNTING FOR COLOR DIFFERENCES IN ILLEGITIMACY

The differentials in illegitimacy between white and nonwhite women are great. This is reflected by all the measures used in this report.

Measure for 1964	White	Non-white	Ratio of nonwhite to white
Illegitimacy rate	11.0	97.2	8.8
First birth illegitimacy rate	7.4	42.9	5.8
Illegitimacy ratio	33.9	245.0	7.2

This section presents some hypotheses that have been suggested to account for these differentials.

First of all, it may be that differences in the timing of marriage after discovery of conception account for an important part of the differences in illegitimacy rates between white and nonwhite women. William Pratt (4) found support for this hypothesis in a study conducted in Detroit. This research was conducted to see whether the rise in illegitimate births and the decline in the age at marriage in recent years might both reflect different adustments to the same underlying trend—rising premarital conceptions.

The sample for his study was drawn from about 20,000 first marriages occurring in Detroit in 1960 (women over 45 years of age were excluded). One in eight white newlyweds and one in two nonwhite newlyweds were included in the sample. Information was collected by mail questionnaires.

TABLE 58–6. NUMBER AND PERCENT DISTRIBUTION OF ILLEGITIMATE LIVE BIRTHS, BY
AGE OF MOTHER: TOTAL OF 35 REPORTING STATES, 1955 AND 1964.

[Refers only to illegitimate births occurring within the reporting area to residents of area. Figures
for age of mother not stated are distributed].

Year and age of mother	Total	White	Non-white	Total	White	Non-white
1964*	Number of illegitimate live births			Percent distribution		
Total	195,068	73,692	121,376	100.0	100.0	100.0
Under 15 years ...	4,426	924	3,502	2.3	1.3	2.9
15-19 years	80,420	29,600	50,820	41.2	40.2	41.9
Under 20 years ...	84,846	30,524	54,322	43.5	41.4	44.8
20-24 years	60,858	26,010	34,848	31.2	35.3	28.7
25-29 years	25,254	9,036	16,218	12.9	12.3	13.4
30-34 years	13,676	4,276	9,400	7.0	5.8	7.7
35-39 years	7,890	2,796	5,094	4.0	3.8	4.2
40 years and over .	2,544	1,050	1,494	1.3	1.4	1.2
1955						
Total	145,615	45,064	100,551	100.0	100.0	100.0
Under 15 years ...	3,253	681	2,572	2.2	1.5	2.6
15-19 years	56,421	17,166	39,255	38.7	38.1	39.0
Under 20 years ...	59,674	17,847	41,827	41.0	39.6	41.6
20-24 years	43,654	14,653	29,001	30.0	32.5	28.8
25-29 years	21,644	6,199	15,445	14.9	13.8	15.4
30-34 years	12,304	3,621	8,683	8.4	8.0	8.6
35-39 years	6,436	2.066	4,370	4.4	4.6	4.3
40 years and over .	1,903	678	1,225	1.3	1.5	1.2

*Based on a 50 percent sample of births.
NOTE: Figures for 1955 based on data shown in Table J in National Office of Vital Statistics,
"Illegitimate Births, United States, 1938-57," by J. Schachter and M. McCarthy, Vital Statistics—
Special Reports, 47, No. 8, Public Healh Service, Washington, D.C., September, 1960.

One of his findings is that white couples are more apt to marry soon after the discovery of conception, while nonwhite couples may wait until after the birth of one or more children before marrying. He further states that:

The dramatic difference between white and nonwhite illegitimate births is as much or more a function of fewer marital resolutions before the birth of the child as it is a function of higher illegitimate conceptions.

I suggest we are in fact witnessing a different cultural pattern in family formation and growth in the nonwhite population, which, if far from universal, is nonetheless sufficiently widespread to merit special study. . . . Overall, it seems to me that far more attention needs to be given to the patterns of family formation and growth in the nonwhite population before firm conclusions as to illegitimacy trends, differentials and their implications can be made.

A second factor that might help to account for the higher nonwhite illegitimacy rate is less frequent induced abortion among Negro women. No reliable estimates have been made of the frequency with which induced abortion occurs, but there has been much discussion of this in recent years because of the health threat it poses. The only research available on this subject was conducted by Alfred Kinsey, (5) and his findings were reported to a conference on abortion sponsored by the Planned Parenthood Federation of America, Inc. He attributed his finding of less frequent induced abortion among Negroes to sociological differences.

There is considerable evidence that socioeconomic composition is an important factor contributing to the white-nonwhite differential in illegitimacy. It is likely that if it were possible

TABLE 58–7. NUMBER AND PERCENT DISTRIBUTION OF ILLEGITIMATE LIVE BIRTHS, BY
COLOR AND BIRTH ORDER: TOTAL OF 35 REPORTING STATES, 1955 AND 1964.

[Refers only to illegitimate births occurring within the reporting area to residents of area. Live-birth order refers to number of children born alive to mother. Figures for live-birth order not stated are distributed].

Year and birth order	Total	White	Nonwhite	Total	White	Nonwhite
1964*	Number of illegitimate births			Percent distribution		
Total	195,068	73,692	121,376	100.0	100.0	100.0
First child	101,557	48,544	53,013	52.1	65.9	43.7
Second child	33,362	10,502	22,860	17.1	14.3	18.8
Third child	19,040	5,494	13,546	9.8	7.5	11.2
Fourth child	12,868	3,752	9,116	6.6	5.1	7.5
Fifth child and over	28,241	5,400	22,841	14.5	7.3	18.8
1955						
Total	145,615	45,064	100,551	100.0	100.0	100.0
First child	71,504	29,570	41,934	49.1	65.6	41.7
Second child	28,164	7,188	20,976	19.3	16.0	20.9
Third child	15,977	3,445	12,532	11.0	7.6	12.5
Fourth child	10,578	1,927	8,651	7.3	4.3	8.6
Fifth child and over	19,392	2,934	16,458	13.3	6.5	16.4

*Based on a 50 percent sample of births.
NOTE: Figures for 1955 based on data shown in Table J in National Office of Vital Statistics, "Illegitimate Births, United States, 1938-57," by J. Schachter and M. McCarthy, Vital Statistics—Special Reports, 47, No. 8, Public Health Service, Washington, D.C., September, 1960.

to control for social class, much of the difference between these two groups would disappear.

Finally, some people have ascribed the differences between white and nonwhite rates of illegitimacy to values and the access to the means of realizing these values in behavior. These values include attitudes toward extramarital intercourse, "forced" marriage, induced abortion, and having an illegitimate child. The variables relating to access include knowledge and availability of contraception, the degree of difficulty in obtaining an induced abortion, and the financial ability to establish a family.

Each of these two types of variables differ for different segments of the population as defined by age, socioeconomic status, place of residence, religion, race, and so forth. But it is also possible that two groups with similar values have different degrees of access to the means of realizing their values, and thus differing rates of illegitimacy. It would require extremely

careful and thorough research to link these variables.

FACTORS ACCOUNTING FOR THE INCREASING ILLEGITIMACY RATE

One factor that may help to account for the rising illegitimacy rates is a decline in the incidence of induced abortion. Alfred Kinsey, (5) in the research discussed earlier, found that for women born during the 40-year period 1890-1930, there was no change in the incidence of premarital pregnancy, but there was a rise in the frequency with which these women ended a pregnancy by abortion. Among ever-married women, he found the lowest rates of abortion among the generation born before 1890. The frequency of abortion rose among women born during the next two decades and then decreased for women born between 1910 and 1929. In his sample he found that between 88 and 95 percent of the premarital pregnancies were ended by induced abortion.

In addition, he noted that the percentage of girls who are having premarital intercourse has increased considerably during the first half of the 20th century. If a higher percentage of girls are having premarital intercourse and if it is more difficult to obtain an abortion, then the number of women having an illegitimate child would increase unless more marry before giving birth. Unfortunately, there is virtually no information available on levels or trends in illegal abortion, and therefore it is not possible to support or refute this hypothesis.

Another factor that may help to account for the rise in illegitimacy is the reduction of sterility associated with venereal disease. This cannot be demonstrated with certainty, but it appears to be a tenable hypothesis, particularly for the nonwhite population. We do know that among nonwhite married women, the prevalence of childlessness was once quite high. Among ever-married nonwhite women 50-54 years of age enumerated in the 1960 census, for example, 28 percent reported that they had never had any children. The proportion was much lower for younger women (14 percent for ever-married nonwhite women 25-29 years of age). It seems likely that this trend toward fewer childless women represents an increase in fecundity, probably due to the reduced prevalence of venereal disease. (6) If there has been an increase in the fecundity of the nonwhite population, it would affect the unmarried population as well as the married and raise the likelihood that premarital intercourse would lead to pregnancy and childbirth.

Such a trend may also have affected illegitimacy rates among certain segments of the white population, particularly the poor and less educated who generally have had less access to adequate medical care.

Again, it should be emphasized that these suggestions are speculative. We have no research findings directly linking an increase in fecundity with an increase in illegitimacy. But in an area in which speculation is much more common than research, the hypothesis of increased fecundity appears to have somewhat more merit than other inadequately supported speculations.

Another factor that may account for the large increase in the illegitimacy rate among nonwhite women during the 1940's is the large-scale migration from southern farms into large cities in many parts of the country. The dissolution of families, crowded living conditions, and generally unfavorable social and economic conditions may have led to greater promiscuity.

William Goode (7) had hypothesized that there tends to be more illegitimacy among groups of the population that have not been completely assimilated; therefore some association between rates of migration and illegitimacy would be expected. In order to get some indication of the effect of migration on illegitimacy, the proportion of migrants into each standard metropolitan statistical area (SMSA) was obtained for the white and nonwhite population between 1955 and 1960. This was correlated with illegitimacy ratios observed in 1964.

For the nonwhite population there was a negative correlation of 0.41 between illegitimacy and migration; for the white population there was a positive correlation of 0.28. Neither of these can be considered meaningful. Clearly more refined measures are needed to test this hypothesis.

None of the factors discussed here can satisfactorily explain the rise in illegitimacy. It is clear, therefore, that more careful and definitive research is needed.

REFERENCES

1. SCHACHTER, J. and McCARTHY, M. *Illegitimate births, United States, 1938–57*, National Office of Vital Statistics: *Vital Statistics—special reports*, September, 1960, *47*, No. 8. Public Health Service. Washington, D.C.
2. HARTLEY, S. M. The amazing rise of illegitimacy in Great Britain. *Social Forces*, June, 1966, *44*, 533–545.
3. GRABILL, W. and PARKE, R., JR. Marriage, fertility and child-spacing. U.S. Bureau of the Census: *Current Population Reports*, July, 1961, Series P-20, No. 108. Wash., D.C.
4. PRATT, W. *Premarital pregnancy in a metropolitan community*. Paper presented at the 1965 meeting of the Population Association of America.
5. KINSEY, A. Illegal abortion in the United States.

In R. W. Roberts (ed.) *The unwed mother* New York: Harper & Row, Publishers, 1966, 196–198.

6. For additional evidence on this point, see Kiser, C. V. Fertility trends and differentials among nonwhites in the United States. *Milbank Memorial Fund Quarterly.* April, 1958, 36:2, 190–196.

7. Goode, W. J. Illegitimacy, anomie, and cultural penetration. *The American Sociological Review,* December, 1961, XXVI, 910–925.

8. Pakter, J., M.D., and Nelson, F. The unmarried mother and her child: the problems and the challenges. *Illegitimacy.* New York: National Council on Illegitimacy, 1965.

9. Hiller, R. W. *A Study of illegitimate birth certificates.* Minnesota Department of Health: A copy of a brief summary of this unpublished study is on file in the Natality Statistics Branch, Division of Vital Statistics, National Center for Health Statistics.

10. *Adoptions among children born in the state of Washington in 1956.* Washington State Department of Health. A copy of this unpublished report is on file in the Natality Statistics Branch, Division of Vital Statistics, National Center for Health Statistics.

11. *Current population reports.* U.S. Bureau of the Census: Series P-20, Nos. 81, 87, 96, 105, 114, 122, 135, and 144. Washington, D.C.

59.

Felix M. Berardo

WIDOWHOOD STATUS IN THE UNITED STATES: PERSPECTIVE ON A NEGLECTED ASPECT OF THE FAMILY LIFE-CYCLE

Widowhood is rapidly becoming a major phenomenon of American society. National census data indicate that there are close to 11 million widowed persons among our population today, the large majority of whom are women.[1] Over the past several decades the widowed female has, in fact, been outdistancing her male counterpart by a continually widening margin. Whereas the number of widowers has remained relatively constant from 1930 to the present, female survivors have shown a substantial rise during this period. Thus, in 1940 there were twice as many widows as there were widowers. During the following decade widows increased by more than 22 percent while the number of widowers rose by only seven percent. By 1960 the ratio of widows to widowers had risen to more than 3½ to 1, and throughout the decade has continued to climb to a present ratio of more than 4 to 1. Currently, there are well over eight and three-quarter million widows in the nation, and their total is expected to continue expanding.[2] Widowhood then is emerging as

This selection is reprinted from: Felix M. Berardo, "Widowhood Status in the United States: Perspective on a Neglected Aspect of the Family Life-Cycle, *The Family Coordinator,* 1968, *17,* 191–203. Reprinted with the permission of the author and publisher.

Scientific Paper 3087. College of Agriculture, Washington State University. Work conducted under Projects 1856 and 1900, Department of Rural Sociology.

[1] The national data, of course, reflect the marital status of individuals at the time of the census enumeration only. It should be noted that people in the status of widowhood today may not be in this status tomorrow. Moreover, many currently married persons were once in the widowhood status. (U.S. Bureau of the Census, 1967, p. 33.)

[2] Three *major* factors are generally cited to account for the growing excess of widows in the United States, namely: (a) mortality among women is lower than among men and, therefore, larger numbers of women survive to advanced years; (b) wives are typically younger than their husbands and, consequently, even without the sex differences in mortality have a greater probability of outliving their husbands; (c) among the widowed, remarriage rates are considerably lower for women than men. Other major factors which also have an impact on widowhood status are the effects of war casualties, depressions, and disease pandemics (Jacobson, 1959, pp. 24–27).

an important area for sociological inquiry because of the growing and extensive population involved. (Unless specified otherwise, the term widowhood as used in this paper will have reference to female survivors and their families only.)

For a variety of reasons, however, widowhood as a topic of study has not engaged the specific interests of *sociological* investigators to any appreciable extent, although there has been occasional recognition of the need for empirical data regarding their patterns of accommodation. Over a decade ago, for example, Kutner and his associates pointed out that "the effects and sequelae of widowhood have received little attention in empirical research. Widows are coming to represent a sizable group in American life and there is a growing need for information regarding their pattern of adjustment." (Kutner, *et. al.*, 1956, p. 19). In the more recent *Handbook of Social Gerontology* one reviewer particularly notes the lack of references to widowhood in the various publications of that specialized field and related areas, remarking: "It is striking that this inevitable and universal phase of life would be so patently neglected as an area of serious study" (Williams, 1961, p. 475). In 1965, a sociologist employed with the federal government made a similar observation, stating: "While much is made of the shock of retirement in gerontological literature, little is made of the shock of bereavement. Both are the common expectation of mankind and each should be studied. But in our society there is a strange silence about death and fear of death that is present with older people" (Kent, 1965, p. 14). Finally, an informal survey of textbooks currently utilized in marriage and family courses reveals that in many instances the topic of widowhood is given only cursory attention and in still others the subject is not even raised. Such apparent disregard and lack of research concerning this special phase of the family life-cycle appears somewhat anomalous, indeed, in light of the fact that three out of every four wives in the United States survive their husbands.

This paper seeks to call specific attention to this neglected aspect of the family life-cycle. It will attempt to accomplish this goal primarily in two ways: (a) by highlighting the acute and problematic aspects of widowhood status through a concentration on significant sociodemographic indicators which characterize the contemporary condition of the widow and her family, and (b) by critically assessing the interdisciplinary scientific efforts concerning the study of widowhood, with particular emphasis on the sociological research orientation. In the latter connection, this paper represents an argument for a more extensive and systematic development of sociological knowledge concerning the phenomenon of widowhood in the United States and by emphasizing some needed areas of research on the social correlates of widowhood status.

SOCIO-DEMOGRAPHIC PROFILE ON AMERICAN WIDOWHOOD

Widowhood has long been known to entail a variety of social problems at the local level, being related to adult and child dependency, poverty, unemployment, illness, and the more significant facts of family disorganization and of women's insecure industrial status (Phelps, 1938). In order to more fully portray the magnitude of the problem in contemporary society it is necessary to present a concise but somewhat abbreviated demographic profile on American widowhood. In addition to serving as a point of information regarding certain baseline data, the picture to be presented hopefully will also provide proper amplification of the current social conditions surrounding female survivors and will set the stage for exploring the sociological dimensions of their status for both the family and society.

It should be noted at the outset that from a statistical standpoint widowhood is largely a problem of the aged woman. As a result of the impact of advances in medical technology, pervasive health programs, etc., on decreasing mortality prior to midlife, widowhood for the most part has been postponed to the latter stages of the family life-cycle. Around the turn of the twentieth century about one in 25 persons was 65 years old or older, as compared to one in 11 in the present decade. Since the gains in longevity have been more rapid for females than for males, the growing proportion of elderly women in our population is accentuating the problem of widowhood. Thus, currently more than three-fifths of the widows in the United States are 65 years of age or over (almost another fourth are between 55-64) and "unless the trends in male and female mortality are sharply reversed, the excess of women over men at the upper ages will increase, and our older population will contain a larger proportion of widows" (Sheldon, 1958, p. 93).

WIDOWHOOD AND INCOME

Because the majority of widows are aged, their economic circumstances are usually below average. A special survey of widows 55 years of age or older, for example, revealed that almost two-thirds of the husbands left a sum total of assets (including cash, savings, life insurance, property value of the home, and other assets) of less than $10,000 to their families; 44 percent left assets of less than $5000. Equally significant, the median income of the wives in the year preceding the survey was less than $2000 (Institute for Life Insurance, 1964). These figures are comparable to some extent with census data on the aged which shows the median income of the widowed as a group to be less than $1200 per year, in comparison to almost $3000 for the aged married. The census data also indicate that widows have substantially lower assets than non-widows in all age groups (Epstein and Murray, 1967).

One thing is clear—the available evidence on income levels lends little support to the occasional stereotype of "the wealthy widow," as a statistically prevalent type among our aged population. In this connection, it is frequently stated that women, as a consequence of outliving their husbands, control a great deal of the inherited wealth in the United States. It is said, for example, that they are beneficiaries of 80 percent of all life insurance policies (National Consumer Finance Association, 1963). It is true that as beneficiaries, women in the United States received more than two-thirds of the nearly $5 billion paid in 1965 following the death of a policyholder. Such gross figures, however, can be misleading. In the study cited earlier, for example, almost three-fourths of the

husbands owned *less* than $5000 in life insurance at the time of their death, and an additional 20 percent owned less than $10,000. Moreover, many of these women have to use what small amounts of insurance their husbands did carry to pay for funeral expenses, medical bills, taxes, mortgages, and so on, leaving them with only small savings on which to survive.

There is no doubt that life insurance has become a principal defense against the insecurity and risk of widowhood in our urban, industrial society with its attendant nuclear family system. It is a concrete form of security which in some instances may help the bereaved family to avoid an embarrassing and reluctant dependence on relatives and/or the state in the case of untimely death. Nevertheless, it has been the experience of investment bankers and the like that few female survivors are capable of handling the economic responsibilities brought about by the husband's death, inasmuch as they know very little about matters of real estate, titles, mortgage, contracts, stocks, bonds, and matters of property[3] (Schwabacher, 1963).

WIDOWHOOD AND EMPLOYMENT

Because they frequently encounter serious economic problems soon after their husbands have passed away, many wives find it necessary to seek employment. This is particularly the case where dependent children are involved; approximately 900,000 female survivors carried this responsibility in 1960. Moreover, at that time over half of all widows under age 35 were either employed or else seeking work. At ages 35-54, this proportion rises to nearly two-thirds (Metropolitan Life, 1966).

[3]Actually, the economic dilemma in which widows often find themselves is frequently brought about as a direct result of the failure of husbands to plan their estates and advise their wives. "The truth is that most men leave their affairs in a jumble. This is not because their lives are unduly complicated, but simply because they can't seem to get around to the task of setting up a program for their families that would automatically go into operation upon their death. Death is unpleasant to think about and always seems remote. The tendency is to put the problem off and plan 'to get to it one of these days'." (*Changing Times*, November, 1961, pp. 9-14). Moreover, many husbands themselves are incapable of making sensible financial decisions and preparations.

While women entering widowhood at the older ages are not as likely to have dependent children in the home, they are nevertheless often faced with a similar problem of self-support, since Social Security benefits provide for the minimum necessities only. Moreover, the obstacles to securing employment at this stage of the life-cycle are often rather difficult to overcome. Typically, these women have been absent from the labor market for several years and are, therefore, at a disadvantage with respect to the educational and occupational demands of current employment. In addition, they are frequently confronted with a subtle but pervasive discrimination on the part of the employers who are not in favor of hiring older jority of all widows, but in particular the aged persons, let alone older women. Since the majority of all widows, but in particular the aged widows, are unemployed, they are unable to support themselves and consequently are partly or wholly dependent on the assistance of children or relatives, and on public or private funds. While the 1965 amendments to Social Security Act broadened and substantially increased benefits available to widows and their dependent children, their economic circumstances still remain far from satisfactory (Palmore, *et. al.*, 1966).

Female survivors who have obtained employment are heavily concentrated in the low-paying jobs. Over one-third are private household or other service workers; one-fifth are clerical and kindred workers, and one-seventh are operatives and kindred workers. Less than one-tenth of all widows are engaged in professional or technical occupations. In any event, research indicates that playing a role in the productive economy is predictive of favorable adaptation to widowhood. Kutner, *et al.*, for example, found that an employed widow in later life tends to be better adjusted, that is, to have higher morale, than both a housewife who has never worked or a retired widow (Kutner, *et al.*, 1956). The acts of preparing for work, carrying out one's tasks, and returning home are viewed as being intimately connected to feelings of personal worth, self-esteem, and significance in life. This has led to the suggestion that "for widowed women, there is a need for a service that will provide occasional jobs, such as babysitting,

service as companions for bedridden persons, and occasional light housekeeping tasks. Many widows have never been in the labor force and have never acquired skills in any other line. These kinds of jobs frequently coincide with their experience as homemakers."[4] (Kutner, *et al.*, 1956, p. 254).

WIDOWHOOD AND ORPHANHOOD

The proportion of children in the United States under 18 years of age who have lost one or both of their natural parents through death has declined markedly since the turn of the century, due to modern advances in medicine and improved health conditions. Nevertheless, orphanhood remains a social problem of considerable magnitude in this country and one that necessitates a variety of services and assistance to accommodate the families affected (Shudde and Epstein, 1955).

Currently there are approximately 3.4 million orphans in the nation and they represent about 4.8 percent of all children under age 18. Among these are more than two million "paternal orphans," that is, children who have lost their fathers through death. The most recent estimates indicate that of all orphans in the nation today, approximately 71 percent have lost their fathers only and about 27 percent have lost their mothers only. Less than three percent have lost both parents (Epstein and Skolnik, 1965). Thus, the burdens of orphanhood are borne primarily by women.

Children who have experienced the trauma of bereavement and/or who have been reared in a one-parent household have been typically depicted as occupying a particularly disadvantageous position due to purported family disruption engendered by such circumstances. The dysfunctional consequences for the personality

---

[4] A federally sponsored program which dovetails rather nicely with the employment needs of older widows who lack specialized technical skills is the recently initiated Foster Grandparent Project developed by the Office of Economic Opportunity. Under this project, the federal government awards grants of money to the states to be used to employ older people as "foster grandparents" to work with and serve as companions for the mentally retarded, physically handicapped, delinquent, emotionally disturbed, and dependent and neglected children in institutions, day care centers, and homes (*Look*, August 23, 1966, pp. 67–71).

development of children involved have been especially emphasized. Researchers sharing this perspective have often "assumed as a working hypothesis that the young person in the broken home who does not go to the extreme of delinquency may still experience problems in his adjustment with peers and teachers, in school relationships, and in the community which are not experienced by young people living in families with both parents present" (Landis, 1953, p. 2). The broader assumption underlying this viewpoint, particularly in the case of the paternal orphan, is that the absence of a proper sex-role model represented by the parent results in inadequate socialization. Similarly, it is assumed that because the mother is forced to shoulder dual parental role obligations, she is not able to adequately supervise and control her children. These circumstances are said to result in a variety of negative consequences, such as delinquency, mental illness, and the like.

The major sociological opinion, then, has endorsed the attributes of a complete family environment. This somewhat traditional viewpoint, however, has been challenged by a number of investigators who stress that the presence of both parents does not automatically guarantee a better child-rearing situation. Rather, it is argued, "the crucial factor in the adjustment of children is the social-psychological success or failure of the family, not whether or not it is legally and physically broken" (Nye, 1957, p. 356). Current research evidence appears to support this contention (Burchinal, 1964). Nye, for example, found that the adjustment of adolescents from *broken* homes was more successful than that of children from *unhappy unbroken homes*. That is, they showed less psychosomatic illness, less delinquency, and better adjustment to parents. Moreover, he found no evidence of greater adjustment problems in "mother only" homes than in remarried or unhappy unbroken homes. As a matter of fact, parent-child relationships were superior in the "solo" mother homes in almost every area of adjustment measured. Perry and Pfuhl (1963) similarly found no significant differences between adolescents in homes broken by death or divorce and those in remarried homes in terms

of delinquent behavior, psychoneurotic tendencies, and school grades. The results of these and similar studies throw into question the assumption that the effects of family dissolution on children are adverse and they suggest that family dissolution, *per se*, is not the most important factor influencing the lives of the adolescents studied. The issue, of course, is by no means settled, and more research is needed which focuses specifically on the social adjustment of children in homes dissolved through the death of a parent.

WIDOWHOOD MORTALITY AND MENTAL HEALTH

That widowhood presents serious problems of personal adjustment and mental health is rather well established. Empirical research has consistently demonstrated that the widowed typically have higher death rates, a greater incidence of mental disorders, and a higher suicide rate than their married counterparts. More specifically:

The Widowed Die Sooner. Analyses of national vital statistics and census data for the United States reveal that the widowed have a significantly higher mortality rate than married persons of the same age, and that among young widowed people there is a particularly high excess of mortality (Kraus and Lilienfeld, 1959). Additional investigations in this country and abroad have supported these findings. Moreover, recent research by Rees and Lutkins (1967) has provided rather dramatic statistical confirmation of the long-standing hypothesis that a death in the family produces an increased post-bereavement mortality rate among close relatives, with the greatest increase in mortality risk occurring among surviving spouses. At present, little is known of the primary causative agents underlying this association between bereavement and mortality. Homogamy, common infection, joint unfavorable environment, and loss of care have all been suggested as possible influences. Moreover, "Personality factors, social isolation, age (old people withstand bereavement better than young), and the nature and magnitude of the loss itself all seem to be important factors. When the bereaved person is supported by a united and affectionate family, when there is something left to live for, when the person has been adequately prepared for the loss, and when it can be fitted into a secure religious or philosophical attitude to life and death there will seldom be much need for professional help. When, however, the bereaved person is left alone in a world which is seen as hostile and insecure, when the future is black and the loss has not been prepared for, help may be needed." (Rees and Lutkins, 1967, p. 3).

Widowhood and Suicide. Durkheim is generally recognized as the first well-known sociologist to stress the connection between widowhood and suicide. "The suicides, occurring at the crisis of widowhood . . . are really due to domestic anomie resulting from the death of husband or wife. A family catastrophe occurs which affects the survivor. He is not adapted to the new situation in which he finds himself and accordingly offers less resistance to suicide" (Durkheim, 1951, p. 259). Numerous investigations have since demonstrated that within a given age group, the suicide rates of the widowed are consistently higher than the married. A review of these studies indicates that suicide —whether attempted or actual—frequently tends to be preceded by the disruption of significant social interaction and reciprocal role relationships through the loss of a mate (Rushing, 1968). Moreover, these studies further reveal that the death of one or both parents in childhood is common among attempted and actual suicide victims; that the incidence of suicide among such persons when they attain adulthood is much greater than that for comparable groups in the general population.

Widowhood, Social Isolation, and Mental Health. That a high correlation exists between marital status and mental illness has been repeatedly noted in the scientific literature. While considerable professional controversy prevails over identification of the exact sequence of the antecedent-consequent conditions which predispose individuals toward various forms of organic and psychogenic disorders, there is little disagreement with the general hypothesis that "the emotional security and social stability afforded by married life makes for low incidence of mental illness" (Adler, 1953, p. 185). Again, the evidence is quite consistent that the wid-

owed experience a substantially higher rate of mental disorders than the still married, particularly among the older populations.

The association between marital status and mental disorders has been shown to be a function of several intervening factors, including age, socioeconomic status, physical condition, and the degree as well as duration of social isolation (Bellen and Hardt, 1958; Lowenthal, 1964, 1965). Problems of social isolation, often accompanied by distressing loneliness, are especially germane to the personal adjustment of aged female survivors, a very high proportion of whom are residing alone as occupants of one-person households. Fried and Stern, (1948) for example, found that almost two-thirds of the widowed in their study were dissatisfied with the single state and were lonesome even after ten years of widowhood. The loss of a husband not only creates many practical problems of living alone, but also produces a social vacuum in the life of the aged widow which is difficult to fill. She may find herself "marooned" in an environment which generally requires paired relationships as a prerequisite to social participation.[5] Consequently, various researchers have found that, compared to married women, widows are more apt to feel economically insecure, unhappy, to suffer from fears of being alone and from loss of self-esteem as women, to exhibit undue anxiety and emotional tensions, and to lack self-confidence. In the case of widows who are still mothers: "There are the objective problems of limited income and the need to find the time and energy for a job to augment it and still be the kind of mother children need in the circumstances—a mother who can maintain a home, discipline and educate young people, and insure their positive emotional growth. Then there are the countless problems of guilt, fear, frustration and loneliness, ever-present and always threatening" (Illgenfritz, 1961, p. 41).

To summarize at this point, it can be seen that a rather dismal picture of widowhood status emerges from the brief socio-demographic profile presented in the preceding pages. Clearly, the majority of women survivors generally have

[5]Blau has demonstrated that the degree of social isolation among older widows is partially conditioned by the prevalence of similar age-sex peer groupings in the social structure (Blau, 1961).

had to face a multiplicity of personal and familial adjustment problems while at the same time attempting to establish a satisfactory adaptation to a new and relatively undefined social role. Their economic position is likely to be insecure; more often than not they will need to seek employment, especially if young children are still in the home, and we only have touched on the various difficulties associated with these conditions. Moreover, in comparison to the still married, the widow faces the possibility of an early mortality, and there is a more than average probability that she will develop some mental disorder or even commit suicide.

Despite all of this, as was noted earlier, widowhood as a significant social problem has not engaged the specific research interest of *sociological* investigators to any great extent (Faunce and Fulton, 1958; Kephart, 1950). In the remainder of this paper, therefore, it may prove fruitful to examine some of the reasons for this inattention and to suggest some areas in which future research might be undertaken. It will be helpful to begin by a brief overview and assessment of the general scope of other disciplinary research perspectives in this area, in particular those of anthropology and psychology.

SCOPE OF RESEARCH ON WIDOWHOOD

Anthropologists, of course, for some time have been describing various facets of death and bereavement and the ritualistic customs and behavior associated with such phenomena among different societies around the world (Bendann, 1930; Krupp and Kligfeld, 1962). Unfortunately, while there appears to be considerable information in the anthropological literature regarding the status of widows, it is scattered among the pages of voluminous monographs which generally focus on larger units of social organization. A library search of various anthropological journals revealed a similar situation. There are apparently no articles devoted *exclusively* to the theoretical or practical aspects of widowhood, although many contain anywhere from a paragraph to two pages of commentary on the subject. Moreover, the relevant data on widowhood tend to be highly descrip-

tive in nature and lacking in systematic treatment. A similar evaluation can be made for the data contained in the Human Relations Area Files.[6] It appears that past anthropological analyses of widowhood have concentrated rather exclusively on its relationship to the economic and kinship systems. Particular emphasis seems to have been placed on patterns of widowhood inheritance, as reflected through the ancient practices of the levirate and sororate marriage arrangements.[7]

PSYCHOLOGICAL ORIENTATION PREDOMINANT

A review of the empirical literature on widowhood discloses that researchers have generally concentrated on the bereavement processes, *per se*. Consequently, they have approached their subject matter primarily, if not exclusively, from a psychological (including both social-psychological and psychoanalytical) frame of reference.[8] The personal, intra-psychic reactions to the shock of "dismemberment" have been particularly stressed.[9] Within this context, case

---

[6] As a part of a current project initiated by the author, a search has been undertaken of the HRAF in order to extract whatever relevant information they contained regarding the status of widows. The search thus far has been, to say the least, rather disappointing. Aside from the categorization difficulties commonly associated with utilizing data from the HRAF, we have frequently found the relevant entries to be sporadic, vague and ambiguous. See: Felix M. Berardo, "Cross-Cultural Perspective on Widowhood," Research Project Outline, Department of Rural Sociology, Washington State University, 1966 (mimeographed). A master's thesis based on data from 44 societies has been completed (Brunton, 1967).

[7] The relevance of anthropological research on widowhood for contemporary industrial societies has not been fully explored. A small but significant start is provided by Goode (1963) in which there is a systematic attempt to analyze the changing status of widows in various societies and the factors associated with this change.

[8] Footnote and bibliographic references to early sources reflecting a psychological approach to death, bereavement, and widowhood may be found in Eliot (1955) and Waller (1938).

[9] A recent comment by Gorer is pertinent here. In reviewing the early as well as current literature in this area, he is led to conclude that: "One short essay by Freud—*Mourning and Melancholia*, written in 1915 and published in 1917—dominates all the psychoanalytical and most of the psychiatric and sociological studies of grief and mourning written since that date. Much of the later work is in the nature of an exegisis on this text" (Gorer, 1965, p. 136).

history analyses of individual conflict and adjustment to annihilation—with specific emphasis on the phenomena of grief, sorrow, and other ccmponents of the mental-emotional mourning process—predominate. Psychiatric diagnoses derived from clinical observations and records follow a similar orientation, especially in connection with investigations of the psychosomatic reactions to bereavement (Parks, 1964, 1965). Recent studies of attitudes toward death may also be characterized as reflecting a predominantly psychological frame of reference (Fulton, 1965; Havighurst and Neugarten, 1961). An expanded discussion of the research undertaken from this point of view will not be presented here, inasmuch as this paper is concerned primarily with exploring the sociological aspects of widowhood. It needs to be emphasized, however, that this orientation is characterized by a general lack of concern with the *social* life of mourners and with their long-term adjustments. This has led one observer to conclude that nearly all "investigators tend to write as though the bereaved were completely alone, with no other occupation in life but to come to terms with and work through their grief [and] this implicit picture of the solitary [person] who has nothing to do but get over his grief has tended to dominate the literature of the last 20 years" (Gorer, 1965, p. 150). Because this approach usually restricts its attention to the mourning and grief reactions of *one* individual in *a* particular family, it usually ignores the *family* mourning process, nor does it commonly treat widowhood as a social condition which has implications for the total family process, as well as for the larger society.

THE SOCIOLOGICAL ORIENTATION

It appears that sociological analyses of death, bereavement, and widowhood comprise a minute proportion of the literature in this area and all too frequently overlap with the psychological in emphasis.[10] That is to say, relatively few investigators have been oriented toward developing the sociological implications of widowhood status or discovering the social and/or environmental factors associated with the adaptive behavior of the widow *and* her family. A large proportion of the sociological research in this area has tended to concentrate on *individual* responses to the immediate crisis event while neglecting the accommodations of the family as a total unit or configuration over time. As a consequence, we know a good deal about the personal adjustment processes involved and rather little about the sociological features of the bereaved family.

Thus, *sociological* monographs concerning the American widowed are conspicuously absent from the literature.[11] Aside from an early (and out of print) publication by social workers, (Richmond and Hall, 1913) a few unpublished theses and dissertations, (Fulcomer, 1942; Harlan, 1951; Fitzelle, 1952) and a handful of lay guidebooks, (Torrey, 1941; Roulston, 1951; Owens, 1951; Langer, 1957; Zalk, 1957; Osborne, 1958; Champagne, 1964) most of the evidence concerning the social correlates of widowhood status is scattered and hidden among a variety of published sources devoted not infrequently to some other query.[12] It is not surprising, therefore, to learn that "no single facet of the literature which deals with fatherless families has ever been comprehensively reviewed by anyone" (Wynn, 1964, p. 198).

One apparent and somewhat paradoxical reason for the dearth of information in this area is that, in recent efforts to give needed attention to the latter stages of the life-cycle, social scientists have tended to submerge the identifications of the widowed through their concentration on the problems of our aged population. Specifically, data on the aged often are not distinguished with respect to widowhood status;

---

[10]Evidence to support this statement was obtained by conducting an informal content analysis of the two most current bibliographies available on death and bereavement (Kalish, 1965; Marks, 1965). If one attempts to classify the individual entries according to their frame of reference, it soon becomes obvious that psychological conceptual frameworks predominate the literature on death, bereavement, and widowhood.

[11]British social scientists, by way of contrast, have been very much interested in the phenomena of widowhood (Gorer, 1965; Wynn, 1964; Aitken-Swan, 1962; Marris, 1958).

[12]Marks, (1965) in compiling a bibliography on the sociology of death has similarly noted that "such empirical knowledge as has been obtained appears in most instances to have resulted from a primary focus on some other field, such as mental health, gerontology, or the sociology of religion. Further, a review of the authors' names will indicate how few of those who are contemporary are also primarily identified as sociologists" (p. 1).

consequently, exact information concerning the widowed becomes difficult to ascertain. Moreover, in most of the research that has been done, differences in levels of functioning as well as differences in backgrounds and experiences are overlooked or ignored; social class and cultural values are typically not differentiated nor considered; and a host of important socioeconomic variables are submerged under the all-inclusive homogeneous category of "the aged" (Jacobson 1959). The fact that a substantial minority of the widowed in the United States does not fall within the usual definitions of the aged population is frequently ignored. About one-fifth of the new widows created each year, for example, are under the age of 45 and their situation is, in many respects, different from those widowed at later ages[13] (Metropolitan Life, 1962). In this same connection, the "divorced, separated, and widowed," are frequently combined and presented as a single statistical category. Such a practice, while it may have certain parsimonious and analytical advantages, nonetheless further obscures the specific data with respect to widowhood.

Another major explanation advanced for the lack of research in this area centers around certain cultural taboos associated with the phenomena of death. Such taboos apparently are inculcated at a relatively young age and their influence is thought to persist throughout the entire life-cycle. As Eliot, one of the pioneers in this field, has commented: "Where death is concerned, there is, in some respects, a heavier load of taboo and resistance than in the case of sex. Yet it is hoped that the relaxation of the conventional repression of death may make it easier to face the fact, to study its social aspects, and to guide our attitudes and our techniques more satisfactorily" (Eliot, 1930, pp.

---

[13]It is perhaps also worth repeating here Waller's early statement: "Because of the many varieties of bereavement, study of a large number of cases would be highly desirable. Contrast the relative uniformity of the divorce situation with the wide variety of bereavement situations which we would need to study in order to generalize effectively . . . its effect necessarily varies with the age of the bereaved, his emotional involvements with the deceased, the nature of the death, the other relationships of the bereaved, and the degree of emancipation of the bereaved person; outside of this universe of factors we have a great range of cultural factors which affect the situation." (Waller, 1938, pp. 491–492).

544-545). Krupp and Kligfeld have noted that there are many factors prevailing in the United States which operate to prevent a direct confrontation with the reality of death:

Much in our American culture conspires to remove death from our minds and even our feelings. In television, the movies, and other expressions of our mores, emphasis is on the preservation of youth and the denial of aging. Death, though threatening and difficult to handle, is made remote. Social Security and the proliferation of nursing homes have facilitated the removal of many elderly and severely sick persons from the family circle. Estranged by our civilization from the basic realities of life (of which death is a part), we have lost contact with the daily struggle for life of animals in the field and forest. We have less and less contact with nature, with the death of livestock, and with the slaughtering of animals for food. Death has become for us foreboding, frightening, repugnant, and mysterious (Krupp and Kligfeld, 1962, p. 226).

Strub has similarly noted the subtle removal of public confrontation with death and its subsequent consequences:

The various supportive institutions and social practices which have developed to make death easier have evolved in such a way as to shield most people from the awareness of death. This seems to have included social scientists. . . . Death, like poverty and hunger, has ceased to be socially visible . . . . Though the afflicted, infirm, and near-dead are still with us, they are shielded from public view . . . . In the past, the use of myth, ritual, religion, and private discussion were all devices for dealing with the highly visible and ever present fact of death. Today, with the relative invisibility of death, conversation may turn to the weather, minor sicknesses, or vacations, where formerly a similar situation might have centered on the sudden death of a friend's or neighbor's child. The socialization process of childhood and youth which formerly included the acceptance of ever present death is no longer as important. The change in the timing of death has created a situation in which the psychological, social, and economic preparations for death are integral aspects of the role associated with advanced age. Essentially it is *only* in the socialization for the role of being aged that the social and psychic preparations for death occur (Straub, 1966, pp. 191–192).

Thus, as a result of the above mentioned factors as well as other considerations, strong resistances are encountered by the investigator attempting to study various aspects of bereavement and widowhood. Waller's observation some years ago that "taboos, prejudices, and fears inhibit the inquirer and the informant, and fear of rebuff has held up extensive investigations in the field," (Waller and Hill, 1951, p. 472) is, to a noticeable extent, still true today.

WIDOWHOOD AS A SOCIAL AND SOCIOLOGICAL PROBLEM

Widowhood must be viewed as a pervasive social problem directly encompassing increasing numbers of women and their families and indirectly affecting many others. Within this context, the husband's demise creates a crisis situation which, to adapt Waller's definition, "strains the resources which families possess, cannot be solved by the repertory of ready-made answers provided by the mores or built up out of the family's previous experience with trouble, and requires the family to find new (and usually expedient) ways of carrying on family operations." Moreover, "once family habits are threatened successfully the influence of the event travels through the family like a bowling ball through a set of tenpins—as one set of habits is disrupted, other sets are affected and there arises the objective possibility of family paralysis" (Waller and Hill, 1951, pp. 456-457). If this type of disruption is to be avoided, and if a successful and long-term adaptation is to be executed, the family must be reorganized as an ongoing social system—roles must be reassigned, status positions shifted, and values and goals reoriented. Although the bereaved family may receive initial support from its kin group in the immediate period prior to or following the husband's death, thereafter it must usually fend for itself both socially and psychologically. Major attention, therefore, needs to be directed toward answering the question: What kinds of social relationships with non-familial persons and groups in the environment need to be developed or maintained which will establish social support for the widow and her family and enable the family to continue functioning despite its loss?

At the more personal level, widowhood requires the development of alternative patterns of behavior if the female survivor is to maintain satisfactory relations with the family, the kin group, and the community, and if she is to establish and sustain an acceptable self-conception—one that will receive approval and which may be appropriately expressed. Women occupying widowhood status experience varying degrees of role ambiguity emanating from vague and contradictory normative expectations concerning appropriate behavior. As a result, the American widow frequently experiences considerable uncertainty and anxiety over reaching decisions concerning such matters as when to terminate the mourning period, how to make others aware of this, when to begin dating again, how long she should wait before considering remarriage, etc. Sociologically, then, the period of widowhood necessitates a reorganization and reintegration of social roles suitable to a new status. The diverse ways through which such role modifications are effectively accomplished, and the manner in which the ambiguous social situation in which the widow finds herself is eventually resolved, represent important areas for empirical inquiry.

CONCLUDING REMARKS

Sociologists have long known that "few events in the life cycle require more extensive changes in activities, responsibilities, and living habits (or cause greater alterations in attitudes, re-ranking of values, and alterations of outlook on life) than does a change from one marital status to another" (Bogue, 1959, p. 212). More specifically, and in terms of the present discussion, they have recognized that the disruption of marriage by the death of a husband has profound repercussions for the widow, her family, and the community. Yet our review of the literature reveals that the special problems that confront the widow both at the time of bereavement and beyond have not undergone extensive *sociological* research. Certainly a rapidly growing population of elderly women, an ever mounting proportion of whom are widowed, would call for a systematic study of their lives, problems, and modes of adaptation. A knowledge of the variations in successful adaptation to widowhood status would have pragmatic consequences with the framework of action-oriented sociologists for educating and preparing individuals and families for dealing with this common experience with better understanding and insight. "Death, even when expected for a long time, is always a shock to the family which has been broken by it. The pain of grief cannot be avoided; but proper preparation will help in facing the work of grief, will lessen the disruption of family life, and will prevent the making of unfortunate decisions during this period of strain. Above all, this preparation will give members of the family insight into ways of helping each other" (Peniston, 1962, p. 16).

In this paper we have concentrated on the widow in American society. The same type of inquiry, however, needs to be undertaken with respect to the widower, about whom scientific information is even less adequate. Currently, there are well over two million widowers in our population, and it can be assumed that the structuring of their adaptation would be different from that of their female counterparts (Berardo, 1967). Unless or until extensive and systematic investigations of widowhood and widowerhood are undertaken and completed, the sociology of isolation will exhibit an unnecessary lag in its development.

REFERENCES

ADLER, LETA M. The relationship of marital status to incidence and recovery from mental illness. *Social Forces*, 1953, *32*, 185–194.

AITKEN-SWAN, JEAN. *Widows in Australia*. Sydney Council of Social Services of New South Wales, 1962.

BELLIN, SEYMOUR S. and HARDT, ROBERT H. Marital status and mental disorders among the aged. *American Sociological Review*, 1958, *23*, 155–162.

BENDANN, EFFIE. *Death customs: an analytical study of burial rites*. New York: Alfred A. Knopf, 1930.

BERARDO, FELIX M. *Social adaptation to widowhood among a rural-urban aged population*. Washington Agricultural Experiment Station Bulletin 689, 1967, College of Agriculture, Washington State University.

BLAU, ZENA S. Structural constraints on friendships in old age. *American Sociological Review*, 1961, *26*, 429–439.

BOGUE, DONALD T. *The population of the United States*. New York: The Free Press, 1959.

BRUNTON, MARJORIE A. *Cross-cultural investigation of the status of widow and widower*. Unpublished master's thesis, Washington State University, 1967.

BURCHINAL, LEE G. Characteristics of adolescents from unbroken, broken, and reconstituted families. *Journal of Marriage and the Family*, 1964, *26*, 44–51.

CHAMPAGNE, M. *Facing life alone—what widows and divorcees should know*. Indianapolis, Ind.: The Bobbs-Merrill Co., Inc., 1964.

DURKHEIM, EMILE. *Suicide: a study in sociology*. New York: The Free Press, 1951.

ELIOT, THOMAS D. Bereavement: inevitable but not insurmountable. In HOWARD BECKER and REUBEN HILL (eds.) *Family marriage and parenthood*. Boston: D. C. Heath & Company (Division of Raytheon Co.), 1955, 641–668.

ELIOT, THOMAS D. The adjustive behavior of bereaved families. *Social Forces*, 1930, *8*, 544–545.

EPSTEIN, LENORE A. and MURRAY, JANET H. *The aged population of the United States*. U.S. Department of Health, Education, and Welfare, Social Security Administration, Office of Research and Statistics, Research Report No. 19, U.S. Government Printing Office, Washington, D.C., 1967.

EPSTEIN, LENORE A. and SKOLNIK, ALFRED M. Social security protection after 30 years. *Social Security Bulletin*, 1965, *28*, 5–17.

FAUNCE, WILLIAM A. and FULTON, ROBERT L. The sociology of death: a neglected area of research. *Social Forces*, 1958, *36*, 205–209.

FITZELLE, G. T. *The personal adjustment of a selected group of widows of fifty-five years and older*. Unpublished doctoral dissertation, Cornell University, 1952.

FRIED, EDRITA G. and STERN, KARL. The situation of the aged within the family. *American Journal of Orthopsychiatry*, 1948, *18*, 31–54.

FULCOMER, DAVID M. *The adjustive behavior of some recently bereaved spouses: a psychosociological study*. Unpublished doctoral dissertation, Northwestern University, 1942.

FULTON, ROBERT (ed.). *Death and identity*. New York: John Wiley & Sons, Inc., 1965.

GORER, GEOFFREY. *Death, grief, and mourning*. Garden City, New York: Anchor Books, Doubleday and Co., Inc., 1965.

GOODE, WILLIAM J. *World revolution and family patterns*. New York: The Free Press, 1963.

HARLAN, WILLIAM H. *Isolation and conduct in later life; a study of four-hundred and sixty-four Chicagoans of ages sixty to ninety-five*. Unpublished doctoral dissertation, University of Chicago, 1951.

HAVIGHURST, ROBERT J. and NEUGARTEN, BERNICE L. (eds.). Attitudes toward death in older persons: a symposium. *Journal of Gerontology*, 1961, *16*, 44–66.

How to help your widow. *Changing Times*. November, 1961, 9–14.

HOWARD, ALAN and SCOTT, ROBERT A. Cultural

values and attitudes toward death. *Journal of Existentialism*, 1966, *6*, 161–171

ILGENFRITZ, MARJORIE P. Mothers on their own—widows and divorcees. *Marriage and Family Living*, 1961, *23*, 38–41.

Institute for Life Insurance. *Some data on life insurance ownership and related characteristics of the older population*, 1964, (mimeographed).

JACOBSON, PAUL H. *American marriage and divorce*. New York: Holt, Rinehart & Winston, Inc., 1959.

KALISH, RICHARD A. *Death and bereavement: an annotated social science bibliography*. Offered in the March-April, 1965, issue of the *SK&F Psychiatric Reporter*, published by Smith Kline and French Laboratories, 1500 Spring Garden Street, Philadelphia.

KENT, DONALD P. *Aging—fact and fancy*. U.S. Department of Health, Education, and Welfare, Welfare Administration, Office of Aging, OA No. 224, U.S Government Printing Office, Washington, D.C., 1965.

KEPHART, WILLIAM M. Status after death. *American Sociological Review*, 1950, *15*, 635–643.

KRAUS, ARTHUR S. and LILIENFELD, ABRAHAM M. The widowed die sooner. *Journal of Chronic Diseases*, 1959, *10*, 207.

KRUPP, GEORGE R. and KLIGFELD, BERNARD. The bereavement reaction: a cross-cultural evaluation. *Journal of Religion and Health*, 1962, *1*, 222–246.

KUTNER, BERNARD, FANSHEL, D., TOGO, A. M. and LANGNER, T. S. *Five-hundred over sixty*. New York: Russell Sage Foundation, 1956.

LANDIS, PAUL H. *The broken home in teenage adjustments*. Washington Agricultural Experiment Station Bulletin No. 542, 1953, now Washington State University.

LANGER, MARION. *Learning to live as a widow*. New York: Julian Messner, 1957.

LOWENTHAL, MARJORIE F. Social isolation and mental illness in old age. *American Sociological Review*, 1964, *29*, 54–70.

LOWENTHAL, MARJORIE F. Antecedents of isolation and mental illness in old age. *Archives of General Psychiatry*, 1965, *12*, 245–254.

Love is being needed. *Look*, August 23, 1966, 67–71.

MARKS, RENEE V. *The sociology of death: a selected bibliography*. Department of Epidemiology, School of Public Health, The University of Michigan, 1965 (mimeographed).

MARRIS, PETER. *Widows and their families*. London: Routledge and Kegan Paul, 1958.

Metropolitan Life Insurance Company. The American widow. *Statistical Bulletin*, 1962, *43*, 1–4.

Metropolitan Life Insurance Company. Orphanhood—a continuing problem. *Statistical Bulletin*, 1966, *47*, 3–5.

Metropolitan Life Insurance Company. Widows and widowhood. *Statistical Bulletin*, 1966, *47*, 3–6.

NYE, F. IVAN. Child adjustment in broken and in unhappy, unbroken homes. *Marriage and Family Living*, 1957, *19*, 356–361.

National Consumer Finance Association. *Finance Facts*. Educational Service Division, Washington, D.C., January, 1963, 1.

OSBORNE, ERNEST. *When you lose a loved one*. New York: Public Affairs Committee, Inc., Pamphlet No. 269, July, 1958.

OWENS J. Z. *Widows can be happy*. New York: Greenberg, 1951.

PARKES, MURRAY C. Bereavement and mental illness, part I, a clinical study of grief of bereaved psychiatric patients. *British Journal of Medical Psychology*, 1965, *38*, 13–26.

PARKES, MURRAY C. Effects of bereavement on physical and mental health—a study of the medical records of widows, *British Medical Journal*, 1964, *2*, 1–15.

PALMORE, ERDMAN, STANLEY, GERTRUDE L., and CORMIER, ROBERT H. *Widows with children under social security*. The 1963 National Survey of widows with Children Under OASDHI. U. S. Department of Health, Education, and Welfare, Social Security Administration, Office of Research and Statistics, Research Report No. 16, U. S. Government Printing Office, Washington, D.C., 1966.

PENISTON, D. HIGH. The importance of "death education" in family life. *The Family Life Coordinator*, 1962, *11*, 15–18.

PERRY, JOSEPH P., JR., and PHUHL, ERDWIN H., JR. Adjustment of children in "solo" and "remarriage" homes. *Marriage and Family Living*, 1963, *25*, 221–223.

PHELPS, HAROLD A. *Contemporary social problems* (rev. ed.). Englewood Cliffs, N.J.: Prentice-Hall, Inc., 1938, *15*, 516–540.

REES, W. DEWI and LUTKINS, SYLVIA G. Mortality of bereavement. *British Medical Journal*, 1967, *4*, 13–16.

RICHMOND, MARY and HALL, JOHN. *A study of nine-hundred and eighty-five widows*. New York: Russell Sage Foundation, 1913.

ROULSTON, MAJORIE H. *You can start all over: a guide to the widow and divorcee*. New York: Harper & Row, Publishers, 1951.

RUSHING, WILLIAM A. Deviance, interpersonal relations, and suicide. *Human Relations*, (forthcoming).

RUSHING, WILLIAM A. Individual behavior and suicide. In JACK P. GIBBS (ed.), *Suicide*. New York: Harper and Row, Publishers, 1968, ch. 4.

SCHWABACHER, ALBERT E., JR. The repository of wealth. In SEYMOUR M. FARBER and ROGER H. L. WILSON (eds.), *The potential of woman*. New York: McGraw-Hill Book Company, 1963, 241–254.

SHELDON, HENRY D. *The older population of the United States.* New York: John Wiley & Sons, Inc., 1958.

SHUDDE, LOUIS O. and EPSTEIN, LENORE A. Orphanhood—a diminishing problem. *Social Security Bulletin,* 1955, *18,* 17–19.

STUB, HOLGER R. Family structure and the social consequences of death. In JEANNETTE R. FORTA and EDITH S. DECK (eds.) *A sociological framework for patient care.* New York: John Wiley & Sons, Inc., 1966, 191–200.

TORREY, TONI. *Wisdom for widows.* New York: E. P. Dutton & Co., Inc., 1941.

U. S. Bureau of the Census. *Statistical abstract of the United States: 1967,* (88th Edition). Washington, D.C., 1967, p. 33, Table 32, Marital Status of the Population, by Sex: 1890–1966.

WALLER, WILLARD. *The family: a dynamic interpretation.* New York: The Cordon Company, 1938.

WALLER, WILLARD. *The family: A dynamic interpretation* (rev. ed. by Reuben Hill). New York: The Dryden Press, 1951.

WILLIAMS, RICHARD W. Changing status, roles, and relationships. In CLARK TIBBITS (ed.), *Handbook of social gerontology.* Chicago: University of Chicago Press, 1961, 261–297.

WYNN, MARGARET. *Fatherless families.* London: Michael Joseph Limited, 1964.

ZALK, LOUIS. *How to be a successful widow.* New York: Fleet Publishing Co., 1957.

60.

PAUL C. GLICK

BACHELORS AND SPINSTERS

If bachelors are defined as single men 35 years old and over and spinsters as single women 30 years old and over, about three million persons in 1960 were bachelors and three million were spinsters. Perhaps four or five million of these six million may never marry. About five percent were members of religious orders; about 10 percent of the bachelors and five percent of the spinsters resided involuntarily in institutions—over one-half of whom were in mental hospitals. Probably most of the remainder would have preferred to marry, if they had had the chance to do so. This judgment is based on the very sharp decline during recent decades in the proportion of persons who will marry. Of all young adults in 1960, probably all but three or four percent will eventually marry; this is only about one-third the corresponding level for those who reached adulthood one generation earlier.

This selection is reprinted from: Paul C. Glick, "Marriage, Socio-economic Status and Health," in Egon Szabady (ed.), *World Views of Population Problems,* Budapest: Hungarian Academy of Sciences, 1968, 127–137 [excerpt].

Reprinted with the permission of the author and publisher.

Spinsters more often than bachelors demonstrate qualities that are high on the educational and economic scale. Spinsters who could marry are probably often motivated against doing so by an aversion for downward socioeconomic mobility in marriage. Bachelors probably include a substantial proportion who, for various reasons, lack the personal competence to convince an acceptable woman to marry them.

One-half of the young bachelors and spinsters in 1960 were still living with their father or mother or both. About 20 to 40 percent of them kept up a home apart from relatives. Spinsters were much more likely than bachelors to live with a brother or sister, whereas bachelors were much more likely than spinsters to be sharing the home of nonrelatives.

Virtually all of the rich men eventually marry. Only two percent of middle-aged men with incomes of $10,000 and over in 1960 were single, as compared with 20 percent of those with less than $10,000. Probably the man's initiative in marriage diminishes, and the woman's initiative increases, as the man's income rises. Women of middle age with incomes between $5000 and

$10,000 were the least likely to have married, and those with still higher incomes were less likely to have married than those with incomes under $5000. Virtually all of the women with no income eventually marry or cease to earn income after marriage, only three percent of women of middle age without income being spinsters.

CHAPTER XV

Some Family Problems

THIS CHAPTER presents two articles dealing with special problems in the family. The first is by Joan K. Jackson, and deals with the difficulties a family faces when there is an alcoholic present. Alcoholism is a personal problem, but it has serious ramifications for the lives of others who must adapt to and live with an alcoholic. In addition to the psychological stress, alcoholism often places economic strains on the family. In the case of low or moderate income families, the cost of alcohol can cut seriously into the budget. When the husband is the alcoholic, it may interfere with his ability to hold a job and hence result in an unpredictable income.

The second article presented is of quite a different nature, dealing with the problems that occur in a family when there is a retarded chid. Children can be problems to their parents in many ways, but when they are unable to function normally because of their mental abilities they become a particular burden and sometimes an embarrassment for their parents and their siblings. The burdens of a retarded child take many forms. In some cases parents may carry great guilt that the retardation is their fault. Some types of mentally retarded children have relatively short life expectancy so that parents must constantly live with the knowledge that they will lose a child. Other parents must live with the tension of whether to have a child placed in a mental hospital. It is difficult not to suffer great guilt if the decision is made to have a child institutionalized, but keeping a child of sub-marginal mental abilities can virtually enslave parents within the home. The care of a mentally retarded child may require attention that makes other siblings feel that they are neglected. Perhaps the amazing thing is that many families do adjust and learn to cope with mental retardation, but the multitude of problems that mental retardation presents never permits adjustment to be easy.

There are many special problems that families often face and these two chapters are presented merely as examples. Mental illness in the family may be analogous to alcoholism. Similarly, if a parent is a gambler, or is detached from the family by virtue of wanting to have a separate and exciting life, or where deviance occurs in parallel form, the situation of adaptation to the society of the family as a unit may be a serious problem. Children may be problems in ways parallel to the mentally retarded. The child that becomes deviant in any of a number of ways may cause similar types of embarrassments and demand extraordinary attention from the family. More general problems of the family have already been discussed in several of the chapters, and implicitly one general way of approaching the study of families is through family problems and their resolution. This approach essentially has a model of some adjustment pattern for families, even though the model may be loosely defined within broad limits.

61.

Joan K. Jackson

ALCOHOLISM AND THE FAMILY

Fifty years ago the members of an alcoholic's family were regarded as innocent victims of the willful self-indulgence of an irresponsible, weak, and sinful person. The drunkard was seen as someone for the family to hide, the police to control, and the clergy to reform. The family was to be pitied and shown charity. The "why" of alcoholism was explained by these attitudes, the "what to do" followed logically enough, while failure to change the alcoholic was readily interpretable. Research on alcoholism and the family, if it could be called such, was of the survey kind meant to provide ammunition for social reformers inveighing against the "evils of drink."

Today alcoholism is in the process of being culturally redefined. It is being viewed increasingly as an illness. In this attitudinal context, it follows that alcoholism has a discoverable etiology, course, and treatment, and is a suitable object for systematic research. Members of the alcoholic's family are no longer regarded simply as innocent victims but may be seen, for instance, as etiological agents or as complicating the illness. At times, it seems as though this latter trend has advanced to the point where the alcoholic emerges as the innocent victim of his family. However, there is as yet little evidence that the new cultural attitudes will permit a clearer view of the behavior of alcoholics or provide better tools for understanding the interaction of alcoholism and the family.

This selection is reprinted from Joan K. Jackson, "Alcoholism and the Family," in David J. Pittman and Charles R. Snyder (eds.), *Society, Culture, and Drinking Patterns,* New York: John Wiley & Sons, Inc., 1962, 472–492 [a segment of the original article is omitted].

Reprinted with the permission of the author and John Wiley & Sons, Inc.

The investigation upon which this paper is based was supported in part by Senior Research Fellowship SF262 from the United States Public Health Service and by State of Washington Initiative 171 Funds for Research in Biology and Medicine.

The alcoholic and his family are typically caught between these old and new definitions of the situation in their attempts to conceptualize and resolve their difficulties. The majority of alcoholics and their families still think of alcoholism as willful and as warranting social condemnation. At the same time, the view that alcoholism is an illness is gaining acceptance. Both sets of attitudes may have an important influence upon family interaction and behavior. For those who seek to understand alcoholism, such cultural attitudes may profoundly affect what is observed and how observations are interpreted, theoretically and programmatically.

A REVIEW OF RESEARCH FINDINGS ON ALCOHOLISM AND THE FAMILY

To date there is no research which could legitimately be called "alcoholism and the family" in the full sense of the phrase. Before such research can occur it must be possible to study the family as a unit. It is still rare to find families in which the alcoholic and all members of the family are willing to be subjects or informants As a result, the majority of research has focused on one family member or has dealt with one family member's perception of the situation. Most commonly the center of attention is the alcoholic's wife, rather than the alcoholic husband and father.

The Alcoholic Husband and Father

The role of the alcoholic in the family unit has not been studied systematically. The published literature contains little in the way of research on his perception of the family situation, of his interactions with family members, and of his ongoing experience in the family. This is particularly peculiar because it is almost impossible in interviewing a married or divorced alcoholic to keep him off the subject. A doctoral dissertation by the present writer (19) contained a chapter on this subject. It was noted that the hospitalized alcoholics appeared to think of their family relationships almost entirely in utilitarian terms of money and service. For instance, if they brought home their pay and did chores around the house, they felt that their wives should be satisfied; at the same time, their demands on their wives for understanding and emotional support appeared to be excessive.

Fox (11), on the basis of observations of a large number of alcoholics in treatment, wrote a discerning description of the alcoholic's part in the marital relationship. It was the chief aim of the compulsive drinker to continue drinking, and the chief aim of the spouse to prevent it. The unpredictability of the alcoholic makes him hard to live with. In rapid succession he may be charming, cruel, aloof, withdrawn, fawning, and hostile. His claims for special treatment and his conviction that he should be free of all responsibilities lead almost inevitably to conflict with his spouse. Family members tend to be the targets for most of his hostility and to be held responsible for most of his difficulties.

Bullock and Mudd (6) clinically observed that the alcoholic spouse has problems in expressing anger constuctively in the marriage setting. Additional problems with his wife center around economic dependency on the wife, resentment over attention given to the children, and jealousy over the relations of his wife with parental families and friends. Most alcoholic husbands expressed dissatisfaction with their marriages in relation to the attitudes and behavior of their wives.

Bacon (2) has suggested that excessive drinking is more incompatible with the institution of marriage than with any other. The supposition is that the personality and role problems which led to alcoholism tend to debar marriage or to become intensified if marriage occurs. The institution of marriage, which has primary importance in establishing intimate, affectional relationships, is thought to be uncongenial to the types of personalities who become alcoholics.

Mowrer's (31) study, based on case studies of alcoholics and of their wives, and of controls, indicated that the status of the male alcoholic in marriage tends to become inferior to that of the wife. Sexual relationships tend to be unsatisfactory because of the inadequacies of both partners. By way of conclusion, there is the suggestion that family attitudes towards the alcoholic tend to result from the alcoholism.

THE ALCOHOLIC WIFE AND MOTHER

There are no empirical studies of the alcoholic wife's effect on the family. Clinicians, however, have published some observations.

Fox (11) has the impression that the alcoholic wife is able to hide her drinking from her husband longer than a male alcoholic could hide it from his wife. Because the cultural attitudes towards alcoholism in women are more stringent, the alcoholic woman is more concerned about hiding her drinking. The structure of the housewife's workday permits more frequent drinking, and most of her tasks can be accomplished despite a state of mild intoxication. It is also Fox's observation that the children of an alcoholic mother can hardly be shielded from the impact of drinking. Deep and lasting feelings of rejection tend to occur.

THE CHILDREN OF ALCOHOLICS

In common with much other family research, children, in studies relating to alcoholism, have not been regarded as playing important roles in the ongoing behavior of the alcoholic's family (10). The literature on children has been concerned with the effect of alcoholism on their development. Only Bacon (2) and the present writer (21) have noted that children play a role in the alcoholic's difficulties. Both suggest that fatherhood tends to intensify the alcoholic's problems. In an earlier study (19), the writer found that parenthood is one of the life events which is commonly associated with a sudden and marked increase in the number of the alcoholism behaviors listed by Jellinek (23).

Roe (36) studied the rate of alcoholism and the over-all adjustment in adulthood of the children of alcoholics raised by foster parents as compared with a control group of other foster children. Her findings led to the almost permanent retirement of the hypothesis that alcoholism is biologically inherited.

Newell (32), in a speculative article, raised interesting hypotheses about the psychological effects upon a child of having an alcoholic parent. Unfortunately these hypotheses have been ignored by those engaged in empirical research. She suggested that the children of alcoholics are placed in a situation very similar to that of the experimental animals who are tempted toward rewards and then continually frustrated, whose environment continually changes in a manner over which they have no control. Under such circumstances experimental animals have convulsions or nervous breakdowns.

We know little of what happens to the children of alcoholics. However, Baker (3) notes that children are almost always under emotional strain when they have an alcoholic parent. She comments on the common tendency among such children to feel more affection for the alcoholic than for the non-alcoholic parent, probably because the alcoholic parent is rewarding when sober, while the non-alcoholic parent tends to be irritable and rejecting under the constant situational pressure. Fox (11) points out that the sons of alcoholic males find it difficult to establish stable identifications and are often beset by ambivalent feelings throughout life. The daughter may side with the mother and blame the father or vice versa. Both sons and daughters may identify masculine independence with drunkenness. In the face of society's attitudes towards excessive drinking, they feel deep shame and humiliation. The present writer, on the basis of observations of an Alanon Family Group, noted that children are more affected than any other family member by living with an alcoholic. Personalities are formed in a social milieu which is markedly unstable, torn with dissension, culturally deviant, and socially disapproved. The children must model themselves on adults who play their roles in a distorted fashion. The alcoholic shows little adequate adult behavior. The non-alcoholic parent attempts to play the roles of both father and mother, often failing to do either well.

The child of an alcoholic is bound to have problems in learning who he is, what is expected of him, and what he can expect from others. Almost inevitably his parents behave inconsistently towards him. His self-conception evolves in a situation in which the way others act towards him has more to do with the current events in the family than with the child's nature. His alcoholic parent feels one way about him when he is sober, another when drunk, and yet another during the hangover stage. What the child can expect from his parents depends on the phase of the drinking cycle as well as on where he stands in relation to each parent at any given time. Only too frequently he is used in the battle between them. The wives of alcoholics are concerned that they find themselves disliking, punishing, or depriving the children preferred by the father and those who resemble him. Similarly, the child who is preferred by or resembles the mother is often hurt by the father. If the child tries to stay close to both parents he is caught in an impossible situation. Each parent resents the affection the other receives while demanding that the child show affection to both.

The children do not understand what is happening. The very young ones do not know that their families are different from other families. When they become aware of the difference, the children are torn between their own loyalty and the views of their parents that others hold. When neighbors ostracize them, the children are bewildered about what they did to bring about this result. Even those who are not ostracized become isolated; they hesitate to bring their friends to a home where their parent is likely to be drunk. Moreover, the tendency of the child to examine his own behavior for reasons for parental alcoholism is very often reinforced inadvertently by his mother. When it is feared that the father is leading up to a drinking episode, the children are put on their best behavior. When the drinking episode occurs, it is not surprising that the children feel that they have somehow done something to precipitate it.

Yet some of the children of alcoholics appear relatively undisturbed. The personality damage appears to be least when the non-alcoholic parent is aware of the problems they face, gives them emotional support, refrains from using them against the alcoholic, tries to be consistent and has insight into her own problems with the alcoholic. It also appears to mitigate some of the child's confusion if alcoholism is explained to him by a parent who accepts alcoholism as an illness.

The Alcoholic Marriage

There has been very little research bearing directly upon the alcoholic and his wife. The works of Gliedman and his associates (14,15), Mitchell (30), Ballard (4), Mowrer (31), Bullock and Mudd (6), and Strayer (39) are exceptions. These researchers focused on the interactions of the spouses, whereas, as a general rule, the non-alcoholic spouse is the focus of attention and the alcoholic remains in the background.

Ballard and Mitchell studied couples composed of male alcoholics and their non-alcoholic wives and compared them with control couples whose marriages were also conflicted. The experience of a stressful marital situation was thereby held constant.

Ballard found that on clinical scales the wives of alcoholics showed few differences from the wives in the control group. If anything, they appeared to be better adjusted. The major difference between the alcoholic and non-alcoholic couples was in the relative adjustment of the partners. In the alcoholic marriages the wife appeared less disturbed whereas in non-alcoholic marriages the husband appeared better adjusted. The wives of alcoholics seem to assume masculine roles, to place emphasis on repression, and to avoid responses which suggest a tendency to "act out." Ballard goes on to specify the ways in which the interaction of the personalities of husbands and wives could provide mutual gratifications and defensive reassurances.

Mitchell dealt specifically with the husband-wife pairs of the same groups as those studied by Ballard. He found that alcoholics and their wives were more sensitive to each other than were the partners in marriages where alcoholism was not a problem. Mitchell suggests that this may be a derivative of a marital situation in which both partners are very vigilant of each other's feelings and behavior in order to maintain the relationship and to meet the practical exigencies of family life. In the evaluation of the role relationship of the alcoholic and his wife, power, control, and dominance appeared to be areas of crucial significance. The wives were overwhelmingly viewed as the most dominant figures within the marriage. Both partners had more difficulty than the controls in handling hostility. Mitchell's research led to the conclusion that a major problem in marriages in which alcoholism is present is for the spouses to be able to differentiate their roles. "At the level of interpersonal perception they seem unclear as to what they can expect from each other; who does what, by what authority, at what time and with whom is the core problem in their relationship." (30, p. 557.)

Bullock and Mudd, studying the same couples as had Ballard and Mitchell, reported that both spouses tend to bring personality problems to the marriage and that these problems become intensified during marriage. The failure of each spouse to gratify the overdetermined needs of the other is viewed as the major factor in the marital conflict.

Gliedman and his associates studied nine couples undergoing treatment for the alcoholism of the husband. These investigators agree with Ballard that the wives of alcoholics are better organized than the husbands. The wives in their study tended to be dissatisfied with themselves and their husbands generally, while the husbands, when they were sober, felt satisfied with their wives. Serious sexual difficulties were found in eight of the nine marriages. With treatment the greatest change came in the marital milieu.

The Wives of Alcoholics

Research on the wives of alcoholics has taken two major directions—the psychological and the sociological. The psychological approach conceptualizes the family as a unit composed of interacting personalities. The majority of the psychological literature deals with a description and analysis of the personality of the alcoholic's wife. Her behavior towards her husband is regarded as an expression of this personality or as a product of the interactions between her personality and that of her husband. Little is said about the alcoholic's impact on her behavior and personality, but there is considerable speculation about the impact of the wife on the alcoholic.

Students of the alcoholic's wife do not state explicitly that she is the cause of her husband's alcoholism or of its persistence. The reader is often left with this impression, however. Hypotheses concerning complementarity of personalities between the alcoholic and his wife have not been proven, although considerable data have been accumulated on the subject. Some research has tested only the non-alcoholic in each marital pair and has then gone on to speculate on the role of the wife's personality in interaction with that of the unstudied alcoholic. Even when both spouses have been studied, the conclusions about their interactions more often have been based upon group averages than upon data derived from the study of the pairs as social units.

In most of the psychological literature, there is implicit the notion of a constant personality reflected in situations but not altered by them. Despite the existence of a considerable body of psychological theory about the responses of personality to stress and about personality change in therapy, the literature on alcoholism and on the spouses of alcoholics seems to have remained bound to psychological tests and to particular points in time. Notwithstanding the paucity of findings on tests that search for "the alcoholic personality," there is a search for a common personality that can be called "the wife of an alcoholic." There are, indeed, similarities in the behavior of alcoholics and their spouses. However, the contribution which the personality of each spouse makes to the onset, peristence, and alleviation of alcoholism will remain in the realm of speculation until we have firmer knowledge of the etiology of alcoholism, its course, and of its remedy.

The sociological approach to research on the wives of alchoholics reflects, in contrast, basic sociological concerns with the social unit called the family—its structure, functions, and processes. The emphasis is on the behavior of the social unit, the institutionalized norms which govern it, and the behavior of members acting in their institutionalized roles. Sociologists are concerned, in short, with institutional behavior, with social acts. They are more interested in the social behavior which occurs under certain types of social conditions than in the question of behavioral normality or abnormality. Thus, when commonalities are found in the behavior of the wives of alcoholics, the sociologist turns for explanation to common features of family structure and processes and to common features of the situations which impinge on the family or in which the family is involved. Yet the sociological approach is also open to criticism in the present context. Generally, there is a tendency to ignore personality factors and to concentrate on social roles as if the social structure and situation completely dictated the behavior of the alcoholic's wife. Obviously this yields a very incomplete picture of the wife's behavior.

All studies to date have dealt with the wives of alcoholics who were seeking help, regardless of the duration of the seeking or the motivation behind it. No two studies have had comparable samples. Yet there is no reason to believe that wives who, say, seek help through Alanon Family Groups are similar to wives who go to marriage counseling clinics, or to those who join their spouses in psychiatric treatment at an alcoholism clinic. Nor can it be assumed that they have much in common with those who seek psychiatric aid for themselves or who end up in mental institutions. Wives of alcoholics who do not seek help or who divorce their alcoholic spouses have not been studied. Hence we do not know if the apparent contradictions in certain research findings are attributable to differences in research techniques, sample sources, or the wives themselves.

Most research on the wives of alcoholics is concerned with the psychopathology of the wife —the disagreement in the literature centers on the degree and nature of the wife's disturbance. Gliedman and his associates (14, 15) and Ballard (4) found the wives in the marital pairs they studied to be better organized than their husbands. Ballard found them to be less disturbed than the control pairs caught in conflicted marriages. Price (35, p. 623), while noting deeper insecurities, conceded that some wives of alcoholics "gave the appearance of being completely adequate, capable women . . . ." The majority of investigators, however, have found them to be extremely disturbed people.

In this latter vein, Futterman (12) concluded that the alcoholic's wife unconsciously encourages her husband's alcoholism because of her own needs. He suggested that the needs are so great that, should the husband become sober, the wife often decompensates and begins to show symptoms of neurotic disturbance. Mac-Donald (29) and Wellman (43) concur in this view. Whalen (44), Lewis (27), and Price (35) have substantially the same view. Whalen delineates four types of personalities commonly found among the wives of alcoholics who come to social agencies for help. Like Futterman, she believes that certain types of women marry alcoholics in order to satisfy deep unconscious needs to be married to weak, inadequate, and dependent males. Price and Lewis differ on the nature of the disturbance, although they agree that it is present. They found the wives of alcoholics to be nervous, hostile, basically dependent people, although on the surface they appear to be adequate. They were unable to cope with the drinking of their husbands and accepted no responsibility for it. The women studied by Lewis and Price appeared to be insecure people at the outset of their marriages who expected their husbands to be strong, dependable, and responsible. They continued to demand that their husbands meet their needs for this type of spouse, thereby making their husbands feel less adequate and, eventually, behave in a less adequate way.

Kalashian (24), Cork (9), and the present writer (21) agree that, during the alcoholism of the husband, the wife tends to be psychologically disturbed. They do not agree with those who contend that, if the husband achieves sobriety, the wife is likely to decompensate; and they have queried the wife's vested interest in maintaining her husband's alcoholism, as well as the basis of her disturbance. Along with Gliedman and his associates, these researchers have noted that the wives they saw were deeply involved in having their husbands achieve sobriety. For instance, only one of the wives seen by the writer over an eight-year period showed an increase in disturbance of more than a temporary nature when the husband's alcoholism became inactive and, apparently, permanently so. On the contrary, the wives' adjustment typically appears to have improved in most respects.

This is not to deny, however, that the onset of sobriety precipitates additional disturbances on the part of all family members. However, the disturbances can be viewed as resulting either from rigidity in personalities or from rigidity in family patterns and processes, or both. When the onset of sobriety is viewed in the context of the total family crisis, rather than as an isolated piece of family history, one may suppose that much of the behavior on the part of the wife which appears to be dysfunctional for the recovery of the alcoholic plays an important part in maintaining the integration and stability of the family as a social unit. An example of this is the wife's reluctance to relinquish her dominance until sobriety is well established and appears to be permanent.

The writer (18) has also raised questions in an earlier report about the ways in which the nature, extent, and duration of the stressful situation contribute to the extent and nature of the wife's disturbance. The behavior of both the alcoholic and his wife is similar in many ways to that of people who are involved in situations characterized by marked and rapid role changes, by social disapproval, by lack of clear-cut definitions for appropriate behavior, by social isolation, by situational ambiguity, and by recurrent auxiliary crises—all of which are ingredients of the family alcoholism crisis.

THE HUSBANDS OF ALCOHOLIC WOMEN

There have been no systematic studies of the husbands of alcoholic women. Lisansky (28), in a study of women alcoholics, found that a sample drawn from a penal state farm typically had husbands who themselves were often in jail, and that abusiveness, irregular employment, and heavy drinking were common. This was not at all characteristic of the husbands of a sample of women alcoholics drawn from an outpatient clinic.

Fox (11) and Bacon (2) comment on their impressions that there is a greater tendency for husbands to leave alcoholic wives than for wives to leave alcoholic husbands. Fox suggests that this results from the tendency of women to mother and sympathize with husbands, from the greater permissiveness towards male drinking in our culture, and from the woman's economic dependence on her husband. Bacon speculates that women in our society have more of an emotional investment in marriage than men. More of their socialization has been directed towards fulfilling the marital and familial roles. In addition, since women have fewer associations than men, the danger of losing such a crucial one is supposedly more threatening. The cultural expectations of the wife's role also permit a woman more readily to remain with an alcoholic husband than a man to remain with an alcoholic wife. Recent research by Bowerman (5) would appear to lend support to Bacon's position. In a study of normal subjects, it was found that the personality adjustment of the wife tended to be seen by her as subordinate to family goals, while for husbands, personal-centered and family-centered goals were of equal importance.

ALCOHOLISM AS A CUMULATIVE CRISIS FOR THE FAMILY

In recent research, the present writer focused on the alcoholic's family and on the time interval between the onset of the illness and its resolution. The data for the first phase of this research, to be discussed here, consist of verbatim recordings of the regular meetings of one Alanon Family Group during the period 1951 to the present. The basic data thus consist of statements by the wives of alcoholics about their perceptions of the behavior of family members in the past and the present. Such a group stresses the wife's behavior and attitudes and is interested in the alcoholic's behavior largely as background material. An orientation of this kind obviously imposes limits on the sorts of data available for study. In addition, more information was available on regular members than on those who rarely attended meetings. Hence the study deals with women who were either strongly motivated or who derived important satisfactions from group participation. The second phase of the study, now in progress, consists of a follow-up of the 157 women who attended the group during this period of study. It involves intensive interviews with these women concerning their families' experiences with alcoholism, the administering of psychological tests, and study of a control group composed of friends of these Alanon members who have had no direct family experience with alcoholism.

In this work, the family's behavior in regard to the alcoholism of the husband and father has been approached as a special case of the theory of family crises. The theoretical background may be summarized as follows: When persons live together over a period of time, patterns evolve of relating to one another and of behaving as a unit. In a family, a division of function occurs and roles interlock. For the family to function smoothly, each person must play his roles in a predictable manner and according to the expectations of others in the family. When the family as a whole is functioning smoothly, individual members of the family also tend to function well. Each member is aware of where he fits, what he is expected to do, and what he can expect from others in the family. When these expectations are not met, repercussions are felt by each family member and the family as a whole ceases to function smoothly. A crisis is underway.

Family crises tend to follow a similar pattern, regardless of the nature of the precipitant. Usually there is an initial denial that a problem exists. The family tries to continue in its usual behavior patterns until it is obvious that these patterns are no longer effective. A downward slump in organization occurs at this point. Roles are played with less enthusiasm, and there is an increase in tensions and strained relationships. Finally, an improvement occurs as some technique of adjustment proves successful; family organization becomes stabilized at a new level. At each stage of the crisis, there is a reshuffling of roles among family members; there are changes in status and prestige, changes in "self" and "other" images, shifts in family solidarity and self-sufficiency and in the visibility of the crisis to outsiders. In the course of the crisis, considerable mental conflict is engendered in all family members, and personality distortion occurs (42). These are the elements which are uniform regardless of the type of family crisis. The phases of the crisis vary in length and intensity depending upon its nature and the nature of the individuals involved in it.

When one of the adults in a family becomes an alcoholic, the over-all pattern of the crisis takes a form similar to that of other family crises, but there are usually recurrent subsidiary crises which complicate the over-all situation and attempts at its resolution. Shame, unemployment, impoverishment, desertion and return, nonsupport, infidelity, imprisonment, illness, and progressive dissension also occur. For certain other types of family crises, there may be cultural prescriptions for socially appropriate behavior and for procedures which will terminate the crisis—but this is not the case for alcoholism.

Culturally, alcoholism is subsumed under a general category of undesirable deviant behavior. The culture assumes that if a family is adequate, its members will behave in accordance with social norms. Thus, in efforts to handle problems associated with deviancy, the family labors under a pall of blame. They feel guilty, ashamed, inadequate, and, above all, isolated from social support. Where the husband is an alcoholic this burden falls disproportionately on the wife who, in her own and in society's view, has failed in her major roles. The situation is further complicated in that the culture offers no guideposts to behavior for the family containing a deviant, other than the expectation that the family should bring the deviant back into line. The cultural norms governing how family members should feel and behave with respect to one another are in direct conflict with the prescriptions for how members of the society in general should behave in relation to social deviants. As a result, family members are constantly in conflict about their behavior. If the family accepts the view that the deviant behavior should be labeled illness, the confusion and conflict is likely to be compounded further when this view is not accepted by the sick person, their acquaintances, or those to whom they turn for help (38). The family of an alcoholic thus finds itself in a socially unstructured situation and must find techniques for handling the crisis through trial and error behavior, without social support. In many respects, there are marked similarities between the type of crisis precipitated by alcoholism and those precipitated by mental illness (45).

Alcoholism seldom emerges full-blown overnight. It is usually heralded by widely spaced incidents of excessive drinking, each of which sets off a small family crisis. Both spouses try to account for the episode and then to avoid or alter the family behavior and situations which appear to have caused the drinking. In their search for explanations, they try to define the situation as controllable, understandable, and "perfectly normal." Between drinking episodes, both feel guilty about their behavior and about their impact on each other. Each tries to be an "ideal spouse" to the other. Gradually, not only the drinking problem but also the other problems in the marriage are denied or side-stepped.

It takes some time before the wife realizes that the drinking is neither normal nor controllable behavior. It takes the alcoholic considerably longer to come to the same conclusion. The cultural view that alcoholics are skid-row bums who are constantly inebriated also serves to cloud the realities of the situation. Friends compound the confusion; if the wife compares her husband with them, some show parallels to his behavior and others marked contrast. She wavers between defining his behavior as "normal" and as "not normal." If she consults friends, they tend to discount her concern, thus facilitating her tendency to deny that a problem exists and adding to her guilt about thinking disloyal thoughts about her husband.

As Yarrow (45) has pointed out in her work on mental illness and the family, part of the wife's problem in recognizing the illness is that her husband's behavior is unfamiliar, incongruent, and unlikely in terms of social expectations. The cultural expectations and assumptions about behavior screen out certain perceptions and provide her with limited tools for interpreting the evidence. In the case of alcoholism, the sporadic nature of the drunken behavior and the intervals of apparently "normal" behavior tend to prolong the process of defining the behavior as "not normal." During this initial stage the family is very concerned about the social visibility of the drinking behavior. They feel that they surely would be ostracized if the extent of the drinking were known. To protect themselves against discovery, the family begins to cut down on their social activities and to withdraw into the home. Yarrow has noted the parallels between the behavior in this stage and minority group behavior.

The second stage begins when the family defines the alcoholic's drinking behavior as "not normal." At this point, frantic efforts are made to eliminate the problem. Lacking clear-cut cultural prescriptions for what to do in a situation like this, the efforts are of the trial-and-error variety. In rapid succession, the wife threatens to leave the husband, babies him during hangovers, drinks with him, hides or empties his bottles, curtails money, tries to understand his problem, keeps his liquor handy for him, and nags him. Yet, all efforts to change the situation fail. The family gradually becomes so preoccupied with the problem of discovering how to keep father sober that long-term family goals recede into the background. At the same time, the isolation of the family reaches its peak of intensity. Extreme isolation magnifies the importance of all intrafamily interactions and events. Almost all thought becomes drinking-centered; drinking comes to symbolize all conflicts between the spouses, and even mother-child conflicts are regarded as indirect derivatives of the drinking behavior. Attempts to keep the social visibility of the behavior at the lowest possible level increase. Moreover, the alienation of husband and wife accelerates. Each feels resentful of the other. Each feels misunderstood and unable to understand. Both search frantically for the reasons for the drinking, believing that if the reasons could be discovered, all family members could gear their behavior so as to make the drinking unnecessary.

There seems to follow, however, a stage of disorganization which could also be entitled "What's the use?" The wife feels increasingly inadequate as a wife, mother, woman, and person. She feels she has failed to make a happy and united home for her husband and children. Her husband's frequent comments to the effect that her behavior causes his drinking, and her own concerns that this may be true intensify the process of self-devaluation. Nothing seems effective in stabilizing the alcoholic. Efforts to change the situation become, at best, sporadic. Behavior is geared to relieve tensions rather than to achieve goals. The family gives up trying to understand the alcoholic. They do not care if the neighbors know about the drinking. The children are told that their father is a drunk. They are no longer required to show

him affection or respect. The myth that father still has an important status in the family is dropped when he no longer supports them, is imprisoned, caught in infidelity, or disappears for long periods of time. The family ceases to care about its self-sufficiency and begins to resort to public agencies for help, thereby losing self-respect. For her part, the wife becomes very concerned about her sanity. She finds herself engaging in tension-relieving behavior which she knows is without goal. She is aware that she feels tense, anxious, and hostile. She regards her precrisis self as "the real me" and becomes very frightened at how she has changed.

When some major or minor subsidiary crisis occurs, the family is forced to take survival action. At this point, many wives leave their husbands. The major characteristic of this stage is that the wife "takes over." The alcoholic is ignored or is assigned the status of the most recalcitrant child. When the wife's obligations to her husband conflict with those to her children, she decides in favor of the children. Family ranks are closed progressively and the father is excluded.

As a result of the changed family organization, father's behavior constitutes less of a problem. Hostility towards him diminishes as the family no longer expects him to change, while feelings of pity, exasperation, and protectiveness arise. Such reorganization has a stabilizing effect on the children. They find their environment and their mother more consistent. Their relationship to their father is more clearly defined. Guilt and anxiety diminish as they come to accept their mother's view that drinking is not caused by any behavior of family members. Long-term family goals and planning begin again. Help from public agencies is accepted as necessary and no longer impairs family self-respect. With the taking over of family control, the wife gradually regains her sense of worth. Her concerns about her emotional health decrease.

Yet, despite the greater stabilization, subsidiary crises multiply. The alcoholic is violent or withdraws more often; income becomes more uncertain; imprisonments and hospitalizations occur more frequently. Each crisis is temporarily disruptive to the new family organization. The symbolization of these events as being caused by alcoholism, however, prevents the complete disruption of the family. The most disruptive type of crisis occurs if the husband recognizes that he has a drinking problem and makes an effort to get help. Hope is mobilized. The family attempts to open its ranks again in order to give him the maximum chance for recovery. Roles are partially reshuffled and attempts at attitude change are made, only to be disrupted again if treatment is unsuccessful.

The problems involved in marital separation from the alcoholic are similar to the problems involved in separation for any other reason, but certain problems may be intensified. The wife who could count on some support from her husband in the earlier stages of his alcoholism, even though such support was manipulative in character, can no longer be sure of any support. Also, the mental conflict about deserting a sick man must be resolved, as well as the wife's feelings of responsibility for his alcoholism. The family which has experienced violence from the alcoholic is concerned that separation may intensify the violence. When the decision is made to separate because of the drinking, the alcoholic often gives up drinking for a while, thereby removing what is apparently the major reason for the separation.

Other events, however, make separation possible. The wife learns that the family can function tolerably well without her husband. Taking over control bolsters her self-confidence; her orientation shifts from inaction to action. The wife also has become familiar with public agencies which can provide help, and she has overcome her shame about using them. Without the father, the family actually tends to reorganize rather smoothly. Having closed ranks against him, the family members feel free of the disruptions he used to create in the family. This kind of reorganization is impeded, however, if the alcoholic continues to attempt reconciliation or feels he must "get even" with the family for deserting him.

The whole family may become united when the husband achieves sobriety, whether or not separation has preceded, but, for the husband and wife facing a sober marriage after many years of an alcoholic marriage, the expectations for marriage without alcoholism are unrealistic and idealistic. Many problems arise. The wife has managed the family for years and now her husband wishes to be reinstated as head of the house. Usually the first role he reestablishes is that of breadwinner. With the resumption of this role, he feels that the family should reinstate him immediately in all his former roles. Difficulties inevitably follow. The children, for example, are often unable to accept his resumption of the father role. Their mother has been mother and father to them for so long that it takes time to get used to consulting their father. Often the father tries to manage this change overnight and the very pressure he puts on the children towards this end defeats him.

Again, in this situation, the wife who finds it difficult to believe that her husband is sober permanently is often unwilling to relinquish her control of family affairs even though she knows that this is necessary to her husband's sobriety. She remembers when his failures to handle responsibility were catastrophic to the family. Used to avoiding any issues which might upset the husband, the wife often has difficulty discussing problems openly. If she permits him to resume his role of father, she often feels resentful of his intrusion into territory she has come to regard as her own. If he makes any decisions which are detrimental to the family, her former feelings of superiority may be mobilized and affect her relationship with him. Yet gradually the difficulties related to alcoholism recede into the past, and family adjustment at some level is achieved. The drinking problem shows up only sporadically, most probably when the time comes for a decision about permitting the children to drink or when pressure is put on the husband to drink at a party.

In summation, research has suggested that there may be distinct stages of family behavior associated with alcoholism in the husband and father. Some of the families studied have passed through all the noted stages to a satisfactory conclusion, while others have traversed only part of the route. Others have shown no movement to date. Families also vary as to the length of time spent in any one stage. The stages themselves may be summarized briefly as follows: (a) attempts to deny the problem; (b) attempts to eliminate the problem; (c) disorganization; (d) attempts to reorganize in spite of the problem; (e) efforts to escape the problem; (f) reorganization of part of the family; and (g) recovery and reorganization of the whole family.

Finally, it bears mention in this context that the writer (22) has also analyzed the changes in family structure with special emphasis on changes in the role and status of the husband and father. The analysis indicates that the alcoholic's status is gradually downgraded when he does not fulfill family and cultural expectations and as other family members assume his traditional roles in order to keep the unit as a whole functioning. Indeed, the alcoholic's major role in some families appears to be that of a spur to the solidarity of the rest of the family who react against him.

IMPLICATIONS

In general, the literature bearing upon alcoholism and the family has been written by persons whose major research interest is the phenomenon of alcoholism itself, or by persons directly or indirectly involved in the amelioration of alcoholism. Even when reports have been primarily research oriented, they tend not to take into account potentially relevant literature other than that directly related to alcoholism, and usually refer only to studies by persons with the same professional identification. Such parochial approaches bode ill both for the acquisition of reliable knowledge by those already interested and for the stimulation of research interest in others.

Gains in knowledge will be made when research on alcoholism and the family is guided by theory and when it is built upon broader awareness of what is already known. There is, for example, a considerable body of information on institutional and family crises. In conceptualizing the experiences of families in which there is an alcoholic, it is illuminating to view what happens to families and their members under social conditions with ingredients similar to those of the alcoholism crisis. Provocative questions arise about the extent to which the alcoholism situation is unique. These lead to further questions about which variables are dependent or independent and to speculation about the etiology, nature, normality, or abnormality of emotional states found in the members of the alcoholic's family at any given point in time.

In this connection, sociologists such as Koos (26), Angell (1), Kamarovsky (25), Cavan (7), and Cavan and Ranck (8) have studied the impact of the depression and of unemployment on family behavior and structure as well as on family members. These investigators found that the status of the father tended to decline when he was no longer the wage earner and that his roles were taken over by other family members. Families often closed ranks against him and the wife frequently became the dominant figure. In this situation, the father lost more roles than he added, and this left him feeling uncertain of himself and of his position in his family. This loss of roles by the father tended to be accompanied by intense self-criticism, feelings of guilt and shame, and sensitivity to criticism both real and imagined. While roles were in the process of being reshuffled, the family suffered from confusion, and the members experienced great anxiety, hostility, and guilt. The realignment of roles often involved a blurring of the differences between husband and father and wife and mother roles and hence in masculine and feminine behavior. It was no longer possible to predict who had responsibility for doing what. Tasks were performed poorly or not at all. Members of the family who were in the process of assuming new roles or dropping old ones found themselves in conflict when their expectations of their roles did not coincide with what others expected from them. Until new family routines became customary and new role definitions were agreed upon, the family and its members behaved in a disorganized fashion.

In the families studied during the depression, re-employment of the father brought on a crisis for the family similar to the crisis brought on by the sobriety of the alcoholic. As the father attempted to resume his former status, family roles had to be reshuffled again. It was rare, however, that he was able to resume his former status entirely. The family had worked out new patterns of relationships which had become routine and comfortable and which were resistant to change, partly because they were no longer at the level of consciousness. In a similar vein, Nye's (33, 34) findings on the consequences of re-employment of the mother both for family behavior and for the psychological comfort of family members is illuminating because the impact of a crisis involving a phenomenon so different from alcoholism is so similar. Likewise, the studies of Stolz (37) and Hill (17) concerning the effect of the return of the war veteran to the family are provocative in their implications for students of alcoholism and the family.

Some of the questions raised by such studies—questions which have been alluded to at various points in this chapter—are: Is the dominance so frequently attributed to the wives of alcoholics an expression of inherent personality attributes of the wife, or is it in some measure a by-product of taking over the roles of husband and father which have been left unfulfilled and without which the family could not survive intact? Is the blurring of sexual identities in the alcoholic and his marital partner the consequence of inadequate sexual identification as an enduring aspect of their personalities, or is the blurring to some extent the structural outcome of a family in which traditionally sex-linked roles have been reshuffled? How much of the confusion in family behavior can be attributed to the structural changes going on in the family, to inadequate adult personalities, or to alcoholism *per se?* To what extent is the reticence to restore to the recovered alcoholic aspects of the husband and father roles a product of family processes and past family adaptations to a vacant father status? To what extent is this reticence based upon personality-engendered hostility towards the alcoholic on the part of family members and upon unconscious wishes to impede his recovery because of personality gratifications stemming from persistence of the illness? Finally, is the disturbance shown by wives when their husbands recover attributable to the loss of such gratifications or to the structural necessity of a realignment of roles?

Further examples of differently focused research which has potentially significant implications for understanding the behavior of family members who are trying to adapt to the alcoholic are to be found in the writings of Tyhurst and his associates (41) and of Glass (13). The former studied the behavior of persons under circumstances involving significant changes in their life situations—circumstances such as disaster, retirement, and migration. The subjects of the research were not in treatment situations. From this research the concept of "transition states" was formulated, defined as "the social and psychological circumstances of being in a state of going from one situation to another." Stages of patterned behavior and emotional states were found in people while they made such transitions. Tyhurst and his associates conclude that emotional disturbance in a transition state is normal—normal in the sense that is is usual, and normal in the sense that a lack of emotional disturbance bodes poorly for the successful adjustment of the person in the future. Signs of emotional disturbance, which were very much in evidence, and which could have been given diagnostic labels had the individual been evaluated apart from his total context, were not equivalent to mental illness.

For his part, Glass wrote about soldiers in combat. In discussing how persons reacted to stress situations for which they had not been trained and which they perceived as unstructured and uncertain, Glass suggests hypotheses for students of alcoholism and the responses of family members. He writes (13, pp. 194–195: "The form or type of psychological non-effective behavior displayed in combat is not determined so much by the individual's personality characteristics as it is dictated either by the practical circumstances of the battle situation or by group acceptance of such symptoms or behavior . . . . Pertinent combat circumstances include the intensity and duration of the battle . . . the degree of support given individuals by buddies, group cohesiveness and leadership."

The family of an alcoholic, including the alcoholic himself, apparently goes through a series of social and psychological transition states made without cultural guideposts, without social and emotional support for individuals, and in a milieu of lowered family cohesiveness. What is the range of behavior to be found under such conditions? Tyhurst's position that feeling states and behavior arise which would lead to the diagnosis of emotional pathology if seen apart from their situational and time dimensions is very provocative. Does the behavior of the family and of its individual members vary according to the degree of family isolation, previous family integration, and training in meeting crises? The sociological literature on the family would support such a hypothesis. More generally, it is to be hoped that future research on alcoholism and the family will be not only more rigorous and interdisciplinary in character, but also better articulated with existing theory and knowledge.

REFERENCES

1. ANGELL, ROBERT C. *The family encounters the depression,* New York: Charles Scribner's Sons, 1936.
2. BACON, SELDEN D. Excessive drinking and the institution of the family. In *Alcohol, Science and Society.* New Haven, Conn.: Journal of Studies on Alcohol, 1945.
3. BAKER, SYBIL M. Social case work with inebriates. In *Alcohol, Science and Society.* New Haven, Conn.: Journal of Studies on Alcohol, 1945.
4. BALLARD, ROBERT G. The interaction between marital conflict and alcoholism as seen through MMPI's of marriage partners, *Amer. J. of Orthopsychiat.,* 1959, 29:528–546.
5. BOWERMAN, CHARLES E. Adjustment in marriage: over-all and in specific areas. *Sociol. Soc. Res.,* 1957, 41:257–263.
6. BULLOCK, SAMUEL C. and MUDD, EMILY H. The interaction of alcoholic husbands and their non-alcoholic wives during counselling. *Amer. J. of Orthopsychiat.,* 1959, 29:519–527.
7. CAVAN, RUTH S. Unemployment—crisis of the common man. *Marr. and Family Living,* 1959, 21:139–146.
8. ——, and RANCK, KATHERINE H. *The family and the depression.* Chicago: University of Chicago Press, 1938.
9. CORK, MARGARET R. Case work in a group setting with wives of alcoholics. *The Social Worker,* 1956, XIV, 1–6.
10. EHRMANN, WINSTON WALLACE. A review of family research in 1957. *Marr. and Family Living,* 1958, 20:384–396.
11. FOX, RUTH. The alcoholic spouse. In V. W. EISENSTEIN (ed.), *Neurotic interaction in marriage.* New York: Basic Books, 1956.
12. FUTTERMAN, S. Personality trends in wives of alcoholics. *J. of Psychiat. Social Work,* 1953, 23:37–41.
13. GLASS, A. Observations upon epidemiology of mental illness in troops during warfare. In *Symposium on preventive and social psychiatry.* Washington, D.C.: Walter Reed Army Medical Center, 1957, 185–198.
14. GLIEDMAN, LESTER H., NASH, HELEN T. and WEBB, W. L. Group psychotherapy of male alcoholics and their wives. *Dis. Nerv. Syst.,* 1956, 17:1–4.
15. GLIEDMAN, LESTER H., ROSENTHAL, DAVID, FRANK, JEROME D. and NASH, HELEN T. Group therapy of alcoholics with concurrent group meetings of their wives. *Quart. J. Stud. Alc.,* 1956, 17:655–670.
16. HEY, RICHARD N., and MUDD, EMILY H. Recurring Problems in Marriage Counselling, *Marr. and Family Living,* 21:127–129, 1959.
17. HILL, REUBEN, *Families under stress.* New York: Harper & Row, Publishers, 1949.
18. JACKSON, JOAN K. The adjustment of the family to the crisis of alcoholism. *Quart. J. Stud. Alc.,* 1954, 15:562–586.
19. ——. *Social adjustment preceding, during and following the onset of alcoholism.* Unpublished doctoral dissertation, University of Washington, 1955.
20. ——, The adjustment of the family to alcoholism. *Marr. and Family Living,* 1956, 18:361–369.
21. ——. Alcoholism and the family. *Ann. Amer. Acad. Pol. Soc. Sci.,* 1958, 315:90–98.
22. ——. Family structure and alcoholism. *Mental Hygiene,* 1959, 43:403–406.
23. JELLINEK, E. M. Phases of alcohol addiction. *Quart. J. Stud. Alc.,* 1952, 13:673–684.
24. KALASHIAN, MARION M. Working with the wives of alcoholics in an out-patient clinic setting. *Marr. and Family Living,* 1959, 21:130–133.
25. KAMAROVSKY, MIRRA. *The unemployed man and his family.* New York: Dryden Press, 1940.
26. KOOS, EARL L. *Families in trouble.* New York: King's Crown Press, 1946.
27. LEWIS, MARGARET L. The initial contact with wives of alcoholics. *Social Casework,* January, 1954.
28. LISANSKY, EDITH S. Alcoholism in women: social and psychological concomitants: I. social history data. *Quart. J. Stud. Alc.,* 1957, 18:588–623.
29. MacDONALD, DONALD E. Mental disorders in wives of alcoholics. *Quart. J. Stud. Alc.,* 1956, 17:282–287.
30. MITCHELL, HOWARD E. Interpersonal perception theory applied to conflicted marriages in which alcoholism is and is not a problem, *Amer. J. Orthopsychiat.,* 1959, 29:547–559.

31. MOWRER, HARRIET R. A psychocultural analysis of the alcoholic. *Amer. Sociol. Rev.*, 1940, 5:546–557.

32. NEWELL, NANCY. Alcoholism and the father image. *Quart. J. Stud. Alc.*, 1950, 11:92–96.

33. NYE, F. IVAN. Social and psychological correlates of the employment of mothers: an introduction (mimeographed). Pullman, Wash.: State University of Washington, 1959.

34. ———. Employment status and maternal adjustment to children. Delivered at the annual meetings of the Amer. Sociol. Society, Chicago, 1959.

35. PRICE, GLADYS M. A study of the wives of 20 alcoholics, *Quart. J. Stud. Alc.*, 1945, 5:620–627.

36. ROE, ANNE. The adult adjustment of children of alcoholic parents raised in foster homes. *Quart. J. Stud. Alc.*, 1944, 5:378–393.

37. STOLZ, LOIS M. *Father relations of war-born children.* Stanford, Calif.: Stanford University Press. 1954.

38. STRAUS, ROBERT. Medical practice and the alcoholic. *Ann. Amer. Acad. Pol. Soc. Sci.*, 1958, 315:117–124

39. STRAYER, ROBERT, Treatment of client and spouse by the same caseworker. *Quart. J. Stud. Alc.*, 1959, 20:86–102.

40. STRYKER, SHELDON, Symbolic Interaction as an Approach to Family Research, *Marr. and Family Living*, 21:111–119, 1959.

41. TYHURST, J. The role of transition states—including disasters—in mental illness. In *Symposium on preventive and social psychiatry.* Washington, D.C.: Walter Reed Army Medical Center, 1957, 149–167.

42. WALLER, WILLARD. *The family: a dynamic interpretation* (revised by REUBEN HILL). New York: Dryden Press, 1951, 453–461.

43. WELLMAN, WAYNE M. Toward an etiology of alcoholism: why young men drink too much. *Canad. Med. Ass. J.*, 1955, 73:717–725.

44. WHALEN, THELMA. Wives of alcoholics: four types observed in a family service agency. *Quart. J. Stud. Alc.*, 1953, 14:632–641.

45. YARROW, MARIAN R., SCHWARTZ, CHARLOTTE G., MURPHY, HARRIET S. and DEASY, LEILA C. The psychological meaning of mental illness in the family. *J. Soc. Issues*, 1955, 11:12–24.

62.

BERNARD FARBER

MENTAL RETARDATION AND FAMILY INTEGRATION

INTRODUCTION

Ordinarily, parents can take either of two courses with respect to their severely mentally retarded child: they can keep the child at home or send him to an institution, usually a state institution. The course they follow depends upon a variety of factors—their own views on parental responsibility, the doctor's opinion, costs of keeping the child at home, the reputation of the institution, possible effects on the retarded child and his siblings, and the opinions of friends, relatives, and neighbors.

This selection is reprinted from: Bernard Farber, *Effects of a Severely Mentally Retarded Child on Family Integration,* Monographs of the Society for Research in Child Development, Inc., 1959, 24, No. 2 [excerpted from pp. 5–11, 12–16, 76–81].

Copyright, 1959, The Society for Research in Child Development. Reprinted with the permission of the author and publisher.

One of the factors to be considered in determining whether a severely retarded child should be institutionalized is the degree to which he affects adversely the members of the family. The aim of this investigation is to describe various conditions influencing the effect of a severely mentally retarded child on family integration.

The conceptual scheme used in guiding the research will be described below. First, the concept of family integration will be discussed and then the process by which the mentally retarded child affects the family will be considered. This process will be described as an arrest in the life-cycle of the family. The process of arrest in the family cycle will be used to explain how such independent variables as age and sex of the retarded child, sex of the normal siblings, social status of the parents, community participation of the parents, and institutionalization of the retarded child affect family integration.

Concept of Family Integration

Family integration is regarded as consisting of two factors: the consensus of its members as to domestic values and a lack of role tension in the interpersonal relations between family members (15, cf. 6). The continued existence of the family as a group depends upon the successful performance of certain tasks such as socialization of parents and children, maintenance of a domicile, and economic activities. Successful performance of these tasks can be viewed as ends or values in family life (cf. 36, p. 203). These ends are evaluated in decision-making and establishing routines and are ranked by the family members in order of preference. The preference hierarchies describe the potentialities and tendencies of future action of the individuals as family members.

Sometimes, in spite of a high degree of consensus in ranking domestic values, family members fail to coordinate their roles effectively. The system of roles can then be said to be in a state of tension, and the character of interpersonal relations is affected. In the communication which accompanies the role tension, tempers may flare, arguments may occur, affectionate demonstrations may cease, decisions may be imposed, the family members may become sullen. As these behaviors become the expected instead of the exceptional action in the association, they tend to be attributed by the actor to the other person or to himself as integral parts of the actual self. Conformity to role expectations is then considered superficial and difficult. Role tension thus may be regarded in terms of the degree of tension, anxiety, and frustration generated in the process of developing and playing given roles and is characterized by an interstimulation of hostile responses (11).

It is assumed that in the highly integrated family (a) the individual members develop domestic and community roles while maintaining a sense of personal integrity and (b) family members meet crises without loss of commitment to one another and with a minimum of disruption of their domestic careers.

The Life-Cycle and Integration of the Family with a Severely Mentally Retarded Child

Family integration as consisting of consensus on values and a lack of tension in the system of roles is a static description of the family as a system of social relations at a given time. Family social relations, however, are obviously of long-term duration and under continual change.

This investigation is concerned with the problem of relating family relations described statically as integration of values and roles at a given time to family relations as they change over a long period of time.

The change in family relations over a long period of time is discussed below as the life cycle of the family. Hypotheses relating the retarded child to family integration will be derived on the basis of the way in which the retarded child seems to affect the family cycle. In this section, therefore, the concept of family cycle and effects of a retarded child on the family cycle will be described.

In sociological studies of the family, the concept of the life cycle has led to increased understanding of processes by which families are integrated (e.g., 19, 34, 41). Generally, contemporary American families can be described roughly as passing through the following stages in their life cycle:

(a) The married couple.
(b) The family whose youngest child is of preschool age.
(c) The family with a preadolescent youngest child.
(d) The family with an adolescent youngest child.
(e) The family in which all children are adults.
(f) The family in which all children are married.

Specific norms and activities are characteristic of each of these stages in the family life cycle (34, 41). The involvement of the family members in these norms and activities is considered as important in determining the extent of family integration. The application of the life cycle concept to families with a severely mentally retarded child may reveal insights into the integration of these families.

Another concept seems necessary, however,

to explain *how* a mentally retarded child affects the family life cycle, which in turn affects family integration. The concept chosen is that of career. Career has been used traditionally in the context of work and occupations, but the character of marriage and the family in contemporary society increases the number of alternatives that the course of a person's home life may take. With the breakdown of the three-generation household, family roles are not as fixed and static as they once were. It, therefore, seems justified to apply the career concept to family life.

A career is regarded as a progression by an individual through a series of roles. As a subjective counterpart of changes in role, a career is also a sequence of self-identifications by an individual. The basis for the career development is that each shift in roles seems to be accompanied by a change in the standpoint of viewing reference groups (47) and persons (54) (if not by a replacement of these with new reference groups). In changing his viewpoint of reference groups and persons, the individual identifies himself differently and tries to develop roles appropriate to this modification in identification (17). The individual's career is thus under continual development (18).

The family as a system of domestic careers is related to the concept of family integration, defined in the previous section, in the following ways: (a) Consensus on domestic values describes the extent to which the family members agree on a common set of goals toward which their careers are oriented. (b) The tension in the system of roles indicates the relative failure of family members to coordinate their interaction at a given time.

The course of the mentally retarded child's family life is different from that of his brothers and sisters. The object of the conceptual scheme presented in this section is to show how the peculiar career of the mentally retarded child affects the life cycle of his family and, consequently, family integration.

The Family Life Cycle and Individual Careers. If the family is viewed as a system of careers, a marked shift in one career in the system affects the other careers. However, it is apparent that shifts in some kinds of careers in the family system generally have greater consequences for family integration than others. It is assumed here that the parents are ordinarily the principal coordinators of family life. The effects of shifts in the careers of children, insofar as they affect family integration, are assumed to affect the other children primarily through an adjustment of the parents to this shift (48, p. 139). In adjusting their roles to the shift in the career of one child, the parents would then change their relationship to the other children and to each other. This discussion does not imply that the career development of one child does not affect the socialization of another, but that this problem is considered secondary in a consideration of general family integration.

As an ideal type, the family is viewed, therefore, as a series of triads, each triad representing a mother-father-child relationship. Two components for all the triads in the family will be in common (the mother and father). The number of triads in a family equals the number of children in that family. The representation of the total family as a series of triads permits the examination of each triad as a unit of analysis.

A stage in the family cycle can be defined by marked changes in the career of any family member. Any marked change in the career of one member will demand an adjustment of roles of the other members in the triad to this career change. Change in one triad should then affect other triads. The entire patterning of roles will thus have to be modified. Therefore, the point of reference in describing movement in the family life cycle may be the father, the mother, or the child, whoever undergoes a marked shift in his career line. If the child starts school, he is the stimulus for movement in the family cycle; if the father retires, the shift in his career is the stimulus; as the child takes over the roles of the adolescent, again the other members of the family must modify their conduct and self identifications. Hence, through the interaction of careers, the family life cycle proceeds from one stage to the next in the family in which all the members are normal (18).

Having described the social process in the family as it would exist ideally, we shall turn to the family with a severely mentally retarded child, in which there is a marked departure from the ideal.

Arrest in the Family Cycle. The presence of a severely mentally retarded child in the family is regarded here as a factor in the arrest of the family cycle (cf. 4, pp. 542-543). This assumption is made on the following basis:

1. In their interaction with their children, parents tend to assign a status to the child commensurate with the capabilities they impute to the child.

a. The roles embodied in the status are classified on the basis of an age grading. By definition, normally, mental age is approximately equal to chronological age.

b. Age grading in a culture is regarded as a psychological rather than a biological variable. (E.g., the chronologically middle-aged severely retarded individual is generally regarded as a "boy" or "girl" by those with whom he interacts.) One religious group, the Hutterites, excludes the mentally retarded from adult responsibility by canceling baptism requirements, thereby giving them a moral status of children (14).

2. As the child proceeds in his career, the parents normally tend to shift correspondingly in their self-conceptions and roles. With respect to their normal children, ideally, parents continually redefine their roles, obligations, and values to adjust to the changing role of the child. With respect to their retarded children, the parental role is fairly constant. Regardless of his birth order in the family, the severely mentally retarded child eventually becomes the youngest child socially (26).

In terms of its activities, the family with a severely retarded child at home would not emerge from the preadolescent stage in its life cycle. The severely retarded child would not engage in dating and courtship, belong to organizations, seek part-time employment, or take part in other activities characteristic of adolescents. In his progressive movement to the youngest-child status in the family, the severely retarded child would thus not merely slow down movement in the family cycle, but would also prevent the development of the later stages in the cycle.

Arrest in the Family Cycle and Family Integration. The family with a retarded child lives in a community of families with normal family cycles. Especially when normal children are in school, parents with a retarded child face different problems from others in the community at that age (cf. 13). Interests differ, time spent in household administration and child care differs, baby sitting arrangements differ. Interaction with other parents whose children are of comparable chronological age would be modified by the presence of the retarded child. Hence, arrest in the career of the child caused by his mental defect affects the development of the parents' domestic and community career, and the value system of one or both of the parents may undergo change. With a constant testing of the appropriateness of various family values, the parents may come to disagree in their ranking of ends. In the process there may be a decline in the mutual dependence of the careers of the husband and wife.

However, arrest in the family cycle is felt not merely in the disruption of domestic careers with potential dissensus described above. More obviously, arrest in the family cycle provides a situation in which anticipated roles are frustrated. There is the initial shock, at which time parents have described themselves in exploratory interviews as living in a void, having nothing to live for, wishing for death. After that, as several parents have phrased it, they learn to live with their problem. Career frustration, thus, may continue to be a factor into the parent's old age. The parent's adjustment and personal commitment to his domestic roles at any time are hereby impeded.

Difference in the meaning of the arrest of the retarded child in his life career to his parents and siblings seems of central importance in assessing the effects of the child on family relations. In accordance with the view of the family as a series of triads, the parents would generally perceive the arrest of the retarded child's life career in the context of the life careers of all the family members and be affected in the marital relationship by gross deficiencies in the development of the child's life career. We can call the parents career-oriented. On the other hand the siblings in the other triads would view arrest of the retarded child's life career in terms of its immediate effects on their own family roles and would be especially sensitive to the retarded child's behavior at a given time. We can describe the normal child as role-oriented.

As independent variables, sex of the retarded child and social status of the parents are regarded as major determinants in the parents' definition of the retarded child's actual and ideal life career. Degree of dependence of the retarded child and sex of the normal sibling, however, are seen as independent variables in determining the effect of the retarded child on the normal sibling's role. The age of the retarded child enters into both the parents' conception of the retarded child's life career and the normal sibling's role.

The relationship between family integration and the independent variables will be discussed more fully in the section on Hypotheses.

Counteracting Arrest in the Family Cycle. In addition to the circumstances described above which influence the degree of arrest in the family cycle, two other considerations will be taken into account in the investigation of conditions which affect integration in a family with a severely mentally retarded child. These conditions are (a) institutionalization and (b) the parents' contact with persons outside their own nuclear family (i.e., family of procreation).

If the problem of whether to institutionalize a retarded child were stated only in terms of the extreme arrest in the family cycle, the answer would have to be always to institutionalize the child. That is, if arrest in the family cycle with its accompanying decrease in family integration is a function of the adjustment of the parents and normal siblings to the mentally retarded child, the less that family members have to do with the child, generally, the less severe would be the child's effect on them.

There are, however, two factors to consider. The first factor is the degree of arrest in the family cycle. In this factor, the independent variables discussed above (such as age and sex of the retarded child, social status, and degree of dependence) are regarded as important. The second factor is the relationship of the normal family members with the rest of the community (i.e., all social systems external to the nuclear family). The second factor is based on the assumption that, given a certain degree of arrest

in the family cycle, various community contacts will help or hinder the family members in their integration with one another. The independent variables concerning community effects on family integration will be discussed in the next section. Thus, both degree of arrest in the family cycle and community relations will be taken into account in studying the problem of whether to institutionalize the retarded child.

Family Integration and External Social Systems. With the truncation of the family cycle, all of the family members must reorient their life with respect to the retarded child. In the reorientation, the social concepts in family life and the norms surrounding these concepts change in meaning. When the chronologically older child is severely retarded, "older sibling" does not connote the same thing as it ordinarily does. "Playing" with a retarded child is not the same as "playing" with a normal child of the same age. "Discipline" of a retarded child does not have the same connotations as "discipline" of a normal child.

With the sharpening of differences in social concepts and their implicit norms between families with a retarded child and those without one, the distinction between supportive and nonsupportive community relations becomes important.

Supportive persons in the community would be those who are willing to interact with the family members on the basis of the reoriented definitions of social concepts. Ordinarily, those persons and institutions stressing general values of parental obligation and love for children would reinforce the revised family norms. Religious groups and extended family would tend to support these norms.

Nonsupportive persons in the community would be those who interact with families with a retarded child primarily within the framework of the traditional or conventional social concepts. They have not revised their concepts of age and sex norms, play, growth, or the distant future. Involvement in these groups by members of families with retarded children would create doubt and anxiety over the propriety of the revised social concepts.

Supportive persons in the community would thus enhance family integration in the adjustment to arrest in the family cycle. Nonsupportive persons would hinder the family's integration.

REVIEW OF LITERATURE

In this investigation, family integration is regarded as the dependent variable. The independent variables are age and sex of the retarded child, sex of the normal siblings, social status, mother's view of dependence of the retarded child, supportive and nonsupportive community relations, and whether the child lives at home or in an institution. Arrest in the family cycle is regarded as the process by which the independent variables affect family integration. In this section, the research literature on the implications of the independent variables for family integration will be reviewed.

FAMILY INTEGRATION

The reaction of families to the depression in the 1930's provided the impetus to the study of the relationship between crisis and family integration. Since then, the focus of family integration studies has shifted to crises in mental and physical illness.

Studies of the reaction of the family to the depression pointed out that postdepression integration was a function of earlier adaptable adjustment (1, 8, 30) and the value systems of the parents (6). In a similar kind of analysis, Hill explained adjustment to the crisis of military service separation and reunion on the basis of the family's recuperative capacity (24). In these studies, the nature of the event producing the crisis was easily identified—loss of a job or income, military separation and reunion. The problem for study was whether postcrisis integration could be predicted from precrisis organization of the family. The inference made was that certain identifiable families could devise strategies for counteracting the crisis while others could not.

Recent studies on family integration have focused upon the situation in which the family members cannot easily define the event precipitating the crisis. The family with an alcoholic father faces a series of events about which decisions must be made. Situations arise which have

no ideal solution, but which may lead to various risks and further unpredictability (25). Similarly, the family with a father who is mentally ill is faced with a series of decisions, with each alternative carrying its own risk (9). The goal of recent family integration investigations is to conceptualize the process by which crisis and reaction to crisis occurs (e.g., 12). With the crisis process conceptualized adequately, questions can be raised about variation in the severity of crises—how one kind of crisis has a more severe effect on family integration than another and the conditions under which the severity of the crises may vary.

THE PRESENCE OF A HANDICAPPED CHILD IN THE FAMILY AS CRISIS PRODUCING

There is an accumulation of evidence that the presence of a handicapped child in the home creates a crisis for the nonhandicapped family members. The research, however, has generally been restricted to the investigation of kinds or number of problems present in families with handicapped children. Roe found problems of adjustment among families with a cerebral palsied child (40). In a study on an Australian sample, Schonell and Watts uncovered many "family upsets" in families with a child with an IQ of 55 or under (43). Various other studies report on the feelings of frustration, projection, doubts, fears, guilt feelings, and other behavior indicating personal maladjustment of the parents of mentally retarded children (10, 20, 22, 27, 38, 42, 50, 53, 55, 57, 59).

An exception to investigations focusing on an inventory of problems is the study by Korkes of parents of mentally ill children (33). Korkes found that the parents' conception of the nature of their child's mental illness affected the amount and kind of communication between husband and wife. The results of her exploratory study suggest that parents who define the cause of their child's mental illness as independent of themselves are less affected adversely than parents who blame themselves. Her findings also indicate that previously minor disturbances in family life are magnified by the presence of the child who is mentally ill.

Parents of retarded children probably are less able than parents of children who are mentally ill to define the cause of the child's illness as independent of themselves. While the existence of disruption of family routines, plans, and activities associated with the presence of a handicapped child is well-documented, the process by which this disruption occurs has not been investigated adequately.

CONCEPTS RELATING TO INDEPENDENT VARIABLES

Each independent variable is significant in this study because of the way it reflects a variation in the rate of movement or the kind of situations accompanying the truncated family cycle. Concepts which have bearing on the dependent variables are age and birth order, sex and social status, dependence, community participation, and relation with in-laws and parents.

Age and Birth Order. The relationship between birth order and role of a normal child has been shown in several studies. In interviews with mothers of kindergarten children, Sears and his associates found that the mother tended to view herself as the primary disciplinarian of the youngest child and her husband as the primary disciplinarian of the oldest child (44, p. 409). Similarly, an investigation of high school and college students by Henry showed that the father is seen as the principal disciplinarian by the oldest child while the mother is perceived as the principal disciplinarian by the youngest child (23; cf. 28). In relating birth order and aggressiveness, Sears found that oldest children were more aggressive toward their parents than middle or youngest children (44, p. 417; cf. 29).

In his study of large families, Bossard describes the "oldest child" role in the family (5). By the oldest child role, he means family roles delegating to a child the responsibility for caring for, protecting, and/or teaching his siblings. This role Bossard finds most often expected of the oldest child—usually the oldest daughter. Bossard's report on personal adjustment, however indicates that generally the oldest child in the large family is rated as more poorly adjusted than his siblings. The inference may be drawn that the oldest child role is not conducive to high personal adjustment.

The significance of the research on birth order for the present study is that according to the process of arrest in the family cycle, socially, the normal child tends progressively to assume an older child role in relation to the retarded child. In this connection, Shere found that the parents of 30 pairs of twins, one of which was cerebral palsied, tended to overprotect the cerebral palsied twin and to make him a central figure in the family (46). In addition, the parents generally expected their normal child "to assume more responsibilities and to act in a more mature manner" than the observers felt appropriate to their age or actual capabilities. Shere's study also showed that the noncerebral palsied twin was more stubborn, more easily excited, more resistant to authority, more jealous, and less cheerful than the twin with cerebral palsy.

Sex Differences. In his investigation of normal children's perceptions of their parents' attitudes and behavior toward them, Ausubel found that girls in elementary school, to a greater extent than boys, regarded their parents as valuing them "for themselves apart from considerations of relative competence and .ability" (2, p. 179). The results of Zelditch's anthropological study of age and sex roles in the nuclear family in various societies are similar (62). Zelditch's findings show how the boys develop task-oriented roles and girls social-emotional roles in the nuclear family (cf. 52, esp. pp. 1103-1104). The emphasis on social-emotional roles of girls as compared with boys is confirmed in Koch's investigation of elementary school children (29). She found that in comparison with boys the girls were rated as more affectionate and obedient and less resistant.

The investigation by Sears and his associates of mothers of kindergarten children showed that mothers expected their boys, more often than their girls, to (a) go farther in school, (b) perform certain chores around the house, (c) act aggressively toward neighborhood children and not aggressively toward their parents, and (d) fight back if provoked (44, pp. 396-407).

The research literature on sex differences suggests that mental retardation in a boy will have a different meaning for the parents than will mental retardation in a girl (cf. 32).

Dependence. In her discussion of the relative

frequency of high dependence in only children as compared with children with siblings, Stendler concluded tentatively that generally "size of family, *per se* is not an all-important factor" (49). Her concern with the number of children as related to dependence raises the question of sibling rivalry as associated with the presence of a highly dependent child. Studies by Levy, Baldwin, and Sewall indicate that sibling rivalry for the mother's attention arises in maternal overprotection (35) and in the presence of a new infant (3, 45).

With the retarded child generally highly dependent, these studies suggest that the degree to which the mother expects the retarded child to act in a highly dependent role affects the adjustment of the normal siblings (cf. 46).

Social Status. The difference in parents' expectations of their daughters in higher and lower social segments has been noted in various studies. Rabban has found that middle-class girls developed concepts of sex role later than lower-class girls (37). West found that the likelihood of a daughter's attending college was more influenced than a son's by either of her parents having been to college (60, p. 699). Both Komarovsky and Wallin found that college girls were faced with a dilemma in that their parents wanted them to succeed academically, but in dating, the girls had to "play dumb" (31, 56). This dilemma emphasizes the changing conceptions of the female role in middle-class groups as compared with lower-class groups. In middle-class groups, the difference in sex role is becoming blurred. No comparable trend is apparent in literature on lower-class groups (e.g., 61). We would thus expect that the difference in the meaning of mental retardation of boys and girls in higher and lower social statuses would affect parents differently.

Community Participation. Risler, in his exploratory study on isolated families, found that lack of intimate contact with other families tended to facilitate the development of abnormal behavior patterns (39). Weinberg investigated family isolation as a factor in incest behavior (58). Zimmerman and Broderick reported that "successful families have more intimate family friends and have more in common with their friends than unsuccessful families

do" (63). Burgess and Wallin concluded that "socially active persons are more religious and conventional, and more determined to make a success of marriage" (7). These studies are in agreement that participation in the community is related to family integration and mental health.

In his study of divorced women, Goode found, however, that certain community contacts are not conducive to successful marriage—e.g., the husband's being involved too much with "the boys," another woman, or his own parents (21).

Stryker investigated the adjustment of married couples to their parents. His data indicate that women are more likely to be dependent upon their mothers than are men and that the wife's adjustment to her mother tends to be significantly higher than her adjustment to her mother-in-law (51).

We would thus view community participation in terms of the support which this participation gives to the marital relationship. High participation with certain groups and persons would tend to be disruptive of the marriage while participation with others would strengthen the marriage.

. . .

SUMMARY AND CONCLUSIONS

The purpose of this study was to investigate how various conditions concerning the severely retarded child and his family influence the effects of the retarded child on family integration.

SAMPLE

Generally, the families in the sample under investigation were similar in social status to all the families in the Chicago area who were in contact with associations for promoting the welfare of the mentally retarded.

On the basis of a study of factors in the sample selection and of family characteristics pertinent to the present investigation, 240 cases with the following characteristics were included in the study: (a) both parents Caucasian; (b) child regarded as severely mentally deficient by one or both parents; (c) mentally deficient child aged 16 or under; (d) only one child in the family regarded by the parents as severely mentally deficient; (e) mentally deficient child born in the present marriage (f) parents married and living together at the time the study was made.

PROCEDURE

In the early phases of the study, preliminary interviews were conducted with parents of severely retarded children in numerous communities in central Illinois. Eighty-eight families participated in the study during the first year.

After a preliminary analysis of data from central Illinois, the questionnaires and interview forms were modified and families in the Chicago area were interviewed. Generally, the retarded children in these families were "trainable" or below (i.e., IQ 50 or lower).

The interviewing procedure was for two interviewers to visit each family in their home at an appointed time. The husband and wife were interviewed in separate rooms. The interview, which took about two hours to complete, was in two parts, an oral section and a written section. Most of the data used in this monograph were from the written section.

Instruments and questions pertaining to independent variables were sex of the retarded child, social status, a modified Vineland scale, age of retarded child, retarded child at home or in institution, religious preference, frequency of church attendance, frequency of seeing wife's mother, frequency of seeing husband's mother, neighborliness scale, frequency of seeing friends, and parents' activity in formal organizations.

Instruments pertaining to the dependent variables were the index of marital integration and sibling role tension index.

The index of the couples' marital integration at the time of the study was composed of the degree of agreement on a rank-ordering of domestic values by the husband and wife and an estimation of existing marital role tension between them.

The index of sibling role tension used in the study was the rating by the mother for each normal child on personality traits on which the parents also rated themselves and their spouse.

These indices were substantiated through comparison with other information in the interview and with observations made by the interviewers. The Mann-Whitney U test was used in the statistical analysis to determine whether or not hypotheses were confirmed by the data.

To examine effects of family resources in meeting the crisis of having a mentally retarded child, the hypothesis tested was: For all families, regardless of whether the retarded child is a boy or girl, parents with high integration early in the marriage are more highly integrated on the average at the time of the study than are parents whose early integration was low. Assumptions made are that, in families in which all children, regardless of sex or normal intelligence, marriage integration tends to remain at a fairly constant level in the early and middle years of marriage (16) and that an estimate of the integration in the early years of marriage provides an indication of the probable integration at the time of the study if no retarded child had been born.

To estimate the degree of early marital integration, the writer used a battery of marital prediction items found statistically significant in at least three previous marriage prediction studies in addition to statements in which the parents evaluated the early stage of their marriage.

It was found that for families with a severely mentally retarded child, the degree of marital integration prior to the birth of the retarded child influenced the degree of marital integration at the time of the study. As a result of these findings, whenever possible, integration early in the marriage was held constant in testing hypotheses.

RESULTS AND DISCUSSION

The results which have been obtained for the 240 families are summarized below.

Findings concerning the marital relationship of the parents were:

a. Generally, the marital integration of parents of mentally retarded boys at home was lower than that of parents of mentally retarded girls. An analysis of the data by social class showed that the presence of a retarded boy in lower-class families had a more acute effect on the parents' marriage than the presence of a retarded girl. In middle-class families, however, the sex of the retarded child was not related to the degree of marital integration of the parents. These results were presumed to stem from differences in parental expectations of the life careers of boys and girls and from the greater stress placed on sex differences among lower-class families than among middle-class families.

b. As the severely mentally retarded boy grew older, he generally had an increasingly disruptive effect on his parents' marriage.

c. The extent of marital integration of the parents was not markedly affected by the degree of dependence of the retarded child perceived by the mother.

d. When the severely retarded child was institutionalized, the differential effects on the marital relationship of having a retarded boy or girl tended to disappear. There was little difference between the degree of marital integration of parents with a retarded girl at home, those with a retarded girl in an institution, and those with a retarded boy in an institution. According to the analysis, the marital integration of all of these parents tended to be higher than that of parents with a retarded boy at home. It was concluded that, in general, placing a retarded boy in an institution had a beneficial effect on the parents' marital relationship.

Results on the integration of siblings in the family indicated that:

a. Contrary to findings on the marital integration of parents, the retarded child's sex and the family's social status did not influence markedly the adjustment of normal siblings to their family roles.

b. The retarded child's brothers and sisters were adversely affected by a high degree of dependence of the retarded child. These results suggested that the pressures of caring for the retarded child and the responsibility placed on the retarded child's siblings adversely influenced the normal sibling's adjustment in relation to his mother. Additional support for this interpretation was provided by the finding that younger retarded children affected the adjustment of their siblings more than did older retarded children.

c. On the average, the normal sister was helped by placing the retarded child in an institution. Institutionalizing the retarded child did not seem to help the normal brothers. The brothers were slightly higher in adjustment than their sisters in families with a retarded child at home. However, when normal brothers and sisters of institutionalized children were compared, the maladjustment of brothers was generally greater than that of sisters.

Differences in the findings for normal brothers and sisters suggested that sex roles in the family be taken into account in assessing the effects of a retarded child on his family. Taken together with the responses to the open-ended questions, the findings on normal brothers indicated that

placing the retarded child in an institution seemed to expand the normal brother's role in the home and create many additional points of stress and conflict between the normal boy and his mother. The sister, who had been delegated duties concerning the retarded child and housework, was relieved of many responsibilities by the removal of the retarded child from the home. Her family role was hence contracted and many points of conflict between mother and daughter were removed.

A comparison of factors affecting the marital relationship with those affecting siblings highlights the contrasting ways in which the parents and normal children are influenced by a retarded child. In contrast to the results on parents, social class and sex of the retarded child did not show differences in siblings' integration that were statistically significant. The dependence of the retarded child did influence the siblings but not the parents. The siblings were adversely affected by a young retarded child, the parents by an older one. The cumulative data on social class, sex and age of the retarded child, and dependence of the retarded child thus support the contention that marital integration is affected mainly by variation in anticipated or actual life careers of the retarded children while siblings' integration is affected primarily by short-run shifts in their role.

Findings on the relationship between community participation and marital integration are summarized below.

Because families with retarded children have to develop norms which are peculiarly their own, two kinds of community relations were considered. One kind was called supportive interaction and the other nonsupportive. Supportive interaction was regarded as that interaction in which there was much sympathetic understanding and a reassurance that the parents' revision of roles in handling the retarded child is appropriate or "right." In contrast, nonsupportive interaction would be that interaction in which sympathetic understanding and encouragement were lacking.

Religious association and frequent relations with the wife's mother were regarded as supportive to the parents with a retarded child at home.

a. In the results concerning religious association, there was little difference in the marital integration of Catholics with a retarded boy at home and those with a boy in an institution. In contrast, among non-Catholics, the marriages of parents with a retarded boy at home were more adversely affected than those with a boy in an institution. Thus, the data suggest that participation in the Catholic church and/or Catholic definitions of home and family life were supportive. The results on the frequency of church attendance without regard to religious denomination, however, were inconclusive.

b. It was found that frequent interaction with the wife's mother was related to high marital integration. This relationship was found regardless of whether the mother perceived the retarded child as dependent or independent. Hence, it seemed that the emotional support of the wife's mother rather than her assistance in caring for the child was responsible for facilitating high marital integration.

Generally, the hypotheses relating to supportive interaction were significant for parents of boys but not of girls. These results are consistent with those on the relative impact of retarded boys and girls on the marriage. If having a retarded boy has a more disruptive effect than having a retarded girl, then supportive interaction should be more influential in counteracting this more severe effect. If having a retarded girl has little disruptive effect in general, supportive interaction in these families should have little influence as a strategy for counteracting the presence of the retarded child.

Frequent interaction with the husband's mother, a high degree of neighboring, frequent participation with friends, and activity in formal organizations were considered as nonsupportive interaction.

a. Seeing the husband's mother frequently was associated with low marital integration. This result was consistent with studies for families without retarded children. This finding provides additional support for the contention that, in the relations with in-laws, it is the quality of interaction rather than assistance given in caring for the retarded child which determines the effects of the in-laws on marital integration.

b. Frequent participation with friends and neighbors was related to low marital integration for women who had relatively poor marital risks. Probably, these women were the most susceptible to nonsupportive interaction with others. Their high participation with friends and neighbors may have also stemmed from a desire to escape from household responsibilities.

c. Men who were active in formal organizations not pertaining to religion or mental retardation tended to have a relatively low marital integration. High participation in formal organizations probably resulted from a desire of the men to be away from home and, in turn, aggravated difficulties in their marriage.

Hypotheses on nonsupportive interaction were only partially confirmed. Clear support by the data was found for the family's interaction with the wife's mother-in-law, but the results for the remaining hypotheses were not so definite.

Practical Implications. Taken together, the results concerning the hypotheses in this study present important considerations in deciding upon institutionalization of the retarded child. Effects of age, sex, and dependence of the retarded child in combination with the presence of normal brothers and sisters and the social status and religion of the family determine the impact of the presence of the retarded child on the family. The parent cannot, of course, predict the future effect of the child on family relations precisely. Yet, the results of the study can serve as guideposts: the parent can expect that a retarded boy, especially after the age of nine, will probably have a disruptive effect on marital relations; he can anticipate personality problems for the sister who is given many responsibilities for the child; the parent must be aware of the degree to which the family has its own resources and supportive interaction in facing crisis situations; and he can expect the degree of helplessness of the retarded to affect the personality of his normal children adversely.

Theoretical Implications. From a theoretical viewpoint, the general support of hypotheses suggests that regarding the mentally retarded child as affecting family integration through inducing an arrest in the family cycle is a fruitful approach to the study of family relations of handicapped children. From a more abstract theoretical position, the results of the investigation indicate some potentialities of (a) relating a static description of family integration to a dynamic one (i.e., to a description of the coordination of the life careers of the family members) in providing testable hypotheses concerning a social problem, (b) viewing family social structure as a series of mother-father-child triads, (c) evaluating differential effects of family crisis on parents and children.

SUGGESTED STUDIES

In the present study, deductions were made on the basis of a symbolic model of the family and past research on the family. These deductions were then considered as hypotheses. Thus, the theory and hypotheses were stated in a gross way, with little empirical work on the family with a retarded child as a guide. The verification of these hypotheses in the present investigation should serve as a starting point for further refinement of theory and hypotheses. For example, precisely which changes in parental expectations for normal sons and daughters occur when the retarded child is institutionalized? This problem implies a change in role and in communication for all family members. A second example would be how parents redefine their expectations of the life careers of all family members when their child is diagnosed as mentally retarded. What are ethnic, social class, and religious differences in this respect? The relationships between subculture and adjustment to crisis would have to be thoroughly examined. On the whole, these studies should provide a refinement of motivation concepts in the study of the family cycle and its arrest.

REFERENCES

1. ANGELL, R. C. *The family encounters the depression.* New York: Scribners, 1936.
2. AUSUBEL, D. P., *et al.* Perceived parent attitudes as determinants of children's ego structure. *Child Development,* 1954, *25,* 173–183.
3. BALDWIN, A. L. Changes in parental behavior during pregnancy: an experiment in longitudinal analysis. *Child Development,* 1947, *18,* 29–39.
4. BENDA, C. E. *Developmental disorders of mentation and cerebral palsies.* New York: Grune & Stratton, 1952.
5. BOSSARD, J., & BOLL, ELEANOR. *The large family system.* Philadelphia: University of Pennsylvania Press, 1956.
6. BURGESS, E. W., *et al.* The restudy of the documents analyzed by Angell in *The family encounters the depression.* New York: Social Science Research Council, ca. 1942. (Hectographed)
7. BURGESS, E. W., & WALLIN, P. *Engagement and marriage.* Philadelphia: J. B. Lippincott Co., 1953.
8. CAVAN, RUTH S., & RANCK, KATHERINE H. *The family and the depression.* Chicago: University of Chicago Press, 1938.

9. CLAUSEN, J. A., & YARROW, MARIAN RADKE (Issue editors). The impact of mental illness on the family. *Journal of Social Issues,* 1955, *II,* issue 4.
10. COLEMAN, J. C. Group therapy with parents of mentally deficient children. *American Journal of Mental Deficiency,* 1953, *57,* 700–704.
11. COTTRELL, L. S., JR. The adjustment of the individual to his age and sex roles. *American Sociological Review,* 1942, *7,* 617–620.
12. DAVIS, F. Definitions of time and recovery in paralytic polio convalescence. *American Journal of Sociology,* 1956, *61,* 582–587.
13. DOLL, E. A. Counseling parents of severely mentally retarded children. *Journal of Clinical Psychology,* 1953, *9,* 114–117.
14. EATON, J. W., & WEIL, R. J. *Culture and mental disorders.* New York: The Free Press, 1955.
15. FARBER, B. An index of marital integration. *Sociometry,* 1957, *20,* 117–134.
16. FARBER, B., & BLACKMAN, L. S. Marital role tensions and number and sex of children. *American Sociological Review,* 1956, *21,* 596–601.
17. FOOTE, N. N. Identification as the basis for a theory of motivation. *American Sociological Review,* 1951, *16,* 14–21.
18. FOOTE, N. N. Matching of husband and wife in phases of development. *Transactions of the Third World Congress of Sociology,* 1956, *4,* 24–34.
19. GLICK, P. The life-cycle of the family. *Marriage and Family Living,* 1955, *17,* 3–9.
20. GOLDSTEIN, H. *Report number two on study projects for trainable mentally handicapped children.* Springfield, Ill.: Superintendent of Public Instruction, 1956.
21. GOODE, W. J. *After divorce.* New York: The Free Press, 1956.
22. GREBLER, ANNA MARIE. Parental attitudes toward mentally retarded children. *American Journal of Mental Deficiency,* 1952, *56,* 475–483.
23. HENRY, A. F. Sibling structure and perception of the disciplinary roles of parents. *Sociometry,* 1957, *20,* 67–74.
24. HILL, R. *Families under stress.* New York: Harper & Row, Publishers, 1949.
25. JACKSON, JOAN K. The adjustment of the family to alcoholism. *Marriage & Family Living,* 1956, *18,* 361–369.
26. JENNE, W. C., & FARBER, B. Interaction between severely mentally retarded children and their normal siblings. Paper read at Inst. Res. Excep. Child. Conference, Allerton Park, Ill., May, 1957.
27. KATZ, G. H. Should the child be sent to an institution. *Nervous Child,* 1946, *5,* 172–177.
28. KING, S. H., & HENRY, A. F. Aggression and cardiovascular reactions related to parental

control over behavior. *Journal of Abnormal and Social Psychology*, 1955, 50, 206–210.

29. KOCH, HELEN L. The relation of certain family constellation characteristics and the attitudes of children toward adults. *Child Development*, 1955, 26, 13–40.

30. KOMAROVSKY, MIRRA. *The unemployed man and his family*. New York: Dryden, 1940.

31. KOMAROVSKY, MIRRA. Cultural contradictions and sex roles. *American Journal of Sociology*, 1946, 52, 184–189.

32. KOMAROVSKY, MIRRA. Functional analysis of sex roles. *American Sociological Review*, 1950, 15, 508–516.

33. KORKES, LENORE. *A study of the impact of mentally ill children upon their families*. Trenton, N. J.: New Jersey Dept. of Institutions & Agencies, ca. 1955. (Mimeographed)

34. LANSING, J. B., & KISH, L. Family life cycle as an independent variable. *American Sociological Review*, 1957,, 512–518.

35. LEVY, D. M. *Maternal overprotection*. New York: Columbia University Press, 1943.

36. PARSONS, T., SHILS, E. A. & OLDS, J. Values, motives, and systems of action. In T. Parsons & E. A. Shils (eds.), *Toward a general theory of action*. Cambridge, Mass.: Harvard University Press, 1951, 47–275.

37. RABBAN, M. Sex-role indentification in young children in two diverse social groups. *Genetic Psychology Monograph*, 1950, 42, 81–158.

38. *Report on study projects for trainable mentally handicapped children*. Issued by Superintendent of Public Instruction, State of Ill., Springfield, Ill., 1954.

39. RISLER, W. P. Familiocentrism. Unpublished master's thesis, University of Chicago, 1942.

40. ROE, H. The psychological effects of having a cerebral palsied child in the family. Unpublished doctoral dissertation, Columbia University, 1952.

41. ROHRER, W. C., & SCHMIDT, J. F. *Family type and social participation*. College Park, Maryland: Agricultural Experiment Station, Univer. of Maryland, Misc. Publ. 196, 1954.

42. ROSEN, L. Selected aspects in the development of the mother's understanding of her mentally retarded child. *American Journal of Mental Deficiency*, 1955, 59, 522–528.

43. SCHONELL, F. J. & WATTS, B. H. A first survey of the effects of a subnormal child on the family unit. *American Journal of Mental Deficiency*, 1956, 61, 210–219.

44. SEARS, R. R. MACCOBY, E. E., & LEVIN, H. *Patterns of child rearing*. Evanston: Row, Peterson, 1957.

45. SEWELL, S. Two studies in sibling rivalry: I. Some causes of jealousy in young children. *Smith College Studies in Social Work*, 1930, I, 6–22.

46. SHERE, MARIE. An evaluation of the social and emotional development of the cerebral palsied twin. Unpublished doctoral dissertation, University of Illinois, 1954.

47. SHIBUTANI, T. Reference groups as perspectives. *American Journal of Sociology*, 1955, 60, 562–569.

48. SIMMEL, G. (K. Wolff, trans.) *The sociology of Georg Simmel*. New York: The Free Press, 1950.

49. STENDLER, CELIA BURNS. Possible causes of overdependency in young children. *Child Development*, 1954, 25, 125–146.

50. STONE, MARGUERITE M. Parental attitudes to retardation. *American Journal of Mental Deficiency*, 1948, 53, 363–372.

51. STRYKER, S. The adjustment of married offspring to their parents. *American Sociological Review*, 1955, 20, 149–154.

52. TERMAN, L. M., & TYLER, LEONA E. Psychological sex differences. In L. Carmichael (ed.), *Manual of child psychology*. New York: John Wiley & Sons, Inc., 1954, 1064–1114.

53. THORNE, F. C., & ANDREWS, J. S. Unworthy parental attitudes toward mental defectives. *American Journal of Mental Deficiency*, 1946, 50, 411–418.

54. TURNER, R. H. Role-taking, role standpoint, and reference-group behavior. *American Journal of Sociology*, 1956, 61, 316–328.

55. WALKER, GALE H. Some considerations of parental reactions to institutionalization of defective children. *American Journal of Mental Deficiency*, 1949, 54, 108–114.

56. WALLIN, P. Cultural contradictions and sex roles: a repeat study. *American Sociological Review*, 1950, 15, 288-293.

57. WARDELL, WINIFRED. Case work with parents of mentally deficient children. *American Journal of Mental Deficiency*, 1947, 52, 91–97.

58. WEINBERG, S. K. *Incest behavior*. New York: Citadel Press, 1955.

59. WEINGOLD, J. T., & HORMUTH, R. P. Group guidance of parents of mentally retarded children. *Journal of Clinical Psychology*, 1935, 9, 118-124.

60. WEST, PATRICIA SALTER. Social mobility among college graduates. In R. Bendix & S. M. Lipset (eds.), *Class, status and power*. New York: The Free Press, 1953, 465–480.

61. WHYTE, W. F. A slum sex code. *American Journal of Sociology*, 1943, 49, 24–31.

62. ZELDITCH, M. Role differentiation in the nuclear family: a comparative study. In T. Parsons & R. F. Bales (eds.), *Family, socialization and interaction process*. New York: The Free Press, 1955, 307–351.

63. ZIMMERMAN, C. C., & BRODERICK, C. B. The nature and role of informal family groups, *Marriage & Family Living*, 1954, 16, 107–111.

CHAPTER XVI

The Prospects of the Family

STUDENTS OF THE FAMILY frequently speculate about the family of the future. It is an interesting exercise, and indirectly it is a way in which the student may analyze what he predicts will be the "evolution" of society. If he perceives the whole of society moving in a direction of rationality, then he may expect that relations of a more rational nature will also be involved in future families. Such expectations about the future of society are implicit in formulations of theories about child raising, and in the dissemination of these theories by professionals and private and government agencies to the general public. Stated most simply, for example, one may see such a process postulated as follows: Assume anxiety in the adult population is judged as bad. Then, assume further that anxious children grow into anxious adults. Therefore, child rearing should not include approaches that make children anxious. Then, how about implementation? If, for example, a theory maintains that early toilet training makes children anxious, early toilet training would by the logic of the situation be discouraged and relegated to the status of unenlightened practices. Another theory may propose that permissive responses on the part of the parents, with no punishment, reduce the anxiety of the child—so only the unenlightened would punish the child. This simple-minded exaggeration of what may happen is only for illustrative purposes, as the historical analysis of "What happened?" is obviously much more complex. As we noted in the early materials in this volume, most events and circumstances must be viewed as multiply determined and are in turn multiple determiners of other events. Still, some things appear to carry more weight than others in trying to analyze what will happen in the future. History tends to be written in terms of the personal lives of men and the listing of events, but more useful history attempts to summarize forces and processes also.

Similarly, the discussion of the future of the family must be couched in terms of an accurate description of the situation as it exists today, but must also include consideration of the values and other forces that will help shape the future. The student must be most careful not to let his own personal values cloud the issues. The desire to see the world as "better" may make a student perceive the trends he would prefer. Similarly, in a personal situation a student may perceive the situation quite differently than if he is an external observer. For example, in the blossom of youth a young lady may see her involvements with men as exciting, educational, broadening, and "real" since, after all, she is a mature person experiencing life, all of which may be so in fact. By contrast, years later in observing her daughter in the same situation, she may judge the daughter as immature, irresponsible, hedonistic, and incapable of appropriate decisions and control. The situation is not dissimilar to reactions with regard to formulations of the law: Is law to govern me, or to control the irrationality of others? There is a pervasive question involving values that must be taken into account in analyzing society. Are most of society's members willing to attribute to others the same processes and values they have, i.e., are they truly objective? Are they more accurate in perceiving the motives of others than they are in examining their own? How shall the expectations of order for the society and freedom for the individual be reconciled? Can the societies of the future develop systems that satisfy both apparent needs? Will the family, if it is assumed to be a necessary base for generating and socializing new members for society, be forced to adopt new forms or modify old ones?

If there is to be "One World," what will it be like and what types of families will live in it? And even if "One World" becomes the end-point, what about the many generations in-between living in different cultures, changing at different rates, not necessarily in the same directions? Is it fruitful to maintain a global framework of anlaysis, or is it more productive to approach specific pragmatic concerns at cultural or sub-cultural level? Who should make the policies, if policies are indeed made by identifiable entities? Professionals? Governments? Religions? Families? Individuals? The image of the "Nature of man" is implicit in all such analyses of the world of the future and the family of the future, and sociologists must attempt in their speculations to make such values explicit as much as possible.

Most Americans are ideologically committed to the institution of the family. To be more specific, many of us are committed to a nostalgic-traditional view of the family. Some tend to view changes that are occurring in family structures with considerable alarm and describe the process of change as one in which the family is "weakening" or "disintegrating." Perhaps a more appropriate approach is to view changes in family structures and role relationships as necessary adaptations to broader changes that are occurring in the total society. These changes may produce new styles of family life that are more commensurate with emerging concepts of human rights. Whether this is true or not, our cultural values that are so deeply committed to a traditional image of the family have probably inhibited our ability to think rationally about the future of the family in a very creative way. Responses to variations of familial structures are often emotional rather than analytic with respect to the total fabric of society.

The first selection in this chapter, "Family Patterns and Human Rights" by William J. Goode, breaks with much traditional thought about the family. Goode is concerned with two questions: (1) What kinds of family patterns would maximize the fulfillment of individual human rights; and (2) Given maximum individual human rights, what would be the effect on family patterns. He sees a very clear relationship between the emerging evolution of human rights and family patterns. In one sense, the traditional authority of the family has been weakened, but this has resulted in significant gains in individual freedom and choice. Moreover, Goode argues, it may be that the changes that are occurring toward greater freedom within the family are serving as the catalyst for the emergence of greater human freedom in every other arena of society.

Reuben Hill, in his article titled "The American Family of the Future," suggests four ways in which we may gain insight about the future family: (1) extrapolating current trends, (2) drawing inferences from systematic studies of three generations of contemporary families, (3) drawing inferences as to the impact of technology and invention, and (4) systematically studying what family experts are saying. Hill concludes that none of these approaches supports an alarmist conclusion that the family is disintegrating. To the contrary, he sees the family of the future characterized by an upgrading in amenities, more flexibility in organization, and more competence in planning and decision-making.

The final selection, "The Future of the Family Revisited" by John Edwards, contrary to what the title sounds like, is not a refutation of Hill's position. Rather, he shares with Hill the view that the family of the future is not in so great a jeopardy as many have argued. Edwards questions whether such factors as loss of functions in the family, increased physical mobility, and emphasis on materialistic values are resulting in a general decline in the strength and quality of family life. Rather, he sees a greater interdependence and interpenetration of the family with other spheres of life. Families of the future are likely to serve the needs of the family members more adequately and marriage may be contracted more on the basis of reason rather than on impulse or habit.

None of the articles presented here takes a grim or alarmist view of the family of the future. At the same time, none of the authors sees the family of the future as a carbon copy of the contemporary family. If one reads between the lines, it is apparent that all three foresee the possibility of rather significant change. If one accepts the thesis of Goode that the family is both the locus and a catalyst for greater personal freedom, we may anticipate change in the direction of greater flexibility in family patterns as well as greater tolerance for patterns that most people would now view as deviant and unacceptable. It seems unlikely that the next quarter of a century will produce anything as radical as a law that makes marriage (like a driver's license) renewable every two years or so. Nor does it seem likely that we will see a law that prohibits a married couple from having a child until they have been married for a certain number of years. But we may very well find that "trial marriages" or casual arrangements will be viewed as acceptable behavioral patterns, anticipatory of marriage. Divorce rates may accelerate, but this may prove to be a less serious problem than it is today because young married couples may be more likely to refrain from early parenthood for a number of reasons, including the development of independent careers for both the husband and wife, greater emphasis on individual "fulfillment" and experiences, as well as the recognition of the risk that is involved in marriage. Whatever the future brings, it seems almost certain that the older generation will view the younger generation with some alarm. But if history has taught us anything, and the analyses presented in this chapter are at all on target, we can anticipate that the institution of the family will survive in some form.

63.

WILLIAM J. GOODE

FAMILY PATTERNS AND HUMAN RIGHTS

The fight for human rights is fraught with perils, not the least of which is that those to whom we wish to grant these freedoms may reject the gift, since they enjoy their chains.

The central psychological problem in extending human rights to disadvantaged groups is that what is one man's right must be another man's obligation. If I am an authoritarian father, my wife and children gain some freedom only if I give up what I now consider my rights. To urge *others* to grant freedom to their slaves, to share the right of decision with their subordinates, is of course easy if we ourselves are not scheduled to give up any of our own privileges, but our ethical position becomes thereby somewhat dubious.

The central sociological problem is to ascertain empirically just what are the social systems or social patterns which will maximize the protection of human rights. This is an almost completely neglected area of research, so that the question cannot really be answered from the data now available. When we do have the answer, we must be prepared to face the harsh possibility, so often the result of precise scientific inquiry, that we shall then consider the costs of achieving or maintaining such a system to be excessive.

Meanwhile, however, it costs little to explore the problem, to clarify it by descriptive and analytic steps. Perhaps thereby we can ascertain at least the dimensions of the task. My ultimate set of questions, which guide this exploration but which must remain unanswered until we have more adequate data, are these:

1. What kinds of family patterns are most likely to support a full implementation of human rights?

This selection is reprinted from: William J. Goode, "Family Patterns and Human Rights," *International Social Science Journal*, 1966, *23*, 41–54.

Copyright, *International Social Science Journal*, UNESCO. Reprinted with the permission of the author and publisher.

2. What kinds of family patterns would the full implementation of a human rights programme create?

More technically formulated, we are asking whether the family patterns of a society, and the extent to which it protects human rights, vary at random with reference to one another; or whether they correlate in any way.

I should like to ignore the thorny task of defining human rights here, to prevent the tedious detours and fruitless debates about social philosophy that will very likely ensue, but my central empirical problem is partially defined by my conception of human rights as a specific part of the social structure, as indeed a social sub-system itself. Therefore, I shall briefly address the problem. I hope, however, that the reader will not stop long to argue with me about what are the basic human rights—and of course on this matter the basic charter of Human Rights offers an excellent guide—but will instead focus on the social structural patterns that support those rights.

The cultural heritage of every civilization contains such kernels of moral wisdom, such all-encompassing definitions of human rights, usually phrased as a moral injunction. One of these, which has its counterpart in perhaps all major civilizations—and, I hasten to remind you, actually applied in none—will serve my analytic purposes here as the core meaning of civic rights. (It has obvious limitations as a definition of family rights.) This injunction tells us to treat the stranger as our brother.

Such exhortations are necessarily cryptic. The prophet does not mean, of course, that we should treat the stranger as we in fact treat our brother, but rather as we ought to treat our brother. Presumably, in the realm of civic rights this would mean that we ought to protect and even cherish those (the strangers) whose opinions are different from our own, who

606 / *The Prospects of the Family*

might be in our economic power or under our political rule. Economic exploitation, arbitrary political condemnation or conquest, repression of artistic, political, or religious expression, prohibitions against geographical or social mobility—all these would appear to be forbidden by such an injunction.

I am here less concerned with whether such a moral preachment contains an adequate programme of human rights, than with (a) the clear fact that some central planks in any defensible human rights programme *are* to be found in such a capsule statement; and (b) any such programme requires a vast expenditure of human energy to implement it. At the microstructural level of the family, for example, the inculcation of such moral sentiments as a set of role obligations, and not simply a set of empty sentiments to be mouthed on appropriate ritual occasions, requires a special kind of child rearing. It is so difficult that even in countries where these rights are relatively well established, such as the United States of America, (a) only a modest majority or a large minority will uphold them, and (b) violations of these rights occur every day.

The difficulty of transforming such 'rights on paper' into role obligations which parents successfully persuade the child to accept may be seen dramatically in the contrast between national constitutions and the respect for human rights in most countries. The egalitarian social philosophies that were expressed by the American and French revolutions had such an impact on the Western nations that almost all the hundreds of constitutions and civil codes promulgated since the beginning of the nineteenth century have contained guarantees of free elections, free speech, freedom of religious practice, and freedom from arbitrary arrest or seizure of property, but in only a few countries have these rights been generally secure, and in none have they been absolutely secure.

This difficulty may be sensed, if not clearly understood, by commenting that most of the freedoms that are called 'human rights' in fact violate the common sense of the average person in most countries. It seems as irrational to the man in the street as it does to the despot to permit a group to publish wrong-headed

opinions, to organize political opposition to the party in power, or to utter blasphemies. Doubtless, most employers throughout history have felt that their employees 'ought' to support them politically. Justice has meant even-handed impartiality in the legal ideals of all nations, but common sense has always urged that only a cold or foolish man would betray his friends or family by judging against their cause. It seems to run counter to common sense for a man in power to step down merely because he has lost an election. The right of base-born men to rise to high position through merit is an ideal proclaimed in many societies and epochs, but upper-class families have felt it was simple common sense to protect the ineptitude of their own members against such rivals.

Yet it is a tragic irony that common sense is wrong. The force that is used to uphold it is misplaced and, especially in the modern era, futile. Slavery and colonialism have corrupted both the exploiter and the exploited, and the removal of these evils has profited both. Secure freedom of speech and religion, far from creating turmoil and instability, develops an adaptable, resilient social structure, which survives long after the highly controlled totalitarian or despotic régimes have crashed.

When the élite families protect their inept sons by denying entrance to the able from other social strata they guarantee their own downfall, often by revolution. In a most fundamental sense, the idealism of human rights is practical, and the common sense of repression and exploitation is unwise, but the family experiences in most societies do not persuade children that this is true.

I should like to add, parenthetically, that neither political science nor sociology has as yet been able to state how a nation can transform its old authoritarian régime into one of liberty.[1] There may well be particular social structural requirements, especially in the short run, before such freedoms can be guaranteed. One might argue, for example, that complete freedom of speech in Ghana might at this time

---

[1] In this connexion, see the illuminating essay by S. M. Lipset, 'Establishing National Authority,' in his *The First New Nation* (New York: Basic Books, 1963, 15–60).

create political chaos, or that England can afford this freedom while Indonesia cannot.

Just what those social-structural conditions are, however, is a separate problem which we cannot investigate here.

I noted earlier the kernel of the psychological problem of extending human rights to a given group, i.e., that each right is someone else's obligation, that to grant a right requires that someone loses what he had formerly considered his right. This problem has an obvious political form as well, that those who are to yield or grant a right are now in possession of that privilege precisely because of their political power, and thus can and usually do resist. Classical China, for example, gave to the eldest male the legal prerogative of making most decisions regarding any member of his family, from mate choice to divorce. The exploitation of any group is never based solely on custom or habit, but is always backed by force, defined as legitimate by the ruling group.

Indeed, it is precisely this resistance that so frequently makes a revolution necessary. Those who rule will not yield, and they have not sufficient wisdom to see that superior force will be arrayed against them. Traditional wisdom is a poor guide in a time of revolution.

And this is an era of revolution, unprecedented in world history. Its aims, and the great social forces that have swept over government throughout the world, have largely centred on human rights. Whether they will turn out to be genuine revolutions, or only transfers of power from one group to another, cannot be known at present, but I predict that the rest of the century will witness the consolidation and establishment of human rights at a rate that no other historical epoch has ever experienced.

In country after country the old stratification system is being rejected. Men demand, as never before, the right to a voice in their governments, the right to have their children educated, the right to be heard. They will not accept a slave or colonial status. They have raised their aspirations beyond any standard in the past, except that of a few industrialized countries and the élite of classical Western republics, such as Athens, Rome, or Florence.

It cannot be a surprise to the sociological theorist, then, that so much of this revolutionary wave has attempted to change family patterns. From at least the time of Plato two and a half millenniums ago, wise men have suggested that if human rights are to be guaranteed, if each human being is to be granted an adequate opportunity for the full development of his talents, the family system must be altered.

Every rigid stratification system, erecting barriers against the able poor, has relied on a highly controlled family system as its base, whether we look in the past at Tokugawa, Japan, or in the present at India. The family system is the keystone of every stratification system. Very likely, every utopia conceived by man has in imagination changed the existing family system. Every wise man has also said that to transform a society it is necessary to rear the children differently, to socialize them for a new set of role obligations.

Since those who are concerned with human rights are not likely to be in positions of power, and therefore are more likely to view with alarm than to point with pride to accomplishments, it is perhaps useful to assert that at least in this one crucial area of human rights a considerable revolution is taking place. Though the facts noted here are well known to students of social change, and have been documented in great detail elsewhere, it is worth while to summarize some of the areas in which human rights relative to family patterns have been extended over the past half century.[2] Let me simply list the main points of change here.

Mate choice. Prior to the Chinese Revolution of 1911, it is safe to say, most marriages in the world were arranged by the parents of the couple. A high but unknown proportion of the girls who married were given little or no choice because they were married in their early 'teens. Since that time, and at an increasing tempo since the Second World War, young people in every major area of the world have gradually come to have a voice in this important decision.

Bride price or dowry. Linked with parental arrangement of marriages in most societies was some type of dowry or bride price. These were not typically purchases, of course, but merely

[2] William J. Goode, *World Revolution and Family Patterns* (New York: The Free Press, 1964).

reflected the economic stake of the elders in the alliance between families. As young people have come to make their own choices, they have also begun to reject such exchanges, thereby achieving a greater freedom of choice in their own lives.

Inter-caste and inter-class marriage. Barriers to inter-caste and inter-class marriages have been rooted in custom as well as law. In almost all parts of the world the legal barriers have been eliminated, and custom has been eroded, too, under the impact of the freedom of choice given to young people. That most marriages will continue to be intra-caste and intra-class goes without saying, but the individual has a wider range of alternatives open than a half century ago.

Control by elders and other kin. Most social systems, including those of great nations such as China, India, Japan and the Arab countries, permitted by law and custom a rather wide control by elders over the young. These areas included geographical mobility, occupational choice, the level of education to be achieved, the allocation of income, and the participation in religious rituals, not to mention more trivial matters. Of course, even in the most industrialized of nations the network of kin plays an important role in the lives of married couples, but in most countries the adult now has a greater freedom in choosing which relatives he will support or listen to. In these respects, India remains perhaps most laggard among the great nations. In perhaps no country can young adults ignore their elders without personal cost, but in most they can obtain jobs without the blessing of their elders, and need not remain in tutelage until their elders die.

Inheritance. Although it may be asserted that any inheritance system which permits much property to pass from one generation to the next within the same family gives an advantage to one set of people and thereby restricts the freedom of another set, some steps toward freedom in this area may be noted. In traditional societies, there is little testamentary freedom, since the direction of inheritance is clear and fixed: e.g., equal inheritance among sons in China, primogeniture among *samurai* in Tokugawa, Japan, inheritance by brothers from the

brothers of the previous generation in India, and so on. However, the modern civil codes have increasingly granted testamentary freedom. In addition, most of these great societies omitted the female almost altogether. Islam did not, of course, but the girl received a half-share. The newer civil codes have moved steadily toward granting equal inheritance to all children, and widows have come to be recognized even in societies that were once only patrilineal.

Contraception. The right to choose whether one will bear children, or how many, has until recently been granted to only a minority of the world's population. That some will wish to bear many children in order to obey a religious injunction need not be questioned, but equally no advocate of human rights would wish to condemn a couple to having more children than they wish. The threat of over-population has stimulated many campaigns which are gradually opening this area of choice to the peoples of the world. It is also worth mentioning here that this is especially an area in which women have not been permitted any choice, although the burden of children was theirs. Numerous studies have shown that even in areas of high birth rates most women are generally willing, and more than men are, to limit their families.

Abortion. Most countries continue to deny the right of the woman, in the event of an unwanted pregnancy, to end it. This freedom has been most widely granted in the Communist countries and in Japan, with somewhat less tolerance in the Scandinavian nations. Various arguments are currently used to support the prohibition against free choice in this area, although without question open debate about the issue is much more acceptable than a generation ago.

Divorce. It is surely a denial of choice if individuals are forced to remain in a marriage they dislike, and at the present time almost all of the world's population is permitted by law to divorce. In India, brahmins were not permitted to divorce, though some divorce did occur, and lower castes did have that permission. Of course, in India as in other nations permitting no divorce the husband typically had or has other alternatives open to him, such as concubines, second wives, and so on. The Westerner should keep in mind, however, that some nations and cultures did permit divorce before the modern era. Islam traditionally gave the husband great freedom to divorce, and divorce rates were very high among the farmers in Tokugawa and Meiji, Japan. Both of these were patrilineal societies. Matrilineal societies have ordinarily been relatively permissive regarding divorce.

Egalitarianism within the family. Although there is little quantitative evidence on this point, almost all observers seem to agree that in almost all nations the woman has been given greater authority, respect and freedom within the family, and this relaxing of a patriarchal tradition has also improved the position of children. As will be noted later, the ideology of familial egalitarianism has its source in a broader stream of radical thought, and its impact can be observed in most countries. One of the most striking consequences of this change has been that women have come to be permitted to occupy responsible positions outside the family. Again it is difficult to quantify such matters, but it seems likely that egalitarianism in the occupational sphere has spread most rapidly in the socialist countries. It must be emphasized that I am not referring to 'women in the labour force.' After all, women have borne heavy burdens in all epochs and countries. Rather, I am pointing to a radically different phenomenon, the right of a woman to obtain a job (and the training necessary for it) and to be promoted within it, on the basis of her own merits without the permission of her husband or father. Needless to say, this factor supports egalitarianism within the family, since it reduces the dependence of women on the males, but it also creates a new respect for the woman as an individual.

Of course, with reference to all of these, the new civil codes are more advanced than the actual behaviour and attitudes of the populations concerned. The codes and new administrative rules are written by a new élite, who intend to lead these populations toward new types of family relations, but the process is relatively slow.

Moreover, it is not clear just how far such changes can go, whatever the ideological campaigns or the economic pressures. All such moves are purchased at some costs, and these may rise too high to be tolerated. It seems unlikely, for example, that any society can completely eliminate the parent-child bond as a way of creating the new civic man without particularistic ties to hamper the political programme. I doubt, too, that any society will in our lifetime be able to create genuine egalitarian relations between men and women.

In addition, we must keep in mind that each of these freedoms is a loss to someone, and most of them reduce the individual's emotional and even financial security. For the former, there may be no structural substitute. For the latter, various types of social welfare and pension programmes may suffice.

Even after taking note of these qualifications, we must concede, nevertheless, that the trends noted are steps toward the securing of human rights. Granted, they do not at first glance seem to be so dramatic or spectacular as the freeing of slaves or the abolition of a feudal system. On the other hand, those liberations may in fact have consequences similar to those of such grander political acts. If one could construct a numerical index, I would predict that the extensions of human rights to women and children in their domestic and occupational roles would loom as large as any other single step in the contemporary fight for human rights —certainly, far more real progress than has occurred in the areas of freedom of speech, religion, and publication, or the right of free elections or assembly. That step added as much or more to the economic production of the nations in which it has taken place and, very likely, at levels which we cannot easily explore here, helped to lay a firmer foundation for human rights in still other areas.

One of these levels does deserve brief attention here, which is that most of these extensions of human rights in the family area have not occurred only passively, but have been impelled by a positive and radical ideology of the family, which grows from but feeds back into a radical ideology of human relations in society.

The ideology of the conjugal family, as it is expressed in debates about family trends over much of the world, asserts the worth of the individual against the claims of caste, clan, or social stratum. It proclaims egalitarianism and the right to take part in important decisions. It urges new rights for women and children, and for adult males against the traditional claims of their elder kin. It demands the right to change exploitative relations among people.

In the West, its roots lie in the philosophic tradition that accompanied and interpreted the ascetic segment of the Protestant Revolution, and that runs counter to central philosophic elements of the Lutheran sects. Its fundamental human roots are still more universal, in that it radically asserts the rights of all to enjoy human freedom, i.e., choices among real alternatives. That no society and no family system wholly lives up to these principles goes without saying, but the contemporary pressures toward those goals are hardly to be denied.

However, we cannot evade the more problematic questions which I raised at the beginning of this paper. Even if most family systems of the world are moving toward granting more human rights to their members, can we assert that any particular kinds of family patterns or relations will produce a higher percentage of adults who will support the claims of their fellow citizens to the full enjoyment of human rights in the broader civic realm? Or, in a less cautious formulation, is it likely that the early experiences of the child in the family have *no* relationship with the willingness of the later adult to grant tolerance, freedom, and protection to others? Or, in a more utopian query, what type of family pattern would be most likely to produce adults who could live up to the really difficult role obligations that are demanded by the full extension of human rights to all?

The difficult task of socialization is not the inculcation of a love for one's personal freedom, which may be an easy goal: after all, any animal prefers at the outset to be free. But training children to support others' freedom and rights requires a more complex psychological and social pattern. Does any type of family pattern do that? Perhaps we might begin by taking note of a speculation often made by social philosophers and sociologists, essentially

that extreme familism denies human rights to others. That is, when individuals are reared largely within the family and derive almost all of their satisfactions there, they are likely to over-value the ingroup—the ethnic group, the tribe, the region. Consequently, they feel free to treat outsiders as of little value, not deserving of any protection. An extreme form of this unwillingness to grant human rights to others may be found in many peasant regions. A well-analysed example is to be found in Edward C. Banfield's perceptive analysis of a southern Italian village.[3]

This suggestion, which we may explore at a later point, that immersion in the family unit fosters intense ethnocentric attitudes that run counter to the role obligations of human rights, also receives some slight support from the finding that children are more likely to be democratic in their social behaviour if they spend more of their time with peers (who have roughly equal power) than with parents, who have superior power (we shall, however, consider this point).

This general hypothesis seems to be roughly correct, if not precisely stated, and of course many essays in the Western world have called on this and prior generations to abjure their loyalties to family and clan, in order to embrace a loyalty to all humanity.

However, the renunciation of extreme familism is hardly sufficient as a directive for rearing children who will support human rights. Speculatively, one would suppose that a high degree of permissiveness and egalitarianism within the family would be more likely to produce individuals who could not adjust easily to a repressive political system, or who would not create such a system. Much evidence on this point has accumulated since the publication of Horkheimer's collection of investigations entitled *Studien über Autorität und Familie* in 1936.[4]

Without attempting to summarize a consid-

---

[3]Edward C. Banfield, *The Moral Basis of a Backward Society* (New York: The Free Press, 1958), especially chapters 5 and 6.

[4]*Forschungsberichte aus dem Institute für Sozialforschung* (Paris: Félix Alcan, 1936).

erable mass of data and critiques,[5] well known to the student of human rights, let me simply remind you of the central suggestions in those studies. By and large, they have asked the question, what kinds of socialization experiences create the type of personality that is most prone to deny human rights to Jews, Negroes and other ethnic groups? However, the answers suggest parallel hypotheses about the denial of human rights generally.

Authoritarian control of the family by the father is correlated with such traits as these: deification of the parent, high evaluation of the father role, the child's passive adjustment to the present situation, the suppression of the child's aggression, suppression of sexual impulses in the child, and the fostering of dependency in the child. 'Democratic' attitudes of fathers correlate with egalitarian treatment of children, encouragement of their independence, and affection as a means of control.[6]

Adults who exhibit intolerance of others' rights are more likely than other adults to have grown up under authoritarian parental control and, of course, to continue that tradition with their own children. The stereotyping that is so characteristic of those who consider people who differ from themselves as having few redeeming traits is emphasized by parental efforts to ascribe fixed, clearly distinct, traits to the two sexes; indeed, the more authoritarian the mother's attitudes, the greater the children's imitation of the like-sex parent.[7]

Additional suggestions as to the kinds of family relations that might maximize the support of human rights can be derived from Allport's description of the 'tolerant' personality,[8] which summarizes the findings of many studies. Perhaps central is the necessity of family interaction based on security and love, rather than threat, and that concedes the right of individuals to have pleasure without guilt. Under a régime of threat, the child—and later, the adult —feels the need to have precise instructions, for fear of making errors and being punished for it. There is, then, an intolerance of ambiguity, whereas in a society that guarantees human rights the individual must be able to interact with others without at all knowing exactly what they will do in turn; more important and more specific, the individual does not have to interact with them as members of neat categories, such as 'Communist,' 'deviationist,' 'bourgeois formalist,' 'decadent imperialist,' 'Jew,' 'Moslem,' and so on. Similarly, in such families, individuals are conceded to have their own unique traits, and not to be forced rigidly into the categories of 'male' and 'female'—for example, chores might be shared on the basis of need and capacity, rather than sex.

Given greater security in affection, and the right to have pleasure without guilt, the individual's tolerance of frustration is greater, and his need to attack others when things go wrong will be less. Thus, he is less likely to approve any denial of human rights to those who differ in political or other beliefs. In more technical terms he will have less repressed aggression, and less need to displace it against people who have not directly harmed him.

Certain family experiences do seem to correlate with some of the attitudes necessary for democratic participation in civic life.[9] Generally, a higher percentage of the people in countries granting more secure human rights feel that they were free as children to participate in family decisions. This finding parallels Allport's suggestion that in the family which fos-

[5]The best-known study in English is T. W. Adorno, E. Frenkel-Brunswik, D. J. Levinson and R. N. Sanford, *The Authoritarian Personality* (New York: Harper & Row, Publishers, 1950). See the critiques in Richard Christie and Marie Jahoda (eds.), *Studies in the Scope and Method of the Authoritarian Personality* (New York: The Free Press, 1953).

[6]R. Nichols, 'A Factor Analysis of Parental Attitudes of Fathers,' *Child Development*, 1962, 33, 797–8.

[7]W. Hartup, 'Some Correlates of Parental Imitation in Young Children,' *Child Development*, 1962, 33, 94.

[8]Needless to say, Allport himself objects to the pale qualities of the term 'tolerant' but no good English word exists which conveys the meaning of 'supporting human rights.' Perhaps there is no such word in other Western languages, either. See Gordon W. Allport, *The Nature of Prejudice* (New York: Doubleday & Co., Inc., 1958), especially chapter 27. See also chapters 10 and 25.

[9]Gabriel A. Almond and Sidney Verba, *The Civic Culture* (Boston: Little Brown, and Company, 1965), 274–6, 284, 286–7.

ters tolerance in a child the junior members are permitted to be critical. They need not dread the superior power of the parent.[10]

In addition, Almond and Verba report that a higher percentage also felt that they actually had some influence on these decisions, and were free to complain about matters if they did not like them. Correspondingly, a higher percentage actually did complain.

These findings also parallel the findings of several studies in the United States of America, showing that there is higher tolerance of deviance and a greater willingness to give civic rights to people with radical opinions, toward the upper social strata, whether this is defined by education or by holding positions of leadership. For it is also in such strata that the ideology and practice of sharing family decisions is more widely found.[11] Toward the upper strata, a higher percentage of adults felt that as children they were able to complain, and did so.

Those who participated in family decisions also feel more competent as adults to influence their own governments.[12] It is worth noting that this correlation is weaker within the higher educational levels, where other types of experiences may supplement any lack of participation within the family itself.

Bearing in mind that we are not searching for the most effective ways of developing the superego in the child, but a particular superego content, let us further suggest (on the basis of research outside the family, but supported by investigations carried out by Kurt Lewin, Ronald Lippitt and many others over the past ten years in a wide range of organizational settings) that a collaborative style of rearing is more likely to create adults who respect the wishes and contributions of others. By contrast, the autocracy that a Luther rejects in his father and his church simply re-emerges in his own pattern of repression as well as in his notion of fixed statuses and duties imposed by fiat.

One of the likely consequences of the collaborative style, in which parents and children co-operate to solve problems, is the development of faith or trust in other people. This, in turn, as most readers know, is negatively correlated with authoritarianism. Faith in people, it is interesting to note here, appears to be highest in countries in which human rights are more secure.[13]

A complex relationship exists between these factors and love. The manipulation of love is one of the most effective techniques for developing a strong superego, but there is some evidence that the threat of love withdrawal creates many psychological problems. Among these is a distrust of others. If love is dependent, for example, on performance, performance may be high but regression is also a possible outcome. It seems likely that the security of parental love must be great enough to permit the child to face aggression by parent or outsider without great anxiety. The ability to face hostility without any inner compulsion to aggress against those who oppose; or without any inner compulsion to bow to that opposition when it is powerful (seeking love by compliance) can be most effectively based on security in parental love.

This security would appear to be based, in turn, on conveying to the child that he is loved as a unique person, not because of his status as elder or younger, male or female. The recognition that each member of the family is unique, with his or her own needs and demands, rather than merely a set of ascribed statuses, should contribute to the generalized feeling that other individuals are also unique: they need not be manipulated to serve one's own needs, or rejected as outcasts.

Such a security has an added by-product of some consequence in the broader area of human rights. When adults or children fail to live up to the norms they themselves claim to accept, it is unlikely that they can face that fact, or improve their behavior, if they can develop some kind of legitimation or rationalization for the discrepancy. As has been widely demonstrated, those who discriminate against others often assert non-discriminatory norms, and avoid

---

[10]Allport, *op. cit.*, 399–400.

[11]On the class differences in the support of civil liberties, see Samuel A. Stouffer, *Communism, Conformity and Civil Liberties* (Gloucester, Mass.: Peter Smith, 1963), especially chapter 2 and appendix E.

[12]Almond and Verba, *op. cit.*, 284.

---

[13]Almond and Verba, *op. cit.*, 212–4.

---

confronting the divergence between their behaviour and their norms. Thus they protect themselves against the strain of actually living up to those standards in the civic realm. It is unlikely that many individuals can achieve such a confrontation unless they have been given a considerable internal security, specifically a feeling that they are loved in spite of moral lapses.

This last point is linked, in turn, with a widely held psychodynamic notion, that self-acceptance is the strongest foundation for the acceptance of others. The child whose parents hammer into him a sense of his pervasive and continual moral failure is much less likely to accept himself as well as others. Reciprocally, those who as adults are authoritarian are more likely than others to express low evaluations of their own parents.[14] With reference to an hypothesis stated earlier, that intense familism is likely to be associated with an unwillingness to grant human rights to strangers, it should be noted that the personal autonomy arising from security permits the individual to be able to leave the family, to feel secure outside it, to trust even the stranger.

Finally, a collaborative style of family relations requires that youngsters take into account the needs and feelings of others. They become, therefore, more skilled at empathy. The authoritarian is less able to intuit correctly the attitudes and emotions of others. Correspondingly, it is not surprising that children from more democratic homes tend to be more popular among their peers than are children from authoritarian homes.[15]

But though such suggestions may be correct, and certainly deserve to be tested and made more precise by cross-cultural research, to persuade parents in many countries to change their ways is a difficult task. It is easier to push a highway through a jungle, or to purify a water supply, than to alter the details of family relations, as we know already from the repeated failures of birth control campaigns. Traditional parents are not more willing to share their authority with their children than are husbands to yield control over their wives. It is likely that the contemporary transformations in the political, economic, and social macrostructures of most nations will ultimately have more impact on the microstructure of the family than will any particular programme aimed at changing those internal relations of the family.

Equally ambiguous are the relations between personality variables and those of the larger social structure. No one has as yet succeeded in showing that personalities of particular types will create particular kinds of societies. Although adults who were reared under the ideal conditions sketched above would probably be more inclined to support human rights, it is not clear that traditional patriarchal, even authoritarian, family relations necessarily create authoritarian political and social structures. Perhaps the German family system contributed, as so many analysts claimed, to Nazism, but the Swiss, Dutch, French, Swedish and Belgian families were hardly less patriarchal or authoritarian.[16]

Nor can we cite as evidence the efforts of totalitarian régimes to control their family systems in order to gain support for their political system. Specifically, systems of high political control often do try to subordinate the individual directly to the state, by-passing the family where possible; and they also try to enlist the family members in campaigns to bring the apathetic or dissident members in line.

Such events prove, however, no more than that revolutionary leaders will use whatever instrumentalities they can command. Whether their hypotheses were correct is a separate matter for study. At present we do not know that these particular family experiences helped to produce adults who would wish to impose a repressive political control over others.

I think that these qualifications and doubts

---

[14]J. Cooper and J. Lewis, 'Parent Evaluation as Related to Social Ideology and Academic Achievement,' *Journal of Genetic Psychology*, 1962, *101*, 135.

[15]J. Howard Kauffman, 'Interpersonal Relations in the Traditional and Emergent Families Among Midwest Mennonites,' *Marriage and Family Living*, August, 1961, *23*, 251.

[16]In this connexion, see the complexities suggested by comparisons among British, German and American child-rearing patterns, in Lipset, *op. cit.*, 277–81, especially his suggestion that perhaps a different type of personality is needed for stable democracy in different kinds of societies.

need not arouse pessimism as to the future of human rights in the world. For though the revolutions in many countries have merely substituted a tight political control in place of the old-fashioned, looser despotism, almost all of these new programmes have promised freedom, and derive much of their support from an ideology of human rights. Ultimately, they will have to fulfil the terms of that implicit contract.

Perhaps, at a still more fundamental level, the family patterns that are being preached in these countries and the trends that are now visible are precisely those most likely to produce a next generation which would rebel still more strongly against political repression, and would support more firmly a programme of human rights. Thus, the revolutionary ideologies of egalitarianism do more than accentuate those trends toward human rights in the limited area of family relations, but reciprocally, the new patterns of family relations will also produce individuals who are more likely to put into effect and uphold a broad programme of human rights. It is possible, then, that the changes in family patterns over the past half century are not only important in themselves; they may also act as a catalyst that will eventually transform the massive flux of modern revolution into a clear movement toward greater human freedom.

64.

REUBEN HILL

THE AMERICAN FAMILY OF THE FUTURE

Previewing what the American family of the future will be like necessitates something of a world perspective through acquaintance by study and personal observation with the similarities and differences in family patterns by class, ethnic background, and region in various countries of the world.

Although the structural forms of marriage and the family vary from society to society and within the regions and class strata of societies, the functions carried out by families show high similarities. Moreover, the trends in form and functioning appear very similar in all of the industrializing countries of the world. Household size, location of power in decision-making, marriage forms, age and sex roles, rules for residence, inheritance, and methods of reckoning kinship continue to show marked variations, although these differences too are narrowing. But the functional assignments of socializing, motivating, and restoring family members in what Parsons has termed the area of "tension management" appear common to each of the societies which the present author has studied. In none of these countries is the family regarded as functionless; indeed, it is highly visible as a flourishing institution in most of the world.

The author's point of view, therefore, is less one of despair about the contemporary family and more one of admiration and respect for its flexibility, its resilience, and its capacity for survival and growth in such varied social and cultural settings. The continued development and elaboration of the family within the relatively affluent and beneficent environment of urban, industrial America hardly seems problematic. Certainly our society is far from the most hostile social and economic order yet encountered by marriage and family institutions. Moreover, when viewed historically as a phenomenon of Western civilization, more options

This selection is reprinted from: Reuben Hill, "The American Family of the Future," *Journal of Marriage and the Family*, 1964, *26*, 20–28.

Reprinted with the permission of the author and publisher.

This paper was originally presented at the annual meeting of the National Council on Family Relations, Denver, Colorado, August 21–23, 1963.

are probably open to families today to experiment, invent, and innovate than in any previous epoch.

Four methods may be delineated for projecting the contemporary American family into the future: extrapolation from current family trends; inferences from differences among three generations of contemporary families; inferences from the impact of current inventions on the family; and inferences from the writings and researches of family specialists. This paper will attempt some projections using each of these methods and will close with a set of objectives for the American family of the future.

EXTRAPOLATION FROM TRENDS INTO THE FUTURE

Projection of current trends in marriage and the family into the future involves predictions in the following areas: trends with respect to proportion married (higher), age at marriage (younger), family size (larger), divorce and separation (higher), remarriage (higher), births out of wedlock (higher), premarital intercourse (higher), power structure (more equalitarian), division of tasks and responsibilities (more flexibility), communication, affectional patterns, delegation of family functions, childrearing beliefs (developmental), and policies and practices (permissive).

This method of projecting into the future is hazardous because some trends are short-term ones tied to the economic climate of prosperity that so affects marriage, birth, and divorce rates. To predict with some certainty, it would be necessary to specify what the state of the economy is going to be—maintenance of full employment, continued economic growth, or stabilized economy.

The projection method is also hazardous because many trends are not necessarily linear. Completed family size has been dropping for 250 years in the United States, and it continued to drop during the high baby boom of the 1940's and 1950's, but it has just turned the corner, with 1954 as the probable low point at 2.4 children. The cohort of women born from 1916-20 who close their reproductive cycle from 1960-64 have had 2.9 children, whereas the

women born from 1931-37 have had or expect to have had 3.2 children by the time they reach age 45. Extrapolation into the future is difficult with 250 years of decline and a very recent upward turn. Will large families of six or more children be the rule 50 years from now? The trend in ideal family size suggests not; this trend indicates that families will have more nearly between three and four children, with 85 percent of couples regarding this size as ideal. To take another trend, age at marriage for men has dropped from 26.1 in 1890 to 22.8 in 1960, but the decrease was ever so gradual from 1890 to 1940, with no drop during the Depression decade at all, and most of the drop was from 1940-50, with no decrease since 1950. Headlines to the contrary, age for women has not dropped in the past decade and has not varied more than one-half year in 40 years. Americans may be marrying at an age level that is unlikely to drop further, but linear extrapolation might lead to the suggestion of American men marrying at the ages men are married in India if the trend were carried forward in linear fashion. It is instructive to recall the startling projections made by Lewis Terman from his data about virginity at marriage:

> In contrast with the slow tempo of many cultural changes, the trend toward premarital sex experience is proceeding with extraordinary rapidity. . . . In the case of husbands the incidence of virginity at marriage is 50.6 percent in the oldest group and only 13.6 percent in the youngest. The corresponding drop for wives is from 86.5 percent to 31.7 percent. If the drop should continue at the average rate shown for those born since 1890, virginity at marriage will be close to the vanishing point for males born after 1930 and for females born after 1940. It is more likely that the rate of change will be somewhat retarded as the zero point is approached and that an occasional virgin will come to the marriage bed for a few decades beyond the dates indicated by the curves. It will be of no small interest to see how long the cultural ideal of virgin marriage will survive as a moral code after its observance has passed into history.[1]

Needless to say, empirical studies on the age groups born in the 1940's and thus predicted to be completely nonvirginal do not confirm Ter-

_____
[1]Lewis M. Terman, *Psychological Factors in Marital Happiness* (New York: McGraw-Hill Book Company, 1938, 321–22).

man's predictions; the trends are not necessarily linear.

Power structure shifts are likewise difficult to extrapolate. Fewer families today are father-centered in decision-making; the trend is toward equalitarian patterns. A recent survey of several thousand families in Ohio and North Carolina finds roughly 50 percent of families democratic-equalitarian with regard to parent-adolescent decision-making and only 34 percent father-centered and autocratic-authoritarian. A representative sample of Detroit families suggests that 46 percent are equalitarian, with about 22 percent male dominant and 22 percent female dominant. But as extrapolation proceeds, is the result to be 100 percent equalitarians in the future? During most of their lives, children are relatively puny contributors to decision-making. Will not parents be authoritarian with respect to children into adolescence while being equalitarian with respect to husband-wife participation in decisions? Will equalitarian mean more shared decision-making or more segregation of decisions in which the wife makes most of the household and child-care decisions and the husband makes many of the financial decisions most of the time? A quick assessment indicates that this method of extrapolating on trends (which has failed in the past) would be an exciting but dangerous method to use in identifying the family of the future unless assumptions about the social and economic order were made crystal-clear and predictions were charted accordingly.

PROJECTION FROM GENERATIONAL CHANGES

A second method carries some of the same hazards but justifies attention; namely, the projection of changes perceived by studying three generations of the same family as the author and his colleagues have done in the metropolitan Minneapolis-St. Paul area. The method consists of examining the consistent differences which persist over three generations into the married-child generation—regarding the families of this latter generation as the best indications of what the American family of the future will be like. The sample studied consists of intact

families linked through three generations and living within 50 miles of Minneapolis-St. Paul who were obtained from area probability samples of the metropolitan area. One hundred grandparent families (ages 60-80), 100 parent families (ages 40-60), and 100 married-children families (ages 20-30) survived five interviews extending over a year's period. These families are ecologically dispersed, distributed by social class and economic levels, but somewhat more stable residentially than comparable families without three-generation linkages.

A number of changes over the three generations are notable: In average years of schooling completed, each generation surpasses its predecessor by an impressive margin, especially in the case of husbands. The superiority in education of wives over their husbands has decreased with each generation (grandparents, eight vs. six, parents, 11 vs. nine, and married children, 12.4 vs. 12.6). No longer is the wife as likely to be the more educated and literate member of the family.

Age at marriage has declined from 25.8 for grandfather to 23.6 for son to 21.9 for grandson, and from 21 for grandmother to 19.9 for granddaughter, showing a smaller age gap between spouses in the newest generation, two years vs. five years.

The number of children born and their spacing is curvilinear, with the parent generation (married during the Depression) having progressively longer intervals between births, from 18 months to five years compared with intervals of more nearly two years for the grandparent and married-child generations. The grandparent generation closed its family at 5.2 children, with over a fourth bearing eight or more children. The last child was born after 15 years of marriage, which stretched childbearing over a long period. The parent generation closed its family at 3.5 children, with over half in the two and three child categories. Their last child was born after ten years of marriage, shortening the childbearing span by more than four years over the preceding generation. The married-child generation still has over 20 years of possible childbearing ahead but has already produced more than two-thirds the number of the parent generation, averaging 2.4 children to date. It will surpass the parent generation but will close its family earlier as a result of closer spacing in the early years.

Comparing the occupational careers of the three generations, the impression emerges of acceleration in upgrading in the youngest generation. The married-child generation starts below the parent generation in less skilled jobs at the beginning of its career, but once under way in their chosen vocation, within a few years after marriage, their rate of advancement is clearly faster than their parents' was during the corresponding phase of their careers. By contrast with both, the grandparent generation suffered the lowest start and the slowest movement upward over their entire working lives. In each successive generation, more of the wives have worked the first several years of marriage, and more have returned to work as their children have grown up. In the married-child generation, 60 percent of wives are working in the first years of marriage as compared with 20 percent of wives at the beginning of marriage in the parent generation, and although still in the childbearing period, 40 percent of the wives in the married-child generation married six to ten years are employed. The impact of the working wife on level of income, home ownership, and acquisition of durable goods is enormous.

In all economic matters, the married-child generation appears destined to outstrip the previous generations based on the achievements of each generation during the first ten years of marriage. Eighty percent of the married-child generation has already exceeded the grandparent generation by becoming homeowners, an achievement reached by that proportion of the parent generation only after 20 years of marriage. In acquisition of durable goods, the married-child generation has overtaken the grandparent generation and is at the point in its inventory where the parent generation was after 35 years of marriage. The same can be said for bathroom and bedroom spaces in the home and other amenities. This has not been done at the expense of protective insurances or retirement provisions, for the married-child generation is well along in the acquisition of a portfolio of insurances and investments. Over 50 percent

have retirement provisions over and beyond social security, and 95 percent have life insurance. This generation starts its marriage with 82 percent covered, which is higher than their grandparents ever reached and as high as their parents achieved after 30 years of marriage.

Nelson Foote,[2] in examining these findings, characterized the phenomenon of change over the generations as "acceleration"—not just linear upward movement, but changes occurring at an accelerated rate: upgrading in education, in occupational composition toward professionalization, in income, in employment of wives, in upgrading of housing and the durable goods inventory, and in progressive improvement in protective insurances and investments—all at an accelerated rate. Each generation has become more innovative, as is indicated by the receptiveness to adoption of new home products earlier in marriage.

Certain other differences may seem more relevant to the description of the family of the future since they refer to the family's value orientations, organization, and problem-solving behaviors. In value orientations, the study drew from Brim's Cognitive Value Scales,[3] which were ingeniously devised from proverbial-type statements about life in several dimensions: fatalism, impulsivity, pessimism, and time orientation. The two older generations are predominantly fatalistic, prudential, optimistic, and present- or past-oriented; whereas the married-child generation is the least fatalistic and is prudential, moderately optimistic, and oriented to the future rather than to the present or past. Using Blood's[4] scaling of Evelyn Duvall's typologies of ideologies about parenthood and childhood which he formed into a Developmental-Traditionalism Scale, the grandparents are clearly the most traditional of the three generations, averaging less than half developmental responses: the parent generation is more developmental, with several parents falling on the clearly developmental side of the scale. The married-child

[2]Personal correspondence with the author.
[3]See appendix B in Orville G. Brim, Jr., *et al., Personality and Decision Processes* (Stanford: Stanford University Press, 1962, 309–12).
[4]Robert O Blood, Jr., *A Teacher's Manual For Use With Anticipating Your Marriage* (New York: The Free Press, 1956, 46–47).

generation is, as might be expected, the most developmental of all, with the longest range and the highest average score. The higher education of the third generation and its greater accessibility to parent-education materials may account for its greater espousal of developmental beliefs.

In family organization, marked differences appear in the authority patterns, the division of labor, and the marital integration of families by generation. In authority patterns, the shift to equalitarian patterns is greatest from the grandparent to the parent generation, but it holds up in the married-child generation. In division of tasks, there is more sharing of tasks and less specialization in the married-child generation as well as less attention to the conventions about what is men's work and women's work. Eighty-three percent of couples did some role crossing in this generation, compared to 60 percent in the grandparent generation.

Consensus on family values improves, but role integration deteriorates by generation; marital communication is especially low in the grandparent generation where role integration is highest. In the observations in the joint interview with husband and wife, in which differences between the spouses were generated by posing difficult questions which they were expected to answer as a pair, the interviewers found a greater readiness to enter into conflict among the youngest generation. The parent generation was loath to enter into conflict and slow to express hostility toward one another but proved to be lower on achieved consensus on the issues raised. The pattern of the youngest generation was frequently one of identifying differences, engaging in conflict, and then locating a basis for agreement with one party undertaking to smooth over the differences and seeking to "save face." Altogether, the interviewers found the youngest generation the most colorful and interesting—the couples of this generation were both most likely to experience conflict and to express hostility, but they were also most likely to conclude with consensus and gestures of affection.

Finally, the planning and problem-solving performance of the three generations over the year's period of observation was studied. In each successive generation, the number of plans expressed was greater, the number of actions taken during the year greater, and the proportion of preplanned actions greater. Here the differences may only reflect the stage in family development of the representatives of each generation. The married-child generation makes many plans and carries out many actions because it is in an expanding phase of need. What is interesting, however, is that the so-called "flighty" young generation is the most likely to preplan its purchases, its residential moves, and its other consumer actions, with 51 percent of its actions during the year preplanned compared with 44 percent in the grandparent generation. Moreover, the components of rational decision-making are more faithfully met in the married-child generation than in its antecedents. That is, the child generation is more likely than the more seasoned generations to search for information outside the immediate family, to weigh satisfaction among alternatives, and to take into account long-term as well as short-term consequences.

Surely these data are adequate to demonstrate the possibilities of utilizing generational changes as the basis for capturing the American family of the future. From this analysis a picture emerges of increasing effectiveness, professional competence, and economic well-being, of greater courage in risk-taking accompanied by greater planning, of greater flexibility in family organization with greater communication and greater conflict between spouses. There is little evidence in this generation of the phenomenon of reaction-formation which is supposed to explain the turn to the right politically. This is a generation which has enjoyed the material amenities and has already chosen to elaborate the nonmaterial values of home and children. Their educational aspirations for their children are the highest of the generations.

THE IMPACT OF INVENTIONS

The third method for capturing the future family involves speculation about the impact of inventions on the family. (With the imagination and skill of Meyer Nimkoff and his eminent colleague, the late W. F. Ogburn, whose work on inventions is now classic, this method might pay off.) The assumption here is that household conveniences designed to save time will have specified effects on family patterns. Among the many timesavers that have been invented and merchandised are the clothes dryer, the TV dinner and other kinds of processed foods, and automatic cookers. Then, to take up the time saved, time-fillers have been invented, such as television, now fully diffused among the entire population; hi-fi; do-it-yourself tools; and go-primitive-in-your-own-backyard-barbecuing types of inventions.

This particular method for identifying the future is exciting but hazardous, for the invention of timesavers results in increasing the quality of service but not in more leisure time, so that the sheer number of hours employed in housekeeping has not decreased markedly except for gainfully employed women who take advantage of these devices to save time. Inventions instead seem to increase the family's level of living before they reduce homemaking time: wearing a clean shirt daily instead of making it last three days is now the norm. There is also some evidence that families have turned away from the accumulation of durable timesavers, time-fillers, and comforts to make *children* the articles of consumption that they wish to enjoy. Some families have gone so far as to reject comforts and timesavers in order to live under simpler conditions.

Extrapolating to the family of the future by extending changes that inventions are intended to bring about may overstate the impact of these inventions. In the past we have overestimated the speed with which certain inventions would be merchandised and underestimated the toughness of the fabric of family habits. We probably overlooked the interaction between consumer and invention in shaping the use to which an invention is put.

THE FAMILY SPECIALIST'S FUTURE FAMILY

The fourth method for dealing in futures is most novel of all but may not provide any prediction regarding the American family of the future. This method starts with the fraternity of professionals engaged in marriage and family research and education. It asks what the future

of the American family would be if the family inadvertently advocated, through the choice of problems selected for research and for discussion in textbooks and classes, were to be taken seriously by the whole country and used as a basis for upgrading American families. This method is dealt with last so that it may be pondered longer. As active agents in shaping the future of the American family by their writing, teaching, and counseling, what variety of family forms and functions are family professionals advocating?

A content analysis of the indexes of a number of marriage and family textbooks published this year has been compared by this writer with the emphases in the first marriage text, published 30 years ago. Examination has also been made of the research problems published in *Marriage and Family Living* for the past five years for other evidences of current concerns. The table prepared by Nye and Bayer[5] showing ing the independent and dependent variables employed in marriage and family research from 1947-61 in 456 publications has been utilized. Finally, attention has been given to the properties which have been operationalized into scales and indexes and which Murray Straus has evaluated in his abstracts of family measurements.[6] The author has attempted to rephrase the most frequently mentioned concerns in the textbooks into miniature objectives which add up to major clusters. A parallel listing of research problems most frequently treated has also been made.

It can be seen that the research problems treated are for the most part instrumental in type. Given the family objective, the research tells what the correlates are which will have to be manipulated to achieve the research objectives or tells the consequences of manapulating the dependent variables. Thus there are many items such as Correlates of Marital Adjustment, Consequences of Different Childrearing Practices, or Consequences of Premarital Sex Relations.

[5]F. Ivan Nye and Alan E. Bayer, "Some Recent Trends in Family Research," *Social Forces*, March, 1963, *41*, 294.

[6]Murray A. Straus, "Measuring Families," in *Handbook of Marriage and The Family*, ed. by Harold T. Christensen (Chicago: Rand McNally, 1964).

TABLE 64–1. A RANKING OF OBJECTIVES FOR THE AMERICAN FAMILY FROM FREQUENCY OF ATTENTION IN TEXTBOOKS AND RESEARCH

First Marriage Textbook (1934)

I. Better Understanding of Sex and Reproduction (33 percent)
  Pregnancy and childbirth
  Conception and contraception
  Anatomy of sex
  Psychology of sex
  Menopause
  Infertility
  Homosexuality
  Masturbation
II. Control of Communicable Diseases and Inherited Disabilities (18 percent)
  Venereal diseases
  Cancer, heart disease, diabetes, glaucoma
  Hereditary disabilities, epilepsy, hemophilia, psychoses.
III. Better Functioning Families (17 percent)
  Parental competence in infant and child care and training
  More equitable division of power and duties
  Better family adjustment
IV. Better Mate Selection and Screening of Unmarriageables (17 percent)
  Better use of courtship and engagement (avoid breach of promise suits)
  Marriage not for everyone
  Later age at marriage
V. More Effective and Companionable Marriages (14 percent)
  Better financial planning
  Better adjusted marriages
  More stability, less divorce
  Better sex adjustment
  Better use of honeymoon

Published Empirical Research, MFL, 1958–63

I. Better Functioning Families (45 percent)
  Comparative family structures and their consequences in other societies
  Correlates of effective family-size control
  Correlates of different types of power structures
  Causes and consequences of maternal employment
  In-law and kinship interactions
  Family structure and child adjustment
  Consequences of different childrearing practices
  Correlates of family integration
  Developmental changes in the family over the life span
II. Improved Preventive and Remedial Services (20 percent)
  Techniques and consequences of marriage and family education
  Methods and consequences of marriage and family counseling
III. More Effective and Companionable Marriages (15 percent)
  Correlates of marital satisfaction and adjustment

Correlates of marital communication and marital interaction
  Correlates of types of sex role allocations
  Consequences of sex role expectations and conflicts
  Consequences of religious factors
  Correlates of sex adjustment
  Consequences of extramarital relations
IV. Better Mate Selection and Screening of Unmarriageables (15 percent)
  Consequences of differences in timing of marriage, late marriage vs. early marriage
  Dating patterns and consequences
  Courtship progress
  Experiments and controls in mate selection by class, religion, and ethnic groups
  Correlates of romanticism
  Controls and consequences of premarital sex behavior
V. Sex and Sexuality (5 percent)
  Sex deviation patterns
  Sex attitudes
  Sex drive
  Conditions and properties of unwed mothers

Three 1963 Marriage Textbooks

I. Better Mate Selection (34 percent)
  More realistic motives for marriage
  Later age for marriage, maturity
  Considerations of marriageability
  Use of dating for developing competence in interpersonal relations
  Use of engagement for testing compatibility
  More mutuality in sex relations, less exploitation
  Single high or single permissive standard for premarital sex
  Homogamous over heterogamous combinations
II. More Companionable and Competent Marriages (33 percent)
  Better adjusted, happier, and more satisfied marriages (11 percent)
  Less divorce, but remarriage acceptable
  Maintenance of companionship in marriage
  Better planning for contingencies, better decisions
  Better preparation for pregnancy and parenthood
  More constructive use of conflict
  More use of marriage counseling and family-life education
III. Better Functioning Families (17 percent)
  Greater competence in childrearing, more developmental views
  More equitable division of power between sexes and ages
  More mutuality and sharing of home tasks, less conformity to conventional sex roles
  Improved in-law and kinship relations
  More effective family-size control at optimum size

IV. Better Understanding of Sex and Reproduction
(14 percent)
Better information about:
Conception and contraception
Infertility and sterility
Techniques of coitus
Pregnancy and childbirth
Psychology of sex

Research Variables Operationalized Into Scales and Indexes (Straus, *Family Measurement Abstracts, 1963*) *263 Measures*

I. Family, Parent-Child, and Child Properties (52 percent)
Parent-child control and authority
Parent-child adjustment
Parent-child affection and support
Parental activity with children
Family integration

Family solidarity
Family adjustment
Family authority of power
Family division of duties
Familism-individualism
Traditional-developmental beliefs about parenthood and children
Marital happiness
Family-kinship interaction
Parental attentiveness to children
Family acceptance of community

II. Properties of the Marriage (32 percent)
Marital adjustment
Marital agreement
Marital authority
Marital empathy
Marital projection of agreement
Marital tension
Marital communication
Marital community of interest

III. Properties of the Premarital Pair (16 percent)
Romanticism
Marital role expectations
Engagement adjustment
Courtship involvement and progress
Conformity to moral codes

What does this method indicate about family workers' concerns and interests? The first marriage textbook put heaviest emphasis on Better Understanding of Sex and Reproduction (33 percent) and Control of Communicable Diseases and Inherited Disabilities (18 percent); 30 years later it is almost assumed that these objectives are achieved. Disease control, including venereal disease control, is absent from the 1963 texts, and virtually no research by family researchers treats it; hereditary issues are no longer problematic. Better Understanding of Sex and Reproduction is in last place in the 1963 texts, and the anatomy of sex and issues of masturbation, homosexuality, and the menopause are no longer seen as deserving of attention.

In 1963, in contrast, first place goes to a host of objectives under the cluster of Better Mate Selection (34 percent)—particularly to the screening out of unmarriageables, a preventive-type objective. Agreement seems to exist on the objectives of screening out immature personalities and slowing up couples with insufficient acquaintance or of incompatible backgrounds and temperaments; the effort seems directed at making it more difficult to enter marriage. Longer and more effective courtships and engagements are advocated for testing and pre-

viewing the marriage relationship. Exploitation in sex relations and in dating is deplored, and mutuality and companionship in dating and courtship are favored. But disagreement arises over whether a single code of high premarital sex morality or of permissiveness should be encouraged among young people today—some proof that Terman's prediction has not yet been achieved. Timing marriage after schooling has been completed is preferred, but the high quality of many college marriages and some high-school marriages necessitates the qualification, "It all depends. . . ." In general, marriage of people with similar backgrounds is advocated, but the success of many international, interethnic, and interfaith marriages, and the evidence that all marriages are to some degree "mixed marriages" are facts which temper this preference.

In second place, with very nearly as much attention in the 1963 texts as Better Mate Selection, is the cluster, More Companionable and Competent Marriages (33 percent). In 1934 the same cluster appeared in last place, but it won 14 percent of the author's attention. The chief attention in this cluster is focused on better adjusted, more satisfied, and happier marriages. Whereas in 1934 this problem was seen as a function of good sex adjustment, and psychological compatibility with good financial planning, in 1963 the researches cited include over 200 different factors related at least once to good marriage adjustment. Nye and Bayer show 193 different analyses of the correlates of marital success. Indeed, marital success outnumbers any other dependent variable in their inventory. They state that if one were to join the analyses of dating success, courtship success, and marital success together, they would find that one-quarter of the analyses reported over the 14-year period deal with the success or failure of the marital relationship or the preliminary interaction preceding such success or failure. Surely this is one cluster of objectives —Better Adjusted Marriages—where family professionals hope to affect the family of the future.

The balance of the miniature objectives are highly related to marital adjustment, more companionship in marriage, and better preparation for pregnancy and parenthood. But there is some uncertainty among writers as to how much conflict is constructive for families. Although essential agreement exists on the values of family stability, divorce and remarriage have been regarded as a healthier alternative for spouses and even children to continued unhappy marriage if marriage counseling fails. Family-life education and marriage counseling are also openly fostered, and the implications of this trend for the future family are broad.

In 1934 a higher rank was given to the cluster of objectives, Better Functioning Families, than in 1963, although the frequency of mention is about identical (17 percent). The ideology preferred for parents is developmental, the policies and practices permissive, and the power structure equalitarian. A more flexible division of tasks, more mutuality and sharing of home tasks with interchangeability of men's and women's tasks appears to be advocated rather than conformity to conventional sex roles. The only moot questions in the objectives of this cluster have to do with timing of participation of children in decision-making and the severity of discipline for different age levels. Family-size control is treated in 1934 as a matter of sex knowledge involving the methods and techniques of contraception, but in 1963 it is treated

as a family function to be mastered by arriving at agreement on number of children desired, spacing, and methods to be used. Some attention is given to conflicting beliefs of religious groups on the matter of methods.

In undertaking this content analysis of the 1963 textbooks, the author has been impressed by the research documentation which underpins the bulk of the treatment: the authors are selective of the problems they treat with an eye on the audience, but they are increasingly careful in their documentation of all generalizations. It is of interest, therefore, to see what differences are found between the listing of emphases in the marriage texts and in the research publications. Research emphases are less provincially limited to America than the textbooks which have been prepared for marriage and family classes. These researchers permit the placing of American family patterns in cross-national perspective. The ranking of variables as important to study by researchers interchanges the clusters Improved Family Functions and Better Mate Selection, in comparison with the textbook writers. Some research problems studied are not given much attention in the textbooks: causes and consequences of maternal employment, family structure and child adjustment, family integration, methods and consequences of marriage and family counseling, consequences of extramarital sex relations, and conditions and characteristics of unwed mothers. The order with which research has been attentive to what is important to study puts heavy accent on issues which lend themselves to programs of upgrading families quite as well as to building a body of theory.

These materials have been scrutinized for the dependent variables most frequently chosen for study in research on the one hand, and the topic headings in leading texts on the other. There has been some hazard in doing this; namely, that neither researchers nor authors have said, "These are our goals for the family." They are implicit rather than explicit goals, goals identified through the selection of emphases in research and teaching. The yield of this study is both in its indications of new emergents and of things missing. In-law and kinship interaction concerns have emerged which were absent a decade ago—family and social network, family and neighborhood, and family and community studies. Other relationships have gone untouched: sibling relations, stepchild and stepparent relations, and analysis of one-parent families. Are all families intact, nuclear units of first marriages without horizontal relations between children?

Another question which arises is whether the several implied objectives are compatible: Are the goals for premarital pairs compatible with those for married pairs, and in turn for families and family-kin relations? Are there discontinuities in implied goals from one stage of development to the next? Are the goals of individuals, unvoiced in this series of researches, compatible with the goals for marriage and the family?

CONCLUSION

A rough summary follows of the properties and procedures which family-field professionals, according to their writings and researches, seem to want perpetuated in families of the future.

1. The mate-selection machinery should be reorganized to encourage couples of reasonably similar backgrounds to meet and be tested for compatibility through a prolonged courtship and engagement.
2. Premarital sex relations should be no more intimate than the consciences of the couple can tolerate and the courting relation can sustain psychologically.
3. Premarital examinations, counseling, and education should help prepare the couple for marriage, postponing and returning to circulation those who are not ready.
4. The objectives of marriage should include the continued matching and stimulating of companionship, mutual understanding, common interests and joint activities, as well as building a system of planning and problem-solving.
5. With the coming of children and the activating of the parental roles, attention to family issues of needs of dependents competes with the needs in the marital relation for which preparation is indicated.
6. The chief objectives for the family phase can be listed as mastering the family tasks of each stage, including family-size control, physical maintenance, socialization, and gratification of emotional needs, and providing the motivation and morale necessary for the stimulation and development of personality potentials of all members.
7. To attain this high plane of family achieve-

ment, an effective group organization must be built and a competent family leadership must be trained. The accent in family organization should be on integrating objectives, good internal communication, clarity of role definitions, and patterns of problem-solving and decision-making. Leadership qualities needed stress interpersonal competence, of which autonomy, empathy, judgment, creativity, and selfmastery are highly relevant to marital and family success.

In projecting plans for NCFR during the next 25 years, recruitment of a membership increasingly sensitive to the needs and organizational properties of families is increasingly important. The day of taking the family for granted should be drawn to a close in America. Family specialists must consider what concerted effort they can make to help *all families* in a program of *family development,* which in a democratic society can be seen as a progressive upgrading of families comparable to urban development, economic development, and community development. Such a program is intended to be in contrast to the concepts of family adjustment or preservation of families which imply some restoration of the status quo. Families should be viewed as more than accommodating and adapting units; indeed, they should be seen as capable of transcending their present dimensions in realizing their goals and objectives, in growing and developing over time. The author advocates this program of family development not as a sentimental movement such as Americans mount on Mother's Day, which is more ritualistic than durable, nor as a militant movement European style, but as a sober recognition that only through a program of development can excellence be achieved in family living.

The capacity of families to take up the slack in the social order has limits which should not be tested by continued negligence. The tremendous resilience and recuperative strengths of families must be fostered and developed. The formulation of national policies which deal with America's millions of families as a precious national resource in social organization should be undertaken by this generation. This task will have the support of findings from hundreds of research studies and the approval of the great majority of families rearing children today.

65.

JOHN N. EDWARDS

THE FUTURE OF THE FAMILY REVISITED

Familial change and institutional interpenetration are subjects which have attracted the continued but sporadic attention of sociologists and scientists.[1] For the most part observers of the family in essence, have considered the interchange between various institutional sectors and the family a one-sided affair. Familial change is perceived, in other words, as resulting from social changes in other institutional spheres with few, if any, reciprocal effects. A considerable amount of evidence has been and can be marshalled to substantiate this interpretation. Yet, one of the consequences of adopting this prevailing view is that it has frequently resulted in the formulation of a unifactorial "theory" or

in the development of a theory of such a general nature that it has little heuristic and predictive utility. Ogburn and Nimkoff's[2] citation of technological innovations as the determinants of functional losses typifies the unifactorial approach, while Burgess'[3] suggestion that familial changes are the consequences of alterations in economic conditions and societal ideology is indicative of the level of abstraction with which change has been treated.

In addition to their predilection for unifactorial and highly general formulations, it has been noted that our earlier analysts of the family and social change were far from dispassionate observers. Either by implication or explicitly, the majority of writers during the 1940's took a stance on our perennial, theoretical antistrophe between persistence and change.[4] With few exceptions, social and family change was treated as a unique and disturbing occurrence. The views of these sociologists were not only tainted with traditional nostalgia in the midst of generalized and rapid change but reflected an over-rigid model of society which was then current.

Despite an increased awareness of the limitations of prior discussions of changes in the American family, many of the issues recently have been raised anew. Hobart, in contending that the family serves as a humanizing influence in modern society, suggests four significant changes being undergone: functional losses, increased personal mobility, declining status ascription, and the continued ascendency of materialistic values.[5] Although there is a certain

This selection is reprinted from: John N. Edwards, "The Future of the Family Revisited," *Journal of Marriage and the Family,* 1967, 29, 505–511.

Reprinted with the permission of the author and publisher.

[1]See, for example, William F. Ogburn, *Social Change* (New York: The Viking Press, Inc., 1922); William F. Ogburn and Meyer F. Nimkoff, *Technology and the Changing Family* (New York: Houghton Mifflin Company, 1955); Pitirim A. Sorokin, *The Crisis of Our Age* (New York: E. P. Dutton & Co., Inc., 1941); Carle C. Zimmerman, *Family and Civilization* (New York: Harper & Row, Publishers, 1947); Margaret P. Redfield, "The American Family: Consensus and Freedom," *American Journal of Sociology,* November, 1946, 52, 175–183; Ernest Burgess, "The Family in a Changing Society," *American Journal of Sociology,* May, 1948, 53, 417–422; Lawrence K. Frank, "Social Change and the Family," *Annals of the American Academy of Political and Social Science,* March, 1932, *160,* 94–102; Joseph K. Folsom, *The Family and Democratic Society* (New York: John Wiley & Sons, Inc., 1934); Ruth N. Anshen, "The Family in Transition," in *The Family: Its Function and Destiny* ed. by Ruth N. Anshen (New York: Harper & Row, Publishers, 1959, 3–19); Sidney M. Greenfield, "Industrialization and the Family in Sociological Theory," *American Journal of Sociology,* November, 1961, 312–322; Meyer F. Nimkoff, "Biological Discoveries and the Future of the Family: A Reappraisal," *Social Forces,* December, 1962, *41,* 121–127; and Reuben Hill, "The American Family of the Future," *Journal of Marriage and the Family,* February, 1964, *26,* 20–28.

[2]Ogburn and Nimkoff, *op. cit.*

[3]Burgess, *op. cit.*

[4]Sorokin and Zimmerman during this period were two outstanding proponents of the theme of family decay and deterioration.

[5]Charles W. Hobart, "Commitment, Value Conflict and the Future of The American Family," *Marriage and Family Living,* November, 1963, 25, 405–412.

amount of confusion at times as to whether these are consequences or causes of change, all of these factors have been isolated as important explanatory variables by previous theorists of familial change. In combining these four factors, Hobart argues that they have led to a profound value predicament in which the primary commitment and meaning of the family are being lost. Material abundance and our present commitment to its expenditure, he maintains, threaten the centrality of "human" values and our prospects of "self-realization." Consequently, if the current trends persist, it is possible "that something more or less than man might emerge to carry on something more or less than human society."[6]

Within the limited compass of this paper, this interpretation of the variables will be examined and an attempt will be made to indicate, whenever appropriate, their limitations as explanations of change. In doing so, the efficacy of these variables as explanations of change, whether employed singly or in concert, will be evaluated. Secondly, an alternative interpretation of marriage and the family will be suggested as a base line for the development of future theories of change.

VARIABLES OF FAMILIAL CHANGE

Loss of Functions

Hobart, in discussing the American family's loss of functions, points to the provision of companionship and emotional security as the basic function and reason for family formation today. Without question, many of the former functions such as economic production, education, protection, and recreation have been shifted to other institutional spheres or, at the very least, their content and form as they are carried out by the American family have been altered. Juxtaposed against this is evidence which suggests that the attractiveness of family formation has increased over the decades. However, Hobart's assertion that Americans seek divorce when they fail to attain a sufficient level of companionship and emotional security lacks empirical support. The precipitating influences in

the initiation of divorce proceedings are, in fact, a matter of some debate. In making such an assertion, Hobart appears to be in accord with Ogburn that "the dilemma of the modern family is due to its loss of function"[7] and that family instability and disintegration are a consequence.

In the words of Barrington Moore, the American family today may have "obsolete and barbaric features,"[8] but family units have persisted and the vast majority continue to persist despite the ongoing loss of functions. Durkheim's classic proposition concerning social differentiation is most suggestive in this connection. Increasing specialization and differentiation, concomitants of societal complexity, Durkheim contended, lead to an increment in interdependence.[9] This is no less true of familial functions than it is of the division of labor. Our present family system, organized around whatever tasks, is more highly interdependent with other institutional sectors than previously. Even the various totalitarian experiments with the eradication of family functions, including those of childrearing and socialization, tentatively suggest the ultimate functionality of the family in societal maintenance, regardless of its specific structure and functions.[10] It thus would appear that the issue of functional losses as a source or indication of instability is a misleading one. It is indeed questionable if family instability (divorce and separation) can be eliminated or reduced however many or few functions the family performs. The issue for any theory of

---

[6]*Ibid.*, 409.

[7]William F. Ogburn, "The Changing Functions of the Family," in *Selected Studies in Marriage and the Family*, ed. by Robert F. Winch, Robert McGinnis, and Herbert R. Barringer (New York: Holt, Rinehart, & Winston, Inc., 1962, 159–163).

[8]Barrington Moore, "Thoughts on the Future of the Family," in *Identity and Anxiety*, ed. by Maurice R. Stein, Arthur J. Vidich, and David M. White (New York: The Free Press, 1960, 394).

[9]Emile Durkheim, *The Division of Labor in Society* (New York: The Free Press, 1947).

[10]Nicholas S. Timasheff, "The Attempt to Abolish the Family in Russia," in *The Family*, ed. by Norman W. Bell and Ezra F. Vogel (New York: The Free Press, 1960, 55–63). Reiss has argued that Timasheff's interpretation of the Russian failure to eradicate the family may be based on a logical fallacy. See Ira L. Reiss, "The Universality of the Family: A Conceptual Analysis," *Journal of Marriage and the Family*, November, 1965, 27, 443–453.

family change seems to be, rather, the identification of the specific direction of interdependence and the concomitants which accompany and lead to increased interdependence.

INCREASED PERSONAL MOBILITY

The relatively high rate of spatial mobility within industrialized society, according to Hobart, affects the family in at least three ways: (1) it precipitates a larger amount of crises and adjustments, (2) it breaks the family from its external supports such as friendship and kinship groups, and (3) it weakens the proscriptions against divorce as a means of resolving family difficulties.[11] Increased personal or spatial mobility undoubtedly occasions the need for more adjustments. Generally such mobility is related to changes in work and, at times, to shifts in family status. The transitions attendant to these alternations are not to be underestimated. Yet, as the Rapoports indicate, conflicts **and stresses** are not necessarily multiplied by these transitions.[12] They may, in actuality, have desirable consequences. As a result of mobility, the functions of the family are by no means residual but become an inextricable background in the free choice of work and career. The prescriptions of work may allow, in turn, considerable latitude in the organization of family structure that was not formerly possible. The pursuit of higher education by women has enabled them to share occupational positions with their spouses and, in so doing, their involvement in the structuring of the family as well as in economic activities has been intensified.

The contention that the American family lacks external support during crisis periods is a corollary of the notion that the nuclear family is isolated in an urban situation. There are now a number of empirical indications which contradict or at least modify this view. Data from a Cleveland study, presented by Sussman, suggest that, in spite of extensive spatial mobility, nuclear families operate within a matrix of mutual kin assistance.[13] It is, in fact, during periods of crises that the aid of kin is most likely to be offered and accepted. Axelrod's research in Detroit indicates that relatives rather than non-relatives are the most important type of informal group association.[14] Babchuk and Bates, in a study of primary relations, also suggest that a large number of close friendships are maintained on a nonlocal and non-face-to-face basis.[15] On the whole, the evidence indicates that the high rate of annual movement by families has a relatively negligible effect on their external supports and does not, as often contended, weaken the informal controls of primary groups. It is patent that family transitions of one sort or another have always existed. The possibility that mobility as a crisis point in family life has merely superseded others is not to be discounted; but, if this is true, the impact of mobility on the family still remains to be demonstrated.

DECLINING ASCRIBED RELATIONSHIPS

In identifying the decline of traditionally defined or ascribed relationships as another element in the weakening of family bonds, Hobart concedes that the emphasis on achieved relationships fosters greater choice in establishing social relations. He argues, though, that the cross-sex contact, particularly in voluntary associations, subjects the marriage bond to greater stress.[16] To view voluntary organizations as potential agents for family dissolution is to oversimplify and distort the complexity of these organizations. Expressive voluntary groups (a dance club, for example) and those whose memberships are comprised of both sexes may serve to reinforce family relations. By their very nature, expressive associations are organized to supply immediate and personal gratification to

[11]Hobart, *op. cit.*, 406.
[12]Robert Rapoport and Rhona Rapoport, "Work and Family in Contemporary Society", *American Sociological Review*, June, 1965, 30, 381–394.
[13]Marvin B. Sussman, "The Isolated Nuclear Family: Fact or Fiction?" *Social Problems*, Spring, 1959, 6, 333–340. Similar findings based on New Haven, Connecticut, data are contained in Marvin B. Sussman, "The Help Pattern in the Middle-Class Family," *American Sociological Review*, February, 1953, 18, 22–28.
[14]Morris Axelrod, "Urban Structure and Social Participation," *American Sociological Review*, February, 1956, 21, 13–18.
[15]Nicholas Babchuk and Alan P. Bates, "The Primary Relations of Middle-Class Couples: A Study in Male Dominance," *American Sociological Review*, June, 1963, 28, 377–385.
[16]Hobart, *op. cit.*, 406–407.

their respective members. Their focus is, in other words, integrative at an individual level, while instrumental groups (such as the Chamber of Commerce) provide integration at a communal level. Particularly where expressive organizations are bisexual in composition, solidarity may be enhanced.[17]

It is, on the other hand, among these organizations which attract their constituencies from only one sex or the other that the probability of affiliation disturbing familial equilibrium is increased. In the one-sex groups, family members become geographically dispersed and may expend considerable amounts of time apart from one another. Even still, a number of relevant studies suggests that these are exceptional cases.[18] A sizable proportion of the population is not affiliated with any type of voluntary association. Moreover, among those who do belong, their participation is neither extensive nor intensive. Americans, all folklore to the contrary, are not a nation of joiners, and it is thus difficult to perceive achieved relationships as a threat to family and marital solidarity.

In conceiving the proliferation of associations and achieved relationships as causes of dissolution and change, there is also an implicit assumption made about the nature of man. Basically, in positing cross-sex contact as a disruptive force, man is viewed as primarily a sexual being. Presumably, social control of the sexual drive is tenuous and exposure to the opposite sex is sufficient to deteriorate this control altogether. Since every society is interested in controlling sexual outlets to some extent, it is particularly imperative for an industrialized society which severely limits such outlets to segregate the sexes. This conception of man is not only incompatible with most sociological theories, but it is ultimately an untenable position. Even if we grant that adultery is a widespread experience, there remains the intricate, and as yet unaccomplished, task of sorting out extramarital involvement from other causes of instability.

ASCENDENCY OF MATERIALISTIC VALUES

Materialistic values are seen as fundamentally incongruous with the more important values of the family; therefore, value confusion and instability result. The resolution of the present value confusion, Hobart notes, is doubly important for the family in that it is one of the basic socializing agents and it symbolizes many of the more fundamental humane values. Either human values must become preeminent in American society or the values of success, efficiency, and prosperity will continue to alter the family institution and eventually erode it. Hobart suggests, in this regard, that a value revolution is essential for continued societal survival. Such a revolution, he argues, cannot be a mere emergence of a consistent value hierarchy but must be a total displacement of our now-prevailing economic values. Although current trends appear to make such a revolution remote, the position set forth by Hobart is in essence optimistic. As a key to renewed commitment to marriage, he suggests that, increasingly, individuals in our affluent society are becoming more important for what they are, rather than for what they are capable of doing. Individuals are perceived and cared for in terms of their intrinsic value, rather than their extrinsic and utilitarian worth. Thus, despite the current prominence of utilitarian values, it is felt that the family is evolving in a new direction.[19]

THE FAMILY TODAY AND TOMORROW

To this juncture, I have attempted to point out several limitations in invoking functional loss, spatial mobility, and the emphasis on achieved relationships as explanations for familial change. I should like, at this point, to offer an alterna-

[17]The integrative impact of voluntary organizations is discussed at length in Nicholas Babchuk and John N. Edwards, "Voluntary Associations and the Integration Hypothesis," *Sociological Inquiry*, Spring, 1965, 35, 149–162.

[18]For instance, see Charles Wright and Herbert Hyman, "Voluntary Association Memberships of American Adults: Evidence from National Sample Surveys," *American Sociological Review*, June, 1958, 23, 284–294; John Foskett, "Social Structure and Social Participation," *American Sociological Review*, August, 1955, 20, 431–438; Wendell Bell and Maryanne Force, "Urban Neighborhood Types and Participation in Formal Associations," *American sociological Review*, February, 1956, 21, 25–34; and John Scott, Jr., "Membership and Participation in Voluntary Associations," *American Sociological Review*, June, 1957, 22, 315–326.

[19]Hobart, *op. cit.*, 407–412.

tive interpretation of contemporary marriage and family living as a base line for further analysis, since it is quite apparent with the data now at hand that there is some measure of disagreement. Specific alternative explanatory variables of change will not be indicated; it is equally important in the formulation of any future theories of change, however, that we avoid stereotyping our present situation as we have done with the rural family of the past. In offering this admittedly tentative and sketchy analysis, Hobart's excellent example is followed by focusing on value orientations.

A basic underlying theme of American culture, Jules Henry has noted, is a preoccupation with pecuniary worth or value that is a consequence of what he terms "technological driveness."[20] Though our institutional structure is highly interdependent, the point is that our economic system and its values have become so pervasive that American life can be characterized as being driven by the constant creation of new wants and desires. Each new want— with considerable impetus from advertising— aids in the destruction of self-denial and impulse control, both virtues of a previous era. Where an economic system has no ceiling or production limits, all hesitation to indulgence must be overcome. And overcome it is, as witnessed by the tremendous growth of the advertising industry.

The preoccupation with pecuniary worth appears to be a necessary complement to a social system dominated by its economic institutional sphere. The nature of an economy of such a social system is that rewards must be transferable and negotiable; hence, the institutionalization of a monetary system. Whether one is selling the products of his labors or his personality and training, tangible rewards are mandatory. No doubt the efficacy of religious thought has suffered for this reason. Eternal damnation is not sufficiently definite, nor the prospect of heaven sufficiently imminent, to normatively persuade many who exist in a society where most rewards are quantified. Quantified rewards and our nearly obsessive concern with them are not identical with status achievement which

other writers have cited as a crucial factor in the dissolution of the family. Status achievement may take many forms, of which the accumulation of monetary rewards is only one manifestation. The point is, rather, that the prospect of quantified rewards has become so pervasive in our society that it permeates virtually all social relationships including that between husband and wife and the progeny. The nonrewarding character of unlimited procreation has partially contributed to the diminution of that function and family size. To speak of "human obsolescence" and to consider the treatment accorded the elderly in our society are also evidence of the importance attached to tangibly rewarded behavior. In many instances it is not too much of an overstatement to consider as objects those that have not yet developed exchangeable resources (the young) and those who have exhausted theirs (the elderly). Even those occupying the middle ground, however, are not necessarily in an enviable position, for their relationships often lack all but a vestige of emotional interchange.

Insofar as marriage and the family are concerned, the first difficulties arising from this emphasis on pecuniary rewards are encountered in the dating process. The emergence of the rating and dating complex, Waller suggested, has fostered exploitative relationships in dating.[21] In such a relationship each partner attempts to maximize his or her returns with the least amount of concessions. Control and therefore the maximization of rewards are vested in that individual who has the least investment in the situation. Were it not a serious matter, it would be ironical that low commitment should be so highly rewarded. Indeed it is significant and symptomatic of contemporary society that rewards from this type of relationship should be consciously and avidly pursued. The exploitative nature of dating, were it merely confined to dating, would be less problematic. Due to the lengthy dating period, ranging from the preteen years to the early twenties, this orientation becomes reinforced through repetition. It cannot fail, therefore, to

[20]Jules Henry, *Culture Against Man* (New York: Random House, Inc., 1963).

[21]Willard Waller and Reuben Hill, *The Family: A Dynamic Interpretation* (New York: Holt, Rinehart & Winston, Inc., 1951), 131–157.

have an impact on marital relationships, particularly in the first years of marriage, the period when couples are most vulnerable to divorce.

Marital relationships, ideally at least, are defined in our society as relationships involving mutual sacrifice, sharing, and giving. Magoun states in this regard: "Anyone going into marriage with the expectation of being thanked for bringing home the bacon—even against dismaying odds—or for shining the ancestral silver tea service til it glistens from the buffet in little pinwheels of light, is headed for heartache."[22] And heartache is precisely what a large proportion of marriages, not only those that terminate in divorce but also the so-called normal marriages, garner. With monotonous repetition we are conditioned, primarily as a result of the pervasiveness of our economic institutions, to react to situations in a manner designed to elicit rewards. When the potential of tangible rewards is absent, interaction tends to be halting and random. Through the conditioning of the economic system and the lengthy continuation of this basic orientation during the dating process, the newly married are grossly unprepared for the prescriptions of marriage.

Recent findings amply illustrate this trend. The marriages of what Cuber refers to as the "significant Americans" are predominantly utilitarian in nature. The partners of these marriages are primarily interested in what each derives from the relationship. There is little concern with mutual sacrifice and sharing other than that which is essential to the maintenance of the marital bond. Moreover, the types of rewards sought in these marriages are not psychic or emotional but those which enhance material security. In fact, these marriages are, as Cuber points out, characterized by continual conflict, passivity, and a lack of vitality. Only a minority of the marriages approximate the cultural ideal of an intimate, emotional attachment between partners that results in mutual concern and sharing; and it is these marriages which are most vulnerable to divorce.[23] Thus, it would

appear that, like the devil, the family in contemporary, industrialized society must take the hindmost. As an institution it is unorganized and, therefore, lacks the influence that may be exercised by those institutions which are. Through necessity it must be flexible and adaptable; those that are not fail.[24]

A central proposition of functional analysis is that a change in one element of an integrated system leads to changes in other elements. The major impetus for social change in our society has been and continues to be our dynamic economic institutions, which seek to create ever new wants and markets for their products and services. Due to its decreasing size, the family's adaptability for change has kept pace. From many perspectives the various social alterations, such as the employment of women, have resulted in greater independence and increased potentialities for individual family members. In other respects, of course, the changes have been dysfunctional. As we have tried to indicate, the disparity that now exists between the ideal marriage and the real is considerable—just as considerable as it probably was in the past. Future alterations are of a high order of probability, particularly adjustments pertaining to the normative emphasis on material rewards and the affective character of marriage. Still, the desinence of the family appears to be a phantasm born of the anxiety accompanying rapid social change.

If, indeed, contemporary marriages are based more on what the marital partners *are* rather than what they *do* as Hobart suggests, the major disjunctive feature of current family life is that what individuals *are* is primarily reward-seeking organisms. This commitment to economic values is logically incompatible with the values of family life, but it is not a source of major dislocation or dissolution of the family group.

Given this condition, what future has our present family system? Earlier industrialization has relieved a major proportion of our female population from the more onerous activities associated with household mangement. In spite

[22]F. Alexander Magoun, *Love and Marriage* (New York: Harper & Row, Publishers, 1956, 44).
[23]John F. Cuber and Peggy B. Harroff, *The Significant Americans: A Study of Sexual Behavior Among the Affluent* (New York: Appleton-Century, 1965).

[24]Clark E. Vincent, "Familia Spongia: The Adaptive Function," *Journal of Marriage and the Family,* February, 1966, 28, 29–36.

of the unprecedented opportunity for experimentation, women in general have found it to be a frustrating era. Either they have found a combination of childrearing and outside activities unrewarding or they have felt that the channels for careers remain severely limited. Ongoing social change with respect to career expansion has been marked, nonetheless, and it is highly probable that the tempo will be increased.

This may have major significance for future marital relationships. The tremendous expansiveness of the insurance industry signifies, to some at least, the import attached to the economic aspects of marriage. This is again highlighted by the frequency with which insurance enters into divorce suits. More importantly, it is clear that marriage for men is more desirable, if not perhaps more necessary, than it is for women. Bernard's study of remarriage adequately illustrates the greater dependence which men have on the marital relationship; women, especially those that are economically secure, are less likely to remarry.[25] With increased avenue for more satisfying gainful employment, women will be afforded an enhanced alternative to wedlock. The generalized societal expectations regarding the desirability of marriage for everyone is quite pervasive, to be sure. But marriage, to put it simply, has become a habit—a habit which many young women with attractive career alternatives are beginning to question, however.

Economic overabundance, it is submitted, in the long run will have a repressive effect on the rate of marriage. The recognition of alternatives to wedlock, as that concerning alternatives to premarital chastity, will not occasion sudden behavioral consequences. But change is overdue. When women, already imbued with the economic ethos, fully realize their equality in this sphere, much of the *raison d'etre* of marriage will no longer be present. This is not to say, it should be emphasized, that family formation will precipitously decline; it is merely contended that the consequences of our reward-seeking orientation will become more evident, and this will be reflected in the marriage rate.

[25]Jessie Bernard, *Remarriage* (New York: The Dryden Press, 1956, 55, 62–63).

In other words, one of the present structural supports which buttresses the attractiveness of the marital relationship will cease to exist. Women will no longer find economic dependence a virtue and worthy byproduct of marriage, for, given the opportunity, they will succeed for themselves as ably as any male might.

Numerous other current trends support this contention. The availability of reliable contraceptive devices, the expectations regarding small family size, and the declining influence and authority of men all suggest that the supports for the marital bond are weakening. Educational opportunities for women and the impetus these provide for the pursuance of careers are another consideration. Universities and colleges will probably attract even larger numbers of women in the future, as they have done for each of the last seven decades. Although most of these women may anticipate marriage eventually, more equitable hiring practices and salaries guaranteed by the Civil Rights Act of 1964 will alter this to some extent. The current popularized literature on the single state also dramatizes the interest in alternatives to marriage.

As stated earlier, the family is not and is not likely to be a nonfunctional entity. The prominence of affective behavior in familial relationships as an ideal appears to be a central support for the continuance of these relationships. Still, just how important affective behavior will remain for individuals and how well these needs will be met in the family stand as primary issues in family research. It is illuminating that study after study to date has found that interaction among couples tends to be halting.[26] It is difficult to conceive of warm, intimate, and emotional relationships being maintained over time when vital interaction is almost non-existent. Perhaps even sporadic episodes of spontaneous communication are sufficient to sustain these relationships, but the accessibility of legal outlets suggests that, without these and other

[26]Robert S. Ort, "A Study of Role-Conflicts as Related to Happiness in Marriage," *Journal of Abnormal and Social Psychology*, October, 1950, 45, 691–699; Peter C. Pineo, "Disenchantment in the Later Years of Marriage," *Marriage and Family Living*, February, 1961, 23, 2–11; and Cuber and Haroff, *op. cit.*

structural supports, many marriages will terminate in divorce.

Despite the many elements of organizational life that are incompatible with our more humane values, bureaucratic structures in many respects recognize the desirability of maintaining intimate familial relationships. W. H. Whyte has noted, in his inimitable analysis of bureaucracies, the attempt to integrate the wife into the organizational structure.[27] In many ways and in many corporations, of course, this is a defensive act. Even as a mechanism of defense, though, this maneuver implicitly recognizes the wife's role as a supportive agent. Regardless of corporate motivation, the attempted integration of wives into the system can have beneficial consequences for the family. Where such an attempt is not made, the abyss between the economic and family group is only widened. Naturally, from the viewpoint of many individuals, this is not an ideal solution. It is, nonetheless, an alternative—an alternative upon which improvement may be made and, in view of increasing societal bureaucratization, one which demands attention.

A man and women marrying today can contemplate, in the majority of cases, over 40 years' duration of the relationship, encompass-

[27]William H. Whyte, Jr., *The Organization Man* (New York: Doubleday & Co., Inc., 1957).

ing over one-half of their lives. In a society in which group membership is extremely transitory, this represents a significant departure. Because of its duration and its small size, the individual has no greater opportunity in influencing the character and quality of a group.

What we are presently witnessing, moreover, is not a revolution of societal values or the demise and increased instability of the American family. Rather, given the current preeminence of economic orientations in our value system, the marital union and family are becoming more highly interdependent with the economic sphere. Cross-culturally and historically, the family, irrespective of its particular structure and functions, has been and is primarily an instrumental group from a societal perspective. It is not accidental, therefore, that marriage in most societies is based on considerations other than an affective and human orientation. That this is less true in the United States is not an indication of incipient instability but intimates that we are engaged in a radical experiment of familism. It is an experiment in which we are seeking to integrate a new individualism with the other more highly organized institutions. Insofar as our value orientations are dominated by economic values, marriages and family formation in the future are more likely to be based on reason rather than the impulse of habit.

Index of Names

Index of Subjects

BOOK MANUFACTURE

Marriage and the Family: A Comprehensive Reader was typeset at Kopecky Typesetting, Inc. Printing by offset and binding was by Kingsport Press, Inc. John Goetz designed the internal material. Charles Kling & Associates designed the cover. The paper is Perkins & Squier's Glatfelter Old Forge. The type is Caledonia with Baskerville and Caledonia display.